T0185202

More information about this subseries at http://www.springer.com/series/1244

Lecture Notes in Artificial Intelligence 12699

Subseries of Lecture Notes in Computer Science

Series Editors

Randy Goebel
  University of Alberta, Edmonton, Canada
Yuzuru Tanaka
  Hokkaido University, Sapporo, Japan
Wolfgang Wahlster
  DFKI and Saarland University, Saarbrücken, Germany

Founding Editor

Jörg Siekmann
  DFKI and Saarland University, Saarbrücken, Germany

André Platzer · Geoff Sutcliffe (Eds.)

Automated Deduction – CADE 28

28th International Conference on Automated Deduction
Virtual Event, July 12–15, 2021
Proceedings

 Springer

Editors
André Platzer
Carnegie Mellon University
Pittsburgh, PA, USA

Geoff Sutcliffe
University of Miami
Coral Gables, FL, USA

ISSN 0302-9743 ISSN 1611-3349 (electronic)
Lecture Notes in Artificial Intelligence
ISBN 978-3-030-79875-8 ISBN 978-3-030-79876-5 (eBook)
https://doi.org/10.1007/978-3-030-79876-5

LNCS Sublibrary: SL7 – Artificial Intelligence

© The Editor(s) (if applicable) and The Author(s) 2021. This book is an open access publication.
Open Access This book is licensed under the terms of the Creative Commons Attribution 4.0 International
License (http://creativecommons.org/licenses/by/4.0/), which permits use, sharing, adaptation, distribution
and reproduction in any medium or format, as long as you give appropriate credit to the original author(s) and
the source, provide a link to the Creative Commons license and indicate if changes were made.
The images or other third party material in this book are included in the book's Creative Commons license,
unless indicated otherwise in a credit line to the material. If material is not included in the book's Creative
Commons license and your intended use is not permitted by statutory regulation or exceeds the permitted use,
you will need to obtain permission directly from the copyright holder.
The use of general descriptive names, registered names, trademarks, service marks, etc. in this publication
does not imply, even in the absence of a specific statement, that such names are exempt from the relevant
protective laws and regulations and therefore free for general use.
The publisher, the authors and the editors are safe to assume that the advice and information in this book are
believed to be true and accurate at the date of publication. Neither the publisher nor the authors or the editors
give a warranty, expressed or implied, with respect to the material contained herein or for any errors or
omissions that may have been made. The publisher remains neutral with regard to jurisdictional claims in
published maps and institutional affiliations.

This Springer imprint is published by the registered company Springer Nature Switzerland AG
The registered company address is: Gewerbestrasse 11, 6330 Cham, Switzerland

Preface

This volume contains the proceedings of the 28th International Conference on Automated Deduction (CADE-28). CADE is the major forum for the presentation of research in all aspects of automated deduction, including foundations, applications, implementations, and practical experience. CADE-28 was hosted by Carnegie Mellon University, Pittsburgh, USA, 11–16 July 2021, but held online due to the COVID-19 pandemic. CADE-28 emphasized the breadth of topics that are of interest, including applications in and beyond STEM, and the use/contribution of automated deduction in AI.

The Program Committee (PC) accepted 36 papers (29 full papers and 7 system descriptions) out of 76 submissions (59 full papers, 4 short papers, and 13 system descriptions). Each submission was reviewed by at least three Program Committee members or their external reviewers. The criteria for evaluation were originality and significance, technical quality, comparison with related work, quality of presentation, and reproducibility of experiments.

The program of the conference included four invited talks:

- Liron Cohen (Ben-Gurion University, Israel): "Non-well-founded Deduction for Induction and Coinduction"
- Guido Governatori (CSIRO, Australia): "Computational Law: Automated Reasoning in the Legal Domain"
- Mooly Sagiv (Tel Aviv University, Israel): "Formal Reasoning about Decentralized Financial Applications"
- Markus Rabe (Google, USA): "What are the Limits of Neural Networks for Automated Reasoning?"

The conference hosted several workshops, tutorials, and competitions:

- Workshop: 10th International Workshop on Theorem Proving Components for Educational Software.
- Workshop: Proof eXchange for Theorem Proving.
- Workshop: Parallel and Distributed Automated Reasoning.
- Workshop: 17th International Workshop on Termination.
- Workshop: Logical Frameworks and Meta-Languages - Theory and Practice.
- Workshop: 3rd International Workshop on Automated Reasoning: Challenges, Applications, Directions, Exemplary Achievements.
- Tutorial: Program Validation and Verification in PVS. Paolo Masci (NIA), Mariano Moscato (NIA), César Munoz (NASA), Aaron Dutle (NASA), and Tanner Slagel (NASA).
- Tutorial: Practice of First-Order Reasoning. Stephan Schulz (DHBW), Adam Pease (Articulate Software), and Geoff Sutcliffe (University of Miami).
- Tutorial: Learning to Prove: Machine Learning for Better SAT and QSAT Solvers. Sean Holden (University of Cambridge).

- Tutorial: Proof-Theoretical Analysis of Non-Fregean Logic. Szymon Chlebowski, Marta Gawek, Dorota Leszczyńska-Jasion, and Agata Tomczyk (Adam Mickiewicz University).
- Competition: 28th CADE ATP System Competition. Geoff Sutcliffe (University of Miami) and Martin Desharnais (Vrije Universiteit Amsterdam).
- Competition: Termination Competition 2021. Albert Rubio (UPC Barcelona) and Akihisa Yamada (AIST Tsukuba).

In addition to the best paper awards, three CADE awards were presented at the conference:

- The Herbrand Award for Distinguished Contributions to Automated Reasoning (for 2020 and 2021).
- The Thoralf Skolem Awards for CADE papers that have passed the test of time by being the most influential papers in the field, for papers from CADE-5 (1980), CADE-11 (1992), CADE-17 (2000), and CADE-23 (2011).
- The (newly established) Bill McCune PhD Award for a PhD thesis' substantive contributions to the field of Automated Reasoning.

Thanks go to the many people without whom the conference would not have been possible - the authors, participants, invited spakers, members of the PC and their subreviewers, conference chairs, local organizers, the workshop/tutorial/competitions chair, the publicity chair, the CADE trustees, the board of the Association for Automated Reasoning, the staff at Springer, and the EasyChair team. CADE-28 gratefully received support from the Automated Reasoning Group at Amazon Web Services, The Journal of Artificial Intelligence, Imandra Inc., and Springer.

July 2021   André Platzer
                                                                                                    Geoff Sutcliffe

Organization

Program Committee

Peter Baumgartner	CSIRO, Australia
Bernhard Beckert	Karlsruhe Institute of Technology, Germany
Christoph Benzmüller	Freie Universität Berlin, Germany
Armin Biere	Johannes Kepler University, Austria
Nikolaj Bjorner	Microsoft Research, USA
Jasmin Blanchette	Vrije Universiteit Amsterdam, The Netherlands
Maria Paola Bonacina	Università degli Studi di Verona, Italy
Agata Ciabattoni	Vienna University of Technology, Austria
Koen Claessen	Chalmers University of Technology, Sweden
Hans de Nivelle	Nazarbayev University, Kazakhstan
Stéphane Demri	CNRS, LMF, France
Huimin Dong	Sun Yat-sen University, China
Gilles Dowek	Inria and ENS Paris-Saclay, France
Mnacho Echenim	Grenoble Alpes University, France
Pascal Fontaine	Université de Liège, Belgium
Nathan Fulton	IBM, USA
Silvio Ghilardi	Università degli Studi di Milano, Italy
Jürgen Giesl	RWTH Aachen University, Germany
Rajeev Gore	The Australian National University, Australia
Nao Hirokawa	Japan Advanced Institute of Science and Technology, Japan
Moa Johansson	Chalmers University of Technology, Sweden
Dejan Jovanović	SRI International, USA
Cezary Kaliszyk	University of Innsbruck, Austria
Laura Kovacs	Vienna University of Technology, Austria
Tomer Libal	American University of Paris, France
Assia Mahboubi	Inria, France
Cláudia Nalon	University of Brasília, Brazil
Vivek Nigam	Huawei Technologies, China
Tobias Nipkow	Technical University of Munich, Germany
Frank Pfenning	Carnegie Mellon University, USA
Giles Reger	University of Manchester, UK
Andrew Reynolds	University of Iowa, USA
Philipp Rümmer	Uppsala University, Sweden
Katsuhiko Sano	Hokkaido University, Japan
Renate A. Schmidt	University of Manchester, UK
Stephan Schulz	DHBW Stuttgart, Germany
Viorica Sofronie-Stokkermans	University Koblenz-Landau, Germany

Martin Suda	Czech Technical University in Prague, Czech Republic
Tanel Tammet	Tallinn University of Technology, Estonia
Sophie Tourret	Inria, France
Christian Urban	King's College London, UK
Uwe Waldmann	Max Planck Institute for Informatics, Germany
Yoni Zohar	Stanford University, USA

Subreviewers

Ruba Alassaf	Michael Kirsten
Johannes Åman Pohjola	Patrick Koopmann
Paolo Baldi	Hanna Lachnitt
Haniel Barbosa	Florian Lanzinger
Lee Barnett	Dominique Larchey-Wendling
Filip Bártek	Jonathan Laurent
Ahmed Bhayat	Alexander Leitsch
Lionel Blatter	Chencheng Liang
Pierre Boutry	Andrea Mazzullo
Martin Bromberger	Aart Middeldorp
James Brotherston	Dale Miller
Claudia Cauli	Julien Narboux
Anupam Das	Ulf Norell
Jeremy Dawson	Mizuhito Ogawa
Emanuele De Angelis	Miroslav Olšák
Stefan Dollase	Hitoshi Omori
Manuel Eberl	Jens Otten
Santiago Escobar	Xavier Parent
Michael Färber	Dirk Pattinson
Mathias Fleury	Lawrence Paulson
Carsten Fuhs	Nicolas Peltier
Thibault Gauthier	Michael Rawson
Alessandro Gianola	Adrian Rebola Pardo
Yuri Gil Dantas	Giselle Reis
Christoph Haase	Simon Robillard
Ludovic Henrio	Jonas Schiffl
Jera Hensel	Claudia Schon
Stepan Holub	Hans-Jörg Schurr
Ullrich Hustadt	Ying Sheng
Jan Jakubuv	Jonni Virtema
Peter Jipsen	Alexander Weigl
Daniela Kaufmann	Emre Yolcu
Daisuke Kimura	Marco Ziener

Conference Chairs

Marijn Heule   Carnegie Mellon University, USA
Iliano Cervesato   Carnegie Mellon University, USA

Local Organizers

Marijn Heule   Carnegie Mellon University, USA
André Platzer   Carnegie Mellon University, USA
Iliano Cervesato   Carnegie Mellon University, USA

Workshop/Tutorial/Competitions Chair

Alexander Steen   University of Luxembourg, Luxembourg

Publicity Chair

Sophie Tourret   Inria, France

Board of Trustees of CADE Inc.

Christoph Benzmüller   Freie Universität Berlin, Germany
  (Vice-president)
Jasmin Blanchette   Vrije Universiteit Amsterdam, The Netherlands
  (IJCAR 2022 PC Co-chair)
Pascal Fontaine   University of Liège, Belgium
Marijn Heule   Carnegie Mellon University, USA
Laura Kovács   Vienna University of Technology, Austria
Aart Middeldorp   University of Innsbruck, Austria
Neil Murray (Treasurer)   State University of New York, USA
André Platzer   Carnegie Mellon University, USA
  (CADE-28 PC Co-chair)
Andrew Reynolds   University of Iowa, USA
Philipp Rümmer (Secretary)   Uppsala University, Sweden
Renate A. Schmidt   University of Manchester, UK
Stephan Schulz   DHBW Stuttgart, Germany
Christoph Weidenbach   Max Planck Institute for Informatics, Germany
  (President)

Board of the Association for Automated Reasoning

Christoph Benzmüller (CADE)   Freie Universität Berlin, Germany
Uli Furbach (Vice-president)   Universität Koblenz-Landau, Germany
Jürgen Giesl (CADE)   RWTH Aachen University, Germany
Philipp Rümmer (Secretary)   Uppsala University, Sweden
Sophie Tourret   Inria, France
  (Newsletter Editor)

Contents

Implementation and Application

ATP and AI

System Descriptions

Invited Talks

Non-well-founded Deduction for Induction and Coinduction

Liron Cohen [ID]

Dept. of Computer Science, Ben-Gurion University, Be'er Sheva, Israel
cliron@cs.bgu.ac.il
https://www.cs.bgu.ac.il/~cliron/

Abstract. Induction and coinduction are both used extensively within mathematics and computer science. Algebraic formulations of these principles make the duality between them apparent, but do not account well for the way they are commonly used in deduction. Generally, the formalization of these reasoning methods employs inference rules that express a general *explicit* (co)induction scheme. Non-well-founded proof theory provides an alternative, more robust approach for formalizing *implicit* (co)inductive reasoning. This approach has been extremely successful in recent years in supporting implicit inductive reasoning, but is not as well-developed in the context of coinductive reasoning. This paper reviews the general method of non-well-founded proofs, and puts forward a concrete natural framework for (co)inductive reasoning, based on (co)closure operators, that offers a concise framework in which inductive and coinductive reasoning are captured as we intuitively understand and use them. Through this framework we demonstrate the enormous potential of non-well-founded deduction, both in the foundational theoretical exploration of (co)inductive reasoning and in the provision of proof support for (co)inductive reasoning within (semi-)automated proof tools.

1 Introduction

The principle of *induction* is a key technique in mathematical reasoning that is widely used in computer science for reasoning about recursive data types (such as numbers or lists) and computations. Its dual principle—the principle of *coinduction* [49,69,70]—is not as widespread, and has only been investigated for a few decades, but still has many applications in computer science, e.g. [42,56,39,52,82,55,57]. It is mainly used for reasoning about coinductive data types (codata), which are data structures containing non-well-founded elements, e.g., infinite streams or trees. One prominent application of coinduction is as a generic formalism for reasoning about state-based dynamical systems, which typically contain some sort of circularity. It is key in proofs of the bisimulation of state-transition systems (i.e., proving that two systems are behaviorally equivalent) and is a primary method for reasoning about concurrent systems [53].

A duality between induction and coinduction is observed when formulating them within an algebraic, or categorical, framework, e.g., [71,64,70,69]. Whereas

© The Author(s) 2021
A. Platzer and G. Sutcliffe (Eds.): CADE 2021, LNAI 12699, pp. 3–24, 2021.
https://doi.org/10.1007/978-3-030-79876-5_1

induction corresponds to a least-fixed-point semantics (or initial algebras), coin-duction corresponds to a greatest-fixed-point semantics (or final coalgebras). However, such an algebraic formulation does not account well for the way these principles are commonly used in deduction, where they are usually applied in different ways: induction to prove properties of certain collections, and coinduction to show equivalences between processes and systems.

Since the principle of induction is so well-known, induction methods are relatively well-developed. They are available in most (semi-)automated deduction systems, and tools for the formal verification of software and hardware such as theorem provers. Generally, implementations of the induction method employ one or more inference rules that express a general *explicit* induction scheme that holds for the elements being reasoned over. That is, to prove that some property, say P, holds for all elements in an inductively defined set, we (i) show that it holds for the initial elements, and (ii) show that P is preserved in the inductive generation of new elements. A side-effect of such implementations is that in applying inductive reasoning, the induction invariant must be provided *explicitly*. While advanced provers offer powerful facilities for producing and manipulating inductive goals, this still poses a major automation challenge. This formalization of the induction principle uses the classical notion of formal proofs invoked in standard theorem provers. There, proofs are *well-founded* trees, starting at the goal and reaching axioms while proceeding by applications of inference rules.

A more robust and natural alternative formalization of inductive reasoning is *implicit induction*, which avoids the need for explicitly specifying induction invariants. This form of reasoning is enabled by extending the standard notion of well-founded, finite proof trees into non-well-founded proof trees, where the presence of cycles can be exploited instead of cluttering the proof with explicit inductive invariants. For example, to prove $P(x)$ using implicit induction, one repeatedly decomposes the goal into subgoals that are either provable in the standard way (via well-founded subtrees) or reducible back to $P(x)$. This alternative has deep historic roots (originating in Fermat's infinite-descent method) and recently has seen a flourishing of its proof theory via *cyclic proof systems*.

Non-well-founded proof theory and its cyclic fragment (comprising only of finite and *regular* proofs) have been extremely successful in recent years in supporting implicit inductive reasoning. For one, the non-well-founded approach has been used to obtain (optimal) cut-free completeness results for highly expressive logics, such as the μ-calculus [3,35,34,37] and Kleene algebra [32,33], providing further evidence of its utility for automation. Other works focus on the structural proof theory of non-well-founded systems, where these promote additional insights into standard proof-theoretical questions by separating local steps of deductive inference from global well-foundedness arguments. In particular, syntactic cut elimination for non-well-founded systems has been studied extensively in the linear logic settings [41,7]. Much work has been devoted to the formal study of explicit versus implicit forms of induction in various logical settings including the μ-calculus [72,75,7,62], systems for arithmetics [74,31], and first-order logics with inductive definitions [19,14,19]. The latter offers a system parameterized by a set of inductive predicates with associated rules, rather than a single rule for induction as with the others. The cyclic machinery has also been used to effectively search for proofs of inductive properties and automatically verify properties of inductive programs, especially in the context of separation logic [78,68,16,17,18].

Unlike induction, the coinduction principle has not been so fully and naturally incorporated into major theorem provers, but it has gained importance and attention in recent years. As noted by Basold, Komendantskaya, and Li: "it may be surprising that *automated proof search for coinductive predicates* in first-order logic does not have a coherent and comprehensive theory, even after three decades..." [8]. Automated provers, to the best of our knowledge, currently do not offer any support for coinduction, and while coinductive data types have been implemented in interactive theorem provers (a.k.a. proof assistants) such as Coq [11,47,83], Nuprl [30], Isabelle [13,81,12,38], Agda [1], Lean [4], and Dafny [54], the treatment of these forms of data is often partial. These formalizations, as well as other formal frameworks that support the combination of induction and coinduction, e.g., [80,61,6,46], generally rely on making (co)invariants explicit within proofs. But just as inductive reasoning is naturally captured via proof cycles, cyclic systems seem to be particularly well-suited for also encompassing the implicit notion of coinduction. Nonetheless, while non-well-founded proof theory has been very successful in supporting inductive reasoning, this proof method has not been equally incorporated and explored in the context of coinductive reasoning. Some notable cyclic systems that do support coinduction in various settings include [67,58,72,36,2]. Another related framework is that of Coq's parameterized coinduction [47,83], which offers a different, but highly related, implicit nature of proofs (based on patterns within parameters, rather than within proof sequents).

This paper reviews the general method of non-well-founded proof theory, focusing on its use in capturing both implicit inductive and coinductive reasoning. Throughout the paper we focus on one very natural and simple logical framework to demonstrate the benefits of the approach—that of the *transitive (co)closure logic*. This logic offers a succinct and intuitive dual treatment to induction and coinduction, while still supporting their common practices in deduction, making it great for prototyping. More specifically, it has the benefits of (1) conciseness: no need for a separate language or interpretation for definitions, nor for fully general least/greatest-fixed-point operators; (2) intuitiveness: the concept of transitive closure is basic, and the dual closure is equally simple to grasp, resulting in a simpler metatheory; (3) illumination: similarities, dualities, and differences between induction and coinduction are clearly demonstrated; and (4) naturality: local reasoning is rudimentary, and the global structure of proofs directly reflects higher-level reasoning. The framework presented is based on ongoing work by Reuben Rowe and the author, some of which can be found in [26,29,28,23]. We conclude the paper by briefly discussing two major open research questions in the field of non-well-founded theory: namely, the need for a user-friendly implementation of the method into modern proof assistants, in order to make it applicable and to facilitate advancements in automated proof search and program verification, and the task of determining the precise relationship between systems for cyclic reasoning and standard systems for explicit reasoning.

2   The Principles of Induction and Coinduction

A duality between the induction principle and the coinduction principle is clearly observed when formulating them within an algebraic, or categorical, framework. This section reviews such a general algebraic formalization (Section 2.1), and then presents transitive (co)closure logic, which will serve as our running example throughout this paper as it provides simple, yet very intuitive, inductive and coinductive notions (Section 2.2).

2.1   Algebraic Formalization of Induction and Coinduction

Both the induction principle and the coinduction principle are usually defined algebraically via the concept of fixed points, where the definitions vary in different domains such as order theory, set theory or category theory. We opt here for a set-theoretical representation for the sake of simplicity, but more general representations, e.g., in a categorical setting, are also well-known [71].

Let $\Psi : \wp(D) \to \wp(D)$ be a monotone operator on sets for some fixed domain D (where $\wp(D)$ denotes the power set of D). Since $(\wp(D), \subseteq)$ is a complete lattice, by the Knaster–Tarski theorem, both the least-fixed point and greatest-fixed point of Ψ exist. The least-fixed point (μ) is given by the intersection of all its *prefixed* points—that is, those sets A satisfying $\Psi(A) \subseteq A$—and, dually, the greatest-fixed point (ν) is given by the union of all its *postfixed* points—that is, those sets A satisfying $A \subseteq \Psi(A)$. These definitions naturally yield corresponding induction and coinduction principles.

Induction Principle: $\Psi(A) \subseteq A \implies \mu(\Psi) \subseteq A$
Coinduction Principle: $A \subseteq \Psi(A) \implies A \subseteq \nu(\Psi)$

The induction principle states that $\mu(\Psi)$ is contained in every Ψ-*closed* set, where a set A is called Ψ-closed if, for all $a \in A$ and $b \in D$, $(a, b) \in \Psi(A)$ implies $b \in A$ (which means that $\mu(\Psi) = \bigcap\{A \mid \Psi(A) \subseteq A\}$). The coinduction principle dually states that $\nu(\Psi)$ contains every Ψ-*consistent* set, where a set A is called Ψ-consistent if, for all $a \in A$, there is some $b \in D$ such that both $(a, b) \in \Psi(A)$ and $b \in A$ (which means that $\nu(\Psi) = \bigcup\{A \mid A \subseteq \Psi(a)\}$).

The intuition behind an inductively defined set is that of a "bottom-up" construction. That is, one starts with a set of initial elements and then applies the constructor operators finitely many times. One concrete example of an inductively defined set is that of finite lists, which can be constructed starting from the empty list and one constructor operator that adds an element to the head of the list. The finiteness restriction stems from the fact that induction is the smallest subset that can be constructed using the operators. Using the induction principle, one can show that all elements of an inductively defined set satisfy a certain property, by showing that the property is preserved for each constructor operator. A coinductively defined set is also constructed by starting with a set of initial elements and applying the constructor operators, *possibly infinitely many times*. One example, which arises from the same initial element and constructors as the inductive set of lists, is that of possibly infinite lists, i.e. the set that also contains infinite streams. The fact that we can apply the operators infinitely many times is due to coinduction being the largest subset that can (potentially) be constructed using the operators. Using the coinduction principle, one can show that an element is in a coinductively defined set.

2.2 Transitive (Co)closure Operators

Throughout the paper we will use two instances of fixed points that provide a minimal framework which captures applicable forms of inductive and coinductive reasoning in an intuitive manner, and is more amenable for automation than the full theory of fixed points. This section introduces these fixed points and discusses the logical framework obtained by adding them to first-order logic.

Definition 1 ((Post-)Composition Operator). *Given a binary relation, X, Ψ_X is an operator on binary relations that post-composes its input with X, that is $\Psi_X(R) = X \cup (X \circ R) = \{(a,c) \mid (a,c) \in X \vee \exists b \,. \, (a,b) \in X \wedge (b,c) \in R\}$.*

Because unions and compositions are monotone operators over a complete lattice, so are composition operators, and therefore both $\mu(\Psi_X)$ and $\nu(\Psi_X)$ exist. A pair of elements, (a,b), is in $\mu(\Psi_X)$ when b is in every X-closed set that can be reached by some X-steps from a, which is equivalent to saying that there is a finite (non-empty) chain of X steps from a to b. A pair of elements, (a,b), is in $\nu(\Psi_X)$ when there exists a set A that contains a such that the set $A \setminus \{b\}$ is X-consistent, which is equivalent to saying that either there is a finite (non-empty) chain of X steps from a to b, or there is an infinite chain of X steps starting from a.

The $\mu(\Psi_X)$ operator is in fact the standard transitive closure operator. Extending first-order logic (FOL) with the addition of this transitive closure operator results in the well-known transitive closure logic (a.k.a. ancestral logic), a generic, minimal logic for expressing finitary[1] inductive structures [48,73,5,24,25,23]. Transitive closure (TC) logic was recently extended with a dual operator, called transitive co-closure, that corresponds to $\nu(\Psi_X)$ [27]. The definition below presents the syntax and semantics of the extended logic, called Transitive (co)Closure logic, or TcC logic.

Definition 2 (TcC Logic). *For σ a first-order signature, let s, t and P range over terms and predicate symbols over σ (respectively), and let M be a structure for σ, and ν a valuation in M.*

Syntax. *The language $\mathcal{L}_{TcC}$ (over σ) is given by the following grammar:*

$$\varphi, \psi ::= s = t \mid P(t_1, \ldots, t_n) \mid \neg\varphi \mid \varphi \wedge \psi \mid \varphi \vee \psi \mid \varphi \rightarrow \psi \mid \forall x \,. \, \varphi \mid \exists x \,. \, \varphi \mid$$
$$(TC_{x,y}\,\varphi)(s,t) \mid (TC^{op}_{x,y}\,\varphi)(s,t)$$

---

[1] See [40] for a formal definition of "finitary" inductive definitions.

*where the variables x, y in the formulas $(TC_{x,y}\,\varphi)(s,t)$ and $(TC^{op}_{x,y}\,\varphi)(s,t)$
are distinct and are bound in the subformula φ.*

Semantics. *The satisfaction relation $M, \nu \models \varphi$ extends the standard satisfaction
relation of classical first-order logic with the following clauses:*

$$M, \nu \models (TC_{x,y}\,\varphi)(s,t) \Leftrightarrow$$
$$\exists (\boldsymbol{d}_i)_{i \leq n} \,.\, d_1 = \nu(s) \wedge d_n = \nu(t) \wedge \forall i < n \,.\, M, \nu[x := d_i, y := d_{i+1}] \models \varphi$$

$$M, \nu \models (TC^{op}_{x,y}\,\varphi)(s,t) \Leftrightarrow$$
$$\exists (\boldsymbol{d}_i)_{i > 0} \,.\, d_1 = \nu(s) \wedge \forall i > 0 \,.\, d_i = \nu(t) \vee M, \nu[x := d_i, y := d_{i+1}] \models \varphi$$

*where $\nu[x_1 := d_n, \dots, x_n := d_n]$ denotes the valuation that maps x_i to d_i and
behaves as ν otherwise; $\varphi\left\{\frac{t_1}{x_1}, \dots, \frac{t_n}{x_n}\right\}$ denotes simultaneous substitution;
and $(\boldsymbol{d}_i)_{i \leq n}$ and $(\boldsymbol{d}_i)_{i > 0}$ denote, respectively, non-empty finite and (countably)
infinite sequences of elements from the domain.*

Intuitively, the formula $(TC_{x,y}\,\varphi)(s,t)$ asserts that there is a (possibly empty)
finite φ-path from s to t, while the formula $(TC^{op}_{x,y}\,\varphi)(s,t)$ asserts that either
there is a (possibly empty) finite φ-path from s to t, or an infinite φ-path starting
at s. For simplicity of presentation we take here the reflexive forms of the closure
operators, which yields the following correspondence.[2]

Proposition 1. *Let $[\![\varphi]\!]^{M,\nu}_{x,y} := \{(a,b) \mid M, \nu[x := a, y := b] \models \varphi\}$.*

(i) $M, \nu \models (TC_{x,y}\,\varphi)(s,t) \quad \Leftrightarrow \quad \nu(s) = \nu(t)$ or $(\nu(s), \nu(t)) \in \mu(\Psi_{[\![\varphi]\!]^{M,\nu}_{x,y}})$.

(ii) $M, \nu \models (TC^{op}_{x,y}\,\varphi)(s,t) \quad \Leftrightarrow \quad \nu(s) = \nu(t)$ or $(\nu(s), \nu(t)) \in \nu(\Psi_{[\![\varphi]\!]^{M,\nu}_{x,y}})$.

Note that, unlike the situation in standard fixed-point logics, the two closure
operators are not inter-definable. The TC operator is definable in arithmetics
(i.e. in Peano Arithmetics, PA), but the TC^{op} operator is not.

Thus, TcC logic is subsumed by fixed-point logics, such as the first-order
μ-calculus [64], but the concept of the transitive (co)closure is intuitively simpler
than that of general fixed-point operators, and it does not require any syntactic
restrictions to ensure monotonicity. In fact, due to its complexity and generality,
the investigation of the full first-order μ-calculus tends to focus only on variants
and fragments, and is mainly concentrated on the logical and model-theoretic
aspects, lacking a comprehensive proof theory.[3] Another reason for focusing on
these (co)closure operators is that they allow for the embedment of many forms of
inductive and coinductive reasoning within one concise logical framework. Thus,
while other extensions of FOL with inductive definitions are *a priori* parametrized
by a set of inductive definitions [59,60,79,19], bespoke induction principles do

---

[2] The definition of the post-composition operator can be reformulated to incorporate
the reflexive case, however, we opt to keep the more standard definition.

[3] Proof theory has been developed for the propositional modal μ-calculus fragment [51],
and recently also for matching μ-logic [20,21,22] which generalizes the μ-calculus.

not need to be added to TcC logic; instead, applicable (co)induction schemes are available within a single, unified language. This conciseness allows the logic to be formally captured using one fixed set of inference rules, and thus makes it particularly amenable for automation. Moreover, in TcC logic, the same signature is shared for both inductive and coinductive data, making certain aspects of the relationship between the two principles more apparent.

Defining infinite structures via the coclosure operators in TcC logic leads to a symmetric foundation for functional languages where inductive and coinductive data types can be naturally mixed. For example, using the standard list constructors (the constant nil and the (infix) binary function symbol '::') and their axiomatization, the collections of finite lists, possibly infinite lists, and infinite lists (i.e., streams) are straightforwardly definable as follows.

$$\mathsf{List}(\sigma) := (TC_{x,y} \exists a.\ x = a :: y)(\sigma, \mathsf{nil})$$
$$\mathsf{List}^{\infty}(\sigma) := (TC_{x,y}^{\mathsf{op}} \exists a.\ x = a :: y)(\sigma, \mathsf{nil})$$
$$\mathsf{Stream}(\sigma) := (TC_{x,y}^{\mathsf{op}} \exists a.\ x = a :: y \wedge y \neq \mathsf{nil})(\sigma, \mathsf{nil}) \wedge \sigma \neq \mathsf{nil}$$

TcC logic also naturally captures properties of, and functions on, streams [29].

3 Non-well-founded Deduction for Induction

This section presents the general method of non-well-founded proof theory (Section 3.1), and then provides a concrete example of a non-well-founded proof system for inductive reasoning in the setting of the transitive closure (Section 3.2), where the implicit form of inductive reasoning is then compared against the explicit one. Note that this section first presents the proof theory only for TC logic, which is the inductive fragment of TcC logic, i.e., the one based only on the transitive closure operator.

3.1 Non-well-founded Proof Theory

The method of *non-well-founded proofs* provides an alternative approach to explicit inductive reasoning by exploiting the fact that there are no infinite descending chains of elements of well-ordered sets. Clearly, not all non-well-founded proof trees constitute a valid proof, i.e. a proof of the validity of the conclusion in the root. A proof tree that simply has one loop over the conclusion or one that repeatedly uses the substitution or permutation rules to obtain cycles are examples of non-well-founded proof trees that one would not like to consider as valid. Thus, a non-well-founded proof tree is allowed to be infinite, but to be considered as a valid proof, it has to obey an additional requirement that prevents such unsound deductions. Hence, non-well-founded proofs are subject to the restriction that every infinite path in the proof admits some infinite descent. Intuitively, the descent is witnessed by tracing syntactic elements, terms or formulas, for which we can give a correspondence with elements of a well-founded set. In this respect, non-well-founded proof theory enables a separation between local steps of deductive inference and global well-foundedness arguments, which are encoded in traces of terms or formulas through possibly infinite derivations.

Below we present proof systems in the style of sequent calculus. Sequents are expressions of the form $\Gamma \Rightarrow \Delta$, for finite sets of formulas Γ and Δ. We write Γ, φ as a shorthand for $\Gamma \cup \{\varphi\}$, and $\mathsf{fv}(\Gamma)$ for the set of free variables of the formulas in Γ. A sequent $\Gamma \Rightarrow \Delta$ is valid if and only if the formula $\bigwedge_{\varphi \in \Gamma} \varphi \to \bigvee_{\psi \in \Delta} \psi$ is.

Let $\mathcal{S}$ be a collection of inference rules. First, we define the notion of a non-well-founded proof tree, a *pre-proof*, based on $\mathcal{S}$.

Definition 3 (Pre-proofs). *A pre-proof in $\mathcal{S}$ is a possibly infinite derivation tree formed using the inference rules of $\mathcal{S}$. A path in a pre-proof is a possibly infinite sequence of sequents, $s_0, s_1, \ldots (, s_n)$, such that s_0 is the root sequent of the proof, and s_{i+1} is a premise of s_i in the derivation tree for each $i < n$.*

As mentioned, not every pre-proof is a proof: only those in which there is some notion of infinite descent in every infinite branch, which allows one to formalize inductive arguments. To make this concrete, one picks some syntactic element, which can be formulas or terms, to be tracked through a pre-proof. We call such elements *traced elements*. The intuition behind picking the traced elements is that eventually, when we are given a pre-proof, we could trace these elements through the infinite branches, and map them into some well-founded set. This is what underpins the soundness of the non-well-founded method, as explained below. Given certain traced elements, we inductively define a notion of trace pairs which corresponds to the appearances of such traced elements within applications of the inference rules throughout the proof. That is, for traced elements, τ, τ', and a rule with conclusion s and a premise s' such that τ appears in s and τ' appears in s', (τ, τ') is said to be a *trace pair* for (s, s') for certain rule applications, and there has to be at least one case identified as a *progressing* trace pair. The progression intuitively stands for the cases in which the elements of the trace pair are mapped to strictly decreasing elements of the well-founded set. We provide a concrete example of traced elements and a trace pair definition in the transitive closure setting in Section 3.2.

Definition 4 (Traces). *A trace is a (possibly infinite) sequence of traced elements. We say that a trace $\tau_1, \tau_2, \ldots (, \tau_n)$ follows a path $s_1, s_2, \ldots (, s_m)$ in a pre-proof $\mathcal{P}$ if, for some $k \geq 0$, each consecutive pair of formulas (τ_i, τ_{i+1}) is a trace pair for (s_{i+k}, s_{i+k+1}). If (τ_i, τ_{i+1}) is a progressing pair, then we say that the trace progresses at i, and we say that the trace is infinitely progressing if it progresses at infinitely many points.*

Proofs, then, are pre-proofs which satisfy a global trace condition.

Definition 5 (Infinite Proofs). *A proof is a pre-proof in which every infinite path is followed by some infinitely progressing trace.*

We denote by $\mathcal{S}^\infty$ the non-well-founded proof system based on the rules in $\mathcal{S}$.

The general soundness argument for such infinite systems follows from a combination of standard local soundness of the inference rules in $\mathcal{S}$ together

$$\frac{}{\Gamma \Rightarrow \Delta, (TC_{x,y}\, \varphi)(s,s)} \, (TC_{ref}) \qquad \frac{\Gamma \Rightarrow \Delta, \varphi\{\frac{s}{x}, \frac{r}{y}\} \quad \Gamma \Rightarrow \Delta, (TC_{x,y}\, \varphi)(r,t)}{\Gamma \Rightarrow \Delta, (TC_{x,y}\, \varphi)(s,t)} \, (TC_R)$$

$$\frac{\Gamma, s = t \Rightarrow \Delta \quad \Gamma, \varphi\{\frac{s}{x}, \frac{z}{y}\}, \boxed{(TC_{x,y}\, \varphi)(z,t)} \Rightarrow \Delta}{\Gamma, (TC_{x,y}\, \varphi)(s,t) \Rightarrow \Delta} \, (TC_L^{im})$$

$$\frac{\Gamma, \psi(x), \varphi(x,y) \Rightarrow \Delta, \psi\{\frac{y}{x}\}}{\Gamma, \psi\{\frac{s}{x}\}, (TC_{x,y}\, \varphi)(s,t) \Rightarrow \Delta, \psi\{\frac{t}{x}\}} \, (TC_L^{ex})$$

where in (TC_L^{im}), $z \notin \mathsf{fv}(\Gamma, \Delta, (TC_{x,y}\, \varphi)(s,t))$, and in (TC_L^{ex}), $x \notin \mathsf{fv}(\Gamma, \Delta)$ and $y \notin \mathsf{fv}(\Gamma, \Delta, \psi)$.

Fig. 1: Proof rules for the TC operator

with a global soundness argument via an infinite descent-style construction, due to the presence of infinitely progressing traces for each infinite path in a proof. One assumes for contradiction that the conclusion of the proof is invalid, which, by the local soundness of the rules, entails the existence of an infinite sequence of counter-models, going along an infinite branch. Then, one demonstrates a mapping of these models into a well-founded set, $(D, <)$, which decreases while following the sequence of counter-models, and strictly decreases when going over progression points. But then, by the global trace condition, there exists an infinitely descending chain in D, which of course yields a contradiction.

While a full infinitary proof system is clearly not effective, effectiveness can be obtained by restricting consideration to the *cyclic* proofs, i.e., those that are finitely representable. These are the *regular* infinite proof trees, which contain only finitely many *distinct* subtrees. Intuitively, the cycles in the proofs capture the looping nature of inductive arguments and, thereby, the cyclic framework provides the basis for an effective system for automated inductive reasoning. A possible way of formalizing such proof graphs is as standard proof trees containing open nodes, called buds, to each of which is assigned a syntactically equal internal node of the proof, called a companion (see, e.g., [19, Sec.7] for a formal definition).

Definition 6 (Cyclic Proofs). *The cyclic proof system S^ω is the subsystem of S^∞ comprising of all and only the finite and regular infinite proofs (i.e., those proofs that can be represented as finite, possibly cyclic, graphs).*

3.2   Explicit vs. Implicit Induction in Transitive Closure Logic

Since we focus on the formal treatment of induction in this section, we here present the proof systems for TC logic, i.e., the logic comprising only the TC operator extension. Both proof systems presented are extensions of $\mathcal{LK}_=$, the sequent calculus for classical first-order logic with equality [44]. [4]

Figure 1 presents proof rules for the TC operator. Rules (TC_{ref}), (TC_R) assert the reflexivity and the transitivity of the TC operator, respectively. Rule

---

[4] Here $\mathcal{LK}_=$ includes a substitution rule, which was not a part of the original systems.

(TC_L^{ex}) can be intuitively read as follows: if the extension of ψ is φ-closed, then it is also closed under the reflexive transitive closure of φ. Rule (TC_L^{im}) is in a sense a case-unfolding argument, stating that to prove something about the reflexive transitive closure of φ, one must prove it for the base case (i.e., $s = t$) and also prove it for one arbitrary decomposition step (i.e., where the φ-path is decomposed to the first step and the remaining path).

The explicit (well-founded) proof system S_{TC} is based on rules (TC_{ref}), (TC_R) and (TC_L^{ex}). The implicit (non-well-founded) proof system S_{TC}^{∞} is based on rules (TC_{ref}), (TC_R) and (TC_L^{im}), and its cyclic subsystem is denoted by S_{TC}^{ω}. In S_{TC}^{∞}, the traced elements are TC formulas on the left-hand side of the sequents, and the points of progression are highlighted in blue in Figure 1. The soundness of the S_{TC}^{∞} system is then underpinned by mapping each model of an TC formula of the form $(TC_{x,y}\,\varphi)(s,t)$ to the minimal length of the φ-path between s and t.

Rules (TC_L^{ex}) and (TC_L^{im}) both offer a unified treatment of inductive reasoning, in the sense that bespoke induction principles do not need to be added to the systems. A big advantage of the implicit system is that it can ameliorate the major challenge in automating inductive reasoning of finding the induction invariant *a priori*. Indeed, a major difference between these two induction rules is the presence of the induction invariant. In (TC_L^{ex}), unlike in (TC_L^{im}), there is an explicit appearance of the induction invariant, namely ψ. Instead, in S_{TC}^{∞}, the induction invariant, which is often stronger than the goal one is attempting to prove, can (usually) be inferred via the cycles in the proof.

Since TC logic subsumes arithmetics, by Gödel's result, the system S_{TC}, while sound, is incomplete with respect to the standard semantics.[5] Nonetheless, the full non-well-founded proof system S_{TC}^{∞} is sound and (cut-free) complete for TC logic [28,26]. Furthermore, the cyclic subsystem S_{TC}^{ω} subsumes the explicit system S_{TC}.

4   Adding Coinductive Reasoning

This section extends the non-well-founded proof theory of TC logic from Section 3.2 to support the transitive coclosure operator, and thus the full TcC logic (Section 4.1). We then provide an illustrative example of the use of the resulting framework, demonstrating its potential for automated proof search (Section 4.2).

4.1   Implicit Coinduction in Transitive (Co)closure Logic

The implicit (non-well-founded) proof system for TcC logic, denoted S_{TcC}^{∞}, is an extension of the system S_{TC}^{∞}, obtained by the addition of the proof rules for the TC^{op} operator presented in Figure 2. Again, rules (TC_{ref}^{op}), (TC_R^{op}) state the reflexivity and transitivity of the TC^{op} operator, respectively, and rule (TC_L^{op}) is a case-unfolding argument. However, unlike the case for the TC^{op} operator in which rule (TC_L^{im}) can be replaced by a rule that decomposes the path from the

---

[5] S_{TC} is sound and complete with respect to a generalized form of Henkin semantics [23].

$$\frac{}{\Gamma \Rightarrow \Delta, (TC_{x,y}^{\mathsf{op}}\, \varphi)(s,s)}\ (TC_{ref}^{\mathsf{op}}) \qquad \frac{\Gamma \Rightarrow \Delta, \varphi\left\{\frac{s}{x}, \frac{r}{y}\right\} \quad \Gamma \Rightarrow \Delta, \boxed{(TC_{x,y}^{\mathsf{op}}\, \varphi)(r,t)}}{\Gamma \Rightarrow \Delta, (TC_{x,y}^{\mathsf{op}}\, \varphi)(s,t)}\ (TC_R^{\mathsf{op}})$$

$$\frac{\Gamma, s = t \Rightarrow \Delta \quad \Gamma, \varphi\left\{\frac{s}{x}, \frac{z}{y}\right\}, (TC_{x,y}^{\mathsf{op}}\, \varphi)(z,t) \Rightarrow \Delta}{\Gamma, (TC_{x,y}^{\mathsf{op}}\, \varphi)(s,t) \Rightarrow \Delta}\ (TC_L^{\mathsf{op}})$$

where in (TC_L^{op}), $z \notin \mathsf{fv}(\Gamma, \Delta, (TC_{x,y}^{\mathsf{op}}\, \varphi)(s,t))$.

Fig. 2: Proof rules for the TC^{op} operator

end, in rule (TC_L^{op}) it is critical that the decomposition starts at the first step (as there is no end point). Apart from the additional inference rules, $\mathsf{S}_{\mathsf{TcC}}^{\infty}$ also extends the traced elements to include TC^{op} formulas, which are traced on the right-hand side of the sequents, and the points of progression are highlighted in pink in Figure 2.

Interestingly, the two closure operators are captured proof-theoretically using inference rules with *the exact same structure*. The difference proceeds from the way the decomposition of the corresponding formulas is traced in a proof derivation: for induction, TC formulas are traced on the left-hand sides of the sequents; for coinduction, TC^{op} formulas are traced on the right-hand sides of sequents. Thus, traces of TC formulas show that certain infinite paths *cannot* exist (induction is well-founded), while traces of TC^{op} formulas show that other infinite paths *must* exist (coinduction is productive). This formation of the rules for the (co)closure operators is extremely useful with respect to automation, as the rules are *locally uniform*, thus enabling the same treatment for induction and coinduction, but are also *globally dual*, ensuring that the underlying system handles them appropriately (at the limit). Also, just like the case for induction, the coinduction invariant is not explicitly mentioned in the inference rules.

The full non-well-founded system $\mathsf{S}_{\mathsf{TcC}}^{\infty}$ is sound and (cut-free) complete with respect to the semantics of TcC logic [27]. It has been shown to be powerful enough to capture non-trivial examples of mixed inductive and coinductive reasoning (such as the transitivity of the substream relation), and to provide a smooth integration of induction and coinduction while also highlighting their similarities. To exemplify the naturality of the system, Figure 3 demonstrates a proof that the transitive closure is contained within the transitive co-closure. The proof has a single cycle (and thus a single infinite path), but, following this path, there is both a trace, consisting of the TC formulas highlighted in blue, and a co-trace, consisting of the TC^{op} formulas highlighted in pink (the progression points are marked with boxes). Thus, the proof can be seen both as a proof by induction and as a proof by coinduction.

4.2 Applications in Automated Proof Search

The cyclic reasoning method seems to have enormous potential for the automation of (co)inductive reasoning, which has not been fully realized. Most notably, as

$$(TC_{x,y}\,\varphi)(u,v) \Rightarrow (TC^{op}_{x,y}\,\varphi)(u,v)$$
$$\overline{(TC_{x,y}\,\varphi)(w,v) \Rightarrow (TC^{op}_{x,y}\,\varphi)(w,v)} \;(\text{Sub})$$

$$\overline{\varphi\left\{\tfrac{u}{x},\tfrac{w}{y}\right\},(TC_{x,y}\,\varphi)(w,v) \Rightarrow \varphi\left\{\tfrac{u}{x},\tfrac{w}{y}\right\}}\;(\text{Ax}) \qquad \overline{\varphi\left\{\tfrac{u}{x},\tfrac{w}{y}\right\},(TC_{x,y}\,\varphi)(w,v) \Rightarrow \boxed{(TC^{op}_{x,y}\,\varphi)(w,v)}}\;(\text{Wk})$$

$$\varphi\left\{\tfrac{u}{x},\tfrac{w}{y}\right\},\boxed{(TC_{x,y}\,\varphi)(w,v)} \Rightarrow (TC^{op}_{x,y}\,\varphi)(u,v) \qquad (TC^{op}_R)$$

$$\frac{}{\Rightarrow (TC^{op}_{x,y}\,\varphi)(u,u)}\;(TC^{op}_{ref})$$
$$\frac{}{u = v \Rightarrow (TC^{op}_{x,y}\,\varphi)(u,v)}\;(\text{Eq})$$

$$(TC^{im}_L)$$
$$\longrightarrow (TC_{x,y}\,\varphi)(u,v) \Rightarrow (TC^{op}_{x,y}\,\varphi)(u,v) \longleftarrow$$

Fig. 3: Proof that the TC^{op} operator subsumes the TC operator

mentioned, cyclic systems can facilitate the discovery of a (co)induction invariant, which is a primary challenge for mechanized (co)inductive reasoning.[6] Thus, in implicit systems, the (co)inductive arguments and hypotheses may be encoded in the cycles of a proof, in the sense that when developing the proof, one can start with the goal and incrementally adjust the invariant as many times as necessary. Roughly speaking, one can perform lazy unfolding of the (co)closure operators to a point in which a cycle can be obtained, taking advantage of non-local information retrieved in other branches of the proof.

The implications of these phenomena for proof search can be examined using proof-theoretic machinery to analyze and manipulate the structures of cyclic proofs. For example, when verifying properties of mutually defined relations, the associated explicit (co)induction principles are often extremely complex. In the cyclic framework, such complex explicit schemes generally correspond to overlapping cycles. Exploring such connections between hard problems that arise from explicit invariants and the corresponding structure of cyclic proofs, can facilitate automated proof search. The cyclic framework offers yet another benefit for verification in that it enables the separation of the two critical properties of a program, namely liveness (termination) and safety (correctness). Thus, while proving a safety property (validity of a formula), one can extract liveness arguments via infinite descent.

4.2.1   Program Equivalence in the TcC Framework

The use of the (co)closure operators in the TcC framework seems to be particularly well-suited for formal verification, as these operators can be used to simultaneously express the operational semantics of programs and the structure of the (co)data manipulated by them. Use of the same constructors for both features of the program constitutes an improvement over current formal frameworks, which

---

[6] Some verification approaches can discover inductive invariants automatically [43,45], or direct their construction based on the property being verified [63,50], but they do not currently support coinductive reasoning.

rest := fix rest(f).λn. if n > 0 then (output n; rest f (n − 1)) else f 0

f := fix f(n). let v = (output n; input()) * 2 in (if v ≠ 0 then f else rest f) (v + n)

g := fix g(m). output (2 * m); let v = input() in if v = 0 then rest g (2 * m) else g (v + n)

RES :=

$$(TC_{\langle u_1,u_2\rangle,\langle v_1,v_2\rangle}\ (u_1 > 0 \wedge v_1 = u_1 - 1 \wedge u_2 = u_1 :: v_2) \vee (u_1 = v_1 = 0 \wedge u_2 = v_2))(\langle n,s\rangle, \langle 0,s'\rangle)$$

$$\psi_f := \exists i, w.\ x_2 = i :: w \wedge$$
$$[(i * 2 \neq 0 \wedge y_1 = i * 2 + x_1 \wedge w = x_1 :: y_2) \vee (i = y_1 = 0 \wedge \text{RES}(x_1, w, x_1 :: y_2))]$$

$$\psi_g := \exists i, w.\ x_2 = i :: w \wedge$$
$$[(i \neq 0 \wedge y_1 = i + x_1 \wedge w = (2 * x_1) :: y_2) \vee (i = y_1 = 0 \wedge \text{RES}(2 * x_1, w, (2 * x_1) :: y_2))]$$

SPEC : $$(TC^{op}_{\langle x_1,x_2\rangle,\langle y_1,y_2\rangle}\ \psi_f)(\langle 2 * m, s\rangle, \langle \perp, \perp\rangle) \iff (TC^{op}_{\langle x_1,x_2\rangle,\langle y_1,y_2\rangle}\ \psi_g)(\langle m, s\rangle, \langle \perp, \perp\rangle)$$

Fig. 4: The recursive programs and their formalization in TcC

usually employ qualitatively different formalisms to describe the operational semantics of programs and the associated data.[7] For instance, although many formalisms employ separation logic to describe the data structures manipulated by programs (e.g., the Cyclist prover [18]), they also encode the relationships between the program's memory and its operational behavior via bespoke symbolic-execution inference rules [10,65].

To demonstrate the capabilities and benefits of the TcC framework for verification and automated proof search, we present the following example, posed in [47, Sec. 3]. The example consists of proving that the two recursive programs given in Figure 4 (weakly) simulate one another. Both programs continually read the next input, compute the double of the sum of all inputs seen so far, and output the current sum. On input zero, both programs count down to zero and start over. The goal is to formally verify that $g(m)$ is equivalent to $f(2m)$. However, as noted in [47], a formal proof of this claim via the standard Tarskian coinduction principle is extremely laborious. This is mainly because one must come up with an appropriate "simulation relation" that contains all the intermediate execution steps of f and g, appropriately matched, which must be fully defined before we can even start the proof.

The (co)closure operators offer a formalization of the problem which is very natural and amenable to automation, formalizing the programs by encoding all (infinite) traces of f and g as streams of input/output events. Hence, the simulation amounts to the fact that each such stream for f can be simulated by g, and vice versa. The bottom part of Figure 4 shows the formalization of the specification in TcC logic, where the encoding of each program is a natural simplification that can easily (and automatically) be obtained from either structural operational semantics or Floyd–Hoare-style axiomatic semantics. We use $\perp$ as a designated unreachable element (i.e., an element not related to any other element). The fact

---

[7] Notable exceptions include [66,76,20,21,22], which take a similar approach but invoke second-order elements.

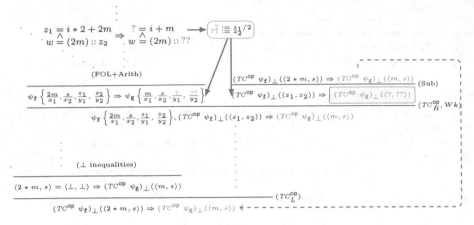

Fig. 5: Structure of the proof of one direction of SPEC

that the (co)closure operators can be applied to complex formulas that include, for example, quantifiers, disjunctions and nesting of the (co)closure operators, enables a concise, natural presentation without resorting to complex case analysis. This offers a significant *a priori* simplification of the formula we provide to the proof system (and, in turn, to a prover), even before starting the proof-search procedure.

The cyclic proof system, in turn, enables a natural treatment of the coinductive reasoning involved in the proof, in a way that is particularly amenable to automation. Figure 5 outlines the structure of the proof of one direction of the equivalence defined in SPEC. For conciseness, the subscripts $\langle x_1, x_2 \rangle, \langle y_1, y_2 \rangle$ are omitted from all TC^{op} formulas and we use $(TC^{op} \varphi)_\perp(\langle u, v \rangle)$ as a shorthand for $(TC^{op} \varphi)(\langle u, v \rangle, \langle \perp, \perp \rangle)$. The proof is compact and the local reasoning is standard: namely, the unfolding of the TC^{op} operator. The proof begins with a single unfolding of the TC^{op} formula on the left and then proceeds with its unfolding on the right. The key observation is that the instantiation of the unfolding on the right (i.e., the choice of the term r in Rule (TC_R^{op})) can be automatically inferred from the terms of the left unfolding, by unification. Thus, when applying Rule (TC_R^{op}), one does not have to guess the intermediate term (in this case, $\langle z_1/2, z_2 \rangle$); instead, the term can be automatically inferred from the equalities in the subproof of the single-step implication, as illustrated by the green question marks in Figure 5.

Finally, to formally establish the correctness of our simplified formalization, one needs to prove that, for example, the abstract $\mathtt{RES}(n, s, s')$ is indeed equivalent to the concrete program restart on f and on g. This can be formalized and proved in a straightforward manner, as the proof has a dual structure and contains a TC cycle. This further demonstrates the compositionality of TcC framework, as such an inductive subproof is completely independent of the general, outer coinductive TC^{op} cycle.

5 Perspectives and Open Questions

As mentioned, the approach of non-well-founded proof theory holds great potential for improving the state-of-the-art in formal support for automated inductive and coinductive reasoning. But the investigation of cyclic proof systems is far from complete, and much work is still required to provide a full picture. This section concludes by describing two key research questions, one concerning the applicability of the framework and the other concerning the fundamental theoretical study of the framework.

5.1 Implementing Non-well-founded Machinery

Current theorem provers offer little or no support for implicit reasoning. Thus, major verification efforts are missing its great potential for lighter, more legible and more automated proofs. The main implementation of cyclic reasoning can be found in the cyclic theorem prover Cyclist [18], which is a *fully automated* prover for inductive reasoning based on the cyclic framework developed in [15,16,19]. Cyclist has been very successful in formal verification in the setting of separation logic. Cyclic inductive reasoning has also been partially implemented into the Coq proof assistant through the development of external libraries and functional schemas [77]. Both implementations do not support coinductive reasoning, however.

To guarantee soundness, and decide whether a cyclic pre-proof satisfies the global trace condition, most cyclic proof systems feature a mechanism that uses a construction involving an inclusion between Büchi automata (see, for example, [15,74]). This mechanism can be (and has been) applied successfully in automated frameworks, but it lacks the transparency and flexibility that one needs in *interactive* theorem proving. For example, encoding proof validity into Büchi automata makes it difficult to understand why a cyclic proof is invalid in order to attempt to fix it. Therefore, to fully integrate cyclic reasoning into modern *interactive* theorem provers in a useful manner, an intrinsic criterion for soundness must be developed, which does not require the use of automata but instead operates directly on the proof tree.

5.2 Relative Power of Explicit and Implicit Reasoning

In general, explicit schemes for induction and coinduction are subsumed by their implicit counterparts. The converse, however, does not hold in general. In [19], it was conjectured that the explicit and cyclic systems for FOL with inductive definitions are equivalent. Later, they were indeed shown to be equivalent *when containing arithmetics* [19], where the embedding of the cyclic system in the explicit one relied on an encoding of the cycles in the proof. However, it was also shown, via a concrete counter-example, that in the general case the cyclic system is strictly stronger than the explicit one [9]. But a careful examination of this counter-example reveals that it only refutes a weak form of the conjecture, according to which the inductive definitions available in both systems are the same. That is, if the explicit system is extended with other inductive predicates, the counter-example for the equivalence no longer holds. Therefore, the less strict formulation of the question—namely, whether for any proof in the cyclic system there is a proof in the explicit system *for some set of inductive predicates*—has not yet been resolved. In particular, in the TcC setting, while the equivalence under arithmetics also holds, the fact that there is no *a priori* restriction on the (co)inductive predicates one is allowed to use makes the construction of a similar counter-example in the general case much more difficult. In fact, the explicit and cyclic systems may even coincide for TcC logic.

Even in cases where explicit (co)induction can capture implicit (co)induction (or a fragment of it), there are still open questions regarding the manner in which this capturing preserves certain patterns. A key question is whether the capturing can be done while preserving important properties such as proof modularity. Current discourse contains only partial answers to such questions [75,77,68] which should be investigated thoroughly and systematically. The uniformity provided by the closure operators in the TcC setting can facilitate a study of this subtle relationship between implicit and explicit (co)inductive reasoning.

Acknowledgements. As mentioned in the introduction, the TcC framework is based on a wonderful ongoing collaboration with Reuben Rowe. The author is also extremely grateful to Andrei Popescu and Shachar Itzhaky for their contributions to the framework.

References

1. Andreas Abel and Brigitte Pientka. Well-founded Recursion with Copatterns and Sized Types. *Journal of Functional Programming*, 26:e2, 2016.
2. Bahareh Afshari and Graham E. Leigh. Circular Proofs for the Modal Mu-Calculus. *Pamm*, 16:893–894, 2016.
3. Bahareh Afshari and Graham E. Leigh. Cut-free Completeness for Modal Mu-calculus. In *Proceedings of the 32nd Annual ACM/IEEE Symposium on Logic in Computer Science, LICS 2017*, pages 1–12, 2017.
4. Jeremy Avigad, Mario Carneiro, and Simon Hudon. Data Types as Quotients of Polynomial Functors. In J. Harrison, J. O'Leary, and A. Tolmach, editors, *10th International Conference on Interactive Theorem Proving (ITP '19)*, volume 141 of *Leibniz International Proceedings in Informatics*, pages 6:1–6:19, Dagstuhl, 2019.
5. Arnon Avron. Transitive Closure and the Mechanization of Mathematics. In F. D. Kamareddine, editor, *Thirty Five Years of Automating Mathematics*, volume 28 of *Applied Logic Series*, pages 149–171. Springer, Netherlands, 2003.
6. David Baelde. Least and Greatest Fixed Points in Linear Logic. *ACM Trans. Comput. Logic*, 13(1):2:1–2:44, Jan 2012.
7. David Baelde, Amina Doumane, and Alexis Saurin. Infinitary Proof Theory: the Multiplicative Additive Case. In *Proceedings of the 25th EACSL Annual Conference on Computer Science Logic, CSL 2016*, pages 42:1–42:17, 2016.
8. Henning Basold, Ekaterina Komendantskaya, and Yue Li. Coinduction in Uniform: Foundations for Corecursive Proof Search with Horn Clauses. In L. Caires, editor, *Programming Languages and Systems*, pages 783–813, Cham, 2019.

9. Stefano Berardi and Makoto Tatsuta. Classical System of Martin-Löf's Inductive Definitions Is Not Equivalent to Cyclic Proof System. In *Proceedings of the 20th International Conference on Foundations of Software Science and Computation Structures, FOSSACS 2017*, pages 301–317, Berlin, Heidelberg, 2017.

10. Josh Berdine, Cristiano Calcagno, and Peter W. O'Hearn. Symbolic Execution with Separation Logic. In K. Yi, editor, *Programming Languages and Systems*, pages 52–68, Berlin, Heidelberg, 2005.

11. Yves Bertot and Ekaterina Komendantskaya. Inductive and Coinductive Components of Corecursive Functions in Coq. *Electronic Notes in Theoretical Computer Science*, 203(5):25 – 47, 2008. Proceedings of the Ninth Workshop on Coalgebraic Methods in Computer Science (CMCS 2008).

12. Jasmin C. Blanchette, Aymeric Bouzy, Andreas Lochbihler, Andrei Popescu, and Dmitriy Traytel. Friends with Benefits. In H. Yang, editor, *Programming Languages and Systems*, pages 111–140, Berlin, Heidelberg, 2017.

13. Jasmin C. Blanchette, Johannes Hölzl, Andreas Lochbihler, Lorenz Panny, Andrei Popescu, and Dmitriy Traytel. Truly Modular (Co)datatypes for Isabelle/HOL. In G. Klein and R. Gamboa, editors, *Interactive Theorem Proving*, pages 93–110, Cham, 2014.

14. James Brotherston. Cyclic Proofs for First-Order Logic with Inductive Definitions. In Bernhard Beckert, editor, *Automated Reasoning with Analytic Tableaux and Related Methods*, pages 78–92, Berlin, Heidelberg, 2005. Springer Berlin Heidelberg.

15. James Brotherston. Formalised Inductive Reasoning in the Logic of Bunched Implications. In Hanne Riis Nielson and Gilberto Filé, editors, *Proceedings of Static Analysis, 14th International Symposium, SAS 2007, Kongens Lyngby, Denmark, August 22-24, 2007*, pages 87–103, 2007.

16. James Brotherston, Richard Bornat, and Cristiano Calcagno. Cyclic Proofs of Program Termination in Separation Logic. In *Proceedings of the 35th ACM SIGPLAN-SIGACT Symposium on Principles of Programming Languages, POPL 2008*, pages 101–112, 2008.

17. James Brotherston, Dino Distefano, and Rasmus Lerchedahl Petersen. Automated Cyclic Entailment Proofs in Separation Logic. In Nikolaj Bjørner and Viorica Sofronie-Stokkermans, editors, *Automated Deduction – CADE-23*, pages 131–146, Berlin, Heidelberg, 2011. Springer Berlin Heidelberg.

18. James Brotherston, Nikos Gorogiannis, and Rasmus L. Petersen. A Generic Cyclic Theorem Prover. In R. Jhala and A. Igarashi, editors, *Programming Languages and Systems*, pages 350–367, Berlin, Heidelberg, 2012.

19. James Brotherston and Alex Simpson. Sequent Calculi for Induction and Infinite Descent. *Journal of Logic and Computation*, 21(6):1177–1216, 2010.

20. Xiaohong Chen and Grigore Roşu. Matching μ-Logic. In *2019 34th Annual ACM/IEEE Symposium on Logic in Computer Science (LICS)*, pages 1–13, 2019.

21. Xiaohong Chen and Grigore Roşu. Matching μ-Logic: Foundation of K Framework. In M. Roggenbach and A. Sokolova, editors, *8th Conference on Algebra and Coalgebra in Computer Science (CALCO)*, volume 139 of *Leibniz International Proceedings in Informatics*, pages 1:1–1:4, Dagstuhl, 2019.

22. Xiaohong Chen, Minh-Thai Trinh, Nishant Rodrigues, Lucas Peña, and Grigore Roşu. Towards A Unified Proof Framework for Automated Fixpoint Reasoning Using Matching Logic. In *PACMPL Issue OOPSLA 2020*, pages 1–29. ACM/IEEE, Nov 2020.

23. Liron Cohen. Completeness for Ancestral Logic via a Computationally-Meaningful Semantics. In Renate A. Schmidt and Cláudia Nalon, editors, *Proceedings of the*

26th International Conference on Automated Reasoning with Analytic Tableaux and Related Methods, TABLEAUX 2017, pages 247–260, Cham, 2017.

24. Liron Cohen and Arnon Avron. Ancestral Logic: A Proof Theoretical Study. In Ulrich Kohlenbach, Pablo Barceló, and Ruy de Queiroz, editors, *Logic, Language, Information, and Computation*, volume 8652 of *Lecture Notes in Computer Science*, pages 137–151. Springer, 2014.

25. Liron Cohen and Arnon Avron. The Middle Ground–Ancestral Logic. *Synthese*, 196:2671–2693, 2015.

26. Liron Cohen and Reuben N. S. Rowe. Uniform Inductive Reasoning in Transitive Closure Logic via Infinite Descent. In *Proceedings of the 27th EACSL Annual Conference on Computer Science Logic, CSL 2018*, pages 16:1–16:17, 2018.

27. Liron Cohen and Reuben N. S. Rowe. Integrating Induction and Coinduction via Closure Operators and Proof Cycles. In N. Peltier and V. Sofronie-Stokkermans, editors, *Automated Reasoning*, volume 21, pages 375–394, Cham, 2020.

28. Liron Cohen and Reuben N. S. Rowe. Non-Well-Founded Proof Theory of Transitive Closure Logic. *ACM Trans. Comput. Logic*, 21(4), August 2020.

29. Liron Cohen, Reuben N. S. Rowe, and Yoni Zohar. Towards Automated Reasoning in Herbrand Structures. *Journal of Logic and Computation*, 29(5):693–721, 2019.

30. Robert L. Constable, Stuart F. Allen, and Mark Bromley et al. *Implementing mathematics with the Nuprl proof development system*. Prentice-Hall, Inc., Upper Saddle River, NJ, USA, 1986.

31. Anupam Das. On the logical complexity of cyclic arithmetic. *Logical Methods in Computer Science*, Volume 16, Issue 1, January 2020.

32. Anupam Das and Damien Pous. A Cut-Free Cyclic Proof System for Kleene Algebra. In Renate A. Schmidt and Cláudia Nalon, editors, *Proceedings of the 26th International Conference Automated Reasoning with Analytic Tableaux and Related Methods, TABLEAUX 2017*, pages 261–277, 2017.

33. Anupam Das and Damien Pous. Non-Wellfounded Proof Theory for (Kleene+Action)(Algebras+Lattices). In Dan Ghica and Achim Jung, editors, *Proceedings of the 27th EACSL Annual Conference on Computer Science Logic, CSL 2018*, volume 119, pages 19:1–19:18. Schloss Dagstuhl–Leibniz-Zentrum fuer Informatik, 2018.

34. Christian Dax, Martin Hofmann, and Martin Lange. A Proof System for the Linear Time μ-Calculus. In S. Arun-Kumar and Naveen Garg, editors, *FSTTCS 2006: Foundations of Software Technology and Theoretical Computer Science*, pages 273–284, Berlin, Heidelberg, 2006. Springer Berlin Heidelberg.

35. Amina Doumane. Constructive Completeness for the Linear-time μ-calculus. In *Proceedings of the 32nd Annual ACM/IEEE Symposium on Logic in Computer Science, LICS 2017*, pages 1–12, 2017.

36. Amina Doumane. *On the Infinitary Proof Theory of Logics with Fixed Points*. PhD thesis, 06 2017.

37. Amina Doumane, David Baelde, Lucca Hirschi, and Alexis Saurin. Towards Completeness via Proof Search in the Linear Time μ-Calculus: The Case of Büchi Inclusions. In *Proceedings of the 31st Annual ACM/IEEE Symposium on Logic in Computer Science*, LICS '16, page 377–386, New York, NY, USA, 2016. Association for Computing Machinery.

38. Sólrún Halla Einarsdóttir, Moa Johansson, and Johannes Åman Pohjola. Into the Infinite - Theory Exploration for Coinduction. In Jacques Fleuriot, Dongming Wang, and Jacques Calmet, editors, *Artificial Intelligence and Symbolic Computation*, pages 70–86, Cham, 2018. Springer International Publishing.

39. Jörg Endrullis, Helle Hvid Hansen, Dimitri Hendriks, Andrew Polonsky, and Alexandre Silva. Coinductive Foundations of Infinitary Rewriting and Infinitary Equational Logic. *Logical Methods in Computer Science*, Volume 14, Issue 1, January 2018.
40. Solomon Feferman. Finitary Inductively presented Logics. *Studies in Logic and the Foundations of Mathematics*, 127:191–220, 1989.
41. Jérôme Fortier and Luigi Santocanale. Cuts for Circular Proofs: Semantics and Cut-elimination. In S. Ronchi D. Rocca, editor, *Computer Science Logic 2013 (CSL 2013)*, volume 23 of *Leibniz International Proceedings in Informatics (LIPIcs)*, pages 248–262, Dagstuhl, Germany, 2013.
42. Vladimir Gapeyev, Michael Y Levin, and Benjamin C Pierce. Recursive Subtyping Revealed. *Journal of Functional Programming*, 12(6):511–548, 2002.
43. Pranav Garg, Christof Löding, P Madhusudan, and Daniel Neider. ICE: A Robust Framework for Learning Invariants. In Armin Biere and Roderick Bloem, editors, *International Conference on Computer Aided Verification*, pages 69–87, Cham, 2014. Springer, Springer International Publishing.
44. Gerhard Gentzen. Untersuchungen über das Logische Schließen. I. *Mathematische Zeitschrift*, 39(1):176–210, 1935.
45. Arie Gurfinkel and Alexander Ivrii. K-Induction without Unrolling. In *Proceedings of the 17th Conference on Formal Methods in Computer-Aided Design*, FMCAD '17, page 148–155, Austin, Texas, 2017. FMCAD Inc.
46. Quentin Heath and Dale Miller. A Proof Theory for Model Checking. *J. Autom. Reasoning*, 63(4):857–885, 2019.
47. Chung-Kil Hur, Georg Neis, Derek Dreyer, and Viktor Vafeiadis. The Power of Parameterization in Coinductive Proof. In *Proceedings of the 40th Annual ACM SIGPLAN-SIGACT Symposium on Principles of Programming Languages*, POPL '13, page 193–206, New York, NY, USA, 2013.
48. Neil Immerman. Languages that Capture Complexity Classes. *SIAM Journal on Computing*, 16(4):760–778, 1987.
49. Bart Jacobs and Jan Rutten. A Tutorial on (Co) Algebras and (Co) Induction. *Bulletin of the European Association for Theoretical Computer Science*, 62:222–259, 1997.
50. Aleksandr Karbyshev, Nikolaj Bjørner, Shachar Itzhaky, Noam Rinetzky, and Sharon Shoham. Property-Directed Inference of Universal Invariants or Proving Their Absence. *J. ACM*, 64(1), March 2017.
51. Dexter Kozen. Results on the Propositional μ-Calculus. In M. Nielsen and E. M. Schmidt, editors, *Automata, Languages and Programming*, pages 348–359, Berlin, Heidelberg, 1982.
52. Dexter Kozen and Alexandra Silva. Practical Coinduction. *Mathematical Structures in Computer Science*, 27(7):1132–1152, 2017.
53. Clemens Kupke and Jurriaan Rot. Expressive Logics for Coinductive Predicates. In M. Fernández and A. Muscholl, editors, *28th EACSL Annual Conference on Computer Science Logic (CSL 2020)*, volume 152 of *Leibniz International Proceedings in Informatics*, pages 26:1–26:18, Dagstuhl, 2020.
54. Rustan Leino and Michal Moskal. Co-Induction Simply: Automatic Co-Inductive Proofs in a Program Verifier. Technical Report MSR-TR-2013-49, Microsoft Research, July 2013.
55. Xavier Leroy. A Formally Verified Compiler Back-End. *J. Autom. Reason.*, 43(4):363–446, December 2009.
56. Xavier Leroy and Hervé Grall. Coinductive Big-Step Operational Semantics. *Information and Computation*, 207(2):284–304, 2009.

57. Thomas Letan and Yann Régis-Gianas. Freespec: Specifying, verifying, and executing impure computations in coq. In *Proceedings of the 9th ACM SIGPLAN International Conference on Certified Programs and Proofs*, CPP 2020, page 32–46, New York, NY, USA, 2020. Association for Computing Machinery.

58. Dorel Lucanu and Grigore Roşu. CIRC: A Circular Coinductive Prover. In Till Mossakowski, Ugo Montanari, and Magne Haveraaen, editors, *International Conference on Algebra and Coalgebra in Computer Science*, pages 372–378. Springer, 2007.

59. Per Martin-Löf. Hauptsatz for the Intuitionistic Theory of Iterated Inductive Definitions. In J. E. Fenstad, editor, *Proceedings of the Second Scandinavian Logic Symposium*, volume 63 of *Studies in Logic and the Foundations of Mathematics*, pages 179–216. Elsevier, 1971.

60. Raymond McDowell and Dale Miller. Cut-elimination for a Logic with Definitions and Induction. *Theoretical Computer Science*, 232(1-2):91–119, 2000.

61. Alberto Momigliano and Alwen Tiu. Induction and Co-Induction in Sequent Calculus. In Stefano Berardi, Mario Coppo, and Ferruccio Damiani, editors, *International Workshop on Types for Proofs and Programs*, pages 293–308. Springer, 2003.

62. Rémi Nollet, Christine Tasson, and Alexis Saurin. PSPACE-Completeness of a Thread Criterion for Circular Proofs in Linear Logic with Least and Greatest Fixed Points. In Serenella Cerrito and Andrei Popescu, editors, *Proceedings of the 27th International Conference on Automated Reasoning with Analytic Tableaux and Related Methods, TABLEAUX 2019*, pages 317–334. Springer, 2019.

63. Oded Padon, Kenneth L. McMillan, Aurojit Panda, Mooly Sagiv, and Sharon Shoham. Ivy: Safety Verification by Interactive Generalization. In *Proceedings of the 37th ACM SIGPLAN Conference on Programming Language Design and Implementation*, PLDI '16, page 614–630, NY, USA, 2016.

64. David Michael Ritchie Park. Finiteness is Mu-Ineffable. *Theor. Comput. Sci.*, 3(2):173–181, 1976.

65. John C. Reynolds. Separation Logic: A Logic for Shared Mutable Data Structures. In *Proceedings 17th Annual IEEE Symposium on Logic in Computer Science*, pages 55–74. IEEE, 2002.

66. Grigore Roşu, Andrei Stefanescu, Stefan Ciobâca, and Brandon M. Moore. One-Path Reachability Logic. In *Proceedings of the 28th Annual ACM/IEEE Symposium on Logic in Computer Science*, LICS '13, page 358–367, USA, 2013.

67. Grigore Roşu and Dorel Lucanu. Circular Coinduction: A Proof Theoretical Foundation. In Alexander Kurz, Marina Lenisa, and Andrzej Tarlecki, editors, *Proceedings of Algebra and Coalgebra in Computer Science, CALCO'09*, pages 127–144. Springer, 2009.

68. Reuben N. S. Rowe and James Brotherston. Automatic Cyclic Termination Proofs for Recursive Procedures in Separation Logic. In *Proceedings of the 6th ACM SIGPLAN Conference on Certified Programs and Proofs, CPP 2017, Paris, France, January 16–17, 2017*, pages 53–65, 2017.

69. Jan Rutten. Universal Coalgebra: a Theory of Systems. *Theoretical computer science*, 249(1):3–80, 2000.

70. Jan Rutten. *The Method of Coalgebra: Exercises in Coinduction*. Amsterdam: CWI, Netherlands, 2019.

71. Davide Sangiorgi and Jan Rutten. *Advanced Topics in Bisimulation and Coinduction*. Cambridge University Press, USA, 1st edition, 2011.

72. Luigi Santocanale. A Calculus of Circular Proofs and Its Categorical Semantics. In Mogens Nielsen and Uffe Engberg, editors, *Proceedings of the 5th International Con-*

ference on Foundations of Software Science and Computation Structures, FOSSACS 2002, pages 357–371, Berlin, Heidelberg, 2002. Springer Berlin Heidelberg.

73. Stewart Shapiro. *Foundations without Foundationalism: A Case for Second-order Logic*, volume 17. Clarendon Press, 1991.

74. Alex Simpson. Cyclic Arithmetic Is Equivalent to Peano Arithmetic. In *Proceedings of the 20th International Conference on Foundations of Software Science and Computation Structures - Volume 10203*, page 283–300, Berlin, Heidelberg, 2017.

75. Christoph Sprenger and Mads Dam. On the Structure of Inductive Reasoning: Circular and Tree-shaped Proofs in the μ-Calculus. In *Proceedings of Foundations of Software Science and Computational Structures, 6th International Conference, FOSSACS 2003*, pages 425–440, 2003.

76. Andrei Ştefănescu, Ştefan Ciobâcă, Radu Mereuta, Brandon M. Moore, Traian Florin Şerbănută, and Grigore Roşu. All-Path Reachability Logic. In G. Dowek, editor, *Rewriting and Typed Lambda Calculi*, pages 425–440, Cham, 2014.

77. Sorin Stratulat. Structural vs. Cyclic Induction: A Report on Some Experiments with Coq. In *2016 18th International Symposium on Symbolic and Numeric Algorithms for Scientific Computing (SYNASC)*, pages 29–36, 2016.

78. Gadi Tellez and James Brotherston. Automatically Verifying Temporal Properties of Pointer Programs with Cyclic Proof. In *Proceedings of the 26th International Conference on Automated Deduction, CADE 26, Gothenburg, Sweden, August 6–11, 2017*, pages 491–508, 2017.

79. Alwen Tiu. *A Logical Framework For Reasoning About Logical Specifications*. PhD thesis, Penn. State University, 2004.

80. Alwen Tiu and Alberto Momigliano. Cut Elimination for a Logic with Induction and Co-induction. *Journal of Applied Logic*, 10(4):330–367, 2012.

81. Dmitriy Traytel, Andrei Popescu, and Jasmin C. Blanchette. Foundational, Compositional (Co)datatypes for Higher-Order Logic: Category Theory Applied to Theorem Proving. In *2012 27th Annual IEEE Symposium on Logic in Computer Science*, pages 596–605, 2012.

82. Li-yao Xia, Yannick Zakowski, Paul He, Chung-Kil Hur, Gregory Malecha, Benjamin C. Pierce, and Steve Zdancewic. Interaction Trees: Representing Recursive and Impure Programs in Coq. *Proc. ACM Program. Lang.*, 4(POPL), December 2019.

83. Yannick Zakowski, Paul He, Chung-Kil Hur, and Steve Zdancewic. An Equational Theory for Weak Bisimulation via Generalized Parameterized Coinduction. In *Proceedings of the 9th ACM SIGPLAN International Conference on Certified Programs and Proofs*, CPP 2020, page 71–84, NY, USA, 2020.

Open Access This chapter is licensed under the terms of the Creative Commons Attribution 4.0 International License (`http://creativecommons.org/licenses/by/4.0/`), which permits use, sharing, adaptation, distribution and reproduction in any medium or format, as long as you give appropriate credit to the original author(s) and the source, provide a link to the Creative Commons license and indicate if changes were made.

The images or other third party material in this chapter are included in the chapter's Creative Commons license, unless indicated otherwise in a credit line to the material. If material is not included in the chapter's Creative Commons license and your intended use is not permitted by statutory regulation or exceeds the permitted use, you will need to obtain permission directly from the copyright holder.

Towards the Automatic Mathematician

Markus N. Rabe[iD] and Christian Szegedy[iD]

Google Research
Mountain View, California, USA
{mrabe,szegedy}@google.com

Abstract. Over the recent years deep learning has found successful applications in mathematical reasoning. Today, we can predict fine-grained proof steps, relevant premises, and even useful conjectures using neural networks. This extended abstract summarizes recent developments of machine learning in mathematical reasoning and the vision of the N2Formal group at Google Research to create an automatic mathematician. The second part discusses the key challenges on the road ahead.

Keywords: Automated reasoning · machine learning · mathematical reasoning · theorem proving · natural language understanding.

1 Introduction

The combination of machine learning and mathematical reasoning goes back at least to the 2000s when Stephan Schulz pioneered ideas to use machine learning to control the search process [44], and Josef Urban used machine learning to select relevant axioms [46,47]. With the advent of deep learning, interest in the area surged, as deep learning promises to enable the automatic discovery of new knowledge from data, while requiring minimal engineering. This suddenly offered a flurry of new possibilities also for theorem proving.

One of the most challenging and impactful tasks in automated theorem proving is *premise selection*, that is to find relevant premises from a large body of available theorems/axioms. Many classical reasoning systems do not scale well into thousands of potentially relevant facts, but some pioneering results by Urban et al. [47] proposed fast machine learning techniques using manually engineered features. However, with the inroads of deep learning, it has become clear that large quality improvements are possible by utilizing deep learning techniques. DeepMath [24] demonstrated that premise selection could be tackled with deep learning, directly (i.e., without feature engineering) applying neural networks to the text of the premise and that of the (negated) conjecture.

In DeepMath, both premise and conjecture are embedded into a vector space by a (potentially expensive) neural network and then a second (preferably cheap) neural network compares the embedding of the current state to each available premise to judge whether the premise is useful. Loos et al. [36] for the first time, demonstrated that the same approach as DeepMath yields substantial improvements as an internal guidance method within a first-order automated theorem prover.

© The Author(s) 2021
A. Platzer and G. Sutcliffe (Eds.): CADE 2021, LNAI 12699, pp. 25–37, 2021.
https://doi.org/10.1007/978-3-030-79876-5_2

Neural Theorem Provers. Emboldened by these early works and by break-throughs in deep learning, several groups extended interactive theorem provers[1] for the use in deep learning research, including Gamepad [23], HOList [5], Coq-Gym [54], GPT-f [39], and recently TacticZero [51]. A typical tactic application predicted by these systems looks as follows (here in HOL Light syntax):

$$\underbrace{\texttt{REWRITE\_TAC}}_{tactic\ name}\ \underbrace{\texttt{[PREMISE1 ; PREMISE2]}}_{list\ of\ premises}$$

This specific tactic expects the given premises to be equalities, with which it attempts to rewrite subexpressions in the current proof goal. The hard part about predicting good tactics is to select the right list of premises from all the previously proven theorems. Some tactics also include free-form expressions, which can be a challenge as well.

In contrast to approaches using lightweight machine learning approaches (e.g. [13,25,26,38,31]), neural theorem provers aim to replicate the human approach to proving theorems in ITPs, searching only through a relatively small number (e.g., hundreds) of proof steps that are very promising. To get high-quality proof steps, increasingly large neural networks (currently up to 774M parameters [39]) are trained on human proofs, or with reinforcement learning.

Already, neural theorem provers can prove a significant portion (up to 70% [4]) of test theorems and some have found proofs that are shorter and more elegant than the proofs that human mathematicians have formalized in these systems. For example, for the theorem CLOSURE_CONVEX_INTER_AFFINE, proven with over 40 tactic calls in HOL Light [20], HOList/DeepHOL has found a proof with just two tactic calls:

```
let CLOSURE_CONVEX_INTER_AFFINE = prove
  ('!s t:real^N->bool.
      convex s /\ affine t /\ ~(relative_interior s INTER t = {})
      ==> closure(s INTER t) = closure(s) INTER t',

    SIMP_TAC [INTER_COMM; AFFINE_IMP_CONVEX;
              CLOSURE_INTER_CONVEX; RELATIVE_INTERIOR_AFFINE]

    THEN

    ASM_MESON_TAC [RELATIVE_INTERIOR_EQ_CLOSURE; INTER_COMM;
                   RELATIVE_INTERIOR_UNIV; IS_AFFINE_HULL]);;
```

---

[1] The focus has been on interactive theorem provers as they are general enough to capture most of mathematics in theory, and several large-scale formalization efforts of the last decades have demonstrated that involved theories can be formalized in practice [28,14,19]. Also ITPs offer relatively short proofs compared to other automated reasoning tools, which allows us to use stronger neural networks for the same computational budget.

Similarly, Polu et al. reported several cases where they found proofs with their neural theorem prover GPT-f that were shorter and more elegant than than those found by humans [39].

Neural Solvers. Closely related to neural theorem provers are methods that, instead of predicting proof steps, directly predict the solution to mathematical problems. A first impressive example was proposed by Selsam et al., who showed that graph neural networks can predict satisfying assignments of small Boolean formulas [45]. Lample and Charton have demonstrated that also higher-level representations, such as the integral of a formula, can be predicted directly using a Transformer [29]. They exploited the fact that for some mathematical operations, such as taking the integral, the inverse operation (taking the derivative) is much easier. Hence, they can train on predicting generated formulas from their derivative without needing a tool that can generate the integral in the first place. Recently, Hahn et al. demonstrated that also classical verification problems, such as LTL satisfiability, can be solved directly with Transformers, beating existing tuned algorithms on their own dataset in some cases [18].

2   Towards the Automatic Mathematician

We are convinced that the success of neural theorem provers and neural solvers is only the beginning of a larger development in which deep learning will revolutionize automated reasoning, and have set out to build an *automatic mathematician.* Ideally, we could simply talk to an automatic mathematician like a colleague, and it would be able to contribute to mathematical research, for example by publishing papers without human support.

An automatic mathematician would thus go far beyond theorem proving, as it would have to formulate and explore its own theories and conjectures, and be able to communicate in natural language. Yet, we believe that neural theorem provers are an important instrument of our plan, as they allow us to evaluate (generated) conjectures, which grounds the learning process in mathematically correct reasoning steps. And because neural theorem provers build on existing interactive theorem provers, they already come with a nucleus of formalized mathematics that we believe might be necessary to bootstrap the understanding of mathematics. In the following, we review some of the main challenges on the path towards an automatic mathematician and first approaches to address them.

2.1   Neural Network Architectures

Naturally, we need neural network architectures that can "understand" formulas, that is, make useful predictions based on formulas. The main question for the design of neural networks appears to be *whether* and, if yes, *how* to exploit the tree structure of formulas.

Exploiting the Structure of Formulas. It is tempting to believe that the embeddings of formulas should represent their semantics. Hence, many authors have suggested to process formulas with tree-structured recurrent neural networks (TreeRNNs), which compute embeddings of expressions from the embeddings of their subexpressions, as this resembles the bottom-up way we define their semantics (e.g., [11,1,23,54]). That intuition, however, may be misleading. In our experiments, bottom-up TreeRNNs have performed significantly worse than top-down architectures (followed by a max-pool aggregation) [37]. This suggests that, to make good predictions based on formulas, it is important to consider subformulas in their context, which bottom-up TreeRNNs cannot do easily.

Sequence Models. The alternative to representing the formula structure in the neural architecture is to interpret formulas simply as sequences of characters or symbols and apply sequence models. Early works using sequence modeling relied on convolutional networks (simple convolutional networks [24] and wave-nets [36,5]), which compared favorably to gated recurrent architectures like LSTM/GRU. With the recent rise of the Transformer architecture [48] sequence models have caught up to those that exploit the formula structure and yielded excellent performance in various settings [29,41,52,39,18].

Sequence models come with two major advantages: First, it is straightforward to not only read formulas, but also generate formulas, which is surprisingly challenging with TreeRNNs or graph neural networks. This allows us to directly predict proof steps as strings [39,52], and to tackle a wider range of mathematical reasoning tasks, such as predicting the integral of a formula [29], satisfying traces for formulas in linear temporal logics [18], or even more creative tasks, such as missing assumptions and conjectures [41].[2] Second, transformer models have shown a surprising flexibility and promise a uniform way to process not only formulas, but also natural language, and even images [10]. This could prove crucial for processing natural language mathematics, which frequently contains formulas, text, and diagrams, and any model processing papers would need to understand how they relate to each other. Transformers certainly set a high bar for the flexibility, generality, and performance of future neural architectures.

Large Models. Scaling up language models to larger and larger numbers of parameters has steadily improved their results [27,22]. Also when we use language models for mathematics, we have observed that larger models tend to improve the quality of predictions [39,41]. GPT-3 has shown that certain abilities, such as basic arithmetic, appear to only materialize in models with at least a certain number of parameters [6]. If this turns out to be true for other abilities, this raises the question how large models have to be to exhibit human-level mathematical reasoning abilities.

---

[2] Yet, there are still cases where hard-coding some formula structure in transformer architectures can improve the results, as shown, for example, by Wu et al. [21,35,18], which suggests that transformers are not the end of the story regarding formula understanding.

There is also the question of how exactly to scale up models. The mere number of parameters may not be as important as how we use them. More efficient alternatives to simply scaling up the transformer architecture might help with the problem to make large models accessible to more researchers (e.g., [32]).

2.2 Training Methodology

Neural networks have shown the ability to learn even advanced reasoning tasks via supervised learning, given the right training data. However, for many interesting tasks, we do not have such data and hence the question is how to train neural networks for tasks for which we have only limited data or no data at all.

Reinforcement Learning. Reinforcement learning can be seen as a way to reduce the amount of human-written proof data needed to learn a strong theorem prover. By training on the proofs generated by the system itself, we can improve its abilities to some extent, and the perhaps strongest neural theorem provers often use some form reinforcement learning (e.g., up to 70% of the proofs in HOL Light [4]). But, for an open-ended training methodology, we need a system that can effectively explore new and interesting theories, without getting lost in irrelevant branches of mathematics. Partial progress has been made in training systems without access to human-written proofs [4,51], and to generate conjectures to train on in a reinforcement learning setting [12], but the problem is wide-open.

Pretraining. In natural language understanding it is already common practice to pretrain transformers on a large body text before fine-tuning them on the final task, especially when only limited data is available for that task. Even though the pretraining data is only loosely related to the final tasks, transformers benefit a lot from pretraining, as it contains general world knowledge and useful inductive biases [9]. Polu et al. have shown that the same can be observed when pretraining transformers on natural language texts from arXiv [39].

Self-supervised Training. The GPT models for natural language have shown that self-supervised language modeling (i.e., only "pre"training without training on any particular task) alone can equip transformers with surprising abilities [42,6]. Mathematical reasoning abilities, including type inference, predicting missing assumptions and conjecturing, can be learned in a very similar way by training transformers to predict missing subexpressions (skip-tree training) [41].

Lample et al. devised several clever approaches to train transformers when data is not directly available. In unsupervised translation training transformers successfully learn to translate between different natural languages starting only with monolingual corpora and without any corresponding pairs of sentences [30]. This approach was even generalized to learn to translate between programming languages without corresponding pairs of programs in different languages [43]. The application of these unsupervised translation ideas to mathematics is tempting, but we experienced that their straight-forward application does not lead to good results. Also Wang et al. [49] report mixed results.

Learning to Retrieve Relevant Information. If we apply standard language models to mathematics, e.g., to predict the next proof step, we expect them to store all the information necessary to make good predictions in their parameters. As the large transformer models have shown (see, e.g., GPT [42,6]), this approach actually works pretty well for natural language question answering, and also for mathematical benchmarks it has been surprisingly successful [41,39,53]. However, there may be a limit to this approach in cases where we expect detailed, consistent, and up-to-date predictions. Guu et al. [17] introduced a hybrid of transformer and retrieval model, REALM, which learns to retrieve Wikipedia articles that are relevant to a given question and extract useful information from the article. REALM is trained self-supervised to retrieve multiple articles and try to use each of them individually to make predictions. The article that led to the best prediction is deemed to be the most relevant, and is used to train the retrieval query for future training iterations. This approach has been extended in follow-up work [33,2,34,3] and appears to be a promising approach also to retrieve the relevant context, such as definitions, possible premises, and even related proofs, for mathematical reasoning.

2.3   Instant Utilization of New Premises

Theorem proving has a key difference compared to other reinforcement learning settings: whenever we reach one of the goals, i.e., prove a theorem, we can use that goal as a premise for future proof attempts. Any learning method applied in a reinforcement learning setting for theorem proving thus needs the ability to adapt to this growing action space, and ideally does not need to be retrained at all when a new theorem becomes available to be used.

Premise selection approaches that are built on retrieval, such as DeepMath [24,36] and HOList [5,37], offer this ability: When a new theorem is proven, we can add it to the list of premises that can be retrieved and future retrieval queries can return the statement. This appears to work well, even when the provers are applied to a new set of theorems, as demonstrated by the DeepHOL prover when it was applied to the unseen Flyspeck theorem database [5]. We can even exploit this kind of generalization for exploration and bootstrap neural theorem provers without access to human proofs as training data [4].

A new challenge arises from the use of language models for theorem proving. Theorem provers using transformers currently have no dedicated retrieval module, and instead predict the statements or names of premises as part of the tactic string (cf. [39]). In our experience this does not provide the required generalization to unseen premises without retraining. (Though there are experiments that suggest that it might be possible [8].) Future approaches will have to find a way to combine the strong reasoning skills and generative abilities of Transformer models with the ability to use new premises without retraining.

2.4   Natural Language

We believe that, perhaps counterintuitively, natural language plays a central role in automated reasoning. The most direct reason is that only a small part of mathematics has been formalized so far, and a pragmatic approach to tap into much more training data is to find a way to learn from natural language mathematics (books and papers on mathematical topics). In this section, however, we want to look beyond the question of feasibility and training data, and discuss the broad advantages of a natural language approach to mathematics.

Accessibility. A bridge between natural and formal mathematics could help to make the system much more accessible, by not requiring the users to learn a specific formal language. This might open up mathematics to a much wider audience, enabling advanced mathematical assistants (think WolframAlpha [50]), and tools for education.

Vice versa, an advanced automatic mathematician without the ability to explain their reasoning in natural language might be hard to understand. Even if the system's predictions and theories are correct, sophisticated, and relevant, we might not be able to use them to inform our own understanding if the notions the system comes up with are only available as vast synthetic formal objects.

Conjecturing, Theory Exploration, and Interestingness. Various approaches have been suggested to produce new conjectures, including heuristic filters [40], deriving rules from data [7], and learning and sampling from a distribution of theorems using language modeling [41].

A particularly interesting idea is the use of adversarial training to generate conjectures (e.g., [12]). Here, two neural networks compete against each other— one with the aim to prove statements and the other with the aim to suggest hard-to-prove statements, somewhat akin to generative adversarial nets [15]. The idea is that the competition between the two networks generates a curriculum of harder and harder problems to solve and also automatically explores new parts of mathematics (as old parts get easier over time). However, there seems to be a catch: Once the network that suggests problems has figured out how to define a one-way function, it becomes very easy to produce an unlimited number of hard problems, such as to find an input to the SHA256 function that produces a certain output hash. This class of problems is almost impossible to solve, and thus likely leads the process into a dead-end.

Once again, natural language seems to be a possible answer. Using the large body of natural language mathematics could help to equip machine learning models with a notion of what human mathematicians find *interesting*, and focus on these areas.

Grounding Language Models. Autoformalization does not only produce formal objects as a desired outcome, it also serves the dual purpose to improve language models. Checking the models' outputs and feeding back their correctness as a training signal would provide valuable grounding for their understanding.

Of course, the gap between formalized and informal mathematics is huge: it will likely require a considerable level of effort to automatically create high quality formalizations. Also, we believe that we will likely need a very high quality theorem prover to bootstrap any autoformalization system. However, recent progress in neural language processing [9,42], unsupervised translation [30,43] and also neural network based symbolic mathematics [29,41,18,39] makes this path seem increasingly feasible and appealing in the long run.

3   Conclusion

In this extended abstract, we surveyed recent results in neural theorem proving and our mission to build an artificial mathematician, as well as some of the challenges on this path. While there is no guarantee that we can overcome these challenges, and there might be challenges that we cannot even anticipate yet, mere partial success to our mission could help the formal methods community with tools to simplify the formalization process, and impact adjacent areas, such as verification, program synthesis, and natural language understanding.

In a 2018 survey among AI researchers, the median prediction for when machines "routinely and autonomously prove mathematical theorems that are publishable in top mathematics journals today, including generating the theorems to prove" was in the 2060s [16]. However, over the last years, deep learning has already beaten a lot of expectations (at least ours) as to what is possible in automated reasoning. There are still several challenges to be solved, some of which we laid out in this abstract, but we believe that creating a truly intelligent artificial mathematician is within reach and will happen on a much shorter time frame than many experts expect.

References

1. Arabshahi, F., Singh, S., Anandkumar, A.: Combining symbolic expressions and black-box function evaluations in neural programs. In: 6th International Conference on Learning Representations, ICLR 2018, Vancouver, BC, Canada, April 30 - May 3, 2018, Conference Track Proceedings. OpenReview.net (2018), https://openreview.net/forum?id=Hksj2WWAW
2. Asai, A., Hashimoto, K., Hajishirzi, H., Socher, R., Xiong, C.: Learning to retrieve reasoning paths over wikipedia graph for question answering. In: 8th International Conference on Learning Representations, ICLR 2020, Addis Ababa, Ethiopia, April 26-30, 2020. OpenReview.net (2020), https://openreview.net/forum?id=SJgVHkrYDH
3. Balachandran, V., Vaswani, A., Tsvetkov, Y., Parmar, N.: Simple and efficient ways to improve REALM. CoRR **abs/2104.08710** (2021), https://arxiv.org/abs/2104.08710
4. Bansal, K., Loos, S.M., Rabe, M.N., Szegedy, C.: Learning to reason in large theories without imitation. CoRR **abs/1905.10501** (2019), http://arxiv.org/abs/1905.10501

5. Bansal, K., Loos, S.M., Rabe, M.N., Szegedy, C., Wilcox, S.: Holist: An environment for machine learning of higher order logic theorem proving. In: Chaudhuri, K., Salakhutdinov, R. (eds.) Proceedings of the 36th International Conference on Machine Learning, ICML 2019, 9-15 June 2019, Long Beach, California, USA. Proceedings of Machine Learning Research, vol. 97, pp. 454–463. PMLR (2019), http://proceedings.mlr.press/v97/bansal19a.html

6. Brown, T.B., Mann, B., Ryder, N., Subbiah, M., Kaplan, J., Dhariwal, P., Neelakantan, A., Shyam, P., Sastry, G., Askell, A., Agarwal, S., Herbert-Voss, A., Krueger, G., Henighan, T., Child, R., Ramesh, A., Ziegler, D.M., Wu, J., Winter, C., Hesse, C., Chen, M., Sigler, E., Litwin, M., Gray, S., Chess, B., Clark, J., Berner, C., McCandlish, S., Radford, A., Sutskever, I., Amodei, D.: Language models are few-shot learners. In: Larochelle, H., Ranzato, M., Hadsell, R., Balcan, M., Lin, H. (eds.) Advances in Neural Information Processing Systems 33: Annual Conference on Neural Information Processing Systems 2020, NeurIPS 2020, December 6-12, 2020, virtual (2020)

7. Brunton, S.L., Proctor, J.L., Kutz, J.N.: Discovering governing equations from data by sparse identification of nonlinear dynamical systems. Proceedings of the National Academy of Sciences **113**(15), 3932–3937 (2016). https://doi.org/10.1073/pnas.1517384113

8. Cao, N.D., Izacard, G., Riedel, S., Petroni, F.: Autoregressive entity retrieval. In: 9th International Conference on Learning Representations, ICLR 2021. OpenReview.net (2021)

9. Devlin, J., Chang, M., Lee, K., Toutanova, K.: BERT: pre-training of deep bidirectional transformers for language understanding. In: Burstein, J., Doran, C., Solorio, T. (eds.) Proceedings of the 2019 Conference of the North American Chapter of the Association for Computational Linguistics: Human Language Technologies, NAACL-HLT 2019, Minneapolis, MN, USA, June 2-7, 2019, Volume 1 (Long and Short Papers). pp. 4171–4186. Association for Computational Linguistics (2019). https://doi.org/10.18653/v1/n19-1423

10. Dosovitskiy, A., Beyer, L., Kolesnikov, A., Weissenborn, D., Zhai, X., Unterthiner, T., Dehghani, M., Minderer, M., Heigold, G., Gelly, S., Uszkoreit, J., Houlsby, N.: An image is worth 16x16 words: Transformers for image recognition at scale. In: 9th International Conference on Learning Representations, ICLR 2021. OpenReview.net (2021)

11. Evans, R., Saxton, D., Amos, D., Kohli, P., Grefenstette, E.: Can neural networks understand logical entailment? In: 6th International Conference on Learning Representations, ICLR 2018, Vancouver, BC, Canada, April 30 - May 3, 2018, Conference Track Proceedings. OpenReview.net (2018), https://openreview.net/forum?id=SkZxCk-0Z

12. Firoiu, V., Aygün, E., Anand, A., Ahmed, Z., Glorot, X., Orseau, L., Zhang, L., Precup, D., Mourad, S.: Training a first-order theorem prover from synthetic data. CoRR **abs/2103.03798** (2021), https://arxiv.org/abs/2103.03798

13. Gauthier, T., Kaliszyk, C., Urban, J.: TacticToe: Learning to reason with HOL4 tactics. In: Eiter, T., Sands, D. (eds.) LPAR-21, 21st International Conference on Logic for Programming, Artificial Intelligence and Reasoning, Maun, Botswana, May 7-12, 2017. EPiC Series in Computing, vol. 46, pp. 125–143. EasyChair (2017), https://easychair.org/publications/volume/LPAR-21

14. Gonthier, G., Asperti, A., Avigad, J., Bertot, Y., Cohen, C., Garillot, F., Roux, S.L., Mahboubi, A., O'Connor, R., Biha, S.O., Pasca, I., Rideau, L., Solovyev, A., Tassi, E., Théry, L.: A machine-checked proof of the odd order theorem. In: Blazy,

S., Paulin-Mohring, C., Pichardie, D. (eds.) Interactive Theorem Proving - 4th International Conference, ITP 2013, Rennes, France, July 22-26, 2013. Proceedings. Lecture Notes in Computer Science, vol. 7998, pp. 163–179. Springer (2013). https://doi.org/10.1007/978-3-642-39634-2_14

15. Goodfellow, I.J., Pouget-Abadie, J., Mirza, M., Xu, B., Warde-Farley, D., Ozair, S., Courville, A.C., Bengio, Y.: Generative adversarial nets. In: Ghahramani, Z., Welling, M., Cortes, C., Lawrence, N.D., Weinberger, K.Q. (eds.) Advances in Neural Information Processing Systems 27: Annual Conference on Neural Information Processing Systems 2014, December 8-13 2014, Montreal, Quebec, Canada. pp. 2672–2680 (2014)

16. Grace, K., Salvatier, J., Dafoe, A., Zhang, B., Evans, O.: Viewpoint: When will AI exceed human performance? evidence from AI experts. J. Artif. Intell. Res. **62**, 729–754 (2018). https://doi.org/10.1613/jair.1.11222

17. Guu, K., Lee, K., Tung, Z., Pasupat, P., Chang, M.: Retrieval augmented language model pre-training. In: Proceedings of the 37th International Conference on Machine Learning, ICML 2020, 13-18 July 2020, Virtual Event. Proceedings of Machine Learning Research, vol. 119, pp. 3929–3938. PMLR (2020), http://proceedings.mlr.press/v119/guu20a.html

18. Hahn, C., Schmitt, F., Kreber, J.U., Rabe, M.N., Finkbeiner, B.: Teaching temporal logics to neural networks. In: 9th International Conference on Learning Representations, ICLR 2021. OpenReview.net (2021)

19. Hales, T., Adams, M., Bauer, G., Dang, T.D., Harrison, J., Le Truong, H., Kaliszyk, C., Magron, V., McLaughlin, S., Nguyen, T.T., et al.: A formal proof of the Kepler conjecture. In: Forum of Mathematics, Pi. vol. 5, p. e2. Cambridge University Press (2017)

20. Harrison, J.: HOL Light: A tutorial introduction. In: Srivas, M.K., Camilleri, A.J. (eds.) Formal Methods in Computer-Aided Design, First International Conference, FMCAD '96, Palo Alto, California, USA, November 6-8, 1996, Proceedings. Lecture Notes in Computer Science, vol. 1166, pp. 265–269. Springer (1996)

21. Hellendoorn, V.J., Sutton, C., Singh, R., Maniatis, P., Bieber, D.: Global relational models of source code. In: 8th International Conference on Learning Representations, ICLR 2020, Addis Ababa, Ethiopia, April 26-30, 2020. OpenReview.net (2020), https://openreview.net/forum?id=B1lnbRNtwr

22. Henighan, T., Kaplan, J., Katz, M., Chen, M., Hesse, C., Jackson, J., Jun, H., Brown, T.B., Dhariwal, P., Gray, S., Hallacy, C., Mann, B., Radford, A., Ramesh, A., Ryder, N., Ziegler, D.M., Schulman, J., Amodei, D., McCandlish, S.: Scaling laws for autoregressive generative modeling. CoRR **abs/2010.14701** (2020), https://arxiv.org/abs/2010.14701

23. Huang, D., Dhariwal, P., Song, D., Sutskever, I.: Gamepad: A learning environment for theorem proving. In: 7th International Conference on Learning Representations, ICLR 2019, New Orleans, LA, USA, May 6-9, 2019. OpenReview.net (2019), https://openreview.net/forum?id=r1xwKoR9Y7

24. Irving, G., Szegedy, C., Alemi, A.A., Eén, N., Chollet, F., Urban, J.: Deepmath - deep sequence models for premise selection. In: Lee, D.D., Sugiyama, M., von Luxburg, U., Guyon, I., Garnett, R. (eds.) Advances in Neural Information Processing Systems 29: Annual Conference on Neural Information Processing Systems 2016, December 5-10, 2016, Barcelona, Spain. pp. 2235–2243 (2016)

25. Jakubuv, J., Urban, J.: ENIGMA: efficient learning-based inference guiding machine. In: Geuvers, H., England, M., Hasan, O., Rabe, F., Teschke, O. (eds.) Intelligent Computer Mathematics - 10th International Conference, CICM 2017, Edinburgh, UK, July 17-21, 2017, Proceedings. Lecture Notes in Computer Science,

vol. 10383, pp. 292–302. Springer (2017). https://doi.org/10.1007/978-3-319-62075-6_20

26. Kaliszyk, C., Urban, J., Michalewski, H., Olsák, M.: Reinforcement learning of theorem proving. In: Bengio, S., Wallach, H.M., Larochelle, H., Grauman, K., Cesa-Bianchi, N., Garnett, R. (eds.) Advances in Neural Information Processing Systems 31: Annual Conference on Neural Information Processing Systems 2018, NeurIPS 2018, December 3-8, 2018, Montréal, Canada. pp. 8836–8847 (2018)

27. Kaplan, J., McCandlish, S., Henighan, T., Brown, T.B., Chess, B., Child, R., Gray, S., Radford, A., Wu, J., Amodei, D.: Scaling laws for neural language models (2020), https://arxiv.org/abs/2001.08361

28. Klein, G., Elphinstone, K., Heiser, G., Andronick, J., Cock, D., Derrin, P., Elkaduwe, D., Engelhardt, K., Kolanski, R., Norrish, M., Sewell, T., Tuch, H., Winwood, S.: seL4: formal verification of an OS kernel. In: Matthews, J.N., Anderson, T.E. (eds.) Proceedings of the 22nd ACM Symposium on Operating Systems Principles 2009, SOSP 2009, Big Sky, Montana, USA, October 11-14, 2009. pp. 207–220. ACM (2009). https://doi.org/10.1145/1629575.1629596

29. Lample, G., Charton, F.: Deep learning for symbolic mathematics. In: 8th International Conference on Learning Representations, ICLR 2020, Addis Ababa, Ethiopia, April 26-30, 2020. OpenReview.net (2020), https://openreview.net/forum?id=S1eZYeHFDS

30. Lample, G., Conneau, A., Denoyer, L., Ranzato, M.: Unsupervised machine translation using monolingual corpora only. In: 6th International Conference on Learning Representations, ICLR 2018, Vancouver, BC, Canada, April 30 - May 3, 2018, Conference Track Proceedings. OpenReview.net (2018), https://openreview.net/forum?id=rkYTTf-AZ

31. Lederman, G., Rabe, M.N., Seshia, S., Lee, E.A.: Learning heuristics for quantified boolean formulas through reinforcement learning. In: 8th International Conference on Learning Representations, ICLR 2020, Addis Ababa, Ethiopia, April 26-30, 2020. OpenReview.net (2020), https://openreview.net/forum?id=BJluxREKDB

32. Lepikhin, D., Lee, H., Xu, Y., Chen, D., Firat, O., Huang, Y., Krikun, M., Shazeer, N., Chen, Z.: GShard: Scaling giant models with conditional computation and automatic sharding. In: International Conference on Learning Representations, ICLR. OpenReview.net (2021)

33. Lewis, M., Ghazvininejad, M., Ghosh, G., Aghajanyan, A., Wang, S., Zettlemoyer, L.: Pre-training via paraphrasing. In: Larochelle, H., Ranzato, M., Hadsell, R., Balcan, M., Lin, H. (eds.) Advances in Neural Information Processing Systems 33: Annual Conference on Neural Information Processing Systems 2020, NeurIPS 2020, December 6-12, 2020, virtual (2020)

34. Lewis, P.S.H., Perez, E., Piktus, A., Petroni, F., Karpukhin, V., Goyal, N., Küttler, H., Lewis, M., Yih, W., Rocktäschel, T., Riedel, S., Kiela, D.: Retrieval-augmented generation for knowledge-intensive NLP tasks. In: Larochelle, H., Ranzato, M., Hadsell, R., Balcan, M., Lin, H. (eds.) Advances in Neural Information Processing Systems 33: Annual Conference on Neural Information Processing Systems 2020, NeurIPS 2020, December 6-12, 2020, virtual (2020)

35. Li, W., Yu, L., Wu, Y., Paulson, L.C.: IsarStep: A benchmark for high-level mathematical reasoning. In: 9th International Conference on Learning Representations, ICLR 2021. OpenReview.net (2021)

36. Loos, S.M., Irving, G., Szegedy, C., Kaliszyk, C.: Deep network guided proof search. In: Eiter, T., Sands, D. (eds.) LPAR-21, 21st International Conference on Logic for Programming, Artificial Intelligence and Reasoning, Maun, Botswana, May

7-12, 2017. EPiC Series in Computing, vol. 46, pp. 85–105. EasyChair (2017), https://easychair.org/publications/paper/ND13

37. Paliwal, A., Loos, S.M., Rabe, M.N., Bansal, K., Szegedy, C.: Graph representations for higher-order logic and theorem proving. In: The Thirty-Fourth AAAI Conference on Artificial Intelligence, AAAI 2020, The Thirty-Second Innovative Applications of Artificial Intelligence Conference, IAAI 2020, The Tenth AAAI Symposium on Educational Advances in Artificial Intelligence, EAAI 2020, New York, NY, USA, February 7-12, 2020. pp. 2967–2974. AAAI Press (2020), https://aaai.org/ojs/index.php/AAAI/article/view/5689

38. Piotrowski, B., Urban, J.: Atpboost: Learning premise selection in binary setting with ATP feedback. In: Galmiche, D., Schulz, S., Sebastiani, R. (eds.) Automated Reasoning - 9th International Joint Conference, IJCAR 2018, Held as Part of the Federated Logic Conference, FloC 2018, Oxford, UK, July 14-17, 2018, Proceedings. Lecture Notes in Computer Science, vol. 10900, pp. 566–574. Springer (2018). https://doi.org/10.1007/978-3-319-94205-6_37

39. Polu, S., Sutskever, I.: Generative language modeling for automated theorem proving. CoRR **abs/2009.03393** (2020), https://arxiv.org/abs/2009.03393

40. Puzis, Y., Gao, Y., Sutcliffe, G.: Automated generation of interesting theorems. In: Sutcliffe, G., Goebel, R. (eds.) Proceedings of the Nineteenth International Florida Artificial Intelligence Research Society Conference, Melbourne Beach, Florida, USA, May 11-13, 2006. pp. 49–54. AAAI Press (2006), http://www.aaai.org/Library/FLAIRS/2006/flairs06-009.php

41. Rabe, M.N., Lee, D., Bansal, K., Szegedy, C.: Mathematical reasoning via self-supervised skip-tree training. In: International Conference on Learning Representations, ICLR. OpenReview.net (2021)

42. Radford, A., Wu, J., Child, R., Luan, D., Amodei, D., Sutskever, I.: Language models are unsupervised multitask learners. In: OpenAI Blog (2018)

43. Rozière, B., Lachaux, M., Chanussot, L., Lample, G.: Unsupervised translation of programming languages. In: Larochelle, H., Ranzato, M., Hadsell, R., Balcan, M., Lin, H. (eds.) Advances in Neural Information Processing Systems 33: Annual Conference on Neural Information Processing Systems 2020, NeurIPS 2020, December 6-12, 2020, virtual (2020)

44. Schulz, S.: Learning search control knowledge for equational theorem proving. In: Baader, F., Brewka, G., Eiter, T. (eds.) KI 2001: Advances in Artificial Intelligence, Joint German/Austrian Conference on AI, Vienna, Austria, September 19-21, 2001, Proceedings. Lecture Notes in Computer Science, vol. 2174, pp. 320–334. Springer (2001). https://doi.org/10.1007/3-540-45422-5_23

45. Selsam, D., Lamm, M., Bünz, B., Liang, P., de Moura, L., Dill, D.L.: Learning a SAT solver from single-bit supervision. In: 7th International Conference on Learning Representations, ICLR 2019, New Orleans, LA, USA, May 6-9, 2019. OpenReview.net (2019), https://openreview.net/forum?id=HJMC_iA5tm

46. Urban, J.: MPTP - motivation, implementation, first experiments. J. Autom. Reason. **33**(3-4), 319–339 (2004). https://doi.org/10.1007/s10817-004-6245-1

47. Urban, J., Sutcliffe, G., Pudlák, P., Vyskocil, J.: Malarea SG1- machine learner for automated reasoning with semantic guidance. In: Armando, A., Baumgartner, P., Dowek, G. (eds.) Automated Reasoning, 4th International Joint Conference, IJCAR 2008, Sydney, Australia, August 12-15, 2008, Proceedings. Lecture Notes in Computer Science, vol. 5195, pp. 441–456. Springer (2008). https://doi.org/10.1007/978-3-540-71070-7_37

48. Vaswani, A., Shazeer, N., Parmar, N., Uszkoreit, J., Jones, L., Gomez, A.N., Kaiser, L., Polosukhin, I.: Attention is all you need. In: Guyon, I., von Luxburg, U., Bengio, S., Wallach, H.M., Fergus, R., Vishwanathan, S.V.N., Garnett, R. (eds.) Advances in Neural Information Processing Systems 30: Annual Conference on Neural Information Processing Systems 2017, December 4-9, 2017, Long Beach, CA, USA. pp. 5998–6008 (2017)
49. Wang, Q., Brown, C.E., Kaliszyk, C., Urban, J.: Exploration of neural machine translation in autoformalization of mathematics in Mizar. In: Blanchette, J., Hritcu, C. (eds.) Proceedings of the 9th ACM SIGPLAN International Conference on Certified Programs and Proofs, CPP 2020, New Orleans, LA, USA, January 20-21, 2020. pp. 85–98. ACM (2020). https://doi.org/10.1145/3372885.3373827
50. WolframAlpha: WolframAlpha (2016), http://www.wolframalpha.com/
51. Wu, M., Norrish, M., Walder, C., Dezfouli, A.: Tacticzero: Learning to prove theorems from scratch with deep reinforcement learning. CoRR **abs/2102.09756** (2021), https://arxiv.org/abs/2102.09756
52. Wu, Y., Jiang, A., Ba, J., Grosse, R.B.: INT: An inequality benchmark for evaluating generalization in theorem proving. In: 9th International Conference on Learning Representations, ICLR 2021. OpenReview.net (2021)
53. Wu, Y., Rabe, M., Li, W., Ba, J., Grosse, R., Szegedy, C.: LIME: Learning inductive bias for primitives of mathematical reasoning. In: Proceedings of International Conference on Machine Learning (to appear) (2021)
54. Yang, K., Deng, J.: Learning to prove theorems via interacting with proof assistants. In: Chaudhuri, K., Salakhutdinov, R. (eds.) Proceedings of the 36th International Conference on Machine Learning, ICML 2019, 9-15 June 2019, Long Beach, California, USA. Proceedings of Machine Learning Research, vol. 97, pp. 6984–6994. PMLR (2019), http://proceedings.mlr.press/v97/yang19a.html

Open Access This chapter is licensed under the terms of the Creative Commons Attribution 4.0 International License (http://creativecommons.org/licenses/by/4.0/), which permits use, sharing, adaptation, distribution and reproduction in any medium or format, as long as you give appropriate credit to the original author(s) and the source, provide a link to the Creative Commons license and indicate if changes were made.

The images or other third party material in this chapter are included in the chapter's Creative Commons license, unless indicated otherwise in a credit line to the material. If material is not included in the chapter's Creative Commons license and your intended use is not permitted by statutory regulation or exceeds the permitted use, you will need to obtain permission directly from the copyright holder.

Logical Foundations

Tableau-based Decision Procedure for Non-Fregean Logic of Sentential Identity*

Joanna Golińska-Pilarek[1], Taneli
Huuskonen[1], and Michał Zawidzki[2,3]

[1] Faculty of Philosophy, University of Warsaw, 3 Krakowskie Przedmiescie St. 00-927
Warsaw, Poland
[2] Department of Computer Science, University of Oxford, Oxford OX1 3QD, UK
[3] Department of Logic, University of Lodz, 3/5 Lindleya St., 90-131 Łódź, Poland
j.golinska@uw.edu.pl
taneli@poczta.onet.pl
michal.zawidzki@cs.ox.ac.uk

Abstract. Sentential Calculus with Identity (SCI) is an extension of
classical propositional logic, featuring a new connective of identity between formulas. In SCI two formulas are said to be identical if they share
the same denotation. In the semantics of the logic, truth values are distinguished from denotations, hence the identity connective is strictly
stronger than classical equivalence. In this paper we present a sound,
complete, and terminating algorithm deciding the satisfiability of SCI-
formulas, based on labelled tableaux. To the best of our knowledge, it
is the first implemented decision procedure for SCI which runs in NP,
i.e., is complexity-optimal. The obtained complexity bound is a result of
dividing derivation rules in the algorithm into two sets: *decomposition*
and *equality* rules, whose interplay yields derivation trees with branches
of polynomial length with respect to the size of the investigated formula.
We describe an implementation of the procedure and compare its performance with implementations of other calculi for SCI (for which, however,
the termination results were not established). We show possible refinements of our algorithm and discuss the possibility of extending it to other
non-Fregean logics.

Keywords: Sentential Calculus with Identity · non-Fregean logics · labelled tableaux · decision procedure · termination · computational complexity.

1 Introduction

In this paper, we present a decision procedure for the non-Fregean sentential
calculus with identity SCI. The contribution of the paper is twofold. First of
all, this is the first implemented and complexity-optimal decision procedure for

* Research reported in this paper is supported by the National Science Centre, Poland
(grant number: UMO-2017/25/B/HS1/00503).

© The Author(s) 2021
A. Platzer and G. Sutcliffe (Eds.): CADE 2021, LNAI 12699, pp. 41–57, 2021.
https://doi.org/10.1007/978-3-030-79876-5_3

SCI, although several deduction systems for SCI have already been presented in the literature. Second, our decision procedure is constructed in the paradigm of labelled tableaux, which makes the whole approach more robust to modifications and extensions to other non-Fregean logics.

Non-Fregean logic is an alternative to both classical and many non-classical systems whose semantics identifies semantical correlates of sentences with their logical values. According to the classical approach in model theory, semantical structures (realities) correspond to the language that is meant to describe them, and therefore, symbols and expressions of that language, such as individual constants or relational symbols, have their denotations in these structures (respectively, objects or relations between objects). However, sentences are treated differently, as they are interpreted in models only in terms of logical values or other semantical relations such as satisfaction or truth. This classical approach allows us to answer the very basic logical question of whether the sentences are logically equivalent; however, it does not provide any tool that would allow to check whether the sentences describe or refer to the same situation, or have the same meaning. Thus, the main motivation for non-Fregean logic was the need for an extensional and two-valued logic that could be used to represent semantical denotations of sentences that – depending on the underlying philosophical theory of language or the reality to which a logic is supposed to refer – could be understood as situations, states of affairs, meanings, etc. In order to express (non)identities or other interactions between the referents of sentences, at least the universe of denotations of sentences needs to be added to the semantics and the new *identity* connective to the language.

The minimal two-valued non-Fregean propositional logic SCI (*Sentential Calculus with Identity*), introduced by Suszko (see [21]), is an extension of classical propositional logic with a new binary connective of identity ($\equiv$) and axioms reflecting its fundamental properties. The identity connective represents the identity of the denotations of sentences, and so, an expression '$\varphi \equiv \psi$' should be read as 'the sentences φ and ψ describe the same «thing»'. The semantics for SCI is based on structures determined by a universe of the denotations of sentences, a set of facts (those denotations that actually hold), and operations corresponding to all the connectives. The identity connective is then interpreted as an operation representing an equivalence relation that additionally satisfies the extensionality property. In the non-Fregean approach the identity and equivalence connectives are in general not equivalent: two sentences with the same truth value can have different denotations. Take, for instance, the following three statements:

A 'There is an effective method for determining whether an arbitrary formula of classical propositional logic is a theorem of that logic.'
B 'Classical propositional logic is finitely axiomatizable, has a recursive set of recursive rules and enjoys the finite model property.'
C 'Classical propositional logic is Post consistent.'

A, B, C are all (necessarily) true as theorems of mathematical logic. Therefore, they are pairwise logically equivalent, that is, all three equivalences: A $\leftrightarrow$ B, B $\leftrightarrow$ C, and A $\leftrightarrow$ C hold. One can fairly claim that A and B refer to the same fact, so A ≡ B, but C has clearly a different semantic correlate than both A and B, as decidability is independent of Post consistency. Thus, we have A ≢ C and B ≢ C.

It is known that the class of all non-equivalent non-Fregean propositional logics satisfying the laws of classical logic is uncountable [7], and some of these logics are equivalent to the well-known non-classical logics (e.g., modal logics S4 and S5, many-valued logics). Higher-order non-Fregean logics are very expressive. In particular, a logic obtained from SCI by adding propositional quantifiers is undecidable and can express many mathematical theories, e.g., Peano arithmetic, the theory of groups, rings, and fields [8]. Furthermore, non-classical and deviant modifications of SCI have been developed and extensively studied in the literature, in particular intuitionistic logics [17,14,4], modal and epistemic logics [15,16], logics with non-classical identity [13], paraconsistent [6,9]. The non-Fregean approach could turn out to be more adequate than the classical one in cognitive science or natural language processing. Moreover, non-Fregean logic could serve as a general framework for comparing different aspects of logics with incompatible languages and semantics and help in addressing the question of which class of logics handles logical symbols in the most adequate way from the perspective of natural language.

In the original works by Suszko and Bloom the deduction system for SCI was defined in the Hilbert style [1,2]. Sound and complete deduction systems which are better suited for automated theorem proving were constructed later: Gentzen sequent calculi [18,22,23,3] and dual tableau systems [5,19,10]. A detailed presentation of all of them can be found in [10]. The main disadvantage of the aforementioned systems is that they are not decision procedures, while SCI is decidable and in particular in NP [2, Theorem 2.3]. Although the system by Wasilewska [22] can be seen as a meta-tool for deciding validity of SCI-formulas, it is equipped with external meta-machinery that is not a part of the system itself. As a result, it constitutes another proof for decidability of SCI, rather than being a decision procedure in the classical sense of the term, that is suitable for computer implementations. In [11] a tableau-based algorithm for SCI was presented as a work-in-progress. The decision procedure presented in this paper is a result of a substantial remodelling of the preliminary system introduced in [11], for which we prove soundness and completeness, present surprisingly straightforward proofs of termination and membership in NP, and provide an implementation.

In this paper, we present a new deduction system T_{SCI} for the logic SCI, based on labelled tableaux. To the best of our knowledge, it is the first decision procedure for SCI. Moreover, its upper complexity bound, that is NP, matches the complexity class of the satisfiability problem for SCI, thus, making the algorithm complexity-optimal. T_{SCI} is built in the paradigm of labelled tableaux. The language of deduction is an extension of the SCI-language with two sorts of labels representing the denotations of formulas (i.e., «facts» and «non-facts») as well as with the equality and the inequality relation that can hold between labels. (In)Equality formulas occurring in a derivation tree provide additional information on identity or distinctness of the denotations of formulas. In Section 2, we provide a formal overview of the logic SCI, in Section 3, we introduce the tableau algorithm $\mathsf{T_{SCI}}$ and prove its soundness, completeness, and termination, establish that it is complexity-optimal with respect to SCI-satisfiability, and show a possible refinement thereof. In Section 4, we discuss an implementation of $\mathsf{T_{SCI}}$ and compare it with an older prover based on a heuristic, unproven algorithm. Conclusions and directions of further research are presented in Section 5.

2 SCI

Syntax Let $\mathcal{L}_{\mathsf{SCI}}$ be a language of the logic SCI with the alphabet $\langle \mathsf{AF}, \neg, \rightarrow, \equiv \rangle$, where $\mathsf{AF} = \{\mathsf{p}, \mathsf{q}, \mathsf{r}, \dots\}$ is a denumerable set of *atomic formulas*. The set FOR of SCI-*formulas* is defined by the following abstract grammar:

$$\varphi ::= \mathsf{p} \mid \neg\varphi \mid \varphi \rightarrow \varphi \mid \varphi \equiv \varphi,$$

where $\mathsf{p} \in \mathsf{AF}$.

Axiomatization The logic SCI is axiomatized by the following set of truth-functional (1–3) and identity (4–8) axiom schemes:

1. $\varphi \rightarrow (\psi \rightarrow \varphi)$
2. $(\varphi \rightarrow (\psi \rightarrow \chi)) \rightarrow ((\varphi \rightarrow \psi) \rightarrow (\varphi \rightarrow \chi))$
3. $(\neg\varphi \rightarrow \neg\psi) \rightarrow (\psi \rightarrow \varphi)$
4. $\varphi \equiv \varphi$
5. $\varphi \equiv \psi \rightarrow \neg\varphi \equiv \neg\psi$
6. $\varphi \equiv \psi \rightarrow (\chi \equiv \theta \rightarrow (\varphi \rightarrow \chi) \equiv (\psi \rightarrow \theta))$
7. $\varphi \equiv \psi \rightarrow (\chi \equiv \theta \rightarrow (\varphi \equiv \chi) \equiv (\psi \equiv \theta))$
8. $\varphi \equiv \psi \rightarrow (\varphi \rightarrow \psi)$.

Semantics Let $U \neq \emptyset$, $D \subset U$, and let $\tilde{\neg} : U \longrightarrow U$, $\tilde{\rightarrow} : U \times U \longrightarrow U$, and $\tilde{\equiv} : U \times U \longrightarrow U$ be functions on U. An SCI-*model* is a structure $\mathcal{M} = \langle U, D, \tilde{\neg}, \tilde{\rightarrow}, \tilde{\equiv} \rangle$, where U and D are called, respectively, *universe* and *set of designated values*, and the following conditions are satisfied for all $a, b \in U$:

$$\tilde{\neg}a \in D \qquad \text{iff} \qquad a \notin D \tag{1}$$

$$a\tilde{\rightarrow}b \in D \qquad \text{iff} \qquad a \notin D \text{ or } b \in D \tag{2}$$

$$a\tilde{\equiv}b \in D \qquad \text{iff} \qquad a = b. \tag{3}$$

A *valuation* in an SCI- model $\mathcal{M} = \langle U, D, \tilde{\neg}, \tilde{\rightarrow}, \tilde{\equiv} \rangle$ is a function $V : \mathsf{FOR} \longrightarrow U$ such that for all $\varphi, \psi \in \mathsf{FOR}$ it holds that $V(\neg\varphi) = \tilde{\neg}V(\varphi)$ and $V(\varphi \# \psi) = V(\varphi)\tilde{\#}V(\psi)$, for $\# \in \{\rightarrow, \equiv\}$. An element $a \in U$ such that $a = V(\varphi)$ is called the *denotation of* φ. Interestingly, SCI-model can be defined alternatively as a triple $\mathcal{M} = \langle U, D, V \rangle$, where a valuation $V : \mathsf{FOR} \longrightarrow U$ needs to satisfy the conditions analogous to (1)–(3) (for instance, $V(\neg\varphi) \in D$ iff $V(\varphi) \notin D$ etc.). In the original approach V may as well be defined only for atomic formulas and then lifted up homomorphically to the set of all formulas, like in classical propositional logic. In the latter setting it is not the case, as a valuation defined solely for atoms does usually not have a unique extension to all formulas. We say that a formula φ is *satisfied* in an SCI-model $\mathcal{M} = \langle U, D, \tilde{\neg}, \tilde{\rightarrow}, \tilde{\equiv} \rangle$ and a valuation V in $\mathcal{M}$, and refer to it as $\mathcal{M}, V \models_{\mathsf{SCI}} \varphi$, if its denotation belongs to D. We call a formula φ *satisfiable* if it is satisfied in some SCI-model by some valuation. We say that a formula φ is *true* in a model $\mathcal{M} = \langle U, D, \tilde{\neg}, \tilde{\rightarrow}, \tilde{\equiv} \rangle$, and refer to it as $\mathcal{M} \models_{\mathsf{SCI}} \varphi$, whenever it is satisfied in $\mathcal{M}$ by all the valuations in $\mathcal{M}$. We call a formula φ *valid*, and refer to it as $\models_{\mathsf{SCI}} \varphi$, if it is true in all SCI-models. Note that over the class of models where D and $U \setminus D$ are singletons SCI collapses to classical propositional logic. In fact all formulas which are SCI-instances of formulas valid in classical propositional are also valid in SCI. It suffices, however, to take a three-element model to tell $\leftrightarrow$ and $\equiv$ apart, as shown in the following example.

Example 1. Although the formula $\neg\neg p \leftrightarrow p$ is a tautology of classical propositional logic, the formula $\neg\neg p \equiv p$ is not valid in SCI. Indeed, consider an SCI-model $\mathcal{M} = \langle U, D, \tilde{\neg}, \tilde{to}, \tilde{\equiv} \rangle$, where $U = \{0, 1, 2\}$, $D = \{1, 2\}$, and the operations $\tilde{\neg}, \tilde{\rightarrow}, \tilde{\equiv}$ are defined by:

$$\tilde{\neg} a = \begin{cases} 0, & \text{if } a \neq 0, \\ 1, & \text{otherwise.} \end{cases} \quad a \tilde{\rightarrow} b = \begin{cases} 0, & \text{if } a \neq 2 \text{ and} \\ & b = 0, \\ 2, & \text{if } a = b, \\ 1, & \text{otherwise.} \end{cases} \quad a \tilde{\equiv} b = \begin{cases} 0, & \text{if } a \neq b \\ a, & \text{if } a = b \text{ and} \\ & a \neq 0, \\ 1, & \text{otherwise.} \end{cases}$$

It is easy to verify that such a structure is an SCI-model. Then, the following hold:

- $\tilde{\neg}\tilde{\neg} 2 = 1$, and so, $\mathcal{M}$ and a valuation V in $\mathcal{M}$ such that $V(p) = 2$ falsify the formula $\neg\neg p \equiv p$,
- $1 \tilde{\rightarrow} 2 = 1$, but $\tilde{\neg} 2 \tilde{\rightarrow} \tilde{\neg} 1 = 2$, and so, the formula $(p \rightarrow q) \equiv (\neg q \rightarrow \neg p)$ is not true in $\mathcal{M}$.

What is also characteristic of SCI is that identical formulas can be interchanged within other formulas with not only truth preservation, but also identity preservation. For instance, if $p \equiv (p \rightarrow q)$, then $p \equiv ((p \rightarrow q) \rightarrow q)$, $p \equiv (((p \rightarrow q) \rightarrow q) \rightarrow q)$ and so on. On the other hand, identity of two formulas does not automatically yield identity of their subformulas. For example, if $\neg p \equiv \neg q$, it does not necessarily mean that $p \equiv q$. It is worth noting that in SCI we lack the usual equivalence between treating $\wedge$, $\vee$, and $\leftrightarrow$ as abbreviations involving $\neg$ and $\rightarrow$ and treating them as independent connectives whose mutual relations are established axiomatically. For instance, when $\neg(\varphi \rightarrow \neg\psi)$ is just a notational variant for $\varphi \wedge \psi$, then $(\varphi \wedge \psi) \equiv \neg(\varphi \rightarrow \neg\psi)$ is, of course, SCI-valid; however, it would not be the case if we regarded $\wedge$ as a separate connective. Nevertheless, extending our results to other connectives introduced as independent logical constants is a matter of routine.

3 Tableaux

In this section, we provide a characterization of a sound, complete and terminating *labelled* tableau system for the logic SCI, which we call T_{SCI}.

Let L^+, L^- be countably infinite disjoint sets and let $L = L^+ \cup L^-$. We will call an expression $w : \varphi$ a *labelled formula*, where $w \in L$ and $\varphi \in FOR$, and w will be called a *label*. We will abbreviate the set of all labelled formulas by LF. Any labels superscribed with '+' are restricted to belong to L^+ and labels superscribed with '−' to belong to L^-. Labels without a superscript are not restricted. Intuitively, w stands for the denotation of φ in an intended model. Labels with '+' in the superscript denote elements of D, whereas labels with superscribed '−' represent elements of $U \setminus D$. Thus, expressions of the form $w = v$ or $w \neq v$ reflect, respectively, the equality or distinctness of two denotations. By Id^+, Id^- we denote the sets of, respectively, all equalities and all inequalities of labels. Finally, we let $Id = Id^+ \cup Id^-$.

A *tableau* generated by the system for the logic SCI is a *derivation tree* whose nodes are assigned labelled formulas and (in)equality expressions. A simple path $\mathcal{B}$ from the root to a leaf in a tableau $\mathcal{T}$ is called *branch of $\mathcal{T}$*. We will identify a branch $\mathcal{B}$ with the set of labelled formulas and (in)equalities occurring on $\mathcal{B}$.

The rules of our tableau system have the following general form: $\frac{\Phi}{\Psi_1 | ... | \Psi_n}$, where Φ is the set of *premises* and each Ψ_i, for $i \in \{1, ..., n\}$, is a set of *conclusions*. Intuitively, the '|' symbol should be read as a meta-disjunction. A rule with only one set of conclusions is called a *non-branching* rule. A rule with several sets of conclusions is a *branching rule*. In T_{SCI} all rules where Ψ_i, for $i \in \{1, ..., n\}$ contain labelled formulas are called *decomposition rules*. All rules with a single equality statement as the conclusion are called *equality rules*. The remaining rules, in which $\perp$ occurs as the conclusion, are referred to as *closure rules*. If we have a decomposition rule (R) with $w : \varphi$ as its premise, then (R) is *applicable* to $w : \varphi$ occurring on a branch $\mathcal{B}$ if it has not been applied to $w : \varphi$ on $\mathcal{B}$ before. Otherwise $w : \varphi$ is called (R)-*expanded* on $\mathcal{B}$. For an equality rule (R) with Φ as the set of premises and $w = v$ as the conclusion, (R) is applicable to $\Phi \subseteq \mathcal{B}$ if $w = v$ is not present on $\mathcal{B}$. Otherwise Φ is (R)-expanded on $\mathcal{B}$. Intuitively, if a set of premises Φ is (R)-expanded on $\mathcal{B}$, then applying (R) to Φ would not add any new information to $\mathcal{B}$.

A branch $\mathcal{B}$ of a tableau $\mathcal{T}$ is extended by applying rules of the system to sets of labelled formulas and (in)equality statements that are already on $\mathcal{B}$. A label w is *present* on $\mathcal{B}$ if there exists a formula φ such that $w : \varphi$ occurs on $\mathcal{B}$. Otherwise w is *fresh* on $\mathcal{B}$. A branch $\mathcal{B}$ is called *closed* if one of the closure rules has been applied to it, that is, when an inconsistency occurs on $\mathcal{B}$. A branch that is not closed, is *open*. A branch $\mathcal{B}$ is *fully expanded* if it is closed or no rules are applicable on it. A tableau $\mathcal{T}$ is called *closed* if all of its branches are closed. Otherwise $\mathcal{T}$ is called *open*. We call $\mathcal{T}$ fully expanded if all of its branches are fully expanded.

Analytic tableaux are satisfiability checkers, so a *tableau proof* of a formula φ is a closed tableau with a labelled formula $w^- : \varphi$ at its root. A formula is *tableau-valid* if all tableaux with $w^- : \varphi$ at the root are closed. On the other hand, a

$$(\neg^+)\ \frac{w^+ : \neg\varphi}{v^- : \varphi} \qquad (\neg^-)\ \frac{w^- : \neg\varphi}{v^+ : \varphi}$$

$$(\to^+)\ \frac{w^+ : \varphi \to \psi}{\begin{array}{c|c|c} v^- : \varphi & v^- : \varphi & v^+ : \varphi \\ u^- : \psi & u^+ : \psi & u^+ : \psi \end{array}} \qquad (\to^-)\ \frac{w^- : \varphi \to \psi}{\begin{array}{c} v^+ : \varphi \\ u^- : \psi \end{array}}$$

$$(\equiv^+)\ \frac{w^+ : \varphi \equiv \psi}{\begin{array}{c|c} v^+ : \varphi & v^- : \varphi \\ u^+ : \psi & u^- : \psi \\ v^+ = u^+ & v^- = u^- \end{array}} \qquad (\equiv^-)\ \frac{w^- : \varphi \equiv \psi}{\begin{array}{c|c|c|c} v^+ : \varphi & & & v^- : \varphi \\ u^+ : \psi & v^+ : \varphi & v^- : \varphi & u^- : \psi \\ v^+ \neq u^+ & u^- : \psi & u^+ : \psi & v^- \neq u^- \end{array}}$$

$$(\equiv^\neg)\ \frac{\begin{array}{c} \varphi \approx \psi \\ u ; \neg\varphi \\ y : \neg\psi \end{array}}{u = y} \qquad (\equiv^\to)\ \frac{\begin{array}{c} \varphi \approx \psi \\ \chi \approx \theta \\ x : \varphi \to \chi \\ z : \psi \to \theta \end{array}}{x = z} \qquad (\equiv^\equiv)\ \frac{\begin{array}{c} \varphi \approx \psi \\ \chi \approx \theta \\ x : \varphi \equiv \chi \\ z : \psi \equiv \theta \end{array}}{x = z} \qquad (\mathrm{F})\ \frac{\begin{array}{c} w : \varphi \\ v : \varphi \end{array}}{w = v}$$

$$(\mathrm{sym})\ \frac{w = v}{v = w} \qquad (\mathrm{tran})\ \frac{\begin{array}{c} w = v \\ v = u \end{array}}{w = u} \qquad (\perp_1)\ \frac{\begin{array}{c} w = v \\ w \neq v \end{array}}{\perp} \qquad (\perp_2)\ \frac{w^+ = v^-}{\perp}$$

[1] Labels occurring in conclusions of the rules: $(\neg^+)$, $(\neg^-)$, $(\to^+)$, $(\to^-)$, $(\equiv^+)$, $(\equiv^-)$ are fresh on the branch.

[2] The abbreviation $\varphi \approx \psi$ represents the set of three preconditions: $w : \varphi$, $v : \psi$, $w = v$, for some $w, v \in L$. Similarly for $\chi \approx \theta$.

Fig. 1. Tableau system $\mathsf{T_{SCI}}$

formula φ is *tableau-satisfiable* if there exists an open and fully expanded tableau with a labelled formula $w^! : \varphi$ at its root. Note that our notion of tableau-satisfiability matches the usual notion of satisfiability as a failure of finding a proof. Indeed, if a formula φ is not tableau-valid, that is, there exists a tableau with $w^- : \varphi$ at the root which has an open branch, then $\neg\varphi$ is tableau-satisfiable. Thus, the standard duality between validity and satisfiability is reflected in the concepts of tableau-validity and tableau-satisfiability.

3.1 Tableau System for SCI

The rules presented in Figure 1 constitute the tableau system $\mathsf{T_{SCI}}$ for the logic SCI. The decomposition rules $(\neg^+)$, $(\neg^-)$, $(\to^+)$, $(\to^-)$, $(\equiv^+)$, $(\equiv^-)$ reflect the semantics of $\neg$, $\to$ and $\equiv$ defined in the conditions 1–3 from Section 2. Note that an application of any of these rules introduces to a branch fresh labels for each of the subformulas into which the premise formula is decomposed. By that means, all occurrences of subformulas of the input formula φ are assigned their unique labels. A few words of extra commentary on the rule $(\equiv^-)$ are in order. It decomposes a formula involving the $\equiv$ connective, which is assumed to be false. By the semantics of $\equiv$ we know that the constituents of the initial $\equiv$-formula have distinct denotations. If these denotations have different polarities, representing different truth values (disjuncts 2 and 3 in the denominator of the rule), then no additional information has to be stored about the distinctness of these denotations. If, on the other hand, the denotations have the same polarity, representing the same truth value (disjuncts 1 and 4 in the denominator of the rule), then extra information is added, namely that the denotations of both formulas are distinct. The rules $(\equiv^-)$, $(\equiv^\to)$ and $(\equiv^\equiv)$ are tableau-counterparts of the axioms 5, 6, and 7, respectively. The rule (F) ensures that a valuation that can be read off from an open branch is a function, i.e., that all denotations assigned to the same formula on a branch are equal. The rules (sym) and (tran) guarantee that equalities appearing on a branch preserve all properties of the =-relation. Note that an application of a closure rule to a branch is always a result of transformations of equality statements. While executing $\mathsf{T_{SCI}}$ we always apply closure rules eagerly, that is, whenever a closure rule can be applied, it should be applied. An example of a tableau proof generated by $\mathsf{T_{SCI}}$ can be found in Figure 2.

The tableau system $\mathsf{T_{SCI}}$ is a user-friendly and elegant solution to the problem most non-labelled systems for SCI struggle with, namely substitutability of identical formulas within other formulas with identity preservation. In a derivation that can result in yielding conclusions of greater complexity than premises, as shown at the end of Section 2. It often leads to a loss of subformula property in a deduction system. $\mathsf{T_{SCI}}$, on the other hand, reduces the whole reasoning to a simple equality calculus where only identities or non-identities between labels are substantial for the result of a given derivation. It allows us to circumvent the abovementioned problem by replacing it with a question: are labels representing given formulas equal or distinct?

$$w^- : \varphi \equiv \psi \to (\varphi \to \psi)$$
$$\left| (\to^-) \right.$$
$$v^+ : \varphi \equiv \psi$$
$$u^- : \varphi \to \psi$$
$$\left| (\to^-) \right.$$
$$x^+ : \varphi$$
$$y^- : \psi$$
$$\diagup (\equiv^+) \diagdown$$

$z^+ : \varphi$	$z^- : \varphi$
$t^+ : \psi$	$t^- : \psi$
$z^+ = t^+$	$z^- = t^-$
(F) $\|$	$\|$ (F)
$y^- = t^+$	$x^+ = z^-$
$(\bot_2) \|$	$\|(\bot_2)$
$\bot$	$\bot$

Fig. 2. Tableau proof for the axiom $\varphi \equiv \psi \to (\varphi \to \psi)$

3.2   Soundness and Completeness[4]

First, we will prove soundness of the tableau system $\mathsf{T_{SCI}}$.

---

[4] A technical appendix to the paper with all omitted proofs can be found in [12]

Let A, B be finite sets such that $A \subseteq \mathsf{LF}$ and $B \subseteq \mathsf{Id}$. A set $A \cup B$ is said to be satisfied in an SCI-model $\mathcal{M} = \langle U, D, \tilde{\neg}, \tilde{\rightarrow}, \tilde{\equiv} \rangle$ by a valuation V in $\mathcal{M}$ and a function $f : \mathsf{L} \longrightarrow U$ if and only if the following hold: (1) $V(\varphi) = f(w)$, for all $w \in \mathsf{L}$ and $\varphi \in \mathsf{FOR}$ such that $w : \varphi \in A$, (2) $f(w) \in D$ iff $w \in \mathsf{L}^+$, for all labels w that occur in $A \cup B$, (3) $f(w) = f(v)$, for all $w, v \in \mathsf{L}$ such that $w = v \in B$, (4) $f(w) \neq f(v)$, for all $w, v \in \mathsf{L}$ such that $w \neq v \in B$. A set $A \cup B$ is said to be SCI-satisfiable whenever there exist an SCI-model $\mathcal{M} = \langle U, D, \tilde{\neg}, \tilde{\rightarrow}, \tilde{\equiv} \rangle$, a valuation V in $\mathcal{M}$, and a function $f : \mathsf{L} \longrightarrow U$ such that $A \cup B$ is satisfied in $\mathcal{M}$ by V and f.

Proposition 1. *For every satisfiable* SCI-*formula* φ *and for all* $w^+ \in \mathsf{L}^+$ *it holds that* $\{w^+ : \varphi\}$ *is* SCI-*satisfiable.*

Proposition 2. *For all* $w, v \in \mathsf{L}$, $w^+ \in \mathsf{L}^+$, *and* $v^- \in \mathsf{L}^-$, *and for all finite* $X \subseteq \mathsf{LF} \cup \mathsf{Id}$, *the sets* $X \cup \{w = v, w \neq v\}$ *and* $X \cup \{w^+ = v^-\}$ *are not* SCI-*satisfiable.*

Let (R) $\frac{\Phi}{\Psi_1 | \dots | \Psi_n}$, for $n \geq 1$, be a decomposition or equality rule of the tableau system $\mathsf{T}_{\mathsf{SCI}}$. A rule (R) is referred to as *sound* whenever, for every finite set $X \subseteq \mathsf{LF} \cup \mathsf{Id}$, it holds that $X \cup \Phi$ is SCI-satisfiable iff $X \cup \Phi \cup \Psi_i$ is SCI-satisfiable for some $i \in \{1, \dots, n\}$.

Proposition 3. *Decomposition and equality rules of the tableau system* $\mathsf{T}_{\mathsf{SCI}}$ *are sound.*

Theorem 1 (Soundness). *The tableau system* $\mathsf{T}_{\mathsf{SCI}}$ *is sound, that is, if an* SCI *formula* φ *is satisfiable, then* φ *is tableau-satisfiable.*

Proof. We prove the contrapositive. Let $\mathcal{T}$ be a closed $\mathsf{T}_{\mathsf{SCI}}$-tableau with $w^+ : \varphi$ at its root. Then, each branch of $\mathcal{T}$ contains either $w^+ = v^-$ or both $w = v$ and $w \neq v$, for some $w, v \in \mathsf{L}$, $w^+ \in \mathsf{L}^+$, $v^- \in \mathsf{L}^-$. By Proposition 2, both sets $X \cup \{w^+ = v^-\}$ and $X \cup \{w = v, w \neq v\}$ are not SCI-satisfiable, for any finite set $X \subseteq \mathsf{LF} \cup \mathsf{Id}$. By Proposition 3, each application of $\mathsf{T}_{\mathsf{SCI}}$-rules preserves SCI-satisfiability. Hence, going from the bottom to the top of the tree $\mathcal{T}$, on each step of the construction of $\mathsf{T}_{\mathsf{SCI}}$-tableau we get SCI-unsatisfiable sets. Thus, we can conclude that $w^+ : \varphi$ is not SCI-satisfiable, and thus by Proposition 1 we obtain that φ is not SCI-satisfiable. Therefore, each satisfiable SCI-formula φ is tableau-satisfiable. $\square$

To prove completeness of the system $\mathsf{T}_{\mathsf{SCI}}$ we need to show that if, for a given formula φ, $\mathsf{T}_{\mathsf{SCI}}$ does not yield a tableau proof, then φ is not valid, i.e., there exists a countermodel $\mathcal{M} = \langle U, D, V \rangle$ such that $\mathcal{M} \not\models \varphi$.

Suppose that we want to obtain a tableau-proof for a formula φ. To that end, we run the $\mathsf{T}_{\mathsf{SCI}}$-tableau algorithm with a labelled formula $\mathbf{w}^- : \varphi$ at the root of the tableau, for $\mathbf{w}^- \in \mathsf{L}^-$. Suppose that it yields an open tableau as a result. It means that the tableau contains an open and fully expanded branch $\mathcal{B}$. We will demonstrate how to construct a structure $\mathcal{M}_{\mathcal{B}} = \langle U, D, \tilde{\neg}, \tilde{\rightarrow}, \tilde{\equiv} \rangle$ using information stored on $\mathcal{B}$ and show that it actually is an SCI-countermodel falsifying φ. Let $\mathsf{L}_\mathcal{B}^+$ be the set of all labels superscribed with '+' occurring on $\mathcal{B}$, let $\mathsf{L}_\mathcal{B}^-$ be the set of all labels superscribed with '−' occurring on $\mathcal{B}$ and let $\mathsf{L}_\mathcal{B} = \mathsf{L}_\mathcal{B}^+ \cup \mathsf{L}_\mathcal{B}^-$. Moreover, let $\mathsf{FOR}_\mathcal{B}$ be the set of all SCI-formulas φ such that $w : \varphi$ occurs on $\mathcal{B}$, for some $w \in \mathsf{L}_\mathcal{B}$. Note that all elements of $\mathsf{FOR}_\mathcal{B}$ are subformulas of φ. Before we characterize the construction of $\mathcal{M}_\mathcal{B}$, we define a binary relation $\sim \subseteq \mathsf{L}_\mathcal{B} \times \mathsf{L}_\mathcal{B}$ in the following way:

$$w \sim v \qquad \text{iff} \qquad w = v \text{ occurs on } \mathcal{B}.$$

Proposition 4. *The relation $\sim$ is an equivalence relation and* $(\mathsf{L}_\mathcal{B}^+ \times \mathsf{L}_\mathcal{B}^-) \cap \sim\, = \emptyset$.

Let $\mathsf{ML}_\mathcal{B}^+$ be a set resulting from choosing exactly one label from each element of $(\mathsf{L}_\mathcal{B}^+)_{/\sim}$. Sets $\mathsf{ML}_\mathcal{B}^-$ and $\mathsf{ML}_\mathcal{B}$ are defined analogically with the assumption that $\mathbf{w}^- \in \mathsf{ML}_\mathcal{B}^-$, where $\mathbf{w}^-$ is such that $\mathbf{w}^- : \varphi$ is at the root of an open tableau. Of course, neither of these sets is uniquely determined.

Proposition 5. *For all $\psi \in \mathsf{FOR}$ and $w, v \in \mathsf{L}_\mathcal{B}$ the following holds:*

if both $w : \psi$ and $v : \psi$ belong to $\mathcal{B}$, then $w \sim v$.

We say that $w \in \mathsf{ML}_\mathcal{B}$ is $(\neg)$-*closed* whenever there are $\psi \in \mathsf{FOR}$, $u \in \mathsf{ML}_\mathcal{B}$, and $v, t \in \mathsf{L}_\mathcal{B}$ such that $w \sim v$, $u \sim t$ and labelled formulas $v : \psi$, $t : \neg\psi$ belong to $\mathcal{B}$. Let $w, v \in \mathsf{ML}_\mathcal{B}$ and $\# \in \{\to, \equiv\}$. The pair (w, v) is said to be $(\#)$-*closed* whenever there exist $\psi, \theta \in \mathsf{FOR}$, $u \in \mathsf{ML}_\mathcal{B}$, and $t, x, y \in \mathsf{L}_\mathcal{B}$ such that $w \sim t$, $v \sim x$, $u \sim y$ and labelled formulas $t : \psi$, $x : \theta$, $y : (\psi\#\theta)$ occur on the branch $\mathcal{B}$.

The *branch structure* $\mathcal{M}_\mathcal{B} = \langle U, D, \tilde{\neg}, \tilde{\to}, \tilde{\equiv} \rangle$ is defined as follows:

- $D = \{w^+ \mid w^+ \in \mathsf{ML}_\mathcal{B}^+\} \cup \{\mathbf{w}^+\}$, where $\mathbf{w}^+ \notin \mathsf{L}_\mathcal{B}$
- $U = D \cup \mathsf{ML}_\mathcal{B}^-$.

It follows from the above that $U \setminus D = \mathsf{ML}_\mathcal{B}^-$. The operations $\tilde{\neg}, \tilde{\to}, \tilde{\equiv}$ are defined for all $w, v \in U$ in the following way:

$$\tilde{\neg}w \stackrel{df}{=} \begin{cases} u \in U, & \text{if there are } \psi \in \mathsf{FOR} \text{ and } v, t \in \mathsf{L}_\mathcal{B} \text{ such that } w = v,\, u = t, \\ & v : \psi, \text{ and } t : \neg\psi \text{ are on } \mathcal{B} \\ \mathbf{w}^+, & \text{if } w \text{ is not } (\neg)\text{-closed and } w \notin D \\ \mathbf{w}^-, & \text{otherwise} \end{cases}$$

$$w\tilde{\to}v \stackrel{df}{=} \begin{cases} u \in U, & \text{if there are } \psi, \theta \in \mathsf{FOR} \text{ and } t, x, y \in \mathsf{L}_\mathcal{B} \text{ such that } w = t, \\ & v = x,\, u = y,\, t : \psi,\, x : \theta, \text{ and } y : (\psi \to \theta) \text{ are on } \mathcal{B} \\ \mathbf{w}^+, & \text{if } v = \mathbf{w}^+ \text{ or both } (w = \mathbf{w}^+ \text{ and } v \in D), \text{ or it holds that} \\ & (w, v) \text{ is not } (\to)\text{-closed and either } w \notin D \text{ or } v \in D \\ \mathbf{w}^-, & \text{otherwise} \end{cases}$$

$$w\tilde{\equiv}v \stackrel{df}{=} \begin{cases} u \in U, & \text{if there are } \psi, \theta \in \mathsf{FOR} \text{ and } t, x, y \in \mathsf{L}_\mathcal{B} \text{ such that } w = t, \\ & v = x,\, u = y,\, t : \psi,\, x : \theta, \text{ and } y : (\psi \equiv \theta) \text{ are on } \mathcal{B} \\ \mathbf{w}^+, & \text{if } w = v \text{ and either } w = \mathbf{w}^+ \text{ or the pair } (w, v) \text{ is not} \\ & (\equiv)\text{-closed} \\ \mathbf{w}^-, & \text{otherwise} \end{cases}$$

Due to the properties of the sets $\mathsf{ML}_\mathcal{B}^+$ and $\mathsf{ML}_\mathcal{B}^-$, we obtain:

Proposition 6. *The sets D and $U \setminus D$ are non-empty and $D \cap (U \setminus D) = \emptyset$.*

The following series of results ensure that the operations $\tilde{\neg}$, $\tilde{\rightarrow}$, and $\tilde{\equiv}$ reflect the semantics of SCI.

Proposition 7. $\tilde{\neg}$ *is a function on U and for all $w \in U$:*

$(*)$ $\tilde{\neg} w \in D$ *iff* $w \notin D$.

Proposition 8. $\tilde{\rightarrow}$ *is a function on U and for all $w, v \in U$, the following holds:*

$(*)$ $w \tilde{\rightarrow} v \in D$ *iff* $w \notin D$ *or* $v \in D$.

Proposition 9. $\tilde{\equiv}$ *is a function on U and for all $w, v \in U$ the following holds:*

$(*)$ $w \tilde{\equiv} v \in D$ *iff* $w = v$.

Propositions 6–9 imply:

Proposition 10. *The structure $\mathcal{M}_B$ is an SCI-model.*

In what follows, the structure $\mathcal{M}_B$ will be referred to as *branch model*.

Now, let $V : \mathsf{FOR} \longrightarrow U$ be a function such that for all $p \in \mathsf{AF}$:

$$V(p) = \begin{cases} u \in \mathsf{ML}_B, & \text{if there is } w \in \mathsf{L}_B \text{ such that } w : p \in B \text{ and } w \sim u \\ \mathbf{w}^+, & \text{otherwise} \end{cases}$$

and for all $\psi, \theta \in \mathsf{FOR}$ the following hold:

$$V(\neg\psi) = \tilde{\neg} V(\psi)$$
$$V(\psi \# \theta) = V(\psi) \tilde{\#} V(\theta), \text{ for } \# \in \{\rightarrow, \equiv\}.$$

Proposition 11. *The function V is well defined and it is a valuation in $\mathcal{M}_B$.*

Proposition 12. *For all $\psi \in \mathsf{FOR}$ and $w \in \mathsf{L}_B$ it holds that:*

$(*)$ *If $w : \psi \in B$, then $w \sim V(\psi)$.*

Theorem 2 (Completeness). *The tableau system $\mathsf{T}_{\mathsf{SCI}}$ is complete, that is, if a formula φ is SCI-valid, then φ has a tableau proof.*

Proof. Let φ be a valid SCI-formula. Suppose that φ does not have a tableau proof. Then, each $\mathsf{T}_{\mathsf{SCI}}$-tableau with $\mathbf{w}^- : \varphi$ at its root is open. Let B be an open and fully expanded branch of an open tableau for $\mathbf{w}^- : \varphi$. By Proposition 10, the structure $\mathcal{M}_B = \langle U, D, \tilde{\neg}, \tilde{\rightarrow}, \tilde{\equiv} \rangle$ is an SCI-model. Let V be a valuation in $\mathcal{M}_B$ defined as before Proposition 11 Then, by Proposition 12, $\mathbf{w}^- \sim V(\varphi)$, and hence $V(\varphi) \notin D$. Thus, φ is not true in $\mathcal{M}_B$, which contradicts the assumption that φ is SCI-valid. $\qquad\square$

3.3 Termination

It turns out that the system presented in Section 3.1 terminates without any external blocking mechanisms involved which would impose some additional restrictions on rule-application. The only caveat that has to be added to the system is the one that we have already expressed, namely that no rule (R) can be applied to the set of premises that is (R)-expanded.

Theorem 3. *The tableau system* T_{SCI} *is terminating.*

Proof. The argument hinges on two observations. First, the decomposition rules are the only rules that introduce fresh labels to a branch $\mathcal{B}$ of a T_{SCI}-tableau $\mathcal{T}$, and, as mentioned before, on a branch $\mathcal{B}$ each occurrence of a subformula of the initial formula φ is assigned its unique label. Thus, since an application of any of the above rules decreases the complexity of the processed formula and the rule cannot be applied twice to the same premise, the total number of labels occurring on a branch does not exceed the size of φ measured as the number of all occurrences of subformulas of φ (henceforth denoted by $|\varphi|$). Secondly, the equality rules can only add equalities between labels to a branch, provided that such an equality statement is not already present thereon. The maximal number of such equalities is quadriatic in the total number of labels occurring on a branch. Thus, for each SCI-formula φ, on any branch $\mathcal{B}$ of a T_{SCI}-tableau for φ, rules are applied at most $|\varphi| + |\varphi|^2 + 1$ times, where '1' in the formula represents an application of a closure rule. This makes the whole derivation finite. □

Corollary 1. *For each* SCI-*formula* φ *every branch* $\mathcal{B}$ *of a* T_{SCI}-*tableau derivation for* φ *is of polynomial size with respect to the size of* φ.

Since SCI contains classical propositional logic, it inherits the NP-lower bound for the satisfiability problem therefrom. Together with membership of SCI-satisfiability in NP it gives the following:

Theorem 4. T_{SCI} *is a complexity-optimal decision procedure for the* NP-*complete problem of* SCI-*satisfiability.*

Proof. Immediate from Corollary 1 and the fact that each branching rule of T_{SCI} is finitely branching. □

3.4 Limiting the Number of Labels

To boost the performance of the system T_{SCI} we propose a refinement thereof. It consists in limiting the number of fresh labels introduced to a tableau by decomposition rules by introducing an additional condition called *urfather blocking*

Given a formula φ for which we construct a T_{SCI}-tableau $\mathcal{T}$, for each subformula ψ of φ, let's call the first occurrence of a labelled formula $w : \psi$ on a branch $\mathcal{B}$ of $\mathcal{T}$ the ψ-*urfather on* $\mathcal{B}$. The system $T_{SCI} + (UB)$ (*tableau system for* SCI *with urfather blocking*) is composed of the rules of T_{SCI} and an additional constraint:

(UB) For each labelled formula $w : \varphi$ that occurs on a branch $\mathcal{B}$, no decomposition rule can be applied to $w : \varphi$ unless it is the φ-urfather on $\mathcal{B}$.

It turns out that augmenting $\mathsf{T_{SCI}}$ with (UB) does not lead to any unwanted consequences such as giving up the completeness.

Proposition 13. *For every SCI-formula φ, if φ has a $\mathsf{T_{SCI}}$-tableau proof, then φ has $\mathsf{TC_{SCI}} + (UB)$-tableau proof.*

Theorem 5. $\mathsf{T_{SCI}} + (\mathsf{UB})$ *is sound, complete, terminating, and complexity-optimal for SCI-satisfiability.*

Proof. The soundness of $\mathsf{T_{SCI}} + (\mathsf{UB})$ straightforwardly follows from the soundness of $\mathsf{T_{SCI}}$ and the fact that both systems share the full set of rules. The argument for termination of $\mathsf{T_{SCI}} + (UB)$ and complexity-optimality of $\mathsf{T_{SCI}} + (UB)$ for SCI-satisfiability goes along the same lines as the proofs of Theorems 3 and 4, and rests on the fact that, for each formula φ, a $\mathsf{T_{SCI}} + (\mathsf{UB})$-tableau contains at most as many labels as a $\mathsf{T_{SCI}}$-tableau. The completeness of $TSCI + (UB)$ is a direct consequence of Proposition 13 and Theorem 2. $\square$

4 Implementation

4.1 Overview

We have written proof-of-concept type implementations of the labelled tableau system described in the present article and its variant with urfather blocking, as well as a dual-tableau-based theorem prover for SCI based on the system from [5]. Since the last system does not enjoy the termination property, the implementation relies on heuristics in this respect. All three provers are implemented in the Haskell language using similar programming techniques in a casual manner, without any serious attempt to optimize the code or to test it extensively, as the programs are only intended as temporary aids to ongoing research.

In testing, the labelled-tableau provers turned out to need drastically more computing resources even in many quite modest test cases. For instance, the axiom $((\mathsf{p} \equiv \mathsf{q}) \wedge (\mathsf{r} \equiv \mathsf{s})) \rightarrow ((\mathsf{p} \equiv \mathsf{r}) \equiv (\mathsf{q} \equiv \mathsf{s}))$ generates a labelled tableau of depth 37 consisting of 619 nodes, which urfather blocking reduces to depth 33 and 555 nodes, while the tree of the dual-tableau prover has depth 18 and only 67 nodes. The difference appears to be mostly due to the large branching factor of the identity rules of the labelled-tableau system. However, in some test cases the labelled-tableau system yields a smaller tree than the other prover. In general, the labelled tableau method seems to tolerate relatively well formulas consisting of a large number of very simple identitities.

4.2 Technical Notes

Unlike the abstract tree described above, each node of which contains only a single labelled formula, each node of the tree built by the program contains a list of all the labelled formulas encountered so far on the branch. This allows the program to freely manipulate the list to keep track of what rules have already been applied to which formulas. There are three main types of nodes: normal nodes, identity nodes, and leaves. First, the decomposition rules are applied in normal nodes. Once they have been applied to exhaustion, the tree is extended with identity nodes, in which the identity rules are applied. At any point, one of the closure rules ($\bot_1$) or ($\bot_2$) can be applied to append a special closure leaf node. An open leaf node is appended whenever there are no more rules to apply in an identity node and the branch remains open.

4.3   Test Results

We found a randomly generated provable SCI-formula that turned out to be somewhat challenging to an earlier prover. The formula, which we will call the φ here, looks as follows:

$$(((q \equiv p) \to (p \to r)) \equiv ((p \to (p \leftrightarrow p)) \equiv p))$$
$$\to (((r \wedge p) \leftrightarrow (p \equiv p)) \vee ((p \wedge p) \vee \neg q))$$

We denote by ψ the formula obtained by replacing each occurrence of p in φ by φ itself. We defined a provability-preserving transformation T that turns an SCI-formula into a Horn clause consisting of very simple identities.

We present the results of attempting to prove the formulas φ, $\neg\varphi$, ψ, $\neg\psi$, $T(\varphi)$, and $T(\neg\varphi)$. These are chosen to illustrate some of the variety of outcomes we observed. As noted above, φ is provable, and therefore also ψ and $T(\varphi)$ are provable. The results are of the form *depth/size*, where *depth* is the maximal branch length and *size* is the number of nodes in the entire tree. There are entries for the dual-tableau-based prover (DT_{SCI}), the current labelled-tableau prover (T_{SCI}), and the same with the urfather blocking condition ($T_{SCI} + (UB)$). Several entries are missing due to exhaustion of memory (the programs were tested on a machine with 8GB of RAM; adding several gigabytes of swap space did not make a difference).

Formula	DT_{SCI}		T_{SCI}		$T_{SCI} + (UB)$	
	depth	**size**	**depth**	**size**	**depth**	**size**
φ	27	299	37	4724	32	4659
$\neg\varphi$	12	42	202	111539	106	95724
ψ	61	17729	–	–	46	3023804
$\neg\psi$	42	602	–	–	–	–
$T(\varphi)$	–	–	143	40230	106	34158
$T(\neg\varphi)$	–	–	529	52789	490	46153

5   Conclusions

In this paper we introduced the system T_{SCI} which is the first complexity-optimal decision procedure for the logic SCI devised in the paradigm of labelled tableaux.

T_{SCI} is conceptually simple and directly reflects the semantics of the logic. The reasoning performed in T_{SCI} has two components: decomposition and equality reasoning. Interestingly, it is the latter that is responsible for closing tableau branches, and thus, yielding tableau proofs for formulas. In this respect T_{SCI} is based on similar conceptual foundations as calculi generated by the tableau-synthesis framework from [20].We provided an implementation of T_{SCI} and a variant with urfather blocking, and we compared their performance with the performance of another implemented deduction system for SCI which has not been proven to be terminating or complete. There was no unique winner; the new system was better at dealing with formulas with complex networks of identities, while the old, unproven system handled other types of formulas better. Urfather blocking yielded modest reductions in depth and total size.

In future research we want to address three main problems. First, we would like to optimize our tableau algorithm by introducing further refinements to it, such as decreasing the branching factor of the rule $(\rightarrow^+)$ and, by that means, making it "information-deleting". Some preliminary results on the implementation of T_{SCI} with the modified rule $(\rightarrow^+)$ show a promising reduction of the size of generated tableaus. Moreover, we plan to search for heuristics and rule-application strategies which would, too, allow to minimize the size of tableaux yielded by T_{SCI} for certain classes of formulas. It seems that it is not always necessary to fully decompose the input formula before performing any equality reasoning, if a contradiction is to be reached on a branch. Secondly, we would like to develop the dual-tableau systems from [5] and [10] to full-fledged decision procedures, implement them, and compare the performance of all three algorithms on an extensive set of various SCI-formulas. Thirdly, we intend to extend the labelled tableaux-based approach presented in this paper to other non-Fregean logics, both classical (such as modal non-Fregean logics) and deviant (such as intuitionistic or many-valued non-Fregean logics, or Grzegorczyk's logic). Finally, we would like to take a closer look at various normal forms of SCI formulas, one of which was mentioned in Section 4, and decide in what cases it pays off to transform a formula into a normal form before running a decision procedure, rather than running it directly on the initial formula.

References

1. Bloom, S.L., Suszko, R.: Semantics for the sentential calculus with identity. Studia Logica 28(1), 77–81 (1971). https://doi.org/10.1007/BF02124265
2. Bloom, S.L., Suszko, R.: Investigations into the sentential calculus with identity. Notre Dame Journal of Formal Logic 13(3), 289–308 (1972). https://doi.org/10.1305/ndjfl/1093890617
3. Chlebowski, S.: Sequent calculi for SCI. Studia Logica 106, 541–563 (2018). https://doi.org/10.1007/s11225-017-9754-8
4. Chlebowski, S., Leszczyńska-Jasion, D.: An investigation into intuitionistic logic with identity. Bulletin of the Section of Logic 48(4), 259–283 (2019). https://doi.org/10.18778/0138-0680.48.4.02

5. Golińska-Pilarek, J.: Rasiowa-sikorski proof system for the non-Fregean sentential logic SCI. Journal of Applied Non-Classical Logics **17**(4), 511–519 (2007). https://doi.org/10.3166/jancl.17.511-519
6. Golińska-Pilarek, J.: On the minimal non-Fregean Grzegorczyk's logic. Studia Logica **104**(2), 209–234 (2016). https://doi.org/10.1007/s11225-015-9635-y
7. Golińska-Pilarek, J., Huuskonen, T.: Number of extensions of non-Fregean logics. Journal of Philosophical Logic **34**(2), 193–206 (2005). https://doi.org/10.1007/s10992-004-6366-3
8. Golińska-Pilarek, J., Huuskonen, T.: Non-Fregean propositional logic with quantifiers. Notre Dame Journal of Formal Logic **57**(2), 249–279 (2016). https://doi.org/10.1215/00294527-3470547
9. Golińska-Pilarek, J., Huuskonen, T.: A mystery of Grzegorczyk's logic of descriptions. In: Garrido, A., Wybraniec-Skardowska, U. (eds.) The Lvov-Warsaw School. Past and Present, pp. 731–745. Studies in Universal Logic, Springer Nature (2018). https://doi.org/10.1007/978-3-319-65430-0_51
10. Golińska-Pilarek, J., Welle, M.: Deduction in non-Fregean propositional logic SCI. Axioms **8**, 115 (2019). https://doi.org/10.3390/axioms8040115
11. Golińska-Pilarek, J., Zawidzki, M.: Tableau-based decision procedure for the logic SCI. In: Gigante, N., Mari, F., Orlandini, A. (eds.) Proceedings of the 1st Workshop on Artificial Intelligence and Formal Verification, Logic, Automata, and Synthesis, co-located with the 18th International Conference of the Italian Association for Artificial Intelligence, OVERLAY@AI*IA 2019, Rende, Italy, November 19-20, 2019. CEUR Workshop Proceedings, vol. 2509, pp. 23–28 (2019)
12. Golińska-Pilarek, J., Huuskonen, T., Zawidzki, M.: Tableau-based decision procedure for non-fregean logic of sentential identity (2021), arXiv: 2104.14697
13. Ishii, T.: Propositional calculus with identity. Bulletin of the Section of Logic **27**(3), 96–104 (1998)
14. Lewitzka, S.: ϵ_I: : An intuitionistic logic without Fregean Axiom and with predicates for truth and falsity. Notre Dame Journal of Formal Logic **50**(3), 275–301 (2009). https://doi.org/10.1215/00294527-2009-012
15. Lewitzka, S.: ϵ_K: a non-Fregean logic of explicit knowledge. Studia Logica **97**(2), 233–264 (2011). https://doi.org/10.1007/s11225-011-9304-8
16. Lewitzka, S.: Denotational semantics for modal systems S3 S5 extended by axioms for propositional quantifiers and identity. Studia Logica **103**(3), 507–544 (2015). https://doi.org/10.1007/s11225-014-9577-9
17. Łukowski, P.: Intuitionistic sentential calculus with classical identity. Bulletin of the Section of Logic **19**(4), 147–150 (1990)
18. Michaels, A.: A uniform proof procedure for SCI tautologies. Studia Logica **33**(3), 299–310 (1974). https://doi.org/10.1007/BF02123284
19. Orłowska, E., Golińska-Pilarek, J.: Dual Tableaux: Foundations, Methodology, Case Studies, Trends in Logic, vol. 33. Springer, Dordrecht (2011). https://doi.org/10.1007/978-94-007-0005-5
20. Schmidt, R.A., Tishkovsky, D.: Automated synthesis of tableau calculi. Logical Methods in Computer Science **7**(2) (2011). https://doi.org/10.2168/LMCS-7(2:6)2011
21. Suszko, R.: Abolition of the Fregean axiom. In: Parikh, R. (ed.) Logic Colloquium. Lecture Notes in Mathematics, vol. 453, pp. 169–239 (1975). https://doi.org/10.1007%2FBFb0064874
22. Wasilewska, A.: A sequence formalization for SCI. Studia Logica **35**(3), 213–217 (1976). https://doi.org/10.1007/BF02282483

23. Wasilewska, A.: DFC-algorithms for Suszko logic and one-to-one Gentzen type formalizations. Studia Logica **43**(4), 395–404 (1984). https://doi.org/10.1007/BF00370509

Open Access This chapter is licensed under the terms of the Creative Commons Attribution 4.0 International License (http://creativecommons.org/licenses/by/4.0/), which permits use, sharing, adaptation, distribution and reproduction in any medium or format, as long as you give appropriate credit to the original author(s) and the source, provide a link to the Creative Commons license and indicate if changes were made.

The images or other third party material in this chapter are included in the chapter's Creative Commons license, unless indicated otherwise in a credit line to the material. If material is not included in the chapter's Creative Commons license and your intended use is not permitted by statutory regulation or exceeds the permitted use, you will need to obtain permission directly from the copyright holder.

Learning from Łukasiewicz and Meredith: Investigations into Proof Structures

Christoph Wernhard[1] and Wolfgang Bibel[2]

[1] Berlin, Germany info@christophwernhard.com
[2] Technical University Darmstadt, Darmstadt, Germany
bibel@gmx.net

Abstract. The material presented in this paper contributes to establishing a basis deemed essential for substantial progress in Automated Deduction. It identifies and studies global features in selected problems and their proofs which offer the potential of guiding proof search in a more direct way. The studied problems are of the wide-spread form of "axiom(s) and rule(s) imply goal(s)". The features include the well-known concept of lemmas. For their elaboration both human and automated proofs of selected theorems are taken into a close comparative consideration. The study at the same time accounts for a coherent and comprehensive formal reconstruction of historical work by Łukasiewicz, Meredith and others. First experiments resulting from the study indicate novel ways of lemma generation to supplement automated first-order provers of various families, strengthening in particular their ability to find short proofs.

1 Introduction

Research in Automated Deduction, also known as Automated Theorem Proving (ATP), has resulted in systems with a remarkable performance. Yet, deep mathematical theorems or otherwise complex statements still withstand any of the systems' attempts to find a proof. The present paper is motivated by the thesis that the reason for the failure in more complex problems lies in the local orientedness of all our current methods for proof search like resolution or connection calculi in use.

In order to find out more global features for directing proof search we start out here to study the structures of proofs for complex formulas in some detail and compare human proofs with those generated by systems. Complex formulas of this kind have been considered by Łukasiewicz in [19]. They are complex in the sense that current systems require tens of thousands or even millions of search steps for finding a proof if any, although the length of the formulas is very short indeed. How come that Łukasiewicz found proofs for those formulas although he could never carry out more than, say, a few hundred search steps by hand? Which global strategies guided him in finding those proofs? Could we discover such strategies from the formulas' global features?

By studying the proofs in detail we hope to come closer to answers to those questions. Thus it is proofs, rather than just formulas or clauses as usually in

© The Author(s) 2021
A. Platzer and G. Sutcliffe (Eds.): CADE 2021, LNAI 12699, pp. 58–75, 2021.
https://doi.org/10.1007/978-3-030-79876-5_4

ATP, which is in the focus of our study. In a sense we are aiming at an ATP-oriented part of Proof Theory, a discipline usually pursued in Logic yet under quite different aspects. This meta-level perspective has rarely been taken in ATP for which reason we cannot rely on the existing conceptual basis of ATP but have to build an extensive conceptual basis for such a study more or less from scratch.

This investigation thus analyzes structures of, and operations on, proofs for formulas of the form "axiom(s) and rule(s) imply goal(s)". It renders condensed detachment, a logical rule historically introduced in the course of studying these complex proofs, as a restricted form of the Connection Method (CM) in ATP. All this is pursued with the goal of enhancing proof search in ATP in mind. As noted, our investigations are guided by a close inspection into proofs by Łukasiewicz and Meredith. In fact, the work presented here amounts at the same time to a very detailed reconstruction of those historical proofs.

The rest of the paper is organized as follows: In Sect. 2 we introduce the problem and a formal human proof that guides our investigations and compare different views on proof structures. We then reconstruct in Sect. 3 the historical method of *condensed detachment* in a novel way as a restricted variation of the CM where proof structures are represented as terms. This is followed in Sect. 4 by results on reducing the size of such proof terms for application in proof shortening and restricting the proof search space. Section 5 presents a detailed feature table for the investigated human proof, and Sect. 6 shows first experiments where the features and new techniques are used to supplement the inputs of ATP systems with lemmas. Section 7 concludes the paper. Supplementary technical material including proofs is provided in the report [37]. Data and tools to reproduce the experiments are available at http://cs.christophwernhard.com/cd.

2   Relating Formal Human Proofs with ATP Proofs

In 1948 Jan Łukasiewicz published a formal proof of the completeness of his shortest single axiom for the implicational fragment (**IF**), that is, classical propositional logic with implication as the only logic operator [19]. In his notation the implication $p \rightarrow q$ is written as Cpq. Following Frank Pfenning [27] we formalize **IF** on the meta-level in the first-order setting of modern ATP with a single unary predicate P to be interpreted as something like "provable" and represent the propositional formulas by terms using the binary function symbol i for implication. We will be concerned with the following formulas.

Nickname [28][29, p. 319]	Łukasiewicz's notation	First-order representation
Simp	$CpCqp$	$\forall pq\, \mathsf{P}(\mathsf{i}(p, \mathsf{i}qp))$
Peirce	$CCCpqpp$	$\forall pq\, \mathsf{P}(\mathsf{i}(\mathsf{i}(\mathsf{i}pq), p), p)$
Syll	$CCpqCCqrCpr$	$\forall pqr\, \mathsf{P}(\mathsf{i}(\mathsf{i}pq, \mathsf{i}(\mathsf{i}qr, \mathsf{i}pr)))$
Syll Simp	$CCpqrCqr$	$\forall pqr\, \mathsf{P}\mathsf{i}(\mathsf{i}(\mathsf{i}pq, r), \mathsf{i}qr)$
Łukasiewicz	$CCCpqrCCrpCsp$	$\forall pqrs\, \mathsf{P}(\mathsf{i}(\mathsf{i}(\mathsf{i}pq, r), \mathsf{i}(\mathsf{i}rp, \mathsf{i}sp)))$

IF can be axiomatized by the set of the three axioms *Simp*, *Peirce* and *Syll*, known as *Tarski-Bernays Axioms*. Alfred Tarski in 1925 raised the problem to

Fig. 1. *ŁDS* along with its five unifiable connections.

characterize **IF** by a single axiom and solved it with very long axioms, which led to a search for the *shortest* single axiom, which was found with the axiom nicknamed after him in 1936 by Łukasiewicz [19]. In 1948 he published his derivation that *Łukasiewicz* entails the three Tarski-Bernays Axioms, expressed formally by the *method of substitution and detachment*. Detachment is also familiar as *modus ponens*. Łukasiewicz's proof involves 34 applications of detachment. Among the Tarski-Bernays axioms *Syll* is by far the most challenging to prove, hence his proof centers around the proof of *Syll*, with *Peirce* and *Simp* spinning off as side results. Carew A. Meredith presented in [24] a "very slight abridgement" of Łukasiewicz's proof, expressed in his framework of *condensed detachment* [28], where the performed substitutions are no longer explicitly presented but implicitly assumed through unification. Meredith's proof involves only 33 applications of detachment. In our first-order setting, detachment can be modeled with the following meta-level axiom.

$$Det \overset{\text{def}}{=} \forall xy \, (\mathsf{P}x \wedge \mathsf{P}\mathsf{i}xy \to \mathsf{P}y).$$

In *Det* the atom $\mathsf{P}x$ is called the *minor premise*, $\mathsf{P}\mathsf{i}xy$ the *major premise*, and $\mathsf{P}y$ the *conclusion*. Let us now focus on the following particular formula.

$$ŁDS \overset{\text{def}}{=} Łukasiewicz \wedge Det \to Syll.$$

"Problem *ŁDS*" is then the problem of determining the validity of the first order formula *ŁDS*. In view of the CM [1,2,3], a formula is valid if there is a spanning and complementary set of connections in it. In Fig. 1 *ŁDS* is presented again, nicknames dereferenced and quantifiers omitted as usual in ATP, with the five unifiable connections in it. Observe that p, q, r, s on the left side of the main implication are variables, while $\mathsf{p}, \mathsf{q}, \mathsf{r}$ on the right side are Skolem constants. Any CM proof of *ŁDS* consists of a number of instances of the five shown connections. Meredith's proof, for example, corresponds to 491 instances of *Det*, each linked with three instances of its five incident connections.

Figure 2 compares different representations of a short formal proof with the *Det* meta axiom. There is a single axiom, *Syll Simp*, and the theorem is $\forall pqrstu \, \mathsf{Pi}(p, \mathsf{i}(q, \mathsf{i}(r, \mathsf{i}(s, \mathsf{i}(t, \mathsf{i}us)))))$. Figure 2a shows the structure of a CM proof. It involves seven instances of *Det*, shown in columns $D_1, \ldots, D_7$. The major premise $\mathsf{P}\mathsf{i}x_iy_i$ is displayed there on top of the minor premise $\mathsf{P}x_i$, and the (negated) conclusion $\neg \mathsf{P}y_i$, where x_i, y_i are variables. Instances of the axiom appear as literals $\neg \mathsf{P}a_i$, with a_i a shorthand for the term $\mathsf{i}(\mathsf{i}(\mathsf{i}p_iq_i, r_i), \mathsf{i}q_ir_i)$. The rightmost literal $\mathsf{P}g$ is a shorthand for the Skolemized theorem. The clause instances are linked through edges representing connection instances. The edge

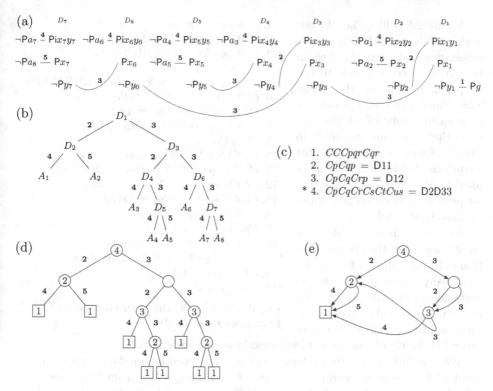

Fig. 2. A proof in different representations.

labels identify the respective connections as in Fig. 1. An actual connection proof is obtained by supplementing this structure with a substitution under which all pairs of literals related through a connection instance become complementary.

Figure 2b represents the *tree* implicit in the CM proof. Its inner nodes correspond to the instances of *Det*, and its leaf nodes to the instances of the axiom. Edges appear ordered to the effect that those originating in a major premise of *Det* are directed to the left and those from a minor premise to the right. The goal clause Pg is dropped. The resulting tree is a *full binary tree*, i.e., a binary tree where each node has 0 or 2 children. We observe that the ordering of the children makes the connection labeling redundant as it directly corresponds to the tree structure.

Figure 2c presents the proof in Meredith's notation. Each line shows a formula, line 1 the axiom and lines 2–4 derived formulas, with proofs annotated in the last column. Proofs are written as terms in Polish notation with the binary function symbol D for *detachment* where the subproofs of the major and minor premise are supplied as first and second, resp., argument. Formula 4, for example, is obtained as conclusion of *Det* applied to formula 2 as major premise and as minor premise another formula that is not made explicit in the presentation, namely the conclusion of *Det* applied to formula 3 as both, major and minor premises. An asterisk marks the goal theorem.

Figure 2d is like Fig. 2b, but with a different labeling: Node labels now refer to the line in Fig. 2c that corresponds to the subproof rooted at the node. The blank node represents the mentioned subproof of the formula that is not made explicit in Fig. 2b. An inner node represents a condensed detachment step applied to the subproof of the major premise (left child) and minor premise (right child).

Figure 2e shows a DAG (directed acyclic graph) representation of Figure 2d. It is the unique maximally factored DAG representation of the tree, i.e., it has no multiple occurrences of the same subtree. Each of the four proof line labels of Fig. 2c appears exactly once in the DAG.

1. $CCCpqrCCrpCsp$
2. $CCCpqpCrp$ = DDD1D111n
3. $CCCpqrCqr$ = DDD1D1D121n
4. $CpCCpqCrq$ = D31
5. $CCCpqCrsCCCqtsCrs$ = DDD1D1D1D141n
6. $CCCpqCrsCCpsCrs$ = D51
7. $CCpCqrCCCpsrCqr$ = D64
8. $CCCCCpqrtCspCCrpCsp$ = D71
9. $CCpqCpq$ = D83
10. $CCCCrpCtpCCCpqrsCuCCCpqrs$ = D18
11. $CCCCpqrCsqCCCqtsCpq$ = DD10.10.n
12. $CCCCpqrCsqCCCqtpCsq$ = D5.11
13. $CCCCpqrsCCsqCpq$ = D12.6
14. $CCCpqrCCrpp$ = D12.9
15. $CpCCpqq$ = D3.14
16. $CCpqCCCprqq$ = D6.15
*17. $CCpqCCqrCpr$ = DD13.D16.16.13
*18. $CCCpqpp$ = D14.9
*19. $CpCqp$ = D33

Fig. 3. Proof MER, Meredith's refinement [24] of Łukasiewicz's proof [19].

We conclude this introductory section with reproducing Meredith's refinement of Łukasiewicz's completeness proof in Fig. 3, taken from [24]. Since we will often refer to this proof, we call it MER. There is a single axiom (1), which is *Łukasiewicz*. The proven theorems are *Syll* (17), *Peirce* (18) and *Simp* (19). In addition to line numbers also the symbol n appears in some of the proof terms. Its meaning will be explained later on in the context of Def. 19. For now, we can read n just as "1". Dots are used in the Polish notation to disambiguate numeric identifiers with more than a single digit.

3   Condensed Detachment and a Formal Basis

Following [4], the idea of condensed detachment can be described as follows: Given premises $F \to G$ and H, we can conclude G', where G' is the most general result that can be obtained by using a substitution instance H' as minor premise with the substitution instance $F' \to G'$ as major premise in modus ponens. Condensed detachment was introduced by Meredith in the mid-1950s as an evolution of the earlier *method of substitution and detachment*, where the involved substitutions were explicitly given. The original presentations of condensed detachment are informal by means of examples [28,17,29,25], formal specifications have been given later [16,13,4]. In ATP, the rendering of condensed detachment by hyperresolution with the clausal form of axiom *Det* is so far the prevalent view. As overviewed in [23,31], many of the early successes of ATP were based on condensed detachment. Starting from the hyperresolution view, structural aspects of condensed detachment have been considered by Robert Veroff [34] with the use of term representations of proofs and *linked* resolution. Results of ATP systems on deriving the Tarski-Bernays axioms from *Łukasiewicz* are reported in [27,39,22,23,11]. Our goal in this section is to provide a formal framework that makes the achievements of condensed detachment accessible from a modern ATP view. In particular, the incorporation of unification, the interplay of nested structures with explicitly and implicitly associated formulas, sharing of structures through lemmas, and the availability of proof structures as terms.

Our notation follows common practice [6] (e.g., $s \geq t$ expresses that t subsumes s, and $s \trianglerighteq t$ that t is a subterm of s) with some additions [37]. For formulas F we write the universal closure as $\forall F$, and for terms s, t, u we use $s[t \mapsto u]$ to denote s after simultaneously replacing all occurrences of t with u.

3.1   Proof Structures: D-Terms, Tree Size and Compacted Size

In this section we consider only the purely structural aspects of condensed detachment proofs. Emphasis is on a twofold view on the proof structure, as a tree and as a DAG (directed acyclic graph), which factorizes multiple occurrences of the same subtree. Both representation forms are useful: the compacted DAG form captures that lemmas can be repeatedly used in a proof, whereas the tree form facilitates to specify properties in an inductive manner. We call the tree representation of proofs by terms with the binary function symbol D *D-terms*.

Definition 1. (i) We assume a distinguished set of symbols called *primitive D-terms*. (ii) A *D-term* is inductively specified as follows: (1.) Any primitive D-term is a D-term. (2.) If d_1 and d_2 are D-terms, then $D(d_1, d_2)$ is a D-term. (iii) The set of primitive D-terms occurring in a D-term d is denoted by $\mathcal{P}rim(d)$. (iv) The set of all D-terms that are not primitive is denoted by $\mathcal{D}$.

A D-term is a full binary tree (i.e, a binary tree in which every node has either 0 or 2 children), where the leaves are labeled with symbols, i.e., primitive D-terms. An example D-term is

$$d \stackrel{\text{def}}{=} D(D(1,1), D(D(1, D(1,1)), D(1, D(1,1)))), \tag{i}$$

which represents the structure of the proof shown in Fig. 2 and can be visualized by the full binary tree of Fig. 2d after removing all labels with exception of the leaf labels. The proof annotations in Fig. 2c and Fig. 3 are D-terms written in Polish notation. The expression D2D33 in line 4 of Fig. 2, for example, stands for the D-term $D(2, D(3, 3))$. $\mathcal{P}rim(D(2, D(3, 3))) = \{2, 3\}$.

A finite tree and, more generally, a finite set of finite trees can be represented as DAG, where each node in the DAG corresponds to a subtree of a tree in the given set. It is well known that there is a unique *minimal* such DAG, which is maximally factored (it has no multiple occurrences of the same subtree) or, equivalently, is minimal with respect to the number of nodes, and, moreover, can be computed in linear time [7]. The number of nodes of the minimal DAG is the number of distinct subtrees of the members of the set of trees. There are two useful notions of measuring the size of a D-term, based directly on its tree representation and based on its minimal DAG, respectively.

Definition 2. (i) The *tree size* of a D-term d, in symbols t-size(d), is the number of occurrences of the function symbol D in d. (ii) The *compacted size* of a D-term d is defined as c-size(d) $\stackrel{\text{def}}{=}$ $|\{e \in \mathcal{D} \mid d \trianglerighteq e\}|$. (iii) The *compacted size* of a finite set D of D-terms is defined as c-size(D) $\stackrel{\text{def}}{=}$ $|\{e \in \mathcal{D} \mid d \in D \text{ and } d \trianglerighteq e\}|$.

The tree size of a D-term can equivalently be characterized as the number of its inner nodes. The compacted size of a D-term is the number of its distinct compound subterms. It can equivalently be characterized as the number of the inner nodes of its minimal DAG. As an example consider the D-term d defined in formula (i), whose minimal DAG is shown in Fig. 2e. The tree size of d is t-size(d) $= 7$ and the compacted size of d is c-size(d) $= 4$, corresponding to the cardinality of the set $\{e \in \mathcal{D} \mid d \trianglerighteq e\}$ of compound subterms of d, i.e., $\{D(1,1), D(1, D(1,1)), D(D(1, D(1,1)), D(1, D(1,1))), d\}$.

As will be explicated in more detail below, each occurrence of the function symbol D in a D-term corresponds to an instance of the meta-level axiom *Det* in the represented proof. Hence the tree size measures the number of instances of *Det* in the proof. Another view is that each occurrence of D in a D-term corresponds to a condensed detachment step, without re-using already proven lemmas. The compacted size of a D-term is the number of its distinct compound subterms, corresponding to the view that the size of the proof of a lemma is only counted once, even if it is used multiply. Tree size and compacted size of D-terms appear in [34] as *CDcount* and *length*, respectively.

3.2 Proof Structures, Formula Substitutions and Semantics

We use a notion of *unifier* that applies to a set of pairs of terms, as convenient in discussions based on the CM [1,9,8].

Definition 3. Let M be a set of pairs of terms and let σ be a substitution. (i) σ is said to be a *unifier* of M if for all $\{s, t\} \in M$ it holds that $s\sigma = t\sigma$. (ii) σ is called a *most general unifier* of M if σ is a unifier of M and for all unifiers σ' of M it holds that $\sigma' \geq \sigma$. (iii) σ is called a *clean most general unifier* of M if it is a most general unifier of M and, in addition, is idempotent and satisfies $\mathcal{D}om(\sigma) \cup \mathcal{VR}ng(\sigma) \subseteq Var(M)$.

The additional properties required for *clean* most general unifiers do not hold for all most general unifiers.[3] However, the unification algorithms known from the literature produce *clean* most general unifiers [9, Remark 4.2]. If a set of pairs of terms has a unifier, then it has a most general unifier and, moreover, also a *clean* most general unifier.

Definition 4. (i) If M is a set of pairs of terms that has a unifier, then mgu(M) denotes some clean most general unifier of M. M is called *unifiable* and mgu(M) is called *defined* in this case, otherwise it is called *undefined*. (ii) We make the convention that proposition, lemma and theorem statements implicitly assert their claims only for the case where occurrences of mgu in them are defined.

---

[3] The inaccuracy observed by [13] in early formalizations of condensed detachment can be attributed to disregarding the requirement $\mathcal{D}om(\sigma) \cup \mathcal{VR}ng(\sigma) \subseteq Var(M)$.

Since we define $\mathsf{mgu}(M)$ as a *clean* most general unifier, we are permitted to make use of the assumption that it is idempotent and that all variables occurring in its domain and range occur in M. Convention 4.ii has the purpose to reduce clutter in proposition, lemma and theorem statements.

The structural aspects of condensed detachment proofs represented by D-terms, i.e., full binary trees, will now be supplemented with associated formulas. Condensed detachment proofs, similar to CM proofs, involve different instances of the input formulas (viewed as quantifier-free, e.g., clauses), which may be considered as obtained in two steps: first, "copies", that is, variants with fresh variables, of the input formulas are created; second a substitution is applied to these copies. Let us consider now the first step. The framework of D-terms permits to give the variables in the copies canonical designators with an index subscript that *identifies the position in the structure*, i.e., in the D-term, or tree.

Definition 5. For all positions p and positive integers i let x_p^i and y_p denote pairwise different variables.

Recall that positions are path specifiers. For a given D-term d and leaf position p of d the variables x_p^i are for use in a formula associated with p which is the copy of an axiom. Different variables in the copy are distinguished by the upper index i. If p is a non-leaf position of d, then y_p denotes the variable in the conclusion of the copy of Det that is represented by p. In addition, y_p for leaf positions p may occur in the antecedents of the copies of Det. The following substitution shift_p is a tool to systematically rename position-associated variables while preserving the internal relationships between the index-referenced positions.

Definition 6. For all positions p define the substitution shift_p as follows: $\mathsf{shift}_p \overset{\text{def}}{=} \{y_q \mapsto y_{p.q} \mid q \text{ is a position}\} \cup \{x_q^i \mapsto x_{p.q}^i \mid i \geq 1 \text{ and } q \text{ is a position}\}$.

The application of shift_p to a term s effects that p is prepended to the position indexes of all the position-associated variables occurring in s. The association of axioms with primitive D-terms is represented by mappings which we call *axiom assignments*, defined as follows.

Definition 7. An *axiom assignment* α is a mapping whose domain is a set of primitive D-terms and whose range is a set of terms whose variables are in $\{x_\epsilon^i \mid i \geq 1\}$. We say that α is *for* a D-term d if $\mathcal{D}om(\alpha) \supseteq \mathcal{P}rim(d)$.

We define a shorthand for a form of *Łukasiewicz* that is suitable for use as a range element of axiom assignments. It is parameterized with a position p.

$$\textit{Łukasiewicz}_p \overset{\text{def}}{=} \mathsf{i}(\mathsf{i}(\mathsf{i}(x_p^1, x_p^2), x_p^3), \mathsf{i}(\mathsf{i}(x_p^3, x_p^1), \mathsf{i}(x_p^4, x_p^1))). \tag{ii}$$

The mapping $\{1 \mapsto \textit{Łukasiewicz}_\epsilon\}$ is an axiom assignment for all D-terms d with $\mathcal{P}rim(d) = \{1\}$. The second step of obtaining the instances involved in a proof can be performed by applying the most general unifier of a pair of terms that constrain it. The tree structure of D-terms permits to associate exactly one such pair with each term position. Inner positions represent detachment steps and leaf positions instances of an axiom according to a given axiom assignment. The following definition specifies these constraining pairs.

Definition 8. Let d be a D-term and let α be an axiom assignment for d. For all positions $p \in \mathcal{P}os(d)$ define the pair of terms $\mathsf{pairing}_\alpha(d, p) \overset{\text{def}}{=} \{y_p, \alpha(d|_p)\mathsf{shift}_p\}$ if $p \in \mathcal{L}eaf\mathcal{P}os(d)$ and $\{y_{p.1}, \mathsf{i}(y_{p.2}, y_p)\}$ if $p \in \mathcal{I}nner\mathcal{P}os(d)$.

A unifier of the set of pairings of all positions of a D-term d equates for a leaf position p the variable y_p with the value of the axiom assignment α for the primitive D-term at p, after "shifting" variables by p. This "shifting" means that the position subscript ϵ of the variables in the axiom argument term $\alpha(d|_p)$ is replaced by p, yielding a dedicated copy of the axiom argument term for the leaf position p. For inner positions p the unifier equates $y_{p.1}$ and $\mathsf{i}(y_{p.2}, y_p)$, reflecting that the major premise of Det is proven by the left child of p.

The substitution induced by the pairings associated with the positions of a D-term allow to associate a specific formula with each position of the D-term, called the *in-place theorem (IPT)*. The case where the position is the top position ϵ is distinguished as *most general theorem (MGT)*.

Definition 9. For D-terms d, positions $p \in \mathcal{P}os(d)$ and axiom assignments α for d define the *in-place theorem (IPT)* of d at p for α, $Ipt_\alpha(d, p)$, and the *most general theorem (MGT)* of d for α, $Mgt_\alpha(d)$, as (i) $Ipt_\alpha(d, p) \overset{\text{def}}{=} \mathsf{P}(y_p\mathsf{mgu}(\{\mathsf{pairing}_\alpha(d, q) \mid q \in \mathcal{P}os(d)\}))$. (ii) $Mgt_\alpha(d) \overset{\text{def}}{=} Ipt_\alpha(d, \epsilon)$.

Since *Ipt* and *Mgt* are defined on the basis of mgu, they are undefined if the set of pairs of terms underlying the respective application of mgu is not unifiable. Hence, we apply the convention of Def. 4.ii for mgu also to occurrences of *Ipt* and *Mgt*. If *Ipt* and *Mgt* are defined, they both denote an atom whose variables are constrained by the *clean* property of the underlying application of mgu. The following proposition relates IPT and MGT with respect to subsumption.

Proposition 10. *For all D-terms d, positions $p \in \mathcal{P}os(d)$ and axiom assignments α for d it holds that $Ipt_\alpha(d, p) \geq Mgt_\alpha(d|_p)$.*

By Prop. 10, the IPT at some position p of a D-term d is subsumed by the MGT of the subterm $d|_p$ of d rooted at position p. An intuitive argument is that the only constraints that determine the most general unifier underlying the MGT are induced by positions of $d|_p$, that is, *below p* (including p itself). In contrast, the most general unifier underlying the IPT is determined by *all* positions of d.

The following lemma expresses the core relationships between a proof structure (a D-term), a proof substitution (accessed via the IPT) and semantic entailment of associated formulas.

Lemma 11. *Let d be a D-term and let α be an axiom assignment for d. Then for all $p \in \mathcal{P}os(d)$ it holds that: (i) If $p \in \mathcal{L}eaf\mathcal{P}os(d)$, then $\forall \mathsf{P}(\alpha(d|_p)) \models Ipt_\alpha(d, p)$. (ii) If $p \in \mathcal{I}nner\mathcal{P}os(d)$, then $Det \wedge Ipt_\alpha(d, p.1) \wedge Ipt_\alpha(d, p.2) \models Ipt_\alpha(d, p)$.*

Based on this lemma, the following theorem shows how *Detachment* together with the axioms in an axiom assignment entail the MGT of a given D-term.

Theorem 12. *Let d be a D-term and let α be an axiom assignment for d. Then $Det \wedge \bigwedge_{p \in \mathcal{L}eaf\mathcal{P}os(d)} \forall \mathsf{P}(\alpha(d|_p)) \models \forall Mgt_\alpha(d)$.*

Theorem 12 states that *Det* together with the axioms referenced in the proof, that is, the values of α for the leaf nodes of d considered as universally closed atoms, entail the universal closure of the MGT of d for α. The universal closure of the MGT is the formula exhibited in Meredith's proof notation in the lines with a trailing D-term, such as lines 2–19 in Fig. 3.

4   Reducing the Proof Size by Replacing Subproofs

The term view on proof trees suggests to shorten proofs by rewriting subterms, that is, replacing occurrences of subproofs by other ones, with three main aims: (1) To shorten given proofs, with respect to the tree size or the compacted size. (2) To investigate given proofs whether they can be shortened by certain rewritings or are closed under these. (3) To develop notions of redundancy for use in proof search. A proof fragment constructed during search may be rejected if it can be rewritten to a shorter one.

It is obvious that if a D-term d' is obtained from a D-term d by replacing an occurrence of a subterm e with a D-term e' such that t-size$(e) \geq$ t-size(e'), then also t-size$(d) \geq$ t-size(d'). Based on the following ordering relations on D-terms, which we call *compaction orderings*, an analogy for reducing the *compacted* size instead of the tree size can be stated.

Definition 13. For D-terms d, e define (i) $d \geq_c e \overset{\text{def}}{=} \{f \in \mathcal{D} \mid d \rhd f\} \supseteq \{f \in \mathcal{D} \mid e \rhd f\}$. (ii) $d >_c e \overset{\text{def}}{=} d \geq_c e$ and $e \not\geq_c d$.

The relations $d \geq_c e$ and $d >_c e$ compare D-terms d and e with respect to the superset relationship of their sets of those strict subterms that are compound terms. For example, $D(D(D(1,1),1),1) >_c D(1,D(1,1))$ because $\{D(1,1), D(D(1,1),1)\} \supseteq \{D(1,1)\}$.

Theorem 14. *Let d, d', e, e' be D-terms such that e occurs in d, and $d' = d[e \mapsto e']$. It holds that (i) If $e \in \mathcal{D}$ and $e \geq_c e'$, then c-size$(d) \geq$ c-size(d'). (ii) If $e >_c e'$, then sc-size$(d) >$ sc-size(d'), where, for all D-terms d sc-size$(d) \overset{\text{def}}{=} \sum_{d \rhd e}$ c-size(e).*

Theorem 14.i states that if d' is the D-term obtained from d by simultaneously replacing *all* occurrences of a compound D-term e with a "c-smaller" D-term e', i.e., $e \geq_c e'$, then the compacted size of d' is less or equal to that of d. As stated with the supplementary Theorem 14.ii, the sc-size is a measure that strictly decreases under the strict precondition $e >_c e'$, which is useful to ensure termination of rewriting. The following proposition characterizes the number of D-terms that are smaller than a given D-term w.r.t the compaction ordering $\geq_c$.

Proposition 15. *For all D-terms d it holds that $|\{e \mid d \geq_c e$ and $\mathcal{P}rim(e) \subseteq \mathcal{P}rim(d)\}| = ($c-size$(d) - 1 + |\mathcal{P}rim(d)|)^2 + |\mathcal{P}rim(d)|$.*

By Prop. 15, for a given D-term d, the number of D-terms e that are smaller than d with respect to $\geq_c$ is only quadratically larger than the compacted size of d and thus also than the tree size of d. Hence techniques that inspect all these smaller D-terms for a given D-term can efficiently be used in practice.

According to Theorem 12, a condensed detachment proof, i.e., a D-term d and an axiom assignment α, proves the MGT of d for α along with instances of the MGT. In general, replacing subterms of d should yield a proof of at least these theorems. That is, a proof whose MGT subsumes the original one. The following theorem expresses conditions which ensure that subterm replacements yield a proof with a MGT that subsumes original one.

Theorem 16. *Let d, e be D-terms, let α be an axiom assignment for d and for e, and let $p_1, \ldots, p_n$, where $n \geq 0$, be positions in $\mathcal{P}os(d)$ such that for all $i, j \in \{1, \ldots, n\}$ with $i \neq j$ it holds that $p_i \not\leq p_j$. If for all $i \in \{1, \ldots, n\}$ it holds that $Ipt_\alpha(d, p_i) \geq Mgt_\alpha(e)$, then $Mgt_\alpha(d) \geq Mgt_\alpha(d[e]_{p_1}[e]_{p_2} \ldots [e]_{p_n})$.*

Theorem 16 states that simultaneously replacing a number of occurrences of possibly different subterms in a D-term by the same subterm with the property that its MGT subsumes each of the IPTs of the original occurrences results in an overall D-term whose MGT subsumes that of the original overall D-term. The following theorem is similar, but restricted to a single replaced occurrence and with a stronger precondition. It follows from Theorem 16 and Prop. 10.

Theorem 17. *Let d, e be D-terms and let α be an axiom assignment for d and for e. For all positions $p \in \mathcal{P}os(d)$ it then holds that if $Mgt_\alpha(d|_p) \geq Mgt_\alpha(e)$, then $Mgt_\alpha(d) \geq Mgt_\alpha(d[e]_p)$.*

Simultaneous replacements of subterm occurrences are essential for reducing the compacted size of proofs according to Theorem 14. For replacements according to Theorem 17 they can be achieved by successive replacements of individual occurrences. In Theorem 16 simultaneous replacements are explicitly considered because the replacement of one occurrence according to this theorem can invalidate the preconditions for another occurrence. Theorem 17 can be useful in practice because the precondition $Mgt_\alpha(d|_p) \geq Mgt_\alpha(e)$ can be evaluated on the basis of α, e and *just the subterm $d|_p$ of d*, whereas determining $Ipt_\alpha(d, p)$ for Theorem 16 requires also consideration of the *context* of p in d. Based on Theorems 16 and 14 we define the following notions of reduction and regularity.

Definition 18. Let d be a D-term, let e be a subterm of d and let α be an axiom assignment for d. For D-terms e' the D-term $d[e \mapsto e']$ is then obtained by *C-reduction* from d for α if $e >_c e'$, $Mgt_\alpha(e')$ is defined, and for all positions $p \in \mathcal{P}os(d)$ such that $d|_p = e$ it holds that $Ipt_\alpha(d, p) \geq Mgt_\alpha(e')$. The D-term d is called *C-reducible* for α if and only if there exists a D-term e' such that $d[e \mapsto e']$ is obtained by C-reduction from d for α. Otherwise, d is called *C-regular*.

If d' is obtained from d by C-reduction, then by Theorem 16 and 14 it follows that $Mgt_\alpha(d) \geq Mgt_\alpha(d')$, c-size$(d) \geq$ c-size(d') and sc-size$(d) >$ sc-size(d'). C-regularity differs from well known concepts of regularity in clausal tableaux (see, e.g., [14]) in two respects: (1) In the comparison of two nodes on a branch (which is done by subsumption as in tableaux with universal variables) for the upper node the stronger instantiated IPT is taken and for the lower node the more weakly instantiated MGT. (2) C-regularity is not based on relating two nested subproofs, but on comparison of all occurrences of a subproof with respect to all proofs that are smaller with respect to the compaction ordering.

Proofs may involve applications of *Det* where the conclusion Py is actually independent from the minor premise Px. Any axiom can then serve as a trivial minor premise. Meredith expresses this with the symbol n as second argument of the respective D-term. Our function simp-n simplifies D-terms by replacing subterms with n accordingly on the basis of the preservation of the MGT.

Definition 19. If d is a D-term and α is an axiom assignment for d, then the *n-simplification of d with respect to* α is the D-term simp-n$_\alpha(d)$, where simp-n is the following function: simp-n$_\alpha(d) \stackrel{\text{def}}{=} d$, if d is a primitive D-term; simp-n$_\alpha(\mathsf{D}(d_1, d_2)) \stackrel{\text{def}}{=} \mathsf{D}(\text{simp-n}_{\alpha'}(d_1), \mathsf{n})$ if $Mgt_{\alpha'}\mathsf{D}(d_1, \mathsf{n}) = Mgt_\alpha\mathsf{D}(d_1, d_2)$, where $\alpha' = \alpha \cup \{\mathsf{n} \mapsto \mathsf{k}\}$ for a fresh constant k; simp-n$_\alpha(\mathsf{D}(d_1, d_2)) \stackrel{\text{def}}{=} \mathsf{D}(\text{simp-n}_\alpha(d_1), \text{simp-n}_\alpha(d_2))$, else.

5 Properties of Meredith's Refined Proof

Our framework renders condensed detachment as a restricted form of the CM. This view permits to consider the expanded proof structures as binary trees or D-terms. On this basis we obtain a natural characterization of proof properties in various categories, which seem to be the key towards reducing the search space in ATP. Table 1 shows such properties for each of the 34 structurally different subproofs of proof MER (Fig. 3). Column **M** gives the number of the subproof in Fig. 3. We use the following short identifiers for the observed properties:

Structural Properties of the D-Term. These properties refer to the respective subproof as D-term or full binary tree. **DT, DC, DH**: Tree size, compacted size, height. **DK**$_L$, **DK**$_R$: "Successive height", that is, the maximal number of successive edges going to the left (right, resp.) on any path from the root to a leaf. **DP**: Is "prime", that is, **DT** and **DC** are equal. **DS**: Relationship between the subproofs of major and minor premise. Identity is expressed with =, the subterm and superterm relationships with $\lhd$ and $\rhd$, resp., and the compaction ordering relationship (if none of the other relationships holds) with $<_c$ and $>_c$. In addition it is indicated if a subproof is an axiom or n. **DD**: "Direct sharings", that is, the number of incoming edges in the DAG representation of the overall proof of all theorems. **DR**: "Repeats", that is, the total number of occurrences in the set of expanded trees of all roots of the DAG.

Properties of the MGT. These properties refer to the argument term of the MGT of the respective subproof. **TT, TH**: Tree size (defined as for D-terms) and height. **TV**: Number of different variables occurring in the term. **TO**: Is "organic" [21], that is, the argument term has no strict subterm s such that P(s) itself is a theorem. We call an atom *weakly organic* (indicated by a gray bullet) if it is not organic and the argument term is of the form i(p, t) where p is a variable that does not occur in the term t and P(t) is organic. For axiomatizations of fragments of propositional logic, *organic* can be checked by a SAT solver.

Regularity. RC: The respective subproof as D-term is C-regular (see Def. 18).

	M	DT	DC	DH	DK_L	DK_R	DP	DS	DD	DR	TT	TC	TH	TV	TO	RC	MT	MC	IT_U	IT_M	IH_U	IH_M
1.1	1	0	0	0	0	0	•	–	17	554	6	6	3	4	•	•	0	0	4451	203	18	11
2. D11		1	1	1	1	1	•	1=1	1	45	8	7	4	5	•	•	1	1	1640	220	17	12
3. D12		2	2	2	1	2	•	1◁	1	45	11	8	4	6	•	•	2	2	1881	252	17	12
4. D31		3	3	3	2	2	•	▷1	1	45	5	5	4	4	◦	•	3	3	689	92	16	11
5. D4n	2	4	4	4	3	2	•	▷n	1	45	4	4	3	3	•	•	4	4	688	91	15	10
6. D15		5	5	5	3	2	•	1◁	1	45	6	5	3	4	•	•	5	5	1667	198	15	10
7. D16		6	6	6	3	3	•	1◁	1	45	7	6	4	5	•	•	6	6	1802	208	16	11
8. D17		7	7	7	3	4	•	1◁	1	45	9	7	4	6	•	•	7	7	2648	303	16	11
9. D81		8	8	8	3	4	•	▷1	1	45	5	5	4	4	◦	•	8	8	1032	119	15	10
10. D9n	3	9	9	9	3	4	•	▷n	5	45	4	4	3	3	•	•	9	9	1031	118	14	9
11. D10.1	4	10	10	10	4	4	•	▷1	2	37	4	4	3	3	•	•	10	10	448	60	13	9
12. D1.11		11	11	11	4	4	•	1◁	1	23	7	7	5	5	•	•	11	11	498	73	14	10
13. D1.12		12	12	12	4	4	•	1◁	1	23	12	8	5	6	•	•	12	12	1157	168	14	10
14. D1.13		13	13	13	4	4	•	1◁	1	23	10	9	6	7	•	•	13	[12,13]	1050	159	15	11
15. D1.14		14	14	14	4	5	•	1◁	1	23	10	6	8	8	•	•	14	[12,14]	1657	246	15	11
16. D15.1		15	15	15	4	5	•	▷1	1	23	9	8	5	6	◦	•	15	[12,15]	684	100	14	10
17. D16.n	5	16	16	16	4	5	•	▷n	2	23	8	7	4	5	•	•	16	[12,16]	683	99	13	9
18. D17.1	6	17	17	17	4	5	•	▷1	3	18	7	6	3	4	•	•	17	[12,17]	395	56	12	8
19. D18.11	7	28	18	18	5	5	–	▷	1	14	7	6	4	4	•	•	14	[12,14]	209	61	11	9
20. D19.1	8	29	19	19	6	5	–	▷1	2	14	9	8	5	5	•	•	15	[12,15]	132	38	10	8
21. D1.20	10	30	20	20	6	5	–	1◁	2	10	12	9	5	6	•	•	16	[12,16]	158	47	10	8
22. D21.21		61	21	21	6	5	–	=	1	5	10	9	5	6	◦	•	[23,33]	[12,17]	53	16	9	7
23. D22.n	11	62	22	22	6	5	–	▷n	1	5	9	8	4	5	•	•	[23,34]	[12,18]	52	15	8	6
24. D17.23	12	79	23	23	6	5	–	◁	2	5	9	8	4	5	•	•	[23,51]	[12,23]	57	16	7	5
25. D24.18	13	97	24	24	6	5	–	▷	2	2	7	6	4	4	•	•	[23,69]	[12,24]	27	17	6	5
26. D20.10	9	39	20	20	7	5	–	▷	2	4	3	2	2	2	•	–	8	6	27	7	6	4
27. D24.26	14	119	25	24	7	5	–	$>_c$	2	3	5	5	3	3	•	•	[23,91]	[12,25]	24	7	6	4
28. D10.27	15	129	26	25	7	5	–	◁	1	2	3	3	3	2	•	•	[23,101]	[12,26]	19	12	6	5
29. D18.28	16	147	27	26	7	5	–	◁	2	2	5	5	4	3	•	•	[23,36]	[12,26]	19	12	6	5
30. D29.29		295	28	27	7	6	–	=	1	1	10	7	5	4	•	•	[23,239]	[12,27]	13	13	5	5
31. D25.30		393	30	28	7	7	–	$<_c$	1	1	7	7	5	4	•	•	[23,121]	[12,29]	13	13	5	5
32. D31.25	17	491	31	29	7	7	–	▷	0	1	5	5	3	3	•	•	[23,191]	[12,30]	5	5	3	3
33. D27.26	18	159	26	25	7	5	–	▷	0	1	3	3	3	2	•	•	15	11	3	3	3	3
34. D10.10	19	19	10	10	4	4	–	=	0	1	2	2	2	2	•	•	7	6	2	2	2	2

Table 1. Properties of all subproofs of the proof MER [24] shown in Fig. 3.

Comparisons with all Proofs of the MGT. These properties relate to the set of all proofs (as D-terms) of the MGT of the respective subproof. **MT**, **MC**: Minimal tree size and minimal compacted size of a proof. These values can be hard to determine such that in Table 1 they are often only narrowed down by an integer interval. To determine them, we used the proof MER, proofs obtained with techniques described in Sect. 6, and enumerations of all D-terms with defined MGT up to a given tree size or compacted size.

Properties of Occurrences of the IPTs. The respective subproof has **DR** occurrences in the set of expanded trees of the roots of the DAG, where each occurrence has an IPT. The following properties refer to the multiset of argument terms of the IPTs of these occurrences. IT_U, IT_M: Maximal tree size and rounded median of the tree size. IH_U, IH_M: Maximal height and rounded median of the height. In Table 1 these values are much larger than those of the corresponding columns for the MGT, i.e, **TT** and **TH**, illustrating Prop. 10.

6   First Experiments

First experiments based on the framework developed in the previous sections are centered around the generation of lemmas where not just formulas but, in the form of D-terms, also proofs are taken into account. This leads in general to preference of small proofs and to narrowing down the search space by re-

Lemmas	#	Time	Prover	Time	DC	DT	DH
1.			Łukasiewicz*		32	435	29
2.			Meredith		31	491	29
3.			Prover9	37 s	94	304,890	40
4.			Prover9*	37 s	83	8,217	38
5.			Prover9* depth ≤ 7	6 s	102	19,113	48
6.	PrimeCore(17)	17	Prover9*	30 s	44	763	28
7.	ProofSubproof(93,7)	291	78 s	Prover9*	3 s	51	1,405	31
8.	ProofSubproof(93,7)	291	78 s	CMProver	2 s	30	394	29
9.	ProofSubproof(100,8)	330	94 s	CMProver	4 s	30	535	29
10.			Reduction of (8.)		48	191	24

Table 2. Proof dimensions of various proofs of problem $ŁDS$.

stricted structuring principles to build proofs. The experiments indicate novel potential calculi which combine aspects from lemma-based generative, bottom-up, methods such as hyperresolution and hypertableaux with structure-based approaches that are typically used in an analytic, goal-directed, way such as the CM. In addition, ways to generate lemmas as preprocessing for theorem proving are suggested, in particular to obtain short proofs. This resulted in a refinement of Łukasiewicz's proof [19], whose compacted size is by one smaller than that of Meredith's refinement [24] and by two than Łukasiewicz's original proof.

Table 2 shows compacted size **DC**, tree size **DT** and height **DH** of various proofs of $ŁDS$. Asterisks indicate that n-simplification was applied with reducing effect on the system's proof. Proof (1.) is the one by Łukasiewicz [19], translated into condensed detachment, proof (2.) is proof MER (Fig. 3) [24]. Rows (3.)–(5.) show results from *Prover9*, where in (5.) the value of `max_depth` was limited to 7, motivated by column **TH** of Table 1. Proof (4.) illustrates the effect of n-simplification.[4] For proofs (6.)–(9.) additional axioms were supplied to *Prover9* and *CMProver* [5,35,36], a goal-directed system that can be described by the CM. Columns indicate the lemma computation method, the number of lemmas supplied to the prover and the time used for lemma computation. Method *PrimeCore* adds the MGTs of subproof 18 from Table 1 and all its subproofs as lemmas. Subproof 18 is the largest subproof of proof MER that is prime and can be characterized on the basis of the axiom – almost uniquely – as a proof that is prime, whose MGT has no smaller prime proof and has the same number of different variables as the axiom, i.e., 4, and whose size, given as parameter, is 17. Method *ProofSubproof* is based on detachment steps with a D-term and a subterm of it as proofs of the premises, which, as column **DS** of Table 1 shows, suffices to justify all except of two proof steps in MER. It proceeds in some analogy to the given clause algorithm on lists of D-terms: If d is the given D-term, then the *inferred D-terms* are all D-terms that have a defined MGT and are of the form $D(d, e)$ or $D(e, d)$, where e is a subterm of d. To determine which of the inferred D-terms are kept, values from Table 1 were taken as guide, including **RC** and **TO**. The first parameter of *ProofSubproof* is the number of iterations of the "given D-term loop". Proof (9.) can be combined with *Peirce* and *Syll* to the overall proof with compacted size 32, one less than MER. The maximal value of DK_L is shown as second parameter, because, when limited to 7, proof (9.)

---

[4] All machine results refer to a system with Intel i7-8550U CPU and 16 GB RAM. Results for further systems: *KRHyper** [26]: 1.610 s, **DC**: 73; *E 2.5* [30]: 30 s, proof length 91; *Vampire 5.4.1* [33] `-mode casc -t 300`: 128 s, proof length 144.

cannot be found. Proof (10.), which has a small tree size, was obtained from (8.) by rewriting subproofs with a variation of C-reduction that rewrites single term occurrences, considering also D-terms from a precomputed table of small proofs.

7   Conclusion

Starting out from investigating Łukasiewicz's classic formal proof [19], via its refinement by Meredith [24] we arrived at a formal reconstruction of Meredith's condensed detachment as a special case of the CM. The resulting formalism yields proofs as objects of a very simple and common structure: full binary trees which, in the tradition of term rewriting, appear as terms, D-terms, as we call them. To form a full proof, formulas are associated with the nodes of D-terms: axioms with the leaves and lemmas with the remaining nodes, implicitly determined from the axioms through the node position and unification. The root lemma is the most general proven theorem. Lemmas also relate to compressed representations of the binary trees, for example as DAGs, where the re-use of a lemma directly corresponds to sharing the structure of its subproof. For future work we intend to position our approach also in the context of earlier works on proofs, proof compression and lemma introduction, e.g., [38,12], and think of compressing D-Terms in forms that are stronger than DAGs, e.g., by tree grammars [18].

The combination of formulas and explicitly available proof structures naturally leads to theorem proving methods that take structural aspects into account, in various ways, as demonstrated by our first experiments. This goes beyond the common clausal tableau realizations of the CM, which in essence operate by enumerating uncompressed proof structures. The discussed notions of regularity and lemma generation methods seem immediately suited for further investigations in the context of first-order theorem proving in general. For other aspects of the work we plan a stepwise generalization by considering further single axioms for the implicational fragment **IF** [21,19,32], single axioms and axiom pairs for further logics [32], the about 200 condensed detachment problems in the LCL domain of the TPTP, problems which involve multiple non-unit clauses, and adapting D-terms to a variation of binary resolution instead of detachment. In the longer run, our approach aims at providing a basis for approaches to theorem proving with machine learning (e.g. [10,15]). With the reification of proof structures more information is available as starting point. As indicated with our exemplary feature table for Meredith's proof, structural properties are considered thereby from a global point of view, as a source for narrowing down the search space in many different ways in contrast to just the common local view "from within a structure", where the narrowing down is achieved for example by focusing on a "current branch" during the construction of a tableau. A general lead question opened up by our setting is that for exploring relationships between properties of proof structures and the associated formulas in proofs of meaningful theorems. One may expect that characterizations of these relationships can substantially restrict the search space for finding proofs.

Acknowledgments. We appreciate the competent comments of all the referees.

References

1. Bibel, W.: Automated Theorem Proving. Vieweg, Braunschweig (1982). https://doi.org/10.1007/978-3-322-90102-6, second edition 1987
2. Bibel, W.: Deduction: Automated Logic. Academic Press, London (1993)
3. Bibel, W., Otten, J.: From Schütte's formal systems to modern automated deduction. In: Kahle, R., Rathjen, M. (eds.) The Legacy of Kurt Schütte, chap. 13, pp. 215–249. Springer (2020). https://doi.org/10.1007/978-3-030-49424-7_13
4. Bunder, M.W.: A simplified form of condensed detachment. J. Log., Lang. Inf. **4**(2), 169–173 (1995). https://doi.org/10.1007/BF01048619
5. Dahn, I., Wernhard, C.: First order proof problems extracted from an article in the Mizar mathematical library. In: Bonacina, M.P., Furbach, U. (eds.) FTP'97. pp. 58–62. RISC-Linz Report Series No. 97–50, Joh. Kepler Univ., Linz (1997), https://www.logic.at/ftp97/papers/dahn.pdf
6. Dershowitz, N., Jouannaud, J.: Notations for rewriting. Bull. EATCS **43**, 162–174 (1991)
7. Downey, P.J., Sethi, R., Tarjan, R.E.: Variations on the common subexpression problem. JACM **27**(4), 758–771 (1980). https://doi.org/10.1145/322217.322228
8. Eder, E.: Relative Complexities of First Order Calculi. Vieweg, Braunschweig (1992). https://doi.org/10.1007/978-3-322-84222-0
9. Eder, E.: Properties of substitutions and unification. J. Symb. Comput. **1**(1), 31–46 (1985). https://doi.org/10.1016/S0747-7171(85)80027-4
10. Färber, M., Kaliszyk, C., Urban, J.: Machine learning guidance for connection tableaux. J. Autom. Reasoning **65**(2), 287–320 (2021). https://doi.org/10.1007/s10817-020-09576-7
11. Fitelson, B., Wos, L.: Missing proofs found. J. Autom. Reasoning **27**(2), 201–225 (2001). https://doi.org/10.1023/A:1010695827789
12. Hetzl, S., Leitsch, A., Reis, G., Weller, D.: Algorithmic introduction of quantified cuts. Theor. Comput. Sci. **549**, 1–16 (2014). https://doi.org/10.1016/j.tcs.2014.05.018
13. Hindley, J.R., Meredith, D.: Principal type-schemes and condensed detachment. Journal of Symbolic Logic **55**(1), 90–105 (1990). https://doi.org/10.2307/2274956
14. Hähnle, R.: Tableaux and related methods. In: Robinson, A., Voronkov, A. (eds.) Handb. of Autom. Reasoning, vol. 1, chap. 3, pp. 101–178. Elsevier (2001). https://doi.org/10.1016/b978-044450813-3/50005-9
15. Jakubuv, J., Chvalovský, K., Olšák, M., Piotrowski, B., Suda, M., Urban, J.: ENIGMA Anonymous: Symbol-independent inference guiding machine (system description). In: Peltier, N., Sofronie-Stokkermans, V. (eds.) IJCAR 2020. LNCS, vol. 12167, pp. 448–463. Springer (2020). https://doi.org/10.1007/978-3-030-51054-1_29
16. Kalman, J.A.: Condensed detachment as a rule of inference. Studia Logica **42**, 443–451 (1983). https://doi.org/10.1007/BF01371632
17. Lemmon, E.J., Meredith, C.A., Meredith, D., Prior, A.N., Thomas, I.: Calculi of pure strict implication. In: Davis, J.W., Hockney, D.J., Wilson, W.K. (eds.) Philosophical Logic, pp. 215–250. Springer Netherlands, Dordrecht (1969). https://doi.org/10.1007/978-94-010-9614-0_17, reprint of a technical report, Canterbury University College, Christchurch, 1957
18. Lohrey, M.: Grammar-based tree compression. In: Potapov, I. (ed.) DLT 2015. LNCS, vol. 9168, pp. 46–57. Springer (2015). https://doi.org/10.1007/978-3-319-21500-6_3

19. Łukasiewicz, J.: The shortest axiom of the implicational calculus of propositions. In: Proc. of the Royal Irish Academy. vol. 52, Sect. A, No. 3, pp. 25–33 (1948), http://www.jstor.org/stable/20488489, republished in [20], p. 295–305
20. Łukasiewicz, J.: Selected Works. North Holland (1970), edited by L. Borkowski
21. Łukasiewicz, J., Tarski, A.: Untersuchungen über den Aussagenkalkül. Comptes rendus des séances de la Soc. d. Sciences et d. Lettres de Varsovie **23** (1930), English translation in [20], p. 131–152
22. Lusk, E.L., McCune, W.W.: Experiments with ROO, a parallel automated deduction system. In: Fronhöfer, B., Wrightson, G. (eds.) Parallelization in Inference Systems. LNCS (LNAI), vol. 590, pp. 139–162. Springer (1992). https://doi.org/10.1007/3-540-55425-4_6
23. McCune, W., Wos, L.: Experiments in automated deduction with condensed detachment. In: Kapur, D. (ed.) CADE-11. LNCS (LNAI), vol. 607, pp. 209–223. Springer (1992). https://doi.org/10.1007/3-540-55602-8_167
24. Meredith, C.A., Prior, A.N.: Notes on the axiomatics of the propositional calculus. Notre Dame J. of Formal Logic **4**(3), 171–187 (1963). https://doi.org/10.1305/ndjfl/1093957574
25. Meredith, D.: In memoriam: Carew Arthur Meredith (1904–1976). Notre Dame J. of Formal Logic **18**(4), 513–516 (10 1977). https://doi.org/10.1305/ndjfl/1093888116
26. Pelzer, B., Wernhard, C.: System description: E-KRHyper. In: Pfenning, F. (ed.) CADE-21. LNCS (LNAI), vol. 4603, pp. 503–513. Springer (2007). https://doi.org/10.1007/978-3-540-73595-3_37
27. Pfenning, F.: Single axioms in the implicational propositional calculus. In: Lusk, E., Overbeek, R. (eds.) CADE-9. LNCS (LNAI), vol. 310, pp. 710–713. Springer (1988). https://doi.org/10.1007/BFb0012869
28. Prior, A.N.: Logicians at play; or Syll, Simp and Hilbert. Australasian Journal of Philosophy **34**(3), 182–192 (1956). https://doi.org/10.1080/00048405685200181
29. Prior, A.N.: Formal Logic. Clarendon Press, Oxford, 2nd edn. (1962). https://doi.org/10.1093/acprof:oso/9780198241560.001.0001
30. Schulz, S., Cruanes, S., Vukmirović, P.: Faster, higher, stronger: E 2.3. In: Fontaine, P. (ed.) CADE 27. pp. 495–507. No. 11716 in LNAI, Springer (2019). https://doi.org/10.1007/978-3-030-29436-6_29
31. Ulrich, D.: A legacy recalled and a tradition continued. J. Autom. Reasoning **27**(2), 97–122 (2001). https://doi.org/10.1023/A:1010683508225
32. Ulrich, D.: Single axioms and axiom-pairs for the implicational fragments of R, R-Mingle, and some related systems. In: Bimbó, K. (ed.) J. Michael Dunn on Information Based Logics, Outstanding Contributions to Logic, vol. 8, pp. 53–80. Springer (2016). https://doi.org/10.1007/978-3-319-29300-4_4
33. Vampire Team: Vampire, online: https://vprover.github.io/, accessed Feb 5, 2021
34. Veroff, R.: Finding shortest proofs: An application of linked inference rules. J. Autom. Reasoning **27**(2), 123–139 (2001). https://doi.org/10.1023/A:1010635625063
35. Wernhard, C.: The *PIE* system for proving, interpolating and eliminating. In: Fontaine, P., Schulz, S., Urban, J. (eds.) PAAR 2016. CEUR Workshop Proc., vol. 1635, pp. 125–138. CEUR-WS.org (2016), http://ceur-ws.org/Vol-1635/paper-11.pdf
36. Wernhard, C.: Facets of the *PIE* environment for proving, interpolating and eliminating on the basis of first-order logic. In: Hofstedt, P., Abreu, S., John, U., Kuchen, H., Seipel, D. (eds.) DECLARE 2019. LNCS (LNAI), vol. 12057, pp. 160–177 (2020). https://doi.org/10.1007/978-3-030-46714-2_11

37. Wernhard, C., Bibel, W.: Learning from Łukasiewicz and Meredith: Investigations into proof structures (extended version). CoRR **abs/2104.13645** (2021), https://arxiv.org/abs/2104.13645
38. Woltzenlogel Paleo, B.: Atomic cut introduction by resolution: Proof structuring and compression. In: Clarke, E.M., Voronkov, A. (eds.) LPAR-16. LNCS, vol. 6355, pp. 463–480. Springer (2010). https://doi.org/10.1007/978-3-642-17511-4_26
39. Wos, L., Winker, S., McCune, W., Overbeek, R., Lusk, E., Stevens, R., Butler, R.: Automated reasoning contributes to mathematics and logic. In: Stickel, M.E. (ed.) CADE-10. pp. 485–499. Springer (1990). https://doi.org/10.1007/3-540-5288 5-7_109

Open Access This chapter is licensed under the terms of the Creative Commons Attribution 4.0 International License (http://creativecommons.org/licenses/by/4.0/), which permits use, sharing, adaptation, distribution and reproduction in any medium or format, as long as you give appropriate credit to the original author(s) and the source, provide a link to the Creative Commons license and indicate if changes were made.

The images or other third party material in this chapter are included in the chapter's Creative Commons license, unless indicated otherwise in a credit line to the material. If material is not included in the chapter's Creative Commons license and your intended use is not permitted by statutory regulation or exceeds the permitted use, you will need to obtain permission directly from the copyright holder.

Efficient Local Reductions to Basic Modal Logic*

Fabio Papacchini[1] , Cláudia Nalon[2] ,
Ullrich Hustadt[1] , and Clare Dixon[4]

[1] Department of Computer Science, University of Liverpool, UK,
{Fabio.Papacchini,U.Hustadt}@liverpool.ac.uk
[2] Department of Computer Science, University of Brasília, nalon@unb.br
[3] Department of Computer Science, University of Manchester,
clare.dixon@manchester.ac.uk

Abstract. We present novel reductions of the propositional modal logics
KB, KD, KT, K4 and K5 to Separated Normal Form with Sets of Modal
Levels. The reductions result in smaller formulae than the well-known
reductions by Kracht and allow us to use the local reasoning of the prover
K$_S$P to determine the satisfiability of modal formulae in these logics. We
show experimentally that the combination of our reductions with the
prover K$_S$P performs well when compared with a specialised resolution
calculus for these logics and with the built-in reductions of the first-order
prover SPASS.

1 Introduction

The main motivation for reducing problems in one logic (the source logic) to
'equivalent' problems in another logic (the target logic) is to exploit results and
tools for the target logic to solve theoretical or practical problems in the source
logic. For propositional modal logics this approach has been researched extensively for reductions of the satisfiability problem in these logics to the satisfiability problem in 'stronger' logics such as first-order logic [10,20], the second-order
theory of n successors [6], simple type theory [4], and regular grammar logics [19].

An alternative approach is to reduce propositional modal logics to a 'weaker'
logic, in particular, the basic modal logic K. For extensions of K with one of the
axioms B, D, alt$_1$, T, and 4, Kracht [12] defines reduction functions of their global
and local satisfiability problem to the corresponding problem in K and proves
their correctness. He also defines a reduction function for K5, the extension
of K with 5, to K4, but this reduction is incorrect as not all theorems of K4
are theorems of K5. Several features of Kracht's approach are relevant to our
work. First, as is not uncommon in modal logic, he treats the modal operator
$\diamondsuit$ as abbreviation for $\neg\square\neg$, that is, $\square$ is the only modal operator occurring
in modal formulae. Second, the basic idea underlying his reduction functions

---

* C. Dixon was partially supported by the EPSRC funded RAI Hubs FAIR-SPACE
(EP/R026092/1) and RAIN (EP/R026084/1), and the EPSRC funded programme
Grant S4 (EP/N007565/1).

© The Author(s) 2021
A. Platzer and G. Sutcliffe (Eds.): CADE 2021, LNAI 12699, pp. 76–92, 2021.
https://doi.org/10.1007/978-3-030-79876-5_5

is for a given modal formula φ to generate sufficiently many instances Δ of a modal axiom Λ so that φ is $K\Lambda$-satisfiable iff $\varphi \wedge \Delta$ is K-satisfiable. Third, Kracht is only concerned with preservation of the computational complexity of the satisfiability problem under consideration, as well as the preservation of other theoretical properties. For instance, the local satisfiability problem in the modal logics covered by Kracht is PSPACE-complete. So, it is sufficient to ensure that Δ is polynomial in size with respect to φ. As Kracht himself concludes, his method offers a uniform way of transferring results about one modal logic to another, but may not be as useful for practical applications.

In [16,15] we have introduced a new normal form for basic multi-modal logic, called Separated Normal Form with Modal Levels, SNF_{ml}, that uses labelled modal clauses. These labels refer to the level within a tree Kripke structure at which a modal clause holds. This can be seen as a compromise between approaches that label formulae with worlds at unspecified level [1,3] and approaches that label formulae with paths [5,23]. A combination of a normal form transformation for modal formulae and a resolution-based calculus for labelled modal clauses can then be used to decide local and global satisfiability in basic modal logic. In [17,18] we have presented K_SP, an implementation of that calculus, together with an experimental evaluation that indicates that K_SP performs well if propositional variables are evenly spread across a wide range of modal levels within the formulae one wants to decide.

A feature of SNF_{ml} is its use of additional propositional symbols as 'surrogates' for subformulae of a modal formula φ. In the following we take advantage of the availability of those surrogates to provide a novel transformation from extensions of K with a single one of the axioms B, D, T, 4 and 5 to SNF_{ml}. Another novel aspect is that we modify the normal form so that it uses sets of modal levels as labels instead of a single modal level. In K we only need a definition of a surrogate at the modal level at which the corresponding subformula occurs in φ. But in KB, KT, K4 and K5, we need a definition at every reachable modal level, of which there can be many. We call the resulting normal form, *Separated Normal Form with Sets of Modal Levels*, SNF_{sml}.

The structure of the paper is as follows. In Section 2 we recap common concepts of propositional modal logic including its syntax and semantics. Section 3 defines SNF_{sml} and the reductions of K, KB, KD, KT, K4 and K5 to SNF_{sml}. Correctness is proved in Section 4. Related work is discussed in Section 5. In Section 6 we compare the performance of a combination of our reductions and the modal-layered resolution calculus implemented in prover K_SP with resolution calculi specifically designed for the logics under consideration and with translation-based approaches built into the first-order theorem prover SPASS.

2 Preliminaries

The language of modal logic is an extension of the language of propositional logic with a unary modal operator $\Box$ and its dual $\Diamond$. More precisely, given a denumerable set of *propositional symbols*, $P = \{p, p_0, q, q_0, t, t_0, \ldots\}$ as well as

propositional *constants* **true** and **false**, *modal formulae* are inductively defined
as follows: Constants and propositional symbols are modal formulae. If φ and ψ
are modal formulae, then so are $\neg\varphi$, $(\varphi \wedge \psi)$, $(\varphi \vee \psi)$, $(\varphi \rightarrow \psi)$, $\Box\varphi$, and $\Diamond\varphi$.
We also assume that $\wedge$ and $\vee$ are associative and commutative operators and
consider, e.g., $(p \vee (q \vee r))$ and $(r \vee (q \vee p))$ to be identical formulae. We often omit
parentheses if this does not cause confusion. By $\text{var}(\varphi)$ we denote the set of all
propositional symbols occurring in φ. This function straightforwardly extends
to finite sets of modal formulae. A *modal axiom (schema)* is a modal formula ψ
representing the set of all instances of ψ.

A *literal* is either a propositional symbol or its negation; the set of literals is
denoted by L. We denote by $\neg l$ the *complement* of the literal $l \in L$, that is, $\neg l$
denotes $\neg p$ if l is the propositional symbol p, and $\neg l$ denotes p if l is the literal
$\neg p$. A *modal literal* is either $\Box l$ or $\Diamond l$, where $l \in L$.

A *(normal) modal logic* is a set of modal formulae which includes all propo-
sitional tautologies, the axiom schema $\Box(\varphi \rightarrow \psi) \rightarrow (\Box\varphi \rightarrow \Box\psi)$, called the
axiom K, is closed under modus ponens (if $\vdash \varphi$ and $\vdash \varphi \rightarrow \psi$ then $\vdash \psi$) and the
rule of necessitation (if $\vdash \varphi$ then $\vdash \Box\varphi$).

K is the weakest modal logic, that is, the logic given by the smallest set
of modal formulae constituting a normal modal logic. By KΣ we denote an
extensions of K by a set Σ of axioms.

The standard semantics of modal logics is the *Kripke semantics* or *possible
world semantics*. A *Kripke frame* F is an ordered pair $\langle W, R \rangle$ where W is a
non-empty set of *worlds* and R is a binary (accessibility) relation over W. A
Kripke structure M over P is an ordered pair $\langle F, V \rangle$ where F is a Kripke frame
and the *valuation* V is a function mapping each propositional symbol in P to
a subset $V(p)$ of W. We say $M = \langle F, V \rangle$ is *based on the frame* F. A *rooted
Kripke structure* is an ordered pair $\langle M, w_0 \rangle$ with $w_0 \in W$. To simplify notation,
in the following we write $\langle W, R, V \rangle$ and $\langle W, R, V, w_0 \rangle$ instead of $\langle \langle W, R \rangle, V \rangle$ and
$\langle \langle \langle W, R \rangle, V \rangle, w_0 \rangle$, respectively.

Satisfaction (or truth) of a formula at a world w of a Kripke structure $M = \langle W, R, V \rangle$ is inductively defined by:

$\langle M, w \rangle \models$ **true**; $\langle M, w \rangle \not\models$ **false**;

$\langle M, w \rangle \models p$ iff $w \in V(p)$, where $p \in P$;

$\langle M, w \rangle \models \neg\varphi$ iff $\langle M, w \rangle \not\models \varphi$;

$\langle M, w \rangle \models (\varphi \wedge \psi)$ iff $\langle M, w \rangle \models \varphi$ and $\langle M, w \rangle \models \psi$;

$\langle M, w \rangle \models (\varphi \vee \psi)$ iff $\langle M, w \rangle \models \varphi$ or $\langle M, w \rangle \models \psi$;

$\langle M, w \rangle \models (\varphi \rightarrow \psi)$ iff $\langle M, w \rangle \models \neg\varphi$ or $\langle M, w \rangle \models \psi$;

$\langle M, w \rangle \models \Box\varphi$ iff for every v, $w \, R \, v$ implies $\langle M, v \rangle \models \varphi$;

$\langle M, w \rangle \models \Diamond\varphi$ iff there is v, $w \, R \, v$ and $\langle M, v \rangle \models \varphi$.

If $\langle M, w \rangle \models \varphi$ holds then M is a *model* of φ, φ is *true at w in M* and M *satisfies*
φ. A modal formula φ is *satisfiable* iff there exists a Kripke structure M and a
world w in M such that $\langle M, w \rangle \models \varphi$. A modal formula φ is *globally true* or *valid*
in a Kripke structure M if it is true at all worlds of M; it is *valid* if it is valid in
all Kripke structures.

Name	Axiom	Frame Property	
D	$\Box\varphi \to \Diamond\varphi$	Serial	$\forall v \exists w. v \, R \, w$
T	$\Box\varphi \to \varphi$	Reflexive	$\forall w. w \, R \, w$
B	$\varphi \to \Box\Diamond\varphi$	Symmetric	$\forall vw. v \, R \, w \to w \, R \, v$
4	$\Box\varphi \to \Box\Box\varphi$	Transitive	$\forall uvw.(u \, R \, v \wedge v \, R \, w) \to u \, R \, w$
5	$\Diamond\varphi \to \Box\Diamond\varphi$	Euclidean	$\forall uvw.(u \, R \, v \wedge u \, R \, w) \to v \, R \, w$

Table 1. Modal axioms and relational frame properties

In the following we are interested in extensions of K with the axiom schemata shown in Table 1. Each of these axiom schemata defines a class of Kripke frames where the accessibility relation R satisfies the first-order property stated in the table. Given a normal modal logic L with corresponding class of frames $\mathfrak{F}$, we say a modal formula φ is *L-satisfiable* iff there exists a frame $F \in \mathfrak{F}$, a valuation V and a world $w_0 \in F$ such that $\langle F, V, w_0 \rangle \models \varphi$.

A *path rooted at w of length k*, $k \geq 0$, in a frame $F = \langle W, R \rangle$ is a sequence $\vec{w} = (w_0, w_1, \ldots, w_k)$ where for every i, $1 \leq i \leq k$, $w_{i-1} \, R \, w_i$. We say that the path $(w_0, w_1, \ldots, w_k)$ *connects* w_0 and w_k. For a path $\vec{w} = (w_0, \ldots, w_k)$ and world w_{k+1} with $w_k \, R \, w_{k+1}$, $\vec{w} \circ w_{k+1}$ denotes the path $(w_0, \ldots, w_k, w_{k+1})$. A path (w_0) of length 0 is identified with its root w_0. We denote the set of all paths rooted at a world w_0 in F by $\vec{F}[w_0]$ and the set of all paths by $\vec{F}$. The function $\mathsf{trm} : \vec{F} \to W$ maps every path $\vec{w} = (w_0, \ldots, w_k)$ to its terminal world w_k while the function $\mathsf{len} : \vec{F} \to \mathbb{N}$ maps every path $\vec{w} = (w_0, w_1, \ldots, w_k)$ to its length k.

A rooted Kripke structure $M = \langle W, R, V, w_0 \rangle$ is a *rooted tree Kripke structure* iff R is a tree, that is, a directed acyclic connected graph where each node has at most one predecessor, with *root* w_0. It is a *rooted tree Kripke model* of a modal formula φ iff $\langle W, R, V, w_0 \rangle \models \varphi$. In a rooted tree Kripke structure with root w_0 for every world $w_k \in W$ there is exactly one path $\vec{w}$ connecting w_0 and w_k; the *modal level of w_k (in M)*, denoted by $\mathsf{ml}_M(w_k)$, is given by $\mathsf{len}(\vec{w})$.

Let $F = \langle W, R \rangle$ be a Kripke frame with $w \in W$. The *unravelling $F^u[w]$ of F at w* is the frame $\langle \vec{W}, \vec{R} \rangle$ where:

- $\vec{W} = \vec{F}[w]$ is the set of all rooted paths at w in F;
- for all $\vec{v}, \vec{w} \in \vec{W}$, if $\vec{w} = \vec{v} \circ w$ for some $w \in W$, then $\vec{v} \, \vec{R} \, \vec{w}$.

Let $F = \langle W, R \rangle$ and $F' = \langle W', R' \rangle$ be two Kripke frames. A function $f : W \mapsto W'$ is a *p-morphism* (or a *bounded morphism*) from F to F' if the following holds:

- if $v \, R \, w$, then $f(v) \, R' \, f(w)$.
- if $f(u) \, R' \, w$, then there exists $v \in W$ s.t. $f(v) = w$ and $u \, R \, v$.

Analogously for Kripke models. For $F = \langle W, R \rangle$, $M' = \langle F, V', w_0 \rangle$, and $M = \langle F^u[w_0], V, (w_0) \rangle$, the function trm is a p-morphism from M to M'.

When considering local satisfiability, the following holds (see, [8]):

Theorem 1. *Let φ be a modal formula. Then φ is K-satisfiable iff there is a finite rooted tree Kripke structure $M = \langle F, V, w_0 \rangle$ such that $\langle M, w_0 \rangle \models \varphi$.*

$$\varphi \wedge \varphi \Rightarrow \varphi \qquad \varphi \wedge \neg\varphi \Rightarrow \textbf{false} \qquad \Box\textbf{true} \Rightarrow \textbf{true} \qquad \neg\textbf{true} \Rightarrow \textbf{false} \quad \neg\neg\varphi \Rightarrow \varphi$$

$$\varphi \vee \varphi \Rightarrow \varphi \qquad \varphi \vee \neg\varphi \Rightarrow \textbf{true} \qquad \Diamond\textbf{false} \Rightarrow \textbf{false} \qquad \neg\textbf{false} \Rightarrow \textbf{true}$$

$$\varphi \wedge \textbf{true} \Rightarrow \varphi \quad \varphi \wedge \textbf{false} \Rightarrow \textbf{false} \quad \varphi \vee \textbf{false} \Rightarrow \varphi \qquad \varphi \vee \textbf{true} \Rightarrow \textbf{true}$$

Table 2. Rewriting Rules for Simplification

For the normal form transformation presented in the next section we assume that any modal formula φ has been simplified by exhaustively applying the rewrite rules in Table 2 and is in Negation Normal Form (NNF), that is, a formula where only propositional symbols are allowed in the scope of negations. We say that such a formula is in *simplified NNF*.

3   Layered Normal Form with Sets of Levels

A formula to be tested for satisfiability is first transformed into a normal form called *Separated Normal Form with Sets of Modal Levels*, SNF_{sml}, whose language extends that of modal logic with labels consisting of sets of modal levels. Informally, we write $S : \varphi$, where S is a set of natural numbers, to denote that a formula φ is true at modal levels $ml \in S$. We write $\star : \varphi$ instead of $\mathbb{N} : \varphi$.

We introduce some notation that will be used in the following. Let $S^+ = \{l+1 \in \mathbb{N} \mid l \in S\}$, $S^- = \{l-1 \in \mathbb{N} \mid l \in S\}$, and $S^{\geq} = \{n \mid n \geq \min(S)\}$, where $\min(S)$ is the least element in S. Note that the restriction of the elements being in $\mathbb{N}$ implies that S^- cannot contain negative numbers.

The labels in SNF_{sml} work as a kind of *weak* universal operator, allowing us to talk about formulae that are satisfied at all worlds in a given set of modal levels. Formally, we restrict ourselves to rooted tree Kripke structures $M = \langle W, R, V, w_0 \rangle$ and if S is a set of modal levels, then by $M[S]$ we denote the set of worlds that are at a modal level in S, that is, $M[S] = \{w \in W \mid ml_M(w) \in S\}$. The satisfaction of labelled formulae in a rooted tree Kripke structure M is then defined as follows:

$$M \models S : \varphi \text{ iff for every world } w \in M[S], \text{ we have } \langle M, w \rangle \models \varphi.$$

If $M \models S : \varphi$, then we say that $S : \varphi$ holds in M. Note that if $S = \emptyset$, then $M \models S : \varphi$ trivially holds. For a set Φ of labelled formulae, $M \models \Phi$ iff $M \models S : \varphi$ for every $S : \varphi$ in Φ, and we say Φ is K-*satisfiable*.

A labelled modal formula is then an SNF_{sml} clause iff it is of one of the following forms:

- Literal clause $S : \bigvee_{b=1}^{r} l_b$
- Positive modal clause $S : l' \rightarrow \Box l$
- Negative modal clause $S : l' \rightarrow \Diamond l$

where $S \subseteq \mathbb{N}$ and l, l', l_b are propositional literals with $1 \leq b \leq r, r \in \mathbb{N}$. Positive and negative modal clauses are together known as *modal clauses*. We regard a literal clause as a set of literals, that is, two clauses are the same if they contain the same set of literals.

We assume that the set P of propositional symbols is partitioned into two infinite sets Q and T such that for every modal formula ψ we have $\mathsf{var}(\psi) \subset Q$ and there exists a propositional symbol $t_\psi \in T$ uniquely associated with ψ.

Given a modal formula φ in simplified NNF and $L \in \{\mathsf{K}, \mathsf{KB}, \mathsf{KD}, \mathsf{KT}, \mathsf{K4}, \mathsf{K5}\}$, then we can obtain a set Φ_L of clauses in SNF_{sml} such that φ is L-satisfiable iff Φ_L is K-satisfiable as $\Phi_L = \{\{0\} : t_\varphi\} \cup \rho_L(\{0\} : t_\varphi \to \varphi)$, where ρ_L is defined as follows:

$$\rho_L(S : t \to \mathbf{true}) = \emptyset$$

$$\rho_L(S : t \to \mathbf{false}) = \{S : \neg t\}$$

$$\rho_L(S : t \to (\psi_1 \wedge \psi_2)) = \{S : \neg t \vee \eta(\psi_1), S : \neg t \vee \eta(\psi_2)\} \cup \delta_L(S, \psi_1) \cup \delta_L(S, \psi_2)$$

$$\rho_L(S : t \to \psi) = \{S : \neg t \vee \psi\}$$

$$\text{if } \psi \text{ is a disjunction of literals}$$

$$\rho_L(S : t \to (\psi_1 \vee \psi_2)) = \{S : \neg t \vee \eta(\psi_1) \vee \eta(\psi_2)\} \cup \delta_L(S, \psi_1) \cup \delta_L(S, \psi_2)$$

$$\text{if } \psi_1 \vee \psi_2 \text{ is not a disjunction of literals}$$

$$\rho_L(S : t \to \Diamond\psi) = \{S : t \to \Diamond\eta(\psi)\} \cup \delta_L(S^+, \psi)$$

$$\rho_L(S : t \to \Box\psi) = P_L(S : t \to \Box\psi) \cup \Delta_L(S : t \to \Box\psi)$$

where η and δ_L are defined as follows:

$$\eta(\psi) = \begin{cases} \psi, & \text{if } \psi \text{ is a} \\ & \text{literal} \\ t_\psi, & \text{otherwise} \end{cases} \qquad \delta_L(S, \psi) = \begin{cases} \emptyset, & \text{if } \psi \text{ is a} \\ & \text{literal} \\ \rho_L(S : t_\psi \to \psi), & \text{otherwise} \end{cases}$$

and functions P_L, Δ_L are defined as shown in Table 3. The function η maps a propositional literal ψ to itself while it maps every other modal formula ψ to a new propositional symbol $t_\psi \in T$ uniquely associated with ψ. We call t_ψ the *surrogate* of ψ or simply a surrogate. The functions P_{KB} and P_{K5} introduce additional propositional symbols, called *supplementary propositional symbols*, $t_{\Box\neg t_{\Box\psi}} \in T$ and $t_{\Diamond t_{\Box\psi}} \in T$, respectively, that do not correspond to subformulae of the formula we are transforming.

Intuitively, P_{KB} is based on the following consideration: Take a world w in a Kripke structure M with a symmetric accessibility relation R. If there exists a world v with $w\,R\,v$ such that $\langle M, v \rangle \models \Box\psi$, then $\langle M, w \rangle \models \psi$. Now, take the contrapositive of that statement: If $\langle M, w \rangle \not\models \psi$, then for every world v with $w\,R\,v$, $\langle M, v \rangle \not\models \Box\psi$. Equivalently, $\langle M, w \rangle \models \psi$ or $\langle M, w \rangle \models \Box\neg\Box\psi$. This is expressed by the formula $\eta(\psi) \vee t_{\Box\neg t_{\Box\psi}}$. For P_{K5}, the formula $t_{\Diamond t_{\Box\psi}} \to \Box t_{\Diamond t_{\Box\psi}}$ expresses an instance of axiom schema 5, $\Diamond\varphi \to \Box\Diamond\varphi$, with $\varphi = \Box\psi$, i.e., $\Diamond\Box\psi \to \Box\Diamond\Box\psi$. The contrapositive of axiom schema 5 is $\Diamond\Box\varphi \to \Box\varphi$, equivalent to $\neg\Diamond\Box\varphi \vee \Box\varphi$. For $\varphi = \psi$ this is expressed by the formula $\neg t_{\Diamond t_{\Box\psi}} \vee t_{\Box\psi}$. For the formula $\neg t_{\Diamond t_{\Box\psi}} \to \Box\neg t_{\Box\psi}$, consider $\neg\Diamond\Box\psi$. By duality of $\Box$ and $\Diamond$, this is

L	$P_L(S : t_{\Box\psi} \to \Box\psi)$	$\Delta_L(S : t_{\Box\psi} \to \Box\psi)$
K	$S : t_{\Box\psi} \to \Box\eta(\psi)$	$\delta_L(S^+, \psi)$
KT	$S : t_{\Box\psi} \to \Box\eta(\psi), S : \neg t_{\Box\psi} \vee \eta(\psi)$	$\delta_L(S \cup S^+, \psi)$
KD	$S : t_{\Box\psi} \to \Box\eta(\psi), S : t_{\Box\psi} \to \Diamond\eta(\psi)$	$\delta_L(S^+, \psi)$
KB	$S : t_{\Box\psi} \to \Box\eta(\psi),$ $S^- : \eta(\psi) \vee t_{\Box\neg t_{\Box\psi}}, S^- : t_{\Box\neg t_{\Box\psi}} \to \Box\neg t_{\Box\psi}$	$\delta_L(S^- \cup S^+, \psi)$
K4	$S^{\geq} : t_{\Box\psi} \to \Box\eta(\psi), S^{\geq} : t_{\Box\psi} \to \Box t_{\Box\psi}$	$\delta_L((S^+)^{\geq}, \psi)$
K5	$\star : t_{\Box\psi} \to \Box\eta(\psi),$ $\star : \neg t_{\Diamond t_{\Box\psi}} \vee t_{\Box\psi}, \star : t_{\Diamond t_{\Box\psi}} \to \Diamond t_{\Box\psi},$ $\star : \neg t_{\Diamond t_{\Box\psi}} \to \Box\neg t_{\Box\psi}, \star : t_{\Diamond t_{\Box\psi}} \to \Box t_{\Diamond t_{\Box\psi}}$	$\delta_L(\star, \psi)$

Table 3. Transformation of $\Box$-formulae in modal logic L

equivalent to $\neg\neg\Box\neg\Box\psi$ and $\Box\neg\Box\psi$. So, $\neg\Diamond\Box\psi \to \Box\neg\Box\psi$ in every normal modal logic, not only K5. The remaining labelled formulae introduced by P_{KB} and P_{K5} ensure that supplementary propositional symbols are defined. For the remaining logics the additional clauses are also based directly on the axiom schemata.

To simplify presentation in the following, we define a function η_f as follows:

$$\eta_f(\varphi_1 \wedge \varphi_2) = \eta(\varphi_1) \wedge \eta(\varphi_2) \qquad \eta_f(\varphi_1 \vee \varphi_2) = \eta(\varphi_1) \vee \eta(\varphi_2)$$
$$\eta_f(\Box\varphi) = \Box\eta(\varphi) \qquad \eta_f(\Diamond\varphi) = \Diamond\eta(\varphi)$$

and we treat the two clauses $S : \neg t_{\psi_1 \wedge \psi_2} \vee \eta(\psi_1)$ and $S : \neg t_{\psi_1 \wedge \psi_2} \vee \eta(\psi_2)$ resulting from the normal form transformation of $\psi_1 \wedge \psi_2$ as a single 'clause' $S : \neg t_{\psi_1 \wedge \psi_2} \vee \eta_f(\psi_1 \wedge \psi_2)$. We also interchangeably write $S : \neg t_{\Box\psi} \vee \eta_f(\Box\psi)$ for $S : t_{\Box\psi} \to \eta_f(\Box\psi)$ and, analogously, $S : \neg t_{\Diamond\psi} \vee \eta_f(\Diamond\psi)$ for $S : t_{\Diamond\psi} \to \eta_f(\Diamond\psi)$. We then call any clause of the form $S : \neg t_\psi \vee \eta_f(\psi)$ a *definitional clause*.

Definition 1. *Let Φ be a set of* SNF$_{sml}$ *clauses. We say $t_\psi \in T$ occurs at level ml in Φ iff either*

(a) *there exists a clause $S : \vartheta$ in Φ with $ml \in S$ such that ϑ is a propositional formula and t_ψ occurs positively in ϑ, or*
(b) *there exists a clause $S : t_{\Box\psi} \to \Box t_\psi$ in Φ with $ml - 1 \in S$, or*
(c) *there exists a clause $S : t_{\Diamond\psi} \to \Diamond t_\psi$ in Φ with $ml - 1 \in S$.*

Definition 2. *Let Φ be a set of* SNF$_{sml}$ *clauses. Then Φ is definition-complete iff for every $t_\psi \in T$ and every level ml, if t_ψ occurs at level ml in Φ then there exists a clause $S : \neg t_\psi \vee \eta_f(\psi)$ in Φ with $ml \in S$.*

Theorem 2. *Let $L \in \{K, KB, KD, KT, K4, K5\}$. Then $\Phi_L = \{\{0\} : t_\varphi\} \cup \rho_L(\{0\} : t_\varphi \to \varphi)$ is definition-complete.*

Proof. By induction over the computation of Φ_L. It is straightforward to see that the transformation of labelled formulae $S : t \to (\psi_1 \wedge \psi_2)$ and $S : t \to (\psi_1 \vee \psi_2)$ only introduces surrogates at levels in S and Δ_L then adds definitional clauses for those surrogates. The transformation of a labelled formula $S : t_{\Diamond\psi} \to \Diamond\psi$ may introduce a surrogate at levels in S^+ and $\delta_L(S^+, \psi)$ then adds definitional clauses for those surrogates. The transformation of a labelled formula $S : t_{\Box\psi} \to \Box\psi$ depends on the logic L. We can see that for every level at which a new surrogate occurs in $P_L(S : t_{\Box\psi} \to \Box\psi)$, then $\Delta_L(S : t_{\Box\psi} \to \Box\psi)$ contains a definitional clause for it at that level.

4   Correctness

Due to space constraints we only prove the correctness of the transformation for KB. We first state several lemmata that are used in the correctness proofs for all logics.

Lemma 1. *Let Φ be a set of definitional clauses such that every t_ψ occurring in Φ is an element of T and all other propositional symbols occurring in Φ are in Q. Let $M = \langle W, R, V, w_0 \rangle$ be a rooted Kripke structure. Let $\langle \vec{W}, \vec{R} \rangle$ be the unravelling of $\langle W, R \rangle$ at w_0. Let $\vec{M} = \langle \vec{W}, \vec{R}, \vec{V_\Sigma}, (w_0) \rangle$ be a Kripke structure such that*

- $\vec{V_\Sigma}(p) = \{ \vec{w} \in \vec{W} \mid trm(\vec{w}) \in V(p) \}$ *for every propositional symbol $p \in Q$, and*
- $\vec{V_\Sigma}(t_\psi) = \{ \vec{w} \in \vec{W} \mid \langle \vec{M}, \vec{w} \rangle \models \psi \}$ *for every surrogate $t_\psi \in T \cap var(\Phi)$.*

Then $\vec{M} \models \Phi$.

Lemma 2. *Let φ be a L-satisfiable modal formula in simplified NNF where L is a normal modal logic and let $\Phi = \{ \{0\} : t_\varphi \} \cup \rho_K(\{0\} : t_\varphi \to \varphi)$. Let $M = \langle W, R, V, w_0 \rangle$ be a rooted K model of φ. Let $\langle \vec{W}, \vec{R} \rangle$ be the unravelling of $\langle W, R \rangle$ at w_0. Let $\vec{M} = \langle \vec{W}, \vec{R}, \vec{V}, (w_0) \rangle$ be a Kripke structure such that*

- $\vec{V}(p) = \{ \vec{w} \in \vec{W} \mid trm(\vec{w}) \in V(p) \}$ *for every propositional symbol $p \subset var(\varphi)$, and*
- $\vec{V}(t_\psi) = \{ \vec{w} \in \vec{W} \mid \langle \vec{M}, \vec{w} \rangle \models \psi \}$ *for every surrogate $t_\psi \in T \cap var(\Phi)$.*

Then $\vec{M} \models \Phi$.

Lemma 3. *Let $M = \langle W, R, V, w_0 \rangle$ be a rooted Kripke structure. Let $\langle \vec{W}, \vec{R} \rangle$ be the unravelling of $\langle W, R \rangle$ at w_0. Let $\vec{M} = \langle \vec{W}, \vec{R}, \vec{V_\Sigma}, (w_0) \rangle$ where $\vec{V_\Sigma}(p) = \{ \vec{w} \in \vec{W} \mid trm(\vec{w}) \in V(p) \}$ for every propositional symbol $p \in Q$.*

Then for every modal formula ψ over Q and for every world $\vec{w} \in \vec{W}$, $\langle \vec{M}, \vec{w} \rangle \models \psi$ iff $\langle M, trm(\vec{w}) \rangle \models \psi$.

Lemma 4. *Let φ be a modal formula in simplified NNF. Let $\Phi_K = \{ \{0\} : t_\varphi \} \cup \rho_K(\{0\} : t_\varphi \to \varphi)$. Let Φ with $\Phi_K \subseteq \Phi$ be a definition-complete set of SNF_{sml} clauses, let $M = \langle W, R, V, w_0 \rangle$ be a tree K model of Φ and let $M' = \langle W, R', V, w_0 \rangle$ be such that*

(4a) $R \subseteq R'$;

(4b) for every modal clause $S : t_{\Box\psi} \to \Box\eta(\psi)$ in Φ and every world $w \in M[S]$,
$\langle M', w \rangle \models t_{\Box\psi} \to \Box\eta(\psi)$;

(4c) for every modal clause $S : t_{\Box\psi} \to \Box t_\psi$ in Φ and all worlds $v, w \in W$, if
    (i) $w \in M[S]$ and (ii) $wR'v$ then (iii) there exists a clause $S' : \neg t_\psi \vee \eta_f(\psi)$
    in Φ with $v \in M[S']$.

Then $\langle M', w_0 \rangle \models \varphi$.

Theorems 3 and 4 now state the correctness of our transformation for KB.

Theorem 3. *Let φ be a modal formula in simplified NNF. Let $\Phi_B = \{\{0\} : t_\varphi\} \cup \rho_{KB}(\{0\} : t_\varphi \to \varphi)$. If φ is KB-satisfiable, then Φ_B is K-satisfiable.*

Proof. The main idea is to show that given a rooted KB model of φ, then a small variation of its unravelling is a rooted tree K model of Φ_B.

Let $M = \langle W, R, V, w_0 \rangle$ be a rooted KB model of φ with $\langle M, w_0 \rangle \models \varphi$ and symmetric relationship R. Let $\langle \vec{W}, \vec{R} \rangle$ be the unravelling of $\langle W, R \rangle$ at w_0. Let $\vec{M}_B = \langle \vec{W}, \vec{R}, \vec{V}_B, (w_0) \rangle$ where

- $\vec{V}_B(p) = \{\vec{w} \in \vec{W} \mid \mathsf{trm}(\vec{w}) \in V(p)\}$ for every propositional symbol $p \in \mathsf{var}(\varphi)$,
- $\vec{V}_B(t_\psi) = \{\vec{w} \in \vec{W} \mid \langle \vec{M}_B, \vec{w} \rangle \models \psi\}$ for every surrogate $t_\psi \in \mathsf{var}(\Phi_B) \setminus \mathsf{var}(\varphi)$ introduced by rewriting, and
- $\vec{V}_B(t_{\Box\neg t_{\Box\psi}}) = \{\vec{w} \in \vec{W} \mid \langle \vec{M}_B, \vec{w} \rangle \models \Box\neg\Box\psi\}$ for every supplementary propositional symbol $t_{\Box\neg t_{\Box\psi}}$ introduced in the normal form transformation of a labelled formula $S : t_{\Box\psi} \to \Box\psi$.

Note that $\vec{V}_B$ is well-defined as for every surrogate $t_\psi \in T$, ψ only contains propositional symbols in Q. Let $\Phi_K = \{\{0\} : t_\varphi\} \cup \rho_K(\{0\} : t_\varphi \to \varphi)$.

We now consider the clauses occurring in Φ_B and show that they hold in $\vec{M}_B$. By Lemma 2 it follows that $\vec{M}_B \models \Phi_K$. Also, all definitional clauses in $\Phi_B \setminus \Phi_K$ are true in $\vec{M}_B$ by Lemma 1.

Next consider clauses of the form

$$(1)\ S' : \eta(\psi) \vee t_{\Box\neg t_{\Box\psi}} \qquad (2)\ S' : t_{\Box\neg t_{\Box\psi}} \to \Box\neg t_{\Box\psi}$$

where $t_{\Box\psi}$ is a surrogate for $\Box\psi$. These are not in Φ_K. We show both are true in $\vec{M}_B$. We do so by first considering that $t_{\Box\neg t_{\Box\psi}}$ is true at a world and then that it is false.

Case (a): Let $\vec{w} \in \vec{M}_B[S']$ with $\langle \vec{M}_B, \vec{w} \rangle \models t_{\Box\neg t_{\Box\psi}}$. Clearly, $\langle \vec{M}_B, \vec{w} \rangle \models \eta(\psi) \vee t_{\Box\neg t_{\Box\psi}}$. Also, by definition of $\vec{M}_B$, $\langle M_B, \vec{w} \rangle \models \Box\neg\Box\psi$. So, for every $\vec{v} \in \vec{W}$ with $\vec{w} \vec{R} \vec{v}$, $\langle \vec{M}_B, \vec{v} \rangle \models \neg\Box\psi$. As $t_{\Box\psi}$ is a surrogate for $\Box\psi$, by definition of $\vec{V}_B$, $\vec{v} \notin \vec{V}_B(t_{\Box\psi})$ and $\langle \vec{M}_B, \vec{v} \rangle \models \neg t_{\Box\psi}$. Thus, $\langle \vec{M}_B, \vec{w} \rangle \models \Box\neg t_{\Box\psi}$ and, by the semantics of implication, $\langle \vec{M}_B, \vec{w} \rangle \models t_{\Box\neg t_{\Box\psi}} \to \Box\neg t_{\Box\psi}$.

Case (b): Let $\vec{w} \in \vec{M}_B[S']$ with $\langle \vec{M}_B, \vec{w} \rangle \not\models t_{\Box\neg t_{\Box\psi}}$. Clearly, by the semantics of implication, $\langle \vec{M}_B, \vec{w} \rangle \models t_{\Box\neg t_{\Box\psi}} \to \Box\neg t_{\Box\psi}$. Also, by definition of $\vec{V}_B$, $\vec{w} \notin \vec{V}_B(t_{\Box\neg t_{\Box\psi}})$ implies $\langle \vec{M}_B, \vec{w} \rangle \not\models \Box\neg\Box\psi$ which in turn implies $\langle \vec{M}_B, \vec{w} \rangle \models \Diamond\Box\psi$. So, there exists $\vec{v} \in \vec{W}$ with $\vec{w}\vec{R}\vec{v}$ and $\langle \vec{M}_B, \vec{v} \rangle \models \Box\psi$. Since trm is a p-morphism from

$\vec{M}_B$ to M, $\mathrm{trm}(\vec{w}) \, R \, \mathrm{trm}(\vec{v})$. Since R is symmetric, we also have $\mathrm{trm}(\vec{v}) \, R \, \mathrm{trm}(\vec{w})$ and by construction of $\vec{M}_B$, for $\vec{u} = \vec{v} \circ \mathrm{trm}(\vec{w})$ we have $\vec{v} \, \vec{R} \, \vec{u}$. Since $\langle \vec{M}_B, \vec{v} \rangle \models \Box\psi$, $\langle \vec{M}_B, \vec{u} \rangle \models \psi$. As trm is a p-morphism and $\langle M, \mathrm{trm}(\vec{u}) \rangle \models \psi$ and since $\mathrm{trm}(\vec{w}) = \mathrm{trm}(\vec{u})$, $\langle M, \mathrm{trm}(\vec{w}) \rangle \models \psi$. By Lemma 3, from $\langle M, \mathrm{trm}(\vec{w}) \rangle \models \psi$ we obtain $\langle \vec{M}_B, \vec{w} \rangle \models \psi$. If ψ is a literal, then $\eta(\psi) = \psi$ and $\langle M, \vec{w} \rangle \models \eta(\psi)$. If ψ is not a literal, then $\eta(\psi) = t_\psi$ and from $\langle \vec{M}_B, \vec{w} \rangle \models \psi$, by definition of $\vec{V}_B$, $\vec{w} \in \vec{V}_B(t_\psi)$ and $\langle \vec{M}_B, \vec{w} \rangle \models t_\psi$. So, $\langle M, \vec{w} \rangle \models \eta(\psi) \vee t_{\Box\neg t_{\Box\psi}}$.

Thus, in both cases, for arbitrary $\vec{w} \in \vec{M}_B[S']$, $\eta(\psi) \vee t_{\Box\neg t_{\Box\psi}}$ and $t_{\Box\neg t_{\Box\psi}} \to \Box\neg t_{\Box\psi}$ and therefore Clauses (1) and (2) are true in $\vec{M}_B$.

Theorem 4. *Let φ be a modal formula in simplified NNF. Let $\Phi_B = \{\{0\} : t_\varphi\} \cup \rho_{KB}(\{0\} : t_\varphi \to \varphi)$. If Φ_B is K-satisfiable, then φ is KB-satisfiable.*

Proof. The main idea is to show that given a rooted tree K model of Φ_B, its symmetric closure is a rooted KB model of φ.

Let $M = \langle W, R, V, w_0 \rangle$ be a rooted tree K model of Φ_B. Let $M^B = \langle W, R^B, V^B, w_0 \rangle$ be a structure such that

(a) R^B is the symmetric closure of R, that is, R^B is the smallest relation on W such that $R \subseteq R^B$ and for every $v, w \in W$, $v \, R^B \, w$ implies $w \, R^B \, v$;

(b) $V^B(p) = V(p)$ for every propositional symbol.

Let $\Phi_K = \{\{0\} : t_\varphi\} \cup \rho_K(\{0\} : t_\varphi \to \varphi)$. We show that $M^B \models \Phi_B$ satisfies the three preconditions of Lemma 4. By Lemma 4 this in turn implies that $M^B \models \varphi$.

- Condition (4a) holds as $R \subseteq R^B$.
- For Condition (4b) let (3) $S : t_{\Box\psi} \to \Box\eta(\psi)$ be a modal clause in Φ_B. Then Φ_B also contains the additional clauses (4) $S^- : \eta(\psi) \vee t_{\Box\neg t_{\Box\psi}}$ and (5) $S^- : t_{\Box\neg t_{\Box\psi}} \to \Box\neg t_{\Box\psi}$. Let $w \in M[S]$. We have to show that (6) $\langle M^B, w \rangle \models t_{\Box\psi} \to \Box\eta(\psi)$. Assume $\langle M^B, w \rangle \models t_{\Box\psi}$. As $V^B(t_{\Box\psi}) = V(t_{\Box\psi})$ this implies $\langle M, w \rangle \models t_{\Box\psi}$. Let $v \in W$ such that $w \, R^B \, v$.

   Case (a): Assume $w \, R \, v$. As $\langle M, w \rangle \models t_{\Box\psi}$ and $\langle M, w \rangle \models t_{\Box\psi} \to \Box\eta(\psi)$, we have $\langle M, w \rangle \models \Box\eta(\psi)$. As $w \, R \, v$, $\langle M, v \rangle \models \eta(\psi)$. As $\eta(\psi)$ is a literal and $V^B = V$ we obtain $\langle M^B, v \rangle \models \eta(\psi)$. So, $\langle M^B, w \rangle \models t_{\Box\psi} \to \Box\eta(\psi)$.

   Case (b): Assume v is not reachable from w via R. Then $w R^B v$ was introduced by the symmetric closure operation on R and we must have $v \, R \, w$. That is, v is a R-predecessor of w and from $w \in M[S]$ it follows that $v \in M[S^-]$. So, (7) $\langle M, v \rangle \models \eta(\psi) \vee t_{\Box\neg t_{\Box\psi}}$ and (8) $\langle M, v \rangle \models t_{\Box\neg t_{\Box\psi}} \to \Box\neg t_{\Box\psi}$. From $v \, R \, w$, $\langle M, w \rangle \models t_{\Box\psi}$ and (8), it follows that $\langle M, v \rangle \models \neg t_{\Box\neg t_{\Box\psi}}$. This together with (7) implies $\langle M, v \rangle \models \eta(\psi)$. As $\eta(\psi)$ is a literal and $V^B = V$ we obtain $\langle M^B, v \rangle \models \eta(\psi)$. So, $\langle M^B, w \rangle \models t_{\Box\psi} \to \Box\eta(t_\psi)$.

   Case (a) and Case (b) together show that Property (6) holds.

- For Condition (4c) let (9) $S : t_{\Box\psi} \to \Box t_\psi$ be in Φ_B, $v, w \in W$, $\mathrm{ml}_M(w) = ml \in S$ (i.e., $w \in M[S]$) and $w \, R^B \, v$. We need to show that there exists a clause $S' : \neg t_\psi \vee \eta_f(\psi)$ in Φ_B with $v \in M[S']$.

   As in the previous case $w \, R^B \, v$ implies either $w \, R \, v$ or $v \, R \, w$. In the first case $\mathrm{ml}_M(v) = ml + 1$ while in the second case $\mathrm{ml}_M(v) = ml - 1$.

As Φ_B contains Clause (9), t_ψ occurs at level $ml+1$ in Φ_B. By definition of ρ_{KB}, Φ_B also contains the clause (10) $S^- : t_\psi \vee t_{\Box\neg\Box_\psi}$. As $ml \in S$, $ml-1 \in S^-$ and therefore t_ψ also occurs at level $ml - 1$ in Φ_B. By Theorem 2, Φ_B is definition-complete, so there must be a clause $S' : \neg t_\psi \vee \eta_f(\psi)$ in Φ_B such that $ml + 1$ and $ml - 1$ in S'.

Theorem 5. *Let φ be a modal formula in simplified NNF, $L \in \{K, KB, KD, KT, K4, K5\}$, and $\Phi_L = \{\{0\} : t_\varphi\} \cup \rho_L(\{0\} : t_\varphi \to \varphi)$. Then φ is L-satisfiable iff Φ_L is K-satisfiable.*

5   Comparison With Related Work

The approaches most closely related to ours are Kracht's reductions of normal modal logics to basic modal logic [11,12], the global modal resolution calculus [14], and Schmidt and Hustadt's axiomatic translation principle for translations of normal modal logics to first-order logic [24].

The first significant difference to our approach is that Kracht's reductions and the axiomatic translation exclude the modal operator $\Diamond$ from the language and only consider the modal operator $\Box$.

In order to present Kracht's approach, we need some additional notions. Let $\mathsf{sf}(\varphi)$, $\mathsf{dg}(\varphi)$, and $|S|$ denote the set of all subformulae of φ, the maximum nesting of modal operators in φ, and the cardinality of the set S, respectively. Let $\Diamond^0\psi = \Box^0\psi = \Box^{<1}\psi = \psi$, $\Box^{<n+1}\psi = (\psi \wedge \Box\Box^{<n}\psi)$, $\Box^{n+1}\psi = \Box\Box^n\psi$, and $\Diamond^{n+1}\psi = \Diamond\Diamond^n\psi$. We can then define a reduction function ρ_L^K for a normal modal logic L in $\{KB, KD, KT, K4\}$ as follows:

$$\rho_L^K(\varphi) = \begin{cases} \varphi \wedge \Box^{<|\mathsf{sf}(\varphi)|+1}P_{K4}^K(\varphi), & \text{for } L = K4 \\ \varphi \wedge \Box^{<\mathsf{dg}(\varphi)+1}P_L^K(\varphi) & \text{otherwise} \end{cases}$$

where $P_{KB}^K(\varphi) = \{\neg\psi \to \Box\neg\Box\psi \mid \Box\psi \in \mathsf{sf}(\varphi)\}$ $P_{KD}^K(\varphi) = \{\neg\Box\textbf{false}\}$

$P_{K4}^K(\varphi) = \{\Box\psi \to \Box\Box\psi \mid \Box\psi \in \mathsf{sf}(\varphi)\}$ $P_{KT}^K(\varphi) = \{\Box\psi \to \psi \mid \Box\psi \in \mathsf{sf}(\varphi)\}$

Kracht shows that φ is L-satisfiable iff $\rho_L^K(\varphi)$ is K-satisfiable. There are three differences to our approach. First, $P_L^K(\varphi)$ will include an axiom instance for every occurrence of a subformula $\neg\Box\psi$, equivalent to $\Diamond\neg\psi$, in φ. In contrast, our approach requires no logic specific treatment of such subformulae. Second, the use of $\Box^{<n}P_L^K(\varphi)$ in ρ_L^K means that the axiom instance is available at every modal level. This means, for example, that for $\vartheta_1 = \Diamond^{100}(\neg p \wedge \Box p)$, the formula $\rho_{KT}^K(\vartheta_1)$ contains the axiom instance $\Box p \to p$ over 100 times, although it is only required at the level at which $\Box p$ occurs. Third, this is further compounded if the formula ψ in $\Box\psi$ is itself a complex formula. We try to avoid that by using a surrogate propositional symbol t_ψ instead, but this will only have a positive effect if the definitional clauses for t_ψ do not have to be repeated.

The global modal resolution (GMR) calculus operates on SNF_K clauses, that is, clauses of the form

$$\Box^*(\textbf{start} \to \bigvee_{b=1}^r l_b) \qquad \Box^*(\textbf{true} \to \bigvee_{b=1}^r l_b) \qquad \Box^*(l' \to \Box l) \qquad \Box^*(l' \to \neg\Box l)$$

[EUC1]	$\square^*(l_1 \to \neg\square\neg l)$		[EUC2]	$\square^*(l \to \square l_2)$	
$\square^*(\mathbf{true} \to \neg l_1 \vee t_{\diamond l})$	$\square^*(t_{\diamond l} \to \neg\square\neg l)$		$\square^*(t_{\diamond l} \to \square l_2)$	$\square^*(t_{\diamond l} \to \neg\square\neg l)$	
$\square^*(\neg t_{\diamond l} \to \square\neg l)$	$\square^*(t_{\diamond l} \to \square t_{\diamond l})$		$\square^*(\neg t_{\diamond l} \to \square\neg l)$	$\square^*(t_{\diamond l} \to \square t_{\diamond l})$	

Table 4. Inference rules in [14] for K5 (EUC1 and EUC2).

where l, l', l_b are propositional literals with $1 \leq b \leq r$, $r \in \mathbb{N}$, and $\square^*$ is the universal operator. The calculus has specific inference rules for normal modal logics such as KB, KD, KT, K4, K5. Table 4 shows the two additional rules for K5, the only logic for which there are rules for both $\square$ and $\neg\square\neg$, i.e., $\diamond$. These inference rules can be seen to perform an 'on-the-fly' computation of a transformation. Note that the clauses produced by P_{K5} differ from those produced by GMR for K5. Implicitly, our results here also show that it should be possible to eliminate EUC1 from the GMR calculus.

For the axiomatic translation, we only present the function P_L^{RS} that computes the logic dependent first-order clausal formulae that are part of the overall translation.

$$P_{\mathsf{KB}}^{\mathsf{RS}}(\square\psi) = \{\forall x(\neg Q_{\square\psi}(y) \vee \neg R(x,y) \vee Q_{\psi}(x)) \mid \square\psi \in \mathsf{sf}(\varphi)\}$$

$$P_{\mathsf{KD}}^{\mathsf{RS}}(\square\psi) = \{\forall x(\neg Q_{\square\psi}(x) \vee Q_{\neg\square\neg\psi}(x)) \mid \square\psi \in \mathsf{sf}(\varphi)\}$$

$$P_{\mathsf{KT}}^{\mathsf{RS}}(\square\psi) = \{\forall x(\neg Q_{\square\psi}(x) \vee Q_{\psi}(x)) \mid \square\psi \in \mathsf{sf}(\varphi)\}$$

$$P_{\mathsf{K4}}^{\mathsf{RS}}(\square\psi) = \{\forall xy(\neg Q_{\square\psi}(x) \vee \neg R(x,y) \vee Q_{\square\psi}(y)) \mid \square\psi \in \mathsf{sf}(\varphi)\}$$

$$P_{\mathsf{K5}}^{\mathsf{RS}}(\square\psi) = \{\forall xy(\neg Q_{\square\psi}(y) \vee \neg R(x,y) \vee Q_{\square\psi}(x)),$$
$$\forall xy(\neg Q_{\square\neg\square\psi}(y) \vee \neg R(x,y) \vee Q_{\square\neg\square\psi}(x)) \mid \square\psi \in \mathsf{sf}(\varphi)\}$$

The predicate symbols Q_{ψ} correspond to our surrogate symbols t_{ψ}. The clausal formulae used in the treatment of KT and K4 are translations of the SNF_{ml} clauses we use (or vice versa). KB and K5 are handled in a different way as the first-order clausal formulae refer directly the accessibility relation and can therefore more easily express the transfer of information to a predecessor world. The universal quantification over worlds also means that the constraints expressed by the formulae hold at all modal levels without the need of any repetition.

In Section 6 we will also use the relational and semi-functional translation of modal logics to first-order logic combined with structural transformation to clause normal form. In both approaches $\square\psi$ is translated as $\forall xy(\neg Q_{\square\psi}(x) \vee \neg R(x,y) \vee Q_{\psi}$, while $\diamond\psi$ becomes $\forall x\exists y(\neg Q_{\diamond\psi}(x) \vee R(x,y))$ and $\forall x\exists \alpha(\neg Q_{\diamond\psi}(x) \vee R(x,[x\alpha]))$ in the relational and semi-functional translation, respectively. Then, depending on the modal logics, further formulae representing the semantic properties of the accessibility R are added. For the relational translation these will simply be the formulae in the fourth column of Table 1. The semi-functional translation uses collections of partial accessibility function in addition to the accessibility relation. A predicate def is used to represent on which worlds a partial accessibility function is defined. For each modal logic there is then again a background theory consisting of formulae over def and R that represents the properties of the underlying accessibility relation which is added to the translation of a formula. For example, for K5 the background theory is: $\forall xy \forall \alpha \beta ((\neg \text{def}(x) \vee \text{def}(y)) \wedge (\neg \text{def}(w_0) \vee R(w_0, [w_0 \alpha])) \wedge (\neg \text{def}(x) \vee \neg \text{def}(y) \vee R([x\alpha], [y\beta])))$, where w_0 is a constant representing the root world in a rooted Kripke structure.

6   Evaluation

We have compared the performance of the following approaches: (i) the combination of our reductions with the modal-layered resolution (MLR) calculus for SNF_{ml} clauses [15] implemented in the modal theorem prover K$_S$P, with three different refinements for resolution inferences on labelled propositional clauses; (ii) the global modal resolution (GMR) calculus, also implemented in K$_S$P, with three different refinements for resolution inferences on propositional clauses; (iii) the combinations of the relational and semi-functional translation of modal logics to first-order logic with ordered first-order resolution implemented in the first-order theorem prover SPASS. In total this gives us eight different approaches to compare. The axiomatic translation is currently not implemented in SPASS. Other provers, such as LEO-III [26], LWB [9], MleanCoP [21], do not have built-in support for the full range of logics considered here. LoTREC 2.0 [7] supports all the logics, but is not intended as automatic theorem prover.

The modal-layered resolution calculus operates on SNF_{ml} clauses, that is, clauses of the form

$$ml : \bigvee_{b=1}^{r} l_b \qquad ml : l' \to \Box l \qquad ml : l' \to \Diamond l$$

where $ml \in \mathbb{N} \cup \{\star\}$ and l, l', l_b are propositional literals with $1 \leq b \leq r$, $r \in \mathbb{N}$. In the implementation of the reductions presented in Section 3, we take a SNF_{sml} clause $S : \psi$ simply as an abbreviation of the set of SNF_{ml} clauses $\{ml : \psi \mid ml \in S\}$. Note that this also means that we will have to repeat similar resolution inferences for different modal levels.

K$_S$P [13] implements the reductions presented in Section 3 as well as a normal form transformation of modal formulae to sets of SNF_K clauses. It implements both the MLR and the GMR calculus. Resolution inferences between (labelled) propositional clauses can either be unrestricted (`cplain` option), restricted by an ordering (`cord` option), that is, clauses can only be resolved on their maximal literals with respect to an ordering chosen by the prover in such a way to preserve completeness, restricted to negative resolution (`cneg` option), that is, one of the premises in an inference has to be a negative clause, or restricted to positive resolution. We do not include the last option in our evaluation as it typically performs worse. K$_S$P also implements a range of simplification rules that are applied to modal formulae before their transformation to normal form. Of those we have enabled pure literal elimination (`early_ple` option), simplification using the Box Normal Form [22] and Prenex Normal Form (`bnfsimp` and `prenex`

Logic	Status	Total	KSP (GMR calculus, cneg)	KSP (GMR calculus, cord)	KSP (GMR calculus, cplain)	KSP (MLR calculus, cneg)	KSP (MLR calculus, cord)	KSP (MLR calculus, cplain)	SPASS (semi-functional)	SPASS (relational)
K	Sat	180	110	139	93	141	**155**	132	92	97
K	Unsat	180	154	**156**	151	154	**156**	153	134	122
KD	Sat	180	125	143	118	141	**155**	133	107	103
KD	Unsat	180	154	**156**	151	154	**156**	153	136	130
KT	Sat	100	53	**60**	37	46	56	26	47	39
KT	Unsat	260	233	236	225	230	**238**	220	222	199
KB	Sat	122	28	35	41	49	**89**	22	31	23
KB	Unsat	238	186	196	197	207	**211**	205	159	169
K4	Sat	161	33	39	38	68	**125**	36	0	0
K4	Unsat	199	124	112	146	**168**	165	163	109	35
K5	Sat	60	**14**	10	9	7	10	4	7	0
K5	Unsat	300	251	246	**259**	255	254	246	255	124
All	Sat	803	363	426	336	452	**590**	353	284	262
All	Unsat	1357	1102	1102	1129	1168	**1180**	1140	1015	779

Table 5. Experimental results on LWB benchmark collection

options) [17]. For clause processing, unit resolution and pure elimination are enabled (`unit`, `lhs_unit`, and `ple` options).

SPASS 3.9 [27,28] supports automated reasoning in extended modal logics, including all logics considered here, PDL-like modal logics as well as description logics. It includes eight different translations of modal logics to first-order logic. In our evaluation we have used the relational translation and the semi-functional translation. For the local satisfiability problem in KB to K5, for the relational translation we have added the first-order frame properties given in Table 1 while for the semi-functional translation we have added the background theories devised by Nonnengart [20]. For the transformation to first-order clausal form, we have enabled renaming of quantified subformulae. The only inference rules used are ordered resolution and ordered factoring, the reduction rules used are condensing, backward subsumption and forward subsumption. For the relational and semi-functional translation for K, KB, KD, and KT we thereby obtain a decision procedure, while for the other logics we do not. For K4 and K5, the fragment of first-order clausal logic corresponding to the semi-functional translation of modal formula and their background theories is decidable by ordered resolution with selection [25]. However, the non-trivial ordering and selection function required is not currently implemented in SPASS.

For our evaluation we have chosen the LWB basic modal logic benchmark collection [2], with 20 formulae in each of 18 parameterised classes. For K, all formulae in 9 classes are satisfiable while all formulae in the other 9 classes are unsatisfiable. In their negation normal form, 63% of modal operators are □ and

37% are $\Diamond$ operators. We have used the collection for each of the six logics. If a formula is unsatisfiable in K then it remains unsatisfiable in the other five logics, while the opposite is not true. As we move to logics other than K, it is also no longer the case that all formulae in a class have the same satisfiability status.

The third column in Table 5 indicates the total number of satisfiable and unsatisfiable formulae for each logic. In the last two lines of the table we sum up the results for all logics. The last eight columns in the table show how many formulae each of the approaches were able to solve with a time limit of 100 CPU seconds for each formula. Benchmarking was performed on a PC with an AMD Ryzen 5 5600X CPU @ 4.60GHz max and 32GB main memory using Fedora release 33 as operating system.

As we can see, the new reductions combined with the modal-layered resolution (MLR) calculus and ordered resolution refinement (cord) perform best, achieving the highest number of solved formulae in 8 out of 12 individual categories in the table, on two of those equal with the global modal resolution (GMR) calculus. On 3 categories, GMR outperfoms MLR. On both satisfiable and unsatisfiable formulae in K5 this can be seen as evidence that 'on-the-fly' transformation offers a (slight) advantage over our approach given that the additional clauses hold universally in both approaches. For SPASS we see a clear advantage of the semi-functional translation over the relational one, on both satisfiable and unsatisfiable formulae.

7   Conclusion and Future Work

We have presented new reductions of propositional modal logics KB, KD, KT, K4, K5 to Separated Normal Form with Sets of Modal Levels. We have shown experimentally that these reductions allow us to reason effectively in these logics.

The obvious next step is to consider extensions of the basic modal logic K with combinations of the axioms B, D, T, 4, and 5. Unfortunately, a simple combination of the reductions for each of the axioms is not sufficient to obtain a satisfiability-preserving reduction for the such modal logics. An example is the simple formula $\neg p \wedge \Diamond\Diamond\Box p$ which is KB4-unsatisfiable. If we define

$$P_{KB4}(S : t_{\Box\psi} \to \Box\psi) = P_{KB}(S : t_{\Box\psi} \to \Box\psi) \cup P_{K4}(S : t_{\Box\psi} \to \Box\psi)$$
$$\Delta_{KB4}(S : t_{\Box\psi} \to \Box\psi) = \delta_{KB4}(\star, \psi),$$

that is, P_{KB4} is the union of P_{KB} and P_{K4}, then the clause set obtained from $\{\{0\} : t_0\} \cup \rho_{KB4}(\{0\} : t_0 \to \neg p \wedge \Diamond\Diamond\Box p)$ is K-satisfiable. The same issue also occurs in the axiomatic translation of modal logics to first-order logic where the translation for KB4 is not simply the combination of the translations for KB and K4 [24, Theorem 5.6]. We are currently exploring solutions to this problem.

Regarding practical applications, it would be advantageous to have an implementation of a calculus that operates directly SNF_{sml} clauses. This would greatly reduce the number of inference steps performed on satisfiable formulae and simplify proof search in general. Again, such an implementation is future work.

References

1. Balbiani, P., Demri, S.: Prefixed tableaux systems for modal logics with enriched languages. In: IJCAI 1997. pp. 190–195. Morgan Kaufmann (1997)
2. Balsiger, P., Heuerding, A., Schwendimann, S.: A benchmark method for the propositional modal logics K, KT, S4. J. Autom. Reasoning **24**(3), 297–317 (2000)
3. Basin, D., Matthews, S., Vigano, L.: Labelled propositional modal logics: Theory and practice. J. Log. Comput. **7**(6), 685–717 (1997)
4. Benzmüller, C., Paulson, L.C.: Multimodal and intuitionistic logics in simple type theory. Log. J. IGPL **18**(6), 881–892 (2010)
5. Fitting, M.: Prefixed tableaus and nested sequents. Ann. Pure Appl. Log. **163**(3), 291–313 (2012)
6. Gabbay, D.M.: Decidability results in non-classical logics: Part I. Ann. Math. Log. **8**, 237–295 (1975)
7. Gasquet, O., Herzig, A., Longin, D., Sahade, M.: LoTREC: Logical tableaux research engineering companion. In: TABLEAUX 2005. LNCS, vol. 3702, pp. 318–322. Springer (2005). https://doi.org/10.1007/11554554_25
8. Halpern, J.Y., Moses, Y.: A guide to completeness and complexity for modal logics of knowledge and belief. Artif. Intell. **54**(3), 319–379 (1992)
9. Heuerding, A., Jäger, G., Schwendimann, S., Seyfried, M.: The Logics Workbench LWB: A snapshot. Euromath Bulletin **2**(1), 177–186 (1996)
10. Horrocks, I., Hustadt, U., Sattler, U., Schmidt, R.A.: Computational modal logic. In: Blackburn, P., van Benthem, J., Wolter, F. (eds.) Handbook of Modal Logic, chap. 4, pp. 181–245. Elsevier (2006)
11. Kracht, M.: Reducing modal consequence relations. J. Log. Comput. **11**(6), 879–907 (2001)
12. Kracht, M.: Notes on the space requirements for checking satisfiability in modal logics. In: Advances in Modal Logic 4, pp. 243–264. King's College Publications (2003)
13. Nalon, C.: K$_S$P (2021), https://cic.unb.br/~nalon/#software
14. Nalon, C., Dixon, C.: Clausal resolution for normal modal logics. J. Algorithms **62**, 117–134 (2007)
15. Nalon, C., Dixon, C., Hustadt, U.: Modal resolution: Proofs, layers, and refinements. ACM Trans. Comput. Log. **20**(4), 23:1–23:38 (2019)
16. Nalon, C., Hustadt, U., Dixon, C.: A modal-layered resolution calculus for K. In: TABLEAUX 2015. LNCS, vol. 9323, pp. 185–200. Springer, Heidelberg (2015). https://doi.org/10.1007/978-3-319-24312-2_13
17. Nalon, C., Hustadt, U., Dixon, C.: K$_S$P: A resolution-based prover for multimodal K. In: IJCAR 2016. LNCS, vol. 9706, pp. 406–415. Springer, Heidelberg (2016). https://doi.org/10.1007/978-3-319-40229-1_28
18. Nalon, C., Hustadt, U., Dixon, C.: K$_S$P: Architecture, refinements, strategies and experiments. J. Autom. Reason. **64**(3), 461–484 (2020)
19. Nguyen, L.A., Szalas, A.: Exptime tableau decision procedures for regular grammar logics with converse. Studia Logica **98**(3), 387–428 (2011)
20. Ohlbach, H.J., Nonnengart, A., de Rijke, M., Gabbay, D.M.: Encoding two-valued nonclassical logics in classical logic. In: Robinson, A., Voronkov, A. (eds.) Handbook of Automated Reasoning, chap. 21, pp. 1403–1485. Elsevier (2001)
21. Otten, J.: MleanCoP: A connection prover for first-order modal logic. In: IJCAR 2014. LNCS, vol. 8562, pp. 269–276. Springer (2014). https://doi.org/10.1007/978-3-319-08587-6_20

22. Pan, G., Sattler, U., Vardi, M.Y.: BDD-based decision procedures for the modal logic K. J. Appl. Non-Class. Log. **16**(1-2), 169–208 (2006)
23. Schmidt, R.A.: Decidability by resolution for propositional modal logics. J. Autom. Reasoning **22**(4), 379–396 (1999)
24. Schmidt, R.A., Hustadt, U.: The axiomatic translation principle for modal logic. ACM Trans. Comput. Log. **8**(4), 19 (2007)
25. Schmidt, R.A., Hustadt, U.: First-order resolution methods for modal logics. In: Programming Logics: Essays in Memory of Harald Ganzinger. LNCS, vol. 7797, pp. 345–391. Springer (2013). https://doi.org/10.1007/978-3-642-37651-1_15
26. Steen, A., Benzmüller, C.: The higher-order prover Leo-III. In: ECAI 2020. Frontiers in Artificial Intelligence and Applications, vol. 325, pp. 2937–2938. IOS Press (2020). https://doi.org/10.3233/FAIA200462
27. The SPASS Team: Spass 3.9 (2016), http://www.spass-prover.org/
28. Weidenbach, C.: Combining superposition, sorts and splitting. In: Robinson, J.A., Voronkov, A. (eds.) Handbook of Automated Reasoning, pp. 1965–2013. Elsevier and MIT Press (2001)

Open Access This chapter is licensed under the terms of the Creative Commons Attribution 4.0 International License (http://creativecommons.org/licenses/by/4.0/), which permits use, sharing, adaptation, distribution and reproduction in any medium or format, as long as you give appropriate credit to the original author(s) and the source, provide a link to the Creative Commons license and indicate if changes were made.

The images or other third party material in this chapter are included in the chapter's Creative Commons license, unless indicated otherwise in a credit line to the material. If material is not included in the chapter's Creative Commons license and your intended use is not permitted by statutory regulation or exceeds the permitted use, you will need to obtain permission directly from the copyright holder.

Isabelle's Metalogic: Formalization and Proof Checker*

Tobias Nipkow and Simon Roßkopf

Technical University of Munich, Munich, Germany

Abstract. Isabelle is a generic theorem prover with a fragment of higher-order logic as a metalogic for defining object logics. Isabelle also provides proof terms. We formalize this metalogic and the language of proof terms in Isabelle/HOL, define an executable (but inefficient) proof term checker and prove its correctness w.r.t. the metalogic. We integrate the proof checker with Isabelle and run it on a range of logics and theories to check the correctness of all the proofs in those theories.

1 Introduction

One of the selling points of proof assistants is their trustworthiness. Yet in practice soundness problems do come up in most proof assistants. Harrison [11] distinguishes errors in the logic and errors in the implementation (and cites examples). Our work contributes to the solution of both problems for the proof assistant Isabelle [31]. Isabelle is a generic theorem prover: it implements $\mathcal{M}$, a fragment of intuitionistic higher-order logic, as a metalogic for defining object logics. Its most developed object logic is HOL and the resulting proof assistant is called Isabelle/HOL [25,24]. The latter is the basis for our formalizations.

Our first contribution is the first complete formalization of Isabelle's metalogic. Thus our work applies to all Isabelle object logics, e.g. not just HOL but also ZF. Of course Paulson [30] describes $\mathcal{M}$ precisely, but only on paper. More importantly, his description does not cover polymorphism and type classes, which were introduced later [26]. The published account of Isabelle's proof terms [4] is also silent about type classes. Yet type classes are a significant complication (as, for example, Kunčar and Popescu [18] found out).

Our second contribution is a verified (against $\mathcal{M}$) and executable checker for Isabelle's proof terms. We have integrated the proof checker with Isabelle. Thus we can guarantee that every theorem whose proof our proof checker accepts is provable in our definition of $\mathcal{M}$. So far we are able to check the correctness of moderately sized theories across the full range of logics implemented in Isabelle.

Although Isabelle follows the LCF-architecture (theorems that can only be manufactured by inference rules) it is based on an infrastructure optimized for

---

* Supported by Wirtschaftsministerium Bayern under DIK-2002-0027//DIK0185/03 and DFG GRK 2428 ConVeY

© The Author(s) 2021

A. Platzer and G. Sutcliffe (Eds.): CADE 2021, LNAI 12699, pp. 93–110, 2021.
https://doi.org/10.1007/978-3-030-79876-5_6

performance. In particular, this includes multithreading, which is used in the kernel and has once lead to a soundness issue[1] . Therefore we opt for the "certificate checking" approach (via proof terms) instead of verifying the implementation.

This is the first work that deals directly with what is implemented in Isabelle as opposed to a study of the metalogic that Isabelle is meant to implement. Instead of reading the implementation you can now read and build on the more abstract formalization in this paper. The correspondence of the two can be established for each proof by running the proof checker.

Our formalization reflects the ML implementation of Isabelle's terms and types and some other data structures. Thus a few implementation choices are visible, e.g. De Bruijn indices. This is necessary because we want to integrate our proof checker as directly as possible with Isabelle, with as little unverified glue code as possible, for example no translation between De Bruijn indices and named variables. We refer to this as our *intentional implementation bias*. In principle, however, one could extend our formalization with different representations (e.g. named terms) and prove suitable isomorphisms. Our work is purely proof theoretic; semantics is out of scope.

The formalization can be found in the Archive of Formal Proofs[28].

2   Related Work

Harrison [11] was the first to verify some of HOL's metatheory and an implementation of a HOL kernel in HOL itself. Kumar *et al.* [13] formalized HOL including definition principles, proved its soundness and synthesized a verified kernel of a HOL prover down to the machine language level. Abrahamsson [2] verified a proof checker for the OpenTheory [12] proof exchange format for HOL.

Wenzel [38] showed how to interpret type classes as predicates on types. We follow his approach of reflecting type classes in the logic but cannot remove them completely because of our intentional implementation bias (see above). Kunčar and Popescu [15,16,17,18] focus on the subtleties of definition principles for HOL with overloading and prove that under certain conditions, type and constant definitions preserve consistency. Åman Pohjola *et al.* [1] formalize [15,18].

Adams [3] presents HOL Zero, a basic theorem prover for HOL that addresses the problem of how to ensure that parser and pretty-printer do not misrepresent formulas.

Let us now move away from Isabelle and HOL. Sozeau *et al.* [36] present the first implementation of a type checker for the kernel of Coq that is proved correct in Coq with respect to a formal specification. Carneiro [6] has implemented a highly performant proof checker for a multi-sorted first order logic and is in the process of verifying it in its own logic.

We formalize a logic with bound variables, and there is a large body of related work that deals with this issue (e.g. [37,21,7]) and a range of logics and systems with special support for handling bound variables (e.g. [33,34,35]). We found that De Bruijn indices worked reasonably well for us.

---

[1] https://mailmanbroy.in.tum.de/pipermail/isabelle-dev/2016-December/007251.html

3   Preliminaries

Isabelle types are built from type variables, e.g. $'a$, and (postfix) type constructors, e.g. $'a$ *list*; the function type arrow is $\Rightarrow$. Isabelle also has a type class system explained later. The notation $t :: \tau$ means that term t has type τ. Isabelle/HOL provides types $'a$ *set* and $'a$ *list* of sets and lists of elements of type $'a$. They come with the following vocabulary: function *set* (conversion from lists to sets), (#) (list constructor), (@) (append), $|xs|$ (length of list xs), $xs \; ! \; i$ (the ith element of xs starting at 0), *list-all2* $p \; [x_1, \ldots, x_m] \; [y_1, \ldots, y_n] = (m = n \; \wedge \; p \; x_1 \; y_1 \; \wedge \; \ldots \; \wedge \; p \; x_n \; y_n)$ and other self-explanatory notation.

The *Field* of a relation r is the set of all x such that $(x,\_)$ or $(\_,x)$ is in r.

There is also the predefined data type

datatype $'a$ *option* = *None* | *Some* $'a$

The type $\tau_1 \rightharpoonup \tau_2$ abbreviates $\tau_1 \Rightarrow \tau_2$ *option*, i.e. partial functions, which we call *maps*. Maps have a domain and a range:

$$dom \; m = \{a \mid m \; a \neq None\} \qquad ran \; m = \{b \mid \exists a. \; m \; a = Some \; b\}.$$

Logical equivalence is written = instead of $\longleftrightarrow$.

4   Types and Terms

A *name* is simply a string. Variables have type *var*; their inner structure is immaterial for the presentation of the logic.

The logic has three layers: terms are classified by types as usual, but in addition types are classified by *sorts*. A *sort* is simply a set of class names. We discuss sorts in detail later.

Types (typically denoted by T, U, ...) are defined like this:

datatype *typ* = *Ty* name (*typ list*) | *Tv* var sort

where *Ty* $\kappa \; [T_1,\ldots,T_n]$ represents the Isabelle type $(T_1,\ldots,T_n) \; \kappa$ and *Tv* $a \; S$ represents a type variable a of sort S — sorts are directly attached to type variables. The notation $T \rightarrow U$ is short for *Ty* "*fun*" $[T,U]$, where "*fun*" is the name of the function type constructor.

Isabelle's terms are simply typed lambda terms in De Bruijn notation:

datatype *term* = *Ct* name typ | *Fv* var typ | *Bv* nat | *Abs* typ term | $(\cdot)$ term term

A term (typically r, s, t, u ...) can be a typed constant *Ct* $c \; T$ or free variable *Fv* $v \; T$, a bound variable *Bv* n (a De Brujin index), a typed abstraction *Abs* $T \; t$ or an application $t \cdot u$.

The term-has-type proposition has the syntax $Ts \vdash_\tau t : T$ where Ts is a list of types, the context for the type of the bound variables.

$$\_ \vdash_\tau Ct \_ T : T \qquad \_ \vdash_\tau Fv \_ T : T \qquad \frac{i < |Ts|}{Ts \vdash_\tau Bv \; i : Ts \; ! \; i}$$

$$\frac{T \ \# \ Ts \vdash_\tau t : T'}{Ts \vdash_\tau Abs \ T \ t : T \to T'}$$

$$\frac{Ts \vdash_\tau u : U \qquad Ts \vdash_\tau t : U \to T}{Ts \vdash_\tau t \cdot u : T}$$

We define $\vdash_\tau t : T = [] \vdash_\tau t : T$.

Function $fv :: term \Rightarrow (var \times typ) \ set$ collects the free variables in a term. Because bound variables are indices, $fv \ t$ is simply the set of all $(v, \ T)$ such that $Fv \ v \ T$ occurs in t. The type is an integral part of a variable.

A *type substitution* is a function ϱ of type $var \Rightarrow sort \Rightarrow typ$. It assigns a type to each type variable and sort pair. We write $\varrho \ \$\$ \ T$ or $\varrho \ \$\$ \ t$ for the overloaded function which applies such a type substitution to all type variables (and their sort) occurring in a type or term. The *type instance* relation is defined like this:

$$T_1 \lesssim T_2 = (\exists \varrho. \ \varrho \ \$\$ \ T_2 = T_1)$$

We also need to β-contract a term $Abs \ T \ t \cdot u$ to something like "t with $Bv \ 0$ replaced by u". We define a function $subst\text{-}bv$ such that $subst\text{-}bv \ u \ t$ is that β-contractum. The definition of $subst\text{-}bv$ is shown in the Appendix and can also be found in the literature (e.g. [23]).

In order to abstract over a free (term) variable there is a function $bind\text{-}fv$ $(v, T) \ t$ that (roughly speaking) replaces all occurrences of $Fv \ v \ T$ in t by $Bv \ 0$. Again, see the Appendix for the definition. This produces (if $Fv \ v \ T$ occurs in t) a term with an unbound $Bv \ 0$. Function $Abs\text{-}fv$ binds it with an abstraction:

$Abs\text{-}fv \ v \ T \ t = Abs \ T \ (bind\text{-}fv \ (v, \ T) \ t)$

While this section described the syntax of types and terms, they are not necessarily wellformed and should be considered pretypes/preterms. The wellformedness checks are described later.

5   Classes and Sorts

Isabelle has a built-in system of type classes [22] as in Haskell 98 except that class constraints are directly attached to variable names: our $Tv \ a \ [C,D,\ldots]$ corresponds to Haskell's (C a, D a, ...) => ... a ....

A *sort* is Isabelle's terminology for a set of (class) names, e.g. $\{C,D,\ldots\}$, which represent a conjunction of class constraints. In our work, variables S, S' etc. stand for sorts.

Apart from the usual application in object logics, type classes also serve an important metalogical purpose: they allow us to restrict, for example, quantification in object logics to object-level types and rule out meta-level propositions.

Isabelle's type class system was first presented in a programming language context [29,27]. We give the first machine-checked formalization. The central data structure is a so-called *order-sorted signature*. Intuitively, it is comprised of a set of class names, a partial subclass ordering on them and a set of *type constructor signatures*. A type constructor signature $\kappa :: (S_1, \ \ldots, \ S_k) \ c$ for a type constructor κ states that applying κ to types $T_1, \ldots, T_k$ such that T_i has sort S_i (defined below) produces a type of class c. Formally:

type_synonym $osig = ((name \times name) \ set \times (name \rightharpoonup (class \rightharpoonup sort \ list)))$

To explain this formalization we start from a pair $(sub, tcs) :: osig$ and recover the informal order-sorted signature described above. The set of classes is simply the *Field* of the sub relation. The tcs component represents the set of all type constructor signatures $\kappa :: (Ss) \ c$ (where Ss is a list of sorts) such that $tcs \ \kappa =$ **Some** dm and $dm \ c =$ **Some** Ss. Representing $\kappa :: (Ss) \ c$ as a triple, we define

$$TCS = \{(\kappa, Ss, c) \mid \exists \, domf. \ tcs \ \kappa = \textbf{Some} \ domf \land domf \ c = \textbf{Some} \ Ss\}$$

TCS is the translation of tcs, the data structure close to the implementation, to an equivalent but more intuitive version TCS that is close to the informal presentations in the literature.

The subclass ordering sub can be extended to a subsort ordering as follows:

$$S_1 \leq_{sub} S_2 = (\forall \, c_2 \in S_2. \ \exists \, c_1 \in S_1. \ c_1 \leq_{sub} c_2)$$

The smaller sort needs to subsume all the classes in the larger sort. In particular $\{c_1\} \leq_{sub} \{c_2\}$ iff $(c_1, c_2) \in sub$.

Now we can define a predicate *has-sort* that checks whether, in the context of some order-sorted signature (sub, tcs), a type fulfills a given sort constraint:

$$\frac{S \leq_{sub} S'}{\textit{has-sort} \ (sub, \ tcs) \ (Tv \ a \ S) \ S'}$$

$$\frac{tcs \ \kappa = \textbf{Some} \ dm \qquad \forall \, c \in S. \ \exists \, Ss. \ dm \ c = \textbf{Some} \ Ss \land \textit{list-all2} \ (\textit{has-sort} \ (sub, \ tcs)) \ Ts \ Ss}{\textit{has-sort} \ (sub, \ tcs) \ (Ty \ \kappa \ Ts) \ S}$$

The rule for type variables uses the subsort relation and is obvious. A type $(T_1, \ldots, T_n) \ \kappa$ has sort $\{c_1, \ldots\}$ if for every c_i there is a signature $\kappa :: (S_1, \ldots, S_n) \ c_i$ and *has-sort* $(sub, tcs) \ T_j \ S_j$ for $j = 1, \ldots, n$.

We *normalize* a sort by removing "superfluous" class constraints, i.e. retaining only those classes that are not subsumed by other classes. This gives us unique representatives for sorts which we call *normalized*:

$normalize\text{-}sort \ sub \ S = \{c \in S \mid \neg \ (\exists \, c' \in S. \ (c', c) \in sub \land (c, c') \notin sub)\}$
$normalized\text{-}sort \ sub \ S = (normalize\text{-}sort \ sub \ S = S)$

We work with normalized sorts because it simplifies the derivation of efficient executable code later on.

Now we can define wellformedness of an $osig$:

$wf\text{-}osig \ (sub, \ tcs) = (wf\text{-}subclass \ sub \land wf\text{-}tcsigs \ sub \ tcs)$

A sublass relation is wellformed if it is a partial order where reflexivity is restricted to its *Field*. Wellformedness of type constructor signatures (*wf-tcsigs*) is more complex. We describe it in terms of TCS derived from tcs (see above). The conditions are the following:

– The following property requires a) that for any $\kappa :: (...)c_1$ there must be a $\kappa :: (...)c_2$ for every superclass c_2 of c_1 and b) *coregularity* which guarantees the existence of principal types [29,10].

$\forall\,(\kappa,\,Ss_1,\,c_1)\in TCS.$
   $\forall\,c_2.\,(c_1,\,c_2)\in sub \longrightarrow$
      $(\exists\,Ss_2.\,(\kappa,\,Ss_2,\,c_2)\in TCS \wedge$ *list-all2* $(\lambda S_1\,S_2.\,S_1 \leq_{sub} S_2)\,Ss_1\,Ss_2)$

– A type constructor must always take the same number of argument types:

$\forall\,\kappa\,Ss_1\,c_1\,Ss_2\,c_2.$
   $(\kappa,\,Ss_1,\,c_1)\in TCS \wedge (\kappa,\,Ss_2,\,c_2)\in TCS \longrightarrow |Ss_1| = |Ss_2|$

– Sorts must be normalized and must exists in *sub*:

$\forall\,(\kappa,\,Ss,\,c)\in TCS.\,\forall\,S\in set\,Ss.$ *wf-sort* $sub\,S$
   where *wf-sort* $sub\,S = ($*normalized-sort* $sub\,S \wedge S \subseteq$ *Field* $sub)$

These conditions are used in a number of places to show that the type system is well behaved. For example, *has-sort* is upward closed:

wf-osig $(sub,\,tcs) \wedge$ *has-sort* $(sub,\,tcs)\,T\,S \wedge S \leq_{sub} S'$
$\longrightarrow$ *has-sort* $(sub,\,tcs)\,T\,S'$

6 Signatures

A *signature* consist of a map from constant names to their (most general) types, a map from type constructor names to their arities, and an order-sorted signature:

type_synonym *signature* $= (name \rightharpoonup typ) \times (name \rightharpoonup nat) \times osig$

The three projection functions are called *const-type*, *type-arity* and *osig*. We now define a number of wellformedness checks w.r.t. a signature Σ. We start with wellformedness of types, which is pretty obvious:

$$\frac{\textit{type-arity}\ \Sigma\ \kappa = \textit{Some}\ |Ts| \qquad \forall\,T\in set\ Ts.\ \textit{wf-type}\ \Sigma\ T}{\textit{wf-type}\ \Sigma\ (\textit{Ty}\ \kappa\ Ts)}$$

$$\frac{\textit{wf-sort}\ (\textit{subclass}\ (\textit{osig}\ \Sigma))\ S}{\textit{wf-type}\ \Sigma\ (\textit{Tv}\ a\ S)}$$

Wellformedness of a term essentially just says that all types in the term are wellformed and that the type T' of a constant in the term must be an instance of the type T of that constant in the signature: $T' \lesssim T$.

$$\frac{\textit{wf-type}\ \Sigma\ T}{\textit{wf-term}\ \Sigma\ (\textit{Fv}\ v\ T)} \qquad \textit{wf-term}\ \Sigma\ (\textit{Bv}\ n)$$

$$\frac{\textit{const-type}\ \Sigma\ s = \textit{Some}\ T \qquad \textit{wf-type}\ \Sigma\ T' \qquad T' \lesssim T}{\textit{wf-term}\ \Sigma\ (\textit{Ct}\ s\ T')}$$

$$\frac{\textit{wf-term}\ \Sigma\ t \qquad \textit{wf-term}\ \Sigma\ u}{\textit{wf-term}\ \Sigma\ (t \cdot u)}$$

$$\frac{\textit{wf-type}\ \Sigma\ T \qquad \textit{wf-term}\ \Sigma\ t}{\textit{wf-term}\ \Sigma\ (\textit{Abs}\ T\ t)}$$

These rules only check whether a term conforms to a signature, not that the contained types are consistent. Combining wellformedness and $\vdash_\tau$ yields well-typedness of a term:

wt-term Σ t = (*wf-term* Σ $t \wedge (\exists\, T.\ \vdash_\tau t : T))$

Wellformedness of a signature $\Sigma = (ctf,\ arf,\ oss)$ where $oss = (sub,\ tcs)$ is defined as follows:

wf-sig Σ =
$((\forall\, T \in ran\ ctf.\ \textit{wf-type}\ \Sigma\ T) \wedge \textit{wf-osig}\ oss \wedge dom\ tcs = dom\ arf\ \wedge$
$(\forall\, \kappa\ dm.\ tcs\ \kappa = Some\ dm \longrightarrow (\forall\, Ss \in ran\ dm.\ arf\ \kappa = Some\ |Ss|)))$

In words: all types in *ctf* are wellformed, *oss* is wellformed, the type constructors in *tcs* are exactly those that have an arity in *arf*, for every type constructor signature $(\kappa,\ Ss,\ \_)$ in *tcs*, κ has arity $|Ss|$.

7 Logic

Isabelle's metalogic $\mathcal{M}$ is an extension of the logic described by Paulson [30]. It is a fragment of intuitionistic higher-order logic. The basic types and connectives of $\mathcal{M}$ are the following:

Concept	Representation	Abbreviation
Type of propositions	*Ty* "prop" []	*prop*
Implication	*Ct* "imp" (*prop* $\to$ *prop* $\to$ *prop*)	$\Longrightarrow$
Universal quantifier	*Ct* "all" (($T \to$ *prop*) $\to$ *prop*)	$\bigwedge_T$
Equality	*Ct* "eq" ($T \to T \to$ *prop*)	$\equiv_T$

The type subscripts of $\bigwedge$ and $\equiv$ are dropped in the text if they can be inferred.

Readers familiar with Isabelle syntax must keep in mind that for readability we use the symbols $\bigwedge$, $\Longrightarrow$ and $\equiv$ for the *encodings* of the respective symbols in Isabelle's metalogic. We avoid the corresponding metalogical constants completely in favour of HOL's $\forall$, $\longrightarrow$, = and inference rule notation.

The provability judgment of $\mathcal{M}$ is of the form $\Theta,\Gamma \vdash t$ where Θ is a theory, Γ (the hypotheses) is a set of terms of type *prop* and t a term of type *prop*.

A *theory* is a pair of a signature and a set of axioms:

type_synonym *theory* = *signature* $\times$ *term set*

The projection functions are *sig* and *axioms*. We extend the notion of wellformedness from signatures to theories:

wf-theory $(\Sigma,\ axs)$ =
(*wf-sig* $\Sigma \wedge (\forall\, p \in axs.\ \textit{wt-term}\ \Sigma\ p \wedge \vdash_\tau p : \textit{prop}) \wedge \textit{is-std-sig}\ \Sigma \wedge \textit{eq-axs} \subseteq axs)$

The first two conjuncts need no explanation. Predicate *is-std-sig* (not shown) requires the signature to have certain minimal content: the basic types ($\to$, *prop*) and constants ($\equiv$, $\bigwedge$, $\Longrightarrow$) of $\mathcal{M}$ and the additional types and constants for type class reasoning from Section 7.3. Our theories also need to contain a minimal set of axioms. The set *eq-axs* is an axiomatic basis for equality reasoning and will be explained in Section 7.2.

We will now discuss the inference system in three steps: the basic inference rules, equality and type class reasoning.

7.1   Basic Inference Rules

The *axiom rule* states that wellformed type-instances of axioms are provable:

$$\frac{\textit{wf-theory } \Theta \qquad t \in \textit{axioms } \Theta \qquad \textit{wf-inst } \Theta \; \varrho}{\Theta, \Gamma \vdash \varrho \; \$\$ \; t}$$

where $\varrho :: var \Rightarrow sort \Rightarrow typ$ is a type substitution and $\$\$$ denotes its application (see Section 4). The types substituted into the type variables need to be wellformed and conform to the sort constraint of the type variable:

wf-inst $(\Sigma, \textit{axs}) \; \varrho =$
$(\forall v \; S. \; \varrho \; v \; S \neq \textit{Tv } v \; S \longrightarrow \textit{has-sort } (\textit{osig } \Sigma) \; (\varrho \; v \; S) \; S \wedge \textit{wf-type } \Sigma \; (\varrho \; v \; S))$

The conjunction only needs to hold if ϱ actually changes something, i.e. if $\varrho \; v \; S \neq \textit{Tv } v \; S$. This condition is not superfluous because otherwise *has-sort oss* $(\textit{Tv } v \; S) \; S$ and *wf-type* $\Sigma \; (\textit{Tv } v \; S)$ only hold if S is wellformed w.r.t Σ.

Note that there are no extra rules for general instantiation of type or term variables. Type variables can only be instantiated in the axioms. Term instantiation can be performed using the forall introduction and elimination rules.

The *assumption rule* allows us to prove terms already in the hypotheses:

$$\frac{\textit{wf-term } (\textit{sig } \Theta) \; t \qquad \vdash_\tau t : \textit{prop} \qquad t \in \Gamma}{\Theta, \Gamma \vdash t}$$

Both $\bigwedge$ and $\Longrightarrow$ are characterized by introduction and elimination rules:

$$\frac{\textit{wf-theory } \Theta \qquad \Theta, \Gamma \vdash t \qquad (x, T) \notin \textit{FV } \Gamma \qquad \textit{wf-type } (\textit{sig } \Theta) \; T}{\Theta, \Gamma \vdash \bigwedge_T (\textit{Abs-fv } x \; T \; t)}$$

$$\frac{\Theta, \Gamma \vdash \bigwedge_T (\textit{Abs } T \; t) \qquad \vdash_\tau u : T \qquad \textit{wf-term } (\textit{sig } \Theta) \; u}{\Theta, \Gamma \vdash \textit{subst-bv } u \; t}$$

$$\frac{\textit{wf-theory } \Theta \qquad \Theta, \Gamma \vdash u \qquad \textit{wf-term } (\textit{sig } \Theta) \; t \qquad \vdash_\tau t : \textit{prop}}{\Theta, \Gamma - \{t\} \vdash t \Longrightarrow u}$$

$$\frac{\Theta, \Gamma_1 \vdash t \Longrightarrow u \qquad \Theta, \Gamma_2 \vdash t}{\Theta, \Gamma_1 \cup \Gamma_2 \vdash u}$$

where $\textit{FV } \Gamma = (\bigcup_{t \in \Gamma} \textit{fv } t)$.

7.2   Equality

Most rules about equality are not part of the inference system but are axioms (the set *eq-axs* mentioned above). Consequences are obtained via the axiom rule. The first three axioms express that $\equiv$ is reflexive, symmetric and transitive:

$$x \equiv x \qquad x \equiv y \implies y \equiv x \qquad x \equiv y \implies y \equiv z \implies x \equiv z$$

The next two axioms express that terms of type *prop* (A and B) are equal iff they are logically equivalent:

$$A \equiv B \implies A \implies B \qquad (A \implies B) \implies (B \implies A) \implies A \equiv B$$

The last equality axioms are congruence rules for application and abstraction:

$$f \equiv g \implies x \equiv y \implies (f \cdot x) \equiv (g \cdot y)$$
$$\bigwedge (\textit{Abs } T \ ((f \cdot \textit{Bv } 0) \equiv (g \cdot \textit{Bv } 0))) \implies \textit{Abs } T \ (f \cdot \textit{Bv } 0) \equiv \textit{Abs } T \ (g \cdot \textit{Bv } 0)$$

Paulson [30] gives a slightly different congruence rule for abstraction, which allows to abstract over an arbitrary, free x in f, g. We are able to derive this rule in our inference system.

Finally there are the lambda calculus rules. There is no need for α conversion because α-equivalent terms are already identical thanks to the De Brujin indices for bound variables. For β and η conversion the following rules are added. In contrast to the rest of this subsection, these are not expressed as axioms.

$$\frac{\textit{wf-theory } \Theta \qquad \textit{wt-term (sig } \Theta) \ (\textit{Abs } T \ t) \qquad \textit{wf-term (sig } \Theta) \ u \qquad \vdash_\tau u : T}{\Theta, \Gamma \vdash (\textit{Abs } T \ t \cdot u) \equiv \textit{subst-bv } u \ t} \ (\beta)$$

$$\frac{\textit{wf-theory } \Theta \qquad \textit{wf-term (sig } \Theta) \ t \qquad \vdash_\tau t : T \to T'}{\Theta, \Gamma \vdash \textit{Abs } T \ (t \cdot \textit{Bv } 0) \equiv t} \ (\eta)$$

Rule (β) uses the substitution function *subst-bv* as explained in Section 4 (and defined in the Appendix).

Rule (η) requires a few words of explanation. We do not explicitly require that t does not contain *Bv 0*. This is already a consequence of the precondition that $\vdash_\tau t : T \to T'$: it implies that t is closed. For that reason it is perfectly unproblematic to remove the abstraction above t.

7.3   Type Class Reasoning

Wenzel [38] encoded class constraints of the form "type T has class c" in the term language as follows. There is a unary type constructor named *"itself"* and T *itself* abbreviates *Ty "itself"* [T]. The notation $TYPE_{T \ \textit{itself}}$ is short for *Ct "type"* (T *itself*) where *"type"* is the name of a new uninterpreted constant. You should view $TYPE_{T \ \textit{itself}}$ as the term-level representation of type T.

Next we represent the predicate "is of class c" on the term level. For this we define some fixed injective mapping *const-of-class* from class to constant names.

For each new class c a new constant *const-of-class* c of type T *itself* → *prop* is added. The term *Ct* (*const-of-class* c) (T *itself* → *prop*) · $TYPE_{T\ itself}$ represents the statement "type T has class c". This is the inference rule deriving such propositions:

$$\frac{\begin{array}{c} \textit{wf-theory } \Theta \\ \textit{const-type } (\textit{sig } \Theta) \ (\textit{const-of-class } C) = \textit{Some } ('a \textit{ itself} \rightarrow \textit{prop}) \\ \textit{wf-type } (\textit{sig } \Theta) \ T \qquad \textit{has-sort } (\textit{osig } (\textit{sig } \Theta)) \ T \ \{C\} \end{array}}{\Theta,\Gamma \vdash \textit{Ct } (\textit{const-of-class } C) \ (T \textit{ itself} \rightarrow \textit{prop}) \cdot \textit{TYPE}_{T \ itself}}$$

This is how the *has-sort* inference system is integrated into the logic.

This concludes the presentation of $\mathcal{M}$. We have shown some minimal sanity properties, incl. that all provable terms are of type *prop* and wellformed:

Theorem 1. $\Theta,\Gamma \vdash t \longrightarrow \vdash_\tau t : \textit{prop} \wedge \textit{wf-term } (\textit{sig } \Theta) \ t$

The attentive reader will have noticed that we do not require unused hypotheses in Γ to be wellformed and of type *prop*. Similarly, we only require *wf-theory* Θ in rules that need it to preserve wellformedness of the terms and types involved. To restrict to wellformed theories and hypotheses we define a top-level provability judgment that requires wellformedness:

$\Theta,\Gamma \Vdash t = (\textit{wf-theory } \Theta \wedge (\forall h \in \Gamma. \ \textit{wf-term } (\textit{sig } \Theta) \ h \wedge \vdash_\tau h : \textit{prop}) \wedge \Theta,\Gamma \vdash t)$

8   Proof Terms and Checker

Berghofer and Nipkow [4] added proof terms to Isabelle. We present an executable checker for these proof terms that is proved sound w.r.t. the above formalization of the metalogic. Berghofer and Nipkow also developed a proof checker but it was unverified and checked the generated proof terms by feeding them back through Isabelle's unverified inference kernel.

It is crucial to realize that all we need to know about the proof term checker is the soundness theorem below. The internals are, from a soundness perspective, irrelevant, which is why we can get away with sketching them informally. This is in contrast to the logic itself, which acts like a specification, which is why we presented it in detail.

This is our data type of proof terms:

datatype *proofterm* = *PAxm term* (((*var* × *sort*) × *typ*) *list*) | *PBound nat*
  | *Abst typ proofterm* | *AbsP term proofterm* | *Appt proofterm term*
  | *AppP proofterm proofterm* | *OfClass typ name* | *Hyp term*

These proof terms are not designed to record proofs in our inference system, but to mirror the proof terms generated by Isabelle. Nevertheless, the constructors of our proof terms correspond roughly to the rules of the inference system. *PAxm* contains an axiom and a type substitution. This substitution is encoded as an association list instead of a function. *AbsP* and *Abst* correspond to introduction of $\Longrightarrow$ and $\bigwedge$, *AppP* and *Appt* correspond to the respective eliminations. *Hyp* and *PBound* relate to the assumption rule, where *Hyp* refers to a free assumption while *PBound* contains a De Brujin index referring to an assumption added during the proof by an *AbsP* constructor. *OfClass* denotes a proof that a type belongs to a given type class.

Isabelle looks at terms modulo $\alpha\beta\eta$-equivalence and therefore does not save β or η steps, while they are explicit steps in our inference system. Therefore we have no constructors corresponding to the (β) and (η) rules. The remaining equality axioms are naturally handled by the *PAxm* constructor.

In the rest of the section we discuss how to derive an executable proof checker. Executability means that the checker is defined as a set of recursive functions that Isabelle's code generator can translate into one of a number of target languages, in particular its implementation language SML [5,9,8].

Because of the approximate correspondence between proof term constructors and inference rules, implementing the proof checker largely amounts to providing executable versions of each inference rule, as in LCF: each rule becomes a function that checks the side conditions, and if they are true, computes the conclusion from the premises given as arguments. The overall checker is a function

replay :: *theory* $\Rightarrow$ *proofterm* $\Rightarrow$ *term option*

In particular we need to make the inductive wellformedness checks for sorts, types and terms, signatures and theories executable. Mostly, this amounts to providing recursive versions of inductive definitions and proving them equivalent.

We now discuss some of the more difficult implementation steps. To model Isabelle's view of terms modulo $\alpha\beta\eta$-equivalence, we $\beta\eta$ normalize our terms (α-equivalence is for free thanks to De Brujin notation) during the reconstruction of the proof. A lengthy proof shows that this preserves provability (we do not go into the details):

wf-theory Θ $\wedge$ *finite* Γ $\wedge$ ($\forall A \in \Gamma.$ *wt-term* (*sig* Θ) $A \wedge \vdash_\tau A$: *prop*) $\wedge$ $\Theta,\Gamma \vdash t \wedge$
beta-eta-norm t = *Some* $u \longrightarrow \Theta,\Gamma \vdash u$

Isabelle's code generator needs some help handling the maps used in the (order-sorted) signatures. We provide a refinement of maps to association lists. Another problematic point is the definition of the type instance relation ($\lesssim$), which contains an (unbounded) existential quantifier. To make this executable, we provide an implementation which tries to compute a suitable type substitution. In another step, we refine the type substitution to an association list as well.

In the end we obtain a proof checker

check-proof Θ P p = (*wf-theory* Θ $\wedge$ *replay* Θ P = *Some* p)

that checks theory Θ and checks if proof P proves the given proposition p. The latter check is important because the Isabelle theorems that we check contain both a proof and a proposition that the theorem claims to prove. Function *check-proof* checks this claim. As one of our main results, we can prove the correctness of our checker:

Theorem 2. *check-proof* Θ P p $\longrightarrow$ $\Theta,$*set* $(hyps\ P)$ $\Vdash$ p

The proof itself is conceptually simple and proceeds by induction over the structure of proof terms. For each proof constructor we need to show that the corresponding inference rule leads to the same conclusion as its functional version used by *replay*. Most of the proof effort goes into a large library of results about terms, types, signatures, substitutions, wellformedness etc. required for the proof, most importantly the fact that $\beta\eta$ normalization preserve provability.

9   Size and Structure of the Formalization

All material presented so far has been formalized in Isabelle/HOL. The definition of the inference system (incl. types, terms etc.) resides in a separate theory *Core* that depends only on the basic library of Isabelle/HOL. It takes about 300 LOC and is fairly high level and readable – we presented most of it. This is at least an order or magnitude smaller than Isabelle's inference kernel (which is not clearly delineated) – of course the latter is optimized for performance. Its abstract type of theorems alone takes about 2,500 LOC, not counting any infrastructure of terms, types, unification etc.

The whole formalization consists of 10,000 LOC. The main components are:

- Almost half the formalization (4,700 LOC) is devoted to providing a library of operations on types and terms and their properties. This includes, among others, executable functions for type checking, different types of substitutions, abstractions, the wellformedness checks and β and η reductions.
- Proving derived rules of our inference system takes up 3,000 LOC. A large part of this is deriving rules for equality and the β and η reductions. Weakening rules are also derived.
- Making the wellformedness checks for (order-sorted) signatures and theories as well as the type instance checks executable takes 1,800 LOC.
- Definition and correctness proof for the checker builds on the above material and take only about 500 additional LOC.

10   Integration with Isabelle

As explained above, Isabelle generates SML code for the proof checker. This code has its own definitions of types, terms etc. and needs to be interfaced with the corresponding data structures in Isabelle. This step requires 150 lines of handwritten SML code (*glue code*) that translates Isabelle's data structures into the corresponding data structures in the generated proof checker such that we can feed them into *check-proof*. We cannot verify this code and therefore aim to keep it as small and simple as possible. This is the reason for the previously mentioned *intentional implementation bias* we introduced in our formalization. We describe now how the various data types are translated. We call a translation trivial if it merely replaces one constructor by another, possibly forgetting some information.

The translation of types and terms is trivial as their structure is almost identical in the two settings. For Isabelle code experts it should be mentioned that the two **term** constructors **Free** and **Var** in Isabelle (which both represent free variables but **Var** can be instantiated by unification) are combined in type *var* of the formalization which we left unspecified but which in fact looks like this: **datatype** *var* = *Free name* | *Var indexname*. This is purely to trivialize the glue code, in our formalization *var* is totally opaque.

Proof term translation is trivial except for two special cases. Previously proved lemmas become axioms in the translation (see also below) and so-called "oracles" (typically the result of unfinished proofs, i.e. "sorry" on the user level) are rejected (but none of the theories we checked contain oracles). Also remember that the translation of proofs is not safety critical because all that matters is that in the end we obtain a correct proof of the claimed proposition.

We also provide functions to translate relevant content from the background theory: axioms and (order-sorted) signatures. This mostly amounts to extracting association lists from efficient internal data structures. Translating the axioms also involves translating some alternative internal representation of type class constraints into their standard form presented in Sect. 7.3.

The checker is integrated into Isabelle by calling it every time a new named theorem has been proved. The set of theorems proved so far is added to the axiomatic basis for this check. Cyclic dependencies between lemmas are ruled out by this ordering because every theorem is checked before being added to the axiomatic basis. However, an explicit cyclicity check is not part of the formalization (yet), which speaks only about checking single proofs.

11   Running the Proof Checker

We run this modified Isabelle with our proof checker on multiple theories in various object logics contained in the Isabelle distribution. A rough overview of the scope of the covered material for some logics and the required running times can be found in the following table. The running times are the total times for running Isabelle, not just the proof checking, but the latter takes 90% of the time. All tests were performed on a Intel Core i7-9750H CPU running at 2.60GHz and 32GB of RAM.

Logic	LOC	Time
FOL	4,500	45 secs
ZF	55,000	25 mins
HOL	10,000	26 mins

We can check the material in several smaller object logics in their entirety. One of the larger such logics is first-order logic (FOL). These logics do not develop any applications but FOL comes with proof automation and theories testing that automation, in particular Pelletier's collection of problems that were considered challenges in their day [32]. Because the proofs are found automatically, the resulting proof terms will typically be quite complex and good test material for a proof checker.

The logic ZF (Zermelo-Fraenkel set theory) builds on FOL but contains real applications and is an order of magnitude larger than FOL. We are able to check all material formalized in ZF in the Isabelle distribution.

Isabelle's most frequently used and largest object logic is HOL. We managed to check about 12% of the `Main` library. This includes the basic logic and the libraries of sets, functions, orderings, lattices and groups. The formalizations are non-trivial and make heavy use of Isabelle's type classes.

Why can we check about five times as many lines of code in ZF compared to HOL? Profiling revealed that the proof checker spends a lot of time in functions that access the signature, especially the wellformedness checks. The primary reasons: inefficient data structures (e.g. association lists) and thus the running time depends heavily on size of signature and increases with every new constant, type and class. To make matters worse, there is no sharing of any kind in terms/types and their wellformedness checks. Because ZF is free of polymorphism and type classes, these wellformedness checks are much simpler.

12   Trust Assumptions

We need to trust the following components outside of the formalization:

- The verification (and code generation) of our proof checker in Isabelle/HOL. This is inevitable, one has to trust some theorem prover to start with. We could improve the trustworthiness of this step by porting our proofs to the verified HOL prover by Kumar *et el.* [13] but its code generator produces CakeML [14], not SML.
- The unverified glue code in the integration of our proof checker into Isabelle (Sect. 10).

Because users currently cannot examine Isabelle's internal data structures that we start from, they have to trust Isabelle's front end that parses and transforms some textual input file into internal data structures. One could add a (possibly verified) presentation layer that outputs those internal representations into a readable format that can be inspected, while avoiding the traps Adams [3] is concerned with.

13   Future Work

Our primary focus will be on scaling up the proof checker to not just deal with all of HOL but with real applications (including itself!). There is a host of avenues for exploration. Just to name a few promising directions: more efficient data structures than association lists (e.g. via existing frameworks [19,20]); caching of wellformedness checks for types and terms; exploiting sharing within terms and types (tricky because our intentionally simple glue code creates copies); working with the compressed proof terms [5] that Isabelle creates by default instead of uncompressing them as we do now.

We will also upgrade the formalization of our checker from individual theorems sets of theorems, explicitly checking cyclic dependencies (which are currently prevented by the glue code, see Sect. 10).

A presentation layer as discussed in Sect. 12 would not just allow the inspection of the internal representation of the theories but could also be extended to the proofs themselves, thus permitting checkers to be interfaced with Isabelle on a textual level instead of internal data structures.

It would also be nice to have a model-theoretic semantics for $\mathcal{M}$. We believe that the work by Kunčar and Popescu [15,16,17,18] could be adapted from HOL to $\mathcal{M}$. This would in particular yield semantically justified cyclicity checks for constant and type definitions which we currently treat as axioms because a purely syntactic justification is unclear.

Acknowledgements

We thank Kevin Kappelmann, Magnus Myreen, Larry Paulson, Andrei Popescu, Makarius Wenzel and the anonymous reviewers for their comments.

A   Appendix

subst-bv u t = subst-bv2 t 0 u

subst-bv2 (Bv i) n u = (if i < n then Bv i else if i = n then u else Bv (i − 1))
subst-bv2 (Abs T t) n u = Abs T (subst-bv2 t (n + 1) (lift u 0))
subst-bv2 (f · t) n u = subst-bv2 f n u · subst-bv2 t n u
subst-bv2 t _ _ = t

lift (Bv i) n = (if n ≤ i then Bv (i + 1) else Bv i)
lift (Abs T t) n = Abs T (lift t (n + 1))
lift (f · t) n = lift f n · lift t n
lift t _ = t

bind-fv T t = bind-fv2 T 0 t

bind-fv2 var n (Fv v T) = (if var = (v, T) then Bv n else Fv v T)
bind-fv2 var n (Abs T t) = Abs T (bind-fv2 var (n + 1) t)
bind-fv2 var n (f · u) = bind-fv2 var n f · bind-fv2 var n u
bind-fv2 _ _ t = t

References

1. Åman Pohjola, J., Gengelbach, A.: A mechanised semantics for HOL with ad-hoc overloading. In: Albert, E., Kovács, L. (eds.) LPAR 2020: 23rd International Conference on Logic for Programming, Artificial Intelligence and Reasoning. EPiC Series in Computing, vol. 73, pp. 498–515. EasyChair (2020), https://doi.org/10.29007/413d

2. Abrahamsson, O.: A verified proof checker for higher-order logic. J. Log. Algebraic Methods Program. **112**, 100530 (2020), https://doi.org/10.1016/j.jlamp.2020.100530

3. Adams, M.: HOL Zero's solutions for Pollack-inconsistency. Lect. Notes in Comp. Sci., vol. 9807, pp. 20–35. Springer (2016), https://doi.org/10.1007/978-3-319-43144-4_2

4. Berghofer, S., Nipkow, T.: Proof terms for simply typed higher order logic. In: Harrison, J., Aagaard, M. (eds.) Theorem Proving in Higher Order Logics. Lect. Notes in Comp. Sci., vol. 1869, pp. 38–52. Springer (2000)

5. Berghofer, S., Nipkow, T.: Executing higher order logic. In: Callaghan, P., Luo, Z., McKinna, J., Pollack, R. (eds.) Types for Proofs and Programs (TYPES 2000). Lect. Notes in Comp. Sci., vol. 2277, pp. 24–40. Springer (2002)

6. Carneiro, M.M.: Metamath Zero: Designing a theorem prover prover. In: Benzmüller, C., Miller, B.R. (eds.) Intelligent Computer Mathematics, CICM 2020. Lect. Notes in Comp. Sci., vol. 12236, pp. 71–88. Springer (2020), https://doi.org/10.1007/978-3-030-53518-6_5

7. Gheri, L., Popescu, A.: A formalized general theory of syntax with bindings: Extended version. J. Automated Reasoning **64**(4), 641–675 (2020), https://doi.org/10.1007/s10817-019-09522-2

8. Haftmann, F., Krauss, A., Kunčar, O., Nipkow, T.: Data refinement in Isabelle/HOL. In: Blazy, S., Paulin-Mohring, C., Pichardie, D. (eds.) Interactive Theorem Proving (ITP 2013). Lect. Notes in Comp. Sci., vol. 7998, pp. 100–115. Springer (2013)

9. Haftmann, F., Nipkow, T.: Code generation via higher-order rewrite systems. In: Blume, M., Kobayashi, N., Vidal, G. (eds.) Functional and Logic Programming (FLOPS 2010). Lect. Notes in Comp. Sci., vol. 6009, pp. 103–117. Springer (2010)

10. Haftmann, F., Wenzel, M.: Constructive type classes in isabelle. In: Altenkirch, T., McBride, C. (eds.) Types for Proofs and Programs, TYPES 2006. Lect. Notes in Comp. Sci., vol. 4502, pp. 160–174. Springer (2006), https://doi.org/10.1007/978-3-540-74464-1_11

11. Harrison, J.: Towards self-verification of HOL Light. In: Furbach, U., Shankar, N. (eds.) Proceedings of the third International Joint Conference, IJCAR 2006. Lect. Notes in Comp. Sci., vol. 4130, pp. 177–191. Springer, Seattle, WA (2006)

12. Hurd, J.: OpenTheory: Package management for higher order logic theories. In: Reis, G., Théry, L. (eds.) Workshop on Programming Languages for Mechanized Mathematics Systems (ACM SIGSAM PLMMS 2009). pp. 31–37 (2009)

13. Kumar, R., Arthan, R., Myreen, M.O., Owens, S.: Self-formalisation of higher-order logic — semantics, soundness, and a verified implementation. J. Automated Reasoning **56**(3), 221–259 (2016), https://doi.org/10.1007/s10817-015-9357-x

14. Kumar, R., Myreen, M.O., Norrish, M., Owens, S.: CakeML: A verified implementation of ML. In: Principles of Programming Languages (POPL). pp. 179–191. ACM Press (Jan 2014), https://doi.org/10.1145/2535838.2535841

15. Kunčar, O., Popescu, A.: A consistent foundation for Isabelle/HOL. In: Urban, C., Zhang, X. (eds.) Interactive Theorem Proving, ITP 2015. Lect. Notes in Comp. Sci., vol. 9236, pp. 234–252. Springer (2015), https://doi.org/10.1007/978-3-319-22102-1_16

16. Kunčar, O., Popescu, A.: Comprehending Isabelle/HOL's consistency. In: Yang, H. (ed.) Programming Languages and Systems, ESOP 2017. Lect. Notes in Comp. Sci., vol. 10201, pp. 724–749. Springer (2017), https://doi.org/10.1007/978-3-662-54434-1_27

17. Kunčar, O., Popescu, A.: Safety and conservativity of definitions in HOL and Isabelle/HOL. Proc. ACM Program. Lang. **2**(POPL), 24:1–24:26 (2018), `https://doi.org/10.1145/3158112`

18. Kunčar, O., Popescu, A.: A consistent foundation for Isabelle/HOL. J. Automated Reasoning **62**(4), 531–555 (2019), `https://doi.org/10.1007/s10817-018-9454-8`

19. Lammich, P., Lochbihler, A.: The Isabelle collections framework. In: Kaufmann, M., Paulson, L.C. (eds.) Interactive Theorem Proving, ITP 2010. Lect. Notes in Comp. Sci., vol. 6172, pp. 339–354. Springer (2010), `https://doi.org/10.1007/978-3-642-14052-5_24`

20. Lochbihler, A.: Light-weight containers for isabelle: Efficient, extensible, nestable. In: Blazy, S., Paulin-Mohring, C., Pichardie, D. (eds.) Interactive Theorem Proving, ITP 2013. Lect. Notes in Comp. Sci., vol. 7998, pp. 116–132. Springer (2013), `https://doi.org/10.1007/978-3-642-39634-2_11`

21. Journal of Automated Reasonig: Special Issue: Theory and Applications of Abstraction, Substitution and Naming, vol. 49. Springer (Aug 2012), `https://link.springer.com/journal/10817/volumes-and-issues/49-2`

22. Nipkow, T.: Order-sorted polymorphism in Isabelle. In: Huet, G., Plotkin, G. (eds.) Logical Environments. pp. 164–188. Cambridge University Press (1993)

23. Nipkow, T.: More Church-Rosser proofs (in Isabelle/HOL). J. Automated Reasoning **26**, 51–66 (2001)

24. Nipkow, T., Klein, G.: Concrete Semantics with Isabelle/HOL. Springer (2014), `http://concrete-semantics.org`

25. Nipkow, T., Paulson, L., Wenzel, M.: Isabelle/HOL — A Proof Assistant for Higher-Order Logic, Lect. Notes in Comp. Sci., vol. 2283. Springer (2002)

26. Nipkow, T., Paulson, L.C.: Isabelle-91. In: Kapur, D. (ed.) Automated Deduction - CADE-11. Lect. Notes in Comp. Sci., vol. 607, pp. 673–676. Springer (1992), `https://doi.org/10.1007/3-540-55602-8_201`

27. Nipkow, T., Prehofer, C.: Type reconstruction for type classes. J. Functional Programming **5**(2), 201–224 (1995)

28. Nipkow, T., Roßkopf, S.: Isabelle's metalogic: Formalization and proof checker. Archive of Formal Proofs (Apr 2021), `https://isa-afp.org/entries/Metalogic_ProofChecker.html`, Formal proof development

29. Nipkow, T., Snelting, G.: Type classes and overloading resolution via order-sorted unification. In: Hughes, J. (ed.) Proc. 5th ACM Conf. Functional Programming Languages and Computer Architecture. Lect. Notes in Comp. Sci., vol. 523, pp. 1–14. Springer (1991)

30. Paulson, L.C.: The foundation of a generic theorem prover. J. Automated Reasoning **5**, 363–397 (1989)

31. Paulson, L.C.: Isabelle: A Generic Theorem Prover, Lect. Notes in Comp. Sci., vol. 828. Springer (1994)

32. Pelletier, F.: Seventy-five problems for testing automatic theorem provers. J. Automated Reasoning **2**, 191–216 (06 1986), `https://doi.org/10.1007/BF02432151`

33. Pfenning, F.: Elf: A language for logic definition and verified metaprogramming. In: Logic in Computer Science (LICS 1989). pp. 313–322. IEEE Computer Society Press (1989)

34. Pfenning, F., Schürmann, C.: System description: Twelf - A meta-logical framework for deductive systems. In: Ganzinger, H. (ed.) Automated Deduction, CADE-16. Lect. Notes in Comp. Sci., vol. 1632, pp. 202–206. Springer (1999), `https://doi.org/10.1007/3-540-48660-7_14`

35. Pientka, B.: Beluga: Programming with dependent types, contextual data, and contexts. In: Blume, M., Kobayashi, N., Vidal, G. (eds.) Functional and Logic Programming, FLOPS 2010. Lect. Notes in Comp. Sci., vol. 6009, pp. 1–12. Springer (2010), https://doi.org/10.1007/978-3-642-12251-4_1

36. Sozeau, M., Boulier, S., Forster, Y., Tabareau, N., Winterhalter, T.: Coq Coq correct! Verification of type checking and erasure for Coq, in Coq. Proc. ACM Program. Lang. 4(POPL), 8:1–8:28 (2020), https://doi.org/10.1145/3371076

37. Urban, C.: Nominal techniques in Isabelle/HOL. J. Automated Reasoning 40, 327–356 (2008), https://doi.org/10.1007/s10817-008-9097-2

38. Wenzel, M.: Type classes and overloading in higher-order logic. In: Gunter, E.L., Felty, A.P. (eds.) Theorem Proving in Higher Order Logics, TPHOLs'97. Lect. Notes in Comp. Sci., vol. 1275, pp. 307–322. Springer (1997), https://doi.org/10.1007/BFb0028402

Open Access This chapter is licensed under the terms of the Creative Commons Attribution 4.0 International License (http://creativecommons.org/licenses/by/4.0/), which permits use, sharing, adaptation, distribution and reproduction in any medium or format, as long as you give appropriate credit to the original author(s) and the source, provide a link to the Creative Commons license and indicate if changes were made.

The images or other third party material in this chapter are included in the chapter's Creative Commons license, unless indicated otherwise in a credit line to the material. If material is not included in the chapter's Creative Commons license and your intended use is not permitted by statutory regulation or exceeds the permitted use, you will need to obtain permission directly from the copyright holder.

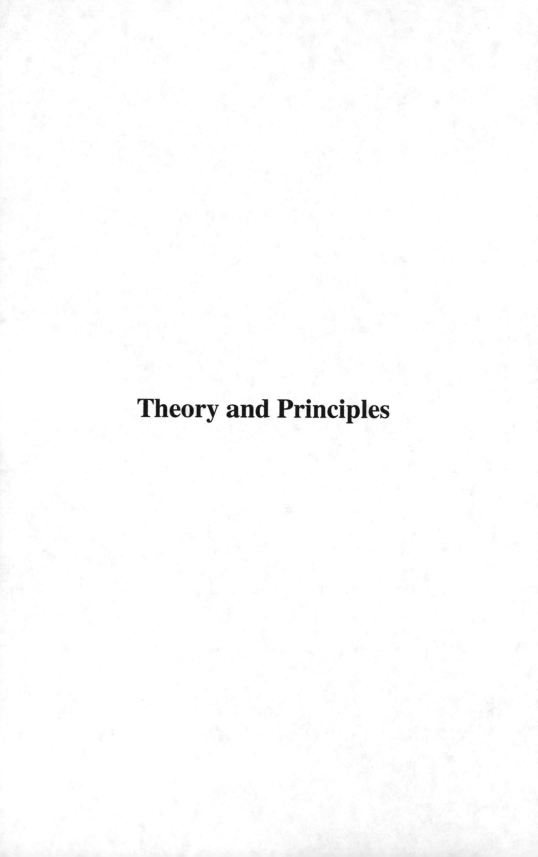

Theory and Principles

The ksmt Calculus Is a δ-complete Decision Procedure for Non-linear Constraints[*]

Franz Brauße[2], Konstantin Korovin[2], Margarita V. Korovina[3],
and Norbert Th. Müller[1]

[1] Abteilung Informatikwissenschaften, Universität Trier, Trier, Germany
[2] The University of Manchester, Manchester, UK
[3] A.P. Ershov Institute of Informatics Systems, Novosibirsk, Russia
brausse@informatik.uni-trier.de, konstantin.korovin@manchester.ac.uk

Abstract. ksmt is a CDCL-style calculus for solving non-linear constraints over the real numbers involving polynomials and transcendental functions. In this paper we investigate properties of the ksmt calculus and show that it is a δ-complete decision procedure for bounded problems. We also propose an extension with local linearisations, which allow for more efficient treatment of non-linear constraints.

1 Introduction

Solving non-linear constraints is important in many applications, including verification of cyber-physical systems, software verification, proof assistants for mathematics [25,21,2,1,15,6]. Hence there has been a number of approaches for solving non-linear constraints, involving symbolic methods [16,23,29,18] as well as numerically inspired ones, in particular for dealing with transcendental functions [13,30], and combinations of symbolic and numeric methods [7,11,12].

In [7] we introduced the ksmt calculus for solving non-linear constraints over a large class of functions including polynomial, exponential and trigonometric functions. The ksmt calculus[4] combines CDCL-style reasoning [28,22,3] over the reals based on conflict resolution [19] with incremental linearisations of non-linear functions using methods from computable analysis [31,24]. Our approach is based on computable analysis and exact real arithmetic which avoids limitations of double precision computations caused by rounding errors and instabilities in numerical methods. In particular, satisfiable and unsatisfiable results returned by ksmt are exact as required in many applications. This approach also supports implicit representations of functions as solutions of ODEs and PDEs [26].

It is well known that in the presence of transcendental functions the constraint satisfiability problem is undecidable [27]. However if we only require solutions up to some specified precision δ, then the problem can be solved algorithmically on bounded instances and that is the motivation behind δ-completeness,

---

[*] This research was partially supported by an Intel research grant, the DFG grant WERA MU 1801/5-1 and the RFBR-JSPS 20-51-5000 grant.
[4] Implementation is available at http://informatik.uni-trier.de/~brausse/ksmt/

© The Author(s) 2021
A. Platzer and G. Sutcliffe (Eds.): CADE 2021, LNAI 12699, pp. 113–130, 2021.
https://doi.org/10.1007/978-3-030-79876-5_7

which was introduced in [13]. In essence a δ-complete procedure decides if a formula is unsatisfiable or a δ weakening of the formula is satisfiable.

In this paper we investigate theoretical properties of the ksmt calculus, and its extension δ-ksmt for the δ-SMT setting. Our main results are as follows:

1. We introduced a notion of ϵ-*full linearisations* and prove that all ϵ-full runs of ksmt are terminating on bounded instances.
2. We extended the ksmt calculus to the δ-satisfiability setting and proved that δ-ksmt is a δ-*complete decision procedure* for bounded instances.
3. We introduced an algorithm for computing ϵ-full *local linearisations* and integrated it into δ-ksmt. Local linearisations can be used to considerably narrow the search space by taking into account local behaviour of non-linear functions avoiding computationally expensive global analysis.

In Section 3, we give an overview about the ksmt calculus and introduce the notion of ϵ-full linearisation used throughout the rest of the paper. We also present a completeness theorem. Section 4 introduces the notion of δ-completeness and related concepts. In Section 5 we introduce the δ-ksmt adaptation, prove it is correct and δ-complete, and give concrete effective linearisations based on a uniform modulus of continuity. Finally in Section 6, we introduce local linearisations and show that termination is independent of computing uniform moduli of continuity, before we conclude in Section 7.

2 Preliminaries

The following conventions are used throughout this paper. By $\| \cdot \|$ we denote the maximum-norm $\|(x_1, x_2, \ldots, x_n)\| = \max\{|x_i| : 1 \le i \le n\}$. When it helps clarity, we write finite and infinite sequences $\boldsymbol{x} = (x_1, \ldots, x_n)$ and $\boldsymbol{y} = (y_i)_i$ in bold typeface. We are going to use open balls $B(\boldsymbol{c}, \epsilon) = \{\boldsymbol{x} : \|\boldsymbol{x} - \boldsymbol{c}\| < \epsilon\} \subseteq \mathbb{R}^n$ for $\boldsymbol{c} \in \mathbb{R}^n$ and $\epsilon > 0$ and $\bar{A}$ to denote the closure of the set $A \subseteq \mathbb{R}^n$ in the standard topology induced by the norm. By $\mathbb{Q}_{>0}$ we denote the set $\{q \in \mathbb{Q} : q > 0\}$. For sets X, Y, a (possibly partial) function from X to Y is written as $X \to Y$. We use the notion of compactness: a set A is compact iff every open cover of A has a finite subcover. In Euclidean spaces this is equivalent to A being bounded and closed [32].

Basic Notions of Computable Analysis

Let us recall the notion of computability of functions over real numbers used throughout this paper. A rational number q is an n-*approximation* of a real number x if $\|q - x\| \le 2^{-n}$. Informally, a function f is *computed* by a function-oracle Turing machine $M_f^?$, where $?$ is a placeholder for the oracle representing the argument of the function, in the following way. The real argument x is represented by an oracle function $\varphi : \mathbb{N} \to \mathbb{Q}$, for each n returning an n-approximation φ_n of x. For simplicity, we refer to φ by the sequence $(\varphi_n)_n$. When run with argument $p \in \mathbb{N}$, $M_f^\varphi(p)$ computes a rational p-approximation of $f(x)$ by querying its oracle φ for approximations of x. Let us note that the definition of the oracle machine does not depend on the concrete oracle, i.e., the oracle can be seen as a parameter. In case only the machine without a concrete oracle is of interest, we write $M_f^?$. We refer to [17] for a precise definition of the model of computation by function-oracle Turing machines which is standard in computable analysis.

Definition 1 ([17]). *Consider $x \in \mathbb{R}^n$. A name for x is a rational sequence $\varphi = (\varphi_k)_k$ such that $\forall k : \|\varphi_k - x\| \leq 2^{-k}$. A function $f : \mathbb{R}^n \to \mathbb{R}$ is computable iff there is a function-oracle Turing machine $M_f^?$ such that for all $x \in \operatorname{dom} f$ and names φ for x, $|M_f^\varphi(p) - f(x)| \leq 2^{-p}$ holds for all $p \in \mathbb{N}$.*

This definition is closely related to interval arithmetic with unrestricted precision, but enhanced with the guarantee of convergence and it is equivalent to the notion of computability used in [31]. The class of computable functions contains polynomials and transcendental functions like sin, cos, exp, among others. It is well known [17,31] that this class is closed under composition and that computable functions are continuous. By continuity, a computable function $f : \mathbb{R}^n \to \mathbb{R}$ total on a compact $D \subset \mathbb{R}^n$ has a computable *uniform modulus of continuity* $\mu_f : \mathbb{N} \to \mathbb{N}$ on D [31, Theorem 6.2.7], that is,

$$\forall k \in \mathbb{N} \, \forall y, z \in D : \|y - z\| \leq 2^{-\mu(k)} \implies |f(y) - f(z)| \leq 2^{-k}. \tag{2.1}$$

A uniform modulus of continuity of f expresses how changes in the value of f depend on changes of the arguments in a uniform way.

3 The ksmt Calculus

We first describe the ksmt calculus for solving non-linear constraints [7] informally, and subsequently recall the main definitions which we use in this paper. The ksmt calculus consists of transition rules, which, for any formula in linear separated form, allow deriving lemmas consistent with the formula and, in case of termination, produce a satisfying assignment for the formula or show that it is unsatisfiable. A quantifier-free formula is in separated linear form $\mathcal{L} \cup \mathcal{N}$ if $\mathcal{L}$ is a set of clauses over linear constraints and $\mathcal{N}$ is a set of non-linear atomic constraints; this notion is rigorously defined below.

In the ksmt calculus there are four transition rules applied to its states: Assignment refinement (A), Conflict resolution (R), Backjumping (B) and Linearisation (L). The final ksmt states are sat and unsat. A non-final ksmt state is a triple $(\alpha, \mathcal{L}, \mathcal{N})$ where α is a (partial) assignment of variables to rationals. A ksmt derivation starts with an initial state where α is empty and tries to extend this assignment to a solution of $\mathcal{L} \cup \mathcal{N}$ by repeatedly applying the Assignment refinement rule. When such assignment extension is not possible we either obtain a linear conflict which is resolved using the conflict resolution rule, or a non-linear conflict which is resolved using the linearisation rule.

The main idea behind the linearisation rule is to approximate the non-linear constraints around the conflict using linear constraints in such a way that the

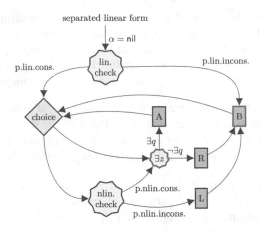

Fig. 1. Core of `ksmt` calculus. Derivations terminate in red nodes.

conflict will be shifted into the linear part where it will be resolved using conflict resolution. Application of either of these two rules results in a state containing a clause evaluating to false under the current assignment. This is followed by either application of the backjumping rule, which undoes assignments or by termination in case the formula is unsat. In this procedure, only the assignment and linear part of the state change and the non-linear part stays fixed.

Notations. Let $\mathcal{F}_{\text{lin}}$ consist of rational constants, addition and multiplication by rational constants; $\mathcal{F}_{\text{nl}}$ denotes an arbitrary collection of non-linear computable functions including transcendental functions and polynomials over the reals. We consider the structure $(\mathbb{R}, \langle \mathcal{F}_{\text{lin}} \cup \mathcal{F}_{\text{nl}}, \mathcal{P} \rangle)$ where $\mathcal{P} = \{<, \leq, >, \geq, =, \neq\}$ and a set of variables $V = \{x_1, x_2, \ldots, x_n, \ldots\}$. We will use, possibly with indices, x to denote variables and q, c, e for rational constants. Define terms, predicates and formulas over V in the standard way. An *atomic linear constraint* is a formula of the form: $q + c_1 x_1 + \ldots + c_n x_n \diamond 0$ where $q, c_1, \ldots, c_n \in \mathbb{Q}$ and $\diamond \in \mathcal{P}$. Negations of atomic formulas can be eliminated by rewriting the predicate symbol $\diamond$ in the standard way, hence we assume that all literals are positive. A *linear constraint* is a disjunction of atomic linear constraints, also called *(linear) clause*. An *atomic non-linear* constraint is a formula of the form $f(\boldsymbol{x}) \diamond 0$, where $\diamond \in \mathcal{P}$ and f is a composition of computable non-linear functions from $\mathcal{F}_{\text{nl}}$ over variables $\boldsymbol{x}$. Throughout this paper for every computable real function f we use $M_f^?$ to denote a function-oracle Turing machine computing f. We assume quantifier-free formulas in *separated linear form* [7, Definition 1], that is, $\mathcal{L} \cup \mathcal{N}$ where $\mathcal{L}$ is a set of linear constraints and $\mathcal{N}$ is a set of non-linear atomic constraints. Arbitrary quantifier-free formulas can be transformed equi-satisfiably into separated linear form in polynomial time [7, Lemma 1]. Since in separated linear form all non-linear constraints are atomic we will call them just *non-linear constraints*.

Let $\alpha : V \to \mathbb{Q}$ be a partial variable assignment. The interpretation $[\![\boldsymbol{x}]\!]^{\alpha}$ of a vector of variables $\boldsymbol{x}$ under α is defined in a standard way as component-wise application of α. Define the notation $[\![t]\!]^\alpha$ as evaluation of term t under assignment α, that can be partial, in which case $[\![t]\!]^\alpha$ is treated symbolically. We extend $[\![\cdot]\!]^\alpha$ to predicates, clauses and CNF in the usual way and true, false denote the constants of the Boolean domain. The evaluation $[\![t \diamond 0]\!]^\alpha$ for a predicate $\diamond$ and a term t results in true or false only if all variables in t are assigned by α.

In order to formally restate the calculus, the notions of linear resolvent and linearisation are essential. A resolvent $R_{\alpha,\mathcal{L},z}$ on a variable z is a set of linear constraints that do not contain z, are implied by the formula $\mathcal{L}$ and which evaluate to false under the current partial assignment α; for more details see [19,7].

Definition 2. *Let P be a non-linear constraint and let α be an assignment with $[\![P]\!]^\alpha = \mathsf{false}$. A linearisation of P at α is a linear clause C with the properties:*

1. $\forall \beta : [\![P]\!]^\beta = \mathsf{true} \implies [\![C]\!]^\beta = \mathsf{true}$, *and*
2. $[\![C]\!]^\alpha = \mathsf{false}$.

Wlog. we can assume that the variables of C are a subset of the variables of P. Let us note that any linear clause C represents the complement of a rational polytope R and we will use both interchangeably. Thus for a rational polytope R, $\boldsymbol{x} \notin R$ also stands for a linear clause. In particular, any linearisation excludes a rational polytope containing the conflicting assignment from the search space.

Transition rules. For a formula $\mathcal{L}_0 \cup \mathcal{N}$ in separated linear form, the initial ksmt state is $(\mathsf{nil}, \mathcal{L}_0, \mathcal{N})$. The calculus consists of the following transition rules from a state $S = (\alpha, \mathcal{L}, \mathcal{N})$ to S':

(A) *Assignment.* $S' = (\alpha :: z \mapsto q, \mathcal{L}, \mathcal{N})$ iff $[\![\mathcal{L}]\!]^\alpha \neq \mathsf{false}$ and there is a variable z unassigned in α and $q \in \mathbb{Q}$ with $[\![\mathcal{L}]\!]^{\alpha::z \mapsto q} \neq \mathsf{false}$.
(R) *Resolution.* $S' = (\alpha, \mathcal{L} \cup R_{\alpha,\mathcal{L},z}, \mathcal{N})$ iff $[\![\mathcal{L}]\!]^\alpha \neq \mathsf{false}$ and there is a variable z unassigned in α with $\forall q \in \mathbb{Q} : [\![\mathcal{L}]\!]^{\alpha::z \mapsto q} = \mathsf{false}$ and $R_{\alpha,\mathcal{L},z}$ is a resolvent.
(B) *Backjump.* $S' = (\gamma, \mathcal{L}, \mathcal{N})$ iff $[\![\mathcal{L}]\!]^\alpha = \mathsf{false}$ and there is a maximal prefix γ of α such that $[\![\mathcal{L}]\!]^\gamma \neq \mathsf{false}$.
(L) *Linearisation.* $S' = (\alpha, \mathcal{L} \cup \{L_{\alpha,P}\}, \mathcal{N})$ iff $[\![\mathcal{L}]\!]^\alpha \neq \mathsf{false}$, there is P in $\mathcal{N}$ with $[\![P]\!]^\alpha = \mathsf{false}$ and there is a linearisation $L_{\alpha,P}$ of P at α.
(F^{sat}) *Final sat.* $S' = \mathsf{sat}$ if all variables are assigned in α, $[\![\mathcal{L}]\!]^\alpha = \mathsf{true}$ and none of the rules $(A), (R), (B), (L)$ is applicable.
(F^{unsat}) *Final unsat.* $S' = \mathsf{unsat}$ if $[\![\mathcal{L}]\!]^{\mathsf{nil}} = \mathsf{false}$. In other words a trivial contradiction, e.g., $0 > 1$ is in $\mathcal{L}$.

A path (or a run) is a derivation in a ksmt. A procedure is an effective (possibly non-deterministic) way to construct a path.

Termination. If no transition rule is applicable, the derivation terminates. For clarity, we added the explicit rules (F^{sat}) and (F^{unsat}) which lead to the final states. This calculus is sound [7, Lemma 2]: if the final transition is (F^{sat}), then α is a solution to the original formula, or (F^{unsat}), then a trivial contradiction $0 > 1$ was derived and the original formula is unsatisfiable. The calculus also makes progress by reducing the search space [7, Lemma 3].

$$\mathcal{C} = \underbrace{(y \leq 1/x)}_{P} \wedge (x/4 + 1 \leq y)$$
$$\wedge (y \leq 4 \cdot (x - 1))$$
$$\wedge \left((x \leq \tfrac{12}{19}) \vee (y \leq \tfrac{19}{12})\right)$$
$$\wedge \left((x \leq \tfrac{220}{223}) \vee (y \leq \tfrac{223}{220})\right)$$
$$\wedge (\tfrac{4}{3} \leq x) \wedge (x \leq \tfrac{220}{223})$$
$$\wedge (\tfrac{4}{3} \leq \tfrac{220}{223})$$

Linearisation of P on conflicts (x, y) at α here:

- choose $d := (1/[\![x]\!]^\alpha + [\![y]\!]^\alpha)/2,$
- $C = (x \leq 1/d \ \vee \ y \leq d)$

rule	α	note
(A)	$x \mapsto 2$	
(A)	$x \mapsto 2,\ y \mapsto \frac{8}{3}$	(3a)
(L)	$x \mapsto 2,\ y \mapsto \frac{8}{3}$	(3b)
(B)	$x \mapsto 2$	
(A)	$x \mapsto 2,\ y \mapsto \frac{84}{55}$	(4a)
(L)	$x \mapsto 2,\ y \mapsto \frac{84}{55}$	(4b)
(B)	$x \mapsto 2$	
(R)	$x \mapsto 2$	on y
(B)		
(R)		on x
(F^{unsat})		unsat

Fig. 2. unsat example run of ksmt using interval linearisation [7].

An example run of the ksmt calculus is presented in Figure 2. We start in a state with a non-linear part $\mathcal{N} = \{y \leq 1/x\}$, which defines the pink area and the linear part $\mathcal{L} = \{(x/4 + 1 \leq y), (y \leq 4 \cdot (x - 1))\}$, shaded in green. Then we successively apply ksmt rules excluding regions around candidate solutions by linearisations, until we derive linearisations which separates the pink area from the green area thus deriving a contradiction.

Remark 1. In general a derivation may not terminate. The only cause of non-termination is the linearisation rule which adds new linear constraints and can be applied infinitely many times. To see this, observe that ksmt with only the rules $(A), (R), (B)$ corresponds to the conflict resolution calculus which is known to be terminating [19,20]. Thus, in infinite ksmt runs the linearisation rule (L) is applied infinitely often. This argument is used in the proof of Theorem 1 below. Let us note that during a run the ksmt calculus neither conflicts nor lemmas can be generated more than once. In fact, any generated linearisation is not implied by the linear part, prior to adding this linearisation.

3.1 Sufficient Termination Conditions

In this section we will assume that $(\alpha, \mathcal{L}, \mathcal{N})$ is a ksmt state obtained by applying ksmt inference rules to an initial state. As in [13] we only consider bounded instances. In many applications this is a natural assumption as variables usually range within some (possibly large) bounds. We can assume that these bounds are made explicit as linear constraints in the system.

Definition 3. *Let F be the formula $\mathcal{L}_0 \wedge \mathcal{N}$ in separated linear form over variables $x_1, \ldots, x_n$ and let B_i be the set defined by the conjunction of all clauses* in $\mathcal{L}_0$ univariate in x_i, for $i = 1, \ldots, n$; in particular, if there are no univariate linear constraints over x_i then $B_i = \mathbb{R}$. We call F a bounded instance if:

- $D_F := \bigtimes_{i=1}^{n} B_i$ is bounded, and
- for each non-linear constraint $P : f(x_{i_1}, \ldots, x_{i_k}) \diamond 0$ in $\mathcal{N}$ with $i_j \in \{1, \ldots, n\}$ for $j \in \{1, \ldots, k\}$ it holds that $\overline{D_P} \subseteq \operatorname{dom} f$ where $D_P := \bigtimes_{j=1}^{k} B_{i_j}$.

By this definition, already the linear part of bounded instances explicitly defines a bounded set by univariate constraints. Consequently, the set of solutions of F is bounded as well.

In Theorem 1 we show that when we consider bounded instances and restrict linearisations to so-called ϵ-full linearisations, then the procedure terminates. We use this to show that the ksmt-based decision procedure we introduce in Section 5 is δ-complete.

Definition 4. Let $\epsilon > 0$, P be a non-linear constraint over variables $\boldsymbol{x}$ and let α be an assignment of $\boldsymbol{x}$. A linearisation C of P at α is called ϵ-full iff for all assignments β of $\boldsymbol{x}$ with $[\![\boldsymbol{x}]\!]^\beta \in B([\![\boldsymbol{x}]\!]^\alpha, \epsilon)$, $[\![C]\!]^\beta = \mathsf{false}$.

A ksmt run is called ϵ-full for some $\epsilon > 0$, if all but finitely many linearisations in this run are ϵ-full.

The next theorem provides a basis for termination of ksmt-based decision procedures for satisfiability.

Theorem 1. Let $\epsilon > 0$. On bounded instances, ϵ-full ksmt runs are terminating.

Proof. Let $F : \mathcal{L}_0 \wedge \mathcal{N}$ be a bounded instance and $\epsilon > 0$. Towards a contradiction assume there is an infinite ϵ-full derivation $(\alpha_0, \mathcal{L}_0, \mathcal{N}), \ldots, (\alpha_n, \mathcal{L}_n, \mathcal{N}), \ldots$ in the ksmt calculus. Then, by definition of the transition rules, $\mathcal{L}_k \subseteq \mathcal{L}_l$ for all k, l with $0 \leq k \leq l$. According to Remark 1 in any infinite derivation the linearisation rule must be applied infinitely many times. During any run of ksmt the set of non-linear constraints $\mathcal{N}$ is fixed and therefore there is a non-linear constraint P in $\mathcal{N}$ over variables $\boldsymbol{x}$ to which linearisation is applied infinitely often. Let $(\alpha_{i_1}, \mathcal{L}_{i_1}, \mathcal{N}), \ldots, (\alpha_{i_n}, \mathcal{L}_{i_n}, \mathcal{N}), \ldots$ be a corresponding subsequence in the derivation such that $C_{i_1} \in \mathcal{L}_{i_1+1}, \ldots, C_{i_n} \in \mathcal{L}_{i_n+1}, \ldots$ are ϵ-full linearisations of P. Consider two different linearisation steps $k, \ell \in \{i_j : j \in \mathbb{N}\}$ in the derivation where $k < \ell$. By the precondition of rule (L) applied in step ℓ we have $[\![\mathcal{L}_\ell]\!]^{\alpha_\ell} \neq \mathsf{false}$. In particular the linearisation $C_k \in \mathcal{L}_{k+1} \subseteq \mathcal{L}_\ell$ of P constructed in step k does not evaluate to false under α_ℓ. Since the set of variables in C_k is a subset of those in P, $[\![C_k]\!]^{\alpha_\ell} \neq \mathsf{false}$ implies $[\![C_k]\!]^{\alpha_\ell} = \mathsf{true}$. By assumption, the linearisation C_k is ϵ-full, thus from Definition 4 it follows that $[\![\boldsymbol{x}]\!]^{\alpha_\ell} \notin B([\![\boldsymbol{x}]\!]^{\alpha_k}, \epsilon)$. Therefore the distance between $[\![\boldsymbol{x}]\!]^{\alpha_k}$ and $[\![\boldsymbol{x}]\!]^{\alpha_\ell}$ is at least ϵ. However, every conflict satisfies the variable bounds defining D_F, so there could be only finitely many conflicts with pairwise distance at least ϵ. This contradicts the above.

Concrete algorithms to compute ϵ-full linearisations are presented in Sections 5 and 6.

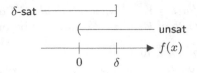

Fig. 3. The overlapping cases in the δ-SMT problem $f(x) \leq 0$.

4 δ-decidability

In the last section, we proved termination of the ksmt calculus on bounded instances when linearisations are ϵ-full. Let us now investigate how ϵ-full linearisations of constraints involving non-linear computable functions can be constructed. To that end, we assume that all non-linear functions are defined on the closure of the bounded space D_F defined by the bounded instance F.

So far we described an approach which gives exact results but at the same time is necessarily incomplete due to undecidability of non-linear constraints in general. On the other hand, non-linear constraints usually can be approximated using numerical methods allowing to obtain approximate solutions to the problem. This gives rise to the bounded δ-SMT problem [13] which allows an overlap between the properties δ-sat and unsat of formulas as illustrated by Figure 3. It is precisely this overlap that enables δ-decidability of bounded instances.

Let us recall the notion of δ-decidability, adapted from [13].

Definition 5. *Let F be a formula in separated linear form and let $\delta \in \mathbb{Q}_{>0}$. We inductively define the δ-weakening F_δ of F.*

- *If F is linear, let $F_\delta := F$.*
- *If F is a non-linear constraint $f(x) \diamond 0$, let*

$$
F_\delta := \begin{cases}
f(\boldsymbol{x}) - \delta \diamond 0, & \text{if } \diamond \in \{<, \leq\} \\
f(\boldsymbol{x}) + \delta \diamond 0, & \text{if } \diamond \in \{>, \geq\} \\
|f(\boldsymbol{x})| - \delta \leq 0, & \text{if } \diamond \in \{=\} \\
(f(\boldsymbol{x}) < 0 \vee f(\boldsymbol{x}) > 0)_\delta, & \text{if } \diamond \in \{\neq\}.
\end{cases}
$$

- *Otherwise, F is $A \circ B$ with $\circ \in \{\wedge, \vee\}$. Let $F_\delta := (A_\delta \circ B_\delta)$.*

δ-*deciding F designates computing*

$$
\begin{cases}
\text{unsat}, & \text{if } [\![F]\!]^\alpha = \text{false for all } \alpha \\
\delta\text{-sat}, & \text{if } [\![F_\delta]\!]^\alpha = \text{true for some } \alpha.
\end{cases}
$$

In case both answers are valid, the algorithm may output any.

An assignment α with $[\![F_\delta]\!]^\alpha = \text{true}$ we call a δ-satisfying assignment for F.

For non-linear constraints P this definition of the δ-weakening P_δ corresponds exactly to the notion of δ-weakening $P^{-\delta}$ used in the introduction of δ-decidability [14, Definition 4.1].

Remark 2. The δ-weakening of a non-linear constraint $f(x) \neq 0$ is a tautology.

We now consider the problem of δ-deciding quantifier-free formulas in separated linear form. The notion of δ-decidability is slightly stronger than in [13] in the sense that we do not weaken linear constraints. Consider a formula F in separated linear form. As before, we assume variables x to be bounded by linear constraints $x \in D_F$. We additionally assume that for all non-linear constraints $P : f(x) \diamond 0$ in $\mathcal{N}$, f is defined on $\overline{D_P}$ and, in order to simplify the presentation, throughout the rest of paper we will assume only the predicates $\diamond \in \{>, \geq\}$ are part of formulas, since the remaining ones $<, \leq, =$ can easily be expressed by the former using simple arithmetic transformations, and by Remark 2 predicates $\neq$ are irrelevant for δ-deciding formulas.

An algorithm is δ-*complete*, if it δ-decides bounded instances [13].

5 δ-ksmt

Since δ-decidability as introduced above adapts the condition when a formula is considered to be satisfied to δ-sat, this condition has to be reflected in the calculus, which we show solves the bounded δ-SMT problem in this section. Adding the following rule (F_δ^{sat}) together with the new final state δ-sat to ksmt relaxes the termination conditions and turns it into the extended calculus we call δ-ksmt.

(F_δ^{sat}) *Final δ-sat.* If $(\alpha, \mathcal{L}, \mathcal{N})$ is a δ-ksmt state where α is a total assignment and $[\![\mathcal{L} \wedge \mathcal{N}_\delta]\!]^\alpha = \text{true}$, transition to the δ-sat state.

The applicability conditions on the rules (L) and (F_δ^{sat}) individually are not decidable [27,5], however, when we compute them simultaneously, we can effectively apply one of these rules, as we will show in Lemma 3. In combination with ϵ-fullness of the computed linearisations (Lemma 4), this leads to Theorem 3, showing that δ-ksmt is a δ-complete decision procedure.

Let us note that if we assume $\delta = 0$ then δ-ksmt would just reduce to ksmt as (F^{sat}) and (F_δ^{sat}) become indistinguishable, but in the following we always assume $\delta > 0$.

In the following sub-section, we prove that terminating derivations of the δ-ksmt calculus lead to correct results. Then, in Section 5.2, we present a concrete algorithm for applying rules (L) and (F_δ^{sat}) and show its linearisations to be ϵ-full, which is sufficient to ensure termination, as shown in Theorem 1. These properties lead to a δ-complete decision procedure. In Section 6 we develop a more practical algorithm for ϵ-full linearisations that does not require computing a uniform modulus of continuity.

5.1   Soundness

In this section we show soundness of the δ-ksmt calculus, that is, validity of its derivations. In particular, this implies that derivability of the final states unsat, δ-sat and sat directly corresponds to unsatisfiability, δ-satisfiability and satisfiability of the original formula, respectively.

Lemma 1. *For all δ-ksmt derivations of $S' = (\alpha', \mathcal{L}', \mathcal{N})$ from a state $S = (\alpha, \mathcal{L}, \mathcal{N})$ and for all total assignments β, $[\![\mathcal{L} \wedge \mathcal{N}]\!]^\beta = [\![\mathcal{L}' \wedge \mathcal{N}]\!]^\beta$.*

Proof. Let β be a total assignment of the variables in $\mathcal{L} \wedge \mathcal{N}$. Since the set of variables remains unchanged by δ-ksmt derivations, β is a total assignment for $\mathcal{L}' \wedge \mathcal{N}$ as well. Let $S' = (\alpha', \mathcal{L}', \mathcal{N})$ be derived from $S = (\alpha, \mathcal{L}, \mathcal{N})$ by a single application of one of δ-ksmt rules. By the structure of S', its derivation was not caused by neither (F^{unsat}), (F^{sat}) or (F_δ^{sat}). For rules (A) and (B) there is nothing to show since $\mathcal{L} = \mathcal{L}'$. If (R) caused $S \mapsto S'$, the claim holds by soundness of arithmetical resolution. Otherwise (L) caused $S \mapsto S'$ in which case the direction $\Rightarrow$ follows from the definition of a linearisation (condition 1 in Definition 2) while the other direction trivially holds since $\mathcal{L} \subseteq \mathcal{L}'$.

The condition on derivations of arbitrary lengths then follows by induction. $\square$

Lemma 2. *Let $\delta \in \mathbb{Q}_{>0}$. Consider a formula $G = \mathcal{L}_0 \wedge \mathcal{N}$ in separated linear form and let $S = (\alpha, \mathcal{L}, \mathcal{N})$ be a δ-ksmt state derivable from the initial state $S_0 = (nil, \mathcal{L}_0, \mathcal{N})$. The following hold.*

- *If rule (F^{unsat}) is applicable to S then G is unsatisfiable.*
- *If rule (F_δ^{sat}) is applicable to S then α is a δ-satisfying assignment for G, hence G is δ-satisfiable.*
- *If rule (F^{sat}) is applicable to S then α is a satisfying assignment for G, hence G is satisfiable.*

Proof. Let formula G and states S_0, S be as in the premise. As S is not final in δ-ksmt, only ksmt rules have been applied in deriving it. The statements for rules (F^{unsat}) and (F^{sat}) thus hold by soundness of ksmt [7, Lemma 2].

Assume (F_δ^{sat}) is applicable to S, that is, $[\![\mathcal{L} \wedge \mathcal{N}_\delta]\!]^\alpha$ is true. Then, since $\mathcal{L}_0 \subseteq \mathcal{L}$, we conclude that α satisfies $\mathcal{L}_0 \wedge \mathcal{N}_\delta$ which, according to Definition 5, equals G_δ. Therefore α is a δ-satisfying assignment for G. $\square$

Since the only way to derive one of the final states unsat, δ-sat and sat from the initial state in δ-ksmt is by application of the rule (F^{unsat}), (F_δ^{sat}) and (F^{sat}), respectively, as corollary of Lemmas 1 and 2 we obtain soundness.

Theorem 2 (Soundness). *Let $\delta \in \mathbb{Q}_{>0}$. The δ-ksmt calculus is sound.*

5.2 δ-completeness

We proceed by introducing Algorithm 1 computing linearisations and deciding which of the rules (F_δ^{sat}) and (L) to apply. These linearisations are then shown to be ϵ-full for some $\epsilon > 0$ depending on the bounded instance. By Theorem 1, this property implies termination, showing that δ-ksmt is a δ-complete decision procedure.

Given a non-final δ-ksmt state, the function NLINSTEP$_\delta$ in Algorithm 1 computes a δ-ksmt state derivable from it by application of (F_δ^{sat}) or (L). This is done by evaluating the non-linear functions and adding a linearisation ℓ based on their uniform moduli of continuity as needed. To simplify the algorithm, it assumes total assignments as input. It is possible to relax this requirement, e.g., by invoking rules (A) or (R) instead of returning δ-sat for partial assignments.

Algorithm 1 (NLINSTEP_δ) Algorithm computing a δ-ksmt derivation according to either rule (L) or (F_δ^{sat}) from a state $(\alpha, \mathcal{L}, \mathcal{N})$ where α is total. The functions f are assumed to be computed by machines $M_f^?$ and μ_f to be a computable uniform modulus of continuity of f.

function $\text{LINEARISE}_\delta(f, \boldsymbol{x}, \diamond, \alpha)$
    compute $p \geq -\lfloor \log_2(\min\{1, \delta/4\}) \rfloor$
    $\varphi \leftarrow (n \mapsto [\![\boldsymbol{x}]\!]^\alpha)$
    $\epsilon \leftarrow 2^{-\mu_f(p)}$
    $\tilde{y} \leftarrow M_f^\varphi(p)$
    if $\tilde{y} \diamond -\delta/2$ **then**
        return None
    end if
    return $(\boldsymbol{x} \notin B([\![\boldsymbol{x}]\!]^\alpha, \epsilon))$
end function

function $\text{NLINSTEP}_\delta(\alpha, \mathcal{L}, \mathcal{N})$
    for $P : (f(\boldsymbol{x}) \diamond 0)$ in $\mathcal{N}$ **do**
        $\ell \leftarrow \text{LINEARISE}_\delta(f, \boldsymbol{x}, \diamond, \alpha)$
        if $\ell \neq$ None **then**
            return $(\alpha, \mathcal{L} \cup \{\ell\}, \mathcal{N})$ ▷ (L)
        end if
    end for
    return δ-sat   ▷ (F_δ^{sat})
end function

Lemma 3. *Let $\delta \in \mathbb{Q}_{>0}$ and let $S = (\alpha, \mathcal{L}, \mathcal{N})$ be a δ-ksmt state where α is total and $[\![\mathcal{L}]\!]^\alpha = \text{true}$. Then $\text{NLINSTEP}_\delta(\alpha, \mathcal{L}, \mathcal{N})$ computes a state derivable by application of either (L) or (F_δ^{sat}) to S.*

Proof. In the proof we will use notions from computable analysis, as defined in Section 2. Let $(\alpha, \mathcal{L}, \mathcal{N})$ be a state as in the premise and let $P : f(\boldsymbol{x}) \diamond 0$ be a non-linear constraint in $\mathcal{N}$. Let $M_f^?$ compute f as in Algorithm 1. The algorithm computes a rational approximation $\tilde{y} = M_f^{([\![\boldsymbol{x}]\!]^\alpha)_i}(p)$ of $f([\![\boldsymbol{x}]\!]^\alpha)$ where $p \geq -\lfloor \log_2(\min\{1, \delta/4\}) \rfloor \in \mathbb{N}$. $[\![\mathcal{L}]\!]^\alpha = \text{true}$ implies $[\![\boldsymbol{x}]\!]^\alpha \in D_P \subseteq \text{dom} f$, thus the computation of $\tilde{y}$ terminates. Since $M_f^?$ computes f, $\tilde{y}$ is accurate up to $2^{-p} \leq \delta/4$, that is, $\tilde{y} \in [f([\![\boldsymbol{x}]\!]^\alpha) \pm \delta/4]$. By assumption $\diamond \in \{>, \geq\}$, thus

1. $\tilde{y} \diamond -\delta/2$ implies $f([\![\boldsymbol{x}]\!]^\alpha) \diamond -\delta$, which is equivalent to $[\![P_\delta]\!]^\alpha = \text{true}$, and
2. $\neg(\tilde{y} \diamond -\delta/2)$ implies $\neg(f([\![\boldsymbol{x}]\!]^\alpha) \diamond -\delta/2 + \delta/4)$, which in turn implies $[\![P]\!]^\alpha = \text{false}$ and the applicability of rule (L).

For Item 1 no linearisation is necessary and indeed the algorithm does not linearise P. Otherwise (Item 2), it adds the linearisation $(\boldsymbol{x} \notin B([\![\boldsymbol{x}]\!]^\alpha, \epsilon))$ to the linear clauses. Since $[\![\boldsymbol{x}]\!]^\alpha \in D_P$ by Eq. (2.1) we obtain that $0 \notin B(f(\boldsymbol{z}), \delta/4)$ holds, implying $\neg(f(\boldsymbol{z}) \diamond 0)$, for all $\boldsymbol{z} \in B([\![\boldsymbol{x}]\!]^\alpha, \epsilon) \cap \overline{D_P}$. Hence, $(\boldsymbol{x} \notin B([\![\boldsymbol{x}]\!]^\alpha, \epsilon))$ is a linearisation of P at α.

In case $\text{NLINSTEP}_\delta(\alpha, \mathcal{L}, \mathcal{N})$ returns δ-sat, the premise of Item 1 holds for every non-linear constraint in $\mathcal{N}$, that is, $[\![\mathcal{N}_\delta]\!]^\alpha = \text{true}$. By assumption $[\![\mathcal{L}]\!]^\alpha = \text{true}$, hence the application of the (F_δ^{sat}) rule deriving δ-sat is possible in δ-ksmt. $\qquad\square$

Lemma 4. *For any bounded instance $\mathcal{L}_0 \wedge \mathcal{N}$ there is a computable $\epsilon \in \mathbb{Q}_{>0}$ such that any δ-ksmt run starting in $(\text{nil}, \mathcal{L}_0, \mathcal{N})$, where applications of (L) and (F_δ^{sat}) are performed by NLINSTEP_δ, is ϵ-full.*

Proof. Let $P : f(\boldsymbol{x}) \diamond 0$ be a non-linear constraint in $\mathcal{N}$. Since $\mathcal{L}_0 \wedge \mathcal{N}$ is a bounded instance, $D_P \subseteq \mathbb{R}^n$ is also bounded. Let $\epsilon_P := 2^{-\mu_f(p)}$ where $p \geq$

$-\lfloor \log_2(\min\{1, \delta/4\}) \rfloor \in \mathbb{N}$ as in Algorithm 1. As μ_f is a uniform modulus of continuity, the inequalities in the following construction hold on the whole domain $\overline{D_P}$ of f and do not depend on the concrete assignment α where the linearisation is performed. Since $\log_2$ and μ_f are computable, so are p and ϵ_P. There are finitely many non-linear constraints P in $\mathcal{N}$, therefore the linearisations the algorithm NLINSTEP$_\delta$ computes are ϵ-full with $\epsilon = \min\{\epsilon_P : P \text{ in } \mathcal{N}\} > 0$.

We call δ-ksmt derivations when linearisation are computed using Algorithm 1 δ-ksmt with full-box linearisations, or δ-ksmt-fb for short. As the runs computed by it are ϵ-full for $\epsilon > 0$, by Theorem 1 they terminate.

Theorem 3. *δ-ksmt-fb is a δ-complete decision procedure.*

Proof. δ-ksmt-fb is sound (Theorem 2) and terminates on bounded instances (Theorem 1 and Lemma 4).

6   Local ϵ-full Linearisations

In practice, when the algorithm computing ϵ-full linearisations described in the previous section is going to be implemented, the question arises of how to get a good uniform modulus of continuity μ_f for a computable function f. Depending on how f is given, there may be several ways of computing it. Implementations of exact real arithmetic, e.g., iRRAM [24] and Ariadne [2], are usually based on the formalism of function-oracle Turing machines (see Definition 1) which allow to compute with representations of computable functions [10] including implicit representations of functions as solutions of ODEs/PDEs [26,9]. If f is only available as a function-oracle Turing machine $M_f^?$ computing it, a modulus μ_f valid on a compact domain can be computed, however, in general this is not possible without exploring the behaviour of the function on the whole domain, which in many cases is computationally expensive. Moreover, since μ_f is uniform, $\mu_f(n)$ is constant throughout D_F, independent of the actual assignment α determining where f is evaluated. Yet, computable functions admit *local* moduli of continuity that additionally depend on the concrete point in their domain. In most cases these would provide linearisations with ϵ larger than that determined by μ_f leading to larger regions being excluded, ultimately resulting in fewer linearisation steps and general speed-up. Indeed, machines producing finite approximations of $f(x)$ from finite approximations of x internally have to compute some form of local modulus to guarantee correctness. In this section, we explore this approach of obtaining linearisations covering a larger part of the function's domain.

In order to guarantee a positive bound on the local modulus of continuity extracted directly from the run of the machine $M_f^?$ computing f, it is necessary to employ a restriction on the names of real numbers $M_f^?$ computes on. The set of names should in a very precise sense be "small", i.e., it has to be compact. The very general notion of names used in Definition 1 is too broad to satisfy this criterion since the space of rational approximations is not even locally compact. Here, we present an approach using practical names of real numbers as sequences of dyadic rationals of lengths restricted by accuracy. For that purpose, we introduce another representation [31] of $\mathbb{R}$, that is, the surjective mapping $\xi : \mathbb{D}_\omega \to \mathbb{R}$. Here, $\mathbb{D}_\omega$ denotes the set of infinite sequences φ of dyadic rationals with bounded length. If φ has a limit (in $\mathbb{R}$), we write $\lim \varphi$.

Definition 6. – *For $k \in \omega$ let $\mathbb{D}_k := \mathbb{Z} \cdot 2^{-(k+1)} = \{m/2^{k+1} : m \in \mathbb{Z}\} \subset \mathbb{Q}$ and let $\mathbb{D}_\omega := \times_{k \in \omega} \mathbb{D}_k$ be the set of all sequences $(\varphi_k)_k$ with $\varphi_k \in \mathbb{D}_k$ for all $k \in \omega$. By default, $\mathbb{D}_\omega$ is endowed with the Baire space topology, which corresponds to that induced by the metric*

$$d : (\varphi, \psi) \mapsto \begin{cases} 0 & \textit{if } \varphi = \psi \\ 1/\min\{1 + n : n \in \omega, \varphi_n \neq \psi_n\} & \textit{otherwise.} \end{cases}$$

– *Define $\xi : \mathbb{D}_\omega \to \mathbb{R}$ as the partial function mapping $\varphi \in \mathbb{D}_\omega$ to $\lim \varphi$ iff $\forall i, j : |\varphi_i - \varphi_{i+j}| \leq 2^{-(i+1)}$. Any $\varphi \in \xi^{-1}(x)$ is called a ξ-name of $x \in \mathbb{R}$.*
– *The representation $\rho : (x_k)_k \mapsto x$ mapping names $(x_k)_k$ of $x \in \mathbb{R}$ to x as per Definition 1 is called* Cauchy representation.

Using a standard product construction we can easily generalise the notion of ξ-names to ξ^n-names of $\mathbb{R}^n$. When clear from the context, we will drop n and just write ξ to denote the corresponding generalised representation $\mathbb{D}^n_\omega \to \mathbb{R}^n$.

Computable equivalence between two representations not only implies that there are continuous maps between them but also that names can computably be transformed [31]. Since the Cauchy representation itself is continuous [4] we derive continuity of ξ, which is used below to show compactness of preimages $\xi^{-1}(X)$ of compact sets $X \subseteq \mathbb{R}$ under ξ. All proofs can be found in [8].

Lemma 5. *The following properties hold for ξ.*

1. *ξ is a representation of $\mathbb{R}^n$: it is well-defined and surjective.*
2. *Any ξ-name of $x \in \mathbb{R}^n$ is a Cauchy-name of x.*
3. *ξ is computably equivalent to the Cauchy representation.*
4. *ξ is continuous.*

The converse of Item 2 does not hold. An example for a Cauchy-name of $0 \in \mathbb{R}$ is the sequence $(x_n)_n$ with $x_n = (-2)^{-n}$ for all $n \in \omega$, which does not satisfy $\forall i, j : |x_i - x_{i+j}| \leq 2^{-(i+1)}$. However, given a name of a real number, we can compute a corresponding ξ-name, this is one direction of the property in Item 3. As a consequence of Item 2 a function-oracle machine $M^?$ computing $f : \mathbb{R}^n \to \mathbb{R}$ according to Definition 1 can be run on ξ-names of $x \in \mathbb{R}^n$ leading to valid Cauchy-names of $f(x)$. Note that this proposition does not require $M^?_f$ to compute a ξ-name of $f(x)$. Any rational sequence rapidly converging to $f(x)$ is a valid output. This means, that the model of computation remains unchanged with respect to the earlier parts of this paper. It is the set of names the machines are operated on, which is restricted. This is reflected in Algorithm 2 by computing dyadic rational approximations $\tilde{x}_k$ of $[x]^\alpha$ such that $\tilde{x}_k \in \mathbb{D}^n_k$ instead of keeping the name of $[x]^\alpha$ constant as has been done in Algorithm 1.

Algorithm 2 (Local linearisation) Algorithm δ-deciding $P : f(\boldsymbol{x}) \diamond 0$ and − in case unsat − computing a linearisation at α or returning "None" and in this case α satisfies P_δ. The function f is computed by machine $M_f^?$.

---

function LINEARISELOCAL$_\delta(f, \boldsymbol{x}, \diamond, \alpha)$
    $\varphi \leftarrow (m \mapsto \mathrm{approx}(\llbracket \boldsymbol{x} \rrbracket^\alpha, m))$ $\triangleright$ then φ is a ξ-name of $\llbracket \boldsymbol{x} \rrbracket^\alpha$
    compute $p \geq -\lfloor \log_2(\min\{1, \delta/4\}) \rfloor$
    run $M_f^\varphi(p + 2)$, record its output $\tilde{y}$ and its maximum query $k \in \omega$ to φ
    if $\tilde{y} \diamond -\delta/2$ **then**
        return None
    else
        return $(\boldsymbol{x} \notin B(\llbracket \boldsymbol{x} \rrbracket^\alpha, 2^{-k}))$
    end if
end function

In particular, in Theorem 4 we show that linearisations for the (L_δ) rule can be computed by Algorithm 2, which – in contrast to LINEARISE$_\delta$ in Algorithm 1 – does not require access to a procedure computing an upper bound μ_f on the uniform modulus of continuity of the non-linear function $f \in \mathcal{F}_{\mathrm{nl}}$ valid on the entire bounded domain. It not just runs the machine $M_f^?$, but also observes the queries M_f^φ poses to its oracle in order to obtain a local modulus of continuity of f at the point of evaluation. The function $\mathrm{approx}(\boldsymbol{x}, m) := \lfloor \boldsymbol{x} \cdot 2^{m+1} \rceil / 2^{m+1}$ used to define Algorithm 2 computes a dyadic approximation of $\boldsymbol{x}$, with $\lfloor \cdot \rceil : \mathbb{Q}^n \to \mathbb{Z}^n$ denoting a rounding operation, that is, it satisfies $\forall \boldsymbol{q} : \|\lfloor \boldsymbol{q} \rceil - \boldsymbol{q}\| \leq \frac{1}{2}$. On rationals (our use-case), $\lfloor \cdot \rceil$ is computable by a classical Turing machine.

Definition 7 ([31, Definition 6.2.6]). *Let $f : \mathbb{R}^n \to \mathbb{R}$ and $\boldsymbol{x} \in \mathrm{dom}\, f$. A function $\gamma : \mathbb{N} \to \mathbb{N}$ is called a (local) modulus of continuity of f at $\boldsymbol{x}$ if for all $p \in \mathbb{N}$ and $\boldsymbol{y} \in \mathrm{dom}\, f$, $\|\boldsymbol{x} - \boldsymbol{y}\| \leq 2^{-\gamma(p)} \implies |f(\boldsymbol{x}) - f(\boldsymbol{y})| \leq 2^{-p}$ holds.*

We note that in most cases a local modulus of continuity of f at $\boldsymbol{x}$ is smaller than the best uniform modulus of f on its domain, since it only depends on the local behaviour of f around x. One way of computing a local modulus of f at $\boldsymbol{x}$ is using the function-oracle machine $M_f^?$ as defined next.

Definition 8. *Let $M_f^?$ compute $f : \mathbb{R}^n \to \mathbb{R}$ and let $\boldsymbol{x} \in \mathrm{dom}\, f$ have Cauchy-name φ. The function $\gamma_{M_f^?, \varphi} : p \mapsto \max\{0, k : M_f^\varphi(p + 2) \text{ queries index } k \text{ of } \varphi\}$ is called* the effective local modulus of continuity induced by $M_f^?$ at φ.

The effective local modulus of continuity of f at a name φ of $\boldsymbol{x} \in \mathrm{dom}\, f$ indeed is a local modulus of continuity of f at $\boldsymbol{x}$ [17, Theorem 2.13]. Algorithm 2 computes ϵ-full linearisations by means of the effective local modulus [8], as stated next.

Lemma 6. *Let $P : f(\boldsymbol{x}) \diamond 0$ be a non-linear constraint in $\mathcal{N}$ and α be an assignment of $\boldsymbol{x}$ to rationals in $\mathrm{dom}\, f$. Whenever $C = \mathrm{LINEARISELOCAL}_\delta(f, \boldsymbol{x}, \diamond, \alpha)$ and $C \neq \mathsf{None}$, C is an ϵ-full linearisation of P at α, with ϵ corresponding to the effective local modulus of continuity induced by $M_f^?$ at a ξ-name of $\llbracket \boldsymbol{x} \rrbracket^\alpha$.*

Thus, the function LINEARISELOCAL$_\delta$ in Algorithm 2 is a drop-in replacement for LINEARISE$_\delta$ in Algorithm 1 since the condition on returning a linearisation of P versus accepting P_δ is identical. The linearisations however differ in the radius ϵ, which now, according to Lemma 6, corresponds to the effective local modulus of continuity. The resulting procedure we call NLINSTEPLOCAL$_\delta$. One of its advantages over NLINSTEP$_\delta$ is running $M_f^?$ on ξ-names instead of Cauchy-names, is that they form a compact set for bounded instances, unlike the latter. This allows us to bound $\epsilon > 0$ for the computed ϵ-full local linearisations of otherwise arbitrary δ-ksmt runs. A proof of the following Lemma showing compactness of preimages $\xi^{-1}(X)$ of compact sets $X \subseteq \mathbb{R}$ under ξ is given in [8].

Lemma 7. *Let $X \subset \mathbb{R}^n$ be compact. Then the set $\xi^{-1}(X) \subset \mathbb{D}_\omega^n$ of ξ-names of elements in X is compact as well.*

The proof involves showing $\xi^{-1}(X)$ to be closed and uses the fact that for each component φ_k of names $(\varphi_k)_k$ of $x \in X$ there are just finitely many choices from $\mathbb{D}_k$ due to the restriction of the length of the dyadics. This is not the case for the Cauchy representation used in Definition 1 and it is the key for deriving existence of a strictly positive lower bound ϵ on the ϵ-fullness of linearisations.

Theorem 4. *Let $\delta \in \mathbb{Q}_{>0}$. For any bounded instance $\mathcal{L}_0 \wedge \mathcal{N}$ there is $\epsilon > 0$ such that any δ-ksmt run starting in $(nil, \mathcal{L}_0, \mathcal{N})$, where applications of (L) and (F_δ^{sat}) are performed according to NLINSTEPLOCAL$_\delta$, is ϵ-full.*

Proof. Assume $\mathcal{L}_0 \wedge \mathcal{N}$ is a bounded instance. Set $\epsilon := \min\{\epsilon_P : P \in \mathcal{N}\}$, where ϵ_P is defined as follows. Let $P : f(x) \diamond 0$ in $\mathcal{N}$. Then the closure $\overline{D_P}$ of the bounded set D_P is compact. Let E be the set of ξ-names of elements of $\overline{D_P} \subseteq \mathrm{dom}\, f$ (see Definition 6) and for any $\varphi \in E$ let k_φ be defined as $\gamma_{M_f^?, \varphi}(p)$ (see Definition 8) where p is computed from δ as in Algorithm 2 and is independent of φ. Since the preimage of each k_φ is open, the function $\varphi \mapsto k_\varphi$ is continuous. By Lemma 7 the set E is compact, thus, there is $\psi \in E$ such that $2^{-k_\psi} = \inf\{2^{-k_\varphi} : \varphi \in E\}$. Set $\epsilon_P := 2^{-k_\psi}$. The claim then follows by Lemma 6. $\qquad \square$

Thus we can conclude.

Corollary 1. *δ-ksmt with local linearisations is a δ-complete decision procedure.*

7 Conclusion

In this paper we extended the the ksmt calculus to the δ-satisfiability setting and proved that the resulting δ-ksmt calculus is a δ-complete decision procedure for solving non-linear constraints over computable functions which include polynomials, exponentials, logarithms, trigonometric and many other functions used in applications. We presented algorithms for constructing ϵ-full linearisations ensuring termination of δ-ksmt. Based on methods from computable analysis we presented an algorithm for constructing local linearisations. Local linearisations exclude larger regions from the search space and can be used to avoid computationally expensive global analysis of non-linear functions.

References

1. Bard, J., Becker, H., Darulova, E.: Formally verified roundoff errors using SMT-based certificates and subdivisions. In: ter Beek, M.H., McIver, A., Oliveira, J.N. (eds.) Formal Methods - The Next 30 Years - Third World Congress, FM 2019, Proceedings. LNCS, vol. 11800, pp. 38–44. Springer (2019)
2. Benvenuti, L., Bresolin, D., Collins, P., Ferrari, A., Geretti, L., Villa, T.: Assume–guarantee verification of nonlinear hybrid systems with Ariadne. International Journal of Robust and Nonlinear Control 24(4), 699–724 (2014)
3. Bonacina, M.P., Graham-Lengrand, S., Shankar, N.: Conflict-driven satisfiability for theory combination: Transition system and completeness. J. Autom. Reason. 64(3), 579–609 (2020)
4. Brattka, V., Hertling, P.: Topological properties of real number representations. Theor. Comput. Sci. 284(2), 241–257 (2002)
5. Brattka, V., Hertling, P., Weihrauch, K.: A Tutorial on Computable Analysis, pp. 425–491. Springer New York, New York, NY (2008)
6. Brauße, F., Khasidashvili, Z., Korovin, K.: Selecting stable safe configurations for systems modelled by neural networks with ReLU activation. In: Ivrii, A., Strichman, O. (eds.) 2020 Formal Methods in Computer Aided Design, FMCAD 2020. pp. 119–127. IEEE (2020)
7. Brauße, F., Korovin, K., Korovina, M.V., Müller, N.T.: A CDCL-style calculus for solving non-linear constraints. In: Herzig, A., Popescu, A. (eds.) Frontiers of Combining Systems - 12th International Symposium, FroCoS 2019, Proceedings. LNCS, vol. 11715, pp. 131–148. Springer (2019)
8. Brauße, F., Korovin, K., Korovina, M.V., Müller, N.T.: The ksmt calculus is a δ-complete decision procedure for non-linear constraints. CoRR abs/2104.13269 (2021)
9. Brauße, F., Korovina, M.V., Müller, N.T.: Towards using exact real arithmetic for initial value problems. In: Mazzara, M., Voronkov, A. (eds.) Perspectives of System Informatics - 10th International Andrei Ershov Informatics Conference, PSI 2015, in Memory of Helmut Veith, Revised Selected Papers. LNCS, vol. 9609, pp. 61–74. Springer (2015)
10. Brauße, F., Steinberg, F.: A minimal representation for continuous functions. CoRR abs/1703.10044 (2017)
11. Cimatti, A., Griggio, A., Irfan, A., Roveri, M., Sebastiani, R.: Incremental linearization for satisfiability and verification modulo nonlinear arithmetic and transcendental functions. ACM Trans. Comput. Log. 19(3), 19:1–19:52 (2018)
12. Fontaine, P., Ogawa, M., Sturm, T., Vu, X.: Subtropical satisfiability. In: Dixon, C., Finger, M. (eds.) Frontiers of Combining Systems - 11th International Symposium, FroCoS 2017, Proceedings. LNCS, vol. 10483, pp. 189–206. Springer (2017)
13. Gao, S., Avigad, J., Clarke, E.M.: δ-complete decision procedures for satisfiability over the reals. In: Gramlich, B., Miller, D., Sattler, U. (eds.) Automated Reasoning - 6th International Joint Conference, IJCAR 2012, Proceedings. LNCS, vol. 7364, pp. 286–300. Springer (2012)
14. Gao, S., Avigad, J., Clarke, E.M.: Delta-decidability over the reals. In: Proceedings of the 27th Annual IEEE Symposium on Logic in Computer Science, LICS 2012. pp. 305–314. IEEE Computer Society (2012)
15. Hales, T.C., Adams, M., Bauer, G., Dang, D.T., Harrison, J., Hoang, T.L., Kaliszyk, C., Magron, V., McLaughlin, S., Nguyen, T.T., Nguyen, T.Q., Nipkow, T., Obua, S., Pleso, J., Rute, J.M., Solovyev, A., Ta, A.H.T., Tran, T.N., Trieu,

D.T., Urban, J., Vu, K.K., Zumkeller, R.: A formal proof of the Kepler conjecture. CoRR **abs/1501.02155** (2015)

16. Jovanovic, D., de Moura, L.: Solving non-linear arithmetic. ACM Commun. Comput. Algebra **46**(3/4), 104–105 (2012)

17. Ko, K.: Complexity Theory of Real Functions. Birkhäuser / Springer (1991)

18. Korovin, K., Kosta, M., Sturm, T.: Towards conflict-driven learning for virtual substitution. In: Gerdt, V.P., Koepf, W., Seiler, W.M., Vorozhtsov, E.V. (eds.) Computer Algebra in Scientific Computing - 16th International Workshop, CASC 2014, Proceedings. LNCS, vol. 8660, pp. 256–270. Springer (2014)

19. Korovin, K., Tsiskaridze, N., Voronkov, A.: Conflict resolution. In: Gent, I.P. (ed.) Principles and Practice of Constraint Programming - CP 2009, 15th International Conference, CP 2009, Proceedings. LNCS, vol. 5732, pp. 509–523. Springer (2009)

20. Korovin, K., Voronkov, A.: Solving systems of linear inequalities by bound propagation. In: Bjørner, N., Sofronie-Stokkermans, V. (eds.) Automated Deduction - CADE-23 - 23rd International Conference on Automated Deduction, Proceedings. LNCS, vol. 6803, pp. 369–383. Springer (2011)

21. Kurátko, J., Ratschan, S.: Combined global and local search for the falsification of hybrid systems. In: Legay, A., Bozga, M. (eds.) Formal Modeling and Analysis of Timed Systems - 12th International Conference, FORMATS 2014, Proceedings. LNCS, vol. 8711, pp. 146–160. Springer (2014)

22. de Moura, L.M., Jovanovic, D.: A model-constructing satisfiability calculus. In: Giacobazzi, R., Berdine, J., Mastroeni, I. (eds.) Verification, Model Checking, and Abstract Interpretation, 14th International Conference, VMCAI 2013, Proceedings. LNCS, vol. 7737, pp. 1–12. Springer (2013)

23. de Moura, L.M., Passmore, G.O.: Computation in real closed infinitesimal and transcendental extensions of the rationals. In: Bonacina, M.P. (ed.) Automated Deduction - CADE-24 - 24th International Conference on Automated Deduction, Proceedings. LNCS, vol. 7898, pp. 178–192. Springer (2013)

24. Müller, N.T.: The iRRAM: Exact arithmetic in C++. In: Blanck, J., Brattka, V., Hertling, P. (eds.) Computability and Complexity in Analysis, 4th International Workshop, CCA 2000, Selected Papers. LNCS, vol. 2064, pp. 222–252. Springer (2000)

25. Platzer, A.: Logical Foundations of Cyber-Physical Systems. Springer (2018)

26. Pour-El, M.B., Richards, J.I.: Computability in analysis and physics. Perspectives in Mathematical Logic, Springer (1989)

27. Richardson, D.: Some undecidable problems involving elementary functions of a real variable. J. Symb. Log. **33**(4), 514–520 (1968)

28. Silva, J.P.M., Sakallah, K.A.: GRASP - a new search algorithm for satisfiability. In: Rutenbar, R.A., Otten, R.H.J.M. (eds.) Proceedings of the IEEE/ACM International Conference on Computer-Aided Design, ICCAD 1996. pp. 220–227. IEEE Computer Society / ACM (1996)

29. Tiwari, A., Lincoln, P.: A search-based procedure for nonlinear real arithmetic. Formal Methods Syst. Des. **48**(3), 257–273 (2016)

30. Tung, V.X., Khanh, T.V., Ogawa, M.: raSAT: An SMT solver for polynomial constraints. In: Olivetti, N., Tiwari, A. (eds.) Automated Reasoning - 8th International Joint Conference, IJCAR 2016, Proceedings. LNCS, vol. 9706, pp. 228–237. Springer (2016)

31. Weihrauch, K.: Computable Analysis – An Introduction. Texts in Theoretical Computer Science. An EATCS Series, Springer (2000)

32. Willard, S.: General Topology. Addison-Wesly (1970)

Open Access This chapter is licensed under the terms of the Creative Commons Attribution 4.0 International License (http://creativecommons.org/licenses/by/4.0/), which permits use, sharing, adaptation, distribution and reproduction in any medium or format, as long as you give appropriate credit to the original author(s) and the source, provide a link to the Creative Commons license and indicate if changes were made.

The images or other third party material in this chapter are included in the chapter's Creative Commons license, unless indicated otherwise in a credit line to the material. If material is not included in the chapter's Creative Commons license and your intended use is not permitted by statutory regulation or exceeds the permitted use, you will need to obtain permission directly from the copyright holder.

Universal Invariant Checking of Parametric Systems with Quantifier-free SMT Reasoning

Alessandro Cimatti [ID], Alberto Griggio [ID], and Gianluca Redondi [ID]

Fondazione Bruno Kessler, Trento, Italy
{cimatti, griggio, gredondi}@fbk.eu

Abstract. The problem of invariant checking in parametric systems –
which are required to operate correctly regardless of the number and
connections of their components – is gaining increasing importance in
various sectors, such as communication protocols and control software.
Such systems are typically modeled using quantified formulae, describing the behaviour of an unbounded number of (identical) components,
and their automatic verification often relies on the use of decidable fragments of first-order logic in order to effectively deal with the challenges
of quantified reasoning.

In this paper, we propose a fully automatic technique for invariant checking of parametric systems which does not rely on quantified reasoning. Parametric systems are modeled with array-based transition systems, and our method iteratively constructs a quantifier-free abstraction
by analyzing, with SMT-based invariant checking algorithms for non-
parametric systems, increasingly-larger finite instances of the parametric
system. Depending on the verification result in the concrete instance, the
abstraction is automatically refined by leveraging candidate lemmas from
inductive invariants, or by discarding previously computed lemmas.

We implemented the method using a quantifier-free SMT-based IC3
as underlying verification engine. Our experimental evaluation demonstrates that the approach is competitive with the state of the art, solving
several benchmarks that are out of reach for other tools.

Keywords: Parametric Systems · Array-based transitions systems ·
Abstraction-refinement · SMT

1 Introduction

Parametric systems consist of a finite but unbounded number of components. Examples include communication protocols (e.g. leader election), feature systems,
or control algorithms in various application domains (e.g. railways interlocking
logics). The key challenge is to prove the correctness of the parametric system
for all possible configurations corresponding to instantiations of the parameters.

Parametric systems can be described as symbolic array-based transition systems [10], where the dependence on the configuration is expressed with first-order
quantifiers in the initial condition and the transition relation of the model.

© The Author(s) 2021
A. Platzer and G. Sutcliffe (Eds.): CADE 2021, LNAI 12699, pp. 131–147, 2021.
https://doi.org/10.1007/978-3-030-79876-5_8

In this paper, we propose a fully automated approach for solving the universal invariant problem of array-based systems. The distinguishing feature is that the approach, grounded in SMT, does not require dealing with quantified theories, with obvious computational advantages. The algorithm implements an abstraction-refinement loop, where the abstract space is a quantifier-free transition system over some SMT theories. Our inspiration and starting point is the Parameter Abstraction of [3,15], which we extend in two directions. First, we modify the definition of the abstraction, by introducing a set of different *environment variables*, which intuitively overapproximate the behaviour of all the instances not precisely tracked by the abstraction, and by introducing a special *stuttering transition* in which the environment is allowed to change non-deterministically. Second, we combine the abstraction with a method for *automatically* inferring candidate universal lemmas, which are used to strengthen the abstraction in case of spurious counterexamples. The candidate lemmas are obtained by generalization from the spuriousness proof carried out in a finite-domain instantiation of the concrete system. However, we do not require quantified reasoning to prove that they universally hold; rather, the algorithm takes into account the fact that candidate lemmas may turn out not to be universally valid. In such cases, the method is able to automatically discover such bad lemmas and discard them, by examining increasingly-higher-dimension bounded instances of the parametric system.

We implemented the method in a tool called LAMBDA. At its core, LAMBDA leverages modern model checking approaches for quantifier-free infinite-state systems, i.e. the SMT-based approach of IC3 with implicit abstraction [4], in contrast to other approaches [19] where the abstract space is Boolean. In our experimental evaluation, we compared LAMBDA with the state-of-the-art tools MCMT [11] and CUBICLE [7]. The results show the advantage of the approach, that is able to solve multiple benchmarks that are out of reach for its competitors.

The rest of the paper is structured as follows. In Section 2 we present some logical background, and in Section 3 we describe array-based systems. We give an informal overview of the algorithm in Section 4. In Section 5 we define the abstraction and state its formal properties. In Section 6 we discuss the approach to concretization and refinement, and we present the techniques for inferring candidate lemmas. We discuss the related work in Section 7, and we present our experimental evaluation in Section 8. Finally, in Section 9 we draw some conclusions and present directions for future work. For lack of space, the proofs of our theoretical results, as well as further details on our experiments, are reported in an extended techical report [5].

2   Preliminaries

Our setting is standard first order logic. A theory $\mathcal{T}$ in the SMT sense is a pair $\mathcal{T} = (\Sigma, \mathcal{C})$, where Σ is a first order signature and $\mathcal{C}$ is a class of models over Σ. A theory $\mathcal{T}$ is closed under substructure if its class $\mathcal{C}$ of structures is such that whenever $\mathcal{M} \in \mathcal{C}$ and $\mathcal{N}$ is a substructure of $\mathcal{M}$, then $\mathcal{N} \in \mathcal{C}$. We use the standard notions of Tarskian interpretation (assignment, model, satisfiability, validity, logical consequence). We refer to 0-arity predicates as Boolean variables, and to 0-arity uninterpreted functions as (theory) variables. A literal is an atom or its negation. A clause is a disjunction of literals. A formula is in conjunctive normal form (CNF) iff it is a conjuction of clauses. If $x_1, ..., x_n$ are variables and ϕ is a formula, we might write $\phi(x_1, ..., x_n)$ to indicate that all the variables occurring free in ϕ are in $x_1, ..., x_n$.

If ϕ is a formula, t is a term and v is a variable which occurs free in ϕ, we write $\phi[v/t]$ for the substitution of every occurrence of v with t. If $\underline{t}$ and $\underline{v}$ are vectors of the same length, we write $\phi[\underline{v}/\underline{t}]$ for the simultaneous substitution of each v_i with the corresponding term t_i. We use an if-then-else notation for formulae. We write **if** ϕ_1 **then** ψ_1 **elif** ϕ_2 **then** ψ_2 **elif** $...\psi_{n-1}$ **else** ψ_n to denote the formula $(\phi_1 \rightarrow \psi_1) \wedge ((\neg\phi_1 \wedge \phi_2) \rightarrow \psi_2) \wedge ... ((\neg\phi_1 ... \neg\phi_{n-1} \wedge \neg\phi_n) \rightarrow \psi_n)$.

Given a set of variables $\underline{v}$, we denote with $\underline{v}'$ the set $\{v'|v \in \underline{v}\}$. A symbolic transition system is a triple $(\underline{v}, I(\underline{v}), T(\underline{v}, \underline{v}'))$, where $\underline{v}$ is a set of variables, and $I(\underline{v})$, $T(\underline{v}, \underline{v}')$ are first order formulae over some signature. An assignment to the variables in $\underline{v}$ is a state. A state s is initial iff it is a model of $I(\underline{v})$, i.e. $s \models I(\underline{v})$. The states s, s' denote a transition iff $s \cup s' \models T(\underline{v}, \underline{v}')$, also written $T(s, s')$. A path is a sequence of states $s_0, s_1, ...$ such that s_0 is initial and $T(s_i, s'_{i+1})$ for all i. We denote paths with π, and with $\pi[j]$ the j-th element of π. A state s is reachable iff there exists a path π such that $\pi[i] = s$ for some i. A variable v is frozen iff for all π, i it holds that $\pi[i](v) = \pi[0](v)$. In the following, when we define a frozen variable v, we assume that this is done by having a constraint $v' = v$ as a top-level conjunct of the transition formula. A formula $\phi(\underline{v})$ is an invariant of the transition system $C = (\underline{v}, I(\underline{v}), T(\underline{v}, \underline{v}'))$ iff it holds in all the reachable states. Following the standard model checking notation, we denote this with $C \models \phi(\underline{v})$.[1] A formula $\phi(\underline{v})$ is an inductive invariant for C iff $I(\underline{v}) \models \phi(\underline{v})$ and $\phi(\underline{v}) \wedge T(\underline{v}, \underline{v}') \models \phi(\underline{v}')$.

3 Modeling Parametric Systems as Array-based Transition Systems

In order to describe parametric systems, we adapt from [10] the notion of array-based systems. In the following, we fix a theory of indexes $\mathcal{T}_I = (\Sigma_I, \mathcal{C}_I)$ and a theory of elements $\mathcal{T}_E = (\Sigma_E, \mathcal{C}_E)$. In order to model the parameters, we require that the class $\mathcal{C}_I$ is closed under substructure. Then with A_I^E we denote the theory whose signature is $\Sigma = \Sigma_I \cup \Sigma_E \cup \{[.]\}$, and a model for it is given by a set of total functions from a model of $\mathcal{T}_I$ to a model of $\mathcal{T}_E$. In general, we can have several array theories with multiple sorts for indexes and elements.

---

[1] Note that we use the symbol $\models$ with three different denotations: if ϕ, ψ are formulae, $\phi \models \psi$ denotes that ψ is a logical consequence of ϕ; if μ is an interpretation, and ψ is a formula, $\mu \models \psi$ denotes that μ is a model of ψ; if C is a transition system, $C \models \psi$ denotes that ψ is an invariant of C.

For simplicity, we fix only an *index* sort and an *elem* sort. In the following, an array-based transition system

$$C = (a, \iota(a), \tau(a, a'))$$

is a symbolic transition system, with the additional constraints that:

- a is a variable of sort *index* $\mapsto$ *elem*. We use a single variable for the sake of simplicity: additional variables of arbitrary type (also of index or element type) can be added without loss of generality.
- $\iota(a)$ is a first-order formula of the form $\forall \underline{i}.\phi(\underline{i}, a[\underline{i}])$, where $\underline{i}$ is of index sort and ϕ is a quantifier-free formula.
- $\tau(a, a')$ is a finite disjunction of formulae, $\vee_{k=1}^{n} \tau_k$, such that every τ_k is a formula of the following type (with $\underline{i}, \underline{j}$ of index sort):

$$\exists \underline{i} \forall \underline{j}.\psi(\underline{i}, \underline{j}, a[\underline{i}], a[\underline{j}], a'[\underline{i}], a'[\underline{j}])$$

  with ψ a quantifier-free formula.

This syntactic requirement subsumes the common guard and update formalism used for the description of parametric systems, used e.g in [10, 12, 15].

In the following, we shall refer to the disjuncts τ_k of τ as *transition rules* (or simply *rules* when clear from the context).

An array-based transition system can be seen as a family of transition systems, one for each cardinality of the finite models $\mathcal{M}_I$ of $\mathcal{T}_I$. In the following, given d an integer, we denote with C^d *the finite instance of C of size d* obtained by instantiating the quantifiers of C over a set of fresh index variables of cardinality d (considered implicitly different from each other). Note that this C^d is a *symmetric presentation* [15]: if $\underline{c} = \{c_1, \ldots, c_d\}$ are the fresh index variables, and σ is a permutation of $\underline{c}$, we have that, for every formula $\phi(\underline{c}, a[\underline{c}])$, $C^d \models \phi(\underline{c}, a[\underline{c}]) \Leftrightarrow C^d \models \phi(\sigma(\underline{c}), a[\sigma(\underline{c})])$.

Example 1 (Mutex Protocol for Ring Topology). Here we describe a simple protocol for accessing a shared resource, with processes in a ring-shaped topology. As an index theory, we use the finite sets of integers. As an element theory, we use both the Booleans and an enumerated data type of two elements, namely $\{idle, critical\}$. The array variable t, with sort *index* $\mapsto$ *boolean*, is true in an index variable x if x holds the token. The variable s, with sort *index* $\mapsto \{idle, critical\}$ holds the current state of the process. In addition, we have an integer frozen variable *length*, which represents the length of the ring. The transition system is described by the following formulae:

Initial states. Initially, only one process holds the token, and every process is idle. We model this initial process with an additional constant *init_token* of sort *index*. Moreover, each index is bounded by the value of *length*. The initial formula is:

$$\forall j.p[j] = idle \wedge j \geq 1 \wedge j \leq length \wedge length > 0$$

$$\wedge \begin{cases} \textbf{if } j = init\_token \textbf{ then } t[j] = true \\ \textbf{else } t[j] = false \end{cases}$$

Transition rule 1. A process which holds the token can enter the critical section:

$$\exists i.s[i] = idle \wedge t[i] = true \wedge s'[i] = critical \wedge t'[i] = t[i] \wedge$$
$$\forall j, j \neq i.(s'[j] = s[j] \wedge t'[j] = t[j])$$

Transition rule 2. A process exits from the critical section and passes the token to the process at its right:

$$\exists i. \wedge s[i] = critical \wedge s'[i] = idle \wedge t'[i] = false \wedge$$

$$\forall j, j \neq i. \begin{cases} \textbf{if } j = 1 \wedge i = length \textbf{ then } s'[j] = s[j] \wedge t'[j] = true \\ \textbf{elif } j = i + 1 \wedge i < length \textbf{ then } s'[j] = s[j] \wedge t'[j] = true \\ \textbf{else } s'[j] = s[j] \wedge t'[j] = t[j] \end{cases}$$

3.1 Universal invariant problem for array-based systems

In the following, given an array-based transition system

$$C = (a, \iota(a), \tau(a, a')),$$

the *universal invariant problem* is the problem of proving (or disproving) that a formula of the form $\Phi \overset{\text{def}}{=} \forall \underline{i}.\phi(\underline{i}, a[\underline{i}])$ is an invariant for C.

Guard Strengthening In order to prove that $\forall \underline{i}.\phi(\underline{i}, a[\underline{i}])$ is an invariant of a system $C = (a, \iota(a), \tau(a, a'))$, we can first strengthen the rules of C by adding the candidate invariant in conjunction with the transition relation, and then prove that the formula is an invariant of the newly-restricted system. This induction principle is justified by the following proposition:

Proposition 1 (Guard strenghtening [15]) *Let $C = (a, \iota(a), \tau(a, a'))$ be a transition system and let Φ be $\forall \underline{i}.\phi(\underline{i}, a[\underline{i}])$. Let $C_\Phi = (a, \iota(a), \tau(a, a') \wedge \Phi)$ be the guard-strengthening of C with respect to Φ. Then, if Φ is an invariant of C_Φ, it is also an invariant of C.*

Prophecy variables The universal quantifiers in the candidate invariant can be replaced with fresh frozen variables, called *prophecy variables*, that intuitively contain the indexes of the processes witnessing the violation of the property.

Proposition 2 (Removing quantifiers [19]) *Let $C = (a, \iota(a), \tau(a, a'))$ be an array-based system. The formula $\forall \underline{i}.\phi(\underline{i}, a[\underline{i}])$ is an invariant for C iff the formula $\phi(\underline{p}, a[\underline{p}])$ is an invariant for $C_{+\underline{p}} = (a \cup \underline{p}, \iota(a), \tau(a, a'))$, where $\underline{p}$ is a set of fresh frozen variables of index sort.*

For better readability, in the following we will omit the subscript $+\underline{p}$. Moreover, we assume that the index variables universally quantified in the candidate invariant are considered to be different. This does not limit expressiveness, and simplifies our discourse. Therefore, the prophecy variables induced by a candidate invariant are considered to be *implicitly different*.

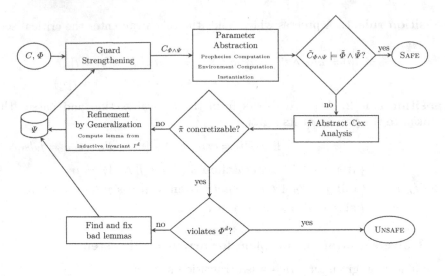

Fig. 1. An overview of the algorithm. C is an array-based transition system; Φ is a quantified candidate invariant; $\Psi \overset{\text{def}}{=} \{\psi_1, \ldots \psi_n\}$ is the set of candidate lemmas; $C_{\Phi \wedge \Psi}$ is a quantified transition system resulting from the strengthening of C; $\tilde{C}_{\Phi \wedge \Psi}$ is a quantifier-free transition system.

4   Overview of the Method

In the following, let an array-based transition system $C \overset{\text{def}}{=} (a, \iota(a), \tau(a, a'))$, and a candidate universal invariant $\Phi \overset{\text{def}}{=} \forall \underline{i}.\phi(\underline{i}, a[\underline{i}])$ for C be given.

We now summarize the algorithm that attempts to solve the universal invariant problem for C and Φ. The algorithm, depicted in Figure 1, iterates trying either to construct an abstraction sufficiently precise to prove the property (exit with SAFE), or to find a finite instantiation of the problem exhibiting a concrete counterexample (exit with UNSAFE). The abstract space is quantifier-free, and obtained by instantiating the universally quantified formulae over two sets of index variables: the prophecy variables, which arise from the candidate invariant (as explained in Proposition 2), and are denoted with $\underline{p}$; and the *environmental* variables, denoted with $\underline{x}$, which arise from the transition formula and are intended to represent the environment surrounding the p indexes, interacting with them in the behaviour leading to the violation. While prophecy variables are frozen, thus representing the same indexes for the whole run, environmental variables are free to change at each time step, hence producing possibly spurious behaviours. The algorithm maintains a set of *candidate lemmas* $\Psi \overset{\text{def}}{=} \{\Psi_i\}_i$, composed of universally quantified formulae, that are used to strengthen the property and to tighten the abstraction. Initially, Ψ is empty. In the following, if C^d is a finite instance of C and Φ is a candidate universal invariant, with Φ^d we denote the formula obtained from Φ by instantiating the quantifiers in variables used for the domain of cardinality d.

At each iteration, we carry out the following high-level steps (described in detail in the next sections):

- the property Φ to be proved is conjoined with the candidate lemmas in Ψ, and its quantifiers are moved in prenex form;[2]
- we construct the guard-strengthening $C_{\Phi \wedge \Psi}$ (cfr. Proposition 1), conjoining $\Phi \wedge \Psi$ to the transition rules of C;
- we compute our modified Parameter Abstraction of $C_{\Phi \wedge \Psi}$ (defined in §5.1). First, we define the necessary prophecy variables p and environmental variables $\underline{x}$. Then, we instantiate the quantifiers obtaining the quantifier-free array transition system $\tilde{C}_{\Phi \wedge \Psi}$.
- we (try to) solve the invariant checking problem $\tilde{C}_{\Phi \wedge \Psi} \models \tilde{\Phi} \wedge \tilde{\Psi}$ by calling a model checker for quantifier-free transition systems. $\tilde{\Phi} \wedge \tilde{\Psi}$ is obtained from $\Phi \wedge \Psi$ by removing quantifiers with prophecy variables, as in Proposition 2
- if the model checker concludes that there is no violation, then Φ holds in C (for the properties of the Parameter Abstraction), and we exit with SAFE.
- otherwise, we try to check whether the property violation in the abstract space corresponds to a real counterexample. We do so by checking whether the current property $\Phi \wedge \Psi$ is falsified in C^d, a suitable finite instance of C. That is, we check whether $C^d \models (\Phi \wedge \Psi)^d$.
- if $C^d \models (\Psi \wedge \Phi)^d$, then the abstraction must be tightened. When the verification of the finite instance succeeds, an inductive invariant I^d is produced, which is used to compute (candidate) lemmas by generalization from d to the universal case.
- if $C^d \not\models (\Psi \wedge \Phi)^d$, two cases are possible. First, we check if the (instantiation of the) property Φ is indeed violated. If so, we exit with UNSAFE, and we produce a concrete counterexample to the original problem, finitely witnessed in C^d.
- However, it is also possible that C^d does not violate Φ^d, but it falsifies some lemmas. In fact, the candidate lemmas obtained at previous iterations, by generalization on C^{d^-} with $d^- \neq d$, may not hold universally in C. In that case, the bad lemmas must be fixed, and the iteration is restarted.

When the algorithm terminates with UNSAFE, we are able to exhibit a finite counterexample trace in a finite instance of C violating the property. When the algorithm terminates with safe, then the property holds in C. The result is obtained by the following chain of implications: from Theorem 3, stated in the next section, we have that $\tilde{C}_{\Phi \wedge \Psi} \models \tilde{\Phi} \wedge \tilde{\Psi}$ implies $C_{\Phi \wedge \Psi} \models \tilde{\Phi} \wedge \tilde{\Psi}$. From Proposition 2, we have that $C_{\Phi \wedge \Psi} \models \Phi \wedge \Psi$. Therefore, from Proposition 1, we have $C \models \Phi \wedge \Psi$. In particular, we have $C \models \Phi$.

5   Modified Parameter Abstraction

We describe here our Parameter Abstraction. The first version of this approach was introduced in [3], and later formalized in [15]. In the following, we describe

---

[2] In the following, with $\Phi \wedge \Psi$ we denote the prenex form $\Phi \wedge \bigwedge_i \Psi_i$

a novel version of the abstraction, and how it can be applied to array-based transition systems. The main novelty is that, instead of using a special abstract index "$*$" that overapproximates the behaviour of the system in the array locations that are not explicitly tracked, we use n *environmental (index) variables* which are not abstracted, but are allowed to change nondeterministically in some transitions. This can be achieved by the usage of an additional **stuttering transition**: this rule allows the environmental variables to change value arbitrarily, while not changing the values of the array in the prophecies.

5.1   Abstraction Computation

Let an array-based transition system C and a universal invariant Φ be given[3]. By conjoining Φ to the transition rules in C, we obtain C_Φ, the guard strengthening of C with respect to Φ. Then, we define two sets of variables: the prophecy variables $\underline{p}$, in number determined by Proposition 2, and the environmental variables $\underline{x}$, in number determined by the greatest existential quantification depth in the transition rules of C_Φ. While the prophecies are frozen variables, the interpretation of the environmental variables is not fixed. Moreover, we assume that the values taken by $\underline{p}$ and $\underline{x}$ are different. We now define $\tilde{C}$, the parameter abstraction of C.

Initial formula Let $\iota(a)$ be $\forall \underline{i}.\phi(\underline{i}, a[\underline{i}])$, the initial formula of C in prenex form, with $\phi(\underline{i}, a[\underline{i}])$ quantifier-free. The initial formula of the abstract system is a quantifier-free first order formula, denoted $\tilde{\iota}(\underline{p}, a[\underline{p}])$ obtained by instantiating all the universal quantifiers in ι over the set of prophecy variables $\underline{p}$.

Transition formula The transition formula of C_Φ is still represented by a disjunction of formulae of the form[4]

$$\tau(a, a') \stackrel{\text{def}}{=} \exists \underline{i} \forall \underline{j}.\psi(\underline{i}, \underline{j}, a[\underline{i}], a[\underline{j}], a'[\underline{i}], a'[\underline{j}]).$$

For simplicity, we can assume that we have only one rule $\tau(a, a')$. First, we compute the set of all substitutions of the $\underline{i}$ over $\underline{p} \cup \underline{x}$, and we consider the set of formulae $\{\tilde{\tau}_j(\underline{p}, \underline{x}, a, a')\}$, where j ranges over the substitutions, and $\tilde{\tau}_j$ is the result of applying the substitution to τ.

Then, for each formula in the set $\{\tilde{\tau}_j\}$, we instantiate the universal quantifiers over the set $\underline{p} \cup \underline{x}$, obtaining a quantifier-free formula over prophecy and environmental variables.

Moreover, we consider an additional transition formula, called the **stuttering transition**, defined by:

$$\tilde{\tau}_S \stackrel{\text{def}}{=} \bigwedge_{p \in \underline{p}} a'[p] = a[p] \wedge p' = p$$

---

[3] These represent the system and the property in input to each iteration of the loop.
[4] Possibly by performing trivial logical manipulations to distribute the guard strengthening inside the rules.

The disjunction of all the abstracted transition formulae is the transition formula $\tilde{\tau}$. So, we can now define the transition system

$$\tilde{C} \stackrel{\text{def}}{=} (\{a, \underline{p}, \underline{x}\}, \tilde{\iota}(\underline{p}, a[\underline{p}]), \tilde{\tau}(\underline{p}, \underline{x}, a[\underline{p} \cup \underline{x}], a'[\underline{p} \cup \underline{x}])).$$

Example 2. We apply the abstraction procedure to the transition rule 2 of the token in the ring protocol of Example 1.

Since the invariant is the formula $\forall i, j. \neg(s[i] = critical \wedge s[j] = critical)$ it follows that we have two prophecy variables p_1, p_2. Recall that the invariant itself is added to the transition as an additional conjunct. Since the existential quantification depth is one, we have only one environment variable x_1. In the abstraction system we obtain three transition formulae from the original transition; we report the one indexed by the substitution mapping i into x_1; such a formula is equivalent to the following:

$$s[x_1] = crit \wedge t[x_1] = true \wedge s'[x_1] = idle \wedge t'[x_1] = false \wedge$$

$$\bigwedge_{j \in \{p_1, p_2\}} \begin{cases} \textbf{if } j = 1 \wedge x_1 = length \textbf{ then } s'[j] = s[j] \wedge t'[j] = false \\ \textbf{elif } j = x_1 + 1 \wedge x_1 < length \textbf{ then } s'[j] = s[j] \wedge t'[j] = false \\ \textbf{else } s'[j] = s[j] \wedge t'[j] = t[j] \end{cases}$$

$$\bigwedge_{\substack{i,j \in \{p_1, p_2, x_1\} \\ i \neq j}} \neg(s[i] = critical \wedge s[j] = critical)$$

5.2 Stuttering Simulation

We define here the stuttering simulation induced by our version of the Parameter Abstraction. The proof of the main theorem can be found in the appendix. The stuttering is induced by $\tilde{\tau}_S$: this is a weaker version than the simulation induced by [15], yet it is sufficient for preserving invariants.

Definition 1 (Stuttering simulation) *Given two symbolic transition systems $C_1 = (\underline{x_1}, \iota_1, \tau_1)$ and $C_2 = (\underline{x_2}, \iota_2, \tau_2)$, with sets of states S_1 and S_2, a stuttering simulation $\mathcal{S}$ is a relation $\mathcal{S} \subset S_1 \times S_2$, such that:*

- *for every $s_1 \in S_1$ such that $s_1 \models \iota_1$, there exists some $s_2 \in S_2$ such that $(s_1, s_2) \in \mathcal{S}$ and $s_2 \models \iota_2$;*
- *for every $(s_1, s_2) \in \mathcal{S}$, and for every $s_1' \in S_1$ such that $s_1 \cup s_1' \models \tau_1$, there exists either some $s_2' \in S_2$ such that $(s_1', s_2') \in \mathcal{S}$ and $s_2 \cup s_2' \models \tau_2$, or some $(s_2', s_2'') \in S_2 \times S_2$ such that $(s_1', s_2'') \in \mathcal{S}$, and $s_2 \cup s_2' \models \tau_2$, $s_2' \cup s_2'' \models \tau_2$.*

If such a relation exists, we say that C_2 stutter simulates C_1.

We write $\mathcal{S}(s_1)$ for $\{s_2 | (s_1, s_2)\} \in \mathcal{S}$. We recall that stutter simulation preserves reachability, i.e. if C_2 stutter simulates C_1, then if s_1 is reachable in C_1 then the set $\mathcal{S}(s_1)$ is reachable in C_2. Formally, the stuttering simulation induced by the Parameter Abstraction is defined as follows.

Definition 2 (Simulation) *Let C be the original transition system and let $\tilde{C}$ be its Parameter Abstraction. Let s and $\tilde{s}$ denote states of C and $\tilde{C}$, respectively. We define $\mathcal{S}$ as follows:*

$$\mathcal{S}(s, \tilde{s}) \text{ iff } s(a)[i] = \tilde{s}(a)[i] \text{ for all } i \in \bigcup_{p \in \underline{p}} \tilde{s}(p).$$

Intuitively, we require that in the concrete state s and the abstract state $\tilde{s}$, the array is interpreted in the same way for all the locations referred by the prophecy variables. We then have the following:

Theorem 3. *The relation $\mathcal{S}$ is a stuttering simulation between C and $\tilde{C}$. Moreover, if $\tilde{C} \models \Phi(\underline{p}, a[\underline{p}])$, then $C \models \Phi(\underline{p}, a[\underline{p}])$.*

6 Refinement

If $\Phi(\underline{p}, a[\underline{p}])$ does not hold in $\tilde{C}$, in general we cannot conclude anything, since the abstraction could be too coarse. So, if an abstract counterexample is encountered, we try to explore a small instance of the system to see if this counterexample occurs in it. To choose the appropriate size, our algorithm keeps a counter d, whose value is equal to the size to explore. Initially, d is equal to the number of (universally-quantified) index variables in the property Φ.[5] When an abstract counterexample is encountered, we check whether $C^d \models (\Phi \wedge \Psi)^d$. For this check, we use a model checker able to return, in case of success, an inductive invariant I^d. From the inductive invariant we compute some first order formulae J which will be a new set of candidate lemmas. We will see later how to obtain this generalization. After computing the new lemmas, we set $d = d + 1$. If a concrete counterexample is found, then there are two cases: (i) the counterexample falsifies the original property, and we exit from the algorithm with a concrete counterexample; (ii) the counterexample falsifies some lemmas; in this case we remove the lemma and restart the loop (without changing d).

6.1 From Invariants to Universal Lemmas

Definition 3 *Let d be an integer, and let I^d be a set of clauses containing d variables. A generalization of I^d is a first-order formula J such that, when evaluating the quantifiers in J in a domain with precisely d elements, we obtain a formula equivalent to I^d.*

We use the following technique for generalization. Suppose that I^d is in CNF, and that we used $c_1, \dots, c_d$ as variables for an instance with d elements. Then, $I^d = \mathcal{C}_1 \wedge \cdots \wedge \mathcal{C}_n$ is a conjunction of clauses. From each of those clauses we

---

[5] Recall that we assume that quantified index variables are required to be different. Therefore, the property holds vacuously on instances of size smaller than the number of index variables in Φ.

will obtain a new candidate lemma. Let $AllDiff(\underline{i})$ be the formula which states that all variables in $\underline{i}$ are different from each other. Since every C^d is given by a symmetric presentation [15], we have that, for every $i \in \{1, \ldots, n\}$, $C^d \models \forall i_1, \ldots, i_h.AllDiff(i_1, \ldots, i_h) \rightarrow C_i(i_1, \ldots, i_h)$, where the quantifiers range over $c_1, \ldots, c_d$ and $h \leq d$ is the number of variables which occur in C_i. This means that $J \stackrel{\text{def}}{=} \bigwedge_i \forall \underline{i}.AllDiff(\underline{i}) \rightarrow C_i(\underline{i})$ is a generalization of I^d. In our algorithm, we add the set $\{\forall \underline{i}.C_i(\underline{i})\}_{i=1}^n$ of new candidate lemmas to Ψ. Note that we omitted the formula $AllDiff$ for our assumption on the different values of index variables.

Fixing Unsound Lemmas Unfortunately, we know a priori that a lemma holds only for the instance from which it was generalized. In general, its universal generalization obtained as outlined above might not hold in the system.

Suppose that the formula ψ_1 is a candidate lemma, obtained by generalization after the successful verification of an instance of size d. Suppose that later, a counterexample for ψ_1 is found by exploring a different instance $C^{d'}$ (with $d' > d$). This means that the lemma ψ_1 does not hold universally, but only for some finite instances of the system (including C^d), and not in general. In this case, we simply remove ψ_1 from the set of candidate lemmas Ψ, thus effectively weakening our working property (from $\Phi \wedge \Psi$ to $\Phi \wedge (\Psi \setminus \{\psi_1\})$). While this may cause a particular (abstract) counterexample to be encountered more than once during the main loop of the algorithm, since the finite instances are explored monotonically and their size d is increased after every successful verification of a bounded instance, the overall procedure still makes progress by exploring increasingly-large instances of the system. The hope is that eventually the algorithm will discover enough good lemmas that block the abstract counterexample. This notion of (weak) progress is justified by the following:

Proposition 4 *Let $\tilde{\pi}$ be an abstract counterexample, Ψ be the current set of universally quantified lemmas, and d be the size of the bounded instance to explore. During every execution of the algorithm, the same triple $(\tilde{\pi}, \Psi, d)$ never occurs twice.*

7 Related Work

Parametric verification is a challenging problem, and there is a large body of work in the literature devoted to this problem. Here, we (necessarily) focus on the approaches that are most related to ours.

Several methods are based on quantifier elimination using decidable fragments of first order logic, with notable examples in [7, 10, 22]. These methods guarantee a high degree of automation, but typically impose strong syntactic requirements in the input problem, and may suffer from scalability issues. A second popular approach is based on abstraction and abstraction refinement. Within this family of abstractions, earlier versions of the Paramater Abstraction [3, 15] have been used successfully also for industrial protocols [24]. The main drawback is that the degree of automation is limited, and substantial expertise is required to obtain the desired results. The first steps of our abstraction algorithm are inspired by the ones in [19] and [15]. The key difference from [19] is that in that work the abstract transition system $\tilde{C}$ is given by an eager propositional abstraction, with the axioms of the background theories recovered by the usage of some schemata. Here we retain the theory of arrays in the abstract space $\tilde{C}$. Moreover, differently from both [15] and [19], our procedure includes an automatic refinement of the abstraction in a counterexample-driven manner.

Ivy [20, 22] implements both semi-automatic invariant checking with decidable logics (namely, Effectively Propositional Logic – EPR) and compositional abstraction with eager axioms [19]. MYPYVY [13,14] is a model checker inspired by the language of Ivy. It implements a version of IC3 capable of dealing with universal formulas [13]; the algorithm is completely automatic, but it is still based on quantifier elimination via reduction to decidable logics. In a more recent work, MYPYVY has gained the capability of inferring invariants with quantifier alternations, using a procedure that combines separators and first-order logic [14]. At the moment, our framework is capable of handling only universally quantified invariants. On the other hand, our approach is not limited to EPR, but it can in principle handle formulae with arbitrary SMT theories.

Exploring small instances of a parameterized system for candidate lemmas is a popular approach for parametric verification. In [8], this idea is used to over-approximate backward reachable states inside an algorithm which combines backward search and quantifier elimination. In [16], a finite-instance exploration is used together with a theorem prover to check the validity of candidate lemmas. In [17], candidate invariants are obtained from the set of reachable states of small instances. Similarly to our approach, these lemmas are used to strengthen an earlier version of the parameter abstraction. However, human intervention is still needed for the refinement.

A similar approach is presented in [23], where lemmas are obtained from a generalization of the proof of the property in a small instance of the protocol. The main difference with our technique, besides the methods used to extract such invariants, is the following: in [23], the authors show that to prove that a property (conjoined with lemmas) is inductive for all N, it is enough to prove that it is inductive for a particular N_0, which is computable from the number of variables in the description of the system. This result is obtained from the imposed syntactic structure of the system. On the other hand, we impose less structure, and we rely on proving the property in an abstract version (and not a concrete instance) of the system. Moreover, our approach is integrated in an abstraction/refinement loop, which is missing from [23].

Another SMT-based approach for parametric verification is in [12]. The method is based on a reduction of invariant checking to the satisfiability of non-linear Constrained Horn Clauses (CHCs). Besides differing substantially in the overall approach, the method is more restrictive in the input language, and handles invariants only with a specific syntactic structure.

The use of prophecy variables for inferring universally quantified invariants has been explored also in non-parametric contexts, such as [18]. The main difference with our work is that [18] focuses on finding quantified invariants for quantifier-free transition systems with arrays, rather than array-based systems with quantifiers. The overall abstraction-refinement approach is also substantially different.

8 Experimental Evaluation

We have implemented our algorithm in a tool called LAMBDA (for **L**earning **A**bstractions fro**M** Bounde**D** **A**nalysis). LAMBDA is written in Python, and uses the SMT-based IC3 with implicit predicate abstraction of [4] as underlying quantifier-free verification engine.[6] LAMBDA accepts as input array-based systems specified either in the language of MCMT [11] or in VMT format (a light-weight extension of SMT-LIB to model transition systems [25]). In case of successful termination, LAMBDA generates either a counterexample trace (for violated properties) in a concrete instance of the parametric system, or a quantified inductive invariant that proves the property for any instance of the system. In the latter case, LAMBDA can also generate proof obligations that can be independently checked with an SMT solver supporting quantifiers, such as Z3 [21] or CVC4 [2]. More specifically, the quantified inductive invariant can be generated by LAMBDA by simply universally quantifying all the (index) variables in the inductive invariant generated for $\tilde{C}$, and conjoining it with the lemmas Ψ discovered during the main loop iterations. Computing such an invariant is immediate after the termination of the algorithm, and does not require additional reasoning.

In order to evaluate the effectiveness of our method, we have compared LAMBDA with two state-of-the-art tools for the verification of array-based systems, namely CUBICLE [7] and MCMT. We could not include MYPYVY in the comparison, due to the many differences in input languages and modeling formalisms, which make an automatic translation of the benchmarks very difficult. We would also have liked to compare with the technique of [12], however the prototype tool mentioned in the paper doesn't seem to be available.

For our evaluation, we have collected a total of 116 benchmarks, divided in three different groups:

Protocols consists of 42 instances taken from the MCMT or the CUBICLE distributions, and used in previous works on verifcation of array-based systems. We have used all the instances which were available in both input formats, and we have split benchmarks containing multiple properties into different files.

DynArch consists of 57 instances of verification problems of dynamic architectures, taken from [6]. These benchmarks make use of arithmetic constraints on

---

[6] In our implementation, we use the theory of integers as an index theory. At first, this may seem odd, since we should consider all finite subsets of the integers. However, this is not a problem, since the satisfiability of a quantifier-free UFLIA formula is equivalent to its satisfiability in a finite index model.

Table 1. Summary of experimental results.

Benchmark family	# of instances	Lambda		MCMT		Cubicle	
		Solved	Unique	Solved	Unique	Solved	Unique
Protocols	42	34	3	24	0	30	1
DynArch	57	48	5	48	5	–	–
Trains	17	17	–	–	–	–	–

index terms, which are not supported by CUBICLE. Therefore, we could only compare LAMBDA with MCMT on them.

Trains consists of 17 instances derived by (a simplified version of) verification problems on railway interlocking logics [1]. These benchmarks make use of several features that are not fully supported by CUBICLE and MCMT (such as non-functional updates in the transition relation, transition rules with more than one universally-quantified variable, real-valued variables). None of such restrictions applies to LAMBDA, which in general accepts models with significatly fewer syntactic constraints than CUBICLE and MCMT. Since these instances are inspired by relevant real-world verification problems, we believe that it is interesting to include them in the evaluation even though we could only run LAMBDA on them.

Our implementation, all the benchmarks, and the scripts for reproducing the results are available at http://es.fbk.eu/people/griggio/papers/cade21-lambda.tar.gz. We have run our experiments on a cluster of machines with a 2.90GHz Intel Xeon Gold 6226R CPU running Ubuntu Linux 20.04.1, using a time limit of 1 hour and a memory limit of 4GB for each instance. We have used the default settings for MCMT, whereas for CUBICLE we have also enabled the BRAB algorithm.[7] A summary of the results of our evaluation are presented in Table 1. More details are provided in our extended version [5].

Overall, LAMBDA is very competitive with the state of the art, and in fact it solves the largest number of instances (even when disregarding the Trains group, which cannot be handled by the other tools).When considering the Protocols group, CUBICLE is often significantly faster than LAMBDA, especially on easier problems, thanks to its explicit-state exploration component (part of the BRAB algorithm). However, the symbolic techniques used by LAMBDA allow it to generally scale better to larger, more challenging problems: in the end, LAMBDA solves 4 more instances than CUBICLE, and 10 more than MCMT. The situation is different for the DynArch group, in which LAMBDA and MCMT solve the same number of instances. However, it is interesting to observe that both tools can solve 5 instances that the other tool cannot solve; more in general, it seems that the two approaches have somewhat complementary strengths. Moreover, as already stated above, the fact that LAMBDA imposes significantly less syntactic restrictions than the other two tools considered allowed it to handle all the instances of the Trains group, which cannot be easily modeled in the languages of MCMT or CUBICLE.

---

[7] The results reported were obtained using `-brab` 2; we have however experimented also with other (small) values for `-brab`, without noticing any significant difference.

Finally, we wish to remark that we have generated SMT proof obligations for checking the correctness of all the (universally quantified) inductive invariants produced by LAMBDA, and checked them with both CVC4 and Z3. None of the solvers reported any error, and overall the combination of the two solvers was able to successfully verify all the proof obligations for 65 of the 67 instances reported as safe.[8] We believe that the fact that we can easily produce proof obligations that can be independently checked is another strength of our approach. This is in contrast to the approach of CUBICLE, where generating proof obligations is nontrivial [9].

9 Conclusions

In this paper we tackled the problem of universal invariant checking for parametric systems. We proposed a fully-automated abstraction-refinement approach, based on quantifier-free reasoning. The abstract model, that stutter simulates the concrete model, is a quantifier-free symbolic transition system refined by (the instantiation of) candidate universal lemmas. These are obtained by analyzing the proofs of validity of the property in a finite instance of the parametric system. We experimentally evaluated an implementation on standard benchmarks from the literature. The results show the effectiveness of the method, also in comparison with state-of-the-art tools (CUBICLE, MCMT). We are able to prove, in a fully automated manner and without manual intervention, several benchmarks that are considered challenging. In the future, we plan to work on generalization, to improve the ability of inferring the right lemmas from a small instance, and to find more effective ways to filter out bad candidates. On the theoretical side, we will investigate the relation between the termination of the algorithm and decidable classes of parametric systems (e.g. those that enjoy a cut-off property). Finally, we will work on the verification of temporally extended properties which are also preserved by stuttering simulations (such as fragments of Linear Temporal Logic).

References

1. Amendola, A., Becchi, A., Cavada, R., Cimatti, A., Griggio, A., Scaglione, G., Susi, A., Tacchella, A., Tessi, M.: A model-based approach to the design, verification and deployment of railway interlocking system. In: Margaria, T., Steffen, B. (eds.) Leveraging Applications of Formal Methods, Verification and Validation: Applications - 9th International Symposium on Leveraging Applications of Formal Methods, ISoLA 2020, Rhodes, Greece, October 20-30, 2020, Proceedings, Part III. Lecture Notes in Computer Science, vol. 12478, pp. 240–254. Springer (2020)
2. Barrett, C.W., Conway, C.L., Deters, M., Hadarean, L., Jovanovic, D., King, T., Reynolds, A., Tinelli, C.: CVC4. In: CAV. Lecture Notes in Computer Science, vol. 6806, pp. 171–177. Springer (2011)

---

[8] In the remaining two cases, both solvers returned **unknown** when trying to prove the validity of some of the proof obligations.

3. Chou, C.T., Mannava, P.K., Park, S.: A simple method for parameterized verification of cache coherence protocols. In: Hu, A.J., Martin, A.K. (eds.) Formal Methods in Computer-Aided Design. pp. 382–398. Springer Berlin Heidelberg, Berlin, Heidelberg (2004)
4. Cimatti, A., Griggio, A., Mover, S., Tonetta, S.: Infinite-state invariant checking with IC3 and predicate abstraction. Formal Methods Syst. Des. **49**(3), 190–218 (2016)
5. Cimatti, A., Griggio, A., Redondi, G.: Universal Invariant Checking of Parametric Systems with Quantifier-Free SMT Reasoning (extended version). Tech. rep., Fondazione Bruno Kessler (2021), https://es-static.fbk.eu/people/griggio/papers/cade21extended.pdf
6. Cimatti, A., Stojic, I., Tonetta, S.: Formal specification and verification of dynamic parametrized architectures. In: Havelund, K., Peleska, J., Roscoe, B., de Vink, E.P. (eds.) Formal Methods - 22nd International Symposium, FM 2018, Held as Part of the Federated Logic Conference, FloC 2018, Oxford, UK, July 15-17, 2018, Proceedings. Lecture Notes in Computer Science, vol. 10951, pp. 625–644. Springer (2018)
7. Conchon, S., Goel, A., Krstic, S., Mebsout, A., Zaïdi, F.: Cubicle: A Parallel SMT-based Model Checker for Parameterized Systems. In: Parthasarathy, M., Seshia, S.A. (eds.) CAV 2012: Proceedings of the 24th International Conference on Computer Aided Verification. Lecture Notes in Computer Science, Springer Verlag, Berkeley, California, USA (July 2012)
8. Conchon, S., Goel, A., Krstic, S., Mebsout, A., Zaïdi, F.: Invariants for finite instances and beyond. In: Formal Methods in Computer-Aided Design, FMCAD 2013, Portland, OR, USA, October 20-23, 2013. pp. 61–68. IEEE (2013)
9. Conchon, S., Mebsout, A., Zaïdi, F.: Certificates for parameterized model checking. In: FM. Lecture Notes in Computer Science, vol. 9109, pp. 126–142. Springer (2015)
10. Ghilardi, S., Nicolini, E., Ranise, S., Zucchelli, D.: Towards smt model checking of array-based systems. In: Armando, A., Baumgartner, P., Dowek, G. (eds.) Automated Reasoning. pp. 67–82. Springer Berlin Heidelberg, Berlin, Heidelberg (2008)
11. Ghilardi, S., Ranise, S.: Backward reachability of array-based systems by SMT solving: Termination and invariant synthesis. Log. Methods Comput. Sci. **6**(4) (2010)
12. Gurfinkel, A., Shoham, S., Meshman, Y.: Smt-based verification of parameterized systems. In: Proceedings of the 2016 24th ACM SIGSOFT International Symposium on Foundations of Software Engineering. p. 338–348. FSE 2016, Association for Computing Machinery, New York, NY, USA (2016)
13. Karbyshev, A., Bjørner, N., Itzhaky, S., Rinetzky, N., Shoham, S.: Property-directed inference of universal invariants or proving their absence. In: Kroening, D., Păsăreanu, C.S. (eds.) Computer Aided Verification. pp. 583–602. Springer International Publishing, Cham (2015)
14. Koenig, J.R., Padon, O., Immerman, N., Aiken, A.: First-order quantified separators. In: Donaldson, A.F., Torlak, E. (eds.) Proceedings of the 41st ACM SIGPLAN International Conference on Programming Language Design and Implementation, PLDI 2020, London, UK, June 15-20, 2020. pp. 703–717. ACM (2020)
15. Krstic, S.: Parametrized system verification with guard strengthening and parameter abstraction (2005)
16. Li, Y., Duan, K., Jansen, D.N., Pang, J., Zhang, L., Lv, Y., Cai, S.: An automatic proving approach to parameterized verification. ACM Trans. Comput. Logic **19**(4) (Nov 2018)

17. Lv, Y., Lin, H., Pan, H.: Computing invariants for parameter abstraction. In: 2007 5th IEEE/ACM International Conference on Formal Methods and Models for Codesign (MEMOCODE 2007). pp. 29–38 (2007)
18. Mann, M., Irfan, A., Griggio, A., Padon, O., Barrett, C.W.: Counterexample-guided prophecy for model checking modulo the theory of arrays. CoRR **abs/2101.06825** (2021)
19. McMillan, K.L.: Eager abstraction for symbolic model checking. In: Chockler, H., Weissenbacher, G. (eds.) Computer Aided Verification. pp. 191–208. Springer International Publishing, Cham (2018)
20. McMillan, K.L., Padon, O.: Ivy: A multi-modal verification tool for distributed algorithms. In: Lahiri, S.K., Wang, C. (eds.) Computer Aided Verification. pp. 190–202. Springer International Publishing, Cham (2020)
21. de Moura, L.M., Bjørner, N.: Z3: an efficient SMT solver. In: TACAS. Lecture Notes in Computer Science, vol. 4963, pp. 337–340. Springer (2008)
22. Padon, O., McMillan, K.L., Panda, A., Sagiv, M., Shoham, S.: Ivy: Safety verification by interactive generalization. SIGPLAN Not. **51**(6), 614–630 (Jun 2016)
23. Pnueli, A., Ruah, S., Zuck, L.D.: Automatic deductive verification with invisible invariants. In: Margaria, T., Yi, W. (eds.) Tools and Algorithms for the Construction and Analysis of Systems, 7th International Conference, TACAS 2001 Held as Part of the Joint European Conferences on Theory and Practice of Software, ETAPS 2001 Genova, Italy, April 2-6, 2001, Proceedings. Lecture Notes in Computer Science, vol. 2031, pp. 82–97. Springer (2001)
24. Talupur, M., Tuttle, M.R.: Going with the flow: Parameterized verification using message flows. In: 2008 Formal Methods in Computer-Aided Design. pp. 1–8 (2008)
25. VMT-LIB. http://www.vmt-lib.org

Open Access This chapter is licensed under the terms of the Creative Commons Attribution 4.0 International License (http://creativecommons.org/licenses/by/4.0/), which permits use, sharing, adaptation, distribution and reproduction in any medium or format, as long as you give appropriate credit to the original author(s) and the source, provide a link to the Creative Commons license and indicate if changes were made.

The images or other third party material in this chapter are included in the chapter's Creative Commons license, unless indicated otherwise in a credit line to the material. If material is not included in the chapter's Creative Commons license and your intended use is not permitted by statutory regulation or exceeds the permitted use, you will need to obtain permission directly from the copyright holder.

Politeness and Stable Infiniteness: Stronger Together

Ying Sheng[1]($\boxtimes$) , Yoni Zohar[1] , Christophe Ringeissen[2] , Andrew Reynolds[3] , Clark Barrett[1] , and Cesare Tinelli[3]

[1] Stanford University, Stanford, CA, USA
[2] Université de Lorraine, CNRS, Inria, LORIA, F-54000 Nancy, France
[3] The University of Iowa, Iowa City, IA, USA

Abstract. We make two contributions to the study of polite combination in satisfiability modulo theories. The first is a separation between politeness and strong politeness, by presenting a polite theory that is not strongly polite. This result shows that proving strong politeness (which is often harder than proving politeness) is sometimes needed in order to use polite combination. The second contribution is an optimization to the polite combination method, obtained by borrowing from the Nelson-Oppen method. The Nelson-Oppen method is based on guessing arrangements over shared variables. In contrast, polite combination requires an arrangement over *all* variables of the shared sorts. We show that when using polite combination, if the other theory is stably infinite with respect to a shared sort, only the shared variables of that sort need be considered in arrangements, as in the Nelson-Oppen method. The time required to reason about arrangements is exponential in the worst case, so reducing the number of variables considered has the potential to improve performance significantly. We show preliminary evidence for this by demonstrating a speed-up on a smart contract verification benchmark.

1 Introduction

Solvers for satisfiability modulo theories (SMT) [5] are used in a wide variety of applications. Many of these applications require determining the satisfiability of formulas with respect to a *combination* of background theories. In order to make reasoning about combinations of theories modular and easily extensible, a combination framework is essential. Combination frameworks provide mechanisms for automatically deriving a decision procedure for the combined theories by using the decision procedures for the individual theories as black boxes. To integrate a new theory into such a framework, it then suffices to focus on the decoupled decision procedure for the new theory alone, together with its interface to the generic combination framework.

In 1979, Nelson and Oppen [16] proposed a general framework for combining theories with disjoint signatures. In this framework, a quantifier-free formula in

© The Author(s) 2021
A. Platzer and G. Sutcliffe (Eds.): CADE 2021, LNAI 12699, pp. 148–165, 2021.
https://doi.org/10.1007/978-3-030-79876-5_9

the combined theory is purified to a conjunction of formulas, one for each theory. Each pure formula is then sent to a dedicated theory solver, along with a guessed arrangement (a set of equalities and disequalities that capture an equivalence relation) of the variables shared among the pure formulas. For completeness [15], this method requires all component theories to be stably infinite. While many important theories are stably infinite, some are not, including the widely-used theory of fixed-length bit-vectors. To address this issue, the polite combination method was introduced by Ranise et al. [17], and later refined by Jovanovic and Barrett [12]. In polite combination, one theory must be *polite*, a stronger requirement than stable-infiniteness, but the requirement on the other theory is relaxed: specifically, it need not be stably infinite. The price for this generality is that unlike the Nelson-Oppen method, polite combination requires guessing arrangements over *all* variables of certain sorts, not just the shared ones. At a high level, polite theories have two properties: smoothness and finite witnessability (see Section 2). The polite combination theorem in [17] contained an error, which was identified in [12]. A fix was also proposed in [12], which relies on stronger requirements for finite witnessability. Following Casal and Rasga [8], we call this strengthened version *strong finite witnessability*. A theory that is both smooth and strongly finitely witnessable is called *strongly polite*.

This paper makes two contributions. First, we give an affirmative answer to the question of whether politeness and strong politeness are different notions, by giving an example of a theory that is polite but not strongly polite. The given theory is over an empty signature and has two sorts, and was originally studied in [8] in the context of shiny theories. Here we state and prove the separation of politeness and strong politeness, without using shiny theories. Proving that a theory is strongly polite is harder than proving that it is just polite. This result shows that the additional effort is sometimes needed in order to be able to use the combination theorem from [12]. We show that for empty signatures, at least two sorts are needed to present a polite theory that is not strongly polite. However, for the empty signature with only one sort, there is a finitely witnessable theory that is not strongly finite witnessable. Such a theory cannot be smooth.

Second, we explore different polite combination scenarios, where additional information is known about the theories being combined. In particular, we improve the polite combination method for the case where one theory is strongly polite w.r.t. a set S of sorts and the other is stably infinite w.r.t. a subset $S' \subseteq S$ of the sorts. For such cases, we show that it is possible to perform Nelson-Oppen combination for S' and polite combination for $S \setminus S'$. This means that for the sorts in S', only shared variables need to be considered for the guessed arrangement, which can considerably reduce its size. We also show that the set of shared variables can be reduced for a couple of other variations of conditions on the theories. Finally, we present a preliminary case study using a challenge benchmark from a smart contract verification application. We show that the reduction of shared variables is evident and significantly improves the solving time. Verification of smart contracts using SMT (and the analyzed benchmark in particular) is the main motivation behind the second contribution of this paper.

Related Work: Polite combination is part of a more general effort to replace the stable infiniteness symmetric condition in the Nelson-Oppen approach with a weaker condition. Other examples of this effort include the notions of *shiny* [21], *parametric* [13], and *gentle* [11] theories. Gentle, shiny, and polite theories can be combined à la Nelson-Oppen with any arbitrary theory. Shiny theories were introduced by Tinelli and Zarba [21] as a class of mono-sorted theories. Based on the same principles as shininess, politeness is particularly well-suited to deal with theories expressed in many-sorted logic. Polite theories were introduced by Ranise et al. [17] to provide a more effective combination approach compared to parametric and shiny theories, the former requiring solvers to reason about cardinalities and the latter relying on expensive computations of minimal cardinalities of models. Shiny theories were extended to many-sorted signatures in [17], where there is a sufficient condition for their equivalence with polite theories. For the mono-sorted case, a sufficient condition for the equivalence of shiny theories and strongly polite theories was given by Casal and Rasga [7]. In later work [8], the same authors proposed a generalization of shiny theories to many-sorted signatures different from the one in [17], and proved that it is equivalent to strongly polite theories with a decidable quantifier-free fragment. The strong politeness of the theory of algebraic datatypes [4] was proven in [18]. That paper also introduced *additive witnesses*, that provided a sufficient condition for a polite theory to be also strongly polite. In this paper we present a theory that is polite but not strongly polite. In accordance with [18], the witness that we provide for this theory is not additive.

The paper is organized as follows. Section 2 provides the necessary notions from first-order logic and polite theories. Section 3 discusses the difference between politeness and strong politeness and shows they are not equivalent. Section 4 gives the improvements for the combination process under certain conditions, and Section 5 demonstrates the effectiveness of these improvements for a challenge benchmark. [4]

2 Preliminaries

2.1 Signatures and Structures

We briefly review the usual definitions of many-sorted first-order logic with equality (see [10,19] for more details). A *signature* Σ consists of a set $\mathcal{S}_\Sigma$ (of *sorts*), a set $\mathcal{F}_\Sigma$ of function symbols, and a set $\mathcal{P}_\Sigma$ of predicate symbols. We assume $\mathcal{S}_\Sigma$, $\mathcal{F}_\Sigma$ and $\mathcal{P}_\Sigma$ are countable. Function symbols have arities of the form $\sigma_1 \times \ldots \times \sigma_n \to \sigma$, and predicate symbols have arities of the form $\sigma_1 \times \ldots \times \sigma_n$, with $\sigma_1, \ldots, \sigma_n, \sigma \in \mathcal{S}_\Sigma$. For each sort $\sigma \in \mathcal{S}_\Sigma$, $\mathcal{P}_\Sigma$ includes an *equality symbol* $=_\sigma$ of arity $\sigma \times \sigma$. We denote it by $=$ when σ is clear from context. When $=_\sigma$ are the only symbols in Σ, we say that Σ is *empty*. If two signatures share no symbols except $=_\sigma$ we call them *disjoint*. We assume an underlying countably

---

[4]   Due to space constraints, some proofs are omitted. They can be found in an extended version at https://arxiv.org/abs/2104.11738.

infinite set of variables for each sort. Terms, formulas, and literals are defined in the usual way. For a Σ-formula ϕ and a sort σ, we denote the set of free variables in ϕ of sort σ by $vars_\sigma(\phi)$. This notation naturally extends to $vars_S(\phi)$ when S is a set of sorts. $vars(\phi)$ is the set of all free variables in ϕ. We denote by $QF(\Sigma)$ the set of quantifier-free Σ-formulas.

A Σ-*structure* is a many-sorted structure that provides semantics for the symbols in Σ (but not for variables). It consists of a *domain* σ^A for each sort $\sigma \in \mathcal{S}_\Sigma$, an interpretation f^A for every $f \in \mathcal{F}_\Sigma$, as well as an interpretation P^A for every $P \in \mathcal{P}_\Sigma$. We further require that $=_\sigma$ be interpreted as the identity relation over σ^A for every $\sigma \in \mathcal{S}_\Sigma$. A Σ-*interpretation* $\mathcal{A}$ is an extension of a Σ-structure with interpretations for some set of variables. For any Σ-term α, α^A denotes the interpretation of α in $\mathcal{A}$. When α is a set of Σ-terms, $\alpha^A = \{x^A \mid x \in \alpha\}$. Satisfaction is defined as usual. $\mathcal{A} \models \varphi$ denotes that $\mathcal{A}$ satisfies φ.

A Σ-*theory* $\mathcal{T}$ is a class of all Σ-structures that satisfy some set Ax of Σ-sentences. For each such set Ax, we say that $\mathcal{T}$ is *axiomatized* by Ax. A Σ-interpretation whose variable-free part is in $\mathcal{T}$ is called a $\mathcal{T}$-interpretation. A Σ-formula ϕ is $\mathcal{T}$-satisfiable if $\mathcal{A} \models \phi$ for some $\mathcal{T}$-interpretation $\mathcal{A}$. A set A of Σ-formulas is $\mathcal{T}$-satisfiable if $\mathcal{A} \models \phi$ for every $\phi \in A$. Two formulas ϕ and ψ are $\mathcal{T}$-*equivalent* if they are satisfied by the same $\mathcal{T}$-interpretations.

Note that for any class $\mathcal{C}$ of Σ-structures there is a theory $\mathcal{T}_\mathcal{C}$ that *corresponds* to it, with the same satisfiable formulas: the Σ-theory axiomatized by the set Ax of Σ-sentences that are satisfied in every structure of $\mathcal{C}$. In the examples that follow, we define theories $\mathcal{T}_\mathcal{C}$ implicitly by specifying only the class $\mathcal{C}$, as done in the SMT-LIB 2 standard [2]. This can be done without loss of generality.

Example 1. Let Σ_{List} be a signature of finite lists containing the sorts elem_1, elem_2, and list, as well as the function symbols cons of arity $\text{elem}_1 \times \text{elem}_2 \times \text{list} \rightarrow \text{list}$, car_1 of arity $\text{list} \rightarrow \text{elem}_1$, car_2 of arity $\text{list} \rightarrow \text{elem}_2$, cdr of arity $\text{list} \rightarrow \text{list}$, and nil of arity list. The Σ_{List}-theory $\mathcal{T}_{\text{List}}$ corresponds to an SMT-LIB 2 theory of algebraic datatypes [2,4], where elem_1 and elem_2 are interpreted as some sets (of "elements"), and list is interpreted as finite lists of pairs of elements, one from elem_1 and the other from elem_2. cons is a list constructor that takes two elements and a list, and inserts the two elements at the head of the list. The pair $(\text{car}_1(l), \text{car}_2(l))$ is the first entry in l, and $\text{cdr}(l)$ is the list obtained from l by removing its first entry. nil is the empty list. □

Example 2. The signature Σ_{Int} includes a single sort int, all numerals $0, 1, \ldots$, the function symbols $+$, $-$ and $\cdot$ of arity $\text{int} \times \text{int} \rightarrow \text{int}$ and the predicate symbols $<$ and $\leq$ of arity $\text{int} \times \text{int}$. The Σ_{Int}-theory $\mathcal{T}_{\text{Int}}$ corresponds to integer arithmetic in SMT-LIB 2, and the interpretation of the symbols is the same as in the standard structure of the integers. The signature Σ_{BV4} includes a single sort BV4 and various function and predicate symbols for reasoning about bit-vectors of length 4 (such as & for bit-wise *and*, constants of the form 0110, etc.). The Σ_{BV4}-theory $\mathcal{T}_{\text{BV4}}$ corresponds to SMT-LIB 2 bit-vectors of size 4, with the expected semantics of constants and operators. □

Let Σ_1, Σ_2 be signatures, $\mathcal{T}_1$ a Σ_1-theory, and $\mathcal{T}_2$ a Σ_2-theory. The *combination* of $\mathcal{T}_1$ and $\mathcal{T}_2$, denoted $\mathcal{T}_1 \oplus \mathcal{T}_2$, consists of all $\Sigma_1 \cup \Sigma_2$-structures $\mathcal{A}$, such that $\mathcal{A}^{\Sigma_1}$ is in $\mathcal{T}_1$ and $\mathcal{A}^{\Sigma_2}$ is in $\mathcal{T}_2$, where $\mathcal{A}^{\Sigma_i}$ is the reduct of $\mathcal{A}$ to Σ_i for $i \in \{1, 2\}$.

Example 3. Let $\mathcal{T}_{\text{IntBV4}}$ be $\mathcal{T}_{\text{Int}} \oplus \mathcal{T}_{\text{BV4}}$. It is the combined theory of integers and bit-vectors. It has all the sorts and operators from both theories. If we rename the sorts elem_1 and elem_2 of Σ_{List} to int and BV4, respectively, we can obtain a theory $\mathcal{T}_{\text{ListIntBV4}}$ defined as $\mathcal{T}_{\text{IntBV4}} \oplus \mathcal{T}_{\text{List}}$. This is the theory of lists of pairs, where each pair consists of an integer and a bit-vector of size 4.   □

The following definitions and theorems will be useful in the sequel.

Theorem 1 (Theorem 9 of [19]). *Let Σ be a signature, and A a set of Σ-formulas that is satisfiable. Then there exists an interpretation $\mathcal{A}$ that satisfies A, in which $\sigma^{\mathcal{A}}$ is countable whenever it is infinite.*[5]

Definition 1 (Arrangement). *Let V be a finite set of variables whose sorts are in S and let $\{V_\sigma \mid \sigma \in S\}$ be a partition of V such that V_σ is the set of variables of sort σ in V. A formula δ is an arrangement of V if*

$$\delta = \bigwedge_{\sigma \in S} (\bigwedge_{(x,y) \in E_\sigma} (x = y) \wedge \bigwedge_{x,y \in V_\sigma, (x,y) \notin E_\sigma} (x \neq y)) ,$$

where E_σ is some equivalence relation over V_σ for each $\sigma \in S$.

The following theorem from [12] is a variant of a theorem from [20].

Theorem 2 (Theorem 2.5 of [12]). *For $i = 1, 2$, let Σ_i be disjoint signatures, $S_i = \mathcal{S}_{\Sigma_i}$ with $S = S_1 \cap S_2$, $\mathcal{T}_i$ be a Σ_i-theory, Γ_i be a set of Σ_i-literals, and $V = vars(\Gamma_1) \cap vars(\Gamma_2)$. If there exist a $\mathcal{T}_1$-interpretation $\mathcal{A}$, a $\mathcal{T}_2$ interpretation $\mathcal{B}$, and an arrangement δ_V of V such that: 1. $\mathcal{A} \models \Gamma_1 \cup \delta_V$; 2. $\mathcal{B} \models \Gamma_2 \cup \delta_V$; and 3. $|A_\sigma| = |B_\sigma|$ for every $\sigma \in S$, then $\Gamma_1 \cup \Gamma_2$ is $\mathcal{T}_1 \oplus \mathcal{T}_2$-satisfiable.*

2.2   Polite Theories

We now give the background definitions necessary for both Nelson-Oppen and polite combination. In what follows, Σ is an arbitrary (many-sorted) signature, $S \subseteq \mathcal{S}_\Sigma$, and $\mathcal{T}$ is a Σ-theory. We start with stable infiniteness and smoothness.

Definition 2 (Stably Infinite). *$\mathcal{T}$ is stably infinite with respect to S if every quantifier-free Σ-formula that is $\mathcal{T}$-satisfiable is also satisfiable in a $\mathcal{T}$-interpretation $\mathcal{A}$ in which $\sigma^{\mathcal{A}}$ is infinite for every $\sigma \in S$.*

Definition 3 (Smooth). *$\mathcal{T}$ is smooth w.r.t. S if for every quantifier-free formula ϕ, $\mathcal{T}$-interpretation $\mathcal{A}$ that satisfies ϕ, and function κ from S to the class of cardinals such that $\kappa(\sigma) \geq |\sigma^{\mathcal{A}}|$ for every $\sigma \in S$, there exists a $\mathcal{T}$-interpretation $\mathcal{A}'$ that satisfies ϕ with $|\sigma^{\mathcal{A}'}| = \kappa(\sigma)$ for every $\sigma \in S$.*

---

[5] In [19] this was proven more generally, for ordered sorted logics.

We identify singleton sets with their single elements when there is no ambiguity (e.g., when saying that a theory is smooth w.r.t. a sort σ).

We next define politeness and related concepts, following the presentation in [18]. Let ϕ be a quantifier-free Σ-formula. A Σ-interpretation $\mathcal{A}$ *finitely witnesses* ϕ *for* $\mathcal{T}$ *w.r.t.* S (or, is a *finite witness of* ϕ *for* $\mathcal{T}$ *w.r.t.* S), if $\mathcal{A} \models \phi$ and $\sigma^{\mathcal{A}} = vars_{\sigma}(\phi)^{\mathcal{A}}$ for every $\sigma \in S$. We say that ϕ is *finitely witnessed for* $\mathcal{T}$ *w.r.t.* S if it is either $\mathcal{T}$-unsatisfiable or has a finite witness for $\mathcal{T}$ w.r.t. S. We say that ϕ is *strongly finitely witnessed for* $\mathcal{T}$ *w.r.t.* S if $\phi \wedge \delta_V$ is finitely witnessed for $\mathcal{T}$ w.r.t. S for every arrangement δ_V of V, where V is any set of variables whose sorts are in S. A function $wit : QF(\Sigma) \to QF(\Sigma)$ is a *(strong) witness for* $\mathcal{T}$ *w.r.t.* S if for every $\phi \in QF(\Sigma)$ we have that: 1. ϕ and $\exists \overrightarrow{w}. wit(\phi)$ are $\mathcal{T}$-equivalent for $\overrightarrow{w} = vars(wit(\phi)) \setminus vars(\phi)$; and 2. $wit(\phi)$ is (strongly) finitely witnessed for $\mathcal{T}$ w.r.t. S. $\mathcal{T}$ is *(strongly) finitely witnessable* w.r.t. S if there exists a computable (strong) witness for $\mathcal{T}$ w.r.t. S. $\mathcal{T}$ is *(strongly) polite w.r.t.* S if it is smooth and (strongly) finitely witnessable w.r.t. S.

3   Politeness and Strong Politeness

In this section, we study the difference between politeness and strong politeness. Since the introduction of strong politeness in [12], it has been unclear whether it is strictly stronger than politeness, that is, whether there exists a theory that is polite but not strongly polite. We present an example of such a theory, answering the open question affirmatively. This result is followed by further analysis of notions related to politeness. This section is organized as follows. In Section 3.1 we reformulate an example given in [12], showing that there are witnesses that are not strong witnesses. We then present a polite theory that is not strongly polite in Section 3.2. The theory is over a signature with two sorts that is otherwise empty. We show in Section 3.3 that politeness and strong politeness are equivalent for empty signatures with a single sort. Finally, we show in Section 3.4 that this equivalence does not hold for finite witnessability alone.

3.1   Witnesses vs. Strong Witnesses

In [12], an example was given for a witness that is not strong. We reformulate this example in terms of the notions that are defined in the current paper, that is, witnessed formulas are not the same as strongly witnessed formulas (Example 4), and witnesses are not the same as strong witnesses (Example 5).

Example 4. Let Σ_0 be a signature with a single sort σ and no function or predicate symbols, and let $\mathcal{T}_0$ be a Σ_0-theory consisting of all Σ_0-structures with at least two elements. Let ϕ be the formula $x = x \wedge w = w$. This formula is finitely witnessed for $\mathcal{T}_0$ w.r.t. σ, but not strongly. Indeed, for $\delta_V \equiv (x = w)$, $\phi \wedge \delta_V$ is not finitely witnessed for $\mathcal{T}_0$ w.r.t. σ: a finite witness would be required to have only a single element and would therefore not be a $\mathcal{T}_0$-interpretation.   □

The next example shows that witnesses and strong witnesses are not equivalent.

Example 5. Take Σ_0, σ, and $\mathcal{T}_0$ as in Example 4, and define $wit(\phi)$ as the function $(\phi \wedge w_1 = w_1 \wedge w_2 = w_2)$ for fresh w_1, w_2. The function is a witness for $\mathcal{T}_0$ w.r.t. σ. However, it is not a strong witness for $\mathcal{T}$ w.r.t. σ.   □

Although the theory $\mathcal{T}_0$ in the above examples does serve to distinguish formulas and witnesses that are and are not strong, it cannot be used to do the same for theories themselves. This is because $\mathcal{T}_0$ is, in fact, strongly polite, via a different witness function.

Example 6. The function $wit'(\phi) = (\phi \wedge w_1 \neq w_2)$, for some $w_1, w_2 \notin vars_\sigma(\phi)$, is a strong witness for $\mathcal{T}_0$ w.r.t. S, as proved in [12].   □

A natural question, then, is whether there is a theory that can separate the two notions of politeness. The following subsection provides an affirmative answer.

3.2   A Polite Theory that is not Strongly Polite

Let Σ_2 be a signature with two sorts σ_1 and σ_2 and no function or predicate symbols (except $=$). Let $\mathcal{T}_{2,3}$ be the Σ_2-theory from [8], consisting of all Σ_2-structures $\mathcal{A}$ such that either $|\sigma_1^{\mathcal{A}}| = 2 \wedge |\sigma_2^{\mathcal{A}}| \geq \aleph_0$ or $|\sigma_1^{\mathcal{A}}| \geq 3 \wedge |\sigma_2^{\mathcal{A}}| \geq 3$ [8].[6]

$\mathcal{T}_{2,3}$ is polite, but is not strongly polite. Its smoothness is shown by extending any given structure with new elements as much as necessary.

Lemma 1. $\mathcal{T}_{2,3}$ *is smooth w.r.t.* $\{\sigma_1, \sigma_2\}$.

For finite witnessability, consider the function wit defined as follows:

$$wit(\phi) := \phi \wedge x_1 = x_1 \wedge x_2 = x_2 \wedge x_3 = x_3 \wedge y_1 = y_1 \wedge y_2 = y_2 \wedge y_3 = y_3 \quad (1)$$

for fresh variables x_1, x_2, and x_3 of sort σ_1 and y_1, y_2, and y_3 of sort σ_2. It can be shown that wit is a witness for $\mathcal{T}_{2,3}$ but there is no strong witness for it.

Lemma 2. $\mathcal{T}_{2,3}$ *is finitely witnessable w.r.t.* $\{\sigma_1, \sigma_2\}$.

Lemma 3. $\mathcal{T}_{2,3}$ *is not strongly finitely witnessable w.r.t.* $\{\sigma_1, \sigma_2\}$.

Lemmas 1 to 3 have shown that $\mathcal{T}_{2,3}$ is polite but is not strongly polite. And indeed, using the polite combination method from [12] with this theory can cause problems. Consider the theory $\mathcal{T}_{1,1}$ that consists of all Σ_2-structures $\mathcal{A}$ such that $|\sigma_1^{\mathcal{A}}| = |\sigma_2^{\mathcal{A}}| = 1$. Clearly, $\mathcal{T}_{1,1} \oplus \mathcal{T}_{2,3}$ is empty, and hence no formula is $\mathcal{T}_{1,1} \oplus \mathcal{T}_{2,3}$-satisfiable. However, denote the formula $true$ by Γ_1 and the formula $x = x$ by Γ_2 for some variable x of sort σ_1. Then $wit(\Gamma_2)$ is $x = x \wedge \bigwedge_{i=1}^{3} x_i = x_i \wedge y_i = y_i$. Let δ be the arrangement $x = x_1 = x_2 = x_3 \wedge y_1 = y_2 = y_3$. It can be shown that $wit(\Gamma_2) \wedge \delta$ is $\mathcal{T}_{2,3}$-satisfiable and $\Gamma_1 \wedge \delta$ is $\mathcal{T}_{1,1}$-satisfiable. Hence the combination method of [12] would consider $\Gamma_1 \wedge \Gamma_2$ to be $\mathcal{T}_{1,1} \oplus \mathcal{T}_{2,3}$-satisfiable, which is impossible. Hence the fact that $\mathcal{T}_{2,3}$ is not strongly polite propagates all the way to the polite combination method.[7]

---

[6] In [8], the first condition is written $|\sigma_1^{\mathcal{A}}| \geq 2$. We use equality as this is equivalent and we believe it makes things clearer.

[7] Notice that $\mathcal{T}_{2,3}$ can be axiomatized using the following set of axioms, given the definitions in Figure 1: $\left\{ \psi_{\geq 2}^{\sigma_1}, \psi_{\geq 3}^{\sigma_2} \right\} \cup \{ \psi_{=2}^{\sigma_1} \rightarrow \neg\psi_{=n}^{\sigma_2} \mid n \geq 3 \}$

$$distinct(x_1, \ldots, x_n) := \bigwedge_{1 \leq i < j <= n} x_i \neq x_j$$

$$\psi^{\sigma}_{\geq n} := \exists x_1, \ldots, x_n.distinct(x_1, \ldots, x_n)$$

$$\psi^{\sigma}_{\leq n} := \exists x_1, \ldots, x_n.\forall y. \bigvee_{i=1}^{n} y = x_i$$

$$\psi^{\sigma}_{=n} := \psi^{\sigma}_{\geq n} \wedge \psi^{\sigma}_{\leq n}$$

Fig. 1. Cardinality formulas for sort σ. All variables are assumed to have sort σ.

Remark 1. An alternative way to separate politeness from strong politeness using $T_{2,3}$ can be obtained through shiny theories, as follows. Shiny theories were introduced in [21] for the mono-sorted case, and were generalized to many-sorted signatures in two different ways in [8] and [17]. In [8], $T_{2,3}$ was introduced as a theory that is shiny according [17], but not according to [8]. Theorem 1 of [8] states that their notion of shininess is equivalent to strong politeness for theories in which the satisfiability problem for quantifier-free formulas is decidable. Since this is the case for $T_{2,3}$, and since it is not shiny according to [8], we get that $T_{2,3}$ is not strongly polite. Further, Proposition 18 of [17] states that every shiny theory (according to their definition) is polite. Hence we get that $T_{2,3}$ is polite but not strongly polite.

We have (and prefer) a direct proof based only on politeness, without a detour through shininess. Note also that [8] dealt only with strongly polite theories and did not study the weaker notion of polite theories. In particular, the fact that strong politeness is different from politeness was not stated nor proved there.

3.3   The Case of Mono-sorted Polite Theories

Theory $T_{2,3}$ includes two sorts but is otherwise empty. In this section, we show that requiring two sorts is essential for separating politeness from strong politeness in otherwise empty signatures. That is, we prove that politeness implies strong politeness otherwise. Let Σ_0 be the signature with a single sort σ and no function or predicate symbols (except $=$). We show that smooth Σ_0-theories have a certain form and conclude strong politeness from politeness.

Lemma 4. *Let T be a Σ_0-theory. If T is smooth w.r.t. σ and includes a finite structure, T is axiomatized by $\psi^{\sigma}_{\geq n}$ from Figure 1 for some $n > 0$.*

Proposition 1. *If T is a Σ_0-theory that is polite w.r.t. σ, then it is strongly polite w.r.t. σ.*

Remark 2. We again note (as we did in Remark 1) that an alternative way to obtain this result is via shiny theories, using [17], which introduced polite theories, as well as [7], which compared strongly polite theories to shiny theories in the mono-sorted case. Specifically, in the presence of a single sort, Proposition 19 of [17] states that:

(∗)   if the question of whether a polite theory over a finite signature contains a finite structure is decidable, the theory is shiny.

In turn, Proposition 1 of [7] states that:

(∗∗) every shiny theory over a mono-sorted signature with a decidable satisfiability problem for quantifier-free formulas is also strongly polite.

It can be shown that the question of whether a polite Σ_0-theory contains a finite structure is decidable. It can also be shown that satisfiability of quantifier-free formulas is decidable for such theories. Using (∗) and (∗∗), we get that in Σ_0-theories, politeness implies strong politeness. As above (Remark 1), we prefer a direct route for showing this result, without going through shiny theories.

3.4   Mono-sorted Finite Witnessability

We have seen that for Σ_0-theories, politeness and strong politeness are the same. Now we show that smoothness is crucial for this equivalence, i.e., that there is no such equivalence between finite witnessability and strong finite witnessability. Let $\mathcal{T}_{\text{Even}}^{\infty}$ be the Σ_0-theory of all Σ_0-structures $\mathcal{A}$ such that $|\sigma^{\mathcal{A}}|$ is even or infinite.[8] Clearly, this theory is not smooth.

Lemma 5. $\mathcal{T}_{\text{Even}}^{\infty}$ is not smooth w.r.t. σ.

We can construct a witness *wit* for $\mathcal{T}_{\text{Even}}^{\infty}$ as follows. Let ϕ be a quantifier-free Σ_0-formula, and let E be the set of all equivalence relations over $vars(\phi) \cup \{w\}$ for some fresh variable w. Let $even(E)$ be the set of all equivalence relations in E with an even number of equivalence classes. Then, $wit(\phi)$ is $\phi \wedge \bigvee_{e \in even(E)} \delta_e$, where for each $e \in even(E)$, δ_e is the arrangement induced by e:

$$\bigwedge_{(x,y) \in e} x = y \;\wedge\; \bigwedge_{x,y \in vars(\phi) \cup \{w\} \wedge (x,y) \notin e} x \neq y$$

It can be shown that *wit* is indeed a witness, and that $\mathcal{T}_{\text{Even}}^{\infty}$ has no strong witness, with a proof similar to that of Lemma 3.

Lemma 6. $\mathcal{T}_{\text{Even}}^{\infty}$ is finitely witnessable w.r.t. σ.

Lemma 7. $\mathcal{T}_{\text{Even}}^{\infty}$ is not strongly finitely witnessable w.r.t. σ.

4   A Blend of Polite and Stably-Infinite Theories

In this section, we show that the polite combination method can be optimized to reduce the search space of possible arrangements. In what follows, Σ_1 and Σ_2 are disjoint signatures, $S = \mathcal{S}_{\Sigma_1} \cap \mathcal{S}_{\Sigma_2}$, $\mathcal{T}_1$ is a Σ_1-theory, $\mathcal{T}_2$ is a Σ_2-theory, Γ_1 is a set of Σ_1-literals, and Γ_2 is a set of Σ_2-literals.

---

[8] Notice that $\mathcal{T}_{\text{Even}}^{\infty}$ can be axiomatized using the set $\{\neg\psi_{=2n+1}^{\sigma} \mid n \in \mathbb{N}\}$.

The Nelson-Oppen procedure reduces the $\mathcal{T}_1 \oplus \mathcal{T}_2$-satisfiability of $\Gamma_1 \cup \Gamma_2$ to the existence of an arrangement δ over the set $V = vars_S(\Gamma_1) \cap vars_S(\Gamma_2)$, such that $\Gamma_1 \cup \delta$ is $\mathcal{T}_1$-satisfiable and $\Gamma_2 \cup \delta$ is $\mathcal{T}_2$-satisfiable. The correctness of this reduction relies on the fact that both theories are stably infinite w.r.t. S. In contrast, the polite combination method only requires a condition (namely strong politeness) from one of the theories, while the other theory is unrestricted and, in particular, not necessarily stably infinite. In polite combination, the $\mathcal{T}_1 \oplus \mathcal{T}_2$-satisfiability of $\Gamma_1 \cup \Gamma_2$ is again reduced to the existence of an arrangement δ, but over a different set $V' = vars_S(wit(\Gamma_2))$, such that $\Gamma_1 \cup \delta$ is $\mathcal{T}_1$-satisfiable and $wit(\Gamma_2) \cup \delta$ is $\mathcal{T}_2$-satisfiable, where wit is a strong witness for $\mathcal{T}_2$ w.r.t. S. Thus, the flexibility offered by polite combination comes with a price. The set V' is potentially larger than V as it contains *all* variables with sorts in S that occur in $wit(\Gamma_2)$, not just those that also occur in Γ_1. Since the search space of arrangements over a set grows exponentially with its size, this difference can become crucial. If $\mathcal{T}_1$ happens to be stably infinite w.r.t. S, however, we can fall back to Nelson-Oppen combination and only consider variables that are shared by the two sets. But what if $\mathcal{T}_1$ is stably infinite only w.r.t. to some proper subset $S' \subset S$? Can this knowledge about $\mathcal{T}_1$ help in finding some set V'' of variables between V and V', such that we need only consider arrangements of V''? In this section we prove that this is possible by taking V'' to include only the variables of sorts in S' that are shared between Γ_1 and $wit(\Gamma_2)$, and all the variables of sorts in $S \setminus S'$ that occur in $wit(\Gamma_2)$. We also identify several weaker conditions on $\mathcal{T}_2$ that are sufficient for the combination theorem to hold.

4.1   Refined Combination Theorem

To put the discussion above in formal terms, we recall the following theorem.

Theorem 3 ([12]). *If $\mathcal{T}_2$ is strongly polite w.r.t. S with a witness wit, then the following are equivalent: 1. $\Gamma_1 \cup \Gamma_2$ is $(\mathcal{T}_1 \oplus \mathcal{T}_2)$-satisfiable; 2. there exists an arrangement δ_V over V, such that $\Gamma_1 \cup \delta_V$ is $\mathcal{T}_1$-satisfiable and $wit(\Gamma_2) \cup \delta_V$ is $\mathcal{T}_2$-satisfiable, where $V = \bigcup_{\sigma \in S} V_\sigma$, and $V_\sigma = vars_\sigma(wit(\Gamma_2))$ for each $\sigma \in S$.*

Our goal is to identify general cases in which information regarding $\mathcal{T}_1$ can help reduce the size of the set V. We extend the definitions of stably infinite, smooth, and strongly finitely witnessable to two sets of sorts rather than one. Roughly speaking, in this extension, the usual definition is taken for the first set, and some cardinality-preserving constraints are enforced on the second set.

Definition 4. *Let Σ be a signature, S_1, S_2 two disjoint subsets of S_Σ, and $\mathcal{T}$ a Σ-theory.*

$\mathcal{T}$ is (strongly) stably infinite w.r.t. (S_1, S_2) if for every quantifier-free Σ-formula ϕ and $\mathcal{T}$-interpretation $\mathcal{A}$ satisfying ϕ, there exists a $\mathcal{T}$-interpretation $\mathcal{B}$ such that $\mathcal{B} \models \phi$, $|\sigma^\mathcal{B}|$ is infinite for every $\sigma \in S_1$, and $|\sigma^\mathcal{B}| \leq |\sigma^\mathcal{A}|$ ($|\sigma^\mathcal{B}| = |\sigma^\mathcal{A}|$) for every $\sigma \in S_2$.

$\mathcal{T}$ is smooth w.r.t. (S_1, S_2) if for every quantifier-free Σ-formula ϕ, $\mathcal{T}$-interpretation $\mathcal{A}$ satisfying ϕ, and function κ from S_1 to the class of cardinals

such that $\kappa(\sigma) \geq |\sigma^A|$ *for each* $\sigma \in S_1$, *there exists a* $\mathcal{T}$-*interpretation* $\mathcal{B}$ *that satisfies* ϕ, *with* $|\sigma^B| = \kappa(\sigma)$ *for each* $\sigma \in S_1$, *and with* $|\sigma^B|$ *infinite whenever* $|\sigma^A|$ *is infinite for each* $\sigma \in S_2$.

$\mathcal{T}$ *is* strongly finitely witnessable *w.r.t.* (S_1, S_2) *if there exists a computable function wit* : $QF(\Sigma) \to QF(\Sigma)$ *such that for every quantifier-free* Σ-*formula* ϕ: *1.* ϕ *and* $\exists \overrightarrow{w}.\, wit(\phi)$ *are* $\mathcal{T}$-*equivalent for* $\overrightarrow{w} = vars(wit(\phi)) \setminus vars(\phi)$; *and 2. for every* $\mathcal{T}$-*interpretation* $\mathcal{A}$ *and arrangement* δ *of any set of variables whose sorts are in* S_1, *if* $\mathcal{A}$ *satisfies* $wit(\phi) \wedge \delta$, *then there exists a* $\mathcal{T}$-*interpretation* $\mathcal{B}$ *that finitely witnesses* $wit(\phi) \wedge \delta$ *w.r.t.* S_1 *and for which* $|\sigma^B|$ *is infinite whenever* $|\sigma^A|$ *is infinite, for each* $\sigma \in S_2$.

Our main result is the following.

Theorem 4. *Let* $S^{si} \subseteq S$ *and* $S^{nsi} = S \setminus S^{si}$. *Suppose* $\mathcal{T}_1$ *is stably infinite w.r.t.* S^{si} *and one of the following holds:*

1. $\mathcal{T}_2$ *is strongly stably infinite w.r.t.* (S^{si}, S^{nsi}) *and strongly polite w.r.t.* S^{nsi} *with a witness wit.*
2. $\mathcal{T}_2$ *is stably infinite w.r.t.* (S^{si}, S^{nsi}), *smooth w.r.t.* (S^{nsi}, S^{si}), *and strongly finitely witnessable w.r.t.* S^{nsi} *with a witness wit.*
3. $\mathcal{T}_2$ *is stably infinite w.r.t.* S^{si} *while smooth and strongly finitely-witnessable w.r.t.* (S^{nsi}, S^{si}) *with a witness wit.*

Then the following are equivalent: 1. $\Gamma_1 \cup \Gamma_2$ *is* $(\mathcal{T}_1 \oplus \mathcal{T}_2)$-*satisfiable; 2. There exists an arrangement* δ_V *over* V *such that* $\Gamma_1 \cup \delta_V$ *is* $\mathcal{T}_1$-*satisfiable, and* $wit(\Gamma_2) \cup \delta_V$ *is* $\mathcal{T}_2$-*satisfiable, where* $V = \bigcup_{\sigma \in S} V_\sigma$, *with* $V_\sigma = vars_\sigma(wit(\Gamma_2))$ *for every* $\sigma \in S^{nsi}$ *and* $V_\sigma = vars_\sigma(\Gamma_1) \cap vars_\sigma(wit(\Gamma_2))$ *for every* $\sigma \in S^{si}$.

All three items of Theorem 4 include assumptions that guarantee that the two theories agree on cardinalities of shared sorts. For example, in the first item, we first shrink the S^{nsi}-domains of the T_2-model using strong finite witnessability, and then expand them using smoothness. But then, to obtain infinite domains for the S^{si} sorts, stable infiniteness is not enough, as we need to maintain the cardinalities of the S^{nsi} domains while making the domains of the S^{si} sorts infinite. For this, the stronger property of strong stable infiniteness is used.

The formal proof of this theorem is provided in Section 4.2, below. Figure 2 is a visualization of the claims in Theorem 4. The theorem considers two variants of strong finite witnessability, two variants of smoothness, and three variants of stable infiniteness. For each of the three cases of Theorem 4, Figure 2 shows which variant of each property is assumed. The height of each bar corresponds to the strength of the property. In the first case, we use ordinary strong finite witnessability and smoothness, but the strongest variant of stable infiniteness; in the second, we use ordinary strong finite witnessability with the new variants of stable infiniteness and smoothness; and for the third, we use ordinary stable infiniteness and the stronger variants of strong finite witnessability and smoothness. The order of the bars corresponds to the order of their usage in the proof of each case. The stage at which stable infiniteness is used determines the required

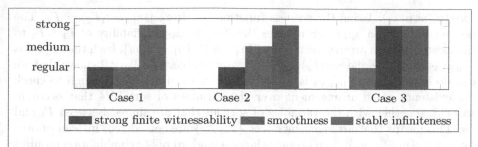

Fig. 2. Theorem 4. The height of each bar corresponds to the strength of the property. The bars are ordered according to their usage in the proof.

strength of the other properties: whatever is used before is taken in ordinary form, and whatever is used after requires a stronger form.

Going back to the standard definitions of stable infiniteness, smoothness, and strong finite witnessability, we get the following corollary by using case 1 of the theorem and noticing that smoothness w.r.t. S implies strong stable infiniteness w.r.t. any partition of S.

Corollary 1. *Let $S^{si} \subseteq S$ and $S^{nsi} = S \setminus S^{si}$. Suppose $\mathcal{T}_1$ is stably infinite w.r.t. S^{si} and $\mathcal{T}_2$ is strongly finitely witnessable w.r.t. S^{nsi} with witness wit and smooth w.r.t. S. Then, the following are equivalent:*
1. $\Gamma_1 \cup \Gamma_2$ is $(\mathcal{T}_1 \oplus \mathcal{T}_2)$-satisfiable; 2. there exists an arrangement δ_V over V such that $\Gamma_1 \cup \delta_V$ is $\mathcal{T}_1$-satisfiable and $wit(\Gamma_2) \cup \delta_V$ is $\mathcal{T}_2$-satisfiable, where $V = \bigcup_{\sigma \in S} V_\sigma$, with $V_\sigma = vars_\sigma(wit(\Gamma_2))$ for $\sigma \in S^{nsi}$ and $V_\sigma = vars_\sigma(\Gamma_1) \cap vars_\sigma(wit(\Gamma_2))$ for $\sigma \in S^{si}$.

Finally, the following result, which is closest to Theorem 3, is directly obtained from Corollary 1, since the strong politeness of $\mathcal{T}_2$ w.r.t. $S^{si} \cup S^{nsi}$ implies that it is strongly finitely witnessable w.r.t. S^{nsi} and smooth w.r.t. $S^{si} \cup S^{nsi}$.

Corollary 2. *Let $S^{si} \subseteq S$ and $S^{nsi} = S \setminus S^{si}$. If $\mathcal{T}_1$ is stably infinite w.r.t. S^{si} and $\mathcal{T}_2$ is strongly polite w.r.t. S with a witness wit, then the following are equivalent: 1. $\Gamma_1 \cup \Gamma_2$ is $(\mathcal{T}_1 \oplus \mathcal{T}_2)$-satisfiable; 2. there exists an arrangement δ_V over V such that $\Gamma_1 \cup \delta_V$ is $\mathcal{T}_1$-satisfiable and $wit(\Gamma_2) \cup \delta_V$ is $\mathcal{T}_2$-satisfiable, where $V = \bigcup_{\sigma \in S} V_\sigma$, with $V_\sigma = vars_\sigma(wit(\Gamma_2))$ for each $\sigma \in S^{nsi}$ and $V_\sigma = vars_\sigma(\Gamma_1) \cap vars_\sigma(wit(\Gamma_2))$ for each $\sigma \in S^{si}$.*

Compared to Theorem 3, Corollary 2 partitions S into S^{si} and S^{nsi} and requires that $\mathcal{T}_1$ be stably infinite w.r.t. S^{si}. The gain from this requirement is that the set V_σ is potentially reduced for $\sigma \in S^{si}$. Note that unlike Theorem 4 and Corollary 1, Corollary 2 has the same assumptions regarding $\mathcal{T}_2$ as the original Theorem 3 from [12]. We show its potential impact in the next example.

Example 7. Consider the theory $\mathcal{T}_{\text{ListIntBV4}}$ from Example 3. Let Γ_1 be $x = 5 \wedge v = 0000 \wedge w = w \mathbin{\&} v$, and let Γ_2 be $a_0 = cons(x, v, a_1) \wedge \bigwedge_{i=1}^{n} a_i =$

$cons(y_i, w, a_{i+1})$. Using the witness function wit from [18], $wit(\Gamma_2) = \Gamma_2$. The polite combination approach reduces the $\mathcal{T}_{\text{ListIntBV4}}$-satisfiability of $\Gamma_1 \wedge \Gamma_2$ to the existence of an arrangement δ over $\{x, v, w\} \cup \{y_1, \ldots, y_n\}$, such that $\Gamma_1 \wedge \delta$ is $\mathcal{T}_{\text{IntBV4}}$-satisfiable and $wit(\Gamma_2) \wedge \delta$ is $\mathcal{T}_{\text{List}}$-satisfiable. Corollary 2 shows that we can do better. Since $\mathcal{T}_{\text{IntBV4}}$ is stably infinite w.r.t. $\{\text{int}\}$, it is enough to check the existence of an arrangement over the variables of sort BV4 that occur in $wit(\Gamma_2)$, together with the variables of sort int that are shared between Γ_1 and Γ_2. This means that arrangements over $\{x, v, w\}$ are considered, instead of over $\{x, v, w\} \cup \{y_1, \ldots, y_n\}$. As n becomes large, standard polite combination requires considering exponentially more arrangements, while the number of arrangements considered by our combination method remains the same.   □

4.2   Proof of Theorem 4

The left-to-right direction is straightforward, using the reducts of the satisfying interpretation of $\Gamma_1 \cup \Gamma_2$ to Σ_1 and Σ_2. We now focus on the right-to-left direction, and begin with the following lemma, which strengthens Theorem 1, obtaining a many-sorted Löwenheim-Skolem Theorem, where the cardinality of the finite sorts remains the same.

Lemma 8. *Let Σ be a signature, $\mathcal{T}$ a Σ-theory, φ a Σ-formula, and $\mathcal{A}$ a $\mathcal{T}$-interpretation that satisfies ϕ. Let $S_\Sigma = S_\mathcal{A}^{fin} \uplus S_\mathcal{A}^{inf}$, where $\sigma^\mathcal{A}$ is finite for every $\sigma \in S_\mathcal{A}^{fin}$ and $\sigma^\mathcal{A}$ is infinite for every $\sigma \in S_\mathcal{A}^{inf}$. Then there exists a $\mathcal{T}$-interpretation $\mathcal{B}$ that satisfies φ such that $|\sigma^\mathcal{B}| = |\sigma^\mathcal{A}|$ for every $\sigma \in S_\mathcal{A}^{fin}$ and $\sigma^\mathcal{B}$ is countable for every $\sigma \in S_\mathcal{A}^{inf}$.*

The proof of Theorem 4 continues with the following main lemma.

Lemma 9 (Main Lemma). *Let $S^{si} \subseteq S$ and $S^{nsi} = S \setminus S^{si}$, Suppose $\mathcal{T}_1$ is stably infinite w.r.t. S^{si} and that one of the three cases of Theorem 4 holds. Further, assume there exists an arrangement δ_V over V such that $\Gamma_1 \cup \delta_V$ is $\mathcal{T}_1$-satisfiable, and $wit(\Gamma_2) \cup \delta_V$ is $\mathcal{T}_2$-satisfiable, where $V = \bigcup_{\sigma \in S} V_\sigma$, with $V_\sigma = vars_\sigma(wit(\Gamma_2))$ for each $\sigma \in S^{nsi}$ and $V_\sigma = vars_\sigma(\Gamma_1) \cap vars_\sigma(wit(\Gamma_2))$ for each $\sigma \in S^{si}$. Then, there is a $\mathcal{T}_1$-interpretation $\mathcal{A}$ that satisfies $\Gamma_1 \cup \delta_V$ and a $\mathcal{T}_2$-interpretation $\mathcal{B}$ that satisfies $wit(\Gamma_2) \cup \delta_V$ such that $|\sigma^\mathcal{A}| = |\sigma^\mathcal{B}|$ for all $\sigma \in S$.*

Proof: Let $\psi_2 := wit(\Gamma_2)$. Since $\mathcal{T}_1$ is stably infinite w.r.t. S^{si}, there is a $\mathcal{T}_1$-interpretation $\mathcal{A}$ satisfying $\Gamma_1 \cup \delta_V$ in which $\sigma^\mathcal{A}$ is infinite for each $\sigma \in S^{si}$. By Theorem 1, we may assume that $\sigma^\mathcal{A}$ is countable for each $\sigma \in S^{si}$. We consider the first case of Theorem 4 (the others are omitted due to space constraints). Suppose $\mathcal{T}_2$ is strongly stably infinite w.r.t. (S^{si}, S^{nsi}) and strongly polite w.r.t. S^{nsi}. Since $\mathcal{T}_2$ is strongly finitely-witnessable w.r.t. S^{nsi}, there exists a $\mathcal{T}_2$-interpretation $\mathcal{B}$ that satisfies $\psi_2 \cup \delta_V$ such that $\sigma^\mathcal{B} = V_\sigma^\mathcal{B}$ for each $\sigma \in S^{nsi}$. Since $\mathcal{A}$ and $\mathcal{B}$ satisfy δ_V, we have that for every $\sigma \in S^{nsi}$, $|\sigma^\mathcal{B}| = |V_\sigma^\mathcal{B}| = |V_\sigma^\mathcal{A}| \leq |\sigma^\mathcal{A}|$. $\mathcal{T}_2$ is also smooth w.r.t. S^{nsi}, and so there exists a $\mathcal{T}_2$-interpretation $\mathcal{B}'$ satisfying $\psi_2 \cup \delta_V$ such that $|\sigma^{\mathcal{B}'}| = |\sigma^\mathcal{A}|$ for each

$\sigma \in S^{nsi}$. Finally, $\mathcal{T}_2$ is strongly stably infinite w.r.t. (S^{si}, S^{nsi}), so there is a $\mathcal{T}_2$-interpretation $\mathcal{B}''$ that satisfies $\psi_2 \cup \delta_V$ such that $\sigma^{\mathcal{B}''}$ is infinite for each $\sigma \in S^{si}$ and $\left|\sigma^{\mathcal{B}''}\right| = \left|\sigma^{\mathcal{B}'}\right| = \left|\sigma^{\mathcal{A}}\right|$ for each $\sigma \in S^{nsi}$. By Lemma 8, we may assume that $\sigma^{\mathcal{B}''}$ is countable for each $\sigma \in S^{si}$. Thus, $\left|\sigma^{\mathcal{B}''}\right| = \left|\sigma^{\mathcal{A}}\right|$ for each $\sigma \in S$.   □

We now conclude Theorem 4: Let $\mathcal{T} := \mathcal{T}_1 \oplus \mathcal{T}_2$. Lemma 9 gives us a $\mathcal{T}_1$ interpretation $\mathcal{A}$ with $\mathcal{A} \models \Gamma_1 \cup \delta_V$ and a $\mathcal{T}_2$ interpretation $\mathcal{B}$ with $\mathcal{B} \models \psi_2 \cup \delta_V$, and $\left|\sigma^{\mathcal{A}}\right| = \left|\sigma^{\mathcal{B}}\right|$ for $\sigma \in S$. Set $\Gamma_1' := \Gamma_1 \cup \delta_V$ and $\Gamma_2' := \psi_2 \cup \delta_V$. Then, $V_\sigma = vars_\sigma(\Gamma_1') \cap vars_\sigma(\Gamma_2')$ for $\sigma \in S$. Now, $\mathcal{A} \models \Gamma_1' \cup \delta_V$ and $\mathcal{B} \models \Gamma_2' \cup \delta_V$. Also, $\left|\sigma^{\mathcal{A}}\right| = \left|\sigma^{\mathcal{B}}\right|$ for $\sigma \in S$. By Theorem 2, $\Gamma_1' \cup \Gamma_2'$ is $\mathcal{T}$-satisfiable. In particular, $\Gamma_1 \cup \{\psi_2\}$ is $\mathcal{T}$-satisfiable, and hence also $\Gamma_1 \cup \{\exists \overline{w}.\psi_2\}$, with $\overline{w} = vars(wit(\Gamma_2)) \setminus vars(\Gamma_2)$. Finally, $\exists \overline{w}.wit(\Gamma_2)$ is $\mathcal{T}_2$-equivalent to Γ_2, hence $\Gamma_1 \cup \Gamma_2$ is $\mathcal{T}$-satisfiable.   □

5   Preliminary Case Study

The results presented in Section 4 was motivated by a set of smart contract verification benchmarks. We obtained these benchmarks by applying the open-source Move Prover verifier [22] to smart contracts found in the open-source Diem project [9]. The Move prover is a formal verifier for smart contracts written in the Move language [6] and was designed to target smart contracts used in the Diem blockchain [1]. It works via a translation to the Boogie verification framework [14], which in turn produces SMT-LIB 2 benchmarks that are dispatched to SMT solvers. The benchmarks we obtained involve datatypes, integers, Booleans, and quantifiers. Our case study began by running CVC4 [3] on the benchmarks. For most of the benchmarks that were solved by CVC4, theory combination took a small percentage of the overall runtime of the solver, accounting for 10% or less in all but 1 benchmark. However, solving that benchmark took 81 seconds, of which 20 seconds was dedicated to theory combination.

We implemented an optimization to the datatype solver of CVC4 based on Corollary 2. With the original polite combination method, every term that originates from the theory of datatypes with another sort is shared with the other theories, triggering an analysis of the arrangements of these terms. In our optimization, we limit the sharing of such terms to those of Boolean sort. In the language of Corollary 2, $\mathcal{T}_1$ is the combined theory of Booleans, uninterpreted functions, and integers, which is stably infinite w.r.t. the uninterpreted sorts and integer sorts. $\mathcal{T}_2$ is an instance of the theory of datatypes, which is strongly polite w.r.t. its element sorts, which in this case are the sorts of $\mathcal{T}_1$.

A comparison of an original and optimized run on the difficult benchmark is shown in Figure 3. As shown, the optimization reduces the total running time by 75%, and the time spent on theory combination in particular by 83%. To further isolate the effectiveness of our optimization, we report the number of terms that each theory solver considered. In CVC4, constraints are not flattened, so shared *terms* are processed instead of shared variables. Each theory solver

	total (s)	comb (s)	DT	INT	UFB	shared
optimized	34.9	3.4	236.1	212.1	78.4	125.8
original	81.5	20.3	116.0	281.0	123.9	163.5

Fig. 3. Runtimes (in seconds) and number of terms (in thousands) added to the data structures of DT, INT, UFB, and the number of shared terms (shared).

maintains its own data structure for tracking equality information. These data structures contain terms belonging to the theory that either come from the input assertions or are shared with another theory. A data structure is also maintained that contains all shared terms belonging to any theory. The last 4 columns of Figure 3 count the number of times (in thousands) a term was added to the equality data structure for the theory of datatypes (DT), integers (INT), and uninterpreted functions and Booleans (UFB), as well as to the the shared term data structure (shared). With the optimization, the datatype solver keeps more inferred assertions internally, which leads to an increase in the number of additions of terms to its data structure. However, sharing fewer terms, reduces the number of terms in the data structures for the other theories. Moreover, while the total number of terms considered remains roughly the same, the number of shared terms decreases by 24%. This suggests that although the workload on the individual theory solvers is roughly similar, a decrease in the number of shared terms in the optimized run results in a significant improvement in the overall runtime. Although our evidence is only anecdotal at the moment, we believe this benchmark is highly representative of the potential benefits of our optimization.

6   Conclusion

This paper makes two contributions. First, we separated politeness and strong politeness, which shows that sometimes, the (typically harder) task of finding a strong witness is not a waste of effort. Then, we provided an optimization to the polite combination method, which applies when one of the theories in the combination is stably infinite w.r.t. a subset of the sorts.

We envision several directions for future work. First, the sepration of politeness from strong politeness demonstrates a need to identify sufficient criteria for the equivalence of these notions — such as, for instance, the *additivity* criterion introduced by Sheng et al. [18]. Second, polite combination might be optimized by applying the witness function only to part of the purified input formula. Finally, we plan to extend the initial implementation of this approach in CVC4 and evaluate its impact based on more benchmarks.

References

1. Amsden, Z., Arora, R., Bano, S., Baudet, M., Blackshear, S., Bothra, A., Cabrera, G., Catalini, C., Chalkias, K., Cheng, E., Ching, A., Chursin, A., Danezis, G., Giacomo, G.D., Dill, D.L., Ding, H., Doudchenko, N., Gao, V., Gao, Z., Garillot, F., Gorven, M., Hayes, P., Hou, J.M., Hu, Y., Hurley, K., Lewi, K., Li, C., Li, Z., Malkhi, D., Margulis, S., Maurer, B., Mohassel, P., de Naurois, L., Nikolaenko, V., Nowacki, T., Orlov, O., Perelman, D., Pott, A., Proctor, B., Qadeer, S., Rain, Russi, D., Schwab, B., Sezer, S., Sonnino, A., Venter, H., Wei, L., Wernerfelt, N., Williams, B., Wu, Q., Yan, X., Zakian, T., Zhou, R.: The Diem Blockchain. https://developers.diem.com/docs/technical-papers/the-diem-blockchain-paper/ (2019)
2. Barrett, C., Fontaine, P., Tinelli, C.: The SMT-LIB Standard: Version 2.6. Tech. rep., Department of Computer Science, The University of Iowa (2017), available at www.SMT-LIB.org
3. Barrett, C.W., Conway, C.L., Deters, M., Hadarean, L., Jovanovic, D., King, T., Reynolds, A., Tinelli, C.: CVC4. In: Gopalakrishnan, G., Qadeer, S. (eds.) Computer Aided Verification - 23rd International Conference, CAV 2011, Snowbird, UT, USA, July 14-20, 2011. Proceedings. Lecture Notes in Computer Science, vol. 6806, pp. 171–177. Springer (2011), https://doi.org/10.1007/978-3-642-22110-1_14
4. Barrett, C.W., Shikanian, I., Tinelli, C.: An abstract decision procedure for a theory of inductive data types. Journal on Satisfiability, Boolean Modeling and Computation 3(1-2), 21–46 (2007)
5. Barrett, C.W., Tinelli, C.: Satisfiability modulo theories. In: Clarke, E.M., Henzinger, T.A., Veith, H., Bloem, R. (eds.) Handbook of Model Checking, pp. 305–343. Springer (2018), https://doi.org/10.1007/978-3-319-10575-8_11
6. Blackshear, S., Cheng, E., Dill, D.L., Gao, V., Maurer, B., Nowacki, T., Pott, A., Qadeer, S., Rain, Russi, D., Sezer, S., Zakian, T., Zhou, R.: Move: A language with programmable resources. https://developers.diem.com/docs/technical-papers/move-paper/ (2019)
7. Casal, F., Rasga, J.: Revisiting the equivalence of shininess and politeness. In: McMillan, K.L., Middeldorp, A., Voronkov, A. (eds.) Logic for Programming, Artificial Intelligence, and Reasoning - 19th International Conference, LPAR-19, Stellenbosch, South Africa, December 14-19, 2013. Proceedings. Lecture Notes in Computer Science, vol. 8312, pp. 198–212. Springer (2013), https://doi.org/10.1007/978-3-642-45221-5_15
8. Casal, F., Rasga, J.: Many-sorted equivalence of shiny and strongly polite theories. J. Autom. Reason. 60(2), 221–236 (2018), https://doi.org/10.1007/s10817-017-9411-y
9. diem: https://github.com/diem/diem
10. Enderton, H.B.: A mathematical introduction to logic. Academic Press (2001)
11. Fontaine, P.: Combinations of theories for decidable fragments of first-order logic. In: Ghilardi, S., Sebastiani, R. (eds.) Frontiers of Combining Systems, 7th International Symposium, FroCoS 2009, Trento, Italy, September 16-18, 2009. Proceedings. Lecture Notes in Computer Science, vol. 5749, pp. 263–278. Springer (2009), https://doi.org/10.1007/978-3-642-04222-5_16
12. Jovanovic, D., Barrett, C.W.: Polite theories revisited. In: Fermüller, C.G., Voronkov, A. (eds.) Logic for Programming, Artificial Intelligence, and Reasoning - 17th International Conference, LPAR-17, Yogyakarta, Indonesia, October 10-15, 2010. Proceedings. Lecture Notes in Computer Science, vol. 6397, pp. 402–416. Springer (2010), https://doi.org/10.1007/978-3-642-16242-8_29

13. Krstic, S., Goel, A., Grundy, J., Tinelli, C.: Combined satisfiability modulo parametric theories. In: Grumberg, O., Huth, M. (eds.) Tools and Algorithms for the Construction and Analysis of Systems, 13th International Conference, TACAS 2007, Held as Part of the Joint European Conferences on Theory and Practice of Software, ETAPS 2007 Braga, Portugal, March 24 - April 1, 2007, Proceedings. Lecture Notes in Computer Science, vol. 4424, pp. 602–617. Springer (2007), https://doi.org/10.1007/978-3-540-71209-1_47

14. Leino, K.R.M.: This is Boogie 2. manuscript KRML **178**(131), 9 (2008), https://www.microsoft.com/en-us/research/publication/this-is-boogie-2-2/

15. Nelson, G.: Techniques for program verification. Tech. Rep. CSL-81-10, Xerox, Palo Alto Research Center (1981)

16. Nelson, G., Oppen, D.C.: Simplification by cooperating decision procedures. ACM Trans. Program. Lang. Syst. **1**(2), 245–257 (1979), https://doi.org/10.1145/357073.357079

17. Ranise, S., Ringeissen, C., Zarba, C.G.: Combining data structures with nonstably infinite theories using many-sorted logic. In: Gramlich, B. (ed.) Frontiers of Combining Systems, 5th International Workshop, FroCoS 2005, Vienna, Austria, September 19-21, 2005, Proceedings. Lecture Notes in Computer Science, vol. 3717, pp. 48–64. Springer (2005), extended technical report is available at https://hal.inria.fr/inria-00070335/

18. Sheng, Y., Zohar, Y., Ringeissen, C., Lange, J., Fontaine, P., Barrett, C.W.: Politeness for the theory of algebraic datatypes. In: Peltier, N., Sofronie-Stokkermans, V. (eds.) Automated Reasoning - 10th International Joint Conference, IJCAR 2020, Paris, France, July 1-4, 2020, Proceedings, Part I. Lecture Notes in Computer Science, vol. 12166, pp. 238–255. Springer (2020), https://doi.org/10.1007/978-3-030-51074-9_14

19. Tinelli, C., Zarba, C.G.: Combining decision procedures for sorted theories. In: Alferes, J.J., Leite, J.A. (eds.) Logics in Artificial Intelligence, 9th European Conference, JELIA 2004, Lisbon, Portugal, September 27-30, 2004, Proceedings. Lecture Notes in Computer Science, vol. 3229, pp. 641–653. Springer (2004)

20. Tinelli, C., Zarba, C.G.: Combining decision procedures for sorted theories. In: Alferes, J.J., Leite, J.A. (eds.) Logics in Artificial Intelligence, 9th European Conference, JELIA 2004, Lisbon, Portugal, September 27-30, 2004, Proceedings. Lecture Notes in Computer Science, vol. 3229, pp. 641–653. Springer (2004), https://doi.org/10.1007/978-3-540-30227-8_53

21. Tinelli, C., Zarba, C.G.: Combining nonstably infinite theories. J. Autom. Reason. **34**(3), 209–238 (2005), https://doi.org/10.1007/s10817-005-5204-9

22. Zhong, J.E., Cheang, K., Qadeer, S., Grieskamp, W., Blackshear, S., Park, J., Zohar, Y., Barrett, C.W., Dill, D.L.: The Move prover. In: Lahiri, S.K., Wang, C. (eds.) Computer Aided Verification - 32nd International Conference, CAV 2020, Los Angeles, CA, USA, July 21-24, 2020, Proceedings, Part I. Lecture Notes in Computer Science, vol. 12224, pp. 137–150. Springer (2020), https://doi.org/10.1007/978-3-030-53288-8_7

165   Y. Sheng et al.

Open Access This chapter is licensed under the terms of the Creative Commons Attribution 4.0 International License (http://creativecommons.org/licenses/by/4.0/), which permits use, sharing, adaptation, distribution and reproduction in any medium or format, as long as you give appropriate credit to the original author(s) and the source, provide a link to the Creative Commons license and indicate if changes were made.

The images or other third party material in this chapter are included in the chapter's Creative Commons license, unless indicated otherwise in a credit line to the material. If material is not included in the chapter's Creative Commons license and your intended use is not permitted by statutory regulation or exceeds the permitted use, you will need to obtain permission directly from the copyright holder.

Equational Theorem Proving Modulo

Dohan Kim$^{(\boxtimes)}$ and Christopher Lynch

Clarkson University, Potsdam, NY, USA
{dohkim,clynch}@clarkson.edu

Abstract. Unlike other methods for theorem proving modulo with constrained clauses [12, 13], equational theorem proving modulo with constrained clauses along with its simplification techniques has not been well studied. We introduce a basic paramodulation calculus modulo equational theories E satisfying certain properties of E and present a new framework for equational theorem proving modulo E with constrained clauses. We propose an inference rule called Generalized E-Parallel for constrained clauses, which makes our inference system completely basic, meaning that we do not need to allow any paramodulation in the constraint part of a constrained clause for refutational completeness. We present a saturation procedure for constrained clauses based on relative reducibility and show that our inference system including our contraction rules is refutationally complete.

1 Introduction

Equations occur frequently in many areas of mathematics, logics, and computer science. Equational theorem proving [6, 8, 19, 22] is, in general, concerned with proving mathematical or logical statements in first-order clause logic with equality. While resolution [24] has been successful for theorem proving for first-order clause logic without equality, it has some limitations to deal with the equality predicate. For example, when dealing with the equality predicate using resolution, one must add the congruence axioms explicitly for each predicate and function symbol in order to express the properties of equality [8, 22].

Paramodulation [23] is based on the replacement of equals by equals, in order to improve the efficiency of resolution in equational theorem proving. However, paramodulation, in general, often produces a large amount of unnecessary clauses, so the search space for a refutation expands very rapidly. Therefore, various improvements have been developed for paramodulation. For example, it was shown that the functional reflexivity equations used by the traditional paramodulation rule [23] are not needed, and paramodulation into variables does not need to be allowed (see [8]).

Basic paramodulation [9,20] restricts paramodulation by forbidding paramodulation at (sub)terms introduced by substitutions from previous inference steps, and uses orderings on terms and literals in order to further restrict paramodulation inferences. In [21, 26], basic paramodulation had been extended to basic paramodulation modulo associativity and commutativity (AC) axioms.

© The Author(s) 2021
A. Platzer and G. Sutcliffe (Eds.): CADE 2021, LNAI 12699, pp. 166–182, 2021.
https://doi.org/10.1007/978-3-030-79876-5_10

(See [25] also for basic paramodulation modulo the associativity (A) axiom.) Basic paramodulation modulo AC uses the symbolic constraints, overcoming a drawback of traditional paramodulation modulo AC (see [7,27]) that often generates many slightly different permuted variants of clauses. For example, more than a million conclusions can possibly be generated by paramodulating the equation $x + x + x = x$ into the clause $P(y_1 + y_2 + y_3 + y_4)$ for which $+$ is an AC symbol, since a minimal complete set of AC-unifiers for $x + x + x$ and $y_1 + y_2 + y_3 + y_4$ contains more than a million AC-unifiers [21, 26]. On the other hand, one only needs a single conclusion $P(x) \, \| \, x + x + x \approx^?_{AC} y_1 + y_2 + y_3 + y_4$ for the above inference using basic paramodulation modulo AC with an equality constraint.

In this paper, we present a new basic paramodulation calculus modulo equational theories E (including $E = AC$) parameterized by a suitable E-compatible ordering $\succ$. Our main inference rule for basic paramodulation modulo E is given (roughly) as follows:

$$\frac{C \vee s \approx t \, \| \, \phi_1 \qquad D \vee L[s'] \, \| \, \phi_2}{C \vee D \vee L[t] \, \| \, s \approx^?_E s' \wedge \phi_1 \wedge \phi_2}$$

The equality constraints are inherited and the accumulated E-unification problems are kept in the constraint part of conclusion. Instead of generating as many conclusions as minimal and complete E-unifiers of two terms s and s', a single conclusion is generated with its constraint keeping the E-unification problem of s and s'. Another key inference rule in our basic paramodulation calculus modulo E is the Generalized E-Parallel (or E-Parallel) rule, adapted from our recent work on basic narrowing modulo [18]. This rule allows our basic paramodulation calculus to adapt the free case (i.e. $E = \emptyset$) to the modulo E case (i.e. $E \neq \emptyset$).[1] For example, suppose that we have three clauses $1 : a + b \approx c$, $2 : a + (b + x) \approx c + x$, and $3 : (a + a) + (b + b) \not\approx c + c$, where $+$ is an AC symbol with $+ \succ a \succ b \succ c$. We use the E-Parallel rule from clause 1 and 2 and obtain the clause $4 : a + (b + (a + b)) \approx c + c$, which derives a contradiction with clause 3 because $a + (b + (a + b)) \approx_{AC} (a + a) + (b + b)$ (i.e. the equality constraint is satisfiable). The details of this inference rule are discussed in Section 4.

Throughout this paper, we assume that (i) we are given an E-compatible reduction ordering $\succ$ on terms with the subterm property that is E-total on ground terms, (ii) E has a finitary and complete unification algorithm, and (iii) E-congruence classes are finite. (If E satisfies condition (i), then E is necessarily *regular* [2].) With these assumptions of E, we can deal uniformly with different equational theories E in our framework and show that our inference system including our contraction rules is refutationally complete.

The known practical theories satisfying the above assumptions of E are AC and finite *permutation theories* [1, 17]. (For example, if one considers an ACI symbol $+$ using our approach, then AC should be a modulo E part and the idempotency axiom $(I : x + x \approx x)$ should be a part of the input formulas.) Although associative (A)-unification is infinitary, our approach is also applicable

---

[1] If $E = \emptyset$, then we may disregard the Generalized E-Parallel (or E-Parallel) rule along with the E-Completion rule and replace E-unification with syntactic unification.

to the case where $E = A$ in practice, since there is a tool for A-unification which is guaranteed to terminate with a finite and complete set of A-unifiers for a significantly large class of A-unification problems (see [14]).

The longer version of this paper is found in [16].

2 Preliminaries

We assume that the reader has some familiarity with rewrite systems [3] (including the *extended rewrite system* for R *modulo* E (i.e. R, E) [11, 15]) and unification [4]. We use the standard terminology of paramodulation [6,9,22].

We denote by $T(\mathcal{F}, \mathcal{X})$ the set of terms over a finite set of function symbols $\mathcal{F}$ and a denumerable set of variables $\mathcal{X}$. An *equation* is an expression $s \approx t$, where s and t are (first-order) terms built from $T(\mathcal{F}, \mathcal{X})$. A *literal* is either an equation L (a *positive literal*) or a negative equation $\neg L$ (a *negative literal*). A *clause* is a finite multiset of literals, written as a disjunction of literals $\neg A_1 \vee \cdots \vee \neg A_m \vee B_1 \vee \cdots \vee B_n$ or as an implication $\Gamma \to \Delta$, where the multiset Γ is called the *antecedent* and the multiset Δ is called the *succedent* of the clause. (Recall that a *multiset* is an unordered collection with possible duplicate elements.)

An *equational theory* is a set of equations. (In this paper, an equational theory and a set of axioms are used interchangeably.) We denote by $\approx_E$ the least congruence on $T(\mathcal{F}, \mathcal{X})$ that is closed under substitutions and contains a set of equations E. If $s \approx_E t$ for two terms s and t, then s and t are *E-equivalent*.

A (strict) ordering $\succ$ on terms is *monotonic* if $s \succ t$ implies $u[s]_p \succ u[t]_p$ for all s, t, u and positions p. An ordering $\succ$ on terms is *stable under substitutions* if $s \succ t$ implies $s\sigma \succ t\sigma$ for all s, t, and substitutions σ. An ordering $\succ$ on terms is a *rewrite ordering* if it is monotonic and stable under substitutions. A well-founded rewrite ordering is a *reduction ordering*. An ordering $\succ$ on terms has the *subterm property* if $t[s]_p \succ s$ for all s, t, and $p \neq \lambda$. (In this paper, λ denotes the top position.) A *simplification ordering* is a rewrite ordering with the subterm property. An ordering $\succ$ on terms is *E-compatible* if $s \succ t$, $s \approx_E s'$, and $t \approx_E t'$ implies $s' \succ t'$ for all s, s', t and t'. An ordering $\succ$ on ground terms is *E-total* if $s \not\approx_E t$ implies $s \succ t$ or $t \succ s$ for all ground terms s and t.

Given a multiset S and an E-compatible ordering $\succ$ on S, we say that x is *maximal* (resp. *strictly maximal*) in S if there is no $y \in S$ (resp. $y \in S \setminus \{x\}$) with $y \succ x$ (resp. $y \succeq x$).

Clauses may also be considered as multisets of occurrences of equations. An occurrence of an equation $s \approx t$ in the antecedent of a clause is the multiset $\{\{s, t\}\}$, and in the succedent it is the multiset $\{\{s\}, \{t\}\}$. We denote ambiguously all those orderings on terms, equations and clauses by $\succ$.

An equational theory is *permutative* if each equation in the theory contains the same symbols on both sides with the same number of occurrences. The *depth* of a term t is defined as $depth(t) = 0$ if t is a variable or a constant and $depth(f(s_1, \ldots, s_n)) = 1 + \max\{depth(s_i) \mid 1 \leq i \leq n\}$. We say that an *equational theory has maximum depth at most k* if the maximum depth of all terms in the equations in the theory is less than or equal to k.

A *(Herbrand) interpretation* I is a congruence on ground terms. I *satisfies* (is a *model* of) a ground clause $\Gamma \to \Delta$, denoted by $I \models \Gamma \to \Delta$, if $I \not\supseteq \Gamma$ or $I \cap \Delta \neq \emptyset$. In this case, we say that $\Gamma \to \Delta$ is *true* in I. A ground clause C *follows* from a set of ground clauses $\{C_1, \ldots, C_k\} \models C$ if C is true in every model of $\{C_1, \ldots, C_k\}$.

3   Constrained Clauses

Definition 1 (Constrained clauses) [22,26] A *constrained clause* is a pair $C \,\|\, \phi$, where C is a clause and ϕ is an equality constraint consisting of a conjunction of the form $s \approx_E^? t$ for terms s and t. The set of solutions of a constraint ϕ, denoted by $Sol(\phi)$, is the set of the ground substitutions defined inductively as:

$$Sol(\phi_1 \wedge \phi_2) = Sol(\phi_1) \cap Sol(\phi_2),$$
$$Sol(s \approx_E^? t) = \{\sigma \mid s\sigma \text{ and } t\sigma \text{ are } E\text{-equivalent}\},$$

A constraint ϕ is *satisfiable* if it admits at least one solution.

A constrained clause with an unsatisfiable constraint is a tautology. If every ground substitution with domain $Vars(\phi)$ of $C \,\|\, \phi$ is a solution of ϕ, then ϕ is a tautological constraint. An unconstrained clause can also be considered as a constrained clause with a tautological constraint.

The main technical difficulties in lifting a reduced ground inference to an inference at the clause level in a basic paramodulation inference system involve a ground clause of the form $C\sigma := D\sigma \vee x\sigma \approx t\sigma$ with $C := D \vee x \approx t \,\|\, \phi$ and $\sigma \in Sol(\phi)$, where $x\sigma \Rightarrow t\sigma \in R$ for a given ground rewrite system R. This motivates the following definition of irreducibility to lift a reduced ground inference to an inference at the clause level in our inference system. (See [9] also for *order-irreducibility* in the free case.)

Definition 2 (Order-irreducibility) Given a ground rewrite system R and an equational theory E, a ground literal $L[l']_p$ is *order-reducible* (at position p) by R, E with $l \Rightarrow r \in R$ if $l' \approx_E l, l \succ r$ and $L \succ l \approx r$. A literal $L[s]$ is *order-irreducible in s* by R, E if $L[s]$ is not order-reducible at any position of s.

In Definition 2, the condition $L \succ l \approx r$ is always true when L is a negative literal or else l' does not occur at the top (i.e. $p = \lambda$) of the largest term of L.

Definition 3 (Reduced ground instances) Given a ground rewrite system R and an equational theory E, $C\sigma$ is a *ground instance* of $C \,\|\, \phi$ if σ is a solution of ϕ (i.e. $\sigma \in Sol(\phi)$). It is a *reduced ground instance* of $C \,\|\, \phi$ w.r.t. R, E if σ is a solution of ϕ and each ground literal $L[x\sigma]$ in $C\sigma$ is order-irreducible in $x\sigma$ by R, E for each variable $x \in Vars(C)$. In this case, σ is a *reduced solution* of $C \,\|\, \phi$ w.r.t. R, E.

Definition 4 (A model of a constrained clause) An interpretation I *satisfies* (is a *model* of) a constrained clause $C \,\|\, \phi$, denoted by $I \models C \,\|\, \phi$, if it satisfies every ground instance of $C \,\|\, \phi$ (i.e. every $C\sigma$ for which σ is a solution of ϕ).

Definition 5 (Reductiveness, weak reductiveness, semi-reductiveness, and weak maximality) An equation $s \approx t$ is *reductive* (resp. *weakly reductive*) for $C \,\|\, \phi :=$ $D \vee s \approx t \,\|\, \phi$ if there exists a ground instance $C\sigma$ such that $s\sigma \approx t\sigma$ is strictly maximal (resp. maximal) in $C\sigma$ with $s\sigma \succ t\sigma$. The clause $C \,\|\, \phi$ is simply called *reductive* if there exists a reductive equation $s \approx t$ for $C \,\|\, \phi$. A negative equation $u \not\approx v$ is *semi-reductive* (resp. *weakly reductive*) for $C \,\|\, \phi := D \vee u \not\approx v \,\|\, \phi$ if there exists a ground instance $C\sigma$ such that $u\sigma \succ v\sigma$ (resp. $u\sigma \succ v\sigma$ and $u\sigma \not\approx v\sigma$ is maximal in $C\sigma$). A literal L is *weakly maximal* for $C \,\|\, \phi := D \vee L \,\|\, \phi$ if there exists a ground instance $C\sigma$ such that $L\sigma$ is maximal in $C\sigma$.

4   Inference Rules

The inference rules in our inference system are parameterized by a selection function $\mathcal{S}$ and an E-compatible reduction ordering $\succ$ with the subterm property that is E-total on ground terms, where $\mathcal{S}$ selects at most one (occurrence of a) negative literal in the clause part C of each (constrained) clause $C \,\|\, \phi$. For technical convenience, if a literal L is selected in C, then we also say that L is selected in $C \,\|\, \phi$. In our inference rules, a literal in a clause $C \,\|\, \phi$ is involved in some inference if it is selected in C (by $\mathcal{S}$) or nothing is selected and it is maximal in C (cf. [8]). The following Basic Paramodulation rule is our main inference rule for equational theorem proving modulo E, where only the maximal sides of literals in clauses are involved in inferences by this rule. We rename variables in the premises in our inference rules if necessary so that no variable is shared between premises (i.e. standardized apart).

Basic Paramodulation

$$\frac{C \vee s \approx t \,\|\, \phi_1 \qquad D \vee L[s'] \,\|\, \phi_2}{C \vee D \vee L[t] \,\|\, s \approx^?_E s' \wedge \phi_1 \wedge \phi_2} \quad \text{if}$$

1. s' is not a variable,
2. $s \approx t$ is reductive for the left premise, and C contains no selected literal,
3. either one of the following three conditions is met:
   (a) L is selected in the right premise, and
       L is of the form $u[s'] \not\approx v$ and is semi-reductive for the right premise.
   (b) nothing is selected in the right premise, and
       L is of the form $u[s'] \approx v$ and is reductive for the right premise.
   (c) nothing is selected in the right premise, and
       L is of the form $u[s'] \not\approx v$ and is weakly reductive for the right premise.

Equality Resolution

$$\frac{C \vee s \not\approx t \,\|\, \phi}{C \,\|\, s \approx^?_E t \wedge \phi} \quad \text{if}$$

$s \not\approx t$ is selected, or else nothing is selected and $s \not\approx t$ is weakly maximal for the premise.

E-Factoring

$$\frac{C \vee s \approx t \vee s' \approx t' \,\|\, \phi}{C \vee t \not\approx t' \vee s' \approx t' \,\|\, s \approx_E^? s' \wedge \phi} \quad \text{if}$$

$s \approx t$ is weakly reductive for the premise, and C contains no selected literal.

E-Completion

$$\frac{C \vee s \approx t \,\|\, \phi}{C \vee e_1[t]_p \approx e_2 \,\|\, s \approx_E^? s' \wedge \phi} \quad \text{if}$$

1. $e_1[s']_p \approx e_2 \in E$ and $p \neq \lambda$, where s' is not a variable,
2. $s \approx t$ is reductive for the premise, and C contains no selected literal.

The above *E-Completion* rule is an adaptation of the *E-closure* [27] rule using equality constraints (cf. *E-extension* [5]).

E-Parallel

$$\frac{C \vee s \approx t \,\|\, \phi_1 \qquad D \vee l \approx r \,\|\, \phi_2}{C \vee D\sigma \vee l\sigma \approx r\theta \,\|\, \phi_1 \wedge \phi_2} \quad \text{if}$$

1. $s \approx t$ is reductive for the left premise, and C contains no selected literal,
2. $l \approx r$ is reductive for the right premise, and D contains no selected literal,
3. both l and s are not variables,
4. $\sigma = \{x \mapsto s\}$ and $\theta = \{x \mapsto t\}$ for some variable $x \in Vars(l) \cap Vars(r)$ with $x \notin Vars(\phi_2)$,
5. there is a term u' with $u' \approx_E l\sigma$, such that u' is R, E-reducible with $R = \{l \Rightarrow r, s \Rightarrow t\}$ only at the top position (i.e. no strict subterm of u' is R, E-reducible).

Generalized E-Parallel

$$\frac{C \vee s \approx t \,\|\, \phi_1 \qquad D \vee l \approx r \,\|\, \phi_2}{C \vee D\sigma \vee l\sigma \approx r\theta \,\|\, \phi_1 \wedge \phi_2} \quad \text{if}$$

1. $s \approx t$ is reductive for the left premise, and C contains no selected literal,
2. $l \approx r$ is reductive for the right premise, and D contains no selected literal,
3. both l and s are not variables,
4. $e_1[u] \approx e_2 \in E$, where u is not a variable,
5. $\sigma = \{x \mapsto u[s]_p\}$ and $\theta = \{x \mapsto u[t]_p\}$ for some variable $x \in Vars(l) \cap Vars(r)$ with $x \notin Vars(\phi_2)$ and some position p,

6. there is a term u' with $u' \approx_E l\sigma$, such that u' is R, E-reducible with $R = \{l \Rightarrow r, s \Rightarrow t\}$ only at the top position.

We mark each clause produced by the Generalized E-Parallel (or E-Parallel) rule as "protected" so that it is protected from our contraction rules discussed in Section 5. (We simply say each marked clause is a protected clause.) Protected clauses behave the same way as other clauses in our inference rules, but our contraction rules are not applied to protected clauses (see Section 5 for details).

We may also use *predicate terms* [6] $P(t_1, \ldots, t_n)$ in our inference system, where a predicate term cannot be a proper subterm of any term. Note that a predicate term $P(t_1, \ldots, t_n)$ can be expressed as an equation $P(t_1, \ldots, t_n) \approx \top$, where $\top$ is a special constant symbol minimal in the ordering $\succ$ and P is considered as a function symbol. (In this sense, $\neg P(t_1, \ldots, t_n)$ can be expressed as $P(t_1, \ldots, t_n) \not\approx \top$.) In the remainder of this paper, by $\mathcal{BP}$ we denote the inference system consisting of the Basic Paramodulation, Equality Resolution, E-Factoring, E-Completion, and the Generalized E-Parallel rule. If E is a permutative theory with maximum depth at most 2 (e.g. $E = A, C$, or AC), then we use the simpler E-Parallel rule instead of the Generalized E-Parallel rule in $\mathcal{BP}$ (see Lemma 6).

Example 1. Let $+$ be an AC symbol (in infix notation) with $+ \succ a \succ b \succ 0$ and consider the following inconsistent set of clauses 1: $x + 0 \approx x$, 2: $a + a \approx 0$, 3: $b + b \approx 0$, and 4: $(a + b) + (a + b) \not\approx 0$. Now we show how the empty clause (with a satisfiable constraint) is derived:

5: $(x + y) + z \approx x + 0 \,\|\, y + z \approx^?_{AC} a + a$ (E-Completion with 2 using the associativity axiom $x + (y + z) \approx (x + y) + z$.)

6: $((b + b) + y) + z \approx 0 + 0 \,\|\, y + z \approx^?_{AC} a + a$ (E-Parallel with 3 into 5. In condition 5 of the E-Parallel rule, term u' corresponds to $(b + y) + (b + z)$ here.)

7: $0 + 0 \not\approx 0 \,\|\, ((b + b) + y) + z \approx^?_{AC} (a + b) + (a + b) \wedge y + z \approx^?_{AC} a + a$ (Basic Paramodulation with 6 into 4)

8: $x \not\approx 0 \,\|\, x + 0 \approx^?_{AC} 0 + 0 \wedge ((b+b)+y)+z \approx^?_{AC} (a+b)+(a+b) \wedge y+z \approx^?_{AC} a+a$ (Basic Paramodulation with 1 into 7)

9: $\Box \,\|\, x \approx^?_{AC} 0 \wedge x + 0 \approx^?_{AC} 0 + 0 \wedge ((b+b)+y)+z \approx^?_{AC} (a+b)+(a+b) \wedge y+z \approx^?_{AC} a + a$ (Equality Resolution on 8)

In contrast, the existing approaches for basic paramodulation modulo AC [21, 26] use clauses 2 and 4, for example, and produce clause 5': $0 + x \not\approx 0 \,\|\, x \approx^?_{AC} b+b$ and then clause 6': $0 + y \not\approx 0 \,\|\, x \approx^?_{AC} b+b \wedge y \approx^?_{AC} 0$ by their inference rules. Then 6' is used to derive a contradiction with 1. It can be viewed that 6' is obtained from 5' by an indirect paramodulation with 3 in the constraint part. In our approach, we simply block clauses like 5' from further inferences (see Definition 12), and no direct or indirect paramodulation is allowed in the constraint part of any clause.

Example 2. Consider $S = \{f(g(x)) \approx x, a \approx b, c \not\approx g(b)\}$ and $E = \{f(g(g(a))) \approx c\}$ with $f \succ g \succ a \succ b$, where E is a regular theory with maximum depth 3. The Generalized E-Parallel rule with premises $f(g(x)) \approx x$ and $a \approx b$ produces the conclusion $f(g(g(a))) \approx g(b)$. (Choose l as $f(g(x))$, s as a, and u as $g(a)$ in the Generalized E-Parallel rule.) Then it is used to derive a contradiction with clause $c \not\approx g(b)$ since $f(g(g(a))) \approx_E c$.

In the above example, a suitable E-compatible reduction ordering $\succ$ on ground terms is obtained in such a way that given two ground terms, we rewrite each occurrence of c in each ground term into $f(g(g(a)))$ at the same position with (the occurrence of) c and then use the standard *lexicographic path ordering* [3,22] for comparing (rewritten) ground terms without any occurrence of c. Then we may compare terms with variables by considering ground substitutions and using this ordering on ground terms.

In what follows, by the Parallel rule we mean the E-Parallel or the Generalized E-Parallel rule. First, observe that we cannot derive a contradiction in both Examples 1 and 2 using inference rules in $\mathcal{BP}$ without the Parallel rule. The intuition behind the Parallel rule is that above all, a reductive ground clause corresponds to a reductive ground conditional rewrite rule [19] with positive and negative conditions. Therefore, roughly speaking, the premises of the Parallel rule are reductive conditional rewrite rules with positive and negative conditions. (The Parallel rule applies to only reductive clauses.) Now the conclusion of the Parallel rule combines two steps: (i) instantiating a "problematic" variable in a special and restricted way, and (ii) selectively rewriting an instantiated term if conditions are met. (Therefore, conditions C is included in the conclusion.) A problematic variable is often determined by a built-in equational theory E. It is mostly a variable produced by an E-Completion inference (see Example 1) for AC cases, which is the counterpart of an extension variable for AC-extension [7,27].

Observe that the Generalized E-Parallel rule is more general than the E-Parallel rule. If p is always the top position for the Generalized E-Parallel rule, then they are equivalent. This is the case for permutative theories with maximum depth at most 2 (e.g. $E = A, C$, or AC).

Lemma 6 *If E is a permutative theory with maximum depth at most 2, then the E-Parallel rule and the Generalized E-Parallel rule are equivalent, i.e., they generate the same conclusion for the same input premises.*

Note that the E-Completion and the Parallel rule are not always needed for every built-in equational theory E. The following example is a simple variant of the *reachability problem* [15] modulo a *permutation theory* [1,17], where $\neg P(f(c, b, b, d, e))$ is the query from the initial configuration $P(f(a, b, c, d, e))$. We may view E in the following example as all permutations of variables x_1, x_2, x_3, x_4, and x_5, since the symmetric group S_5 is generated by two cycles $(1\,2)$ and $(1\,2\,3\,4\,5)$.

Example 3. Let $E = \{f(x_1, x_2, x_3, x_4, x_5) \approx f(x_2, x_1, x_3, x_4, x_5), f(x_1, x_2, x_3, x_4, x_5) \approx f(x_2, x_3, x_4, x_5, x_1)\}$ with $P \succ f \succ a \succ b \succ c \succ d \succ e$ and consider the following set of clauses 1: $\neg P(f(c, b, b, d, e))$, 2: $P(f(a, b, c, d, e))$, and 3: $f(a, b, x, y, z) \approx f(b, b, x, y, z)$. Basic Paramodulation with 3 into 2 yields clause 4: $P(f(b,b,x,y,z)) \,\|\, f(a,b,x,y,z) \approx_E^? f(a,b,c,d,e)$. By apply-ing Basic Paramodulation with 1 and 4 (using $P(f(c,b,b,d,e)) \not\approx \top$ and $P(f(b,b,x,y,z)) \approx \top \,\|\, f(a,b,x,y,z) \approx_E^? f(a,b,c,d,e))$ and then applying Equality Resolution, we have clause 5: $\Box \,\|\, f(b,b,x,y,z) \approx_E^? f(c,b,b,d,e) \wedge f(a,b,x,y,z) \approx_E^? f(a,b,c,d,e)$. The equality constraint in 5 is satisfiable and we have a contradiction. Note that clause 4 schematizes the set of ground clauses $\{P(f(b,b,c,d,e)), P(f(b,b,c,e,d)), P(f(b,b,d,c,e)), P(f(b,b,d,e,c)), P(f(b,b,e, c,d)), P(f(b,b,e,d,c))\}$.

5   Redundancy Criteria and Contraction Techniques

Definition 7 (Relative reducibility) Given an equational theory E, a ground instance $C\sigma_1$ of $C \,\|\, \phi_1$ is *reduced relative to* a ground instance $D\sigma_2$ of $D \,\|\, \phi_2$ if for any rewrite system R, $C\sigma_1$ is a reduced ground instance of $C \,\|\, \phi_1$ w.r.t. R, E whenever $D\sigma_2$ is a reduced ground instance of $D \,\|\, \phi_2$ w.r.t. R, E.

In what follows, the relation $\trianglelefteq$ on terms represents the subterm relation, i.e., $s \trianglelefteq t$ if s is a subterm of t. The relation $\sqsubseteq$ on sets of terms is defined as follows: $\{s_1, \ldots, s_m\} \sqsubseteq \{t_1, \ldots, t_n\}$ if for all $1 \le i \le m$, there is some $1 \le j \le n$ such that $s_i \trianglelefteq t_j$, and $\emptyset \sqsubseteq X$ for any set of terms X. Given a clause $C \,\|\, \phi$, we denote by $Ran(\sigma|_{Vars(C)})$ for some $\sigma \in Sol(\phi)$ the range of the restriction of σ to the set of variables $Vars(C)$ if $Vars(C) \neq \emptyset$. If C is a ground clause with a tautological constraint (e.g. the empty constraint), then we set $Ran(\sigma|_{Vars(C)}) = \emptyset$. (Note that any ground substitution is a solution of a tautological constraint.)

We say that a clause $C \,\|\, \phi$ is a clause with a *succedent top variable* [21] w.r.t. $\sigma \in Sol(\phi)$ if there is a variable $x \in Vars(C) \cap Vars(\phi)$ only appearing in equations $x \approx t$ of the succedent of C with $x\sigma \succ t\sigma$ for some t. The following lemma, which directly follows from Definition 7, is a sufficient syntactic condition for $C\sigma_1$ being reduced relative to $D\sigma_2$ in Definition 7 if $D \,\|\, \phi_2$ is not a clause with a succedent top variable w.r.t. σ_2. If $D \,\|\, \phi_2$ is a clause with a succedent top variable x w.r.t. some $\sigma_2 \in Sol(\phi_2)$, then one may (partially) instantiate x in D with σ_2 if possible, so that one may use the syntactic condition for checking whether $C\sigma_1$ is reduced relative to $D\sigma_2$ as in the following lemma.

Lemma 8 *Given an equational theory E, a ground instance $C\sigma_1$ of $C \,\|\, \phi_1$ is reduced relative to a ground instance $D\sigma_2$ of $D \,\|\, \phi_2$ if $Ran(\sigma_1|_{Vars(C)}) \sqsubseteq Ran(\sigma_2|_{Vars(D)})$ and $D \,\|\, \phi_2$ is not a clause with a succedent top variable w.r.t. σ_2.*

In what follows, we denote by $E^{\prec C}$ (resp. $R^{\prec C}$) the set of ground instances of equations in E (resp. the set of ground rewrite rules in R) smaller than the ground clause C (w.r.t. $\succ$), and by S modulo E a set of clauses S with a built-in equational theory E.

Definition 9 (Redundancy) A clause $C \,\|\, \phi$ is *redundant* in S modulo E (w.r.t. relative reducibility) if for every ground instance $C\sigma$, there exist ground instances $C_1\sigma_1,\ldots,C_k\sigma_k$ of clauses $C_1 \,||\, \phi_1,\ldots,C_k \,||\, \phi_k$ in S reduced relative to $C\sigma$, such that $C\sigma \succ C_i\sigma_i$, $1 \leq i \leq k$, and $\{C_1\sigma_1,\ldots,C_k\sigma_k\} \cup R^{\prec C\sigma} \cup E^{\prec C\sigma} \models C\sigma$ for any ground rewrite system R contained in $\succ$. (In this case, we also say that each $C\sigma$ is *redundant* in S modulo E (w.r.t. relative reducibility).)

Definition 10 (Basic E-simplification) An equation $l \approx r$ *simplifies* a clause $C \vee L[l']_p \,||\, \phi$ into $C \vee L[r\rho]_p \,||\, \phi$ if the following conditions are met:
(i) p is a non-variable position;
(ii) there is a substitution ρ such that $l\rho \approx_E l'$, $L[l'] \succ l\rho \approx r\rho$, $Vars(l\rho) \supseteq Vars(r\rho)$, $l\rho \succ r\rho$, and $C \vee L[l']_p \,||\, \phi$ is neither protected nor a clause with a succedent top variable w.r.t. any $\sigma \in Sol(\phi)$.

Lemma 11 *If an equation $l \approx r$ simplifies a clause $C \vee L[l']_p \,||\, \phi$ into $C \vee L[r\rho]_p \,||\, \phi$ as in Definition 10, then $C \vee L[l']_p \,||\, \phi$ is redundant in S modulo E, where $S = \{l \approx r, C \vee L[r\rho]_p \,||\, \phi\}$.*

The following definition extends the blocking rule in the free case (see [9]) to the modulo case, where a blocked clause does not contribute to finding a refutation during a theorem proving derivation w.r.t. $\mathcal{BP}$ (see Definition 16) starting with an initial set of unconstrained clauses.

Definition 12 (Basic E-blocking) A clause $C \,||\, \phi$ is *blocked* in S modulo E if the following conditions are met:
(i) $C \,||\, \phi$ is not a clause with a succedent top variable w.r.t. any $\tau \in Sol(\phi)$;
(ii) there is a variable $x \in Vars(C) \cap Vars(\phi)$ such that for every $\sigma \in Sol(\phi)$, there exist ground instances $C_1\sigma_1,\ldots,C_k\sigma_k$ of clauses $C_1 \,||\, \phi_1,\ldots,C_k \,||\, \phi_k$ in S reduced relative to $C\sigma$, such that $C\sigma \succ C_i\sigma_i$, $1 \leq i \leq k$, and $\{C_1\sigma_1,\ldots,C_k\sigma_k\} \cup E^{\prec C\sigma} \models x\sigma \approx s$ with $x\sigma \succ s$ for some ground term s.

Definition 13 (Basic E-instance) A clause $C \,||\, \phi$ is a *basic E-instance* in S modulo E if the following conditions are met:
(i) $C \,||\, \phi$ is protected;
(ii) there is a protected clause $D \,||\, \psi \in S$ such that for every ground instance $C\sigma$ (resp. $D\tau$) of $C \,||\, \phi$ (resp. $D \,||\, \psi$), there is a ground instance $D\tau$ (resp. $C\sigma$) of $D \,||\, \psi$ (resp. $C \,||\, \phi$) such that they are reduced relative to each other with $C\sigma = D\tau$.

Observe that protected clauses are produced in a restricted way (e.g. see condition 5 in the E-Parallel rule) and if two protected clauses are the same up to variable renaming, then they are basic E-instances of each other and they do not need to be distinguished.

Definition 14 (Redundancy of an inference) An inference π with conclusion $D \,||\, \phi$ is *redundant* in S modulo E (w.r.t. relative reducibility) if $D \,||\, \phi$ is blocked or a basic E-instance in S modulo E, or for every ground instance $\pi\sigma$ with maximal premise C and conclusion $D\sigma$, there exist ground instances $C_1\sigma_1,\ldots,C_k\sigma_k$ of clauses $C_1 \,||\, \phi_1,\ldots,C_k \,||\, \phi_k$ in S reduced relative to $D\sigma$, such that $C \succ C_i\sigma_i$, $1 \leq i \leq k$, and $\{C_1\sigma_1,\ldots,C_k\sigma_k\} \cup R^{\prec C} \cup E^{\prec C} \models D\sigma$ for any ground rewrite system R contained in $\succ$.

The following lemma immediately follows from Definition 9 and the observation that if $\{C_1\sigma_1, \ldots, C_k\sigma_k\} \cup E^{\prec C\sigma} \models C\sigma$, then $\{C_1\sigma_1, \ldots, C_k\sigma_k\} \cup R^{\prec C\sigma} \cup E^{\prec C\sigma} \models C\sigma$ for any ground rewrite system R contained in $\succ$, which serves as a sufficient condition for redundancy of clauses. Also, if an (unconstrained) clause C properly subsumes an (unconstrained) clause $C' \vee D$ in the classical sense, where C and C' are the same up to variable renaming, then it is easy to see that $C' \vee D$ is redundant in $\{C\}$ modulo E.

Lemma 15 *A clause $C \,\|\, \phi$ is redundant in S modulo E if for every ground instance $C\sigma$, there exist ground instances $C_1\sigma_1, \ldots, C_k\sigma_k$ of clauses $C_1 \,\|\, \phi_1, \ldots, C_k \,\|\, \phi_k$ in S reduced relative to $C\sigma$, such that $C\sigma \succ C_i\sigma_i$, $1 \leq i \leq k$, and $\{C_1\sigma_1, \ldots, C_k\sigma_k\} \cup E^{\prec C\sigma} \models C\sigma$.*

Definition 16 (Theorem proving derivation) A *theorem proving derivation* is a sequence of sets of clauses $S_0 = S, S_1, \ldots$ such that:
(i) Deduction: $S_i = S_{i-1} \cup \{C \,\|\, \phi\}$ for some $C \,\|\, \phi$ if it can be deduced from premises in S_{i-1} by applying an inference rule in $\mathcal{BP}$ or basic E-simplification.
(ii) Deletion: $S_i = S_{i-1} \setminus \{D \,\|\, \psi\}$ for some $D \,\|\, \psi$ if it is not protected, and is redundant or blocked in S_{i-1} modulo E.

The set S_∞ of *persistent clauses* is defined as $\bigcup_i (\bigcap_{j \geq i} S_j)$, which is called the *limit* of the derivation. A theorem proving derivation $S_0, S_1, S_2, \ldots$ is *fair* [6] w.r.t. the inference system $\mathcal{BP}$ if every inference π by $\mathcal{BP}$ with premises in S_∞ is redundant in $\bigcup_j S_j$ modulo E.

Definition 17 (Saturation w.r.t. relative reducibility) Given an equational theory E, we say that S modulo E is *saturated* under $\mathcal{BP}$ w.r.t. relative reducibility if every inference by $\mathcal{BP}$ with premises in S is redundant in S modulo E.

In what follows, we say that a clause $C \,\|\, \phi$ is *non-protected redundant* (resp. *non-protected blocked*) in S modulo E if it is not protected and is redundant (resp. blocked) in S modulo E. (If $C \,\|\, \phi$ is non-protected redundant in S modulo E, then we also say that each ground instance $C\sigma$ of $C \,\|\, \phi$ is *non-protected redundant* in S modulo E.)

Lemma 18 *(i) If $S \subseteq S'$, then any clause which is non-protected redundant or non-protected blocked in S modulo E is also non-protected redundant or non-protected blocked in S' modulo E.*
(ii) Let $S \subseteq S'$ such that all clauses in $S' \setminus S$ are non-protected redundant or non-protected blocked in S' modulo E. Then (ii.1) any clause which is non-protected redundant or non-protected blocked in S' modulo E is also non-protected redundant or non-protected blocked in S modulo E, and (ii.2) any inference which is redundant in S' modulo E is also redundant in S modulo E.

Lemma 19 *Let $S_0, S_1, \ldots$ be a fair theorem proving derivation w.r.t. $\mathcal{BP}$ such that S_0 is a set of unconstrained clauses. Then S_∞ modulo E is saturated under $\mathcal{BP}$ w.r.t. relative reducibility.*

Proof. If S_∞ contains the empty clause, then it is immediate that S_∞ modulo E is saturated under $\mathcal{BP}$ w.r.t. relative reducibility, so we assume that the empty clause is not in S_∞.

If a clause $C \parallel \phi$ is deleted in a theorem proving derivation, then we see that it is non-protected redundant or non-protected blocked in some S_j modulo E. It is also non-protected redundant or non-protected blocked in $\bigcup_j S_j$ modulo E by Lemma 18(i). Similarly, every clause in $\bigcup_j S_j \setminus S_\infty$ is non-protected redundant or non-protected blocked in $\bigcup_j S_j$ modulo E.

Now by fairness of the derivation, every inference π by $\mathcal{BP}$ with premises in S_∞ is redundant in $\bigcup_j S_j$ modulo E. Then by Lemma 18(ii.2) and the above, π is also redundant in S_∞ modulo E. Thus, S_∞ modulo E is saturated under $\mathcal{BP}$ w.r.t. relative reducibility. □

6 Refutational Completeness

The soundness of $\mathcal{BP}$ (w.r.t. a fair theorem proving derivation) is straightforward, i.e., $S_i \cup E \models S_{i+1} \cup E$ for all $i \geq 0$. If the empty clause is in some S_j, then $S_0 \cup E$ is unsatisfiable by the soundness of $\mathcal{BP}$. The following theorem states that $\mathcal{BP}$ with our contraction rules (i.e. basic E-simplification and basic E-blocking) is refutationally complete. In order to prove the following theorem, we adapt a variant of *model construction techniques* [7–9,21,27]. In this section, we assume that the equality is the only predicate by expressing other predicates (i.e. predicate terms) as (predicate) equations as discussed in Section 4.

Theorem 20 *Let $S_0, S_1, \ldots$ be a fair theorem proving derivation w.r.t. $\mathcal{BP}$ such that S_0 is a set of unconstrained clauses. Then $S_0 \cup E$ is unsatisfiable if and only if the empty clause is in some S_j.*

Definition 21 (Model construction) Let S be a set of (constrained) clauses. We use induction on $\succ$ to define the sets $Rules_C$, R_C, E_C, and I_C, for all ground instances C of clauses in S. Let C be such a ground instance of a clause in S and suppose that $Rules_{C'}$ has been defined for all ground instances C' of clauses in S for which $C \succ C'$. Then we define by $R_C = \bigcup_{C \succ C'} Rules_{C'}$ and by E_C the set of ground instances $e_1 \approx e_2$ of equations in E, such that $C \succ e_1 \approx e_2$, and e_1 and e_2 are both irreducible by R_C. We also define by I_C the interpretation $(R_C \cup E_C)^*$ (i.e. the least congruence containing $R_C \cup E_C$).

Now let $C := D \vee s \approx t$ be a reduced ground instance of a clause in S w.r.t. R_C such that C is not an instance of a clause with a selected literal. Then C produces the set of ground rewrite rules $Rules_C = \{u \Rightarrow t \mid u \approx_E s \text{ and } u \text{ is irreducible by } R_C\}$ if the following conditions are met: (1) $I_C \not\models C$ (resp. $I_C \not\models D$) if C is an instance of a non-protected clause (resp. protected clause), (2) $I_C \not\models t \approx t'$ for every $s' \approx t'$ in D with $s' \approx_E s$, (3) $s \approx t$ is reductive for C, and (4) there exists u with $u \approx_E s$ for which u is irreducible by R_C. We say that C is *productive* and *produces* $Rules_C$ if it satisfies all of the above conditions. Otherwise, $Rules_C = \emptyset$. Finally, we define $R_S = \bigcup_C R_C$, $E_S = \bigcup_C E_C$, and $I_S = (R_S \cup E_S)^*$.

We may include the special non-productive ground clause $tt \approx tt$ in S for the above (inductive) definition, where $tt \approx tt$ is assumed to be greater than all ground instances of clauses in $S \cup E$ w.r.t. $\succ$ other than $tt \approx tt$ itself (see [21,27]). (If C is the strictly maximal ground instance among ground instances of clauses in S and is productive, then R_S may not include $Rules_C$ by the above inductive definition of R_C without $tt \approx tt$.) In what follows, we say that a ground instance $\pi\sigma$ of an inference π with premises in S is *reduced* if each premise and conclusion of $\pi\sigma$ is a reduced ground instance of a clause in $S \cup E$ w.r.t. R_S, E_S.

Definition 22 (Redundancy w.r.t. R_S, E_S) A clause $C \,||\, \phi$ is *redundant* in S modulo E w.r.t. R_S, E_S if for every reduced ground instance $C\sigma$ w.r.t. R_S, E_S, there exist reduced ground instances $C_1\sigma_1, \ldots, C_k\sigma_k$ of clauses $C_1 \,||\, \phi_1 \ldots C_k \,||\, \phi_k$ in S w.r.t. R_S, E_S, such that $C\sigma \succ C_i\sigma_i$, $1 \le i \le k$, and $\{C_1\sigma_1, \ldots, C_k\sigma_k\} \cup R_S^{\prec C\sigma} \cup E^{\prec C\sigma} \models C\sigma$. (In this case, we also say that each $C\sigma$ is *redundant* in S modulo E w.r.t. R_S, E_S.)

An inference π with conclusion $D \,||\, \phi$ is *redundant* in S modulo E w.r.t. R_S, E_S if $D \,||\, \phi$ is blocked or a basic E-instance in S modulo E, or for every reduced ground instance $\pi\sigma$ with maximal premise C and conclusion $D\sigma$, there exist reduced ground instances $C_1\sigma_1, \ldots, C_k\sigma_k$ of clauses $C_1 \,||\, \phi_1, \ldots, C_k \,||\, \phi_k$ in S w.r.t. R_S, E_S, such that $C \succ C_i\sigma_i$, $1 \le i \le k$, and $\{C_1\sigma_1, \ldots, C_k\sigma_k\} \cup R_S^{\prec C} \cup E^{\prec C} \models D\sigma$.

Definition 23 (Saturation w.r.t. R_S, E_S) Given an equational theory E, we say that S modulo E is *saturated* under $\mathcal{BP}$ w.r.t. R_S, E_S if every inference by $\mathcal{BP}$ with premises in S is redundant in S modulo E w.r.t. R_S, E_S.

Lemma 24 *(i) There are no overlaps among the left-hand sides of rules in R_S.*
(ii) A term t is reducible by R_S if and only if it is reducible by R_S, E_S at the same position.
(iii) For every $l \Rightarrow r, s \Rightarrow t \in R_S$, if $l \approx_E s$, then r and t are the same term.
(iv) R_S/E_S is terminating.
(v) For ground terms u and v, if $I_S \models u \approx v$, then $u \downarrow_{R_S, E_S} v$.
(vi) If a ground instance $C\theta := D\theta \lor l\theta \approx r\theta$ of a clause $C \,||\, \phi := D \lor l \approx r \,||\, \phi$ is productive, then it is a reduced ground instance of $C \,||\, \phi$ w.r.t. R_S, E_S.

The proofs of (i), (ii), and (iii) in Lemma 24 follow from the construction of R_S in Definition 21. For (iv), since R_S is contained in an E-compatible reduction ordering $\succ$ on terms that is E-total on ground terms, R_S/E_S is terminating. Meanwhile, Lemma 24(v) describes the ground *Church-Rosser property* [19] of R_S, E_S. Since R_S/E_S is terminating by (iv), this shows that R_S, E_S is ground convergent modulo E_S. In the following, we assume that any saturated clause set under $\mathcal{BP}$ is obtained from an initial set of clauses without constraints.

Lemma 25 *Let S modulo E be saturated under $\mathcal{BP}$ w.r.t. R_S, E_S not containing the empty clause and let C be a reduced ground instance of a clause in S w.r.t. R_S, E_S or a ground instance of an equation in E. Then C is true in I_S. More specifically,*

(i) C is not an instance of a blocked clause in S modulo E.
(ii) If C is redundant in S modulo E w.r.t. R_S, E_S, then it is true in I_S.
(iii) If C is an instance of a clause with a selected literal, then it is true in I_S.
(iv) If C contains a maximal negative literal (w.r.t. $\succ$) and is not an instance of a clause with a selected literal, then it is true in I_S.
(v) If C is an instance of an equation in E, then it is true in I_S.
(vi) If C is an instance of a protected clause or a basic E-instance of it, then it is true in I_S.
(vii) If C is non-productive, then it is true in I_S.
(viii) If $C := C' \vee s \approx t$ is productive and produces $Rules_C$ with $s \Rightarrow t \in Rules_C$, then C' is false and C is true in I_S.

We leave it to the reader to verify the following lemma using the definitions of redundancy of an inference w.r.t. relative reducibility and w.r.t. R_S, E_S, along with Lemma 19.

Lemma 26 *Let $S_0, S_1, \ldots$ be a fair theorem proving derivation w.r.t. $\mathcal{BP}$ such that S_0 is a set of unconstrained clauses. Then S_∞ modulo E is saturated under $\mathcal{BP}$ w.r.t. $R_{S_\infty}, E_{S_\infty}$.*

Theorem 27 *Let $S_0, S_1, \ldots$ be a fair theorem proving derivation w.r.t. $\mathcal{BP}$ such that S_0 is a set of unconstrained clauses. If S_∞ does not contain the empty clause, then $I_{S_\infty} \models S_0 \cup E$ (i.e., $S_0 \cup E$ is satisfiable).*

Proof. By Lemma 26, we know that S_∞ modulo E is saturated under $\mathcal{BP}$ w.r.t. $R_{S_\infty}, E_{S_\infty}$. Let C be a ground instance of an equation in E or a ground instance of a clause C' in S_0. By Lemma 25(v), if C is a ground instance of an equation in E, then it is true in I_{S_∞}. Therefore, we assume that C is not a ground instance of an equation in E. Suppose first that $C := C'\sigma'$ is a reduced ground instance of $C' \in S_0$ w.r.t. $R_{S_\infty}, E_{S_\infty}$. Then there are two cases to consider. If $C' \in S_\infty$, then C is true in I_{S_∞} by Lemma 25. Otherwise, if $C' \notin S_\infty$, then C' is (non-protected) redundant in some S_j modulo E w.r.t. relative reducibility because $C' \in S_0$ (with the empty constraint) is neither protected nor can it be a blocked clause in some S_j modulo E. Thus, C' is (non-protected) redundant in $\bigcup_j S_j$ modulo E w.r.t. relative reducibility, and hence is (non-protected) redundant in S_∞ modulo E w.r.t. relative reducibility by Lemma 18. It follows that there exist ground instances $C_1\sigma_1, \ldots, C_k\sigma_k$ of clauses $C_1 \| \phi_1, \ldots, C_k \| \phi_k$ in S_∞ reduced relative to C, such that $C \succ C_i\sigma_i, 1 \leq i \leq k$, and $\{C_1\sigma_1, \ldots, C_k\sigma_k\} \cup R^{\prec C} \cup E^{\prec C} \models C$ for any ground rewrite system R contained in $\succ$. Since C is a reduced ground instance of C' w.r.t. $R_{S_\infty}, E_{S_\infty}$, we see that $C_i\sigma_i, 1 \leq i \leq k$, are also reduced ground instances w.r.t. $R_{S_\infty}, E_{S_\infty}$ by Definition 7 and are true in I_{S_∞} by Lemma 25. Similarly, $R_{S_\infty}^{\prec C}$ and $E^{\prec C}$ are true in I_{S_∞} by Lemma 25, and hence we may infer that C is also true in I_{S_∞}.

Now suppose that $C := C'\sigma'$ is a reducible ground instance of $C' \in S_0$ w.r.t. $R_{S_\infty}, E_{S_\infty}$. Let σ'' be a ground substitution such that $x\sigma'' = x\sigma'{\downarrow}_{R_{S_\infty}, E_{S_\infty}}$ for each $x \in Vars(C')$. Since $C'\sigma''$ is a reduced ground instance of $C' \in S_0$ w.r.t. $R_{S_\infty}, E_{S_\infty}$, $C'\sigma''$ is true in I_{S_∞} by the previous paragraph, and hence C is also true in I_{S_∞}. $\qquad\square$

We may now present the proof that $\mathcal{BP}$ with our contraction rules is refutationally complete.

Proof of Theorem 20 Let $S_0, S_1, \ldots$ be a fair theorem proving derivation w.r.t. $\mathcal{BP}$ such that S_0 is a set of unconstrained clauses. If the empty clause is in some S_j, then $S_0 \cup E$ is unsatisfiable by the soundness of $\mathcal{BP}$. Otherwise, if the empty clause is not in S_k for all k, then by the soundness of $\mathcal{BP}$, S_∞ does not contain the empty clause, and hence $S_0 \cup E$ is satisfiable by Theorem 27.   □

7   Conclusion

We have presented a basic paramodulation calculus modulo and provided a framework for equational theorem proving modulo equational theories E satisfying some properties of E using constrained clauses, where a constrained clause may schematize a set of unconstrained clauses by keeping E-unification problems in its constraint part. Our results imply that we can deal uniformly with different equational theories E in our equational theorem proving modulo framework. We only need a single refutational completeness proof for our basic paramodulation calculus modulo E for different equational theories E.

Our contraction techniques (i.e. basic E-simplification and basic E-blocking) for constrained clauses can also be applied uniformly for different equational theories E satisfying some properties of E in our equational theorem proving modulo framework. Since a constrained clause may schematize a set of unconstrained clauses, the simplification or deletion of a constrained clause may correspond to the simplification or deletion of a set of unconstrained clauses. We have proposed a saturation procedure for constrained clauses based on relative reducibility and showed the refutational completeness of our inference system using a saturated clause set (w.r.t. $\succ$).

Some possible improvements remain to be done. One of the main issues is the broadening the scope of our equational theorem proving modulo E to more equational theories E. This can be achieved by dropping or weakening some ordering requirements of $\succ$ (e.g. monotonicity of $\succ$) for a basic paramodulation calculus modulo E, while maintaining the refutational completeness of the calculus (cf. [10]). This can also be achieved by finding suitable E-compatible orderings for more equational theories E. In fact, we provided an E-compatible simplification ordering $\succ$ on terms that is E-total on ground terms for finite permutation theories E in [17], which allows us to provide a refutationally complete equational theorem proving with built-in permutation theories using the results of this paper. Since permutations play an important role in mathematics and many fields of science including computer science, we believe that developing applications for equational theorem proving with built-in permutation theories is another promising future research direction.

References

1. Avenhaus, J.: Efficient Algorithms for Computing Modulo Permutation Theories. In: Basin, D., Rusinowitch, M. (eds.) Automated Reasoning - IJCAR 2004, Cork, Ireland, July 4–8. pp. 415–429. Springer, Berlin, Heidelberg (2004)
2. Baader, F.: Combination of compatible reduction orderings that are total on ground terms. In: Winskel, G. (ed.) Proceedings of the Twelfth Annual IEEE Symposium on Logic in Computer Science. pp. 2–13. IEEE Computer Society Press, Warsaw, Poland (1997)
3. Baader, F., Nipkow, T.: Term Rewriting and All That. Cambridge University Press, Cambridge, UK (1998)
4. Baader, F., Snyder, W.: Unification Theory. In: Handbook of Automated Reasoning, chap. 8, pp. 445 – 532. Volume I, Elsevier, Amsterdam (2001)
5. Bachmair, L., Dershowitz, N.: Completion for rewriting modulo a congruence. Theoretical Computer Science **67**(2), 173 – 201 (1989)
6. Bachmair, L., Ganzinger, H.: Rewrite-based Equational Theorem Proving with Selection and Simplification. J. Log. Comput. **4**(3), 217–247 (1994)
7. Bachmair, L., Ganzinger, H.: Associative-commutative superposition. In: Dershowitz, N., Lindenstrauss, N. (eds.) Conditional and Typed Rewriting Systems. pp. 1–14. Springer, Berlin, Heidelberg (1995)
8. Bachmair, L., Ganzinger, H.: Equational Reasoning in Saturation-Based Theorem Proving. In: Bibel, W., Schmitt, P. (eds.) Automated Deduction. A basis for applications, chap. 11, p. 353–397. Volume I, Kluwer, Dordrecht, Netherlands (1998)
9. Bachmair, L., Ganzinger, H., Lynch, C., Snyder, W.: Basic Paramodulation. Information and Computation **121**(2), 172 – 192 (1995)
10. Bofill, M., Rubio, A.: Paramodulation with Non-Monotonic Orderings and Simplification. Journal of Automated Reasoning **50**, 51–98 (2013)
11. Dershowitz, N., Plaisted, D.A.: Rewriting. In: Handbook of Automated Reasoning, chap. 9, pp. 535 – 610. Volume I, Elsevier, Amsterdam (2001)
12. Dowek, G.: Polarized Resolution Modulo. In: Calude, C.S., Sassone, V. (eds.) Theoretical Computer Science. pp. 182–196. Springer, Berlin, Heidelberg (2010)
13. Dowek, G., Hardin, T., Kirchner, C.: Theorem Proving Modulo. Journal of Automated Reasoning **31**(1), 33–72 (2003)
14. Durán, F., Eker, S., Escobar, S., Martí-Oliet, N., Meseguer, J., Talcott, C.: Associative Unification and Symbolic Reasoning Modulo Associativity in Maude. In: Rusu, V. (ed.) Rewriting Logic and Its Applications. pp. 98–114. Springer, Cham (2018)
15. Escobar, S., Sasse, R., Meseguer, J.: Folding variant narrowing and optimal variant termination. The Journal of Logic and Algebraic Programming **81**(7), 898 – 928 (2012)
16. Kim, D., Lynch, C.: Equational Theorem Proving Modulo (2021), Technical Report, Web link: https://people.clarkson.edu/~clynch/PAPERS/etpm.pdf
17. Kim, D., Lynch, C.: An RPO-based ordering modulo permutation equations and its applications to rewrite systems. In: 6th International Conference on Formal Structures for Computation and Deduction, FSCD 2021, Buenos Aires, Argentina (Virtual Conference), July 17–24, to appear. vol. 195, pp. 19:1–19:17. LIPIcs (2021), preprint: http://people.clarkson.edu/~dohkim/tech_reports/ERPO.pdf
18. Kim, D., Lynch, C., Narendran, P.: Reviving Basic Narrowing Modulo. In: Herzig, A., Popescui, A. (eds.) Frontiers of Combining Systems. pp. 313–329. Springer, Cham, Switzerland (2019)

19. Kirchner, C., Kirchner, H.: Rewriting, Solving, Proving (1999), Preliminary version: http://citeseerx.ist.psu.edu/viewdoc/summary?doi=10.1.1.144.5349
20. Nieuwenhuis, R., Rubio, A.: Basic superposition is complete. In: Krieg-Brückner, B. (ed.) ESOP '92. pp. 371–389. Springer, Berlin, Heidelberg (1992)
21. Nieuwenhuis, R., Rubio, A.: Paramodulation with Built-in AC-Theories and Symbolic Constraints. Journal of Symbolic Computation **23**(1), 1 – 21 (1997)
22. Nieuwenhuis, R., Rubio, A.: Paramodulation-based theorem proving. In: Handbook of Automated Reasoning, chap. 7, pp. 371–443. Volume I, Elsevier, Amsterdam (2001)
23. Robinson, G., Wos, L.: Paramodulation and theorem-proving in first-order theories with equality. In: Meltzer, B., Michie, D. (eds.) Machine Intelligence 4, pp. 133–150. American Elsevier, New York (1969)
24. Robinson, J.A.: A machine-oriented logic based on the resolution principle. J. ACM **12**(1), 23–41 (1965)
25. Rubio, A.: Theorem Proving modulo Associativity. In: Büning, H.K. (ed.) Computer Science Logic. pp. 452–467. Springer, Berlin, Heidelberg (1996)
26. Vigneron, L.: Associative-Commutative Deduction with Constraints. In: Bundy, A. (ed.) Automated Deduction - CADE-12. pp. 530–544. Springer, Berlin (1994)
27. Wertz, U.: First-order theorem proving modulo equations. Tech. Rep. MPI-I-92-216, Max-Planck-Institut für Informatik, Saarbrücken (1992)

Open Access This chapter is licensed under the terms of the Creative Commons Attribution 4.0 International License (http://creativecommons.org/licenses/by/4.0/), which permits use, sharing, adaptation, distribution and reproduction in any medium or format, as long as you give appropriate credit to the original author(s) and the source, provide a link to the Creative Commons license and indicate if changes were made.

The images or other third party material in this chapter are included in the chapter's Creative Commons license, unless indicated otherwise in a credit line to the material. If material is not included in the chapter's Creative Commons license and your intended use is not permitted by statutory regulation or exceeds the permitted use, you will need to obtain permission directly from the copyright holder.

Unifying Decidable Entailments in Separation Logic with Inductive Definitions

Mnacho Echenim[1] , Radu Iosif[2] , and Nicolas Peltier[1]

[1] Univ. Grenoble Alpes, CNRS, LIG, F-38000 Grenoble France
[2] Univ. Grenoble Alpes, CNRS, VERIMAG, F-38000 Grenoble France

Abstract. The entailment problem $\varphi \models \psi$ in Separation Logic [12,15], between separated conjunctions of equational ($x \approx y$ and $x \not\approx y$), spatial ($x \mapsto (y_1, \ldots, y_\kappa)$) and predicate ($p(x_1, \ldots, x_n)$) atoms, interpreted by a finite set of inductive rules, is undecidable in general. Certain restrictions on the set of inductive definitions lead to decidable classes of entailment problems. Currently, there are two such decidable classes, based on two restrictions, called *establishment* [10,13,14] and *restrictedness* [8], respectively. Both classes are shown to be in 2EXPTIME by the independent proofs from [14] and [8], respectively, and a many-one reduction of established to restricted entailment problems has been given [8]. In this paper, we strictly generalize the restricted class, by distinguishing the conditions that apply only to the left- (φ) and the right- (ψ) hand side of entailments, respectively. We provide a many-one reduction of this generalized class, called *safe*, to the established class. Together with the reduction of established to restricted entailment problems, this new reduction closes the loop and shows that the three classes of entailment problems (respectively established, restricted and safe) form a single, unified, 2EXPTIME-complete class.

1 Introduction

Separation Logic [12,15] (SL) was primarily introduced for writing concise Hoare logic proofs of programs that handle pointer-linked recursive data structures (lists, trees, etc). Over time, SL has evolved into a powerful logical framework, that constitutes the basis of several industrial-scale static program analyzers [3,2,5], that perform scalable compositional analyses, based on the principle of *local reasoning*: describing the behavior of a program statement with respect only to the small (local) set of memory locations that are changed by that statement, with no concern for the rest of the program's state.

Given a set of memory locations (e.g., addresses), SL formulæ describe *heaps*, that are finite partial functions mapping finitely many locations to records of locations. A location ℓ is *allocated* if it occurs in the domain of the heap. An atom $x \mapsto (y_1, \ldots, y_\kappa)$ states that there is only one allocated location, associated with x, that moreover refers to the tuple of locations associated with $(y_1, \ldots, y_\kappa)$, respectively. The *separating conjunction* $\phi * \psi$ states that the heap can split into two parts, with disjoint domains, that make ϕ and ψ true, respectively. The separating conjunction is instrumental in supporting local reasoning, because the disjointness between the (domains of the) models of its arguments ensures that no update of one heap can actually affect the other.

© The Author(s) 2021
A. Platzer and G. Sutcliffe (Eds.): CADE 2021, LNAI 12699, pp. 183–199, 2021.
https://doi.org/10.1007/978-3-030-79876-5_11

Reasoning about recursive data structures of unbounded sizes (lists, trees, etc.) is possible via the use of predicate symbols, whose interpretation is specified by a user-provided *set of inductive definitions* (SID) of the form $p(x_1, \ldots, x_n) \Leftarrow \pi$, where p is a predicate symbol of arity n and the free variables of the formula π are among the parameters $x_1, \ldots, x_n$ of the rule. Here the separating conjunction ensures that each un-folding of the rules, which substitute some predicate atom $p(y_1, \ldots, y_n)$ by a formula $\pi[x_1/y_1, \ldots, x_n/y_n]$, corresponds to a way of building the recursive data structure. For instance, a list is either empty, in which case its head equals its tail pointer, or is built by first allocating the head, followed by all elements up to but not including the tail, as stated by the inductive definitions $\mathsf{ls}(x, y) \Leftarrow x \approx y$ and $\mathsf{ls}(x, y) \Leftarrow \exists z . x \mapsto (z) * \mathsf{ls}(z, y)$.

An important problem in program verification, arising during the construction of Hoare-style correctness proofs of programs, is the discharge of verification conditions of the form $\phi \models \psi$, where ϕ and ψ are SL formulæ, asking whether every model of ϕ is also a model of ψ. These problems, called *entailments*, are, in general, undecidable in the presence of inductively defined predicates [11,1].

A first decidable class of entailments, described in [10], involves three restrictions on the SID rules: *progress*, *connectivity* and *establishment*. Intuitively, the progress (P) condition states that every rule allocates exactly one location, the connectivity (C) condition states that the set of allocated locations has a tree-shaped structure, and the es-tablishment (E) condition states that every existentially quantified variable from a rule defining a predicate is (eventually) allocated in every unfolding of that predicate. A 2EXPTIME algorithm was proposed for testing the validity of PCE entailments [13,14] and a matching 2EXPTIME-hardness lower bound was provided shortly after [6].

Later work relaxes the establishment condition, necessary for decidability [7], by proving that the entailment problem is still in 2EXPTIME if the establishment condition is replaced by the *restrictedness* (R) condition, which requires that every disequality $(x \not\approx y)$ involves at least one free variable from the left-hand side of the entailment, propagated through the unfoldings of the inductive system [8]. Interestingly, the rules of a progressive, connected and restricted (PCR) entailment may generate data structures with "dangling" (i.e. existentially quantified but not allocated) pointers, which was not possible with PCE entailments.

In this paper, we generalize PCR entailments further, by showing that the connec-tivity and restrictedness conditions are needed only on the right-hand side of the en-tailment, whereas the only condition required on the left-hand side is progress (which can usually be enforced by folding or unfolding definitions). Our results thus allow for "asymetric" entailments, i.e., one can test whether the structures described by induc-tive rules that are (almost) arbitrary fulfill some restricted formula. Although the class of data structures that can be described is much larger, we show that this new class of entailments, called *safe*, is also 2EXPTIME-complete, by a many-one reduction of the validity of safe entailments to the validity of PCE entailments. A second contribution of the paper is the cross-certification of the two independent proofs of the 2EXPTIME upper bounds, for the PCE [6,14,8] and PCR [8] classes of entailments, respectively, by closing the loop. Namely, the reduction given in this paper enables the translation of any of the three entailment problems into an equivalent problem in any other class, while preserving the 2EXPTIME upper bound. This is because all the reductions are polynomial in the overall size of the SID and singly-exponential in the maximum size of the rules in the SID. The theoretical interest of the reduction is that it makes the proof of decidability and of the complexity class much shorter and clearer. It also has some practical advantages, since it allows one to re-use existing implementations designed for established systems instead of having to develop entirely new automated reasoning systems. Due to space restrictions, some of the proofs are omitted. All proofs can be found in [9].

2 Definitions

For a (partial) function $f : A \to B$, we denote by $\mathrm{dom}(f)$ and $\mathrm{rng}(f)$ its domain and range, respectively. For a relation $R \subseteq A \times A$, we denote by R^* the reflexive and transitive closure of R.

Let κ be a fixed natural number throughout this paper and let P be a countably infinite set of *predicate symbols*. Each predicate symbol $p \in$ P is associated a unique arity, denoted $ar(p)$. Let V be a countably infinite set of *variables*. For technical convenience, we also consider a special constant $\bot$, which will be used to denote "empty" record fields. Formulæ are built inductively, according to the following syntax:

$$\phi :- x \not\approx x' \mid x \approx x' \mid x \mapsto (y_1, \ldots, y_\kappa) \mid p(x_1, \ldots, x_n) \mid \phi_1 * \phi_2 \mid \phi_1 \vee \phi_2 \mid \exists x . \phi_1$$

where $p \in$ P is a predicate symbol of arity $n = ar(p)$, $x, x', x_1, \ldots, x_n \in$ V are variables and $y_1, \ldots, y_\kappa \in$ V $\cup \{\bot\}$ are *terms*, i.e. either variables or $\bot$.

The set of variables freely occurring in a formula ϕ is denoted by $\mathrm{fv}(\phi)$, we assume by α-equivalence that the same variable cannot occur both free and bound in the same formula ϕ, and that distinct quantifiers bind distinct variables. The *size* $|\phi|$ of a formula ϕ is the number of occurrences of symbols in ϕ. A formula $x \approx x'$ or $x \not\approx x'$ is an *equational atom*, $x \mapsto (y_1, \ldots, y_\kappa)$ is a *points-to atom*, whereas $p(x_1, \ldots, x_n)$ is a *predicate atom*. Note that $\bot$ cannot occur in an equational or in a predicate atom. A formula is *predicate-less* if no predicate atom occurs in it. A *symbolic heap* is a formula of the form $\exists x . *_{j=1}^{m} \alpha_j$, where each α_i is an atom and x is a possibly empty vector of variables.

Definition 1. *A variable* x *is* allocated *by a symbolic heap* ϕ *iff* ϕ *contains a sequence of equalities* $x_1 \approx x_2 \approx \ldots \approx x_{n-1} \approx x_n$, *for* $n \geq 1$, *such that* $x = x_1$ *and* $x_n \mapsto (y_1, \ldots, y_\kappa)$ *occurs in* ϕ, *for some variables* $x_1, \ldots, x_n$ *and some terms* $y_1, \ldots, y_\kappa \in$ V $\cup \{\bot\}$.

A *substitution* is a partial function mapping variables to variables. If σ is a substitution and ϕ is a formula, a variable or a tuple, then $\phi\sigma$ denotes the formula, the variable or the tuple obtained from ϕ by replacing every free occurrence of a variable $x \in \mathrm{dom}(\sigma)$ by $\sigma(x)$, respectively. We denote by $\{\langle x_i, y_i \rangle \mid i \in [\![1, n]\!]\}$ the substitution with domain $\{x_1, \ldots, x_n\}$ that maps x_i to y_i, for each $i \in [\![1, n]\!]$.

A *set of inductive definitions* (SID) $\mathcal{R}$ is a finite set of implications (or rules) of the form $p(x_1, \ldots, x_n) \Leftarrow \pi$, where $p \in$ P, $n = ar(p)$, $x_1, \ldots, x_n$ are pairwise distinct variables and π is a quantifier-free symbolic heap. The predicate atom $p(x_1, \ldots, x_n)$ is the *head* of the rule and $\mathcal{R}(p)$ denotes the subset of $\mathcal{R}$ consisting of rules with head $p(x_1, \ldots, x_n)$ (the choice of $x_1, \ldots, x_n$ is not important). The variables in $\mathrm{fv}(\pi) \setminus \{x_1, \ldots, x_n\}$ are called the *existential variables of the rule*. Note that, by definition, these variables are not explicitly quantified inside π and that π is quantifier-free. For simplicity, we denote by $p(x_1,\ldots,x_n) \Leftarrow_{\mathcal{R}} \pi$ the fact that the rule $p(x_1,\ldots,x_n) \Leftarrow \pi$ belongs to $\mathcal{R}$. The *size of* $\mathcal{R}$ is defined as $|\mathcal{R}| \overset{\text{def}}{=} \sum_{p(x_1,\ldots,x_n)\Leftarrow_{\mathcal{R}}\pi} |\pi| + n$ and its *width* as $\mathrm{w}(\mathcal{R}) \overset{\text{def}}{=} \max_{p(x_1,\ldots,x_n)\Leftarrow_{\mathcal{R}}\pi} |\pi| + n$.

We write $p \succeq_{\mathcal{R}} q$, $p,q \in \mathsf{P}$ iff $\mathcal{R}$ contains a rule of the form $p(x_1,\ldots,x_n) \Leftarrow \pi$, and q occurs in π. We say that p *depends on* q if $p \succeq_{\mathcal{R}}^* q$. For a formula ϕ, we denote by $\mathcal{P}(\phi)$ the set of predicate symbols q, such that $p \succeq_{\mathcal{R}}^* q$ for some predicate p occurring in ϕ.

Given formulæ ϕ and ψ, we write $\phi \Leftarrow_{\mathcal{R}} \psi$ if ψ is obtained from ϕ by replacing an atom $p(u_1,\ldots,u_n)$ by $\pi\{\langle x_1,u_1\rangle,\ldots,\langle x_n,u_n\rangle\}$, where $\mathcal{R}$ contains a rule $p(x_1,\ldots,x_n) \Leftarrow \pi$. We assume, by a renaming of existential variables, that the set $(\mathrm{fv}(\pi)\setminus\{x_1,\ldots,x_n\})\cap \mathrm{fv}(\phi)$ is empty. We call ψ an *unfolding* of ϕ iff $\phi \Leftarrow_{\mathcal{R}}^* \psi$.

We now define the semantics of SL. Let $\mathcal{L}$ be a countably infinite set of *locations* containing, in particular, a special location $\bot\!\!\!\bot$. A *structure* is a pair $(\mathfrak{s},\mathfrak{h})$, where:

- $\mathfrak{s}$ is a partial function from $\mathsf{V}\cup\{\bot\}$ to $\mathcal{L}$, called a *store*, such that $\bot \in \mathrm{dom}(\mathfrak{s})$ and $\mathfrak{s}(x) = \bot\!\!\!\bot \iff x = \bot$, for all $x \in \mathsf{V}\cup\{\bot\}$, and
- $\mathfrak{h}: \mathcal{L} \to \mathcal{L}^\kappa$ is a finite partial function, such that $\bot\!\!\!\bot \notin \mathrm{dom}(\mathfrak{h})$.

If $x_1,\ldots,x_n$ are pairwise distinct variables and $\ell_1,\ldots,\ell_n \in \mathcal{L}$ are locations, we denote by $\mathfrak{s}[x_i \leftarrow \ell_i \mid 1 \le i \le n]$ the store $\mathfrak{s}'$ defined by $\mathrm{dom}(\mathfrak{s}') = \mathrm{dom}(\mathfrak{s})\cup\{x_1,\ldots,x_n\}$, $\mathfrak{s}'(y) = \ell_i$ if $y = x_i$ for some $i \in [\![1,n]\!]$, and $\mathfrak{s}'(y) = \mathfrak{s}(x)$ otherwise. If $x_1,\ldots,x_n \notin \mathrm{dom}(\mathfrak{s})$, then the store $\mathfrak{s}'$ is called an *extension* of $\mathfrak{s}$ to $\{x_1,\ldots,x_n\}$.

Given a heap $\mathfrak{h}$, we define $\mathrm{ref}(\mathfrak{h}) \overset{\text{def}}{=} \bigcup_{l\in\mathrm{dom}(\mathfrak{h})}\{\ell_i \mid \mathfrak{h}(\ell) = (\ell_1,\ldots,\ell_\kappa), i \in [\![1,\kappa]\!]\}$ and $\mathrm{loc}(\mathfrak{h}) \overset{\text{def}}{=} \mathrm{dom}(\mathfrak{h})\cup\mathrm{ref}(\mathfrak{h})$. Two heaps $\mathfrak{h}_1$ and $\mathfrak{h}_2$ are *disjoint* iff $\mathrm{dom}(\mathfrak{h}_1)\cap\mathrm{dom}(\mathfrak{h}_2) = \emptyset$, in which case $\mathfrak{h}_1 \uplus \mathfrak{h}_2$ denotes the union of $\mathfrak{h}_1$ and $\mathfrak{h}_2$, undefined whenever $\mathfrak{h}_1$ and $\mathfrak{h}_2$ are not disjoint.

Given an SID $\mathcal{R}$, $(\mathfrak{s},\mathfrak{h}) \models_{\mathcal{R}} \phi$ is the least relation between structures and formulæ such that whenever $(\mathfrak{s},\mathfrak{h}) \models_{\mathcal{R}} \phi$, we have $\mathrm{fv}(\phi) \subseteq \mathrm{dom}(\mathfrak{s})$ and the following hold:

$(\mathfrak{s},\mathfrak{h}) \models_{\mathcal{R}} x \approx x'$	if $\mathrm{dom}(\mathfrak{h}) = \emptyset$ and $\mathfrak{s}(x) = \mathfrak{s}(x')$
$(\mathfrak{s},\mathfrak{h}) \models_{\mathcal{R}} x \not\approx x'$	if $\mathrm{dom}(\mathfrak{h}) = \emptyset$ and $\mathfrak{s}(x) \neq \mathfrak{s}(x')$
$(\mathfrak{s},\mathfrak{h}) \models_{\mathcal{R}} x \mapsto (y_1,\ldots,y_\kappa)$	if $\mathrm{dom}(\mathfrak{h}) = \{\mathfrak{s}(x)\}$ and $\mathfrak{h}(\mathfrak{s}(x)) = \langle\mathfrak{s}(y_1),\ldots,\mathfrak{s}(y_\kappa)\rangle$
$(\mathfrak{s},\mathfrak{h}) \models_{\mathcal{R}} \phi_1 * \phi_2$	if there exist disjoint heaps $\mathfrak{h}_1$ and $\mathfrak{h}_2$ such that $\mathfrak{h} = \mathfrak{h}_1 \uplus \mathfrak{h}_2$ and $(\mathfrak{s},\mathfrak{h}_i) \models_{\mathcal{R}} \phi_i$, for both $i = 1,2$
$(\mathfrak{s},\mathfrak{h}) \models_{\mathcal{R}} \phi_1 \vee \phi_2$	if $(\mathfrak{s},\mathfrak{h}) \models_{\mathcal{R}} \phi_i$, for some $i = 1,2$
$(\mathfrak{s},\mathfrak{h}) \models_{\mathcal{R}} \exists x . \phi$	if there exists $\ell \in \mathcal{L}$ such that $(\mathfrak{s}[x \leftarrow \ell],\mathfrak{h}) \models \phi$
$(\mathfrak{s},\mathfrak{h}) \models_{\mathcal{R}} p(x_1,\ldots,x_n)$	if $p(x_1,\ldots,x_n) \Leftarrow_{\mathcal{R}} \phi$, and there exists a store $\mathfrak{s}_e$ coinciding with $\mathfrak{s}$ on $\{x_1,\ldots,x_n\}$, such that $(\mathfrak{s}_e,\mathfrak{h}) \models \phi$

Given formulæ ϕ and ψ, we write $\phi \models_{\mathcal{R}} \psi$ whenever $(\mathfrak{s},\mathfrak{h}) \models_{\mathcal{R}} \phi \Rightarrow (\mathfrak{s},\mathfrak{h}) \models_{\mathcal{R}} \psi$, for all structures $(\mathfrak{s},\mathfrak{h})$ and $\phi \equiv_{\mathcal{R}} \psi$ for $(\phi \models_{\mathcal{R}} \psi$ and $\psi \models_{\mathcal{R}} \phi)$. We omit the subscript $\mathcal{R}$ whenever these relations hold for any SID. It is easy to check that, for all formulæ ϕ_1,ϕ_2,ψ, it is the case that $(\phi_1 \vee \phi_2) * \psi \equiv (\phi_1 * \psi) \vee (\phi_2 * \psi)$ and $(\exists x.\phi_1) * \phi_2 \equiv \exists x . \phi_1 * \phi_2$. Consequently, each formula can be transformed into an equivalent finite disjunction of symbolic heaps.

Definition 2. *An* entailment problem *is a triple* $\mathfrak{P} \stackrel{\text{def}}{=} \phi \vdash_{\mathcal{R}} \psi$, *where* ϕ *is a quantifier-free formula,* ψ *is a formula and* $\mathcal{R}$ *is an SID. The problem* $\mathfrak{P}$ *is* valid *iff* $\phi \models_{\mathcal{R}} \psi$. *The* size *of the problem* $\mathfrak{P}$ *is defined as* $|\mathfrak{P}| \stackrel{\text{def}}{=} |\phi| + |\psi| + |\mathcal{R}|$ *and its* width *is defined as* $\mathrm{w}(\mathfrak{P}) \stackrel{\text{def}}{=} \max(|\phi|, |\psi|, \mathrm{w}(\mathcal{R}))$.

Note that considering ϕ to be quantifier-free loses no generality, because $\exists x.\phi \models_{\mathcal{R}} \psi \iff \phi \models_{\mathcal{R}} \psi$.

3   Decidable Entailment Problems

The class of general entailment problems is undecidable, see Theorem 5 below for a refinement of the initial undecidability proofs [11,1]. A first attempt to define a natural decidable class of entailment problems is described in [10] and involves three restrictions on the SID rules, formally defined below:

Definition 3. *A rule* $p(x_1, \ldots, x_n) \Leftarrow \pi$ *is:*
1. progressing *(P) iff* $\pi = x_1 \mapsto (y_1, \ldots, y_\kappa) * \rho$ *and* ρ *contains no points-to atoms,*
2. connected *(C) iff it is progressing,* $\pi = x_1 \mapsto (y_1, \ldots, y_\kappa) * \rho$ *and every predicate atom in* ρ *is of the form* $q(y_i, \boldsymbol{u})$, *for some* $i \in [\![1, \kappa]\!]$,
3. established *(E) iff every existential variable* $x \in \mathrm{fv}(\pi) \setminus \{x_1, \ldots, x_n\}$ *is allocated by every predicate-less unfolding* $\pi \Leftarrow^*_{\mathcal{R}} \phi$.
An SID $\mathcal{R}$ *is P (resp. C, E) for a formula* ϕ *iff every rule in* $\bigcup_{p \in \mathcal{P}(\phi)} \mathcal{R}(p)$ *is P (resp. C,E). An entailment problem* $\phi \vdash_{\mathcal{R}} \psi$ *is left- (resp. right-) P (resp. C, E) iff* $\mathcal{R}$ *is P (resp. C, E) for* ϕ *(resp.* ψ*). An entailment problem is P (resp. C, E) iff it is both left- and right-P (resp. C, E).*

The decidability of progressing, connected and left-established entailment problems is an immediate consequence of the result of [10]. Moreover, an analysis of the proof [10] leads to an elementary recursive complexity upper bound, which has been recently tighten down to 2EXPTIME-complete [14,8,6]. In the following, we refer to Table 1 for a recap of the complexity results for the entailment problem. The last line is the main result of the paper and corresponds to the most general (known) decidable class of entailment problems (Definition 8).

Table 1. Decidability and Complexity Results for the Entailment Problem ($\checkmark$ means that the corresponding condition holds on the left- and right-hand side of the entailment)

Reference	Progress	Connected	Established	Restricted	Complexity
Theorem 4	$\checkmark$	$\checkmark$	left	-	2EXP-co.
Theorem 5	$\checkmark$	left	$\checkmark$	-	undec.
[7, Theorem 6]	$\checkmark$	$\checkmark$	-	-	undec.
[8, Theorem 32]	$\checkmark$	$\checkmark$	-	$\checkmark$	2EXP-co.
Theorem 31	$\checkmark$	right	-	right	2EXP-co.

The following theorem is an easy consequence of previous results [6].

Theorem 4. *The progressing, connected and left-established entailment problem is* *2EXPTIME-complete. Moreover, there exists a decision procedure that runs in time* $2^{2^{O(w(\mathfrak{P})^8 \cdot \log|\mathfrak{P}|)}}$ *for every instance $\mathfrak{P}$ of this problem.*

A natural question arises in this context: which of the restrictions from the above theorem can be relaxed and what is the price, in terms of computational complexity, of relaxing (some of) them? In the light of Theorem 5 below, the connectivity restriction cannot be completely dropped. Further, if we drop the establishment condition, the problem becomes undecidable [7, Theorem 6], even if both the left/right progress and connectivity conditions apply.

Theorem 5. *The progressing, left-connected and established entailment problem is undecidable.*

The second decidable class of entailment problems [8] relaxes the connectivity condition and replaces the establishment with a syntactic condition (that can be checked in polynomial time in the size of the SID), while remaining 2EXPTIME-complete. Informally, the definition forbids (dis)equations between existential variables in symbolic heaps or rules: the only allowed (dis)equations are of the form $x \bowtie y$ where x is a free variable (viewed as a constant in [8]). The definition given below is essentially equivalent to that of [8], but avoids any reference to constants; instead it uses a notion of $\mathcal{R}$-positional functions, which helps to identify existential variables that are always replaced by a free variable from the initial formula during unfolding.

An $\mathcal{R}$-*positional function* maps every n-ary predicate symbol p occurring in $\mathcal{R}$ to a subset of $[\![1,n]\!]$. Given an $\mathcal{R}$-positional function λ and a formula ϕ, we denote by $V_\lambda(\phi)$ the set of variables x_i such that ϕ contains a predicate atom $p(x_1,\ldots,x_n)$ with $i \in \lambda(p)$. Note that V_λ is stable under substitutions, i.e. $V_\lambda(\phi\sigma) = (V_\lambda(\phi))\sigma$, for each formula ϕ and each substitution σ.

Definition 6. *Let ψ be a formula and $\mathcal{R}$ be an SID. The* fv-profile *of the pair $(\psi, \mathcal{R})$ is the $\mathcal{R}$-positional function λ such that the sets $\lambda(p)$, for $p \in \mathsf{P}$, are the maximal sets satisfying the following conditions:*

1. *$V_\lambda(\psi) \subseteq \mathrm{fv}(\psi)$.*
2. *For all predicate symbols $p \in \mathcal{P}(\psi)$, all rules $p(x_1,\ldots,x_n) \Leftarrow \pi$ in $\mathcal{R}$, all predicate atoms $q(y_1,\ldots,y_m)$ in π and all $i \in \lambda(q)$, there exists $j \in \lambda(p)$ such that $x_j = y_i$.*

The fv-profile of $(\psi, \mathcal{R})$ is denoted by $\lambda_{\mathcal{R}}^{\psi}$.

Intuitively, given a predicate $p \in \mathsf{P}$, the set $\lambda_{\mathcal{R}}^{\psi}(p)$ denotes the formal parameters of p that, in every unfolding of ψ, will always be substituted by variables occurring freely in ψ. It is easy to check that $\lambda_{\mathcal{R}}^{\psi}$ can be computed in polynomial time w.r.t. $|\psi| + |\mathcal{R}|$, using a straightforward greatest fixpoint algorithm. The algorithm starts with a function mapping every predicate p of arity n to $[\![1,n]\!]$ and repeatedly removes elements from the sets $\lambda(p)$ to ensure that the above conditions hold. In the worst case, we may have eventually $\lambda(p) = \emptyset$ for all predicate symbols p.

Definition 7. *Let λ be an $\mathcal{R}$-positional function, and V be a set of variables. A formula ϕ is λ-restricted (λ-R) w.r.t. V iff the following hold:*

1. *for every disequation $y \not\approx z$ in ϕ, we have $\{y,z\} \cap V \neq \emptyset$, and*
2. $V_\lambda(\phi) \subseteq V$.

A *rule* $p(x_1, \ldots, x_n) \Leftarrow x \mapsto (y_1, \ldots, y_\kappa) * \rho$ *is:*
- *λ-connected (λ-C) iff for every atom $q(z_1, \ldots, z_m)$ occurring in ρ, we have $z_1 \in V_\lambda(p(x_1, \ldots, x_n)) \cup \{y_1, \ldots, y_\kappa\}$,*
- *λ-restricted (λ-R) iff ρ is λ-restricted w.r.t. $V_\lambda(p(x_1, \ldots, x_n))$.*

An *SID* $\mathcal{R}$ is P *(resp. λ-C, λ-R) for a formula ϕ iff every rule in $\bigcup_{p \in \mathcal{P}(\phi)} \mathcal{R}(p)$ is P (resp. λ-C, λ-R).*

An *SID* $\mathcal{R}$ *is λ-C (λ-R) for a formula ϕ iff every rule in $\bigcup_{p \in \mathcal{P}(\phi)} \mathcal{R}(p)$ is λ-C (λ-R).* An *entailment problem $\phi \vdash_{\mathcal{R}} \psi$ is left- (right-) λ-C, (λ-R) iff $\mathcal{R}$ is λ-C (λ-R) for ϕ (ψ), where λ is considered to be $\lambda_{\mathcal{R}}^{\phi}$ ($\lambda_{\mathcal{R}}^{\psi}$). An entailment problem is λ-C (λ-R) iff it is both left- and right-λ-C (λ-R).*

The class of progressing, λ-connected and λ-restricted entailment problems has been shown to be a generalization of the class of progressing, connected and left-established problems, because the latter can be reduced to the former by a many-one reduction [8, Theorem 13] that runs in time $|\mathfrak{P}| \cdot 2^{O(w(\mathfrak{P})^2)}$ on input $\mathfrak{P}$ (Figure 1) and preserves the problem's width asymptotically.

Fig. 1. Many-one Reductions between Decidable Entailment Problems

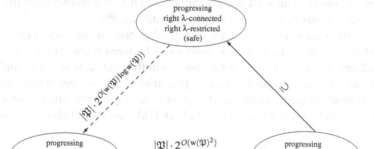

In the rest of this paper we close the loop by defining a syntactic extension of λ-progressing, λ-connected and λ-restricted entailment problems and by showing that this extension can be reduced to the class of progressing, connected and left-established entailment problems by a many-one reduction. The new fragment is defined as follows:

Definition 8. *An entailment problem $\phi \vdash_{\mathcal{R}} \psi$ is safe if, for $\lambda \stackrel{\text{def}}{=} \lambda_{\mathcal{R}}^{\psi}$, the following hold:*
1. *every rule in $\mathcal{R}$ is progressing,*
2. *ψ is λ-restricted w.r.t. $\text{fv}(\phi)$,*
3. *all the rules from $\bigcup_{p \in \mathcal{P}(\psi)} \mathcal{R}(p)$ are λ-connected and λ-restricted.*

Note that there is no condition on the formula ϕ, or on the rules defining the predicates occurring only in ϕ, other than the progress condition. The conditions in Definition 8 ensure that all the disequations occurring in any unfolding of ψ involve at least one variable that is free in ϕ. Further, the heaps of the model of ψ must be *forests*, i.e. unions of trees, the roots of which are associated with the first argument of the predicate atoms in ψ or to free variables from ϕ.

A typical yet very simple example of such an entailment is the so-called "reversed list" problem that consists in checking that any list segment $\mathtt{revls}(z,y)$ defined in the reverse direction (from the tail to the head) is a list segment $\mathtt{ls}(x,y)$ in the usual sense (defined inductively from head to tail). This corresponds to the entailment problem $\mathtt{revls}(z,y) \vdash_{\mathcal{R}} \exists x.\mathtt{ls}(x,y)$ where $\mathcal{R}$ contains the following rules:

$$\mathtt{ls}(x,y) \Leftarrow x \mapsto (y) \qquad\qquad \mathtt{revls}(z,y) \Leftarrow z \mapsto (y)$$
$$\mathtt{ls}(x,y) \Leftarrow x \mapsto (z) * \mathtt{ls}(z,y) \qquad \mathtt{revls}(z,y) \Leftarrow z \mapsto (y) * \mathtt{revls}(u,z)$$

This problem is considered as challenging for proof search-based automated reasoning procedures (see, e.g., [4,16]). The antecedent does not fulfill the connectivity condition, but the subsequent does, hence the entailment is safe. Similar, more complex examples can be defined, for instance a list can be constructed by interleaving elements at odd or even positions. Another example is the case of a data structure containing an unbounded number of acylic lists (e.g., a list of acyclic lists). Such a data structure does not fulfill the restricteness condition, since one needs to compare the pointers occurring along each list to the point at the end. Checking, for instance, that the concatenation of two lists of acyclic lists is again a list of (possibly cyclic) lists is a problem that fits into the safe class and can thus be effectively checked by our algorithm.

We refer the reader to Figure 1 for a general picture of the entailment problems considered so far and of the many-one reductions between them, where the reduction corresponding to the dashed arrow is the concern of the next section. Importantly, since all reductions are many-one, taking time polynomial in the size and exponential in the width of the input problem, while preserving its width asymptotically, the three classes from Figure 1 can be unified into a single (2EXPTIME-complete) class of entailments.

4   Reducing Safe to Established Entailments

In a model of a safe SID (Definition 8), the existential variables introduced by the replacement of predicate atoms with corresponding rule bodies are not required to be allocated. This is because safe SIDs are more liberal than established SIDs and allow heap structures with an unbounded number of dangling pointers. As observed in [8], checking the validity of an entailment (w.r.t a restricted SID) can be done by considering only those structures in which the dangling pointers point to pairwise distinct locations. The main idea of the hereby reduction of safe to established entailment problems is that any such structure can be extended by allocating all dangling pointers separately and, moreover, the extended structures can be defined by an established SID.

In what follows, we fix an arbitrary instance $\mathfrak{P} = \phi \vdash_{\mathcal{R}} \psi$ of the safe entailment problem (Definition 8) and denote by $\lambda \stackrel{\text{def}}{=} \lambda_{\mathcal{R}}^{\psi}$ the fv-profile of $(\psi, \mathcal{R})$ (Definition 6). Let $\boldsymbol{w} \stackrel{\text{def}}{=} (w_1, \ldots, w_v)$ be the vector of free variables from ϕ and ψ, where the order of variables is not important and assume w.l.o.g. that $v > 0$. Let $\mathcal{P}_l \stackrel{\text{def}}{=} \mathcal{P}(\phi)$ and

$\mathcal{P}_r \stackrel{\text{def}}{=} \mathcal{P}(\psi)$ be the sets of predicate symbols that depend on the predicate symbols occurring in the left- and right-hand side of the entailment, respectively. We assume that ϕ and ψ contain no points-to atoms and that $\mathcal{P}_l \cap \mathcal{P}_r = \emptyset$. Again, these assumptions lose no generality, because a points-to atom $u \mapsto (v_1, \ldots, v_\kappa)$ can be replaced by a predicate atom $p(u, v_1, \ldots, v_\kappa)$, where p is a fresh predicate symbol associated with the rule $p(x, y_1, \ldots, y_\kappa) \Leftarrow x \mapsto (y_1, \ldots, y_\kappa)$. Moreover the condition $\mathcal{P}_l \cap \mathcal{P}_r \neq \emptyset$ may be enforced by considering two copies of each predicate, for the left-hand side and for the right-hand side, respectively. Finally, we assume that every rule contains exactly μ existential variables, for some fixed $\mu \in \mathbb{N}$; this condition can be enforced by adding dummy literals $x \approx x$ if needed.

We describe a reduction of $\mathfrak{P}$ to an equivalent progressing, connected, and left-established entailment problem. The reduction will extend heaps, by adding $\nu + \mu$ record fields. We shall therefore often consider heaps and points-to atoms having $\kappa + \nu + \mu$ record fields, where the formal definitions are similar to those given previously. Usually such formulæ and heaps will be written with a prime. These additional record fields will be used to ensure that the constructed system is connected, by adding all the existential variables of a given rule (as well as the variables in $w_1, \ldots, w_\nu$) into the image of the location allocated by the considered rule. Furthermore, the left-establishment condition will be enforced by adding predicates and rules in order to allocate all the locations that correspond to existential quantifiers and that are not already allocated, making such locations point to a dummy vector $\perp \stackrel{\text{def}}{=} (\perp, \ldots, \perp)$, of length $\kappa + \nu + \mu$, where $\perp$ is the special constant denoting empty heap entries. To this aim, we shall use a predicate symbol $\perp$ associated with the rule $\perp(x) \Leftarrow x \mapsto \perp$. Note that allocating all these locations will entail (by definition of the separating conjunction) that they are distinct, thus the addition of such predicates and rules will reduce the number of satisfiable unfoldings. However, due to the restrictions on the use of disequations[3], we shall see that this does not change the status of the entailment problem.

Definition 9. *For any total function $\gamma \colon L \to L$ and any tuple $\boldsymbol{\ell} = \langle \ell_1, \ldots, \ell_n \rangle \in L^n$, we denote by $\gamma(\boldsymbol{\ell})$ the tuple $\langle \gamma(\ell_1), \ldots, \gamma(\ell_n) \rangle$. If $\mathfrak{s}$ is a store, then $\gamma(\mathfrak{s})$ denotes the store with domain $\mathrm{dom}(\mathfrak{s})$, such that $\gamma(\mathfrak{s})(x) \stackrel{\text{def}}{=} \gamma(\mathfrak{s}(x))$, for all $x \in \mathrm{dom}(\mathfrak{s})$. Consider a heap $\mathfrak{h}$ such that for all $\ell \neq \ell' \in \mathrm{dom}(\mathfrak{h})$, we have $\gamma(\ell) \neq \gamma(\ell')$. Then $\gamma(\mathfrak{h})$ denotes the heap with domain $\mathrm{dom}(\gamma(\mathfrak{h})) = \{\gamma(\ell) \mid \ell \in \mathrm{dom}(\mathfrak{h})\}$, such that $\gamma(\mathfrak{h})(\gamma(\ell)) \stackrel{\text{def}}{=} \gamma(\mathfrak{h}(\ell))$, for all $\ell \in \mathrm{dom}(\mathfrak{h})$.*

The following lemma identifies conditions ensuring that the application of a mapping to a structure (Definition 9) preserves the truth value of a formula.

Lemma 10. *Given a set of variables V, let α be a formula that is λ-restricted w.r.t. V, such that $\mathcal{P}(\alpha) \subseteq \mathcal{P}_r$ and let $(\mathfrak{s}, \mathfrak{h})$ be an $\mathcal{R}$-model of α. For every mapping $\gamma \colon L \to L$ such that $\gamma(\ell) = \gamma(\ell') \Rightarrow \ell = \ell'$ holds whenever either $\{\ell, \ell'\} \subseteq \mathrm{dom}(\mathfrak{h})$ or $\{\ell, \ell'\} \cap \mathfrak{s}(V) \neq \emptyset$, we have $(\gamma(\mathfrak{s}), \gamma(\mathfrak{h})) \models_{\mathcal{R}} \alpha$.*

If γ is, moreover, injective, then the result of Lemma 10 holds for any formula:

Lemma 11. *Let α be a formula and let $(\mathfrak{s}, \mathfrak{h})$ be an $\mathcal{R}$-model of α. For every injective mapping $\gamma \colon L \to L$ we have $(\gamma(\mathfrak{s}), \gamma(\mathfrak{h})) \models_{\mathcal{R}} \alpha$.*

---

[3] Point (1) of Definition 7 in conjunction with point (2) of Definition 8.

Fig. 2. Heap Expansion and Truncation

4.1 Expansions and Truncations

We introduce a so-called *expansion* relation on structures, as well as a *truncation* operation on heaps. Intuitively, the expansion of a structure is a structure with the same store and whose heap is augmented with new allocated locations (each pointing to $\bot$) and additional record fields, referring in particular to all the newly added allocated locations. These locations are introduced to accommodate all the existential variables of the predicate-less unfolding of the left-hand side of the entailment (to ensure that the obtained entailment is left-established). Conversely, the truncation of a heap is the heap obtained by removing these extra locations. We also introduce the notion of a γ-expansion which is a structure whose image by γ is an expansion.

We recall that, throughout this and the next sections, $w = (w_1, \ldots, w_\nu)$ denotes the vector of free variables occurring in the problem, which is assumed to be fixed throughout this section and that $\{w_1, \ldots, w_\nu, \bot\} \subseteq \mathrm{dom}(\mathfrak{s})$, for every store $\mathfrak{s}$ considered here. Moreover, we assume w.l.o.g. that $w_1, \ldots, w_\nu$ do not occur in the considered SID $\mathcal{R}$ and denote by μ the number of existential variables in each rule of $\mathcal{R}$. We refer to Figure 2 for an illustration of the definition below:

Definition 12. *Let* $\gamma : L \to L$ *be a total mapping. A structure* $(\mathfrak{s}, \mathfrak{h}')$ *is a* γ-*expansion (or simply an* expansion *if* $\gamma = id$*) of some structure* $(\mathfrak{s}, \mathfrak{h})$*, denoted by* $(\mathfrak{s}, \mathfrak{h}') \rhd_\gamma (\mathfrak{s}, \mathfrak{h})$*, if* $\mathfrak{h} : L \to L^\kappa$, $\mathfrak{h}' : L \to L^{\kappa+\mu+\nu}$ *and there exist two disjoint heaps,* $\mathrm{main}(\mathfrak{h}')$ *and* $\mathrm{aux}(\mathfrak{h}')$*, such that* $\mathfrak{h}' = \mathrm{main}(\mathfrak{h}') \uplus \mathrm{aux}(\mathfrak{h}')$ *and the following hold:*
1. *for all* $\ell_1, \ell_2 \in \mathrm{dom}(\mathrm{main}(\mathfrak{h}'))$*, if* $\gamma(\ell_1) = \gamma(\ell_2)$ *then* $\ell_1 = \ell_2$,
2. $\gamma(\mathrm{dom}(\mathrm{main}(\mathfrak{h}'))) = \mathrm{dom}(\mathfrak{h})$,
3. *for each* $\ell \in \mathrm{dom}(\mathrm{main}(\mathfrak{h}'))$*, we have* $\mathfrak{h}'(\ell) = \langle \boldsymbol{a}, \mathfrak{s}(\boldsymbol{w}), b_1^\ell, \ldots, b_\mu^\ell \rangle$*, for some locations* $b_1^\ell, \ldots, b_\mu^\ell \in L$ *and* $\gamma(\boldsymbol{a}) = \mathfrak{h}(\gamma(\ell))$.
4. *for each* $\ell \in \mathrm{dom}(\mathrm{aux}(\mathfrak{h}'))$*, we have* $\mathfrak{h}'(\ell) = \bot\!\bot$ *and there exists a location* $\ell' \in \mathrm{dom}(\mathrm{main}(\mathfrak{h}'))$ *such that* $\mathrm{main}(\mathfrak{h}')(\ell')$ *is of the form* $\langle \boldsymbol{a}, \ell, b_1^{\ell'}, \ldots, b_\mu^{\ell'} \rangle$ *where* ℓ *is a tuple of locations and* $\ell = b_i^{\ell'}$*, for some* $i \in [\![1, \mu]\!]$*. The element* ℓ' *is called the* connection *of* ℓ *in* $\mathfrak{h}'$ *and is denoted by* $\mathrm{C}_{\mathfrak{h}'}(\ell)$.[4]

Let $(\mathfrak{s}, \mathfrak{h}')$ be a γ-expansion of $(\mathfrak{s}, \mathfrak{h})$ and let $\ell \in \mathrm{dom}(\mathrm{main}(\mathfrak{h}'))$ be a location. Since $\nu > 0$ and for all $i \in [\![1, \nu]\!]$, $\mathfrak{s}(w_i)$ occurs in $\mathfrak{h}'(\ell)$, and since we assume that $\mathfrak{s}(w_i) \neq \bot\!\bot = \mathfrak{s}(\bot)$ for every $i \in [\![1, \nu]\!]$, necessarily $\mathrm{main}(\mathfrak{h}')(\ell) \neq \bot\!\bot$. This entails that the decomposition

---

[4] Note that ℓ' does not depend on γ, and if several such locations exist, then one is chosen arbitrarily.

$\mathfrak{h}' = \mathrm{main}(\mathfrak{h}') \uplus \mathrm{aux}(\mathfrak{h}')$ is unique: $\mathrm{main}(\mathfrak{h}')$ and $\mathrm{aux}(\mathfrak{h}')$ are the restrictions of $\mathfrak{h}'$ to the locations ℓ in $\mathrm{dom}(\mathfrak{h}')$ such that $\mathfrak{h}'(\ell) \neq \underline{\perp}$ and $\mathfrak{h}'(\ell) = \underline{\perp}$, respectively. In the following, we shall thus freely use the notations $\mathrm{aux}(\mathfrak{h}')$ and $\mathrm{main}(\mathfrak{h}')$, for arbitrary heaps $\mathfrak{h}'$.

Definition 13. *Given a heap $\mathfrak{h}'$, we denote by $\mathrm{trunc}(\mathfrak{h}')$ the heap $\mathfrak{h}$ defined as follows:* $\mathrm{dom}(\mathfrak{h}) \overset{\mathrm{def}}{=} \mathrm{dom}(\mathfrak{h}') \setminus \{\ell \in \mathrm{dom}(\mathfrak{h}') \mid \mathfrak{h}'(\ell) = \underline{\perp}\}$ *and for all $\ell \in \mathrm{dom}(\mathfrak{h})$, if $\mathfrak{h}'(\ell) = (\ell_1, \ldots, \ell_{\kappa+\nu+\mu})$, then $\mathfrak{h}(\ell) \overset{\mathrm{def}}{=} (\ell_1, \ldots, \ell_\kappa)$.*

Note that, if $\mathfrak{h} = \mathrm{trunc}(\mathfrak{h}')$ then $\mathfrak{h} : L \to L^\kappa$ and $\mathfrak{h}' : L \to L^{\kappa+\mu+\nu}$ are heaps of different out-degrees. In the following, we silently assume this fact, to avoid cluttering the notation by explicitly specifying the out-degree of a heap.

Example 14. Assume that $L = \mathbb{N}$, $\nu = \mu = 1$. Let $\mathfrak{s}$ be a store such that $\mathfrak{s}(w_1) = 0$. We consider:

$$\mathfrak{h} \overset{\mathrm{def}}{=} \{\langle 1,2 \rangle, \langle 2,2 \rangle\},$$
$$\mathfrak{h}'_1 \overset{\mathrm{def}}{=} \{\langle 1,(2,0,1) \rangle, \langle 2,(2,0,3) \rangle, \langle 3,(\perp,\perp,\perp) \rangle\},$$
$$\mathfrak{h}'_2 \overset{\mathrm{def}}{=} \{\langle 1,(3,0,1) \rangle, \langle 2,(4,0,3) \rangle, \langle 3,(\perp,\perp,\perp) \rangle\}.$$

We have $(\mathfrak{s},\mathfrak{h}'_1) \rhd_{id} (\mathfrak{s},\mathfrak{h})$ and $(\mathfrak{s},\mathfrak{h}'_2) \rhd_\gamma (\mathfrak{s},\mathfrak{h})$, with $\gamma \overset{\mathrm{def}}{=} \{\langle 1,1 \rangle, \langle 2,2 \rangle, \langle 3,2 \rangle, \langle 4,2 \rangle\}$. Also, $\mathrm{trunc}(\mathfrak{h}'_1) = \{\langle 1,2 \rangle, \langle 2,2 \rangle\} = \mathfrak{h}$ and $\mathrm{trunc}(\mathfrak{h}'_2) = \{\langle 1,3 \rangle, \langle 2,4 \rangle\}$. Note that $\mathfrak{h}$ has out-degree $\kappa = 1$, whereas $\mathfrak{h}'_1$ and $\mathfrak{h}'_2$ have out-degree 3. ∎

Lemma 15. *If $(\mathfrak{s},\mathfrak{h}') \rhd_\gamma (\mathfrak{s},\mathfrak{h})$ then $\mathfrak{h} = \gamma(\mathrm{trunc}(\mathfrak{h}'))$, hence $(\mathfrak{s},\mathfrak{h}') \rhd_{id} (\mathfrak{s},\mathrm{trunc}(\mathfrak{h}'))$.*

The converse of Lemma 15 does not hold in general, but it holds under some additional conditions:

Lemma 16. *Consider a store $\mathfrak{s}$, let $\mathfrak{h}'$ be a heap and let $\mathfrak{h} \overset{\mathrm{def}}{=} \mathrm{trunc}(\mathfrak{h}')$. Let $D_2 \overset{\mathrm{def}}{=} \{\ell \in \mathrm{dom}(\mathfrak{h}') \mid \mathfrak{h}'(\ell) = \underline{\perp}\}$ and $D_1 \overset{\mathrm{def}}{=} \mathrm{dom}(\mathfrak{h}') \setminus D_2$. Assume that:*
1. *for every location $\ell \in D_1$, $\mathfrak{h}(\ell)$ is of the form $(\ell_1, \ldots, \ell_\kappa)$ and $\mathfrak{h}'(\ell)$ is of the form $(\ell_1, \ldots, \ell_\kappa, \mathfrak{s}(w), \ell'_1, \ldots, \ell'_\mu)$;*
2. *every location $\ell \in D_2$ has a connection in $\mathfrak{h}'$.*
Then $(\mathfrak{s},\mathfrak{h}') \rhd_{id} (\mathfrak{s},\mathfrak{h})$.

4.2 Transforming the Consequent

We first describe the transformation for the right-hand side of the entailment problem, as this transformation is simpler.

Definition 17. *We associate each n-ary predicate $p \in \mathcal{P}_r$ with a new predicate $\widehat{p}$ of arity $n + \nu$. We denote by $\widehat{\alpha}$ the formula obtained from α by replacing every predicate atom $p(x_1, \ldots, x_n)$ by $\widehat{p}(x_1, \ldots, x_n, w)$, where $w = (w_1, \ldots, w_\nu)$.*

Definition 18. *We denote by $\widehat{\mathcal{R}}$ the set of rules of the form:*

$$\widehat{p}(x_1, \ldots, x_n, w) \Leftarrow x_1 \mapsto (y_1, \ldots, y_\kappa, w, z_1, \ldots, z_\mu)\sigma * \widehat{\rho}\sigma * \xi_I * \chi_\sigma$$

where:

- $p(x_1,\ldots,x_n) \Leftarrow x_1 \mapsto (y_1,\ldots,y_\kappa) * \rho$ is a rule in $\mathcal{R}$ with $p \in \mathcal{P}_r$,
- $z_1,\ldots,z_\mu$ are variables not occurring in $\mathrm{fv}(\rho) \cup \{x_1,\ldots,x_n,y_1,\ldots,y_\kappa,w_1,\ldots,w_\nu\}$,
- σ is a substitution with $\mathrm{dom}(\sigma) \subseteq \mathrm{fv}(\rho) \setminus \{x_1\}$ and $\mathrm{rng}(\sigma) \subseteq \{w_1,\ldots,w_\nu\}$,
- $\xi_I \overset{def}{=} *_{i \in I} \bot(z_i)$, with $I \subseteq \{1,\ldots,\mu\}$,
- $\chi_\sigma \overset{def}{=} *_{x \in \mathrm{dom}(\sigma)} x \approx x\sigma$.

We denote by $\mathcal{R}_r$ the set of rules in $\widehat{\mathcal{R}}$ that are connected[5].

Note that the free variables w are added as parameters in the rules above, instead of some arbitrary tuple of fresh variables ω, of the same length as w. This is for the sake of conciseness, since these parameters ω will be systematically mapped to w.

Example 19. Assume that $\psi = \exists x . p(x,w_1)$, with $\nu = 1, \mu = 1$ and $\lambda(p) = \{2\}$. Assume also that p is associated with the rule: $p(u_1,u_2) \Leftarrow u_1 \mapsto u_1 * q(u_2)$. Observe that the rule is λ-connected, but not connected. Then $\mathrm{dom}(\sigma) \subseteq \{u_2\}, \mathrm{rng}(\sigma) \subseteq \{w_1\}$ and $I \subseteq \{1\}$, so that $\widehat{\mathcal{R}}$ contains the following rules:

$$(1)\ p(u_1,u_2,w_1) \Leftarrow u_1 \mapsto (u_1,w_1,z_1) * q(u_2)$$
$$(2)\ p(u_1,u_2,w_1) \Leftarrow u_1 \mapsto (u_1,w_1,z_1) * q(u_2) * \bot(z_1)$$
$$(3)\ p(u_1,u_2,w_1) \Leftarrow u_1 \mapsto (u_1,w_1,z_1) * q(w_1) * u_2 \approx w_1$$
$$(4)\ p(u_1,u_2,w_1) \Leftarrow u_1 \mapsto (u_1,w_1,z_1) * q(w_1) * \bot(z_1) * u_2 \approx w_1$$

Rules (1) and (2) are not connected, hence do not occur in $\mathcal{R}_r$. Rules (3) and (4) are connected, hence occur in $\mathcal{R}_r$. Note that (4) is established, but (3) is not. ∎

We now relate the SIDs $\mathcal{R}$ and $\mathcal{R}_r$ by the following result:

Lemma 20. *Let α be a formula that is λ-restricted w.r.t. $\{w_1,\ldots,w_\nu\}$ and contains no points-to atoms, with $\mathcal{P}(\alpha) \subseteq \mathcal{P}_r$. Given a store $\mathfrak{s}$ and two heaps $\mathfrak{h}$ and $\mathfrak{h}'$, such that $(\mathfrak{s},\mathfrak{h}') \triangleright_{id} (\mathfrak{s},\mathfrak{h})$, we have $(\mathfrak{s},\mathfrak{h}') \models_{\mathcal{R}_r} \widehat{\alpha}$ if and only if $(\mathfrak{s},\mathfrak{h}) \models_{\mathcal{R}} \alpha$.*

4.3 Transforming the Antecedent

We now describe the transformation operating on the left-hand side of the entailment problem. For technical convenience, we make the following assumption:

Assumption 21. *We assume that, for every predicate $p \in \mathcal{P}_l$, every rule of the form $p(x_1,\ldots,x_n) \Leftarrow \pi$ in $\mathcal{R}$ and every atom $q(x'_1,\ldots,x'_m)$ occurring in π, $x'_1 \notin \{x_1,\ldots,x_n\}$.*

This is without loss of generality, because every variable $x'_1 \in \{x_1,\ldots,x_n\}$ can be replaced by a fresh variable z, while conjoining the equational atom $z \approx x'_1$ to π. Note that the obtained SID may no longer be connected, but this is not problematic, because the left-hand side of the entailment is not required to be connected anyway.

Definition 22. *We associate each pair (p,X), where $p \in \mathcal{P}_l$, $ar(p) = n$ and $X \subseteq [\![1,n]\!]$, with a fresh predicate symbol p_X, such that $ar(p_X) = n + \nu$. A decoration of a formula α containing no points-to atoms, such that $\mathcal{P}(\alpha) \subseteq \mathcal{P}_l$, is a formula obtained by replacing each predicate atom $\beta \overset{def}{=} q(y_1,\ldots,y_m)$ in α by an atom of the form $q_{X_\beta}(y_1,\ldots,y_m,w)$, with $X_\beta \subseteq [\![1,m]\!]$. The set of decorations of a formula α is denoted by $D(\alpha)$.*

---

[5] Note that all the rules in $\widehat{\mathcal{R}}$ are progressing.

The role of the set X in a predicate atom $p_X(x_1,\ldots,x_n,\boldsymbol{w})$ will be explained below. Note that the set of decorations of an atom α is always finite.

Definition 23. *We denote by* $D(\mathcal{R})$ *the set of rules of the form*

$$p_X(x_1,\ldots,x_n,\boldsymbol{w}) \Leftarrow x_1 \mapsto (y_1,\ldots,y_\kappa,\boldsymbol{w},z_1,\ldots,z_\mu)\sigma * \rho' * *_{i\in I}\bot(z_i),$$

where:

- $p(x_1,\ldots,x_n) \Leftarrow x_1 \mapsto (y_1,\ldots,y_\kappa) * \rho$ *is a rule in* $\mathcal{R}$ *and* $X \subseteq [\![1,n]\!]$;
- $\{z_1,\ldots,z_\mu\} = (\mathrm{fv}(\rho) \cup \{y_1,\ldots,y_\kappa\}) \setminus \{x_1,\ldots,x_n\}$,
- σ *is a substitution, with* $\mathrm{dom}(\sigma) \subseteq \{z_1,\ldots,z_\mu\}$ *and* $\mathrm{rng}(\sigma) \subseteq \{x_1,\ldots,x_n,w_1,\ldots,w_\nu,$ $z_1,\ldots,z_\mu\}$;
- ρ' *is a decoration of* $\rho\sigma$;
- $I \subseteq \{1,\ldots,\mu\}$ *and* $z_i \notin \mathrm{dom}(\sigma)$, *for all* $i \in I$.

Lemma 24. *Let* α *be a formula containing no points-to atom, with* $\mathcal{P}(\alpha) \subseteq \mathcal{P}_l$, *and let* α' *be a decoration of* α. *If* $(\mathfrak{s},\mathfrak{h}') \models_{D(\mathcal{R})} \alpha'$ *and* $(\mathfrak{s},\mathfrak{h}') \rhd_{id} (\mathfrak{s},\mathfrak{h})$, *then* $(\mathfrak{s},\mathfrak{h}) \models_{\mathcal{R}} \alpha$.

At this point, the set X for predicate symbol p_X is of little interest: atoms are simply decorated with arbitrary sets. However, we shall restrict the considered rules in such a way that for every model $(\mathfrak{s},\mathfrak{h})$ of an atom $p_X(x_1,\ldots,x_{n+\nu})$, with $n = ar(p)$, the set X denotes a set of indices $i \in [\![1,n]\!]$ such that $\mathfrak{s}(x_i) \in \mathrm{dom}(\mathfrak{h})$. In other words, X will denote a set of formal parameters of p_X that are allocated in every model of p_X.

Definition 25. *Given a formula* α, *we define the set* $Alloc(\alpha)$ *as follows:* $x \in Alloc(\alpha)$ *iff* α *contains either a points-to atom of the form* $x \mapsto (y_1,\ldots,y_{\kappa+\mu+\nu})$, *or a predicate atom* $q_X(x'_1,\ldots,x'_{m+\nu})$ *with* $x'_i = x$ *for some* $i \in X$.

Note that, in contrast with Definition 1, we do not consider that $x \in Alloc(\alpha)$, for those variables x related to a variable from $Alloc(\alpha)$ by equalities.

Definition 26. *A rule* $p_X(x_1,\ldots,x_{n+\nu}) \Leftarrow \pi$ *in* $D(\mathcal{R})$ *with* $n = ar(p)$ *with* $\rho = x_1 \mapsto$ $(y_1,\ldots,y_k,\boldsymbol{w},z_1,\ldots,z_\mu) * \rho'$ *is well-defined if the following conditions hold:*

1. $\{x_1\} \subseteq Alloc(p_X(x_1,\ldots,x_{n+\nu})) \subseteq Alloc(\pi)$;
2. $\mathrm{fv}(\pi) \subseteq Alloc(\pi) \cup \{x_1,\ldots,x_{n+\nu}\}$.

We denote by $\mathcal{R}_l$ *the set of well-defined rules in* $D(\mathcal{R})$.

We first state an important properties of $\mathcal{R}_l$.

Lemma 27. *Every rule in* $\mathcal{R}_l$ *is progressing, connected and established.*

We now relate the systems $\mathcal{R}$ and $\mathcal{R}_l$ by the following result:

Definition 28. *A store* $\mathfrak{s}$ *is quasi-injective if, for all* $x,y \in \mathrm{dom}(\mathfrak{s})$, *the implication* $\mathfrak{s}(x) = \mathfrak{s}(y) \Rightarrow x = y$ *holds whenever* $\{x,y\} \not\subseteq \{w_1,\ldots,w_\nu\}$.

Lemma 29. *Let* L *be an infinite subset of* $\mathcal{L}$. *Consider a formula* α *containing no points-to atom, with* $\mathcal{P}(\alpha) \subseteq \mathcal{P}_l$, *and let* $(\mathfrak{s},\mathfrak{h})$ *be an* $\mathcal{R}$-*model of* α, *where* $\mathfrak{s}$ *is quasi-injective, and* $(\mathrm{rng}(\mathfrak{s}) \cup \mathrm{loc}(\mathfrak{h})) \cap L = \emptyset$. *There exists a decoration* α' *of* α, *a heap* $\mathfrak{h}'$ *and a mapping* $\gamma : L \to \mathcal{L}$ *such that:*

- $(\mathfrak{s}, \mathfrak{h}') \rhd_\gamma (\mathfrak{s}, \mathfrak{h})$,
- *if* $\ell \notin L$ *then* $\gamma(\ell) = \ell$,
- $\mathrm{loc}(\mathfrak{h}') \setminus \mathrm{rng}(\mathfrak{s}) \subseteq L$,
- $\mathrm{dom}(\mathrm{aux}(\mathfrak{h}')) \subseteq L$ *and*
- $(\mathfrak{s}, \mathfrak{h}') \models_{\mathcal{R}_l} \alpha'$.

Furthermore, if $\mathfrak{s}(u) \in \mathrm{dom}(\mathfrak{h}') \setminus \{\mathfrak{s}(w_i) \mid 1 \leq i \leq \nu\}$ *then* $u \in \mathit{Alloc}(\alpha')$.

4.4   Transforming Entailments

We define $\widehat{\mathcal{R}} \overset{\text{def}}{=} \mathcal{R}_l \cup \mathcal{R}_r$. We show that the instance $\phi \vdash_{\mathcal{R}} \psi$ of the safe entailment problem can be solved by considering an entailment problem on $\widehat{\mathcal{R}}$ involving the elements of $D(\phi)$ (see Definition 22). Note that the rules from $\mathcal{R}_l$ are progressing, connected and established, by Lemma 27, whereas the rules from $\mathcal{R}_r$ are progressing and connected, by Definition 18. Hence, each entailment problem $\phi' \vdash_{\widehat{\mathcal{R}}} \widehat{\psi}$, where $\phi' \in D(\phi)$, is progressing, connected and left-established.

Lemma 30. $\phi \models_{\mathcal{R}} \psi$ *if and only if* $\bigvee_{\phi' \in D(\phi)} \phi' \models_{\widehat{\mathcal{R}}} \widehat{\psi}$.

Proof. "$\Rightarrow$" Assume that $\phi \models_{\mathcal{R}} \psi$ and let $\phi' \in D(\phi)$ be a formula, $(\mathfrak{s}, \mathfrak{h}')$ be an $\widehat{\mathcal{R}}$-model of ϕ' and $\mathfrak{h} \overset{\text{def}}{=} \mathrm{trunc}(\mathfrak{h}')$. By construction, $(\mathfrak{s}, \mathfrak{h}')$ is an $\mathcal{R}_l$-model of ϕ'. By definition of $D(\phi)$, ϕ' is a decoration of ϕ. Let $D_2 \overset{\text{def}}{=} \{\ell \in \mathrm{dom}(\mathfrak{h}') \mid \mathfrak{h}'(\ell) = \perp\}$, $D_1 \overset{\text{def}}{=} \mathrm{dom}(\mathfrak{h}') \setminus D_2$, and consider a location $\ell \in \mathrm{dom}(\mathfrak{h}')$. By definition, ℓ must be allocated by some rule in $\mathcal{R}_l$. If ℓ is allocated by a rule of the form given in Definition 23, then necessarily $\mathfrak{h}'(\ell)$ is of the form $(\ell_1, \ldots, \ell_\kappa, \mathfrak{s}(w), \ell'_1, \ldots, \ell'_\mu)$ and $\ell \in D_1$. Otherwise, ℓ is allocated by the predicate $\perp$ and we must have $\ell \in D_2$ by definition of the only rule for $\perp$. Since this predicate must occur within a rule of the form given in Definition 23, ℓ necessarily occurs in the μ last components of the image of a location in D_1, hence admits a connection in $\mathfrak{h}'$. Consequently, by Lemma 16 $(\mathfrak{s}, \mathfrak{h}') \rhd (\mathfrak{s}, \mathfrak{h})$, and by Lemma 24, $(\mathfrak{s}, \mathfrak{h}) \models_{\mathcal{R}} \phi$. Thus $(\mathfrak{s}, \mathfrak{h}) \models_{\mathcal{R}} \psi$, and by Lemma 20, $(\mathfrak{s}, \mathfrak{h}') \models_{\mathcal{R}_r} \widehat{\psi}$, thus $(\mathfrak{s}, \mathfrak{h}') \models_{\widehat{\mathcal{R}}} \widehat{\psi}$.

"$\Leftarrow$" Assume that $\bigvee_{\phi' \in D(\phi)} \phi' \models_{\widehat{\mathcal{R}}} \widehat{\psi}$ and let $(\mathfrak{s}, \mathfrak{h})$ be a $\mathcal{R}$-model of ϕ. Since the truth values of ϕ and ψ depend only on the variables in $\mathrm{fv}(\phi) \cup \mathrm{fv}(\psi)$, we may assume, w.l.o.g., that $\mathfrak{s}$ is quasi-injective. Consider an infinite set $L \subseteq \mathcal{L}$ such that $(\mathrm{rng}(\mathfrak{s}) \cup \mathrm{loc}(\mathfrak{h})) \cap L = \emptyset$. By Lemma 29, there exist a heap $\mathfrak{h}'$, a mapping $\gamma : L \to \mathcal{L}$ and a decoration ϕ' of ϕ such that $\gamma(\ell) = \ell$ for all $\ell \notin L$, $(\mathfrak{s}, \mathfrak{h}') \rhd_\gamma (\mathfrak{s}, \mathfrak{h})$ and $(\mathfrak{s}, \mathfrak{h}') \models \phi'$. Since $\mathrm{rng}(\mathfrak{s}) \cap L = \emptyset$, we also have $\gamma(\mathfrak{s}) = \mathfrak{s}$. Then $(\mathfrak{s}, \mathfrak{h}') \models \widehat{\psi}$. Let $\mathfrak{h}_1 \overset{\text{def}}{=} \mathrm{trunc}(\mathfrak{h}')$. Since $(\mathfrak{s}, \mathfrak{h}') \rhd_\gamma (\mathfrak{s}, \mathfrak{h})$, by Lemma 15 we have $(\mathfrak{s}, \mathfrak{h}') \rhd_{id} (\mathfrak{s}, \mathfrak{h}_1)$, and by Lemma 20, $(\mathfrak{s}, \mathfrak{h}_1) \models \psi$. By Lemma 15 we have $\mathfrak{h} = \gamma(\mathfrak{h}_1)$. Since ψ is λ-restricted w.r.t. $\{w_1, \ldots, w_n\}$, we deduce by Lemma 10 that $(\mathfrak{s}, \mathfrak{h}) \models \psi$. $\qquad\square$

This leads to the main result of this paper:

Theorem 31. *The safe entailment problem is 2EXPTIME-complete.*

Proof. The 2EXPTIME-hard lower bound follows from [8, Theorem 32], as the class of progressing, λ-connected and λ-restricted entailment problems is a subset of the safe entailment class. For the 2EXPTIME membership, Lemma 30 describes a many-one reduction to the progressing, connected and established class, shown to be in 2EXP-TIME, by Theorem 4. Considering an instance $\mathfrak{P} = \phi \vdash_{\mathcal{R}} \psi$ of the safe class, Lemma 30 reduces this to checking the validity of $|D(\phi)|$ instances of the form $\phi' \vdash_{\widehat{\mathcal{R}}} \widehat{\psi}$, that are all progressing, connected and established, by Lemma 27. Since a formula $\phi' \in D(\phi)$ is obtained by replacing each predicate atom $p(x_1, \ldots, x_n)$ of ϕ by $p_X(x_1, \ldots, x_n, \boldsymbol{w})$ and there are at most 2^n such predicate atoms, it follows that $|D(\phi)| = 2^{O(\mathrm{w}(\mathfrak{P}))}$. To obtain 2EXPTIME-membership of the problem, it is sufficient to show that each of the progressing, connected and established instances $\phi' \vdash_{\widehat{\mathcal{R}}} \widehat{\psi}$ can be built in time $|\mathfrak{P}| \cdot 2^{O(\mathrm{w}(\mathfrak{P}) \cdot \log \mathrm{w}(\mathfrak{P}))}$. First, for each $\phi' \in D(\phi)$, by Definition 22, we have $|\phi'| \leq |\phi| \cdot (1 + v) \leq |\phi| \cdot (1 + \mathrm{w}(\mathfrak{P})) = |\phi| \cdot 2^{O(\log \mathrm{w}(\mathfrak{P}))}$. By Definition 17, we have $|\widehat{\phi}| \leq |\phi| \cdot (1 + v) = |\phi| \cdot 2^{O(\log \mathrm{w}(\mathfrak{P}))}$. By Definition 23, $D(\mathcal{R})$ can be obtained by enumeration in time that depends linearly of

$$|D(\mathcal{R})| \leq |\mathcal{R}| \cdot 2^{\mu} \cdot (n + v + \mu)^v \leq |\mathcal{R}| \cdot 2^{\mathrm{w}(\mathfrak{P}) + \mathrm{w}(\mathfrak{P}) \cdot \log \mathrm{w}(\mathfrak{P})} = |\mathfrak{P}| \cdot 2^{O(\mathrm{w}(\mathfrak{P}))}$$

This is because the number of intervals I is bounded by 2^{μ} and the number of substitutions σ by $(n + v + \mu)^v$, in Definition 23. By Definition 25, checking whether a rule is well-defined can be done in polynomial time in the size of the rule, hence in $2^{O(\mathrm{w}(\mathfrak{P}))}$, so the construction of $\mathcal{R}$ takes time $|\mathfrak{P}| \cdot 2^{O(\mathrm{w}(\mathfrak{P}) \log \mathrm{w}(\mathfrak{P}))}$. Similarly, by Definition 23, the set $\widehat{\mathcal{R}}$ is constructed in time

$$|\widehat{\mathcal{R}}| \leq |\mathcal{R}| \cdot 2^{\mu} \cdot \mathrm{w}(\mathfrak{P})^v \leq |\mathcal{R}| \cdot 2^{\mathrm{w}}(\mathfrak{P}) \cdot 2^{\mathrm{w}(\mathfrak{P}) \cdot \log \mathrm{w}(\mathfrak{P})} = |\mathfrak{P}| \cdot 2^{O(\mathrm{w}(\mathfrak{P}))}$$

Moreover, checking that a rule in $\widehat{\mathcal{R}}$ is connected can be done in time polynomial in the size of the rule, hence the construction of $\mathcal{R}_c$ takes time $2^{O(\mathrm{w}(\mathfrak{P}) \log \mathrm{w}(\mathfrak{P}))}$. Then the entire reduction takes time $2^{O(\mathrm{w}(\mathfrak{P}) \log \mathrm{w}(\mathfrak{P}))}$, which proves the 2EXPTIME upper bound for the safe class of entailments.   □

5   Conclusion and Future Work

Together with the results of [10,14,6,8], Theorem 31 draws a clear and complete picture concerning the decidability and complexity of the entailment problem in Separation Logic with inductive definitions. The room for improvement in this direction is probably very limited, since Theorem 31 pushes the frontier quite far. Moreover, virtually any further relaxation of the conditions leads to undecidability.

A possible line of future research which could be relevant for applications would be to consider inductive rules constructing simultaneously several data structures, which could be useful for instance to handle predicates comparing two structures, but it is clear that very strong conditions would be required to ensure decidability. We are also interested in defining effective, goal-directed, proof procedures (i.e., sequent or tableaux calculi) for testing the validity of entailment problems. Thanks to the reduction devised in the present paper, it is sufficient to focus on systems that are progressing, connected and left-established. We are also trying to extend the results to entailments with formulæ involving data with infinite domains, either by considering a theory of locations (e.g., arithmetic on addresses), or, more realistically, by considering additional sorts for data.

References

1. Timos Antonopoulos, Nikos Gorogiannis, Christoph Haase, Max I. Kanovich, and Joël Ouaknine. Foundations for decision problems in separation logic with general inductive predicates. In Anca Muscholl, editor, *FOSSACS 2014, ETAPS 2014, Proceedings*, volume 8412 of *Lecture Notes in Computer Science*, pages 411–425, 2014.
2. Josh Berdine, Byron Cook, and Samin Ishtiaq. Slayer: Memory safety for systems-level code. In Ganesh Gopalakrishnan andShaz Qadeer, editor, *Computer Aided Verification - 23rd International Conference, CAV 2011, Snowbird, UT, USA, July 14-20, 2011. Proceedings*, volume 6806 of *LNCS*, pages 178–183. Springer, 2011.
3. Cristiano Calcagno, Dino Distefano, Jérémy Dubreil, Dominik Gabi, Pieter Hooimeijer, Martino Luca, Peter W. O'Hearn, Irene Papakonstantinou, Jim Purbrick, and Dulma Rodriguez. Moving fast with software verification. In Klaus Havelund, Gerard J. Holzmann, and Rajeev Joshi, editors, *NASA Formal Methods - 7th International Symposium, NFM 2015, Pasadena, CA, USA, April 27-29, 2015, Proceedings*, volume 9058 of *LNCS*, pages 3–11. Springer, 2015.
4. Duc-Hiep Chu, Joxan Jaffar, and Minh-Thai Trinh. Automatic induction proofs of data-structures in imperative programs. In David Grove and Stephen M. Blackburn, editors, *Proceedings of the 36th ACM SIGPLAN Conference on Programming Language Design and Implementation, Portland, OR, USA, June 15-17, 2015*, pages 457–466. ACM, 2015. URL: https://doi.org/10.1145/2737924.2737984, doi:10.1145/2737924.2737984.
5. Kamil Dudka, Petr Peringer, and Tomás Vojnar. Predator: A practical tool for checking manipulation of dynamic data structures using separation logic. In Ganesh Gopalakrishnan and Shaz Qadeer, editors, *Computer Aided Verification - 23rd International Conference, CAV 2011, Snowbird, UT, USA, July 14-20, 2011. Proceedings*, volume 6806 of *LNCS*, pages 372–378. Springer, 2011.
6. Mnacho Echenim, Radu Iosif, and Nicolas Peltier. Entailment checking in separation logic with inductive definitions is 2-exptime hard. In *LPAR 2020: 23rd International Conference on Logic for Programming, Artificial Intelligence and Reasoning, Alicante, Spain, May 22-27, 2020*, volume 73 of *EPiC Series in Computing*, pages 191–211. EasyChair, 2020.
7. Mnacho Echenim, Radu Iosif, and Nicolas Peltier. Entailment is Undecidable for Symbolic Heap Separation Logic Formulae with Non-Established Inductive Rules. working paper or preprint, September 2020. URL: https://hal.archives-ouvertes.fr/hal-02951630.
8. Mnacho Echenim, Radu Iosif, and Nicolas Peltier. Decidable entailments in separation logic with inductive definitions: Beyond establishment. In *CSL 2021: 29th International Conference on Computer Science Logic*, EPiC Series in Computing. EasyChair, 2021.
9. Mnacho Echenim, Radu Iosif, and Nicolas Peltier. Unifying decidable entailments in separation logic with inductive definitions, 2021. arXiv:2012.14361.
10. Radu Iosif, Adam Rogalewicz, and Jiri Simacek. The tree width of separation logic with recursive definitions. In *Proc. of CADE-24*, volume 7898 of *LNCS*, 2013.
11. Radu Iosif, Adam Rogalewicz, and Tomás Vojnar. Deciding entailments in inductive separation logic with tree automata. In Franck Cassez and Jean-François Raskin, editors, *ATVA 2014, Proceedings*, volume 8837 of *Lecture Notes in Computer Science*, pages 201–218. Springer, 2014.
12. Samin S Ishtiaq and Peter W O'Hearn. Bi as an assertion language for mutable data structures. In *ACM SIGPLAN Notices*, volume 36, pages 14–26, 2001.
13. Jens Katelaan, Christoph Matheja, and Florian Zuleger. Effective entailment checking for separation logic with inductive definitions. In Tomás Vojnar and Lijun Zhang, editors, *TACAS 2019, Proceedings, Part II*, volume 11428 of *Lecture Notes in Computer Science*, pages 319–336. Springer, 2019.

14. Jens Pagel and Florian Zuleger. Beyond symbolic heaps: Deciding separation logic with inductive definitions. In *LPAR-23*, volume 73 of *EPiC Series in Computing*, pages 390–408. EasyChair, 2020.
15. J.C. Reynolds. Separation Logic: A Logic for Shared Mutable Data Structures. In *Proc. of LICS'02*, 2002.
16. Quang-Trung Ta, Ton Chanh Le, Siau-Cheng Khoo, and Wei-Ngan Chin. Automated lemma synthesis in symbolic-heap separation logic. *Proc. ACM Program. Lang.*, 2(POPL):9:1–9:29, 2018. URL: https://doi.org/10.1145/3158097, doi:10.1145/3158097.

Open Access This chapter is licensed under the terms of the Creative Commons Attribution 4.0 International License (http://creativecommons.org/licenses/by/4.0/), which permits use, sharing, adaptation, distribution and reproduction in any medium or format, as long as you give appropriate credit to the original author(s) and the source, provide a link to the Creative Commons license and indicate if changes were made.

The images or other third party material in this chapter are included in the chapter's Creative Commons license, unless indicated otherwise in a credit line to the material. If material is not included in the chapter's Creative Commons license and your intended use is not permitted by statutory regulation or exceeds the permitted use, you will need to obtain permission directly from the copyright holder.

Subformula Linking for Intuitionistic Logic with Application to Type Theory

Kaustuv Chaudhuri [iD]

Inria & LIX/Ecole polytechnique, Palaiseau, France
kaustuv.chaudhuri@inria.fr, https://chaudhuri.info

Abstract. Subformula linking is an interactive theorem proving technique that was initially proposed for (classical) linear logic. It is based on truth and context preserving rewrites of a conjecture that are triggered by a user indicating *links* between subformulas, which can be done by direct manipulation, without the need of tactics or proof languages. The system guarantees that a true conjecture can always be rewritten to a known, usually trivial, theorem. In this work, we extend subformula linking to intuitionistic first-order logic with simply typed lambda-terms as the term language of this logic. We then use a well known embedding of intuitionistic type theory into this logic to demonstrate one way to extend linking to type theory.

1 Introduction

Suppose you want to prove a conjecture such as:

$$\left(\forall x.\, \exists y.\, a(f(x), y)\right) \wedge \left(\forall z.\, a(f(f(c)), z) \supset b(z)\right) \supset \exists u.\, b(f(u))$$

or to find replacements for the ?s that would allow a dependent type such as the following to be inhabited:

$$\Pi u{:}(\Pi x{:}a.\, \Pi y{:}(b\,x).\, c\,x\,y).\, \Pi v{:}(\Pi x{:}a.\, b\,x).\, \Pi w{:}a.\, (c\,?\,?).$$

In a mainstream interactive theorem proving system you would attempt it by giving instructions to a carefully constructed proof verification engine using a *formal proof language*, often with a *read-eval-print* loop for immediate feedback. Your instructions would guide the verifier through the twists and turns of a formal derivation until it is satisfied that all formal obligations have been established. Your language of instructions could be tactics-based (such as in Coq), or it could be a programming language itself (such as in HOL-Light or Agda); it could also have a formal *structure* or be *declarative* (such as Isabelle/Isar).[1] Despite these superficial differences, all such systems can broadly be called *linguistic* because the internal state of the verifier can only be modified by means of the formal

---

[1] These are just illustrative examples of mainstream proof systems and should not be read as assigning them a position of privilege or authority.

© The Author(s) 2021
A. Platzer and G. Sutcliffe (Eds.): CADE 2021, LNAI 12699, pp. 200–216, 2021.
https://doi.org/10.1007/978-3-030-79876-5_12

proof language (and the whims—or semantics, if you prefer—of the interpreter of the language).

An alternative to such a linguistic system would be a system of *direct manipulation*, wherein there is a tangible representation of the state of the verifier that one can modify directly using such tools as one's fingers, pointing devices, or eye movements. The verifier's job is then to make sure that the direct manipulation attempts are allowed when they are logically permissible and prevented when they are not. A prominent example of such a direct manipulation system is the *proof by pointing* technique [3], where mouse clicks on the representation of a proof state (in a version of Coq) are given a meaning: a click on a connective deep in a formula is interpreted as a sequence of Coq tactics that bring the connective to the top, at which point it could be made to interact with the other hypotheses or the conclusion in the usual manner.

A generalization of this idea, called *proof by linking*, was proposed in [4]. It allows the user not only to point but also to *link* different subformulas, say with a multi-touch input device or with a drag-and-drop metaphor. There are two immediate benefits of linking over pointing: (1) the surrounding context of a formula is not destroyed because the linked subformulas are not brought to the top, and (2) the interaction mode is easier to describe to complete novices. For instance, a novice could be instructed to "match the atoms" for the first example above, in which case they might start by attempting the following link:

$$(\forall x. \, \exists y. \, a(f(x), y)) \wedge (\forall z. \, \underline{a(f(f(c)), z)} \supset b(z)) \supset \exists u. \, b(f(u)).$$

The linking procedure would interpret this link as a desire to "bring" the source atom "to" the destination atom. Without touching any other part of the conjecture except the smallest subformula containing both the source and the destination of the link, the conjecture would be *rewritten* to a different one:

$$\exists x. \, \forall y. \, \forall z. \, \Big((a(f(x), y) \supset a(f(f(c)), z)) \supset b(z)\Big) \supset \exists u. \, b(f(u)).$$

The surrounding context of the link is preserved as nothing is brought to the top; instead, the source moves through the formula tree to meet the destination. The rewrites that underlie the transformation are *provability preserving*: if the rewritten conjecture is provable, then so is the original conjecture. Eventually, the conjecture (if true) would be reduced to a trivial theorem such as $\top$. Note that the novice user does not need to know *any* proof language to draw these links, not even a conceptual proof system such as the sequent calculus.

The original *proof by linking* technique was proposed for classical linear logic and freely exploited the *calculus of structures* [17]. In this paper we show how to adapt the technique to intuitionistic logics and intuitionistic type theories, where the calculus of structures is not so well behaved [18,8] (or, in the case of dependent type theory, entirely missing), and where preserving the context of the rewrites is a more delicate task. We do this by first defining the technique for intuitionistic first-order logic over λ-terms, and then we use an existing complete (shallow) embedding of dependent type theory in this logic [6,15]. A secondary contribution is to give some insight into what a deep inference formalism might look like for dependent type theory.

2   Subformula Linking for Intuitionistic First-Order Logic

This section will serve both as an introduction to the subformula linking procedure, and as evidence that the technique can be applied to intuitionistic logics. Let us do this in two phases: first for the the propositional fragment, and then extended with first-order quantification.

2.1   The Propositional Fragment

We will use the following grammar of *formulas* (written $A, B, \dots$), where *atomic formulas* are written in lowercase $(a, b, \dots)$.

$$A, B, \dots ::= a \mid A \wedge B \mid \top \mid A \vee B \mid \bot \mid A \supset B$$

Following usual conventions, the connectives $\wedge$ and $\vee$ are left-associative, while $\supset$ is right-associative; the binding priority from strongest to weakest is $\wedge, \vee, \supset$.

The true formulas of this calculus can be defined in terms of derivability in a variety of formal systems such as with the sequent calculus LJ or G3ip [11]. In this paper the precise sequent calculus is not of primary concern; however, we will use the notation $\Gamma \vdash C$ where Γ is a multiset of formulas to denote that the formula C is derivable from the assumptions Γ using any such calculus.

A *positively signed formula context* (written $\mathcal{C}\{\}$) is a formula with a single occurrence of a hole $\{\}$ in the place where a positively signed subformula may occur; it is defined mutually recursively with an *negatively signed formula context* (written $\mathcal{A}\{\}$) by the following grammar, where $* \in \{\wedge, \vee\}$.

$$\mathcal{C}\{\} ::= \{\} \mid A * \mathcal{C}\{\} \mid \mathcal{C}\{\} * B \mid A \supset \mathcal{C}\{\} \mid \mathcal{A}\{\} \supset B$$
$$\mathcal{A}\{\} ::= A * \mathcal{A}\{\} \mid \mathcal{A}\{\} * B \mid A \supset \mathcal{A}\{\} \mid \mathcal{C}\{\} \supset B$$

The *replacement* of the hole in $\mathcal{C}\{\}$ (resp. $\mathcal{A}\{\}$) with a formula A yields a new formula, which we write as $\mathcal{C}\{A\}$ (resp. $\mathcal{A}\{A\}$). For instance, if $\mathcal{C}\{\}$ is $a \wedge ((b \supset \{\}) \vee d)$, then $\mathcal{C}\{c \supset \bot\}$ is $a \wedge ((b \supset (c \supset \bot)) \vee d)$.

Theorem 1. *Suppose that* $A \vdash B$. *Then:*

- *for any positively signed context* $\mathcal{C}\{\}$, *it is the case that* $\mathcal{C}\{A\} \vdash \mathcal{C}\{B\}$; *and*
- *for any negatively signed context* $\mathcal{A}\{\}$, *it is the case that* $\mathcal{A}\{B\} \vdash \mathcal{A}\{A\}$.

Proof. Induction on the structure of the contexts $\mathcal{C}\{\}$ or $\mathcal{A}\{\}$. □

In order to define the subformula linking procedure for this calculus, we work with *interaction formulas*; an interaction formula is a formula where:

Terminal rules

$$\frac{\mathcal{C}\{\top\}}{\mathcal{C}\{a \triangleright a\}} \ \text{in} \qquad \frac{\mathcal{C}\{A \supset B\}}{\mathcal{C}\{A \triangleright B\}} \ \text{rel}$$

(the conclusion of rel is understood as not overlapping that of in)

Positively signed rules

$$\frac{\mathcal{C}\{(A \triangleright B) \wedge F\}}{\mathcal{C}\{A \triangleright (B \wedge F)\}} \ \triangleright\wedge_1 \qquad \frac{\mathcal{C}\{F \wedge (A \triangleright B)\}}{\mathcal{C}\{A \triangleright (F \wedge B)\}} \ \triangleright\wedge_2$$

$$\frac{\mathcal{C}\{(A \triangleright B) \wedge (F \supset B)\}}{\mathcal{C}\{(A \vee F) \triangleright B\}} \ \vee\triangleright_1 \qquad \frac{\mathcal{C}\{(F \supset B) \wedge (A \triangleright B)\}}{\mathcal{C}\{(F \vee A) \triangleright B\}} \ \vee\triangleright_2$$

$$\frac{\mathcal{C}\{(A \circ B) \supset F\}}{\mathcal{C}\{A \triangleright (B \supset F)\}} \ \triangleright\supset_1 \qquad \frac{\mathcal{C}\{F \supset (A \triangleright B)\}}{\mathcal{C}\{A \triangleright (F \supset B)\}} \ \triangleright\supset_2$$

$$\frac{\mathcal{C}\{A \triangleright B\}}{\mathcal{C}\{A \triangleright (B \vee F)\}} \ \triangleright\vee_1 \qquad \frac{\mathcal{C}\{A \triangleright B\}}{\mathcal{C}\{A \triangleright (F \vee B)\}} \ \triangleright\vee_2$$

$$\frac{\mathcal{C}\{A \triangleright B\}}{\mathcal{C}\{(A \wedge F) \triangleright B\}} \ \wedge\triangleright_1 \qquad \frac{\mathcal{C}\{A \triangleright B\}}{\mathcal{C}\{(F \wedge A) \triangleright B\}} \ \wedge\triangleright_2 \qquad \frac{\mathcal{C}\{F \wedge (A \triangleright B)\}}{\mathcal{C}\{(F \supset A) \triangleright B\}} \ \supset\triangleright$$

Negatively signed rules

$$\frac{\mathcal{A}\{(A \circ B) \vee F\}}{\mathcal{A}\{A \circ (B \vee F)\}} \ \circ\vee_1 \qquad \frac{\mathcal{A}\{F \vee (A \circ B)\}}{\mathcal{A}\{A \circ (F \vee B)\}} \ \circ\vee_2$$

$$\frac{\mathcal{A}\{A \circ B\}}{\mathcal{A}\{A \circ (B \wedge F)\}} \ \circ\wedge_1 \qquad \frac{\mathcal{A}\{A \circ B\}}{\mathcal{A}\{A \circ (F \wedge B)\}} \ \circ\wedge_2$$

$$\frac{\mathcal{A}\{(A \triangleright B) \supset F\}}{\mathcal{A}\{A \circ (B \supset F)\}} \ \circ\supset_1 \qquad \frac{\mathcal{A}\{F \supset (A \circ B)\}}{\mathcal{A}\{A \circ (F \supset B)\}} \ \circ\supset_2$$

(plus all the symmetric variants)

Fig. 1. Inference rules for interaction formulas

– either a *single* occurrence of $\supset$ is replaced with $\triangleright$,
– or a *single* occurrence of $\wedge$ is replaced with $\circ$.

We will define an inference system for interaction formulas that consist of inference rules with a single conclusion and a single premise, both of which are either formulas or interaction formulas. The inference rule represents an admissible rule of intuitionistic logic: if the premise is a theorem, then so is the conclusion. The full collection of rules is shown in fig. 1. There are three kinds of rules, explained below in an upwards (conclusion to premises) reading.

– *Terminal rules* are used to terminate a $\triangleright$-interaction in a positively signed context. In the case where the $\triangleright$-interaction links two occurrences of the

Interaction creation rules   Contraction

$$\frac{\mathcal{C}\{A \triangleright B\}}{\mathcal{C}\{A \supset B\}} \triangleright \qquad \frac{\mathcal{A}\{A \circ B\}}{\mathcal{A}\{A \wedge B\}} \circ \qquad\qquad \frac{\mathcal{C}\{A \supset A \supset F\}}{\mathcal{C}\{A \supset F\}} \text{ cont}$$

Simplification rules

$$\frac{\mathcal{C}\{\top\}}{\mathcal{C}\{A \supset \top\}} \qquad \frac{\mathcal{C}\{B\}}{\mathcal{C}\{\top \supset B\}} \qquad \frac{\mathcal{C}\{\top\}}{\mathcal{C}\{\bot \supset B\}}$$

$$\frac{\mathcal{C}\{F\}}{\mathcal{C}\{\top \wedge F\}} \quad \frac{\mathcal{C}\{F\}}{\mathcal{C}\{F \wedge \top\}} \quad \frac{\mathcal{A}\{F\}}{\mathcal{A}\{\bot \vee F\}} \quad \frac{\mathcal{A}\{F\}}{\mathcal{A}\{F \vee \bot\}}$$

$$\frac{\mathcal{A}\{\bot\}}{\mathcal{A}\{\bot \wedge F\}} \quad \frac{\mathcal{A}\{\bot\}}{\mathcal{A}\{F \wedge \bot\}} \quad \frac{\mathcal{C}\{\top\}}{\mathcal{C}\{\top \vee F\}} \quad \frac{\mathcal{C}\{\top\}}{\mathcal{C}\{F \vee \top\}}$$

Fig. 2. Link creation, contraction, and simplification. The conclusion in each case must not be an interaction formula.

same atom, the result is $\top$; otherwise the $\triangleright$ turns back into $\supset$. These are the only rules that can transition out of interaction formulas.

- *Positively signed rules* operate on a $\triangleright$-interaction in a positively signed context. The rules are written in fig. 1 in such a way that the subformulas A and B are brought together in the premise, and occurrences of F (if they exist) are side formulas.

- *Negatively signed rules* operate on a $\circ$-interaction in an negatively signed context. Fig. 1 only shows one of the two symmetric variants for each case; the other variant is built by permuting A with B and transposing the operands of $\circ$. For instance, $\circ\vee_1$ has the following symmetric variant.

$$\frac{\mathcal{A}\{(A \circ B) \vee F\}}{\mathcal{A}\{(A \vee F) \circ B\}} \circ\vee_{1'}$$

We will use primes to systematically name the symmetric variants of rules.

Proposition 2 (Soundness). *Interpreting $\triangleright$ as $\supset$ and $\circ$ as $\wedge$, each rule of fig. 1 with premise P and conclusion Q has the property that $P \vdash Q$.*

Proof. Straightforward consequence of theorem 1. $\qquad\qquad\qquad\qquad\qquad$ □

Two further administrative steps remain to complete the technique. First, since the rules of fig. 1 always contain an interaction formula in the conclusion, we need to add some rules that can conclude ordinary (non-interaction) formulas. Since we read each inference rule from conclusion to premise, we will call these the *interaction creation* rules, which are shown in the first part of fig. 2. To incorporate non-linearity, we add a separate contraction rule; this keeps the interaction creation rules simple, but it needs to be explicitly invoked. These interaction creation rules are obviously sound under the interpretation of proposition 2.

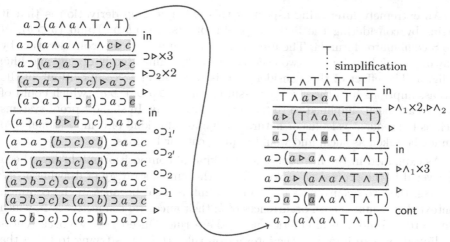

Fig. 3. Lnip derivation fragment for the S-combinator

The final step is to detect when a proof is complete. Since every inference rule presented so far has a single premise, we will say that a proof is complete when the final (again reading bottom to top) premise is, effectively, $\top$. What do we mean by "effectively"? One candidate definition could be that a purely algorithmic procedure can detect when a proof is finished in linear time. For instance, we can say that a proof is complete if its premise can be established using only the *simplification rules* shown in the second part of fig. 2. These rules may be applied in any arbitrary order and at any time. An implementation of the technique may choose to apply these simplification rules on the fly.

Definition 3. *The collection of rules in figures 1 and 2 will be known as the proof system* Lnip. *If A and B are formulas or interaction formulas, we write* $A \xrightarrow{\text{Lnip}} B$ *to mean that either A = B or there is an* Lnip *derivation where the topmost rule has premise A and the bottom-most rule has conclusion B.*   □

Theorem 4 (Completeness of Lnip). *If* $\vdash F$, *then* $\top \xrightarrow{\text{Lnip}} F$.

Proof (Sketch). There are many ways to prove this, both syntactic and semantic. An instructive syntactic proof goes as follows. For a small variant of the G3ip sequent calculus [11], we show that every inference rule is admissible in Lnip under a suitable formula interpretation of sequents. Thus, any sequent proof is recoverable in terms of Lnip inferences. We then just appeal to completeness of the sequent calculus.   □

Example 5. A Lnip derivation of the S-combinator formula, $(a \supset b \supset c) \supset (a \supset b) \supset a \supset c$, is shown in fig. 3. The interaction connectives ▷ and ∘ take the precedence and associativity of ⊃ and ∧ respectively. The locus where a Lnip rule is applied is depicted with a highlight. Of course, the S-combinator formula cannot be proved without appealing to contraction at least once, which is seen by the appeal to cont in the derivation.

An extremely interesting aspect of this example Lnip derivation is that it begins by considering the first two assumptions, $(a \supset b \supset c)$ and $(a \supset b)$, of the S-combinator formula. The user might have indicated this consideration by drawing a *link* between the two occurrences of b, highlighted in orange and blue in fig. 3. The effect of this consideration is to perform a "composition" of the two assumptions into the stronger assumption $(a \supset a \supset \top \supset c)$, which could of course have been simplified to $(a \supset a \supset c)$ immediately. In shallow proof systems such as the sequent calculus or natural deduction this kind of compositional step cannot be taken as such, and would require cuts or lemmas.

As explained in the introduction, this kind of composition might have been discovered in the process of exploration by the simple strategy of drawing a *link* between the two occurrences of b. Such a link is legal because in the common context that contains both occurrences of b, their ancestral connective is $\supset$, which can be turned into a $\triangleright$ interaction using the $\triangleright$ rule. Once these two occurrences are linked, we can interpret the interaction rules (fig. 1) as trying to bring the two ends of the link closer. Indeed, in each of the rules of fig. 1, we can say that one of the ends of the link is in the formula A and the other is in the formula B. We are therefore ready to formulate the linking procedure.

Definition 6 (Subformula Linking Procedure). *Repeat the following sequence of steps until the conjecture formula (i.e., end-formula) F is transformed to $\top$ (success), no fruitful progress can be made (failure), or the proof attempt is aborted by the user.*

1. *(Optional) Ask the user to indicate negatively signed subformulas of F that need to be contracted using the* cont *rule.*

2. *Ask the user to indicate two different subformulas of F; this is the* link.

3. *If the first common ancestor connective of the two linked subformulas is a $\supset$ that occurs in a positively signed context, use the $\triangleright$ rule to turn it into a $\triangleright$; likewise, if the ancestor is a $\wedge$ in an negatively signed context, use the $\circ$ rule to turn it into a $\circ$. If neither case applies, then the user indicated an invalid link, so we return immediately to step 2.*

4. *Use the interaction rules (fig. 1) in such a way that the endpoints of the link stay in the same interaction from conclusion to premise.*

5. *Eventually, one of the terminal rules* in *or* rel *will be applicable to remove the interaction; at this point we say that the link is* resolved.

6. *After resolving a link, the simplification rules may be applied eagerly in an arbitrary order.*

The most important step in the inner loop of the procedure is step 4. The rules for interaction are not unambiguous because the conclusions of different rules can overlap. Let us start by examining the positively signed rules; as an example, consider the interaction $\mathcal{C}\{(F \supset A) \triangleright (G \supset B)\}$, with the understanding that the endpoints of the indicated link in step 2 are present in A and B. There are two possible ways to resolve this link:

$$\frac{\dfrac{\mathcal{C}\{F \wedge (G \supset (A \rhd B))\}}{\mathcal{C}\{F \wedge (A \rhd (G \supset B))\}} \; {\scriptstyle \rhd\supset_2}}{\mathcal{C}\{(F \supset A) \rhd (G \supset B)\}} \; {\scriptstyle \supset\rhd} \qquad \frac{\dfrac{\mathcal{C}\{G \supset (F \wedge (A \rhd B))\}}{\mathcal{C}\{G \supset ((F \supset A) \rhd B)\}} \; {\scriptstyle \supset\rhd}}{\mathcal{C}\{(F \supset A) \rhd (G \supset B)\}} \; {\scriptstyle \rhd\supset_2}$$

Does the choice matter? Yes, because the formulas $F \wedge (G \supset H)$ and $G \supset (F \wedge H)$ are not intuitionistically equivalent; indeed, the former strictly entails the latter. Hence, one of the two alternatives produces a strictly stronger—and potentially unprovable!—premise. Which one should the procedure pick?

This ambiguity also existed in the original formulation of the formula linking procedure for classical linear logic [4], and we can use the same answer used in that work. The key insight is that many of the ambiguous cases can be resolved by a simple analysis of *polarities*. A detailed discussion of polarity (and the oft-associated *focusing* discipline [1]) is not relevant to this work, however.[2] We will instead just use the observation that some of the interaction rules of fig. 1 are *asynchronous*, meaning that the premise of the rule is equiderivable as the conclusion—assuming we replace $\rhd$ and $\circ$ with $\supset$ and $\wedge$ respectively—while other rules are *synchronous*, which means that the premise strictly entails the conclusion. For the specific example above, the $\rhd\supset_2$ rule is asynchronous, because the order of assumptions in an implication is immaterial (at least in intuitionistic logic), while the $\supset\rhd$ rule is synchronous since its conclusion cannot justify the premise. We can draw up this table for all the positively signed rules.

asynchronous rules:	$\rhd\wedge_1$, $\rhd\wedge_2$, $\vee\rhd_1$, $\vee\rhd_2$, $\rhd\supset_1$, $\rhd\supset_2$
synchronous rules:	$\rhd\vee_1$, $\rhd\vee_2$, $\wedge\rhd_1$, $\wedge\rhd_2$, $\supset\rhd$

Whenever there is a choice between a synchronous and an asynchronous rule to apply first (reading from bottom to top), we should pick the asynchronous rule, since that does not destroy derivability. If we have a choice of two asynchronous rules, then the choice is immaterial, as derivability is preserved regardless; the procedure can pick arbitrarily. Different choices would just lead to associative-commutative variants of the same ultimate premise. Finally, for a choice between two synchronous rules, we can consider all such pairs from the table above to see that the choice is immaterial: all choices have the same result.

The story is not quite as simple for the negatively signed rules of fig. 1, where every single rule would be synchronous by our definition. Unlike in the positively signed case, here we have a critical pair.

$$\frac{\dfrac{\mathcal{A}\{(F \supset (A \circ B)) \vee G\}}{\mathcal{A}\{((F \supset A) \circ B) \vee G\}} \; {\scriptstyle \circ\supset_{2'}}}{\mathcal{A}\{(F \supset A) \circ (B \vee G)\}} \; {\scriptstyle \circ\vee_1} \qquad \frac{\dfrac{\mathcal{A}\{F \supset (A \circ B) \vee G\}}{\mathcal{A}\{F \supset (A \circ (B \vee G))\}} \; {\scriptstyle \circ\vee_1}}{\mathcal{A}\{(F \supset A) \circ (B \vee G)\}} \; {\scriptstyle \circ\supset_{2'}}$$

As before, the premises are not equiderivable. Resolving this ambiguity is going to be as hard as fully automated proof search, which will therefore not be recursively

---

[2] Our choice of connectives here has only negative polarity connectives except $\exists$ and $\vee$. In intuitionistic logic it is also possible to have a positive $\wedge$ and atoms of both polarities [5,10], but this generality is not necessary for the present work.

Terminal rules

$$\frac{\mathcal{C}\{\vec{s} \doteq \vec{t}\}}{\mathcal{C}\{a \cdot \vec{s} \rhd a \cdot \vec{t}\}} \text{ in}$$

Quantifier rules

$$\frac{\mathcal{C}\{\forall x.\,(A \rhd B)\}}{\mathcal{C}\{A \rhd \forall x.\,B\}} \rhd\forall \qquad \frac{\mathcal{C}\{\exists x.\,(A \rhd B)\}}{\mathcal{C}\{(\forall x.\,A) \rhd B\}} \forall\rhd \qquad \frac{\mathcal{A}\{\forall y.\,(A \circ B)\}}{\mathcal{A}\{A \circ \forall y.\,B\}} \circ\forall$$

$$\frac{\mathcal{C}\{\exists y.\,(A \rhd B)\}}{\mathcal{C}\{A \rhd \exists y.\,B\}} \rhd\exists \qquad \frac{\mathcal{C}\{\forall x.\,(A \rhd B)\}}{\mathcal{C}\{(\exists x.\,A) \rhd B\}} \exists\rhd \qquad \frac{\mathcal{A}\{\exists y.\,(A \circ B)\}}{\mathcal{A}\{A \circ \exists y.\,B\}} \circ\exists$$

(in each rule, $x \# B$ and $y \# A$)

Simplification and instantiation rules

$$\frac{\mathcal{C}\{\top\}}{\mathcal{C}\{\forall x.\,\top\}} \qquad \frac{\mathcal{C}\{\top\}}{\mathcal{C}\{x \doteq x\}} \text{ refl} \qquad \frac{\mathcal{C}\{\vec{s} \doteq \vec{t}\}}{\mathcal{C}\{f \cdot \vec{s} \doteq f \cdot \vec{t}\}} \text{ cong} \qquad \frac{\mathcal{C}\{t \text{ term}\} \quad \mathcal{C}\{[t/x]A\}}{\mathcal{C}\{\exists x.\,A\}} \text{ inst}$$

Fig. 4. System Lni: rules for quantifiers and terms

solvable as soon as we introduce quantifiers. The subformula linking procedure needs further guidance from the user to resolve the ambiguity. A variant of this ambiguity can also be found in the original subformula linking work for classical linear logic [4]; there, the solution was to make the links *directed*. Then, whenever there is a choice to be made—which will necessarily have to be a choice between one subformula containing the *source* of the link and the other containing the *destination*—the procedure can choose to perform the rule corresponding to the *destination first*. In the above critical pair, for instance, if A contained the source and B the destination, then we would perform the $\circ\vee_1$ step first (i.e., follow the left derivation). This choice is made to evoke the intuition that *the source is brought to the destination*; the context of the destination swallows the context of the source.

Definition 7 (Directed Subformula Linking Procedure). *We modify the procedure of definition 6 by making the links in step 2 directed, and in the resolution step 4 we break synchronous/synchronous ties for negatively signed rules by performing the rule for the destination first.*

2.2   Quantifiers

Extending Lnip with first-order quantifiers can be done in a number of ways. Here we present a parsimonious extension that avoids any up front commitments with regard to the strength of the term language. Our terms (written $s, t, \dots$) have the following grammar:

$$s, t, \dots ::= x \mid f \cdot \vec{s}$$

where we write $\vec{s}$ to stand for a list of terms $[s_1, s_2, \ldots, s_n]$. We use $x, y, \ldots$ to range over variables and $\mathsf{f}, \mathsf{g}, \ldots$ to range over function symbols, and we abbreviate $\mathsf{f} \cdot []$ to f. We also extend atomic formulas: they are now written $a \cdot \vec{s}$ where a is a predicate symbol, and we again abbreviate $a \cdot []$ to a. To formulas and contexts we now add the two quantifiers, $\forall$ and $\exists$, to give the following extended grammars, where $* \in \{\wedge, \vee\}$ and $Q \in \{\forall, \exists\}$.

$$A, B, \ldots ::= a \cdot \vec{s} \mid A \wedge B \mid \top \mid A \vee B \mid \bot \mid A \supset B \mid \forall x.\, A \mid \exists x.\, A$$
$$\mathcal{C}\{\} ::= \{\} \mid A * \mathcal{C}\{\} \mid \mathcal{C}\{\} * B \mid Qx.\mathcal{C}\{\} \mid A \supset \mathcal{C}\{\} \mid \mathcal{A}\{\} \supset B$$
$$\mathcal{A}\{\} ::= A * \mathcal{A}\{\} \mid \mathcal{A}\{\} * B \mid Qx.\mathcal{A}\{\} \mid A \supset \mathcal{A}\{\} \mid \mathcal{C}\{\} \supset B$$

We write $\mathcal{C}\{t \text{ term}\}$ to assert that the term t is well-formed for the hole in $\mathcal{C}\{\}$, i.e., all the (free) variables of t are bound by some quantifier that the hole in $\mathcal{C}\{\}$ is in the scope of. We also write $x \# t$ or $x \# A$ to indicate that the variable x is not free in t or A respectively. Finally, the capture-avoiding substitution of t for x in a term u or formula A is written $[t/x]u$ or $[t/x]A$ respectively. The replacement of formulas in contexts, on the other hand, is not capture-avoiding $\mathcal{C}\{A\}$; instead, this replacement is considered to be well-formed whenever every free variable x of A has the property that $\mathcal{C}\{x \text{ term}\}$.

In order to give ourselves maximum freedom in the definition of the first-order extension, we will use the additional binary predicate symbol $\doteq$ to denote equality. Given two lists of terms $\vec{s} = [s_1, \ldots, s_n]$ and $\vec{t} = [t_1, \ldots, t_n]$ of equal length, we will write $\vec{s} \doteq \vec{t}$ to stand for $(s_1 \doteq t_1) \wedge \cdots \wedge (s_n \doteq t_n)$ if $n > 0$ and for $\top$ otherwise. Using this additional predicate, the terminal rule in of Lnip is modified to account for the term arguments.

Definition 8 (System Lni). *The system Lni is an extension of Lnip by removing the in rule of Lnip and adding the rules of fig. 4.*

Theorem 9 (Completeness of Lni). *If $\vdash F$ in a complete sequent calculus for first-order intuitionistic logic (e.g., G3i [11]) then $\top \xrightarrow{\text{Lni}} F$.*

Proof (Sketch). We can follow the same strategy as for theorem 4. Note that for any term t, the rules refl and cong suffice to reduce $\mathcal{C}\{t \doteq t\}$ to $\mathcal{C}\{\top\}$. A transitivity rule for $\doteq$ is not needed: no $\doteq$ is created in an negatively signed context. $\square$

Example 10. Two example Lni derivations are shown in fig. 5.

(a) This is a derivation for a provable formula where the user may have linked the two occurrences of a. Observe that the simplification rules $\{\text{cong}, \text{inst}, \text{refl}\}$ help to implement first-order unification under a mixed quantifier prefix. However, since Lni simplification rules can be applied at any time, we can solve unification problems incrementally, in tandem with logical reasoning.

(b) This is a derivation for an unprovable formula containing an illegal quantifier exchange, where once again the indicated link is between the two occurrences of a. This derivation cannot be completed because there is no instantiation for x for which $\forall w.\, x \doteq w$ is true.

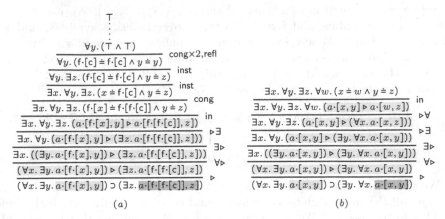

Fig. 5. Two example Lni derivations

3 Incorporating Arity-Typed λ-Terms

To make the calculus Lni of the previous section suitable to host a type theory as an object language, we will need to generalize from first-order terms to general λ-terms. We will follow a standard technique known variously as *higher-order abstract syntax* (HOAS) [12] or *λ-tree syntax* [7] that treats the *pure* λ-calculus—together with $\alpha\beta\eta$-equality as its equational theory—to represent object languages. To keep things computable, we will use simply typed λ-terms with only one basic type, which is sometimes known as *arity typing*. Arity types $(\alpha, \beta, \dots)$ and terms $(s, t, \dots)$ have the following grammar.

$$\alpha, \beta, \dots ::= \star \mid \alpha \to \beta \qquad h ::= x \mid \mathsf{k} \qquad s, t, \dots ::= h \cdot \vec{s} \mid \lambda x{:}\alpha.\, t$$

where $x, y, \dots$ range over variables, and sans-serif identifiers such as k range over term constants. For formulas, we also change the quantifiers $Qx.\, F$ to their arity typed forms $Qx{:}\alpha.\, F$, where $Q \in \{\forall, \exists\}$.

We keep λ-terms in canonical *spine form*, where the head (h) of an application is identified and separated; in more usual notation, $h \cdot [s_1, \dots, s_n]$ would be written as the iterated application $(\cdots(h\, s_1) \cdots s_n)$. The definition of substitution, $[t/x]s$, must be modified to retain spine forms, which is usually done by removing redexes on the fly; for example (using @ as an auxiliary operation):

$$[t/x]\mathsf{k} = \mathsf{k} \cdot [] \qquad [t/x]x = t \qquad [t/x]y = y \cdot [] \quad \text{(where } x \text{ and } y \text{ are different)}$$

$$[t/x](\lambda y{:}\alpha.\, s) = \lambda y{:}\alpha.\, [t/x]s$$

$$[t/x](h \cdot [s_1, \dots, s_n]) = ([t/x]h) @ [[t/x]s_1, \dots, [t/x]s_n]$$

$$(\lambda x{:}\alpha.\, s) @ [t_1, t_2, \dots, t_n] = ([t_1/x]s) @ [t_2, \dots, t_n]$$

$$(h \cdot [s_1, \dots, s_m]) @ [t_1, \dots, t_n] = h \cdot [s_1, \dots, s_m, t_1, \dots, t_n]$$

Most of the inference rules of system Lni generalize easily to this setting. The immediate differences will be with respect to the simplification rules. For the inst rule, we use a variant judgement $\mathcal{C}\{t : \alpha\}$ to mean that the λ-term t is well-typed at type α based on the type assumptions of its free variables that are bound in the scope of the hole in $\mathcal{C}\{\}$. It is possible to view this judgement as being defined by inference rules; for instance (for $Q \in \{\forall, \exists\}$):

$$\frac{}{\mathcal{C}\{Qx{:}\alpha.\,\mathcal{C}'\{x : \alpha\}\}} \qquad \frac{\mathcal{C}\{\forall x{:}\alpha.\,(t : \beta)\}}{\mathcal{C}\{(\lambda x{:}\alpha.\,t) : \alpha \to \beta\}}$$

$$\frac{\mathcal{C}\{h : \alpha_1 \to \cdots \to \alpha_n \to \beta\} \quad \mathcal{C}\{s_i : \alpha_i\}}{\mathcal{C}\{(h{\cdot}[s_1, \ldots, s_n]) : \beta\}}$$

The rules refl and cong of Lni are replaced with:

$$\frac{\mathcal{C}\{\vec{s} \doteq \vec{t}\}}{\mathcal{C}\{h{\cdot}\vec{s} \doteq h{\cdot}\vec{t}\}} \ \text{cong} \qquad \frac{\mathcal{C}\{\forall x{:}\alpha.\,(s \doteq t)\}}{\mathcal{C}\{(\lambda x{:}\alpha.\,s) \doteq (\lambda x{:}\alpha.\,t)\}} \ \text{abs}$$

$$\frac{\mathcal{C}\{(\lambda x{:}\alpha.\,h{\cdot}[s_1, \ldots, s_n, x]) \doteq (\lambda x{:}\alpha.\,t)\}}{\mathcal{C}\{h{\cdot}[s_1, \ldots, s_n] \doteq (\lambda x{:}\alpha.\,t)\}} \ \eta\text{-exp} \qquad \text{(and its symm. variant)}$$

Definition 11 (System Lniλ). *The system Lniλ is a modification of Lni with the ∇ rules, cong, abs, η-exp, and in above.*

Theorem 12 (Completeness of Lniλ). *For any formula F in the language of first-order logic over λ-terms but without any occurrence of $\doteq$, if $\vdash F$ in a complete sequent calculus then $\top \xrightarrow{\ Lni\lambda\ } F$.*

Proof (Sketch). Once again, this is a straightforward extension of the proof of theorem 9. Since there are no occurrences of $\doteq$ in F, and in particular no occurrence of it in a negatively signed context, the rules cong, abs and η-exp are sufficient to implement $\alpha\beta\eta$-equivalence. $\square$

4 Application: Embedding Intuitionistic Type Theories

The first-order language over arity-typed λ-terms of the previous section has enough expressive power for a complete encoding of any pure type system [6,15]. To keep things simple in this paper, we will demonstrate the case for LF (aka $\lambda\Pi$) using the *simple* embedding from [15]. Expressions in LF belong to one of the following three syntactic categories: *kinds*, *types*, or *terms*.

$$K ::= \text{type} \mid \Pi x{:}A.\,K \qquad \text{(kinds)}$$
$$A, B, \ldots ::= \text{a } M_1 \cdots M_n \mid \Pi x{:}A.\,B \qquad \text{(types)}$$
$$M, N, \ldots ::= x \mid \text{k} \mid \lambda x{:}A.\,M \mid M\,N \qquad \text{(terms)}$$

The LF type system is formally specified using inference rules in [9] and will not be repeated here. Instead, we will directly present a complete encoding of LF expressions using the language of Lniλ.

The encoding proceeds in two steps. First, we transform the dependently typed terms of LF into their simply typed forms, normalizing them as necessary. However, since LF terms can mention their types, we simultaneously transform LF types into simple types. This transformation erases not just the type dependencies but also the identities of the types by collapsing all of them to the same base type $\star$.

Definition 13. *The forgetful map ϕ specified below transforms LF terms into* Lniλ *λ-terms and LF types and kinds into* Lniλ *types.*

$$
\begin{aligned}
\phi(\mathsf{k}) &= \mathsf{k}\cdot[] & \phi(\mathsf{a}\ M_1 \cdots M_n) &= \star \\
\phi(x) &= x\cdot[] & \phi(\Pi x{:}A.\ B) &= \phi(A) \to \phi(B) \\
\phi(\lambda x{:}A.\ M) &= \lambda x{:}\phi(A).\ \phi(M) & \phi(\mathsf{type}) &= \star \\
\phi(M\ N) &= \phi(M) @ [\phi(N)] & \phi(\Pi x{:}A.\ K) &= \phi(A) \to \phi(K)
\end{aligned}
$$

The second stage of the transformation recovers the information that was lost in the ϕ map by means of one atomic propositions, has. Using this we define a mapping $[\![\ ]\!]$ that transforms types and kinds to formulas in such a way that if $M : A$ holds then $[\![A]\!]\phi(M)$ is true.

Definition 14. *The mapping $[\![\ ]\!]$ transforms an LF type/kind and a* Lniλ *λ-terms into a* Lniλ *formula, specified recursively as follows.*

$$
\begin{aligned}
[\![\mathsf{a}\ M_1 \cdots M_n]\!]m &= \mathsf{has}\cdot[m, \mathsf{a}\cdot[\phi(M_1), \ldots, \phi(M_n)]] \\
[\![\mathsf{type}]\!]m &= \mathsf{has}\cdot[m, \mathsf{type}] \\
[\![\Pi x{:}A.\ J]\!]m &= \forall x{:}\phi(A).\ [\![A]\!]x \supset [\![J]\!](m @ [x])
\end{aligned}
$$

(where J can be a LF type or kind).

Proposition 15 (Completeness [15]). *If the judgement $x_1{:}J_1, \ldots, x_n{:}J_n \vdash M : A$ is derivable in LF [9], then the following formula is provable in* Lniλ*:*
$\forall x_1{:}\phi(J_1).\ [\![J_1]\!](x_1\cdot[]) \supset \cdots \supset \forall x_n{:}\phi(J_n).\ [\![J_n]\!](x_n\cdot[]) \supset [\![A]\!]\phi(M).$ □

The converse of proposition 15 does not necessarily hold, since the forgetful map ϕ is injective, not surjective.[3] In particular, since the encoding of atomic types forgets the term arguments, we have that $\phi(\lambda x{:}A_1.\ s) = \phi(\lambda x{:}A_2.\ s)$ if $\phi(A_1) = \phi(A_2)$; however, the latter does not guarantee that $A_1 = A_2$. Thus, $[\![\Pi x{:}A_1.\ B]\!]\phi(\lambda x{:}A_2.\ s)$ may hold even when $A_1 \neq A_2$. To guarantee surjectivity, we must use the *canonical LF* variant of the LF type theory where the type ascription on λ is omitted and the type system is made bidirectional [19]; this will guarantee that only Π-types will ascribe types to bound variables, removing the issue highlighted above.

---

[3] This issue, pointed out in [16], is a mistake in earlier papers such as [6,15].

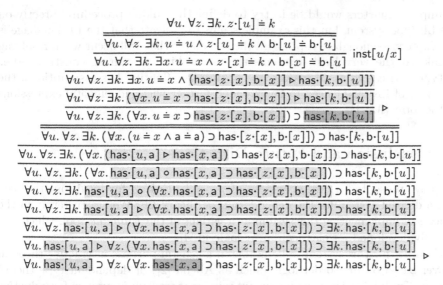

Fig. 6. A Lniλ derivation of an embedded LF type (example 16). Some type ascriptions are elided, and doubled lines denote simplifications.

Example 16. Consider the following LF type $A \triangleq \Pi u{:}a.\, \Pi z{:}(\Pi x{:}a.\, b\, x).\, b\, u$. By definition 14, we have:

$$[\![A]\!]k = \forall u{:}\star.\, \mathsf{has}{\cdot}[u, a] \supset$$
$$\forall z{:}\star \to \star.\, (\forall x{:}\star.\, \mathsf{has}{\cdot}[x, a] \supset \mathsf{has}{\cdot}[z{\cdot}[x], b{\cdot}[x]]) \supset$$
$$\mathsf{has}{\cdot}[k, b{\cdot}[u]].$$

Fig. 6 has an example Lniλ derivation of this formula where k is existentially quantified. As usual, highlights are used to indicate the two links the user indicated in the two ▷ rules. The derivation can be complete with the instantiation $[z{\cdot}[u]/k]$; this means that the LF type A is inhabited by some LF term M for which $\phi(M) = z{\cdot}[u]$.

Note that the fact that we have not discovered a LF term for k using the Lniλ derivation is not a problem. Given a Lniλ term k for which $[\![A]\!]k$ is derivable, it is possible to find a term M for which $\phi(M) = k$ and $M : A$ holds in LF. One way to do this would be to use *bidirectional type checking* [14,19] to recreate—deterministically—the missing LF types.

While the encoding of LF in Lniλ suffices to implement the proof by linking technique, it is a leaky encoding. As the derivation in fig. 6 proceeds, the conjecture resembles the image of the $[\![\ ]\!]$ map less and less; in particular, the conjecture starts to accumulate things that are not fundamentally present in the LF type system, such as term equations, conjunctions, and existential quantifiers. The purported novice user mentioned in the introduction thus needs to be familiar with at least two languages: LF and (a somewhat esoteric variant of) first-order logic. One way to improve matters would be to try to define the linking procedure directly on the LF type system, but this example seems to indicate that the LF language is not expressive enough to capture all the structures that will occur when resolving a link. At the very least, it seems that some kind of pairing construct—i.e., Σ-types—is essential. Moreover, to capture free floating has assumptions, the language of LF might need to be extended further with judgemental expressions of the form $\langle M{:}A \rangle$.

5   Conclusion and Future Directions

We have presented a formal system of *proof by linking* for intuitionistic logic and a derived system for the dependent type theory LF. We are currently in the process of implementing this system as a variant of the *Profound* tool, which was initially developed for classical linear logic in [4].

In order for this system to be usable in a general purpose interactive theorem prover based on first-order logic (such as Abella [2]) or dependent type theory (such as Twelf [13]), the most important missing ingredient is support for inductive definitions and reasoning by induction. The first step in a proof by structural induction is to indicate which assumption(s) will drive the analysis, which is closer to a *pointing* than a *linking*. Thus, proof by linking and pointing will need to co-exist.

A further improvement that would be made as a matter of course in an implementation would be the use of a unification engine to remove the clutter of $\doteq$ formulas. It is worth investigating (in future work) if the linking metaphor can also be used for algebraic operations on terms based on $\doteq$. In many systems $\doteq$-assumptions can be used to rewrite terms, which is readily incorporated into the linking scheme: just link a term to one side of a $\doteq$. We can in fact see it as variants of the inst rule:

$$\frac{\mathcal{C}\{[t/x]\mathcal{C}'\{\top\}\}}{\mathcal{C}\{\exists x.\,\mathcal{C}'\{x \doteq t\}\}} \qquad \frac{\mathcal{A}\{[t/x]\mathcal{A}'\{\top\}\}}{\mathcal{A}\{\forall x.\,\mathcal{A}'\{x \doteq t\}\}}$$

It is worth investigating if such variants of inst can make the embedding of LF into Lniλ less leaky.

Note that proof by linking, like proof by pointing, can easily be incorporated as a tactic in an existing proof system. After all, each of the inference rules of Lniλ is logically motivated, and can therefore be established as a certifying tactic. The quality of the formal proof terms produced in this way will be poor since most proof term languages are not designed for deep rewriting – indeed, the proof term for each Lniλ inference rule may have a size that is exponential in that of the conjecture. It is perhaps better to see proof by linking as a *proof exploration* tool for quickly testing out logical properties of a conjecture before attempting a traditional structured proof. In the hands of an expert user, this exploration mode can also help to discover useful lemmas to bridge the gap between an existing collection of proved theorems and a desired target theorem.

References

1. J.-M. Andreoli. Logic Programming with Focusing Proofs in Linear Logic. *Journal of Logic and Computation*, 2(3):297–347, 1992.
2. D. Baelde, K. Chaudhuri, A. Gacek, D. Miller, G. Nadathur, A. Tiu, and Y. Wang. Abella: A system for reasoning about relational specifications. *Journal of Formalized Reasoning*, 7(2), 2014.
3. Y. Bertot, G. Kahn, and L. Théry. Proof by pointing. In *Theoretical Aspects of Computer Software*, pages 141–160, 1994.
4. K. Chaudhuri. Subformula linking as an interaction method. In S. Blazy, C. Paulin-Mohring, and D. Pichardie, editors, *4th Conference on Interactive Theorem Proving (ITP)*, volume 7998 of *LNCS*, pages 386–401. Springer, July 2013.
5. K. Chaudhuri, F. Pfenning, and G. Price. A logical characterization of forward and backward chaining in the inverse method. *Journal of Automated Reasoning*, 40(2-3):133–177, Mar. 2008.
6. A. Felty and D. Miller. Encoding a dependent-type λ-calculus in a logic programming language. In *CADE*, volume 449 of *LNAI*, pages 221–235. Springer, 1990.
7. A. Gacek, D. Miller, and G. Nadathur. A two-level logic approach to reasoning about computations. *Journal of Automated Reasoning*, 49(2):241–273, 2012.
8. N. Guenot. *Nested Deduction in Logical Foundations for Computation*. Ph.d. thesis, Ecole Polytechnique, 2013.
9. R. Harper, F. Honsell, and G. Plotkin. A framework for defining logics. *Journal of the ACM*, 40(1):143–184, 1993.
10. C. Liang and D. Miller. Focusing and polarization in linear, intuitionistic, and classical logics. *Theoretical Computer Science*, 410(46):4747–4768, 2009.
11. S. Negri and J. von Plato. *Structural Proof Theory*. Cambridge University Press, 2001.
12. F. Pfenning and C. Elliott. Higher-order abstract syntax. In *ACM-SIGPLAN Conference on Programming Language Design and Implementation (PLDI)*, pages 199–208. ACM Press, June 1988.
13. F. Pfenning and C. Schürmann. System description: Twelf — A meta-logical framework for deductive systems. In H. Ganzinger, editor, *16th International Conference on Automated Deduction (CADE)*, number 1632 in LNAI, pages 202–206, Trento, 1999. Springer.
14. B. C. Pierce and D. N. Turner. Local type inference. *ACM Transactions of Programming Language Systems*, 22(1):1–44, 2000.
15. Z. Snow, D. Baelde, and G. Nadathur. A meta-programming approach to realizing dependently typed logic programming. In *Principles and Practices of Declarative Programming (PPDP)*, pages 187–198, 2010.
16. M. Southern. *A Framework for Reasoning about LF Specifications*. PhD thesis, University of Minnesota, Mar. 2021. Defended; final version to appear.
17. L. Straßburger. *Linear Logic and Noncommutativity in the Calculus of Structures*. PhD thesis, Technische Universität Dresden, 2003.
18. A. Tiu. A local system for intuitionistic logic. In *Logic for Programming, Artificial Intelligence, and Reasoning (LPAR)*, volume 4246 of *LNCS*, pages 242–256. Springer, 2006.
19. K. Watkins, I. Cervesato, F. Pfenning, and D. Walker. A concurrent logical framework I: The propositional fragment. In *Post-proceedings of TYPES 2003 Workshop*, number 3085 in LNCS. Springer, 2003.

Open Access This chapter is licensed under the terms of the Creative Commons Attribution 4.0 International License (http://creativecommons.org/licenses/by/4.0/), which permits use, sharing, adaptation, distribution and reproduction in any medium or format, as long as you give appropriate credit to the original author(s) and the source, provide a link to the Creative Commons license and indicate if changes were made.

The images or other third party material in this chapter are included in the chapter's Creative Commons license, unless indicated otherwise in a credit line to the material. If material is not included in the chapter's Creative Commons license and your intended use is not permitted by statutory regulation or exceeds the permitted use, you will need to obtain permission directly from the copyright holder.

Efficient SAT-based Proof Search
in Intuitionistic Propositional Logic

Camillo Fiorentini[✉]

Department of Computer Science, Università degli Studi di Milano, Milan, Italy

Abstract. We present an efficient proof search procedure for Intuitionistic Propositional Logic which involves the use of an incremental SAT-
solver. Basically, it is obtained by adding a restart operation to the system `intuit` by Claessen and Rosén, thus we call our implementation
`intuitR`. We gain some remarkable advantages: derivations have a simple
structure; countermodels are in general small; using a standard benchmarks suite, we outperform `intuit` and other state-of-the-art provers.

1 Introduction

The `intuit` theorem prover by Claessen and Rosén [2] implements an efficient
decision procedure for Intuitionistic Propositional Logic (IPL) based on a Satisfiability Modulo Theories (SMT) approach. Given an input formula α, the
clausification module of `intuit` computes a sequent $\sigma = R, X \Rightarrow g$ equivalent
to α with respect to IPL-validity, where R, X and g have a special form: R is
a set of clauses, X is a set of implications $(a \rightarrow b) \rightarrow c$, with a, b, c atoms, g
is an atom. The decision procedure at the core of `intuit` searches for a Kripke
model $\mathcal{K}$ such that at its root all the formulas in R and X are forced and g is
not forced; we call $\mathcal{K}$ a countermodel for σ, since it witnesses the non-validity
of σ in IPL. The search is performed via a proper variant of the DPLL($\mathcal{T}$) procedure [12], whose top-level loop exploits an incremental SAT-solver. This leads
to a highly performant decision strategy; actually, on the basis of a standard
benchmarks suite, `intuit` outperforms two of the state-of-the-art provers for
IPL, namely fCube [5] and `intHistGC` [11]. At first sight, the `intuit` decision
procedure seems to be far away from the traditional techniques for deciding IPL
validity; on the other hand, the in-depth investigation presented in [10] unveils
a close and surprising connection between the `intuit` approach based on SMT
and the known proof-theoretic methods. The crucial point is that the main loop
of the decision procedure mimics a standard root-first proof search strategy for
the sequent calculus LJT$_{\text{SAT}}$ [10] (see Fig. 7), a variant of Dyckhoff's calculus
LJT [3]. In [10] the `intuit` decision procedure is re-formulated so that, given a
sequent σ, it outputs either a derivation of σ in LJT$_{\text{SAT}}$ or a countermodel for σ.

Here we continue this investigation to better take advantage of the interplay
between the SMT perspective and proof-theoretic methods. At first, we have enhanced the Haskell `intuit` code[1] by implementing the derivation/countermodel

---

[1] Available at `https://github.com/koengit/intuit`.

© The Author(s) 2021
A. Platzer and G. Sutcliffe (Eds.): CADE 2021, LNAI 12699, pp. 217–233, 2021.
https://doi.org/10.1007/978-3-030-79876-5_13

extraction procedures discussed in [10]. We experimented some unexpected and weird phenomena: derivations are often convoluted and contain applications of the cut rule which cannot be trivially eliminated; countermodels in general contain lots of redundancies. To overcome these issues, we have redesigned the decision procedure. Differently from `intuit`, in the main loop we keep all the worlds of the countermodel under construction. Whenever the generation of a new world fails, the current model is emptied and the computation restarts with a new iteration of the main loop. We call the obtained prover `intuitR` (intuit with Restart). We gain some remarkable advantages. Firstly, the proof search procedure has a plain and intuitive presentation, consisting of two nested loops (see the flowchart in Fig. 3). Secondly, derivations have a linear structure, formalized by the calculus $C^{\rightarrow}$ in Fig. 1; basically, a derivation in $C^{\rightarrow}$ is a cut-free derivation in LJT_{SAT} having only one branch. Thirdly, the countermodels obtained by `intuitR` are in general smaller than the ones obtained by `intuit`, since restarts cross out redundant worlds. We have replicated the experiments in [2] (1200 benchmarks): as reported in the table in Fig. 9 and in the scatter plot in Fig. 11, `intuitR` has better performances than `intuit`. The `intuitR` implementation and other additional material (e.g., the omitted proofs, a detailed report on experiments) can be downloaded at `https://github.com/cfiorentini/intuitR`.

2   Preliminary Notions

Formulas, denoted by lowercase Greek letters, are built from an infinite set of propositional variables V, the constant $\perp$ and the connectives $\wedge$, $\vee$, $\rightarrow$; the formula $\alpha \leftrightarrow \beta$ stands for $(\alpha \rightarrow \beta) \wedge (\beta \rightarrow \alpha)$. Elements of the set $V \cup \{\perp\}$ are called *atoms* and are denoted by lowercase Roman letters, uppercase Greek letters denote sets of formulas. A *(classical) interpretation* M is a subset of V, identifying the propositional variables assigned to true. By $M \models \alpha$ we mean that α is true in M; moreover, $M \models \Gamma$ iff $M \models \alpha$ for every $\alpha \in \Gamma$. We write $\Gamma \vdash_c \alpha$ iff, for every interpretation M, $M \models \Gamma$ implies $M \models \alpha$. A formula α is CPL-valid (valid in Classical Propositional Logic) iff $\emptyset \vdash_c \alpha$.

A (rooted) Kripke model for IPL (Intuitionistic Propositional Logic) is a quadruple $\langle W, \leq, r, \vartheta \rangle$ where W is a finite and non-empty set (the set of *worlds*), $\leq$ is a reflexive and transitive binary relation over W, the world r (the *root* of $\mathcal{K}$) is the minimum of W w.r.t. $\leq$, and $\vartheta : W \mapsto 2^V$ (the *valuation* function) is a map obeying the persistence condition: for every pair of worlds w_1 and w_2 of $\mathcal{K}$, $w_1 \leq w_2$ implies $\vartheta(w_1) \subseteq \vartheta(w_2)$. The valuation ϑ is extended into a *forcing* relation between worlds and formulas as follows:

$w \Vdash p$ iff $p \in \vartheta(w)$, $\forall p \in V$ $w \not\Vdash \perp$ $w \Vdash \alpha \wedge \beta$ iff $w \Vdash \alpha$ and $w \Vdash \beta$

$w \Vdash \alpha \vee \beta$ iff $w \Vdash \alpha$ or $w \Vdash \beta$ $w \Vdash \alpha \rightarrow \beta$ iff $\forall w' \geq w$, $w' \Vdash \alpha$ implies $w' \Vdash \beta$.

By $w \Vdash \Gamma$ we mean that $w \Vdash \alpha$ for every $\alpha \in \Gamma$. A formula α is IPL-valid iff, for every Kripke model $\mathcal{K}$ we have $r \Vdash \alpha$ (here and below r designates the root of $\mathcal{K}$). Thus, if there exists a model $\mathcal{K}$ such that $r \not\Vdash \alpha$, then α is not IPL-valid; we call $\mathcal{K}$ a *countermodel* for α, written $\mathcal{K} \not\models \alpha$, and we say that α is *counter-satisfiable*. We write $\Gamma \vdash_i \delta$ iff, for every model $\mathcal{K}$, $r \Vdash \Gamma$ implies $r \Vdash \delta$; thus,

$$\frac{R \vdash_c g}{R, X \Rightarrow g} \; \text{cpl}_0 \qquad \frac{R, A \vdash_c b \qquad R, \varphi, X \Rightarrow g}{R, X \Rightarrow g} \; \text{cpl}_1 \qquad \begin{array}{l} (a \to b) \to c \in X \\ A \subseteq V \\ \varphi \; = \; \bigwedge(A \setminus \{a\}) \to c \end{array}$$

Fig. 1. The sequent calculus $C^\to$; $R, X \Rightarrow g$ is an r-sequent.

α is IPL-valid iff $\emptyset \vdash_i \alpha$. Let σ be a sequent of the form $\Gamma \Rightarrow \delta$; σ is IPL-valid iff $\Gamma \vdash_i \delta$. By $\mathcal{K} \not\models \sigma$ we mean that $r \Vdash \Gamma$ and $r \not\Vdash \delta$. Note that such a model $\mathcal{K}$ witnesses that σ is not IPL-valid; we say that $\mathcal{K}$ is a *countermodel* for σ and that σ is *counter-satisfiable*.

Clausification We review the main concepts about the clausification procedure described in [2]. *Flat clauses* φ and *implication clauses* λ are defined as

$$\begin{array}{ll} \varphi := \bigwedge A_1 \to \bigvee A_2 \mid \bigvee A_2 & \emptyset \subset A_k \subseteq V \cup \{\bot\}, \text{ for } k \in \{1,2\} \\ \lambda := (a \to b) \to c & a \in V, \{b,c\} \subseteq V \cup \{\bot\} \end{array}$$

where $\bigwedge A_1$ and $\bigvee A_2$ denote the conjunction and the disjunction of the atoms in A_1 and A_2 respectively ($\bigwedge\{a\} = \bigvee\{a\} = a$). Henceforth, $\bigwedge \emptyset \to \bigvee A_2$ must be read as $\bigvee A_2$; moreover, $R, R_1, \ldots$ denote sets of flat clauses; $X, X_1, \ldots$ sets of implication clauses; $A, A_1, \ldots$ sets of atoms. The `intuit` procedure relies on the following property (see Lemma 2 in [10]):

Lemma 1. *For every set of flat clauses R and every atom g, $R \vdash_i g$ iff $R \vdash_c g$.*

In the decision procedure, flat clauses are actively used only in classical reasoning. A pair (R, X) is $\to$-*closed* iff, for every $(a \to b) \to c \in X$, $b \to c \in R$. An *r-sequent* (reduced sequent) is a sequent $\Gamma \Rightarrow g$ where g is an atom, $\Gamma = R \cup X$ and (R, X) is $\to$-closed. Given a formula α, the clausification procedure yields a triple (R, X, g) such that $R, X \Rightarrow g$ is an r-sequent and:

(1) $\vdash_i \alpha$ iff $R, X \vdash_i g$; (2) $\mathcal{K} \not\models R, X \Rightarrow g$ implies $\mathcal{K} \not\models \alpha$, for every $\mathcal{K}$. [2]

Thus, IPL-validity of formulas can be reduced to IPL-validity of r-sequents.

3 The Calculus $C^\to$

The sequent calculus $C^\to$ consists of the rules cpl_0 and cpl_1 from Fig. 1. Rule cpl_0 (axiom rule) can only be applied if the condition $R \vdash_c g$ holds, rule cpl_1 requires that $R, A \vdash_c b$ holds. In rule cpl_1, $(a \to b) \to c$ is the *main formula* and A the *local assumptions*; note that A is any set of propositional variables (not necessarily containing a). Derivations are defined as usual (see e.g. [14]);

---

[2] In [2] the clausification procedure outputs a triple (R, X, g) satisfying (1) and (2); the $\to$-closure of (R, X) is performed at the beginning of the decision procedure (for every $(a \to b) \to c \in X$, the clause $b \to c$ is added to R).

$$\cfrac{R_{m-1}, A_{m-1} \vdash_c b_{m-1} \qquad \cfrac{R_m \vdash_c g}{R_m, X \Rightarrow g}}{R_{m-1}, X \Rightarrow g}\, \lambda_{m-1}$$

$$\vdots$$

$$\cfrac{R_0, A_0 \vdash_c b_0 \qquad \cfrac{R_1, A_1 \vdash_c b_1 \qquad \cfrac{R_2, X \Rightarrow g}{}\,\lambda_1}{R_1, X \Rightarrow g}\,\lambda_0}{R_0, X \Rightarrow g}$$

$$\lambda_k = (a_k \to b_k) \to c_k \in X, \qquad \varphi_k = \bigwedge(A_k \setminus \{a_k\}) \to c_k, \qquad R_{k+1} = R_k \cup \{\varphi_k\}$$

Fig. 2. Derivation of $R_0, X \Rightarrow g$ in $C^{\to}$ ($0 \le k \le m-1$).

by $\vdash_{C^{\to}} \sigma$ we mean that there exists a derivation of the r-sequent σ in $C^{\to}$. In showing derivations, we leave out rule names and we display the main formulas of cpl_1 applications. Soundness of rule cpl_1 relies on the following property:

(a) If $R, A \vdash_c b$, then $R, (a \to b) \to c \vdash_i \varphi$, where $\varphi = \bigwedge(A \setminus \{a\}) \to c$.

Indeed, let $R, A \vdash_c b$. By Lemma 1 $R, A \vdash_i b$, thus $R, A \setminus \{a\} \vdash_i a \to b$. It follows that $R, (a \to b) \to c, A \setminus \{a\} \vdash_i c$, hence $R, (a \to b) \to c \vdash_i \varphi$. By Lemma 1 and (a), the soundness of $C^{\to}$ follows:

Proposition 1. $\vdash_{C^{\to}} R, X \Rightarrow g$ *implies* $R, X \vdash_i g$.

A derivation of $\sigma_0 = R_0, X \Rightarrow g$ has the plain form shown in Fig. 2: it only contains the branch of sequents $\sigma_k = R_k, X \Rightarrow g$ where the sets R_k are increasing. Nevertheless, the design of a root-first proof search strategy for $C^{\to}$ is not obvious. Let σ_0 be the r-sequent to be proved; we try to bottom-up build the derivation in Fig. 2 by running a loop where, at each iteration $k \ge 0$, we search for a derivation of σ_k. It is convenient to firstly check whether $R_k \vdash_c g$ so that, by applying rule cpl_0, we immediately get a derivation of σ_k. If this is not the case, we should pick an implication λ_k from X and guess a proper set of local assumptions A_k in order to bottom-up apply rule cpl_1.

$$\cfrac{R_k, b_k \vdash_c b_k \qquad R_k, X \Rightarrow g}{R_k, X \Rightarrow g}\,\lambda_k$$

$\lambda_k = (a_k \to b_k) \to c_k \in X,\ b_k \to c_k \in R_k$
$A_k = \{b_k\},\ \varphi_k = b_k \to c_k,\ R_{k+1} = R_k$

If we followed a blind choice, the procedure would be highly inefficient; for instance, the application of rule cpl_1 shown on the left triggers a non-terminating loop. Instead, we pursue this strategy: we search for a countermodel for σ_k; if we succeed, then $R_k, X \nvdash_i g$ and, being $R_0 \subseteq R_k$, we conclude that $R_0, X \nvdash_i g$ and proof search ends. Otherwise, from the failure we learn the proper λ_k and A_k to be used in the application of rule cpl_1; in next iteration, proof search restarts with the sequent σ_{k+1}, where R_{k+1} is obtained by adding the learned clause φ_k to R_k. To check classical provability, we exploit a SAT-solver; each time the solver is invoked, the set R_k has increased, thus it is advantageous to use an incremental SAT-solver.

Countermodels Henceforth we define Kripke models by specifying the interpretations associated with its worlds. Let W be a finite set of interpretations with minimum M_0, namely: $M_0 \subseteq M$ for every $M \in W$. By $\mathcal{K}(W)$ we denote the Kripke model $\langle W, \leq, M_0, \vartheta \rangle$ where $\leq$ coincides with the subset relation $\subseteq$ and ϑ is the identity map, thus $M \Vdash p$ (in $\mathcal{K}(W)$) iff $p \in M$. We introduce the following *realizability relation* $\triangleright_W$ between W and implication clauses:

$$M \triangleright_W (a \to b) \to c \quad \text{iff} \quad (a \in M) \text{ or } (b \in M) \text{ or } (c \in M) \text{ or }$$
$$(\exists M' \in W \text{ s.t. } M \subset M' \text{ and } a \in M' \text{ and } b \notin M').$$

By $M \triangleright_W X$ we mean that $M \triangleright_W \lambda$ for every $\lambda \in X$. Countermodels of r-sequents can be characterized as follows:

Proposition 2. *Let $\sigma = R, X \Rightarrow g$ be an r-sequent and let W be a finite set of interpretations with minimum M_0. Then, $\mathcal{K}(W) \not\models \sigma$ iff:
(i) $g \notin M_0$; (ii) for every $M \in W$, $M \models R$ and $M \triangleright_W X$.*

4   The Procedure proveR

The strategy outlined in Sec. 3 is implemented by the decision procedure proveR (prove with Restart) defined by the flowchart in Fig. 3. The call proveR(R,X,g) returns Valid if the r-sequent $\sigma = R, X \Rightarrow g$ is IPL-valid, CountSat otherwise; by tracing the computation, we can build a $C^{\to}$-derivation of σ in the former case, a countermodel for σ in the latter. We exploit a single incremental SAT-solver s: clauses can be added to s but not removed; by R(s) we denote the set of clauses stored in s. The solver s has associated a set of propositional variables U(s) (the universe of s); we assume that every clause φ supplied to s is built over U(s) (namely, every variable occurring in φ belongs to U(s)). The SAT-solver is required to support the following operations:

- newSolver()
  Create a new SAT-solver.
- addClause(s, φ) // s is a SAT-solver, φ a flat clause built over U(s)
  Add the clause φ to s.
- satProve(s, A, g) // s is a SAT-solver, $A \subseteq$ U(s), $g \in$ U(s) $\cup \{\bot\}$
  Call s to decide whether R(s), $A \vdash_c g$ (A is a set of local assumptions). The solver outputs one of the following answers:
  - Yes(A'): thus, $A' \subseteq A$ and R(s), $A' \vdash_c g$;
  - No(M): thus, $A \subseteq M \subseteq$ U(s) and $M \models$ R(s) and $g \notin M$.
  In the former case it follows that R(s), $A \vdash_c g$, in the latter R(s), $A \nvdash_c g$.

The procedure newSolver(R), defined using the primitive operations, creates a new SAT-solver containing all the clauses in R. The computation of the call proveR(R, X, g) consists of the following steps:

(S0) A new SAT-solver s storing all the clauses in R is created.

(S1) A loop starts *(main loop)* with empty W.

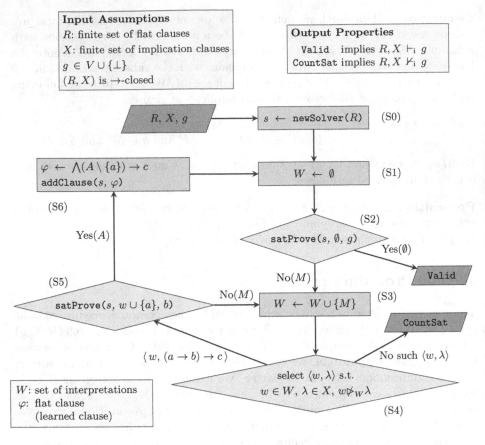

Fig. 3. Computation of proveR(R, X, g).

(S2) The SAT-solver s is called to check whether R(s) $\vdash_c$ g. If the answer is Yes($\emptyset$), the computation stops yielding Valid. Otherwise, the output is No(M) and the computation continues at Step (S3).

(S3) A loop starts *(inner loop)* by adding the interpretation M computed at Step (S2) to the set W (thus, $W = \{M\}$).

(S4) We have to select a pair $\langle w, \lambda \rangle$ such that $w \in W$, $\lambda \in X$ and $w \not\vdash_W \lambda$. If such a pair does not exist, the procedure ends with output CountSat. Otherwise, the computation continues at Step (S5).

(S5) Let $\langle w, (a \rightarrow b) \rightarrow c \rangle$ be the pair selected at Step (S4). The SAT-solver s is called to check whether R(s), w, a $\vdash_c$ b. If the result is No(M), then a new iteration of the inner loop is performed where M is added to W. Otherwise, the answer is Yes(A) and the computation continues at Step (S6); we call A the *learned assumptions* and $\langle w, (a \rightarrow b) \rightarrow c \rangle$ the *learned pair*.

(S6) The clause φ (the *learned clause*) is added to the solver s and the computation restarts from Step (S1) with a new iteration of the main loop.

Note that during the computation no new variables are created, thus $U(s)$ can be defined as the set of propositional variables occurring in $R \cup X \cup \{g\}$. We show that the call `proveR`(R,X,g) is correct, namely: if R, X, g match the Input Assumptions, then the Output Properties hold (see Fig. 3). We stipulate that:

- R_k denotes the set $R(s)$ at the beginning of iteration k of the main loop;
- φ_k denotes the clause learned at iteration k of the main loop;
- $W_{k,j}$ denotes the set W at iteration k of the main loop and just after Step (S3) of iteration j of the inner loop.
- $\sim_c$ denotes classical equivalence, namely: $\alpha \sim_c \beta$ iff $\vdash_c \alpha \leftrightarrow \beta$.

We prove some properties about the computation of `proveR`(R, X, g).

(P1) Let $k, j \geq 0$ be such that $W_{k,j}$ is defined. Then:
  (i) The set $W_{k,j}$ has a minimum element M_0 and $g \notin M_0$.
  (ii) For every $M \in W_{k,j}$, $M \models R_k$.
  (iii) If $W_{k,j+1}$ is defined, then $W_{k,j} \subset W_{k,j+1}$.
(P2) For every $0 \leq h < k$ such that φ_k is defined, $\varphi_h \not\sim_c \varphi_k$.

Let $W_{k,0} = \{M\}$; one can easily check that, setting $M_0 = M$, (i) holds. Point (ii) follows by the fact that each M in $W_{k,j}$ comes from an answer $No(M)$, thus $M \models R_k$. Let $W_{k,j+1}$ be defined and let $W_{k,j+1} = W_{k,j} \cup \{M\}$, with M computed at step (S5); there is $w \in W_{k,j}$ and $\lambda = (a \to b) \to c \in X$ such that $w \not\rhd_{W_{k,j}} \lambda$ and $w \cup \{a\} \subseteq M$ and $b \notin M$. We cannot have $M \in W_{k,j}$, otherwise, since $w \subseteq M$ and $a \in M$ and $b \notin M$, we would get $w \rhd_{W_{k,j}} \lambda$, a contradiction. Thus $M \notin W_{k,j}$, and this proves (iii).

Let $0 \leq h < k$ be such that φ_k is defined, let $\langle w_k, \lambda_k = (a_k \to b_k) \to c_k \rangle$ and A_k be the pair and the assumptions learned at iteration k respectively; note that $A_k \subseteq w_k \cup \{a_k\}$. Since $R_h \cup \{\varphi_h\} = R_{h+1} \subseteq R_k$, we have $\varphi_h \in R_k$; by (P1)(ii), it holds that $w_k \models R_k$, hence $w_k \models \varphi_h$. We show that $w_k \not\models \varphi_k$, and this proves (P2). Since $\langle w_k, \lambda_k \rangle$ has been selected at Step (S4), $c_k \notin w_k$; by the fact that $\varphi_k = \bigwedge(A_k \setminus \{a_k\}) \to c_k$ and $A_k \setminus \{a_k\} \subseteq w_k$, we conclude $w_k \not\models \varphi_k$.

Exploiting the above properties, we prove the correctness of `proveR`, also showing how to extract derivations and countermodels from computations.

Proposition 3. *The call* `proveR`(R,X,g) *is correct.*

Proof. We start by proving that the computation never diverges. By (P2), the learned clauses φ_k are pairwise not classically equivalent; since each φ_k is built over the finite set $U(s)$, at most $2^{|U(s)|}$ such clauses can be generated, and this proves the termination of the main loop. Since every interpretation M in W is a subset of $U(s)$, by (P1)(iii) the termination of the inner loop follows.

Let $\sigma = R, X \Rightarrow g$. If `proveR`$(R,X,g)$ returns `CountSat`, then the computation ends at Step (S4) since no pair $\langle w, \lambda \rangle$ can be selected. By (P1), the current set W satisfies the assumptions (i),(ii) of Prop. 2; accordingly, $\mathcal{K}(W)$ is a countermodel for σ, thus $R, X \not\vdash_i g$. If `proveR`(R,X,g) outputs `Valid`, then there exists $m \geq 0$ such that, at Step (S2) of iteration m of the main loop, the

SAT-solver yields Yes($\emptyset$), hence $R_m \vdash_c g$. For every iteration k in $0 \dots m-1$ of the main loop, let $\langle w_k, \lambda_k = (a_k \to b_k) \to c_k \rangle$ be the learned pair and A_k the learned assumptions (thus, R_k, $A_k \vdash_c b_k$). We can apply rule cpl_1 as follows:

$$\frac{R_k, A_k \vdash_c b_k \qquad R_{k+1}, X \Rightarrow g}{R_k, X \Rightarrow g} \lambda_k \qquad \begin{array}{l} \varphi_k = \bigwedge (A_k \setminus \{a_k\}) \to c_k \\ R_0 = R, \quad R_{k+1} = R_k \cup \{\varphi_k\} \end{array}$$

Accordingly, we can build the derivation of $R, X \Rightarrow g$ displayed in Fig. 2 and, by Prop. 1, we conclude $R, X \vdash_i g$.　　$\square$

As a corollary, we get the completeness of the calculus $C^{\to}$:

Proposition 4. *For every r-sequent $\sigma = R, X \Rightarrow g$, $\vdash_{C^{\to}} \sigma$ iff $R, X \vdash_i g$.*

We give two examples of computations using formulas from the ILTP (Intuitionistic Logic Theorem Proving) library [13].

Example 1. Let χ be the first instance of problem class SYJ201 from the ILTP library [13], where $\eta_{ij} = p_i \leftrightarrow p_j$ and $\gamma = p_1 \wedge p_2 \wedge p_3$:

$$\chi = ((\eta_{12} \to \gamma) \wedge (\eta_{23} \to \gamma) \wedge (\eta_{31} \to \gamma)) \to \gamma$$

The clausification of χ yields the triple $(R_0, X, \tilde{g})$, where X contains the implication clauses $\lambda_0, \dots, \lambda_5$ defined in Fig. 4 and R_0 the following 17 clauses (we mark by a tilde the fresh variables introduced during clausification): [3]

$$\tilde{p}_0 \to \tilde{p}_4, \quad \tilde{p}_3 \to p_2, \quad \tilde{p}_3 \to p_3, \quad \tilde{p}_4 \to p_1, \quad \tilde{p}_4 \to \tilde{p}_3, \quad \tilde{p}_5 \to \tilde{p}_4, \quad \tilde{p}_8 \to \tilde{p}_4,$$
$$\tilde{p}_1 \wedge \tilde{p}_2 \to \tilde{p}_0, \quad \tilde{p}_6 \wedge \tilde{p}_7 \to \tilde{p}_5, \quad \tilde{p}_9 \wedge \tilde{p}_{10} \to \tilde{p}_8, \quad p_1 \wedge p_2 \wedge p_3 \to \tilde{g},$$
$$p_1 \to \tilde{p}_2, \quad p_1 \to \tilde{p}_9, \quad p_2 \to \tilde{p}_1, \quad p_2 \to \tilde{p}_7, \quad p_3 \to \tilde{p}_6, \quad p_3 \to \tilde{p}_{10}.$$

The trace of the computation of proveR(R_0,X,$\tilde{g}$) is shown in Fig. 4. Each row displays the validity tests performed by the SAT-solver and the computed answers. If the result is No(_), the last two columns show the worlds w_k in the current set W and, for each w_k, the list of λ such that $w_k \not\Vdash_W \lambda$; the pair selected at Step (S4) is underlined. For instance, after call (0) we have $W = \{w_0\}$ and $w_0 \not\Vdash_W \lambda_k$ for every $0 \le k \le 5$; the selected pair is $\langle w_0, \lambda_0 \rangle$. After call (1), the set W is updated by adding the world w_1 and $w_1 \not\Vdash_W \lambda_3$, $w_1 \not\Vdash_W \lambda_5$ and $w_0 \not\Vdash_W \lambda_k$ for every $2 \le k \le 5$ (since $w_1 \in W$, we get $w_0 \rhd_W \lambda_0$); the selected pair is $\langle w_1, \lambda_3 \rangle$. Whenever the SAT-solver outputs Yes(A), we display the learned clause φ_k. The SAT-solver is invoked 15 times and there are 6 restarts. Fig. 4 also shows the derivation of $R_0, X \Rightarrow \tilde{g}$ extracted from the computation.　　$\Diamond$

Example 2. Let ψ be the second instance of problem class SYJ207 from the ILTP library [13], where $\eta_{ij} = p_i \leftrightarrow p_j$ and $\gamma = p_1 \wedge p_2 \wedge p_3 \wedge p_4$:

$$\psi = ((\eta_{12} \to \gamma) \wedge (\eta_{23} \to \gamma) \wedge (\eta_{34} \to \gamma) \wedge (\eta_{41} \to \gamma)) \to (p_0 \vee \neg p_0 \vee \gamma)$$

---

[3] With intuit, the set R_0 consists of the 11 clauses in the first two rows; the remaining 6 clauses are added when the $\to$-closure of (R_0, X) is performed (see footnote 2).

$\lambda_0 = (p_3 \to p_2) \to \tilde{p}_7$ $\quad \lambda_1 = (p_3 \to p_1) \to \tilde{p}_9$ $\quad \lambda_2 = (p_2 \to p_3) \to \tilde{p}_6$

$\lambda_3 = (p_2 \to p_1) \to \tilde{p}_2$ $\quad \lambda_4 = (p_1 \to p_3) \to \tilde{p}_{10}$ $\quad \lambda_5 = (p_1 \to p_2) \to \tilde{p}_1$

$w_0 = \emptyset$ $\quad w_1 = \{p_3, \tilde{p}_6, \tilde{p}_{10}\}$ $\quad w_2 = \{p_2, \tilde{p}_1, \tilde{p}_7, \tilde{p}_{10}\}$ $\quad w_3 = \{p_3, \tilde{p}_2, \tilde{p}_6, \tilde{p}_{10}\}$

$w_4 = \{p_1, \tilde{p}_2, \tilde{p}_6, \tilde{p}_9\}$ $\quad w_5 = \{\tilde{p}_1, \tilde{p}_7, \tilde{p}_9\}$ $\quad w_6 = w_5 \cup \{p_2\}$ $\quad w_7 = \{p_1, \tilde{p}_2, \tilde{p}_7, \tilde{p}_9\}$

	@SAT	Answer	W	λ s.t. $w \nvdash_W \lambda$
Start	(0) $R_0 \vdash_c^? \tilde{g}$	No(w_0)	$\underline{w_0}$	$\lambda_0, \ldots, \lambda_5$
	(1) $R_0, w_0, p_3 \vdash_c^? p_2$	No(w_1)	$\underline{w_1}$	λ_3, λ_5
			w_0	$\lambda_2, \ldots, \lambda_5$
	(2) $R_0, w_1, p_2 \vdash_c^? p_1$	Yes($\{p_2, \tilde{p}_6\}$)		$\varphi_0 = \tilde{p}_6 \to \tilde{p}_2$
Rest 1	(3) $R_1 \vdash_c^? \tilde{g}$	No(w_2)	$\underline{w_2}$	λ_1
	(4) $R_1, w_2, p_3 \vdash_c^? p_1$	Yes($\{p_3, \tilde{p}_1\}$)		$\varphi_1 = \tilde{p}_1 \to \tilde{p}_9$
Rest 2	(5) $R_2 \vdash_c^? \tilde{g}$	No(w_3)	$\underline{w_3}$	λ_5
	(6) $R_2, w_3, p_1 \vdash_c^? p_2$	Yes($\{p_1, \tilde{p}_{10}\}$)		$\varphi_2 = \tilde{p}_{10} \to \tilde{p}_1$
Rest 3	(7) $R_3 \vdash_c^? \tilde{g}$	No(w_4)	$\underline{w_4}$	λ_0
	(8) $R_3, w_4, p_3 \vdash_c^? p_2$	Yes($\{p_3\}$)		$\varphi_3 = \tilde{p}_7$
Rest 4	(9) $R_4 \vdash_c^? \tilde{g}$	No(w_5)	$\underline{w_5}$	$\lambda_2, \lambda_3, \lambda_4$
	(10) $R_4, w_5, p_2 \vdash_c^? p_3$	No(w_6)	$\underline{w_6}$	λ_4
			w_5	λ_4
	(11) $R_4, w_6, p_1 \vdash_c^? p_3$	Yes($\{p_1, \tilde{p}_1\}$)		$\varphi_4 = \tilde{p}_1 \to \tilde{p}_{10}$
Rest 5	(12) $R_5 \vdash_c^? \tilde{g}$	No(w_7)	$\underline{w_7}$	λ_2
	(13) $R_5, w_7, p_2 \vdash_c^? p_3$	Yes($\{p_2\}$)		$\varphi_5 = \tilde{p}_6$
Rest 6	(14) $R_6 \vdash_c^? \tilde{g}$	Yes($\emptyset$)		**Valid**

$$
\cfrac{
  \cfrac{
    \cfrac{
      \cfrac{
        \cfrac{
          \cfrac{
            \cfrac{
              R_0, p_2, \tilde{p}_6 \vdash_c p_1 \quad R_1, X \Rightarrow \tilde{g}
            }{R_0, X \Rightarrow \tilde{g}} \lambda_3
            \quad R_1, p_3, \tilde{p}_1 \vdash_c p_1 \quad R_2, X \Rightarrow \tilde{g}
          }{\ } \lambda_1
          \quad R_2, p_1, \tilde{p}_{10} \vdash_c p_2 \quad R_3, X \Rightarrow \tilde{g}
        }{\ } \lambda_5
        \quad R_3, p_3 \vdash_c p_2 \quad R_4, X \Rightarrow \tilde{g}
      }{\ } \lambda_0
      \quad R_4, p_1, \tilde{p}_1 \vdash_c p_3 \quad R_5, X \Rightarrow \tilde{g}
    }{\ } \lambda_4
    \quad R_5, p_2 \vdash_c p_3 \quad R_6, X \Rightarrow \tilde{g}
  }{\ } \lambda_2
  \quad R_6 \vdash_c \tilde{g}
}{\ }
$$

Fig. 4. Computation of $\mathtt{proveR}(R_0, X, \tilde{g})$, see Ex. 1.

$$\lambda_0 = (p_4 \to p_3) \to \tilde{p}_{11} \qquad \lambda_1 = (p_4 \to p_1) \to \tilde{p}_{13} \qquad \lambda_2 = (p_3 \to p_4) \to \tilde{p}_{10}$$
$$\lambda_3 = (p_3 \to p_2) \to \tilde{p}_8 \qquad \lambda_4 = (p_2 \to p_3) \to \tilde{p}_7 \qquad \lambda_5 = (p_2 \to p_1) \to \tilde{p}_2$$
$$\lambda_6 = (p_1 \to p_4) \to \tilde{p}_{14} \qquad \lambda_7 = (p_1 \to p_2) \to \tilde{p}_1 \qquad \lambda_8 = (p_0 \to \bot) \to \tilde{g}$$
$$w_0 = \emptyset \quad w_1 = \{p_4, \tilde{p}_{10}, \tilde{p}_{14}\} \quad w_2 = \{p_3, \tilde{p}_7, \tilde{p}_{11}, \tilde{p}_{14}\} \quad w_3 = \{p_4, \tilde{p}_8, \tilde{p}_{10}, \tilde{p}_{14}\}$$
$$w_4 = w_3 \cup \{p_2, \tilde{p}_1\} \quad w_5 = w_4 \cup \{p_0, \tilde{g}\} \quad w_6 = \{p_1, \tilde{p}_2, \tilde{p}_8, \tilde{p}_{10}, \tilde{p}_{13}\}$$
$$w_7 = \{p_4, \tilde{p}_1, \tilde{p}_8, \tilde{p}_{10}, \tilde{p}_{14}\} \quad w_8 = w_7 \cup \{p_2\} \quad w_9 = w_7 \cup \{p_0, \tilde{g}\}$$

	@SAT	Answer	W	λ s.t. $w \not\vdash_W \lambda$
Start	(0) $R_0 \vdash_c^? \tilde{g}$	No(w_0)	$\underline{w_0}$	$\underline{\lambda_0}, \dots, \lambda_8$
	(1) $R_0, w_0, p_4 \vdash_c^? p_3$	No(w_1)	$\underline{w_1}$	$\underline{\lambda_3}, \lambda_4, \lambda_5, \lambda_7, \lambda_8$
			w_0	$\lambda_2, \dots, \lambda_8$
	(2) $R_0, w_1, p_3 \vdash_c^? p_2$	Yes($\{p_3, \tilde{p}_{10}\}$)		$\varphi_0 = \tilde{p}_{10} \to \tilde{p}_8$
Rest 1	(3) $R_1 \vdash_c^? \tilde{g}$	No(w_2)	$\underline{w_2}$	$\underline{\lambda_1}, \lambda_5, \lambda_7, \lambda_8$
	(4) $R_1, w_2, p_4 \vdash_c^? p_1$	Yes($\{p_4, \tilde{p}_{11}\}$)		$\varphi_1 = \tilde{p}_{11} \to \tilde{p}_{13}$
Rest 2	(5) $R_2 \vdash_c^? \tilde{g}$	No(w_3)	$\underline{w_3}$	$\underline{\lambda_4}, \lambda_5, \lambda_7, \lambda_8$
	(6) $R_2, w_3, p_2 \vdash_c^? p_3$	No(w_4)	$\underline{w_4}$	$\underline{\lambda_8}$
			w_3	λ_7, λ_8
	(7) $R_2, w_4, p_0 \vdash_c^? \bot$	No(w_5)	w_5	$\emptyset$
			w_4	$\emptyset$
			w_3	λ_7
	(8) $R_2, w_3, p_1 \vdash_c^? p_2$	Yes($\{p_1, \tilde{p}_{14}\}$)		$\varphi_2 = \tilde{p}_{14} \to \tilde{p}_1$
Rest 3	(9) $R_3 \vdash_c^? \tilde{g}$	No(w_6)	$\underline{w_6}$	$\underline{\lambda_0}, \lambda_4, \lambda_8$
	(10) $R_3, w_6, p_4 \vdash_c^? p_3$	Yes($\{p_4, \tilde{p}_{13}\}$)		$\varphi_3 = \tilde{p}_{13} \to \tilde{p}_{11}$
Rest 4	(11) $R_4 \vdash_c^? \tilde{g}$	No(w_7)	$\underline{w_7}$	$\underline{\lambda_4}, \lambda_5, \lambda_6$
	(12) $R_4, w_7, p_2 \vdash_c^? p_3$	No(w_8)	$\underline{w_8}$	$\underline{\lambda_8}$
			w_7	λ_8
	(13) $R_4, w_8, p_0 \vdash_c^? \bot$	No(w_9)	w_9	$\emptyset$
	CountSat		w_8	$\emptyset$
			w_7	$\emptyset$

$\mathcal{K}(\{w_7, w_8, w_9\})$

Generated by our implementation of intuit

Fig. 5. Computation of proveR($R_0, X, \tilde{g}$), see Ex. 2.

```
 1  procedure prove(R, X, g)
 2  |    // Same Input Ass. and Output Prop. as for intuitR (Fig. 3)
 3  |    s ← newSolver(R);    τ ← prAux(X, ∅, g)
 4  |    if τ = Yes(∅) then return Valid else return CountSat
 5  |    procedure prAux(X̃, Ã, q)
 6  |    |    // Output: Yes(A) or No(M), where A ⊆ Ã and M ⊆ Ã
 7  |    |    τ₀ ← satProve(s, Ã, q)
 8  |    |    if τ₀ = Yes(A) then  return Yes(A)
 9  |    |    else  // τ₀ = No(M)
10  |    |    |    for λ = (a → b) → c ∈ X s.t. a ∉ M and b ∉ M and c ∉ M do
11  |    |    |    |    τ₁ ← prAux(X̃ \ {λ}, M ∪ {a}, b)
12  |    |    |    |    if τ₁ = Yes(A) then
13  |    |    |    |    |    φ ← ⋀(A \ {a}) → c;    addClause(s, φ)
14  |    |    |    |    |    return prAux(X̃, Ã, q)
15  |    |    |    return No(M)
16 end
```

Fig. 6. The prove procedure of intuit [2,10].

We proceed as in Ex. 1. The clausification procedure yields $(R_0, X, \tilde{g})$, where X consists of the implication clauses $\lambda_0, \ldots, \lambda_8$ in Fig. 5 and the set R_0 contains the 24 flat clauses below:

$$p_0 \to \tilde{g}, p_1 \to \tilde{p}_2, \ p_1 \to \tilde{p}_{13}, \ p_2 \to \tilde{p}_1, p_2 \to \tilde{p}_8, \ p_3 \to \tilde{p}_7, p_3 \to \tilde{p}_{11}, \ p_4 \to \tilde{p}_{10}, \ p_4 \to \tilde{p}_{14},$$
$$\tilde{p}_0 \to \tilde{p}_5, \ \tilde{p}_3 \to p_3, \ \tilde{p}_3 \to p_4, \ \tilde{p}_4 \to p_2, \ \tilde{p}_4 \to \tilde{p}_3, \ \tilde{p}_5 \to p_1, \ \tilde{p}_5 \to \tilde{p}_4, \ \tilde{p}_6 \to \tilde{p}_5, \ \tilde{p}_9 \to \tilde{p}_5$$
$$\tilde{p}_1 \wedge \tilde{p}_2 \to \tilde{p}_0, \ \tilde{p}_7 \wedge \tilde{p}_8 \to \tilde{p}_6, \ \tilde{p}_{10} \wedge \tilde{p}_{11} \to \tilde{p}_9, \ \tilde{p}_{13} \wedge \tilde{p}_{14} \to \tilde{p}_{12}, \ \tilde{p}_{12} \to \tilde{p}_5, \ \gamma \to \tilde{g}.$$

The execution of proveR($R_0, X, \tilde{g}$) (see Fig. 5) requires 14 calls to the SAT-solver and 4 restarts. After the last call we get $W = \{w_7, w_8, w_9\}$ and $w_k \triangleright_W X$ for every $w_k \in W$, thus the computation ends yielding CountSat. The model $\mathcal{K}(W)$, depicted at the bottom left of the figure, is a countermodel for $R_0, X \Rightarrow \tilde{g}$ and for ψ (see Sec. 2).   ◇

5   Related Work and Experimental Results

We compare the procedure proveR of intuitR with its intuit counterpart, namely the procedure prove defined in Fig. 6. Here we comply with the presentation in [10], equivalent to the original one in [2]. The recursive auxiliary function prAux plays the role of the main loop of proveR (but in proveR the set of atoms $\tilde{A}$ is not used); the loop inside prAux corresponds to the inner loop of proveR. [4] We point out some major differences. Firstly, in prAux the interpretations M computed by the SAT-solver are not collected; in the loop, only the interpretation M computed at line 8 is considered, thus at the beginning of each

---

[4] Actually intuit implements a variant of prAux where as much as possible clauses φ are added to the solver.

$$\frac{R \vdash_c q}{R, X \Rightarrow q} \, cpl_0 \qquad \frac{R_1, b \to c, X, A \Rightarrow b \qquad R_2, \varphi, X, (a \to b) \to c \Rightarrow q}{R_1, R_2, X, (a \to b) \to c \Rightarrow q} \, ljt$$

$$\frac{R_1, X_1 \vdash_i \varphi \qquad \varphi, R_2, X_2 \Rightarrow q}{R_1, R_2, X_1, X_2 \Rightarrow q} \, cut \qquad \begin{array}{c} A \subseteq V, \; q \in V \cup \{\bot\} \\ \varphi \; = \; \bigwedge(A \setminus \{a\}) \to c \end{array}$$

Fig. 7. The calculus LJT_{SAT}.

iteration just the "local" conditions of the test $M \not\vdash_W \lambda$ are checked (line 10). Secondly, the call $\mathtt{satProve}(s, \, w \cup \{a\}, \, b)$ to the SAT-solver at Step (S5) is replaced by the recursive call $\mathtt{prAux}(\tilde{X} \setminus \{\lambda\}, \, M \cup \{a\}, \, b)$ at line 11; as a consequence, we cannot build derivations by applying rule cpl_1. As thoroughly discussed in [10], the calculus underlying $\mathtt{intuit}$ is the sequent calculus LJT_{SAT} in Fig. 7, obtained from $C^{\to}$ by replacing the rule cpl_1 with the more general rule ljt and introducing a cut rule. Rule ljt can be seen as a generalization of Dyckhoff's implication-left rule from the calculus LJT (alias G4ip) [3,14]. We remark that a $C^{\to}$-derivation is isomorphic to a cut-free LJT_{SAT}-derivation where, in every application of rule ljt, the left-premise has a trivial proof (just apply rule cpl_0). In [10] it is shown how countermodels and LJT_{SAT}-derivations can be extracted from $\mathtt{prove}$ computations. In brief, countermodels are obtained by considering some of the interpretations coming from $No(\_)$ answers; countermodels are in general bigger than the ones built by $\mathtt{proveR}$, where at each restart the model is emptied. As an example, let $\sigma_0 = R_0, X \Rightarrow \tilde{g}$ be defined as in Ex. 2; the computation of $\mathtt{prove}(R_0, X, \tilde{g})$ requires 31 calls to the SAT-solver (24 $No(\_)$ answers) and the computed countermodel for σ_0 has 6 worlds (see Fig. 5); instead, $\mathtt{proveR}(R_0, X, \tilde{g})$ requires 14 calls and the countermodel has 3 worlds. Derivation extraction presents some awkward aspects. The key insight is that, for every recursive call $\mathtt{prAux}(\tilde{X}, \tilde{A}, q)$ occurring in the computation of $\mathtt{prove}(R, X, g)$, if $\mathtt{prAux}(\tilde{X}, \tilde{A}, q)$ returns $Yes(A)$ (where $A \subseteq \tilde{A}$), then we can build an LJT_{SAT}-derivation of a sequent $R, R', A, \tilde{X} \Rightarrow q$, where R' contains some of the clauses added to the SAT-solver. The derivation is built either by applying the rule cpl_0 if $\mathtt{prAux}$ ends at line 8, or else by applying rule ljt, exploiting the derivations obtained by the recursive calls at lines 11 and 14. Accordingly, the main call $\mathtt{prove}(R, X, g)$ yields a derivation of $R, R', X \Rightarrow g$. The crucial point is that the redundant clauses φ in R' satisfy $R, X \vdash_i \varphi$ (this ultimately follows by property (a) in Sec. 3), thus we can eliminate them by applying the cut rule.

Example 3. Let $\sigma_0 = R_0, X \Rightarrow \tilde{g}$ be defined as in Ex. 1; $\mathtt{prove}(R_0, X, \tilde{g})$ yields the LJT_{SAT}-derivation $\mathcal{D}_0$ of $R_2, \varphi_4, X \Rightarrow \tilde{g}$ in Fig. 8. By applying the cut rule three times, we get an LJT_{SAT}-derivation of σ_0. We stress that the $C^{\to}$-derivation of σ_0 obtained with $\mathtt{intuitR}$ (see Fig. 4) has a simpler structure. $\qquad\square$

Finally, we remark that the clauses φ computed in $\mathtt{prAux}$ do not enjoy property (P2) (Sec. 4); we have experimented cases where such clauses are even duplicated (e.g., with formulas from class SYJ205 of ILTP library).

$$\cfrac{R_0, p_2, \tilde{p}_6 \vdash_c p_1}{R_0, X_{\{0,3\}}, p_2, \tilde{p}_6 \Rightarrow p_1} \qquad \cfrac{\cfrac{R_1, p_1, \tilde{p}_{10} \vdash_c p_2}{R_1, X_{\{0,5\}}, p_1, \tilde{p}_{10} \Rightarrow p_2} \quad \cfrac{R_2, p_3 \vdash_c p_2}{R_2, X_{\{0\}}, p_3 \Rightarrow p_2}}{R_1, X_{\{0\}}, p_3 \Rightarrow p_2} \lambda_5$$
$$\hat{\sigma} \;=\; R_0, X_{\{0\}}, p_3 \Rightarrow p_2 \qquad \lambda_3 = (p_2 \to p_1) \to \tilde{p}_2$$

$$\vdots$$
shown
above

$$\cfrac{R_3, p_3 \vdash_c p_1}{R_3, X_{\{1\}}, p_3 \Rightarrow p_1} \quad \cfrac{\cfrac{R_4, p_1, \tilde{p}_1 \vdash_c p_3}{R_4, X_{\{2,4\}}, p_1, \tilde{p}_1 \Rightarrow p_3}}{R_4, X_{\{2\}}, p_2 \Rightarrow p_3} \quad \cfrac{\cfrac{R_5, p_2 \vdash_c p_3}{R_5, X_{\{2\}}, p_2 \Rightarrow p_3}}{R_5, X \Rightarrow \tilde{g}} \lambda_4 \quad \cfrac{R_6 \vdash_c \tilde{g}}{R_6, X \Rightarrow \tilde{g}} \lambda_2$$

$$\hat{\sigma} \qquad \lambda_1 = (p_3 \to p_1) \to \tilde{p}_9$$

$$\cfrac{R_3, \varphi_4, X \Rightarrow \tilde{g}}{R_2, \varphi_4, X \Rightarrow \tilde{g}} \quad \lambda_0 = (p_3 \to p_2) \to \tilde{p}_7$$

$$\lambda_2 = (p_2 \to p_3) \to \tilde{p}_6 \qquad \lambda_4 = (p_1 \to p_3) \to \tilde{p}_{10} \qquad \lambda_5 = (p_1 \to p_2) \to \tilde{p}_1$$
$$\varphi_0 = \tilde{p}_6 \to \tilde{p}_2 \quad \varphi_1 = \tilde{p}_{10} \to \tilde{p}_1 \quad \varphi_2 = \tilde{p}_7 \quad \varphi_3 = \tilde{p}_9 \quad \varphi_4 = \tilde{p}_1 \to \tilde{p}_{10} \quad \varphi_5 = \tilde{p}_6$$
$$X_I = X \setminus \{\lambda_k \mid k \in I\} \quad R_{k+1} = R_k \cup \{\varphi_k\}$$

Fig. 8. Derivation $\mathcal{D}_0$ of $R_2, \varphi_4, X \Rightarrow \tilde{g}$ in $\mathrm{LJT_{SAT}}$ (see Ex. 3).

Experimental results We have implemented `intuitR` in Haskell on the top of `intuit`: we have replaced the function `prove` with `proveR` and added some features (e.g., trace of computations, construction of derivations/countermodels); as in `intuit`, we exploit the module MiniSat, a Haskell bundle of the MiniSat SAT-solver [4] (but in principle we can use any incremental SAT-solver). We compare `intuitR` with `intuit` and with two of the state-of-the-art provers for IPL by replicating the experiments in [2]. The first prover is `fCube` [5]; it is based on a standard tableaux calculus and exploits a variety of simplification rules [6] that can significantly reduce branching and backtracking. The second prover is `intHistGC` [11]; it relies on a sequent calculus with histories and uses dependency directed backtracking for global caching to restrict the search space; we run it with its best flags (`-b -c -c3`). All tests were conducted on a machine with an Intel i7-8700 CPU@3.20GHz and 16GB memory. We considered the benchmarks provided with `intuit` implementation, including the ILTP library, the `intHistGC` benchmarks and the API problems introduced by `intuit` developers. This amounts to a total of 1200 problems, 498 `Valid` and 702 `CountSat`; we used a 600s (seconds) timeout. Fig. 9 reports the more significant results, among which the classes where at least a prover fails and the classes where `intuitR` performs poorly. In all the tests, the time required by clausification is negligible. Even though no optimized data structure has been implemented, `intuitR` solve more problems than its competitors; in families SYJ201 (`Valid` formulas) and SYJ207 (`CountSat` formulas) `intuitR` outperforms its rivals, in all the other cases, except the families EC, negEC and portia, `intuitR` is comparable to the best prover (which is `intuit` in most cases). The most remarkable improvement with respect to `intuit` occurs with class SYJ212 (see Fig. 10), where `intuit` timings are fluc-

Class (number of problems)	intuitR	intuit	fCube	intHistGC
SYJ201(50)	50 (2.259)	50 (11.494)	50 (259.776)	50 (39.466)
SYJ202(38)	10* (49.265)	10* (50.658)	9* (176.984)	6* (324.673)
SYJ203(50)	50 (0.250)	50 (0.335)	50 (1.671)	50 (0.293)
SYJ204(50)	50 (0.442)	50 (0.477)	50 (0.972)	50 (0.203)
SYJ205(50)	50 (0.500)	50 (0.730)	50 (1.317)	50 (4.129)
SYJ206(50)	50 (0.303)	50 (0.348)	50 (0.759)	50 (0.112)
SYJ207(50)	50 (2.291)	50 (109.919)	50 (138.546)	50 (1014.476)
SYJ208(38)	38 (5.225)	38 (5.479)	29* (2.755)	38 (497.715)
SYJ209(50)	50 (0.226)	50 (0.278)	50 (1.690)	50 (0.254)
SYJ210(50)	50 (0.272)	50 (0.252)	50 (0.988)	50 (0.288)
SYJ211(50)	50 (0.462)	50 (1.251)	50 (1.073)	50 (63.686)
SYJ212(50)	50 (0.669)	42* (587.794)	50 (2.698)	50 (1.624)
EC(100)	100 (2.738)	100 (0.821)	100 (6.183)	100 (0.651)
negEC(100)	100 (3.614)	100 (1.116)	100 (13.733)	100 (5.807)
cross(4)	4 (0.100)	4 (0.097)	4 (3.417)	2* (0.005)
jm_cross(4)	4 (0.120)	4 (0.090)	4 (5.404)	3* (4.324)
jm_lift(3)	3 (0.170)	3 (0.133)	3 (6.847)	2* (0.028)
lift(3)	3 (0.119)	3 (0.102)	3 (6.494)	2* (0.012)
mapf(4)	4 (0.187)	4 (0.400)	4 (446.921)	3* (0.043)
portia(100)	100 (32.878)	100 (22.596)	100 (3255.818)	100 (3200.135)
negportia(100)	100 (7.956)	100 (8.309)	98* (3826.011)	100 (28.289)
negportiav2(100)	100 (8.081)	100 (8.411)	98* (1264.103)	100 (3212.293)
nishimura2(28)	28 (9.784)	28 (12.285)	27* (141.326)	28 (7.616)
Unsolved	28	36	43	38

Fig. 9. For each prover, we report the number of solved problems within 600s timeout and between brackets the total time in seconds required for the solved problems. The best prover is highlighted, a star reports that there are some unsolved problems.

tuating. To give a close comparison, let us consider the case $k = 25$; clausification produces 246 flat clauses and 100 implications clauses (176 atoms). Our intuit implementation requires 11214 calls to the SAT-solvers (10181 No($_-$)) and the computed countermodel has 1955 worlds. Instead, intuitR requires 45 calls to the SAT-solvers, 8 restarts and yields a countermodel consisting of 4 worlds; the set W contains 26 worlds before the first restart, one world before the remaining ones. With all the benchmarks the models generated during the computation are small (typically, big models occur before the first restart); however, differently from [7,8,9], we cannot guarantee that countermodels have minimum depth or minimum number of worlds. To complete the picture, the scatter plot in Fig. 11 compares intuitR and intuit on all the benchmarks.

k	intuitR	intuit
1 .. 24	< 0.01	< 0.1
25	0.007	0.691
26	0.007	25.064
27	0.007	0.020
28	0.008	0.083
29	0.009	8.412
30	0.008	-

k	intuitR	intuit
31	0.007	8.724
32	0.007	4.216
33	0.012	0.034
34	0.010	2.445
35	0.033	77.226
36	0.018	0.038
37	0.016	22.445
38	0.017	-

k	intuitR	intuit
39	0.020	0.404
40	0.016	0.838
41	0.027	-
42	0.020	0.785
43	0.036	435.324
44	0.026	0.098
45	0.070	0.639
46 .. 50	≤ 0.07	-

Problem k:

$$(\ldots((\neg\neg p_1 \leftrightarrow p_2) \leftrightarrow p_3) \leftrightarrow \ldots \leftrightarrow p_k) \leftrightarrow (\ldots((p_1 \leftrightarrow p_2) \leftrightarrow p_3) \leftrightarrow \ldots \leftrightarrow p_k) \qquad \neg\alpha := \alpha \rightarrow \bot$$

Fig. 10. Timings for problems $k = 1..50$ of SYJ212 (`CountSat`), - means timeout (600s).

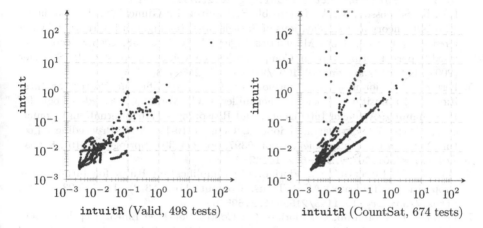

intuitR (Valid, 498 tests)   **intuitR** (CountSat, 674 tests)

Fig. 11. Comparison between `intuitR` and `intuit` (1172 problems, the 28 problems where both provers run out of time have been omitted); time axis are logarithmic, the 8 red squares indicates that `intuit` has exceeded the timeout.

To conclude, we point out that `intuitR` can be extended to deal with some superintuitionistic logics [1]. For instance, let us consider the Göedel-Dummett logic GL, characterized by linear models; at any step of the computation of `proveR`, the model $\mathcal{K}(W)$ must be kept linear. Whenever the insertion of a new world to W breaks linearity, we follow a "restart with learning" strategy [12]: let $\gamma = (a \rightarrow b) \vee (b \rightarrow a)$ be the instance of the GL-axiom falsified at the root of $\mathcal{K}(W)$; we restart by taking γ as "learned axiom", so to avoid the repetition of the flaw. However, we cannot add γ to the SAT-solver, because γ is not a clause, but the clausification of γ, namely the clauses $\tilde{q}_1 \vee \tilde{q}_2$, $\tilde{q}_1 \wedge a \rightarrow b$, $\tilde{q}_2 \wedge b \rightarrow a$, where $\tilde{q}_1$ and $\tilde{q}_2$ are fresh atoms; despite the language of the SAT-solver must be extended, the process converges. The other generalizations suggested in [2] (modal logics, fragments of first-order logic) seem to be more challenging.

Acknowledgments. I am grateful to the reviewers for their valuable suggestions. This work has been funded by the INdAM-GNCS project 2020 "Estensioni del *Property-based Testing* di e con linguaggi di programmazione dichiarativa".

References

1. Chagrov, A.V., Zakharyaschev, M.: Modal Logic, Oxford logic guides, vol. 35. Oxford University Press (1997)
2. Claessen, K., Rosén, D.: SAT Modulo Intuitionistic Implications. In: Davis, M., Fehnker, A., McIver, A., Voronkov, A. (eds.) Logic for Programming, Artificial Intelligence, and Reasoning - 20th International Conference, LPAR-20 2015, Suva, Fiji, November 24-28, 2015, Proceedings. Lecture Notes in Computer Science, vol. 9450, pp. 622–637. Springer (2015), https://doi.org/10.1007/978-3-662-48899-7_43
3. Dyckhoff, R.: Contraction-free sequent calculi for intuitionistic logic. J. Symb. Log. **57**(3), 795–807 (1992), https://doi.org/10.2307/2275431
4. Eén, N., Sörensson, N.: An Extensible SAT-solver. In: Giunchiglia, E., Tacchella, A. (eds.) Theory and Applications of Satisfiability Testing, 6th International Conference, SAT 2003. Santa Margherita Ligure, Italy, May 5-8, 2003 Selected Revised Papers. Lecture Notes in Computer Science, vol. 2919, pp. 502–518. Springer (2003), https://doi.org/10.1007/978-3-540-24605-3_37
5. Ferrari, M., Fiorentini, C., Fiorino, G.: fCube: An Efficient Prover for Intuitionistic Propositional Logic. In: Fermüller, C.G., Voronkov, A. (eds.) Logic for Programming, Artificial Intelligence, and Reasoning - 17th International Conference, LPAR-17, Yogyakarta, Indonesia, October 10-15, 2010. Proceedings. Lecture Notes in Computer Science, vol. 6397, pp. 294–301. Springer (2010), https://doi.org/10.1007/978-3-642-16242-8_21
6. Ferrari, M., Fiorentini, C., Fiorino, G.: Simplification Rules for Intuitionistic Propositional Tableaux. ACM Trans. Comput. Log. **13**(2), 14:1–14:23 (2012), https://doi.org/10.1145/2159531.2159536
7. Ferrari, M., Fiorentini, C., Fiorino, G.: Contraction-Free Linear Depth Sequent Calculi for Intuitionistic Propositional Logic with the Subformula Property and Minimal Depth Counter-Models. J. Autom. Reason. **51**(2), 129–149 (2013), https://doi.org/10.1007/s10817-012-9252-7
8. Fiorentini, C.: An ASP Approach to Generate Minimal Countermodels in Intuitionistic Propositional Logic. In: Kraus, S. (ed.) Proceedings of the Twenty-Eighth International Joint Conference on Artificial Intelligence, IJCAI 2019, Macao, China, August 10-16, 2019. pp. 1675–1681. ijcai.org (2019), https://doi.org/10.24963/ijcai.2019/232
9. Fiorentini, C., Ferrari, M.: Duality between unprovability and provability in forward refutation-search for intuitionistic propositional logic. ACM Trans. Comput. Log. **21**(3), 22:1–22:47 (2020), https://doi.org/10.1145/3372299
10. Fiorentini, C., Goré, R., Graham-Lengrand, S.: A Proof-Theoretic Perspective on SMT-Solving for Intuitionistic Propositional Logic. In: Cerrito, S., Popescu, A. (eds.) Automated Reasoning with Analytic Tableaux and Related Methods - 28th International Conference, TABLEAUX 2019, London, UK, September 3-5, 2019, Proceedings. Lecture Notes in Computer Science, vol. 11714, pp. 111–129. Springer (2019), https://doi.org/10.1007/978-3-030-29026-9_7
11. Goré, R., Thomson, J., Wu, J.: A History-Based Theorem Prover for Intuitionistic Propositional Logic Using Global Caching: IntHistGC System Description. In: Demri, S., Kapur, D., Weidenbach, C. (eds.) Automated Reasoning - 7th International Joint Conference, IJCAR 2014, Held as Part of the Vienna Summer of Logic, VSL 2014, Vienna, Austria, July 19-22, 2014. Proceedings. Lecture Notes in Computer Science, vol. 8562, pp. 262–268. Springer (2014), https://doi.org/10.1007/978-3-319-08587-6_19

12. Nieuwenhuis, R., Oliveras, A., Tinelli, C.: Solving SAT and SAT Modulo Theories: From an abstract Davis–Putnam–Logemann–Loveland procedure to DPLL(T). J. ACM **53**(6), 937–977 (2006), https://doi.org/10.1145/1217856.1217859
13. Raths, T., Otten, J., Kreitz, C.: The ILTP problem library for intuitionistic logic. J. Autom. Reason. **38**(1-3), 261–271 (2007), https://doi.org/10.1007/s10817-006-9060-z
14. Troelstra, A.S., Schwichtenberg, H.: Basic proof theory, Second Edition, Cambridge tracts in theoretical computer science, vol. 43. Cambridge University Press (2000)

Open Access This chapter is licensed under the terms of the Creative Commons Attribution 4.0 International License (http://creativecommons.org/licenses/by/4.0/), which permits use, sharing, adaptation, distribution and reproduction in any medium or format, as long as you give appropriate credit to the original author(s) and the source, provide a link to the Creative Commons license and indicate if changes were made.

The images or other third party material in this chapter are included in the chapter's Creative Commons license, unless indicated otherwise in a credit line to the material. If material is not included in the chapter's Creative Commons license and your intended use is not permitted by statutory regulation or exceeds the permitted use, you will need to obtain permission directly from the copyright holder.

Proof Search and Certificates for Evidential Transactions

Vivek Nigam[1], Giselle Reis[2], Samar Rahmouni[2], and Harald Ruess[3]

[1] Huawei Munich Research Center, Munich, Germany vivek.nigam@gmail.com
[2] Carnegie Mellon University, Ar-Rayyan, Qatar giselle@cmu.edu,
srahmoun@andrew.cmu.edu [3] fortiss GmbH, Munich, Germany ruess@fortiss.org

Abstract. Attestation logics have been used for specifying systems with policies involving different principals. Cyberlogic is an attestation logic used for the specification of Evidential Transactions (ETs). In such transactions, evidence has to be provided supporting its validity with respect to given policies. For example, visa applicants may be required to demonstrate that they have sufficient funds to visit a foreign country. Such evidence can be expressed as a Cyberlogic proof, possibly combined with non-logical data (*e.g.*, a digitally signed document). A key issue is how to construct and communicate such evidence/proofs. It turns out that attestation modalities are challenging to use established proof-theoretic methods such as focusing. Our first contribution is the refinement of Cyberlogic proof theory with knowledge operators which can be used to represent knowledge bases local to one or more principals. Our second contribution is the identification of an executable fragment of Cyberlogic, called Cyberlogic programs, enabling the specification of ETs. Our third contribution is a sound and complete proof system for Cyberlogic programs enabling proof search similar to search in logic programming. Our final contribution is a proof certificate format for Cyberlogic programs inspired by Foundational Proof Certificates as a means to communicate evidence and check its validity.

Keywords: Attestation Logics · Proof Search · Sequent Calculus

1 Introduction

Attestation logics [1,14,21,15,6,5,29] have been used for the specification of policies of distributed systems, such as access control systems [1], distributed authorization policies [14,21], and evidential transactions (ETs) [15,5,6,6,29]. In these logics, one specifies policies involving attestation formulas of the form $K :\triangleright F$, where K is a principal (or agent) in the system.

Cyberlogic is an attestation logic for ETs. In Cyberlogic, cryptographic keys K are identified with specific authorities, and attestations $K :\triangleright A$ express the fact that principal K attests to statement A. For example, K may be a visa-granting authority and A the statement that the visa requester is authorized

© The Author(s) 2021
A. Platzer and G. Sutcliffe (Eds.): CADE 2021, LNAI 12699, pp. 234–251, 2021.
https://doi.org/10.1007/978-3-030-79876-5_14

to enter the specified country by the end of the year and at most once. An evidential transaction might issue a visa given that proof of sufficient funds has been provided in the form of a digital certificate whose validity can then be verified by customs authorities upon entry.

Formally, evidence in ETs can be expressed as a Cyberlogic proof. To carry out an ET, a Cyberlogic proof demonstrating policy compliance shall be produced and communicated. ETs therefore enable trust in, for example, distributed exchanges in electronic commerce, by enabling the exchange of various forms of *verifiable evidence*, such as evidence of funds in the visa example above.

The problem of producing attestation logic proofs (and proof objects) has not been given enough attention so far. Attestation logics have been formalized as Hilbert-style proof systems [1,15] that do not have the sub-formula property and therefore are not suitable for proof search. Other works on authorization logics [14,21] have proposed sequent calculi which do possess the sub-formula property. However, the search space is too great to enable efficient proof search.

The established proof-theoretic method for proof search is *focusing* [3,18]. Focusing distinguishes between inference rules that have "don't know" and "don't care" non-determinism to prune the proof search space. Interestingly, focused proof systems [7,18] provide a proof-theoretical justification for backward and forward-chaining, two proof-search strategies for Horn clauses (logic programs). Such justification, however, breaks when programs contain modalities, such as attestation modalities, *i.e.*, formulas of the form $K :\!\!\rhd F$. This is because focusing is lost whenever any of these formulas is encountered and therefore, improvements to the search space because of focusing is not so significant for attestation logics.

Our main goal is the study of Cyberlogic's proof theory in order to enable proof search (similar to the search involved in logic programming) and the generation of proof certificates for the communication of evidence in ETs.

Our first contribution, detailed in Section 2, is a Gentzen style proof system for Cyberlogic that admits cut elimination. A feature of the proof system is that it enables the combination of evidence represented as logical derivations as well as digital evidence, *e.g.*, signed hashes of documents, financial statements, medical records. The logic also includes a knowledge operator for sets of principals.

Our second contribution, detailed in Section 3, is the identification of a fragment of Cyberlogic, called Cyberlogic programs, akin to Horn clauses used in logic programming. This is motivated by the ongoing work on building distributed logic programming engines for ETs which extend existing engines [10] with attestations of the form $K :\!\!\rhd A$.

Our third contribution, also detailed in Section 3, addresses the challenge of how to efficiently construct Cyberlogic program proofs. We propose a focused inspired proof system for Cyberlogic programs and prove that it is sound and complete in this fragment. This system enables more efficient proof search.

Our last contribution, detailed in Section 4, addresses the challenge of how to efficiently communicate evidence. We propose a proof certificate format for Cyberlogic programs inspired by Foundational Proof Certificates (FPCs) [9]. FPCs enable the reconstruction of proofs by using simple logic programs as guides. This

$$\overline{\Gamma, A \longrightarrow A} \; \text{init} \qquad \frac{\text{evidence}_\mathsf{K} A}{\Gamma \longrightarrow \mathsf{K} :\!\triangleright A} \; \text{ext} \qquad \overline{\Gamma \longrightarrow \top} \; \top_r \qquad \overline{\Gamma, \bot \longrightarrow C} \; \bot_l$$

$$\frac{\Gamma, F_1, F_2 \longrightarrow G}{\Gamma, F_1 \wedge F_2 \longrightarrow G} \; \wedge_l \qquad \frac{\Gamma \longrightarrow F_1 \quad \Gamma \longrightarrow F_2}{\Gamma \longrightarrow F_1 \wedge F_2} \; \wedge_r \qquad \frac{\Gamma, F_1 \longrightarrow G \quad \Gamma, F_2 \longrightarrow G}{\Gamma, F_1 \vee F_2 \longrightarrow G} \; \vee_l \qquad \frac{\Gamma \longrightarrow F_i}{\Gamma \longrightarrow F_1 \wedge F_2} \; \vee_{r_i}$$

$$\frac{\Gamma, F_1 \supset F_2 \longrightarrow F_1 \quad \Gamma, F_2 \longrightarrow G}{\Gamma, F_1 \supset F_2 \longrightarrow G} \; \supset_l \qquad \frac{\Gamma, F_1 \longrightarrow F_2}{\Gamma \longrightarrow F_1 \supset F_2} \; \supset_r$$

$$\frac{\Gamma, \forall x. F, F[t/x] \longrightarrow G}{\Gamma, \forall x. F \longrightarrow G} \; \forall_l \qquad \frac{\Gamma \longrightarrow F[\alpha/x]}{\Gamma \longrightarrow \forall x. F} \; \forall_r \qquad \frac{\Gamma, F[\alpha/x] \longrightarrow G}{\Gamma, \exists x. F \longrightarrow G} \; \exists_l \qquad \frac{\Gamma \longrightarrow F[t/x]}{\Gamma \longrightarrow \exists x. F} \; \exists_r$$

$$\frac{\Gamma, F \longrightarrow \mathsf{K} :\!\triangleright G}{\Gamma, \mathsf{K} :\!\triangleright F \longrightarrow \mathsf{K} :\!\triangleright G} \; :\!\triangleright_l \qquad \frac{\Gamma \longrightarrow F}{\Gamma \longrightarrow \mathsf{K} :\!\triangleright F} \; :\!\triangleright_r \qquad \frac{\Gamma, \mathsf{kb}_\mathcal{Q} F, F \longrightarrow G}{\Gamma, \mathsf{kb}_\mathcal{Q} F \longrightarrow G} \; \mathsf{kb}_l \qquad \frac{\Gamma \mid_\mathcal{Q} \longrightarrow F}{\Gamma \longrightarrow \mathsf{kb}_\mathcal{Q} F} \; \mathsf{kb}_r$$

Fig. 1. $\mathsf{CL}_\mathcal{K}$ – Cyberlogic proof system for $\mathcal{K} = \{\mathsf{K}_1, \ldots, \mathsf{K}_n\}$. Here A is an atomic formula, $\mathcal{Q} \subseteq \mathcal{K}$, and $\Gamma \mid_\mathcal{Q} = \{\mathsf{kb}_{\mathcal{Q}'} F \mid \mathsf{kb}_{\mathcal{Q}'} F \in \Gamma \wedge \mathcal{Q}' \subseteq \mathcal{Q}\}$. Moreover, in rules $\exists_L$ and $\forall_R$, α is a fresh constant not appearing in Γ nor F.

means that such certificates can elide parts that can be easily reconstructed or which one is willing to reconstruct.

2 Cyberlogic Proof Theory

Cyberlogic [29] is an intuitionistic modal logic which can be used for specifying ETs. The logic is parametrized by a finite set of principals $\mathcal{K} = \{\mathsf{K}_1, \ldots, \mathsf{K}_n\}$, which are used in formulas as follows:

- $\mathsf{K}_i :\!\triangleright F$: meaning that principal K_i attests the (Cyberlogic) formula F;
- $\mathsf{kb}_\mathcal{Q} F$, where $\mathcal{Q} \subseteq \mathcal{K}$: meaning that all principals in $\mathcal{Q}$ know F, or, alternatively, that the combined knowledge of principals in $\mathcal{Q}$ imply F; and
- $\mathsf{evidence}_{\mathsf{K}_i} A$: standing for an external evidence signed by principal K_i.

External evidences are left unspecified since they fall outside the logical scope and depend on the ET being formalized. For example, $\mathsf{evidence}_{\mathsf{K}_i} A$ could be signed hashes of tickets, financial statments, medical records, etc. In Cyberlogic the evidence associated with an ET is a combination of a formal proof (in sequent calculus) and a collection of external evidences.

Cyberlogic formulas are constructed according to the following grammar:

$$F, G ::= A \mid F \wedge G \mid F \vee G \mid F \supset G \mid \top \mid \bot \mid \mathsf{K} :\!\triangleright F \mid \mathsf{kb}_\mathcal{Q} F \mid \forall x. F \mid \exists x. F$$

where A is an atom, $\mathsf{K} \in \mathcal{K}$, and $\mathcal{Q} \subseteq \mathcal{K}$. The formula $\mathsf{K} :\!\triangleright F$ is read as "principal K attests F" and acts like the *says* modality in lax logics [13,27]. The formula $\mathsf{kb}_\mathcal{Q} F$ is read as "principals in $\mathcal{Q}$ know F" and is inspired by the *knows* modality used in linear authorization logics [14,21]. Different from that logic, Cyberlogic allows the direct specification of knowledge shared by multiple principals, as illustrated in Example 1.

Cyberlogic sequents are of the shape $\Gamma \longrightarrow G$, where Γ is a multiset of formulas. The Cyberlogic proof system, $\mathsf{CL}_\mathcal{K}$, is depicted in Figure 1. Rules for the intuitionistic connectives $\wedge, \vee, \supset, \forall, \exists$ are as in LJ [30]. The new rules are the ones involving assertions $\mathsf{K} :\!\!\rhd F$ and $\mathsf{kb}_\mathcal{Q}$. Note that a "built-in" contraction of the main formula is needed on the left premise of $\supset_l$ and the premise of $\forall_l$, as expected in intuitionistic logics. Also, the rule kb_l has an explicit contraction on the premise. These contractions are needed for cut admissibility (Theorem 2).

Rules $:\!\!\rhd_l$ and $:\!\!\rhd_r$ specify that $:\!\!\rhd$ is a lax modality [27,21,24]. The intuition behind $:\!\!\rhd_l$ is: if an assertion G of a principal K is provable using F, then it is also provable if K attests F. Rule $:\!\!\rhd_r$ specifies that principals are rational, i.e., they can always attest formulas that are derivable. Differently from existing systems with lax modalities, $\mathsf{CL}_\mathcal{K}$ has the rule ext. This rule allows a proof of an attestation $\mathsf{K} :\!\!\rhd A$ to be completed whenever a principal provides evidence evidence$_\mathsf{K} A$ for the claim A. This formalizes the intuition that principals may use digital evidence signed by their private key. We leave the definition of evidence unspecified as it depends on the intended ET specified.

Rules kb_l and kb_r refine Cyberlogic by enabling the collection of logical theories known by a set of principals. Such theories act as *knowledge bases*. Rule kb_l specifies that any common knowledge can be part of a knowledge base. The interesting rule is kb_r, which specifies that $\mathsf{kb}_\mathcal{Q} F$ can only be proved using the local knowledge or evidence provided by principals in $\mathcal{Q}$. This is formally captured by restricting Γ in kb_r's premise to the set $\Gamma |_\mathcal{Q} = \{\mathsf{kb}_{\mathcal{Q}'} F \mid \mathsf{kb}_{\mathcal{Q}'} F \in \Gamma \wedge \mathcal{Q}' \subseteq \mathcal{Q}\}$. This is a powerful construct that increases the expressiveness of Cyberlogic. In particular, it is straightforward to specify that certain assertions can be concluded from the shared knowledge of a set of principals.

Proposition 1. *The following sequents are provable in $\mathsf{CL}_\mathcal{K}$ for all $\mathsf{K} \in \mathcal{K}$ and formulas F_1, F_2. $F_1 \equiv F_2$ represents the sequents $(F_1 \longrightarrow F_2)$ and $(F_2 \longrightarrow F_1)$:*

1. $F \longrightarrow \mathsf{K} :\!\!\rhd F$

2. $\mathsf{kb}_\mathcal{Q} F \longrightarrow F$

3. $\mathsf{kb}_{\{\mathsf{K}\}} F \longrightarrow \mathsf{K} :\!\!\rhd F$

4. $\mathsf{K} :\!\!\rhd \mathsf{K} :\!\!\rhd F \equiv \mathsf{K} :\!\!\rhd F$

5. $\mathsf{kb}_{\mathcal{Q}'} F \longrightarrow \mathsf{kb}_\mathcal{Q} F$, *if $\mathcal{Q}' \subseteq \mathcal{Q}$. In particular, $\mathsf{kb}_{\mathcal{Q}_1} \mathsf{kb}_{\mathcal{Q}_2} F \longrightarrow \mathsf{kb}_{\mathcal{Q}_1 \cup \mathcal{Q}_2} F$.*

6. $\mathsf{kb}_{\mathcal{Q}_1} F \wedge \mathsf{kb}_{\mathcal{Q}_2} F \longrightarrow \mathsf{kb}_{\mathcal{Q}_1 \cup \mathcal{Q}_2} F$

7. $\mathsf{K} :\!\!\rhd (F_1 \wedge F_2) \equiv \mathsf{K} :\!\!\rhd F_1 \wedge \mathsf{K} :\!\!\rhd F_2$

8. $\mathsf{kb}_\mathcal{Q} (F_1 \wedge F_2) \equiv \mathsf{kb}_\mathcal{Q} F_1 \wedge \mathsf{kb}_\mathcal{Q} F_2$

9. $(\mathsf{K} :\!\!\rhd F_1 \vee \mathsf{K} :\!\!\rhd F_2) \longrightarrow \mathsf{K} :\!\!\rhd (F_1 \vee F_2)$

10. $\mathsf{kb}_\mathcal{Q} A \vee \mathsf{kb}_\mathcal{Q} B \longrightarrow \mathsf{kb}_\mathcal{Q} (A \vee B)$

11. $\mathsf{K} :\!\!\rhd (F_1 \supset F_2) \longrightarrow (\mathsf{K} :\!\!\rhd F_1 \supset \mathsf{K} :\!\!\rhd F_2)$

12. $\mathsf{kb}_\mathcal{Q} (F_1 \supset F_2) \longrightarrow (\mathsf{kb}_\mathcal{Q} F_1 \supset \mathsf{K} :\!\!\rhd F_2)$

13. $\mathsf{K} :\!\!\rhd (\nabla x.F) \equiv \nabla x. \mathsf{K} :\!\!\rhd F$, $\nabla \in \{\forall, \exists\}$

14. $\mathsf{kb}_\mathcal{Q} (\nabla x.F) \equiv \nabla x. \mathsf{kb}_\mathcal{Q} F$, $\nabla \in \{\forall, \exists\}$

Moreover, the following sequents are not provable if $\mathsf{K}_1 \neq \mathsf{K}_2$ and $\mathcal{Q}_1 \neq \mathcal{Q}_2$:

1. $\mathsf{K} :\!\!\rhd F \nrightarrow F$

2. $F \nrightarrow \mathsf{kb}_\mathcal{Q} F$

3. $\mathsf{K} :\!\!\rhd F \nrightarrow \mathsf{kb}_{\{\mathsf{K}\}} F$

4. $\mathsf{K}_1 :\!\!\rhd (\mathsf{K}_2 :\!\!\rhd F) \nrightarrow \mathsf{K}_2 :\!\!\rhd (\mathsf{K}_1 :\!\!\rhd F)$

5. $\mathsf{kb}_{\mathcal{Q}_1} (\mathsf{kb}_{\mathcal{Q}_2} F) \nrightarrow \mathsf{kb}_{\mathcal{Q}_2} (\mathsf{kb}_{\mathcal{Q}_1} F)$

6. $\mathsf{kb}_{\mathcal{Q}_1 \cup \mathcal{Q}_2} F \nrightarrow \mathsf{kb}_{\mathcal{Q}_i} F$, $i \in \{1, 2\}$

7. $\mathsf{kb}_{\mathcal{Q}_1 \cup \mathcal{Q}_2} F \nrightarrow \mathsf{kb}_{\mathcal{Q}_1} F \wedge \mathsf{kb}_{\mathcal{Q}_2} F$

8. $\mathsf{kb}_\mathcal{Q} \mathsf{K} :\!\!\rhd A \nrightarrow \mathsf{K} :\!\!\rhd \mathsf{kb}_\mathcal{Q} A$

9. $\mathsf{K} :\!\!\rhd \mathsf{kb}_\mathcal{Q} A \nrightarrow \mathsf{kb}_\mathcal{Q} \mathsf{K} :\!\!\rhd A$

In the remainder of the paper, we elide the set of principals $\mathcal{K}$ whenever it can be deduced from the context.

Example 1. **(Shared Knowledge)** The ability to use kb with multiple principals allows the derivation of facts that depend on the combination of knowledge of multiple principals. Consider that principal K_1 knows A and $B \supset C$, and principal K_2 knows $A \supset B$, then the following sequent is provable in CL:

$$\mathsf{kb}_{\{K_1\}}A, \mathsf{kb}_{\{K_1\}}B \supset C, \mathsf{kb}_{\{K_2\}}A \supset B \longrightarrow \mathsf{kb}_{\{K_1, K_2\}}C$$

Remark 1. The original Cyberlogic paper [5] (and technical report [4]) proposed two kinds of attestations, :▷ and ▷, to distinguish when an attestation is derived from a digital evidence or logical inferences. This combination, however, does not yield to a proof system with the cut-elimination property [28].

The meta-theory of CL has been analysed using the L-framework [25], which uses rewriting logic to automatically derive structural proofs of sequent calculi properties [26]. The following lemma was used in the proofs of cut-elimination and invertibility.

Lemma 1. *If $\Gamma, K :\triangleright F \longrightarrow G$, then $\Gamma, F \longrightarrow G$.*

The proof proceeds by structural induction on the derivation of $\Gamma, K :\triangleright F \longrightarrow G$. The proof has been mechanically checked using the the L-framework with some few cases proved by hand.

As expected, $\supset_r, \wedge_r, \wedge_l, \vee_l, \forall_r, \exists_l$ are invertible whereas $\vee_r, \supset_l, \forall_l, \exists_r$ are not invertible. In addition, the rules $:\triangleright_l$ and kb_l are invertible whereas the $:\triangleright_r$ and kb_r are not invertible.

Lemma 2. *If $\Gamma, K :\triangleright F \longrightarrow K :\triangleright G$ then $\Gamma, F \longrightarrow K :\triangleright G$.*

This is a simple corollary of Lemma 1. Invertibility of kb_l is straighforward because of the contraction of the main formula.

Rules $:\triangleright_r$ and kb_r are not invertible. The counter examples are:

$$[:\triangleright_r] \quad K :\triangleright a \longrightarrow K :\triangleright a \text{ but } K :\triangleright a \not\longrightarrow a$$
$$[\mathsf{kb}_r] \quad a, a \supset \mathsf{kb}_K b \longrightarrow \mathsf{kb}_K b \text{ but } \not\longrightarrow b$$

Weakening is height perserving admissible in CL.

Theorem 1 (Identity expansion). *$F \longrightarrow F$ is provable in CL for any cyberlogic formula F.*

The proof is by structural induction on F.

Theorem 2 (Cut elimination). *If $\Gamma \longrightarrow F$ and $\Gamma, F \longrightarrow C$, then $\Gamma \longrightarrow C$.*

The proof proceeds by a nested induction on the structure of the proofs of $\Gamma \longrightarrow F$ and $\Gamma, F \longrightarrow C$, and the formula F. The noteworthy cases are the ones where cut needs to permute over kb rules. For kb_l, contraction of the main formula is needed, and the permutation over kb_r can be done only if cut is principal on the left (which is a lemma that can be proved). Details about these transformations are in Appendix A.

3   Cyberlogic Programs

Cyberlogic programs are fragment of CL which resembles Horn clauses in logic programming. Section 3.2 proposes a proof search operational semantics for cyberlogic programs and proves its soundness and completeness. The proof search discipline relies on ideas from focusing [3]. Focused proof systems for LJ [18] provide a proof theoretical justification of forward and backward chaining search. Each technique is enforced by the choice of polarity of atomic formulas: positive atoms lead to forward chaining and negative atoms lead to backward chaining. This correspondence, however, does not extend to cyberlogic due to attestation formulas $K :\!\rhd A$ which cause focusing to be lost [21]. Consider the following example where the formula under focus is in brackets:

$$\frac{K_1 :\!\rhd a \longrightarrow [K_1 :\!\rhd a] \quad K_1 :\!\rhd a, [K_2 :\!\rhd b] \longrightarrow K_2 :\!\rhd b}{K_1 :\!\rhd a, [K_1 :\!\rhd a \supset K_2 :\!\rhd b] \longrightarrow K_2 :\!\rhd b} \supset_l$$

In focused proof systems, forward chaining can be enforced by disallowing focus to be lost on the right formula in the left premise, *i.e.* $[K_1 :\!\rhd a]$. However, if $:\!\rhd_r$ is applied to this sequent the premise would be $K_1 :\!\rhd a \longrightarrow a$, which is not provable (see Proposition 1). In fact, $[K_1 :\!\rhd a]$ must lose focus on the right for the proof to be completed. Therefore, if $:\!\rhd$ modalities are used in logic programs, other strategies for proof search need to be analysed.

3.1   Cyberlogic Program Syntax

Cyberlogic programs can be divided into goals, knowledge bases, common knowledge, and attestation clauses.

Goals (G) Cyberlogic programs are used to derive a goal G, defined as:

$$G ::= \top \mid K :\!\rhd \mathsf{kb}_\varrho A \mid G_1 \wedge G_2 \mid \exists x.G$$

where A is an atomic formula. The restriction of $:\!\rhd \mathsf{kb}_\varrho$ to atoms does not reduce the expressiveness of goals, given the equivalences in Proposition 1.

Knowledge Bases (B): A knowledge base, written $\mathsf{kb}_{\{K_i\}}\Gamma$, of a principal $K_i \in \mathcal{K}$ is a set of formulas Γ not containing the connectives $:\!\rhd$ or kb. Here, $\mathsf{kb}_{\{K_i\}}\Gamma$ represents the set of formulas $\{\mathsf{kb}_{\{K_i\}}F \mid F \in \Gamma\}$.

Intuitively, a knowledge base $\mathsf{kb}_{\{K_i\}}\Gamma$ can be interpreted as K_i's local knowledge. This means that K_i may use its own prover to derive new facts. For example, if Γ is a collection of Horn-clauses, then K_i may deploy a Prolog engine to derive some goal. Alternatively if Γ is a set of formulas in CNF form, then K_i may use resolution provers. The absence of modal connectives in knowledge bases has important impacts on the design of the proof certificate described in Section 4, as those may rely on existing certificates for different provers [9].

Common Knowledge (C): Common knowledge are knowledge bases that are known to all principals, written as $\mathsf{kb}_\emptyset\, \Gamma$. Since $\emptyset \subseteq \mathcal{Q}$ for every $\mathcal{Q}$, these formulas remain in the context when applying kb_r. In this sense they contain first order formulas that may be used by all principals.

Attestation Formulas (D): Formulas of the form $\mathsf{K} :\!\triangleright \mathsf{kb}_\mathcal{Q} A$ are derived by attestation formulas of the form below where for all $1 \leq i \leq n$, $\mathsf{K}_i \in \mathcal{K}$, $\mathcal{Q}_i \subseteq \mathcal{K}$, and $A_1, \ldots, A_n, A$ are atomic formulas and $\vec{X}$ are bounded by universal quantifiers:

$$\forall \vec{X}.(\mathsf{kb}_{\mathcal{Q}_1}(\mathsf{K}_1 :\!\triangleright A_1) \wedge \cdots \wedge \mathsf{kb}_{\mathcal{Q}_n}(\mathsf{K}_n :\!\triangleright A_n) \wedge G \supset \mathsf{K} :\!\triangleright (\mathsf{kb}_\emptyset A))$$
$$\forall \vec{X}.(\mathsf{kb}_{\mathcal{Q}_1}(\mathsf{K}_1 :\!\triangleright A_1) \wedge \cdots \wedge \mathsf{kb}_{\mathcal{Q}_n}(\mathsf{K}_n :\!\triangleright A_n) \wedge G \supset \mathsf{K} :\!\triangleright (\mathsf{kb}_{\{\mathsf{K}\}} A))$$

Intuitively, an attestation formula belongs to a principal, namely K in the right-hand side of $\supset$. Such formulas derive K's attestation of an atomic formula which is its own knowledge ($\mathsf{kb}_{\{\mathsf{K}\}} A$), or common knowledge ($\mathsf{kb}_\emptyset A$). This means that K's attestation formulas cannot derive knowledge belonging to other principals. Furthermore to derive an attestation, one can use the knowledge base of other principals, *i.e.* the formulas $\mathsf{kb}_{\mathcal{Q}_i}(\mathsf{K}_i :\!\triangleright A_i)$ or additional goals, *i.e.* G. Finally notice that $\mathsf{K} :\!\triangleright (\mathsf{kb}_\emptyset A)$ and $\mathsf{K} :\!\triangleright (\mathsf{kb}_{\{\mathsf{K}\}} A)$ are attestation formulas themselves, where the left-hand side of $\supset$ is empty (denoting $\top$).

The difference between formulas $\mathsf{K} :\!\triangleright A$ and $\mathsf{K} :\!\triangleright (\mathsf{kb}_{\{\mathsf{K}\}} A)$ is subtle. Note that the former can be derived using the evidence rule ext, while the latter cannot. $\mathsf{K} :\!\triangleright (\mathsf{kb}_{\{\mathsf{K}\}} A)$ is K's attestation that A follows from its local knowledge base. It is possible to specify that A can be derived from an external evidence, but this has to be made explicit by an attestation formula, *e.g.*, $\mathsf{kb}_{\{\mathsf{K}\}}(\mathsf{K} :\!\triangleright A) \supset \mathsf{K} :\!\triangleright (\mathsf{kb}_{\{\mathsf{K}\}} A)$. Note that this formula is not a tautology.

We are interested in proving goals from attestation formulas, knowledge bases, and common knowledge, which are formally represented by cyberlogic program sequents defined as follows.

Definition 1 (Cyberlogic Program Sequents (CPS)). *A cyberlogic program sequent* (CPS) *is a sequent* $\mathcal{C}, \mathcal{B}, \mathcal{D} \longrightarrow G$, *where* $\mathcal{B}$ *is a set of knowledge bases,* $\mathcal{C}$ *is a set of common knowledge formulas,* $\mathcal{D}$ *is a set of attestation formulas, and* G *is a goal formula.*

Example 2. **(Local Computations)** This example illustrates the use of kb to specify when parts of a derivation can be proved locally using a principal's knowledge. Consider that the following clause

$$\mathsf{kb}_{\{\mathsf{K}_1\}}(\mathsf{K}_1 :\!\triangleright F_1) \wedge \mathsf{kb}_{\{\mathsf{K}_2\}}(\mathsf{K}_2 :\!\triangleright F_2) \supset \mathsf{K} :\!\triangleright \mathsf{kb}_{\{\mathsf{K}\}} G$$

specifies that for K to attest G, K_1 and K_2 have to attest F_1 and F_2 respectively, using *their own local theories, common knowledge, or evidence.* This means that computations carried out by K_1 and K_2 to derive their assertions $\mathsf{K}_1 :\!\triangleright F_1$ and $\mathsf{K}_2 :\!\triangleright F_2$ respectively, do not depend on other principals and therefore, the search for these derivations can be performed locally.

Example 3. (**Levels of Trust**) This example illustrates the use of kb to specify that some evidence should only be trusted if derived from trusted sources. Consider three principals $\mathcal{K} = \{K_T, K_U, K\}$ where K trusts evidence from K_T, but not all evidence from K_U. Then the following clause

$$kb_{\{K,K_T\}}(K :\triangleright critical(ok)) \wedge kb_{\mathcal{K}}(K :\triangleright nonCritical(ok)) \supset K :\triangleright kb_{\emptyset}(all(ok))$$

specifies that K can attest that everything is ok as a common knowledge if all the non-critical and critical elements are ok. However, the check of critical parts can only be performed by principals K trusts, namely K itself or K_T. Information from K_U's knowledge bases cannot be used in the proof of critical(ok).

Example 4. (**Simplified Visa**) Consider a visa issuing scenario where an applicant applies to a consulate (cons) for an entry visa. This is an example of an ET as, to obtain the visa, evidence has to be provided that, for example, the applicant has no crime records, or that they have sufficient funds. We illustrate how such an ET can be specified in Cyberlogic.

The formula below labelled **main** specifies conditions for a visa to be issued:

> **main:** $\forall Id.\forall Doc.\forall V.(kb_{\{cons\}}(cons :\triangleright visitOk(Id, Doc))$
> $\wedge\ kb_{\{cons\}}(cons :\triangleright prepVisa(Id, V))$
> $\wedge\ cons :\triangleright kb_{\{cons\}}(suffin(Doc)) \wedge police :\triangleright kb_{\{police\}}(noCrimeRec(Id))$
> $\supset cons :\triangleright kb_{cons}(issVisa(Id, Doc, V)))$

The transaction for cons issuing a visa V to an applicant Id requires cons to attest validity of Id's visit by itself (visitOk(Id, Doc)) and Id's criminal record with the help of the police (noCrimeRec(Id)). In addition, cons also needs to attest Id's financial status (suffin(Doc)).

The following two clauses expand on how cons can attest suffin(Doc): either via an employment contract or a bank statement.

> **cont:** $kb_{\{cons\}}(\forall Doc.\forall Cont.(empContract(Doc, Cont) \wedge valid(Cont)$
> $\supset suffin(Doc)))$
>
> **bankStmt:** $\forall Doc.\forall Stmt.(kb_{\{cons\}}(cons :\triangleright bankStmt(Doc, Stmt))$
> $\wedge bank :\triangleright kb_{\{bank\}}(valid(Stmt)) \supset cons :\triangleright kb_{\{cons\}}(suffin(Doc)))$

The formula labeled **cont** belongs to cons's knowledge base. This means that cons can check the validity of an employment contract without evidence from other principals. For example, valid(Cont) may check the contract duration and salary. The formula labeled **bankStmt**, on the other hand, takes the bank statement Stmt from the given documents, Doc, and requires the bank to validate it using its knowledge base. This makes sense as Id's financial records are sensitive and do not need to be disclosed to anyone else apart from her financial institute.

These clauses also illustrate the subtle difference between goal formulas $K :\triangleright kb_{\{K\}}F$ and knowledge base formulas $kb_{\{K\}}K :\triangleright F$. For example, in the **main** clause, the fact that applicant has come to their appointment at the consulate does not depend on other agents and that is why we use a knowledge base formula. The same applies to the visa preparation. On the other hand, the fact that applicant has sufficient funds may require evidence from other parties, *e.g.*, the applicant's bank. Therefore this is specified as a goal.

Goal decomposition

$$\frac{}{\Theta;\Lambda;\Delta \longrightarrow [\top]}\ \top_r \qquad \frac{\Theta;\Lambda;\Delta \longrightarrow [G_1] \quad \Theta;\Lambda;\Delta \longrightarrow [G_2]}{\Theta;\Lambda;\Delta \longrightarrow [G_1 \wedge G_2]}\ \wedge_r \qquad \frac{\Theta;\Lambda;\Delta \longrightarrow [G[t/x]]}{\Theta;\Lambda;\Delta \longrightarrow [\exists x.G]}\ \exists_r$$

$$\frac{\Theta;\Lambda;[\Delta] \longrightarrow \mathsf{K} :\!\!\triangleright \mathsf{kb}_\varrho A}{\Theta;\Lambda;\Delta \longrightarrow [\mathsf{K} :\!\!\triangleright \mathsf{kb}_\varrho A]}\ G \Rightarrow :\!\triangleright_l \qquad \frac{\Theta \mid_\varrho^* \longrightarrow A}{\Theta;\Lambda;\Delta \longrightarrow [\mathsf{K} :\!\!\triangleright \mathsf{kb}_\varrho A]}\ :\!\triangleright_r + \mathsf{kb}_r + \mathsf{kb}_l$$

$:\!\triangleright_l$ application

$$\frac{\Theta, \mathsf{kb}_\varrho A;\Lambda;[\Delta] \longrightarrow \mathsf{K} :\!\!\triangleright \mathsf{kb}_{\varrho'} A'}{\Theta;\Lambda;[\Delta, \mathsf{K} :\!\!\triangleright \mathsf{kb}_\varrho A] \longrightarrow \mathsf{K} :\!\!\triangleright \mathsf{kb}_{\varrho'} A'}\ :\!\triangleright_l$$

$$\frac{\Theta;[\Lambda];\Delta^\dagger \longrightarrow \mathsf{K} :\!\!\triangleright \mathsf{kb}_\varrho A}{\Theta;\Lambda;[\Delta^\dagger] \longrightarrow \mathsf{K} :\!\!\triangleright \mathsf{kb}_\varrho A}\ :\!\triangleright_l \Rightarrow \mathsf{att} \qquad \frac{\Theta;\Lambda;\Delta^\dagger \longrightarrow [\mathsf{K} :\!\!\triangleright \mathsf{kb}_\varrho A]}{\Theta;\Lambda;[\Delta^\dagger] \longrightarrow \mathsf{K} :\!\!\triangleright \mathsf{kb}_\varrho A}\ :\!\triangleright_l \Rightarrow G$$

Attestation formula decomposition

$$\frac{\Theta;\Lambda;\Delta \longrightarrow [G\sigma] \quad \Theta;\Lambda;[\Delta, \mathsf{K} :\!\!\triangleright \mathsf{kb}_\varrho A\sigma] \longrightarrow \mathsf{K}' :\!\!\triangleright \mathsf{kb}_{\varrho'} A' \quad \Theta \mid_{\varrho_1};\cdot;\cdot \longrightarrow [\mathsf{K}_1 :\!\!\triangleright A_1\sigma] \quad \cdots \quad \Theta \mid_{\varrho_n};\cdot;\cdot \longrightarrow [\mathsf{K}_n :\!\!\triangleright A_n\sigma]}{\Theta;[\Lambda, \forall \vec{X}.(\mathsf{kb}_{\varrho_1}(\mathsf{K}_1 :\!\!\triangleright A_1) \wedge \cdots \wedge \mathsf{kb}_{\varrho_n}(\mathsf{K}_n :\!\!\triangleright A_n) \wedge G \supset \mathsf{K} :\!\!\triangleright \mathsf{kb}_\varrho A)];\Delta \longrightarrow \mathsf{K}' :\!\!\triangleright \mathsf{kb}_{\varrho'} A'}\ \mathsf{att}$$

$\mathsf{K} :\!\triangleright A$ decomposition

$$\frac{\mathsf{evidence}_\mathsf{K} A}{\Theta;\cdot;\cdot \longrightarrow [\mathsf{K} :\!\!\triangleright A]}\ \mathsf{ext} \qquad \frac{\Theta^* \longrightarrow A}{\Theta;\cdot;\cdot \longrightarrow [\mathsf{K} :\!\!\triangleright A]}\ :\!\triangleright_r + \mathsf{kb}_l$$

First-order reasoning:

All first-order rules from CL on $\Theta^* \longrightarrow A$ sequents

Fig. 2. $\mathsf{CL}_\mathcal{P}$ – Sequent calculus for cyberlogic programs. A, A' and A_i are atoms, $\Delta^\dagger$ is such that for all $\mathsf{K}' :\!\!\triangleright \mathsf{kb}'_\varrho A' \in \Delta^\dagger$, $\mathsf{K}' \neq \mathsf{K}$, and $\Theta^* = \{F \mid \mathsf{kb}_\varrho F \in \Theta\}$.

3.2 CPS Proof Search

Proof search of CPS can be divided into the following phases: goal decomposition, $:\!\triangleright_l$ application, attestation formula decomposition, $\mathsf{K} :\!\triangleright A$ decomposition, and first-order reasoning. We define a (focusing inspired) sequent calculus for the CPS fragment, called $\mathsf{CL}_\mathcal{P}$ (Figure 2) for enforcing this proof search discipline. Sequents in $\mathsf{CL}_\mathcal{P}$ have the following shape: $\Theta;\Lambda;\Delta \longrightarrow F$, where Θ contains kb formulas, Λ contains attestation formulas, Δ contains formulas of the form $\mathsf{K} :\!\triangleright \mathsf{kb}_\varrho A$, and F is either a goal formula, $\mathsf{kb}_\varrho(\mathsf{K} :\!\triangleright A)$, $\mathsf{K} :\!\triangleright A$ or A, where A is an atom. Moreover, the part of the sequent containing the formula that is being decomposed will be enclosed in square brackets. This will help distinguishing the phases mentioned above.

Lemma 3. *The kb_r rules permutes down every left rule in the CPS fragment.*

Proof. First we note that, in the CPS fragment, $\wedge$, $\vee$, $\forall$, and kb formulas on the left do not have kb modalities as subformulas. We look at the case of kb_l, as the others follow a similar argument.

Since F is not a kb formula, then $F \notin (\Gamma, \mathsf{kb}_{Q'}F, F) \mid_Q$. Therefore we can conclude that $(\Gamma, \mathsf{kb}_{Q'}F, F) \mid_Q = (\Gamma, \mathsf{kb}_{Q'}F) \mid_Q$ and the permutation is:

$$
\cfrac{\cfrac{\overset{\varphi}{(\Gamma, \mathsf{kb}_{Q'}F, F) \mid_Q \longrightarrow G}}{\Gamma, \mathsf{kb}_{Q'}F, F \longrightarrow \mathsf{kb}_Q G} \; \mathsf{kb}_r}{\Gamma, \mathsf{kb}_{Q'}F \longrightarrow \mathsf{kb}_Q G} \; \mathsf{kb}_l
\qquad \rightsquigarrow \qquad
\cfrac{\overset{\varphi}{(\Gamma, \mathsf{kb}_{Q'}F) \mid_Q \longrightarrow G}}{\Gamma, \mathsf{kb}_{Q'}F \longrightarrow \mathsf{kb}_Q G} \; \mathsf{kb}_r
$$

The case for $:\!\rhd_l$ holds vacuously, as it is impossible to have $:\!\rhd_l$ immediately below kb_r since the former requires the right formula to be of the shape $\mathsf{K} :\!\rhd$.

The remaining case is $\supset_l$. Observe that in the CPS fragment, the formula F_2 in $F_1 \supset F_2$ is of the form $\mathsf{K} :\!\rhd \mathsf{kb}_{Q'}A$. Therefore, $(\Gamma, F_2) \mid_Q = \Gamma \mid_Q$. Also, $(\Gamma, F_1 \supset F_2) \mid_Q = \Gamma \mid_Q$. Thus the permutation is:

$$
\cfrac{\Gamma \longrightarrow F_1 \quad \cfrac{\overset{\varphi}{(\Gamma, F_2) \mid_Q \longrightarrow G}}{\Gamma, F_2 \longrightarrow \mathsf{kb}_Q G} \; \mathsf{kb}_r}{\Gamma, F_1 \supset F_2 \longrightarrow \mathsf{kb}_Q G} \; \supset_l
\qquad \rightsquigarrow \qquad
\cfrac{\overset{\varphi}{(\Gamma, F_1 \supset F_2) \mid_Q \longrightarrow G}}{\Gamma, F_1 \supset F_2 \longrightarrow \mathsf{kb}_Q G} \; \mathsf{kb}_r
$$

$\square$

Notice that it is crucial for attestation formulas to have a $:\!\rhd$ modality formula on the consequent, otherwise Lemma 3 would not hold. As seen below, this lemma is key to proving completeness of the proof search procedure for CPS.

Theorem 3 (Soundness and completeness of $\mathsf{CL}_{\mathcal{P}}$). $\Theta; \Lambda; \Delta \longrightarrow [F]$ *in* $\mathsf{CL}_{\mathcal{P}}$ *if and only if* $\Theta, \Lambda, \Delta \longrightarrow F$ *in* CL

Proof. Soundness is straightforward: a proof in $\mathsf{CL}_{\mathcal{P}}$ can be transformed into a proof in CL by using the same logical rules (possibly expanded – *e.g.* att becomes a sequence of $\forall_l + \supset_l + \wedge_r + \mathsf{kb}_r$) and skipping the phase transition rules $\Rightarrow$ (which only change the syntax of the sequent, but not its content).

Completeness is achieved by reasoning about invertibility and permutability of inference rules in the specific case of CPS. We argue that each phase can be performed in the proposed order.

Goal decomposition The goal formula can be eagerly decomposed until becoming $\mathsf{K} :\!\rhd \mathsf{kb}_Q A$ before applying other rules because: $\top_r$ and $\wedge_r$ are invertible, and in the absence of $\forall_r$ and $\exists_l$, $\exists_r$ permutes down every rule. Once the right side formula is $\mathsf{K} :\!\rhd \mathsf{kb}_Q A$, there are two options to continue: (1) change to $:\!\rhd_l$ application phase, or (2) apply rules $:\!\rhd_r + \mathsf{kb}_r + \mathsf{kb}_l$ in Figure 1.

The first case is discussed below. In the second case, we need to argue that kb_r may be applied immediately above $:\!\rhd_r$. Once $:\!\rhd_r$ is applied, we could choose a formula from the context to continue with. However, kb_r permutes down all left rules for the CPS fragment, as shown in Lemma 3. Therefore any proof that continues with a formula in Θ, Λ, or Δ above $:\!\rhd_r$ can be transformed into a proof where kb_r is applied immediately above $:\!\rhd_r$. Since kb_l is invertible, it can be applied to exhaustion safely.

$:\!\rhd_l$ **application** After eagerly decomposing the goal, $:\!\rhd_l$ can be applied to exhaustion since it is an invertible rule (Lemma 2).

Attestation formula decomposition This phase contains only one rule, namely att, which encompasses $\forall_l$, $\supset_l$, $\wedge_r$, and kb_r. The quantifier rule can always be delayed until its subformula is needed, and $\wedge_r$ is an invertible rule, therefore these can be chained together without loss of completeness. Due to Lemma 3, the application of kb_r can be permuted down for the CPS fragment and thus it is safe to apply the rule as soon as possible.

The two top premises of att force the proof search to go back to applying invertible rules, which does not break completeness.

$K :\rhd A$ decomposition Once this state is reached, Θ is left with kb formulas whose subformulas are in first-order logic (i.e., no modalities). In this case, one can either close the proof with an external evidence, or apply $:\rhd_r + kb_l$ to release the atom on the right side. The eager application of kb_l is justified due to its invertibility. It can also be delayed until this point because it permutes up $\supset_l$ and $:\rhd_r$ in CL, and it permutes up kb_r in the CPS fragment (Lemma 3).

First-order reasoning From this point onwards, there are no modalities in the sequent so it will be proved using only first-order reasoning.   □

4   Proof Certificates

Cyberlogic programs may be used to derive facts about attestation (goals), using pure logical reasoning (knowledge bases), principal delegation (attestation formulas), and external evidence. Once a goal is derived, evidence shall be available so that any interested party can verify that the proof is correct. Verifiable evidence means that entities do not need to trust each other's proof producing process, as long as they can check the proofs using their own trusted processes.

Given a cyberlogic program sequent of the shape: $\Theta; \Lambda; \Delta \longrightarrow G$ one could take its full sequent calculus proof in $CL_{\mathcal{P}}$ as evidence. If the interested parties know the calculus, checking validity of proofs reduces to checking the valid application of each rule. However, these proofs are too fine grained, and contain many uninteresting details that can be easily inferred. Proof certificates elide such details, and keep only the crucial steps for proof reconstruction.

Proof certificates for cyberlogic are defined inspired by λ-terms and *foundational proof certificates* [8,20] (FPC). FPC is a framework for checking proofs in different formalisms using a small trusted kernel. The proposed kernels are the sequent calculus focused systems LKF and LJF [18] for LK and LJ respectively, augmented with predicates for guiding proof search [9]. The definition of proof certificates for a proof system $\mathcal{S}$ relies on two parts: (1) a translation of $\mathcal{S}$'s formulas into LKF or LJF formulas; and (2) a correspondence of $\mathcal{S}$ proofs (or proof steps) to LKF or LJF proof steps. Given these two elements, a proof certificate for a proof of F in $\mathcal{S}$ consists of a predicate which guides a proof of F's translation in LKF or LJF. The following proof formats can be checked in FPC: resolution, λ-terms, Horn clauses, Frege proofs, matings, tableaux, etc.

Defining LKF or LJF FPCs for cyberlogic is challenging due to the modalities $:\rhd$ and kb, and digital evidences. LKF has been used to check proofs in modal logics [19], but the translation of modal formulas into LK formulas used the

$$\frac{}{\mathsf{top} : \Theta; \Lambda; \Delta \longrightarrow [\top]} \; \top_r \qquad \frac{\Xi : \Theta; \Lambda; \Delta \longrightarrow [G[t/x]]}{\Xi : \Theta; \Lambda; \Delta \longrightarrow [\exists x. G]} \; \exists_r$$

$$\frac{\Xi_1 : \Theta; \Lambda; \Delta \longrightarrow [G_1] \quad \Xi_2 : \Theta; \Lambda; \Delta \longrightarrow [G_2]}{\mathsf{split}(\Xi_1, \Xi_2) : \Theta; \Lambda; \Delta \longrightarrow [G_1 \wedge G_2]} \; \wedge_r$$

$$\frac{\Xi : \Theta; \Lambda; [\Delta] \longrightarrow \mathsf{K} :\triangleright \mathsf{kb}_\varrho A}{\mathsf{toSays_L}(\Xi) : \Theta; \Lambda; \Delta \longrightarrow [\mathsf{K} :\triangleright \mathsf{kb}_\varrho A]} \; G \Rightarrow :\triangleright_l \qquad \frac{\Psi : \Theta \mid_\varrho^* \longrightarrow A}{\mathsf{fol}(\Psi) : \Theta; \Lambda; \Delta \longrightarrow [\mathsf{K} :\triangleright \mathsf{kb}_\varrho A]} \; :\triangleright_r + \mathsf{kb}_r + \mathsf{kb}_l$$

$$\frac{\Xi : \Theta, \mathsf{kb}_\varrho A; \Lambda; [\Delta] \longrightarrow \mathsf{K} :\triangleright \mathsf{kb}_{\varrho'} A'}{\Xi : \Theta; \Lambda; [\Delta, \mathsf{K} :\triangleright \mathsf{kb}_\varrho A] \longrightarrow \mathsf{K} :\triangleright \mathsf{kb}_{\varrho'} A'} \; :\triangleright_l$$

$$\frac{\Xi : \Theta; [\Lambda]; \Delta^\dagger \longrightarrow \mathsf{K} :\triangleright \mathsf{kb}_{\dot\varrho} A}{\mathsf{toAtt}(\Xi) : \Theta; \Lambda; [\Delta^\dagger] \longrightarrow \mathsf{K} :\triangleright \mathsf{kb}_\varrho A} \; :\triangleright_l \Rightarrow \mathsf{att} \qquad \frac{\Xi : \Theta; \Lambda; \Delta^\dagger \longrightarrow [\mathsf{K} :\triangleright \mathsf{kb}_\varrho A]}{\mathsf{toGoal}(\Xi) : \Theta; \Lambda; [\Delta^\dagger] \longrightarrow \mathsf{K} :\triangleright \mathsf{kb}_\varrho A} \; :\triangleright_l \Rightarrow G$$

$$\frac{\begin{array}{c} \Xi' : \Theta; \Lambda; \Delta \longrightarrow [G\sigma] \quad \Xi'' : \Theta; \Lambda; [\Delta, \mathsf{K} :\triangleright \mathsf{kb}_\varrho A\sigma] \longrightarrow \mathsf{K}' :\triangleright \mathsf{kb}_{\varrho'} A' \\ \Xi_1 : \Theta \mid_{\varrho_1}; \cdot; \cdot \longrightarrow [\mathsf{K}_1 :\triangleright A_1 \sigma] \quad \cdots \quad \Xi_n : \Theta \mid_{\varrho_n}; \cdot; \cdot \longrightarrow [\mathsf{K}_n :\triangleright A_n \sigma] \\ \mathsf{att}(i, \sigma, [\Xi_1, ..., \Xi_n], \Xi', \Xi'') : \end{array}}{\Theta; [\Lambda, i : \forall \vec{X}.(\mathsf{kb}_{\varrho_1}(\mathsf{K}_1 :\triangleright A_1) \wedge \cdots \wedge \mathsf{kb}_{\varrho_n}(\mathsf{K}_n :\triangleright A_n) \wedge G \supset \mathsf{K} :\triangleright \mathsf{kb}_\varrho A)]; \Delta \longrightarrow \mathsf{K}' :\triangleright \mathsf{kb}_{\varrho'} A'} \; \mathsf{att}$$

$$\frac{\mathsf{evidence_K}(E, A)}{\mathsf{ext}(E) : \Theta; \cdot; \cdot \longrightarrow [\mathsf{K} :\triangleright A]} \; \mathsf{ext} \qquad \frac{\Psi : \Theta^* \longrightarrow A}{\mathsf{fol}(\Psi) : \Theta; \cdot; \cdot \longrightarrow [\mathsf{K} :\triangleright A]} \; :\triangleright_r + \mathsf{kb}_l$$

Fig. 3. $\mathsf{CL}_\mathcal{P}^a$ – $\mathsf{CL}_\mathcal{P}$ kernel for verifying $\mathsf{CL}_\mathcal{P}$ proof certificates of Cyberlogic programs. $\Delta^\dagger$ is such that for all $\mathsf{K}' :\triangleright \mathsf{kb}'_\varrho A' \in \Delta^\dagger$, $\mathsf{K}' \neq \mathsf{K}$ and $\Theta^* = \{F \mid \mathsf{kb}_\varrho F \in \Theta\}$.

modalities' semantic definition. Instead, we propose a modular $\mathsf{CL}_\mathcal{P}$ kernel which allows facts derived from knowledge bases or external evidence to be checked by the appropriate engine or entity.

The $\mathsf{CL}_\mathcal{P}$ kernel $\mathsf{CL}_\mathcal{P}^a$ (Figure 3) is constructed by augmenting sequents with a certificate Ξ (a term indicating how the proof must proceed) and indices for the formulas in Λ. A certificate for a proof of $\Theta; \Lambda; \Delta \longrightarrow G$ is $\Xi : \Theta; \Lambda_I; \Delta \longrightarrow G$, where Ξ is a term built from the predicates used in $\mathsf{CL}_\mathcal{P}^a$, and Λ_I is a mapping from indices to formulas in Λ. The indices are used in Ξ. The checking of a cyberlogic sequent $\Theta; \Lambda; \Delta \longrightarrow G$ with certificate Ξ starts from the sequent $\Xi : \Theta; \Lambda_I; \Delta \longrightarrow [G]$. Certificates denoted by the letter Ψ can represent proofs in other formalisms and may be checked by another engine. The predicates in Ξ are used for the following purposes during a derivation in $\mathsf{CL}_\mathcal{P}^a$.

First of all, they indicate how the proof should continue when there are multiple choices. For example, if the sequent is of the form $\Theta; \Lambda; \Delta \longrightarrow [\mathsf{K} :\triangleright \mathsf{kb}_\varrho A]$, then Ξ must be one of $\mathsf{toSays_L}(\_)$ or $\mathsf{fol}(\_)$, indicating whether to work on $:\triangleright$ modalities on the left, or finish the proof with first-order reasoning, respectively.

Secondly, certificates relay information at the appropriate moment. For example, $\mathsf{split}(\_, \_)$ contains the certificates for each of the branches on a splitting rule, and $\mathsf{ext}(\_)$ includes an external evidence for proposition A. Note that there is no certificate for $\exists_R$ since these can be instantiated with meta-variables, and unification can be verified when the proof is completed.

The certificate for rule att is more interesting. It includes the index i of the attestation formula to be decomposed, the substitution σ for the $\forall$ quantifier, and certificates for each premise. Note that each $\Xi_1, ... \Xi_n$ must be $\mathsf{ext}(\_)$ or $\mathsf{fol}(\_)$.

Example 5. Consider Example 4, and let the indices of the formulas be their labels: **main**, **cont**, and **bankStmt**. The certificate for a proof that alice can get a visa is $\Xi : \mathbf{cont}; \mathbf{main}, \mathbf{bankStmt}; \cdot \longrightarrow \mathsf{cons} : \rhd \mathsf{kb}_{\{\mathsf{cons}\}} \mathsf{issVisa}(\mathsf{alice}, \mathsf{doc}, \mathsf{visa})$. Where Ξ is:

$$\mathsf{att}(\mathbf{main}, \{\mathsf{Id} \mapsto \mathsf{alice}, \mathsf{Doc} \mapsto \mathsf{doc}, \mathsf{V} \mapsto \mathsf{visa}\}, [\mathsf{fol}(\Psi_{\mathsf{visitOk}}), \mathsf{fol}(\Psi_{\mathsf{prepVisa}})], \Xi_G, \Xi_0)$$

The certificates Ψ_{visitOk} and Ψ_{prepVisa} are first-order logic proof certificates from derivations using the consulate's own knowledge base.

Certificate Ξ_0 corresponds to att's premise where the conclusion of **main** is added to the context. This branch can be closed by removing the modalities, so $\Xi_0 = \mathsf{toGoal}(\mathsf{fol}(\mathsf{id}))$, where id is a first-order logic directive to close the proof. Certificate Ξ_G guides the proof of the new goal:

$$\mathsf{cons} : \rhd \mathsf{kb}_{\{\mathsf{cons}\}}(\mathsf{sufFin}(\mathsf{doc})) \wedge \mathsf{police} : \rhd \mathsf{kb}_{\{\mathsf{police}\}}(\mathsf{noCrimeRec}(\mathsf{alice}))$$

and thus $\Xi_G = \mathsf{split}(\Xi_{\mathsf{fin}}, \Xi_{\mathsf{crime}})$. Ξ_{fin} depends on how cons decides to check for sufficient funds. It could rely on the bank and use the attestation formula **bankStmt**, in which case Ξ_{fin} has the shape

$$\mathsf{toSays}_\mathsf{L}(\mathsf{toAtt}(\mathsf{att}(\mathbf{bankStmt}, \_, \_, \_, \_)))$$

Or it could use **cont** from its knowledge base, in which case Ξ_{fin} would be $\mathsf{fol}(\_)$.

5   Related Work

Attestation logics have been proposed for the specification of policies of several distributed systems [14,21,15,5,29,1]. We have been inspired by some of this work in the design of Cyberlogic. Actually, Cyberlogic was proposed some decades ago [29,5], but until now its proof theory had not been carefully investigated. In particular, there were no statements on cut-elimination. Additionally, we have been inspired by the previous works on authorization logics [14,21,15] to extend Cyberlogic with knowledge operators.

The main contribution of our work is the study of proof search and proof certificates for attestation logics with knowledge operators.

In previous work [14] in intuitionistic authorization logic, knowledge was restricted to one principal. As demonstrated in Example 1, allowing for multiple principal knowledge databases ensures collaboration in reasoning.

Proof search for attestation logics is not adequately addressed in the literature. Either the proposed proof systems are Hilbert-style [1,2,17] which do not enjoy the sub-formula property and therefore are not suitable for proof search, or they are sequent calculus proof system, but not focused proof systems [14,21,29,5,16]. [14] only speculates that logic programming languages can be used to carry out proof search for fragments of attestation logic. We confirm this speculation with the definition of Cyberlogic programs.

Our main inspiration for proof certificate is the work on foundational proof certificates [9]. However, the existing work did not consider proof certificates for attestation logics. Closer to our objective is the work of Libal and Volpe [19], which define proof certificates for modal logics by encoding (the semantics of) these logics in LKF. Our work instead proposes proof certificates directly in Cyberlogic. This means that we are able to capitalize on rules, such as attestation rules, to build more compact certificates. Another difference is that our proof certificates may contain (pointers to) extra-logical evidence.

Cyberlogic has been formalized in Coq [11], encoding evidential transactions for Schengen Visa applications. Our approach is different in that it lays a proof theoretic foundation to Cyberlogic. In particular, proof search is formally justified as well as the representation of Cyberlogic proofs as FPCs.

Logic programming engines, such as ETB [10], have been proposed for programming ETs. However, these engines do not (yet) support attestations, such as $K :\triangleright F$, local knowledge, such as $kb_Q F$, nor the use of digital certificates. We believe that this work can greatly profit from the foundations laid by this paper.

Finally, works [15,6] propose the use of evidence for authorization. Specifically, [16] show that a fragment of their system is decidable in linear time. It would be interesting to investigate how this fragment relates to Cyberlogic programs, and whether proof certificates as defined in this work can be applied to the decidable fragment. This is left for future work.

6   Conclusions

This paper lays the proof-theoretic foundations for Cyberlogic, an attestation logic for evidential transactions, and refine Cyberlogic with epistemic modalities. We identify a fragment of Cyberlogic, Cyberlogic programs, and propose a proof system similar to focused proof systems for enabling sound and complete proof search. The necessary permutations for completeness rely on the careful interplay between attestation, $:\triangleright$, and knowledge modalities, kb_Q. We then propose a concise proof certificate format for proofs of Cyberlogic programs.

This paper is the first step for a framework enabling evidential transactions that we are currently implementing. In particular, we are extending Distributed Datalog engines available in [10] to support Cyberlogic. Moreover, we are integrating such engines with PKI infrastructure, available in, for example, Distributed Ledger Technologies. This means that evidence, both in the form of digital evidence and logical derivations in the form of FPCs, can be stored and audited through the Ledger Technologies.

We are currently investigating extensions to Cyberlogic programs to include other modalities, such as temporal and epistemic [23,12] while still preserving its good proof search properties. We have also started to study conditions for when two attestation rules can be introduced in any order. If two clauses can be introduced in any order, then they can also be introduced in parallel. Therefore, this would provide proof-theoretic justification for proof search optimization. This could be used, for example, for proposing refinements to dependency graphs used for evaluating distributed logic programming [22] which take principals into account. These results will impact the maintenance of evidential transactions, whose applications can have important consequences to, *e.g.*, certification in automotive and avionics domains.

Acknowledgment: We would like to thank Dian Balta, Natarajan Shankar and Tewodros Beyene for useful discussions and valuable feedback on earlier versions of this paper. This project has received funding from the European Union's Horizon 2020 research and innovation programme under grant agreement No 830892 and from BayernCloud 3, AZ: 20-13-3410.I-01A-2017. Nigam is partially supported CNPq grant 303909/2018-8.

A   Cut-elimination

Proof. (Sketch) The proof follows the usual Gentzen strategy of reducing the cuts' grade and rank. The interesting cases are rank reduction over kb rules.

In the case of kb_l, contraction of the main formula is needed for the permutation to work. If this was not the case, we could not conclude $\Gamma, A \longrightarrow G$ from $\Gamma, \mathsf{kb}_{\mathcal{Q}} A \longrightarrow G$. The transformations are:

$$
\cfrac{\cfrac{\cfrac{\varphi_1}{\Gamma, \mathsf{kb}_{\mathcal{Q}} A, A \longrightarrow C}}{\Gamma, \mathsf{kb}_{\mathcal{Q}} A \longrightarrow C}\,\mathsf{kb}_l \quad \cfrac{\varphi_2}{\Gamma, \mathsf{kb}_{\mathcal{Q}} A, C \longrightarrow G}}{\Gamma, \mathsf{kb}_{\mathcal{Q}} A \longrightarrow G}\,\mathrm{cut} \quad\rightsquigarrow\quad \cfrac{\cfrac{\cfrac{\varphi_1}{\Gamma, \mathsf{kb}_{\mathcal{Q}} A, A \longrightarrow C} \quad \cfrac{\varphi_2 + \mathrm{weakening}}{\Gamma, \mathsf{kb}_{\mathcal{Q}} A, A, C \longrightarrow G}}{\Gamma, \mathsf{kb}_{\mathcal{Q}} A, A \longrightarrow G}\,\mathrm{cut}}{\Gamma, \mathsf{kb}_{\mathcal{Q}} A, \longrightarrow G}\,\mathsf{kb}_l
$$

$$
\cfrac{\cfrac{\varphi_1}{\Gamma, \mathsf{kb}_{\mathcal{Q}} A \longrightarrow C} \quad \cfrac{\cfrac{\varphi_2}{\Gamma, \mathsf{kb}_{\mathcal{Q}} A, C \longrightarrow G}}{\Gamma, \mathsf{kb}_{\mathcal{Q}} A, C \longrightarrow G}\,\mathsf{kb}_l}{\Gamma, \mathsf{kb}_{\mathcal{Q}} A \longrightarrow G}\,\mathrm{cut} \quad\rightsquigarrow\quad \cfrac{\cfrac{\cfrac{\varphi_1 + \mathrm{weakening}}{\Gamma, \mathsf{kb}_{\mathcal{Q}} A, A \longrightarrow C} \quad \cfrac{\varphi_2}{\Gamma, \mathsf{kb}_{\mathcal{Q}} A, A, C \longrightarrow G}}{\Gamma, \mathsf{kb}_{\mathcal{Q}} A, A \longrightarrow G}\,\mathrm{cut}}{\Gamma, \mathsf{kb}_{\mathcal{Q}} A \longrightarrow G}\,\mathsf{kb}_l
$$

The other interesting case is when we need to permute a cut over a kb_r rule on the right branch:

$$
\cfrac{\cfrac{\varphi_1}{\Gamma \longrightarrow C} \quad \cfrac{\cfrac{\varphi_2}{(\Gamma, C)\mid_{\mathcal{Q}_i} \longrightarrow G}}{\Gamma, C \longrightarrow \mathsf{kb}_{\mathcal{Q}_i} G}\,\mathsf{kb}_r}{\Gamma \longrightarrow \mathsf{kb}_{\mathcal{Q}_i} G}\,\mathrm{cut}
$$

There are two cases to consider:

1. $C \equiv \mathsf{kb}_{\mathcal{Q}_j} C'$ and $\mathcal{Q}_i \preceq \mathcal{Q}_j$: in this case, we can permute the cut over rules on φ_1 (left rules except $\rhd_L$, which is never applicable) until it is principal. This lemma can be proved by case analysis. At this point, the premise on the left branch will be $\Gamma \mid_{\mathcal{Q}_j} \longrightarrow C'$. Then kb_R can be applied to the end-sequent, resulting in:

$$
\cfrac{\cfrac{\varphi_1'}{\Gamma \mid_{\mathcal{Q}_i} \longrightarrow \mathsf{kb}_{\mathcal{Q}_j} C'} \quad \cfrac{\varphi_2'}{\Gamma \mid_{\mathcal{Q}_i}, \mathsf{kb}_{\mathcal{Q}_j} C' \longrightarrow G}}{\cfrac{\Gamma \mid_{\mathcal{Q}_i} \longrightarrow G}{\Gamma \longrightarrow \mathsf{kb}_{\mathcal{Q}_i} G}\,\mathsf{kb}_r}\,\mathrm{cut}
$$

The proof φ_2' is exactly φ_2, since $(\Gamma, \mathsf{kb}_{\mathcal{Q}_j} C') \mid_{\mathcal{Q}_i} \equiv \Gamma \mid_{\mathcal{Q}_i}, \mathsf{kb}_{\mathcal{Q}_j} C'$ when $\mathcal{Q}_i \preceq \mathcal{Q}_j$. The proof φ_1' is obtained from the proof of $\Gamma \mid_{\mathcal{Q}_j} \longrightarrow C'$, since $\Gamma \mid_{\mathcal{Q}_j} \subseteq \Gamma \mid_{\mathcal{Q}_i}$ when $\mathcal{K}_i \preceq \mathcal{Q}_j$.
2. $C \not\equiv \mathsf{kb}_{\mathcal{Q}_j} C'$ or $\mathcal{Q}_i \not\preceq \mathcal{Q}_j$: in this case $C \notin (\Gamma, C) \mid_{\mathcal{Q}_i}$, so kb_r can be applied directly to the end-sequent, and the cut can be removed.

$\square$

References

1. Abadi, M.: Logic in Access Control. In: 18th IEEE Symposium on Logic in Computer Science (LICS) Proceedings. pp. 228–233. IEEE Computer Society (2003). https://doi.org/10.1109/LICS.2003.1210062

2. Abadi, M., Burrows, M., Lampson, B.W., Plotkin, G.D.: A Calculus for Access Control in Distributed Systems. ACM Trans. Program. Lang. Syst. **15**(4), 706–734 (1993). https://doi.org/10.1145/155183.155225

3. Andreoli, J.M.: Logic Programming with Focusing Proofs in Linear Logic. Joural of Logic and Computation **2**(3), 297–347 (1992). https://doi.org/10.1093/logcom/2.3.297

4. Bernat, V.: First-Order Cyberlogic Hereditary Harrop Logic. Tech. rep., SRI International (2006), http://www.lsv.ens-cachan.fr/Publis/PAPERS/PS/Bernat-cyberlogic1.ps

5. Bernat, V., Ruess, H., Shankar, N.: First-order Cyberlogic. Technical Report CSL-SRI-04-03, SRI International Computer Science Laboratory (2004)

6. Blass, A., Gurevich, Y., Moskal, M., Neeman, I.: Evidential Authorization. In: Nanz, S. (ed.) The Future of Software Engineering. pp. 73–99. Springer (2010). https://doi.org/10.1007/978-3-642-15187-3_5

7. Chaudhuri, K., Pfenning, F., Price, G.: A Logical Characterization of Forward and Backward Chaining in the Inverse Method. In: Furbach, U., Shankar, N. (eds.) Automated Reasoning, Third International Joint Conference, IJCAR, Proceedings. pp. 97–111. Springer Berlin Heidelberg (2006). https://doi.org/10.1007/11814771_9

8. Chihani, Z., Miller, D., Renaud, F.: Foundational Proof Certificates in First-Order Logic. In: Bonacina, M.P. (ed.) CADE-24 - 24th International Conference on Automated Deduction. Proceedings. Lecture Notes in Computer Science, vol. 7898, pp. 162–177. Springer (2013). https://doi.org/10.1007/978-3-642-38574-2_11

9. Chihani, Z., Miller, D., Renaud, F.: A Semantic Framework for Proof Evidence. J. Autom. Reasoning **59**(3), 287–330 (2017). https://doi.org/10.1007/s10817-016-9380-6

10. Cruanes, S., Hamon, G., Owre, S., Shankar, N.: Tool Integration with the Evidential Tool Bus. In: Giacobazzi, R., Berdine, J., Mastroeni, I. (eds.) Verification, Model Checking, and Abstract Interpretation, 14th International Conference, VMCAI. Proceedings. pp. 275–294. Springer Berlin Heidelberg (2013). https://doi.org/10.1007/978-3-642-35873-9_18

11. Dargaye, Z., Kirchner, F., Tucci-Piergiovanni, S., Gürcan, O.: Towards Secure and Trusted-by-Design Smart Contracts. In: JFLA (2018)

12. DeYoung, H., Garg, D., Pfenning, F.: An Authorization Logic With Explicit Time. In: Proceedings of the 21st IEEE Computer Security Foundations Symposium, CSF. pp. 133–145. IEEE Computer Society (2008). https://doi.org/10.1109/CSF.2008.15

13. Fairtlough, M., Mendler, M.: Propositional Lax Logic. Inf. Comput. **137**(1), 1–33 (1997). https://doi.org/10.1006/inco.1997.2627

14. Garg, D., Bauer, L., Bowers, K.D., Pfenning, F., Reiter, M.K.: A Linear Logic of Authorization and Knowledge. In: Gollmann, D., Meier, J., Sabelfeld, A. (eds.) Computer Security - ESORICS 2006, 11th European Symposium on Research in Computer Security, Proceedings. pp. 297–312. Springer Berlin Heidelberg (2006). https://doi.org/10.1007/11863908_19

15. Gurevich, Y., Neeman, I.: DKAL: Distributed-Knowledge Authorization Language. Tech. Rep. MSR-TR-2008-09, Microsoft Research (January 2008), https://www.microsoft.com/en-us/research/publication/191tr-dkal-distributed-knowledge-authorization-language/

16. Gurevich, Y., Neeman, I.: DKAL 2 - A Simplified and Improved Authorization Language. Tech. Rep. MSR-TR-2009-11, Microsoft Research (2009), https://www.microsoft.com/en-us/research/publication/200-dkal-2-a-simplified-and-improved-authorization-language/

17. Gurevich, Y., Neeman, I.: Logic of infons: The propositional case. ACM Trans. Comput. Log. **12**(2), 9:1–9:28 (2011). https://doi.org/10.1145/1877714.1877715

18. Liang, C., Miller, D.: Focusing and polarization in linear, intuitionistic, and classical logics. Theor. Comput. Sci. **410**(46), 4747–4768 (2009). https://doi.org/10.1016/j.tcs.2009.07.041

19. Libal, T., Volpe, M.: A general proof certification framework for modal logic. Math. Struct. Comput. Sci. **29**(8), 1344–1378 (2019). https://doi.org/10.1017/S0960129518000440

20. Miller, D.: Foundational Proof Certificates. In: Delahaye, D., Paleo, B.W. (eds.) All about Proofs, Proofs for All, All about Proofs, Proofs for All, vol. Mathematical Logic and Foundations, 55, pp. 150–163. College Publications (2015), https://hal.inria.fr/hal-01239733

21. Nigam, V.: A framework for linear authorization logics. Theor. Comput. Sci. **536**, 21–41 (2014). https://doi.org/10.1016/j.tcs.2014.02.018

22. Nigam, V., Jia, L., Loo, B.T., Scedrov, A.: Maintaining distributed logic programs incrementally. Computer Languages, Systems & Structures **38**(2), 158–180 (2012). https://doi.org/10.1016/j.cl.2012.02.001

23. Nigam, V., Olarte, C., Pimentel, E.: A General Proof System for Modalities in Concurrent Constraint Programming. In: D'Argenio, P.R., Melgratti, H.C. (eds.) CONCUR 2013 - Concurrency Theory - 24th International Conference. Proceedings. Lecture Notes in Computer Science, vol. 8052, pp. 410–424. Springer (2013). https://doi.org/10.1007/978-3-642-40184-8_29

24. Nigam, V., Pimentel, E., Reis, G.: An extended framework for specifying and reasoning about proof systems. J. Log. Comput. **26**(2), 539–576 (2016). https://doi.org/10.1093/logcom/exu029

25. Olarte, C.: L-framework. https://carlosolarte.github.io/L-framework/, accessed on 03-01-2021

26. Olarte, C., Pimentel, E., Rocha, C.: Proving Structural Properties of Sequent Systems in Rewriting Logic. In: Rusu, V. (ed.) Rewriting Logic and Its Applications - 12th International Workshop, WRLA 2018, Held as a Satellite Event of ETAPS, Proceedings. Lecture Notes in Computer Science, vol. 11152, pp. 115–135. Springer (2018). https://doi.org/10.1007/978-3-319-99840-4_7

27. Pfenning, F., Davies, R.: A judgmental reconstruction of modal logic. Mathematical Structures in Computer Science **11**(4), 511–540 (2001). https://doi.org/10.1017/S0960129501003322

28. Reis, G.: Observations about the proof theory of cyberlogic. http://www.gisellereis.com/papers/cyberlogic-report.pdf (2019)

29. Ruess, H., Shankar, N.: Introducing Cyberlogic (2003)

30. Troelstra, A.S., Schwichtenberg, H.: Basic Proof Theory. Cambridge University Press (1996)

Open Access This chapter is licensed under the terms of the Creative Commons Attribution 4.0 International License (http://creativecommons.org/licenses/by/4.0/), which permits use, sharing, adaptation, distribution and reproduction in any medium or format, as long as you give appropriate credit to the original author(s) and the source, provide a link to the Creative Commons license and indicate if changes were made.

The images or other third party material in this chapter are included in the chapter's Creative Commons license, unless indicated otherwise in a credit line to the material. If material is not included in the chapter's Creative Commons license and your intended use is not permitted by statutory regulation or exceeds the permitted use, you will need to obtain permission directly from the copyright holder.

Non-clausal Redundancy Properties [*]

Lee A. Barnett[iD] and Armin Biere[iD]

Johannes Kepler University Linz
Altenbergerstraße 69, 4040 Linz, Austria
{lee.barnett,armin.biere}@jku.at

Abstract. State-of-the-art refutation systems for SAT are largely based on the derivation of clauses meeting some redundancy criteria, ensuring their addition to a formula does not alter its satisfiability. However, there are strong propositional reasoning techniques whose inferences are not easily expressed in such systems. This paper extends the redundancy framework beyond clauses to characterize redundancy for Boolean constraints in general. We show this characterization can be instantiated to develop efficiently checkable refutation systems using redundancy properties for Binary Decision Diagrams (BDDs). Using a form of reverse unit propagation over conjunctions of BDDs, these systems capture, for instance, Gaussian elimination reasoning over XOR constraints encoded in a formula, without the need for clausal translations or extension variables. Notably, these systems generalize those based on the strong Propagation Redundancy (PR) property, without an increase in complexity.

1 Introduction

The correctness and reliability of Boolean satisfiability (SAT) solvers is critical for many applications. For instance SAT solvers are used for verifying hardware and software systems (e.g. [19,28,44]), to search for solutions to open problems in mathematics (e.g. [38,46]), and as subroutines of other logical reasoning tools (e.g. [7,67]). Solvers should be able to provide solution certificates that are easily and externally checkable. For a satisfiable formula, any satisfying assignment is a suitable certificate and typically can be easily produced by a solver. For an unsatisfiable formula, a solver should be able to produce a refutation proof.

Modern SAT solvers primarily refute unsatisfiable formulas using clausal proof systems, such as the popular DRAT system [69] used by the annual SAT competition in recent years [4], or newer systems based on the surprisingly strong Propagation Redundancy (PR) property [33]. Clausal proof systems iteratively extend a formula, typically given in conjunctive normal form (CNF), by adding clauses that are redundant; that is, their addition to the formula does not affect whether it is satisfiable. Systems are distinguished by their underlying redundancy properties, restricted but efficiently-decidable forms of redundancy.

[*] Supported by the Linz Institute of Technology AI Lab funded by the State of Upper Austria, as well as the Austrian Science Fund (FWF) under project W1255-N23, the LogiCS Doctoral College on Logical Methods in Computer Science.

© The Author(s) 2021
A. Platzer and G. Sutcliffe (Eds.): CADE 2021, LNAI 12699, pp. 252–272, 2021.
https://doi.org/10.1007/978-3-030-79876-5_15

Redundancy is a useful notion in SAT as it captures most inferences made by state-of-the-art solvers. This includes clauses implied by the current formula, such as the resolvent of two clauses or clauses learned during conflict-driven clause learning (CDCL) [8,51], as well as clauses which are not implied but derived nonetheless by certain preprocessing and inprocessing techniques [43], such as those based on blocked clauses [42,45,48]. Further, clausal proof systems based on properties like PR include short refutations for several hard families of formulas, such as those encoding the pigeonhole principle, that have no polynomial-length refutations in resolution [2] (see [16] for an overview). These redundancy properties, seen as inference systems, thus potentially offer significant improvements in efficiency, as the CDCL algorithm at the core of most solvers searches only for refutations in resolution [9]. While the recent satisfaction-driven clause learning (SDCL) paradigm has shown some initial success [35,37], it is still unclear how to design solving techniques which take full advantage of this potential.

Conversely, there are existing strong reasoning techniques which similarly exceed the abilities of CDCL alone, but are difficult to express using clausal proof systems. Important examples include procedures for reasoning over CNF formulas encoding pseudo-Boolean and cardinality constraints (see [58]), as well as Gaussian elimination (see [12,61,62,68]), which has been highlighted as a challenge for clausal proof systems [31]. Gaussian elimination, applied to sets of "exclusive-or" (XOR) constraints, is a crucial technique for many problems from cryptographic applications [62], and can efficiently solve, for example, Tseitin formulas hard for resolution [64,66]. This procedure, implemented by CryptoMiniSAT [62], Lingeling [10], and Coprocessor [50] for example, can be polynomially simulated by extended resolution, allowing inferences over new variables, and similar systems (see [56,60]). However due to the difficulty of such simulations they are not typically implemented. Instead solvers supporting these techniques simply prevent them from running when proof output is required, preferring less efficient techniques whose inferences can be more easily represented.

This paper extends the redundancy framework for clausal proof systems to include non-clausal constraints, such as XOR or cardinality constraints, presenting a characterization of redundancy for Boolean functions in general. We demonstrate a particular use of this characterization by instantiating it for functions represented by Binary Decision Diagrams [13], a powerful representation with a long history in SAT solving (e.g. [14,23,24,52,54]) and other areas of automated reasoning (e.g. [15,29,47,57]). We show the resulting refutation systems succinctly express Gaussian elimination while also generalizing existing clausal systems. Results using a prototype implementation confirm these systems allow compact and efficiently checkable refutations of CNF formulas that include embedded XOR constraints solvable by Gaussian elimination.

In the rest of the paper, Section 2 includes preliminaries and Section 3 presents the characterization of redundancy for Boolean functions. Section 4 introduces redundancy properties for BDDs, and Section 5 demonstrates their use for Gaussian elimination. Section 6 presents the results of our preliminary implementation, and Section 7 concludes.

2   Preliminaries

We assume a set of Boolean variables V under a fixed order $\prec$ and use standard SAT terminology. The set of truth values is $B = \{0, 1\}$. An *assignment* is a function $\tau : V \to B$ and the set of assignments is B^V. A function $f : B^V \to B$ is *Boolean*. If $f(\tau) = 1$ for some $\tau \in B^V$ then f is *satisfiable*, otherwise f is *unsatisfiable*. Formulas express Boolean functions as usual, are assumed to be in conjunctive normal form, and are written using capital letters F and G. A clause can be represented by its set of literals and a formula by its set of clauses.

A *partial assignment* is a non-contradictory set of literals σ; that is, if $l \in \sigma$ then $\neg l \notin \sigma$. The *application* of a partial assignment σ to a clause C is written $C|_\sigma$ and defined by: $C|_\sigma = \top$ if every $\tau \in B^V$ that satisfies $\bigwedge_{l \in \sigma} l$ also satisfies C, otherwise $C|_\tau = \{l \mid l \in C \text{ and } l, \neg l \notin \sigma\}$. For example, $(x_1 \vee x_2)|_{\{\neg x_1, x_2\}} = \top$, and $(x_1 \vee x_2)|_{\{\neg x_2, \neg x_3\}} = (x_1)$. Similarly the application of σ to a formula F is written $F|_\sigma$ and defined by: $F|_\sigma = \top$ if $C|_\sigma = \top$ for all $C \in F$, otherwise $F|_\sigma = \{C|_\sigma \mid C \in F \text{ and } C|_\sigma \neq \top\}$. *Unit propagation* is the iterated replacement of F with $F|_{\{l\}}$ for each unit clause $(l) \in F$, until F includes the empty clause $\bot$, or F contains no unit clauses. A formula F implies a clause C by *reverse unit propagation* (RUP) if unit propagation on $F \wedge \neg C$ ends by producing $\bot$ [27].

For a formula F and clause C, if F and $F \wedge C$ are equisatisfiable (both satisfiable or both unsatisfiable) then C is *redundant* with respect to F. Efficiently identifiable redundant clauses are at the foundation of many formula simplification techniques and refutation systems (for instance, see [32,33,37,43]). In general, deciding whether a clause is redundant is complete for the complement of the class DP [6], containing both NP and co-NP [55], so solvers and proof systems rely on polynomially-decidable *redundancy properties* for checking specific instances of redundancy. The following characterization of redundant clauses provides a common framework for formulating such properties.

Theorem 1 (Heule, Kiesl, and Biere [36]). *A clause $C \neq \bot$ is redundant with respect to a formula F if and only if there is a partial assignment ω such that $C|_\omega = \top$ and $F|_\alpha \vDash F|_\omega$, for the partial assignment $\alpha = \{\neg l \mid l \in C\}$.*

The partial assignment ω, usually called a *witness* for C, includes at least one of the literals occurring in C, while α is said to *block* the clause C. Redundancy properties can be defined by replacing $\vDash$ in the theorem above with efficiently-decidable relations R such that $R \subseteq \vDash$. *Propagation redundancy* (PR) [33] replaces $\vDash$ with $\vdash_1$, where $F \vdash_1 G$ if and only if F implies each $D \in G$ by RUP. The property PR gives rise to a refutation system, in which a refutation is a list of clauses $C_1, \ldots, C_n$ and witnesses $\omega_1, \ldots, \omega_n$ such that $C_k|_{\omega_k} = \top$ and $(F \bigwedge_{i=1}^{k-1} C_i)|_{\alpha_k} \vdash_1 (F \bigwedge_{i=1}^{k-1} C_i)|_{\omega_k}$ for all $1 \leq k \leq n$, and $F \bigwedge_{i=1}^{n} C_i \vdash_1 \bot$.

Most redundancy properties used in SAT solving can be understood as restricted forms of propagation redundancy. The RAT property [43] is equivalent to *literal propagation redundancy*, where the witness ω for any clause C may differ from the associated α on only one literal; that is, $\omega = (\alpha \setminus \{\neg l\}) \cup \{l\}$ for some $l \in C$ [36]. The DRAT system [69] is based on RAT, with the added ability to remove clauses from the accumulated formula $F \bigwedge C_i$.

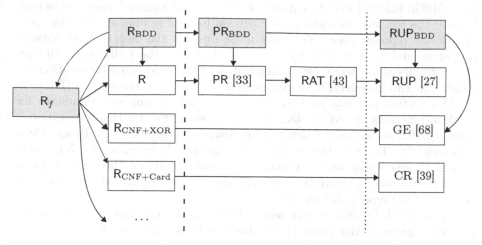

Fig. 1: Different notions of redundancy and their relationships. An arrow from A to B indicates A generalizes B. Properties to the right of the thick dashed line are polynomially checkable; those to the right of the thin dotted line only derive logical consequences. Novel properties defined in this paper are grey.

3   Redundancy for Boolean Functions

Theorem 1 provides a foundation for clausal proof systems by characterizing redundant clauses in a convenient way. However, the restriction to clauses places limitations on these systems, making some forms of non-clausal reasoning difficult to express. For solvers aiming to construct refutations in these systems, this translates directly to restrictions on which solving techniques can be used.

We show this characterization can be broadened to include redundancy for non-clausal constraints, and can be used to define useful redundancy properties and refutation systems. The contributions of this paper are divided into three corresponding levels of generality. The top level, covered in the current section, is the direct extension of Theorem 1 from redundancy for clauses, written R, to redundancy for Boolean functions, written R_f. The middle level, the focus of Section 4, instantiates the resulting Theorem 2 to define the refutation systems RUP_{BDD} and PR_{BDD} based on redundancy for Binary Decision Diagrams. At the bottom level, these systems are shown to easily handle Gaussian elimination (GE) in Section 5, as well as some aspects of cardinality reasoning (CR). The relationships between these notions of redundancy are shown in Figure 1.

Each level of generality is individually important to this work. At the bottom level, the straightforward expression of Gaussian elimination by RUP_{BDD} and PR_{BDD} makes it more feasible for solvers to use this efficient technique with proof production, especially as these systems generalize their clausal analogs already in use. The results in Section 6 confirm the usefulness of RUP_{BDD} for this purpose. At the middle level, we show the notion of redundancy instantiated for BDDs in this way may be capable of other strong forms of reasoning as well. Finally, the top level provides a very general form of redundancy, independent of function representation. This may make possible the design of redundancy properties and refutation systems in contexts where the BDD representation of constraints is too large; for example, it is known that some pseudo-Boolean constraints can in general have exponential size BDD representations [1,41].

This section presents in Theorem 2 a characterization of redundancy for Boolean functions in general. One way of instantiating this characterization is demonstrated in Section 4 where the functions are represented by Binary Decision Diagrams; the resulting refutation systems are shown in Section 5 to easily express Gaussian elimination. However, the applicability of Theorem 2 is much broader, providing a foundation for redundancy-based refutation systems independent of the representation used.

Proofs of theoretical results not included in the text can be found in an extended version of this paper [5]. We begin with the property R_f.

Definition 1. *A Boolean function g is* redundant *with respect to a Boolean function f if the functions f and $f \wedge g$ are both satisfiable, or both unsatisfiable.*

As we will see, extending Theorem 1 to the non-clausal case relies on the notion of a *Boolean transformation*, or just transformation: a function $\varphi : B^V \to B^V$, mapping assignments to assignments. Importantly, for a function f and transformation φ, in fact $f \circ \varphi : B^V \to B$ is a function as well, where as usual $f \circ \varphi(\tau) = f(\varphi(\tau))$. For instance let $F = x_1 \wedge x_2$ and for all $\tau \in B^V$, the transformation φ *flips* x_1, so that $\varphi(\tau)(x_1) = \neg\tau(x_1)$, and *ignores* x_2, that is, $\varphi(\tau)(x_2) = \tau(x_2)$. Then in fact $F \circ \varphi$ is expressed by the formula $\neg x_1 \wedge x_2$.

Composing a function with a transformation can be seen as a generalization of the application of a partial assignment to a formula or clause as defined in the previous section. Specifically, for a partial assignment σ let $\hat{\sigma}$ refer to the following transformation: for any assignment τ, the assignment $\hat{\sigma}(\tau)$ satisfies $\bigwedge_{l \in \sigma} l$, and $\hat{\sigma}$ ignores any $x \in V$ such that $x, \neg x \notin \sigma$. Then for any formula F the formula $F|_\sigma$ expresses exactly the function $F \circ \hat{\sigma}$. In particular, if α is the partial assignment blocking a clause C then notice $C \circ \hat{\alpha}(\tau) = 0$ for all τ, but $\hat{\alpha}$ ignores variables not appearing in C; consequently $\hat{\alpha}(\tau) = \tau$ if τ already falsifies C. Generalizing this idea to transformations that block non-clausal constraints is more complicated. In particular, there may be multiple blocking transformations.

Example 1. Let g be the function $g(\tau) = 1$ if and only if $\tau(a) \neq \tau(b)$ (i.e. g is an XOR constraint). Transformations α_1, α_2 are shown in the table below.

$\tau(a)$	$\tau(b)$	g	$\alpha_1(\tau)(a)$	$\alpha_1(\tau)(b)$	$g \circ \alpha_1$	$\alpha_2(\tau)(a)$	$\alpha_2(\tau)(b)$	$g \circ \alpha_2$
0	0	0	0	0	0	0	0	0
0	1	1	0	0	0	1	1	0
1	0	1	0	0	0	0	0	0
1	1	0	1	1	0	1	1	0

Both transformations ignore all $x \neq a, b$. Notice if $g(\tau) = 0$ then τ is unaffected by either transformation, and $g \circ \alpha_1(\tau) = g \circ \alpha_2(\tau) = 0$ for any assignment τ.

However α_1 and α_2 are different, so that, for example, if $F = \neg a \wedge (b \vee c)$ and τ satisfies the literals $\neg a$, b, and c then $F \circ \alpha_1(\tau) = 1$ but $F \circ \alpha_2(\tau) = 0$.

Motivated by this we define transformations blocking a function as follows.

Definition 2. *A transformation α blocks a function g if $g \circ \alpha$ is unsatisfiable, and for any assignment τ if $g(\tau) = 0$ then $\alpha(\tau) = \tau$.*

Notice any g not equal to the constant function 1 has blocking transformations; for example, by mapping every τ satisfying g to a particular assignment falsifying it. Using this definition, the following theorem shows how the redundancy of a Boolean function g with respect to another function f can be demonstrated. This is a direct generalization of Theorem 1, using a transformation blocking g in the place of the partial assignment blocking a clause, and a transformation ω such that $g \circ \omega$ is the constant function 1 in place of the witnessing assignment.

Theorem 2. *Let f be a function and g a non-constant function. Then g is redundant with respect to f if and only if there exist transformations α and ω such that α blocks g and $g \circ \omega$ is the constant function 1, and further $f \circ \alpha \vDash f \circ \omega$.*

Proof. ($\Rightarrow$) Suppose g is redundant with respect to f and let α be any transformation blocking g. If f is unsatisfiable then $f \circ \alpha$ is as well, so that $f \circ \alpha \vDash f \circ \omega$ holds for any ω. Thus we can take as ω the transformation $\omega(\tau) = \tau^*$ for all $\tau \in B^V$, where τ^* is some assignment satisfying g. If instead f is satisfiable, by redundancy so is $f \wedge g$. Here we can take as ω the transformation $\omega(\tau) = \tau^*$ for all $\tau \in B^V$, where τ^* is some assignment satisfying $f \wedge g$. Then both $f \circ \omega$ and $g \circ \omega$ are the constant function 1, so that $f \circ \alpha \vDash f \circ \omega$ holds in this case as well.

($\Leftarrow$) Suppose α, ω meet the criteria stated in the theorem. We show that g is redundant by demonstrating that if f is satisfiable, then so is $f \wedge g$. Suppose τ is an assignment satisfying f. If also $g(\tau) = 1$, then of course τ satisfies $f \wedge g$. If instead $g(\tau) = 0$, then $\alpha(\tau) = \tau$ as α blocks the function g. Thus $f \circ \alpha (\tau) = f(\alpha(\tau)) = f(\tau) = 1$. As $f \circ \alpha \vDash f \circ \omega$, this means $f(\omega(\tau)) = 1$. As $g \circ \omega$ is the constant function 1 then $g(\omega(\tau)) = 1$, so $\omega(\tau)$ satisfies $f \wedge g$. $\quad\square$

The clausal characterization in Theorem 1 shows that the redundancy of a clause can be evidenced by providing a witnessing assignment and demonstrating that an implication holds, providing a foundation for refutations based on the iterative conjunction of clauses. Theorem 2 above shows that the redundancy of a function in general can be seen in the same way by providing transformations α and ω. Consequently this suggests how to construct refutations based on the iterative conjunction of Boolean functions.

Definition 3. *A sequence $\sigma = (g_1, \alpha_1, \omega_1), \ldots, (g_n, \alpha_n, \omega_n)$ is a redundancy sequence for a Boolean function f if:*

1. α_k blocks g_k and $g_k \circ \omega_k$ is the constant function 1, for all $1 \le k \le n$,
2. $(f \wedge \bigwedge_{i=1}^{k-1} g_i) \circ \alpha_k \vDash (f \wedge \bigwedge_{i=1}^{k-1} g_i) \circ \omega_k$, for all $1 \le k \le n$.

As for clausal redundancy, refutations are intuitively based on the following: if g_1 is redundant with respect to f, and g_2 is redundant with respect to $f \wedge g_1$, then f and $f \wedge g_1 \wedge g_2$ are equisatisfiable; that is, $g_1 \wedge g_2$ is redundant with respect to f. The following holds as a direct consequence.

Proposition 1. *Let f be a Boolean function. If $(g_1, \alpha_1, \omega_1), \ldots, (g_n, \alpha_n, \omega_n)$ is a redundancy sequence for f, and $f \wedge \bigwedge_{i=1}^{n} g_i$ is unsatisfiable, then so is f.*

This shows, abstractly, how redundant Boolean functions can be used as a basis for refutations in the same way as redundant clauses. To define practical, and polynomially-checkable, refutation systems based on non-clausal redundancy in this way, we focus on a representation of Boolean functions that can be used within the framework described above. Specifically, we consider sets of BDDs in conjunction, just as formulas are sets of clauses in conjunction. Clauses are easily expressed by BDDs, and thus this representation easily expresses (CNF) formulas; this is necessary as we are typically interested in proving the unsatisfiability not of functions in general, but of (CNF) formulas. It is important to notice this is only a particular instantiation of Theorem 2, and that other representations of Boolean functions may give rise to useful and efficient systems as well.

BDDs [3,13,49] are compact expressions of Boolean functions in the form of rooted, directed, acyclic graphs consisting of *decision nodes*, each labeled by a variable $x \in V$ and having two children, and two *terminal nodes*, labeled by 0 and 1. The BDD for a function $f : B^V \to B$ is based on its *Shannon expansion*,

$$f = (\neg x \wedge f \circ \hat{\sigma}_0) \vee (x \wedge f \circ \hat{\sigma}_1)$$

where $\sigma_0 = \{\neg x\}$ and $\sigma_1 = \{x\}$, for $x \in V$. As is common we assume BDDs are *ordered* and *reduced*: if a node with variable label x precedes a node with label y in the graph then $x \prec y$, and the graph has no distinct, isomorphic subgraphs. Representation this way is canonical up to variable order, so that no two distinct BDDs with the same variable order represent the same Boolean function [13].

Our use of BDDs for representing non-clausal redundancy relies on the concept of *cofactors* as developed in BDD literature. The functions $f \circ \hat{\sigma}_0$ and $f \circ \hat{\sigma}_1$ are called *literal cofactors* of f by $\neg x$ and x, respectively, and are usually written $f|_{\neg x}$ and $f|_x$. The cofactor of f by a conjunction of literals $c = l_1 \wedge \cdots \wedge l_n$ can be defined similarly, so that $f|_c = f \circ \hat{\sigma}_c$, for the partial assignment $\sigma_c = \{l_1, \ldots, l_n\}$. This notation is the same as for the application of a partial assignment to a clause or formula from Section 2, as the notions coincide. More precisely, if a formula F and BDD f express the same function, so do the formula $F|_{\sigma_c}$ and BDD $f|_c$.

More broadly, for BDDs f and g, a *generalized cofactor* of f by g is a BDD h such that $f \wedge g = h \wedge g$; that is, f and h agree on all assignments satisfying g. This leaves unspecified what value $h(\tau)$ should take when $g(\tau) = 0$, and various different BDD operations have been developed for constructing generalized cofactors [20,21,22] The *constrain* operation [21] produces for f and g, with g not equal to the always false 0 BDD, a generalized cofactor which can be seen as the composition $f \circ \pi_g$, where π_g is the transformation [63]:

$$\pi_g(\tau) = \begin{cases} \tau & \text{if } g(\tau) = 1 \\ \underset{\{\tau' \mid g(\tau')=1\}}{\arg\min} \; d(\tau, \tau') & \text{otherwise.} \end{cases}$$

The function d is defined as follows: $d(\tau, \tau') = \sum_{i=1}^{n} |\tau(x_i) - \tau'(x_i)| \cdot 2^{n-i}$, where $V = \{x_1, \ldots, x_n\}$ with $x_1 \prec \cdots \prec x_n$. Intuitively, d is a measure of distance between two assignments based on the variables on which they disagree, weighted by their position in the variable order. It is important to notice then that the transformation π_g and the resulting $f \circ \pi_g$ depend on the variable order, and may differ for distinct orders. For a conjunction of literals c, though, $f \circ \pi_c = f|_c$ regardless of the order, so that $f|_g$ refers to $f \circ \pi_g$ in general.

As the transformation π_g maps an assignment falsifying the function g to the nearest assignment (with respect to d) satisfying it, a transformation that blocks the function g can surely be obtained as follows.

Lemma 1. *If g is not equal to the constant function 1 then $\pi_{\neg g}$ blocks g.*

This form of generalized cofactor, as computed by the constrain operation, is well suited for use in redundancy-based reasoning as described above, as the transformation $\pi_{\neg g}$ depends only on g. As a consequence, for BDDs f_1 and f_2 in fact $(f_1 \wedge f_2)|_{\neg g} \equiv f_1|_{\neg g} \wedge f_2|_{\neg g}$; that is, the BDD $(f_1 \wedge f_2)|_{\neg g}$ expresses the same function as the BDD for the conjunction $f_1|_{\neg g} \wedge f_2|_{\neg g}$. Thus given a set of BDDs $f_1, \ldots, f_n$ we can represent $(f_1 \wedge \cdots \wedge f_n)|_{\neg g}$ simply by the set of cofactors $f_i|_{\neg g}$ and without constructing the BDD for the conjunction $f_1 \wedge \cdots \wedge f_n$, which is NP-hard in general. In particular, given a formula $F = C_1 \wedge \cdots \wedge C_n$ and a Boolean constraint g, the function $F|_{\neg g}$ can be represented simply by applying the constrain operation to each of the BDDs representing C_i. Therefore, from Theorem 2 we can characterize redundancy for conjunctions of BDDs, written R_{BDD}, as follows.

Proposition 2. *Suppose $f_1, \ldots, f_n$ are BDDs and g is a non-constant BDD. If there is a partial assignment $\{l_1, \ldots, l_k\}$ such that for $\omega = \bigwedge_{i=1}^{k} l_i$,*

$$f_1|_{\neg g} \wedge \cdots \wedge f_n|_{\neg g} \vDash f_1|_\omega \wedge \cdots \wedge f_n|_\omega$$

and $g|_\omega = 1$ then g is redundant with respect to $f_1 \wedge \ldots \wedge f_n$.

4   BDD Redundancy Properties

The previous section provided a characterization of redundancy for Boolean functions, and showed how this could be instantiated for BDDs. In this section we develop polynomially-checkable properties for showing that a BDD is redundant with respect to a conjunction of BDDs, and describe their use in refutation systems for proving the unsatisfiability of formulas.

UnitProp$(f_1, \ldots, f_n)$

1   **repeat**

2   **if** $f_i = 0$ or $f_i = \neg f_j$ for some $1 \leq i, j \leq n$ **then**

3   **return** "conflict"

4   **if** $U(f_i) \neq \emptyset$ for some $1 \leq i \leq n$ **then**

5            $f_j := f_j|_{\bigwedge U(f_i)}$ for all $1 \leq j \leq n$

6   **until** no update to $f_1, \ldots, f_n$

Fig. 2: A procedure for unit propagation over a set of BDDs

As Theorem 1 is used for defining clausal redundancy properties, Proposition 2 gives rise to BDD redundancy properties by replacing $\vDash$ with polynomially-decidable relations. Similar to the use of the unit propagation procedure by the clausal properties RUP and PR, we describe a unit propagation procedure for use with a set of BDDs and derive analogous properties RUP_{BDD} and PR_{BDD}.

For a BDD f, the Shannon expansion shows that if $f|_{\neg l} = 0$ (i.e. $f|_{\neg l}$ is the always false 0 BDD) for some literal l, then $f = l \wedge f_l$, and therefore $f \vDash l$. Then the *units implied by* f, written $U(f)$, can be defined as follows.

Definition 4. $U(f) = \{l \mid \text{var}(l) \in V \text{ and } f|_{\neg l} = 0\}$, for $f : B^V \to B$.

As $f|_{\neg l}$ can be computed in $O(|f|)$, where $|f|$ is the number of nodes in the BDD for f [59], then $U(f)$ can certainly be computed in $O(|V| \cdot |f|) \subseteq O(|f|^2)$, though this can be reduced to $O(|f|)$. We write $\bigwedge U(f)$ to mean $\bigwedge_{l \in U(f)} l$.

Figure 2 provides a sketch of the unit propagation procedure. Whenever $U(f)$ is non-empty for some f in a set of BDDs, each BDD in the set can be replaced with its cofactor by $\bigwedge U(f)$. This approach to unit propagation is largely similar to that of Olivo and Emerson [53], except we consider two conflict situations: if some BDD becomes 0, or if two BDDs are the negations of each other.

For $N = |f_1| + \cdots + |f_n|$ the procedure UnitProp$(f_1, \ldots, f_n)$ can be performed in time $O(N^2)$. In line 5, if f_j and $\bigwedge U(f_i)$ share no variables, then $f_j = f_j|_{\bigwedge U(f_i)}$, otherwise the BDD for $f_j|_{\bigwedge U(f_i)}$ can be constructed in time $O(|f_j|)$ and further $|f_j|_{\bigwedge U(f_i)}| < |f_j|$. This procedure is correct: "conflict" is only returned when $\bigwedge_{i=1}^{n} f_i$ is unsatisfiable (see the extended paper for the proof).

Proposition 3. *If* UnitProp$(f_1, \ldots, f_n)$ *returns "conflict" then* $f_1 \wedge \cdots \wedge f_n \equiv 0$.

UnitProp generalizes the usual unit propagation procedure on a formula: if C is a clause, then $U(C) \neq \emptyset$ implies C is a unit clause and $\bigwedge_{l \in U(C)} l = C$. We extend the relation $\vdash_1$ and the definition of RUP accordingly.

Definition 5. *Let* $f_1, \ldots, f_n$ *and* $g \neq 0$ *be BDDs. Then* $f_1 \wedge \cdots \wedge f_n$ *implies* g *by* RUP_{BDD} *if* UnitProp$(f_1|_{\neg g}, \ldots, f_n|_{\neg g})$ *returns "conflict."*

Example 2. Let $F = \{C_1 = b \vee c, C_2 = a \vee b, C_3 = a \vee c\}$, and assume $a \prec b \prec c$. Consider g as shown in Figure 3, expressing the cardinality constraint $g(\tau) = 1$ if and only if τ satisfies at least two a, b, c; also written $\{a, b, c\} \geq 2$. Figure 3

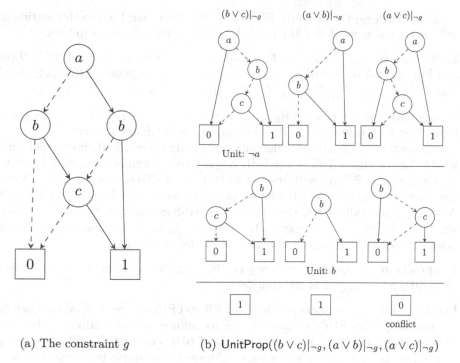

(a) The constraint g (b) UnitProp$((b \vee c)|_{\neg g}, (a \vee b)|_{\neg g}, (a \vee c)|_{\neg g})$

Fig. 3: Example derivation of a constraint g, shown in (a), using RUP$_{\text{BDD}}$. In (b), the top line shows the BDDs for each of the clauses $(b \vee c), (a \vee c), (a \vee b)$ after cofactoring by g. The second line shows each of these BDDs after cofactoring by the unit $\neg a \in U((b \vee c)|_{\neg g})$. Here, the middle BDD becomes simply the unit b, and the third line shows each BDD cofactored by the unit b. In this line, the third BDD has become 0, so a conflict is returned.

shows the updates made throughout UnitProp$(C_1|_{\neg g}, C_2|_{\neg g}, C_3|_{\neg g})$. Notice that $U(C_1|_{\neg g}) = \{\neg a\}$, and $U((C_2|_{\neg g})|_{\neg a}) = \{b\}$. Then $C_3|_{\neg g}$ after cofactoring by $\neg a$ and b becomes the constant BDD 0, so the procedure returns "conflict." As a result, F implies the BDD g by RUP$_{\text{BDD}}$.

We show that RUP$_{\text{BDD}}$ is a redundancy property. Given BDDs $f_1, \ldots, f_n, g$, checking whether g is implied by RUP$_{\text{BDD}}$ primarily consists of the UnitProp procedure, though each $f_i|_{\neg g}$ must first be constructed, which can be done in time $O(|f_i| \cdot |g|)$ [21]. The size of this BDD may in some cases be larger than the size of f_i, though it is typically smaller [21,63] and at worst $|f_i|_{\neg g}| \leq |f_i| \cdot |g|$. Consequently it can be decided in time $O(|g|^2 \cdot N^2)$ whether g is implied by RUP$_{\text{BDD}}$. Finally if g is implied by RUP$_{\text{BDD}}$ then it is redundant with respect to $f_1 \wedge \cdots \wedge f_n$; in fact, it is a logical consequence (proof of the following is available in the extended paper).

Proposition 4. *If* $f_1 \wedge \cdots \wedge f_n \vdash_1 g$, *then* $f_1 \wedge \cdots \wedge f_n \vDash g$.

From RUP_{BDD} the property PR can be directly generalized to this setting as well. Specifically, we define the redundancy property PR_{BDD} as follows.

Definition 6. *Suppose $f_1, \ldots, f_n$ are BDDs and g is a non-constant BDD. Then g is PR_{BDD} with respect to $\bigwedge_{i=1}^{n} f_i$ if there is partial assignment $\{l_1, \ldots, l_k\}$ such that $g|_\omega = 1$ and $\bigwedge_{i=1}^{n} f_i|_{\neg g} \vdash_1 f_j|_\omega$ for all $1 \leq j \leq n$, where $\omega = \bigwedge_{i=1}^{k} l_i$.*

Proposition 2 shows if g is PR_{BDD} with respect to $f = f_1 \wedge \cdots \wedge f_n$ then g is redundant with respect to f, thus PR_{BDD} is a redundancy property.

Notice these properties and derivations directly generalize their clausal equivalents; for example, if C is PR with respect to a formula F, then (the BDD expressing) C is PR_{BDD} with respect to (the set of BDDs expressing) F. Deciding whether a clause C is PR with respect to a formula F is NP-complete [37]. As PR_{BDD} generalizes PR, then PR_{BDD} is NP-hard as well. Further, checking whether g is PR_{BDD} with respect to $f_1 \wedge \cdots \wedge f_n$ by some candidate ω can be done polynomially as argued above, thus the following holds.

Proposition 5. *Deciding whether g is PR_{BDD} with respect to $f_1 \wedge \cdots \wedge f_n$, given the BDDs $g, f_1, \ldots, f_n$, is NP-complete.*

In other words, the decision problems for PR and PR_{BDD} are of equal complexity.

The properties RUP_{BDD} and PR_{BDD} as defined in this section can be used to show that a BDD can be added to a set of BDDs in a satisfiability-preserving way. Of course, any clause has a straightforward and simple representation as a BDD, so that a formula can be easily represented this way as a set of BDDs. As a result RUP_{BDD} and PR_{BDD} can be used as systems for refuting unsatisfiable formulas. In the following, we identify a clause with its representation as a BDD, and a formula with its representation as a set of such BDDs.

To simplify the presentation of derivations based on RUP_{BDD} and PR_{BDD} we introduce an additional redundancy property, allowing derivations to include steps to directly derive certain BDDs *path-wise* in the following way.

Definition 7. *$f_1 \wedge \cdots \wedge f_n$ implies g by RUP_{path} if (1) $f_1 \wedge \cdots \wedge f_n \vdash_1 \neg c$ for every $c = l_1 \wedge \cdots \wedge l_m$ such that $l_1, \ldots, l_m$ is a path from the root of g to the 0 terminal, and (2) $|g| \leq \log_2(|f_1| + \cdots + |f_n|)$.*

If $f_1 \wedge \cdots \wedge f_n$ implies g by RUP_{path} then it is a logical consequence of $f_1 \wedge \cdots \wedge f_n$, as this checks that no assignment satisfies both $\neg g$ and $f_1 \wedge \cdots \wedge f_n$. The number of paths in a BDD g can however be exponential in $|g|$, as in the BDD for an XOR constraint, so the second condition ensures RUP_{path} is polynomially-checkable.

The property RUP_{path} is primarily useful as it allows the derivation of a BDD g whose representation as a set of clauses is included in $\{f_1, \ldots, f_n\}$: if c corresponds to a path to 0 in g, the clause $\neg c$ is included in the direct clausal translation of g. In this context, the restrictive condition (2) in Definition 7 can in fact be removed, since the number of paths in g is then at most n.

Definition 8. *A sequence of BDDs $g_1, \ldots, g_n$ is a RUP_{BDD} derivation from a formula F if $F \wedge \bigwedge_{i=1}^{k-1} g_i$ implies g_k by RUP_{BDD}, or by RUP_{path}, for all $1 \leq k \leq n$. A sequence of BDD and assignment pairs $(g_1, \omega_1), \ldots, (g_n, \omega_n)$ is* *a* $\mathsf{PR}_{\mathsf{BDD}}$ derivation *from a formula F if* $F \wedge \bigwedge_{i=1}^{k-1} g_i$ *implies* g_k *by* $\mathsf{RUP}_{\mathsf{path}}$, *or* ω_k *is a* $\mathsf{PR}_{\mathsf{BDD}}$-*witness for* g_k *with respect to* $F \wedge \bigwedge_{i=1}^{k-1} g_i$, *for all* $1 \leq k \leq n$.

As $\mathsf{RUP}_{\mathsf{BDD}}$, $\mathsf{RUP}_{\mathsf{path}}$, and $\mathsf{PR}_{\mathsf{BDD}}$ are redundancy properties, any $\mathsf{RUP}_{\mathsf{BDD}}$ or $\mathsf{PR}_{\mathsf{BDD}}$ derivation corresponds to a redundancy sequence of the same length.

Example 3. Consider the formula $F = \{a \vee b, a \vee c, b \vee c, a \vee d, b \vee d, c \vee d\}$ and let g be the BDD such that $g(\tau) = 1$ if and only if τ satisfies at least 3 of a, b, c, d; that is, g is the cardinality constraint $\{a, b, c, d\} \geq 3$. As seen in Example 2, the constraint $g_1 = \{a, b, c\} \geq 2$ is $\mathsf{RUP}_{\mathsf{BDD}}$ with respect to F; similarly so are the constraints, $g_2 = \{a, c, d\} \geq 2$, and $g_3 = \{b, c, d\} \geq 2$. Now, $\neg a \in U(g_3|_{\neg g})$: for any τ the assignment $\pi_{\neg g}(\tau)$ satisfies at most 2 of a, b, c, d, and if a is one of them then $\pi_{\neg g}(\tau)$ surely falsifies g_3. As a result, $(g_3|_{\neg g})|_a = 0$. In a similar way $\neg b \in U(g_2|_{\neg g})$. Since $g_1|_{\neg g}$ cofactored by the units $\neg a$ and $\neg b$ is falsified, then $\mathsf{UnitProp}(g_1|_{\neg g}, g_2|_{\neg g}, g_3|_{\neg g})$ returns "conflict." Consequently g is $\mathsf{RUP}_{\mathsf{BDD}}$ with respect to $F \wedge g_1 \wedge g_2 \wedge g_3$, and g_1, g_2, g_3, g is a $\mathsf{RUP}_{\mathsf{BDD}}$ derivation from F.

This example can be generalized to show that $\mathsf{RUP}_{\mathsf{BDD}}$ is capable of expressing an inference rule for cardinality constraints called the *diagonal sum* [40]. For $L = \{l_1, \ldots, l_n\}$ let $L_i = L \setminus \{l_i\}$; the diagonal sum derives $L \geq k + 1$ from the set of all n constraints $L_i \geq k$.

While the properties and refutation systems $\mathsf{RUP}_{\mathsf{BDD}}$ and $\mathsf{PR}_{\mathsf{BDD}}$ easily extend their clausal counterparts, it is important to notice that redundancy-based systems using BDDs can be defined in other ways. For instance, say $\bigwedge_{i=1}^{n} f_i$ implies g by $\mathsf{IMP}_{\mathsf{pair}}$ if $f_i|_{\neg g} \wedge f_j|_{\neg g} = 0$ for some i, j. Then $\mathsf{IMP}_{\mathsf{pair}}$ is polynomially checkable, computing the conjunction for each pair i, j. Moreover, it is clear that $f_1 \wedge f_2 \vDash g$ if and only if $f_1 \wedge f_2$ implies g by $\mathsf{IMP}_{\mathsf{pair}}$. As many logical inference rules have this form, it is possible that systems based on $\mathsf{IMP}_{\mathsf{pair}}$ are very strong.

5   Gaussian Elimination

Next, we show how the Gaussian elimination technique for simplifying XOR constraints embedded in a formula is captured by the redundancy properties defined in the previous section. Specifically, if an XOR constraint X is derivable from a formula F by Gaussian elimination, we show there is a $\mathsf{RUP}_{\mathsf{BDD}}$ derivation from F including the BDD expressing X with only a linear size increase.

An *XOR clause* $[x_1, \ldots, x_n]^p$ expresses the function $f : B^V \rightarrow B$, where $V = \{x_1, \ldots, x_n\}$ and p is 0 or 1, such that $f(\tau) = 1$ if and only if the number of $x_i \in V$ satisfied by τ is equal modulo 2 to p. In other words, p expresses the parity of the positive literals x_i an assignment must satisfy in order to satisfy the XOR clause. As $[x, y, y]^p$ and $[x]^p$ express the same function, we assume no variable occurs more than once in an XOR clause. Notice that $[]^0$ expresses the constant function 1, while $[]^1$ expresses 0.

The Gaussian elimination procedure begins by detecting XOR clauses encoded in a formula F. The *direct encoding* $\mathcal{D}(X)$ of $X = [x_1, \ldots, x_n]^p$ is the collection of clauses of the form $C = \{l_1, \ldots, l_n\}$, where each l_i is either x_i or

$\neg x_i$ and the number of negated literals in each C is not equal modulo 2 to p The formula $\mathcal{D}(X)$ expresses the same function as X, containing the clauses preventing each assignment over the variables in X not satisfying X. As a result, $\mathcal{D}(X)$ implies the BDD expressing X by $\mathsf{RUP}_{\text{path}}$ (see the extended paper for proof).

Lemma 2. $\mathcal{D}(X)$ *implies* X *by* $\mathsf{RUP}_{\text{path}}$, *for* $X = [x_1, \ldots, x_n]^p$.

Similar to the approach of Philipp and Rebola-Pardo [56], we represent Gaussian elimination steps by deriving the addition $X \oplus Y$ of XOR clauses $X = [x_1, \ldots, x_m, z_1, \ldots, z_r]^p$ and $Y = [y_1, \ldots, y_n, z_1, \ldots, z_r]^q$, given by:

$$X \oplus Y = [x_1, \ldots, x_m, y_1, \ldots, y_n]^{p \oplus q}.$$

The following lemma shows that $X \oplus Y$ is $\mathsf{RUP}_{\text{BDD}}$ with respect to $X \wedge Y$; that is, if a $\mathsf{RUP}_{\text{BDD}}$ derivation includes X and Y then $X \oplus Y$ can be derived as well. This is a result of the following observation: while the precise cofactors of X and Y by $\neg(X \oplus Y)$ depend on the variable order $\prec$, they are the negations of one another (proof is included in the extended paper).

Lemma 3. *Let* v *be the* $\prec$*-greatest variable in occurring in exactly one of* X *and* Y, *and assume* v *occurs in* Y. *Then* $X|_{\neg(X \oplus Y)} = X$, *and* $Y|_{\neg(X \oplus Y)} = \neg X$.

The above lemma shows that the procedure $\mathsf{UnitProp}(X|_{\neg X \oplus Y}, Y|_{\neg X \oplus Y})$ returns "conflict" immediately, and as a result $X \oplus Y$ is $\mathsf{RUP}_{\text{BDD}}$ with respect to $f_1 \wedge \cdots \wedge f_n \wedge X \wedge Y$ for any set of BDDs $f_1, \ldots, f_n$.

Define a Gaussian elimination derivation Π from a formula F as a sequence of XOR clauses $\Pi = X_1, \ldots, X_N$, such that for all $1 \leq i \leq N$, either $X_i = X_j \oplus X_k$ for $j, k < i$, or $\mathcal{D}(X_i) \subseteq F$. The size of the derivation is $|\Pi| = \sum_{i=1}^{N} s_i$, where s_i is the number of variables occurring in X_i. We show that Π corresponds to a $\mathsf{RUP}_{\text{BDD}}$ derivation with only a linear size increase. This size increase is a result of the fact that the BDD expressing an XOR clause $X = [x_1, \ldots, x_n]^p$ has size $2n + 1$ (proof of the following theorem is in the extended paper).

Theorem 3. *Suppose* $\Pi = X_1, \ldots, X_N$ *is a Gaussian elimination derivation from a formula* F. *Then there is a* $\mathsf{RUP}_{\text{BDD}}$ *derivation from* F *with size* $O(|\Pi|)$.

A consequence of this theorem is that $\mathsf{RUP}_{\text{BDD}}$ includes short refutations for formulas whose unsatisfiability can be shown by Gaussian elimination. More precisely, suppose a formula F includes the direct representations of an unsatisfiable collection of XOR clauses. Then there is a polynomial-length Gaussian elimination derivation of the unsatisfiable XOR clause $[]^1$ from F [62], and by Theorem 3, a polynomial-length $\mathsf{RUP}_{\text{BDD}}$ derivation of the unsatisfiable BDD 0.

Notably, $\mathsf{RUP}_{\text{BDD}}$ then includes short refutations of, for example, the Tseitin formulas, for which no polynomial-length refutations exist in the resolution system [64,66]. This limitation of resolution holds as well for the clausal RUP system, without the ability to introduce new variables, as it can be polynomially simulated by resolution [9,25]. As the translation into $\mathsf{RUP}_{\text{BDD}}$ used to prove Theorem 3 introduces no new variables, this demonstrates the strength of $\mathsf{RUP}_{\text{BDD}}$ compared to resolution and its clausal analog RUP.

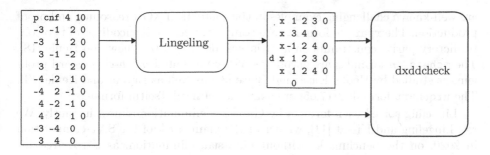

Fig. 4: Usage of the tool dxddcheck, showing an example formula and refutation.

6   Results

To begin to assess the practical usefulness of the systems introduced in Section 4, we have implemented in Python a prototype of a tool called dxddcheck[1] for checking refutations in a subset of $\mathsf{RUP_{BDD}}$. In particular we focus on the result of Section 5, that Gaussian elimination is succinctly captured by $\mathsf{RUP_{BDD}}$.

We ran the SAT solver Lingeling (version bcp) on a collection of crafted unsatisfiable formulas, all of which can be solved using Gaussian elimination. From Lingeling output we extract a list of XOR clause additions and deletions, ending with the addition of the empty clause, as shown in Figure 4. This list is passed directly to dxddcheck, which carries it out as a $\mathsf{DRUP_{BDD}}$ refutation; that is, a $\mathsf{RUP_{BDD}}$ refutation also allowing steps which remove or "delete" BDDs from the set. These deletion steps can be removed without affecting the correctness of the refutation, though their inclusion can decrease the time required for checking it, as is the case with DRUP and RUP.

Formula	number of variables	number of clauses	solving time (s)	proof lines	proof size (KB)	checking time (s)
rpar_50	148	394	0.1	297	7	0.34
rpar_100	298	794	0.1	597	15	1.35
rpar_200	598	1594	0.2	1197	35	6.67
mchess_19	680	2291	0.0	1077	41	4.07
mchess_21	836	2827	0.1	1317	50	5.09
mchess_23	1008	3419	0.1	1581	63	6.42
urquhart-s5-b2	107	742	0.0	150	7	0.95
urquhart-s5-b3	121	1116	0.1	150	9	1.64
urquhart-s5-b4	114	888	0.0	150	8	1.20

For these experiments we used a 1.8 GHz Intel Core i5 CPU with 8 GB of memory. The table shows the time Lingeling took to solve each formula, the number of lines in the constructed proof and its size, and the time dxddcheck took to construct and check the associated $\mathsf{DRUP_{BDD}}$ proof. These benchmarks

---

[1] Source code is available under the MIT license at http://fmv.jku.at/dxddcheck along with the benchmarks used and our experimental data.

are well-known challenging examples in the contexts of XOR reasoning and proof production. The rpar_ n formulas are compact, permuted encodings of two contradictory parity constraints on n variables, described by Chew and Heule [18]. The mchess_ n formulas are encodings of the mutilated $n \times n$-chessboard problem, as studied by Heule, Kiesl, and Biere [34] as well as Bryant and Heule [14]. The urquhart formulas [17,65] are examples of hard Tseitin formulas.

Lingeling solved each formula by Gaussian elimination almost instantly. We ran Lingeling and Kissat [11], winner of the main track of the SAT competition in 2020, on the benchmarks without Gaussian elimination, as is required for producing clausal refutations, using an Intel Xeon E5-2620 v4 CPU at 2.10 GHz. Only rpar_50 was solved in under about 10 hours, producing significantly larger proofs; for instance, Kissat produced a refutation of size 6911 MB.

While methods to construct clausal proofs from Gaussian elimination have been proposed, most are either lacking a public implementation or are limited in scope [18,56]. An exception is the approach very recently proposed by Gocht and Nordström using pseudo-Boolean reasoning [26], with which we are interested in carrying out a thorough comparison of results in the future.

7   Conclusion

We presented a characterization of redundancy for Boolean functions, generalizing the framework of clausal redundancy and efficient clausal proof systems. We showed this can be instantiated to design redundancy properties for functions given by BDDs, and polynomially-checkable refutation systems based on the conjunction of redundant BDDs, including the system PR_{BDD} generalizing the clausal system PR. The system PR_{BDD} also generalizes RUP_{BDD}, which can express Gaussian elimination reasoning without extension variables or clausal translations. The results of a preliminary implementation of a subset of RUP_{BDD} confirms such refutations are compact and can be efficiently checked.

Examples 2 and 3 show RUP_{BDD} reasoning over cardinality constraints, and we are interested in exploring rules such as *generalized resolution* [39,40]. Other forms of non-clausal reasoning may be possible using BDD-based redundancy systems as well. We are particularly interested in exploring the property IMP_{pair}.

While the system RUP_{BDD} derives only constraints implied by the conjunction of the formula and previously derived constraints, PR_{BDD} is capable of *interference-based* reasoning [30], like its clausal analog PR; there are possibly novel, non-clausal reasoning techniques taking advantage of this ability. Further, RUP_{BDD} and PR_{BDD} are based on the conjunction of BDDs, though Theorem 2 is more general and could be used for other ways of expressing Boolean functions. Finally we are interested in developing an optimized tool for checking proofs in the system PR_{BDD}, as well as a certified proof checker.

Acknowledgements. We extend our thanks to Marijn Heule for his helpful comments on an earlier draft of this paper.

References

1. Abío, I., Nieuwenhuis, R., Oliveras, A., Rodríguez-Carbonell, E., Mayer-Eichberger, V.: A new look at BDDs for pseudo-Boolean constraints. Journal of Artificial Intelligence Research **45**, 443–480 (2012). https://doi.org/10.1613/jair.3653
2. Ajtai, M.: The complexity of the pigeonhole principle. Combinatorica **14**(4), 417–433 (1994). https://doi.org/10.1007/BF01302964
3. Akers, S.B.: Binary decision diagrams. IEEE Trans. Computers **27**(6), 509–516 (1978). https://doi.org/10.1109/TC.1978.1675141
4. Balyo, T., Heule, M.J.H., Järvisalo, M.: SAT competition 2016: Recent developments. In: Singh, S.P., Markovitch, S. (eds.) 31st AAAI Conference on Artificial Intelligence. pp. 5061–5063. AAAI Press (2017)
5. Barnett, L.A., Biere, A.: Non-clausal redundancy properties (extended version). Tech. Rep. 21/2, Johannes Kepler University Linz, FMV Reports Series, Institute for Formal Models and Verification, Johannes Kepler University, Altenbergerstr. 69, 4040 Linz, Austria (2021). https://doi.org/10.35011/fmvtr.2021-2
6. Barnett, L.A., Cerna, D., Biere, A.: Covered clauses are not propagation redundant. In: Peltier, N., Sofronie-Stokkermans, V. (eds.) 10th Intl. Joint Conference on Automated Reasoning – IJCAR. LNCS, vol. 12166, pp. 32–47. Springer (2020). https://doi.org/10.1007/978-3-030-51074-9_3
7. Barrett, C., Sebastiani, R., Seshia, S.A., Tinelli, C.: Satisfiability modulo theories. In: Biere, A., Heule, M., van Maaren, H., Walsh, T. (eds.) Handbook of Satisfiability. pp. 1267–1329. IOS Press (2021). https://doi.org/10.3233/FAIA201017
8. Bayardo, R.J., Schrag, R.: Using CSP look-back techniques to solve real-world SAT instances. In: Kuipers, B., Webber, B.L. (eds.) 14th AAAI National Conference on Artificial Intelligence. pp. 203–208. AAAI Press (1997)
9. Beame, P., Kautz, H., Sabharwal, A.: Towards understanding and harnessing the potential of clause learning. Journal of Artificial Intelligence Research **22**(1), 319–351 (2004). https://doi.org/10.1613/jair.1410
10. Biere, A.: CaDiCaL, Lingeling, Plingeling, Treengeling and YalSAT entering the SAT competition 2018. In: Heule, M.J.H., Järvisalo, M., Suda, M. (eds.) Proc. of SAT Competition 2018. pp. 13–14. Department of Computer Science Series of Publications B, University of Helsinki (2018)
11. Biere, A., Fazekas, K., Fleury, M., Heisinger, M.: CaDiCaL, Kissat, Paracooba, Plingeling and Treengeling entering the SAT Competition 2020. In: Balyo, T., Froleyks, N., Heule, M., Iser, M., Järvisalo, M., Suda, M. (eds.) Proc. of SAT Competition 2020 – Solver and Benchmark Descriptions. Department of Computer Science Report Series B, vol. B-2020-1, pp. 51–53. University of Helsinki (2020)
12. Biere, A., Järvisalo, M., Kiesl, B.: Preprocessing in SAT solving. In: Biere, A., Heule, M., van Maaren, H., Walsh, T. (eds.) Handbook of Satisfiability. pp. 391–435. IOS Press (2021). https://doi.org/10.3233/FAIA200992
13. Bryant, R.E.: Graph-based algorithms for Boolean function manipulation. IEEE Transactions on Computers **35**(8), 677–691 (1986). https://doi.org/10.1109/TC.1986.1676819
14. Bryant, R.E., Heule, M.J.H.: Generating extended resolution proofs with a BDD-based SAT solver. In: Groote, J.F., Larsen, K.G. (eds.) 27th Intl. Conference on Tools and Algorithms for the Construction and Analysis of Systems – TACAS. LNCS, vol. 12651, pp. 76–93. Springer (2021). https://doi.org/10.1007/978-3-030-72016-2_5

15. Burch, J.R., Clarke, E.M., Long, D.E., McMillan, K.L., Dill, D.L.: Symbolic model checking for sequential circuit verification. IEEE Trans. Comput. Aided Des. Integr. Circuits Syst. **13**(4), 401–424 (1994). https://doi.org/10.1109/43.275352

16. Buss, S., Thapen, N.: DRAT proofs, propagation redundancy, and extended resolution. In: Janota, M., Lynce, I. (eds.) 22nd Intl. Conference on Theory and Applications of Satisfiability Testing – SAT. LNCS, vol. 11628, pp. 71–89. Springer (2019). https://doi.org/10.1007/978-3-030-24258-9_5

17. Chatalic, P., Simon, L.: Multi-resolution on compressed sets of clauses. In: 12th IEEE Intl. Conference on Tools with Artificial Intelligence – ICTAI. pp. 2–10. IEEE Computer Society (2000). https://doi.org/10.1109/TAI.2000.889839

18. Chew, L., Heule, M.J.H.: Sorting parity encodings by reusing variables. In: Pulina, L., Seidl, M. (eds.) 23rd Intl. Conference on Theory and Applications of Satisfiability Testing – SAT. LNCS, vol. 12178, pp. 1–10. Springer (2020). https://doi.org/10.1007/978-3-030-51825-7_1

19. Clarke, E., Biere, A., Raimi, R., Zhu, Y.: Bounded model checking using satisfiability solving. Formal Methods in System Design **19**(1), 7–34 (2001). https://doi.org/10.1023/A:1011276507260

20. Coudert, O., Berthet, C., Madre, J.C.: Verification of synchronous sequential machines based on symbolic execution. In: Sifakis, J. (ed.) Intl. Workshop on Automatic Verification Methods for Finite State Systems. LNCS, vol. 407, pp. 365–373. Springer (1990). https://doi.org/10.1007/3-540-52148-8_30

21. Coudert, O., Madre, J.C.: A unified framework for the formal verification of sequential circuits. In: IEEE Intl. Conference on Computer-Aided Design – ICCAD. pp. 126–129. IEEE Computer Society (1990). https://doi.org/10.1109/ICCAD.1990.129859

22. Coudert, O., Madre, J.C., Berthet, C.: Verifying temporal properties of sequential machines without building their state diagrams. In: Clarke, E.M., Kurshan, R.P. (eds.) 2nd Intl. Workshop on Computer Aided Verification – CAV. LNCS, vol. 531, pp. 23–32. Springer (1990). https://doi.org/10.1007/BFb0023716

23. Damiano, R.F., Kukula, J.H.: Checking satisfiability of a conjunction of BDDs. In: 40th Design Automation Conference – DAC. pp. 818–823. ACM (2003). https://doi.org/10.1145/775832.776039

24. Franco, J., Kouril, M., Schlipf, J., Ward, J., Weaver, S., Dransfield, M., Vanfleet, W.M.: SBSAT: a state-based, BDD-based satisfiability solver. In: Giunchiglia, E., Tacchella, A. (eds.) 6th Intl. Conference on Theory and Applications of Satisfiability Testing – SAT. LNCS, vol. 2919, pp. 398–410. Springer (2004). https://doi.org/10.1007/978-3-540-24605-3_30

25. Gelder, A.: Verifying RUP proofs of propositional unsatisfiability. In: 10th Intl. Symposium on Artificial Intelligence and Mathematics – ISAIM (2008)

26. Gocht, S., Nordström, J.: Certifying parity reasoning efficiently using pseudo-Boolean proofs. In: 35th AAAI Conference on Artificial Intelligence. AAAI Press (2021), to appear

27. Goldberg, E.I., Novikov, Y.: Verification of proofs of unsatisfiability for CNF formulas. In: Conference on Design, Automation and Test in Europe– DATE. pp. 886–891. IEEE Computer Society (2003). https://doi.org/10.1109/DATE.2003.10008

28. Goldberg, E.I., Prasad, M.R., Brayton, R.K.: Using SAT for combinational equivalence checking. In: Nebel, W., Jerraya, A. (eds.) Conference on Design, Automation and Test in Europe – DATE. pp. 114–121. IEEE Computer Society (2001). https://doi.org/10.1109/DATE.2001.915010

29. Groote, J.F., Tveretina, O.: Binary decision diagrams for first-order predicate logic. J. Log. Algebraic Methods Program. **57**(1-2), 1–22 (2003). https://doi.org/10.1016/S1567-8326(03)00039-0

30. Heule, M., Kiesl, B.: The potential of interference-based proof systems. In: Reger, G., Traytel, D. (eds.) 1st Intl. Workshop on Automated Reasoning: Challenges, Applications, Directions, Exemplary Achievements – ARCADE. EPiC Series in Computing, vol. 51, pp. 51–54. EasyChair (2017)

31. Heule, M.J.H., Biere, A.: All about Proofs, Proofs for All, Mathematical Logic and Foundations, vol. 55, chap. Proofs for Satisfiability Problems, pp. 1–22. College Publications (2015)

32. Heule, M.J.H., Järvisalo, M., Lonsing, F., Seidl, M., Biere, A.: Clause elimination for SAT and QSAT. Journal of Artificial Intelligence Research **53**(1), 127–168 (2015). https://doi.org/10.1613/jair.4694

33. Heule, M.J.H., Kiesl, B., Biere, A.: Short proofs without new variables. In: de Moura, L. (ed.) 26th Intl. Conference on Automated Deduction – CADE. LNCS, vol. 10395, pp. 130–147. Springer (2017). https://doi.org/10.1007/978-3-319-63046-5_9

34. Heule, M.J.H., Kiesl, B., Biere, A.: Clausal proofs of mutilated chessboards. In: Badger, J.M., Rozier, K.Y. (eds.) 11th NASA Formal Methods Symposium – NFM. LNCS, vol. 11460, pp. 204–210. Springer (2019). https://doi.org/10.1007/978-3-030-20652-9_13

35. Heule, M.J.H., Kiesl, B., Biere, A.: Encoding redundancy for satisfaction-driven clause learning. In: Vojnar, T., Zhang, L. (eds.) 25th Intl. Conference on Tools and Algorithms for the Construction and Analysis of Systems – TACAS. LNCS, vol. 11427, pp. 41–58. Springer (2019). https://doi.org/10.1007/978-3-030-17462-0_3

36. Heule, M.J.H., Kiesl, B., Biere, A.: Strong extension-free proof systems. Journal of Automated Reasoning **64**(3), 533–554 (2020). https://doi.org/10.1007/s10817-019-09516-0

37. Heule, M.J.H., Kiesl, B., Seidl, M., Biere, A.: PRuning through satisfaction. In: Strichman, O., Tzoref-Brill, R. (eds.) 13th Intl. Haifa Verification Conference – HVC. LNCS, vol. 10629, pp. 179–194. Springer (2017). https://doi.org/10.1007/978-3-319-70389-3_12

38. Heule, M.J.H., Kullmann, O., Marek, V.W.: Solving and verifying the Boolean Pythagorean triples problem via cube-and-conquer. In: Creignou, N., Le Berre, D. (eds.) 19th Intl. Conference on Theory and Applications of Satisfiability Testing – SAT. LNCS, vol. 9710, pp. 228–245. Springer (2016). https://doi.org/10.1007/978-3-319-40970-2_15

39. Hooker, J.N.: Generalized resolution and cutting planes. Annals of Operations Research **12**, 217–239 (1988). https://doi.org/10.1007/BF02186368

40. Hooker, J.N.: Generalized resolution for 0-1 linear inequalities. Annals of Mathematics and Artificial Intelligence **6**, 271–286 (1992). https://doi.org/10.1007/BF01531033

41. Hosaka, K., Takenaga, Y., Kaneda, T., Yajima, S.: Size of ordered binary decision diagrams representing threshold functions. Theor. Comput. Sci. **180**(1-2), 47–60 (1997). https://doi.org/10.1016/S0304-3975(97)83807-8

42. Järvisalo, M., Biere, A., Heule, M.J.H.: Blocked clause elimination. In: Esparza, J., Majumdar, R. (eds.) 16th Intl. Conference on Tools and Algorithms for the Construction and Analysis of Systems – TACAS. LNCS, vol. 6015, pp. 129–144. Springer (2010). https://doi.org/10.1007/978-3-642-12002-2_10

43. Järvisalo, M., Heule, M.J.H., Biere, A.: Inprocessing rules. In: Gramlich, B., Miller, Dalea nd Sattler, U. (eds.) 6th Intl. Joint Conference on Automated Reasoning – IJCAR. LNCS, vol. 7364, pp. 355–370. Springer (2012). https://doi.org/10.1007/978-3-642-31365-3_28

44. Kaiss, D., Skaba, M., Hanna, Z., Khasidashvili, Z.: Industrial strength SAT-based alignability algorithm for hardware equivalence verification. In: 7th Intl. Conference on Formal Methods in Computer Aided Design – FMCAD. pp. 20–26. IEEE Computer Society (2007). https://doi.org/10.1109/FAMCAD.2007.37

45. Kiesl, B., Seidl, M., Tompits, H., Biere, A.: Super-blocked clauses. In: Olivetti, N., Tiwari, A. (eds.) 8th Intl. Joint Conference on Automated Reasoning – IJCAR. LNCS, vol. 9706, pp. 45–61. Springer (2016). https://doi.org/10.1007/978-3-319-40229-1_5

46. Konev, B., Lisitsa, A.: Computer-aided proof of Erdős discrepancy properties. Artificial Intelligence **224**, 103–118 (2015). https://doi.org/10.1016/j.artint.2015.03.004

47. Kuehlmann, A., Krohm, F.: Equivalence checking using cuts and heaps. In: Yoffa, E.J., Micheli, G.D., Rabaey, J.M. (eds.) 34th Design Automation Conference – DAC. pp. 263–268. ACM (1997). https://doi.org/10.1145/266021.266090

48. Kullmann, O.: On a generalization of extended resolution. Discrete Applied Mathematics **96-97**, 149–176 (1999). https://doi.org/10.1016/S0166-218X(99)00037-2

49. Lee, C.Y.: Representation of switching circuits by binary-decision programs. The Bell System Technical Journal **38**(4), 985–999 (1959)

50. Manthey, N.: Coprocessor 2.0 – a flexible CNF simplifier. In: Cimatti, A., Sebastiani, R. (eds.) 15th Intl. Conference on Theory and Applications of Satisfiability Testing – SAT 2012. LNCS, vol. 7317, pp. 436–441. Springer (2012). https://doi.org/10.1007/978-3-642-31612-8_34

51. Marques-Silva, J.P., Sakallah, K.A.: GRASP - a new search algorithm for satisfiability. In: IEEE Intl. Conference on Computer Aided Design – ICCAD. pp. 220–227. IEEE Computer Society / ACM (1996). https://doi.org/10.1109/ICCAD.1996.569607

52. Motter, D.B., Markov, I.L.: A compressed breadth-first search for satisfiability. In: Mount, D.M., Stein, C. (eds.) 4th Intl. Workshop on Algorithm Engineering and Experiments – ALENEX. LNCS, vol. 2409, pp. 29–42. Springer (2002). https://doi.org/10.1007/3-540-45643-0_3

53. Olivo, O., Emerson, E.A.: A more efficient BDD-based QBF solver. In: Lee, J. (ed.) 17th Intl. Conference on Principles and Practice of Constraint Programming – CP. pp. 675–690. LNCS, Springer (2011). https://doi.org/10.1007/978-3-642-23786-7_51

54. Pan, G., Vardi, M.Y.: Search vs. symbolic techniques in satisfiability solving. In: 7th Intl. Conference on Theory and Applications of Satisfiability Testing – SAT. LNCS, vol. 3542, pp. 235–250. Springer (2004). https://doi.org/10.1007/11527695_19

55. Papadimitriou, C., Yannakakis, M.: The complexity of facets (and some facets of complexity). Journal of Computer and System Sciences **28**(2), 244–259 (1984). https://doi.org/10.1016/0022-0000(84)90068-0

56. Philipp, T., Rebola-Pardo, A.: DRAT proofs for XOR reasoning. In: Michael, L., Kakas, A.C. (eds.) 15th European Conference on Logics in Artificial Intelligence – JELIA. LNCS, vol. 10021, pp. 415–429 (2016). https://doi.org/10.1007/978-3-319-48758-8_27

57. Posegga, J., Ludäscher, B.: Towards first-order deduction based on Shannon graphs. In: Ohlbach, H.J. (ed.) 16th German Conference on Arti-

ficial Intelligence – GWAI. LNCS, vol. 671, pp. 67–75. Springer (1992). https://doi.org/10.1007/BFb0018993

58. Roussel, O., Manquinho, V.: Pseudo-Boolean and cardinality constraints. In: Biere, A., Heule, M., van Maaren, H., Walsh, T. (eds.) Handbook of Satisfiability. pp. 1087–1129. IOS Press (2021). https://doi.org/10.3233/978-1-58603-929-5-695

59. Sieling, D., Wegener, I.: Reduction of OBDDs in linear time. Information Processing Letters **48**(3), 139 – 144 (1993). https://doi.org/10.1016/0020-0190(93)90256-9

60. Sinz, C., Biere, A.: Extended resolution proofs for conjoining BDDs. In: Grigoriev, D., Harrison, J., Hirsch, E.A. (eds.) Computer Science - Theory and Applications, 1st Intl. Computer Science Symposium in Russia – CSR. vol. 3967, pp. 600–611. Springer (2006). https://doi.org/10.1007/11753728_60

61. Soos, M., Gocht, S., Meel, K.S.: Tinted, detached, and lazy CNF-XOR solving and its applications to counting and sampling. In: Lahiri, S.K., Wang, C. (eds.) 32nd Intl. Conference on Computer Aided Verification – CAV. LNCS, vol. 12224, pp. 463–484. Springer (2020). https://doi.org/10.1007/978-3-030-53288-8_22

62. Soos, M., Nohl, K., Castelluccia, C.: Extending SAT solvers to cryptographic problems. In: Kullmann, O. (ed.) 12th Intl. Conference on Theory and Applications of Satisfiability Testing – SAT. pp. 244–257. LNCS, Springer (2009). https://doi.org/10.1007/978-3-642-02777-2_24

63. Touati, H.J., Savoj, H., Lin, B., Brayton, R.K., Sangiovanni-Vincentelli, A.L.: Implicit state enumeration of finite state machines using BDDs. In: IEEE Intl. Conference on Computer-Aided Design – ICCAD. pp. 130–133. IEEE Computer Society (1990). https://doi.org/10.1109/ICCAD.1990.129860

64. Tseitin, G.S.: On the complexity of derivation in propositional calculus. In: Slissenko, A.O. (ed.) Studies in Constructive Mathematics and Mathematical Logic, vol. 2, pp. 115–125. Steklov Mathematical Institute (1970)

65. Urquhart, A.: Hard examples for resolution. Journal of the ACM **34**(1), 209–219 (1987). https://doi.org/10.1145/7531.8928

66. Urquhart, A.: The complexity of propositional proofs. Bulletin of Symbolic Logic **1**(4), 425–467 (12 1995). https://doi.org/10.2307/421131

67. Voronkov, A.: AVATAR: The architecture for first-order theorem provers. In: Biere, A., Bloem, R. (eds.) 26th Intl. Conference on Computer Aided Verification – CAV. LNCS, vol. 8559, pp. 696–710. Springer (2014). https://doi.org/10.1007/978-3-319-08867-9_46

68. Warners, J.P., Maaren, H.V., Warners, J.P., Maaren, H.V.: A two phase algorithm for solving a class of hard satisfiability problems. Operations Research Letters **23**, 81–88 (1998). https://doi.org/10.1016/S0167-6377(98)00052-2

69. Wetzler, N., Heule, M.J.H., Hunt, W.A.: DRAT-trim: Efficient checking and trimming using expressive clausal proofs. In: Sinz, C., Egly, U. (eds.) 17th Intl. Conference on Theory and Applications of Satisfiability Testing – SAT. LNCS, vol. 8561, pp. 422–429. Springer (2014). https://doi.org/10.1007/978-3-319-09284-3_31

Open Access This chapter is licensed under the terms of the Creative Commons Attribution 4.0 International License (http://creativecommons.org/licenses/by/4.0/), which permits use, sharing, adaptation, distribution and reproduction in any medium or format, as long as you give appropriate credit to the original author(s) and the source, provide a link to the Creative Commons license and indicate if changes were made.

The images or other third party material in this chapter are included in the chapter's Creative Commons license, unless indicated otherwise in a credit line to the material. If material is not included in the chapter's Creative Commons license and your intended use is not permitted by statutory regulation or exceeds the permitted use, you will need to obtain permission directly from the copyright holder.

Multi-Dimensional Interpretations for Termination of Term Rewriting

Akihisa Yamada[ID]

National Institute of Advanced Industrial Science and Technology, Tokyo, Japan

Abstract. Interpretation methods constitute a foundation of termination analysis for term rewriting. From time to time remarkable instances of interpretation methods appeared, such as polynomial interpretations, matrix interpretations, arctic interpretations, and their variants. In this paper we introduce a general framework, the multi-dimensional interpretation method, that subsumes these variants as well as many previously unknown interpretation methods as instances. Employing the notion of derivers, we prove the soundness of the proposed method in an elegant way. We implement the proposed method in the termination prover NaTT and verify its significance through experiments.

1 Introduction

Term rewriting [2] is a formalism for reasoning about function definitions or functional programs. For instance, a term rewrite system (TRS) $\mathcal{R}_{\mathtt{fact}}$ [7] consisting of the following rewrite rules defines the factorial function:

$$\mathtt{fact}(\mathtt{0}) \to \mathtt{s}(\mathtt{0}) \quad \mathtt{fact}(\mathtt{s}(x)) \to \mathtt{mul}(\mathtt{s}(x), \mathtt{fact}(\mathtt{p}(\mathtt{s}(x)))) \quad \mathtt{p}(\mathtt{s}(x)) \to x$$

assuming that $\mathtt{s}$, $\mathtt{p}$, and $\mathtt{mul}$ are interpreted respectively as the successor, predecessor, and multiplication functions.

Analyzing whether a TRS *terminates*, meaning that the corresponding functional program responds or the function is well defined, has been an active research area for decades. Consequently, several fully automatic termination provers have been developed, e.g., AProVE [10], T$_T$T$_2$ [20], CiME [5], MU-TERM [23], and NaTT [34], and have been competing in the annual Termination Competitions (TermCOMP) [11].

Throughout their history, interpretation methods [25] have been foundational in termination analysis. They are categorized by the choice of well-founded carriers and the class of functions as which symbols are interpreted. *Polynomial interpretations* [22] use the natural numbers $\mathbb{N}$ as the carrier and interpretations are monotone polynomials, i.e., every variable has coefficient at least 1. Weakly monotone polynomials, i.e., zero coefficients, are allowed in the *dependency pair* method [1]. *Negative constants* are allowed using the max operator [15]. General combinations of polynomials and the max operator are proposed in both the standard [37] and the dependency pair settings [9]. *Negative coefficients* and thus

© The Author(s) 2021

A. Platzer and G. Sutcliffe (Eds.): CADE 2021, LNAI 12699, pp. 273–290, 2021.
https://doi.org/10.1007/978-3-030-79876-5_16

non-monotone polynomials are also allowed, but in a more elaborated theoretical framework [15,9].

These methods share the common carrier $\mathbb{N}$. In contrast, *matrix interpretations* [16,8] choose vectors over $\mathbb{N}$ as the carrier, and interpret symbols as affine maps over it. Although the carrier is generalized, matrix interpretations do not properly generalize polynomial interpretations, since not all polynomials are affine. This gap can be filled by *improved matrix interpretations*, that further generalize the carrier to square matrices [6], so that natural polynomial interpretations can be subsumed by matrix polynomials over 1×1 matrices. In *arctic interpretations* [19], the carrier consists of vectors over arctic naturals ($\mathbb{N} \cup \{-\infty\}$) or integers ($\mathbb{Z} \cup \{-\infty\}$), and interpretations are affine maps over it, where affinity is with respect to the *max/plus semiring*.

Having this many variations would be welcome if you are a user of a termination tool in which someone else has already implemented all of them. It would not be so if you are the developer of a termination tool in which you will have to implement all of them. Also, to ultimately trust termination tools, one needs to formalize proof methods using proof assistants and obtain trusted certifier that validates outputs of termination tools, see, e.g., IsaFoR/CeTA [31] or CoLoR/Rainbow [4] frameworks. Although some interpretation methods have already been formalized [28,30], adding missing variants one by one would cost a significant effort.

In this paper, we introduce a general framework for interpretation methods, which subsumes most of the above-mentioned methods as instances, namely, (max-)polynomial interpretations (with negative constants), (improved) matrix interpretations, and arctic interpretations, as well as a syntactic method called *argument filtering* [1,21]. Moreover, we obtain a bunch of previously unexplored interpretation methods as other instances.

After preliminaries, we start with a convenient fact about *reduction pairs*, a central tool in termination proving with dependency pairs (Section 3).

The first step to the main contribution is the use of *derivers* [24,33], which allow us to abstract away the mathematical details of polynomials or max-polynomials. We will obtain a key soundness result that derivers derive monotone interpretations from monotone interpretations (Section 4).

The second step is to extend derivers to multi-dimensional ones. This setting further generalizes (improved) matrix interpretations, so that max-polynomials, negative constants, and negative entries are allowed (Section 5). It will also be hinted that multi-dimensional derivers can emulate the effect of negative coefficients, although theoretical comparison is left for future work. We also show that our approach subsumes arctic interpretations by adding a treatment for $-\infty$ (Section 6). Although the original formulation by Koprowski and Waldmann [19] has some trickiness, we will show that our simpler formulation is sufficient.

As *strict monotonicity* is crucial for proving termination without dependency pairs, and is still useful with dependency pairs, we will see how to ensure strict monotonicity (Section 7). At this point, the convenient fact we have seen in Section 3 becomes crucial.

Finally, the proposed method is implemented in the termination prover NaTT, and experimental results are reported (Section 8). We evaluate various instances of our method, some corresponding to known interpretation methods and many others not. We choose two new instances to integrate to the NaTT strategy. The new strategy proved the termination of 20 more benchmarks than the old one, and five of them were not proved by any tool in TermCOMP 2020.

2   Preliminaries

We start with *order-sorted* algebras. Let $\mathcal{S} = \langle S, \sqsubseteq \rangle$ be a partially ordered set, where elements in S are called *sorts* and $\sqsubseteq$ is called the *subsort relation*. An $\mathcal{S}$-*sorted set* is an S-indexed family $A = \{A^\sigma\}_{\sigma \in S}$ such that $\sigma \sqsubseteq \tau$ implies $A^\sigma \subseteq A^\tau$. We write $A^{(\sigma_1,\ldots,\sigma_n)}$ for the set $A^{\sigma_1} \times \cdots \times A^{\sigma_n}$. A *sorted map* between $\mathcal{S}$-sorted sets X and A is a mapping f, written $f : X \to A$, such that $x \in X^\sigma$ implies $f(x) \in A^\sigma$.

An $\mathcal{S}$-*sorted signature* is an $S^* \times S$-indexed family $\mathcal{F} = \{\mathcal{F}_{\vec{\sigma},\tau}\}_{\langle \vec{\sigma},\tau \rangle \in S^* \times S}$ of function symbols.[1] When $f \in \mathcal{F}_{(\sigma_1,\ldots,\sigma_n),\tau}$, we say f has *rank* $(\sigma_1,\ldots,\sigma_n) \to \tau$ and *arity* n in $\mathcal{F}$. We may also view sorted sets and signatures as sets: having $a : \sigma \in A$ means $a \in A^\sigma$, and $f : \vec{\sigma} \to \tau \in \mathcal{F}$ means $f \in \mathcal{F}_{\vec{\sigma},\tau}$.

Example 1. Consider sort Nat. We define the following {Nat}-sorted signatures:

- $\mathcal{N} := \{0 : () \to \text{Nat}, \ 1 : () \to \text{Nat}, \ 2 : () \to \text{Nat}, \ \ldots\}$
- $\mathcal{N}_* := \mathcal{N} \cup \{* : (\text{Nat}, \text{Nat}) \to \text{Nat}\}$
- $\mathcal{N}_+ := \mathcal{N} \cup \{+ : (\text{Nat}, \text{Nat}) \to \text{Nat}\}$
- $\mathcal{N}_{\max} := \mathcal{N} \cup \{\max : (\text{Nat}, \text{Nat}) \to \text{Nat}\}$

Let us abbreviate unions of signatures by concatenations of subscripts: for instance $\mathcal{N}_{*+\max}$ denotes $\mathcal{N}_* \cup \mathcal{N}_+ \cup \mathcal{N}_{\max}$. Next consider sorts Neg and Int with Nat, Neg $\sqsubseteq$ Int. We define the following {Nat, Neg, Int}-sorted signatures:

- $\mathcal{Z} := \mathcal{N} \cup \{0 : () \to \text{Neg}, \ -1 : () \to \text{Neg}, \ -2 : () \to \text{Neg}, \ \ldots\}$
- $\mathcal{Z}_* := \mathcal{Z} \cup \mathcal{N}_* \cup \{* : (\text{Neg}, \text{Neg}) \to \text{Nat}, \ * : (\text{Int}, \text{Int}) \to \text{Int}\}$
- $\mathcal{Z}_+ := \mathcal{Z} \cup \mathcal{N}_+ \cup \{+ : (\text{Neg}, \text{Neg}) \to \text{Neg}, \ + : (\text{Int}, \text{Int}) \to \text{Int}\}$
- $\mathcal{Z}_{\max} := \mathcal{Z} \cup \mathcal{N}_{\max} \cup$
  $\{\max : (\text{Nat}, \text{Int}) \to \text{Nat}, \ \max : (\text{Int}, \text{Nat}) \to \text{Nat}, \ \max : (\text{Int}, \text{Int}) \to \text{Int}\}$

For an $\mathcal{S}$-sorted signature $\mathcal{F}$, an $\mathcal{F}$-*algebra* $\langle A, [\cdot] \rangle$ consists of an $\mathcal{S}$-sorted set A called the *carrier* and a family $[\cdot]$ of mappings called the *interpretation* such that $[f] : A^{\vec{\sigma}} \to A^\tau$ whenever $f \in \mathcal{F}_{\vec{\sigma},\tau}$.

Example 2. We consider the following *standard* interpretation $[\![\cdot]\!]$:

$$\cdots \quad [\![-2]\!] := -2 \quad [\![-1]\!] := -1 \quad [\![0]\!] := 0 \quad [\![1]\!] := 1 \quad [\![2]\!] := 2 \quad \cdots$$
$$[\![*]\!](a, b) := a \cdot b \qquad [\![+]\!](a, b) := a + b \qquad [\![\max]\!](a, b) := \max(a, b)$$

Notice that $\langle \mathbb{N}, [\![\cdot]\!] \rangle$ is an $\mathcal{N}_{*+\max}$-algebra and $\langle \mathbb{Z}, [\![\cdot]\!] \rangle$ is a $\mathcal{Z}_{*+\max}$-algebra. Here, the {Nat}-sorted set $\mathbb{N}$ is defined by $\mathbb{N}^{\text{Nat}} := \mathbb{N}$ and the {Nat, Neg, Int}-sorted set $\mathbb{Z}$ is defined by $\mathbb{Z}^{\text{Nat}} := \mathbb{N}$, $\mathbb{Z}^{\text{Neg}} := \{0, -1, -2, \ldots\}$ and $\mathbb{Z}^{\text{Int}} := \mathbb{Z}$.

---

[1] In the literature, sorted signatures are given more assumptions such as monotonicity or regularity. For the purpose of this paper, these assumptions are not necessary.

Sorted Terms: Given an $\mathcal{S}$-sorted signature $\mathcal{F}$ and an $\mathcal{S}$-sorted set $\mathcal{V}$ of *variables*, the $\mathcal{S}$-sorted set $\mathcal{T}(\mathcal{F}, \mathcal{V})$ of *terms* is inductively defined as follows:

- $v \in \mathcal{T}(\mathcal{F}, \mathcal{V})^\sigma$ if $v \in \mathcal{V}^\sigma$;
- $f(s_1, \ldots, s_n) \in \mathcal{T}(\mathcal{F}, \mathcal{V})^\rho$ if $f \in \mathcal{F}_{\vec{\sigma}, \tau}$, $(s_1, \ldots, s_n) \in \mathcal{T}(\mathcal{F}, \mathcal{V})^{\vec{\sigma}}$, and $\tau \sqsubseteq \rho$.

An interpretation $[\cdot]$ is extended over terms as follows: given $\alpha : \mathcal{V} \to A$, $[x]\alpha := \alpha(x)$ if $x \in \mathcal{V}^\sigma$, and $[f(s_1, \ldots, s_n)]\alpha := [f]([s_1]\alpha, \ldots, [s_n]\alpha)$. The $\mathcal{F}$-algebra $\langle \mathcal{T}(\mathcal{F}, \mathcal{V}), \cdot \rangle$ (which interprets f as the mapping that takes $(s_1, \ldots, s_n)$ and returns $f(s_1, \ldots, s_n)$) is called the *term algebra*, and a sorted map $\theta : \mathcal{V} \to \mathcal{T}(\mathcal{F}, \mathcal{V})$ is called a *substitution*. The term obtained by replacing every variable x by $\theta(x)$ in s is thus $s\theta$.

Term Rewriting: This paper is concerned with termination analysis for plain term rewriting. In this setting, there is only one sort $\mathbf{1}$, and we may identify a $\{\mathbf{1}\}$-sorted set A and the set $A^{\mathbf{1}}$. The set of variables appearing in a term s is denoted by $\mathsf{Var}(s)$. A *context* C is a term with a special variable $\square$ occurring exactly once. We denote by $C[s]$ the term obtained by substituting $\square$ by s in C. A *rewrite rule* is a pair of terms l and r, written $l \to r$, such that $l \notin \mathcal{V}$ and $\mathsf{Var}(l) \supseteq \mathsf{Var}(r)$. A *term rewrite system (TRS)* is a set $\mathcal{R}$ of rewrite rules, which induces the *root rewrite step* $\xrightarrow[\mathcal{R}]{\epsilon}$ and the *rewrite step* $\xrightarrow[\mathcal{R}]{}$ as the least relations such that $l\theta \xrightarrow[\mathcal{R}]{\epsilon} r\theta$ and $C[l\theta] \xrightarrow[\mathcal{R}]{} C[r\theta]$, for any rule $l \to r \in \mathcal{R}$, substitution θ, and context C. A TRS $\mathcal{R}$ is *terminating* iff no infinite rewriting $s_1 \xrightarrow[\mathcal{R}]{} s_2 \xrightarrow[\mathcal{R}]{} s_3 \xrightarrow[\mathcal{R}]{} \cdots$ is possible.

The dependency pair (DP) framework [1,14,13] is a *de facto* standard among automated termination provers for term rewriting. Here we briefly recapitulate its essence. The *root symbol* of a term $s = f(s_1, \ldots, s_n)$ is f and is denoted by $\mathsf{root}(s)$. The set of *defined* symbols in $\mathcal{R}$ is $\mathcal{D}_\mathcal{R} := \{\mathsf{root}(l) \mid l \to r \in \mathcal{R}\}$. We assume a fresh *marked* symbol $f^\sharp$ for every $f \in \mathcal{D}_\mathcal{R}$, and write $s^\sharp$ to denote the term $f^\sharp(s_1, \ldots, s_n)$ for $s = f(s_1, \ldots, s_n)$. A *dependency pair* of a TRS $\mathcal{R}$ is a rule $l^\sharp \to r^\sharp$ such that $\mathsf{root}(r) \in \mathcal{D}_\mathcal{R}$ and $l \to C[r] \in \mathcal{R}$ for some context C. The set of all dependency pairs of $\mathcal{R}$ is denoted by $\mathsf{DP}(\mathcal{R})$. A *DP problem* $\langle \mathcal{P}, \mathcal{R} \rangle$ is just a pair of TRSs.

Theorem 1 ([1]). *A TRS $\mathcal{R}$ is terminating iff the DP problem $\langle \mathsf{DP}(\mathcal{R}), \mathcal{R} \rangle$ is finite, i.e., there is no infinite chain $s_0 \xrightarrow[\mathsf{DP}(\mathcal{R})]{\epsilon} t_0 \xrightarrow[\mathcal{R}]{}^* s_1 \xrightarrow[\mathsf{DP}(\mathcal{R})]{\epsilon} t_1 \xrightarrow[\mathcal{R}]{}^* \cdots$.*

A number of techniques called *DP processors* that simplify or decompose DP problems are proposed; see [13] for a list of such processors. Among them, the central technique for concluding the finiteness of DP problems is the *reduction pair* processor, which will be reformulated in the next section.

3   Notes on Reduction Pairs

A reduction pair is a pair $\langle \succsim, \succ \rangle$ of order-like relations over terms with some conditions. Here we introduce two formulations of reduction pairs, one demanding natural assumptions of orderings, and the other, reduction pair seed, demanding only essential requirements. The first formulation is useful when proving properties of reduction pairs, while the latter is useful when devising new reduction pairs. We will show that the two notions are essentially equivalent: one can always extend a reduction pair seed into a reduction pair of the former sense. Existing formulations of reduction pairs lie strictly in between the two.

Definition 1 (reduction pair). *A (quasi-)order pair $\langle \succsim, \succ \rangle$ is a pair of a quasi-order $\succsim$ and an irreflexive relation $\succ \subseteq \succsim$ satisfying* compatibility: $\succsim; \succ; \succsim \subseteq \succ$. *The order pair is* well-founded *if $\succ$ is well-founded.*

A reduction pair *is a well-founded order pair $\langle \succsim, \succ \rangle$ on terms, such that both $\succsim$ and $\succ$ are closed under substitutions, and $\succsim$ is closed under contexts. Here, a relation $\sqsupseteq$ is* closed under substitutions *(resp. contexts) iff $s \sqsupseteq t$ implies $s\theta \sqsupseteq t\theta$ for every substitution θ (resp. $C[s] \sqsupseteq C[t]$ for every context C).*

The above formulation of reduction pairs is strictly subsumed by standard definitions (e.g., [1,14,13]), where $\succ$ is not necessarily a subset of $\succsim$, and compatibility is weakened to either $\succsim; \succ \subseteq \succ$ or $\succ; \succsim \subseteq \succ$. Instead, $\succ$ is required to be transitive but this follows from our assumptions $\succ \subseteq \succsim$ and compatibility: $\succ; \succ \subseteq \succsim; \succ \subseteq \succ$. On one hand, this means that we can safely import existing results of reduction pairs into our formulation.

Theorem 2 (reduction pair processor [14,13]). *Let $\langle \mathcal{P}, \mathcal{R} \rangle$ be a DP problem and $\langle \succsim, \succ \rangle$ be a reduction pair such that $\mathcal{P} \cup \mathcal{R} \subseteq \succsim$. Then the DP problem $\langle \mathcal{P}, \mathcal{R} \rangle$ is finite if and only if $\langle \mathcal{P} \setminus \succ, \mathcal{R} \rangle$ is.*

Example 3. Consider again the TRS $\mathcal{R}_{\mathsf{fact}}$ of the introduction. Proving that $\mathcal{R}_{\mathsf{fact}}$ terminates in the DP framework boils down to finding a reduction pair $\langle \succsim, \succ \rangle$ satisfying (considering *usable rules* [1]):

$$\mathsf{p}(\mathsf{s}(x)) \succsim x \qquad\qquad \mathsf{fact}^\sharp(\mathsf{s}(x)) \succ \mathsf{fact}^\sharp(\mathsf{p}(\mathsf{s}(x)))$$

On the other hand, one may wonder whether Definition 1 might be too restrictive. We justify our formulation by uniformly extending general "reduction pairs" into reduction pairs that comply with Definition 1. This is possible for even more general pairs of relations than standard reduction pairs.

Definition 2 (reduction pair seed). *A* well-founded order seed *is a pair $\langle W, S \rangle$ of relations such that S is well-founded and $S; W \subseteq S^+$. A* reduction pair seed *is a well-founded order seed on terms such that both W and S are closed under substitutions, and W is closed under contexts.*

Now we show that every reduction pair seed $\langle W, S \rangle$ can be extended to a reduction pair $\langle \succsim, \succ \rangle$ such that $W \subseteq \succsim$ and $S \subseteq \succ$. Before that, the assumption $S; W \subseteq S^+$ of Definition 2 is generalized as follows.

Lemma 1. *If $\langle W, S \rangle$ is a well-founded order seed, then $S; W^* \subseteq S^+$.*

Proof. By induction on the number of W steps. □

Theorem 3. *Let $\langle W, S \rangle$ be a well-founded order seed. Then $\langle \succsim, \succ \rangle$ is a well-founded order pair, where $\succsim := (W \cup S)^*$ and $\succ := (W^*; S)^+$.*

Proof. It is trivial that $\succsim$ is a quasi-order and $\succ \subseteq \succsim$ by definition. We show the well-foundedness of $\succ$ as follows: Suppose on the contrary we have an infinite sequence:

$$a_1 \ W^* \ b_1 \ S \ a_2 \ W^* \ b_2 \ S \ a_3 \ W^* \ b_2 \ S \cdots$$

Then using Lemma 1 ($S; W^* \subseteq S^+$) we obtain $a_1 \ W^* \ b_1 \ S^+ \ b_2 \ S^+ \cdots$, which contradicts the well-foundedness of S.

Now we show compatibility. By definition we have $\succsim; \succ \subseteq \succ$, so it suffices to show $\succ; \succsim \subseteq \succ$. By induction we reduce the claim to $\succ; (W \cup S) \subseteq \succ$, that is, both $\succ; W \subseteq \succ$ and $\succ; S \subseteq \succ$. Using $S; W \subseteq S^+ = S; S^*$ we have

$$\begin{aligned}
\succ; W = (W^*; S)^+; W &= (W^*; S)^*; W^*; S; W \\
&\subseteq (W^*; S)^*; W^*; S; S^* \subseteq \succ
\end{aligned}$$

The other case $\succ; S \subseteq \succ$ is easy from the definition. $\square$

Now we obtain the following corollary of Theorem 2 and Theorem 3.

Corollary 1. *Let $\langle \mathcal{P}, \mathcal{R} \rangle$ be a DP problem and $\langle W, S \rangle$ a reduction pair seed such that $\mathcal{P} \cup \mathcal{R} \subseteq W$. Then $\langle \mathcal{P}, \mathcal{R} \rangle$ is finite if and only if $\langle \mathcal{P} \setminus S, \mathcal{R} \rangle$ is.*

Notice that Definition 2 does not demand any order-like property, most notably transitivity. This is beneficial when developing new reduction pairs; for instance, *higher-order recursive path orders* [17] are known to be non-transitive, but form a reduction pair seed with their reflexive closure. Throughout the paper we use Definition 1, since it provides more useful and natural properties of orderings, which becomes crucial in Section 7.

4   Interpretation Methods as Derivers

Interpretation methods construct reduction pairs from $\mathcal{F}$-algebras, where $\mathcal{F}$ is the $\{1\}$-sorted signature of an input TRS or DP problem, and the carrier is a mathematical structure where a well-founded ordering $>$ is known. In the DP framework, weakly monotone $\mathcal{F}$-algebras play an important role.

Definition 3 (weakly monotone algebra). *A mapping $f : A_1 \times \cdots \times A_n \to A$ is monotone with respect to $\sqsupset$ if $f(a_1, \ldots, a_i, \ldots, a_n) \sqsupset f(a_1, \ldots, a_i', \ldots, a_n)$ whenever $a_1 \in A_1, \ldots, a_n \in A_n$, $a_i' \in A_i$, and $a_i \sqsupset a_i'$. A weakly monotone $\mathcal{F}$-algebra $\langle A, [\cdot], \geq, > \rangle$ consists of an $\mathcal{F}$-algebra $\langle A, [\cdot] \rangle$ and an order pair $\langle \geq, > \rangle$ such that every $[f]$ is monotone with respect to $\geq$.*

Example 4. Continuing Example 2, $\langle \mathbb{N}, [\![\cdot]\!], \geq, > \rangle$ is a weakly monotone $\mathcal{N}_{*+\max}$-algebra with the standard ordering $\langle \geq, > \rangle$. Notice that $\langle \mathbb{Z}, [\![\cdot]\!], \geq, > \rangle$ is not a weakly monotone $\mathcal{Z}_{*+\max}$-algebra, since multiplication on integers is not necessarily monotone. Nevertheless, it is a weakly monotone $\mathcal{Z}_{+\max} \cup \mathcal{N}_*$-algebra.

To ease presentation, from now on we assume that $\mathcal{F}$ is a $\{1\}$-sorted signature, while $\mathcal{G}$ is an $\mathcal{S}$-sorted signature. It is easy nevertheless to generalize our results to an arbitrary order-sorted signature $\mathcal{F}$.

Theorem 4 ([14]). *Let $\langle A, [\cdot], \geq, > \rangle$ be a weakly monotone $\mathcal{F}$-algebra such that $>$ is well-founded in A. Then $\langle [\geq], [>] \rangle$ is a reduction pair on $\mathcal{T}(\mathcal{F}, \mathcal{V})$, where $s \sqsupseteq t :\Longleftrightarrow \forall \alpha : \mathcal{V} \to A. [s]\alpha \sqsupseteq [t]\alpha$.*

Moreover, using the term algebra any reduction pair $\langle \succsim, \succ \rangle$ on $\mathcal{T}(\mathcal{F}, \mathcal{V})$ can be seen as a well-founded $\mathcal{F}$-algebra $\langle \mathcal{T}(\mathcal{F}, \mathcal{V}), \cdot, \succsim, \succ \rangle$.

Example 5. Continuing Example 4, $\langle [\geq], [>] \rangle$ forms a reduction pair for signature $\mathcal{N}_{*+\max}$. Notice that it does not for $\mathcal{Z}_{+\max} \cup \mathcal{N}_*$, essentially because $>$ is not well-founded in $\mathbb{Z}$.

In order to prove the finiteness of a given DP problem, we need a weakly monotone $\mathcal{F}$-algebra for the signature $\mathcal{F}$ indicated by this problem, rather than for a predefined signature like $\mathcal{N}_{*+\max}$. We fill the gap by employing the notion of *derivers* [24,33] to derive an $\mathcal{F}$-algebra from one of another signature $\mathcal{G}$.

Definition 4 (deriver). *An $\mathcal{F}/\mathcal{G}$-deriver is a pair of a sort $\delta \in \mathcal{S}$ and a mapping d, such that $d(f) \in \mathcal{T}(\mathcal{G}, \{x_1 : \delta, \ldots, x_n : \delta\})^\delta$ when f has arity n in $\mathcal{F}$. Given a base $\mathcal{G}$-algebra $\langle A, [\cdot] \rangle$, we define the derived $\mathcal{F}$-algebra $\langle A^\delta, d[\cdot] \rangle$ by*

$$d[f](a_1, \ldots, a_n) := [d(f)](x_1 \mapsto a_1, \ldots, x_n \mapsto a_n)$$

Example 6. Define a $\{\mathtt{fact}^\sharp, \mathtt{p}, \mathtt{s} : 1 \to 1\}/\mathcal{Z}_{+\max}$-deriver $\langle \mathtt{Nat}, d \rangle$ by

$$d(\mathtt{fact}^\sharp) := x_1 \qquad d(\mathtt{s}) := x_1 + 1 \qquad d(\mathtt{p}) := \max(x_1 - 1, 0)$$

Note that $d(\mathtt{p})$ has sort $\mathtt{Nat}$, thanks to the rank $(\mathtt{Int}, \mathtt{Nat}) \to \mathtt{Nat}$ of $\max$ in $\mathcal{Z}_{\max}$. The order pair $\langle d[\geq], d[>] \rangle$ satisfies the constraints given in Example 3.

Now we show that an $\mathcal{F}/\mathcal{G}$-deriver yields a weakly monotone $\mathcal{F}$-algebra if the base $\mathcal{G}$-algebra is known to be weakly monotone. Thus, Example 6 proves that $\mathcal{R}_{\mathtt{fact}}$ is terminating. The next result about monotonicity is folklore:

Lemma 2. *A mapping $f : A^n \to A$ is monotone with respect to a quasi-order $\geq$ if and only if $a_1 \geq b_1, \ldots, a_n \geq b_n$ implies $f(a_1, \ldots, a_n) \geq f(b_1, \ldots, b_n)$.*

Proof. The "if" direction is due to the reflexivity of $\geq$, and the "only if" direction is easy by induction on n and the transitivity of $\geq$. □

Then monotonicity is carried over to the interpretation of terms, in the following sense. For two sorted maps $\alpha : X \to A$ and $\beta : X \to A$, we write $\alpha \geq \beta$ to mean that $\alpha(x) \geq \beta(x)$ for any $x \in X^\sigma$ and sort σ.

Lemma 3. *Let $\langle A, [\cdot], \geq, > \rangle$ be a weakly monotone $\mathcal{G}$-algebra and $s \in \mathcal{T}(\mathcal{G}, \mathcal{V})^\sigma$. If $\alpha \geq \beta$ then $[s]\alpha \geq [s]\beta$.*

Proof. By structural induction on s. The claim is trivial if s is a variable. Consider $s = f(s_1, \ldots, s_n)$. We have $[s_i]\alpha \geq [s_i]\beta$ for each $i \in \{1, \ldots, n\}$ by induction hypothesis. With Lemma 2 and the monotonicity of $[f]$, we conclude:

$$[s]\alpha = [f]([s_1]\alpha, \ldots, [s_n]\alpha) \geq [f]([s_1]\beta, \ldots, [s_n]\beta) = [s]\beta \qquad \square$$

Lemma 4. *Let $\langle \delta, d \rangle$ be an $\mathcal{F}/\mathcal{G}$-deriver and $\langle A, [\cdot], \geq, > \rangle$ a weakly monotone $\mathcal{G}$-algebra. Then $\langle A^\delta, d[\cdot], \geq, > \rangle$ is a weakly monotone $\mathcal{F}$-algebra.*

Proof. Suppose that f has arity n in $\mathcal{F}$, and for every $i \in \{1, \ldots, n\}$ that $a_i, b_i \in A^\delta$ and $a_i \geq b_i$. Then from Lemma 3,

$$
\begin{aligned}
d[f](a_1, \ldots, a_n) &= [d(f)](x_1 \mapsto a_1, \ldots, x_n \mapsto a_n) \\
&\geq [d(f)](x_1 \mapsto b_1, \ldots, x_n \mapsto b_n) = d[f](b_1, \ldots, b_n)
\end{aligned}
$$

With Lemma 2 we conclude that every $d[f]$ is monotone with respect to $\geq$, and hence $\langle A^\delta, d[\cdot], \geq, > \rangle$ is a weakly monotone $\mathcal{F}$-algebra. $\qquad \square$

Thus we conclude the soundness of the deriver-based interpretation method:

Theorem 5. *If $\langle \delta, d \rangle$ is a $\mathcal{F}/\mathcal{G}$-deriver, $\langle A, [\cdot], \geq, > \rangle$ is a weakly monotone $\mathcal{G}$-algebra and $>$ is well-founded in A^δ, then $\langle d[\geq], d[>] \rangle$ is a reduction pair.*

Proof. Immediate consequence of Lemma 4 and Theorem 4. $\qquad \square$

It should be clear that Theorem 5 with $\mathcal{G} = \mathcal{Z}_{+\max} \cup \mathcal{N}_*$ subsumes the polynomial interpretation method with negative constants [15, Lemma 4]. Their trick is to turn integers into naturals by applying $\max(\cdot, 0)$, as demonstrated in Example 6 in a syntactic manner. Theorem 5 gives a slightly more general fact that one can mix max and negative constants and still get a reduction pair. As far as the author knows, this fact has not been reported elsewhere, although natural max-polynomials without negative constants are known to yield reduction pairs [9, Section 4.1].

In addition, a syntactic technique known as *argument filtering* [1,21] is also a special case of Theorem 5. In the context of higher-order rewriting, Kop and van Raamsdonk generalized argument filters into *argument functions* [18, Definition 7.7], which, in the first-order case, correspond to derivers with $\mathcal{G}$ being a variant of $\mathcal{F}$. In these applications, base signatures and algebras are not *a priori* known, but are subject to be synthesized and analyzed.

5   Multi-Dimensional Interpretations

The *matrix interpretation method* [8] uses a well-founded weakly monotone algebra $\langle \mathbb{N}^m, [\cdot]_{\mathcal{M}at}, \geqq, \gg \rangle$ over natural vectors, with an affine interpretation:

$$[f]_{\mathcal{M}at}(\vec{a}_1, \ldots, \vec{a}_n) = C_1 \vec{a}_1 + \cdots + C_n \vec{a}_n + \vec{c}$$

where $C_1, \ldots, C_n \in \mathbb{N}^{m \times m}$ and $\vec{c} \in \mathbb{N}^m$, and the following ordering:

Definition 5 ([8,19]). *Given an order pair $\langle \geq, > \rangle$ on A and a dimension $m \in \mathbb{N}$, we define the order pair $\langle \gtrdot, \ggdot \rangle$ on A^m as follows:*

$$(a_1, \ldots, a_m) \gtrdot (b_1, \ldots, b_m) :\Longleftrightarrow a_1 \gtrdot b_1 \wedge a_2 \geq b_2 \wedge \cdots \wedge a_m \geq b_m$$

Improved matrix interpretations [6] consider square matrices instead of vectors, and thus, in principle, matrix polynomials can be considered. Now we generalize these methods by extending derivers to multi-dimensional ones.

Definition 6 (multi-dimensional derivers). *An m-dimensional $\mathcal{F}/\mathcal{G}$-deriver consists of an m-tuple $\vec{\delta} \in \mathcal{S}^m$ of sorts and a mapping $\vec{d}$ such that $\vec{d}(f) \in \mathcal{T}(\mathcal{G}, \mathcal{X})^{\vec{\delta}}$, where $\mathcal{X} := \{x_{i,j} : (\vec{\delta})_j \mid i \in \{1, \ldots, n\}, j \in \{1, \ldots, m\}\}$ if f has arity n in $\mathcal{F}$. Given a $\mathcal{G}$-algebra $\langle A, [\cdot] \rangle$, the derived $\mathcal{F}$-algebra $\langle A^{\vec{\delta}}, \vec{d}[\cdot] \rangle$ is defined by*

$$\vec{d}[f](\vec{a}_1, \ldots, \vec{a}_n) := ([(\vec{d}(f))_1]\alpha, \ldots, [(\vec{d}(f))_m]\alpha)$$

where α is defined by $\alpha(x_{i,j}) := (\vec{a}_i)_j$.

Example 7 ([8, Example 1]). The TRS of the single rule $\mathbf{f}(\mathbf{f}(x)) \to \mathbf{f}(\mathbf{g}(\mathbf{f}(x)))$ can be shown terminating by the following 2-dimensional matrix interpretation:

$$[\mathbf{f}]_{Mat}(\vec{a}) = \begin{pmatrix} 1 & 1 \\ 0 & 0 \end{pmatrix} \vec{a} + \begin{pmatrix} 0 \\ 1 \end{pmatrix} \qquad [\mathbf{g}]_{Mat}(\vec{a}) = \begin{pmatrix} 1 & 0 \\ 0 & 0 \end{pmatrix} \vec{a} + \begin{pmatrix} 0 \\ 0 \end{pmatrix}$$

The 2-dimensional $\{\mathbf{f}, \mathbf{g}\}/\mathcal{N}_+$-deriver $\langle (\mathtt{Nat}, \mathtt{Nat}), \vec{d} \rangle$ defined by

$$\vec{d}(\mathbf{f}) = \begin{pmatrix} x_{11} + x_{12} \\ 1 \end{pmatrix} \qquad \vec{d}(\mathbf{g}) = \begin{pmatrix} x_{11} \\ 0 \end{pmatrix}$$

represents $[\cdot]_{Mat}$ as $\vec{d}[\![\cdot]\!]$, that is, $[\gtrdot]_{Mat} = \vec{d}[\![\gtrdot]\!]$ and $[\ggdot]_{Mat} = \vec{d}[\![\ggdot]\!]$.

Now we prove a counterpart of Theorem 5 for multi-dimensional derivers. The following lemma is one of the main results of this paper, which is somewhat surprisingly easy to prove.

Lemma 5. *For an m-dimensional $\mathcal{F}/\mathcal{G}$-deriver $\langle \vec{\delta}, \vec{d} \rangle$ and a weakly monotone $\mathcal{G}$-algebra $\langle A, [\cdot], \geq, > \rangle$, $\langle A^{\vec{\delta}}, \vec{d}[\cdot], \gtrdot, \ggdot \rangle$ is a weakly monotone $\mathcal{F}$-algebra.*

Proof. Let f have arity n in $\mathcal{F}$ and $\vec{a}_1, \ldots, \vec{a}_n, \vec{b}_1, \ldots, \vec{b}_n \in A^{\vec{\delta}}$ satisfy $\vec{a}_i \gtrdot \vec{b}_i$. Define α and β by $\alpha(x_{i,j}) := (\vec{a}_i)_j$ and $\beta(x_{i,j}) := (\vec{b}_i)_j$. By assumption we have $\alpha \geq \beta$, and with Lemma 3 we have

$$\left(\vec{d}[f](\vec{a}_1, \ldots, \vec{a}_n) \right)_j = [(\vec{d}(f))_j]\alpha \geq [(\vec{d}(f))_j]\beta = \left(\vec{d}[f](\vec{b}_1, \ldots, \vec{b}_n) \right)_j$$

for every $j \in \{1, \ldots, m\}$. Hence $\vec{d}[f](\vec{a}_1, \ldots, \vec{a}_n) \gtrdot \vec{d}[f](\vec{b}_1, \ldots, \vec{b}_n)$, and this concludes the proof due to Lemma 2. $\qquad \square$

Theorem 6. *For a multi-dimensional $\mathcal{F}/\mathcal{G}$-deriver $\langle \vec{\delta}, \vec{d} \rangle$ and a weakly mono-tone $\mathcal{G}$-algebra $\langle A, [\cdot], \geq, > \rangle$ such that $>$ is well-founded in $A^{(\vec{\delta})_1}$, $\langle \vec{d}[\geqq], \vec{d}[\ggg] \rangle$ is a reduction pair.*

Proof. Thanks to Lemma 5 and Theorem 4, it suffices to show that $\ggg$ is well-founded in $A^{\vec{\delta}}$. Suppose on the contrary that there exists an infinite sequence $\vec{a}_1 \ggg \vec{a}_2 \ggg \cdots$ with $\vec{a}_1, \vec{a}_2, \ldots \in A^{\vec{\delta}}$. Then we have $(\vec{a}_1)_1 > (\vec{a}_2)_1 > \cdots$ and $(\vec{a}_1)_1, (\vec{a}_2)_1, \ldots \in A^{(\vec{\delta})_1}$, contradicting the well-foundedness of $>$ in $A^{(\vec{\delta})_1}$. $\qquad \square$

It should be clear that every m-dimensional (improved) matrix interpretation can be expressed as an m-dimensional (or m^2-dimensional) $\mathcal{F}/\mathcal{N}_{*+}$-deriver. There are two more important consequences of Theorem 6: First, we can interpret symbols as non-affine maps even including max-polynomials; and second, since $>$ is not required to be well-founded in $A^{(\vec{\delta})_2}, \ldots, A^{(\vec{\delta})_m}$, examples that previously required non-monotone interpretations—and hence a stronger condition than Theorem 2—can be handled.

Example 8 (Excerpt of `APROVE_08/log`*).* Consider the TRS $\mathcal{R}_l$ consisting of

$$x - 0 \to x \qquad\qquad 0 \, / \, y \to 0$$
$$\mathsf{s}(x) - \mathsf{s}(y) \to x - y \qquad \mathsf{s}(x) \, / \, \mathsf{s}(y) \to (\mathsf{s}(x) - \mathsf{s}(y)) \, / \, \mathsf{s}(y)$$

which defines (for simplicity, rounded up) natural division. Proving $\mathcal{R}_l$ terminating using dependency pairs boils down to finding a reduction pair $\langle \succeq, \succ \rangle$ such that (again considering usable rules)

$$x - 0 \succeq x \qquad \mathsf{s}(x) - \mathsf{s}(y) \succeq x - y \qquad \mathsf{s}(x) \, /^\sharp \, \mathsf{s}(y) \succ (\mathsf{s}(x) - \mathsf{s}(y)) \, /^\sharp \, \mathsf{s}(y)$$

A polynomial interpretation $[\cdot]_{\mathcal{P}ol}$ with negative coefficients such that

$$[0]_{\mathcal{P}ol} = 0 \quad [\mathsf{s}]_{\mathcal{P}ol}(x) = x + 1 \quad [/^\sharp]_{\mathcal{P}ol}(x,y) = x \quad [-]_{\mathcal{P}ol}(x,y) = \max(x - y, 0)$$

satisfies the above constraints, but one must validate the requirements of [15, Theorem 11]. In our setting, an $\mathcal{F}/\mathcal{Z}_{+\max}$-deriver $\langle (\mathsf{Nat}, \mathsf{Neg}), \vec{d} \rangle$ such that

$$\vec{d}(0) = \begin{pmatrix} 0 \\ 0 \end{pmatrix} \quad \vec{d}(\mathsf{s}) = \begin{pmatrix} x_{1,1} + 1 \\ x_{1,2} - 1 \end{pmatrix} \quad \vec{d}(-) = \begin{pmatrix} \max(x_{1,1} + x_{2,2}, 0) \\ 0 \end{pmatrix} \quad \vec{d}(/^\sharp) = \begin{pmatrix} x_{1,1} \\ 0 \end{pmatrix}$$

yields a reduction pair satisfying the above constraints.

The intuition here is that the two dimensional interpretation of $\mathsf{s}^n(0)$ records n in the first coordinate and $-n$ in the second. Hence, one does not have to reconstruct $-n$ from n using the non-monotonic minus operation.

It seems plausible to the author that negative coefficients can be eliminated using the above idea; however, the increase of the dimension leads to more freedom in variables (the variable introduced to represent $-n$ may take values other than that) and so the ordering over terms may be different. It is left for future work to investigate whether this idea always works or not.

6   Arctic Interpretations

An *arctic interpretation* [19] $[\cdot]_{\mathcal{A}}$ is a matrix interpretation on the *arctic semiring*; that is, every interpretation $[f]_{\mathcal{A}}(\vec{x}_1, \ldots, \vec{x}_n)$ is of the form

$$C_1 \otimes \vec{x}_1 \oplus \cdots \oplus C_n \otimes \vec{x}_n \oplus \vec{c} \tag{1}$$

where $\otimes$ and $\oplus$ denote the matrix multiplication and matrix addition in which the scalar addition is replaced by the max operation, and the scalar multiplication by addition; and entries of C_i and $\vec{c}$ are *arctic naturals* ($\mathbb{N}_{-\infty} := \mathbb{N} \cup \{-\infty\}$) or *arctic integers* ($\mathbb{Z}_{-\infty} := \mathbb{Z} \cup \{-\infty\}$). In addition, (1) must be *absolute positive*: $(\vec{c})_1 \geq 0$, so that $\langle \mathbb{N} \times \mathbb{N}_{-\infty}^{m-1}, [\cdot]_{\mathcal{A}}, \geqq, \gg \rangle$ or $\langle \mathbb{N} \times \mathbb{Z}_{-\infty}^{m-1}, [\cdot]_{\mathcal{A}}, \geqq, \gg \rangle$ forms a well-founded weakly monotone algebra.

The above formulation deviates from the original [19] in two ways. First, we do not introduce the special relation such that $-\infty \gg -\infty$. Koprowski and Waldmann demanded this to ensure closure under general substitutions, but such a comparison cannot occur as we only need to consider substitutions that respect the carrier $\mathbb{N} \times \mathbb{Z}_{-\infty}^{m-1}$. Second, for arctic natural interpretations they relax absolute positiveness to *somewhere finiteness*: $(\vec{c})_1 \neq -\infty$ or $(C_i)_{1,1} \neq -\infty$ for some i. However, the two assumptions turn out to be equivalent.

Proposition 1. *Every arctic natural interpretation of form (1) is absolute positive iff it is somewhere finite.*

Proof. Clearly, absolute positiveness implies somewhere finiteness. For the other direction, since $(\vec{c})_1 \neq -\infty$ trivially implies absolute positiveness, suppose that $(\vec{c})_1 = -\infty$ and $(C_i)_{1,1} \neq -\infty$ for some i. We then know $(\vec{y})_1 \geq 0$, where $\vec{y} := C_1 \otimes \vec{x}_1 \oplus \cdots \oplus C_n \otimes \vec{x}_n$. Hence, by $\vec{c}' := (0, (\vec{c})_2, \ldots, (\vec{c})_m)$, we have $[f]_{\mathcal{A}}(\vec{x}_1, \ldots, \vec{x}_n) = \vec{y} \oplus \vec{c}'$, and this representation is absolute positive. $\qquad\square$

One can easily obtain arctic interpretations via multi-dimensional derivers: consider a sort ANat with Nat $\sqsubseteq$ ANat and {Nat, ANat}-sorted signature $\mathcal{N}_{\texttt{+max-}\infty}$, extending $\mathcal{N}_{\texttt{+max}}$ with

$$-\infty : () \to \text{ANat} \qquad + : (\text{ANat}, \text{ANat}) \to \text{ANat}$$

$$\max : (\text{Nat}, \text{ANat}) \to \text{Nat} \quad \max : (\text{ANat}, \text{Nat}) \to \text{Nat} \quad \max : (\text{ANat}, \text{ANat}) \to \text{ANat}$$

and extend the standard interpretation $[\![\cdot]\!]$ accordingly. We omit the easy proof of the following fact and the counterpart for arctic integer interpretations.

Proposition 2. *Every absolute positive arctic natural interpretation $[\cdot]_{\mathcal{A}}$ is represented as $\vec{d}[\![\cdot]\!]$ via an $\mathcal{F}/\mathcal{N}_{\texttt{+max-}\infty}$-deriver $\langle (\text{Nat}, \text{ANat}, \ldots, \text{ANat}), \vec{d} \rangle$.*

Notice that, in practice, this requires us to deal with $-\infty$ by ourselves since there is no standard SMT theory [3] that supports arithmetic with $-\infty$.

7   Strict Monotonicity

Before the invention of dependency pairs [1], strictly monotone algebras were necessary for proving termination by interpretation methods, and they constitute a sound and complete method for proving termination of TRSs.

Definition 7. *A strictly monotone $\mathcal{F}$-algebra is a weakly monotone $\mathcal{F}$-algebra $\langle A, [\cdot], \geq, > \rangle$ such that $\langle A, [\cdot] \rangle$ is monotone with respect to both $\geq$ and $>$.*

Theorem 7 (cf. [36]). *A TRS $\mathcal{R}$ is terminating if and only if there is a strictly monotone well-founded $\mathcal{F}$-algebra $\langle A, [\cdot], \geq, > \rangle$ such that $\mathcal{R} \subseteq [>]$.*

Moreover, strict monotonicity is a desirable property in the DP framework as it allows one to remove not only dependency pairs but also rewrite rules.

Theorem 8 ([12]). *A DP problem $\langle \mathcal{P}, \mathcal{R} \rangle$ is finite if $\langle \mathcal{P} \setminus [>], \mathcal{R} \setminus [>] \rangle$ is, where $\langle A, [\cdot], \geq, > \rangle$ is a strictly monotone well-founded $\mathcal{F}$-algebra such that $\mathcal{P} \cup \mathcal{R} \subseteq [\geq]$.*

We now state a criterion that ensures the strict monotonicity of multi-dimensional interpretation obtained via derivers. Below we write d_i to mean the mapping defined by $d_i(f) := \left(\vec{d}(f) \right)_i$.

Theorem 9. *Let $\langle \vec{\delta}, \vec{d} \rangle$ be an m-dimensional $\mathcal{F}/\mathcal{G}$-deriver and $\langle A, [\cdot], \geq, > \rangle$ a weakly monotone $\mathcal{G}$-algebra. Suppose that when f has arity n in $\mathcal{F}$ and $i \in \{1, \ldots, n\}$, $\alpha(x_{i,1}) > a$ implies $[d_1(f)]\alpha > [d_1(f)]\alpha(x_{i,1} \mapsto a)$ for any $\alpha : \mathcal{X} \to A$ and $a \in A$. Then $\langle A^{\vec{\delta}}, \vec{d}[\cdot], \geqq, \gg \rangle$ is a strictly monotone $\mathcal{F}$-algebra.*

Proof. We only prove strict monotonicity as we already know weak monotonicity by Lemma 5. So suppose that f has arity n in $\mathcal{F}$, $\vec{a}_1, \ldots, \vec{a}_i, \ldots, \vec{a}_n, \vec{a}_i' \in A^{\vec{\delta}}$ and $\vec{a}_i \gg \vec{a}_i'$. For the first coordinate, define α by $\alpha(x_{k,j}) := (\vec{a}_k)_j$. Then, first using the assumption, and then Lemma 3, we conclude

$$
\begin{aligned}
d_1[f](\vec{a}_1 \ldots, \vec{a}_i, \ldots, \vec{a}_n) &= [d_1(f)]\alpha \\
&> [d_1(f)]\alpha(x_{i,1} \mapsto (\vec{a}_i')_1) \\
&\geq [d_1(f)]\alpha(x_{i,1} \mapsto (\vec{a}_i')_1, x_{i,2} \mapsto (\vec{a}_i')_2, \ldots, x_{i,m} \mapsto (\vec{a}_i')_m) \\
&= d_1[f](\vec{a}_1, \ldots, \vec{a}_i', \ldots, \vec{a}_n)
\end{aligned}
$$

For the other coordinates, thanks to the "new" assumption $> \subseteq \geq$ in Definition 1 we have $\vec{a}_i \geqq \vec{a}_i'$. Then the weak monotonicity ensures $\vec{d}[f](\vec{a}_1, \ldots, \vec{a}_i, \ldots \vec{a}_n) \geqq \vec{d}[f](\vec{a}_1, \ldots, \vec{a}_i', \ldots, \vec{a}_n)$, from which we deduce for each $j \in \{2, \ldots, m\}$,

$$
d_j[f](\vec{a}_1, \ldots, \vec{a}_i, \ldots, \vec{a}_n) \geq d_j[f](\vec{a}_1, \ldots, \vec{a}_i', \ldots, \vec{a}_n) \qquad \square
$$

Although the above result and proof do not look surprising, it would be worth noticing that the statement is false in the standard formulation allowing $> \not\subseteq \geq$ (as even in [8]).

Example 9. Consider the following apparently monotone matrix interpretation:

$$[\mathtt{f}]\left(\begin{pmatrix} a_1 \\ a_2 \end{pmatrix}\right) := \begin{pmatrix} 1 & 0 \\ 1 & 0 \end{pmatrix}\begin{pmatrix} a_1 \\ a_2 \end{pmatrix} = \begin{pmatrix} a_1 \\ a_1 \end{pmatrix}$$

If one had $a_1 > b_1$ but $a_1 \not\geq b_1$, then

$$[\mathtt{f}]\left(\begin{pmatrix} a_1 \\ a_2 \end{pmatrix}\right) = \begin{pmatrix} a_1 \\ a_1 \end{pmatrix} \overset{>}{\not\geq} \begin{pmatrix} b_1 \\ b_1 \end{pmatrix} = [\mathtt{f}]\left(\begin{pmatrix} b_1 \\ a_2 \end{pmatrix}\right) \quad \text{even though} \quad \begin{pmatrix} a_1 \\ a_2 \end{pmatrix} \gg \begin{pmatrix} b_1 \\ a_2 \end{pmatrix}.$$

So $[\mathtt{f}]$ would not be monotone with respect to $\gg$.

8 Implementation and Experiments

Multi-dimensional interpretations are implemented in the termination prover NaTT version 2.0^2, using a *template*-based approach.

Definition 8. *An m-dimensional $\mathcal{F}/\mathcal{G}$-deriver template $\langle \vec{\delta}, \vec{d} \rangle$ with $\mathcal{S}$-sorted set $\mathcal{W}$ of template variables is defined as in Definition 6, but allowing $\vec{d}(f) \in \mathcal{T}(\mathcal{G}, \mathcal{W} \cup \mathcal{X})^{\vec{\delta}}$. Its instance according to a substitution $\theta : \mathcal{W} \to \mathcal{T}(\mathcal{G}, \emptyset)$ is the $\mathcal{F}/\mathcal{G}$-deriver $\langle \vec{\delta}, \vec{d\theta} \rangle$, defined by $\vec{d\theta}(f) := (d_1(f)\theta, \dots, d_m(f)\theta)$.*

In the implementation, we fix $\mathcal{G} = \mathcal{Z}_{+\max} \cup \mathcal{N}_*$ and the base weakly monotone $\mathcal{G}$-algebra $\langle \mathbb{Z}, [\![\cdot]\!], \geq, > \rangle$. Given an m-dimensional deriver template $\langle \vec{\delta}, \vec{d} \rangle$ with $\mathcal{W}$, our interest is now to find $\theta : \mathcal{W} \to \mathbb{Z}$ such that $\vec{d\theta}[s] \geq \vec{d\theta}[t]$ for every $(s, t) \in \mathcal{P} \cup \mathcal{R}$ for the DP problem $\langle \mathcal{P}, \mathcal{R} \rangle$ of concern, thanks to Theorem 6. NaTT reduces this problem into an SMT problem and passes it to a backend SMT solver. The page limit is not enough to detail the reduction; in short, the constraint $\vec{d\theta}[s] \gg \vec{d\theta}[t]$ is reduced into a Boolean formula over atoms of form $a * \langle v_1, i_1 \rangle * \cdots * \langle v_n, i_n \rangle \geq b * \langle v_1, i_1 \rangle * \cdots * \langle v_n, i_n \rangle$, where $a, b \in \mathcal{T}(\mathcal{G}, \mathcal{W})$, and $\langle v_1, i_1 \rangle \dots, \langle v_n, i_n \rangle \in (\mathsf{Var}(s) \cup \mathsf{Var}(t)) \times \{1, \dots, m\}$ are seen as variables. Internally NaTT uses a distribution approach [30], whose soundness crucially relies on the fact that the only rank of $*$ is $(\mathsf{Nat}, \mathsf{Nat}) \to \mathsf{Nat}$ in the signature $\mathcal{G}$. Then each atom is further reduced to (1) $a = b$ if $(\vec{\delta})_{i_j} = \mathsf{Int}$ for some j, (2) $a \geq b$ if $|\{j \mid (\vec{\delta})_{i_j} = \mathsf{Neg}\}|$ is even, and (3) $a \leq b$ otherwise. Due to the last step, having coordinates of sort Int leads to a stronger constraint when ordering terms. Finally, the resulting formula, containing only template variables, is passed to the SMT solver Z3 4.8.10 [26] and a satisfying solution $\theta : \mathcal{W} \to \mathbb{Z}$ is a desired substitution.

To verify the practical significance of the method, we evaluated various templates in a simple dependency pair setting. For a function symbol f of arity $n \geq 2$, the k-th coordinate of template $\vec{d}(f)$ is chosen from

- sum: $w + \sum_{i=1}^{n}(b * x_{i,k})$,

Table 1. Evaluation of 2-dimensional templates.

#	Coordinate 1		Coordinate 2		YES	New	Time	Known as
1	sum	Nat	-	-	512	-	00:36:12	polynomial [1]
2	sum	Int	-	-	559	-	00:52:37	negative constant [15]
3	sum-sum	Nat	sum-sum	Nat	636	-	04:18:05	matrix [8]
4	sum-sum	Int	sum	Neg	602	10	04:00:05	new
5	sum-sum	Int	sum-sum	Int	542	0	25:07:04	new
6	sum-sum	Int	max	Neg	585	8	14:58:41	new
7	max	Int	-	-	560	-	00:58:58	max-polynomial [9]³
8	max-max	Nat	max-max	Nat	552	3	12:33:43	arctic natural [19]⁴
9	max-max	Int	max-max	Int	580	2	22:35:29	arctic integer [19]⁴
10	max-max	Nat	sum	Nat	577	0	03:48:46	new
11	max-max	Int	sum	Neg	584	2	06:53:34	new
12	max-sum	Int	sum	Neg	592	4	06:59:22	new
13	heuristic	Int	sum	Neg	648	9	04:55:43	new

- max: $\max_{i=1}^{n} b * (w + x_{i,k})$,
- sum-sum: $w + \sum_{i=1}^{n} \sum_{j=1}^{m} b * x_{i,j}$,
- max-max: $\max_{i=1}^{n} \max_{j=1}^{m} b * (w + x_{i,j})$,
- sum-max: $\sum_{i=1}^{n} \max_{j=1}^{m} b * (w + x_{i,j})$,
- max-sum: $\max_{i=1}^{n} (w + \sum_{j=1}^{m} b * x_{i,j})$, and
- a heuristic choice [35] between sum-sum and max-sum,

where b and w introduce fresh template variables, b ranges over $\{0, 1\}$ and the sort of w is up to further choice. The sort of the first coordinate is turned to Nat by applying $\max(\cdot, 0)$ if necessary.

Experiments are run on the StarExec environment [29], with timeout of 300 seconds. The benchmarks are the 1507 TRSs from the TRS Standard category of the *termination problem database* 11 [32]. Due to the huge search space, we evaluate templates of dimensions up to 2. A part of the results are summarized in Table 1. Full details of the experiments are made available at http://www.trs.cm.is.nagoya-u.ac.jp/NaTT/multi/.

In the table, each coordinate is represented by the template and the sort of w. In terms of the number of successful termination proofs indicated in the "YES" column, the classical matrix interpretations (row #3) are impressively strong. Nevertheless, it is worth considering a negative coordinate (#4) as it gives 10 termination proofs that the previous version of NaTT could not find, indicated in the "New" column. In contrast, considering whole integers in the second coordinate (#5) does not look promising as the runtime grows significantly. Concerning "max", we observe that its use in the second coordinate (#6)

---

³ This template is a subset of integer max-polynomials [9], although the fact that it yields a reduction pair is new.

⁴ In our implementation, negative infinity is not supported. Instead, similar effect is emulated by zero coefficients.

Table 2. Experiments with combined strategies

Strategy	YES	New to NaTT	New to TermCOMP	Time
Old Strategy	861	0	0	3:46:12
With #4	874	13	3	4:14:09
With #13	871	10	1	4:26:14
With #4 and #13	881	20	5	4:49:50

degrades the performance. Using "max" in both coordinates *a la* arctic interpretations (#8, #9) gives a few new termination proofs, but the impact in the runtime is significant in the current implementation. The runtime improves by replacing some occurrences of "max" by "sum" (#10–12), while the power does not seem defected. In terms of the number of termination proofs, the heuristic choice of "sum-sum" and "max-sum" in the first coordinate (#13) performed the best among the evaluated templates.

From these experiments, we pick templates #4 and #13 to incorporate in the NaTT default strategy. The final results are summarized in Table 2. Although the runtime noticeably increases, adding both #4 and #13 gives 20 more examples solved, and five of them (`AProVE_09_Inductive/log` and four in `Transformed_CSR_04/`) were not solved by any tool in the TermCOMP 2020.

9 Conclusion

In this paper we introduced a deriver-based multi-dimensional interpretation method. The author expects that the result makes the relationships between existing interpretation methods cleaner, and eases the task of developing and maintaining termination tools. Moreover, it yields many previously unknown interpretation methods as instances, proving the termination of some standard benchmarks that state-of-the-art termination provers could not.

Theoretical comparison with negative coefficients is left for future work, and the use of $-\infty$ is not implemented yet. Also since this work broadens the search space, it is interesting to heuristically search for derivers rather than fixing some templates. Derivers of higher dimensions seem also interesting to explore. Finally, although the proposed method is implemented in the termination prover NaTT, there is no guarantee that the implementation is correct. In order to certify termination proofs that use multi-dimensional derivers, one must formalize the proofs in this paper, extend the certifiable proof format [27], and implement a verified function to validate such proofs.

Acknowledgments The author would like to thank Aaron Stump and his team for StarExec environment that ran experiments taking 40 days of node within a day. The author also thanks the anonymous reviewers of previous versions of the paper. This work was partly supported by the Austrian Science Fund (FWF) projects Y757 and P27502, and the Japan Science and Technology Agency (JST) project ERATO MMSD.

References

1. Arts, T., Giesl, J.: Termination of term rewriting using dependency pairs. Theor. Compt. Sci. **236**(1–2), 133–178 (2000). https://doi.org/10.1016/S0304-3975(99)00207-8
2. Baader, F., Nipkow, T.: Term rewriting and all that. Cambridge University Press (1998)
3. Barrett, C.W., Tinelli, C.: Satisfiability modulo theories. In: Clarke, E.M., Henzinger, T.A., Veith, H., Bloem, R. (eds.) Handbook of Model Checking, pp. 305–343. Springer (2018). https://doi.org/10.1007/978-3-319-10575-8_11
4. Blanqui, F., Koprowski, A.: CoLoR: a Coq library on well-founded rewrite relations and its application to the automated verification of termination certificates. Math. Struct. Comput. Sci. **21**(4), 827–859 (2011). https://doi.org/10.1017/S0960129511000120
5. Contejean, É., Courtieu, P., Forest, J., Pons, O., Urbain, X.: Automated certified proofs with CiME3. In: Schmidt-Schauß, M. (ed.) RTA 2011. LIPIcs, vol. 10, pp. 21–30. Schloss Dagstuhl–Leibniz-Zentrum fuer Informatik, Dagstuhl, Germany (2011). https://doi.org/10.4230/LIPIcs.RTA.2011.21
6. Courtieu, P., Gbedo, G., Pons, O.: Improved matrix interpretation. In: van Leeuwen, J., Muscholl, A., Peleg, D., Pokorný, J., Rumpe, B. (eds.) SOFSEM 2010. LNCS, vol. 5901, pp. 283–295. Springer (2010). https://doi.org/10.1007/978-3-642-11266-9_24
7. Dershowitz, N.: 33 examples of termination. In: Comon, H., Jouannaud, J.P. (eds.) Term Rewriting. pp. 16–26. Springer (1995). https://doi.org/10.1007/3-540-59340-3_2
8. Endrullis, J., Waldmann, J., Zantema, H.: Matrix interpretations for proving termination of term rewriting. J. Autom. Reason. **40**(2-3), 195–220 (2008). https://doi.org/10.1007/s10817-007-9087-9
9. Fuhs, C., Giesl, J., Middeldorp, A., Schneider-Kamp, P., Thiemann, R., Zankl, H.: Maximal termination. In: Voronkov, A. (ed.) RTA 2008. LNCS, vol. 5117, pp. 110–125. Springer (2008). https://doi.org/10.1007/978-3-540-70590-1_8
10. Giesl, J., Brockschmidt, M., Emmes, F., Frohn, F., Fuhs, C., Otto, C., Plücker, M., Schneider-Kamp, P., Ströder, T., Swiderski, S., Thiemann, R.: Proving termination of programs automatically with AProVE. In: Demri, S., Kapur, D., Weidenbach, C. (eds.) IJCAR 2014. LNCS, vol. 8562, pp. 184–191. Springer (2014). https://doi.org/10.1007/978-3-319-08587-6_13
11. Giesl, J., Rubio, A., Sternagel, C., Waldmann, J., Yamada, A.: The termination and complexity competition. In: Beyer, D., Huisman, M., Kordon, F., Steffen, B. (eds.) TACAS 2019 (3). LNCS, vol. 11429, pp. 156–166. Springer (2019). https://doi.org/10.1007/978-3-030-17502-3_10
12. Giesl, J., Thiemann, R., Schneider-Kamp, P.: The dependency pair framework: Combining techniques for automated termination proofs. In: Baader, F., Voronkov, A. (eds.) LPAR 2004. LNCS, vol. 3452, pp. 301–331. Springer (2004). https://doi.org/10.1007/978-3-540-32275-7_21
13. Giesl, J., Thiemann, R., Schneider-Kamp, P., Falke, S.: Mechanizing and improving dependency pairs. J. Autom. Reason. **37**(3), 155–203 (2006). https://doi.org/10.1007/s10817-006-9057-7
14. Hirokawa, N., Middeldorp, A.: Dependency pairs revisited. In: van Oostrom, V. (ed.) RTA 2004. LNCS, vol. 3091, pp. 249–268. Springer (2004). https://doi.org/10.1007/978-3-540-25979-4_18

15. Hirokawa, N., Middeldorp, A.: Polynomial interpretations with negative coefficients. In: Buchberger, B., Campbell, J.A. (eds.) AISC 2004. LNAI, vol. 3249, pp. 185–198. Springer (2004). https://doi.org/10.1007/978-3-540-30210-0_16
16. Hofbauer, D., Waldmann, J.: Termination of string rewriting with matrix interpretations. In: Pfenning, F. (ed.) RTA 2006. LNCS, vol. 4098, pp. 328–342. Springer (2006). https://doi.org/10.1007/11805618_25
17. Jouannaud, J., Rubio, A.: The higher-order recursive path ordering. In: LICS 1999. pp. 402–411. IEEE Computer Society (1999). https://doi.org/10.1109/LICS.1999.782635
18. Kop, C., van Raamsdonk, F.: Dynamic dependency pairs for algebraic functional systems. Log. Methods Comput. Sci. **8**(2) (2012). https://doi.org/10.2168/LMCS-8(2:10)2012
19. Koprowski, A., Waldmann, J.: Max/plus tree automata for termination of term rewriting. Acta Cybern. **19**(2), 357–392 (2009)
20. Korp, M., Sternagel, C., Zankl, H., Middeldorp, A.: Tyrolean Termination Tool 2. In: Treinen, R. (ed.) RTA 2009. LNCS, vol. 5595, pp. 295–304. Springer (2009). https://doi.org/10.1007/978-3-642-02348-4_21
21. Kusakari, K., Nakamura, M., Toyama, Y.: Argument filtering transformation. In: Nadathur, G. (ed.) PPDP 1999. LNCS, vol. 1702, pp. 47–61. Springer (1999). https://doi.org/10.1007/10704567_3
22. Lankford, D.: Canonical algebraic simplification in computational logic. Tech. Rep. ATP-25, University of Texas (1975)
23. Lucas, S.: MU-TERM: A tool for proving termination of context-sensitive rewriting. In: van Oostrom, V. (ed.) RTA 2004. LNCS, vol. 3091, pp. 200–209. Springer (2004). https://doi.org/10.1007/978-3-540-25979-4_14
24. Lucas, S., Gutiérrez, R.: Automatic synthesis of logical models for order-sorted first-order theories. J. Autom. Reason. **60**(4), 465–501 (2018). https://doi.org/10.1007/s10817-017-9419-3
25. Manna, Z., Ness, S.: On the termination of Markov algorithms. In: the 3rd Hawaii International Conference on System Science. pp. 789–792 (1970)
26. de Moura, L.M., Bjørner, N.: Z3: an efficient SMT solver. In: Ramakrishnan, C.R., Rehof, J. (eds.) TACAS 2008. LNCS, vol. 4963, pp. 337–340. Springer (2008). https://doi.org/10.1007/978-3-540-78800-3_24
27. Sternagel, C., Thiemann, R.: The certification problem format. In: Benzmüller, C., Paleo, B.W. (eds.) UITP 2014. EPTCS, vol. 167, pp. 61–72 (2014). https://doi.org/10.4204/EPTCS.167.8
28. Sternagel, C., Thiemann, R.: Formalizing monotone algebras for certification of termination and complexity proofs. In: Dowek, G. (ed.) RTA-TLCA 2014. LNCS, vol. 8560, pp. 441–455. Springer (2014). https://doi.org/10.1007/978-3-319-08918-8_30
29. Stump, A., Sutcliffe, G., Tinelli, C.: StarExec: A cross-community infrastructure for logic solving. In: Demri, S., Kapur, D., Weidenbach, C. (eds.) IJCAR. LNCS, vol. 8562, pp. 367–373. Springer (2014). https://doi.org/10.1007/978-3-319-08587-6_28
30. Thiemann, R., Schöpf, J., Sternagel, C., Yamada, A.: Certifying the Weighted Path Order (Invited Talk). In: Ariola, Z.M. (ed.) FSCD 2020. LIPIcs, vol. 167, pp. 4:1–4:20. Schloss Dagstuhl–Leibniz-Zentrum für Informatik, Dagstuhl, Germany (2020). https://doi.org/10.4230/LIPIcs.FSCD.2020.4
31. Thiemann, R., Sternagel, C.: Certification of termination proofs using CeTA. In: Berghofer, S., Nipkow, T., Urban, C., Wenzel, M. (eds.) TPHOLs 2009. LNCS,

vol. 5674, pp. 452–468. Springer (2009). https://doi.org/10.1007/978-3-642-03359-9_31

32. The termination problem data base, http://termination-portal.org/wiki/TPDB
33. Watson, T., Goguen, J., Thatcher, J., Wagner, E.: An initial algebra approach to the specification, correctness, and implementation of abstract data types. In: Current Trends in Programming Methodology. Prentice Hall (1976)
34. Yamada, A., Kusakari, K., Sakabe, T.: Nagoya Termination Tool. In: Dowek, G. (ed.) RTA-TLCA 2014. LNCS, vol. 8560, pp. 466–475. Springer (2014). https://doi.org/10.1007/978-3-319-08918-8_32
35. Yamada, A., Kusakari, K., Sakabe, T.: A unified order for termination proving. Sci. Comput. Program. **111**, 110–134 (2015). https://doi.org/10.1016/j.scico.2014.07.009
36. Zantema, H.: Termination of term rewriting: interpretation and type elimination. J. Symb. Comput. **17**(1), 23–50 (1994). https://doi.org/10.1006/jsco.1994.1003
37. Zantema, H.: The termination hierarchy for term rewriting. Appl. Algebr. Eng. Comm. Compt. **12**(1/2), 3–19 (2001). https://doi.org/10.1007/s002000100061

Open Access This chapter is licensed under the terms of the Creative Commons Attribution 4.0 International License (http://creativecommons.org/licenses/by/4.0/), which permits use, sharing, adaptation, distribution and reproduction in any medium or format, as long as you give appropriate credit to the original author(s) and the source, provide a link to the Creative Commons license and indicate if changes were made.

The images or other third party material in this chapter are included in the chapter's Creative Commons license, unless indicated otherwise in a credit line to the material. If material is not included in the chapter's Creative Commons license and your intended use is not permitted by statutory regulation or exceeds the permitted use, you will need to obtain permission directly from the copyright holder.

Finding Good Proofs for Description Logic Entailments using Recursive Quality Measures

Christian Alrabbaa, Franz Baader, Stefan Borgwardt, Patrick Koopmann, and Alisa Kovtunova

Theoretical Computer Science, TU Dresden, Dresden, Germany

Abstract. Logic-based approaches to AI have the advantage that their behavior can in principle be explained to a user. If, for instance, a Description Logic reasoner derives a consequence that triggers some action of the overall system, then one can explain such an entailment by presenting a proof of the consequence in an appropriate calculus. How comprehensible such a proof is depends not only on the employed calculus, but also on the properties of the particular proof, such as its overall size, its depth, the complexity of the employed sentences and proof steps, etc. For this reason, we want to determine the complexity of generating proofs that are below a certain threshold w.r.t. a given measure of proof quality. Rather than investigating this problem for a fixed proof calculus and a fixed measure, we aim for general results that hold for wide classes of calculi and measures. In previous work, we first restricted the attention to a setting where proof size is used to measure the quality of a proof. We then extended the approach to a more general setting, but important measures such as proof depth were not covered. In the present paper, we provide results for a class of measures called recursive, which yields lower complexities and also encompasses proof depth. In addition, we close some gaps left open in our previous work, thus providing a comprehensive picture of the complexity landscape.

1 Introduction

Explainability has developed into a major issue in Artificial Intelligence, particularly in the context of sub-symbolic approaches based on Machine Learning [6]. In contrast, results produced by symbolic approaches based on logical reasoning are "explainable by design" since a derived consequence can be formally justified by showing a proof for it. In practice, things are not that easy since proofs may be very long, and even single proof steps or stated sentences may be hard to comprehend for a user that is not an expert in logic. For this reason, there has been considerable work in the Automated Deduction and Logic in AI communities on how to produce "good" proofs for certain purposes, both for full first-order logic, but also for decidable logics such a Description Logics (DLs) [9]. We mention here only a few approaches, and refer the reader to the introduction of our previous work [2] for a more detailed review.

© The Author(s) 2021
A. Platzer and G. Sutcliffe (Eds.): CADE 2021, LNAI 12699, pp. 291–308, 2021.
https://doi.org/10.1007/978-3-030-79876-5_17

First, there is work that transforms proofs that are produced by an automated reasoning system into ones in a calculus that is deemed to be more appropriate for human consumption [11, 22, 23]. Second, abstraction techniques are used to reduce the size of proofs by introducing definitions, lemmas, and more abstract deduction rules [16, 17]. Justification-based explanations for DLs [10, 14, 28] can be seen as a radical abstraction technique where the abstracted proof consists of a single proof step, from a minimal set of stated sentences that implies a certain consequence directly to this consequence. Finally, instead of presenting proofs in a formal, logical syntax, one can also try to increase readability by translating them into natural language text [12, 25–27] or visualizing them [5].

The purpose of this work is of a more (complexity) theoretic nature. We want to investigate how hard it is to find good proofs, where the quality of a proof is described by a measure m that assigns non-negative rational numbers to proofs. More precisely, as usual we investigate the complexity of the corresponding decision problem, i.e., the problem of deciding whether there is a proof $\mathcal{P}$ with $m(\mathcal{P}) \leq q$ for a given rational number q. In order to abstract from specific logics and proof calculi, we develop a general framework in which proofs are represented as labeled, directed hypergraphs, whose hyperedges correspond to single sound derivation steps. To separate the complexity of generating good proofs from the complexity of reasoning in the underlying logic, we introduce the notion of a *deriver*, which generates a so-called *derivation structure*. This structure consists of possible proof steps, from which all proofs of the given consequence can be constructed. Basically, such a derivation structure can be seen as consisting of all relevant instantiations of the rules of a calculus that can be used to derive the consequence. We restrict the attention to decidable logics and consider derivers that produce derivation structures of polynomial or exponential size. Examples of such derivers are consequence-based reasoners for the DLs $\mathcal{EL}$ [7, 21] and $\mathcal{ELI}$ [9, 18], respectively. In our complexity results, the derivation structure is assumed to be already computed by the deriver,[1] i.e., the complexity of this step is not assumed to be part of the complexity of computing good proofs. Our complexity results investigate the problem along the following orthogonal dimensions: we distinguish between (i) polynomial and exponential derivers; and (ii) whether the threshold value q is encoded in unary or binary. The obtained complexity upper bounds hold for all instances of a considered setting, whereas the lower bounds mean that there is an instance (usually based on $\mathcal{EL}$ or $\mathcal{ELI}$) for which this lower bound can be proved.

In our first work in this direction [2], we focused our attention on *size* as the measure of proof quality. We could show that the above decision problem is NP-complete even for polynomial derivers and unary coding of numbers. For exponential derivers, the complexity depends on the coding of numbers: NP-complete (NExpTime-complete) for unary (binary) coding. For the related measure *tree size* (which assumes that the proof hypergraphs are tree-shaped, i.e. cannot reuse already derived consequences), the complexity turned out to

---

[1] The highly efficient reasoner ELK [21] for (an extension of) $\mathcal{EL}$ actually produces a derivation structure, and thus is a deriver in our sense.

Table 1. Overview over existing and new complexity results for deciding the existence of good proofs, w.r.t. polynomial/exponential derivers and unary/binary encoding of the bound q (known results in gray).

Measure	polynomial unary	polynomial binary	exponential unary	exponential binary
Size	NP [2]	NP [2]	NExpTime [2]	NExpTime [2]
Monotone recursive Φ-measures	$\leq$ P	$\leq$ P [Th.12]	$\leq$ ExpTime	$\leq$ ExpTime [Th.12]
Tree size	P [2]	P	NP [2]	PSpace [Th.17,18]
Depth	P [Th.14]	P	PSpace [Th.16]	ExpTime [Th.14]
Logarithmic depth	P [Cor.15]	P	ExpTime [Cor.15]	ExpTime

be considerably lower, due to the fact that a Dijkstra-like greedy algorithm can be applied. In [3], we generalized the results by introducing a class of measures called Ψ-*measures*, which contains both size and tree size and for which the same complexity upper bounds as for size could be shown for polynomial derivers. We also lifted the better upper bounds for tree size (for polynomial derivers) to *local* Ψ-*measures*, a natural class of proof measures. In this paper, we extend this line of research by providing a more general notion of measures, *monotone recursive* Φ-*measures*, which now also allow to measure the *depth* of a proof. We think that depth is an important measure since it measures how much of the proof tree a (human or automated) proof checker needs to keep in memory at the same time. We analyze these measures not only for polynomial derivers, but this time also consider exponential derivers, thus giving insights on how our complexity results transfer to more expressive logics. In addition to upper bounds for the general class of monotone recursive Φ-measures, we show improved bounds for the specific measures considering depth and tree size, in the latter case improving results from [2]. Overall, we thus obtain a comprehensive picture of the complexity landscape for the problem of finding good proofs for DL and other entailments (see Table 1).

An extended version of this paper with detailed proofs can be found at [4].

2 Preliminaries

Most of our theoretical discussion applies to arbitrary *logics* $\mathcal{L} = (\mathcal{S}_\mathcal{L}, \models_\mathcal{L})$ that consist of a set $\mathcal{S}_\mathcal{L}$ of $\mathcal{L}$-*sentences* and a *consequence relation* $\models_\mathcal{L} \subseteq P(\mathcal{S}_\mathcal{L}) \times \mathcal{S}_\mathcal{L}$ between $\mathcal{L}$-*theories*, i.e. subsets of $\mathcal{L}$-sentences, and single $\mathcal{L}$-sentences. We assume that $\models_\mathcal{L}$ has a semantic definition, i.e. for some definition of "model", $\mathcal{T} \models_\mathcal{L} \eta$ holds iff every model of all elements in $\mathcal{T}$ is also a model of η. We also assume that the *size* $|\eta|$ of an $\mathcal{L}$-sentence η is defined in some way, e.g. by the number of symbols in η. Since $\mathcal{L}$ is usually fixed, we drop the prefix "$\mathcal{L}$-" from now on. For example, $\mathcal{L}$ could be *first-order logic*. However, we are mainly interested in proofs for DLs, which can be seen as decidable fragments of first-order logic [9]. In particular, we use specific DLs to show our hardness results.

$$R_0 \; \frac{}{C \sqsubseteq C} \qquad R_\top \; \frac{}{C \sqsubseteq \top} \qquad R_\sqsubseteq \; \frac{C \sqsubseteq D}{C \sqsubseteq E} : D \sqsubseteq E \in \mathcal{T} \qquad R_{\sqcap,1}^- \; \frac{C \sqsubseteq D \sqcap E}{C \sqsubseteq D}$$

$$R_{\sqcap,2}^- \; \frac{C \sqsubseteq D \sqcap E}{C \sqsubseteq E} \qquad R_\sqcap^+ \; \frac{C \sqsubseteq D \quad C \sqsubseteq E}{C \sqsubseteq D \sqcap E} \qquad R_\exists \; \frac{C \sqsubseteq \exists r.D \quad D \sqsubseteq E}{C \sqsubseteq \exists r.E}$$

Fig. 1. The inference rules for $\mathcal{EL}$ used in ELK [21].

The syntax of DLs is based on disjoint, countably infinite sets N_C and N_R of *concept names* $A, B, \ldots$ and *role names* $r, s, \ldots$, respectively. Sentences of the DL $\mathcal{EL}$, called *general concept inclusions (GCIs)*, are of the form $C \sqsubseteq D$, where C and D are $\mathcal{EL}$-concepts, which are built from concept names by applying the constructors $\top$ (*top*), $C \sqcap D$ (*conjunction*), and $\exists r.C$ (*existential restriction* for a role name r). The DL $\mathcal{ELI}$ extends $\mathcal{EL}$ by the role constructor r^- (*inverse role*). In DLs, finite theories are called *TBoxes* or *ontologies*.

The semantics of DLs is based on first-order interpretations; for details, see [9]. In Figure 1, we depict a simplified version of the inference rules for $\mathcal{EL}$ from [21]. For example, $\{A \sqsubseteq \exists r.B, \; B \sqsubseteq C, \; \exists r.C \sqsubseteq D\} \models A \sqsubseteq D$ is a valid inference in $\mathcal{EL}$. Deciding consequences in $\mathcal{EL}$ is P-complete [7], and in $\mathcal{ELI}$ it is EXPTIME-complete [8].

2.1 Proofs

We formalize proofs as (labeled, directed) *hypergraphs* (see Figures 2, 3), which are tuples (V, E, ℓ) consisting of a finite set V of *vertices*, a finite set E of *(hyper)edges* of the form (S, d) with $S \subseteq V$ and $d \in V$, and a *vertex labeling function* $\ell \colon V \to \mathcal{S}_\mathcal{L}$. Full definitions of such hypergraphs, as well as related notions such as *trees, unravelings, homomorphisms, cycles* can be found in the extended version [4]. For example, there is a homomorphism from Figure 3 to Figure 2, but not vice versa, and Figure 3 is the tree unraveling of Figure 2.

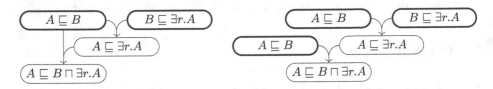

Fig. 2. An acyclic hypergraph/proof   **Fig. 3.** A tree hypergraph/proof

The following definition formalizes basic requirements for hyperedges to be considered valid inference steps from a given finite theory.

Definition 1 (Derivation Structure). *A derivation structure* $\mathcal{D} = (V, E, \ell)$ *over a finite theory* $\mathcal{T}$ *is a hypergraph that is*

– *grounded, i.e. every leaf* v *in* $\mathcal{D}$ *is labeled by* $\ell(v) \in \mathcal{T}$; *and*

— sound, *i.e. for every $(S,d) \in E$, the entailment $\{\ell(s) \mid s \in S\} \models \ell(d)$ holds.*

We define proofs as special derivation structures that derive a conclusion.

Definition 2 (Proof). *Given a conclusion η and a finite theory $\mathcal{T}$, a proof for $\mathcal{T} \models \eta$ is a derivation structure $\mathcal{P} = (V, E, \ell)$ over $\mathcal{T}$ such that*

- *$\mathcal{P}$ contains exactly one sink $v_\eta \in V$, which is labeled by η,*
- *$\mathcal{P}$ is acyclic, and*
- *every vertex has at most one incoming edge, i.e. there is no vertex $w \in V$ s.t. there are $(S_1, w), (S_2, w) \in E$ with $S_1 \neq S_2$.*

A tree proof is a proof that is a tree. A subproof S of a hypergraph H is a subgraph of H that is a proof s.t. the leaves of S are a subset of the leaves of H.

The hypergraphs in Figures 2 and 3 can be seen as proofs in the sense of Definition 2, where the sentences of the theory are marked with a thick border. Both proofs use the same inference steps, but have different numbers of vertices. They both prove $A \sqsubseteq B \sqcap \exists r.A$ from $\mathcal{T} = \{A \sqsubseteq B, \ B \sqsubseteq \exists r.A\}$. The second proof is a tree and the first one a hypergraph without label repetition.

Lemma 3. *Let $\mathcal{P} = (V, E, \ell)$ be a proof for $\mathcal{T} \models \eta$. Then*

1. *all paths in $\mathcal{P}$ are finite and all longest paths in $\mathcal{P}$ have v_η as the target; and*
2. *$\mathcal{T} \models \eta$.*

Given a proof $\mathcal{P} = (V, E, \ell)$ and a vertex $v \in V$, the *subproof of $\mathcal{P}$ with sink v* is the largest subgraph $\mathcal{P}_v = (V_v, E_v, \ell_v)$ of $\mathcal{P}$ where V_v contains all vertices in V that have a path to v in $\mathcal{P}$.

2.2 Derivers

In practice, proofs and derivation structures are constructed by a reasoning system, and in theoretical investigations, it is common to define proofs by means of a calculus. To abstract from these details, we use the concept of a *deriver* as in [2], which is a function that, given a theory $\mathcal{T}$ and a conclusion η, produces the corresponding derivation structure in which we can look for an optimal proof. However, in practice, it would be inefficient and unnecessary to compute the entire derivation structure beforehand when looking for an optimal proof. Instead, we allow to access elements in a derivation structure using an oracle, which we can ask whether given inferences are a part of the current derivation structure. Similar functionality exists for example for the DL reasoner ELK [19], and may correspond to checking whether the inference is an instance of a rule in the calculus. Since reasoners may not be complete for proving arbitrary sentences of $\mathcal{L}$, we restrict the conclusion η to a subset $C_\mathcal{L} \subseteq S_\mathcal{L}$ of supported consequences.

Definition 4 (Deriver). *A deriver $\mathfrak{D}$ is given by a set $C_\mathcal{L} \subseteq S_\mathcal{L}$ and a function that assigns derivation structures to pairs $(\mathcal{T}, \eta)$ of finite theories $\mathcal{T} \subseteq S_\mathcal{L}$ and sentences $\eta \in C_\mathcal{L}$, such that $\mathcal{T} \models \eta$ iff $\mathfrak{D}(\mathcal{T}, \eta)$ contains a proof for $\mathcal{T} \models \eta$. A*

$$\text{CR1} \ \frac{}{K \sqsubseteq A} \ \text{if } A \in K \text{ and } K \text{ appears in } \mathcal{T}'$$

$$\text{CR2} \ \frac{M \sqsubseteq A \text{ for all } A \in K, \ K \sqsubseteq C}{M \sqsubseteq C} \ \text{if } M \text{ appears in } \mathcal{T}'$$

$$\text{CR3} \ \frac{M \sqsubseteq \exists r.L \quad L \sqsubseteq \forall r^-.A}{M \sqsubseteq A} \qquad \text{CR4} \ \frac{L \sqsubseteq \exists r.M \quad L \sqsubseteq \forall r.A}{L \sqsubseteq \exists r.(M \sqcap A)}$$

Fig. 4. The inference rules for $\mathcal{ELI}$ [9]. Given a finite theory $\mathcal{T}$ in a certain normal form, the rules produce a saturated theory $\mathcal{T}'$. Here, K, L, M are conjunctions of concept names, A is a concept name, C is an $\mathcal{ELI}$ concept of the form A, $\exists r.M$, or $\forall r.A$, and r is a role name or the inverse of a role name. In this calculus conjunctions are implicitly viewed as sets, i.e. the order and multiplicity of conjuncts is ignored.

proof $\mathcal{P}$ for $\mathcal{T} \models \eta$ is called admissible *w.r.t. $\mathfrak{D}(\mathcal{T}, \eta)$ if there is a homomorphism $h \colon \mathcal{P} \to \mathfrak{D}(\mathcal{T}, \eta)$. We call $\mathfrak{D}$ a* polynomial deriver *if there exists a polynomial $p(x)$ such that the size of $\mathfrak{D}(\mathcal{T}, \eta)$ is bounded by $p(|\mathcal{T}| + |\eta|)$.* Exponential derivers *are defined similarly by the restriction $|\mathfrak{D}(\mathcal{T}, \eta)| \leq 2^{p(|\mathcal{T}|+|\eta|)}$.*

ELK is an example of a polynomial deriver, that is, for a given $\mathcal{EL}$ theory $\mathcal{T}$ and $\mathcal{EL}$ sentence η, ELK$(\mathcal{T}, \eta)$ contains all allowed instances of the rules shown in Figure 1. As an example for an exponential deriver we use ELI, which uses the rules from Figure 4 and is complete for $\mathcal{ELI}$ theories and conclusions of the form $A \sqsubseteq B$, $A, B \in \mathsf{N_C}$. The oracle access for a deriver $\mathfrak{D}$ works as follows. Let $\mathcal{D} = (V, E, \ell) := \mathfrak{D}(\mathcal{T}, \eta)$ and $V = \{v_1, \ldots, v_m\}$. $\mathcal{D}$ is accessed using the following two functions, where $i, i_1, \ldots, i_l$ are indices of vertices and α is a sentence:

$$[\mathcal{D}](i_1, \ldots, i_l, i) := \begin{cases} \mathsf{true} & \text{if } (\{v_{i_1}, \ldots, v_{i_l}\}, v_i) \in E, \\ \mathsf{false} & \text{otherwise;} \end{cases}$$

$$[\mathcal{D}](i, \alpha) := \begin{cases} \mathsf{true} & \text{if } \ell(v_i) = \alpha, \\ \mathsf{false} & \text{otherwise.} \end{cases}$$

In this paper, we focus on polynomial and exponential derivers, for which we further make the following technical assumptions: 1) $\mathfrak{D}(\mathcal{T}, \eta)$ does not contain two vertices with the same label; 2) the number of premises in an inference is polynomially bounded by $|\mathcal{T}|$ and $|\eta|$; and 3) the size of each label is polynomially bounded by $|\mathcal{T}|$ and $|\eta|$. While 1) is without loss of generality, 2) and 3) are not. If a deriver does not satisfy 2), we may be able to fix this by splitting inference steps. Assumption 3) would not work for derivers with higher complexity, but is required in our setting to avoid trivial complexity results for exponential derivers. We furthermore assume that for polynomial and exponential derivers, the polynomial p from Definition 4 bounding the size of derivation structures is known.

3   Measuring Proofs

To formally study quality measures for proofs, we developed the following definition, which will be instantiated with concrete measures later. Our goal is to find proofs that minimize these measures, i.e. lower numbers are better.

Definition 5 (Φ-Measure). *A (quality) measure is a function* $\mathfrak{m} \colon \mathrm{P}_{\mathcal{L}} \to \mathbb{Q}_{\geq 0}$, *where* $\mathrm{P}_{\mathcal{L}}$ *is the set of all proofs over* $\mathcal{L}$ *and* $\mathbb{Q}_{\geq 0}$ *is the set of non-negative rational numbers. We call* $\mathfrak{m}$ *a* Φ-measure *if, for every* $\mathcal{P} \in \mathrm{P}_{\mathcal{L}}$, *the following hold.*

[P] $\mathfrak{m}(\mathcal{P})$ *is computable in polynomial time in the size of* $\mathcal{P}$.
[HI] *Let* $h \colon \mathcal{P} \to H$ *be any homomorphism, and* $\mathcal{P}'$ *be any subproof of the homomorphic image* $h(\mathcal{P})$ *that is minimal (w.r.t.* $\mathfrak{m}$) *among all such subproofs having the same sink. Then* $\mathfrak{m}(\mathcal{P}') \leq \mathfrak{m}(\mathcal{P})$.

Intuitively, a Φ-measure $\mathfrak{m}$ does not increase when the proof gets smaller, either when parts of the proof are removed (to obtain a subproof) or when parts are merged (in a homomorphic image). For example, $\mathfrak{m}_{\mathsf{size}}((V, E, \ell)) := |V|$ is a Φ-measure, called the *size* of a proof, and we have already investigated the complexity of the following deicision problem for $\mathfrak{m}_{\mathsf{size}}$ in [2].

Definition 6 (Optimal Proof). *Let* $\mathfrak{D}$ *be a deriver and* $\mathfrak{m}$ *be a measure. Given a finite theory* $\mathcal{T}$ *and a sentence* $\eta \in C_{\mathcal{L}}$ *s.t.* $\mathcal{T} \models \eta$, *an admissible proof* $\mathcal{P}$ *w.r.t.* $\mathfrak{D}(\mathcal{T}, \eta)$ *is called* optimal *w.r.t.* $\mathfrak{m}$ *if* $\mathfrak{m}(\mathcal{P})$ *is minimal among all such proofs. The associated decision problem, denoted* $\mathsf{OP}(\mathfrak{D}, \mathfrak{m})$, *is to decide, given* $\mathcal{T}$ *and* η *as above and* $q \in \mathbb{Q}_{\geq 0}$, *whether there is an admissible proof* $\mathcal{P}$ *w.r.t.* $\mathfrak{D}(\mathcal{T}, \eta)$ *with* $\mathfrak{m}(\mathcal{P}) \leq q$.

For our complexity analysis, we distinguish the encoding of q with a subscript (unary/binary), e.g. $\mathsf{OP}_{\mathsf{unary}}(\mathfrak{D}, \mathfrak{m})$.

We first show that if $\mathcal{P}$ is optimal w.r.t. a Φ-measure $\mathfrak{m}$ and $\mathfrak{D}(\mathcal{T}, \eta)$, then the homomorphic image of $\mathcal{P}$ in $\mathfrak{D}(\mathcal{T}, \eta)$ is also a proof. Thus, to decide $\mathsf{OP}(\mathfrak{D}, \mathfrak{m})$ we can restrict our search to proofs that are subgraphs of $\mathfrak{D}(\mathcal{T}, \eta)$.

Lemma 7. *For any deriver* $\mathfrak{D}$ *and* Φ-measure $\mathfrak{m}$, *if there is an admissible proof* $\mathcal{P}$ *w.r.t.* $\mathfrak{D}(\mathcal{T}, \eta)$ *with* $\mathfrak{m}(\mathcal{P}) \leq q$ *for some* $q \in \mathbb{Q}_{\geq 0}$, *then there exists a subproof* $\mathcal{Q}$ *of* $\mathfrak{D}(\mathcal{T}, \eta)$ *for* $\mathcal{T} \models \eta$ *with* $\mathfrak{m}(\mathcal{Q}) \leq q$.

In particular, this shows that an optimal proof always exists.

Corollary 8. *For any deriver* $\mathfrak{D}$ *and* Φ-measure $\mathfrak{m}$, *if* $\mathcal{T} \models \eta$, *then there is an optimal proof for* $\mathcal{T} \models \eta$ *w.r.t.* $\mathfrak{D}$ *and* $\mathfrak{m}$.

Proof. By Definition 4, the derivation structure $\mathfrak{D}(\mathcal{T}, \eta)$ contains at least one proof for $\mathcal{T} \models \eta$. Since $\mathfrak{D}(\mathcal{T}, \eta)$ is finite, there are finitely many proofs for $\mathcal{T} \models \eta$ contained in $\mathfrak{D}(\mathcal{T}, \eta)$. The finite set of all $\mathfrak{m}$-weights of these proofs always has a minimum. Finally, if there were an admissible proof weighing less than this minimum, it would contradict Lemma 7. □

3.1   Monotone Recursive Measures

Since the complexity of $\mathsf{OP}(\mathfrak{D}, \mathfrak{m})$ for Φ-measures in general is quite high [2], in this paper we focus on a subclass of measures that can be evaluated recursively.

Definition 9. *A Φ-measure $\mathfrak{m}$ is recursive if there exist*

- *a leaf function $\mathsf{leaf}_{\mathfrak{m}} \colon \mathcal{S}_{\mathcal{L}} \to \mathbb{Q}_{\geq 0}$ and*
- *a partial edge function $\mathsf{edge}_{\mathfrak{m}}$, which maps (i) the labels $(\mathcal{S}, \alpha)$ of a hyperedge and (ii) a finite multiset $\mathcal{Q}$ of already computed intermediate weights in $\mathbb{Q}_{\geq 0}$ to a combined weight $\mathsf{edge}_{\mathfrak{m}}((\mathcal{S}, \alpha), \mathcal{Q})$*

such that, for any proof $\mathcal{P} = (V, E, \ell)$ with sink v, we have

$$\mathfrak{m}(\mathcal{P}) = \begin{cases} \mathsf{leaf}_{\mathfrak{m}}(\ell(v)) & \text{if } V = \{v\}, \\ \mathsf{edge}_{\mathfrak{m}}(\ell(S, v), \{\mathfrak{m}(\mathcal{P}_w) \mid w \in S\}) & \text{if } (S, v) \in E. \end{cases}$$

Such a measure is monotone *if, for any multiset $\mathcal{Q}$, whenever $q \in \mathcal{Q}$ and $\mathcal{Q}' = (\mathcal{Q} \setminus \{q\}) \cup \{q'\}$ with $q' \leq q$ and both $\mathsf{edge}_{\mathfrak{m}}((\mathcal{S}, \alpha), \mathcal{Q}')$ and $\mathsf{edge}_{\mathfrak{m}}((\mathcal{S}, \alpha), \mathcal{Q})$ are defined, then $\mathsf{edge}_{\mathfrak{m}}((\mathcal{S}, \alpha), \mathcal{Q}') \leq \mathsf{edge}_{\mathfrak{m}}((\mathcal{S}, \alpha), \mathcal{Q})$.*

Intuitively, a recursive measure $\mathfrak{m}$ can be computed in a bottom-up fashion starting with the weights of the leaves given by $\mathsf{leaf}_{\mathfrak{m}}$. The function $\mathsf{edge}_{\mathfrak{m}}$ is used to recursively combine the weights of the direct subproofs into a weight for the full proof. This function is well-defined since in a proof every vertex has at most one incoming edge. We require $\mathsf{edge}_{\mathfrak{m}}$ to be defined only for inputs $((\mathcal{S}, \alpha), \mathcal{Q})$ that actually correspond to a valid proof in $\mathcal{L}$, i.e. where $\mathcal{S} \models_{\mathcal{L}} \alpha$ and $\mathcal{Q}$ consists of the weights of some proofs for the sentences in $\mathcal{S}$. For example, if $\mathfrak{m}$ always yields natural numbers, we obviously do not need $\mathsf{edge}_{\mathfrak{m}}$ to be defined for multisets containing fractional numbers.

In this paper, we are particularly interested in the following monotone recursive Φ-measures.

- The *depth* $\mathfrak{m}_{\mathsf{depth}}$ of a proof is defined by

$$\mathsf{leaf}_{\mathfrak{m}_{\mathsf{depth}}}(\alpha) := 0 \text{ and } \mathsf{edge}_{\mathfrak{m}_{\mathsf{depth}}}((\mathcal{S}, \alpha), \mathcal{Q}) := 1 + \max \mathcal{Q}.$$

- The *tree size* $\mathfrak{m}_{\mathsf{tree}}$ is given by

$$\mathsf{leaf}_{\mathfrak{m}_{\mathsf{tree}}}(\alpha) := 1 \text{ and } \mathsf{edge}_{\mathfrak{m}_{\mathsf{tree}}}((\mathcal{S}, \alpha), \mathcal{Q}) := 1 + \sum \mathcal{Q}.$$

What distinguishes *tree size* from *size* is that vertices are counted multiple times if they are used in several subproofs. The name *tree size* is inspired by the fact that it can be interpreted as the *size* of the tree unraveling of a given proof (cf. Figures 2 and 3). In fact, we show in the extended version [4] that all recursive Φ-measures are invariant under unraveling. This indicates that *tree size*, *depth* and other monotone recursive Φ-measures are especially well-suited for cases where proofs are presented to users in the form of trees. This is for example the case for the proof plugin for Protégé [20].

Lemma 10. Depth *and* tree size *are monotone recursive Φ-measures.*

Algorithm 1: A Dijkstra-like algorithm

Input: A derivation structure $\mathfrak{D}(\mathcal{T}, \eta) = (V, E, \ell)$, a monotone recursive
      Φ-measure $\mathfrak{m}$
Output: An optimal proof of $\mathcal{T} \models \eta$ w.r.t. $\mathfrak{D}(\mathcal{T}, \eta)$ and $\mathfrak{m}$

1   $Q := \emptyset$
2   **foreach** $e \in E$ **do** $k(e) := 0$
3   **foreach** $v \in V$ **do**
4   **if** $\ell(v) \in \mathcal{T}$ **then**
5       $|$ $\mathcal{P}(v) := (\{v\}, \emptyset, \ell|_{\{v\}}); \ Q := Q \cup \{v\}$ `// ℓ(v) is in the theory`
6   **else if** $(\emptyset, v) \in E$ **then**
7       $|$ $\mathcal{P}(v) := (\{v\}, \{(\emptyset, v)\}, \ell|_{\{v\}}); \ Q := Q \cup \{v\}$ `// ℓ(v) is a tautology`
8   **else**
9       $|$ $\mathcal{P}(v) := \text{undefined}$
10 **while** $Q \neq \emptyset$ **do**
11   choose $v \in Q$ with minimal $\mathfrak{m}(\mathcal{P}(v))$ `// P(v) is optimal for ℓ(v)`
12     $Q := Q \setminus \{v\}$
13   **foreach** $e = (S, d) \in E$ with $v \in S$ **do**
14       $k(e) := k(e) + 1$
15   **if** $k(e) = |S|$ **then**   `// all source vertices have been reached`
16         $\mathcal{P} := (S \cup \{d\}, e, \ell_{S \cup \{d\}}) \cup \bigcup_{s \in S} \mathcal{P}(s)$ `// construct new proof`
17   **if** $\mathcal{P}$ is acyclic **then**
18   **if** $\mathcal{P}(d)$ is undefined or $\mathfrak{m}(\mathcal{P}(d)) > \mathfrak{m}(\mathcal{P})$ **then**
19            $|$ $\mathcal{P}(d) := \mathcal{P}; \ Q := Q \cup \{d\}$ `// P is better for ℓ(d)`
20 **return** $\mathcal{P}(v_\eta)$, where $\ell(v_\eta) = \eta$

---

4   Complexity Results

We investigate the decision problem OP for monotone recursive Φ-measures. We first show upper bounds for the general case, and then consider measures for *depth* and *tree size*, for which we obtain even lower bounds. An artificial modification of the *depth* measure gives a lower bound matching the general upper bound even if unary encoding is used for the threshold q.

4.1   The General Case

Algorithm 1 describes a Dijkstra-like approach that is inspired by the algorithm in [13] for finding minimal hyperpaths w.r.t. so-called *additive weighting functions*, which represent a subclass of monotone recursive Φ-measures. The algorithm progressively discovers proofs $\mathcal{P}(v)$ for $\ell(v)$ that are contained in $\mathfrak{D}(\mathcal{T}, \eta)$. If it reaches a new vertex v in this process, this vertex is added to the set Q. In each step, a vertex with minimal weight $\mathfrak{m}(\mathcal{P}(v))$ is chosen and removed from Q. For each hyperedge $e = (S, d) \in E$, a counter $k(e)$ is maintained that is increased whenever a vertex $v \in S$ is chosen. Once this counter reaches $|S|$, we know that all source vertices of e have been processed. The algorithm then constructs a new proof $\mathcal{P}$ for $\ell(d)$ by joining the proofs for the source vertices using the current hyperedge e. This proof $\mathcal{P}$ is then compared to the best previously known proof $\mathcal{P}(d)$ for $\ell(d)$ and $\mathcal{P}(d)$ is updated accordingly. For Line 20, recall that we assumed $\mathfrak{D}(\mathcal{T}, \eta)$ to contain no two vertices with the same label, and hence it contains a unique vertex v_η with label η.

Lemma 11. *For any monotone recursive Φ-measure $\mathfrak{m}$ and deriver $\mathfrak{D}$, Algorithm 1 computes an optimal proof in time polynomial in the size of $\mathfrak{D}(\mathcal{T}, \eta)$.*

Since we can actually compute an optimal proof in polynomial time in the size of the whole derivation structure, it is irrelevant how the upper bound q in the decision problem OP is encoded, and hence the following results follow.

Theorem 12. *For any monotone recursive Φ-measure $\mathfrak{m}$ and polynomial deriver $\mathfrak{D}$, $\mathsf{OP}_{\mathsf{binary}}(\mathfrak{D}, \mathfrak{m})$ is in P. It is in EXPTIME for all exponential derivers $\mathfrak{D}$.*

4.2   Proof Depth

We now consider the measure $\mathfrak{m}_{\mathsf{depth}}$ in more detail. We can show lower bounds of P and EXPTIME for polynomial and exponential derivers, respectively, although the latter only holds for upper bounds q encoded in binary.

Since our definition of $\mathsf{OP}(\mathfrak{D}, \mathfrak{m})$ requires that the input entailment $\mathcal{T} \models \eta$ already holds, we cannot use a straightforward reduction from the entailment problem in $\mathcal{EL}$ or $\mathcal{ELI}$, however. Instead, we show that ordinary proofs $\mathcal{P}$ for $\mathcal{T} \models \eta$ satisfy $\mathfrak{m}(\mathcal{P}) \leq q$ for some q, and then extend the TBox to $\mathcal{T}'$ in order to create an artificial proof $\mathcal{P}'$ with $\mathfrak{m}(\mathcal{P}') > q$. In this way, we ensure that $\mathcal{T}' \models \eta$ holds and can use q to distinguish the artificial from the original proofs.

For $\mathcal{ELI}$, we can use an observation from [9, Example 6.29] for this purpose.

Proposition 13 ([9]).   *For every $q \in \mathbb{Q}_{\geq 0}$ and $\mathcal{ELI}$ sentence of the form $A \sqsubseteq B$, where $A, B \in N_C$, one can construct in time polynomial in q an $\mathcal{ELI}$ theory $\mathcal{T}$ such $\mathcal{T} \models A \sqsubseteq B$, and every proof for $\mathcal{T} \models A \sqsubseteq B$ in ELI is of depth larger than 2^q.*

We can now reduce the entailment problems for $\mathcal{EL}$ and $\mathcal{ELI}$ to obtain the claimed lower bounds.

Theorem 14. *The problems $\mathsf{OP}_{\mathsf{unary}}(\mathsf{ELK}, \mathfrak{m}_{\mathsf{depth}})$ and $\mathsf{OP}_{\mathsf{binary}}(\mathsf{ELI}, \mathfrak{m}_{\mathsf{depth}})$ are P-hard and EXPTIME-hard, respectively.*

Proof. For the P-hardness, we provide a LOGSPACE-reduction from the entailment problem of a GCI $A \sqsubseteq B$ with two concept names A, B from an $\mathcal{EL}$-theory $\mathcal{T}$, which is P-hard [9]. To reduce this problem to $\mathsf{OP}_{\mathsf{unary}}(\mathsf{ELK}, \mathfrak{m}_{\mathsf{tree}})$, we need to find a theory $\mathcal{T}'$ and a number q such that $\mathcal{T}' \models A \sqsubseteq B$ holds, and moreover $\mathcal{T} \models A \sqsubseteq B$ holds iff $\mathsf{ELK}(\mathcal{T}', A \sqsubseteq B)$ contains a proof of $\mathcal{T}' \models A \sqsubseteq B$ of depth $\leq q$ (cf. Lemma 7).

First, observe that, since proofs must be acyclic, the depth of any proof of $A \sqsubseteq B$ from $\mathcal{T}$ is bounded by $q := |\mathsf{ELK}(\mathcal{T}, A \sqsubseteq B)|$, whose size in unary encoding is polynomial in the size of $\mathcal{T}$. We now construct

$$\mathcal{T}' := \mathcal{T} \cup \{A \sqsubseteq A_1, \ A_1 \sqsubseteq A_2, \ldots, A_{q+2} \sqsubseteq B\},$$

where $A_1, \ldots, A_q$ are concept names not occurring in $\mathcal{T}$. Clearly, we have $\mathcal{T}' \models A \sqsubseteq B$. Furthermore, the existence of an admissible proof for $\mathcal{T}' \models A \sqsubseteq B$ of depth at most q is equivalent to $\mathcal{T} \models A \sqsubseteq B$, since any proof that uses the new concept names must take $q + 1$ consecutive steps using rule $\mathsf{R}_{\sqsubseteq}$, i.e. must be of depth $q + 1$. Moreover, we can compute q (in binary representation) and output it in unary representation using a logarithmically space-bounded Turing machine, and similarly for $\mathcal{T}'$. Hence, the above construction constitutes the desired LOGSPACE-reduction.

For the remaining result, we can use similar arguments about the exponential deriver ELI, where entailment is EXPTIME-hard [9]:

- the minimal depth of a proof in an exponential derivation structure is at most exponential, and this exponential bound q can be computed in polynomial time using binary encoding;
- by Proposition 13, there is an $\mathcal{ELI}$ theory $\mathcal{T}$ of size polynomial in the size of the binary encoding of q such that $\mathcal{T} \models A \sqsubseteq B$ and any proof for $\mathcal{T} \models A \sqsubseteq B$ must have at least depth $q + 1$. $\qquad\square$

To demonstrate that the generic upper bounds from Theorem 12 are tight even for unary encoding, we quickly consider the artificial measure $\mathsf{m}_{\log(\text{depth})}$ (*logarithmic depth*), which simply computes the (binary) logarithm of the depth of a given proof. This is also a monotone recursive Φ-measure, since the logarithmic depth contains exactly the same information as the depth itself. It is easy to obtain the following lower bounds from the previous results about $\mathsf{m}_{\text{depth}}$.

Corollary 15. $\mathsf{OP}_{\text{unary}}(\text{ELK}, \mathsf{m}_{\log(\text{depth})})$ *is* P-*hard and* $\mathsf{OP}_{\text{unary}}(\text{ELI}, \mathsf{m}_{\log(\text{depth})})$ *is* EXPTIME-*hard.*

Proof. For any deriver $\mathfrak{D}$, $\mathsf{OP}_{\text{binary}}(\mathfrak{D}, \mathsf{m}_{\text{depth}})$ can be LOGSPACE-reduced to $\mathsf{OP}_{\text{unary}}(\mathfrak{D}, \mathsf{m}_{\log(\text{depth})})$, because in order to find a proof of depth at most q (with q given in binary), one can equivalently look for a proof whose logarithmic depth is bounded by the value $\log q$. The unary encoding of $\log q$ has the same size as the binary encoding of q and can be computed in LOGSPACE by flipping all bits of the binary encoding of q to 1. $\qquad\square$

We now return to $\mathsf{m}_{\text{depth}}$ and cover the remaining case of exponential derivers and unary encoding of the upper bound q.

Theorem 16. $\mathsf{OP}_{\text{unary}}(\mathfrak{D}, \mathsf{m}_{\text{depth}})$ *is in* PSPACE *for any exponential deriver* $\mathfrak{D}$. *It is* PSPACE-*hard for the exponential deriver* $\mathfrak{D} = \text{ELI}$.

Proof. For the upper bound, we employ a depth-first guessing strategy: we guess a proof of depth at most q, where at each time point we only keep one branch of the proof in memory. As the length of this branch is bounded by q, and due to our assumptions on derivers, this procedure only requires polynomial space.

For the lower bound, we provide a reduction from the PSPACE-complete QBF problem (satisfiability of quantified Boolean formulas). Let $Q_1 x_1 Q_2 x_2 \ldots Q_m x_m.\phi$ be a quantified Boolean formula, where for $i \in \{1, \ldots, m\}$, $Q_i \in \{\exists, \forall\}$, and ϕ is a formula over $\{x_1, \ldots, x_m\}$. We assume ϕ to be in negation normal form, that is, negation only occurs directly in front of a variable. We construct an $\mathcal{ELI}$ theory $\mathcal{T}$ and a number q, both of size polynomial in the size of the formula, such that $\mathcal{T} \models A \sqsubseteq B$ holds (cf. Definition 6) and $\mathcal{T}$ has a proof for $A \sqsubseteq B$ of depth q iff the QBF formula is valid. We use two roles r_1, r_2 to deal with the variable valuations, concept names $A_0, \ldots, A_m$ to count the quantifier nesting, and a concept name A_ψ for every sub-formula ψ of ϕ. In addition, we use the concept names A and B occurring in the conclusion, and two concept names B_1 and B_2.

The concept name A initializes the formula at quantifier nesting level 0:

$$A \sqsubseteq A_0$$

For every $i \in \{1, \ldots, m\}$, $\mathcal{T}$ contains the following sentence to select a truth valuation for x_i, increasing the nesting depth in each step.

$$A_{i-1} \sqsubseteq \exists r_1.(A_i \sqcap A_{x_i}) \tag{1}$$

$$A_{i-1} \sqsubseteq \exists r_2.(A_i \sqcap A_{\neg x_i}). \tag{2}$$

To ensure truth valuations are kept along the role-successors, we use the following sentences for every $l \in \{x_i, \neg x_i \mid 1 \le i \le m\}$:

$$A_l \sqsubseteq \forall r_1.A_l \qquad A_l \sqsubseteq \forall r_2.A_l \tag{3}$$

The following GCIs are now used to evaluate ϕ. For every conjunction $\psi = \psi_1 \wedge \psi_2$ occurring in ϕ, we use:

$$A_{\psi_1} \sqcap A_{\psi_2} \sqsubseteq A_\psi, \tag{4}$$

and for every disjunction $\psi = \psi_1 \vee \psi_2$, we use:

$$A_{\psi_1} \sqsubseteq A_\psi \qquad A_{\psi_2} \sqsubseteq A_\psi \tag{5}$$

Finally, the following GCIs are used to propagate the result of the evaluation back towards the start.

$$A_\phi \sqsubseteq B \tag{6}$$

$$A_i \sqcap B \sqsubseteq \forall r_1^-.B \qquad A_i \sqcap B \sqsubseteq \forall r_2^-.B \qquad\qquad\qquad \text{if } Q_i = \exists \tag{7}$$

$$A_i \sqcap B \sqsubseteq \forall r_1^-.B_1 \qquad A_i \sqcap B \sqsubseteq \forall r_2^-.B_2 \qquad B_1 \sqcap B_2 \sqsubseteq B \qquad \text{if } Q_i = \forall \tag{8}$$

One can now show that there exists a proof for $A \sqsubseteq B$ from $\mathcal{T}$ of depth at most q iff the QBF formula is valid, where q is polynomial and determined by the size and structure of ϕ. Finally, we can extend $\mathcal{T}$ with the sentences from Proposition 13 to ensure that $\mathcal{T} \models A \sqsubseteq B$ holds while retaining this equivalence.   □

4.3   The Tree Size Measure

The tree size measure was discussed already in [2], where tight bounds were provided for polynomial derivers and exponential derivers with unary encoding. For the case of exponential derivers with binary encoding, only an EXPTIME upper bound was provided, and the precise complexity left open. We improve this result by showing that $OP_{\text{binary}}(\mathfrak{D}, \mathfrak{m}_{\text{tree}})$ can indeed be decided in PSPACE.

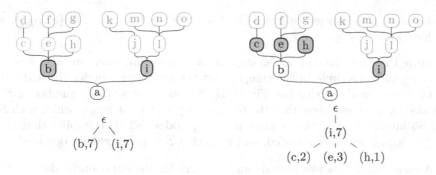

Fig. 5. Illustration of the argument used for Theorem 17. On the top, the partially guessed proof tree for two consecutive steps of the algorithm is shown, where the dark nodes are what is currently kept in memory. On the bottom, we see how the corresponding tuples are organized into a tree satisfying Conditions **S1–S6**.

Theorem 17. *For any exponential deriver* $\mathfrak{D}$, $\mathsf{OP}_{\mathsf{binary}}(\mathfrak{D}, \mathsf{m}_{\mathsf{tree}})$ *is in* PSPACE.

Proof (sketch). We describe a non-deterministic procedure for $\mathsf{OP}_{\mathsf{binary}}(\mathfrak{D}, \mathsf{m}_{\mathsf{tree}})$, in polynomial space. Let $\mathcal{T}$ be a theory, η the goal sentence, and q a rational number in binary encoding. By Lemma 7, it suffices to find a proof $\mathcal{P}$ for $\mathcal{T} \models \eta$ in $\mathfrak{D}(\mathcal{T}, \eta)$ with $\mathsf{m}_{\mathsf{tree}}(\mathcal{P}) \leq q$. The procedure guesses such a proof starting from the conclusion, while keeping in memory a set S of tuples (η', q'), where η' is a sentence and $q' \leq q$ a rational number. Intuitively, such a tuple states: "We still need to guess a proof for η' of tree size at most q'."

1. Initialize $S := \{(\eta, q)\}$.
2. While $S \neq \emptyset$,
    (a) select from S a tuple (η', q') such that for all tuples $(\eta'', q'') \in S$ it holds that $q'' \geq q'$;
    (b) guess a hyperedge $(\{v_1, \ldots, v_m\}, v')$ in $\mathfrak{D}(\mathcal{T}, \eta)$ (using the oracle access described in Section 2.2) and m numbers $q_1, \ldots, q_m$, such that $\ell(v') = \eta'$ and $q_1 + \ldots + q_m + 1 \leq q'$; and
    (c) replace (η', q') in S by the tuples $(\ell(v_1), q_1), \ldots, (\ell(v_m), q_m)$.

There is a proof for $\mathcal{T} \models \eta$ of tree size at most q iff every step in the algorithm is successful. To show that it only requires polynomial space, we show that during the computation, the number of elements in S is always polynomially bounded. For this, we show that the elements in S can always be organized into a tree with the following properties:

S1 the root is labeled with ϵ,
S2 every other node is labeled with a distinct element from S,
S3 every node that is not the root or a leaf has at least 2 children,
S4 every node has at most p children, where p is the maximal number of premises in any inference in $\mathfrak{D}(\mathcal{T}, \eta)$, which we assumed to be polynomial in the input,
S5 every node (η', q') has at most 1 child (η'', q'') that is not a leaf and for this child it holds that $q'' < \frac{q'}{2}$,

S6 for every node labeled (η', q') with children labeled $(\eta_1, q_1), \ldots, (\eta_m, q_m)$, we have $q_1 + \ldots + q_m < q'$.

We prove this by induction on the steps of the algorithm, where in each step, we either replace one tuple in the tree, or put the new tuples under the leaf with the currently smallest value (see Fig.5). By **S3** and because every number in S is bounded by q, we can show that the tree has depth at most $\log_2 q$, which with **S4** and **S5** implies that it has at most $p \cdot \log_2 q$ nodes. **S2** then implies that that $|S| \leq p \cdot \log_2 q$ is always satisfied, and thus that S is polynomially bounded. $\quad\square$

A corresponding lower bound can be found for the exponential deriver ELI by a reduction of the word problem for deterministic Turing machines with polynomial space bound.

Theorem 18. *For the exponential deriver* ELI, $\mathrm{OP}_{\mathsf{binary}}(\mathrm{ELI}, \mathsf{m}_{\mathsf{tree}})$ *is* PSPACE-*hard.*

Proof (sketch). Let $T = (Q, \Gamma, \flat, \Sigma, \delta, q_0, F)$ be a deterministic Turing machine, where Q is the set of states, Γ the tape alphabet, $\flat \in \Gamma$ the blank symbol, $\Sigma \subseteq \Gamma$ the input alphabet, $\delta : Q \times \Gamma \not\rightarrow Q \times \Gamma \times \{-1, 0, +1\}$ the partial transition function, q_0 the initial state, and $F \subseteq Q$ the accepting states. We assume that T is polynomially space bounded, that is, there is a polynomial p such that on input words $w \in \Sigma^*$, T only accesses the first $p(|w|)$ cells of the tape. For a word w, we denote by $w[i]$ its ith letter. For some fixed word w, we construct a theory $\mathcal{T}$ using the following names, where $k = p(|w|)$:

- **Start** marks the inital and **Accept** an accepting configuration;
- to denote that we are in state $q \in Q$, we use a concept name S_q;
- for every $a \in \Gamma$ and $i \in \{0, \ldots, k\}$, we use a concept name A_i^a denoting that the letter a is on tape position i;
- for every $i \in \{0, \ldots, k\}$, we use the concept name P_i^+ to denote that the head is currently on position i, and P_i^- to denote that it is not;
- the role r is used to express the transitions between the configurations.

For convenience, we present the theory not in the required normal form, but aggregate conjunctions on the right. The following sentence describes the initial configuration.

$$\mathsf{Start} \sqsubseteq S_{q_0} \sqcap \prod_{i=0}^{|w|-1} A_i^{w[i]} \sqcap \prod_{i=|w|}^{k} A_i^{\flat} \sqcap P_0^+ \sqcap \prod_{i=1}^{k} P_i^- \tag{9}$$

The transition from one configuration to the next is encoded with the following sentences for every $i \in \{0, \ldots, k\}$ and every $(q, a) \in Q \times \Gamma$ with $\delta(q, a) = (q', b, d)$:

$$S_q \sqcap A_i^a \sqcap P_i^+ \sqsubseteq \exists r.S_{q'} \sqcap \forall r.A_i^b \sqcap \forall r.P_{i+d}^+ \sqcap \prod_{j \in \{0, \ldots, k\} \setminus \{i+d\}} \forall r.P_j^- \tag{10}$$

$$A_i^a \sqcap P_i^- \sqsubseteq \forall r.A_i^a \tag{11}$$

Finally, we use the following sentences to detect accepting configurations and propagate the information of acceptance back to the initial configuration

$$S_f \sqsubseteq \mathsf{Accept} \text{ for all } f \in F, \tag{12}$$

$$\mathsf{Accept} \sqsubseteq \forall r^-.\mathsf{Accept} \tag{13}$$

One can find a number q exponential in k and the size of T s.t. that there is a proof for $\mathcal{T} \models \mathsf{Start} \sqsubseteq \mathsf{Accept}$ with tree size at most q iff T accepts w. Using Proposition 13, we can extend $\mathcal{T}$ to a theory $\mathcal{T}'$ s.t. $\mathcal{T}' \models \mathsf{Start} \sqsubseteq \mathsf{Accept}$, while a proof of tree size q exists iff T accepts w (observe that $\mathsf{m}_{\mathsf{tree}}(\mathcal{P}) \geq \mathsf{m}_{\mathsf{depth}}(\mathcal{P})$ holds for all proofs $\mathcal{P}$). □

5   Conclusion

We have investigated the complexity of finding optimal proofs w.r.t. quality measures that satisfy the property of being *monotone recursive*. Two important examples of this class of measures, *depth* and *tree size*, have been considered in detail in combination with exponential and polynomial derivers. The obtained results are promising: given a deriver, the search for an optimal proof for an entailment can be easier than producing all of the proofs by this deriver. The algorithms used to show the upper bounds can serve as building blocks for finding an optimal proof w.r.t. to a monotone recursive measure automatically.

We conjecture that weighted versions of *tree size* and *depth*, where sentences or inference steps can have associated rational weights, are also monotone recursive, and the generic upper bounds established in this paper can be straightforwardly applied to them. However, a more thorough study is required here, since the complexity of the decision problem depends on the exact way in which the weights are employed. This step towards weighted measures is motivated by user studies [1, 15, 24], demonstrating that different types of sentences and logical inferences can be more or less difficult to understand.

Acknowledgements This work was supported by the DFG in grant 389792660 as part of TRR 248 (https://perspicuous-computing.science), and QuantLA, GRK 1763 (https://lat.inf.tu-dresden.de/quantla).

References

1. Alharbi, E., Howse, J., Stapleton, G., Hamie, A., Touloumis, A.: The efficacy of OWL and DL on user understanding of axioms and their entailments. In: d'Amato, C., Fernández, M., Tamma, V.A.M., Lécué, F., Cudré-Mauroux, P., Sequeda, J.F., Lange, C., Heflin, J. (eds.) ISWC 2017 - 16th International Semantic Web Conference, Proceedings. Lecture Notes in Computer Science, vol. 10587, pp. 20–36. Springer (2017). https://doi.org/10.1007/978-3-319-68288-4_2
2. Alrabbaa, C., Baader, F., Borgwardt, S., Koopmann, P., Kovtunova, A.: Finding small proofs for description logic entailments: Theory and practice. In: Albert, E.,

Kovacs, L. (eds.) LPAR-23: 23rd International Conference on Logic for Programming, Artificial Intelligence and Reasoning. EPiC Series in Computing, vol. 73, pp. 32–67. EasyChair (2020). https://doi.org/10.29007/nhpp

3. Alrabbaa, C., Baader, F., Borgwardt, S., Koopmann, P., Kovtunova, A.: On the complexity of finding good proofs for description logic entailments. In: Borgwardt, S., Meyer, T. (eds.) Proceedings of the 33rd International Workshop on Description Logics (DL 2020). CEUR Workshop Proceedings, vol. 2663. CEUR-WS.org (2020), http://ceur-ws.org/Vol-2663/paper-1.pdf

4. Alrabbaa, C., Baader, F., Borgwardt, S., Koopmann, P., Kovtunova, A.: Finding good proofs for description logic entailments using recursive quality measures (extended technical report) (2021), https://arxiv.org/abs/2104.13138, arXiv:2104.13138 [cs.AI]

5. Alrabbaa, C., Baader, F., Dachselt, R., Flemisch, T., Koopmann, P.: Visualising proofs and the modular structure of ontologies to support ontology repair. In: DL 2020: International Workshop on Description Logics. CEUR Workshop Proceedings, vol. 2663. CEUR-WS.org (2020), http://ceur-ws.org/Vol-2663/paper-2.pdf

6. Arrieta, A.B., Diaz-Rodriguez, N., Ser, J.D., Bennetot, A., Tabik, S., Barbado, A., Garcia, S., Gil-Lopez, S., Molina, D., Benjamins, R., Chatila, R., Herrera, F.: Explainable Artificial Intelligence (XAI): Concepts, taxonomies, opportunities and challenges toward responsible AI. Information Fusion **58**, 82–115 (2020). https://doi.org/10.1016/j.inffus.2019.12.012

7. Baader, F., Brandt, S., Lutz, C.: Pushing the $\mathcal{EL}$ envelope. In: Kaelbling, L.P., Saffiotti, A. (eds.) Proc. of the 19th Int. Joint Conf. on Artificial Intelligence (IJCAI'05). pp. 364–369. Professional Book Center (2005), http://ijcai.org/Proceedings/09/Papers/053.pdf

8. Baader, F., Brandt, S., Lutz, C.: Pushing the $\mathcal{EL}$ envelope further. In: Clark, K., Patel-Schneider, P.F. (eds.) Proc. of the 4th Workshop on OWL: Experiences and Directions. pp. 1–10 (2008), http://webont.org/owled/2008dc/papers/owled2008dc_paper_3.pdf

9. Baader, F., Horrocks, I., Lutz, C., Sattler, U.: An Introduction to Description Logic. Cambridge University Press (2017). https://doi.org/10.1017/9781139025355

10. Baader, F., Suntisrivaraporn, B.: Debugging SNOMED CT using axiom pinpointing in the description logic $\mathcal{EL}^+$. In: Proc. of the 3rd Conference on Knowledge Representation in Medicine (KR-MED'08): Representing and Sharing Knowledge Using SNOMED. CEUR-WS, vol. 410 (2008), http://ceur-ws.org/Vol-410/Paper01.pdf

11. Borgida, A., Franconi, E., Horrocks, I.: Explaining $\mathcal{ALC}$ subsumption. In: ECAI 2000, Proceedings of the 14th European Conference on Artificial Intelligence, Berlin, Germany, August 20-25, 2000. pp. 209–213 (2000), http://www.frontiersinai.com/ecai/ecai2000/pdf/p0209.pdf

12. Fiedler, A.: Natural language proof explanation. In: Mechanizing Mathematical Reasoning, Essays in Honor of Jörg H. Siekmann on the Occasion of His 60th Birthday. pp. 342–363 (2005). https://doi.org/10.1007/978-3-540-32254-2_20

13. Gallo, G., Longo, G., Pallottino, S.: Directed hypergraphs and applications. Discrete Applied Mathematics **42**(2), 177–201 (1993). https://doi.org/10.1016/0166-218X(93)90045-P

14. Horridge, M.: Justification Based Explanation in Ontologies. Ph.D. thesis, University of Manchester, UK (2011), https://www.research.manchester.ac.uk/portal/files/54511395/FULL_TEXT.PDF

15. Horridge, M., Bail, S., Parsia, B., Sattler, U.: Toward cognitive support for OWL justifications. Knowl. Based Syst. **53**, 66–79 (2013). https://doi.org/10.1016/j.knosys.2013.08.021, https://doi.org/10.1016/j.knosys.2013.08.021

16. Horridge, M., Parsia, B., Sattler, U.: Justification oriented proofs in OWL. In: The Semantic Web - ISWC 2010 - 9th International Semantic Web Conference, ISWC 2010, Shanghai, China, November 7-11, 2010, Revised Selected Papers, Part I. pp. 354–369 (2010). https://doi.org/10.1007/978-3-642-17746-0_23

17. Huang, X.: Reconstruction proofs at the assertion level. In: Proceedings of the 12th International Conference on Automated Deduction. p. 738–752. CADE-12, Springer-Verlag (1994). https://doi.org/10.1007/3-540-58156-1_53

18. Kazakov, Y.: Consequence-driven reasoning for horn SHIQ ontologies. In: Boutilier, C. (ed.) IJCAI 2009, Proceedings of the 21st International Joint Conference on Artificial Intelligence, Pasadena, California, USA, July 11-17, 2009. pp. 2040–2045 (2009), http://ijcai.org/Proceedings/09/Papers/336.pdf

19. Kazakov, Y., Klinov, P.: Goal-directed tracing of inferences in $\mathcal{EL}$ ontologies. In: Mika, P., Tudorache, T., Bernstein, A., Welty, C., Knoblock, C.A., Vrandecic, D., Groth, P.T., Noy, N.F., Janowicz, K., Goble, C.A. (eds.) Proc. of the 13th International Semantic Web Conference (ISWC 2014). Lecture Notes in Computer Science, vol. 8797, pp. 196–211. Springer (2014). https://doi.org/10.1007/978-3-319-11915-1_13

20. Kazakov, Y., Klinov, P., Stupnikov, A.: Towards reusable explanation services in Protege. In: Artale, A., Glimm, B., Kontchakov, R. (eds.) Proc. of the 30th Int. Workshop on Description Logics (DL'17). CEUR Workshop Proceedings, vol. 1879 (2017), http://www.ceur-ws.org/Vol-1879/paper31.pdf

21. Kazakov, Y., Krötzsch, M., Simancik, F.: The incredible ELK – from polynomial procedures to efficient reasoning with $\mathcal{EL}$ ontologies. J. Autom. Reasoning **53**(1), 1–61 (2014). https://doi.org/10.1007/s10817-013-9296-3

22. Lingenfelder, C.: Structuring computer generated proofs. In: Proceedings of the 11th International Joint Conference on Artificial Intelligence. Detroit, MI, USA, August 1989. pp. 378–383 (1989), http://ijcai.org/Proceedings/89-1/Papers/060.pdf

23. McGuinness, D.L.: Explaining Reasoning in Description Logics. Ph.D. thesis, Rutgers University, NJ, USA (1996). https://doi.org/10.7282/t3-q0c6-5305

24. Nguyen, T.A.T., Power, R., Piwek, P., Williams, S.: Measuring the understandability of deduction rules for OWL. In: Proceedings of the First International Workshop on Debugging Ontologies and Ontology Mappings, WoDOOM 2012, Galway, Ireland, October 8, 2012. pp. 1–12 (2012), http://www.ida.liu.se/~patla/conferences/WoDOOM12/papers/paper4.pdf

25. Nguyen, T.A.T., Power, R., Piwek, P., Williams, S.: Predicting the understandability of OWL inferences. In: The Semantic Web: Semantics and Big Data, 10th International Conference, ESWC 2013, Montpellier, France, May 26-30, 2013. Proceedings. pp. 109–123 (2013). https://doi.org/10.1007/978-3-642-38288-8_8

26. Schiller, M.R.G., Glimm, B.: Towards explicative inference for OWL. In: Informal Proceedings of the 26th International Workshop on Description Logics, Ulm, Germany, July 23 - 26, 2013. pp. 930–941 (2013), http://ceur-ws.org/Vol-1014/paper_36.pdf

27. Schiller, M.R.G., Schiller, F., Glimm, B.: Testing the adequacy of automated explanations of EL subsumptions. In: Proceedings of the 30th International Workshop on Description Logics, Montpellier, France, July 18-21, 2017. (2017), http://ceur-ws.org/Vol-1879/paper43.pdf

28. Schlobach, S., Cornet, R.: Non-standard reasoning services for the debugging of description logic terminologies. In: Gottlob, G., Walsh, T. (eds.) Proc. of the 18th Int. Joint Conf. on Artificial Intelligence (IJCAI 2003). pp. 355–362. Morgan Kaufmann, Acapulco, Mexico (2003), http://ijcai.org/Proceedings/03/Papers/053.pdf

Open Access This chapter is licensed under the terms of the Creative Commons Attribution 4.0 International License (http://creativecommons.org/licenses/by/4.0/), which permits use, sharing, adaptation, distribution and reproduction in any medium or format, as long as you give appropriate credit to the original author(s) and the source, provide a link to the Creative Commons license and indicate if changes were made.

The images or other third party material in this chapter are included in the chapter's Creative Commons license, unless indicated otherwise in a credit line to the material. If material is not included in the chapter's Creative Commons license and your intended use is not permitted by statutory regulation or exceeds the permitted use, you will need to obtain permission directly from the copyright holder.

Computing Optimal Repairs of Quantified ABoxes w.r.t. Static $\mathcal{EL}$ TBoxes*

Franz Baader⬚, Patrick Koopmann⬚, Francesco Kriegel⬚, and
Adrian Nuradiansyah⬚

Theoretical Computer Science, TU Dresden, Dresden, Germany
firstname.lastname@tu-dresden.de

Abstract. The application of automated reasoning approaches to Description Logic (DL) ontologies may produce certain consequences that
either are deemed to be wrong or should be hidden for privacy reasons.
The question is then how to repair the ontology such that the unwanted
consequences can no longer be deduced. An optimal repair is one where
the least amount of other consequences is removed. Most of the previous approaches to ontology repair are of a syntactic nature in that they
remove or weaken the axioms explicitly present in the ontology, and
thus cannot achieve semantic optimality. In previous work, we have addressed the problem of computing optimal repairs of (quantified) ABoxes,
where the unwanted consequences are described by concept assertions of
the lightweight DL $\mathcal{EL}$. In the present paper, we improve on the results
achieved so far in two ways. First, we allow for the presence of terminological knowledge in the form of an $\mathcal{EL}$ TBox. This TBox is assumed to
be static in the sense that it cannot be changed in the repair process. Second, the construction of optimal repairs described in our previous work
is best case exponential. We introduce an optimized construction that
is exponential only in the worst case. First experimental results indicate
that this reduces the size of the computed optimal repairs considerably.

1 Introduction

Description Logics [3] are a well-investigated family of logic-based knowledge
representation languages, which are frequently used to formalize ontologies for
application domains such as biology and medicine [17]. As the size of ontologies grows, the likelihood of them containing errors increases as well. This is
particularly problematic if the data, stored in the ABox, are automatically extracted from text or other sources using natural language processing or machine
learning. The reasoning services of DL systems [22,12,33,15], which derive implicit consequences from the explicitly represented knowledge, are not only useful
once an ontology is deployed, but can also be employed for debugging purposes
by exhibiting consequences that are not supposed to hold in the application

---

* funded by DFG in project number 430150274 and TRR 248 (cpec, grant 389792660).

© The Author(s) 2021
A. Platzer and G. Sutcliffe (Eds.): CADE 2021, LNAI 12699, pp. 309–326, 2021.
https://doi.org/10.1007/978-3-030-79876-5_18

domain. Another reason why one might want to remove a consequence is that it reveals private information that is supposed to be hidden [14,5]. Once such an unwanted consequence is detected, it is often not easy to see how to repair the ontology in order to get rid of this consequence. Classical repair approaches based on axiom pinpointing [31,29,27,32,21,8] compute maximal subsets of the ontology that do not have the consequence. The obtained result thus strongly depends on the syntactic form of the axioms. For example, it is well-known that, for expressive DLs, a finite set of terminological axioms can be expressed by a single axiom. If the given terminology (TBox) is of this shape, then the only possible classical repair is the empty TBox. To alleviate this problem, repair approaches have been developed that replace certain axioms by weaker ones (in the sense that they have less consequences) instead of removing them completely [18,24,34,6]. However, these approaches usually do not produce optimal repairs. In fact, it was shown in [6] that, even for the inexpressive DL $\mathcal{EL}$, optimal repairs need not exist. The abstract example given there can be rephrased as follows. Assume that the TBox defines humans to be exactly those individuals that have a human parent, and that the ABox says that Sam is a human. After we find out that Sam is in fact not human [9], we want to get rid of the latter assertion, but keep the (correct) consequences saying that Sam has an unbounded chain of ancestors (of undetermined species). If the TBox is assumed to be fixed, then there is no optimal repair of the ABox since we can add only a finite number of parent assertions.

To avoid such problems, our previous work on computing optimal repairs (formulated in the guise of achieving compliance with privacy policies) restricted the attention to the case without TBox. In [5] the ABox was additionally restricted to be a so-called instance store [19], i.e., an ABox without role assertions. The privacy policy (specifying which consequences are to be removed) was given as $\mathcal{EL}$ instance queries. In this setting, optimal repairs always exist and can be computed in exponential time, which is optimal since there may be exponentially many optimal repairs of exponential size.

In [7] these results were extended to ABoxes with role assertions. More precisely, we considered *quantified* ABoxes in which some individuals are anonymized by viewing them as existentially quantified variables. For example, assume that the ABox contains the information that Ben has a parent, Jerry, that is both rich and famous, and we want to remove the consequence $\exists parent.(Rich \sqcap Famous)(BEN)$. Classical repairs can be obtained by removing one of the assertions $Rich(JERRY)$, $Famous(JERRY)$, and $parent(BEN, JERRY)$. If instead we replace the first assertion with $Rich(x)$ and $parent(BEN, x)$ for an existentially quantified variable x, then we retain more consequences. Note that we could not have used an individual name (i.e., constant) $ANNE$ instead of x since information like $Rich(ANNE)$ about Anne does not follow from the original ABox. We show in [7] that in this setting all optimal repairs can be computed by an exponential-time algorithm with access to an NP-oracle. The oracle is needed since our algorithm first computes a superset of the set of optimal repairs, from which non-optimal ones need to be removed using the (NP-complete) entailment test between (potentially exponentially large) quantified ABoxes. We also consider a modified version of entailment (called IQ-entailment) in [7], where quantified ABoxes are compared w.r.t. which $\mathcal{EL}$ instance relationships they imply. Using this notion, no NP-oracle is needed for computing the set of all IQ-optimal repairs since IQ-entailment can be decided in polynomial time.

In the present paper, we improve on these results in two respects. On the one hand, we allow for the presence of terminological knowledge in the form of an $\mathcal{EL}$ TBox, which is assumed to be correct, and thus is not changed by the repair. To deal with a TBox, the approach from [7] for computing optimal repairs must be extended in two ways. First, the ABox needs to be saturated w.r.t. the TBox before applying our repair approach. The saturated ABox has the same consequences as the original one has together with the TBox. In our Ben and Jerry example, assume that the assertion $Rich(JERRY)$ does not belong to the original ABox, but the TBox contains the axiom $Famous \sqsubseteq Rich$. Then the ABox on its own does not have the unwanted consequence $\exists parent.(Rich \sqcap Famous)(BEN)$, but together with the TBox it does. Saturation adds the assertion $Rich(JERRY)$ to the ABox. For arbitrary TBoxes, saturation need not terminate. We consider two ways to remedy this problem: either allow for arbitrary TBoxes, but consider IQ-entailment, or use classical entailment, but consider cycle-restricted TBoxes [1]. In both cases, saturation always terminates; in the former in polynomial and in the latter in exponential time. One might be tempted to assume that, after saturation, one can simply apply the repair approach of [7] unchanged. This is not true, however, since the TBox may re-add assertions that have been removed or replaced by the repair. In our example, where $Rich(JERRY)$ is replaced, but $Famous(JERRY)$ is left untouched in the repair, the repaired ABox together with the TBox would still have the unwanted consequence. Thus, the repair approach needs to be changed to take this possibility into account.

On the other hand, the construction of optimal repairs described in our previous work [5,7], and extended in this paper such that it can deal with TBoxes, is best case exponential. The second contribution of this paper is the design of a new construction, both for classical and IQ-entailment, that is exponential only in the worst case. We also report on first experimental results, which indicate that this reduces the size of the computed optimal repairs considerably.

Detailed proofs of our results can be found in [4].

2   Preliminaries

Throughout this paper, we assume that Σ is a *signature*, which is a disjoint union of sets Σ_O, Σ_C, and Σ_R of *object names*, *concept names*, and *role names*. We use symbols t, u, v, w to denote object names, A, B to denote concept names, and r, s to denote role names, all of them possibly with sub- or superscripts.

As in [7], a *quantified ABox (qABox)* $\exists X. \mathcal{A}$ over Σ consists of a finite subset X of Σ_O, the elements of which are called *variables*, and a *matrix* $\mathcal{A}$, which is a finite set of *concept assertions* $A(u)$ where $u \in \Sigma_O$ and $A \in \Sigma_C$, and of *role assertions* $r(u, v)$ where $u, v \in \Sigma_O$ and $r \in \Sigma_R$. An non-variable object name in

$\exists X.\mathcal{A}$ is called an *individual name*, and the set of all these names is denoted as $\Sigma_I(\exists X.\mathcal{A})$. We further set $\Sigma_O(\exists X.\mathcal{A}) := \Sigma_I(\exists X.\mathcal{A}) \cup X$. Traditional DL ABoxes are qABoxes where $X = \emptyset$; we then write $\mathcal{A}$ instead of $\exists \emptyset.\mathcal{A}$. The matrix of a qABox is such a traditional ABox.

An *interpretation* $\mathcal{I}$ of Σ is a pair $(\Delta^{\mathcal{I}}, \cdot^{\mathcal{I}})$, where the *domain* $\Delta^{\mathcal{I}}$ is a non-empty set and the *interpretation function* $\cdot^{\mathcal{I}}$ maps each $u \in \Sigma_O$ to an element $u^{\mathcal{I}}$ of $\Delta^{\mathcal{I}}$, each $A \in \Sigma_C$ to a set $A^{\mathcal{I}} \subseteq \Delta^{\mathcal{I}}$, and each $r \in \Sigma_R$ to a binary relation $r^{\mathcal{I}}$ over $\Delta^{\mathcal{I}}$. The interpretation $\mathcal{I}$ of Σ is a *model* of a qABox $\exists X.\mathcal{A}$ over Σ if there is an interpretation $\mathcal{J}$ such that $\Delta^{\mathcal{I}} = \Delta^{\mathcal{J}}$, the interpretation functions $\cdot^{\mathcal{I}}$ and $\cdot^{\mathcal{J}}$ coincide on $\Sigma \setminus X$, and $u^{\mathcal{J}} \in A^{\mathcal{J}}$ for each $A(u) \in \mathcal{A}$ as well as $(u^{\mathcal{J}}, v^{\mathcal{J}}) \in r^{\mathcal{J}}$ for each $r(u,v) \in \mathcal{A}$.

Following [7], we define $\mathcal{EL}$ atoms and $\mathcal{EL}$ concept descriptions over Σ by simultaneous induction as follows. An $\mathcal{EL}$ *atom* is either a concept name $A \in \Sigma_C$ or an *existential restriction* $\exists r.C$ for some role name $r \in \Sigma_R$ and an $\mathcal{EL}$ concept description C. An $\mathcal{EL}$ *concept description* is a *conjunction* $\bigsqcap \mathcal{C}$ where $\mathcal{C}$ is a finite set of $\mathcal{EL}$ atoms. An $\mathcal{EL}$ *concept inclusion* is of the form $C \sqsubseteq D$ for $\mathcal{EL}$ concept descriptions C and D, and an $\mathcal{EL}$ *TBox* is a finite set of such concept inclusions. An $\mathcal{EL}$ *concept assertion* is an expression $C(u)$, where C is an $\mathcal{EL}$ concept description and $u \in \Sigma_O$.

For each interpretation $\mathcal{I}$ of Σ, we extend the interpretation function $\cdot^{\mathcal{I}}$ to $\mathcal{EL}$ atoms and $\mathcal{EL}$ concept descriptions in the following manner:

- $(\exists r.C)^{\mathcal{I}} := \{ \delta \mid \text{there exists some } \gamma \text{ such that } (\delta, \gamma) \in r^{\mathcal{I}} \text{ and } \gamma \in C^{\mathcal{I}} \}$,
- $(\bigsqcap \mathcal{C})^{\mathcal{I}} := \bigcap \{ C^{\mathcal{I}} \mid C \in \mathcal{C} \}$ where $\bigcap \emptyset = \Delta^{\mathcal{I}}$.

The interpretation $\mathcal{I}$ is a *model* of the concept inclusion $C \sqsubseteq D$ (the concept assertion $C(u)$) if $C^{\mathcal{I}} \subseteq D^{\mathcal{I}}$ ($u^{\mathcal{I}} \in C^{\mathcal{I}}$), and of the TBox $\mathcal{T}$ if it is a model of each concept inclusion in $\mathcal{T}$.

To make the syntax introduced above more akin to the one usually employed for $\mathcal{EL}$, we denote the empty conjunction $\bigsqcap \emptyset$ as $\top$ (*top concept*), singleton conjunctions $\bigsqcap \{C\}$ as C, and conjunctions $\bigsqcap \mathcal{C}$ for $|\mathcal{C}| \geq 2$ as $C_1 \sqcap \ldots \sqcap C_n$, where $C_1, \ldots, C_n$ is an enumeration of the elements of $\mathcal{C}$ in an arbitrary order. Since we do not distinguish between the singleton conjunction $\bigsqcap \{C\}$ and the atom C, each atom is also a concept description. The set $\mathsf{Sub}(C)$ of *subconcepts* of an $\mathcal{EL}$ concept description C is defined as follows: $\mathsf{Sub}(A) := \{A\}$, $\mathsf{Sub}(\exists r.C) := \{\exists r.C\} \cup \mathsf{Sub}(C)$, and $\mathsf{Sub}(\bigsqcap \mathcal{C}) := \{\bigsqcap \mathcal{C}\} \cup \bigcup \{ \mathsf{Sub}(D) \mid D \in \mathcal{C} \}$. The set $\mathsf{Atoms}(C)$ consists of all atoms contained in $\mathsf{Sub}(C)$. These two notions are extended to TBoxes and sets of concept assertions in the obvious way.

Let α, β be qABoxes, concept inclusions, or concept assertions (possibly not both of the same kind), and $\mathcal{T}$ an $\mathcal{EL}$ TBox. Then we write $\mathcal{I} \models \alpha$ if the interpretation $\mathcal{I}$ is a model of α. We say that α *entails* β w.r.t. $\mathcal{T}$ (written $\alpha \models^{\mathcal{T}} \beta$) if every model of α and $\mathcal{T}$ is a model of β. Furthermore, α and β are *equivalent* w.r.t. $\mathcal{T}$ (written $\alpha \equiv^{\mathcal{T}} \beta$), if $\alpha \models^{\mathcal{T}} \beta$ and $\beta \models^{\mathcal{T}} \alpha$. In case $\mathcal{T} = \emptyset$, we will sometimes write $\models$ instead of $\models^{\emptyset}$. If $\exists \emptyset.\emptyset \models^{\mathcal{T}} C \sqsubseteq D$, then we also write $C \sqsubseteq^{\mathcal{T}} D$ and say that C *is subsumed by* D w.r.t. $\mathcal{T}$; in case $\mathcal{T} = \emptyset$ we simply say that C is subsumed by D. Two $\mathcal{EL}$ concept descriptions are *equivalent* w.r.t. $\mathcal{T}$ (written $C \equiv^{\mathcal{T}} D$) if they subsume each other w.r.t. $\mathcal{T}$. We write $C \sqsubset^{\mathcal{T}} D$ to indicate that $C \sqsubseteq^{\mathcal{T}} D$, but $C \not\equiv^{\mathcal{T}} D$. If $\exists X.\mathcal{A} \models^{\mathcal{T}} C(a)$, then a is called an *instance of* C w.r.t. $\exists X.\mathcal{A}$ and $\mathcal{T}$. For $\mathcal{EL}$, the subsumption and the instance problem are decidable in polynomial time [2]. However, entailment between qABoxes is NP-complete even w.r.t. the empty TBox [7].

We also use the reduced form C^r of $\mathcal{EL}$ concept descriptions C [23], which is obtained by removing redundant subdescriptions (see [7] for details). Adapting the results in [23], one can show that $C \equiv^{\emptyset} C^r$ and that $C \equiv^{\emptyset} D$ implies $C^r = D^r$.

3   A Tale of Two Entailments

DL-based ontologies are usually accessed through appropriate query languages, where for the purpose of this paper it is sufficient to assume that a query language is given by a fragment of first-order logic. Instead of comparing ontologies w.r.t. the models they have, it thus makes sense to compare them w.r.t. the answers to queries they entail [25]. Given such a query language QL and an $\mathcal{EL}$ TBox $\mathcal{T}$, we say that the qABox $\exists X.\mathcal{A}$ QL-*entails* the qABox $\exists Y.\mathcal{B}$ w.r.t. $\mathcal{T}$ (written $\exists X.\mathcal{A} \models_{QL}^{\mathcal{T}} \exists Y.\mathcal{B}$) if for each query $\varphi(x_1, \ldots, x_k) \in$ QL and each tuple of individuals $(a_1, \ldots, a_k)$ we have that $\mathcal{T} \wedge \exists Y.\mathcal{B} \models \varphi(a_1, \ldots, a_k)$ implies $\mathcal{T} \wedge \exists X.\mathcal{A} \models \varphi(a_1, \ldots, a_k)$, where we view the TBox and the ABox as first-order formulae and $\models$ is classical first-order entailment (see [25] for more details). We say that two qABox are QL-*equivalent w.r.t.* $\mathcal{T}$ if they QL-entail each other w.r.t. $\mathcal{T}$, and denote this equivalence relation as $\equiv_{QL}^{\mathcal{T}}$.

For $\mathcal{EL}$ ontologies, one usually considers instance queries (IQ) or conjunctive queries (CQ). The former are given by $\mathcal{EL}$ concept descriptions, viewed as first-order formulae with one free variable. The latter are basically qABoxes of the form $\exists X.\mathcal{A}$, but with the elements of $\Sigma_I(\exists X.\mathcal{A})$ viewed as free variables. Replacing these free variables with a tuple of individuals thus yields a qABox in the sense introduced above. In particular, this means that CQ-entailment corresponds to entailment of the same qABoxes (see [7] for more details regarding the connection between conjunctive queries and qABoxes).

3.1   Classical Entailment and CQ-Entailment

Due to the close connection between conjunctive queries and qABoxes mentioned above, it is easy to see that the classical entailment relation $\models^{\mathcal{T}}$ between qABoxes, as introduced in the previous section, actually coincides with CQ-entailment $\models_{CQ}^{\mathcal{T}}$. To keep the notation more uniform and to distinguish this kind of entailment explicitly from IQ-entailment, we will usually talk about CQ-entailment and write $\models_{CQ}^{\mathcal{T}}$.

Whenever we compare two qABoxes $\exists X.\mathcal{A}$ and $\exists Y.\mathcal{B}$, we assume without loss of generality that they are *renamed apart*, which means that X is disjoint with $\Sigma_O(\exists Y.\mathcal{B})$ and Y is disjoint with $\Sigma_O(\exists X.\mathcal{A})$, and we further assume that the two qABoxes speak about the same set of individual names $\Sigma_I := \Sigma_I(\exists X.\mathcal{A}) \cup \Sigma_I(\exists Y.\mathcal{B})$. For the case of an empty TBox, it was shown in [7] that $\exists X.\mathcal{A} \models_{CQ}^{\emptyset} \exists Y.\mathcal{B}$ iff there is a homomorphism from $\exists Y.\mathcal{B}$ to $\exists X.\mathcal{A}$. A *homomorphism* from

$\sqcap$**-rule.** If $(C_1 \sqcap \cdots \sqcap C_n)(t) \in \mathcal{A}$, then remove this assertion from $\mathcal{A}$, and add the assertions $C_1(t), \cdots, C_n(t)$ to $\mathcal{A}$.

$\exists$**-rule.** If $(\exists r.C)(t) \in \mathcal{A}$, then remove this assertion from $\mathcal{A}$, add the two assertions $r(t,x)$ and $C(x)$ to $\mathcal{A}$, and add x to X, where x is a fresh variable not occurring in $\mathcal{A}$ or X.

$\sqsubseteq$**-rule.** If $t \in \Sigma_0(\exists X.\mathcal{A})$, $C \sqsubseteq D \in \mathcal{T}$, $\mathcal{A} \models C(t)$, and $\mathcal{A} \not\models D(t)$, then add the assertion $D(t)$ to $\mathcal{A}$.

The $\sqcap$-rule has highest priority and the $\sqsubseteq$-rule has lowest priority.

Fig. 1: The CQ-saturation rules.

$\exists Y.\mathcal{B}$ to $\exists X.\mathcal{A}$ is a mapping $h \colon \Sigma_0(\exists Y.\mathcal{B}) \to \Sigma_0(\exists X.\mathcal{A})$ such that $h(a) = a$ for each $a \in \Sigma_\mathsf{I}$, $A(h(u)) \in \mathcal{A}$ for each $A(u) \in \mathcal{B}$, and $r(h(u), h(v)) \in \mathcal{A}$ for each $r(u, v) \in \mathcal{B}$. In order to obtain a similar characterization of entailment for the case of a non-empty TBox $\mathcal{T}$, we need to saturate the given qABox w.r.t. $\mathcal{T}$.

Basically, this saturation performs what is called *the chase* in the database community [26,20,10]. Given an $\mathcal{EL}$ TBox $\mathcal{T}$ and a qABox $\exists X.\mathcal{A}$, it extends the ABox by new assertions that are implied by the TBox. The rules that realize this are described in Fig. 1. Their rôle is two-fold: whereas the $\sqsubseteq$-rule adds new concept assertions that are implied by the ABox together with the TBox, the other two rules break down the complex concept assertions added by this rule into smaller parts.

In general, applying these rules need not terminate; e.g., if applied to the qABox $\exists \emptyset.\{A(a)\}$ for the TBox $\{A \sqsubseteq \exists r.A\}$. There are various sufficient conditions that guarantee termination of the chase [13]. Here, we use a condition introduced in [1] in the context of unification in $\mathcal{EL}$.

Definition 1. *The $\mathcal{EL}$ TBox $\mathcal{T}$ is* cycle-restricted *if there is no non-empty sequence of role names $r_1, \ldots, r_k$ and $\mathcal{EL}$ concept description C such that $C \sqsubseteq^{\mathcal{T}} \exists r_1. \cdots \exists r_k.C$.*

As shown in [1], it can be decided in time polynomial whether a given $\mathcal{EL}$ TBox is cycle-restricted or not. For cycle-restricted TBoxes, CQ-saturation always terminates.

Theorem 2. *Let $\mathcal{T}$ be a cycle-restricted $\mathcal{EL}$ TBox and $\exists X.\mathcal{A}$ a qABox. Then exhaustive application of the CQ-saturation rules terminates in exponential time in the size of $\exists X.\mathcal{A}$ and $\mathcal{T}$, and yields a qABox $\mathsf{sat}_{\mathsf{CQ}}^{\mathcal{T}}(\exists X.\mathcal{A})$ such that the following statements are equivalent for all qABoxes $\exists Y.\mathcal{B}$:*

- *$\exists X.\mathcal{A} \models_{\mathsf{CQ}}^{\mathcal{T}} \exists Y.\mathcal{B}$,*
- *$\mathsf{sat}_{\mathsf{CQ}}^{\mathcal{T}}(\exists X.\mathcal{A}) \models_{\mathsf{CQ}}^{\emptyset} \exists Y.\mathcal{B}$,*
- *there is a homomorphism from $\exists Y.\mathcal{B}$ to $\mathsf{sat}_{\mathsf{CQ}}^{\mathcal{T}}(\exists X.\mathcal{A})$.*

We can show that there are examples where the CQ-saturation of a qABox w.r.t. a cycle-restricted TBox is of exponential size, and thus its computation must take exponential time. Nevertheless, the entailment relation $\models_{\mathsf{CQ}}^{\mathcal{T}}$ can still be decided within NP by adapting results for conjunctive query answering in $\mathcal{EL}$ [30].

⊓-**rule.** If $(C_1 \sqcap \ldots \sqcap C_n)(t) \in \mathcal{A}$, then remove this assertion from $\mathcal{A}$ and add the assertions $C_1(t), \ldots, C_n(t)$ to $\mathcal{A}$.

∃-**rule.** If $(\exists r.C)(t) \in \mathcal{A}$, then remove this assertion from $\mathcal{A}$, add the two assertions $r(t, x_C)$ and $C(x_C)$ to $\mathcal{A}$, and add x_C to X if it is not already there.

⊑-**rule.** If $t \in \Sigma_O(\exists X.\mathcal{A})$, $C \sqsubseteq D \in \mathcal{T}$, $\mathcal{A} \models C(t)$, and $\mathcal{A} \not\models D(t)$, then add the assertion $D(t)$ to $\mathcal{A}$.

The ⊓-rule has higher precedence than the ∃-rule, and the latter has higher precedence than the ⊑-rule.

$$\text{Fig. 2: The IQ-saturation rules.}$$

3.2 IQ-Entailment

Recall that the qABox $\exists X.\mathcal{A}$ IQ-entails the qABox $\exists Y.\mathcal{B}$ w.r.t. the $\mathcal{EL}$ TBox $\mathcal{T}$ if every concept assertion $C(a)$ entailed w.r.t. $\mathcal{T}$ by the latter is also entailed w.r.t. $\mathcal{T}$ by the former. In the following we assume again that these two qABoxes are renamed apart. For the case of an empty TBox, it was shown in [7] that $\exists X.\mathcal{A} \models_{IQ}^{\emptyset} \exists Y.\mathcal{B}$ iff there is a simulation from $\exists Y.\mathcal{B}$ to $\exists X.\mathcal{A}$. A *simulation* from $\exists Y.\mathcal{B}$ to $\exists X.\mathcal{A}$ is a relation $\mathfrak{S} \subseteq \Sigma_O(\exists Y.\mathcal{B}) \times \Sigma_O(\exists X.\mathcal{A})$ such that $(a, a) \in \mathfrak{S}$ for each $a \in \Sigma_I$ and, for each $(u, v) \in \mathfrak{S}$, $A(u) \in \mathcal{B}$ implies $A(v) \in \mathcal{A}$ and $r(u, u') \in \mathcal{B}$ implies that there exists an object $v' \in \Sigma_I \cup X$ such that $(u', v') \in \mathfrak{S}$ and $r(v, v') \in \mathcal{A}$. Since checking the existence of a simulation can be done in polynomial time [16], we conclude that IQ-entailment between qABoxes can be decided in polynomial time for the case of an empty TBox.

To extend these results to the case of a non-empty TBox, we again need to saturate the ABox w.r.t. the TBox. But now the saturation rules, given in Fig. 2, are more parsimonious w.r.t. the introduction of new objects. To be more precise, for each existential restriction $\exists r.C \in \mathsf{Sub}(\mathcal{T})$, we assume that x_C is a fresh variable not contained in the initial qABox $\exists X.\mathcal{A}$. When applying the ∃-rule to an assertion of the form $(\exists r.C)(t)$, we always use this variable for the successor object. Due to this restriction, IQ-saturation always terminates, i.e., it is not necessary to impose any restrictions on the TBox. Also note that IQ-saturation basically generates a qABox representation of what is called the *canonical model* in [25, Section 5.2].

Theorem 3. *Let $\mathcal{T}$ be an $\mathcal{EL}$ TBox and $\exists X.\mathcal{A}$ a qABox. Then exhaustive application of the IQ-saturation rules terminates in polynomial time in the size of $\exists X.\mathcal{A}$ and $\mathcal{T}$, and yields a qABox $\mathsf{sat}_{IQ}^{\mathcal{T}}(\exists X.\mathcal{A})$ such that the following statements are equivalent for all qABoxes $\exists Y.\mathcal{B}$:*

- *$\exists X.\mathcal{A} \models_{IQ}^{\mathcal{T}} \exists Y.\mathcal{B}$,*
- *$\mathsf{sat}_{IQ}^{\mathcal{T}}(\exists X.\mathcal{A}) \models_{IQ}^{\emptyset} \exists Y.\mathcal{B}$,*
- *there is a simulation from $\exists Y.\mathcal{B}$ to $\mathsf{sat}_{IQ}^{\mathcal{T}}(\exists X.\mathcal{A})$.*

Since $\mathsf{sat}_{IQ}^{\mathcal{T}}(\exists X.\mathcal{A})$ can be computed in polynomial time and the existence of a simulation can be decided in polynomial time, this shows that the entailment relation $\models_{IQ}^{\mathcal{T}}$ can be decided in polynomial time.

4   Canonical Repairs

We specify what is to be repaired by a finite set of $\mathcal{EL}$ concept assertions, which we call a repair request. A repair is a qABox that does not have any of these assertions as a consequence. This generalizes previous repair approaches [6] in that more than one consequence specified as unwanted is removed in one step. It also encompasses the notion of a privacy policy, as introduced in [7], which specifies forbidden concepts, with the meaning that one should not be able to derive that any of the individuals occurring in the qABox is an instance of such a concept. We assume that the TBox is static (i.e., may not be changed by the repair) and consider both CQ- and IQ-entailment for comparing qABoxes.

Definition 4. *Let $\mathcal{T}$ be an $\mathcal{EL}$ TBox and* QL $\in \{$CQ, IQ$\}$.

- *An $\mathcal{EL}$ repair request is a finite set of $\mathcal{EL}$ concept assertions.*
- *Given a qABox $\exists X.\mathcal{A}$ and an $\mathcal{EL}$ repair request $\mathcal{R}$, a QL-repair of $\exists X.\mathcal{A}$ for $\mathcal{R}$ w.r.t. $\mathcal{T}$ is a qABox $\exists Y.\mathcal{B}$ such that $\exists X.\mathcal{A} \models_{QL}^{\mathcal{T}} \exists Y.\mathcal{B}$ and $\exists Y.\mathcal{B} \not\models^{\mathcal{T}} C(a)$ for all $C(a) \in \mathcal{R}$.*
- *Such a repair $\exists Y.\mathcal{B}$ is optimal if there is no QL-repair $\exists Z.\mathcal{C}$ of $\exists X.\mathcal{A}$ for $\mathcal{R}$ w.r.t. $\mathcal{T}$ such that $\exists Z.\mathcal{C} \models_{QL}^{\mathcal{T}} \exists Y.\mathcal{B}$ and $\exists Z.\mathcal{C} \not\models_{QL}^{\mathcal{T}} \exists Y.\mathcal{B}$.*

Intuitively, a repair is a qABox that has no new consequences of the specified type (instance relationships or answers to conjunctive queries), and no longer has the consequences forbidden by the repair request. In an optimal repair, a minimal amount of consequences of the specified type is lost. Since there are different options for what to change when repairing a qABox, there may exist several non-equivalent optimal repairs.

In the following, let QL $\in \{$CQ, IQ$\}$ and let $\mathcal{T}$ be a fixed TBox, which is assumed to be cycle-restricted if QL = CQ. In addition, let $\mathcal{R}$ be a repair request and $\exists X.\mathcal{A}$ be the qABox to be QL-repaired for $\mathcal{R}$ w.r.t. $\mathcal{T}$. We assume that $\mathcal{R}$ does not contain an assertion of the form $C(a)$ such that $\top \sqsubseteq^{\mathcal{T}} C$ since the presence of such an assertions would preclude the existence of a repair. If $\mathcal{R}$ satisfies this restriction, then the empty qABox $\exists \emptyset.\emptyset$ is always a repair. However, as mentioned in the introduction, this does not imply that there is an optimal repair. We will show that, for the case of IQ-entailment, optimal repairs always exist. For CQ-entailment, this is the case if the TBox $\mathcal{T}$ is cycle-restricted. In both cases, the set of optimal repairs covers all repairs in the sense that each repair is entailed by some optimal repair.

As mentioned in the introduction, to deal with TBoxes, the approach for computing so-called canonical repairs from [7] needs to be adapted in two ways. First, one needs to QL-saturate the given qABox w.r.t. the TBox. Second, when computing canonical repairs from $\mathsf{sat}_{QL}^{\mathcal{T}}(\exists X.\mathcal{A})$, the construction needs to ensure that the TBox does not reintroduce consequences that have been removed by the repair. The main idea underlying the construction of canonical repairs is to introduce variables as copies of the objects occurring in $\mathsf{sat}_{QL}^{\mathcal{T}}(\exists X.\mathcal{A})$. Such a variable is of the form $y_{u,\mathcal{K}}$, where the first component of the subscript says that this is a copy of the object u. The second component $\mathcal{K}$ is a set of atoms, with the intuitive meaning that $y_{u,\mathcal{K}}$ must *not* be an instance of any element of $\mathcal{K}$. To avoid introducing unnecessary copies, certain restrictions were imposed in [7] on the sets $\mathcal{K}$. We add a further restriction that takes care of the TBox.

To be more precise, let $\mathsf{Sub}(\mathcal{R}, \mathcal{T})$ be the set of subconcepts of concept descriptions occurring in $\mathcal{R}$ or $\mathcal{T}$, and let $\mathsf{Atoms}(\mathcal{R}, \mathcal{T})$ be the set of atoms occurring in $\mathsf{Sub}(\mathcal{R}, \mathcal{T})$. The set $\mathcal{K}$ in a variable $y_{u,\mathcal{K}}$ must be a repair type for u.

Definition 5. *Let* $\exists Y.\mathcal{B} := \mathsf{sat}_{\mathsf{QL}}^{\mathcal{T}}(\exists X.\mathcal{A})$ *and let* u *be an object name occurring in* $\mathcal{B}$. *A repair type for* u *is a subset* $\mathcal{K}$ *of* $\mathsf{Atoms}(\mathcal{R}, \mathcal{T})$ *that satisfies the following:*

1. $\mathcal{B} \models^{\emptyset} C(u)$ *for each atom* $C \in \mathcal{K}$,
2. *if* C, D *are distinct atoms in* $\mathcal{K}$, *then* $C \not\sqsubseteq^{\emptyset} D$,
3. $\mathcal{K}$ *is premise-saturated w.r.t.* $\mathcal{T}$, *i.e., for all* $C \in \mathsf{Sub}(\mathcal{R}, \mathcal{T})$ *with* $\mathcal{B} \models^{\emptyset} C(u)$ *and* $C \sqsubseteq^{\mathcal{T}} D$ *for some* $D \in \mathcal{K}$, *there is* $E \in \mathcal{K}$ *such that* $C \sqsubseteq^{\emptyset} E$.

The first two conditions coincide with the ones in [7]. Basically, 1. says that we only need to remove instance relationships explicitly if they are really there. Condition 2. corresponds to the fact that preventing $D(y_{u,\mathcal{K}})$ as a consequence also prevents $C(y_{u,\mathcal{K}})$ if D subsumes C, and thus $C \in \mathcal{K}$ would be redundant if $D \in \mathcal{K}$. Condition 3. ensures that instance relationships that are removed due to $\mathcal{K}$ cannot be re-introduced by the TBox. It is easy to see that the set of repair types for u can be computed in exponential time.

Similarly to the approach in [7], canonical repairs are induced by seed functions. Such a function determines, for each individual, which instance relationships should be prevented in order to obtain a repair.

Definition 6. *A repair seed function is a function* s *that maps each individual name* $b \in \Sigma_{\mathsf{I}}(\exists X.\mathcal{A})$ *to a repair type* $s(b)$ *for* b *that satisfies the following:*

- *if* $C(b) \in \mathcal{R}$ *and* $\mathsf{sat}_{\mathsf{QL}}^{\mathcal{T}}(\exists X.\mathcal{A}) \models C(b)$, *then* $s(b)$ *contains an atom* D *such that* $C \sqsubseteq^{\emptyset} D$.

Using our general assumption that the repair request $\mathcal{R}$ does not contain a concept assertion $C(a)$ with $\top \sqsubseteq^{\mathcal{T}} C$, we can show that there is always at least one repair seed function. Each repair seed function induces a repair as follows.

Definition 7. *Given a repair seed function* s, *we define the canonical QL-repair* $\mathsf{rep}_{\mathsf{QL}}^{\mathcal{T}}(\exists X.\mathcal{A}, s)$ *induced by* s *as the qABox* $\exists Y.\mathcal{B}$ *where*

1. *the set* Y *consists of the variables* $y_{u,\mathcal{K}}$ *for all object names* u *occurring in* $\mathsf{sat}_{\mathsf{QL}}^{\mathcal{T}}(\exists X.\mathcal{A})$ *and all repair types* $\mathcal{K}$ *for* u, *except for the case where* u *is an individual name and* $\mathcal{K} = s(u)$, *and*
2. *the matrix* $\mathcal{B}$ *consists of the following assertions, where we use* $y_{b,s(b)}$ *as a synonym for the individual name* b:
   - $A(y_{u,\mathcal{K}}) \in \mathcal{B}$ *for each concept assertion* $A(u)$ *in* $\mathsf{sat}_{\mathsf{QL}}^{\mathcal{T}}(\exists X.\mathcal{A})$ *such that* $A \notin \mathcal{K}$,
   - $r(y_{u,\mathcal{K}}, y_{v,\mathcal{L}}) \in \mathcal{B}$ *for each role assertion* $r(u, v)$ *in* $\mathsf{sat}_{\mathsf{QL}}^{\mathcal{T}}(\exists X.\mathcal{A})$ *such that the following holds for each* $\exists r.C \in \mathcal{K}$: *if the matrix of* $\mathsf{sat}_{\mathsf{QL}}^{\mathcal{T}}(\exists X.\mathcal{A})$ *entails* $C(v)$, *then the set* $\mathcal{L}$ *contains an atom that subsumes* C.

Our construction of canonical repairs based on seed functions is sound and complete in the following sense.

Proposition 8. *For each repair seed function s, the induced canonical repair $\mathrm{rep}_{\mathsf{QL}}^{\mathcal{T}}(\exists X.\mathcal{A}, s)$ is a QL-repair of $\exists X.\mathcal{A}$ for $\mathcal{R}$ w.r.t. $\mathcal{T}$. Conversely, if $\exists Y.\mathcal{B}$ is a QL-repair of $\exists X.\mathcal{A}$ for $\mathcal{R}$ w.r.t. $\mathcal{T}$, then there is a repair seed function s such that $\mathrm{rep}_{\mathsf{QL}}^{\mathcal{T}}(\exists X.\mathcal{A}, s) \models_{\mathsf{QL}}^{\mathcal{T}} \exists Y.\mathcal{B}$.*

We define the set of all canonical QL-repairs of $\exists X.\mathcal{A}$ for $\mathcal{R}$ w.r.t. $\mathcal{T}$ as

$$\mathrm{Repairs}_{\mathsf{QL}}^{\mathcal{T}}(\exists X.\mathcal{A}, \mathcal{R}) := \{ \mathrm{rep}_{\mathsf{QL}}^{\mathcal{T}}(\exists X.\mathcal{A}, s) \mid s \text{ is a repair seed function} \}.$$

As an easy consequence of Proposition 8 we obtain that $\mathrm{Repairs}_{\mathsf{QL}}^{\mathcal{T}}(\exists X.\mathcal{A}, \mathcal{R})$ contains all optimal repairs (up to equivalence). However, as in the case without a TBox, it may also contain non-optimal repairs [7]. To compute the set of optimal repairs, one thus needs to remove such non-optimal elements from $\mathrm{Repairs}_{\mathsf{QL}}^{\mathcal{T}}(\exists X.\mathcal{A}, \mathcal{R})$. Since the entailment test required for this is NP-complete for $\mathsf{QL} = \mathsf{CQ}$ and polynomial for $\mathsf{QL} = \mathsf{IQ}$, we obtain the following theorem.

Theorem 9. *There is a (deterministic) algorithm that computes the set of all optimal QL-repairs of $\exists X.\mathcal{A}$ for $\mathcal{R}$ w.r.t. $\mathcal{T}$ and runs in exponential time. If $\mathsf{QL} = \mathsf{CQ}$, then this algorithm needs access to an NP oracle, whereas no such oracle is required for $\mathsf{QL} = \mathsf{IQ}$.*

5 Optimized Repairs

The construction of the canonical repair induced by a seed function described in the previous section usually introduces an exponential number of copies for the objects occurring in the saturated qABox. The following example demonstrates that this is not always necessary to obtain an optimal repair.

Example 10. Let $\mathcal{T} := \emptyset$ and consider the repair request $\{(\exists r.(A_1 \sqcap \ldots \sqcap A_n))(a)\}$ for the qABox $\exists \{x\}.\{r(a, x), A_1(x), \ldots, A_n(x)\}$. There is only one repair seed function s, which assigns $\{\exists r.(A_1 \sqcap \ldots \sqcap A_n)\}$ to a. Both for the CQ and the IQ case, the canonical repair induced by s contains 2^n copies of x, namely all the variables $y_{x,\mathcal{K}}$ for $\mathcal{K} \subseteq \{A_1, \ldots, A_n\}$. However, most of these copies are redundant. In fact, we will see below that there are optimal repairs equivalent to the canonical one that contain only linearly many variables in n, both for the CQ and the IQ case.

The idea is now to construct, for a given seed function, a set of variables that is a (hopefully small) subset of the set Y introduced in Definition 7, which is nevertheless sufficient to obtain a repair equivalent to the canonical one. Note, however, that in general an exponential blow-up cannot be avoided, as already shown in [5] for the case of $\mathcal{EL}$ instance stores. Throughout this section, we assume that QL, $\mathcal{T}$, $\mathcal{R}$, and $\exists X.\mathcal{A}$ satisfy the properties assumed in the previous section. In addition, we assume that the repair request $\mathcal{R}$ is *reduced*, i.e., every concept occurring in a concept assertion in $\mathcal{R}$ is reduced, and if $\mathcal{R}$ contains $C(a)$ and $D(a)$ for distinct concept descriptions C, D, then $C \not\sqsubseteq^{\emptyset} D$, and we further assume that each concept occurring in the TBox $\mathcal{T}$ is reduced. Before we can describe our construction of the set of relevant variables, we must introduce some notation and show an auxiliary result.

Given two sets of concept descriptions $\mathcal{K}$ and $\mathcal{L}$, we say that $\mathcal{L}$ *covers* $\mathcal{K}$ (written $\mathcal{K} \leq \mathcal{L}$) if each concept in $\mathcal{K}$ is subsumed by some concept in $\mathcal{L}$.

Now, let s be a repair seed function and set $\exists Y.\mathcal{B} := \mathrm{rep}_{\mathsf{QL}}^{\mathcal{T}}(\exists X.\mathcal{A}, s)$. Recall that, according to Definition 7, a role assertion $r(y_{t,\mathcal{K}}, y_{u,\mathcal{L}})$ belongs to the matrix $\mathcal{B}$ iff the saturation $\mathrm{sat}_{\mathsf{QL}}^{\mathcal{T}}(\exists X.\mathcal{A})$ contains the role assertion $r(t, u)$ and the repair type $\mathcal{L}$ covers the set $\mathrm{Succ}(\mathcal{K}, r, u) := \{\, C \mid \exists r.C \in \mathcal{K} \text{ and the matrix of } \mathrm{sat}_{\mathsf{QL}}^{\mathcal{T}}(\exists X.\mathcal{A}) \text{ entails } C(u) \,\}$.

If $\mathcal{L}$ does not satisfy this requirement, there might be another repair type $\mathcal{L}'$ such that the canonical repair contains the assertion $r(y_{t,\mathcal{K}}, y_{u,\mathcal{L}'})$, and thus our optimized repair needs to contain an appropriate variable to which $y_{u,\mathcal{L}'}$ can be mapped by a homomorphism or simulation. We generate such variables by looking for repair types $\mathcal{M}$ that cover both $\mathcal{L}$ and $\mathrm{Succ}(\mathcal{K}, r, u)$. The set of all such repair types can effectively be computed, though it might be empty. For our purposes, it is sufficient to use only the ones that are minimal w.r.t. the cover relation $\leq$.

Lemma 11. *The set of all $\leq$-minimal repair types for u that cover $\mathcal{L} \cup \mathrm{Succ}(\mathcal{K}, r, u)$ can be computed in exponential time.*

In general, this computation may produce exponentially many repair types, but this is not always the case. For instance, consider $a = y_{a,s(a)}$ and $y_{x,\emptyset}$ in Example 10. We have $\mathrm{Succ}(s(a), r, x) = \{A_1 \sqcap \ldots \sqcap A_n\}$ and thus the assertion $r(a, y_{x,\emptyset})$ is not in $\mathcal{B}$ since $\emptyset$ clearly does not cover $\mathrm{Succ}(s(a), r, x)$. The $\leq$-minimal repair types covering $\mathrm{Succ}(s(a), r, x)$ are exactly the sets $\{A_i\}$ for $i = 1, \ldots, n$.

In the following, we construct a sequence $Y_0, Y_1, \ldots, Y_m$ of subsets Y_i of Y such that $\exists Y.\mathcal{B}$ is QL-equivalent to its sub-qABox $\exists Y_m.\mathcal{B}_m$ where $\mathcal{B}_m$ contains only those assertions in $\mathcal{B}$ involving object names in $\Sigma_{\mathsf{I}} \cup Y_m$. Recall that we use $y_{a,s(a)}$ as synonyms for the individuals $a \in \Sigma_{\mathsf{I}}$.

We start with the set Y_0, which is empty if $\mathsf{QL} = \mathsf{IQ}$, and equal to the set $\{\, y_{t,\emptyset} \mid t \text{ is an object name occurring in } \mathrm{sat}_{\mathsf{CQ}}^{\mathcal{T}}(\exists X.\mathcal{A}) \,\}$ if $\mathsf{QL} = \mathsf{CQ}$.

The subsequent sets are obtained by exhaustively applying one of the following rules, depending on whether $\mathsf{QL} = \mathsf{CQ}$ or $\mathsf{QL} = \mathsf{IQ}$.

CQ-construction rule. If $y_{t,\mathcal{K}}$ and $y_{u,\mathcal{L}}$ are elements of $\Sigma_{\mathsf{I}} \cup Y_i$, the saturation $\mathrm{sat}_{\mathsf{CQ}}^{\mathcal{T}}(\exists X.\mathcal{A})$ contains the role assertion $r(t, u)$, the repair type $\mathcal{L}$ does not cover $\mathrm{Succ}(\mathcal{K}, r, u)$, and $\mathcal{M}$ is a $\leq$-minimal repair type for u that covers $\mathcal{L} \cup \mathrm{Succ}(\mathcal{K}, r, u)$, but $y_{u,\mathcal{M}}$ is not contained in $\Sigma_{\mathsf{I}} \cup Y_i$, then set $Y_{i+1} := Y_i \cup \{y_{u,\mathcal{M}}\}$.

IQ-construction rule. If $y_{t,\mathcal{K}}$ is an element of $\Sigma_{\mathsf{I}} \cup Y_i$, the saturation $\mathrm{sat}_{\mathsf{IQ}}^{\mathcal{T}}(\exists X.\mathcal{A})$ contains the role assertion $r(t, u)$, and $\mathcal{M}$ is a $\leq$-minimal repair type for u that covers $\mathrm{Succ}(\mathcal{K}, r, u)$, but $y_{u,\mathcal{M}}$ is not contained in $\Sigma_{\mathsf{I}} \cup Y_i$, then set $Y_{i+1} := Y_i \cup \{y_{u,\mathcal{M}}\}$.

The sets Y_i are all subsets of the set Y of variables in the canonical repair. Since each rule application adds a variable, the exhaustive application of rules must terminate after finitely many steps with a set of variables $Y_m \subseteq Y$.

Let us illustrate this construction using Example 10, first for the IQ case. We have $a = y_{a,s(a)} \in \Sigma_I$ and the assertion $r(a,x)$ belongs to the saturation, which is equal to the original qABox. As mentioned above, the $\leq$-minimal repair types covering $\mathsf{Succ}(s(a), r, x)$ are exactly the sets $\{A_i\}$ for $i = 1, \ldots, n$. Thus, repeated applications of the IQ-construction rule add the variables $y_{x,\{A_i\}}$, and the construction ends with $Y_m^{IQ} = \{ y_{x,\{A_i\}} \mid i = 1, \ldots, n \}$. In the CQ case, the initial set of variables is $Y_0^{CQ} = \{ y_{a,\emptyset}, y_{x,\emptyset} \}$. In this example, the CQ-construction rule then generates the same variables as the IQ rule, though this need not be the case in general. We end up with the final set $Y_m^{IQ} \cup Y_0^{CQ}$.

Definition 12. *Let s be a repair seed function and $Y_m \subseteq Y$ be the set of variables obtained by an exhaustive application of the QL-construction rule. The* optimized QL-repair *of $\exists X.\mathcal{A}$ for $\mathcal{R}$ w.r.t. $\mathcal{T}$ induced by s, denoted by $\mathsf{orep}_{QL}^{\mathcal{T}}(\exists X.\mathcal{A}, s)$, is the qABox $\exists Y_m.\mathcal{B}_m$ where the matrix $\mathcal{B}_m$ contains all assertions in $\mathcal{B}$ involving only object names in $\Sigma_I \cup Y_m$.*

Note that, to compute $\mathcal{B}_m$, we need not compute the larger matrix $\mathcal{B}$ first. Instead, we just apply the definition of the matrix in Definition 7 to the object names in $\Sigma_I \cup Y_m$.

In our example, the optimized IQ-repair is the qABox $\exists Y_m^{IQ}.\mathcal{B}_m$ with

$$\mathcal{B}_m = \{ r(a, y_{x,\{A_i\}}) \mid 1 \leq i \leq n \} \cup \{ A_j(y_{x,\{A_i\}}) \mid j \neq i \text{ and } 1 \leq i, j \leq n \}.$$

In the optimized CQ-repair, the quantifier prefix additionally contains the variables $y_{a,\emptyset}$ and $y_{x,\emptyset}$, and the matrix additionally contains the assertions $r(y_{a,\emptyset}, y_{x,\emptyset})$ and $A_i(y_{x,\emptyset})$ for $i = 1, \ldots, n$. Note that, without these assertions, the positive answer to the Boolean conjunctive query $\exists y, z.\, (r(y,z) \wedge A_1(z) \wedge \ldots \wedge A_n(z))$ would be lost.

Coming back to the general case, we first observe that the canonical QL-repair induced by s QL-entails the optimized QL-repair induced by s due to the inclusion relationship between these two qABoxes. The entailment in the other direction also holds, but this is harder to show, in particular for QL = CQ.

Proposition 13. *For each repair seed function s, the optimized QL-repair induced by s QL-entails the canonical QL-repair induced by s.*

Proof sketch. For QL = IQ, the proposition can be proved by showing that the following relation $\mathfrak{S}$ is a simulation from $\exists Y.\mathcal{B}$ to $\exists Y_m.\mathcal{B}_m$:

$$\mathfrak{S} := \{ (y_{t,\mathcal{K}}, y_{t,\mathcal{K}'}) \mid y_{t,\mathcal{K}} \in \Sigma_O(\exists Y.\mathcal{B}),\ y_{t,\mathcal{K}'} \in \Sigma_O(\exists Y_m.\mathcal{B}_m), \text{ and } \mathcal{K}' \leq \mathcal{K} \}.$$

For QL = CQ, we introduce a sequence of mappings $h_0, h_1, \ldots, h_n \colon \Sigma_O(\exists Y.\mathcal{B}) \to \Sigma_O(\exists Y_m.\mathcal{B}_m)$, starting with $h_0(y_{t,\mathcal{K}}) = y_{t,s(t)}$ if $t \in \Sigma_I$ and $s(t) \leq \mathcal{K}$ and $h_0(y_{t,\mathcal{K}}) = y_{t,\emptyset}$ otherwise. The initial mapping h_0 need not be a homomorphism since role assertions may not be preserved. In the step-wise construction of the mappings h_i such defects are corrected, one by one. We can show that this construction always terminates after finitely many steps, yielding a homomorphism h_n from $\exists Y.\mathcal{B}$ to $\exists Y_m.\mathcal{B}_m$. $\square$

Summing up, we have thus shown the following theorem, which implies that the optimized repairs also satisfy the properties stated in Proposition 8.

Theorem 14. *For each repair seed function s, the canonical QL-repair induced by s and the optimized QL-repair induced by s are QL-equivalent.*

6   Evaluation

To find out whether the repair approaches introduced in this paper are in principle viable for non-trivial ontologies, we made experiments for both IQ and CQ-repairs with a first, rather unoptimized implementation. In addition to checking how often the implementation was able to compute a repair within a certain timeout, we also compared the sizes of optimized repairs with those of canonical repairs. We considered two different repair scenarios: repairing a single unwanted consequence for a single individual (S1), and repairing a single unwanted consequence for 10% of the individuals occurring in the ABox (S2). We report here the main results—more details and discussions can be found in [4].

As corpus for our evaluation, we chose the ontologies used in the 2015 OWL Reasoner Competition for the track OWL EL Realisation [28], since they contain a substantial amount of ABox assertions. These 109 ontologies were converted into pure $\mathcal{EL}$ by applying standard transformations and afterwards filtering out unsupported axioms. From these ontologies, we kept those that had at most 100,000 axioms in total. The resulting corpus contained 80 ontologies.

We implemented our methods in Java, using the OWL-API[1] for parsing OWL ontologies, and ELK [22] for precomputing any subsumption relationships entailed with and without the TBox potentially relevant for our repair approach. The code is available online.[2] All experiments were performed on an Intel(R) Core(TM) i5-4590 CPU with 4 cores and 32 GB RAM, of which we assigned 16 GB as maximal heap space to the Java VM.

Since it is a precondition of our repair approach, we first saturated the ontologies using the IQ-saturation rules of Figure 2, and the CQ-saturation rules of Figure 1. The CQ-saturation rules were implemented using the rule engine VLog [11] through the Java facade Rulewerk.[3] As CQ-saturation only terminates for cycle-restricted TBoxes, we only considered those ontologies for the CQ-saturation whose IQ-saturation did not introduce cycles between introduced variables. We used a timeout of 60 minutes for every saturation. This way, we successfully computed IQ-saturations of every ontology, and 62 CQ-saturations.

---

[1] http://owlapi.sourceforge.net
[2] https://github.com/de-tu-dresden-inf-lat/abox-repairs-wrt-static-tbox
[3] https://github.com/knowsys/rulewerk

The size of the saturated ABox was usually not much larger than that of the original one, and always less than two orders of magnitude larger. Interestingly, the successful CQ-saturations were rarely larger than the IQ-saturations, and often even of the same size, because no variables were added.

Scenario S1 was about repairing a single faulty entailment $\mathcal{A} \models^{\mathcal{T}} C(a)$. Since we did not have information about whether any entailments from the considered ontologies are faulty, we generated such assertions randomly. For this, we looked at entailments of the form $\mathcal{A} \models^{\mathcal{T}} C(a)$, where $C \in \mathsf{Sub}(\mathcal{T})$. To make the repair requests more interesting, we furthermore required that C is not of the form A or $\exists r.\top$, where A is a concept name. This requirement already ruled out 54 of the IQ-saturated ontologies, and 44 of the CQ-saturated ontologies, as they did not have any complex entailments of the required form. For Scenario S2, we randomly selected some concept $C \in \mathsf{Sub}(\mathcal{T})$ which had at least one instance (surprisingly, although C was not required to be complex, this ruled out 12 ontologies, including 4 of the CQ-saturated ones), together with a random selection of 10% of the individuals in $\mathcal{A}$, and built the repair request consisting of all assertions $C(a)$ where a ranges over the selected individuals. For both scenarios, we selected a random seed function for the obtained repair request.

For each ontology, scenario, and $\mathsf{QL} \in \{\mathsf{IQ}, \mathsf{CQ}\}$, we attempted to compute optimised QL-repairs for 50 different repair requests. We also tried to compute the set of objects that would be included in the canonical repairs, to get an idea of the impact of our optimisation. For each such repair computation, we used a timeout of 10 minutes. Since all repair requests used only concept descriptions that were already in the input ontology, the number of objects in the canonical repair was independent of the repair request. We thus performed the latter computation only once for each ontology. The success rates were as follows:

- The objects included in the canonical IQ- and CQ-repair could be computed within the timeout and without memory exceptions for respectively only 52.9 % and 62.1 % of the ontologies.
- For S1, we could compute the optimized IQ-repair in 99.9 %, and the optimised CQ-repair in 100.0 % of all attempts.
- For S2, 98.9 % of IQ-repairs and 99.9 % of CQ-repairs were successful.

This shows that the optimizations introduced in Section 5 have a very positive impact on the viability of our repair approach.

Fig. 3 gives more information on the number of objects and assertions in the computed repairs. On the left, we consider canonical and optimised IQ-repairs for scenario S2: specifically, we look at the difference in numbers of individuals occurring in the repair compared to the input ABox. In the middle and on the right, we visualise the difference between the number of assertions in the optimized IQ- and CQ-repairs, compared to the input ABoxes, for the scenarios S1 and S2, respectively. By construction, CQ-repairs cannot contain less assertions than the input ontologies. Sometimes the CQ-repairs were smaller than the corresponding IQ-repairs, which is due to the different saturation methods: variables introduced by the IQ-saturation could be connected to more individuals than for the CQ-saturation.

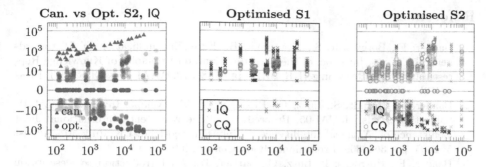

Fig. 3: Evaluation results. On the left, we show the difference of the number of object names in the canonical IQ-repairs (purple triangle) with the same difference, but restricted to objects occurring in assertions, for the optimised IQ-repairs (red circle) for S2. The other two graphs consider optimised IQ- and CQ-repairs for S1 and S2. In each graph, the x-axis shows the number of assertions in the input ontology, and the y-axis the observed difference.

7   Conclusion

This paper presents approaches for repairing DL-based ontologies, in the sense that they allow to get rid of unwanted consequences. In contrast to most of the other work on ontology repair, our goal is to compute *optimal* repairs, i.e., ones that lose the least amount of other consequences. As relevant consequences to be preserved, we consider both answers to conjunctive queries (CQ) and answers to $\mathcal{EL}$ instance queries (IQ). The presented results improve on our previous work in this direction in two respects. First, we allow for the presence of a TBox, which is assumed to be static (i.e., cannot be changed by the repair), whereas before we assumed that the TBox is empty. Second, we develop a more efficient construction of optimal repairs, which is exponential only in the worst case. Our experimental results show that this optimization makes our repair approach viable also for fairly large ontologies, at least for the IQ case.

One question for future research is how to lift the restriction to cycle-restricted TBoxes in the CQ case. Since optimal repairs need not longer exist then, one can ask whether the existence question is decidable, and how to compute optimal repairs if they exist. We have already noticed in our first attempts to tackle this problem that optimal repairs may then become larger than single-exponential.

In this and in our previous work, we have assumed that unwanted consequences are specified as $\mathcal{EL}$ instance relationships. Another interesting open question is whether our results can be generalized to a setting where unwanted consequences are specified as answers to conjunctive queries, as e.g. in [14].[4]

---

[4] Note that no TBox is considered in [14], and the notion of optimality used there is different from ours (see the introduction of [7] for a discussion of the differences).

References

1. Baader, F., Borgwardt, S., Morawska, B.: Extending unification in $\mathcal{EL}$ towards general TBoxes. In: Proc. of the 13th Int. Conf. on Principles of Knowledge Representation and Reasoning (KR 2012). pp. 568–572. AAAI Press/The MIT Press (2012)
2. Baader, F., Brandt, S., Lutz, C.: Pushing the $\mathcal{EL}$ envelope. In: Kaelbling, L.P., Saffiotti, A. (eds.) IJCAI-05, Proceedings of the Nineteenth International Joint Conference on Artificial Intelligence, Edinburgh, Scotland, UK, July 30 - August 5, 2005. pp. 364–369. Professional Book Center (2005)
3. Baader, F., Horrocks, I., Lutz, C., Sattler, U.: An Introduction to Description Logic. Cambridge University Press (2017)
4. Baader, F., Koopmann, P., Kriegel, F., Nuradiansyah, A.: Computing optimal repairs of quantified ABoxes w.r.t. static $\mathcal{EL}$ TBoxes (extended version). LTCS-Report 21-01, Chair of Automata Theory, Institute of Theoretical Computer Science, Technische Universität Dresden, Dresden, Germany (2021), https://lat.inf.tu-dresden.de/research/reports/2021/BaKoKrNu-LTCS-21-01.pdf
5. Baader, F., Kriegel, F., Nuradiansyah, A.: Privacy-preserving ontology publishing for $\mathcal{EL}$ instance stores. In: Calimeri, F., Leone, N., Manna, M. (eds.) Logics in Artificial Intelligence - 16th European Conference, JELIA 2019, Rende, Italy, May 7-11, 2019, Proceedings. Lecture Notes in Computer Science, vol. 11468, pp. 323–338. Springer (2019)
6. Baader, F., Kriegel, F., Nuradiansyah, A., Peñaloza, R.: Making repairs in description logics more gentle. In: Thielscher, M., Toni, F., Wolter, F. (eds.) Principles of Knowledge Representation and Reasoning: Proceedings of the Sixteenth International Conference, KR 2018, Tempe, Arizona, 30 October - 2 November 2018. pp. 319–328. AAAI Press (2018)
7. Baader, F., Kriegel, F., Nuradiansyah, A., Peñaloza, R.: Computing compliant anonymisations of quantified aboxes w.r.t. $\mathcal{EL}$ policies. In: Pan, J.Z., Tamma, V.A.M., d'Amato, C., Janowicz, K., Fu, B., Polleres, A., Seneviratne, O., Kagal, L. (eds.) The Semantic Web - ISWC 2020 - 19th International Semantic Web Conference, Athens, Greece, November 2-6, 2020, Proceedings, Part I. Lecture Notes in Computer Science, vol. 12506, pp. 3–20. Springer (2020)
8. Baader, F., Suntisrivaraporn, B.: Debugging SNOMED CT using axiom pinpointing in the description logic $\mathcal{EL}^+$. In: Proceedings of the International Conference on Representing and Sharing Knowledge Using SNOMED (KR-MED'08). Phoenix, Arizona (2008)
9. Boyle, T.C.: Talk to Me. Bloomsbury Publishing (2021), To appear.
10. Calì, A., Lembo, D., Rosati, R.: On the decidability and complexity of query answering over inconsistent and incomplete databases. In: Neven, F., Beeri, C., Milo, T. (eds.) Proceedings of the Twenty-Second ACM SIGACT-SIGMOD-SIGART Symposium on Principles of Database Systems, June 9-12, 2003, San Diego, CA, USA. pp. 260–271. ACM (2003)
11. Carral, D., Dragoste, I., González, L., Jacobs, C.J.H., Krötzsch, M., Urbani, J.: Vlog: A rule engine for knowledge graphs. In: Ghidini, C., Hartig, O., Maleshkova, M., Svátek, V., Cruz, I.F., Hogan, A., Song, J., Lefrançois, M., Gandon, F. (eds.) The Semantic Web - ISWC 2019 - 18th International Semantic Web Conference. Lecture Notes in Computer Science, vol. 11779, pp. 19–35. Springer (2019)
12. Glimm, B., Horrocks, I., Motik, B., Stoilos, G., Wang, Z.: Hermit: An OWL 2 reasoner. J. Autom. Reason. **53**(3), 245–269 (2014)

13. Grau, B.C., Horrocks, I., Krötzsch, M., Kupke, C., Magka, D., Motik, B., Wang, Z.: Acyclicity notions for existential rules and their application to query answering in ontologies. J. Artif. Intell. Res. **47**, 741–808 (2013)
14. Grau, B.C., Kostylev, E.V.: Logical foundations of linked data anonymisation. J. Artif. Intell. Res. **64**, 253–314 (2019)
15. Haarslev, V., Hidde, K., Möller, R., Wessel, M.: The RacerPro knowledge representation and reasoning system. Semantic Web **3**(3), 267–277 (2012)
16. Henzinger, M.R., Henzinger, T.A., Kopke, P.W.: Computing simulations on finite and infinite graphs. In: 36th Annual Symposium on Foundations of Computer Science, Milwaukee, Wisconsin, USA, 23-25 October 1995. pp. 453–462. IEEE Computer Society (1995)
17. Hoehndorf, R., Schofield, P.N., Gkoutos, G.V.: The role of ontologies in biological and biomedical research: A functional perspective. Brief. Bioinform. **16**(6), 1069–1080 (2015)
18. Horridge, M., Parsia, B., Sattler, U.: Laconic and precise justifications in OWL. In: Sheth, A.P., Staab, S., Dean, M., Paolucci, M., Maynard, D., Finin, T.W., Thirunarayan, K. (eds.) The Semantic Web - ISWC 2008, 7th International Semantic Web Conference, ISWC 2008, Karlsruhe, Germany, October 26-30, 2008. Proceedings. Lecture Notes in Computer Science, vol. 5318, pp. 323–338. Springer (2008)
19. Horrocks, I., Li, L., Turi, D., Bechhofer, S.: The instance store: DL reasoning with large numbers of individuals. In: Haarslev, V., Möller, R. (eds.) Proceedings of the 2004 International Workshop on Description Logics (DL2004), Whistler, British Columbia, Canada, June 6-8, 2004. CEUR Workshop Proceedings, vol. 104. CEUR-WS.org (2004)
20. Johnson, D.S., Klug, A.C.: Testing containment of conjunctive queries under functional and inclusion dependencies. In: Ullman, J.D., Aho, A.V. (eds.) Proceedings of the ACM Symposium on Principles of Database Systems, March 29-31, 1982, Los Angeles, California, USA. pp. 164–169. ACM (1982)
21. Kalyanpur, A., Parsia, B., Horridge, M., Sirin, E.: Finding all justifications of OWL DL entailments. In: Proc. of ISWC'07. Lecture Notes in Computer Science, vol. 4825, pp. 267–280. Springer-Verlag (2007)
22. Kazakov, Y., Krötzsch, M., Simancik, F.: The incredible ELK - from polynomial procedures to efficient reasoning with $\mathcal{EL}$ ontologies. Journal of Automed Reasoning **53**(1), 1–61 (2014)
23. Küsters, R.: Non-standard Inferences in Description Logics, Lecture Notes in Artificial Intelligence, vol. 2100. Springer-Verlag (2001)
24. Lam, J.S.C., Sleeman, D.H., Pan, J.Z., Vasconcelos, W.W.: A fine-grained approach to resolving unsatisfiable ontologies. J. Data Semant. **10**, 62–95 (2008)
25. Lutz, C., Wolter, F.: Deciding inseparability and conservative extensions in the description logic $\mathcal{EL}$. J. Symb. Comput. **45**(2), 194–228 (2010)
26. Maier, D., Mendelzon, A.O., Sagiv, Y.: Testing implications of data dependencies. ACM Trans. Database Syst. **4**(4), 455–469 (1979)
27. Meyer, T., Lee, K., Booth, R., Pan, J.Z.: Finding maximally satisfiable terminologies for the description logic $\mathcal{ALC}$. In: Proc. of the 21st Nat. Conf. on Artificial Intelligence (AAAI 2006). AAAI Press/The MIT Press (2006)
28. Parsia, B., Matentzoglu, N., Gonçalves, R.S., Glimm, B., Steigmiller, A.: The OWL Reasoner Evaluation (ORE) 2015 competition report. Journal of Automed Reasoning **59**(4), 455–482 (2017)

29. Parsia, B., Sirin, E., Kalyanpur, A.: Debugging OWL ontologies. In: Ellis, A., Hagino, T. (eds.) Proc. of the 14th International Conference on World Wide Web (WWW'05). pp. 633–640. ACM (2005)
30. Rosati, R.: On conjunctive query answering in $\mathcal{EL}$. In: Calvanese, D., Franconi, E., Haarslev, V., Lembo, D., Motik, B., Turhan, A., Tessaris, S. (eds.) Proceedings of the 2007 International Workshop on Description Logics (DL2007), Brixen-Bressanone, near Bozen-Bolzano, Italy, 8-10 June, 2007. CEUR Workshop Proceedings, vol. 250. CEUR-WS.org (2007)
31. Schlobach, S., Cornet, R.: Non-standard reasoning services for the debugging of description logic terminologies. In: Gottlob, G., Walsh, T. (eds.) Proc. of the 18th Int. Joint Conf. on Artificial Intelligence (IJCAI 2003). pp. 355–362. Morgan Kaufmann, Los Altos, Acapulco, Mexico (2003)
32. Schlobach, S., Huang, Z., Cornet, R., Harmelen, F.: Debugging incoherent terminologies. J. Automated Reasoning **39**(3), 317–349 (2007)
33. Steigmiller, A., Liebig, T., Glimm, B.: Konclude: System description. J. Web Semant. **27-28**, 78–85 (2014)
34. Troquard, N., Confalonieri, R., Galliani, P., Peñaloza, R., Porello, D., Kutz, O.: Repairing ontologies via axiom weakening. In: McIlraith, S.A., Weinberger, K.Q. (eds.) Proceedings of the Thirty-Second AAAI Conference on Artificial Intelligence, (AAAI-18), the 30th innovative Applications of Artificial Intelligence (IAAI-18), and the 8th AAAI Symposium on Educational Advances in Artificial Intelligence (EAAI-18), New Orleans, Louisiana, USA, February 2-7, 2018. pp. 1981–1988. AAAI Press (2018)

Open Access This chapter is licensed under the terms of the Creative Commons Attribution 4.0 International License (http://creativecommons.org/licenses/by/4.0/), which permits use, sharing, adaptation, distribution and reproduction in any medium or format, as long as you give appropriate credit to the original author(s) and the source, provide a link to the Creative Commons license and indicate if changes were made.

The images or other third party material in this chapter are included in the chapter's Creative Commons license, unless indicated otherwise in a credit line to the material. If material is not included in the chapter's Creative Commons license and your intended use is not permitted by statutory regulation or exceeds the permitted use, you will need to obtain permission directly from the copyright holder.

Generalized Completeness for SOS Resolution and its Application to a New Notion of Relevance

Fajar Haifani[1,2], Sophie Tourret[1,3], and Christoph Weidenbach[1]

[1] Max Planck Institute for Informatics, Saarland Informatics Campus, Saarbrücken
Germany
[2] Graduate School of Computer Science, Saarbrücken, Germany
[3] Université de Lorraine, CNRS, Inria, LORIA, Nancy, France

Abstract. We prove the SOS strategy for first-order resolution to be refutationally complete on a clause set N and set-of-support S if and only if there exists a clause in S that occurs in a resolution refutation from $N \cup S$. This strictly generalizes and sharpens the original completeness result requiring N to be satisfiable. The generalized SOS completeness result supports automated reasoning on a new notion of relevance aiming at capturing the support of a clause in the refutation of a clause set. A clause C is *relevant* for refuting a clause set N if C occurs in every refutation of N. The clause C is *semi-relevant*, if it occurs in some refutation, i.e., if there exists an SOS refutation with set-of-support $S = \{C\}$ from $N \setminus \{C\}$. A clause that does not occur in any refutation from N is *irrelevant*, i.e., it is not semi-relevant. Our new notion of relevance separates clauses in a proof that are ultimately needed from clauses that may be replaced by different clauses. In this way it provides insights towards proof explanation in refutations beyond existing notions such as that of an unsatisfiable core.

1 Introduction

Shortly after the invention of first-order resolution [14] its first complete refinement was established: set-of-support (SOS) resolution [18]. The idea of the SOS strategy is to split a current clause set into two sets, namely N and S and restrict resolution inferences to have one parent from the set-of-support S. Wos et al. [18] proved the SOS strategy complete if N is satisfiable. The motivation by Wos et. al. for the SOS strategy was getting rid of "irrelevant" inferences. If N defines a theory and S contains the negation of a conjecture (goal) to be refuted, the strategy puts emphasis on resolution inferences with the conjecture. This can be beneficial, because resolution is deductively complete (modulo subsumption) [11,13], i.e., resolution inferences solely performed on clauses from N will enumerate *all* semantic consequences, not necessarily only consequences that turn out to be useful in refuting $N \cup S$. Even in more restrictive contexts, the SOS strategy can be shown complete, e.g., if N is saturated by superposition and does not contain the empty clause, then the SOS strategy is also complete

© The Author(s) 2021
A. Platzer and G. Sutcliffe (Eds.): CADE 2021, LNAI 12699, pp. 327–343, 2021.
https://doi.org/10.1007/978-3-030-79876-5_19

in the context of the strong superposition inference restrictions on N and a set-of-support S [2].

In this paper, we generalize and sharpen the original completeness result for the SOS strategy: The resolution calculus with the SOS strategy is complete if and only if there is at least one clause in S that is contained in a resolution refutation from $N \cup S$, Theorem 11. The proof is performed via proof transformation. Any (non SOS) refutation from $N \cup S$ can be transformed into an SOS refutation with SOS S, if the original refutation contains at least one clause from S.

The generalized SOS completeness result supports our new notion of *relevance* that is meant to be a first stop towards explaining the gist of a refutation. A clause $C \in N$ is *relevant* if it is needed for any refutation of the clause set N. The clause C is *semi-relevant* if there is a refutation from N using C and C is *irrelevant* otherwise, Definition 12. Applying our generalized SOS completeness result, a clause $C \in N$ is semi-relevant if and only if there is an SOS refutation from $N \setminus \{C\}$ with SOS $\{C\}$.

The interest in semi-relevant clauses comes from real-world applications. In an industrial scenario where different products are built out of a building set, the overall product portfolio is often defined by a set of clauses (rules). Roughly, every clause describes the integration of some part out of the building set in a product. Different proofs for the existence of some product correspond to different builds of the product. For example, answering a question like "Can we build car x with part y?" from the automotive world boils down to the semi-relevance of the clauses defining part y in a refutation showing the existance of a car x. All German car manufacturers maintain such clause sets defining their product portfolio [6, 17].

Our new notion of relevance is related to other notions capturing aspects of a refutation. A minimal unsatisfiable core of an unsatisfiable clause set contains only semi-relevant clauses. The intersection of all minimal unsatisfiable cores is the set of relevant clauses. The notion of a minimal unsatisfiable core does not provide a test for semi-relevance of a specific clause. There are various notions from the description logic community related to unsatisfiable cores of a translation to first-order and/or to our notion of relevance [1,4,8,16]. An in-depth discussion of these relationships can be found in our description logic workshop paper [7]. The notion of relevant clauses is also related to what has been studied in the field of propositional satisfiability under the name of *lean kernels* [9,10]: Given an unsatisfiable set N of propositional clauses, the lean kernel consists exactly of those clauses that are involved in at least one refutation proof of N in the resolution calculus, and thus, in our terminology, the set of semi-relevant clauses. A different notion of relevance was previously defined in the context of propositional abduction [5]. The authors provide algorithms and complexity results for various abduction settings in the propositional logic context. In addition to the fact that our notion of relevance is defined with respect to first-order clauses, in their context of propositional abduction, if a propositional variable is relevant, it must be satisfiability preserving when added to the theory (clause set). In our case, if a clause $C \in N$ is (semi-)relevant, then N is unsatisfiable and $N \setminus \{C\}$ may be unsatisfiable as well.

The paper is organized as follows. After fixing some notations and notions at the beginning of Section 2 we introduce our proof transformation technique. First on an example, Figure 1, then in general. The following Section 3 proves important properties of the transformation, yielding our generalized completeness result for SOS, Theorem 11. We then link the SOS completeness result to our notion of semi-relevance in Section 4. The paper ends with a summary, a discussion of the contributions, and directions for future work, Section 5.

2 Resolution Proof Transformation

After fixing some common notions and notation, this section introduces our proof transformation technique. First on an example and afterwards on resolution refutations in general.

We assume a first-order language without equality where N denotes a clause set; C, D denote clauses; L, K denote literals; A, B denote atoms; P, Q, R, T denote predicates; t, s terms; f, g, h functions; a, b, c constants; and x, y, z variables, all possibly indexed. Atoms, literals, clauses and clause sets are considered as usual. Clauses are disjunctions of literals. The complement of a literal is denoted by the function comp. Semantic entailment $\models$ considers variables in clauses to be universally quantified. Substitutions σ, τ are total mappings from variables to terms, where $\operatorname{dom}(\sigma) := \{x \mid x\sigma \neq x\}$ is finite and $\operatorname{codom}(\sigma) := \{t \mid x\sigma = t, x \in \operatorname{dom}(\sigma)\}$. A *renaming* σ is a bijective substitution. The application of substitutions is extended to literals, clauses, and sets/sequences of such objects in the usual way. The function mgu denotes the *most general unifier* of two terms, atoms, literals if it exists. We assume that any mgu of two terms or literals does not introduce any fresh variables and is idempotent.

The resolution calculus consists of two inference rules: Resolution and Factoring [14, 15]. The rules operate on a state (N, S) where the initial state for a classical resolution refutation from a clause set N is $(\emptyset, N)$ and for an SOS refutation with clause set N and initial SOS S the initial state is (N, S). We describe the rules in the form of abstract rewrite rules operating on states (N, S). As usual we assume for the resolution rule that the involved clauses are variable disjoint. This can always be achieved by applying renamings to fresh variables.

Resolution $(N, S \uplus \{C \vee K\}) \Rightarrow_{\text{RES}} (N, S \cup \{C \vee K, (D \vee C)\sigma\})$
provided $(D \vee L) \in (N \cup S)$ and $\sigma = \operatorname{mgu}(L, \operatorname{comp}(K))$

Factoring $(N, S \uplus \{C \vee L \vee K\}) \Rightarrow_{\text{RES}} (N, S \cup \{C \vee L \vee K\} \cup \{(C \vee L)\sigma\})$
provided $\sigma = \operatorname{mgu}(L, K)$

The clause $(D \vee C)\sigma$ is called the result of a *Resolution inference* between its parents. The clause $(C \vee L)\sigma$ is called the result of a *Factoring inference* of its parent. A sequence of rule applications $(N, S) \Rightarrow_{RES}^{*} (N, S')$ is called a *resolution derivation.* It is called an *SOS resolution derivation* if $N \neq \emptyset$. In case $\perp \in S'$ it is a called a *(SOS) resolution refutation.*

Theorem 1 (Soundness and Refutational Completeness of (SOS) Resolution [14, 18]). *Resolution is sound and refutationally complete [14]. If for some clause set N and initial SOS S, N is satisfiable and $N \cup S$ is unsatisfiable, then there is a derivation of $\perp$ from (N, S) [18].*

Where a resolution derivation $(N, S) \Rightarrow^*_{\text{RES}} (N, S')$ shows how new clauses can be derived from (N, S), a deduction presents the minimal derivation of a single clause, e.g., the empty clause $\perp$ in case of a refutation. For deductions we require every clause to be used exactly once, so deductions always have a tree form. This is a purely technical restriction, see Corollary 5, that facilitates our deduction transformation technique that then needs not to take care of variable renamings except for input clauses.

Definition 2 (Deduction). *A deduction $\pi_N = [C_1, \dots, C_n]$ of a clause C_n from some clause set N is a finite sequence of clauses such that for each C_i the following holds:*

1.1 C_i is a renamed, variable-fresh version of a clause in N, or
1.2 there is a clause $C_j \in \pi_N$, $j < i$ s.t. C_i is the result of a Factoring inference from C_j, or
1.3 there are clauses $C_j, C_k \in \pi_N$, $j < k < i$ s.t. C_i is the result of a Resolution inference from C_j and C_k,

and for each $C_i \in \pi_N$, $i < n$:

2.1 there exists exactly one factor C_j of C_i with $j > i$, or
2.2 there exists exactly one C_j and C_k such that C_k is a resolvent of C_i and C_j and $i, j < k$.

We omit the subscript N in π_N if the context is clear.

A deduction π' of some clause $C \in \pi$, where π, π' are deductions from N is a subdeduction of π if $\pi' \subseteq \pi$, where for the latter subset relation we identify sequences with multisets. A deduction $\pi_N = [C_1, \dots, C_{n-1}, \perp]$ is called a *refutation.*

Note that variable renamings are only applied to clauses from N such that all clauses from N that are introduced in the deduction are variable disjoint.

Definition 3 (SOS Deduction). *A deduction $\pi_{N \cup S} = [C_1, \dots, C_n]$ is called an SOS deduction if the derivation $(N, S_0) \Rightarrow^*_{\text{RES}} (N, S_m)$ is an SOS derivation where $C'_1, \dots, C'_m$ is the subsequence from $[C_1, \dots, C_n]$ with input clauses removed, $S_0 = S$, and $S_{i+1} = S_i \cup C'_{i+1}$.*

Definition 4 (Overall Substitution of a Deduction). *Given a deduction π of a clause C_n the overall substitution $\tau_{\pi,i}$ of $C_i \in \pi$ is recursively defined by*

1 if C_i is a factor of C_j with $j < i$ and mgu σ, then $\tau_{\pi,i} = \tau_{\pi,j} \circ \sigma$,

2 if C_i is a resolvent of C_j and C_k with $j < k < i$ and mgu σ, then $\tau_{\pi,i} = (\tau_{\pi,j} \circ \tau_{\pi,k}) \circ \sigma$,
3 if C_i is an initial clause, then $\tau_{\pi,i} = \emptyset$,

and the overall substitution of the deduction is $\tau_\pi = \tau_{\pi,n}$. We omit the subscript π if the context is clear.

Overall substitutions are well-defined, because clauses introduced from N into the deduction are variable disjoint and each clause is used exactly once in the deduction. A grounding of an overall substitution τ of some deduction π is a substitution $\tau\delta$ such that codom($\tau\delta$) only contains ground terms and dom(δ) is exactly the variables from codom(τ).

Corollary 5 (Deduction Refutations versus Resolution Refutations).
There exists a resolution refutation $(N, S) \Rightarrow^*_{RES} (N, S' \cup \{\bot\})$ if and only if there exists a deduction refutation $\pi_{(N \cup S)} = [C_1, \ldots, C_{n-1}, \bot]$ where $C_i \in (N \cup S')$ for all i, modulo variable renaming.

We prove the generalized completeness result of SOS by transforming non-SOS refutations into SOS refutations. For illustration of our proof transformation technique, consider the below unsatisfiable set of clauses N. Literals are labeled in N by a singleton set of a unique natural number [12]. We will refer to the literal labels during proof transformation in order to identify resolution and factorization steps. The labels are inherited in a resolution inference and united for the factorized literal in a factoring inference. See the factoring inference on clause (3), Figure 1.

$$N = \{(1){:}\{1\}\neg Q(x_3, f(a)) \vee \{2\}P(f(a)), \quad (2){:}\{3\}\neg P(x_4) \vee \{4\}\neg Q(b, x_4),$$
$$(5){:}\{5\}\neg Q(b,a) \vee \{6\}Q(x_1, f(x_6)),$$
$$(6){:}\{7\}Q(b,x_2) \vee \{8\}R(x_2) \vee \{9\}T(c,x_1),$$
$$(9){:}\{10\}\neg R(x_5), \quad (11){:}\{11\}\neg T(c,b)\}$$

Figure 1 shows a resolution refutation
$$\pi = [(5), (6), (7), (1), (2), (3), (4), (8), (9), (10), (11), (12)]$$
from N. This resolution refutation is also an SOS refutation with SOS $S = \{(2), (5)\}$ and remaining clause set $N \setminus S$. It is not an SOS refutation with SOS $S = \{(5)\}$ and the remaining clause set $N \setminus S$ because the resolution step between clauses (1) and (2) is not an SOS step. The shaded part of the tree belongs to an SOS deduction with $S = \{(5)\}$.

The transformation identifies a clause closest to the leaves of the tree, obtained by resolution, that has one parent that can be derived by the SOS strategy, but the other parent is not in the SOS nor an input clause. For our example with starting SOS $S = \{(5)\}$ this is clause (8). The parent (7) can be derived via SOS from S but the other parent (4) is not part of an SOS derivation. The overall grounding substitution of π is $\tau = \{x_1 \mapsto b, x_2 \mapsto a, x_3 \mapsto b, x_4 \mapsto f(a), x_5 \mapsto a, x_6 \mapsto a\}$. Now the idea of a single transformation step is to perform the

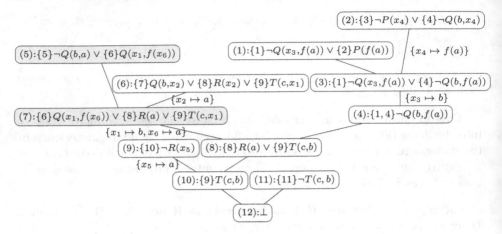

Fig. 1. Refutation of π of N

resolution step on the labelled literal $\{1,4\}\neg Q(b,f(a))$ and the respective literal $\{6\}Q(x_1,f(x_6))$ of the SOS derivable clause (7) already on the respective literals from the input clauses yielding (8), here clauses (1) and (2). To this end the derivation $[(5),(6),(7)]$ is copied with fresh variables, see Figure 2, yielding the clauses (7) and (7′) used in the refutation π' below, see also Figure 3.

$$(5){:}\{5\}\neg Q(b,a) \vee \{6\}Q(x_7,f(x_9)) \qquad (6){:}\{7\}Q(b,x_8) \vee \{8\}R(x_8) \vee \{9\}T(c,x_7)$$
$$\{x_8 \mapsto a\}$$
$$(7){:}\{6\}Q(x_7,f(x_9)) \vee \{8\}R(a) \vee \{9\}T(c,x_7)$$

Fig. 2. The copied subdeductions deriving (7)

The two freshly renamed copies (7) and (7′) are resolved with the respective input clauses (1) and (2). Finally, the rest of the deduction yielding clause (8) is simulated with the resolved input clauses, see Figure 3. Now (8‴) is exactly clause (8) from the original deduction π, but (8‴) is derived by an SOS deduction. The deduction can then be continued the same way it was done in π and in this case will already yield an SOS refutation.

$$\pi' = [(5),(6),(7),(5'),(6'),(7'),(1),(1'),(2),(2'),(8'),(8''),(8'''),$$
$$(9),(10),(11),(12)].$$

The example motivates our use of literal labels. Firstly, they tell us which literals from input clauses need to be resolved: here the literals $\{1\}\neg Q(x_3,f(a))$ and $\{4\}\neg Q(b,x_4)$ that are factorized in π to $\{1,4\}\neg Q(b,f(a))$. Secondly, they guide additional factoring steps in π' during the simulation of the non-SOS part from π: here the factoring between the two literals labelled $\{8\}$ in clause (8′) and

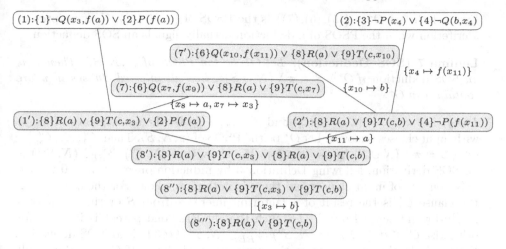

Fig. 3. The new SOS deduction yielding a copy of clause (8)

the two literals with label $\{9\}$ in clause (8″). The transformation always works because the overall grounding substitution of the initial refutation π is preserved by the transformation. It just needs to be extended to the extra variables added by freshly renamed copies of clauses.

The above example shows the importance of keeping track of the occurrences of literals in a deduction. A *labeled literal* is a pair ML where M is a finite non-empty set of natural numbers called the *label* and L is a literal. We identify literals with labeled literals and refer explicitly to the label of a labeled literal by the function lb. The function lb is extended to clauses via union of the respective literal labels. We extend the notion of a clause to that of a labeled clause built on labeled literals in the straightforward way. We call a deduction π_N *label-disjoint* if the clauses from N in the deduction have unique singleton labels. Labels are inherited in a deduction as follows: in case of a resolution inference, the labels of the parent clauses are inherited and in case of the factoring inference, the label of the remaining literal is the union of labels of the factorized literals.

In general, we need to identify the parts of a deduction that are already contained in an SOS deduction, this is called the *partial SOS* of a deduction, Definition 6. Then this information can be used to perform the above transformation on any deduction π.

Definition 6 (PSOS of a Deduction). *Let π be a deduction from $N \uplus S$, then the* partial SOS *(PSOS) O^* of $\langle \pi, N, S \rangle$ is defined as $O^* = \bigcup_{i=0}^{m} O^i$, where $O^0 = S$, $O^{i+1} = O^i \cup \{C_j\}$ provided $C_j \in \pi$, $C_j \notin O^i$ and C_j is either the factor of some clause in O^i or the resolvent of two clauses in π where at least one parent is from O^i, and where O^m is such that there is no longer such a C_j in π.*

The partial SOS is well-defined because the resulting O^* is independent of the sequence O^i used. For example, for the deduction π from N presented in

Figure 1 the set $O^* = \{(5), (6), (7)\}$ is the PSOS of $\langle \pi, N, \{5\} \rangle$. Next we present a criterion when the PSOS of a deduction actually signals an SOS deduction.

Lemma 7 (SOS Deduction). *Let O^* be the PSOS of $\langle \pi, N, S \rangle$. Then π is an SOS deduction if $O^* \setminus S = \pi \setminus (N \cup S)^4$, i.e., all inferred clauses in π are contained in O^*.*

Proof. Let $\pi_{N \cup S} = [C_1, \ldots, C_n]$ and $[C'_1, \ldots, C'_m]$ be the subsequence of $\pi_{N \cup S}$ with input clauses removed. Let O^* be the PSOS of $\langle \pi, N, S \rangle$. Then $[C'_1, \ldots, C'_m] = O^* \setminus S = \pi \setminus (N \cup S)$ by assumption. We show that $(N, S^0) \Rightarrow^*_{RES} (N, S^m)$ is an SOS derivation, following Definition 3 by induction on m. If $m = 0$ then π only consists of input clauses and there is nothing to show. For the case $m = 1$, the clause C'_1 is the result of a factoring inference from S or the result of a resolution inference from $N \cup S$ such that at least one parent is in S as for otherwise $C'_1 \notin (O^* \setminus S)$. So $(N, S^0) \Rightarrow^*_{RES} (N, S^0 \cup \{C'_1\})$ is an SOS derivation. For the induction case, assume the property holds for i. If C'_{i+1} is the result of a factoring inference, then its parent C'' is contained in S^i because otherwise $C'' \in N$ because π being a deduction, and, therefore $C'_{i+1} \notin (O^* \setminus S)$, a contradiction. If C'_{i+1} is the result of a resolution inference, then again all its parents are contained in $N \cup S^i$ because π is a deduction. If both parents are from N, then $C'_{i+1} \notin (O^* \setminus S)$, a contradiction. So, by the induction hypothesis, $(N, S^0) \Rightarrow^*_{RES} (N, S^i) \Rightarrow_{RES} (N, S^{i+1})$ is an SOS derivation. $\square$

The rest of this section is devoted to describing the transformation in detail. In the next section, we then prove the new completeness result for SOS.

Let π be a label-disjoint deduction from $N \cup S$ and let $C_k \in \pi$ be a clause of minimal index such that C_k is the result of a resolution inference from clauses $C_j \in O^*$ and $C_i \notin (N \cup O^*)$. Let τ be an overall ground substitution for π. We transform π into π' by changing the deduction of C_i such that the overall deduction gets "closer" to an SOS derivation and preserves τ. Let

$$
\begin{aligned}
C_j &= C'_j \vee L \\
C_i &= C'_i \vee K \\
C_k &= (C'_i \vee C'_j)\sigma
\end{aligned}
\tag{1}
$$

where $\sigma = \mathrm{mgu}(K, \mathrm{comp}(L))$. Without loss of generality we assume that

$$
\pi = [C_1, \ldots, C_i, C_{i+1}, \ldots, C_j, C_k, C_{k+1}, \ldots, C_n]
\tag{2}
$$

where $[C_1, \ldots, C_i]$ and $[C_{i+1}, \ldots, C_j]$ are subdeductions of π, and the prefixes of these sequences are exactly the introduced renamed copies of input clauses from N that are used to derive C_i and C_j, respectively. The transformed derivation will be

$$
\pi' = [C^1_{i+1}, \ldots, C^1_j, \ldots, C^m_{i+1}, \ldots, C^m_j, D_1, \ldots, D_l, C'_{k+1}, \ldots, C'_n]
\tag{3}
$$

where

---

[4] Here we refer to the removal of all input clauses from O^* and π, respectively.

(a) the subsequences $[C^o_{i+1}, \ldots, C^o_j]$ are freshly variable-renamed copies of the sequence $[C_{i+1}, \ldots, C_j]$ where $m = |\,\text{lb}(K)|$. For the copies $[C^o_{i+1}, \ldots, C^o_j]$ we keep the labels of literals of the original sequence $[C_{i+1}, \ldots, C_j]$ for reference in the transformation. The clauses C^o_j are decomposed into $C'^o_j \vee L'$, in the same way that the clause C_j is decomposed into $C'_j \vee L$. Thus, for each clause from N in the sequence $[C_1, \ldots, C_i]$ containing a literal K' with $\text{lb}(K') \subseteq \text{lb}(K)$ we add a deduction deriving a renamed copy of C^p_j; let δ^p be the renaming substitution from the old to the freshly renamed sequence, then we extend τ to τ' as follows: $\tau'_0 = \tau$, $\tau'_{p+1} = \tau'_p \circ \{x\delta^{p+1} \mapsto t \mid x \in \text{dom}(\delta^{p+1}), t = x\tau\}$ for $1 \leq p \leq m$ yielding the overall new grounding substitution $\tau' = \tau'_m$ for π';

(b) the clauses $D_1, \ldots, D_l$ are generated by simulating the deduction $[C_1, \ldots, C_i]$ eventually producing C_k, up to possible variable renamings: Let C_p be the current clause out of this deduction and let $D_1, \ldots, D_q$ be the clauses generated so far until C_{p-1};

(i) if C_p is an input clause not containing a literal K' with $\text{lb}(K') \subseteq \text{lb}(K)$, then $D_{q+1} = C_p$ and we associate D_{q+1} with C_p;

(ii) if C_p is an input clause containing a literal K' with $\text{lb}(K') \subseteq \text{lb}(K)$, then $D_{q+1} = C_p$ and D_{q+2} is the resolvent between D_{q+1} and a so far unused clause C^o_j on the literals $K' \in D_{q+1}$ and $L' \in C^o_j$ where $\text{lb}(K') \subseteq \text{lb}(K)$ and $\text{lb}(L') = \text{lb}(L)$ and we associate D_{q+2} with C_p;

(iii) if C_p is the resolvent between two clauses $C_{i'}, C_{j'}$ then we perform the respective resolution step between the associated clauses and respective associated literals from $D_{q'}, D_{q''}$ yielding D_{q+1} and associate D_{q+1} with C_p;

(iv) if C_p is the factor on some literal K' with $\text{lb}(K') \subseteq \text{lb}(K)$, then we perform the respective factoring steps $D_{q+1}, \ldots, D_{q+s}$ for respective literals with labels from C'_j, where $s = |C'_j|$ and we associate D_{q+s} with C_p,

(v) if C_p is the factor on some literal K' with $\text{lb}(K') \not\subseteq \text{lb}(K)$, then we perform the respective factoring step on the respective literals with identical labels from clause $D_{q'}$ yielding D_{q+1} and we associate D_{q+1} with C_p;

(c) the clauses $C'_{k+1}, \ldots, C'_n$ are obtained by simulating the generation of clauses $C_{k+1}, \ldots, C_n$ where C_k is substituted with D_l.

Note that by assumption, the generation of clauses $C_{k+1}, \ldots, C_n$ does not depend on clauses $C_1, \ldots, C_i, C_{i+1}, \ldots, C_j$ but only on C_k and the input clauses. We will prove that $C_k\tau = C_k\tau' = D_l\tau'$ which is then sufficient to prove $C_n\tau = C_n\tau' = C'_n\tau'$ and for the above to be well-defined. In general, the clause D_l is not identical to C_k because we introduce fresh variables in π' and do not make any specific assumptions on the unifiers used to derive D_l.

Mapping the transformation to our running example, Figure 1: $C_j = (7)$, $C_i = (4)$, and $C_k = (8)$. We need two copies of (7) because $K = \{1,4\}\neg Q(b, f(a))$ so $m = |\{1,4\}| = 2$ and $L = \{6\}Q(x_1, f(x_6))$.

3   A Generalized Completeness Proof for SOS

In this section, we prove that repeated applications of the transformation introduced in the previous section can actually transform an arbitrary deduction into an SOS deduction, given that at least one clause from the SOS occurs in the original deduction. Firstly, we show that associated clauses of the transformed deduction preserve main properties of the original deduction. The extended substitution is identical to the original substitution on old clauses and the changed part of the deduction ends in exactly the same clause.

Lemma 8 (Properties of Associated Clauses). *Let C_j, C_i, C_k, L, K, π, π', τ, τ' be as defined in (1), (2), and (3), page 334. For each clause C out of $[C_1, \ldots, C_i]$ and clause D associated with C:*

1. $C\tau = C\tau'$,
2. $K'\tau' = L'\tau'$ if $\mathrm{lb}(K') = \mathrm{lb}(L')$ for any K', L' occurring in either π or π',
3. $\mathrm{lb}(C) \setminus \mathrm{lb}(K) = \mathrm{lb}(D) \setminus \mathrm{lb}(C_j'^o)$ and $\mathrm{lb}(C_j'^o) \subseteq \mathrm{lb}(D)$ if there is $K' \in C$ with $\mathrm{lb}(K') \subseteq \mathrm{lb}(K)$,
4. $C\tau \setminus \{K'\tau \in C \mid \mathrm{lb}(K') \subseteq \mathrm{lb}(K)\} = D\tau' \setminus \{L'\tau' \in D\tau' \mid \mathrm{lb}(L') \in \mathrm{lb}(C_j'^o)\}$ and $C_j'^o\tau' \subseteq D\tau'$ if there is $K' \in C$ with $\mathrm{lb}(K') \subseteq \mathrm{lb}(K)$,
5. $C_k\tau = D_l\tau'$.

Proof. 1. By definition of τ' the additional variables in τ' do not occur in C while τ' is identical to τ on the variables of C, hence $C\tau = C\tau'$.

2. By induction on the generation of π'. For the base case, every literal occurring in $N \cup S$ has a unique label and any renamed clause C_m^o for some $C_m \in (N \cup S)$ has the labels kept. So, for any two literals K' and L' in any non inferred clauses in π and π', $K'\tau' = L'\tau'$ when the labels are equal. For the induction step, for inferred clauses, $\mathrm{lb}(K') = \mathrm{lb}(L')$ happens when the label of K' is inherited from L' through an inference. The inference uses an mgu which is compatible with τ' due to τ' being an overall ground substitution, so $K'\tau' = L'\tau'$.

3. We prove this property by induction on the length of the derivation $[C_1, \ldots, C_i]$. Let $C = C_p$, $1 \leq p \leq i$, and let $D_1, \ldots, D_q$ be the clauses generated until C_{p-1} for which, by the induction hypothesis the property already holds.

(i) If C is an input clause not containing a literal K' with $\mathrm{lb}(K') \subseteq \mathrm{lb}(K)$, we have $C = C_p = D_{q+1} = D$ and $\{K' \in C\tau \mid \mathrm{lb}(K') \subseteq \mathrm{lb}(K)\} = \{L' \in D_q\tau' \mid \mathrm{lb}(L') \subseteq \mathrm{lb}(C_j'^o)\} = \emptyset$.

(ii) If C is an input clause containing a literal K' with $\mathrm{lb}(K') \subseteq \mathrm{lb}(K)$ then $D = D_{q+2}$ results from a resolution inference between $C = C_p$ and an unused C_j^o on the literals K' and $L' \in C_j^o$ with $\mathrm{lb}(L') = \mathrm{lb}(L)$. Let $C = C' \vee K'$. Then $D\tau' = (C' \vee C_j'^o)\tau'$ and hence $\mathrm{lb}(C) \setminus \mathrm{lb}(K) = \mathrm{lb}(D) \setminus \mathrm{lb}(C_j'^o)$ because $\mathrm{lb}(C) \cap \mathrm{lb}(C_j^o) = \emptyset$ as π is a label-disjoint deduction and $\mathrm{lb}(C_j) = \mathrm{lb}(C_j^o)$ by construction.

(iii) If C is a resolvent of $C_{i'} = C_{i'}' \vee L_{i'}'$ and $C_{j'} = C_{j'}' \vee L_{j'}'$ on literals $L_{i'}'$, $L_{j'}'$, then $C\tau = C_{i'}'\tau \vee C_{j'}'\tau$, and D_{q+1} is a resolvent of some $D_{q'} = D_{q'}' \vee L_{q'}''$ and $D_{q''} = D_{q''}' \vee L_{q''}''$ associated with $C_{i'}$ and $C_{j'}$ respectively. We have

$\text{lb}(L'_{i'}) = \text{lb}(L''_{q''})$ and $\text{lb}(L'_{j'}) = \text{lb}(L''_{q''})$ and none of these literals has a label from $\text{lb}(K)$ or $\text{lb}(C'^o_j)$. Hence, the conjecture holds by the induction hypothesis.

(iv) If C results from a factoring on K' from C_{p-1}, we get D_{q+s} by a sequence of s factoring inferences from D_{q+1} associated with C_{p-1}. Any factorings on C_{p-1} and D_{q+1} do not change literal labels because we factorize literals of identical label. So, this property holds by the induction hypothesis. This holds regardless of whether $\text{lb}(K') \subseteq \text{lb}(K)$.

4. From Lemma 8.3 we know that $\text{lb}(C) \setminus \text{lb}(K) = \text{lb}(D) \setminus \text{lb}(C'^o_j)$ and $\text{lb}(C'^o_j) \subseteq \text{lb}(D)$ if there is $K' \in C$ with $\text{lb}(K') \subseteq \text{lb}(K)$. Since the labels coincide, using Lemma 8.2, we have $C\tau' \setminus \{K' \in C\tau' \mid \text{lb}(K') \subseteq \text{lb}(K)\} = D\tau' \setminus \{L' \in D\tau' \mid \text{lb}(L') \in \text{lb}(C'^o_j)\}$ and $C'^o_j \tau' \subseteq D\tau'$ if there is $K' \in C$ with $\text{lb}(K') \subseteq \text{lb}(K)$. This hypothesis holds by applying Lemma 8.1 on literals and clauses from π in the equation.

5. The clause C_k is the result of a resolution inference between C_i and C_j upon K and L: $C_k\tau = C'_i\tau \cup C'_j\tau$. By translation and because $\{K' \in C_i \mid \text{lb}(K') \subseteq \text{lb}(K)\} = \{K\}$, the clause C_i is associated with $D_l \in \pi'$ and $C_i\tau \setminus \{K\tau\} = D_l\tau' \setminus \{L' \in D_l\tau' \mid \text{lb}(L') \in \text{lb}(C'^o_j)\}$. Since $C'^o_j\tau' = C'_j\tau = C_j\tau \setminus \{L\tau\}$, we have $\{L'' \in D_l\tau' \mid \text{lb}(L'') \subseteq \text{lb}(L')$ for some $L' \in C'^o_j\} = D_l\tau' \cap C'^o_j \setminus \{L\tau\} = C_j \setminus \{L\tau\}$. So $C_i \setminus \{K\tau\} = D_l\tau' \setminus (D_l\tau' \cap C_j \setminus \{L\tau\}) = D_l\tau' \setminus (C_j \setminus \{L\tau\})$. We can add $C_j\tau \setminus \{L\tau\}$ to both sides and get $C_k\tau = C_i\tau \cup C_j\tau \setminus \{K\tau, L\tau\} \supseteq D_l\tau'$. In addition, since $\text{lb}(K) \subseteq \text{lb}(K)$, this means $C_j\tau = C'^o_j\tau' \subseteq D_q\tau'$. Therefore $C_k\tau = C_i\tau \cup C_j\tau \setminus \{K\tau, L\tau\} = D_l\tau'$. □

Next we need a well-founded measure that decreases with every transformation step and in case of reaching its minimum signals an SOS deduction. Given a clause set N and an initial SOS S, the SOS measure of a deduction π is $\mu(\pi)$ where $\mu(\pi) = \sum_{C_i \in \pi} \mu(C_i, \pi)$ and $\mu(C_i, \pi) = 0$ if $C_i \in N \cup O^*$ otherwise $\mu(C_i, \pi) = 1$.

Lemma 9 (Properties of μ). *Given a clause set N, an initial SOS S, and a deduction π that contains at least one resolution step,*

1. $\mu(\pi) \geq 0$, *and*
2. *if* $\mu(\pi) = 0$ *then* π *is an SOS deduction.*

Proof. 1. Obvious.

2. Towards contradiction, suppose $\pi = [C_1, \ldots, C_n]$ is not an SOS deduction. This means $O^* \setminus S \subsetneq \pi \setminus (N \cup S)$ by Lemma 7. Consider a clause $C_i \in (\pi \setminus (N \cup S)) \setminus (O^* \setminus S)$ of minimal index. Then C_i must be the result of an inference on some C_j and C_k such that both are not in O^*. This means $C_i \notin (N \cup O^*)$. For this clause, μ assigns a nonzero value: $\mu(C_i, \pi) > 0$. Therefore, $\mu(\pi) \neq 0$. □

Next we combine the properties of associated clauses on one transformation step with the properties of the measure resulting in an overall deduction transformation that can be recursively applied and deduces the same clause modulo some grounding.

Lemma 10 (Properties of the Transformation). *Given a deduction π of a clause C_n from $N \cup S$ that contains at least one resolution step such that $\pi \cap S \neq \emptyset$, an overall ground substitution τ of π and the transformed deduction π' of a clause C'_n as defined in (1), (2), and (3) with overall ground substitution τ', we have:*

1. *π' is a deduction from $N \cup S$,*
2. *$C_n \tau = C'_n \tau'$, and*
3. *$\mu(\pi') < \mu(\pi)$.*

Proof. 1. We show that π' is a deduction following Definition 2. These properties will be carried over from π. Observe that, if π_1 is a deduction of C_k from $N \cup S$ and π_2 is a deduction from $N \cup S \cup \{C_k\}$ using C_k only once, their concatenation $\pi_1 \circ \pi_2$ is a deduction from $N \cup S$. Firstly, the subsequences $[C^o_{i+1}, \ldots, C^o_j]$ are deductions of C^o_j from $N \cup S$ since they are only the renamed copies of the subdeduction $[\hat{C}_{i+1}, \ldots C_j]$ of π. Secondly, the subsequence $[C_k, \ldots, C_n]$ is a deduction of C_n from $N \cup S \cup \{C_k\}$ since the clauses after C_k do not use any clauses before C_k by the way π is represented as a sequence. Now, by showing that $[C^1_j, \ldots, C^m_j, D_1, \ldots, D_l, C_k]$ is a deduction of C_k from $N \cup S \cup \{C^o_j\}_{o \in [1,m]}$, the sequence $[D_1, \ldots, D_l]$ would then connect the initial copied sequences and the tailing subsequence. Each C^o_j is used for exactly one resolution inference producing some D_q, the other required clauses are copied, and the later resolution and factoring steps in $[D_1, \ldots, D_l]$ are sound while the deduction properties of $[C_1, \ldots, C_i]$ are preserved in its associated clauses: for an inference where $C_{p'}$ (and $C_{p''}$) generates C_p, we have a unique inference between their associated clauses $D_{q'}, (D_{q''},) D_{q+1}$ where $D_{q'}$ (and $D_{q''}$) generates D_{q+1}, possibly with additional factoring inferences in between. If C_p is an input clause not containing a literal K' with $\mathrm{lb}(K') \subseteq \mathrm{lb}(K)$, then $D_{q+1} = C_p \in N$. The clause D_{q+1} is used in π' as C_p is used in π; if C_p is an input clause containing a literal K' with $\mathrm{lb}(K') \subseteq \mathrm{lb}(K)$, the resolution between D_{q+1} and a so far unused clause C^o_j is sound as K' and $\mathrm{comp}(L')$ are unifiable by τ'. Here, all C^o_j will be eventually used as there are $m = |\mathrm{lb}(K)|$ literals in the clauses from N; if C_p is the resolvent between two clauses $C_{i'}, C_{j'}$ then the respective resolution step between the associated clauses $D_{q'}, D_{q''}$ upon the respective associated literals K' and L' is sound because we can get $K'\tau' = \mathrm{comp}(L')\tau'$ using Lemma 8; if C_p is the factor on some literal K' with $\mathrm{lb}(K') \subseteq \mathrm{lb}(K)$, then the respective factoring steps $D_{q+1}, \ldots, D_{q+s}$ are also sound: each pair of the s associated literals M and M' from C^o_j and $C^{o'}_j$ are unifiable because $M\tau' = M'\tau'$; if C_p is the factor of C_{p-1} upon some literal K' and L' with $\{\mathrm{lb}(K'), \mathrm{lb}(L')\} \not\subseteq \mathrm{lb}(K)$, the respective factoring step on the associated clause $D_{q'}$ is also sound by Lemma 8. Therefore π is a deduction from $N \cup S$.

2. By Lemma 8.5, $C_k \tau = D_l \tau'$. The derivation of clauses $C_k, C_{k+1}, \ldots, C_n$ only depends on the input clauses by assumption. By an inductive argument we get $C_{k+1}\tau = C'_{k+1}\tau'$ yielding $C_n \tau = C'_n \tau'$.

3. The clauses in $[C^o_{i+1}, \ldots, C^o_j]$ have the measure 0 as their original ones in $[C_{i+1}, \ldots, C_j]$ because they are in $N \cup O^*$. The clauses in $[C_k, \ldots, C_n]$ also retain their original measures. The clauses in $[D_1, \ldots, D_l]$ are s.t. $\Sigma^l_{k=1} \mu(\pi', D_k) <$

$\Sigma_{k=1}^{i}\mu(\pi', C_k)$. More specifically, any $C \in [C_1, \ldots, C_i]$ that is not in $N \cup O^*$ (with measure $\mu(C, \pi) \geq 1$) and containing K' with $\mathrm{lb}(K') \subseteq \mathrm{lb}(K)$ is associated with $D_q \in O^* \setminus N$ having the measure $\mu(D_q, \pi') = 0$, while all other clauses in $[D_1, \ldots, D_l]$ are either copied from π with the same measure as before or new in π' but have the measure 0.

By induction on the length of the sequence $[C_1, \ldots, C_i]$ we prove the following property: if D is associated with a clause $C \in [C_1, \ldots, C_i]$ and C contains some literal in $\{K' \mid \mathrm{lb}(K') \subseteq \mathrm{lb}(K)\}$, then $D \in N \cup O^*$ and $\mu(D, \pi') = 0$. Let $C = C_p$. Let $D_1, \ldots, D_q$ be the clauses generated until C_{p-1} s.t. the property already holds.

(i) If C_p is an input clause with no literals in $\{K' \mid \mathrm{lb}(K') \subseteq \mathrm{lb}(K)\}$, it is associated with $D_q = C_p$ s.t. $\mu(C_p, \pi) = \mu(D_q, \pi') = 0$;

(ii) If C_p is an input clause containing $\{K' \mid \mathrm{lb}(K') \subseteq \mathrm{lb}(K)\}$, it is resolved with some $C_j^o \in O^*$ resulting in $D_{q+1} \in O^*$. Here we have $\mu(C_p, \pi) = \mu(D_q, \pi') = 0$;

(iii) If C_p is the resolvent between two clauses $C_{i'}, C_{j'}$ then we perform the respective resolution step between the associated clauses $D_{q'}, D_{q''}$ yielding the clause D_q associated with C_p. If either $C_{i'}$ or $C_{j'}$ contains some literal from $\{K' \mid \mathrm{lb}(K') \subseteq \mathrm{lb}(K)\}$ then C_p contains this literal as well and either $D_{q'} \in O^*$ or $D_{q''} \in O^*$ by the induction hypothesis. So, we get $D_q \in O^*$ and $\mu(D_q, \pi') = 0$. Otherwise, $\mu(D_q, \pi') = \mu(C_p, \pi) = 1$;

(iv) If C_p is the factor of C_{p-1} on some literal K' with $\mathrm{lb}(K') \subseteq \mathrm{lb}(K)$, then we have the respective factoring steps $D_{q+1}, \ldots, D_{q+s}$ where D_{q+1} is associated with C_{p-1}. By the induction hypothesis, $D_{q+1} \in O^*$. Therefore $D_{q+1}, \ldots, D_{q+s} \in O^*$ with $\mu(D_{q+t}, \pi') = 0$ for $1 \leq t \leq s$;

(v) If C_p is the factor of C_{p-1} (associated with D_q) on some literal K' and L' with $\{\mathrm{lb}(K'), \mathrm{lb}(L')\} \not\subseteq \mathrm{lb}(K)$, the factoring happens to the associated clauses in π' with similar measure.

Finally, by the choice of C_i, C_j, and C_k, there must exist at least one C_p with some literal from $\{K' \mid \mathrm{lb}(K') \subseteq \mathrm{lb}(K)\}$ but associated with some D such that $D \in O^*$ from case (iii) or (iv) before. This also means $\mu(D, \pi') = 0$. The clause C_i has this property as it contains K. In addition, any C_p has a nonzero measure because $C_i \not\in N \cup O^*$ and C_p is used to prove C_i. Therefore, we have $\mu(C_p, \pi) > \mu(D, \pi') = 0$. As these clauses are never copied to π', $\mu(\pi') < \mu(\pi)$. $\square$

Eventually, by an inductive argument we prove our main result.

Theorem 11 (Generalized SOS Completeness). *There is an SOS resolution refutation from (N, S) if and only if there is resolution refutation from $N \cup S$ that contains at least one clause from S.*

Proof. "$\Rightarrow$": Obvious: If there is no refutation from $N \cup S$ using a clause S then there can also not be any SOS resolution refutation from (N, S).

"$\Leftarrow$": If there is a deduction refutation π from $N \cup S$ that contains at least one clause from S, then by an inductive argument on μ it can be transformed into an SOS deduction refutation with SOS S, and the result follows by Corollary 5. If $\mu(\pi) = 0$ then π is already an SOS deduction, Lemma 9. For otherwise, we transform the deduction π into a deduction π' according to (1), (2), and (3). A refutation always contains at least one resolution step, so by Lemma 10, π' is also a refutation from $N \cup S$ and $\mu(\pi') < \mu(\pi)$. Eventually, π' can be transformed into a label-disjoint deduction by assigning fresh labels to all used clauses from $N \cup S$. □

As an example for the "$\Rightarrow$" direction consider the propositional logic clause set $N = \{P, \neg P\}$ and SOS $S = \{Q\}$. Obviously, there is no refutation of $N \cup S$ using Q and there is no SOS refutation. Theorem 11 also guarantees that the consecutive application of the proof transformation steps (1), (2), and (3), page 334, results in an effective recursive procedure that transforms non-SOS refutations into SOS refutations.

4   A new Notion of Relevance

The idea of our notion of relevance is to separate clauses that are ultimately needed in a refutation proof called *relevant*, from clauses that are useful called *semi-relevant*, from clauses that are not needed called *irrelevant*.

Definition 12 (Relevance). *Given an unsatisfiable set of clauses N, a clause $C \in N$ is relevant if for all deduction refutations π of N it holds that $C \in \pi$. A clause $C \in N$ is semi-relevant if there exists a deduction refutation π of N in which $C \in \pi$. A clause $C \in N$ is irrelevant if there is no deduction refutation π of N in which $C \in \pi$.*

With respect to our example clause set N from Section 2 and its refutation, Figure 1, clause (5) is semi-relevant but not relevant, because the clauses (1), (2), (6), (9), (11) are already unsatisfiable. The clauses (1), (2), (6), (9), (11) are all relevant.

Lemma 13 (Relevance). *Given an unsatisfiable set of clauses N, the clause $C \in N$ is relevant if and only if $N \setminus \{C\}$ is satisfiable.*

Proof. Obvious: if $N \setminus \{C\}$ is satisfiable there is no resolution refutation and since N is unsatisfiable C must occur in all refutations. If C occurs in all refutations there is no refutation without C so $N \setminus \{C\}$ is satisfiable. □

Lemma 14 (Semi-Relevance Test). *Given a set of clauses N, and a clause $C \in N$, C is semi-relevant if and only if $(N \setminus \{C\}, \{C\}) \Rightarrow^*_{RES} (N \setminus \{C\}, S \cup \{\bot\})$.*

Proof. If $(N \setminus \{C\}, \{C\}) \Rightarrow^*_{RES} (N \setminus \{C\}, S \cup \{\bot\})$ then we have found a refutation containing C. On the other hand, by Theorem 11, Lemma 7 and Corollary 5, if there is a refutation containing C, then there is also an SOS refutation with SOS $\{C\}$. □

An immediate consequence of the above test and completeness of resolution for first-order logic is the following corollary.

Corollary 15 (Complexity of the Semi-Relevance Test). *Testing semi-relevance in first-order logic is semi-decidable. It is decidable for all fragments where resolution constitutes a decision procedure.*

Fragments where our semi-relevance test is guaranteed to terminate are for example first-order fragments enjoying the bounded model property, such as the Bernays-Schoenfinkel fragment [3].

5   Conclusion

We have extended and sharpened the original completeness result for SOS resolution [18], Theorem 11. The generalized SOS completeness result can actually be used to effectively test clauses for semi-relevance in case resolution constitutes a decision procedure for the respective clause set. This is for example the case for all fragments enjoying the bounded model property, such as the Bernays-Schoenfinkel fragment [3]. In general, our approach yields a semi-decision procedure for semi-relevance.

Our proof is based on deductions having an a priori tree structure. However, this is not a principle restriction. It just simplifies the transformation introduced in Section 2: renamings have only to be considered on input clauses. In a setting where proofs forming directed acyclic graphs are considered, renamings have to be carried all over a deduction, adding further technicalities to our transformation.

It is well-known that changing the ordering of resolution steps in a resolution deduction may exponentially increase or exponentially decrease the length of the deduction. Therefore, our transformation of a deduction into an SOS deduction may also yield an exponential growth in the length of the deduction. It may also be the other way round if, e.g, subsumption is added to the transformation. It is also not difficult to find examples where the transformation of Section 2 introduces redundant clauses. Recall that we have not made any assumption with respect to redundancy on deductions. So an open question is whether corresponding results hold on non-redundant deductions and what they actually mean for a respective notion of relevance.

An open problem is the question whether a test for semi-relevance can be established with more restricted resolution calculi such as ordered resolution. In general, the SOS strategy is not complete with ordered resolution. However, it is complete with respect to a clause set saturated by ordered resolution. The technical obstacle here is that a saturated clause set may already contain the empty clause, because for our generalized completeness result and the respective relationship to semi-relevance, the set N may still be unsatisfiable without the clause C to be tested for semi-relevance.

Acknowledgments: This work was funded by DFG grant 389792660 as part of TRR 248. We thank our reviewers for their valuable comments.

References

1. Baader, F., Peñaloza, R.: Axiom pinpointing in general tableaux. J. Log. Comput. **20**(1), 5–34 (2010)
2. Bachmair, L., Ganzinger, H.: Rewrite-based equational theorem proving with selection and simplification. Journal of Logic and Computation **4**(3), 217–247 (1994), revised version of Max-Planck-Institut für Informatik technical report, MPI-I-91-208, 1991
3. Bernays, P., Schönfinkel, M.: Zum entscheidungsproblem der mathematischen logik. Mathematische Annalen **99**, 342–372 (1928)
4. Bourgaux, C., Ozaki, A., Peñaloza, R., Predoiu, L.: Provenance for the description logic elhr. In: Bessiere, C. (ed.) Proceedings of the Twenty-Ninth International Joint Conference on Artificial Intelligence, IJCAI 2020. pp. 1862–1869. ijcai.org (2020)
5. Eiter, T., Gottlob, G.: The complexity of logic-based abduction. Journal of the ACM **42**(1), 3–42 (1995)
6. Fetzer, C., Weidenbach, C., Wischnewski, P.: Compliance, functional safety and fault detection by formal methods. In: Margaria, T., Steffen, B. (eds.) Leveraging Applications of Formal Methods, Verification and Validation: Discussion, Dissemination, Applications - 7th International Symposium, ISoLA 2016, Imperial, Corfu, Greece, October 10-14, 2016, Proceedings, Part II. Lecture Notes in Computer Science, vol. 9953, pp. 626–632 (2016)
7. Haifani, F., Koopmann, P., Tourret, S., Weidenbach, C.: On a notion of relevance. In: Borgwardt, S., Meyer, T. (eds.) Proceedings of the 33rd International Workshop on Description Logics (DL 2020) co-located with the 17th International Conference on Principles of Knowledge Representation and Reasoning (KR 2020), Online Event [Rhodes, Greece], September 12th to 14th, 2020. CEUR Workshop Proceedings, vol. 2663. CEUR-WS.org (2020)
8. Kalyanpur, A., Parsia, B., Horridge, M., Sirin, E.: Finding all justifications of OWL DL entailments. In: Aberer, K., Choi, K., Noy, N.F., Allemang, D., Lee, K., Nixon, L.J.B., Golbeck, J., Mika, P., Maynard, D., Mizoguchi, R., Schreiber, G., Cudré-Mauroux, P. (eds.) The Semantic Web, 6th International Semantic Web Conference, 2nd Asian Semantic Web Conference, ISWC 2007 + ASWC 2007, Busan, Korea, November 11-15, 2007. Lecture Notes in Computer Science, vol. 4825, pp. 267–280. Springer (2007)
9. Kleine Büning, H., Kullmann, O.: Minimal unsatisfiability and autarkies. In: Biere, A., Heule, M., van Maaren, H., Walsh, T. (eds.) Handbook of Satisfiability, Frontiers in Artificial Intelligence and Applications, vol. 185, pp. 339–401. IOS Press (2009)
10. Kullmann, O.: Investigations on autark assignments. Discret. Appl. Math. **107**(1-3), 99–137 (2000)
11. Lee, C.T.: A Completeness Theorem and a Computer Program for Finding Theorems Derivable from Given Axioms. Phd thesis, University of Berkeley, California, Department of Electrical Engineering (1967)
12. Lev-Ami, T., Weidenbach, C., Reps, T.W., Sagiv, M.: Labelled clauses. In: Pfenning, F. (ed.) Automated Deduction - CADE-21, 21st International Conference on Automated Deduction, Bremen, Germany, July 17-20, 2007, Proceedings. LNCS, vol. 4603, pp. 311–327. Springer (2007)
13. Nienhuys-Cheng, S., de Wolf, R.: The equivalence of the subsumption theorem and the refutation-completeness for unconstrained resolution. In: Kanchanasut, K., Lévy, J. (eds.) Algorithms, Concurrency and Knowledge: 1995 Asian Computing Science

Conference, ACSC '95, Pathumthani, Thailand, December 11-13, 1995, Proceedings. Lecture Notes in Computer Science, vol. 1023, pp. 269–285. Springer (1995)

14. Robinson, J.A.: A machine-oriented logic based on the resolution principle. Journal of the ACM **12**(1), 23–41 (January 1965)

15. Robinson, J.A., Voronkov, A. (eds.): Handbook of Automated Reasoning (in 2 volumes). Elsevier and MIT Press (2001)

16. Schlobach, S., Cornet, R.: Non-standard reasoning services for the debugging of description logic terminologies. In: Gottlob, G., Walsh, T. (eds.) IJCAI-03, Proceedings of the Eighteenth International Joint Conference on Artificial Intelligence, Acapulco, Mexico, August 9-15, 2003. pp. 355–362. Morgan Kaufmann (2003)

17. Walter, R., Felfernig, A., Küchlin, W.: Constraint-based and sat-based diagnosis of automotive configuration problems. J. Intell. Inf. Syst. **49**(1), 87–118 (2017)

18. Wos, L., Robinson, G., Carson, D.: Efficiency and completeness of the set of support strategy in theorem proving. Journal of the ACM **12**(4), 536–541 (1965)

Open Access This chapter is licensed under the terms of the Creative Commons Attribution 4.0 International License (http://creativecommons.org/licenses/by/4.0/), which permits use, sharing, adaptation, distribution and reproduction in any medium or format, as long as you give appropriate credit to the original author(s) and the source, provide a link to the Creative Commons license and indicate if changes were made.

The images or other third party material in this chapter are included in the chapter's Creative Commons license, unless indicated otherwise in a credit line to the material. If material is not included in the chapter's Creative Commons license and your intended use is not permitted by statutory regulation or exceeds the permitted use, you will need to obtain permission directly from the copyright holder.

A Unifying Splitting Framework

Gabriel Ebner[1] (✉), Jasmin Blanchette[1,2,3], and Sophie Tourret[2,3]

[1] Vrije Universiteit Amsterdam, Amsterdam, the Netherlands
{g.e.ebner,j.c.blanchette}@vu.nl
[2] Université de Lorraine, CNRS, Inria, LORIA, Nancy, France
{jasmin.blanchette,sophie.tourret}@inria.fr
[3] Max-Planck-Institut für Informatik, Saarland Informatics Campus,
Saarbrücken, Germany
{jasmin.blanchette,stourret}@mpi-inf.mpg.de

Abstract. AVATAR is an elegant and effective way to split clauses in a saturation prover using a SAT solver. But is it refutationally complete? And how does it relate to other splitting architectures? To answer these questions, we present a unifying framework that extends a saturation calculus (e.g., superposition) with splitting and embeds the result in a prover guided by a SAT solver. The framework also allows us to study locking, a subsumption-like mechanism based on the current propositional model. Various architectures are instances of the framework, including AVATAR, labeled splitting, and SMT with quantifiers.

1 Introduction

One of the great strengths of saturation calculi such as superposition [1] is that they avoid case distinctions. Derived clauses hold unconditionally, and the prover can stop as soon as it derives the empty clause, without having to backtrack. The drawback is that these calculi often generate long, unwieldy clauses that slow down the prover. A remedy is to partition the search space by splitting a multiple-literal clause $C_1 \vee \cdots \vee C_n$ into variable-disjoint subclauses C_i. Splitting approaches include splitting with backtracking [24], splitting without backtracking [20], labeled splitting [10], and AVATAR [22].

The SAT-based AVATAR architecture is of particular interest because it is so successful. Voronkov reported that an AVATAR-enabled Vampire could solve 421 TPTP [21] problems that had never been solved before by any system [22, Sect. 9], a mind-boggling number. AVATAR works well in combination with the superposition calculus because it combines superposition's strong equality reasoning with the SAT solver's strong clausal reasoning. It is also appealing theoretically, because it gracefully generalizes traditional saturation provers and yet degenerates to a SAT solver if the problem is propositional.

Example 1. To illustrate the approach, we follow the key steps of an AVATAR-enabled resolution prover on the initial clause set containing $\neg p(a)$, $\neg q(z, z)$, and $p(x) \vee q(y, b)$. The disjunction can be split into $p(x) \leftarrow \{[p(x)]\}$ and $q(y, b) \leftarrow \{[q(y, b)]\}$, where $C \leftarrow \{[C]\}$ indicates that the clause C is enabled only in models in which the associated propositional variable $[C]$ is true. A SAT solver is then

© The Author(s) 2021
A. Platzer and G. Sutcliffe (Eds.): CADE 2021, LNAI 12699, pp. 344–360, 2021.
https://doi.org/10.1007/978-3-030-79876-5_20

run to choose a model $\mathcal{J}$ of $[\mathsf{p}(x)] \vee [\mathsf{q}(y, \mathsf{b})]$. Suppose $\mathcal{J}$ makes $[\mathsf{p}(x)]$ true and $[\mathsf{q}(y, \mathsf{b})]$ false. Then resolving $\mathsf{p}(x) \leftarrow \{[\mathsf{p}(x)]\}$ with $\neg\mathsf{p}(\mathsf{a})$ produces $\bot \leftarrow \{[\mathsf{p}(x)]\}$, which closes the branch. Next, the SAT solver makes the right disjunct true, and resolving $\mathsf{q}(y, \mathsf{b}) \leftarrow \{[\mathsf{q}(y, \mathsf{b})]\}$ with $\neg\mathsf{q}(z, z)$ yields $\bot \leftarrow \{[\mathsf{q}(y, \mathsf{b})]\}$. The SAT solver then reports "unsatisfiable," concluding the refutation.

What about refutational completeness? Far from being a purely theoretical concern, establishing completeness—or finding counterexamples—could yield insights and perhaps lead to an even stronger AVATAR. Before we can answer this open question, we must mathematize splitting. Our starting point is the *saturation framework* by Waldmann, Tourret, Robillard, and Blanchette [23], based on Bachmair and Ganzinger [2]. It covers a wide array of techniques, but "the main missing piece of the framework is a generic treatment of clause splitting" [23, p. 332]. We provide that missing piece, in the form of a *splitting framework*, and use it to show the completeness of an AVATAR-like architecture.

Our framework has five layers, linked by refinement. The first layer consists of a refutationally complete *base calculus*, such as resolution or superposition. It must be presentable as an inference system and a redundancy criterion.

From a base calculus, we derive a *splitting calculus* (Sect. 3). This extends the base calculus with splitting and inherits the base's completeness. It works on A-clauses or A-formulas $C \leftarrow A$, where A is a set of propositional literals.

Using the saturation framework, we can prove the dynamic completeness of an abstract prover, formulated as a transition system, that implements the splitting calculus. However, this ignores a vital component of AVATAR: the SAT solver. AVATAR considers only inferences involving A-formulas whose assertions are true in the current propositional model. The role of the third layer is to reflect this behavior. A *model-guided prover* operates on states of the form $(\mathcal{J}, \mathcal{N})$, where $\mathcal{J}$ is a propositional model and $\mathcal{N}$ is a set of A-formulas (Sect. 4).

The fourth layer introduces AVATAR's *locking* mechanism (Sect. 5). With locking, an A-formula $D \leftarrow B$ can be temporarily disabled by another A-formula $C \leftarrow A$ if C subsumes D, even if $A \not\subseteq B$. Here we make a first discovery: AVATAR-style locking compromises completeness and must be curtailed.

Finally, the fifth layer is an *AVATAR-based prover* (Sect. 6). This refines the locking model-guided prover of the fourth layer with the given clause procedure, which saturates an A-formula set by distinguishing between active and passive A-formulas. Here we make another discovery: Selecting A-formulas fairly is not enough to guarantee completeness. We need a stronger criterion.

In a hypothetical tête-à-tête with the designers of labeled splitting, they might gently point out that by pioneering the use of a propositional model, including locking, they almost invented AVATAR themselves. Likewise, developers of SMT solvers might be tempted to claim that Voronkov merely reinvented SMT. To investigate such questions, we apply our framework to splitting without backtracking, labeled splitting, and SMT with quantifiers (Sect. 7). This gives us a solid basis for comparison as well as some new theoretical results.

A technical report [8] is available with the proofs, several counterexamples, and further details. A formalization using Isabelle/HOL [16] is underway.

2 Preliminaries

Our framework is parameterized by abstract notions of formulas, consequence relations, inferences, and redundancy. We largely follow the conventions of Waldmann et al. [23]. A-formulas generalize Voronkov's A-clauses [22].

Formulas. A set $\mathbf{F}$ of *formulas* is a set that contains a distinguished element $\bot$ denoting falsehood. A *consequence relation* $\models \subseteq (\mathcal{P}(\mathbf{F}))^2$ has the following properties for all $M, N, P, Q \subseteq \mathbf{F}$ and $C, D \in \mathbf{F}$: (D1) $\{\bot\} \models \emptyset$; (D2) $\{C\} \models \{C\}$; (D3) if $M \subseteq N$ and $P \subseteq Q$, then $M \models P$ implies $N \models Q$; (D4) if $M \models P$ and $N \models Q \cup \{C\}$ for every $C \in M$ and $N \cup \{D\} \models Q$ for every $D \in P$, then $N \models Q$. The intended meaning of $M \models N$ is $\bigwedge M \longrightarrow \bigvee N$. From $\models$, we can easily derive a relation understood as $\bigwedge M \longrightarrow \bigwedge N$, as required by the saturation framework.

The $\models$ notation can be extended to allow negation on either side. Let $\mathbf{F}_\sim$ be defined as $\mathbf{F} \uplus \{\sim C \mid C \in \mathbf{F}_\sim\}$ such that $\sim\sim C = C$. Given $M, N \subseteq \mathbf{F}_\sim$, we have $M \models N$ if and only if $\{C \in \mathbf{F} \mid C \in M\} \cup \{C \in \mathbf{F} \mid \sim C \in N\} \models \{C \in \mathbf{F} \mid \sim C \in M\} \cup \{C \in \mathbf{F} \mid C \in N\}$.

Following the saturation framework [23, p. 318], we distinguish between the consequence relation $\models$ used for stating refutational completeness and a possibly stronger consequence relation $\approx$ for soundness. We require that $\approx$ is compact.

Example 2. In clausal first-order logic with equality, the formulas in $\mathbf{F}$ consist of clauses over a signature Σ. Each clause C is a finite multiset of literals $L_1, \ldots, L_n$ written $C = L_1 \vee \cdots \vee L_n$. Each literal L is either an atom or its negation ($\neg$), and each atom is an unoriented equation $s \approx t$. We have $M \models N$ if and only if every Σ-model of M also satisfies at least one clause in N.

Calculi and Derivations. A refutational calculus $(\mathit{Inf}, \mathit{Red})$ combines a set of inferences Inf and a redundancy criterion Red. We refer to Waldmann et al. [23] for the precise definitions. Recall in particular that $\mathit{Inf}(N)$ is the set of inferences from N, $\mathit{Inf}(N, M) = \mathit{Inf}(N \cup M) \setminus \mathit{Inf}(N \setminus M)$, N is *saturated* w.r.t. Inf and Red_I if $\mathit{Inf}(N) \subseteq \mathit{Red}_\mathrm{I}(N)$, and $(\mathit{Inf}, \mathit{Red})$ is *statically (refutationally) complete* (w.r.t. $\models$) if $\bot \in N$ for every $N \models \{\bot\}$ saturated w.r.t. Inf and Red_I.

Let $(X_i)_i$ be a sequence of sets. Its *limit inferior* is $X_\infty = \liminf_{j \to \infty} X_j = \bigcup_i \bigcap_{j \geq i} X_j$, and its *limit superior* is $X^\infty = \limsup_{j \to \infty} X_j = \bigcap_i \bigcup_{j \geq i} X_j$. The elements of X_∞ are called *persistent*. A sequence $(N_i)_i$ over $\mathcal{P}(\mathbf{F})$ is *weakly fair* w.r.t. Inf and Red_I if $\mathit{Inf}(N_\infty) \subseteq \bigcup_i \mathit{Red}_\mathrm{I}(N_i)$ and *strongly fair* if $(\mathit{Inf}(N_i))^\infty \subseteq \bigcup_i \mathit{Red}_\mathrm{I}(N_i)$. Given a relation $\rhd$, a $\rhd$-*derivation* is an infinite sequence such that $x_i \rhd x_{i+1}$ for every i. Finite runs can be extended to derivations via stuttering.

Let $\rhd_{\mathit{Red}_\mathrm{F}} \subseteq (\mathcal{P}(\mathbf{F}))^2$ be the relation such that $M \rhd_{\mathit{Red}_\mathrm{F}} N$ if and only if $M \setminus N \subseteq \mathit{Red}_\mathrm{F}(N)$. The calculus $(\mathit{Inf}, \mathit{Red})$ is *dynamically (refutationally) complete* (w.r.t. $\models$) if for every $\rhd_{\mathit{Red}_\mathrm{F}}$-derivation $(N_i)_i$ that is weakly fair w.r.t. Inf and Red_I and such that $N_0 \models \{\bot\}$, we have $\bot \in N_i$ for some i.

A-Formulas. We fix throughout a countable set $\mathbf{V}$ of *propositional variables* $\mathsf{v}_0, \mathsf{v}_1, \ldots$. For each $\mathsf{v} \in \mathbf{V}$, let $\neg\mathsf{v} \in \neg\mathbf{V}$ denote its negation, with $\neg\neg\mathsf{v} = \mathsf{v}$. We assume that a formula $\mathit{fml}(\mathsf{v}) \in \mathbf{F}$ is associated with each $\mathsf{v} \in \mathbf{V}$. Intuitively, v

approximates $fml(\mathsf{v})$ at the propositional level. This definition is extended so that $fml(\neg\mathsf{v}) = {\sim}fml(\mathsf{v})$. An *assertion* $a \in \mathbf{A} = \mathbf{V} \cup \neg\mathbf{V}$ is either a propositional variable v or its negation $\neg\mathsf{v}$. Given a formula $C \in \mathbf{F}_{\sim}$, let $asn(C)$ denote the set of assertions $a \in \mathbf{A}$ such that $\{fml(a)\} \mathrel{\approx\!\!\!\!\!/\,} \{C\}$ and $\{C\} \mathrel{\approx\!\!\!\!\!/\,} \{fml(a)\}$.

A *propositional interpretation* $\mathcal{J} \subseteq \mathbf{A}$ is a set such that for every $\mathsf{v} \in \mathbf{V}$, exactly one of $\mathsf{v} \in \mathcal{J}$ and $\neg\mathsf{v} \in \mathcal{J}$ holds. We reserve the letter $\mathcal{J}$ for interpretations, and define $fml(\mathcal{J}) = \{fml(a) \mid a \in \mathcal{J}\}$.

An *A-formula* over a set $\mathbf{F}$ of *base formulas* and an assertion set $\mathbf{A}$ is a pair $\mathcal{C} = (C, A) \in \mathbf{AF} = \mathbf{F} \times \mathcal{P}_{\mathrm{fin}}(\mathbf{A})$, written $C \leftarrow A$, where C is a formula and A is a finite set of assertions $\{a_1, \ldots, a_n\}$ understood as an implication $a_1 \wedge \cdots \wedge a_n \longrightarrow C$. We identify $C \leftarrow \emptyset$ with C and define the projection $\lfloor C \leftarrow A \rfloor = C$. Moreover, $\mathcal{N}_{\perp}$ is the set consisting of all A-formulas of the form $\perp \leftarrow A \in \mathcal{N}$. We call such A-formulas *propositional clauses*. Note the use of calligraphic letters (e.g., $\mathcal{C}, \mathcal{N}$) to range over A-formulas and sets of A-formulas.

We say that $C \leftarrow A \in \mathbf{AF}$ is *enabled* in $\mathcal{J}$ if $A \subseteq \mathcal{J}$. A set of A-formulas is *enabled* in $\mathcal{J}$ if all of its members are enabled in $\mathcal{J}$. The *enabled projection* $\mathcal{N}_{\mathcal{J}} \subseteq \lfloor\mathcal{N}\rfloor$ consists of the projections $\lfloor\mathcal{C}\rfloor$ of all A-formulas $\mathcal{C}$ enabled in $\mathcal{J}$. Analogously, the *enabled projection* $Inf_{\mathcal{J}} \subseteq \lfloor Inf \rfloor$ of a set Inf of **AF**-inferences consists of the projections $\lfloor\iota\rfloor$ of all inferences $\iota \in Inf$ whose premises are all enabled in $\mathcal{J}$.

A propositional interpretation $\mathcal{J}$ is a *propositional model* of $\mathcal{N}_{\perp}$, written $\mathcal{J} \models \mathcal{N}_{\perp}$, if $\perp \notin (\mathcal{N}_{\perp})_{\mathcal{J}}$. Moreover, we write $\mathcal{J} \mathrel{\approx\!\!\!\!\!/\,} \mathcal{N}_{\perp}$ if $\perp \notin (\mathcal{N}_{\perp})_{\mathcal{J}}$ or $fml(\mathcal{J}) \mathrel{\approx\!\!\!\!\!/\,} \{\perp\}$. A set $\mathcal{N}_{\perp}$ is *propositionally satisfiable* if there exists an interpretation $\mathcal{J}$ such that $\mathcal{J} \models \mathcal{N}_{\perp}$. In contrast to consequence relations, propositional modelhood $\models$ interprets the set $\mathcal{N}_{\perp}$ conjunctively: $\mathcal{J} \models \mathcal{N}_{\perp}$ is understood as $\mathcal{J} \models \bigwedge \mathcal{N}_{\perp}$.

Finally, we lift $\models$ and $\mathrel{\approx\!\!\!\!\!/\,}$ from $\mathcal{P}(\mathbf{F})$ to $\mathcal{P}(\mathbf{AF})$: $\mathcal{M} \models \mathcal{N}$ if and only if $\mathcal{M}_{\mathcal{J}} \models \lfloor\mathcal{N}\rfloor$ for every $\mathcal{J}$ in which $\mathcal{N}$ is enabled, and $\mathcal{M} \mathrel{\approx\!\!\!\!\!/\,} \mathcal{N}$ if and only if $fml(\mathcal{J}) \cup \mathcal{M}_{\mathcal{J}} \mathrel{\approx\!\!\!\!\!/\,} \lfloor\mathcal{N}\rfloor$ for every $\mathcal{J}$ in which $\mathcal{N}$ is enabled.

Example 3. In the original AVATAR [22], the connection between first-order clauses and assertions takes the form of a function $[\,] : \mathbf{F} \to \mathbf{A}$. The encoding is such that $[\neg C] = \neg[C]$ for every ground unit clause C and $[C] = [D]$ if and only if C is syntactically equal to D up to variable renaming. This can be supported in our framework by letting $fml(\mathsf{v}) = C$ for some C such that $[C] = \mathsf{v}$, for every v.

3   Splitting Calculi

Let $\mathbf{F}$ be a set of base formulas equipped with $\perp$, $\models$, and $\mathrel{\approx\!\!\!\!\!/\,}$. The relation $\mathrel{\approx\!\!\!\!\!/\,}$ is assumed to be nontrivial: (D5) $\emptyset \mathrel{\not\approx\!\!\!\!\!/\,} \emptyset$. Let $\mathbf{A}$ be a set of assertions over $\mathbf{V}$ and $\mathbf{AF}$ be the set of A-formulas over $\mathbf{F}$ and $\mathbf{A}$. Let $(FInf, FRed)$ be a base calculus for $\mathbf{F}$, where $FRed$ is a redundancy criterion that additionally satisfies (1) an inference is $FRed_{\mathrm{I}}$-redundant if one of its premises is $FRed_{\mathrm{F}}$-redundant; (2) $\perp \notin FRed_{\mathrm{F}}(N)$ for every $N \subseteq \mathbf{F}$; and (3) $C \in FRed_{\mathrm{F}}(\{\perp\})$ for every $C \neq \perp$. These requirements can easily be met by a well-designed redundancy criterion [1, Sect. 4.3].

Below, we will define the *splitting calculus* induced by the base calculus. We will see that it not only is statically and dynamically complete w.r.t. $\models$, but also meets stronger, "local completeness" criteria that capture model switching.

The Inference Rules. We start with the mandatory inference rules.

Definition 4. The *splitting inference system SInf* consists of all instances of

$$\frac{(C_i \leftarrow A_i)_{i=1}^n}{D \leftarrow A_1 \cup \cdots \cup A_n} \ \text{BASE} \qquad\qquad \frac{(\bot \leftarrow A_i)_{i=1}^n}{\bot} \ \text{UNSAT}$$

For BASE, the side condition is $(C_n, \ldots, C_1, D) \in FInf$. For UNSAT, the side condition is that $\{\bot \leftarrow A_1, \ldots, \bot \leftarrow A_n\}$ is propositionally unsatisfiable.

In addition, the following optional inference rules can be used:

$$\frac{C \leftarrow A}{\bot \leftarrow \{\neg a_1, \ldots, \neg a_n\} \cup A \quad (C_i \leftarrow \{a_i\})_{i=1}^n} \ \text{SPLIT}$$

$$\frac{(\bot \leftarrow A_i)_{i=1}^n \quad C \leftarrow A}{(\bot \leftarrow A_i)_{i=1}^n} \ \text{COLLECT} \qquad \frac{(\bot \leftarrow A_i)_{i=1}^n \quad C \leftarrow A \cup B}{(\bot \leftarrow A_i)_{i=1}^n \quad C \leftarrow B} \ \text{TRIM}$$

$$\frac{(\bot \leftarrow A_i)_{i=1}^n}{\bot} \ \text{STRONGUNSAT} \qquad \frac{C \leftarrow A}{\bot \leftarrow \{\neg a\} \cup A} \ \text{APPROX} \qquad \frac{}{C \leftarrow A} \ \text{TAUTO}$$

The following side conditions apply. For SPLIT: $C \neq \bot$ is splittable into $C_1, \ldots,$ C_n and $a_i \in asn(C_i)$ for each i. A formula C is *splittable* into two or more formulas $C_1, \ldots, C_n$ if $\{C\} \not\approx \{C_1, \ldots, C_n\}$ and $C \in FRed_F(\{C_i\})$ for each i. For COLLECT: $C \neq \bot$ and $\{\bot \leftarrow A_i\}_{i=1}^n \not\approx \{\bot \leftarrow A\}$. For TRIM: $C \neq \bot$ and $\{\bot \leftarrow A_i\}_{i=1}^n \cup \{\bot \leftarrow A\} \not\approx \{\bot \leftarrow B\}$. For STRONGUNSAT: $\{\bot \leftarrow A_i\}_{i=1}^n \not\approx \{\bot\}$. For APPROX: $a \in asn(C)$. For TAUTO: $\not\approx \{C \leftarrow A\}$.

The three rules identified by double bars are simplifications; they replace their premises with their conclusions in the current A-formula set. The premises' removal is justified by $SRed_F$, defined below. Also note that BASE preserves the soundness of $FInf$ w.r.t. $\approx$ and that the other rules are sound w.r.t. $\approx$.

The SPLIT rule performs an n-way case split on C. Each case C_i is approximated by an assertion a_i. The first conclusion expresses that the case distinction is exhaustive. The n other conclusions assume C_i if its approximation a_i is true. In a clausal prover, typically $C = C_1 \vee \cdots \vee C_n$, where the subclauses C_i have mutually disjoint sets of variables and form a maximal split.

COLLECT and TRIM do some garbage collection. STRONGUNSAT is a variant of UNSAT that uses $\approx$ instead of $\models$. It might correspond to invoking an SMT solver [3] ($\approx$) with a time limit, falling back on a SAT solver ($\models$). APPROX can be used to make any derived A-formula visible to $\approx$. TAUTO allows communication in the other direction, from the SAT solver to the calculus.

Example 5. Suppose the base calculus is first-order resolution [2] and the initial clauses are $\neg p(a)$, $\neg q(z, z)$, and $p(x) \vee q(y, b)$, as in Example 1. SPLIT replaces the last clause by $\bot \leftarrow \{\neg v_0, \neg v_1\}$, $p(x) \leftarrow \{v_0\}$, and $q(y, b) \leftarrow \{v_1\}$. Two BASE inferences then generate $\bot \leftarrow \{v_0\}$ and $\bot \leftarrow \{v_1\}$. Finally, UNSAT generates $\bot$.

The Redundancy Criterion. Next, we lift the base redundancy criterion.

Definition 6. The *splitting redundancy criterion SRed* $= (SRed_I, SRed_F)$ is specified as follows. An A-formula $C \leftarrow A \in \mathbf{AF}$ is redundant w.r.t. $\mathcal{N}$, written $C \leftarrow A \in SRed_F(\mathcal{N})$, if (1) $C \in FRed_F(\mathcal{N}_{\mathcal{J}})$ for every propositional interpretation $\mathcal{J} \supseteq A$ or (2) there exists an A-formula $C \leftarrow B \in \mathcal{N}$ with $B \subset A$. An inference $\iota \in SInf$ is redundant w.r.t. $\mathcal{N}$, written $\iota \in SRed_I(\mathcal{N})$, if (1) ι is a BASE inference and $\{\iota\}_{\mathcal{J}} \subseteq FRed_I(\mathcal{N}_{\mathcal{J}})$ for every $\mathcal{J}$ or (2) ι is an UNSAT inference and $\perp \in \mathcal{N}$.

SRed qualifies as a redundancy criterion. It can justify the deletion of A-formulas that are propositionally tautological. It also allows other simplifications, as long as the assertions on A-formulas used to simplify a given $C \leftarrow A$ are contained in A. If the base criterion $FRed_F$ supports subsumption, this also extends to A-formulas: $D \leftarrow B \in SRed_F(\{C \leftarrow A\})$ if D is strictly subsumed by C and $B \supseteq A$, or if $C = D$ and $B \supset A$.

Local Saturation. It is not difficult to show that if $(FInf, FRed)$ is statically complete, then $(SInf, SRed)$ is statically and hence dynamically complete. However, this result fails to capture a key aspect of most splitting architectures. Since $\triangleright_{SRed_F}$-derivations have no notion of current split branch or model $\mathcal{J}$, they must also perform disabled inferences. To respect enabledness, we need a weaker notion of saturation. If an A-formula set is consistent, it should suffice to saturate w.r.t. a single propositional model. In other words, if no A-formula $\perp \leftarrow A \subseteq \mathcal{J}$ is derivable for some model $\mathcal{J} \models \mathcal{N}_\perp$, the prover should be allowed to give a verdict of "consistent." We will call such model-specific saturations *local*.

Definition 7. A set $\mathcal{N} \subseteq \mathbf{AF}$ is *locally saturated* w.r.t. *SInf* and $SRed_I$ if either $\perp \in \mathcal{N}$ or there exists $\mathcal{J} \models \mathcal{N}_\perp$ such that $\mathcal{N}_{\mathcal{J}}$ is saturated w.r.t. *FInf* and $FRed_I$.

Theorem 8 (Strong static completeness). *Assume $(FInf, FRed)$ is statically complete. Given a set $\mathcal{N} \subseteq \mathbf{AF}$ that is locally saturated w.r.t. SInf and $SRed_I$ and such that $\mathcal{N} \models \{\perp\}$, we have $\perp \in \mathcal{N}$.*

Example 9. Consider the A-clause set $\{\perp \leftarrow \{\neg[\mathsf{p}(x)], \neg[\mathsf{q}(y)]\}, \mathsf{p}(x) \leftarrow \{[\mathsf{p}(x)]\}, \mathsf{q}(y) \leftarrow \{[\mathsf{q}(y)]\}, \neg\mathsf{q}(a)\}$ expressed using AVATAR conventions. It is not saturated for resolution, because the conclusion $\perp \leftarrow \{[\mathsf{q}(y)]\}$ of resolving the last two A-clauses is missing, but it is locally saturated with $\mathcal{J} \supseteq \{[\mathsf{p}(x)], \neg[\mathsf{q}(y)]\}$.

Definition 10. A sequence $(\mathcal{N}_i)_i$ of sets of A-formulas is *locally fair* w.r.t. *SInf* and $SRed_I$ if either $\perp \in \mathcal{N}_i$ for some i or there exists $\mathcal{J} \models (\mathcal{N}_\infty)_\perp$ such that $FInf((\mathcal{N}_\infty)_{\mathcal{J}}) \subseteq \bigcup_i FRed_I((\mathcal{N}_i)_{\mathcal{J}})$.

Theorem 11 (Strong dynamic completeness). *Assume $(FInf, FRed)$ is statically complete. Given a $\triangleright_{SRed_F}$-derivation $(\mathcal{N}_i)_i$ that is locally fair w.r.t. SInf and $SRed_I$ and such that $\mathcal{N}_0 \models \{\perp\}$, we have $\perp \in \mathcal{N}_i$ for some i.*

In Sects. 4 to 6, we will review three transition systems of increasing complexity, culminating with an idealized specification of AVATAR. They will be linked by a chain of stepwise refinements, like pearls on a string. All derivations using these will correspond to $\triangleright_{SRed_F}$-derivations, and their fairness criteria will imply local fairness. Consequently, by Theorem 11, they will all be complete.

4 Model-Guided Provers

AVATAR and other splitting architectures maintain a model of the propositional clauses, which represents the split tree's current branch. We can capture this abstractly by refining $\triangleright_{SRed_F}$-derivations to incorporate a propositional model.

The states are now pairs $(\mathcal{J}, \mathcal{N})$, where $\mathcal{J}$ is a propositional model and $\mathcal{N} \subseteq \mathbf{AF}$. Initial states have the form $(\mathcal{J}, N)$, where $N \subseteq \mathbf{F}$. The *model-guided prover* MG is defined by the following transition rules:

DERIVE $\qquad (\mathcal{J}, \mathcal{N} \uplus \mathcal{M}) \Longrightarrow_{MG} (\mathcal{J}, \mathcal{N} \uplus \mathcal{M}') \quad$ if $\mathcal{M} \subseteq SRed_F(\mathcal{N} \uplus \mathcal{M}')$

SWITCH $\qquad (\mathcal{J}, \mathcal{N}) \Longrightarrow_{MG} (\mathcal{J}', \mathcal{N}) \qquad\qquad$ if $\mathcal{J}' \models \mathcal{N}_\perp$

STRONGUNSAT $\ (\mathcal{J}, \mathcal{N}) \Longrightarrow_{MG} (\mathcal{J}, \mathcal{N} \cup \{\perp\}) \qquad$ if $\mathcal{N}_\perp \not\approx \{\perp\}$

From an $\Longrightarrow_{MG}$-derivation, we obtain an $\triangleright_{SRed_F}$-derivation by simply erasing the $\mathcal{J}$ components. The DERIVE rule can add new A-formulas and delete redundant A-formulas. $\mathcal{J}$ should be a model of $\mathcal{N}_\perp$ most of the time; when it is not, SWITCH can be used to switch model or STRONGUNSAT to finish the refutation.

Example 12. Let us revisit Example 5. Initially, let $\mathcal{J}_0 = \{\neg v_0, \neg v_1\}$. After the split, we have $\neg p(a)$, $\neg q(z, z)$, $p(x) \leftarrow \{v_0\}$, $q(y, b) \leftarrow \{v_1\}$, and $\perp \leftarrow \{\neg v_0, \neg v_1\}$. The natural option is to switch model. We take $\mathcal{J}_1 = \{v_0, \neg v_1\}$. We then derive $\perp \leftarrow \{v_0\}$. Since $\mathcal{J}_1 \not\models \perp \leftarrow \{v_0\}$, we switch to $\mathcal{J}_2 = \{\neg v_0, v_1\}$, where we derive $\perp \leftarrow \{v_1\}$. Finally, we detect that the propositional clauses are unsatisfiable.

We need a fairness criterion for MG that implies local fairness of the underlying $\triangleright_{SRed_F}$-derivation. The latter requires a witness $\mathcal{J}$ but gives us no hint as to where to look for one. Our solution involves a topological concept: $\mathcal{J}$ is a *limit point* in $(\mathcal{J}_i)_i$ if there exists a subsequence $(\mathcal{J}'_i)_i$ of $(\mathcal{J}_i)_i$ such that $\mathcal{J} = \mathcal{J}'_\infty = \mathcal{J}'^\infty$.

Example 13. Let $(\mathcal{J}_i)_i$ be the sequence such that $\mathcal{J}_{2i} \cap \mathbf{V} = \{v_1, v_3, \ldots, v_{2i-1}\}$ (i.e., $v_1, v_3, \ldots, v_{2i-1}$ are true and the other variables are false) and $\mathcal{J}_{2i+1} = (\mathcal{J}_{2i} \setminus \{\neg v_{2i}\}) \cup \{v_{2i}\}$. Although it is not in the sequence, the interpretation $\mathcal{J} \cap \mathbf{V} = \{v_1, v_3, \ldots\}$ is a limit point. The associated split tree is shown in Fig. 1. The direct path from the root to a node $\mathcal{J}_i$ specifies the assertions that are true in $\mathcal{J}_i$.

Example 14. Let $(\mathcal{J}_i)_i$ be such that $\mathcal{J}_0 \cap \mathbf{V} = \emptyset$, $\mathcal{J}_{4i+1} \cap \mathbf{V} = \{v_0\} \cup \{v_{4j+3} \mid j < i\}$, $\mathcal{J}_{4i+2} \cap \mathbf{V} = \{v_0, v_{4i+2}\} \cup \{v_{4j+3} \mid j < i\}$, $\mathcal{J}_{4i+3} \cap \mathbf{V} = \{v_{4j+1} \mid j \leq i\}$, and $\mathcal{J}_{4i+4} \cap \mathbf{V} = \{v_{4j+1} \mid j \leq i\} \cup \{v_{4i+4}\}$. This sequence has two limit points: $\mathcal{J}' = \liminf_{i \to \infty} \mathcal{J}_{4i+1}$ and $\mathcal{J}'' = \liminf_{i \to \infty} \mathcal{J}_{4i+3}$. The split tree is depicted in Fig. 2.

Basic topology tells us that every sequence has a limit point. No matter how erratically the prover switches branches, it will fully explore at least one of them. It then suffices to perform the base *FInf*-inferences fairly in that branch:

Definition 15. An $\Longrightarrow_{MG}$-derivation $(\mathcal{J}_i, \mathcal{N}_i)_i$ is *fair* if either (1) $\perp \in \mathcal{N}_i$ for some i or (2) $\mathcal{J}_i \models (\mathcal{N}_i)_\perp$ for infinitely many indices i and there exists a limit point $\mathcal{J}$ of $(\mathcal{J}_i)_i$ such that $FInf((\mathcal{N}_\infty)_\mathcal{J}) \subseteq \bigcup_i FRed_I((\mathcal{N}_i)_\mathcal{J})$.

Fairness of an $\Longrightarrow_{MG}$-derivation implies local fairness of the underlying $\triangleright_{SRed_F}$-derivation. A well-behaved propositional solver, as in labeled splitting, always gives rise to a single limit point $\mathcal{J}_\infty$, which can be taken for $\mathcal{J}$ in Definition 15.

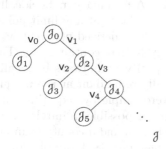

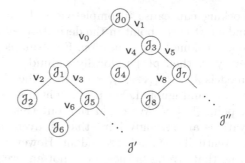

Fig. 1: A split tree with a single infinite branch

Fig. 2: A split tree with two infinite branches

By contrast, an unconstrained solver, as supported by AVATAR, can produce multiple limit points. Then it is more challenging to ensure fairness.

Example 16. Consider the consistent set consisting of $\neg p(x)$, $p(a) \vee q(a)$, and $\neg q(y) \vee p(f(y)) \vee q(f(y))$. Splitting the second clause into $p(a)$ and $q(a)$ and resolving $q(a)$ with the third clause yields $p(f(a)) \vee q(f(a))$. This process can be iterated. Now suppose that v_{2i} and v_{2i+1} are associated with $p(f^i(a))$ and $q(f^i(a))$, respectively. If we split every emerging $p(f^i(a)) \vee q(f^i(a))$ and the SAT solver always makes v_{2i} true first, we end up with the situation of Example 13 and Fig. 1. For the limit point $\mathcal{J}$, all *FInf*-inferences are performed. Thus, the derivation is fair.

Example 17. We build a clause set from two copies of Example 16, where each clause C from each copy $i \in \{1, 2\}$ is extended to $\neg r_i \vee C$. We add the clause $r_1 \vee r_2$ and split it as our first move. From there, each branch imitates Example 16. A SAT solver might jump back and forth, as in Example 14 and Fig. 2. Even if A-clauses get disabled and re-enabled infinitely often, we must perform all nonredundant inferences in at least one of the two limit points ($\mathcal{J}'$ or $\mathcal{J}''$).

5   Locking Provers

Next, we refine the model-guided prover into a locking prover that temporarily locks away A-formulas that are redundant locally w.r.t. some $\mathcal{J}$ but not globally. The states are triples $(\mathcal{J}, \mathcal{N}, \mathcal{L})$, with $\mathcal{L} \subseteq \mathcal{P}_{\text{fin}}(\mathbf{A}) \times \mathbf{AF}$. Intuitively, $(B, C \leftarrow A) \in \mathcal{L}$ means that $C \leftarrow A$ is "locally redundant" in interpretations $\mathcal{J} \supseteq B$. The function $\|\ \|$ erases the locks: $\|\mathcal{L}\| = \{\mathcal{C} \mid (B, \mathcal{C}) \in \mathcal{L} \text{ for some } B\}$. Initial states have the form $(\mathcal{J}, N, \emptyset)$, where $N \subseteq \mathbf{F}$. The *locking prover* is defined by these two rules:

LIFT $(\mathcal{J}, \mathcal{N}, \mathcal{L}) \Longrightarrow_L (\mathcal{J}', \mathcal{N}' \cup \|\mathcal{U}\|, \mathcal{L} \setminus \mathcal{U})$
    if $(\mathcal{J}, \mathcal{N}) \Longrightarrow_{\text{MG}} (\mathcal{J}', \mathcal{N}')$ and $\mathcal{U} = \{(B, C \leftarrow A) \in \mathcal{L} \mid B \not\subseteq \mathcal{J}' \text{ and } A \subseteq \mathcal{J}'\}$

LOCK $(\mathcal{J}, \mathcal{N} \uplus \{C \leftarrow A\}, \mathcal{L}) \Longrightarrow_L (\mathcal{J}, \mathcal{N}, \mathcal{L} \cup \{(B, C \leftarrow A)\})$
    if $B \subseteq \mathcal{J}$ and $C \in FRed_F(\mathcal{N}_{\mathcal{J}'})$ for all $\mathcal{J}' \supseteq A \cup B$

We note that $\Longrightarrow_L$-derivations refine $\Longrightarrow_{\text{MG}}$-derivations, with states $(\mathcal{J}, \mathcal{N}, \mathcal{L})$ mapped to $(\mathcal{J}, \mathcal{N} \cup \|\mathcal{L}\|)$.

Locking can cause incompleteness, because an A-formula can be locally redundant at every point in the derivation and yet not be so at any limit point, thereby breaking local saturation. For example, if we have derived $\mathsf{p}(x) \leftarrow \{\neg\mathsf{v}_k\}$ for every k, then $\mathsf{p}(\mathsf{c})$ is locally redundant in any $\mathcal{J}$ that contains $\neg\mathsf{v}_k$. For the models $\mathcal{J}_i = \{\mathsf{v}_1, \ldots, \mathsf{v}_i, \neg\mathsf{v}_{i+1}, \ldots\}$, the clause $\mathsf{p}(\mathsf{c})$ would always be locally redundant and ignored. Yet $\mathsf{p}(\mathsf{c})$ might not be locally redundant at the unique limit point $\mathcal{J} = \mathbf{V}$. We could rule out this counterexample by requiring that derivations are strongly fair—that is, every inference possible infinitely often must eventually be made redundant. However, we have found a counterexample showing that strong fairness does not ensure completeness [8, Example 46]. It would seem that this counterexample could arise with Vampire if the underlying SAT solver produces this specific sequence of interpretations.

Our solution is as follows. Let $(\mathcal{J}_i, \mathcal{N}_i, \mathcal{L}_i)_i$ be an $\Longrightarrow_\mathsf{L}$-derivation, let $(\mathcal{J}'_j)_j$ be a subsequence of $(\mathcal{J}_i)_i$, and let $(\mathcal{N}'_j)_j$ be the corresponding subsequence of $(\mathcal{N}_i)_i$. To achieve fairness, we now consider $\mathcal{N}'_\infty$, the A-formulas persistent in the unlocked subsequence $(\mathcal{N}'_j)_j$. By contrast, fairness of $\Longrightarrow_\mathsf{MG}$-derivations used $\mathcal{N}_\infty$.

Definition 18. An $\Longrightarrow_\mathsf{L}$-derivation $(\mathcal{J}_i, \mathcal{N}_i, \mathcal{L}_i)_i$ is *fair* if either (1) $\perp \in \bigcup_i \mathcal{N}_i$ or (2) $\mathcal{J}_i \models (\mathcal{N}_i)_\perp$ for infinitely many indices i and there exists a subsequence $(\mathcal{J}'_j)_j$ converging to a limit point $\mathcal{J}$ such that $FInf((\mathcal{N}'_\infty)_\mathcal{J} \cup ((\limsup_{j\to\infty} \lfloor\mathcal{L}'_j\rfloor)_\mathcal{J} \setminus \lfloor\mathcal{L}'^\infty\rfloor)_\mathcal{J}) \subseteq \bigcup_i FRed_\mathrm{I}((\mathcal{N}_i \cup \lfloor\mathcal{L}_i\rfloor)_\mathcal{J})$, where $(\mathcal{N}'_j)_j$ and $(\mathcal{L}'_j)_j$ correspond to $(\mathcal{J}'_j)_j$.

Fairness of an $\Longrightarrow_\mathsf{L}$-derivation implies fairness of the corresponding $\Longrightarrow_\mathsf{MG}$-derivation. The condition on the sets $\mathcal{L}'_j$ ensures that inferences from A-formulas that are locked infinitely often, but not infinitely often with the same lock, are redundant at the limit point. In particular, if we know that each A-formula is locked at most finitely often, then $\limsup_{j\to\infty} \lfloor\mathcal{L}'_j\rfloor = \lfloor\mathcal{L}'^\infty\rfloor$ and the inclusion in the definition above simplifies to $FInf((\mathcal{N}'_\infty)_\mathcal{J}) \subseteq \bigcup_i FRed_\mathrm{I}((\mathcal{N}_i \cup \lfloor\mathcal{L}_i\rfloor)_\mathcal{J})$.

6   AVATAR-Based Provers

AVATAR was unveiled in 2014 by Voronkov [22]. Since then, he and his colleagues studied many options and extensions [3, 17]. A second implementation, in Lean's **super** tactic, is due to Ebner [9]. Here we attempt to capture AVATAR's essence.

The abstract AVATAR-based prover we define in this section extends the locking prover L with a given clause procedure [13]. A-formulas are moved in turn from the passive to the active set, where inferences are performed. The heuristic for choosing the next *given* A-formula to move is guided by timestamps indicating when the A-formulas were derived, to ensure fairness.

Let $\mathbf{TAF} = \mathbf{AF} \times \mathbb{N}$ be the set of *timestamped A-formulas*. Given $\mathcal{N} \subseteq \mathbf{TAF}$, we define $\wr\mathcal{N}\wr = \{\mathcal{C} \mid (\mathcal{C}, t) \in \mathcal{N} \text{ for some } t\}$, and we overload existing notations to erase timestamps. Thus, $\lfloor\mathcal{N}\rfloor = \lfloor\wr\mathcal{N}\wr\rfloor$, $\mathcal{N}_\perp = \wr\mathcal{N}\wr_\perp$, and so on. Note that we use a new set of calligraphic letters (e.g., $\mathcal{C}, \mathcal{N}$) to range over timestamped A-formulas and A-formulas sets. Using the saturation framework [23, Sect. 3], we lift $(SInf, SRed)$ to a calculus $(TSInf, TSRed)$ on $\mathbf{TAF}$ with the tiebreaker order $>$ on timestamps, so that $(\mathcal{C}, t+k) \in TSRed_\mathrm{F}(\{(\mathcal{C}, t)\})$ for any $k > 0$.

A state is a tuple $(\mathcal{J}, \mathcal{A}, \mathcal{P}, \mathcal{Q}, \mathcal{L}) \in \mathcal{P}(\mathbf{A}) \times \mathcal{P}(\mathbf{TAF})^3 \times \mathcal{P}(\mathcal{P}_{\mathrm{fin}}(\mathbf{A}) \times \mathbf{TAF})$, where $\mathcal{A}$, $\mathcal{P}$, and $\mathcal{Q}$ are respectively the sets of *active, passive,* and other (disabled or propositional) timestamped A-formulas, and $\mathcal{L}$ is the set of locked timestamped A-formulas such that (1) $\mathcal{A}_\perp = \mathcal{P}_\perp = \emptyset$, (2) $\mathcal{A} \cup \mathcal{P}$ is enabled in $\mathcal{J}$, and (3) $\mathcal{Q}_{\mathcal{J}} \subseteq \{\perp\}$. The *AVATAR-based prover* AV is defined as follows:

INFER
$(\mathcal{J}, \mathcal{A}, \mathcal{P} \uplus \{\mathcal{C}\}, \mathcal{Q}, \mathcal{L}) \Longrightarrow_{\mathsf{AV}} (\mathcal{J}, \mathcal{A} \cup \{\mathcal{C}\}, \mathcal{P}', \mathcal{Q}', \mathcal{L})$
if $TSInf(\mathcal{A}, \{\mathcal{C}\}) \subseteq TSRed_{\mathrm{I}}(\mathcal{A} \cup \{\mathcal{C}\} \cup \mathcal{P}' \cup \mathcal{Q}')$, $\mathcal{P} \subseteq \mathcal{P}'$, and $\mathcal{Q} \subseteq \mathcal{Q}'$

PROCESS
$(\mathcal{J}, \mathcal{A}, \mathcal{P}, \mathcal{Q}, \mathcal{L}) \Longrightarrow_{\mathsf{AV}} (\mathcal{J}, \mathcal{A}', \mathcal{P}', \mathcal{Q}', \mathcal{L})$
if $\mathcal{A} \supseteq \mathcal{A}'$
and $(\mathcal{A}\backslash\mathcal{A}') \cup (\mathcal{P}\backslash\mathcal{P}') \cup (\mathcal{Q}\backslash\mathcal{Q}') \subseteq TSRed_{\mathrm{F}}(\mathcal{A}' \cup \mathcal{P}' \cup \mathcal{Q}')$

SWITCH
$(\mathcal{J}, \mathcal{A}, \mathcal{P}, \mathcal{Q}, \mathcal{L}) \Longrightarrow_{\mathsf{AV}} (\mathcal{J}', \mathcal{A}', \mathcal{P}' \cup \|\mathcal{U}\|, \mathcal{Q}', \mathcal{L} \setminus \mathcal{U})$
if $\mathcal{J} \not\models \mathcal{Q}_\perp$, $\mathcal{J}' \models \mathcal{Q}_\perp$, $\mathcal{A}' = \{\mathcal{C} \in \mathcal{A} \mid \mathcal{C}$ is enabled in $\mathcal{J}'\}$,
$\mathcal{U} = \{(B, (C \leftarrow A, t)) \in \mathcal{L} \mid B \not\subseteq \mathcal{J}'$ and $A \subseteq \mathcal{J}'\}$, and
$\mathcal{A} \cup \mathcal{P} \cup \mathcal{Q} = \mathcal{A}' \cup \mathcal{P}' \cup \mathcal{Q}'$

STRONGUNSAT
$(\mathcal{J}, \mathcal{A}, \mathcal{P}, \mathcal{Q}, \mathcal{L}) \Longrightarrow_{\mathsf{AV}} (\mathcal{J}, \mathcal{A}, \mathcal{P}, \mathcal{Q} \cup \{(\perp, t)\}, \mathcal{L})$ if $\mathcal{Q}_\perp \not\models \perp$

LOCKA
$(\mathcal{J}, \mathcal{A} \uplus \{(C \leftarrow A, t)\}, \mathcal{P}, \mathcal{Q}, \mathcal{L}) \Longrightarrow_{\mathsf{AV}}$
$(\mathcal{J}, \mathcal{A}, \mathcal{P}, \mathcal{Q}, \mathcal{L} \cup \{(B, (C \leftarrow A, t))\})$
if $B \subseteq \mathcal{J}$ and $C \in FRed_{\mathrm{F}}((\mathcal{A} \cup \mathcal{P})_{\mathcal{J}'})$ for every $\mathcal{J}' \supseteq A \cup B$

There is also a LOCKP rule that is identical to LOCKA except that it starts in the state $(\mathcal{J}, \mathcal{A}, \mathcal{P} \uplus \{(C \leftarrow A, t)\}, \mathcal{Q}, \mathcal{L})$. An AV-derivation is *well timestamped* if every A-formula introduced by a rule is assigned a unique timestamp.

Let $(\mathcal{J}_i, \mathcal{A}_i, \mathcal{P}_i, \mathcal{Q}_i, \mathcal{L}_i)_i$ be an $\Longrightarrow_{\mathsf{AV}}$-derivation. It is easy to see that it refines the $\Longrightarrow_{\mathsf{L}}$-derivation $(\mathcal{J}_i, \lfloor \mathcal{A}_i \cup \mathcal{P}_i \cup \mathcal{Q}_i \rfloor, \lfloor \mathcal{L}_i \rfloor)_i$ and that the saturation invariant $TSInf(\mathcal{A}_i) \subseteq TSRed_{\mathrm{I}}(\mathcal{A}_i \cup \mathcal{P}_i \cup \mathcal{Q}_i \cup \|\mathcal{L}_i\|)$ holds if $\mathcal{A}_0 = \emptyset$.

In contrast with nonsplitting provers, for AV, fairness w.r.t. formulas does not imply fairness w.r.t. inferences. A problematic scenario involves two premises $\mathcal{C}, \mathcal{D}$ of an inference ι and four transitions repeated forever, possibly with other steps interleaved: INFER makes $\mathcal{C}$ active; SWITCH disables it; INFER makes $\mathcal{D}$ active; SWITCH disables it. Even though $\mathcal{C}$ and $\mathcal{D}$ are selected in a strongly fair fashion, ι is never performed. We need an even stronger fairness criterion.

Definition 19. An $\Longrightarrow_{\mathsf{AV}}$-derivation $(\mathcal{J}_i, \mathcal{A}_i, \mathcal{P}_i, \mathcal{Q}_i, \mathcal{L}_i)_i$ is *fair* if (1) $\perp \in \lfloor \bigcup_i \mathcal{Q}_i \rfloor$ or (2) $\mathcal{J}_i \models (\mathcal{Q}_i)_\perp$ for infinitely many indices i and there exists a subsequence $(\mathcal{J}'_j)$ converging to a limit point $\mathcal{J}'_\infty$ such that (3) $\liminf_{j \to \infty} TSInf(\mathcal{A}'_j, \mathcal{P}'_j) = \emptyset$ and (4) $(\limsup_{j \to \infty} \|\mathcal{L}'_j\|)_{\mathcal{J}} \setminus \|\mathcal{L}'^\infty\|_{\mathcal{J}} \subseteq \bigcup_i FRed_{\mathrm{F}}((\mathcal{A}_i \cup \mathcal{P}_i \cup \mathcal{Q}_i \cup \|\mathcal{L}_i\|)_{\mathcal{J}})$.

Condition (3) ensures that all inferences involving passive A-formulas are redundant at the limit point. It would not suffice to require $\mathcal{P}'_\infty = \emptyset$ because A-formulas can move back and forth between $\mathcal{A}$, $\mathcal{P}$, and $\mathcal{Q}$, as we just saw. Condition (4) is similar to the condition on locks in Definition 18. If the $\Longrightarrow_{\mathsf{AV}}$-derivation is fair, the corresponding $\Longrightarrow_{\mathsf{L}}$-derivation is also fair.

Many selection strategies are combinations of basic strategies, such as choosing the smallest formula by weight or the oldest by age. We capture such strategies using selection orders $\prec$. Intuitively, $\mathcal{C} \prec \mathcal{D}$ if the prover will always select $\mathcal{C}$

before $\mathcal{D}$ if both are present. We use two selection orders: $<_{\mathbf{TAF}}$, based on timestamps, must be followed infinitely often; $<_{\mathbf{F}}$ must be followed otherwise. For the first one, we can use $<_{\mathrm{age}}$ defined so that $(\mathcal{C}, t) <_{\mathrm{age}} (\mathcal{C}', t')$ if $t < t'$.

Definition 20. Let X be a set. A *selection order* $\prec$ on X is an irreflexive and transitive relation such that $\{y \mid y \not\succ x\}$ is finite for all $x \in X$.

The intersection of two orders $\prec_1$ and $\prec_2$ corresponds to the nondeterministic alternation between them. The prover may choose either a $\prec_1$-minimal or a $\prec_2$-minimal A-formula, at its discretion.

To ensure completeness, we must restrict the inferences that the prover may perform; otherwise, it could derive infinitely many A-formulas with different assertions, causing it to switch between two branches of the split tree without making progress. Given $\mathcal{N} \subseteq \mathbf{AF}$, let $\lceil \mathcal{N} \rceil = \{A \mid C \leftarrow A \in \mathcal{N}$ for some $C\}$.

Definition 21. A function $F : \mathcal{P}(\mathbf{AF}) \to \mathcal{P}(\mathbf{AF})$ is *strongly finitary* if $\lfloor F(\mathcal{N}) \rfloor$ and $\bigcup \lceil F(\mathcal{N}) \rceil \setminus \bigcup \lceil \mathcal{N} \rceil$ are finite for any $\mathcal{N} \subseteq \mathbf{AF}$ such that $\lfloor \mathcal{N} \rfloor$ is finite.

Intuitively, a strongly finitary function F returns finitely many base formulas and finitely many new assertions, although it may return infinitely many A-formulas. Clearly, $F(\mathcal{N})$ is finite for any finite $\mathcal{N} \subseteq \mathbf{AF}$. If $FInf(N)$ is finite for any finite $N \subseteq \mathbf{F}$, then performing $SInf$-inferences is strongly finitary. Deterministic SPLIT rules, such as AVATAR's, are also strongly finitary. We can lift a strongly finitary F to any $\mathcal{N} \subseteq \mathbf{TAF}$ by taking $F_{\mathbf{TAF}}(\mathcal{N}) = F(\lfloor \mathcal{N} \mathcal{J}) \times \mathbb{N}$. If F and G are strongly finitary, then so is $\mathcal{N} \mapsto F(\mathcal{N}) \cup G(\mathcal{N})$.

Simplification rules used by the prover must be restricted even more to ensure completeness, because they can lead to new splits and assertions. For example, simplifying $\mathsf{p}(x * 0) \vee \mathsf{p}(x)$ to $\mathsf{p}(0) \vee \mathsf{p}(x)$ transforms an unsplittable clause into a splittable one. If simplifications were to produce infinitely many such clauses, the prover might split and switch models forever without making progress.

Definition 22. Let $\prec$ be a well-founded relation on $\mathbf{F}$, and let $\preceq$ be its reflexive closure. A function $S : \mathbf{AF} \to \mathcal{P}(\mathbf{AF})$ is a *strongly finitary simplification bound* for $\prec$ if $\mathcal{N} \mapsto \bigcup_{\mathcal{C} \in \mathcal{N}} S(\mathcal{C})$ is strongly finitary and $\lfloor \mathcal{C}' \rfloor \preceq \lfloor \mathcal{C} \rfloor$ for all $\mathcal{C}' \in S(\mathcal{C})$.

The prover may simplify an A-formula $\mathcal{C}$ to $\mathcal{C}'$ only if $\mathcal{C}' \in S(\mathcal{C})$. It may also delete $\mathcal{C}$. Strongly finitary simplification bounds are closed under unions, allowing the combination of simplification techniques based on $\prec$. For superposition, a natural choice for $\prec$ is the clause order. The key property of strongly finitary simplification bounds is that if we saturate a finite set of A-formulas w.r.t. simplifications, the saturation is also finite.

Example 23. Let $\mathbf{F}$ be the set of first-order clauses and $S(C \leftarrow A) = \{C' \leftarrow A' \mid C'$ is a subclause of C and $A' \subseteq A\}$. Then S is a strongly finitary simplification bound. This S covers many simplification techniques, including elimination of duplicate literals, deletion of resolved literals, and subsumption resolution.

Example 24. If the Knuth–Bendix order [12] is used and all weights are positive, then $S(C \leftarrow A) = \{C' \leftarrow A' \mid C' \prec C$ and $A' \subseteq A\}$ is a strongly finitary simplification bound. This can be used to cover demodulation.

Equipped with the above definitions, we introduce a fairness criterion that is more concrete and easier to apply than fairness of $\Longrightarrow_{AV}$-derivations. We could refine AV further and use this criterion to show the completeness of an imperative procedure such as Voronkov's extended Otter loop [22, Fig. 3], thus showing that Vampire with AVATAR is complete if locking is sufficiently restricted.

Lemma 25. *Let I be a strongly finitary function, and let S be a strongly finitary simplification bound. Then a well-timestamped $\Longrightarrow_{AV}$-derivation $(\mathcal{J}_i, \mathcal{A}_i, \mathcal{P}_i, \mathcal{Q}_i, \mathcal{L}_i)_i$ is fair if all of the following conditions hold:*

1. *$<_{\mathbf{TAF}}$ is a selection order on $\bigcup_i \mathcal{P}_i$, and $<_{\mathbf{F}}$ is a selection order on $\mathbf{F}$;*
2. *$\mathcal{A}_0 = \mathcal{L}_0 = \emptyset$ and $\mathcal{P}_0 \cup \mathcal{Q}_0$ is finite;*
3. *for every INFER transition, either $\mathcal{C}$ is $<_{\mathbf{TAF}}$-minimal in $\mathcal{P}$ or $\lfloor \mathcal{C} \rfloor$ is $<_{\mathbf{F}}$-minimal in $\lfloor \mathcal{P} \rfloor$;*
4. *for every INFER transition, $\mathcal{P}' \cup \mathcal{Q}' \subseteq I_{\mathbf{TAF}}(\mathcal{A} \cup \{\mathcal{C}\})$;*
5. *for every PROCESS transition, $\mathcal{P}' \cup \mathcal{Q}' \subseteq S_{\mathbf{TAF}}(\mathcal{A} \cup \mathcal{P} \cup \mathcal{Q} \cup \lfloor \mathcal{L} \rfloor)$;*
6. *if $\mathcal{J}_i \not\models (\mathcal{Q}_i)_\perp$, then eventually SWITCH or STRONGUNSAT occurs;*
7. *if $\mathcal{P}_i \neq \emptyset$, then eventually INFER, SWITCH or STRONGUNSAT occurs;*
8. *there are infinitely many indices i such that either $\mathcal{P}_i = \emptyset$ or INFER chooses a $<_{\mathbf{TAF}}$-minimal $\mathcal{C}$ at i;*
9. *$(\limsup_{j \to \infty} \lfloor \mathcal{L}'_j \rfloor)_{\mathcal{J}} \setminus \lfloor \mathcal{L}'^\infty \rfloor_{\mathcal{J}} \subseteq \bigcup_i FRed_{\mathbf{F}}((\mathcal{A}_i \cup \mathcal{P}_i \cup \mathcal{Q}_i \cup \lfloor \mathcal{L}_i \rfloor)_{\mathcal{J}})$ for every subsequence converging to a limit point.*

7 Application to Other Architectures

AVATAR may be the most natural application of our framework, but it is not the only one. Below we complete the picture by studying splitting without backtracking, labeled splitting, and SMT with quantifiers.

Splitting without Backtracking. Before AVATAR, Riazanov and Voronkov [20] had already experimented with splitting in Vampire in a lighter variant without backtracking. They based their work on ordered resolution O with selection [2]. Weidenbach [24, end of Sect. 4.5] independently outlined the same technique. The basic idea is to extend the signature Σ with a countable set $\mathbb{P}$ of nullary predicate symbols and to augment the base calculus with a binary splitting rule that replaces a $\Sigma_\mathbb{P}$-clause $C \vee D$ with two $\Sigma_\mathbb{P}$-clauses $C \vee \mathsf{p}$ and $D \vee \neg\mathsf{p}$. Riazanov and Voronkov require that the precedence $\prec$ makes all $\mathbb{P}$-literals smaller than the Σ-literals. Binary splitting is then a simplification. They also extend the selection function of the base calculus to support $\mathbb{P}$-literals. Their *parallel* selection function imitates as much as possible the original selection function.

The calculus $\mathsf{O}_\mathbb{P}$ is closely related to an instance of our framework. Let $\mathbf{F}$ be the set of Σ-clauses, with the empty clause as $\bot$. Let $\mathsf{O} = (FInf, FRed)$ be the base calculus. We take $\mathbf{V} = \mathbb{P}$. Let $\mathsf{LA} = (SInf, SRed)$, whose name stands for *lightweight AVATAR*, be the induced splitting calculus. Lightweight AVATAR amounts to the splitting architecture Cruanes implemented in Zipperposition [7, Sect. 2.5]. Binary splitting can be realized in LA as a SPLIT-like simplification rule. The calculi $O_{\mathbb{P}}$ and LA disagree slightly because $O_{\mathbb{P}}$'s order $\prec$ can break ties using $\mathbb{P}$-literals and because LA can detect unsatisfiability early using the UNSAT rule. Despite its slightly weaker order, LA is tighter than $O_{\mathbb{P}}$ in the sense that saturation w.r.t. $O_{\mathbb{P}}$ implies saturation w.r.t. LA but not vice versa.

Labeled Splitting. Labeled splitting, as originally described by Fietzke and Weidenbach [10] and implemented in SPASS, is a first-order resolution-based calculus with binary splitting that traverses the split tree in a depth-first way, using an elaborate backtracking mechanism inspired by CDCL [15]. It works on states $(\Psi, \mathcal{N})$, where Ψ is a stack storing the current state of the split tree and $\mathcal{N}$ is a set of *labeled clauses*—clauses annotated with finite sets of natural numbers.

We model labeled splitting as an instance of the locking prover L based on the splitting calculus $\mathsf{LS} = (SInf, SRed)$ induced by the resolution calculus $\mathsf{R} = (FInf, FRed)$, where $\models$ and $\approx$ are as in Example 2 and $\mathbf{V} = \bigcup_{i \in \mathbb{N}} \{l_i, r_i, s_i\}$. A-clauses correspond to labeled clauses. Splits are identified by unique *split levels*. Given a split on $C \vee D$ with level k, $l_k \in asn(C)$ and $r_k \in asn(D)$ represent the left and right branches. In practice, the prover would dynamically extend fml to ensure that $fml(l_k) = C$ and $fml(r_k) = D$.

When splitting, if we simply added $\bot \leftarrow \{\neg l_k, \neg r_k\}$, we would always need to consider either $C \leftarrow \{l_k\}$ or $D \leftarrow \{r_k\}$, depending on the interpretation. However, labeled splitting can undo splits when backtracking. Yet fairness would require us to perform inferences with either C or D even when labeled splitting would not. We solve this as follows. Let $\top = {\sim}\bot$. We introduce the variable $s_k \in asn(\top)$ so that we can enable or disable the split. The STRONGUNSAT rule then knows that s_k is true, but we can still switch to propositional models that disable both C and D. A-clauses are then split using the following binary variant of SPLIT:

$$\frac{C \vee D \leftarrow A}{\bot \leftarrow \{\neg l_k, \neg r_k, s_k\} \quad C \leftarrow A \cup \{l_k\} \quad D \leftarrow A \cup \{r_k\}} \text{ SOFTSPLIT}$$

where C and D share no variables and k is the next split level. Unlike AVATAR, labeled splitting keeps the premise and might split it again with another level.

To emulate the original, the locking prover based on LS must repeatedly apply the following three steps in any order until saturation:

1. Apply BASE to perform an inference from the enabled A-clauses. If an enabled $\bot \leftarrow A$ is derived with $A \subseteq \bigcup_i \{l_i, r_i\}$, apply SWITCH or STRONGUNSAT.
2. Apply DERIVE to simplify or delete an enabled A-clause. Use LOCK if necessary to remove the original A-clause. If an enabled $\bot \leftarrow A$ is derived with $A \subseteq \bigcup_i \{l_i, r_i\}$, apply SWITCH or STRONGUNSAT.
3. Apply SOFTSPLIT with split level k on an A-clause $\mathcal{C}$. Then use SWITCH to enable the left branch and apply LOCK on $\mathcal{C}$ with s_k as the lock.

SWITCH is powerful enough to support all of Fietzke and Weidenbach's backtracking rules, but to explore the tree in the same order as they do, we must choose the new model carefully. If a left branch is closed, the model must be updated so as to disable the splits that were not used to close this branch and to enable the right branch. If a right branch is closed, the split must be disabled, and the model must switch to the right branch of the closest enabled split above it with an enabled left branch. If a right branch is closed but there is no split above with an enabled left branch, the entire tree has been visited. Then, a propositional clause $\bot \leftarrow A$ with $A \subseteq \bigcup_i \{s_i\}$ is $\models$-entailed by the A-clause set, and STRONGUNSAT can finish the refutation by exploiting $fml(s_i) = \top$.

The above strategy helps achieve fairness, because it ensures that there exists exactly one limit point. It also uses locks in a well-behaved way. This means we can considerably simplify the notion of fairness for $\Longrightarrow_L$-derivations and obtain a criterion that is almost identical to, but slightly more liberal than, Fietzke and Weidenbach's—thereby re-proving the completeness of labeled splitting.

For terminating derivations, their fairness criterion coincides with ours. For diverging derivations, Fietzke and Weidenbach construct a limit subsequence $(\Phi'_i, \mathcal{N}'_i)_i$ of the derivation $(\Phi_i, \mathcal{N}_i)_i$ and require that every persistent inference in it be made redundant, exactly as we do for $\Longrightarrow_L$-derivations. The subsequence consists of all states that lie on the split tree's unique infinite branch. Locks are well behaved, with $\limsup_{j \to \infty} \|\mathcal{L}'_j\| = \|\mathcal{L}'^\infty\|$, because with the strategy above, once an A-clause is enabled on the rightmost branch, it remains enabled forever. Our definition of fairness allows more subsequences, although this is difficult to exploit without bringing in all the theoretical complexity of AVATAR.

SMT with Quantifiers. Satisfiability modulo theories (SMT) solvers based on DPLL(T) [15] combine a SAT solver with theory solvers. In the classical setup, the theories are decidable, and the SMT solver is a decision procedure for the union of the theories. Some SMT solvers also support quantified formulas via instantiation at the expense of decidability.

Complete instantiation strategies have been developed for various fragments of first-order logic [11,18,19]. In particular, enumerative quantifier instantiation [18] is complete under some conditions. An SMT solver following such a strategy ought to be refutationally complete, but this has never been proved. Although SMT is quite different from the architectures considered above, we can instantiate our framework to show the completeness of an abstract SMT solver. The model-guided prover MG will provide a suitable starting point.

Let $\mathbf{F}$ be the set of first-order Σ-formulas. We represent the SMT solver's underlying SAT solver by the UNSAT rule and complement it with an inference system *FInf* that includes rules for clausification outside quantifiers, theory reasoning, and instantiation. The clausification rules derive C and D from a premise $C \wedge D$, among others; the theory rules derive $\bot$ from some Σ-formula set N such that $N \models \{\bot\}$, ignoring quantifiers; and the instantiation rules derive $\varphi(u)$ from premises $\forall x.\ \varphi(x)$, where u is a ground term. For *FRed*, we take an arbitrary instance of standard redundancy. Its only purpose is to split disjunctions destructively. We define the "theories with quantifiers" calculus $\mathsf{TQ} = (FInf, FRed)$. For $\models$ and $\approx$, we use entailment in the supported theories including quantifiers.

We use the same approximation function as in AVATAR (Example 3). Let us call $C \leftarrow A$ a *subunit* if C is not a disjunction. Whenever a (ground) disjunction $C \vee D \leftarrow A$ emerges, we immediately apply SPLIT. This delegates clausal reasoning to the SAT solver. It then suffices to assume that TQ is complete for subunits.

Theorem 26 (Dynamic completeness). *Assume* TQ *is statically complete for subunit sets. Let* $(\mathcal{J}_i, \mathcal{N}_i)_i$ *be a fair* $\Longrightarrow_{MG}$-*derivation based on* TQ. *If* $\mathcal{N}_0 \models \{\bot\}$ *and* $\mathcal{N}_\infty$ *contains only subunits, then* $\bot \in \mathcal{N}_j$ *for some* j.

Like AVATAR-based provers, SMT solvers will typically not perform all *SInf*-inferences, not even up to *SRed*$_{\mathrm{I}}$. Given $\mathsf{a} \approx \mathsf{b} \leftarrow \{\mathsf{v}_0\}$, $\mathsf{b} \approx c \leftarrow \{\mathsf{v}_1\}$, $\mathsf{a} \approx \mathsf{d} \leftarrow \{\mathsf{v}_2\}$, $c \approx \mathsf{d} \leftarrow \{\mathsf{v}_3\}$, and $\mathsf{a} \not\approx c \leftarrow \{\mathsf{v}_4\}$, an SMT solver will find only one of the conflicts $\bot \leftarrow \{\mathsf{v}_0, \mathsf{v}_1, \mathsf{v}_4\}$ or $\bot \leftarrow \{\mathsf{v}_2, \mathsf{v}_3, \mathsf{v}_4\}$ but not both. For decidable theories, a practical fair strategy is to instantiate quantifiers only if no other rules are applicable.

Our mathematization of AVATAR and SMT with quantifiers exposes their dissimilarities. With SMT, splitting is mandatory, and there is no subsumption or simplification, locking, or active and passive sets. And of course, theory inferences are n-ary and quantifier instantiation is unary, whereas superposition is binary. Nevertheless, their completeness follows from the same principles.

8   Conclusion

Our framework captures splitting calculi and provers in a general way, independently of the base calculus. Users can conveniently derive a dynamic refutational completeness result for a splitting prover based on a given statically refutationally complete calculus. As we developed the framework, we faced some tension between constraining the SAT solver's behavior and the saturation prover's. It seemed preferable to constrain the prover, because the prover is typically easier to modify than an off-the-shelf SAT solver. To our surprise, we discovered counterexamples related to locking, formula selection, and simplification, which may affect Vampire's AVATAR implementation, depending on the SAT solver used. We proposed some restrictions, but alternatives could be investigated.

We found that labeled splitting can be seen as a variant of AVATAR where the SAT solver follows a strict strategy and propositional variables are not reused across branches. A benefit of the strict strategy is that locking preserves completeness. As for the relationship between AVATAR and SMT, there are some glaring differences, including that splitting is necessary to support disjunctions in SMT but fully optional in AVATAR. For future work, we could try to complete the picture by considering other related architectures [4–6,14].

Acknowledgment. Petar Vukmirović greatly helped us design the abstract notions related to A-formulas. Giles Reger patiently explained AVATAR and revealed some of its secrets. Simon Cruanes did the same regarding lightweight AVATAR. Simon Robillard, Andrei Voronkov, Uwe Waldmann, Christoph Weidenbach discussed splitting with us. Haniel Barbosa, Pascal Fontaine, Andrew Reynolds, and Cesare Tinelli explained some fine points of SMT. Natarajan Shankar pointed us to his work on the Shostak procedure. Ahmed Bhayat, Mark Summerfield, Dmitriy Traytel, Petar Vukmirović, and the anonymous reviewers suggested textual improvements. We thank them all.

This research has received funding from the European Research Council (ERC) under the European Union's Horizon 2020 research and innovation program (grant agreement No. 713999, Matryoshka). The research has also received funding from the Nederlandse Organisatie voor Wetenschappelijk Onderzoek (NWO) under the Vidi program (project No. 016.Vidi.189.037, Lean Forward).

References

1. Bachmair, L., Ganzinger, H.: Rewrite-based equational theorem proving with selection and simplification. J. Log. Comput. 4(3), 217–247 (1994)
2. Bachmair, L., Ganzinger, H.: Resolution theorem proving. In: Robinson, A., Voronkov, A. (eds.) Handbook of Automated Reasoning, vol. I, pp. 19–99. Elsevier (2001)
3. Bjø[r]ner, N., Reger, G., Suda, M., Voronkov, A.: AVATAR modulo theories. In: Benzmüller, C., Sutcliffe, G., Rojas, R. (eds.) GCAI 2016. EPiC Series in Computing, vol. 41, pp. 39–52. EasyChair (2016)
4. Bonacina, M.P., Graham-Lengrand, S., Shankar, N.: Satisfiability modulo theories and assignments. In: de Moura, L. (ed.) CADE-26. LNCS, vol. 10395, pp. 42–59. Springer (2017)
5. Bonacina, M.P., Lynch, C., de Moura, L.: On deciding satisfiability by DPLL($\Gamma + T$) and unsound theorem proving. In: Schmidt, R.A. (ed.) CADE-22. LNCS, vol. 5663, pp. 35–50. Springer (2009)
6. Bonacina, M.P., Plaisted, D.A.: SGGS theorem proving: An exposition. In: Schulz, S., de Moura, L., Konev, B. (eds.) PAAR-2014. EPiC Series in Computing, vol. 31, pp. 25–38. EasyChair (2014)
7. Cruanes, S.: Extending Superposition with Integer Arithmetic, Structural Induction, and Beyond. Ph.D. thesis, École polytechnique (2015)
8. Ebner, G., Blanchette, J., Tourret, S.: A unifying splitting framework (technical report). Technical report (2021), https://matryoshka-project.github.io/pubs/splitting_report.pdf
9. Ebner, G., Ullrich, S., Roesch, J., Avigad, J., de Moura, L.: A metaprogramming framework for formal verification. Proc. ACM Program. Lang. 1(ICFP), 34:1–34:29 (2017)
10. Fietzke, A., Weidenbach, C.: Labelled splitting. Ann. Math. Artif. Intell. 55(1–2), 3–34 (2009)
11. Ge, Y., de Moura, L.: Complete instantiation for quantified formulas in satisfiabiliby modulo theories. In: Bouajjani, A., Maler, O. (eds.) CAV 2009. LNCS, vol. 5643, pp. 306–320. Springer (2009)
12. Knuth, D.E., Bendix, P.B.: Simple word problems in universal algebras. In: Leech, J. (ed.) Computational Problems in Abstract Algebra. pp. 263–297. Pergamon Press (1970)
13. McCune, W., Wos, L.: Otter—the CADE-13 competition incarnations. J. Autom. Reason. 18(2), 211–220 (1997)
14. de Moura, L., Jovanović, D.: A model-constructing satisfiability calculus. In: Giacobazzi, R., Berdine, J., Mastroeni, I. (eds.) VMCAI 2013. LNCS, vol. 7737, pp. 1–12. Springer (2013)
15. Nieuwenhuis, R., Oliveras, A., Tinelli, C.: Solving SAT and SAT modulo theories: From an abstract Davis–Putnam–Logemann–Loveland procedure to DPLL(T). J. ACM 53(6), 937–977 (2006)
16. Nipkow, T., Klein, G.: Concrete Semantics: With Isabelle/HOL. Springer (2014)
17. Reger, G., Suda, M., Voronkov, A.: Playing with AVATAR. In: Felty, A.P., Middeldorp, A. (eds.) CADE-25. LNCS, vol. 9195, pp. 399–415. Springer (2015)
18. Reynolds, A., Barbosa, H., Fontaine, P.: Revisiting enumerative instantiation. In: Beyer, D., Huisman, M. (eds.) TACAS 2018. LNCS, vol. 10806, pp. 112–131. Springer (2018)

19. Reynolds, A., Tinelli, C., Goel, A., Krstić, S.: Finite model finding in SMT. In: Sharygina, N., Veith, H. (eds.) CAV 2013. LNCS, vol. 8044, pp. 640–655. Springer (2013)
20. Riazanov, A., Voronkov, A.: Splitting without backtracking. In: Nebel, B. (ed.) IJCAI 2001. pp. 611–617. Morgan Kaufmann (2001)
21. Sutcliffe, G.: The TPTP problem library and associated infrastructure—from CNF to TH0, TPTP v6.4.0. J. Autom. Reason. 59(4), 483–502 (2017)
22. Voronkov, A.: AVATAR: The architecture for first-order theorem provers. In: Biere, A., Bloem, R. (eds.) CAV 2014. LNCS, vol. 8559, pp. 696–710. Springer (2014)
23. Waldmann, U., Tourret, S., Robillard, S., Blanchette, J.: A comprehensive framework for saturation theorem proving. In: Peltier, N., Sofronie-Stokkermans, V. (eds.) IJCAR 2020, Part I. LNCS, vol. 12166, pp. 316–334. Springer (2020)
24. Weidenbach, C.: Combining superposition, sorts and splitting. In: Robinson, A., Voronkov, A. (eds.) Handbook of Automated Reasoning, vol. II, pp. 1965–2013. Elsevier and MIT Press (2001)

Open Access This chapter is licensed under the terms of the Creative Commons Attribution 4.0 International License (http://creativecommons.org/licenses/by/4.0/), which permits use, sharing, adaptation, distribution and reproduction in any medium or format, as long as you give appropriate credit to the original author(s) and the source, provide a link to the Creative Commons license and indicate if changes were made.

The images or other third party material in this chapter are included in the chapter's Creative Commons license, unless indicated otherwise in a credit line to the material. If material is not included in the chapter's Creative Commons license and your intended use is not permitted by statutory regulation or exceeds the permitted use, you will need to obtain permission directly from the copyright holder.

Integer Induction in Saturation

Petra Hozzová[1] ![ORCID], Laura Kovács[1] ![ORCID], and Andrei Voronkov[2,3]

[1] TU Wien, Vienna, Austria
{petra.hozzova, laura.kovacs}@tuwien.ac.at, andrei@voronkov.com
[2] University of Manchester, Manchester, UK
[3] EasyChair, Manchester, UK

Abstract. Integers are ubiquitous in programming and therefore also in applications of program analysis and verification. Such applications often require some sort of inductive reasoning. In this paper we analyze the challenge of automating inductive reasoning with integers. We introduce inference rules for integer induction within the saturation framework of first-order theorem proving. We implemented these rules in the theorem prover VAMPIRE and evaluated our work against other state-of-the-art theorem provers. Our results demonstrate the strength of our approach by solving new problems coming from program analysis and mathematical properties of integers.

1 Introduction

One of the most commonly used data types in imperative/functional programs are integers. For example, iterating over arrays in imperative programs or recursively computing sums in functional programs include integer-valued program variables, as illustrated in Figure 1. While for many uses of integers in programming we only need to consider non-negative integers, there are also applications where integers are essential, for example, reasoning about memory. To formally prove functional correctness of such and similar programs, reasoning about integers is indispensable but so is handling some sort of induction over integers. In this paper we address these two reasoning challenges and fully automate inductive reasoning with integers within saturation-based theorem proving.

Induction in saturation-based theorem proving is a new exciting direction in the automation of induction, recently introduced in [5, 10, 16]. This work focused on induction on inductively defined data types, also called algebraic data types [12], such as natural numbers or lists. However, automating *integer induction*, that is, induction on integers, has not yet been addressed sufficiently.

While natural numbers have a well-founded order and induction over this order is very useful in automated inductive theorem proving, the standard order on integers is not well-founded, so it cannot be directly used as the induction ordering. In this paper we will use the observation that the standard ordering $<$ is well-founded on every set of integers having a lower bound b and likewise, the inverse $>$ of this ordering is well-founded on every set of integers having an upper bound b. This gives us two induction rules on such integer subsets: induction (with the base case b) using $<$ and induction (with the base case b) using $>$,

© The Author(s) 2021
A. Platzer and G. Sutcliffe (Eds.): CADE 2021, LNAI 12699, pp. 361–377, 2021.
https://doi.org/10.1007/978-3-030-79876-5_21

respectively, to prove that a property holds for all integers $\geq b$ and, respectively, $\leq b$. We define these induction rules as *upward, respectively, downward induction rules with symbolic bounds*. We also consider two variations of these rules over integer intervals and refer to such rules as *interval upward, respectively, downward induction rules with symbolic bounds*.

For natural numbers, 0 is an obvious base case candidate, which also turns out to be successful in the theorem proving practice. It is also a natural base case candidate for induction. In this paper we will give some natural problems for which neither 0 nor any concrete integer is a good base case. Our paper focuses on the following three issues:

1. proofs of properties of integers by induction on bounded sets of integers in saturation theorem proving, using (interval) downward/upward induction rules with symbolic bounds;
2. techniques for discovering a suitable base case;
3. implementation techniques.

This paper is organized as follows. In Section 2 we illustrate our approach by considering properties of the functional and imperative programs of Figure 1. Then in Section 3 we define four induction rules over integers, called *(interval) downward, respectively upward, induction rules with symbolic bounds*, and prove their soundness. Section 4 introduces an extension of superposition calculus by our new integer induction rules. We demonstrate that, using this extension, superposition provers can prove integer properties similarly to how humans would do. This extension is especially successful when used together with the AVATAR architecture [19], since AVATAR helps in reasoning efficiently using constraints coming out of the integer induction rules.

We implemented our work in the VAMPIRE theorem prover [13] and compare our implementation with other relevant provers, including VAMPIRE without integer induction (Section 5). Our experiments show that integer induction can solve many new problems that could not so far be solved by any prover. For example, 75 problems coming from program analysis and/or mathematical integer properties could be solved only by VAMPIRE with the new induction rules.

Contributions. This paper makes the following contributions:

- We introduce four new inference rules for automating integer induction: *(interval) downward, respectively upward, induction rules with symbolic bounds* (Section 3).
- Based on these rules, we introduce corresponding inference rules for integer induction in the superposition calculus (Section 4). These rules are formulated in the context of saturation-based theorem proving in a way that avoids an immediate combinatorial explosion of the search space.
- We implement and evaluate the new rules in the theorem prover VAMPIRE. Our experimental results show that our implementation can solve a number of problems previously unsolved by any prover (Section 5).
- We introduce a large collection of new inductive benchmarks, publicly available at `https://github.com/vprover/inductive_benchmarks`.

```
                          assume  0 ≤ pos < A.size

fun sum(n, m) =           i := pos;
  if n = m then n         while i + 1 < A.size do
  else n + sum(n + 1, m);     A[i + 1] := A[i];
                              i := i + 1;
assert                        inv ∀j ∈ Z.(pos ≤ j < i → valₐ(j + 1) = valₐ(j))
∀n, m ∈ Z.(n ≤ m →        end
  2 · sum(n, m) =
  m · (m + 1) − n · (n − 1))  assert
                          ∀j ∈ Z.(pos ≤ j < A.size → valₐ(j) = valₐ(pos))
  (a) Sum of integers
    from [n, m].            (b) Array initialization, with valₐ(j) denoting A[j].
```

Fig. 1. Motivating examples for inductive reasoning with integers.

2 Motivating Examples

2.1 Preliminaries

We assume familiarity with standard many-sorted first-order logic with equality. For details we refer to [13]. Throughout this paper we denote variables by x, y, e, j, n, m, constants by c, c', Skolem constants by σ, all possibly with indices. We denote terms by t, literals by L, formulas by F and clauses by C. We denote the equality predicate by $=$ and write $t_1 \neq t_2$ for the literal $\neg(t_1 = t_2)$.

We will focus on integer induction. To this end, we assume a distinguished *integer sort*, denoted by $\mathbb{Z}$. When we use standard integer predicates $<, \leq, >, \geq$, functions $+, -, \ldots$ and constants $0, 1, 2, \ldots$, we assume that they denote the corresponding interpreted integer predicates and functions with their standard interpretations. All other symbols are uninterpreted. We will write quantifiers like $\forall x \in \mathbb{Z}$ to denote that x has the integer sort.

In what follows, we will sometimes write "this problem requires integer induction". This should not be regarded as a formal statement: this property is not easy to formalize in general and it is possible that some of these problems can be proved by certain combinations of decision procedures, first-order theorem proving with uninterpreted functions, and axiomatization of interpreted functions on integers. However, when we make such statements, one can see that these problems have relatively simple proofs involving induction and cannot be proved by existing provers without induction.

2.2 Examples

To illustrate problems arising in automating integer induction, let us consider the programs of Figure 1. Properties of both programs are specified using assertions expressed in first-order logic, with pre- and post-conditions specified by the keywords **assume** and **assert**, respectively.

Functional programs. The ML-style functional program of Figure 1(a) computes the sum $\mathtt{sum}(n, m)$ of integers in the interval $[n, m]$, that is $\sum_{i=n}^{m} i$, where $m \geq n$. The function definition uses the following axioms of $\mathtt{sum}$:

$$\forall n \in \mathbb{Z}.(\mathtt{sum}(n, n) = n); \tag{1}$$
$$\forall n, m \in \mathbb{Z}.(n \neq m \rightarrow \mathtt{sum}(n, m) = n + \mathtt{sum}(n + 1, m)). \tag{2}$$

We should prove the assertion

$$\forall n, m \in \mathbb{Z}.(n \leq m \rightarrow 2 \cdot \mathtt{sum}(n, m) = m \cdot (m + 1) - n \cdot (n - 1)). \tag{3}$$

Formally proving (3) requires inductive reasoning with both integers and quantifiers. Let $F[x]$ be a formula with one or more occurrences of an integer variable x and b an integer term not containing x. Consider the following formula:

$$F[b] \wedge \forall x \in \mathbb{Z}.(x \leq b \wedge F[x] \rightarrow F[x - 1]) \rightarrow \forall x \in \mathbb{Z}.(x \leq b \rightarrow F[x]). \tag{4}$$

This formula is valid. It is similar to the standard induction on natural numbers, yet with two essential differences. First, we use $x - 1$ instead of $x + 1$ and second, we use the term b where for the standard induction we would use 0. Note that b does not have to be a concrete integer, it can be any term. In the sequel we will refer to such terms b used in induction rules as *symbolic bounds*.

For proving (3) using a theorem prover, we first negate and skolemize (3), obtaining the following formula, where σ_n, σ_m are fresh skolem constants:

$$\sigma_n \leq \sigma_m \wedge 2 \cdot \mathtt{sum}(\sigma_n, \sigma_m) \neq \sigma_m \cdot (\sigma_m + 1) - \sigma_n \cdot (\sigma_n - 1) \tag{5}$$

Modern theorem provers implementing linear integer arithmetic and quantifiers can prove unsatisfiability of (1), (2) and (5) in a relatively straightforward way if we also add an instance of induction rule (4) with

$$F[x] \overset{\text{def}}{=} 2 \cdot \mathtt{sum}(x, \sigma_m) = \sigma_m \cdot (\sigma_m + 1) - x \cdot (x - 1);$$
$$b \overset{\text{def}}{=} \sigma_m.$$

Here and in the sequel $\overset{\text{def}}{=}$ means "equal by definition" or "defined as". If we want to automate this kind of reasoning, the main question is finding the corresponding instance of induction rule (4), that is, finding the induction formula $F[x]$ and the (symbolic) bound b.

Imperative programs. The C-style imperative program of Figure 1(b) initializes an integer-valued array A starting at the index *pos*. We should prove the assertion stating that all array elements at indices greater than or equal to *pos* are equal to each other. Proving such assertions typically requires loop invariants "summarizing" the loop behavior. One such invariant I is shown in the loop after the keyword **inv**. This invariant I could be derived by existing approaches to invariant generation [8, 9].

The assertion of Figure 1(b) is then proved using I, by establishing that the post-condition

$$\forall j \in \mathbb{Z}.(pos \leq j < A.size \to \text{val}_A(j) = \text{val}_A(pos)) \tag{6}$$

is a logical consequence of the invariant I and the negation of the loop condition:

$$\forall j \in \mathbb{Z}.(pos \leq j < i \to \text{val}_A(j+1) = \text{val}_A(j)); \\ \neg(i+1 < A.size). \tag{7}$$

Interestingly, modern theorem provers cannot perform such proofs. Similar to the first example, we can use an induction rule for integers formulated as follows:

$$\big(F[b_1] \wedge \forall x \in \mathbb{Z}.(b_1 \leq x < b_2 \wedge F[x] \to F[x+1])\big) \\ \to \forall x \in \mathbb{Z}.(b_1 \leq x \leq b_2 \to F[x]). \tag{8}$$

If we add an instance of this rule defined as follows:

$$F[x] \stackrel{\text{def}}{=} \text{val}_A(x) = \text{val}_A(pos); \\ b_1 \stackrel{\text{def}}{=} pos; \\ b_2 \stackrel{\text{def}}{=} A.size - 1,$$

then state-of-the-art theorem provers can easily prove that (6) is a logical consequence of (7) and the corresponding instance of (8). For example, Cvc4 [1], Z3 [6] and Vampire prove such an instance in essentially no time. However, similarly to the example of Figure 1(a), in order to find such proofs automatically using the induction rule of (8), we need to be able to discover, during the proof search, the induction formula $F[x]$ and the symbolic bounds b_1, b_2. In what follows, we describe our solution to automating this discovery by integrating integer induction within saturation-based theorem proving.

3 Integer Induction

In this section we define four induction rules, or induction schemas, on integers. Two of them were already considered in Section 2 – namely (4) and (8).

Definition 1 (Downward/Upward Induction). A *downward, respectively upward, induction axiom with symbolic bounds* is any formula of the form

$$F[b] \wedge \forall x.(x \leq b \wedge F[x] \to F[x-1]) \to \forall x.(x \leq b \to F[x]); \quad \textit{(downward)} \\ F[b] \wedge \forall x.(x \geq b \wedge F[x] \to F[x+1]) \to \forall x.(x \geq b \to F[x]), \quad \textit{(upward)}$$

respectively, where $F[x]$ is a formula with one or more occurrences of an integer variable x and b is an integer term not containing x. □

Note that (4) is a downward induction axiom with symbolic bounds.

Definition 2 (Interval Downward/Upward Induction). An *interval downward, respectively upward, induction axiom with symbolic bounds* is any formula of the form

$$F[b_2] \wedge \forall x.(b_1 < x \leq b_2 \wedge F[x] \to F[x-1]) \to \forall x.(b_1 \leq x \leq b_2 \to F[x]); \quad \textit{(down.)}$$
$$F[b_1] \wedge \forall x.(b_1 \leq x < b_2 \wedge F[x] \to F[x+1]) \to \forall x.(b_1 \leq x \leq b_2 \to F[x]), \quad \textit{(up.)}$$

respectively, where $F[x]$ is a formula with one or more occurrences of an integer variable x and b_1, b_2 are integer terms not containing x. $\square$

Note that (8) is an interval upward induction axiom with symbolic bounds. The main motivation for interval induction rules is their utility in reasoning about loops, as illustrated by the example of Figure 1(a). While interval induction can be captured by induction with one bound, it would require additional case analysis, which is not efficient in saturation-based proving practice.

In the sequel, we will refer to the integer terms of b, b_1, b_2 from Definitions 1-2 as *symbolic bounds* and the formulas $F[x]$ from the induction axioms of Definitions 1-2 as *induction formulas*.

Definition 3 (Downward/Upward Induction Rules). The *downward (respectively, upward) induction rule with symbolic bounds*, or simply *downward (respectively, upward) induction rule* is the inference rule whose instances are all downward (respectively, upward) induction axioms with symbolic bounds.

Likewise, the *interval downward (respectively, upward) induction rule with symbolic bounds*, or simply *interval downward (respectively, upward) induction rule* is the inference rule whose instances are all interval downward (respectively, upward) induction axioms with symbolic bounds. $\square$

It is easy to see that the following theorem holds.

Theorem 1 (Soundness). *The (interval) downward/upward induction rules of Definition 3 are sound, that is, all corresponding induction axioms from Definitions 1-2 are valid.* $\square$

4   Integer Induction in Saturation-Based Proof Search

Our next aim is to define analogues of the induction rules introduced in Section 3 that can be used in superposition theorem provers and their saturation algorithms. For a general discussion of superposition and saturation we refer to [13]. In this section we use $\square$ to denote the empty clause and write $\mathrm{CNF}(F)$ to mean (any) clausal normal form of a formula F. We refer to the set of clauses on which a saturation algorithm operates as the *search space*.

The most general way to introduce our new induction rules at the calculus level is to add clausal forms of our new induction axioms to the search space. That is, for every induction axiom F from Section 3, we add the rule

$$\frac{}{\mathrm{CNF}(F)} \; .$$

However, we cannot efficiently implement such a calculus, as any formula with one variable can be used as an induction formula. We will therefore introduce different, more specialized, rules, which still correspond to the previously defined induction rules. The new rules use variations of the following three ideas:

1. Use only simple induction formulas, for example literals;
2. To find an induction formula, generalize a subgoal occurring in the search space. Then the derived induction formula can be immediately used to prove this subgoal;
3. Use (symbolic) bounds that correspond to bounds already occurring in the search space.

The first two ideas were already used in the first papers underlying our approach to induction in saturation theorem proving [10, 16]. For example, they can be implemented by using only induction formulas that are obtained from ground literals $L[t]$ in the search space, where t is a ground term. The corresponding induction formula will be $\neg L[x]$. The idea is that, when we prove the induction formula, $\neg L[x]$ will be resolved against $L[t]$.

The third idea is new. Note that, if we use the first two ideas and the upward induction rule, instead of $\neg L[x]$ we will derive $b \leq x \to \neg L[x]$. When we resolve this against $L[t]$, we obtain the clause $\neg (b \leq t)$. However, if we already previously derived $b \leq t$, we can also resolve away $\neg (b \leq t)$. This gives us the idea to only apply the upward induction rules when we have $b \leq t$.[4]

Based on the three ideas above, we introduce the following four induction rules on clauses. In these rules t is a ground term, b is a constant and $L[x]$ is a literal containing at least one occurrence of a variable x and no other variables. The rules depend on which comparisons among $t \geq b$, $t > b$, $t \leq b$ and $t < b$ already occur in the current search space:

$$\frac{\neg L[t] \vee C \qquad t \geq b}{\mathrm{CNF}\Big(\big(L[b] \wedge \forall x.(x \geq b \wedge L[x] \to L[x+1])\big) \to \forall y.(y \geq b \to L[y])\Big)} \ (\texttt{IntInd}_{\geq})$$

$$\frac{\neg L[t] \vee C \qquad t > b}{\mathrm{CNF}\Big(\big(L[b] \wedge \forall x.(x \geq b \wedge L[x] \to L[x+1])\big) \to \forall y.(y > b \to L[y])\Big)} \ (\texttt{IntInd}_{>})$$

$$\frac{\neg L[t] \vee C \qquad t \leq b}{\mathrm{CNF}\Big(\big(L[b] \wedge \forall x.(x \leq b \wedge L[x] \to L[x-1])\big) \to \forall y.(y \leq b \to L[y])\Big)} \ (\texttt{IntInd}_{\leq})$$

$$\frac{\neg L[t] \vee C \qquad t < b}{\mathrm{CNF}\Big(\big(L[b] \wedge \forall x.(x \leq b \wedge L[x] \to L[x-1])\big) \to \forall y.(y < b \to L[y])\Big)} \ (\texttt{IntInd}_{<})$$

Note that $\texttt{IntInd}_{\geq}$ and $\texttt{IntInd}_{>}$ are upward induction rules, whereas $\texttt{IntInd}_{\leq}$ and $\texttt{IntInd}_{<}$ are downward induction rules. One can also introduce non-ground analogues of these rules but we do not consider them in this paper.

---

[4] Using the AVATAR architecture [19], we can easily obtain valid literals $b \leq t$.

Similarly to the above rules on the clausal level, we also introduce the interval upward/downward induction rules on clauses to be used in saturation algorithms for the superposition calculus. Since these rules are similar to each other, here we only define one rule $\text{IntInd}_{[\geq]}$ for interval upward induction. For a ground term t, constants b_1, b_2, and $L[x]$ a literal containing at least one occurrence of a variable x and no other variables, an interval upward induction rule on clauses:

$$\frac{\neg L[t] \vee C \quad t \geq b_1 \quad t \leq b_2}{\begin{array}{c} \text{CNF}\Big(\big(L[b_1] \wedge \forall x.(b_1 \leq x < b_2 \wedge L[x] \to L[x+1]) \big) \\ \to \forall y.(b_1 \leq y \leq b_2 \to L[y]) \Big) \end{array}} \quad (\text{IntInd}_{[\geq]})$$

In view of Theorem 1, all induction rules of Section 3 are sound. Assuming that our CNF function preserves satisfiability, we conclude that all our induction rules $\text{IntInd}_{\geq}$, $\text{IntInd}_{>}$, $\text{IntInd}_{\leq}$, $\text{IntInd}_{<}$ and $\text{IntInd}_{[\geq]}$ on the clausal level are sound.

Theorem 2 (Soundness). *For every satisfiability preserving CNF function, the induction rules from Definition 3 are sound.* □

Example 1. To illustrate again how the choice of induction formulas allows us to have shorter clauses, consider $\text{IntInd}_{\leq}$. The CNF in its conclusion consists of three clauses:

$$\neg L[b] \vee \sigma \leq b \vee \neg y \leq b \vee L[y]$$
$$\neg L[b] \vee L[\sigma] \vee \neg y \leq b \vee L[y] \quad (9)$$
$$\neg L[b] \vee \neg L[\sigma - 1] \vee \neg y \leq b \vee L[y]$$

These clauses can be resolved against premises of $\text{IntInd}_{\leq}$, yielding the following clauses:

$$\neg L[b] \vee \sigma \leq b \vee C$$
$$\neg L[b] \vee L[\sigma] \vee C \quad (10)$$
$$\neg L[b] \vee \neg L[\sigma - 1] \vee C$$

They have an especially simple form when C is the empty clause $\square$. In this case we have three clauses:

$$\neg L[b] \vee \sigma \leq b$$
$$\neg L[b] \vee L[\sigma] \quad (11)$$
$$\neg L[b] \vee \neg L[\sigma - 1]$$

which subsume the original three longer clauses and are ground. Since they are ground, they can be handled efficiently by AVATAR. □

Example 2. Let us now demonstrate how the downward induction rule $\text{IntInd}_{\leq}$ works for refuting the inductive property (3) from our motivating example of Figure 1(a). We use literals from (5) as the premises of the $\text{IntInd}_{\leq}$ rule. The corresponding instance of the downward induction rule is defined by

$$b \stackrel{\text{def}}{=} \sigma_m;$$
$$t \stackrel{\text{def}}{=} \sigma_n;$$
$$L[x] \stackrel{\text{def}}{=} 2 \cdot \text{sum}(x, \sigma_m) = \sigma_m \cdot (\sigma_m + 1) - x \cdot (x - 1).$$

This instance of `IntInd`$_\le$ is:

$$\frac{2 \cdot \mathsf{sum}(\sigma_n, \sigma_m) \neq \sigma_m \cdot (\sigma_m + 1) - \sigma_n \cdot (\sigma_n - 1) \qquad \sigma_n \le \sigma_m}{\begin{aligned} \mathrm{CNF}\Big(&(2 \cdot \mathsf{sum}(\sigma_m, \sigma_m) = \sigma_m \cdot (\sigma_m + 1) - \sigma_m \cdot (\sigma_m - 1) \\ &\wedge\, \forall x.(x \le \sigma_m \to 2 \cdot \mathsf{sum}(x, \sigma_m) = \sigma_m \cdot (\sigma_m + 1) - x \cdot (x - 1) \\ &\qquad\qquad \to 2 \cdot \mathsf{sum}(x - 1, \sigma_m) = \sigma_m \cdot (\sigma_m + 1) - (x - 1) \cdot ((x - 1) - 1))) \\ &\to \forall y.(y \le \sigma_m \to 2 \cdot \mathsf{sum}(y, \sigma_m) = \sigma_m \cdot (\sigma_m + 1) - y \cdot (y - 1))\Big) \end{aligned}} \quad (\texttt{IntInd}_\le)$$

This single instance of the induction rule does the magic. By adding its conclusion to the search space we can obtain a contradiction in a few steps by applying a few superposition rules and using ground reasoning in linear integer arithmetic with uninterpreted functions (as evidenced by the results for the first problem subset, *x_all* of *sum*, in Table 3).

We finally note that functional correctness of Figure 1(b) is proved by the interval upward induction rule `IntInd`$_{[\ge]}$, in a similar way as above (and as evidenced by the results of Table 3 for *declared_unint_ax-fin_conj-fin* in *val*).   □

What we find especially interesting in Example 2 is that the induction axiom used in it (and discovered by our implementation of induction in VAMPIRE) uses the induction argument that would probably be used by a majority of humans who would try to argue why the program property holds.

5   Implementation and Experiments

5.1   Implementation

We implemented our integer induction rules `IntInd`$_\ge$, `IntInd`$_>$, `IntInd`$_\le$, `IntInd`$_<$ as well as `IntInd`$_{[\ge]}$ and the other corresponding interval induction rules in VAMPIRE. Further, we also implemented a more general induction rule `IntInd` that does not require bounds to be in the search space and uses 0 as the lower or the upper bound. Our implementation in VAMPIRE, consisting of approximately 1,200 lines of new C++ code, is available at https://github.com/vprover/vampire. The size of this additional code is relatively small because VAMPIRE has libraries for indexing and chaining inference rules that could be used off the shelf.

Our (interval) downward/upward induction rules described in Section 4 can be applied when either (i) the comparison literal (e.g., $t \ge b$ for the `IntInd`$_\ge$ rule) is selected and the corresponding clause $\neg L[t] \vee C$ was already selected as an induction candidate before, or (ii) if $\neg L[t] \vee C$ is selected as an induction candidate and the corresponding comparison literal was already selected before. To implement these rules efficiently, we should be able to efficiently retrieve comparison literals and literals selected for induction. To do so, we extended the indexing mechanism of VAMPIRE to index such literals. We do not apply induction when the induction formula $L[x]$ is a comparison having x as a top level argument, for example, $x \le t$, and allow to apply it to all other induction formulas deemed to be suitable by other user-specified options.

<u>assume</u> $e \geq 1$

fun $\text{power}(x, 1) = x$
     $| \ \text{power}(x, e) = x \cdot \text{power}(x, e - 1);$

<u>assert</u> $\forall x, y \in \mathbb{Z}.(\text{power}(x \cdot y, e) = \text{power}(x, e) \cdot \text{power}(y, e))$

Fig. 2. ML-like functional program computing integer powers for positive exponents.

Our (interval) downward/upward induction rules in VAMPIRE are enabled by the new option `--induction int`. The options `--int_induction_interval infinite` and `--int_induction_interval finite` limit the enabled rules to downward/upward only, and interval downward/upward only, respectively. Further, `--int_induction_default_bound on` enables the more general rule which does not require bounds to be in the search space. Our new induction rules can also be controlled by other VAMPIRE options for well-founded/structural induction, such as `--induction_on_complex_terms on`, which enables applying induction on any ground complex term. To improve VAMPIRE's performance for integer induction, we combined our new induction rules with `--induction_on_complex_terms on` and also other options not specific for induction. We extended VAMPIRE with a new mode scheduling various option configurations for integer induction, switched on by the option `--mode portfolio --schedule integer_induction`. Additionally, we introduced the option `--schedule induction` which uses either the integer induction configurations as for `--schedule integer_induction`, or structural induction configurations, or both, depending on the data types used in the problem/property to be proved.

5.2   Benchmarks

We used two sets of examples: (i) benchmark sets LIA and UFLIA from the SMT-LIB collection [2], consisting of, respectively, 607 and 10,137 examples, and (ii) 120 new benchmarks similar to our motivating examples from Section 2.

To the best of our knowledge, the state-of-the-art systems implementing inductive reasoning have so far not yet considered inductive reasoning over integers, with two exceptions: [17], which mainly focuses on induction over inductively defined data types but mentions induction on non-negative integers and [11], which supports inductive reasoning using recursive function definitions without any special treatment for integers.

Since integer induction has not yet attracted enough attention in theorem proving, there is no significant collection of benchmarks for integer induction. To properly carry out experiments, we therefore created a set of *120 new benchmarks* based on variations of our motivating examples from Section 2 and on properties of computing integer powers. One example is the function correctness of the

Set	Variant tag	Description
sum	*x / y*	$\text{sum}(x, y)$ for $x > y$ defined as $x + \text{sum}(x+1, y)$ or $y + \text{sum}(x, y-1)$
	all / geq / leq	the conjecture holds for all x, y where $x \le y$, or only for $x \le y = c$, or only for $c = x \le y$; where $c \in \mathbb{Z}$ is an interpreted constant
val	*declared / defined*	**val** was either not defined, only declared and axiomatized (as in (6)), or defined as a total computable function (as in (14))
	inter / unint / mixed	the axiom and conjecture use concrete interpreted constants, or uninterpreted constants, or a mix of both
	ax-fin/ax-all/ ax-leq/ax-geq	the axiom holds for integers in an interval $[c, c')$, or for all $x \in \mathbb{Z}$, or only for $x \le c$, or only for $x \ge c$; where $c, c' \in \mathbb{Z}$ are constants
	conj-fin/conj- all/conj-leq /conj-geq	the conjecture holds for integers in an interval $[c, c']$, or for all integers, or only for integers $\le c$, or only for integers $\ge c$; where $c, c' \in \mathbb{Z}$ are constants
power	*0 / 1*	**power** defined starting with $\text{power}(x, 0) = 1$ or $\text{power}(x, 1) = x$
	all / pos / neg	the conjecture holds either for all x, y, or only for $x, y \ge 0$, or only for $x, y \le 0$

Table 1. Description of our benchmark set of 120 new examples.

program of Figure 2, which is formalized as follows:

$$\text{axioms:} \quad \forall x \in \mathbb{Z}.(\text{power}(x, 1) = x)$$

$$\forall x, e \in \mathbb{Z}.(2 \le e \rightarrow \text{power}(x, e) = x \cdot \text{power}(x, e - 1)) \quad (12)$$

$$\text{conjecture:} \quad \forall x, y, e.(1 \le e \rightarrow \text{power}(x \cdot y, e) = \text{power}(x, e) \cdot \text{power}(y, e))$$

Our set of 120 new benchmarks is described in Table 1 and available online at:

https://github.com/vprover/inductive_benchmarks

To confirm that our new benchmarks require the use of inductive reasoning, we tested them on the SMT solver Z3 [6] that does not support induction. Z3 could not solve any of the 120 problems from our benchmark set. Names of subsets of our new benchmarks are constructed by joining variant tags described in Table 1. For example, problem (6) belongs to the category *declared_unint_ax-fin_conj-fin* of the set *val*. The following benchmark:

$$\text{axiom:} \quad \forall x \in \mathbb{Z}.(\text{val}(x) = \text{val}(x + 1))$$

$$\text{conjecture:} \quad \forall x, y \in \mathbb{Z}.(\text{val}(x) = \text{val}(y)) \quad (13)$$

belongs to *declared_unint_ax-all_conj-all* of *val* and the below example is from *defined_inter_ax-geq_conj-geq* of *val*:

$$\text{axioms:} \quad \forall x \in \mathbb{Z}.(x \le 0 \rightarrow \text{val}(x) = 0)$$

$$\forall x \in \mathbb{Z}.(0 < x \rightarrow \text{val}(x) = \text{val}(x - 1)) \quad (14)$$

$$\text{conjecture:} \quad \forall x \in \mathbb{Z}.(0 \le x \rightarrow \text{val}(x) = \text{val}(0))$$

While 9 of the benchmarks (all in *val*) use finite intervals in both the assertion and the invariant (*ax-fin_conj-fin*), the remaining 111 benchmarks require inductive reasoning over infinite intervals.

Problem set	Total count	Cvc4	Z3	Vampire	Vampire-I	new compared to Vampire	new compared to Vampire, Cvc4 and Z3
LIA	607	553	435	216	214	10	1
UFLIA	10137	7002	6705	6116	5796	99	44

Table 2. Comparison of solvers on SMT-LIB benchmarks.

5.3 Experimental Setup

We ran our experiments on computers with 32 cores (AMD Epyc 7502, 2.5 GHz) and 1 TB RAM. In all experiments we used the memory limit of 16 GB per problem. For the new benchmarks we used a 300 seconds time limit. For the experiments on the larger LIA and UFLIA sets we used a 10 seconds time limit.

In what follows, Vampire refers to the (default) version of Vampire, as in [10,16]. By Vampire-I we denote our new version of Vampire, using integer induction rules (--induction int). Vampire-I* refers to the portfolio mode of Vampire-I, scheduling various option configurations for integer induction (--mode portfolio --schedule induction).

For *experiments with the new benchmarks*, we note that Vampire without integer induction cannot solve any of the problems. In this set of experiments, we therefore compared Vampire-I to the provers Cvc4 [17] and Acl2 [11], which are, to the best of our knowledge, the only two automated solvers supporting inductive reasoning with integers in addition to reasoning with theories and quantifiers. For Cvc4, we used the *ig* configuration from [17]: --quant-ind --quant-cf --conjecture-gen --conjecture-gen-per-round=3 --full-saturate-quant. For Acl2, we used its default configuration and translated our new problem set into the functional program encoding syntax of Acl2. In the *experiments with the LIA and UFLIA benchmark sets of SMT-LIB*, we also used Z3 [6] in the default configuration.

We ran Cvc4, Z3, Vampire and Vampire-I on problems encoded in the SMT-LIB2 syntax [2]. For running Acl2 on the new benchmarks, we translated problems into the functional program encoding syntax of Acl2.

5.4 Experimental Results

SMT-LIB Benchmarks. First, we evaluated the improvements of integer induction in Vampire-I when compared to Vampire, Cvc4 and Z3 on the LIA and UFLIA sets of SMT-LIB [2]. We aimed to verify that Vampire-I's performance does not deteriorate due to adding integer induction, check whether Vampire-I can solve problems that could not be solved automatically before, and to identify the best values for options related to integer induction. To this end, we picked five different strategies (e.g. using different saturation algorithms and selection functions) and used different combinations of induction options. Table 2 summarizes our results, showcasing that integer induction enabled Vampire-I to

Problem set	Problem subset	Count	ACL2	CVC4	VAMPIRE-I*
	x_all	1	0	0	1
	y_all	1	0	0	1
sum	*x_leq*	5	0	0	4
	y_geq	5	0	5	5
	subset total	12	0	5	11
	declared_mixed_ax-fin_conj-fin	6	0	1	4
	declared_unint_ax-fin_conj-fin	3	0	0	3
	declared_inter_ax-all_conj-all	5	0	0	3
	declared_inter_ax-all_conj-geq	9	0	9	9
	declared_inter_ax-all_conj-leq	9	0	0	9
	declared_inter_ax-geq_conj-geq	13	0	13	10
	declared_inter_ax-leq_conj-leq	13	0	0	11
val	*declared_unint_ax-all_* *	7	0	0	7
	declared_unint_ax-geq_conj-geq	2	0	0	2
	declared_unint_ax-leq_conj-leq	2	0	0	2
	defined_inter_ax-all_conj-all	3	1	0	3
	defined_inter_ax-geq_conj-geq	3	2	3	3
	defined_inter_ax-leq_conj-leq	3	2	0	3
	*defined_unint_* *	6	0	0	6
	subset total	84	5	26	75
	0_all	4	0	0	4
	0_pos	4	0	0	4
	0_neg	4	0	0	4
power	*1_all*	4	0	0	2
	1_pos	4	0	0	4
	1_neg	4	0	0	2
	subset total	24	0	0	20
all sets	combined total	120	5	31	106
all sets	uniquely solved	-	0	3	75

Table 3. Experiments with our new benchmarks from Table 1.

solve over 100 new problems that VAMPIRE could not solve before (last but one column of Table 2). Moreover, 45 of these problems were also new compared to CVC4 and Z3 (last column of Table 2), which most likely means that no theorem prover was able to prove them before.

In problems solved using integer induction, the integer induction rules were applied often: at least one of the interval induction rules was used in nearly 99% of problems, while one of the induction rules with one bound was used in nearly all problems. The interval induction and induction rules were used on average 4559 and 1191 times, respectively. 89% of the proofs employed interval induction (67% upward, 29% downward), while 27% of the proofs used induction with one bound (22% upward, 8% downward). Additionally, over 64% of proofs only required one application of any induction rule.

Experiments with 120 New Benchmarks. Comparison results for VAMPIRE-I, ACL2 and CVC4 on our new benchmarks are displayed in Table 3, aggregated by benchmark subsets, as described in Table 1. We do not show VAMPIRE in the table, since without integer induction it cannot solve any of the problems.

The results show that in some cases ACL2 can perform upward and downward induction on integers, but only when using interpreted constants as a base case (that is, it cannot handle symbolic bounds). However, it can only do so if it also proves termination of the recursively defined function. It also has issues with reasoning about multiplication.

CVC4 has limited support for integer induction: it can apply upward induction but only when the base case is an interpreted constant. Since some problems seem to require induction with symbolic bounds, CVC4 is mostly able to either solve all problems in a subset, or none of them. The only exception is the subset *declared_mixed_ax-fin_conj-fin*, in which CVC4 solves one problem, which can be solved using upward induction with an interpreted constant as the base case.

VAMPIRE-I* does not have any conceptual problems with solving the benchmarks. However, since it uses axioms and inference rules rather than dedicated decision procedures for handling integers, it sometime has issues with solving problems with large integer values. For example, for the infinite interval subset of the *val* benchmark set, the only problems VAMPIRE-I* did not solve were those containing the interpreted constant 100 or -100. Similarly, in the *power* benchmark set, the unsolved problems contained large numbers. Finally, in the *declared_mixed_ax-fin_conj-fin* subset, the two problems VAMPIRE-I* did not solve also required more sophisticated arithmetic reasoning. However, inability of efficiently dealing with large numbers is not an intrinsic problem of superposition theorem provers. Reasoning with quantifiers and theories is still in its infancy and major improvements are underway. For example, there are recent parallel developments in superposition and linear arithmetic [15] that should improve this kind of reasoning in VAMPIRE.

6   Related Work

Previous works on automating induction mainly focused on inductive reasoning for inductively defined data types, for example in inductive theorem provers ACL2 [11], IsaPlanner [7], HipSpec [4], Zeno [18] and Imandra [14]; superposition theorem provers Zipperposition [5] and VAMPIRE [16]; and the SMT solver CVC4 [17]. While most of these solvers support reasoning with integers, only ACL2 and CVC4 implement some form of induction over integers.

The ACL2 approach [11] generates induction schemas based on recursive function calls in the property to be proved. Hence, it can only use induction to solve problems properties of recursively defined functions. On the other hand, the SMT-based setting of CVC4 [17] applies induction by inductive strengthening of SMT properties in combination with subgoal discovery. As noted in Section 5, CVC4 is limited to induction with concrete base cases and upward induction.

While downward integer induction can be considered a straightforward generalization of upward integer induction and does not solve many more problems in our benchmark sets, symbolic bounds provide a very powerful generalization, as witnessed by experimental results. In automated reasoning, the power provided by more general rules comes with the price of uncontrollable blowup of the search space. To harness this power we came up with defining (interval) upward/downward induction rules with symbolic bounds in the superposition calculus in such a way that they result in most cases in the addition of very simple clauses, which can be efficiently handled within the AVATAR architecture.

We believe that variants of our induction rules defined in Section 4 can also be successfully used by SMT solvers. The idea is to apply them, like we do, only when there is a suitable bound in the current candidate model. One can also combine this with the observation made in Example 1: one can resolve added induction formulas against literals already occurring in the search space to add only ground formulas.

The benchmark suite we propose and use in this paper is new and can be used to complement existing benchmarks: the TIP library [3] and the examples of [17]. Our 120 new examples are however more focused on integer properties, whereas [3,17] contain a variety of problems mostly requiring induction over inductively defined types. Specifically, out of more than 500 inductive problems in TIP [3], only 3 use integers and no inductive data types. The examples from [17] contain 311 inductive benchmarks translated into three encodings, (i) using only inductive data types, (ii) using integers instead of natural numbers, but also other inductive data types (such as lists or trees), and (iii) using both integers and natural numbers to express the same properties, alongside other inductive data types. Problems from (iii) are also included in SMT-LIB [2]. Note that there is a substantial difference between our benchmarks and benchmarks from (ii). The latter mostly require inductive reasoning only for inductive data types (or no induction at all): they contain integers but only a few of them require inductive reasoning over integers, while most of our benchmarks require proper integer induction. For example, VAMPIRE can solve 131 of 306 benchmarks in (ii) without using integer induction.

7 Conclusions

We introduced new inference rules for automating inductive reasoning with integers within saturation-based theorem proving. Many problems in program analysis and mathematical problems of integers previously unsolvable by any theorem prover can now be solved completely automatically. We believe our results can progress automated program analysis and automation of mathematics, where integers are universally used.

Acknowledgments. We thank Márton Hajdú and Giles Reger for fruitful discussions. This work was partially funded by the ERC CoG ARTIST 101002685, the ERC StG SYMCAR 639270, the EPSRC grant EP/P03408X/1 and the FWF grant LogiCS W1255-N23.

References

1. Barrett, C., Conway, C.L., Deters, M., Hadarean, L., Jovanović, D., King, T., Reynolds, A., Tinelli, C.: CVC4. In: Gopalakrishnan, G., Qadeer, S. (eds.) Proc. of CAV. LNCS, vol. 6806, pp. 171–177. Springer (2011). https://doi.org/10.1007/978-3-642-22110-1_14
2. Barrett, C., Fontaine, P., Tinelli, C.: The Satisfiability Modulo Theories Library (SMT-LIB). www.SMT-LIB.org (2016)
3. Claessen, K., Johansson, M., Rosén, D., Smallbone, N.: TIP: Tons of Inductive Problems. In: Kerber, M., Carette, J., Kaliszyk, C., Rabe, F., Sorge, V. (eds.) Proc. of CICM. LNCS, vol. 9150, pp. 333–337. Springer (2015). https://doi.org/10.1007/978-3-319-20615-8_23
4. Claessen, K., Johansson, M., Rosén, D., Smallbone, N.: Automating Inductive Proofs using Theory Exploration. In: Bonacina, M.P. (ed.) Proc. of CADE. LNCS, vol. 7898, pp. 392–406. Springer (2013). https://doi.org/10.1007/978-3-642-38574-2_27
5. Cruanes, S.: Superposition with Structural Induction. In: Dixon, C., Finger, M. (eds.) Proc. of FRoCoS. LNCS, vol. 10483, pp. 172–188. Springer (2017). https://doi.org/10.1007/978-3-319-66167-4_10
6. De Moura, L., Bjørner, N.: Z3: An Efficient SMT Solver. In: Ramakrishnan, C.R., Rehof, J. (eds.) Proc. of TACAS. LNCS, vol. 4963, pp. 337–340. Springer (2008). https://doi.org/10.1007/978-3-540-78800-3_24
7. Dixon, L., Fleuriot, J.: Higher Order Rippling in IsaPlanner. In: Slind, K., Bunker, A., Gopalakrishnan, G. (eds.) Proc. of TPHOLs. LNCS, vol. 3223, pp. 83–98. Springer (2004). https://doi.org/10.1007/978-3-540-30142-4_7
8. Fedyukovich, G., Prabhu, S., Madhukar, K., Gupta, A.: Quantified Invariants via Syntax-Guided Synthesis. In: Dillig, I., Tasiran, S. (eds.) Proc. of CAV. LNCS, vol. 11561, pp. 259–277. Springer (2019). https://doi.org/10.1007/978-3-030-25540-4_14
9. Georgiou, P., Gleiss, B., Kovács, L.: Trace Logic for Inductive Loop Reasoning. In: Ivrii, A., Strichman, O. (eds.) Proc. of FMCAD. Conference Series: FMCAD, vol. 1, pp. 255–263 (2020). https://doi.org/10.34727/2020/isbn.978-3-85448-042-6_33
10. Hajdú, M., Hozzová, P., Kovács, L., Schoisswohl, J., Voronkov, A.: Induction with Generalization in Superposition Reasoning. In: Benzmüller, C., Miller, B. (eds.) Proc. of CICM. LNCS, vol. 12236, pp. 123–137. Springer (2020). https://doi.org/10.1007/978-3-030-53518-6_8
11. Kaufmann, M., Manolios, P., Moore, J.S.: Computer-Aided Reasoning: An Approach, vol. 3. Springer (06 2000). https://doi.org/10.1007/978-1-4615-4449-4
12. Kovács, L., Robillard, S., Voronkov, A.: Coming to Terms with Quantified Reasoning. In: Castagna, G., Gordon, A.D. (eds.) Proc. of POPL. ACM SIGPLAN Notices, vol. 52, pp. 260–270. ACM (2017). https://doi.org/10.1145/3093333.3009887
13. Kovács, L., Voronkov, A.: First-Order Theorem Proving and Vampire. In: Sharygina, N., Veith, H. (eds.) Proc. of CAV. LNCS, vol. 8044, pp. 1–35. Springer (2013). https://doi.org/10.1007/978-3-642-39799-8_1
14. Passmore, G., Cruanes, S., Ignatovich, D., Aitken, D., Bray, M., Kagan, E., Kanishev, K., Maclean, E., Mometto, N.: The Imandra Automated Reasoning System. In: Peltier, N., Sofronie-Stokkermans, V. (eds.) Proc. of IJCAR. LNCS, vol. 12167, pp. 464–471. Springer (2020). https://doi.org/10.1007/978-3-030-51054-1_30

15. Reger, G., Schoisswohl, J., Voronkov, A.: Making Theory Reasoning Simpler. In: Groote, J.F., Larsen, K. (eds.) Proc. of TACAS. LNCS, vol. 12652, pp. 164–180. Springer (2021). https://doi.org/10.1007/978-3-030-72013-1_9

16. Reger, G., Voronkov, A.: Induction in Saturation-Based Proof Search. In: Fontaine, P. (ed.) Proc. of CADE. LNCS, vol. 11716, pp. 477–494. Springer (2019). https://doi.org/10.1007/978-3-030-29436-6_28

17. Reynolds, A., Kuncak, V.: Induction for SMT Solvers. In: D'Souza, D., Lal, A., Larsen, K.G. (eds.) Proc. of VMCAI. LNCS, vol. 8931, pp. 80–98. Springer (2015). https://doi.org/10.1007/978-3-662-46081-8_5

18. Sonnex, W., Drossopoulou, S., Eisenbach, S.: Zeno: An Automated Prover for Properties of Recursive Data Structures. In: Flanagan, C., König, B. (eds.) Proc. of TACAS. LNCS, vol. 7214, pp. 407–421. Springer (2012). https://doi.org/10.1007/978-3-642-28756-5_28

19. Voronkov, A.: AVATAR: The Architecture for First-Order Theorem Provers. In: Biere, A., Bloem, R. (eds.) Proc. of CAV. LNCS, vol. 8559, pp. 696–710. Springer (2014). https://doi.org/10.1007/978-3-319-08867-9_46

Open Access This chapter is licensed under the terms of the Creative Commons Attribution 4.0 International License (http://creativecommons.org/licenses/by/4.0/), which permits use, sharing, adaptation, distribution and reproduction in any medium or format, as long as you give appropriate credit to the original author(s) and the source, provide a link to the Creative Commons license and indicate if changes were made.

The images or other third party material in this chapter are included in the chapter's Creative Commons license, unless indicated otherwise in a credit line to the material. If material is not included in the chapter's Creative Commons license and your intended use is not permitted by statutory regulation or exceeds the permitted use, you will need to obtain permission directly from the copyright holder.

Superposition with First-class Booleans and Inprocessing Clausification

Visa Nummelin[1] , Alexander Bentkamp[1] ,
Sophie Tourret[2,3] , and Petar Vukmirović[1]

[1] Vrije Universiteit Amsterdam, Amsterdam, The Netherlands
visa.nummelin@vu.nl   a.bentkamp@vu.nl   p.vukmirovic@vu.nl
[2] Université de Lorraine, CNRS, Inria, LORIA, Nancy, France
sophie.tourret@inria.fr
[3] Max-Planck-Institut für Informatik, Saarland Informatics Campus, Saarbrücken,
Germany

Abstract. We present a complete superposition calculus for first-order logic with an interpreted Boolean type. Our motivation is to lay the foundation for refutationally complete calculi in more expressive logics with Booleans, such as higher-order logic, and to make superposition work efficiently on problems that would be obfuscated when using clausification as preprocessing. Working directly on formulas, our calculus avoids the costly axiomatic encoding of the theory of Booleans into first-order logic and offers various ways to interleave clausification with other derivation steps. We evaluate our calculus using the Zipperposition theorem prover, and observe that, with no tuning of parameters, our approach is on a par with the state-of-the-art approach.

1 Introduction

Superposition is a calculus for equational first-order logic that works on problems given in clausal normal form. Its immense success made preprocessing clausification a predominant mechanism in modern automatic theorem proving. However, this preprocessing is not without drawbacks. Clausification can transform simple problems, such as $s \rightarrow s$ where s is a large formula, in a way that hides its original simplicity from the superposition calculus. Ganzinger and Stuber's superposition-like calculus [13] operates on clauses that contain formulas as well as terms and replaces preprocessing clausification by inprocessing—meaning processing during the operation of the calculus itself. Inprocessing clausification allows superposition's powerful simplification engine to work on formulas. For example, unit equalities can rewrite formulas s and t in $s \leftrightarrow t$ before clausification duplicates the occurrences into $s \rightarrow t$ and $t \rightarrow s$. Whole formulas rather than simple literals can be removed by rules such as subsumption resolution [4].

Another issue with Boolean reasoning in the standard superposition calculus is that, in first-order logic, formulas cannot appear inside terms although this is often desirable for problems coming from software verifiers or proof assistants. Instead, authors of such tools need to resort to translations. Kotelnikov et al.

© The Author(s) 2021
A. Platzer and G. Sutcliffe (Eds.): CADE 2021, LNAI 12699, pp. 378–395, 2021.
https://doi.org/10.1007/978-3-030-79876-5_22

studied effects of these translations in detail. They showed that simple axioms such as the domain cardinality axiom for Booleans ($\forall(x : o). x \approx \top \vee x \approx \bot$) can severely slow down superposition provers. To support more efficient reasoning on problems with first-class Booleans, they describe the FOOL logic, which admits functions that take arguments of Boolean type and quantification over Booleans. They further describe two approaches to reason in FOOL: The first one [17] requires an additional rule in the superposition calculus, whereas the second one [16] is completely based on preprocessing.

Our calculus combines complementary advantages of Ganzinger and Stuber's and of Kotelnikov et al.'s work. Following Kotelnikov et al., our logic (Sect. 2) is similar to FOOL and supports nesting formulas inside terms, as well as quantifying over Booleans. Following Ganzinger and Stuber, our calculus (Sect. 3) reasons with formulas and supports inprocessing clausification.

Our calculus also extends the two approaches. To reduce the number of possible inferences, we generalize Ganzinger and Stuber's Boolean selection functions, which allow us to restrict the Boolean subterms in a clause on which inferences can be performed. The term order requirements of our calculus are less restrictive than Ganzinger and Stuber's. In addition to the lexicographic path order (LPO), we also support the Knuth-Bendix order (KBO) [15], which is known to work better with superposition in practice.

Our proof of refutational completeness (Sect. 4) lays the foundation for complete calculi in more complex logics with Booleans. Indeed, Bentkamp et al. [8] devised a refutationally complete calculus for higher-order logic based on our completeness theorem. Our theorem incorporates a powerful redundancy criterion that allows for a variety of inprocessing clausification methods (Sect. 5).

We implemented our approach in the Zipperposition theorem prover (Sect. 6) and evaluated it on thousands of problems that target our logic ranging from TPTP to SMT-LIB to Sledgehammer-generated benchmarks (Sect. 7). Without fine-tuning, our new calculus performs as well as known techniques. Exploring the strategic choices that our calculus opens should lead to further performance improvements. In addition, we corroborate the claims of Ganzinger and Stuber concerning applicability of formula-based superposition reasoning: We find a set of 17 TPTP problems (out of 1000 randomly selected) that Zipperposition can solve only using the techniques described in this paper. We refer to our technical report [25] for more details on our calculus and the complete completeness proof.

2   Logic

Our logic is a first-order logic with an interpreted Boolean type. It is essentially identical to the UF logic of SMT-LIB [5], including the Core theory, but without if-then-else and let expressions, which can be supported through simple translations. It also closely resembles Kotelnikov et al.'s FOOL [17], which additionally supports if-then-else and let expressions.

Our logic requires an interpreted Boolean type o and allows for an arbitrary number of uninterpreted types. The set of symbols must contain the logical symbols $\top, \bot : o$; $\neg : o \to o$; $\wedge, \vee, \to : (o \times o) \to o$; and the overloaded symbols $\approx, \not\approx : (\tau \times \tau) \to o$ for each type τ. The logical symbols are printed in bold to distinguish them from the notation used for clauses below. Throughout the paper, we write tuples $(a_1, \ldots, a_n)$ as $\bar{a}_n$ or $\bar{a}$.

The set of *terms* is defined inductively as follows. Every variable is a term. If $\mathsf{f} : \bar{\tau}_n \to \upsilon$ is a symbol and $\bar{t}_n : \bar{\tau}_n$ is a tuple of terms, then the application $\mathsf{f}(\bar{t}_n)$ (or simply f if $n = 0$) is a term of type υ. If x is a variable and $t : o$ a Boolean term, then the quantified terms $\forall x.\, t$ and $\exists x.\, t$ are terms of Boolean type. We view quantified terms modulo α-renaming. A *formula* is a term of Boolean type.

The *root* of a term is f if the term is an application $\mathsf{f}(\bar{t}_n)$; it is x if the term is a variable x; and it is $\forall$ or $\exists$ if the term is a quantified term $\forall x.\, t$ or $\exists x.\, t$. A variable occurrence is *free* in a term if it is not bound by $\forall$ or $\exists$. A term is *ground* if it contains no free variables. Substitutions are defined as usual in first-order logic and they rename quantified variables to avoid capture.

A literal $s \dot{\approx} t$ is an equation $s \approx t$ or a disequation $s \not\approx t$. Unlike terms constructed using the function symbols $\approx$ and $\not\approx$, literals are unoriented. A clause $L_1 \vee \cdots \vee L_n$ is a finite multiset of literals L_j. The empty clause is written as $\bot$. Terms t of Boolean type are not literals. They must be encoded as $t \approx \top$ and $t \approx \bot$, which we call *predicate literals*. Both are considered positive literals because they are equations, not disequations.

We have considered excluding negative literals $s \not\approx t$ by encoding them as $(s \approx t) \approx \bot$, following Ganzinger and Stuber. However, this approach requires an additional term order condition to make the conclusion of equality factoring small enough, excluding KBO. To support both KBO and LPO, we allow negative literals. Regardless, our simplification mechanism will allow us to simplify negative literals of the form $t \not\approx \bot$ and $t \not\approx \top$ into $t \approx \top$ and $t \approx \bot$, respectively, thereby eliminating redundant representations of predicate literals.

The semantics is a straightforward extension of standard first-order logic only adding the interpretation of the Boolean type as a two element domain, as in Kotelnikov et al.'s FOOL logic. Some of our calculus rules introduce Skolem symbols, which are intended to be interpreted as witnesses for existentially quantified terms. Still, our semantics treats them as uninterpreted symbols. To achieve a satisfiability-preserving calculus, we assume that these symbols do not occur in the input problem. More precisely, we inductively extend the signature of the input problem by a symbol $\mathsf{sk}_{\forall \bar{y}. \exists z. t} : \bar{\tau} \to \upsilon$ for each term of the form $\exists z.\, t$ over the extended signature, where υ is the type of z and $\bar{y} : \bar{\tau}$ are the free variables occurring in $\exists z.\, t$, in order of first appearance.

3   The Calculus

Following standard superposition, our calculus employs a term order and a literal selection function to restrict the search space. To accommodate for quantified Boolean terms, we impose additional requirements on the term order. To support flexible reasoning with Boolean subterms, in addition to the literal selection function, we introduce a Boolean subterm selection function.

Term Order The calculus is parameterized by a strict well-founded order $\succ$ on ground terms that fulfills: (O1) $u \succ \bot \succ \top$ for any term u that is not $\top$ or $\bot$; (O2) $\forall x.\, t \succ \{x \mapsto u\}t$ and $\exists x.\, t \succ \{x \mapsto u\}t$ for any term u whose only Boolean subterms are $\top$ and $\bot$; (O3) subterm property; (O4) compatibility with contexts (not necessarily below $\forall$ and $\exists$); (O5) totality. The order is extended to literals, clauses, and nonground terms as usual [2]. The nonground order then also enjoys (O6) stability under grounding substitutions.

Ganzinger and Stuber's term order restrictions are similar but incompatible with KBO. Using an encoding of our terms into untyped first-order logic we describe how both LPO and the transfinite variant of KBO [19] can satisfy conditions (O1)–(O6).

Our encoding represents bound variables by De Bruijn indices, which become new constant symbols db_n for $n \in \mathbb{N}$. Quantifiers are represented by two new unary function symbols, also denoted by $\forall$ and $\exists$. All other symbols are simply identified with their untyped counterpart. Regardless of symbol precedence or symbol weights, KBO and LPO enjoy properties (O3)–(O6) when applied to the encoded terms. They are even compatible with contexts below quantifiers.

To satisfy (O1) and (O2), let the precedence for LPO be $\top < \bot < f < \forall < \exists < db_0 < db_1 < \cdots$ where f is any other symbol. For KBO, we can use the same symbol precedence and a symbol weight function $\mathcal{W}$ that assigns each symbol ordinal weights (of the form $\omega a + b$ with $a, b \in \mathbb{N}$), where $\mathcal{W}(\top) = \mathcal{W}(\bot) = 1$, $\mathcal{W}(\forall) = \mathcal{W}(\exists) = \omega$, and $\mathcal{W}(f) \in \mathbb{N} \setminus \{0\}$ for any other symbol f.

Selection and Eligibility Following an idea of Ganzinger and Stuber, we parameterize our calculus with two selection functions: one selecting literals and one selecting Boolean subterms.

Definition 1 (Selection functions). The calculus is parameterized by a literal selection function *FLSel* and a Boolean subterm selection function *FBSel*. The function *FLSel* maps each clause to a subset of its literals. The selection function *FBSel* maps each clause to a subset of its Boolean subterms. The literals *FLSel(C)* and the subterms *FBSel(C)* are *selected* in C. The following restrictions apply: (S1) A literal can only be selected if it is negative or of the form $s \approx \bot$. (S2) A Boolean subterm can only be selected if it is not $\top$, $\bot$, or a variable. (S3) A Boolean subterm can only be selected if its occurrence is not below a quantifier. (S4) The topmost terms on either side of a positive literal cannot be selected.

The interplay of maximality w.r.t. term order, literal and Boolean selection functions gives rise to a new notion of eligibility:

Definition 2 (Eligibility). A literal L is (*strictly*) *eligible* w.r.t. a substitution σ in C if it is selected in C or there are no selected literals and no selected Boolean subterms in C and σL is (strictly) maximal in σC. The eligible subterms of a clause C w.r.t. a substitution σ are inductively defined as follows: (E1) Any selected subterm is eligible. (E2) If a literal $s \approx t$ with $\sigma s \not\preceq \sigma t$ is either eligible and negative or strictly eligible and positive, then s is eligible. (E3) If a subterm is eligible and its root is not $\approx$, $\not\approx$, $\forall$, or $\exists$, all of its direct subterms are also eligible. (E4) If a subterm is eligible and of the form $s \approx t$ or $s \not\approx t$, then s is eligible if $\sigma s \not\preceq \sigma t$ and t is eligible if $\sigma s \not\succeq \sigma t$. The substitution σ is left implicit if it is the identity substitution.

The Core Inference Rules The following inference rules form our calculus:

$$\frac{\overbrace{D' \vee t \approx t'}^{D} \quad C[u]}{\sigma(D' \vee C[t'])} \text{SUP} \qquad \frac{\overbrace{C' \vee u' \approx v' \vee u \approx v}^{C}}{\sigma(C' \vee v \not\approx v' \vee u \approx v')} \text{FACTOR}$$

$$\frac{\overbrace{C' \vee u \not\approx u'}^{C}}{\sigma C'} \text{IRREFL} \qquad \frac{\overbrace{C' \vee s \approx t}^{C}}{\sigma C'} \bot\text{ELIM} \qquad \frac{C[u]}{\sigma C[t']} \text{BOOLRW}$$

$$\frac{C[\forall z.\, v]}{C[\{z \mapsto \mathsf{sk}_{\forall \bar{y}.\, \exists z. \neg v}(\bar{y})\}v]} \forall\text{RW} \qquad \frac{C[\exists z.\, v]}{C[\{z \mapsto \mathsf{sk}_{\forall \bar{y}.\, \exists z. v}(\bar{y})\}v]} \exists\text{RW}$$

$$\frac{C[u]}{C[\bot] \vee u \approx \mathsf{T}} \text{BOOLHOIST} \qquad \frac{C[s \approx t]}{C[\bot] \vee s \approx t} \approx\text{HOIST} \qquad \frac{C[s \not\approx t]}{C[\mathsf{T}] \vee s \approx t} \not\approx\text{HOIST}$$

$$\frac{C[\forall x.\, t]}{C[\bot] \vee \{x \mapsto y\}t \approx \mathsf{T}} \forall\text{HOIST} \qquad \frac{C[\exists x.\, t]}{C[\mathsf{T}] \vee \{x \mapsto y\}t \approx \bot} \exists\text{HOIST}$$

The rules are subject to the following side conditions:

SUP (1) $\sigma = \mathrm{mgu}(t, u)$; (2) u is not a variable; (3) $\sigma t \not\preceq \sigma t'$; (4) $D \prec C[u]$; (5) u is eligible in C w.r.t. σ; (6) $t \approx t'$ is strictly eligible in D w.r.t. σ; (7) the root of t is not a logical symbol; (8) if $\sigma t' = \bot$, the subterm u is at the top level of a positive literal.

FACTOR (1) $\sigma = \mathrm{mgu}(u, u')$; (2) $\sigma u \not\approx t \notin \sigma C$ for any term t; (3) no Boolean subterm and no literal is selected in C; (4) σu is a maximal term in σC; (5) σv is maximal in $\{t \mid \sigma u \approx t \in \sigma C\}$.

IRREFL (1) $\sigma = \mathrm{mgu}(u, u')$; (2) $u \not\approx u'$ is eligible in C w.r.t. σ.

$\bot$ELIM (1) $\sigma = \mathrm{mgu}(s \approx t, \bot \approx \mathsf{T})$; (2) $s \approx t$ is strictly eligible in C w.r.t. σ.

BOOLRW (1) (t, t') is one of the following pairs, where x is a fresh variable: $(\neg\bot, \mathsf{T})$, $(\neg\mathsf{T}, \bot)$, $(\bot \wedge \bot, \bot)$, $(\mathsf{T} \wedge \bot, \bot)$, $(\bot \wedge \mathsf{T}, \bot)$, $(\mathsf{T} \wedge \mathsf{T}, \mathsf{T})$, $(\bot \vee \bot, \bot)$, $(\mathsf{T} \vee \bot, \mathsf{T})$, $(\bot \vee \mathsf{T}, \mathsf{T})$, $(\mathsf{T} \vee \mathsf{T}, \mathsf{T})$, $(\bot \rightarrow \bot, \mathsf{T})$, $(\mathsf{T} \rightarrow \bot, \bot)$, $(\bot \rightarrow \mathsf{T}, \mathsf{T})$, $(\mathsf{T} \rightarrow \mathsf{T}, \mathsf{T})$, $(x \approx x, \mathsf{T})$, $(x \not\approx x, \bot)$; (2) $\sigma = \mathrm{mgu}(t, u)$; (3) u is not a variable; (4) u is eligible in C w.r.t. σ.

$\star$RW (where $\star \in \{\forall, \exists\}$) (1) v is a term that may refer to z; (2) $\bar{y}$ are the free variables occurring in $\forall z.\, v$ and $\exists z.\, v$, respectively, in order of first appearance; (3) the indicated subterm is eligible in C; (4) for $\forall$RW, $C[\mathsf{T}]$ is not a tautology; (5) for $\exists$RW, $C[\bot]$ is not a tautology. (In an implementation, the tautology check can be approximated by checking if the affected literal is of the form $\forall z.\, v \approx \mathsf{T}$ or $\exists z.\, v \approx \bot$.)

BOOLHOIST (1) u is a Boolean term whose root is an uninterpreted predicate; (2) u is eligible in C; (3) u is not a variable; (4) u is not at the top level of a positive literal.

$\star$HOIST (where $\star \in \{\approx, \not\approx, \forall, \exists\}$) (1) the indicated subterm is eligible in C; (2) y is a fresh variable.

Rationale for the Rules Our calculus is a graceful generalization of superposition: if the input clauses do not contain any Boolean terms, it coincides with standard superposition. In addition to the standard superposition rules SUP, FACTOR, and IRREFL, our calculus contains various rules to deal with Booleans. For each logical symbol and quantifier, we must consider the case where it is true and the case where it is false. Whenever possible, we prefer rules that rewrite the Boolean subterm in place (with names ending in Rw). When this cannot be done in a satisfiability-preserving way, we resort to rules hoisting the Boolean subterm into a dedicated literal (with names ending in HOIST). For terms rooted by an uninterpreted predicate, the rule BOOLHOIST only deals with the case that the term is false. If it is true, we rely on SUP to rewrite it to $\top$ eventually.

Example 3. The clause $a \land \neg a \approx \top$ can be refuted by the core inferences as follows. First we derive $a \approx \top$ (displayed on the left) and then we use it to derive $\bot$ (displayed on the right). In this and the following example, we assume eager selection of literals whenever the selection restrictions allow it.

$$\frac{\dfrac{\dfrac{\dfrac{\dfrac{\dfrac{\dfrac{\dfrac{a \land \neg a \approx \top}{\bot \land \neg a \approx \top \lor a \approx \top}\text{BOOLHOIST}}{\bot \land \neg \bot \approx \top \lor a \approx \top \lor a \approx \top}\text{BOOLHOIST}}{\bot \land \top \approx \top \lor a \approx \top \lor a \approx \top}\text{BOOLRW}}{\bot \approx \top \lor a \approx \top \lor a \approx \top}\text{BOOLRW}}{a \approx \top \lor a \approx \top}\bot\text{ELIM}}{\top \not\approx \top \lor a \approx \top}\text{FACTOR}}{a \approx \top}\text{IRREFL}}$$

$$\frac{\dfrac{\dfrac{\dfrac{\dfrac{\dfrac{a \land \neg a \approx \top \quad a \approx \top}{\top \land \neg a \approx \top}\text{SUP}}{\top \land \neg \top \approx \top}\text{SUP}}{\top \land \bot \approx \top}\text{BOOLRW}}{\bot \approx \top}\text{BOOLRW}}{\bot}\bot\text{ELIM}}$$

The derivation illustrates how BOOLHOIST and SUP replace uninterpreted predicates by $\top$ and $\bot$ to allow BOOLRW to eliminate the surrounding logical symbols.

Example 4. The clause $(\exists x. \forall y. y \not\approx x) \approx \top$ can be refuted as follows:

$$\frac{\dfrac{\dfrac{\dfrac{\dfrac{(\exists x. \forall y. y \not\approx x) \approx \top}{(\forall y. y \not\approx \mathsf{sk}_{\exists x. \forall y. y \not\approx x}) \approx \top}\exists\text{Rw}}{\bot \approx \top \lor (y' \not\approx \mathsf{sk}_{\exists x. \forall y. y \not\approx x}) \approx \top}\forall\text{HOIST}}{(y' \not\approx \mathsf{sk}_{\exists x. \forall y. y \not\approx x}) \approx \top}\bot\text{ELIM}}{\bot \approx \top}\not\approx\text{Rw}}{\bot}\bot\text{ELIM}$$

Redundancy Criterion In standard superposition, a clause is defined as redundant if all of its ground instances follow from smaller ground instances of other clauses. We keep this definition, but use a nonstandard notion of ground instances, inspired by constraint superposition [23]. In our completeness proof, this new notion of ground instances ensures that ground instances of the conclusion of $\forall$Rw, $\exists$Rw, $\forall$Hoist, and $\exists$Hoist inferences are smaller than the corresponding instances of their premise by property (O2).

Definition 5 (Redundancy of clauses). The *ground instances* of a clause C are all ground clauses of the form γC where γ is a substitution such that for all variables x, the only Boolean subterms of γx are $\bot$ and $\top$. A ground clause C is *redundant* w.r.t. a ground clause set N if there exist clauses $C_1, \ldots, C_k \in N$ such that $C_1, \ldots, C_k \models C$ and $C \succ C_i$ for all $1 \leq i \leq k$. A nonground clause C is redundant w.r.t. clauses N if C is strictly subsumed by a clause in N or every ground instance of C is redundant w.r.t. ground instances of N.

In standard superposition, an inference is defined as redundant if all its ground instances are, and a ground inference is defined as redundant if its conclusion follows from other clauses smaller than the main premise. We keep this definition as well, but we use a nonstandard notion of ground instances for some of the Boolean rules. In our report, we define a slightly stronger variant of inference redundancy via an explicit ground calculus, but the following notion is also strong enough to justify the few prover optimizations based on inference redundancy we know from the literature (e.g., simultaneous superposition [7]).

Definition 6 (Redundancy of inferences). A *ground instance* of a $\forall$Rw, $\exists$Rw, $\forall$Hoist, or $\exists$Hoist inference is an inference obtained by applying a grounding substitution to premise and conclusion, regardless of whether the result is a valid $\forall$Rw, $\exists$Rw, $\forall$Hoist, or $\exists$Hoist inference. A *ground instance* of an inference ι of other rules is an inference ι' of the same rule such that premises and conclusion of ι' are ground instances of the respective premises and conclusion of ι. For ι', we use selection functions that select the ground literals and Boolean subterms corresponding to the ones selected in the nonground premises. A ground inference with main premise C, side premises $C_1, \ldots, C_n$, and conclusion D is *redundant* w.r.t. N if there exist clauses $D_1, \ldots, D_k \prec C$ in N such that $D_1, \ldots, D_k, C_1, \ldots, C_n \models D$. A nonground inference is redundant if all its ground instances are redundant.

A clause set N is *saturated* if every inference from N is redundant w.r.t. N.

Simplification Rules The redundancy criterion is a graceful generalization of the criterion of standard superposition. Thus, the standard simplification and deletion rules, such as deletion of trivial literals and clauses, subsumption, and demodulation, can be justified. Demodulation below quantifiers is justified if the term order is compatible with contexts below quantifiers.

Some calculus rules can act as simplifications. $\bot$Elim can always be a simplification. Given a clause on which both $\star$Rw and $\star$Hoist apply, where $\star \in \{\forall, \exists\}$, the clause can be replaced by the conclusions of these rules. If $\star$Rw does not apply because of condition 4 or 5, $\star$HOIST alone can be a simplification. Also justified by redundancy, the rules BOOLHOIST and $\star$HOIST can simultaneously replace all occurrences of the eligible subterm they act on. For example, applying $\approx$HOIST to $\mathsf{p}(x \approx y) \approx \mathsf{T} \vee \mathsf{q}(x \approx y) \approx \bot$ yields $\mathsf{p}(\bot) \approx \mathsf{T} \vee \mathsf{q}(\bot) \approx \bot \vee x \approx y$.

While experimenting with our implementation, we have observed that the following simplification rule from Vampire [18] can substantially shorten proofs:

$$\frac{s \not\approx t \vee C[s]}{s \not\approx t \vee C[t]} \text{LOCALRW}$$

In this rule, we require $s \succ t$.

Interpreting literals of the form $s \approx \mathsf{T}$ as $s \not\approx \bot$ and $s \approx \bot$ as $s \not\approx \mathsf{T}$ we can apply the rule even to these positive literals. This especially convenient with rules such as BOOLHOIST. Consider the clause $C = \mathsf{p}^i(\bot) \approx \bot \vee \mathsf{q} \approx \bot$, assume no literal is selected and the Boolean selection function always selects a subterm $\mathsf{p}(\bot)$. Applying BOOLHOIST to C we get $\mathsf{p}(\bot) \approx \mathsf{T} \vee \mathsf{p}^{i-1}(\bot) \approx \bot \vee \mathsf{q} \approx \bot$. This can then be simplified to a tautological clause $\mathsf{p}(\bot) \approx \mathsf{T} \vee \mathsf{p}(\bot) \approx \bot \vee \mathsf{q} \approx \bot$ using $i - 2$ LOCALRW steps. If we did not use LOCALRW, BOOLHOIST would produce $i - 2$ intermediary clauses starting from C, none of which would be recognized as a tautology.

Many rules of our calculus replace subterms with T or $\bot$. After this replacement, resulting terms can be simplified using Boolean equivalences that specify the behavior of logical operations on T and $\bot$. To this end, we use the rule BOOLSIMP [33], similar to simp of Leo-III [27, Sect. 4.2.1]:

$$\frac{C[s]}{C[t]} \text{BOOLSIMP}$$

This rule replaces s with t whenever $s \approx t$ is contained in a predefined set of tautological equations. In addition to all equations that Leo-III uses for simp, we also include more complex ones, such as $(\neg u \to u) \approx u$ and $(u_1 \to \cdots \to u_n \to v_1 \vee \cdots \vee v_m) \approx \mathsf{T}$ where $u_i = v_j$ for some i and j. The exhaustive list is given in our technical report. Using BOOLSIMP and $\bot$ELIM, the twelve steps of Example 3 can be replaced by just two simplification steps.

BOOLSIMP simplifies terms with logical symbol roots if one argument is either T or $\bot$ or if two arguments are identical. Thus, after simplification, BOOLRW applies only in two remaining cases: if all arguments of a logical symbol are distinct variables and if the sides of a (dis)equation are different and unifiable. This observation can be used to streamline the implementation of BOOLRW.

4   Refutational Completeness

Our calculus is dynamically refutationally complete. All the rules that do not introduce Skolem symbols are also sound.

Completeness Theorem 7. *Let S_0 be an unsatisfiable set of clauses. Let $(S_i)_{i=0}^{\infty}$ be a fair derivation—i.e., a derivation where $\bigcup_{i=0}^{\infty} \bigcap_{j=i}^{\infty} S_j$ is saturated. Then $\bot \in S_i$ for some i.*

We outline some key parts of the proof here and refer to our technical report [25] for the details. We first define a ground version of our calculus with standardly inherited redundancy criterion and prove it complete. Devising suitable ground analogues of the rules ∀Rw and ∃Rw was difficult because the arguments of the Skolems depend on the variables occurring in the premise. Therefore, we parameterize the ground calculus by a function that provides ground Skolem terms in the ground versions of these rules. When lifting the completeness result to the nonground level, we instantiate the parameter with a specific function that allows us to lift the ∀Rw and ∃Rw inferences.

To prove the ground calculus complete, we employ the framework for reduction of counterexamples [3]. It requires us to construct an interpretation $\mathcal{I}$ given a saturated unsatisfiable clause set that does not contain $\bot$. Then we must show that any counterexample—i.e., a clause that does not hold in $\mathcal{I}$—can be reduced to a smaller ($\prec$) counterexample by some inference.

The interpretation $\mathcal{I}$ is defined by a normalizing rewrite system as in the standard completeness proof of superposition. To ensure a correct interpretation of Booleans, we incrementally add Boolean rewrite rules along with the rules produced by clauses as usual. If a counterexample can be rewritten by a Boolean rule, we reduce it by a ⋆Rw or ⋆Hoist inference. If it can be rewritten by a rule produced by a clause, we reduce it by a Sup inference.

We derive the dynamic completeness of our nonground calculus using the saturation framework [35]. It gives us a nonground clause set N to work with. We then have to choose the parameters of our ground calculus such that all of its inferences from the grounding of N are redundant or liftable. We show that inferences rewriting below variables are redundant. Other inferences we show to be liftable—i.e., they are a ground instance of some inference from N.

5   Inprocessing Clausification Methods

Our calculus makes preprocessing clausification unnecessary: A problem specified by a formula f can be represented as a clause $f \approx \top$. Our redundancy criterion allows us to add various sets of rules to steer the inprocessing clausification.

Without any additional rules, our core calculus rules perform all the necessary reasoning about formulas. We call this method *inner delayed clausification* because the calculus rules tend to operate on the inner Boolean subterms first.

The *outer delayed clausification* method adds the following rules to the calculus, which are guided by the outermost logical symbols. Let s and t be Boolean terms. Below, we let s^+ range over literals of the form $s \approx \top$ and $s \not\approx \bot$, and s^- over literals of the form $s \approx \bot$ and $s \not\approx \top$.

$$\frac{s^+ \vee C}{oc(s, C)} +\textsc{OuterClaus} \qquad \frac{s^- \vee C}{oc(\neg s, C)} -\textsc{OuterClaus}$$

$$\frac{s \approx t \vee C}{s \approx \bot \vee t \approx \mathsf{T} \vee C \quad s \approx \mathsf{T} \vee t \approx \bot \vee C} \approx \textsc{OuterClaus}$$

$$\frac{s \not\approx t \vee C}{s \approx \bot \vee t \approx \bot \vee C \quad s \approx \mathsf{T} \vee t \approx \mathsf{T} \vee C} \not\approx \textsc{OuterClaus}$$

The rules $+\textsc{OuterClaus}$ and $-\textsc{OuterClaus}$ are applicable to any term s whose root is a logical symbol, whereas the rules $\approx\textsc{OuterClaus}$ and $\not\approx\textsc{OuterClaus}$ are only applicable if neither s nor t is T or $\bot$. Clearly, our redundancy criterion allows us to replace the premise of all $\textsc{Outer}$-$\textsc{Claus}$-rules with their conclusions. Nonetheless, the rules $\approx\textsc{OuterClaus}$ and $\not\approx\textsc{OuterClaus}$ are not used as simplification rules since destructing equivalences disturbs the syntactic structure of the formulas, as noted by Ganzinger and Stuber [13]. The function $oc(s, C)$ analyzes the shape of the formula s and distributes it over the clause C. For example, $oc(s_1 \rightarrow s_2, C) = \{s_1 \approx \bot \vee s_2 \approx \mathsf{T} \vee C\}$, and $oc(\neg(s_1 \vee s_2), C) = \{s_1 \approx \bot \vee C, s_2 \approx \bot \vee C\}$. This function also replaces quantified terms by either a fresh free variable or a Skolem in the body of the quantified term, depending on the polarity. The full definition of $oc(s, C)$ is specified in our technical report.

A third inprocessing clausification method is *immediate clausification*. It first preprocesses the input problem using a standard first-order clausification procedure such as Nonnengart and Weidenbach's [24]. Then, during the proof search, when a clause C appears on which $\textsc{OuterClaus}$ rules could be applied, we apply the standard clausification procedure on the formula $\forall \bar{x}. C$ instead (where $\bar{x}$ are the free variables of C), and replace C with the clausification results. With this method, the formulas are clausified in one step, making intermediate clausification results inaccessible to the simplification machinery.

Renaming Common Formulas Following Tseitin [31], clausification procedures usually rename common formulas to prevent a possible combinatorial explosion caused by naive clausification. In our two delayed clausification methods, we realize this idea using the following rule:

$$\frac{C_1[\sigma_1 f] \quad \cdots \quad C_n[\sigma_n f]}{C_1[\sigma_1 \mathsf{p}(\bar{x})] \quad \cdots \quad C_n[\sigma_n \mathsf{p}(\bar{x})] \quad R_1 \quad \cdots \quad R_m} \textsc{Rename}$$

Here, the formula f has a logical root, $\bar{x}$ are the distinct free variables in f, p is a fresh symbol, σ_i is a substitution, and the clauses $R_1, \ldots, R_m$ are the result of simplifying a *definition clause* $R = \mathsf{p}(\bar{x}) \approx f$ as described below. The rule avoids exponential explosion by replacing n positions in which results of f's clausification will appear into a single position in R. Optimizations such as polarity-aware renaming [24, Sect. 4] also apply to $\textsc{Rename}$.

Several issues arise with RENAME as an inprocessing rule. We need to ensure that in R, $f \succ \mathsf{p}(\bar{x})$, since otherwise demodulation might reintroduce a formula f in the simplified clauses. This can be achieved by giving the fresh symbol p a precedence smaller than that of all symbols initially present in the problem (other than T and $\perp$). To ensure the precedence is well founded, the precedence of p must be greater than that of symbols previously introduced by the calculus. For KBO, we additionally set the weight of p to the minimal possible weight.

For RENAME to be used as a simplification rule, we need to ensure that the conclusions are smaller than the premises. This is trivially true for all clauses other than the clause R. For example, let $C_i = f \approx \mathsf{T}$ (σ_i is the identity). Clearly, R is larger than C_i. However, we can view the definition clause R as two clauses $R^+ = \mathsf{p}(\bar{x}) \approx \perp \vee f \approx \mathsf{T}$ and $R^- = \mathsf{p}(\bar{x}) \approx \mathsf{T} \vee f \approx \perp$. Then, we can apply a single step of the OUTERCLAUS rules to R^+ and R^- (on their subformula f), which further results in clauses $R_1, \ldots, R_m$. Inspecting the OUTERCLAUS rules, it is clear that $m \leq 4$, which makes enforcing this simplification tolerable. Furthermore, as f is simplified in each of $R_1, \ldots, R_m$, they are smaller than any premise C_i.

Another potential source of a combinatorial explosion in our calculus are formulas that occur deep in the arguments of uninterpreted predicates. Consider the clause $C = \mathsf{p}^i(x) \approx \mathsf{T} \vee \mathsf{q}^j(y) \approx \mathsf{T}$ where $i, j > 2$. If the first and the second literal are eligible in C, any clause $\mathsf{p}^{i_1}(x) \approx \mathsf{T} \vee \mathsf{p}^{i_2}(\perp) \approx \mathsf{T} \vee \cdots \vee \mathsf{p}^{i_k}(\perp) \approx \mathsf{T} \vee \mathsf{q}^{j_1}(y) \approx \mathsf{T} \vee \mathsf{q}^{j_2}(\perp) \approx \mathsf{T} \vee \cdots \vee \mathsf{q}^{j_l}(\perp) \approx \mathsf{T}$ (where $i_1 + \cdots + i_k = i$ and $j_1 + \cdots + j_l = j$) , resulting from multiple BOOLHOIST applications, can be obtained in many different ways. This explosion can be avoided using the following rule:

$$\frac{s \approx t \vee C}{\mathsf{p}(\bar{x}) \approx \mathsf{T} \vee C \quad R_1 \quad \cdots \quad R_4} \text{ RENAMEDEEP}$$

where p is a fresh symbol, $\bar{x}$ are all free variables occurring in $s \approx t$, the clauses $R_1, \ldots, R_4$ result from simplifying $R = \mathsf{p}(\bar{x}) \approx (s \approx t)$ as described above, and we impose the same precedence and weight restrictions on p as for RENAME. Finally, we require that both $s \approx t$ and C contain deep Booleans where a Boolean subterm $u|_p$ of a term u is a *deep Boolean* if there are at least two distinct proper prefixes q of the position p such that the root of $u|_q$ is an uninterpreted predicate.

Similarly to RENAME, the definition clause R can be larger than the premise. As OUTERCLAUS-rules might not apply to $s \approx t$, we need a different solution:

$$\frac{C[u]}{C[\perp] \vee u \approx \mathsf{T} \quad C[\mathsf{T}] \vee u \approx \perp} \text{ BOOLHOISTSIMP}$$

In this rule u is a non-variable Boolean subterm, different from T and $\perp$, whose indicated occurrence is not in a literal $u \approx b$ where b is T, $\perp$ or a variable. Clearly, both conclusions of BOOLHOISTSIMP are smaller than the premise. As before, observing that R is equivalent to two clauses $R^+ = \mathsf{p}(\bar{x}) \approx \perp \vee s \approx t$ and $R^- = \mathsf{p}(\bar{x}) \approx \mathsf{T} \vee s \not\approx t$, we simplify R^+ and R^- into clauses that are guaranteed to be smaller than the premise. This is achieved by applying BOOLHOISTSIMP to one of the deep Boolean occurrences in both R^+ and R^-, which produces $R_1, \ldots, R_4$ and reduces the size of resulting clauses enough for them to be smaller than the premise of RENAMEDEEP. The RENAMEDEEP rule can be applied analogously to negative literals $s \not\approx t$.

6 Implementation

Zipperposition [11] is an automatic theorem prover designed for easy prototyping of various extensions of superposition. So far, it has been extended to support induction, arithmetic, and various fragments of higher-order logic. We have implemented our calculus and its extensions described above in Zipperposition.

Zipperposition has long supported λ as the only binder. Because introducing new binders would significantly complicate the implementation, we decided to represent the terms $\forall x. t$ and $\exists x. t$ as $\forall(\lambda x. t)$ and $\exists(\lambda x. t)$, respectively.

We introduced a normalized presentation of predicate literals as either $s \approx \top$ or $s \approx \bot$. As Zipperposition previously encoded them as $s \approx \top$ or $s \not\approx \top$, enforcing the new encoding was a source of tedious implementation effort.

FACTOR inferences happen even when the maximal literal is selected since the discovery of condition (3) as described in Sect. 3 came after the evaluation.

Zipperposition's existing selection functions were not designed with Boolean subterm selection in mind. For instance, a function that selects a literal L with a selectable Boolean subterm s can make s eligible, even if the Boolean selection function did not select s. To mitigate this issue, we can optionally block selection of literals that contain selectable Boolean subterms.

We implemented four Boolean selection functions: selecting the leftmost innermost, leftmost outermost, syntactically largest or syntactically smallest selectable subterm. Ties are broken by selecting the leftmost term. Additionally, we implemented a Boolean selection function that does not select any subterm.

Vukmirović and Nummelin [33, Sect. 3.4] explored inprocessing clausification as part of their pragmatic approach to higher-order Boolean reasoning. They describe in detail how the formula renaming mechanism is implemented. We reuse their mechanism, and simplify definition clauses as described in Sect. 5.

7 Evaluation

The goal of our evaluation was to answer the following questions:

1. How does our approach compare to preprocessing?
2. How do the different inprocessing clausification methods compare?
3. Is there an overhead of our calculus on problems without first-class Booleans?
4. What effect do Boolean selection, LOCALRW, and BOOLHOISTSIMP have?

We filtered TPTP [29] and SMT-LIB [5] to get first-order benchmarks that actually do use the Boolean type. In TPTP THF we found 145 such problems (*TPTP Bool*) and in the UF section of SMT-LIB 5507 such problems. Martin

Desharnais and Jasmin Blanchette generated 1253 Sledgehammer problems that target our logic. To measure the overhead of our calculus, we randomly chose 1000 FOF and CNF problems from the TPTP (*TPTP FO*). Even with this sample the experiment could take up to $(145+5507+1253+1000) \times \#\text{modes} \times 300\,\text{s} \approx 9$ CPU months. On StarExec servers, evaluation roughly took three days under low load. Otherwise evaluating on all 13 000 FOF and CNF problems could have taken 2.5 times longer.

SMT-LIB interprets the symbol ite as the standard if-then-else function [5, Sect. 3.7.1]. Whenever a term $s = \text{ite}(t_1, t_2, t_3)$ of type τ occurs in a problem, we replace s with $f_\tau(t_1, t_2, t_3)$, where f_τ is a fresh symbol denoting the ite function of a particular return type. To comply with SMT-LIB, we add the following axioms: $\forall x\, y.\, f_\tau(\top, x, y) \approx x$ and $\forall x\, y.\, f_\tau(\bot, x, y) \approx y$. SMT-LIB allows the use of let variable bindings [5, Sect. 3.6.1]. We simply replace each variable with its definition in the body of the let bindings.

Currently, among competing superposition-based provers only E and Vampire support first-order logic with interpreted Booleans, and they do so through preprocessing. We could not evaluate Vampire in the first-order mode with FOOL preprocessing because it yielded unsound results on TPTP Bool benchmarks. We were able to run E on all benchmarks, except for the ones in SMT syntax.

We used Zipperposition's first-order portfolio, which invokes the prover sequentially with up to 13 configurations in different time slices. To compare different features, we ran different *modes* that enable a given feature in all of the portfolio configurations. All experiments were performed on the StarExec Iowa servers [28], equipped with Intel Xeon E5-2609 0 CPUs clocked at 2.40 GHz. We set the CPU time limit to 300 s. Figure 1 displays the results. An empty cell indicates that a mode is not evaluated on that benchmark set. An archive with the raw evaluation data is publicly available.[4]

A preprocessing transformation that removes all Boolean subterms occurring as arguments of symbols [34, Sect. 8], similar to Kotelnikov et al.'s FOOL clausification approach [16], is implemented in Zipperposition. To answer question 1, we enabled preprocessing and compared it to our new calculus parameterized with the Boolean selection function that selects the smallest selectable subterm. The mode using our new calculus performs immediate inprocessing clausification, and we call it *base*, while the mode that preprocesses Boolean subterms is denoted by *preprocess* in Figure 1.

The obtained results do not give a conclusive answer to question 1. On both TPTP Bool and Sledgehammer problems, some configuration of our new calculus manages to prove one problem more than preprocessing. On SMT-LIB benchmarks, the best configuration of our calculus matches preprocessing. This shows that our calculus already performs roughly as well as previously known techniques and suggests that it will be able to outperform preprocessing techniques after tuning of its parameters.

For context, we provide the evaluation of E on supported benchmarks. On TPTP FO benchmarks it solves 643 problems, on TPTP Bool benchmarks 144

---

[4] https://doi.org/10.5281/zenodo.4550787

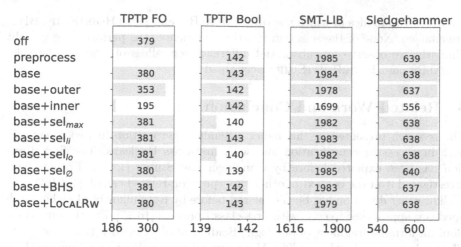

	TPTP FO	TPTP Bool	SMT-LIB	Sledgehammer
off	379			
preprocess		142	1985	639
base	380	143	1984	638
base+outer	353	142	1978	637
base+inner	195	142	1699	556
base+sel$_{max}$	381	140	1982	638
base+sel$_{li}$	381	143	1983	638
base+sel$_{lo}$	381	140	1982	638
base+sel$_{\varnothing}$	380	139	1985	640
base+BHS	381	142	1983	637
base+LocalRw	380	143	1979	638
	186 300	139 142	1616 1900	540 600

Fig. 1: Number of problems solved per benchmark set and Zipperposition mode. The x-axes start from the number of problems solved by all evaluated modes.

problems, and on Sledgehammer benchmarks 674 problems. Note that there is no straightforward way to compare these results with Zipperposition.

Our *base* mode uses immediate inprocessing clausification. To answer question 2, we compared *base* with a variant of *base* with outer delayed clausification (*base+outer*) and with a variant with inner delayed clausification (*base+inner*). In the delayed modes, we invoke the RENAME rule on formulas that are discovered to occur more than four times in the proof state.

The results show that inner delayed clausification, which performs the laziest form of clausification, gives the worst results on most benchmark sets. Outer delayed clausification performs roughly as well as immediate clausification on problems targeting our logic. On purely first-order problems, it performs slightly worse than immediate clausification. However, outer delayed clausification solves 17 problems not solved by immediate clausification on these problems. This suggests that it opens new possibilities for first-order reasoning that need to be explored further with specialized strategies and additional rules.

We found a problem with a conjecture of the form $s \to s$ that only the delayed clausification modes can prove: the TPTP problem SWV122+1. The subformula renaming mechanism of immediate clausification obfuscates this problem, whereas delayed clausification allows BoolSimp to convert the negated conjecture to $\bot$ directly, completing the proof in half a second.

To answer question 3, we compared the mode of Zipperposition in which all rules introduced by our calculus are disabled (*off*) with *base* on purely first-order problems. Our results show that both modes perform roughly the same.

To answer question 4, we evaluated the Boolean selection functions we have implemented: syntactically smallest selectable term (used in *base*), syntactically largest selectable term (sel$_{max}$), leftmost innermost selectable term (sel$_{li}$), leftmost outermost selectable term (sel$_{lo}$), and no Boolean selection (sel$_{\varnothing}$). We also evaluated two modes in which the rules LOCALRW and BOOLHOISTSIMP (BHS) are enabled. None of the selection functions influences the performance greatly. Similarly, we observe no substantial difference regardless of whether the rules LOCALRW and BOOLHOISTSIMP are enabled.

8 Related Work and Conclusion

The research presented in this paper extends superposition in two directions: with inprocessing clausification and with first-class Booleans. The first direction has been explored before by Ganzinger and Stuber [13], and others have investigated it in the context of other superposition-related calculi [1,4,9,20,21].

The other direction has been explored before by Kotelnikov et al., who developed two approaches to cope with first-class Booleans [16,17]. For the quantified Boolean formula fragment of our logic, Seidl et al. developed a translation into effectively propositional logic [26]. More general approaches to incorporate theories into superposition include superposition for finite domains [14], hierarchic superposition [6], and superposition with (co)datatypes [10].

For SMT solvers [22], supporting first-class Booleans is a widely accepted standard [5]. In contrast, the TPTP TFX format [30], intended to promote first-class Booleans in the rest of the automated reasoning community, has yet to gain traction. Software verification tools could clearly benefit from its popularization, as some of them identify terms and formulas in their logic, e.g., Why3 [12].

In conclusion, we devised a refutationally complete superposition calculus for first-order logic with interpreted Booleans. Its redundancy criterion allows us to flexibly add inprocessing clausification and other simplification rules. We believe our calculus is an excellent choice for the basis of new superposition provers: it offers the full power of standard superposition, while supporting rich input languages such as SMT-LIB and TPTP TFX. Even with unoptimized implementation and basic strategies, our calculus matches the performance of earlier approaches. In addition, the freedom it offers in term order, literal and Boolean subterm selection opens possibilities that are yet to be explored. Overall, our calculus appears as a solid foundation for richer logics in which the Boolean type cannot be efficiently preprocessed, such as higher-order logic [8]. In future work, we plan to tune the parameters and would find it interesting to combine our calculus with clause splitting techniques, such as AVATAR [32].

Acknowledgment Martin Desharnais and Jasmin Blanchette generated the Sledgehammer benchmarks. Simon Cruanes helped us with the implementation. The anonymous reviewers, Ahmed Bhayat, Jasmin Blanchette, and Uwe Waldmann suggested textual improvements. The maintainers of StarExec Iowa let us use their service. We thank them all. Nummelin's research has received funding from the Netherlands Organization for Scientific Research (NWO) under the Vidi program (project No. 016.Vidi.189.037, Lean Forward). Bentkamp and Vukmirović's research has received funding from the European Research Council (ERC) under the European Union's Horizon 2020 research and innovation program (grant agreement No. 713999, Matryoshka).

References

[1] Leo Bachmair and Harald Ganzinger. Non-clausal resolution and superposition with selection and redundancy criteria. In Andrei Voronkov, editor, *Logic Programming and Automated Reasoning (LPAR'92)*, volume 624 of *LNCS*, pages 273–284. Springer, 1992.

[2] Leo Bachmair and Harald Ganzinger. Rewrite-based equational theorem proving with selection and simplification. *J. Log. Comput.*, 4(3):217–247, 1994.

[3] Leo Bachmair and Harald Ganzinger. Resolution theorem proving. In John Alan Robinson and Andrei Voronkov, editors, *Handbook of Automated Reasoning*, volume I, pages 19–99. Elsevier and MIT Press, 2001.

[4] Leo Bachmair, Harald Ganzinger, David A. McAllester, and Christopher Lynch. Resolution theorem proving. In *Handbook of Automated Reasoning*, pages 19–99. Elsevier and MIT Press, 2001.

[5] Clark Barrett, Pascal Fontaine, and Cesare Tinelli. The SMT-LIB Standard: Version 2.6. Technical report, Department of Computer Science, The University of Iowa, 2017. Available at www.SMT-LIB.org.

[6] Peter Baumgartner and Uwe Waldmann. Hierarchic superposition with weak abstraction. In Maria Paola Bonacina, editor, *CADE-24*, volume 7898 of *LNCS*, pages 39–57. Springer, 2013.

[7] Dan Benanav. Simultaneous paramodulation. In Mark E. Stickel, editor, *CADE-10*, volume 449 of *LNCS*, pages 442–455. Springer, 1990.

[8] Alexander Bentkamp, Jasmin Blanchette, Sophie Tourret, and Petar Vukmirović. Superposition for full higher-order logic. In André Platzer and Geoff Sutcliffe, editors, *CADE-28*, LNCS. Springer, 2021.

[9] Christoph Benzmüller. Extensional higher-order paramodulation and RUE-resolution. In Harald Ganzinger, editor, *CADE-16*, volume 1632 of *LNCS*, pages 399–413. Springer, 1999.

[10] Jasmin Christian Blanchette, Nicolas Peltier, and Simon Robillard. Superposition with datatypes and codatatypes. In Didier Galmiche, Stephan Schulz, and Roberto Sebastiani, editors, *IJCAR 2018*, volume 10900 of *LNCS*, pages 370–387. Springer, 2018.

[11] Simon Cruanes. *Extending Superposition with Integer Arithmetic, Structural Induction, and Beyond*. Ph.D. thesis, École polytechnique, 2015.

[12] Jean-Christophe Filliâtre and Andrei Paskevich. Why3—where programs meet provers. In Matthias Felleisen and Philippa Gardner, editors, *European Symposium on Programming (ESOP 2013)*, volume 7792 of *LNCS*, pages 125–128. Springer, 2013.

[13] Harald Ganzinger and Jürgen Stuber. Superposition with equivalence reasoning and delayed clause normal form transformation. *Inf. Comput.*, 199(1-2):3–23, 2005.

[14] Thomas Hillenbrand and Christoph Weidenbach. Superposition for bounded domains. In Maria Paola Bonacina and Mark E. Stickel, editors, *Automated Reasoning and Mathematics*, volume 7788 of *LNCS*, pages 68–100. Springer, 2013.

[15] D. E. Knuth and P. B. Bendix. Simple word problems in universal algebras. In J. Leech, editor, *Computational Problems in Abstract Algebra*, pages 263–297. Pergamon Press, 1970.

[16] Evgenii Kotelnikov, Laura Kovács, Martin Suda, and Andrei Voronkov. A clausal normal form translation for FOOL. In Christoph Benzmüller, Geoff Sutcliffe, and Raúl Rojas, editors, *Global Conference on Artificial Intelligence (GCAI 2016)*, volume 41 of *EPiC*, pages 53–71. EasyChair, 2016.

[17] Evgenii Kotelnikov, Laura Kovács, and Andrei Voronkov. A first class Boolean sort in first-order theorem proving and TPTP. In Manfred Kerber, Jacques Carette, Cezary Kaliszyk, Florian Rabe, and Volker Sorge, editors, *Intelligent Computer Mathematics (CICM 2015)*, volume 9150 of *LNCS*, pages 71–86. Springer, 2015.

[18] Laura Kovács and Andrei Voronkov. First-order theorem proving and Vampire. In Natasha Sharygina and Helmut Veith, editors, *Computer Aided Verification (CAV 2013)*, volume 8044 of *LNCS*, pages 1–35. Springer, 2013.

[19] Michel Ludwig and Uwe Waldmann. An extension of the Knuth-Bendix ordering with LPO-like properties. In Nachum Dershowitz and Andrei Voronkov, editors, *Logic Programming and Automated Reasoning (LPAR 2007)*, volume 4790 of *LNCS*, pages 348–362. Springer, 2007.

[20] Zohar Manna and Richard J. Waldinger. A deductive approach to program synthesis. *ACM Trans. Program. Lang. Syst.*, 2(1):90–121, 1980.

[21] Neil V. Murray. Completely non-clausal theorem proving. *Artif. Intell.*, 18(1):67–85, 1982.

[22] Robert Nieuwenhuis, Albert Oliveras, and Cesare Tinelli. Solving SAT and SAT modulo theories: From an abstract Davis–Putnam–Logemann–Loveland procedure to DPLL(T). *J. ACM*, 53(6):937–977, 2006.

[23] Robert Nieuwenhuis and Albert Rubio. Basic superposition is complete. In Bernd Krieg-Brückner, editor, *European Symposium on Programming (ESOP '92)*, volume 582 of *LNCS*, pages 371–389. Springer, 1992.

[24] Andreas Nonnengart and Christoph Weidenbach. Computing small clause normal forms. In *Handbook of Automated Reasoning*, pages 335–367. Elsevier and MIT Press, 2001.

[25] Visa Nummelin, Alexander Bentkamp, Sophie Tourret, and Petar Vukmirović. Superposition with first-class Booleans and inprocessing clausification (technical report). Technical report, 2021. https://matryoshka-project.github.io/pubs/boolsup_report.pdf.

[26] Martina Seidl, Florian Lonsing, and Armin Biere. qbf2epr: A tool for generating EPR formulas from QBF. In Pascal Fontaine, Renate A. Schmidt, and Stephan Schulz, editors, *Practical Aspects of Automated Reasoning (PAAR-2012)*, volume 21 of *EPiC Series in Computing*, pages 139–148. EasyChair, 2012.

[27] Alexander Steen. *Extensional Paramodulation for Higher-order Logic and Its Effective Implementation Leo-III*. Dissertationen zur künstlichen Intelligenz. Akademische Verlagsgesellschaft AKA GmbH, 2018.

[28] Aaron Stump, Geoff Sutcliffe, and Cesare Tinelli. Starexec: A cross-community infrastructure for logic solving. In *IJCAR 2014*, volume 8562 of *LNCS*, pages 367–373. Springer, 2014.

[29] Geoff Sutcliffe. The TPTP problem library and associated infrastructure—from CNF to TH0, TPTP v6.4.0. *J. Autom. Reason.*, 59(4):483–502, 2017.

[30] Geoff Sutcliffe and Evgenii Kotelnikov. TFX: the TPTP extended typed first-order form. In Boris Konev, Josef Urban, and Philipp Rümmer, editors, *Practical Aspects of Automated Reasoning (PAAR-2018)*, volume 2162 of *CEUR Workshop Proceedings*, pages 72–87. CEUR-WS.org, 2018.

[31] Grigori Tseitin. On the complexity of derivation in propositional calculus. In *Automation of reasoning: Classical Papers on Computational Logic*, volume 2, pages 466–483. Springer, 1983.

[32] Andrei Voronkov. AVATAR: the architecture for first-order theorem provers. In *CAV 2014*, volume 8559 of *LNCS*, pages 696–710. Springer, 2014.

[33] Petar Vukmirović and Visa Nummelin. Boolean reasoning in a higher-order superperposition prover. In Pascal Fontaine, Konstantin Korovin, Ilias S. Kotsireas, Philipp Rümmer, and Sophie Tourret, editors, *Practical Aspects of Automated Reasoning (PAAR-2020)*, volume 2752 of *CEUR Workshop Proceedings*, pages 148–166. CEUR-WS.org, 2020.

[34] Petar Vukmirović, Jasmin Blanchette, Simon Cruanes, and Stephan Schulz. Extending a brainiac prover to lambda-free higher-order logic. *Accepted in International Journal on Software Tools for Technology Transfer.*

[35] Uwe Waldmann, Sophie Tourret, Simon Robillard, and Jasmin Blanchette. A comprehensive framework for saturation theorem proving. In Nicolas Peltier and Viorica Sofronie-Stokkermans, editors, *IJCAR 2020*, LNCS. Springer, 2020.

Open Access This chapter is licensed under the terms of the Creative Commons Attribution 4.0 International License (http://creativecommons.org/licenses/by/4.0/), which permits use, sharing, adaptation, distribution and reproduction in any medium or format, as long as you give appropriate credit to the original author(s) and the source, provide a link to the Creative Commons license and indicate if changes were made.

The images or other third party material in this chapter are included in the chapter's Creative Commons license, unless indicated otherwise in a credit line to the material. If material is not included in the chapter's Creative Commons license and your intended use is not permitted by statutory regulation or exceeds the permitted use, you will need to obtain permission directly from the copyright holder.

Superposition for Full Higher-order Logic

Alexander Bentkamp[1] , Jasmin Blanchette[1,2,3] ,
Sophie Tourret[2,3] , and Petar Vukmirović[1]

[1] Vrije Universiteit Amsterdam, Amsterdam, the Netherlands
{a.bentkamp,j.c.blanchette,p.vukmirovic}@vu.nl
[2] Université de Lorraine, CNRS, Inria, LORIA, Nancy, France
sophie.tourret@inria.fr
[3] Max-Planck-Institut für Informatik, Saarland Informatics Campus, Saarbrücken, Germany

Abstract. We recently designed two calculi as stepping stones towards superposition for full higher-order logic: Boolean-free λ-superposition and superposition for first-order logic with interpreted Booleans. Stepping on these stones, we finally reach a sound and refutationally complete calculus for higher-order logic with polymorphism, extensionality, Hilbert choice, and Henkin semantics. In addition to the complexity of combining the calculus's two predecessors, new challenges arise from the interplay between λ-terms and Booleans. Our implementation in Zipperposition outperforms all other higher-order theorem provers and is on a par with an earlier, pragmatic prototype of Booleans in Zipperposition.

1 Introduction

Superposition is a leading calculus for first-order logic with equality. We have been wondering for some years whether it would be possible to gracefully generalize it to extensional higher-order logic and use it as the basis of a strong higher-order automatic theorem prover. Towards this goal, we have, together with colleagues, designed superposition-like calculi for three intermediate logics between first-order and higher-order logic. Now we are finally ready to assemble a superposition calculus for full higher-order logic. The filiation of our new calculus from Bachmair and Ganzinger's standard first-order superposition is as follows:

Standard superposition
Bachmair and Ganzinger [2] (Sup)

Superposition with $\leftrightarrow$ and delayed CNF   Boolean-free λ-free superposition
Ganzinger and Stuber [16] ($\leftrightarrow$Sup)   Bentkamp et al. [7] (λfSup)

Superposition with Booleans   Boolean-free λ-superposition
Nummelin et al. [23] (oSup)   Bentkamp et al. [6] (λSup)

Boolean λ-superposition
This paper (oλSup)

© The Author(s) 2021
A. Platzer and G. Sutcliffe (Eds.): CADE 2021, LNAI 12699, pp. 396–412, 2021.
https://doi.org/10.1007/978-3-030-79876-5_23

Our goal was to devise an efficient calculus for higher-order logic. To achieve it, we pursued two objectives. First, the calculus should be refutationally complete. Second, the calculus should coincide as much as possible with its predecessors oSup and λSup on the respective fragments of higher-order logic (which in turn essentially coincide with Sup on first-order logic). Achieving these objectives is the main contribution of this paper. We made an effort to keep the calculus simple, but often the refutational completeness proof forced our hand to add conditions or special cases.

Like oSup, our calculus oλSup operates on clauses that can contain Boolean subterms, and it interleaves clausification with other inferences. Like λSup, oλSup eagerly $\beta\eta$-normalizes terms, employs full higher-order unification, and relies on a fluid subterm superposition rule (FLUIDSUP) to simulate superposition inferences below applied variables—i.e., terms of the form $y\,t_1\ldots t_n$ for $n \geq 1$.

Because oSup contains several superposition-like inference rules for Boolean subterms, our completeness proof requires dedicated *fluid Boolean subterm hoisting rules* (FLUIDBOOLHOIST, FLUIDLOOBHOIST), which simulate Boolean inferences below applied variables, in addition to FLUIDSUP, which simulates superposition inferences.

Due to restrictions related to the term order that parameterizes superposition, it is difficult to handle variables bound by unclausified quantifiers if these variables occur applied or in arguments of applied variables. We solve the issue by replacing such quantified terms $\forall y.\, t$ by equivalent terms $(\lambda y.\, t) \approx (\lambda y.\, \top)$ in a preprocessing step.

We implemented our calculus in the Zipperposition prover and evaluated it on TPTP and Sledgehammer benchmarks. The new Zipperposition outperforms all other higher-order provers and is on a par with an ad hoc implementation of Booleans in the same prover by Vukmirović and Nummelin [30]. We refer to the technical report [8] for the completeness proof and a more detailed account of the calculus and its evaluation.

2 Logic

Our logic is higher-order logic (simple type theory) with rank-1 polymorphism, Hilbert choice, and functional and Boolean extensionality. Its syntax mostly follows Gordon and Melham [17]. We use the notation $\bar{a}_n$ or $\bar{a}$ to stand for the tuple $(a_1, \ldots, a_n)$ where $n \geq 0$. Deviating from Gordon and Melham, type arguments are explicit, written as $c\langle \bar{\tau}_m \rangle$ for a symbol $c : \Pi\bar{\alpha}_m.\, \upsilon$ and types $\bar{\tau}_m$. In the type signature Σ_{ty}, we require the presence of a nullary Boolean type constructor o and a binary function type constructor $\rightarrow$. In the term signature Σ, we require the presence of the logical symbols $\top$, $\bot$, $\neg$, $\wedge$, $\vee$, $\rightarrow$, $\forall$, $\exists$, $\approx$, and $\not\approx$. The logical symbols are shown in bold to distinguish them from the notation used for clauses below. Moreover, we require the presence of the Hilbert choice operator $\varepsilon \in \Sigma$. Although ε is interpreted in our semantics, we do not consider it a logical symbol. Our calculus will enforce the semantics of ε by an axiom, whereas the semantics of the logical symbols will be enforced by inference rules. We write $\mathcal{V}$ for the set of (term) variables. We use Henkin semantics, in the style of Fitting [15], with respect to which we can prove our calculus refutationally complete. In summary, our logic essentially coincides with the TPTP TH1 format [20].

We generally view terms modulo $\alpha\beta\eta$-equivalence. When defining operations that need to analyze the structure of terms, however, we use a custom normal form as the default representative of a $\beta\eta$-equivalence class: The $\beta\eta Q_\eta$-*normal* form $t{\downarrow}_{\beta\eta Q_\eta}$ of a term t is obtained by bringing the term into η-short β-normal form and finally applying the rewrite rule $Q\langle\tau\rangle\, s \longrightarrow_{Q_\eta} Q\langle\tau\rangle\, (\lambda x.\, s\, x)$ exhaustively whenever s is not a λ-expression. Here and elsewhere, Q stands for either $\forall$ or $\exists$.

On top of the standard higher-order terms, we install a clausal structure that allows us to formulate calculus rules in the style of first-order superposition. A literal $s \approx t$ is an equation $s \approx t$ or disequation $s \not\approx t$ of terms s and t; both equations and disequations are unordered pairs. A clause $L_1 \vee \cdots \vee L_n$ is a finite multiset of literals L_j. The empty clause is written as $\bot$. This clausal structure does not restrict the logic, because an arbitrary term t of Boolean type can be written as the clause $t \approx \top$.

We considered excluding negative literals by encoding them as $(s \approx t) \approx \bot$, following $\leftrightarrow$Sup [16]. However, this approach would make the conclusion of the equality factoring rule (EFACT) too large for our purposes. Regardless, the simplification machinery will allow us to reduce negative literals $t \not\approx \bot$ and $t \not\approx \top$ to $t \approx \top$ and $t \approx \bot$, respectively, thereby eliminating redundant representations of nonequational literals.

We let $\mathrm{CSU}(s,t)$ denote an arbitrary (preferably, minimal) complete set of unifiers for two terms s and t on the set of free variables of the clauses in which s and t occur. To compute such sets, Huet-style preunification [18] is not sufficient, and we must resort to a full unification procedure [19, 29]. To cope with the nontermination of such procedures, we use dovetailing as described by Vukmirović et al. [28, Sect. 5].

Some of the rules in our calculus introduce Skolem symbols, representing objects mandated by existential quantification. We assume that these symbols do not occur in the input problem. More formally, given a problem over a term signature Σ, our calculus operates on a Skolem-extended term signature Σ_{sk} that, in addition to all symbols from Σ, inductively contains symbols $\mathsf{sk}_{\Pi\bar{\alpha}.\,\forall\bar{x}.\,\exists z.\,t\,z} : \Pi\bar{\alpha}.\,\bar{\tau} \to \upsilon$ for all types υ, variables $z : \upsilon$, and terms $t : \upsilon \to o$ over Σ_{sk}, where $\bar{\alpha}$ are the free type variables occurring in t and $\bar{x} : \bar{\tau}$ are the free term variables occurring in t, both in order of first occurrence.

3   The Calculus

The oλSup calculus closely resembles λSup, augmented with rules for Boolean reasoning that are inspired by oSup. As in λSup, superposition-like inferences are restricted to certain first-order-like subterms, the *green subterms*, which we define inductively as follows: Every term t is a green subterm of t, and for all symbols $\mathsf{f} \in \Sigma \setminus \{\forall, \exists\}$, if t is a green subterm of u_i for some i, then t is a green subterm of $\mathsf{f}\langle\bar{\tau}\rangle\,\bar{u}$. For example, the green subterms of $\mathsf{f}\,(\mathsf{g}\,(\neg\mathsf{p}))\,(\forall\langle\tau\rangle\,(\lambda x.\mathsf{q}))\,(y\,\mathsf{a})\,(\lambda x.\mathsf{h}\,\mathsf{b})$ are the term itself, $\mathsf{g}\,(\neg\mathsf{p})$, $\neg\mathsf{p}$, p, $\forall\langle\tau\rangle\,(\lambda x.\mathsf{q})$, $y\,\mathsf{a}$, and $\lambda x.\mathsf{h}\,\mathsf{b}$. We write $s\langle t\rangle$ to denote a term s with a green subterm t and call the first-order-like context $s\langle\ \rangle$ a *green context*.

Following λSup, we call a term t *fluid* if (1) $t{\downarrow}_{\beta\eta Q_\eta}$ is of the form $y\,\bar{u}_n$ where $n \geq 1$, or (2) $t{\downarrow}_{\beta\eta Q_\eta}$ is a λ-expression and there exists a substitution σ such that $t\sigma{\downarrow}_{\beta\eta Q_\eta}$ is not a λ-expression (due to η-reduction). Intuitively, fluid terms are terms whose normal form can change radically as a result of instantiation.

We define deeply occurring variables as in λSup, but exclude λ-expressions directly below quantifiers: A variable *occurs deeply* in a clause C if it occurs inside an argument of an applied variable or inside a λ-expression that is not directly below a quantifier.

Preprocessing. Our completeness theorem requires that quantified variables do not appear in certain higher-order contexts. We use preprocessing to eliminate problematic occurrences of quantifiers. The rewrite rules $\forall_\approx$ and $\exists_\approx$, which we collectively denote by $Q_\approx$, are defined as $\forall\langle\tau\rangle \rightarrow_{\forall_\approx} \lambda y. y \approx (\lambda x.\, \top)$ and $\exists\langle\tau\rangle \rightarrow_{\exists_\approx} \lambda y. y \not\approx (\lambda x.\, \bot)$ where the rewritten occurrence of $Q\langle\tau\rangle$ is unapplied or has an argument of the form $\lambda x.\, v$ such that x occurs as a nongreen subterm of v. If either of these rewrite rules can be applied to a given term, the term is $Q_\approx$-*reducible*; otherwise, it is $Q_\approx$-*normal*.

For example, the term $\lambda y.\, \exists\langle\iota \rightarrow \iota\rangle\,(\lambda x.\, g\,x\,y\,(z\,y)\,(f\,x))$ is $Q_\approx$-normal. A term may be $Q_\approx$-reducible because a quantifier appears unapplied (e.g., $g\,\exists\langle\iota\rangle$); a quantified variable occurs applied (e.g., $\exists\langle\iota \rightarrow \iota\rangle\,(\lambda x.\, x\,a)$); a quantified variable occurs inside a nested λ-expression (e.g., $\forall\langle\iota\rangle\,(\lambda x.\, f\,(\lambda y.\, x)))$; or a quantified variable occurs in the argument of a variable, either a free variable (e.g., $\forall\langle\iota\rangle\,(\lambda x.\, z\,x)$) or a variable bound above the quantifier (e.g., $\lambda y.\, \exists\langle\iota\rangle\,(\lambda x.\, y\,x)$).

A preprocessor $Q_\approx$-normalizes the input problem. Although inferences may produce $Q_\approx$-reducible clauses, we do not $Q_\approx$-normalize during the derivation process itself. Instead, $Q_\approx$-reducible ground instances of clauses will be considered redundant by the redundancy criterion. Thus, clauses whose ground instances are all $Q_\approx$-reducible can be deleted. However, there are $Q_\approx$-reducible clauses, such as $x\,\forall\langle\iota\rangle \approx a$, that nevertheless have $Q_\approx$-normal ground instances. Such clauses must be kept because the completeness proof relies on their $Q_\approx$-normal ground instances.

In principle, we could omit the side condition of the $Q_\approx$-rewrite rules and eliminate all quantifiers. However, the calculus (especially, the redundancy criterion) performs better with quantifiers than with λ-expressions, which is why we restrict $Q_\approx$-normalization as much as the completeness proof allows. Extending the preprocessing to eliminate all Boolean terms as in Kotelnikov et al. [21] does not work for higher-order logic because Boolean terms can contain variables bound by enclosing λ-expressions.

Term Order. The calculus is parameterized by a well-founded strict total order $\succ$ on ground terms satisfying these four criteria: (O1) compatibility with green contexts— i.e., $s' \succ s$ implies $t\langle s'\rangle \succ t\langle s\rangle$; (O2) green subterm property—i.e. $t\langle s\rangle \succeq s$ where $\succeq$ is the reflexive closure of $\succ$; (O3) $u \succ \bot \succ \top$ for all terms $u \notin \{\top, \bot\}$; (O4) $Q\langle\tau\rangle\,t \succ t\,u$ for all types τ, terms t, and terms u such that $Q\langle\tau\rangle\,t$ and u are $Q_\approx$-normal and the only Boolean green subterms of u are $\top$ and $\bot$. The restriction of (O4) to $Q_\approx$-normal terms ensures that term orders fulfilling the requirements exist, but it forces us to preprocess the input problem. We extend $\succ$ to literals and clauses via the multiset extensions in the standard way [2, Sect. 2.4].

For nonground terms, $\succ$ is required to be a strict partial order such that $t \succ s$ implies $t\theta \succ s\theta$ for all grounding substitutions θ. As in λSup, we also introduce a nonstrict variant $\succsim$ for which we require that $t\theta \succeq s\theta$ for all grounding substitutions θ whenever $t \succsim s$, and similarly for literals and clauses.

To construct a concrete order fulfilling these requirements, we define an encoding into untyped first-order terms, and compare these using a variant of the Knuth–Bendix order. In a first step, denoted O, the encoding translates fluid terms t as fresh variables z_t; nonfluid λ-expressions $\lambda x{:}\tau.\, u$ as $\mathsf{lam}(O(\tau), O(u))$; applied quantifiers $Q\langle\tau\rangle(\lambda x{:}\tau.\, u)$ as $Q_1(O(\tau), O(u))$; and other terms $f\langle\bar\tau\rangle\,\bar u_k$ as $f_k(O(\bar\tau), O(\bar u_k))$. Bound variables are encoded as constants db^i corresponding to De Bruijn indices. In a second step, denoted $\mathcal{P}$, the encoding replaces Q_1 by Q'_1 and variables z by z' whenever they occur below lam. For example, $\forall\langle\iota\rangle(\lambda x.\, p\, y\, y\,(\lambda u.\, f\, y\, y\,(\forall\langle\iota\rangle(\lambda v.\, u))))$ is encoded as $\forall_1(\iota, p_3(y, y, \mathsf{lam}(o, f_3(y', y', \forall'_1(\iota, \mathsf{db}^1)))))$. The first-order terms can then be compared using a transfinite Knuth–Bendix order $\succ_{\mathsf{kb}}$ [22]. Let the weight of $\forall_1$ and $\exists_1$ be ω, the weight of T_0 and $\bot_0$ be 1, and the weights of all other symbols be less than ω. Let the precedence $>$ be total and $\bot_0, \mathsf{T}_0$ be the symbols of lowest precedence, with $\bot_0 > \mathsf{T}_0$. Then let $t \succ s$ if $O(\mathcal{P}(t)) \succ_{\mathsf{kb}} O(\mathcal{P}(s))$ and $t \succsim s$ if $O(\mathcal{P}(t)) \succsim_{\mathsf{kb}} O(\mathcal{P}(s))$.

Selection Functions. The calculus is also parameterized by a literal selection function and a Boolean subterm selection function. We define an element x of a multiset M to be $\trianglerighteq$-*maximal* for some relation $\trianglerighteq$ if for all $y \in M$ with $y \trianglerighteq x$, we have $y = x$. It is *strictly* $\trianglerighteq$-maximal if it is $\trianglerighteq$-maximal and occurs only once in M.

The literal selection function *HLitSel* maps each clause to a subset of *selected literals*. A literal may not be selected if it is positive and neither side is $\bot$. Moreover, a literal $L\langle y\rangle$ may not be selected if $y\,\bar{u}_n$, with $n \geq 1$, is a $\succsim$-maximal term of the clause.

The Boolean subterm selection function *HBoolSel* maps each clause C to a subset of *selected subterms* in C. Selected subterms must be green subterms of Boolean type. Moreover, a subterm s must not be selected if $s = \mathsf{T}$, if $s = \bot$, if s is a variable-headed term, if s is at the topmost position on either side of a positive literal, or if s contains a variable y as a green subterm, and $y\,\bar{u}_n$, with $n \geq 1$, is a $\succsim$-maximal term of the clause.

Eligibility. A literal L is *(strictly) eligible* w.r.t. a substitution σ in C if it is selected in C or there are no selected literals and no selected Boolean subterms in C and $L\sigma$ is (strictly) $\succsim$-maximal in $C\sigma$.

The eligible subterms of a clause C w.r.t. a substitution σ are inductively defined as follows: Any selected subterm is eligible. If a literal $L = s \approx t$ with $s\sigma \not\precsim t\sigma$ is either eligible and negative or strictly eligible and positive, then the subterm s is eligible. If a subterm t is eligible and the head of t is not $\approx$ or $\not\approx$, all direct green subterms of t are eligible. If a subterm t is eligible and t is of the form $u \approx v$ or $u \not\approx v$, then u is eligible if $u\sigma \not\precsim v\sigma$ and v is eligible if $u\sigma \not\precsim v\sigma$.

The Core Inference Rules. The calculus consists of the following core inference rules. The first five rules stem from λSup, with minor adaptions concerning Booleans:

$$\frac{\overbrace{D' \vee t \approx t'}^{D} \quad \overbrace{C\langle u\rangle}^{}}{(D' \vee C\langle t'\rangle)\sigma}\ \textsc{Sup} \qquad \frac{\overbrace{C' \vee u \not\approx u'}^{C}}{C'\sigma}\ \textsc{ERes} \qquad \frac{\overbrace{C' \vee u' \approx v' \vee u \approx v}^{C}}{(C' \vee v \not\approx v' \vee u \approx v')\sigma}\ \textsc{EFact}$$

$$\frac{\overbrace{D' \vee t \approx t'}^{D} \quad \overbrace{C\langle u\rangle}^{}}{(D' \vee C\langle z\,t'\rangle)\sigma}\ \textsc{FluidSup} \qquad \frac{\overbrace{C' \vee s \approx s'}^{C}}{C'\sigma \vee s\sigma\,\bar{x}_n \approx s'\sigma\,\bar{x}_n}\ \textsc{ArgCong}$$

SUP 1. u is not fluid; 2. u is not a variable deeply occurring in C; 3. if u is a variable y, there must exist a grounding substitution θ such that $t\sigma\theta \succ t'\sigma\theta$ and $C\sigma\theta \prec C''\sigma\theta$, where $C'' = C\{y \mapsto t'\}$; 4. $\sigma \in \mathrm{CSU}(t, u)$; 5. $t\sigma \not\precsim t'\sigma$; 6. u is eligible in C w.r.t. σ; 7. $C\sigma \not\precsim D\sigma$; 8. $t \approx t'$ is strictly eligible in D w.r.t. σ; 9. $t\sigma$ is not a fully applied logical symbol; 10. if $t'\sigma = \bot$, the subterm u is at the top level of a positive literal.

ERES 1. $\sigma \in \mathrm{CSU}(u, u')$; 2. $u \not\approx u'$ is eligible in C w.r.t. σ.

EFACT 1. $\sigma \in \mathrm{CSU}(u, u')$; 2. $u\sigma \not\precsim v\sigma$; 3. $(u \approx v)\sigma$ is $\succsim$-maximal in $C\sigma$; 4. $u\sigma \not\precsim v\sigma$; 5. nothing is selected in C.

FLUIDSUP 1. u is a variable deeply occurring in C or u is fluid; 2. z is a fresh variable; 3. $\sigma \in \mathrm{CSU}(z\,t, u)$; 4. $(z\,t')\sigma \neq (z\,t)\sigma$; 5.–10. as for SUP.

ARGCONG 1. $n > 0$; 2. σ is the most general type substitution that ensures well-typedness of the conclusion for a given n; 3. $\bar{x}_n$ is a tuple of distinct fresh variables; 4. the literal $s \approx s'$ is strictly eligible in C w.r.t. σ.

The following rules are concerned with Boolean reasoning and originate from oSup. They have been adapted to support polymorphism and applied variables.

$$\frac{C\langle u\rangle}{(C\langle\bot\rangle \vee u \approx \top)\sigma}\ \textsc{BoolHoist} \qquad \frac{\overbrace{C' \vee s \approx s'}^{C}}{C'\sigma}\ \textsc{FalseElim}$$

$$\frac{C\langle u\rangle}{(C\langle\bot\rangle \vee x \approx y)\sigma}\ \textsc{EqHoist} \qquad \frac{C\langle u\rangle}{C\langle t'\rangle\sigma}\ \textsc{BoolRw}$$

$$\frac{C\langle u\rangle}{(C\langle\top\rangle \vee x \approx y)\sigma}\ \textsc{NeqHoist} \qquad \frac{C\langle u\rangle}{C\langle y\,(\mathsf{sk}_{\Pi\bar{\alpha}.\,\forall\bar{x}.\,\exists z.\,\neg y\sigma\,z}\langle\bar{\alpha}\rangle\,\bar{x})\rangle\sigma}\ \textsc{ForallRw}$$

$$\frac{C\langle u\rangle}{(C\langle\bot\rangle \vee y\,x \approx \top)\sigma}\ \textsc{ForallHoist} \qquad \frac{C\langle u\rangle}{C\langle y\,(\mathsf{sk}_{\Pi\bar{\alpha}.\,\forall\bar{x}.\,\exists z.\,y\sigma\,z}\langle\bar{\alpha}\rangle\,\bar{x})\rangle\sigma}\ \textsc{ExistsRw}$$

$$\frac{C\langle u\rangle}{(C\langle\top\rangle \vee y\,x \approx \bot)\sigma}\ \textsc{ExistsHoist}$$

BOOLHOIST 1. σ is a type unifier of the type of u with the Boolean type o (i.e., the identity if u is Boolean or $\{\alpha \mapsto \mathrm{o}\}$ if u is of type α for some type variable α); 2. the head of u is neither a variable nor a logical symbol; 3. u is eligible in C; 4. the occurrence of u is not at the top level of a positive literal.

EQHOIST, NEQHOIST, FORALLHOIST, EXISTSHOIST 1. $\sigma \in \mathrm{CSU}(u,\, x \mathbin{\boldsymbol{\approx}} y)$, $\sigma \in \mathrm{CSU}(u,\, x \mathbin{\boldsymbol{\not\approx}} y)$, $\sigma \in \mathrm{CSU}(u, \boldsymbol{\forall}\langle\alpha\rangle\, y)$, or $\sigma \in \mathrm{CSU}(u, \boldsymbol{\exists}\langle\alpha\rangle\, y)$, respectively; 2. x, y, and α are fresh variables; 3. u is eligible in C w.r.t. σ; 4. if the head of u is a variable, it must be applied and the affected literal must be of the form $u \approx \top$, $u \approx \bot$, or $u \approx v$ where v is a variable-headed term.

FALSEELIM 1. $\sigma \in \mathrm{CSU}(s \approx s', \bot \approx \top)$; 2. $s \approx s'$ is strictly eligible in C w.r.t. σ.

BOOLRW 1. $\sigma \in \mathrm{CSU}(t, u)$ and (t, t') is one of the following pairs, where y is a fresh variable: $(\neg\bot, \top)$, $(\neg\top, \bot)$, $(\bot\wedge\bot, \bot)$, $(\top\wedge\bot, \bot)$, $(\bot\wedge\top, \bot)$, $(\top\wedge\top, \top)$, $(\bot\vee\bot, \bot)$, $(\top\vee\bot, \top)$, $(\bot\vee\top, \top)$, $(\top\vee\top, \top)$, $(\bot\rightarrow\bot, \top)$, $(\top\rightarrow\bot, \bot)$, $(\bot\rightarrow\top, \top)$, $(\top\rightarrow\top, \top)$, $(y \mathbin{\boldsymbol{\approx}} y, \top)$, $(y \mathbin{\boldsymbol{\not\approx}} y, \bot)$; 2. u is not a variable; 3. u is eligible in C w.r.t. σ; 4. if the head of u is a variable, it must be applied and the affected literal must be of the form $u \approx \top$, $u \approx \bot$, or $u \approx v$ where v is a variable-headed term.

FORALLRW, EXISTSRW 1. $\sigma \in \mathrm{CSU}(\boldsymbol{\forall}\langle\beta\rangle\, y, u)$ and $\sigma \in \mathrm{CSU}(\boldsymbol{\exists}\langle\beta\rangle\, y, u)$, respectively, where β is a fresh type variable, y is a fresh term variable, $\bar{\alpha}$ are the free type variables and $\bar{x}$ are the free term variables occurring in $y\sigma$ in order of first occurrence;

2. u is not a variable; 3. u is eligible in C w.r.t. σ; 4. if the head of u is a variable, it must be applied and the affected literal must be of the form $u \approx \top$, $u \approx \bot$, or $u \approx v$ where v is a variable-headed term; 5. for FORALLRW, the indicated occurrence of u is not in a literal $u \approx \top$, and for EXISTSRW, the indicated occurrence of u is not in a literal $u \approx \bot$.

Like SUP, also the Boolean rules must be simulated in fluid terms. The following rules are Boolean counterparts of FLUIDSUP:

$$\frac{C\langle u\rangle}{(C\langle z\bot\rangle \vee x \approx \top)\sigma} \text{ FLUID-BoolHoist} \qquad \frac{C\langle u\rangle}{(C\langle z\top\rangle \vee x \approx \bot)\sigma} \text{ FLUID-LoobHoist}$$

FLUIDBOOLHOIST 1. u is fluid; 2. z and x are fresh variables; 3. $\sigma \in \text{CSU}(z\,x, u)$; 4. $(z\bot)\sigma \neq (z\,x)\sigma$; 5. $x\sigma \neq \top$ and $x\sigma \neq \bot$; 6. u is eligible in C w.r.t. σ.
FLUIDLOOBHOIST Like the above but with $\bot$ replaced by $\top$ in condition 4.

In addition to the inference rules, our calculus relies on two axioms, below. Axiom (EXT), from λSup, embodies functional extensionality; the expression diff$\langle\alpha,\beta\rangle$ abbreviates $\text{sk}_{\Pi\alpha\beta.\,\forall z\,y.\,\exists x.\,z\,x\not\approx y\,x}\langle\alpha,\beta\rangle$. Axiom (CHOICE) characterizes the Hilbert choice operator ε.

$$z\,(\text{diff}\langle\alpha,\beta\rangle\,z\,y) \not\approx y\,(\text{diff}\langle\alpha,\beta\rangle\,z\,y) \vee z \approx y \qquad \text{(EXT)}$$
$$y\,x \approx \bot \vee y\,(\varepsilon\langle\alpha\rangle\,y) \approx \top \qquad \text{(CHOICE)}$$

Rationale for the Rules. Most of the calculus's rules are adapted from its precursors. SUP, ERES, and EFACT are already present in Sup, with slightly different side conditions. Notably, as in λfSup and λSup, SUP inferences are required only into green contexts. Other subterms are accessed indirectly via ARGCONG and (EXT).

The rules BOOLHOIST, EQHOIST, NEQHOIST, FORALLHOIST, EXISTSHOIST, FALSEELIM, BOOLRW, FORALLRW, and EXISTSRW, concerned with Boolean reasoning, stem from oSup, which was inspired by $\leftrightarrow$Sup. Except for BOOLHOIST and FALSEELIM, these rules have a condition stating that "if the head of u is a variable, it must be applied and the affected literal must be of the form $u \approx \top$, $u \approx \bot$, or $u \approx v$ where v is a variable-headed term." The inferences at variable-headed terms permitted by this condition are our form of primitive substitution [1,18], a mechanism that blindly substitutes logical connectives and quantifiers for variables z with a Boolean result type.

Example 1. Our calculus can prove that Leibniz equality implies equality (i.e., if two values behave the same for all predicates, they are equal) as follows:

$$\frac{\dfrac{\dfrac{\dfrac{\dfrac{\dfrac{z\,a \approx \bot \vee z\,b \approx \top}{(x\,a \approx y\,a) \approx \bot \vee \bot \approx \top \vee x\,b \approx y\,b}\text{ EQHoist}}{\top \approx \bot \vee \bot \approx \top \vee w\,a\,b\,b \approx w\,b\,a\,b}\text{ BoolRw}}{\bot \approx \top \vee w\,a\,b\,b \approx w\,b\,a\,b}\text{ FalseElim}}{a \not\approx b \qquad w\,a\,b\,b \approx w\,b\,a\,b}\text{ FalseElim}}{\dfrac{a \not\approx a}{\bot}\text{ ERes}}$$

The EQHOIST inference, applied on $z\,b$, illustrates how our calculus introduces logical symbols without a dedicated primitive substitution rule. Although $\approx$ does not appear in the premise, we still need to apply EQHOIST on $z\,b$ with $\mathrm{CSU}(z\,b, x_0 \approx y_0) = \{\{z \mapsto \lambda v.\, x\,v \approx y\,v,\ x_0 \mapsto x\,b,\ y_0 \mapsto y\,b\}\}$. Other calculi [1, 9, 18, 26] would apply an explicit primitive substitution rule instead, yielding essentially $(x\,a \approx y\,a) \approx \bot \lor (x\,b \approx y\,b) \approx \top$. However, in our approach this clause is subsumed and could be discarded immediately. By hoisting the equality to the clausal level, we bypass the redundancy criterion.

Next, BOOLRW can be applied to $x\,a \approx y\,a$ with $\mathrm{CSU}(x\,a \approx y\,a, y_0 \approx y_0) = \{\{x \mapsto \lambda v.\, w\,a\,v\,v,\ y \mapsto \lambda v.\, w\,v\,a\,v,\ y_0 \mapsto w\,a\,a\,a\}\}$. The two FALSEELIM steps remove the $\bot \approx \top$ literals. Then SUP is applicable with the unifier $\{w \mapsto \lambda x_1\,x_2\,x_3.\, x_2\} \in \mathrm{CSU}(b, w\,a\,b\,b)$, and ERES derives the contradiction.

Like in λSup, the FLUIDSUP rule is responsible for simulating superposition inferences below applied variables, other fluid terms, and deeply occurring variables. Complementarily, FLUIDBOOLHOIST and FLUIDLOOBHOIST simulate the various Boolean inference rules below fluid terms. Initially, we considered adding a fluid version of each rule that operates on Boolean subterms, but we discovered that FLUID-BOOLHOIST and FLUIDLOOBHOIST suffice to achieve refutational completeness.

Example 2. The clause set consisting of $h\,(y\,b) \not\approx h\,(g\,\bot) \lor h\,(y\,a) \not\approx h\,(g\,\top)$ and $a \not\approx b$ highlights the need for FLUIDBOOLHOIST and its companion. The set is unsatisfiable because the instantiation $\{y \mapsto \lambda x.\, g\,(x \approx a)\}$ produces the clause $h\,(g\,(b \approx a)) \not\approx h\,(g\,\bot) \lor h\,(g\,(a \approx a)) \not\approx h\,(g\,\top)$, which is unsatisfiable in conjunction with $a \not\approx b$.

The literal selection function can select either literal in the first clause. ERES is applicable in either case, but the unifiers $\{y \mapsto \lambda x.\, g\,\bot\}$ and $\{y \mapsto \lambda x.\, g\,\top\}$ do not lead to a contradiction. Instead, we need to apply FLUIDBOOLHOIST if the first literal is selected or FLUIDLOOBHOIST if the second literal is selected. In the first case, the derivation is as follows:

$$
\cfrac{
\cfrac{
\cfrac{
a \not\approx b \qquad
\cfrac{
\cfrac{
\cfrac{
\cfrac{h\,(y\,b) \not\approx h\,(g\,\bot) \lor h\,(y\,a) \not\approx h\,(g\,\top)}
{h\,(z'\,b\,\bot) \not\approx h\,(g\,\bot) \lor h\,(z'\,a\,(x'\,a)) \not\approx h\,(g\,\top) \lor x'\,b \approx \top}\ \text{FLUIDBOOLHOIST}}
{h\,(g\,(x'\,a)) \not\approx h\,(g\,\top) \lor x'\,b \approx \top}\ \text{ERES}}
{h\,(g\,(x''\,a \approx x'''\,a)) \not\approx h\,(g\,\top) \lor \bot \approx \top \lor x''\,b \approx x'''\,b}\ \text{EQHOIST}}
{h\,(g\,(a \approx x'''\,a)) \not\approx h\,(g\,\top) \lor \bot \approx \top \lor a \not\approx x'''\,b}\ \text{SUP}}
{h\,(g\,\top) \not\approx h\,(g\,\top) \lor \bot \approx \top \lor a \not\approx a}\ \text{BOOLRW}}
{\bot \approx \top \lor a \not\approx a}\ \text{ERES}}
{\bot \approx \top}\ \text{ERES}}
{\bot}\ \text{FALSEELIM}
$$

The FLUIDBOOLHOIST inference uses the unifier $\{y \mapsto \lambda u.\, z'\,u\,(x'\,u),\ z \mapsto \lambda u.\, z'\,b\,u,\ x \mapsto x'\,b\} \in \mathrm{CSU}(z\,x, y\,b)$. We apply ERES to the first literal of the resulting clause, with unifier $\{z' \mapsto \lambda uv.\, g\,v\} \in \mathrm{CSU}(h\,(z'\,b\,\bot), h\,(g\,\bot))$. Next, we apply EQHOIST with the unifier $\{x' \mapsto \lambda u.\, x''\,u \approx x'''\,u,\ w \mapsto x''\,b,\ w' \mapsto x'''\,b\} \in \mathrm{CSU}(x'\,b, w \approx w')$ to the literal created by FLUIDBOOLHOIST, effectively performing a primitive substitution. The resulting clause can superpose into a $\not\approx$ b with the unifier $\{x'' \mapsto \lambda u.\, u\} \in \mathrm{CSU}(x''\, \mathrm{b}, \mathrm{b})$. The two sides of the interpreted equality in the first literal can then be unified, allowing us to apply BOOLRW with the unifier $\{y \mapsto \mathrm{a}, \; x''' \mapsto \lambda u.\, \mathrm{a}\} \in \mathrm{CSU}(y \approx y, \mathrm{a} \approx x'''\, \mathrm{b})$. Finally, applying ERES twice and FALSEELIM once yields the empty clause.

Remarkably, none of the provers that participated in the CASC-J10 competition can solve this two-clause problem within a minute. Satallax finds a proof after 72 s and LEO-II after over 7 minutes. Our new Zipperposition implementation solves it in 3 s.

The Redundancy Criterion. In first-order superposition, a clause is considered redundant if all its ground instances are entailed by $\prec$-smaller ground instances of other clauses. In essence, this will also be our definition, but we will use a different notion of ground instances and a different notion of entailment.

Given a clause C, let its *ground instances* $\mathcal{G}(C)$ be the set of all clauses of the form $C\theta$ for some substitution θ such that $C\theta$ is ground and $\mathsf{Q}_\approx$-normal, and for all variables x occurring in C, the only Boolean green subterms of $x\theta$ are $\top$ and $\bot$. The rationale of this definition is to ensure that ground instances of the conclusion of FORALLHOIST, EXISTSHOIST, FORALLRW, and EXISTSRW inferences are smaller than the corresponding instances of their premise by property (O4).

The redundancy criterion's notion of entailment is defined via an encoding into a weaker logic, following λfSup and λSup. In this paper, the weaker logic is ground first-order logic with interpreted Booleans—the ground fragment of the logic of oSup. Its signature $(\Sigma_{\mathrm{ty}}, \Sigma_{\mathrm{GF}})$ is derived from our higher-order signature $(\Sigma_{\mathrm{ty}}, \Sigma)$ as follows. The type constructors Σ_{ty} are the same in both signatures, but $\to$ is an uninterpreted type constructor in first-order logic. For each ground instance $\mathsf{f}\langle \bar{\upsilon}\rangle : \tau_1 \to \cdots \to \tau_n \to \tau$ of a symbol $\mathsf{f} \in \Sigma$, we introduce a first-order symbol $\mathsf{f}_j^{\bar{\upsilon}} \in \Sigma_{\mathrm{GF}}$ with argument types $\bar{\tau}_j$ and result type $\tau_{j+1} \to \cdots \to \tau_n \to \tau$, for each j. Moreover, for each ground term $\lambda x.\, t$, we introduce a symbol $\mathrm{lam}_{\lambda x.\, t} \in \Sigma_{\mathrm{GF}}$ of the same type. The symbols $\bot_0, \top_0, \neg_1, \wedge_2, \vee_2, \to_2, \approx_2^\tau$, and $\not\approx_2^\tau$ are identified with the corresponding first-order logical symbols.

We define an encoding $\mathcal{F}$ of $\mathsf{Q}_\approx$-normal ground higher-order terms into this ground first-order logic recursively as follows: $\mathcal{F}(\forall\langle\tau\rangle\,(\lambda x.\, t)) = \forall x.\, \mathcal{F}(t)$ and $\mathcal{F}(\exists\langle\tau\rangle\,(\lambda x.\, t)) = \exists x.\, \mathcal{F}(t)$ for applied quantifiers; $\mathcal{F}(\lambda x.\, t) = \mathrm{lam}_{\lambda x.\, t}$ for λ-expressions; and $\mathcal{F}(\mathsf{f}\langle\bar{\upsilon}\rangle\,\bar{s}_j) = \mathsf{f}_j^{\bar{\upsilon}}(\mathcal{F}(\bar{s}_j))$ for other terms. For quantified variables, we define $\mathcal{F}(x) = x$. Here, $\mathsf{Q}_\approx$-normality is crucial to ensure that bound variables do not occur applied or within λ-expressions. The definition of green subterms is devised such that green subterms correspond to first-order subterms via the encoding $\mathcal{F}$, with the exception of first-order subterms below quantifiers. The encoding $\mathcal{F}$ is extended to clauses by mapping each literal and each side of a literal individually. From the entailment relation $\models$ for the ground first-order logic, we derive an entailment relation $\models_\mathcal{F}$ on $\mathsf{Q}_\approx$-normal ground higher-order clauses by defining $M \models_\mathcal{F} N$ if $\mathcal{F}(M) \models \mathcal{F}(N)$. This relation is weaker than standard higher-order entailment; for example, $\{\mathsf{f} \approx \mathsf{g}\} \not\models_\mathcal{F} \{\mathsf{f}\,\mathsf{a} \approx \mathsf{g}\,\mathsf{a}\}$ (because of the subscripts added by $\mathcal{F}$) and $\{\mathsf{p}\,(\lambda x.\, \top)\} \not\models_\mathcal{F} \{\mathsf{p}\,(\lambda x.\, \neg\,\bot)\}$ (because of the lam symbols used by $\mathcal{F}$).

Using $\models_\mathcal{F}$, we define a clause C to be *redundant* w.r.t. a clause set N if for every $D \in \mathcal{G}(C)$, we have $\{E \in \mathcal{G}(N) \mid E \prec D\} \models_\mathcal{F} D$ or there exists a clause $C' \in N$ such that $C \sqsupset C'$ and $D \in \mathcal{G}(C')$. The tiebreaker $\sqsupset$ can be an arbitrary well-founded partial order on clauses; in practice, we use a well-founded restriction of the ill-founded strict subsumption relation [6, Sect. 3.4]. We denote the set of redundant clauses w.r.t. a clause set N by $Red_C(N)$. Note that $\models_{\mathcal{F}}$ is weak enough to ensure that the ARGCONG inference rule and axiom (EXT) are not immediately redundant and can fulfill their purpose.

For first-order superposition, an inference is considered redundant if for each of its ground instances, a premise is redundant or the conclusion is entailed by clauses smaller than the main premise. For most inference rules, our definition follows this idea, using $\models_{\mathcal{F}}$ for entailment; other rules need nonstandard notions of ground instances and redundancy. The definition of inference redundancy presented below is simpler than the more sophisticated notion in our technical report. Nonetheless, the redundant inferences below are a strict subset of the redundant inferences of our report and thus completeness also holds using the notion below. For the few prover optimizations based on inference redundancy that we know about (e.g., simultaneous superposition [4]), the following criterion suffices.

For SUP, ERES, EFACT, BOOLHOIST, FALSEELIM, EQHOIST, NEQHOIST, and BOOLRW, we define ground instances as usual: *Ground instances* are all inferences obtained by applying a grounding substitution to premises and conclusion such that the result adheres to the conditions of the given rule w.r.t. selection functions that select literals and subterms as in the original premise. For FLUIDSUP and FLUIDBOOLHOIST, we define ground instances in the same way except that we require that ground instances adhere to the conditions of SUP or BOOLHOIST, respectively. For FORALLRW, EXISTSRW, FORALLHOIST, EXISTSHOIST, which do not have ground instances in the sense above, we define a *ground instance* as any inference that is obtained by applying the unifier σ to the premise and then applying a grounding substitution to premise and conclusion, regardless of whether the resulting inference is an inference of our calculus.

For all rules except FLUIDLOOBHOIST and ARGCONG, we define an inference to be *redundant* w.r.t. a clause set N if for each ground instance ι, a premise of ι is redundant w.r.t. $G(N)$ or the conclusion of ι is entailed w.r.t. $\models_{\mathcal{F}}$ by clauses from $G(N)$ that are smaller than the main (i.e., rightmost) premise of ι. For the rules FLUIDLOOB-HOIST and ARGCONG, as well as axioms (EXT) and (CHOICE)—viewed as premiseless inferences—we define an inference to be *redundant* w.r.t. a clause set N if all ground instances of its conclusion are contained in $G(N)$ or redundant w.r.t. $G(N)$. We denote the set of redundant inferences w.r.t. N by $Red_I(N)$.

Simplification Rules. Our redundancy criterion is strong enough to support counterparts of most simplification rules implemented in Schulz's first-order E [25, Sect. 2.3.1 and 2.3.2]. Deletion of duplicated literals, deletion of resolved literals, syntactic tautology deletion, negative simplify-reflect, and clause subsumption adhere to our redundancy criterion. Positive simplify-reflect, equality subsumption, and rewriting (demodulation) of positive and negative literals are supported if they are applied on green subterms or on other subterms that are encoded into first-order subterms by G and $\mathcal{F}$. Semantic tautology deletion can be applied as well, using $\models_{\mathcal{F}}$; moreover, for positive literals, the rewriting clause must be smaller than the rewritten clause.

Under some circumstances, inference rules can be applied as simplifications. The FALSEELIM and BOOLRW rules can be applied as a simplification if σ is the identity. If the head of u is $\forall$, FORALLHOIST and FORALLRW can both be applied and, together, serve as one simplification rule. The same holds for EXISTSHOIST and EXISTSRW if the head of u is $\exists$. For all of these rules, the eligibility conditions can be ignored.

Clausification. Like oSup, our calculus does not require the input problem to be clausified during the preprocessing, and it supports higher-order analogues of the three inprocessing clausification methods introduced by Nummelin et al. *Inner delayed clausification* relies on our core calculus rules to destruct logical symbols. *Outer delayed clausification* adds the following clausification rules to the calculus:

$$\frac{s \approx \top \vee C}{oc(s, C)} \text{PosOuterClaus} \qquad \frac{s \approx \bot \vee C}{oc(\neg s, C)} \text{NegOuterClaus}$$

$$\frac{s \approx t \vee C}{s \approx \bot \vee t \approx \top \vee C \quad s \approx \top \vee t \approx \bot \vee C} \text{EqOuterClaus}$$

$$\frac{s \not\approx t \vee C}{s \approx \bot \vee t \approx \bot \vee C \quad s \approx \top \vee t \approx \top \vee C} \text{NeqOuterClaus}$$

The double bars identify simplification rules (i.e., the conclusions make the premise redundant and can replace it). The first two rules require that s has a logical symbol as its head, whereas the last two require that s and t are Boolean terms other than $\top$ and $\bot$. The function oc distributes the logical symbols over the clause C—e.g., $oc(s \rightarrow t, C) = \{s \approx \bot \vee t \approx \top \vee C\}$, and $oc(\neg(s \vee t), C) = \{s \approx \bot \vee C, t \approx \bot \vee C\}$. It is easy to check that our redundancy criterion allows us to replace the premise of the OUTERCLAUS rules with their conclusion. Nonetheless, we apply EQOUTERCLAUS and NEQOUTERCLAUS as inferences because the premises might be useful in their original form.

Besides the two delayed clausification methods, a third inprocessing clausification method is *immediate* clausification. This clausifies the input problem's outer Boolean structure in one swoop, resulting in a set of higher-order clauses. If unclausified Boolean terms rise to the top during saturation, the same algorithm is run to clausify them.

Unlike delayed clausification, immediate clausification is a black box and is unaware of the proof state other than the Boolean term it is applied to. Delayed clausification, on the other hand, clausifies the term step by step, allowing us to interleave clausification with the strong simplification machinery of superposition provers. It is especially powerful in higher-order contexts: Examples such as $y\,p\,q \not\approx (p \vee q)$ can be refuted directly by equality resolution, rather than via more explosive rules on the clausified form.

4 Refutational Completeness

Our calculus is dynamically refutationally complete for problems in $Q_\approx$-normal form. The full proof can be found in our technical report [8].

Theorem 3 (Dynamic refutational completeness). *Let $(N_i)_i$ be a derivation—i.e., $N_i \setminus N_{i+1} \subseteq Red_C(N_{i+1})$ for all i. Let N_0 be $Q_\approx$-normal and such that $N_0 \models \bot$. Moreover, assume that $(N_i)_i$ is fair—i.e., all inferences from clauses in the limit inferior $\bigcup_i \bigcap_{j \geq i} N_j$ are contained in $\bigcup_i Red_I(N_i)$. Then we have $\bot \in N_i$ for some i.*

Following the completeness proof of λSup, our proof is structured in three levels of logics. For each, we define a calculus and show that it is refutationally complete: ground monomorphic first-order logic with an interpreted Boolean type (GF); the $Q_{\approx}$-normal ground fragment of higher-order logic (GH); and higher-order logic (H).

The logic of the GF level is the ground fragment of oSup's logic. The GF calculus is a ground version of oSup, which Nummelin et al. showed refutationally complete. It consists of ground first-order equivalents of our rules, excluding ARGCONG, FLUID-BOOLHOIST, and FLUIDLOOBHOIST, which are specific to higher-order logic. The counterparts to FORALLHOIST and EXISTSHOIST enumerate ground terms instead of producing free variables, to stay within the ground fragment. For compatibility with the nonground level, the conclusions of FORALLRW and EXISTSRW cannot contain concrete Skolem functions. Instead, the GF calculus is parameterized by a witness function that can assign an arbitrary term to each occurrence of a quantifier in a clause. This witness function is used to retrieve the Skolem terms in the GF equivalents of FORALLRW and EXISTSRW.

On the next level, the GH calculus includes inference rules isomorphic to the GF rules, transferred to higher-order logic via $\mathcal{F}^{-1}$. Moreover, it contains an ARGCONG variant that enumerates ground terms instead of introducing fresh variables, as well as rules enumerating ground instances of axioms (EXT) and (CHOICE). We prove refutational completeness of the GH calculus by constructing a higher-order interpretation based on the model constructed for the completeness proof of the GF level. This proof step is analogous to the corresponding step in λSup's proof, but we must also consider $Q_{\approx}$-normality and the logical symbols.

To lift completeness to the H level, we use the saturation framework of Waldmann et al. [31]. The main proof obligation it leaves us to show is that nonredundant GH inferences can be lifted to corresponding nonground H inferences. For this lifting, we must choose a suitable GH witness function and appropriate GH selection functions for literals and Boolean subterms, given a saturated clause set at the H level and the H selection functions. Then the saturation framework guarantees static refutational completeness w.r.t. Herbrand entailment, which is the entailment relation induced by the grounding function $\mathcal{G}$. We then show that this implies dynamic refutational completeness w.r.t. $\models$ for $Q_{\approx}$-normal initial clause sets.

5   Implementation

We implemented our calculus in the Zipperposition prover [14], whose OCaml source code makes it convenient to prototype calculus extensions. Except for the presence of axioms (EXT) and (CHOICE), the new code gracefully extends Zipperposition's implementation of oSup in the sense that oλSup coincides with oSup on first-order problems. The same cannot be said w.r.t. λSup on Boolean-free problems because of the FLUIDBOOLHOIST and FLUIDLOOBHOIST rules, which are triggered by any applied variable. From the implementation of λSup, we inherit the given clause procedure, which supports infinitely branching inferences, as well as calculus extensions and heuristics [28]. From the implementation of oSup, we inherit the simplification rule BOOLSIMP, a mainstay of our Boolean simplification machinery.

As in the implementation of λSup, we approximate fluid terms as terms that are either nonground λ-expressions or terms of the form $x\,\bar{s}_n$ with $n > 0$. Two slight, accidental discrepancies are that we also count variable occurrences below quantifiers as deep and perform EFACT inferences even if the maximal literal is selected. Since we expect FLUIDBOOLHOIST and FLUIDLOOBHOIST to be highly explosive, we penalize them and all of their offspring. In addition to various λSup extensions [6, Sect. 5], we also use all the rules for Boolean reasoning described by Vukmirović and Nummelin [30] except for the BOOLEF rules.

6 Evaluation

We evaluate the calculus implementation in Zipperposition and compare it with other higher-order provers. Our experiments were performed on StarExec Miami servers equipped with Intel Xeon E5-2620 v4 CPUs clocked at 2.10 GHz. We used all 2606 TH0 theorems from the TPTP 7.3.0 library [27] and 1253 "Judgment Day" problems [12] generated using Sledgehammer (SH) [24] as our benchmark set. An archive containing the benchmarks and the raw evaluation results is publicly available [5].

Calculus Evaluation. In this first part, we evaluate selected parameters of Zipperposition by varying only the studied parameter in a fixed well-performing configuration. This base configuration disables axioms (CHOICE) and (EXT) and the FLUID- rules. It uses the unification procedure of Vukmirović et al. [29] in its complete variant—i.e., the variant that produces a complete set of unifiers. It uses none of the early Boolean rules described by Vukmirović and Nummelin [30]. The preprocessor $Q_\approx$ is disabled as well. All of the completeness-preserving simplification rules listed in Sect. 3 are enabled. The configuration uses immediate clausification. We set the CPU time limit to 30 s in all three experiments.

In the first experiment, we assess the overhead incurred by the FLUID- rules. These rules unify with a term whose head is a fresh variable. Thus, we expected that they needed to be tightly controlled to achieve good performance. To test our hypothesis, we simultaneously modified the parameters of these three rules. In Figure 1, the *off* mode simply disables the rules, the *pragmatic* mode uses a terminating incomplete unification algorithm (the pragmatic variant of Vukmirović et al. [29]), and the *complete* mode uses a complete unification algorithm. The results show that disabling FLUID-rules altogether achieves the best performance. However, on TPTP problems, *complete* finds 35 proofs not found by *off*, and *pragmatic* finds 22 proofs not found by *off*. On Sledgehammer benchmarks, this effect is much weaker, likely because the Sledgehammer benchmarks require less higher-order reasoning: *complete* finds only one new proof over *off*, and *pragmatic* finds only four.

In the second experiment, we explore the clausification methods introduced at the end of Sect. 3: *inner* delayed clausification, *outer* delayed clausification, and *immediate* clausification. The modes *inner* and *outer* employ oSup's RENAME rule, which renames Boolean terms headed by logical symbols using a Tseitin-like transformation if they occur at least four times in the proof state. Vukmirović and Nummelin [30] observed that *outer* clausification can greatly help prove higher-order problems, and we expected

	off	*pragmatic*	*complete*
TPTP	**1642**	1591	1619
SH	**467**	431	437

Fig. 1. Evaluation of FLUID- rules

	inner	*outer*	*immediate*
TPTP	1323	**1670**	1642
SH	406	**470**	467

Fig. 2. Evaluation of clausification method

	off	$p = 64$	$p = 16$	$p = 4$	$p = 1$
TPTP	**1642**	1617	1613	1615	1594
SH	**467**	458	458	459	445

Fig. 3. Evaluation of axiom (CHOICE)

	TPTP	ofSH	SH
CVC4 1.8	1796	680	619
Leo-III 1.5.2	2104	681	621
Vampire 4.5	2131	692	681
Satallax 3.5	2162	573	587
Zip (CASC-J10)	2301	**734**	**736**
New Zip	**2320**	724	720

Fig. 4. Evaluation of all competitive higher-order provers

it to perform well for our calculus, too. The results are shown in Figure 2. The results confirm our hypothesis: The *outer* mode outperforms *immediate* on both TPTP and Sledgehammer benchmarks. The *inner* mode performs worst, but on Sledgehammer benchmarks, it proves 17 problems beyond the reach of the other two. Interestingly, several of these problems contain axioms of the form $\phi \to \psi$, and applying superposition and demodulation to these axioms is preferable to clausifying them.

In the third experiment, we investigate the effect of axiom (CHOICE), which is necessary to achieve refutational completeness. To evaluate (CHOICE), we either disabled it in a configuration labeled *off* or set the axiom's penalty p to different values. In Zipperposition, penalties are propagated through inference and simplification rules and are used to increase the heuristic weight of clauses, postponing the selection of penalized clauses. The results are shown in Figure 3. As expected, disabling (CHOICE), or at least penalizing it heavily, improves performance. Yet enabling (CHOICE) can be crucial: For 19 TPTP problems, the proofs are found when (CHOICE) is enabled and $p = 4$, but not when the rule is disabled. On Sledgehammer problems, this effect is weaker, with only two new problems proved for $p = 4$.

Prover Comparison. In this second part, we compare Zipperposition's performance with other higher-order provers. Like at CASC-J10, the wall-clock time limit was 120 s, the CPU time limit was 960 s, and the provers were run on StarExec Miami. We used the following versions of all systems that took part in the THF division: CVC4 1.8 [3], Leo-III 1.5.2 [26], Satallax 3.5 [13], and Vampire 4.5 [11]. The developers of Vampire have informed us that its higher-order schedule is optimized for running on a single core. As a result, the prover suffers some degradation of performance when running on multiple cores. We evaluate both the version of Zipperposition that took part in CASC-J10 (*Zip*) and the updated version of Zipperposition that supports our new calculus (*New Zip*). Zip's portfolio of prover configurations is based on λSup and techniques described by Vukmirović and Nummelin [30]. New Zip's portfolio is specially designed for our new calculus and optimized for TPTP problems. To assess the performance of Boolean reasoning, we used Sledgehammer benchmarks generated both with native Booleans (SH) and with an encoding into Boolean-free higher-order logic (ofSH). For technical reasons, the encoding also performs λ-lifting, but this minor transformation should have little impact on results [6, Sect. 7].

The results are shown in Figure 4. The two versions of Zipperposition are ahead of all other provers on both benchmark sets. This shows that, with thorough parameter tuning, higher-order superposition outperforms tableaux, which had been the state of the art in higher-order reasoning for a decade. The updated version of New Zip beats Zip on TPTP problems but lags behind Zip on Sledgehammer benchmarks as we have yet to further explore more general heuristics that work well with our new calculus. The Sledgehammer benchmarks fail to demonstrate the superiority of native Booleans reasoning compared with an encoding, and in fact CVC4 and Leo-III perform dramatically better on the encoded Boolean problems, suggesting that there is room for tuning.

7 Conclusion

We have created a superposition calculus for higher-order logic that is refutationally complete. Most of the key ideas have been developed in previous work by us and colleagues, but combining them in the right way has been challenging. A key idea was to $Q_{\approx}$-normalize away inconvenient terms.

Unlike earlier refutationally complete calculi for full higher-order logic based on resolution or paramodulation, our calculus employs a term order, which restricts the proof search, and a redundancy criterion, which can be used to add various simplification rules while keeping refutational completeness. These two mechanisms are undoubtedly major factors in the success of first-order superposition, and it is very fortunate that we could incorporate both in a higher-order calculus. An alternative calculus with the same two mechanisms could be achieved by combining oSup with Bhayat and Reger's combinatory superposition [10]. The article on λSup [6, Sect. 8] discusses related work in more detail.

The evaluation results show that our calculus is an excellent basis for higher-order theorem proving. In future work, we want to experiment further with the different parameters of the calculus (for example, with Boolean subterm selection heuristics) and implement it in a state-of-the-art prover such as E.

Acknowledgment. Uwe Waldmann provided advice and carefully checked the completeness proof. Visa Nummelin led the design of the oSup calculus. Simon Cruanes helped us with the implementation. Martin Desharnais generated the Sledgehammer benchmarks. Christoph Benzmüller, Ahmed Bhayat, Mathias Fleury, Herman Geuvers, Giles Reger, Alexander Steen, Mark Summerfield, Geoff Sutcliffe, and the anonymous reviewers helped us in various ways. We thank them all.

Bentkamp, Blanchette, and Vukmirović's research has received funding from the European Research Council (ERC) under the European Union's Horizon 2020 research and innovation program (grant agreement No. 713999, Matryoshka). Blanchette's research has received funding from the Netherlands Organization for Scientific Research (NWO) under the Vidi program (project No. 016.Vidi.189.037, Lean Forward).

References

[1] Andrews, P.B.: On connections and higher-order logic. J. Autom. Reason. **5**(3), 257–291 (1989)

[2] Bachmair, L., Ganzinger, H.: Rewrite-based equational theorem proving with selection and simplification. J. Log. Comput. **4**(3), 217–247 (1994)

[3] Barrett, C.W., Conway, C.L., Deters, M., Hadarean, L., Jovanovic, D., King, T., Reynolds, A., Tinelli, C.: CVC4. In: CAV. LNCS, vol. 6806, pp. 171–177. Springer (2011)

[4] Benanav, D.: Simultaneous paramodulation. In: Stickel, M.E. (ed.) CADE-10. LNCS, vol. 449, pp. 442–455. Springer (1990)

[5] Bentkamp, A., Blanchette, J., Tourret, S., Vukmirović, P.: Superposition for full higher-order logic (supplementary material), https://doi.org/10.5281/zenodo.4534759

[6] Bentkamp, A., Blanchette, J., Tourret, S., Vukmirović, P., Waldmann, U.: Superposition with lambdas, accepted in J. Autom. Reason. Preprint at https://arxiv.org/abs/2102.00453v1 (2021)

[7] Bentkamp, A., Blanchette, J.C., Cruanes, S., Waldmann, U.: Superposition for lambda-free higher-order logic. In: Galmiche, D., Schulz, S., Sebastiani, R. (eds.) IJCAR 2018. LNCS, vol. 10900, pp. 28–46. Springer (2018)

[8] Bentkamp, A., Blanchette, J.C., Tourret, S., Vukmirović, P.: Superposition for full higher-order logic (technical report). Technical report (2021), https://matryoshka-project.github.io/pubs/hosup_report.pdf

[9] Benzmüller, C., Paulson, L.C., Theiss, F., Fietzke, A.: LEO-II—A cooperative automatic theorem prover for higher-order logic. In: Armando, A., Baumgartner, P., Dowek, G. (eds.) IJCAR 2008. LNCS, vol. 5195, pp. 162–170. Springer (2008)

[10] Bhayat, A., Reger, G.: Set of support for higher-order reasoning. In: Konev, B., Urban, J., Rümmer, P. (eds.) PAAR-2018. CEUR Workshop Proceedings, vol. 2162, pp. 2–16. CEUR-WS.org (2018)

[11] Bhayat, A., Reger, G.: A combinator-based superposition calculus for higher-order logic. In: Peltier, N., Sofronie-Stokkermans, V. (eds.) IJCAR 2020, Part I. LNCS, vol. 12166, pp. 278–296. Springer (2020)

[12] Böhme, S., Nipkow, T.: Sledgehammer: Judgement Day. In: Giesl, J., Hähnle, R. (eds.) IJCAR 2010. LNCS, vol. 6173, pp. 107–121. Springer (2010)

[13] Brown, C.E.: Satallax: An automatic higher-order prover. In: Gramlich, B., Miller, D., Sattler, U. (eds.) IJCAR 2012. LNCS, vol. 7364, pp. 111–117. Springer (2012)

[14] Cruanes, S.: Extending Superposition with Integer Arithmetic, Structural Induction, and Beyond. Ph.D. thesis, École polytechnique (2015)

[15] Fitting, M.: Types, Tableaus, and Gödel's God. Kluwer (2002)

[16] Ganzinger, H., Stuber, J.: Superposition with equivalence reasoning and delayed clause normal form transformation. Information and Computation **199**(1–2), 3–23 (2005)

[17] Gordon, M.J.C., Melham, T.F. (eds.): Introduction to HOL: A Theorem Proving Environment for Higher Order Logic. Cambridge University Press (1993)

[18] Huet, G.P.: A mechanization of type theory. In: Nilsson, N.J. (ed.) IJCAI-73. pp. 139–146. William Kaufmann (1973)

[19] Jensen, D.C., Pietrzykowski, T.: Mechanizing ω-order type theory through unification. Theor. Comput. Sci. **3**(2), 123–171 (1976)

[20] Kaliszyk, C., Sutcliffe, G., Rabe, F.: TH1: The TPTP typed higher-order form with rank-1 polymorphism. In: Fontaine, P., Schulz, S., Urban, J. (eds.) PAAR-2016. CEUR Workshop Proceedings, vol. 1635, pp. 41–55. CEUR-WS.org (2016)

[21] Kotelnikov, E., Kovács, L., Suda, M., Voronkov, A.: A clausal normal form translation for FOOL. In: Benzmüller, C., Sutcliffe, G., Rojas, R. (eds.) GCAI 2016. EPiC, vol. 41, pp. 53–71. EasyChair (2016)

[22] Ludwig, M., Waldmann, U.: An extension of the Knuth-Bendix ordering with LPO-like properties. In: Dershowitz, N., Voronkov, A. (eds.) LPAR-14. LNCS, vol. 4790, pp. 348–362. Springer (2007)

[23] Nummelin, V., Bentkamp, A., Tourret, S., Vukmirović, P.: Superposition with first-class Booleans and inprocessing clausification. In: Platzer, A., Sutcliffe, G. (eds.) CADE-28. LNCS, Springer (2021)

[24] Paulson, L.C., Blanchette, J.C.: Three years of experience with Sledgehammer, a practical link between automatic and interactive theorem provers. In: Sutcliffe, G., Schulz, S., Ternovska, E. (eds.) IWIL-2010. EPiC, vol. 2, pp. 1–11. EasyChair (2012)

[25] Schulz, S.: E - a brainiac theorem prover. AI Commun. **15**(2-3), 111–126 (2002)

[26] Steen, A., Benzmüller, C.: The higher-order prover Leo-III. In: Galmiche, D., Schulz, S., Sebastiani, R. (eds.) IJCAR 2018. LNCS, vol. 10900, pp. 108–116. Springer (2018)

[27] Sutcliffe, G.: The TPTP problem library and associated infrastructure—from CNF to TH0, TPTP v6.4.0. J. Autom. Reason. **59**(4), 483–502 (2017)

[28] Vukmirović, P., Bentkamp, A., Blanchette, J., Cruanes, S., Nummelin, V., Tourret, S.: Making higher-order superposition work. In: Platzer, A., Sutcliffe, G. (eds.) CADE-28. LNCS, Springer (2021)

[29] Vukmirović, P., Bentkamp, A., Nummelin, V.: Efficient full higher-order unification. In: Ariola, Z.M. (ed.) FSCD 2020. LIPIcs, vol. 167, pp. 5:1–5:17. Schloss Dagstuhl—Leibniz-Zentrum für Informatik (2020)

[30] Vukmirović, P., Nummelin, V.: Boolean reasoning in a higher-order superposition prover. In: PAAR-2020. CEUR Workshop Proceedings, vol. 2752, pp. 148–166. CEUR-WS.org (2020)

[31] Waldmann, U., Tourret, S., Robillard, S., Blanchette, J.: A comprehensive framework for saturation theorem proving. In: Peltier, N., Sofronie-Stokkermans, V. (eds.) IJCAR 2020, Part I. LNCS, vol. 12166, pp. 316–334. Springer (2020)

Open Access This chapter is licensed under the terms of the Creative Commons Attribution 4.0 International License (http://creativecommons.org/licenses/by/4.0/), which permits use, sharing, adaptation, distribution and reproduction in any medium or format, as long as you give appropriate credit to the original author(s) and the source, provide a link to the Creative Commons license and indicate if changes were made.

The images or other third party material in this chapter are included in the chapter's Creative Commons license, unless indicated otherwise in a credit line to the material. If material is not included in the chapter's Creative Commons license and your intended use is not permitted by statutory regulation or exceeds the permitted use, you will need to obtain permission directly from the copyright holder.

Implementation and Application

Making Higher-Order Superposition Work

Petar Vukmirović[1], Alexander Bentkamp[1], Jasmin Blanchette[1,2,3],
Simon Cruanes[4], Visa Nummelin[1], and Sophie Tourret[2,3]

[1] Vrije Universiteit Amsterdam, Amsterdam, the Netherlands
{p.vukmirovic,a.bentkamp,j.c.blanchette,visa.nummelin}@vu.nl
[2] Université de Lorraine, CNRS, Inria, LORIA, Nancy, France
sophie.tourret@inria.fr
[3] Max-Planck-Institut für Informatik, Saarbrücken, Germany
[4] Aesthetic Integration, Austin, Texas, USA
simon@imandra.ai

Abstract. Superposition is among the most successful calculi for first-order logic. Its extension to higher-order logic introduces new challenges such as infinitely branching inference rules, new possibilities such as reasoning about formulas, and the need to curb the explosion of specific higher-order rules. We describe techniques that address these issues and extensively evaluate their implementation in the Zipperposition theorem prover. Largely thanks to their use, Zipperposition won the higher-order division of the CASC-J10 competition.

1 Introduction

In recent decades, superposition-based first-order automatic theorem provers have emerged as useful reasoning tools. They dominate at the annual CASC [45] theorem prover competitions, having always won the first-order theorem division. They are also used as backends to proof assistants [13, 25, 35], automatic higher-order theorem provers [42], and software verifiers [17]. The superposition calculus has only recently been extended to higher-order logic, resulting in λ-*superposition* [6], which we developed together with Waldmann, as well as *combinatory superposition* [10] by Bhayat and Reger.

Both higher-order superposition calculi were designed to gracefully extend first-order reasoning. As most steps in higher-order proofs tend to be essentially first-order, extending the most successful first-order calculus to higher-order logic seemed worth trying. Our first attempt at corroborating this conjecture was in 2019: Zipperposition 1.5, based on λ-superposition, finished third in the higher-order theorem division of CASC-27 [47], 12 percentage points behind the winner, the tableau prover Satallax 3.4 [11].

Studying the competition results, we discovered that higher-order tableaux have some advantages over higher-order superposition. To bridge the gap, we developed techniques and heuristics that simulate the behavior of a tableau prover in the context of saturation. We implemented them in Zipperposition 2, which took part in CASC-J10 in 2020. This time, Zipperposition won the division,

© The Author(s) 2021
A. Platzer and G. Sutcliffe (Eds.): CADE 2021, LNAI 12699, pp. 415–432, 2021.
https://doi.org/10.1007/978-3-030-79876-5_24

solving 84% of problems, a whole 20 percentage points ahead of the next best prover, Satallax 3.4. In this paper, we describe the main techniques that explain this reversal of fortunes. They range from preprocessing to backend integration.

Interesting patterns can be observed in various higher-order encodings of problems. We show how we can exploit these to simplify problems (Sect. 3). By working on formulas rather than clauses, tableau techniques take a more holistic view of a higher-order problem. Delaying the clausification through the use of calculus rules that act on formulas achieves the same effect in superposition. We further explore the benefits of this approach (Sect. 4).

The main drawback of λ-superposition compared with combinatory superposition is that it relies on rules that enumerate possibly infinite sets of unifiers. We describe a mechanism that interleaves performing infinitely branching inferences with the standard saturation process (Sect. 5). The prover retains the same behavior as before on first-order problems, smoothly scaling with increasing numbers of higher-order clauses. We also propose some heuristics to curb the explosion induced by highly prolific λ-superposition rules (Sect. 6).

Using first-order backends to finish the proof is common practice in higher-order reasoning. Since λ-superposition coincides with standard superposition on first-order clauses, invoking backends may seem redundant; yet Zipperposition is nowhere as efficient as E [38] or Vampire [28], so invoking a more efficient backend does make sense. We describe how to achieve a balance between allowing native higher-order reasoning and delegating reasoning to a backend (Sect. 7).

Finally, we compare Zipperposition 2 with other provers on all monomorphic higher-order TPTP benchmarks [46] to perform a more extensive evaluation than at CASC (Sect. 8). Our evaluation corroborates the competition results.

2   Background and Setting

We focus on monomorphic higher-order logic, but the techniques can easily be extended with polymorphism. Indeed, Zipperposition already supports some techniques polymorphically.

Higher-Order Logic. We define terms s, t, u, v inductively as free variables F, X, bound variables $x, y, z, \ldots$, constants $\mathsf{f}, \mathsf{g}, \mathsf{a}, \mathsf{b}, \ldots$, applications $s\,t$, and λ-abstractions $\lambda x.\,s$. The syntactic distinction between free and bound variables gives rise to *loose bound variables* (e.g., y in $\lambda x.\,y\,\mathsf{a}$) [32]. We let $s\,\overline{t}_n$ stand for $s\,t_1 \ldots t_n$ and $\lambda \overline{x}_n.\,s$ for $\lambda x_1 \ldots \lambda x_n.\,s$. Every β-normal term can be written as $\lambda \overline{x}_m.\,s\,\overline{t}_n$, where s is not an application; we call s the *head* of the term. If the type of a term t is of the form $\tau_1 \to \cdots \to \tau_n \to o$, where o is the distinguished Boolean type and $n \geq 0$, we call t a *predicate*. A literal l is an equation $s \approx t$ or a disequation $s \not\approx t$. A clause is a finite multiset of literals, interpreted and written disjunctively $l_1 \vee \cdots \vee l_n$. Logical symbols that may occur within terms are written in boldface: $\neg, \wedge, \vee, \to, \leftrightarrow, \ldots$. Predicate literals are encoded as (dis)equations with T based on their sign; for example, $\mathsf{even}(x)$ becomes $\mathsf{even}(x) \approx \mathsf{T}$, and $\neg\,\mathsf{even}(x)$ becomes $\mathsf{even}(x) \not\approx \mathsf{T}$.

Higher-Order Calculi. The λ-superposition calculus is a refutationally complete inference system and redundancy criterion for Boolean-free extensional polymorphic clausal higher-order logic. The calculus relies on *complete sets of unifiers* (*CSUs*). The CSU for s and t with respect to a set of variables V, denoted by $\mathrm{CSU}_V(s, t)$, is a set of unifiers such that for any unifier ϱ of s and t, there exist substitutions $\sigma \in \mathrm{CSU}_V(s, t)$ and θ such that $\varrho(X) = \sigma(\theta(X))$ for all variables $X \in V$. The set X is used to distinguish between important and auxiliary variables. We usually omit it. A pragmatic, incomplete extension of λ-superposition with interpreted Booleans is described by Vukmirović and Nummelin [51]. This forms the basis of most of this work. Recently, a refutationally complete extension was developed by Bentkamp et al. [5]; it is not considered here.

By contrast, the combinatory superposition calculus avoids CSUs by using a form of first-order unification, but essentially it enumerates higher-order terms using rules that instantiate applied variables with partially applied combinators from the complete combinator set $\{\mathsf{S}, \mathsf{K}, \mathsf{B}, \mathsf{C}, \mathsf{I}\}$. This calculus is the basis of Vampire 4.5 [10], which finished closely behind Satallax 3.4 at CASC-J10.

A different, very successful calculus is Satallax's SAT-guided tableaux [2]. Satallax was the leading higher-order prover of the 2010s. Its simple and elegant tableaux avoid deep superposition-style rewriting inferences. Nevertheless, our working hypothesis for the past six years has been that superposition would likely provide a stronger basis for higher-order reasoning. Other competing higher-order calculi include SMT (implemented in CVC4 [3, 4]) and extensional paramodulation (implemented in Leo-III [42]).

Zipperposition. Zipperposition [6, 12] is a higher-order theorem prover based on a pragmatic extension of λ-superposition. It was conceived as a testbed for rapidly experimenting with extensions of first-order superposition, but over time, it has assimilated many of E's techniques and heuristics. Zipperposition 2 also implements combinatory superposition.

Several of our techniques extend the *given clause procedure* [30, Section 2.3], the standard saturation procedure. It partitions the proof state into a set P of *passive* clauses and a set A of *active* clauses. Initially, P contains all input clauses, and A is empty. At each iteration, a *given* clause C from P is moved to A (i.e., it is *activated*), all inferences between C and clauses in A are performed, and the conclusions are added to P. Because Zipperposition fully simplifies clauses only when they are activated, it implements a DISCOUNT-style loop [14].

Experimental Setup. To assess our techniques, we carried out experiments with Zipperposition 2. We used all 2606 monomorphic higher-order problems from the TPTP library [46], version 7.2.0, as benchmarks. Although some techniques support polymorphism, we uniformly used the monomorphic benchmarks. We fixed a *base* configuration of Zipperposition parameters as a baseline for all comparisons. Then, in each experiment, we varied the parameters associated with a specific technique to evaluate it. The experiments were run on StarExec [43] servers, equipped with Intel Xeon E5-2609 CPUs clocked at 2.40 GHz. Unless otherwise stated, we used a CPU time limit of 20 s, roughly the time each configuration is given in the portfolio mode used for CASC. The raw evaluation results are available online.[5]

3   Preprocessing Higher-Order Problems

The TPTP library contains thousands of higher-order problems. Despite their diversity, they have a markedly different flavor from the TPTP first-order problems. Notably, they extensively use the `definition` role to identify universally quantified equations (or equivalences) that define symbols.

Definitions can be replaced by rewrite rules, using the orientation given in the input problem. If there are multiple definitions for the same symbol, only the first one is replaced by a rewrite rule. Then, whenever a clause is picked in the given clause procedure, it will be rewritten using the collected rules. Since the TPTP format enforces no constraints on definitions, rewriting might diverge. To ensure termination, we limit the number of applied rewrite steps. In practice, most TPTP problems are well behaved: Only one definition is given for each symbol, and the definitions are acyclic. Instead of rewriting a clause when it is activated, we can rewrite the input formulas as a preprocessing step. This ensures that the input clauses will be fully simplified when the proving process starts and no defined symbols will occur in clauses, which usually helps the heuristics.

Eagerly unfolding the definitions and β-reducing can eliminate all of a problem's higher-order features, making it amendable to first-order methods. However, this can inflate the problem beyond recognition and compromise the refutational completeness of superposition.

To keep completeness, we can try to orient the definitions using the term order that parameterized superposition and rely on demodulation to simplify the proof state. Usually, the Knuth–Bendix order (KBO) [26] is used. It compares terms by first comparing their weights, which is the sum of all the weights assigned to the symbols it contains. Given a symbol weight assignment $\mathcal{W}$, we can update it so that it orients acyclic definitions from left to right assuming that they are of the form $f\,\overline{X}_m \approx \lambda \overline{y}_n.\,t$, where the only free variables in t are $\overline{X}_m$, no free variable repeats or appears applied in t, and f does not occur in t. Then we traverse the symbols f that are defined by such equations following the dependency relation, starting with a symbol f that does not depend on any other defined symbol. For each f, we set $\mathcal{W}(f)$ to $w + 1$, where w is the maximum weight of the right-hand sides of f's definitions, computed using $\mathcal{W}$. By construction, for each equation the left-hand side is heavier. Thus, the equations are orientable from left to right.

Evaluation and Discussion. The *base* configuration treats axioms annotated with `definition` as rewrite rules, and it preprocesses the formulas using the rewrite rules. We also tested the effects of disabling this preprocessing (−preprocess), disabling the special treatment of `definition` axioms (−RW), and disabling the special treatment of `definition` while using adjusted KBO

---

[5] https://doi.org/10.5281/zenodo.4534829

base	−preprocess	−RW	−RW+KBO
1638	1627	1303	1324

Fig. 1: Effect of the definition rewriting methods

	+LA	−LA
IC	1624	1638
DCI	1496	1531
DCS	1659	**1710**

Fig. 2: Effect of clausification and lightweight AVATAR

weights as described above (−RW+KBO). The results are given in Figure 1. In all of the figures in this paper, each cell gives the number of proved problems; the highest number is typeset in bold. Clearly, treating `definition` axioms as rewrite rules greatly improves performance. Using adjusted KBO weights is not as strong, although it proves 15 problems not proved using other configurations.

4   Reasoning about Formulas

Higher-order logic identifies terms and formulas. To prove a problem, we often need to instantiate a variable with the right predicate. Finding this predicate can be easier if the problem is not clausified. Consider the conjecture $\exists f.\, f\, \mathsf{p}\, \mathsf{q} \leftrightarrow \mathsf{p} \wedge \mathsf{q}$. Expressed in this form, the formula is easy to prove by taking $f := \lambda x\, y.\, x \wedge y$. By contrast, guessing the right instantiation for the negated, clausified form $F\, \mathsf{p}\, \mathsf{q} \not\approx \mathsf{T} \vee \mathsf{p} \not\approx \mathsf{T} \vee \mathsf{q} \not\approx \mathsf{T}, F\, \mathsf{p}\, \mathsf{q} \approx \mathsf{T} \vee \mathsf{p} \approx \mathsf{T},\, F\, \mathsf{p}\, \mathsf{q} \approx \mathsf{T} \vee \mathsf{q} \approx \mathsf{T}$ is more challenging. One of the strengths of higher-order tableau provers is that they do not clausify the input problem. This might explain Satallax's dominance in the THF division of CASC competitions until CASC-J10.

We studied techniques to incrementally clausify formulas during proof search in incomplete [51] and complete [5] extensions of λ-superposition. Both approaches include the same set of (*outer*) *delayed clausification rules* that clausify top-level logical symbols, proceeding outside in; for example, a clause $C' \vee (\mathsf{p} \wedge \mathsf{q}) \not\approx \mathsf{T}$ is transformed into $C' \vee \mathsf{p} \not\approx \mathsf{T} \vee \mathsf{q} \not\approx \mathsf{T}$. The complete approach requires additional inference rules; it also supports *inner* delayed clausification. We focus on the pragmatic, incomplete approach and do not consider inner clausification due to its poor performance [5].

Delayed clausification rules can be used as inference rules (which add conclusions to the passive set) or as simplification rules (which delete premises and add conclusions to the passive set). Inferences are more flexible because they produce all intermediate clausification states, whereas simplifications produce fewer clauses. Since clausifying equivalences can destroy a lot of syntactic structure [18], we never apply simplifying clausification rules on them.

We discuss two tableau-inspired approaches for reasoning about formulas. First, we study how clause-splitting techniques interfere with delayed clausification. Second, we discuss heuristic instantiation of quantifiers during saturation.

Zipperposition supports a lightweight variant of AVATAR [49], an architecture that partitions the search space by splitting clauses into variable-disjoint subclauses. This variant of AVATAR is described by Ebner et al. [15]. Combining lightweight AVATAR and delayed clausification makes it possible to split a clause $(\varphi_1 \vee \cdots \vee \varphi_n) \approx \mathsf{T}$, where the φ_i's are arbitrarily complex formulas that share no free variables with each other, into clauses $\varphi_i \approx \mathsf{T}$.

To finish the proof, it suffices to derive $\perp$ under each assumption $\varphi_i \approx \mathsf{T}$. Since the split is performed at the formula level, this technique resembles tableaux, but it exploits the strengths of superposition, such as its powerful redundancy criterion and simplification machinery, to close the branches.

Interleaving clausification and saturation allows us to simulate another tableau technique. Whenever dynamic clausification replaces the predicate variable x in a clause of the form $(\forall x.\,\varphi) \approx \mathsf{T} \vee C$ with a fresh variable X, resulting in $\varphi\{x \mapsto X\} \approx \mathsf{T} \vee C$, we can create additional clauses in which x is replaced with $t \in \mathit{Inst}$, where Inst is a set of heuristically chosen terms. This set contains λ-abstractions whose bodies are formulas and which occur in activated clauses, and *primitive instantiations* [51]—that is, imitations (in the sense of higher-order unification) of logical symbols that approximate the shape of a predicate that can instantiate a predicate variable.

However, as a new term t can be added to Inst after a clause with a quantified variable of the same type as t has been activated, we must also keep track of the clauses $\varphi\{x \mapsto X\} \approx \mathsf{T} \vee C$, so that when Inst is extended, we instantiate the saved clauses. Conveniently, instantiated clauses are not recognized as subsumed, since Zipperposition uses an optimized but incomplete subsumption algorithm.

Given a disequation $\mathsf{f}\,\bar{s}_n \not\approx \mathsf{f}\,\bar{t}_n$, the *abstraction* of s_i is $\lambda x.\, u \approx v$, where u is obtained by replacing s_i with x in $\mathsf{f}\,\bar{s}_n$ and v is obtained by replacing s_i with x in $\mathsf{f}\,\bar{t}_n$. For $\mathsf{f}\,\bar{s}_n \approx \mathsf{f}\,\bar{t}_n$, the analogous abstraction is $\lambda x.\,\neg\,(u \approx v)$.

Adding abstractions of the conjecture literals to Inst can provide useful instantiations for formulas such as induction principles for datatypes. As the conjecture is negated, the equation's polarity is inverted in the abstraction. Consider the TPTP problem DAT056^2 [44], whose clausified negated conjecture is $\mathsf{ap\,xs\,(ap\,ys\,zs)} \not\approx \mathsf{ap\,(ap\,xs\,ys)\,zs}$, where ap is the append operator defined recursively on its first argument and xs, ys, and zs are of list type. Abstracting xs from the disequation yields $t = \lambda x.\,\mathsf{ap}\,x\,(\mathsf{ap\,ys\,zs}) \approx \mathsf{ap\,(ap}\,x\,\mathsf{ys)\,zs}$, which is added to Inst. Included in the problem is the induction axiom for the list datatype: $\forall p.\,(p\,\mathsf{nil} \wedge (\forall x\,xs.\,p\,xs \to p\,(\mathsf{cons}\,x\,xs))) \to \forall xs.\,p\,xs$, where nil and cons have the usual meanings. Instantiating p with t and using the ap definition, we can prove $\forall x.\,\mathsf{ap}\,x\,(\mathsf{ap\,ys\,zs}) \approx \mathsf{ap\,(ap}\,x\,\mathsf{ys)\,zs}$, from which we easily derive a contradiction.

Evaluation and Discussion. The base configuration uses *immediate clausification* (IC), an approach that applies a standard clausification algorithm [33] both as a preprocessing step and whenever predicate variables are instantiated. Zipperposition's lightweight AVATAR is disabled in the base configuration. To test the merits of delayed clausification, we vary *base*'s parameters along two axes: We choose immediate clausification (IC), delayed clausification as inference (DCI), or delayed clausification as simplification (DCS), and we either enable (+LA) or disable (−LA) the lightweight AVATAR. The base configuration does not use instantiation with terms from Inst.

Figure 2 shows that using delayed clausification as simplification greatly increases the success rate, while using delayed clausification as inference has the opposite effect. Manually inspecting the proofs found by the DCS configuration, we noticed that a main reason for its success is that it does not simplify away equivalences. Overall, the lightweight AVATAR harms performance, but the sets of problems proved with and without it are vastly different. For example, the IC+LA configuration proves 60 problems not proved by IC−LA.

The Boolean instantiation technique presented above requires delayed clausification. To test its effects, we enabled it in the best configuration from Figure 2, DCS−LA. With this change, Zipperposition proves 1744 problems, 36 of which cannot be proved by any other configuration in the same figure. Boolean instantiation is the only way in which Zipperposition 2 can prove higher-order problems requiring reasoning about induction axioms (e.g., DAT056^2).

5   Enumerating Infinitely Branching Inferences

As an optimization and to simplify the implementation, Leo-III [40] and Vampire 4.4 [9] (which uses a predecessor of combinatory superposition) compute only a finite subset of the possible conclusions for inferences that require enumerating a CSU. Not only is this a source of incompleteness, but choosing the cardinality of the computed subset is a difficult heuristic choice. Small sets can result in missing the unifier necessary for the proof, whereas large sets make the prover spend a long time in the unification procedure, generate useless clauses, and possibly get sidetracked into the wrong parts of the search space.

We propose a modification to the given clause procedure to seamlessly interleave unifier computation and proof state exploration. Given a complete unification procedure, which may yield infinite streams of unifiers, our modification fairly enumerates all conclusions of inferences relying on elements of a CSU. Under some reasonable assumptions, it behaves exactly like the standard given clause procedure on purely first-order problems. We also describe heuristics that help achieve a similar performance as when using incomplete, terminating unification procedures without sacrificing completeness.

Given the undecidability of the question as to whether there exists a next CSU element in a stream of unifiers, the request for the next conclusion might not terminate, effectively bringing the theorem prover to a halt. Our modified given clause procedure expects the unification procedure to return a lazily computed stream [34, Sect. 4.2], each element of which is either $\emptyset$ or a singleton set containing a unifier. To avoid getting stuck waiting for a unifier that may not exist, the unification procedure should return $\emptyset$ after it performs a number of operations without finding a unifier.

The complete unification procedure by Vukmirović et al. [52] returns such a stream. Other procedures such as Huet's [22] and Jensen and Pietrzykowski's [23] can easily be adapted to meet this requirement. Based on the stream of unifiers interspersed with $\emptyset$, we can construct a stream of inferences similarly interspersed with $\emptyset$ of which any finite prefixes can be computed in finite time.

To support such streams in the given clause procedure, we extend it to represent the proof state not only by the active (A) and passive (P) clause sets, but also by a priority queue Q containing the inference streams. Each stream is associated with a weight, and Q is sorted in order of increasing weight. Elsewhere [6], Bentkamp et al. described an older version of this extension. Here we present a newer version in more detail, including heuristics to postpone unpromising streams. The pseudocode of the modified procedure is as follows:

function EXTRACTCLAUSE(Q, *stream*)
  maybe_clause ← pop and compute the first element of *stream*
  if *stream* is not empty **then** add *stream* to Q with an increased weight
  return *maybe_clause*

function HEURISTICPROBE(Q)
  (*collected_clauses*, i) ← ($\emptyset$, 0)
  while $i < K_{\text{best}}$ and Q is not empty **do**
    (*maybe_clause*, j) ← ($\emptyset$, 0)
    while $j < K_{\text{retry}}$ and Q is not empty and *maybe_clause* = $\emptyset$ **do**
      stream ← pop the lowest weight stream in Q
      maybe_clause ← EXTRACTCLAUSE(Q, *stream*)
      $j \leftarrow j + 1$
    collected_clauses ← *collected_clauses* $\cup$ *maybe_clause*
    $i \leftarrow i + 1$
  return *collected_clauses*

function FAIRPROBE(Q, *num_oldest*)
  collected_clauses ← $\emptyset$
  oldest_streams ← pop *num_oldest* oldest streams from Q
  for *stream* in *oldest_streams* **do**
    collected_clauses ← *collected_clauses* $\cup$ EXTRACTCLAUSE(Q, *stream*)
  return *collected_clauses*

function FORCEPROBE(Q)
  collected_clauses ← $\emptyset$
  while Q is not empty and *collected_clauses* = $\emptyset$ **do**
    collected_clauses ← FAIRPROBE(Q, $|Q|$)
  if Q and *collected_clauses* are empty **then** *status* ← Satisfiable
  else *status* ← Unknown
  return (*status*, *collected_clauses*)

function GIVENCLAUSE(P, A, Q)
  (*status*, i) ← (Unknown, 0)
  while *status* = Unknown **do**
    if P is not empty **then**
      given ← pop a chosen clause from P and simplify it
      if *given* is the empty clause **then** *status* ← Unsatisfiable

    else
        $A \leftarrow A \cup \{given\}$
        for *stream* in streams of inferences between *given* and *other* $\in A$ **do**
            if *stream* is not empty **then** $P \leftarrow P \cup \textsc{ExtractClause}(Q, stream)$
        $i \leftarrow i + 1$
        if $i \bmod K_{\text{fair}} = 0$ **then** $P \leftarrow P \cup \textsc{FairProbe}(Q, \lfloor i/K_{\text{fair}} \rfloor)$
        else $P \leftarrow P \cup \textsc{HeuristicProbe}(Q)$
    else
        $(status, forced\_clauses) \leftarrow \textsc{ForceProbe}(Q)$
        $P \leftarrow P \cup forced\_clauses$
  return *status*

Initially, all input clauses are put into P, and A and Q are empty. Unlike in the standard given clause procedure, inference results are represented as clause streams. The first element is inserted into P, and the rest of the stream is stored in Q with some positive integer weight computed from the inference rule.

To eventually consider inference conclusions from streams in Q as given clauses, we extract elements from, or *probe*, streams and move any obtained clauses to P. Analogously to the traditional pick–given ratio [30, 37], we use a parameter K_{fair} (by default, $K_{\text{fair}} = 70$) to ensure fairness: Every K_{fair}th iteration, FairProbe probes an increasing number of oldest streams, which achieves dovetailing. In all other iterations, HeuristicProbe attempts to extract up to K_{best} clauses from the most promising streams (by default, $K_{\text{best}} = 7$). In each attempt, the most promising stream in Q is chosen. If its first element is $\emptyset$, the rest of the stream is inserted into Q, and a new stream is chosen. This is repeated until either K_{retry} occurrences of $\emptyset$ have been met (by default, $K_{\text{retry}} = 20$) or the stream yields a singleton set. Setting $K_{\text{retry}} > 0$ increases the chance that HeuristicProbe will return K_{best} clauses, as desired. Finally, if P becomes empty, ForceProbe searches relentlessly for a clause in Q, as a fallback.

The function ExtractClause extracts an element from a nonempty stream not in Q and inserts the remaining stream into Q with an increased weight, calculated as follows. Let n be the number of times the stream was chosen for probing. If probing results in $\emptyset$, the stream's weight is increased by $\max\{2, n - 16\}$. If probing results in a clause C whose penalty is p, the stream's weight is increased by $p \cdot \max\{1, n - 64\}$. The penalty of a clause is a number assigned by Zipperposition based on features such as the depth of its derivation and the rules used in it. The constants 16 and 64 increase the chance that newer streams are picked, which is desirable because their first clauses are expected to be useful.

All three probing functions are invoked by GivenClause, which forms the body of the saturation loop. It differs from the standard given clause procedure in three ways: First, the proof state includes Q in addition to P and A. Second, new inferences involving the given clause are added to Q instead of being performed immediately. Third, inferences in Q are periodically performed lazily to fill P.

GivenClause eagerly stores the first element of a new inference stream in P to imitate the standard given clause procedure. If the underlying unification procedure behaves like the standard first-order unification algorithm on higher-order logic's first-order fragment, our given clause procedure coincides with the standard one. The unification procedure by Vukmirović et al. terminates on the first-order and other fragments [32], and for problems outside these fragments, it immediately returns $\emptyset$ to avoid computing complicated unifiers eagerly.

Evaluation and Discussion. When the unification procedure of Vukmirović et al. was implemented in Zipperposition, it was observed that Zipperposition is the only competing higher-order prover that proves all Church numeral problems from the TPTP, never spending more than 5 seconds on the problem [52].

Consider the TPTP problem NUM800^1, which requires finding a function F such that $F\,c_1\,c_2 \approx c_2 \wedge F\,c_2\,c_3 \approx c_6$, where c_n abbreviates the Church numeral for n, $\lambda s\,z.\,s^n(z)$. To prove it, it suffices to take F to be the multiplication operator $\lambda x\,y\,s\,z.\,x\,(y\,s)\,z$. However, this unifier is only one out of many available for each occurrence of F.

In an independent evaluation setup on the same set of 2606 problems used in this paper, Vukmirović et al. compared a complete, nonterminating variant and a pragmatic, terminating variant of the unification procedure [52, Sect. 7]. The pragmatic variant was used directly—all the inference conclusions were put immediately in P, bypassing Q. The complete variant, which relies on possibly infinite streams and is much more prolific, proved only 15 problems less than the most competitive pragmatic variant. Furthermore, it proved 19 problems not proved by the pragmatic variant. This shows that our given clause procedure, with its heuristics, allows the prover to defer exploring less promising branches of the unification and uses the full power of a complete higher-order unifier search to solve unification problems that cannot be solved by a crippled procedure.

Among the competing higher-order theorem provers, only Satallax uses infinitely branching calculus rules. It maintains a queue of "commands" that contain instructions on how to create a successor state in the tableau. One command describes infinite enumeration of all closed terms of a given function type. Each execution of this command makes progress in the enumeration. Unlike evaluation of streams representing elements of CSU, each command execution is guaranteed to make progress in enumerating the next closed functional term, so there is no need to ever return $\emptyset$.

6   Controlling Prolific Rules

To support higher-order features such as function extensionality and quantification over functions, many refutationally complete calculi employ highly prolific rules. For example, λ-superposition uses a rule FLUIDSUP [6] that very often applies to two clauses if one of them contains a term of the form $F\,\bar{s}_n$, where $n > 0$. We describe three mechanisms to keep rules like these under control.

First, *we limit applicability of the prolific rules.* In practice, it often suffices to apply prolific higher-order rules only to initial or shallow clauses—clauses with a shallow derivation depth. Thus, we added an option to forbid the application of a rule if the derivation depth of any premise exceeds a limit.

Second, *we penalize the streams of expensive inferences.* The weight of each stream is given an initial value based on characteristics of the inference premises such as their derivation depth. For prolific rules such as FLUIDSUP, we increment this value by a parameter K_{incr}. Weights for less prolific variants of this rule, such as DUPSUP [6], are increased by a fraction of K_{incr} (e.g., $\lfloor K_{incr}/3 \rfloor$).

Third, *we defer the selection of prolific clauses.* To select the given clause, most saturating provers evaluate clauses according to some criteria and select the clause with the lowest evaluation. For this choice to be efficient, passive clauses are organized into a priority queue ordered by their evaluations. Like E, Zipperposition maintains multiple queues, ordered by different evaluations, that are visited in a round-robin fashion. It also uses E's two-layer evaluation functions, a variant of which has recently been implemented in Vampire [19]. The two layers are *clause priority* and *clause weight.* Clauses with higher priority are preferred, and the weight is used for tie-breaking. Intuitively, the first layer crudely separates clauses into priority classes, whereas the second one uses heuristic weights to prefer clauses within a priority class. To control the selection of prolific clauses, we introduce new clause priority functions that take into account features specific to higher-order clauses.

The first new priority function PreferHOSteps (PHOS) assigns a higher priority if rules specific to λ- or combinatory superposition were used in the clause derivation. Since most of the other clause priority functions tend to defer higher-order clauses, having a clause queue that prefers the results of higher-order inferences might be necessary to find a proof more efficiently. A simpler function, which prefers clauses containing λ-abstractions, is PreferLambda (PL).

We also introduce the priority function ByNormalizationFactor (BNF), inspired by the observation that a higher-order inference that applies a complicated substitution to a clause is usually followed by a $\beta\eta$-normalization step. If $\beta\eta$-normalization greatly reduces the size of a clause, it is likely that this substitution simplifies the clause (e.g., by removing a variable's arguments). Thus, this function prefers clauses that were produced by $\beta\eta$-normalization, and among those it prefers the ones with larger size reductions.

Another new priority function is PreferShallowAppVars (PSAV). This prefers clauses with lower depths of the deepest occurrence of an applied variable—that is, $C[X\ a]$ is preferred over $C[f\ (X\ a)]$. This function tries to curb the explosion of both λ- and combinatory superposition: Applying a substitution to a top-level applied variable often reduces this applied variable to a term with a constant head, which likely results in a less explosive clause. Among the functions that rely on properties of applied variables we implemented PreferDeepAppVars (PDAV), which returns the priority opposite of PSAV, and ByAppVarNum (BAVN), which prefers clauses with fewer occurrences of applied variables.

Evaluation and Discussion. In the base configuration, Zipperposition visits several clause queues, one of which uses the constant priority function ConstPrio (CP). To evaluate the new priority functions, we replaced the queue ordered by CP with the queue ordered by one of the new functions, leaving the clause weight intact. The results are shown in Figure 3. It shows that the expensive priority

base (CP)	BAVN	PL	PSAV	PHOS	BNF	PDAV
1638	**1640**	1637	1637	1632	1594	1520

Fig. 3: Effect of the priority function on performance

base (∞)	16	8	4	2	1
1638	1619	1621	1618	1612	1610

Fig. 4: Effect of the FLUIDSUP weight increment K_{incr} on performance

functions PHOS and BNF, which require inspecting the proof of clauses, hardly help. Simple functions such as PL are more effective: Compared with *base*, PL loses one problem overall but proves 22 new problems.

FLUIDSUP is disabled in *base* because it is so explosive. To test if increasing inference stream weights makes a difference on the success rate, we enabled FLUIDSUP and used different weight increments K_{incr} for FLUIDSUP inference queues. The results are shown in Figure 4. As expected, using a low increment with FLUIDSUP is detrimental to performance. However, as the column for $K_{incr} = 16$ shows, nor should we use too high an increment, since that delays useful FLUIDSUP inferences. Interestingly, even though the configuration with $K_{incr} = 1$ proves the least problems overall, it proves 7 problems not proved by *base*, which is more than any other configuration we tried.

7   Controlling the Use of Backends

Cooperation with efficient first-order theorem provers is an essential feature of higher-order theorem provers such as Leo-III [40, Sect. 4.4] and Satallax [11]. Those provers invoke first-order backends repeatedly during a proof attempt and spend a substantial amount of time in backend collaboration. Since λ-superposition generalizes a highly efficient first-order calculus, we expect that future efficient λ-superposition implementations will not benefit much from backends. Experimental provers such as Zipperposition can still gain a lot. We present some techniques for controlling the use of backends.

In his thesis [40, Sect. 6.1], Steen extensively evaluates the effects of using different first-order backends on the performance of Leo-III. His results suggest that adding only one backend already substantially improves the performance. To reduce the effort required for integrating multiple backends, we chose Ehoh [50] as our single backend. Ehoh is an extension of the highly optimized superposition prover E with support for higher-order features such as partial application, applied variables, and interpreted Booleans. On the one hand, Ehoh provides the efficiency of E while easing the translation from full higher-order logic: The only missing syntactic feature is λ-abstraction. On the other hand, Ehoh's higher-

base	0.1	0.25	0.5	0.75
1638	**1936**	1935	1934	1923

Fig. 5: Effect of the backend invocation point K_{time}

base	lifting	SKBCI	omitted
1638	**1935**	1867	1855

Fig. 6: Effect of the method used to translate λ-abstractions

base	16	32	64	128	256	512
1638	1936	1935	**1939**	1928	1925	1912

Fig. 7: Effect of the number of selected clauses K_{size}

order reasoning capabilities are limited. Its unification algorithm is essentially first-order and it cannot synthesize λ-abstractions.

In a departure from Leo-III and other cooperative provers, we invoke the backend at most once during a run of the prover. This is because most competitive higher-order provers use a portfolio mode in which many configurations are run for a short time, and we want to leave enough time for native higher-order reasoning. Moreover, multiple backend invocations tend to be wasteful, because currently each invocation starts with no knowledge of the previous ones.

Only a carefully chosen subset of the available clauses are translated and sent to Ehoh. Let I be the set of input clauses. Given a proof state, let $M = P \cup A$, and let M_{ho} denote the subset of M that contains only clauses that were derived using at least one λ-superposition-specific inference rule. We order the clauses in M_{ho} by increasing derivation depth, using syntactic weight to break ties. Then we choose all clauses in I and the first K_{size} clauses from M_{ho} for use with the backend reasoner. We leave out clauses in $M \backslash (I \cup M_{\text{ho}})$ because Ehoh can rederive them. We also expect large clauses with deep derivations to be less useful.

The remaining step is the translation of λ-abstractions. We support two translation methods: λ-lifting [24] and SKBCI combinators [48]. For SKBCI, we omit the combinator definition axioms, because they are very explosive [10]. A third mode simply omits clauses containing λ-abstractions.

Evaluation and Discussion. In Zipperposition, we can adjust the CPU time allotted to Ehoh, Ehoh's own proof search parameters, the point when Ehoh is invoked, the number K_{size} of selected clauses from M_{ho}, and the λ translation method. We fix the time limit to 5 s, use Ehoh in *auto* mode, and focus on the last three parameters. In *base*, collaboration with Ehoh is disabled.

Ehoh is invoked after $K_{\text{time}} \cdot t$ CPU seconds, where $0 \leq K_{\text{time}} < 1$ and t is the total CPU time allotted to Zipperposition. Figure 5 shows the effect of varying K_{time} when $K_{\text{size}} = 32$ and λ-lifting is used. The evaluation confirms that using a highly optimized backend such as Ehoh greatly improves the performance of a less optimized prover such as Zipperposition. The figure indicates that it is preferable to invoke the backend early. We have indeed observed that if the backend

	Uncoop	Coop
CVC4	1810	–
Leo-III	1641	2108
Satallax	2089	2224
Vampire	2096	–
Zipperposition	2223	**2307**

Fig. 8: Comparison of competing higher-order theorem provers

is invoked late, small clauses with deep derivations tend to be present by then. These clauses might have been used to delete important shallow clauses already. But due to their derivation depth, they will not be translated. In such situations, it is better to invoke the backend before the important clauses are deleted.

Figure 6 quantifies the effects of the three λ-abstraction translation methods. We fixed $K_{time} = 0.25$ and $K_{size} = 32$. The clear winner is λ-lifting. Omitting clauses with λ-abstractions performs comparably to SKBCI combinators.

Figure 7 shows the effect of K_{size} on performance, with $K_{time} = 0.25$ and λ-lifting. We find that including a small number of higher-order clauses with the lowest weight performs better than including a large number of such clauses.

8   Comparison with Other Provers

Different choices of parameters lead to noticeably different sets of proved problems. In an attempt to use Zipperposition 2 to its full potential, we have created a portfolio mode that runs up to 50 configurations in parallel during the allotted time. To provide some context, we compare Zipperposition 2 with the latest versions of all higher-order provers that competed at CASC-J10: CVC4 1.8 [4], Leo-III 1.5 [42], Satallax 3.5 [11], and Vampire 4.5 [10]. Note that Vampire's higher-order schedule is optimized for running on a single core.

We use the same 2606 monomorphic higher-order TPTP 7.2.0 problems as elsewhere in this paper, but we try to replicate the CASC setup more faithfully. CASC-J10 was run on 8-core CPUs with a 120 s wall-clock limit and a 960 s CPU limit. Since we run the experiments on 4-core CPUs, we set the wall-clock limit to 240 s and keep the same CPU limit. Leo-III, Satallax, and Zipperposition are cooperative provers. We also run them in uncooperative mode, without their backends, to measure their intrinsic strength. Figure 8 summarizes the results.

Among the cooperative provers, Zipperposition is the one that depends the least on its backend, and its *uncooperative* mode is only one problem behind Satallax's *cooperative* mode. This confirms our hypothesis that λ-superposition is a suitable basis for automatic higher-order reasoning. This also suggests that the implementation of this calculus in a modern first-order superposition prover such as E or Vampire would achieve markedly better results. Moreover, we believe that there are still techniques inspired by tableaux, SAT solving, and SMT solving that could be adapted and integrated in saturation provers.

9   Discussion and Conclusion

Back in 1994, Kohlhase [27, Sect. 1.3] was optimistic about the future of higher-order automated reasoning:

> The obstacles to proof search intrinsic to higher-order logic may well be compensated by the greater expressive power of higher-order logic and by the existence of shorter proofs. Thus higher-order automated theorem proving will be practically as feasible as first-order theorem proving is now as soon as the technological backlog is made up.

For higher-order superposition, the backlog consisted of designing calculus extensions, heuristics, and algorithms that mitigate its weaknesses. In this paper, we presented such enhancements, justified their design, and evaluated them. We explained how each weak point in the higher-order proving pipeline could be improved, from preprocessing to reasoning about formulas, to delaying unpromising or explosive inferences, to invoking a backend. Our evaluation indicates that higher-order superposition is now the state of the art in higher-order reasoning.

Higher-order extensions of first-order superposition have been considered by Bentkamp et al. [6, 7] and Bhayat and Reger [9, 10]. They introduced proof calculi, proved them refutationally complete, and suggested optional rules, but they hardly discussed the practical aspects of higher-order superposition. Extensions of SMT are discussed by Barbosa et al. [3]. Bachmair and Ganzinger [1], Manna and Waldinger [29], and Murray [31] have studied nonclausal resolution calculi.

In contrast, there is a vast literature on practical aspects of first-order reasoning using superposition and related calculi. The literature evaluates various procedures and techniques [21,36], literal and term order selection functions [20], and clause evaluation functions [19,39], among others. Our work joins the select club of papers devoted to practical aspects of higher-order reasoning [8,16,41,53].

As a next step, we plan to implement the described techniques in Ehoh [50], the λ-free higher-order extension of E. We expect the resulting prover to be substantially more efficient than Zipperposition. Moreover, we want to investigate the proofs found by provers such as CVC4 and Satallax but missed by Zipperposition. Finding the reason behind why Zipperposition fails to prove specific problems will likely result in useful new techniques.

Acknowledgment. We are grateful to the maintainers of StarExec for letting us use their service. Ahmed Bhayat and Giles Reger guided us through details of Vampire 4.5. Ahmed Bhayat, Michael Färber, Mathias Fleury, Predrag Janičić, Mark Summerfield, and the anonymous reviewers suggested content, textual, and typesetting improvements. We thank them all.

Vukmirović, Bentkamp, and Blanchette's research has received funding from the European Research Council (ERC) under the European Union's Horizon 2020 research and innovation program (grant agreement No. 713999, Matryoshka). Blanchette and Nummelin's research has received funding from the Netherlands Organization for Scientific Research (NWO) under the Vidi program (project No. 016.Vidi.189.037, Lean Forward) and the Incidental Financial Support scheme.

References

1. Bachmair, L., Ganzinger, H.: Non-clausal resolution and superposition with selection and redundancy criteria. In: Voronkov, A. (ed.) LPAR '92. LNCS, vol. 624, pp. 273–284. Springer (1992)
2. Backes, J., Brown, C.E.: Analytic tableaux for higher-order logic with choice. J. Autom. Reason. **47**(4), 451–479 (2011)
3. Barbosa, H., Reynolds, A., Ouraoui, D.E., Tinelli, C., Barrett, C.W.: Extending SMT solvers to higher-order logic. In: Fontaine, P. (ed.) CADE-27. LNCS, vol. 11716, pp. 35–54. Springer (2019)
4. Barrett, C.W., Conway, C.L., Deters, M., Hadarean, L., Jovanović, D., King, T., Reynolds, A., Tinelli, C.: CVC4. In: Gopalakrishnan, G., Qadeer, S. (eds.) CAV 2011. LNCS, vol. 6806, pp. 171–177. Springer (2011)
5. Bentkamp, A., Blanchette, J., Tourret, S., Vukmirović, P.: Superposition for full higher-order logic. In: Platzer, A., Sutcliffe, G. (eds.) CADE-28. LNCS, Springer (2021), to appear
6. Bentkamp, A., Blanchette, J., Tourret, S., Vukmirović, P., Waldmann, U.: Superposition with lambdas. J. Autom. Reason. To appear, preprint at https://arxiv.org/abs/2102.00453 (2021)
7. Bentkamp, A., Blanchette, J.C., Cruanes, S., Waldmann, U.: Superposition for lambda-free higher-order logic. In: Galmiche, D., Schulz, S., Sebastiani, R. (eds.) IJCAR 2018. LNCS, vol. 10900, pp. 28–46. Springer (2018)
8. Benzmüller, C., Sorge, V., Jamnik, M., Kerber, M.: Can a higher-order and a first-order theorem prover cooperate? In: Baader, F., Voronkov, A. (eds.) LPAR 2004. LNCS, vol. 3452, pp. 415–431. Springer (2004)
9. Bhayat, A., Reger, G.: Restricted combinatory unification. In: Fontaine, P. (ed.) CADE-27. LNCS, vol. 11716, pp. 74–93. Springer (2019)
10. Bhayat, A., Reger, G.: A combinator-based superposition calculus for higher-order logic. In: Peltier, N., Sofronie-Stokkermans, V. (eds.) IJCAR 2020, Part I. LNCS, vol. 12166, pp. 278–296. Springer (2020)
11. Brown, C.E.: Reducing higher-order theorem proving to a sequence of SAT problems. J. Autom. Reason. **51**(1), 57–77 (2013)
12. Cruanes, S.: Extending superposition with integer arithmetic, structural induction, and beyond. Ph.D. thesis, École polytechnique (2015)
13. Czajka, L., Kaliszyk, C.: Hammer for Coq: Automation for dependent type theory. J. Autom. Reason. **61**(1-4), 423–453 (2018)
14. Denzinger, J., Kronenburg, M., Schulz, S.: DISCOUNT—a distributed and learning equational prover. J. Autom. Reason. **18**(2), 189–198 (1997)
15. Ebner, G., Blanchette, J., Tourret, S.: Unifying splitting. In: Platzer, A., Sutcliffe, G. (eds.) CADE-28. LNCS, Springer (2021), to appear
16. Färber, M., Brown, C.E.: Internal guidance for Satallax. In: Olivetti, N., Tiwari, A. (eds.) IJCAR 2016. LNCS, vol. 9706, pp. 349–361. Springer (2016)
17. Filliâtre, J., Paskevich, A.: Why3—where programs meet provers. In: Felleisen, M., Gardner, P. (eds.) ESOP 2013. LNCS, vol. 7792, pp. 125–128. Springer (2013)
18. Ganzinger, H., Stuber, J.: Superposition with equivalence reasoning and delayed clause normal form transformation. In: Baader, F. (ed.) CADE-19. LNCS, vol. 2741, pp. 335–349. Springer (2003)
19. Gleiss, B., Suda, M.: Layered clause selection for theory reasoning (short paper). In: Peltier, N., Sofronie-Stokkermans, V. (eds.) IJCAR 2020, Part I. LNCS, vol. 12166, pp. 402–409. Springer (2020)

20. Hoder, K., Reger, G., Suda, M., Voronkov, A.: Selecting the selection. In: Olivetti, N., Tiwari, A. (eds.) IJCAR 2016. LNCS, vol. 9706, pp. 313–329. Springer (2016)
21. Hoder, K., Voronkov, A.: Comparing unification algorithms in first-order theorem proving. In: Mertsching, B., Hund, M., Aziz, M.Z. (eds.) KI 2009. LNCS, vol. 5803, pp. 435–443. Springer (2009)
22. Huet, G.P.: A unification algorithm for typed lambda-calculus. Theor. Comput. Sci. 1(1), 27–57 (1975)
23. Jensen, D.C., Pietrzykowski, T.: Mechanizing omega-order type theory through unification. Theor. Comput. Sci. 3(2), 123–171 (1976)
24. Johnsson, T.: Lambda lifting: Transforming programs to recursive equations. In: Jouannaud, J. (ed.) FPCA 1985. LNCS, vol. 201, pp. 190–203. Springer (1985)
25. Kaliszyk, C., Urban, J.: HOL(y)Hammer: Online ATP service for HOL Light. Math. Comput. Sci. 9(1), 5–22 (2015)
26. Knuth, D.E., Bendix, P.B.: Simple word problems in universal algebras. In: Leech, J. (ed.) Computational Problems in Abstract Algebra, pp. 263–297. Pergamon (1970)
27. Kohlhase, M.: A mechanization of sorted higher-order logic based on the resolution principle. Ph.D. thesis, Universität des Saarlandes, Saarbrücken, Germany (1994)
28. Kovács, L., Voronkov, A.: First-order theorem proving and Vampire. In: Sharygina, N., Veith, H. (eds.) CAV 2013. LNCS, vol. 8044, pp. 1–35. Springer (2013)
29. Manna, Z., Waldinger, R.: A deductive approach to program synthesis. In: Buchanan, B.G. (ed.) IJCAI-79. pp. 542–551. William Kaufmann (1979)
30. McCune, W., Wos, L.: Otter—the CADE-13 competition incarnations. J. Autom. Reason. 18(2), 211–220 (1997)
31. Murray, N.V.: Completely non-clausal theorem proving. Artif. Intell. 18(1), 67–85 (1982)
32. Nipkow, T.: Functional unification of higher-order patterns. In: Best, E. (ed.) LICS 1993. pp. 64–74. IEEE Computer Society (1993)
33. Nonnengart, A., Weidenbach, C.: Computing small clause normal forms. In: Robinson, J.A., Voronkov, A. (eds.) Handbook of Automated Reasoning, pp. 335–367. Elsevier and MIT Press (2001)
34. Okasaki, C.: Purely functional data structures. Cambridge University Press (1999)
35. Paulson, L.C., Blanchette, J.C.: Three years of experience with Sledgehammer, a practical link between automatic and interactive theorem provers. In: Sutcliffe, G., Schulz, S., Ternovska, E. (eds.) IWIL-2010. EPiC Series in Computing, vol. 2, pp. 1–11. EasyChair (2010)
36. Reger, G., Suda, M., Voronkov, A.: Playing with AVATAR. In: Felty, A.P., Middeldorp, A. (eds.) CADE-25. LNCS, vol. 9195, pp. 399–415. Springer (2015)
37. Schulz, S.: E—a brainiac theorem prover. AI Commun. 15(2-3), 111–126 (2002)
38. Schulz, S., Cruanes, S., Vukmirović, P.: Faster, higher, stronger: E 2.3. In: Fontaine, P. (ed.) CADE-27. LNCS, vol. 11716, pp. 495–507. Springer (2019)
39. Schulz, S., Möhrmann, M.: Performance of clause selection heuristics for saturation-based theorem proving. In: Olivetti, N., Tiwari, A. (eds.) IJCAR 2016. LNCS, vol. 9706, pp. 330–345. Springer (2016)
40. Steen, A.: Extensional paramodulation for higher-order logic and its effective implementation Leo-III. Ph.D. thesis, Free University of Berlin, Dahlem, Germany (2018)
41. Steen, A., Benzmüller, C.: There is no best β-normalization strategy for higher-order reasoners. In: Davis, M., Fehnker, A., McIver, A., Voronkov, A. (eds.) LPAR-20. LNCS, vol. 9450, pp. 329–339. Springer (2015)

42. Steen, A., Benzmüller, C.: The higher-order prover Leo-III. In: Galmiche, D., Schulz, S., Sebastiani, R. (eds.) IJCAR 2018. LNCS, vol. 10900, pp. 108–116. Springer (2018)

43. Stump, A., Sutcliffe, G., Tinelli, C.: Starexec: A cross-community infrastructure for logic solving. In: Demri, S., Kapur, D., Weidenbach, C. (eds.) IJCAR 2014. LNCS, vol. 8562, pp. 367–373. Springer (2014)

44. Sultana, N., Blanchette, J.C., Paulson, L.C.: LEO-II and Satallax on the Sledgehammer test bench. J. Appl. Log. 11(1), 91–102 (2013)

45. Sutcliffe, G.: The CADE ATP System Competition—CASC. AI Magazine 37(2), 99–101 (2016)

46. Sutcliffe, G.: The TPTP problem library and associated infrastructure—from CNF to TH0, TPTP v6.4.0. J. Autom. Reason. 59(4), 483–502 (2017)

47. Sutcliffe, G.: The CADE-27 automated theorem proving system competition—CASC-27. AI Commun. 32(5-6), 373–389 (2019)

48. Turner, D.A.: Another algorithm for bracket abstraction. J. Symb. Log. 44(2), 267–270 (1979)

49. Voronkov, A.: AVATAR: the architecture for first-order theorem provers. In: Biere, A., Bloem, R. (eds.) CAV 2014. LNCS, vol. 8559, pp. 696–710. Springer (2014)

50. Vukmirović, P., Blanchette, J.C., Cruanes, S., Schulz, S.: Extending a brainiac prover to lambda-free higher-order logic. In: Vojnar, T., Zhang, L. (eds.) TACAS 2019, Part I. LNCS, vol. 11427, pp. 192–210. Springer (2019)

51. Vukmirović, P., Nummelin, V.: Boolean reasoning in a higher-order superposition prover. In: Fontaine, P., Korovin, K., Kotsireas, I.S., Rümmer, P., Tourret, S. (eds.) PAAR-2020. CEUR Workshop Proceedings, vol. 2752, pp. 148–166. CEUR-WS.org (2020)

52. Vukmirović, P., Bentkamp, A., Nummelin, V.: Efficient full higher-order unification. In: Ariola, Z.M. (ed.) FSCD. LIPIcs, vol. 167, pp. 5:1–5:17. Schloss Dagstuhl—Leibniz-Zentrum für Informatik (2020)

53. Wisniewski, M., Steen, A., Kern, K., Benzmüller, C.: Effective normalization techniques for HOL. In: Olivetti, N., Tiwari, A. (eds.) IJCAR 2016. LNCS, vol. 9706, pp. 362–370. Springer (2016)

Open Access This chapter is licensed under the terms of the Creative Commons Attribution 4.0 International License (http://creativecommons.org/licenses/by/4.0/), which permits use, sharing, adaptation, distribution and reproduction in any medium or format, as long as you give appropriate credit to the original author(s) and the source, provide a link to the Creative Commons license and indicate if changes were made.

The images or other third party material in this chapter are included in the chapter's Creative Commons license, unless indicated otherwise in a credit line to the material. If material is not included in the chapter's Creative Commons license and your intended use is not permitted by statutory regulation or exceeds the permitted use, you will need to obtain permission directly from the copyright holder.

Dual Proof Generation for Quantified Boolean Formulas with a BDD-based Solver

Randal E. Bryant (✉) ⓘ and Marijn J. H. Heule ⓘ

Computer Science Department
Carnegie Mellon University, Pittsburgh, PA, United States
{Randy.Bryant, mheule}@cs.cmu.edu

Abstract. Existing proof-generating quantified Boolean formula (QBF) solvers must construct a different type of proof depending on whether the formula is false (refutation) or true (satisfaction). We show that a QBF solver based on ordered binary decision diagrams (BDDs) can emit a single *dual proof* as it operates, supporting either outcome. This form consists of a sequence of equivalence-preserving clause addition and deletion steps in an extended resolution framework. For a false formula, the proof terminates with the empty clause, indicating conflict. For a true one, it terminates with all clauses deleted, indicating tautology. Both the length of the proof and the time required to check it are proportional to the total number of BDD operations performed. We evaluate our solver using a scalable benchmark based on a two-player tiling game.

1 Introduction

Adding quantifiers to Boolean formulas, yielding the logic of *quantified Boolean formulas* (QBFs), greatly extends their expressive power [11], but it presents several challenges, including verifying the output of a QBF solver. Unlike a satisfiable Boolean formula, there is no satisfying assignment for a QBF—the formula is simply false or true. Instead, a proof-generating QBF solver must provide a full proof in either case: a *refutation* proof if the formula is false, or a *satisfaction* proof if the formula is true.

Currently, there is little standardization of the proof capabilities or the proof systems supported by different QBF solvers [21]. Some solvers can generate *syntactic* certificates—ones that can be directly checked by a proof checker. For a false formula, these can be expressed in clausal proof frameworks that augment resolution with rules for universal quantification [18]. For a true formula, several QBF solvers can generate term resolution proofs [12], effectively reasoning about a negated version of the input formula represented in disjunctive form. These require the proof checker to support an entirely different set of proof rules.

An even larger number of solvers can generate *semantic* certificates in the form of Herbrand functions for false formulas and Skolem functions for true ones, describing how to instantiate either the universal or the existential variables [21]. These can be used to expand the original formula into a (often much larger) Boolean formula that is checked with a SAT solver [22] or with a high-degree polynomial algorithm [25]. Performing the check often requires far more effort than does running the solver. These approaches, along with others involving syntactic certificates, require at least two passes—one to determine whether the formula is true or false and one to generate the proof.

© The Author(s) 2021
A. Platzer and G. Sutcliffe (Eds.): CADE 2021, LNAI 12699, pp. 433–449, 2021.
https://doi.org/10.1007/978-3-030-79876-5_25

This paper describes a new approach to proof generation for QBF, where the solver generates a *dual proof*, serving as either a refutation or a satisfaction proof depending on whether the solver determines the formula to be false or true. A dual proof consists of a sequence of clause addition and deletion steps, each preserving equivalence to the original formula. If the proof terminates with the addition of the empty clause, then it demonstrates that the original formula was contradictory and therefore false. If the proof terminates with all clauses removed, then it demonstrates that the original formula was equivalent to a tautology and is therefore true. The proofs are expressed in a clausal proof framework that incorporates extended resolution, as well as rules for universal and existential quantification [13, 14].

We have implemented a QBF solver PGBDDQ based on ordered binary decision diagrams (BDDs) that can generate dual proofs as it operates. As optimizations, PGBDDQ can be directed to generate refutation or satisfaction proofs, and these can be somewhat shorter and take less time to check than dual proofs. Refutation proofs follow the traditional format of a series of truth-preserving steps leading to an empty clause. Satisfaction proofs follow the novel format of a series of falsehood-preserving steps leading to an empty set of clauses. This approach for satisfaction proofs has been previously used as part of a QBF preprocessor [13, 14], but, to the best of our knowledge, ours is the first use in a complete QBF solver. Whether dual, refutation, or satisfaction, the proofs generated by PGBDDQ have length proportional to the number of BDD operations and can readily be validated by a simple proof checker.

For the case of refutation proofs, PGBDDQ builds on the work of Jussila, et al. [17], whose BDD-based QBF solver EBDDRES could generate refutation proofs in an extended resolution framework. Whereas their solver, as well as all other published BDD-based QBF solvers [23, 24], require the BDD variable ordering to be the inverse of the quantification ordering, PGBDDQ allows independent choices for the two orderings. As will be shown, this can lead to an exponential advantage on some benchmarks.

We evaluate the performance of PGBDDQ using a scalable benchmark based on a two-player tiling game. We show that, with the right combination of Tseitin variable placement, BDD variable ordering and elimination variable ordering, a BDD-based QBF solver can achieve performance that scales polynomially with the problem size. In these cases, PGBDDQ can readily outperform state-of-the-art search-based solvers, while having the added benefit that it generates a checkable proof.

2 Background Preliminaries

A *literal* l is either a variable y or its complement $\bar{y}$. We denote the underlying variable for literal l as $Var(l)$, while $\bar{l}$ denotes the complement of literal l.

A *clause* is a set of literals, representing the disjunction of a set of complemented and uncomplemented variables. The empty clause, indicating logical falsehood, is written $\bot$. We consider only *proper* clauses, where a literal can only occur once in a clause, and a clause cannot contain both a variable and its complement. Logical truth, or tautology, is denoted $\top$ and represented by an empty set of clauses. For clarity, we write clauses as Boolean formulas, such as $x \wedge y \rightarrow z$ for the clause $\{\bar{x}, \bar{y}, z\}$. As a special case, the unit clause consisting of literal l is simply written as l.

ITE: For Boolean values a, b, and c, the *ITE* operation (short for "If-Then-Else") is defined as: $ITE(a, b, c) = (a \wedge b) \vee (\neg a \wedge c)$. This can be also be written as a conjunction of clauses: $ITE(a, b, c) = (a \rightarrow b) \wedge (\neg a \rightarrow c)$.

QBF: We consider quantified formulas in *prenex normal form* over a set of *input variables* X, with input formula Φ_I having the form $\Phi_I = Q_1 X_1 Q_2 X_2 \cdots Q_m X_m \psi_I$. The *quantifier prefix* $\mathcal{Q}_I = Q_1 X_1 Q_2 X_2 \cdots Q_m X_m$ consists of a series of *quantifier blocks*. Each block j has an associated quantifier $Q_j \in \{\forall, \exists\}$ and a set of variables $X_j \subseteq X$, such that the sets $X_1, X_2, \ldots, X_m$ form a partitioning of X. The formula *matrix* ψ_I is given as a set of clauses referred to as the *input* clauses. An input variable x occurring in some partition X_j is said to be *universal* (respectively, *existential*) when $Q_j = \forall$ (resp., $Q_j = \exists$) and is said to be at *quantification level j*. The type and level of each literal l matches that of its underlying variable $Var(l)$.

Resolution: Let C and D be clauses, where C contains variable y and D contains its complement $\overline{y}$. We also require that there can be no literal $l \in C$, with $l \neq y$, such that $\overline{l} \in D$. The *resolvent* clause is then defined as $Res(C, D) = C \cup D - \{y, \overline{y}\}$. When C and D do not satisfy the above requirements, then $Res(C, D)$ is undefined. This definition does not allow the resolvent to be a tautology.

The resolution operation extends to linear chains and sets of clauses, as well. For a clause sequence $C_1, C_2, \ldots, C_k$, we define its resolvent as:

$$Res(C_1, C_2, \ldots, C_k) = Res(C_1, Res(C_2, \cdots, Res(C_{k-1}, C_k) \cdots))$$

The sequence $C_1, C_2, \ldots, C_k$ is termed the *antecedent*. Again, the operation is undefined if any individual application of the operation is undefined. For a set of clauses ψ, we define $Res(\psi)$ as the set of all resolvents that can be generated from sequences comprised of clauses from ψ with each clause used at most once per sequence.

As a separate notation, for a set of clauses ψ, we let $Res_y(\psi)$ be the set of all defined resolvents $Res(C, D)$ with $C, D \in \psi$, $y \in C$, and $\overline{y} \in D$.

Extension: Extended resolution [28] allows the introduction of *extension variables* to serve as a shorthand notation for other formulas. Generalizing extended resolution to quantified formulas requires additional considerations regarding 1) the distinction between existentially and universally quantified variables, and 2) the position of the extension variables within the quantification ordering. In particular, as extension variables are generated, they must be classified as existential and be inserted into intermediate positions in the ordering [3, 17]. To support this capability, we associate a *quantification level* $\lambda(y)$ with each input and extension variable y. For input variable x, where $x \in X_j$, we define $\lambda(x) = 2j - 1$. Input variables will therefore have odd values for λ. Each extension variable e will be assigned an even value for $\lambda(e)$ according to rules defined below. For literal l, we define $\lambda(l) = \lambda(Var(l))$.

As clauses are added and deleted, and as extension variables are introduced, a formula will be maintained with an overall form

$$\Phi = Q_1 X_1 \exists E_1 Q_2 X_2 \exists E_2 \cdots Q_m X_m \exists E_m \psi \tag{1}$$

where $E_1, E_2, \ldots, E_m$ is a partitioning of the set of extension variables. The quantifier prefix $\mathcal{Q}$ in (1) is therefore an alternation of input and extension variables, with all extension variables being existentially quantified. We can also view the quantifier prefix as simply being a set of variables y, being ordered by the values of $\lambda(y)$, and where y is universal when $\lambda(y) = 2j - 1$ with $Q_j = \forall$. Otherwise, y is existential. We use set notation when referring to the quantifier prefix, recognizing that the partitioning of variables into quantifier blocks and the associated quantifier types, are defined implicitly by the function λ.

Two quantifier prefixes $\mathcal{Q}$ and $\mathcal{Q}'$, each with m input variable blocks, are said to be *compatible* when $Q_j = Q'_j$ for $1 \leq j \leq m$, and $\lambda(y) = \lambda'(y)$ for all $y \in \mathcal{Q} \cap \mathcal{Q}'$, where the unprimed and primed symbols correspond to $\mathcal{Q}$ and $\mathcal{Q}'$, respectively.

Extension introduces existential variable e by adding a set of *defining clauses* θ to the matrix and adding e to the quantifier prefix. Consider QBF $\Phi = \mathcal{Q}\psi$. Let e be a fresh variable (i.e., $e \notin \mathcal{Q}$) and let θ be a set of clauses that are *blocked* on e [5]. That is, each clause in θ must contain either e or $\bar{e}$, and for any clauses $C, D \in \theta$ for which $e \in C$ and $\bar{e} \in D$, there must be some other literal $l \in C$ such that $\bar{l} \in D$, and therefore $Res_e(\theta) = \emptyset$. Define $\Phi' = \mathcal{Q}'\psi'$ as follows. Variable e is assigned quantification level $\lambda(e) = \max\{Even(\lambda(y)) | y \in Var(\theta), y \neq e\}$, where $Var(\theta)$ is defined to be the set of all variables occurring in the clauses in θ. Function $Even$ rounds a number up to the next higher even value, i.e., $Even(a) = 2\lceil a/2 \rceil$. This definition guarantees that $\lambda(e)$ is even and that every variable y occurring in θ will have $\lambda(y) \leq \lambda(e)$. Letting $\mathcal{Q}' = \mathcal{Q} \cup \{e\}$ and $\psi' = \psi \cup \theta$, it can be shown that Φ' is true if and only if Φ is true [17].

Boolean Functions: The *restriction* of Boolean function f with respect to variable x, denoted $f|_x$ is defined as the function that results when variable x is assigned value 1. Similarly, $f|_{\bar{x}}$ is defined as the function that results when x is assigned value 0.

The *Shannon expansion* relates a Boolean function to its restrictions with respect to a variable and its complement. For a function f and variable x:

$$f = ITE(x, f|_x, f|_{\bar{x}})$$
$$= (x \to f|_x) \wedge (\bar{x} \to f|_{\bar{x}}) \tag{2}$$

We will find clausal form (2) to be of use in generating satisfaction proofs.

For Boolean function f and variable x we can define the existential and universal quantifications of f with respect to x as projection operations that eliminate the dependency on x through either disjunction or conjunction:

$$\exists x\, f = f|_x \vee f|_{\bar{x}} \tag{3}$$
$$\forall x\, f = f|_x \wedge f|_{\bar{x}} \tag{4}$$

BDDs: A reduced, ordered binary decision diagram (BDD) provides a canonical form for representing a set of Boolean functions, and an associated set of algorithms for constructing them and testing their properties [1,7,8]. A set of functions is represented as a directed acyclic graph, with each function indicated by a pointer to its root node. We will therefore use the symbol u to refer at times to 1) a node in the BDD, 2) the subgraph of the BDD having u as its root, 3) the function represented by this subgraph, and 4) an extension variable associated with the node.

The ordered BDD representation requires defining a total ordering of the variables. Unlike other BDD-based QBF solvers [17, 23, 24], PGBDDQ allows this ordering to be independent of the ordering of variables in the quantifier prefix. The two leaf nodes are denoted L_0 and L_1, representing the constant functions $\mathbf{0}$ and $\mathbf{1}$, respectively. Each nonterminal node u has an associated variable and two children indicating branches for the two possible values of the variable.

BDD packages support multiple operations for constructing and testing the properties of Boolean functions represented by a BDD. A number of these are based on the *Apply* algorithm [6]. Given root nodes u and v representing functions f and g, respectively, and a Boolean operation (e.g., AND), the algorithm generates a root node w representing the result of applying the operation to those functions (e.g., $f \wedge g$). It operates by traversing its arguments via a series of recursive calls, using a table to cache previously computed results. Variants of the Apply algorithm can also perform restriction and quantification.

QBF Solving with a BDD: With the ability to perform disjunction, conjunction, and quantification of Boolean functions, there is a straightforward algorithm for solving a QBF with a BDD. It starts by computing a representation of the formula matrix using the Apply algorithm with operation $\vee$ for each clause and conjuncting these using the Apply algorithm with operation $\wedge$. Then, quantifiers are eliminated by working from the innermost quantifier block X_m and working outward, using either universal or existential quantifier operations. At the end, the BDD will be reduced to either L_0 indicating that the formula is false, or L_1 indicating that the formula is true. This basic algorithm can be improved by deferring some of the conjunctions and by carefully selecting the order of quantification within each quantifier block [23, 24].

3   Logical Foundations

A *clausal proof* consists of a sequence of steps starting with the clauses in the input formula Φ_I. Each step either adds a set of clauses, and possibly an extension variable, or it removes a set of clauses. These additions and removals define a sequence of QBFs $\Phi_1, \Phi_2, \ldots, \Phi_t$, with $\Phi_1 = \Phi_I$ and each Φ_i of the form $\mathcal{Q}_i \, \psi_i$.

For a refutation proof, each step i must preserve truth, i.e., $\Phi_i \rightarrow \Phi_{i+1}$, and it must end with $\bot \in \psi_t$. This construction serves as a proof that $\Phi_I = \Phi_1 \rightarrow \Phi_2 \rightarrow \cdots \rightarrow \Phi_t = \bot$, and therefore the input formula is false. A satisfaction proof follows the same general format, except that it requires each step i to preserve falsehood: $\Phi_{i+1} \rightarrow \Phi_i$, and it reaches a final result with $\psi_t = \emptyset$. This construction serves as a proof that $\top = \Phi_t \rightarrow \Phi_{t-1} \rightarrow \cdots \rightarrow \Phi_1 = \Phi_I$, and therefore the input formula is true. A *dual* proof requires that each step preserves equivalence: $\Phi_i \leftrightarrow \Phi_{i+1}$, i.e., it is both truth and falsehood preserving. Only the final step with $\psi_t \in \{\bot, \top\}$ determines whether it is a refutation or a satisfaction proof.

3.1   Inference Rules

Table 1 shows the equivalence-preserving inference rules we use in our proofs. These are based on *redundant clauses*—cases where there are two sets of clauses ψ and θ such that $\mathcal{Q} \, \psi \leftrightarrow \mathcal{Q}' \, (\psi \cup \theta)$, for compatible prefixes $\mathcal{Q}$ and $\mathcal{Q}'$. Thus, adding clauses θ to the matrix ψ defines an equivalence-preserving addition rule, while deleting them from the matrix $\psi \cup \theta$ defines an equivalence-preserving removal rule.

Table 1. Inference rules where clause set θ is redundant with respect to the clauses in ψ.

Addition	Removal	Requirements
Resolution addition	Resolution deletion	$\theta \subseteq Res(\psi)$.
Universal reduction	—	$\theta = \{C\}$. l universal. $\lambda(l') < \lambda(l)$ for all existential $l' \in C$. $C \cup \{l\} \in \psi$.
Extension	Existential elimination	y existential. $y \notin Var(\psi)$. $y \in Var(C)$ for all $C \in \theta$. $Res_y(\theta) \subseteq \psi$. $\lambda(y') \leq \lambda(y)$ for all $y' \in Var(\theta)$.

We have already described resolution in Section 2. Universal reduction (also known as "forall reduction" [4, 17]) is the standard rule for eliminating universal variables in a QBF refutation proof [18].

The extension rule forms the basis for adding extension variable $y = e$ and its defining clauses θ. For this case, the clauses in θ are blocked with respect to y, and therefore $Res_y(\theta) = \emptyset$. As a deletion rule, the existential elimination rule is used to remove extension variables and their defining clauses, as well as to remove the existential input variables. It is a generalization of *blocked clause elimination* [5] in that the clauses in θ need not be blocked, as long as ψ contains all of the resolvents with respect to variable y. The redundancies used by the resolution, extension, and existential elimination rules are special cases of the quantified resolution asymmetric tautology (QRAT) property [13, 14].

3.2   Integrating Proof Generation into BDD Operations

As described in [16, 17, 26] and [9], we use a BDD to represent Boolean functions defined by applying Boolean operations to the input variables X. When creating node u, we introduce an extension variable, also referred to as u, with up to four defining clauses. For node u with variable x, and children nodes u_1 and u_0, these clauses encode the formula $u \leftrightarrow ITE(x, u_1, u_0)$. As described in Section 2, we will have $\lambda(u) = \max\{\lambda(x) + 1, \lambda(u_1), \lambda(u_0)\}$.

As in [9], we associate leaf nodes L_0 and L_1 directly with logical values $\bot$ and $\top$. When constructing node u, if either u_1 or u_0 is a leaf node, the defining clauses may be simplified, and some may degenerate to tautologies. By defining $\lambda(\bot) = \lambda(\top) = 0$, we can still use the above formula to define the value of $\lambda(u)$, such that $\lambda(u_1) \leq \lambda(u)$, $\lambda(u_0) \leq \lambda(u)$, and $\lambda(x) < \lambda(u)$. This guarantees that the value of $\lambda(u)$ is greater or equal to that of any node or variable occurring in the subgraph with root u.

For node u, define its *support set* $S(u)$ as the set of variables occurring at some node in the subgraph with root u. Based on our construction, any node u will have $\lambda(u) = 2j$ if and only if there is some j and some x for which $x \in X_j \cap S(u)$, and this property does not hold for any $j' > j$.

As a final notation, let $\theta(u)$ denote the set consisting of the defining clauses for all nodes in the subgraph with root u.

The BDD package implements the set of operations shown in the Table 2. Each generates a result node w, and it also generates sets of clauses forming extended reso-

Table 2. Required BDD Operations. Each generates a root node plus a set of proofs.

Operation	Arguments	Result	Proved Properties	
			Truth Preserving	Falsehood Preserving
FROMCLAUSE	C	$u = \bigvee_{l \in C} l$	$C, \theta(u) \vdash u$	$u, \theta(u) \vdash C$
APPLYAND	u, v	$w = u \wedge v$	$u \wedge v \rightarrow w$	$w \rightarrow u, w \rightarrow v$
APPLYOR	u, v	$w = u \vee v$	$u \rightarrow w, v \rightarrow w$	$w \rightarrow u \vee v$
RESTRICT	u, l	$w = u\vert_l$	$l \wedge u \rightarrow w$	$l \wedge w \rightarrow u$

lution proofs of some properties relating the result to the arguments. As shown, some of these properties are truth preserving, while others are falsehood preserving. In each of these, C indicates a clause, u, v, and w are BDD nodes (or their associated extension variables), and l is a literal of an input variable.

These operations serve the following roles:

- FROMCLAUSE generates the BDD representation u of a clause C. It also generates a set of resolution steps proving that the unit clause u is logically entailed by the input clause and defining clauses: $u \in Res(\{C\} \cup \theta(u))$, and the converse: $C \in Res(\{u\} \cup \theta(u))$.
- APPLYAND generates the BDD representation w of the conjunction of its arguments. It also generates a proof that the extension variables for the argument and result nodes satisfy $u \wedge v \rightarrow w$, as well as a proof of the converse: $w \rightarrow u$ and $w \rightarrow v$, and therefore $w \rightarrow u \wedge v$.
- APPLYOR generates the BDD representation w of the disjunction of its arguments. Its generated proofs include $u \rightarrow w$ and $v \rightarrow w$, implying that $u \vee v \rightarrow w$, as well as the converse: $w \rightarrow u \vee v$.
- RESTRICT generates the restriction w of argument u with respect to literal l. It generates proofs that the operation satisfies *downward* implication: $l \wedge u \rightarrow w$, and also *upward* implication: $l \wedge w \rightarrow u$. This operation has the property that for $x = Var(l)$, variable x will not occur in the subgraph with root w, i.e., $x \notin S(w)$.

4   Integrating Proof Generation into a QBF Solver

PGBDDQ solves a QBF by maintaining a set T of root nodes, which we refer to as "terms." Each term is the result of conjuncting and applying elimination operations to some subset of the input clauses. T initially contains the root nodes for the BDD representations of the input clauses. The solver repeatedly removes one or two terms from T, performs a quantification or conjunction operation, and adds the result to T, except that terms with value L_1 are not added. Quantifiers are eliminated in reverse order, starting with block X_m and continuing through X_1. The process continues until either some generated term is the leaf value L_0, indicating that the formula is false, or the set becomes empty, indicating that the formula is true. The solver simultaneously generates proof steps, including ones that add a unit clause u for each node $u \in T$.

Our presentation describes the general requirements for applying conjunction and elimination operations. These operations can be used to implement the basic method described in Section 2, as well as more sophisticated strategies that defer conjunctions until they are required before performing some of the elimination operations [23, 24].

Universal quantification commutes with conjunction and so can be applied to the terms independently. Applying existential quantification, on the other hand, requires performing conjunction operations until the variables to be quantified occur only in a single term.

4.1 Dual Proof Generation

For both technical and implementation reasons, which we explain below, we require the input formula to have only a single variable in each quantifier block. This restriction can be satisfied by rewriting an arbitrary QBF, such that a quantifier block with k variables is *serialized*, splitting it into a sequence of k distinct quantification levels.

When generating a dual proof, the solver generates steps proving that each update to the set of terms T preserves equivalence with the input formula. More formally, consider a matrix ψ containing the following clauses: 1) unit clause u for each $u \in T$, plus 2) all of the defining clauses $\theta(u)$ for the subgraph rooted by each node $u \in T$. Let $\mathcal{Q}$ be the compatible quantifier prefix formed by augmenting input prefix $\mathcal{Q}_I$ with the extension variables associated with the nodes in these subgraphs. Then each update preserves the invariant that $\mathcal{Q}_I \, \psi_I \leftrightarrow \mathcal{Q} \, \psi$. Furthermore, the solver takes care to systematically delete clauses once they are no longer needed, using the removal rules listed in Table 1. That enables it to finish with an empty set of clauses in the event the formula is true. The initial set of terms T consists of a root node u for each input clause C, and the solver uses the proof that $C, \theta(u) \vdash u$ to justify adding unit clause u to the proof. It then uses this unit clause, plus the proof that $u, \theta(u) \vdash C$ to justify deleting input clause C.

Each step proceeds by generating new terms and by adding and removing clauses in the proof. Suppose the step involves computing results with root nodes $w_1, ..., w_n$ based on argument terms $u_1, ..., u_k$. If any of the result nodes is BDD leaf L_0, then the formula is false. The solver can use truth-preserving rules generated by the BDD operations to justify adding an empty clause. Otherwise, the solver removes the argument terms from T and adds the result nodes, except for any equal to BDD leaf L_1. The solver uses the existing unit clauses plus the truth-preserving rules to justify adding unit clauses for each newly added term. It then uses the falsehood-preserving rules and the newly added unit clauses to justify deleting the unit clauses associated with the argument terms. It must also explicitly generate rules to remove some intermediate clauses that are added during these proof constructions. Other clauses, including the defining clauses for the BDD nodes and the clauses added during the BDD operations get removed by a separate process described in Section 4.2. The net effect for each step then is to replace the argument terms in T by the non-constant result terms, maintaining a unit clause for each term in T as part of the proof.

Conjunction operations. For $u, v \in T$, the solver computes $w = \text{APPLYAND}(u, v)$. For the case where $w = L_0$ the generated truth-preserving proof will be the clause $\overline{u} \vee \overline{v}$, which resolves with unit clauses u and v to generate the empty clause—the solver has proved that the formula is false.

Otherwise, the solver sets T to be $T - \{u, v\} \cup w$. The proof for adding unit clause w follows by resolving the unit clauses u and v with the generated clause $\overline{u} \vee \overline{v} \vee w$, (i.e., $u \wedge v \to w$). The generated clauses $w \to u$ and $w \to v$ each resolve with unit clause w to justify deleting unit clauses u and v.

Universal elimination operation. This operation is performed when $Q_j = \forall$, and by our restriction, we must have $X_j = \{x\}$ for some universal variable x. We also require that the input variables for blocks $X_{j'}$ such that $j' > j$ have already been eliminated.

Since universal quantification commutes with conjunction, the solver can quantify each term individually and let subsequent conjunction operations perform the conjunction indicated in (4). That is, for each $u \in T$ such that $x \in S(u)$, operation RESTRICT is used to compute the two restrictions $w_x = u|_x$ and $w_{\overline{x}} = u|_{\overline{x}}$. These will generate proofs of two downward implications: $l \wedge u \to w_l$ for $l \in \{x, \overline{x}\}$, as well as proofs of two upward implications: $l \wedge w_l \to u$.

If w_l equals leaf node L_0 for either $l = x$ or $l = \overline{x}$, then the corresponding downward implication will be a clause of the form $l \wedge u \to \bot = \overline{l} \vee \overline{u}$. Resolving this with the unit clause u and applying universal reduction generates the empty clause—the solver has proved that the formula is false.

Consider the general case, where neither w_x nor $w_{\overline{x}}$ is a leaf node. The solver sets $T = T \cup \{w_x, w_{\overline{x}}\} - \{u\}$. The downward implications $l \wedge u \to w_l$ can be resolved with unit clause u to yield the clause $l \to w_l$ for $l \in \{x, \overline{x}\}$. We can be certain that $\lambda(w_l) < \lambda(x)$ for both values of l, since $x \notin S(w_l)$. Applying universal reduction to the two generated clauses then yields the unit clauses w_x and $w_{\overline{x}}$. Resolving each unit clause w_l with the upward implication $l \wedge w_l \to u$ gives the clause $l \to u$, for $l \in \{x, \overline{x}\}$. Resolving these with each other justifies deleting unit clause u. Intermediate clauses $\overline{x} \to w$, $x \to w$, $x \to w_x$, and $\overline{x} \to w_{\overline{x}}$ are removed by resolution deletion.

The case where one of the restrictions is the leaf node L_1 is handled similarly to the general case, except that this node is not added to T.

Our implementation applies the conjunction operation to terms w_x and $w_{\overline{x}}$ immediately after they are generated to avoid causing the number of terms to expand by a factor of 2^k when the formula contains a sequence of k universal quantifiers.

Existential elimination operations. This operation is performed when $Q_j = \exists$. We can assume that $X_j = \{x\}$ for some existential variable x. We require that the input variables for blocks $X_{j'}$ such that $j' > j$ have already been eliminated. We also require the conjunction operations to have reduced T to contain at most one node u such that $x \in S(u)$. The solver proceeds as follows to existentially quantify x from u yielding a new term w and creating the justification for adding unit clause w. It also removes unit clause u, as well as some intermediate clauses. Note that w can equal L_1, but not L_0.

1. Compute $u_x = \text{RESTRICT}(u, x)$ and $u_{\overline{x}} = \text{RESTRICT}(u, \overline{x})$, generating proofs of the downward implications $x \wedge u \to u_x$ and $\overline{x} \wedge u \to u_{\overline{x}}$, as well as the upward implications $x \wedge u_x \to u$ and $\overline{x} \wedge u_{\overline{x}} \to u$. Resolving the two downward implications with the unit clause u justifies adding clauses $C_x = x \to u_x$ and $C_{\overline{x}} = \overline{x} \to u_{\overline{x}}$. These clauses form the Shannon expansions (2) of u with respect to variable x.

2. For $l \in \{x, \overline{x}\}$, resolving clause C_l with the upward implication $l \wedge u_l \to u$ justifies adding clauses $x \to u$ and $\overline{x} \to u$. Resolving these with each other justifies deleting unit clause u. This step completes the replacement of u by its Shannon expansion.

3. Apply *clause removal* to remove every clause containing a literal l such that $\lambda(l) > \lambda(x) = 2j - 1$. This is described in Section 4.2.

4. C_x and $C_{\overline{x}}$ are the only clauses remaining that contain either x or $\overline{x}$. Resolving these with each other justifies adding clause $u_x \vee u_{\overline{x}}$. The existential elimination rule can now be applied to justify deleting C_x and $C_{\overline{x}}$, with the result that there will be no further clauses containing any literal l with $\lambda(l) \geq \lambda(x)$.

5. Compute $w = \text{APPLYOR}(u_x, u_{\overline{x}})$, generating three proofs: $u_x \to w$, $u_{\overline{x}} \to w$, and $w \to u_x \vee u_{\overline{x}}$.

6. If w is leaf node L_1, then the falsehood-preserving proof generated by APPLYOR derives the clause $u_x \vee u_{\overline{x}}$. This proof justifies deleting the instance of this clause added in step 5. If w is a nonleaf node, then the first two proofs from Step 5 can be resolved with the clause $u_x \vee u_{\overline{x}}$ to justify adding unit clause w, and the third can be resolved with this unit clause to justify deleting clause $u_x \vee u_{\overline{x}}$. This completes the replacement of u by the disjunction of its two restrictions, as in (3).

7. If w is leaf node L_1, then set T to $T - \{u\}$. Otherwise, set it to $T - \{u\} \cup \{w\}$.

Overall Operation: For a false formula, the solver will terminate with the generation of leaf value L_0 during a conjunction or universal quantification operation. These cases will cause the proof to terminate with the addition of an empty clause. For a true formula, the solver will finish with T equal to the empty set, since it never adds a leaf node to T. A final clause removal operation with quantification level 0 then yields $\psi_t = \emptyset$.

We can see now why we impose the restriction that any quantifier block X_j with $Q_j = \forall$ contain only one variable. Without it, the universal variable elimination operation may not be possible. Suppose $X_j = \{x, x'\}$. Attempting to perform the universal quantification operation on variable x could yield a BDD node w_l, with either $l = x$ or $l = \overline{x}$, that depends on x'. That would require that $\lambda(w_l) > \lambda(x') = \lambda(x)$, and so the universal reduction rule could not be applied. Serializing the universal blocks avoids this difficulty, without limiting the generality of the solver.

4.2   Clause Removal

As a dual proof proceeds, the BDD operations cause clauses to be added as extension variables are introduced and as inferences are made via resolution. Other clauses are added and removed explicitly by the proof steps, including the unit clauses for each term and the intermediate clauses generated by the steps. In order to support having the outcome of the solver be true, the defining and resolution clauses must be removed in order to ultimately end up with an empty set of clauses. The solver must justify their removal, since clause deletion is not, in general, equivalence preserving.

Clause removal is triggered when performing existential quantification, just before applying the variable elimination rule with variable x to remove clauses C_x and $C_{\overline{x}}$ (step 3). We must first ensure that there are no other clauses containing x or $\overline{x}$.

Our method is to remove any clause C containing a literal l for which $\lambda(l) > \lambda(x) = 2j - 1$. Clause removal can proceed by stepping through the clauses in the reverse order from how they were added. If a clause that was added by resolution contains a literal l with $\lambda(l) \geq 2j$, it can be removed via resolution deletion, using the same antecedent as was used when it was added.

Suppose the solver encounters the defining clauses for a node u with $\lambda(u) \geq 2j$. It can be certain that all clauses added by resolution that contain either u or $\bar{u}$ have already been removed, since these must have followed the introduction of u in the clause ordering. Similarly, any parent node v of u must have already had its defining clauses removed, since the defining clauses for v must occur after those for u. The existential elimination rule can therefore be used to remove the defining clauses for u.

Working through the set of clauses in reverse order, the solver may encounter clauses added by resolution and defining clauses containing only literals l with $\lambda(l) < 2j - 1$. These need not be removed, and indeed they can prove useful (clauses added by resolution) or necessary (some defining clauses) for subsequent proof steps. They will be deleted by clause removal during later phases.

We can see now why we impose the restriction that any quantifier block X_j with $Q_j = \exists$ contain only one variable. It enables the use of the λ values to determine which clauses should be removed to eliminate any dependency on existential variable x. Serializing the existential quantifier blocks allows this scheme to work without limiting the generality of the solver.

4.3 Specializing to Refutation or Satisfaction Proofs

Dual proofs have the advantage that they can be generated as a single pass, without knowing in advance whether the formula is true or false. On the other hand, they are, by necessity, somewhat longer and require more time to generate and to check. Another approach is to know (or guess) what the outcome will be and then direct the solver to generate a pure refutation or satisfaction proof. Specializing the proof generation to one of these forms is straightforward, and it can take advantage of more efficient ways to perform some of the quantifications.

A refutation proof need only justify that each step preserves truth. This enables several optimizations. Observe that deleting a clause always preserves truth, because it can only cause the set of satisfying solutions for the matrix to expand. Therefore clause deletion can be performed without any justification and instead be incorporated into the BDD garbage collection process [9]. Second, the BDD package need not generate the falsehood-preserving proofs shown in Table 2, reducing the number of clauses generated. Finally, the existential operation of (3) is inherently truth preserving. BDD packages can implement the quantification of a function by an entire set of variables via a variant of the Apply algorithm. If the quantification of root node u generates result node w, then the solver can run an implication test after the BDD computation has been performed to prove that $u \rightarrow w$, as is done with our SAT solver [9]. This avoids the need to serialize existential quantifier blocks and to have the solver generate low-level proof steps for each existential variable.

Conversely, a satisfaction proof need only justify that each step preserves falsehood. Adding a clause always preserves falsehood, since it can only reduce the set of satisfying solutions for the matrix, and therefore clause addition can be performed without any justification. In addition, the BDD package need not generate the truth-preserving proofs shown in Table 2. Finally, universal quantification can be performed on an entire block of variables producing node w from argument u. The solver can then run an implication test to generate a proof that $w \rightarrow u$.

5 Experimental Results

PGBDDQ[1] is written entirely in Python and consists of around 3350 lines of code, including a BDD package, support for generating extended-resolution proofs, and the overall QBF solver. By comparison, our proof-generating BDD-based SAT solver required around 2130 lines of code [9]. PGBDDQ can generate proofs in either the QRAT format [13, 14] or in a format we call QPROOF that supports just the proof rules given in Table 1. The latter format requires explicit lists of antecedents, and therefore each step can be checked without any search.

The overall control of PGBDDQ is based on a form of bucket elimination [10], where each quantifier block X_j defines a bucket. It starts by generating BDD representations of the input clauses. The resulting terms are inserted into buckets according to the value of $\lambda(u)$ for each root node u. As described in Section 3.2, this value will be $2j$ when u contains a variable from block X_j in its support, and it has no variables at higher quantification levels.

Processing proceeds from the highest numbered bucket downward. For a universal level, quantification is performed for each bucket element individually with the results placed into buckets according to their values for λ. For an existential level, the elements are conjuncted and then existential quantification is performed. The result is placed into a bucket according to its value of λ.

We can see that this approach defers conjunction as long as possible, only operating on terms at some quantification level j that truly depend on one or more variables in X_j. Similar techniques have been used in other BDD-based QBF solvers [23, 24]. However, other implementations place terms into buckets according to the BDD level of their root nodes, requiring the BDD variables to be ordered as the inverse of the quantification ordering. By labeling each node with its value of λ, we can determine the appropriate bucket from the root node without regard to the BDD variable ordering.

We have tested PGBDDQ on a number of scalable benchmark problems, finding it performs well in some cases, scaling polynomially, and poorly in others, scaling exponentially. Here we present results for a problem based on a two-player game. It provides insights into how polynomial scaling can be achieved, as well as the performance of the solver and two checkers.

Two-player games provide a rich set of benchmarks for QBF solvers, with each turn being translated into a quantification level. To encode the game from the perspective of the first player (Player A), A's turns are encoded with existential quantifiers, while the second player's (Player B) turns are encoded with universal quantifiers. The formula will be true if the game has a guaranteed winning strategy for A. The encoding of a game into QBF constrains the two players to only make legal moves. It also expresses the conditions under which A is the winner, namely that the game consist of t consecutive moves, for an odd value of t. Conversely, we can encode the formula where B has a winning strategy by reversing the quantifiers and expressing that the game must consist of an even number of consecutive moves. For a game where no draws are possible, these two formulas will be complementary.

---

[1] A demonstration version, complete with solver, checker, and benchmarks, is available at https://github.com/rebryant/pgbddq-artifact.

Consider a game played on a $1 \times N$ grid of squares with a set of dominos, each of which can cover two squares. Players alternate turns, each placing a domino to cover two adjacent squares. The game completes when no more moves are possible, taking at most $\lfloor N/2 \rfloor$ turns. The first player who cannot place a domino loses. This *linear domino placement* game is isomorphic to the object-removal game "Dawson's Kales" [2]. It can be shown that player B has a winning strategy for $N \in \{0, 1, 15, 35\}$ as well as for all values of the form $34\,i + c$ where $i \geq 0$ and $c \in \{5, 9, 21, 25, 29\}$ [27].

The game is encoded as a QBF by introducing a set of $N - 1$ input variables for each possible move, each corresponding to the boundary between a pair of adjacent squares. A set of $N - 1$ Tseitin variables encodes the board state after each move, and sets of clauses enforce the conditions that 1) each move should cover exactly one boundary, and 2) neither that boundary nor the two adjacent ones should have been covered previously. In all, there are around $N^2/4$ universal input variables, $N^2/4$ existential input variables, and $3N^2/2$ Tseitin variables. The number of clauses grows as $\Theta(N^3)$ due to the quadratic number of clauses to enforce the exactly-one constraints on the input variables for each move.

To achieve polynomial performance, we found that several problem-specific techniques are required. First, the Tseitin variables for a given move are placed in an existential quantifier block immediately following the block for the input variables for the move. This is logically equivalent to the usual convention of placing all Tseitin variables in an innermost quantifier block, but it enables the bucket elimination algorithm to process the clauses for each move in sequence, rather than expanding the formulas in terms of only the input variables at the outset. Second, all variables are ordered for the BDD in "boundary-major" ordering. That is, all variables, including input and Tseitin variables, for the first boundary on the board are included from the first quantification level to the last. The variables for the second boundary follow similarly, and so on for all $N - 1$ boundaries. This ordering has the effect that, when processing the clauses for some move, the variables encoding the next, and previous state for a boundary, as well as the proposed change to its state, are localized within the ordering. Finally, when splitting a quantifier block into a series of single-variable blocks, we ordered them according to their BDD variable ordering. Since the solver eliminates variables in the reverse of their quantifier ordering, this convention causes the disjunction and conjunction operations of Equations (3) and (4) to be performed mainly on subgraphs of the BDD below the variables being quantified. This enables greater use of previously computed results via the operation cache.

Table 3 shows the performance of PGBDDQ, two checkers, and two other QBF solvers on the domino placement game as functions of N. It shows first cases where the encoded player has a winning strategy, and therefore the formula is true, and then cases where the encoded player's opponent has a winning strategy, and therefore the formula is false. Dual proofs were generated for both cases. For measurements with sufficient data points, we show the scaling trends, obtained by performing a linear regression on the logarithms of data generated for each value of N in increments of 5. All measurements were performed on a 4.2 GHz Intel Core i7 (I7-7700K) processor with 32 GB of memory running the MacOS operating system. Times are measured in elapsed seconds.

Table 3. Experimental Results for Dual Proof Generation with Linear Domino Placement Game. The first data series are for proofs of true formulas, and the second are for false formulas. Entries shown as "—" indicate cases where the program exceeded a 7200-second time limit.

N	Winner/	Input	PGBDDQ				Other solvers	
	Player	Clauses	Total Clauses	Solve	Qproof	QRAT-TRIM	DEPQBF	GHOSTQ
10	A/A	666	132,138	3.1	3.3	3.4	0.1	0.0
15	B/B	1,725	628,392	15.2	15.7	43.8	3.8	1.3
20	A/A	3,880	2,572,139	67.3	65.5	605.0	1896.6	57.9
25	B/B	6,637	7,098,146	202.6	199.5	4265.6	—	—
40	A/A	24,010	83,736,352	3358.6	3479.5	—	—	—
Trend		$N^{2.7}$	$N^{4.5}$	$N^{4.8}$	$N^{4.8}$			
10	A/B	664	132,403	3.1	3.2	7.3	0.1	0.0
15	B/A	1,728	629,530	15.2	15.5	108.7	3.6	1.0
20	A/B	3,885	2,580,284	67.2	66.7	1521.5	—	49.1
25	B/A	6,631	7,083,515	205.1	190.0	—	—	6942.2
40	A/B	24,000	83,662,168	3279.2	3457.4	—	—	—
Trend		$N^{2.7}$	$N^{4.5}$	$N^{4.8}$	$N^{4.8}$			

As indicated in the column labeled "Input Clauses," the number of clauses grows as $N^{2.7}$, not quite reaching the asymptotic value of N^3. The number of proof clauses generated by PGBDDQ are nearly the same for both true and false formulas, with growth rates of $N^{4.5}$. The time taken by the solver (labeled "Solve") , and by our own checker ("Qproof") scale at about the same rate as the number of proof clauses.

We also benchmarked the QBF proof checker QRAT-TRIM [13, 14]. This program was already equipped to handle our forms of refutation and satisfaction proofs, and it can handle dual proofs without modification. The only concession to the idiosyncrasies of PGBDDQ was to serialize the universal quantifier blocks in the prefix of false formulas. This is required to enable application of the universal reduction rule. The existential blocks can stay intact, since our only reason to serialize these is to guide the clause removal process. Although the scaling of QRAT-TRIM is poor, it is encouraging that the solver can be verified by a checker that predates it by a number of years.

For comparison, we evaluated the performance of two other QBF solvers on this benchmark: DEPQBF, version 6.0 [20], and GHOSTQ [15, 19]. We found they are both very fast for smaller values of N but then reach a narrow range of values for which they transition from running in just a few seconds to exceeding the timeout limit of 7200 seconds. For DEPQBF, this transition occurs as N ranges from 17 to 21, and for GHOSTQ, as N ranges from 21 to 26. PGBDDQ is much slower for small values of N, but it keeps scaling without hitting a sudden cutoff.

Although we did not run EBDDRES [17], we can use PGBDDQ to evaluate the impact of having the BDD variable ordering be the inverse of the quantifier ordering. Our experiments show that this ordering causes the runtime and proof sizes to scale exponentially in N. With $N = 14$ and B as the player, PGBDDQ runs for 4100 seconds to generate a refutation proof with 114,157,025 clauses. By contrast, a boundary-major ordering requires just 6 seconds and generates a proof with 309,387 clauses.

Table 4. Experimental Results for Specialized Proof Generation with Linear Domino Placement Game. The first data series are for satisfaction proofs, and the second are for refutation proofs.

N	Winner/Player	Input Clauses	Total Clauses	Solve	Qproof
10	A/A	666	90,924	1.8	1.4
20	A/A	3,880	1,516,756	36.4	24.0
30	A/A	11,166	10,466,168	346.0	192.6
40	A/A	24,010	44,874,662	1990.3	1254.8
45	A/A	32,241	74,891,554	4033.4	2760.8
Trend		$N^{2.7}$	$N^{4.4}$	$N^{4.8}$	$N^{4.7}$
10	A/B	664	126,127	2.4	1.8
20	A/B	3,885	1,232,252	27.3	18.6
30	A/B	11,159	7,084,367	180.0	121.6
40	A/B	24,010	26,150,238	773.9	565.0
50	A/B	43,904	85,077,630	2955.4	2151.4
Trend		$N^{2.7}$	$N^{4.0}$	$N^{4.3}$	$N^{4.3}$

Table 4 shows the advantage of generating specialized proofs when the formula is known in advance to be true or false. Comparing the columns labeled "Total Clauses" in Tables 3 and 4, we can see especially that refutation proofs are asymptotically shorter. These can take advantage of the more efficient approach to existential quantification in handling the large number of Tseitin variables. Again, the solution and checking time track the proof sizes. These optimizations allowed us to solve larger instances of the problem—up to $N = 45$ for true instances and $N = 50$ for false ones.

6   Conclusions

We have demonstrated that a QBF solver can emit a single proof as it operates, leading to either an empty clause for a false formula or an empty set of clauses for a true one. Both the proof and the time required to check it scale as the number of BDD operations performed. Moreover, a BDD-based QBF solver can allow the choice of BDD variable ordering to be made independently from the quantifier ordering. This feature can be critical to obtaining performance that scales polynomially with the problem size.

Our prototype is only a start in implementing a fully automated QBF solver. Such a solver must be able to choose a BDD variable ordering based on the input formula structure. It must also be able to identify and move Tseitin variables to earlier positions in the quantifier ordering, generating proof steps justifying that this transformation is equivalence preserving.

The underlying operation of PGBDDQ has potential applications beyond QBF solving. The program could stop the process described in Section 4.1 at any point and generate a QBF that is provably equivalent to the input formula. PGBDDQ could therefore be used as a preprocessor for other solvers, and for other applications that require reasoning about Boolean formulas with quantifiers.

Acknowledgements. The second author is supported by NSF grant CCF-2010951.

References

1. Andersen, H.R.: An introduction to binary decision diagrams. Tech. rep., Technical University of Denmark (October 1997)
2. Berlekamp, E.R., Conway, J.H., Guy, R.K.: Winning Ways for your Mathematical Plays: Volume 1, Second edition. CRC Press (2001)
3. Beyersdorff, O., Chew, L., Janota, M.: Extension variables in QBF resolution. In: AAAI Workshop on Beyond NP (2016)
4. Biere, A.: Resolve and expand. In: Theory and Applications of Satisfiability Testing (SAT). LNCS, vol. 3542, pp. 59–70 (2005)
5. Biere, A., Lonsing, F., Seidl, M.: Blocked clause elimination for QBF. In: Conference on Automated Deduction (CADE). LNCS, vol. 6803, pp. 101–115. Springer (2011)
6. Bryant, R.E.: Graph-based algorithms for Boolean function manipulation. IEEE Trans. Computers **35**(8), 677–691 (1986)
7. Bryant, R.E.: Symbolic Boolean manipulation with ordered binary decision diagrams. ACM Computing Surveys **24**(3), 293–318 (September 1992)
8. Bryant, R.E.: Binary decision diagrams. In: Clarke, E.M., Henzinger, T.A., Veith, H., Bloem, R. (eds.) Handbook of Model Checking, pp. 191–217. Springer (2018)
9. Bryant, R.E., Heule, M.J.H.: Generating extended resolution proofs with a BDD-based SAT solver. In: Tools and Algorithms for the Construction and Analysis of Systems (TACAS) (2021)
10. Dechter, R.: Bucket elimination: A unifying framework for reasoning. Artificial Intelligence **113**(1–2), 41–85 (1999)
11. Garey, M.R., Johnson, D.S.: Computers and Intractability: A Guide to the Theory of NP-Completeness. W. H. Freeman (1979)
12. Giunchiglia, E., Narizzano, M., Tacchella, A.: Clause/term resolution and learning in the evaluation of quantified Boolean formulas. Journal of AI Research **26**, 371–416 (2006)
13. Heule, M.J.H., Seidl, M., Biere, A.: A unified proof system for QBF preprocessing. In: International Joint Conference on Automated Reasoning (IJCAR). LNCS, vol. 8562, pp. 91–106 (2014)
14. Heule, M.J.H., Seidl, M., Biere, A.: Solution validation and extraction for QBF. Journal of Automated Reasoning **58**, 97–125 (2017)
15. Janota, M., Klieber, W., Marques-Silva, J.a.P., Clarke, E.M.: Solving QBF with counterexample guided refinement. Artificial Intelligence **234**, 1–25 (2016)
16. Jussila, T., Sinz, C., Biere, A.: Extended resolution proofs for symbolic SAT solving with quantification. In: Theory and Applications of Satisfiability Testing (SAT). LNCS, vol. 4121, pp. 54–60 (2006)
17. Jussila, T., Sinz, C., Biere, A., Kröning, D., Wintersteiger, C.M.: A first step towards a unified proof checker for QBF. In: Theory and Applications of Satisfiability Testing (SAT). LNCS, vol. 4501, pp. 201–714 (2007)
18. Kleine Büning, H., Karpinski, M., Flögel, A.: Resolution for quantified Boolean formulas. Information and Computation **117**(1), 12–18 (1995)
19. Klieber, W.: GhostQ system description. Journal on Satisfiability, Boolean Modeling, and Computation **11**, 65–72 (2019)
20. Lonsing, F., Egly, U.: DepQBF 6.0: A search-based QBF solver beyond traditional QCDCL. In: Conference on Automated Deduction (CADE). LNCS, vol. 10395, pp. 371–384 (2017)
21. Narizzano, M., Peschiera, C., Pulina, L., Tacchella, A.: Evaluating and certifying QBFs: A comparison of state-of-the-art tools. AI Communications **22**(4), 191–210 (2009)
22. Niemetz, A., Preiner, M., Lonsing, F., Seidl, M., Biere, A.: Resolution-based certificate extraction for QBF. In: Theory and Applications of Satisfiability Testing (SAT). LNCS, vol. 7317, pp. 430–435 (2012)

23. Olivo, O., Emerson, E.A.: A more efficient BDD-based QBF solver. In: Principles and Practice of Constraint Programming (CP). LNCS, vol. 6876, pp. 675–690 (2011)
24. Pan, G., Vardi, M.Y.: Symbolic decision procedures for QBF. In: Principles and Practice of Constraint Programming (CP). LNCS, vol. 3258, pp. 453–467 (2004)
25. Peitl, T., Slivovsky, F., Szeider, S.: Polynomial-time validation of QCDCL certificates. In: Theory and Applications of Satisfiability Testing (SAT). LNCS, vol. 10929, pp. 253–269 (2018)
26. Sinz, C., Biere, A.: Extended resolution proofs for conjoining BDDs. In: Computer Science Symposium in Russia (CSR). LNCS, vol. 3967, pp. 600–611 (2006)
27. Sloane, N.J.A., The OEIS Foundation: The on-line encyclopedia of integer sequences (2012), http://oeis.org/A215721, sequence A215721
28. Tseitin, G.S.: On the complexity of derivation in propositional calculus. In: Automation of Reasoning: 2: Classical Papers on Computational Logic 1967–1970. pp. 466–483. Springer (1983)

Open Access This chapter is licensed under the terms of the Creative Commons Attribution 4.0 International License (http://creativecommons.org/licenses/by/4.0/), which permits use, sharing, adaptation, distribution and reproduction in any medium or format, as long as you give appropriate credit to the original author(s) and the source, provide a link to the Creative Commons license and indicate if changes were made.

The images or other third party material in this chapter are included in the chapter's Creative Commons license, unless indicated otherwise in a credit line to the material. If material is not included in the chapter's Creative Commons license and your intended use is not permitted by statutory regulation or exceeds the permitted use, you will need to obtain permission directly from the copyright holder.

Reliable Reconstruction of Fine-grained Proofs in a Proof Assistant

Hans-Jörg Schurr[1], Mathias Fleury[2,3], and Martin Desharnais[4]

[1] University of Lorraine, CNRS, Inria, and LORIA, Nancy, France
hans-jorg.schurr@inria.fr
[2] Johannes Kepler University Linz, Linz, Austria
mathias.fleury@jku.at
[3] Max-Planck Institute für Informatik, Saarland Informatics Campus, Saarbrücken,
Germany
[4] Universität der Bundeswehr München, München, Germany
martin.desharnais@unibw.de

Abstract. We present a fast and reliable reconstruction of proofs generated by the SMT solver veriT in Isabelle. The fine-grained proof format makes the reconstruction simple and efficient. For typical proof steps, such as arithmetic reasoning and skolemization, our reconstruction can avoid expensive search. By skipping proof steps that are irrelevant for Isabelle, the performance of proof checking is improved. Our method increases the success rate of Sledgehammer by halving the failure rate and reduces the checking time by 13%. We provide a detailed evaluation of the reconstruction time for each rule. The runtime is influenced by both simple rules that appear very often and common complex rules.

Keywords: automatic theorem provers · proof assistants ·
proof verification

1 Introduction

Proof assistants are used in verification and formal mathematics to provide trustworthy, machine-checkable formal proofs of theorems. Proof *automation* reduces the burden of finding proofs and allows proof assistant users to focus on the core of their arguments instead of technical details. A successful approach implemented by "hammers," like Sledgehammer for Isabelle [15], is to heuristically selects facts from the background; use an external automatic theorem prover, such as a satisfiability modulo theories (SMT) solver [12], to filter facts needed to discharge the goal; and to use the filtered facts to find a trusted proof.

Isabelle does not accept proofs that do not go through the assistant's inference kernel. Hence, Sledgehammer attempts to find the fastest internal method that can recreate the proof (*preplay*). This is often a call of the *smt* tactic, which runs an SMT solver, parses the proof, and reconstructs it through the kernel. This reconstruction allows the usage of external provers. The smt tactic was originally developed for the SMT solver Z3 [18, 34].

© The Author(s) 2021
A. Platzer and G. Sutcliffe (Eds.): CADE 2021, LNAI 12699, pp. 450–467, 2021.
https://doi.org/10.1007/978-3-030-79876-5_26

The SMT solver CVC4 [10] is one of the best solvers on Sledgehammer generated problems [14], but currently does not produce proofs for problems with quantifiers. To reconstruct its proofs, Sledgehammer mostly uses the smt tactic based on Z3. However, since CVC4 uses more elaborate quantifier instantiation techniques, many problems provable for CVC4 are unprovable for Z3. Therefore, Sledgehammer regularly fails to find a trusted proof and the user has to write the proofs manually. veriT [19] (Sect. 2) supports these techniques and we extend the smt tactic to reconstruct its proofs. With the new reconstruction (Sect. 3), more smt calls are successful. Hence, less manual labor is required from users.

The runtime of the smt method depends on the runtime of the reconstruction and the solver. To simplify the reconstruction, we do not treat veriT as a black box anymore, but extend it to produce more detailed proofs that are easier to reconstruct. We use detailed rules for simplifications with a combination of propositional, arithmetic, and quantifier reasoning. Similarly, we add additional information to avoid search, e.g., for linear arithmetic and for term normalization. Our reconstruction method uses the newly provided information, but it also has a *step skipping* mode that combines some steps (Sect. 4).

A very early prototype of the extension was used to validate the fine-grained proof format itself [7, Sect. 6.2, second paragraph]. We also published some details of the reconstruction method and the rules [25] before adapting veriT to ease reconstruction. Here, we focus on the new features.

We optimize the performance further by tuning the search performed by veriT. Multiple options influence the execution time of an SMT solver. To fine-tune veriT's search procedure, we select four different combinations of options, or *strategies*, by generating typical problems and selecting options with complementary performance on these problems. We extend Sledgehammer to compare these four selected strategies and suggest the fastest to the user. We then evaluate the reconstruction with Sledgehammer on a large benchmark set. Our new tactic halves the failure rate. We also study the time required to reconstruct each rule. Many simple rules occur often, showing the importance of step skipping (Sect. 5).

Finally, we discuss related work (Sect. 6). Compared to the prototype [25], the smt tactic is now thoroughly tested. We fixed all issues revealed during development and improved the performance of the reconstruction method. The work presented here is integrated into Isabelle version 2021; i.e., since this version Sledgehammer can also suggest veriT, without user interaction. To simplify future reconstruction efforts, we document the proof format and all rules used by veriT. The resulting reference manual is part of the veriT documentation [40].

2   veriT and Proofs

The SMT solver veriT is an open source solver based on the CDCL($\mathcal{T}$) calculus. In proof-production mode, it supports the theories of uninterpreted functions with equality, linear real and integer arithmetic, and quantifiers. To support quantifiers veriT uses quantifier instantiation and extensive preprocessing.

veriT's proof syntax is an extension of SMT-LIB [11] which uses S-expressions and prefix notation. The proofs are refutation proofs, i.e., proofs of ⊥. A proof is an indexed list of steps. Each step has a conclusion clause (cl ..) and is annotated with a rule, a list of premises, and some rule-dependent arguments. veriT distinguishes 90 rules [40]. Subproofs are the key feature of the proof format. They introduce an additional *context*. Contexts are used to reason about binders, e.g., preprocessing steps like transformation under quantifiers.

The conclusions of rules with contexts are always equalities. The context models a substitution into the free variables of the term on the left-hand side of the equality. Consider the following proof fragment that renames the variable name x to vr, as done during preprocessing:

```
(assume a0 (exists (x A) (f x)))
(anchor :step t3 :args (:= x vr))
(step t1 (cl (= x vr)) :rule refl)
(step t2 (cl (= (f x) (f vr))) :rule cong :premises (t1))
(step t3 (cl (= (exists (x A) (f x))
               (exists (vr A) (f vr))) :rule bind)
```

The **assume** command repeats input assertions or states local assumptions. In this fragment the assumption a0 is not used. Subproofs start with the **anchor** command that introduces a context. Semantically, the context is a shorthand for a lambda abstraction of the free variable and an application of the substituted term. Here the context is $x \mapsto$ vr and the step t1 means $(\lambda x.\ x)$ vr = vr. The step is proven by congruence (rule **cong**). Then congruence is applied again (step t2) to prove that $(\lambda x.\ f\ x)$ vr = f vr and step t3 concludes the renaming.

During proof search each module of veriT appends steps onto a list. Once the proof is completed, veriT performs some cleanup before printing the proof. First, a pruning phase removes branches of the proof not connected to the root ⊥. Second, a merge phase removes duplicated steps. The final pass prepares the data structures for the optional term sharing via name annotations.

3   Overview of the veriT-Powered smt Tactic

Isabelle is a generic proof assistant based on an intuitionistic logic framework, *Pure*, and is almost always only used parameterized with a logic. In this work we use only Isabelle/HOL, the parameterization of Isabelle with higher-order logic with rank-1 (top level) polymorphism. Isabelle adheres to the LCF [26] tradition. Its kernel supports only a small number of inferences. Tactics are programs that prove a goal by using only the kernel for inferences. The LCF tradition also means that external tools, like SMT solvers, are not trusted.

Nevertheless, external tools are successfully used. They provide relevant facts or a detailed proof. The Sledgehammer tool implements the former and passes the filtered facts to trusted tactics during preplay. The smt tactic implements the latter approach. The provided proof is checked by Isabelle. We focus on the smt tactic, but we also extended Sledgehammer to also suggest our new tactic.

The smt tactic translates the current goal to the SMT-LIB format [11], runs an SMT solver, parses the proof, and replays it through Isabelle's kernel. To choose the smt tactic the user applies (smt (z3)) to use Z3 and (smt (verit)) to use veriT. We will refer to them as z-smt and v-smt. The proof formats of Z3 and veriT are so different that separate reconstruction modules are needed. The v-smt tactic performs four steps:

1. It negates the proof goal to have a refutation proof and also encodes the goal into first-order logic. The encoding eliminates lambda functions. To do so, it replaces each lambda function with a new function and creates app operators corresponding to function application. Then veriT is called to find a proof.
2. It parses the proof found by veriT (if one is found) and encodes it as a directed acyclic graph with $\bot$ as the only conclusion.
3. It converts the SMT-LIB terms to typed Isabelle terms and also reverses the encoding used to convert higher-order into first-order terms.
4. It traverses the proof graph, checks that all input assertions match their Isabelle counterpart and then reconstructs the proof step by step using the kernel's primitives.

4 Tuning the Reconstruction

To improve the speed of the reconstruction method, we create small and well-defined rules for preprocessing simplifications (Sect. 4.1). Previously, veriT implicitly normalized every step; e.g., repeated literals were immediately deleted. It now produces proofs for this transformation (Sect. 4.2). Finally, the linear-arithmetic steps contain coefficients which allow Isabelle to reconstruct the step without relying on its limited arithmetic automation (Sect. 4.3). On the Isabelle side, the reconstruction module selectively decodes the first-order encoding (Sect. 4.4). To improve the performance of the reconstruction, it skips some steps (Sect. 4.5).

4.1 Preprocessing Rules

During preprocessing SMT solvers perform simplifications on the operator level which are often akin to simple calculations; e.g., $a \times 0 \times f(x)$ is replaced by 0.

To capture such simplifications, we create a list of 17 new rules: one rule per arithmetic operator, one to replace boolean operators such as XOR with their definition, and one to replace n-ary operator applications with binary applications. This is a compromise: having one rule for every possible simplification would create a longer proof. Since preprocessing uses structural recursion, the implementation simply picks the right rule in each leaf case. The example above now produces a prod_simplify step with the conclusion $a \times 0 \times f(x) = 0$. Previously, a single step of the connect_equiv rule collected all those simplifications and no list of simplifications performed by this rule existed. The reconstruction relied an experimentally created list of tactics to be fast enough.

On the Isabelle side, the reconstruction is fast, because we can direct the search instead of trying automated tactics that can also work on other parts of the formula. For example, the simplifier handles the numeral manipulations of the prod_simplify rule and we restrict it to only use arithmetic lemmas.

Moreover, since we know the performed transformations, we can ignore some parts of the terms by *generalizing*, i.e., replacing them by constants [18]. Because generalized terms are smaller, the search is more directed and we are less likely to hit the search-depth limitation of Isabelle's auto tactic as before. Overall, the reconstruction is more robust and easier to debug.

4.2   Implicit Steps

To simplify reconstruction, we avoid any implicit normal form of conclusions. For example, a rule concluding $t \vee P$ for any formula t can be used to prove $P \vee P$. In such cases veriT automatically normalizes the conclusion $P \vee P$ to P. Without a proof of the normalization, the reconstruction has to handle such cases.

We add new proof rules for the normalization and extend veriT to use them. Instead of keeping only the normalized step, both the original and the normalized step appear in the proof. For the example above, we have the step $P \vee P$ and the normalized P. To remove a double negation $\neg\neg t$ we introduce the tautology $\neg\neg\neg t \vee t$ and resolve it with the original clause. Our changes do not affect any other part of veriT. The solver now also prunes steps concluding $\top$.

On the Isabelle side, the reconstruction becomes more regular with fewer special cases and is more reliable. The reconstruction method can directly reconstruct rules. To deal with the normalization, the reconstruction used to first generate the conclusion of the theorem and then ran the simplifier to match the normalized conclusion. This could not deal with tautologies.

We also improve the proof reconstruction of quantifier instantiation steps. One of the instantiation schemes, *conflicting instances* [8,36], only works on clausified terms. We introduce an explicit quantified-clausification rule qnt_cnf issued before instantiating. While this rule is not detailed, knowing when clausification is needed improves reconstruction, because it avoids clausifying unconditionally. The clausification is also shared between instantiations of the same term.

4.3   Arithmetic Reasoning

We use a proof witness to handle linear arithmetic. When the propositional model is unsatisfiable in the theory of linear real arithmetic, the solver creates la_generic steps. The conclusion is a tautological clause of linear inequalities and equations and the justification of the step is a list of coefficients so that the linear combination is a trivially contradictory inequality after simplification (e.g., $0 \geq 1$). Farkas' lemma guarantees the existence of such coefficients for reals. Most SMT solvers, including veriT, use the simplex method [21] to handle linear arithmetic. It calculates the coefficients during normal operation.

The real arithmetic solver also strengthens inequalities on integer variables before adding them to the simplex method. For example, if x is an integer the inequality $2x < 3$ becomes $x \leq 1$. The corresponding justification is the rational coefficient $1/2$. The reconstruction must replay this strengthening.

The complete linear arithmetic proof step $1 < x \lor 2x < 3$ looks like

```
(step t11 (cl (< 1 x) (< (* 2 x) 3))
      :rule la_generic :args (1 (div 1 2)))
```

The reconstruction of an la_generic step in Isabelle starts with the goal $\bigvee_i \neg c_i$ where each c_i is either an equality or an inequality. The reconstruction method first generalizes over the non-arithmetic parts. Then it transforms the lemma into the equivalent formulation $c_1 \Rightarrow \cdots \Rightarrow c_n \Rightarrow \bot$ and removes all negations (e.g., by replacing $\neg a \leqslant b$ with $b > a$).

Next, the reconstruction method multiplies the equation by the corresponding coefficient. For example, for integers, the equation $A < B$, and the coefficient p/q (with $p > 0$ and $q > 0$), it strengthens the equation and multiplies by p to get

$$p \times (A \operatorname{div} q) + p \times (\text{if } B \operatorname{mod} q = 0 \text{ then } 1 \text{ else } 0) \leqslant p \times (B \operatorname{div} q).$$

The if-then-else term (if $B \operatorname{mod} q = 0$ then 1 else 0) corresponds to the strengthening. If $B \operatorname{mod} q = 0$, the result is an equation of the form $A' + 1 \leqslant B'$, i.e., $A' < B'$. No strengthening is required for the corresponding theorem over reals.

Finally, we can combine all the equations by summing them while being careful with the equalities that can appear. We simplify the resulting (in)equality using Isabelle's simplifier to derive $\bot$.

To replay linear arithmetic steps, Isabelle can also use the tactic linarith as used for Z3 proofs. It searches the coefficients necessary to verify the lemma. The reconstruction used it previously [25], but the tactic can only find integer coefficients and fails if strengthening is required. Now the rule is a mechanically checkable certificate.

4.4   Selective Decoding of the First-order Encoding

Next, we consider an example of a rule that shows the interplay of the higher-order encoding and the reconstruction. To express function application, the encoding introduces the first-order function app and constants for encoded functions. The proof rule eq_congruent expresses congruence on a first-order function: $(t_1 \neq u_1) \lor \ldots \lor (t_n \neq u_n) \lor f(t_1, \ldots, t_n) = f(u_1, \ldots, u_n)$. With the encoding it can conclude $f \neq f' \lor x \neq x' \lor \operatorname{app}(f, x) = \operatorname{app}(f', x')$. If the reconstruction unfolds the entire encoding, it builds the term $f \neq f' \lor x \neq x' \lor fx = f'x'$. It then identifies the functions and the function arguments and uses rewriting to prove that if $f = f'$ and $x = x'$, then $fx = f'x'$.

However, Isabelle β-reduces all terms implicitly, changing the term structure. Assume $f := \lambda x.\ x = a$ and $f' := \lambda x.\ a = x$. After unfolding all constructs that encode higher-order terms and after β-reduction, we get $(\lambda x.\ x = a) \neq (\lambda x.\ a = x') \lor (x \neq x') \lor (x = a) = (a = y')$. The reconstruction method cannot identify the functions and function arguments anymore.

Instead, the reconstruction method does not unfold the encoding including app. This eliminates the need for a special case to detect lambda functions. Such a case was used in the previous prototype, but the code was very involved and hard to test (such steps are rarely used).

4.5   Skipping Steps

The increased number of steps in the fine-grained proof format slows down reconstruction. For example, consider skolemization from $\exists x.\ P\ x$. The proof from Z3 uses *one* step. veriT uses *eight* steps—first renaming it to $(\exists x.\ P\ x) = (\exists v.\ P\ v)$ (with a subproof of at least 2 steps), then concluding the renaming to get $(\exists v.\ P\ v)$ (two steps), then $(\exists v.\ P\ v) = P\ (\epsilon v.\ P\ v)$ (with a subproof of at least 2 steps), and finally $P\ (\epsilon v.\ P\ v)$ (two steps).

To reduce the number of steps, our reconstruction skips two kinds of steps. First, it replaces every usage of the or rule by its only premise. Second, it skips the renaming of bound variables. The proof format treats $\forall x.\ P\ x$ and $\forall y.\ P\ y$ as two different terms and requires a detailed proof of the conversion. Isabelle, however, uses De Bruijn indices and variable names are irrelevant. Hence, we replace steps of the form $(\forall x.\ P\ x) \Leftrightarrow (\forall y.\ P\ y)$ by a single application of reflexivity. Since veriT canonizes all variable names, this eliminates many steps.

We can also simplify the idiom "`equiv_pos2; th_resolution`". veriT generates it for each skolemization and variable renaming. Step skipping replaces it by a single step which we replay using a specialized theorem.

On proof with quantifiers, step skipping can remove more than half of the steps—only four steps remain in the skolemization example above (where two are simply reflexivity). However, with step skipping the smt method is not an independent checker that confirms the validity of every single step in a proof.

5   Evaluation

During development we routinely tested our proof reconstruction to find bugs. As a side effect, we produced SMT-LIB files corresponding to the calls. We measure the performance of veriT with various options on them and select five different strategies (Sect. 5.1). We also evaluate the repartition of the tactics used by Sledgehammer for preplay (Sect. 5.2), and the impact of the rules (Sect. 5.3).

We performed the strategy selection on a computer with two Intel Xeon Gold 6130 CPUs (32 cores, 64 threads) and 192 GiB of RAM. We performed Isabelle experiments with Isabelle version 2021 on a computer with two AMD EPYC 7702 CPUs (128 cores, 256 threads) and 2 TiB of RAM.

5.1   Strategies

veriT exposes a wide range of options to fine-tune the proof search. In order to find good combinations of options (*strategies*), we generate problems with Sledgehammer and use them to fine-tune veriT's search behavior. Generating problems also makes it possible to test and debug our reconstruction.

We test the reconstruction by using Isabelle's *Mirabelle* tool. It reads theories and automatically runs Sledgehammer [14] on all proof steps. Sledgehammer calls various automatic provers (here the SMT solvers CVC4, veriT, and Z3 and the superposition prover E [38]) to *filter* facts and chooses the fastest tactic that can prove the goal. The tactic smt is used as a last resort.

Table 1. Options corresponding to the different veriT strategies

Name	Options
default	(no option)
del_insts	--index-sorts --index-fresh-sorts --ccfv-breadth --inst-deletion
	--index-SAT-triggers --inst-deletion-loops --inst-deletion-track-var
ccfv_SIG	--triggers-new --index-SIG --triggers-sel-rm-specific
ccfv_insts	--triggers-new --index-sorts --index-fresh-sorts --triggers-sel-rm-specific
	--triggers-restrict-combine --inst-deletion-loops --index-SAT-triggers
	--inst-deletion-track-vars --ccfv-index=100000 --ccfv-index-full=1000
	--inst-sorts-threshold=100000 --ematch-exp=10000000 --inst-deletion
best	--triggers-new --index-sorts --index-fresh-sorts --triggers-sel-rm-specific

To generate problems for tuning veriT, we use the theories from HOL-Library (an extended standard library containing various developments) and from the formalizations of Green's theorem [2, 3], the Prime Number Theorem [23], and the KBO ordering [13]. We call Mirabelle with only veriT as a fact filter. This produces SMT files for representative problems Isabelle users want to solve and a series of calls to v-smt. For failing v-smt calls three cases are possible: veriT does not find a proof, reconstruction times out, or reconstruction fails with an error. We solved all reconstruction failures in the test theories.

To find good strategies, we determine which problems are solved by several combination of options within a two second timeout. We then choose the strategy which solves the most benchmarks and three strategies which together solve the most benchmarks. For comparison, we also keep the default strategy.

The strategies are shown in Table 1 and mostly differ in the instantiation schemes. The strategy *del_insts* uses instance deletion [6] and uses a breadth-first algorithm to find conflicting instances. All other strategies rely on extended trigger inference [29]. The strategy *ccfv_SIG* uses a different indexing method for instantiation. It also restricts enumerative instantiation [35], because the options --index-sorts and --index-fresh-sorts are not used. The strategy *ccfv_insts* increases some thresholds. Finally, the strategy *best* uses a subset of the options used by the other strategies. Sledgehammer uses *best* for fact filtering.

We have also considered using a scheduler in Isabelle as used in the SMT competition. The advantage is that we do not need to select the strategy on the Isabelle side. However, it would make v-smt unreliable. A problem solved by only one strategy just before the end of its time slice can become unprovable on slower hardware. Issues with z-smt timeouts have been reported on the Isabelle mailing list, e.g., due to an antivirus delaying the startup [27].

5.2   Improvements of Sledgehammer Results

To measure the performance of the v-smt tactic, we ran Mirabelle on the full HOL-Library, the theory Prime Distribution Elementary (PDE) [22], an executable resolution prover (RP) [37], and the Simplex algorithm [30]. We extended Sledgehammer's proof preplay to try all veriT strategies and added instrumentation for

Table 2. Outcome of Sledgehammer calls showing the total success rate (SR, higher is better) of one-liner proof preplay, the number of suggested v-smt (OL_v) and z-smt (OL_z) one-liners, and the number of preplay failures (PF, lower is better), in percentages of the unique goals.

	HOL-Library (13 562 goals)				PNT (1 715 goals)				RP (1 658 goals)				Simplex (1 982 goals)			
	SR	OL_v	OL_z	PF	SR	OL_v	OL_z	PF	SR	OL_v	OL_z	PF	SR	OL_v	OL_z	PF
Fact-filter prover: CVC4																
z-smt	54.5		2.7	1.5	33.1		3.7	0.8	64.8		1.3	0.8	51.6		1.6	0.9
both	55.5	2.5	1.1	0.5	33.6	3.6	0.6	0.3	65.3	1.4	0.4	0.3	52.1	1.1	1.0	0.4
Fact-filter prover: E																
z-smt	55.5		1.1	1.7	36.0		0.3	1.7	61.7		0.7	1.2	49.8		1.4	0.7
both	56.0	0.8	0.7	1.3	36.4	0.6	0.1	1.3	62.1	0.9	0.2	0.8	49.9	0.3	1.3	0.5
Fact-filter prover: veriT																
z-smt	48.5		1.7	1.2	26.1		1.5	0.5	58.2		0.9	0.7	46.7		0.9	1.0
both	49.4	1.6	0.9	0.4	26.5	1.4	0.4	0.2	58.6	1.1	0.3	0.2	47.4	1.0	0.6	0.3
Fact-filter prover: Z3																
z-smt	50.8		2.5	0.8	27.9		2.7	0.4	60.4		0.8	0.7	48.3		0.9	0.3
both	51.3	1.9	1.1	0.3	28.2	2.5	0.5	0.1	60.9	1.1	0.1	0.2	48.4	0.4	0.6	0.2

the time of all tried tactics. Sledgehammer and automatic provers are mostly non-deterministic programs. To reduce the variance between the different Mirabelle runs, we use the deterministic MePo fact filter [33] instead of the better performing MaSh [28] that uses machine learning (and depends on previous runs) and underuse the hardware to minimize contention. We use the default timeouts of 30 seconds for the fact filtering and one second for the proof preplay. This is similar to the Judgment Day experiments [17]. The raw results are available [1].

Success Rate. Users are not interested in which tactics are used to prove a goal, but in how often Sledgehammer succeeds. There are three possible outcomes: (i) a successfully preplayed proof, (ii) a proof hint that failed to be preplayed (usually because of a timeout), or (iii) no proof. We define the success rate as the proportion of outcome (i) over the total number of Sledgehammer calls.

Table 2 gathers the results of running Sledgehammer on all unique goals and analyzing its outcome using different preplay configurations where only z-smt (the baseline) or both v-smt and z-smt are enabled. Any useful preplay tactic should increase the success rate (SR) by preplaying new proof hints provided by the fact-filter prover, reducing the preplay failure rate (PF).

Let us consider, e.g., the results when using CVC4 as fact-filter prover. The success rate of the baseline on the HOL-Library is 54.5% and its preplay failure rate is 1.5%. This means that CVC4 found a proof for 54.5% + 1.5% = 56% of the goals, but that Isabelle's proof methods failed to preplay many of them. In such cases, Sledgehammer gives a proof hint to the user, which has to manually find a functioning proof. By enabling v-smt, the failure rate decreases by two thirds, from 1.5% to 0.5%, which directly increases the success rate by 1 percentage point: new cases where the burden of the proof is moved from the user to the proof assistant. The failure rate is reduced in similar proportions for PNT (63%), RP (63%), and Simplex (56%). For these formalizations, this improvement translates to a smaller increase of the success rate, because the baseline failure rate was smaller to begin with. This confirms that the instantiation technique *conflicting instances* [8, 36] is important for CVC4.

When using veriT or Z3 as fact-filter prover, a failure rate of zero could be expected, since the same SMT solvers are used for both fact filtering and preplaying. The observed failure rate can partly be explained by the much smaller timeout for preplay (1 second) than for fact filtering (30 seconds).

Overall, these results show that our proof reconstruction enables Sledgehammer to successfully preplay more proofs. With v-smt enabled, the weighted average failure rate decreases as follows: for CVC4, from 1.3% to 0.4%; for E, from 1.5% to 1.2%; for veriT, from 1.0% to 0.3%; and for Z3, from 0.7% to 0.3%. For the user, this means that the availability of v-smt as a proof preplay tactic increases the number of goals that can be fully automatically proved.

Saved time. Table 3 shows a different view on the same results. Instead of the raw success rate, it shows the time that is spent reconstructing proofs. Using the baseline configuration, preplaying all formalizations takes a total of 250.1 + 33.4 + 37.2 + 42.8 = 363.5 seconds. When enabling v-smt, some calls to z-smt are replaced by faster v-smt calls and the reconstruction time decreases by 13% to 212.6 + 28.4 + 34.4 + 41.6 = 317 seconds. Note that the per-formalization improvement varies considerably: 15% for HOL-Library, 15% for PNT, 7.5% for RP, and 4.0% for Simplex.

For the user, this means that enabling v-smt as a proof preplay tactic may significantly reduce the verification time of their formalizations.

Impact of the Strategies. We have also studied what happens if we remove a single veriT strategy from Sledgehammer (Table 4). The most important one is *best*, as it solves the highest number of problems. On the contrary, *default* is nearly entirely covered by the other strategies. *ccfv_SIG* and *del_insts* have a similar number where they are faster than Z3, but the latter has more unique goals and therefore, saves more time. Each strategy has some uniquely solved problems that cannot be reconstructed using any other. The results are similar for the other theories used in Table 3.

5.3   Speed of Reconstruction

To better understand what the key rules of our reconstruction are, we recorded the time used to reconstruct each rule and the time required by the solver over all calls attempted by Sledgehammer including the ones not selected. The reconstruction ratio (reconstruction over search time) shows how much slower reconstructing

Table 3. Preplayed proofs (Pr.) and their execution time (s) when using CVC4 as fact-filter prover. Shared proofs are found with and without v-smt and new proofs are found only with v-smt. The proofs and their associated timings are categorized in one-liners using v-smt (OL_v), z-smt (OL_z), or any other Isabelle proof methods (OL_o).

		Total Pr.	Total Time	=	OL_v Time (Pr.)	+	OL_z Time (Pr.)	+	OL_o Time (Pr.)	New proofs OL_v Time (Pr.)
HOL-Library	z-smt	7 409	250.1	=			85.0 (362)	+	165.1 (7 047)	
	both	7 545	212.6	=	27.9 (211)	+	19.6 (152)	+	165.1 (7 047)	34.7 (135)
PNT	z-smt	569	33.4	=			14.8 (64)	+	18.5 (505)	
	both	577	28.4	=	7.7 (54)	+	2.1 (10)	+	18.5 (505)	3.4 (8)
RP	z-smt	1 077	37.2	=			8.7 (22)	+	28.5 (1 055)	
	both	1 085	34.4	=	4.5 (16)	+	1.4 (6)	+	28.5 (1 055)	2.2 (8)
Simplex	z-smt	1 024	42.8	=			6.7 (32)	+	36.0 (992)	
	both	1 033	41.6	=	2.4 (13)	+	3.2 (19)	+	36.0 (992)	3.0 (9)

Table 4. Reconstruction time and number of solved goals when removing a single strategy (HOL-Library results only), using CVC4 as fact filter.

	Shared proofs OL_v		OL_z		New proofs OL_v	
	Time	Proofs	Time	Proofs	Time	Proofs
No *best*	16.5	119	50.6	244	25.9	94
No *ccfv_SIG*	27.0	198	22.6	164	33.5	123
No *ccfv_threshold*	28.3	211	19.6	152	33.9	130
No *del_insts*	27.4	201	21.8	162	32.9	124
No *default*	27.9	207	20.1	156	33.8	134
Baseline	27.9	211	19.6	152	34.7	135

compared to finding a proof is. For the 25% of the proofs, Z3's concise format is better and the reconstruction is faster than proof finding (first quartile: 0.9 for v-smt vs. 0.1 for z-smt). The 99th percentile of the proofs (18.6 vs. 27.2) shows that veriT's detailed proof format reduces the number of slow proofs. The reconstruction is slower than finding proofs on average for both solvers.

Fig. 1 shows the distribution of the time spent on some rules. We remove the slowest and fastest 5% of the applications, because garbage collection can trigger at any moment and even trivial rules can be slow. Fig. 2 gives the sum of all reconstruction times over all proofs. We call `parsing` the time required to parse and convert the veriT proof into Isabelle terms.

Overall, there are two kinds of rules: (1) direct application of a sequence of theorems—e.g., `equiv_pos2` corresponds to the theorem $\neg(a \Leftrightarrow b) \vee \neg a \vee b$—and (2) calls to full-blown tactics—like `qnt_cnf` (Sect. 4.2).

First, direct application of theorems are usually fast, but they occur so often that the cumulative time is substantial. For example, `cong` only needs to unfold assumptions and apply reflexivity and symmetry of equality. However, it appears so often and sometimes on large terms, that it is an important rule.

Second, rules which require full-blown tactics are the slowest rules. For `qnt_cnf` (CNF under quantifiers, see Sect. 4.2), we have not written a specialized tactic, but rely on Isabelle's tableau-based blast tactic. This rule is rather slow, but is rarely used. It is similar to the rule `la_generic`: it is slow on average, but searching the coefficients takes even more time.

We can also see that the time required to check the simplification steps that were formerly combined into the `connect_equiv` rule is not significant anymore.

We have performed the same experiments with the reconstruction of the SMT solver Z3. In contrast to veriT, we do not have the amount of time required for parsing. The results are shown in Figs. 3 and 4. The rule distribution is very different. The `nnf-neg` and `nnf-pos` rules are the slowest rules and take a huge amount of time in the worst case. However, the coarser quantifier instantiation step is on average *faster* than the one produced by veriT. We suspect that reconstruction is faster because the rule, which is only an implication without choice terms, is easier to check (no equality reordering).

6 Related Work

The SMT solvers CVC4 [10], Z3 [34], and veriT [19] produce proofs. CVC4 does not record quantifier reasoning in the proof, and Z3 uses some macro rules. Proofs from SMT solvers have also been used to find unsatisfiability cores [20], and interpolants [32]. They are also useful to debug the solver itself, since unsound steps often point to the origin of bugs. Our work also relates to systems like Dedukti [5] that focuses on translating proof steps, not on replaying them.

Proof reconstruction has been implemented in various systems, including CVC4 proofs in HOL Light [31], Z3 in HOL4 and Isabelle/HOL [18], and veriT [4] and CVC4 [24] in Coq. Only veriT produces detailed proofs for preprocessing and skolemization. SMTCoq [4, 24] currently supports veriT's version 1 of the proof output which has different rules, does not support detailed skolemization rules, and is implemented in the 2016 version of veriT, which has worse performance. SMTCoq also supports bit vectors and arrays.

The reconstruction of Z3 proofs in HOL4 and Isabelle/HOL is one of the most advanced and well tested. It is regularly used by Isabelle users. The Z3 proof reconstruction succeeds in more than 90% of Sledgehammer benchmarks [14, Section 9] and is efficient (an older version of Z3 was used). Performance numbers are reported [16,18] not only for problems generated by proof assistants (including Isabelle), but also for preexisting SMT-LIB files from the SMT-LIB library.

The performance study by Böhme [16, Sect. 3.4] uses version 2.15 of Z3, whereas we use version 4.4.0 which currently ships with Isabelle. Since version 2.15, the proof format changed slightly (e.g., `th-lemma-arith` was introduced), fulfilling some of the wishes expressed by Böhme and Weber [18] to simplify reconstruction. Surprisingly, the `nnf` rules do not appear among the five rules that used the most runtime. Instead, the `th-lemma` and `rewrite` rules were the

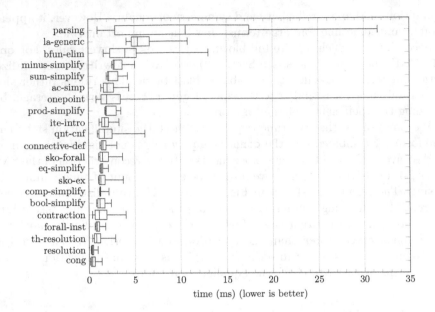

Fig. 1. Timing, sorted by the median, of a subset of veriT's rules. From left to right, the lower whisker marks the 5th percentile, the lower box line the first quartile, the middle of the box the median, the upper box line the third quartile, and the upper whisker the 95th percentile.

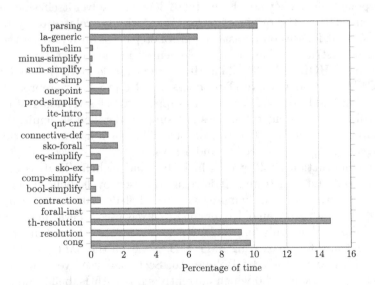

Fig. 2. Total percentage spent on each rule for the SMT solver veriT in the same order as Fig. 1. This graph maps the rules already shown in Fig. 1 to the total amount of time. The slowest rules are th_resolution (14.7%), parsing (10.3%), and cong (9.77%).

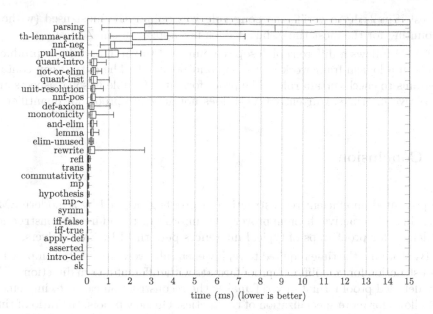

Fig. 3. Timing of some of Z3's rules sorted by median. From left to right, the lower whisker marks the 5th percentile, the lower box line the first quartile, the middle of the box the median, the upper box line the third quartile, and the upper whisker the 95th percentile. nnf-neg's 95th percentile is 87 ms, nnf-pos's is 33 ms, and parsing's is 25 ms.

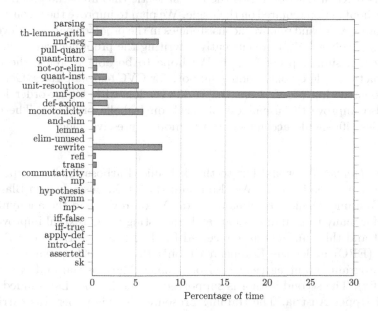

Fig. 4. Total amount of time per rule for the SMT solver Z3. nnf-neg takes 39% of the reconstruction time.

slowest. Similarly to veriT, the `cong` rule was among the most used (without accounting for the most time), but it does not appear in our Z3 tests.

CVC4 follows a different philosophy compared to veriT and Z3: it produces proofs in a logical framework with side conditions [39]. The output can contain programs to check certain rules. The proof format is flexible in some aspects and restrictive in others. Currently CVC4 does not generate proofs for quantifiers.

7   Conclusion

We presented an efficient reconstruction of proofs generated by a modern SMT solver in an interactive theorem prover. Our improvements address reconstruction challenges for proof steps of typical inferences performed by SMT solvers.

By studying the time required to replay each rule, we were able to compare the reconstruction for two different proof formats with different design directions. The very detailed proof format of veriT makes the reconstruction easier to implement and allows for more specialization of the tactics. On slow proofs, the ratio of time to reconstruct and time to find a proof is better for our more detailed format. Integrating our reconstruction in Isabelle halves the number of failures from Sledgehammer and nicely completes the existing reconstruction method with Z3.

Our work is integrated into Isabelle version 2021. Sledgehammer suggests the veriT-based reconstruction if it is the fastest tactic that finds the proof; so users profit without action required on their side. We plan to improve the reconstruction of the slowest rules and remove inconsistencies in the proof format. The developers of the SMT solver CVC4 are currently rewriting the proof generation and plan to support a similar proof format. We hope to be able to reuse the current reconstruction code by only adding support for CVC4-specific rules. Generating and reconstructing proofs from the veriT version with higher-order logic [9] could also improve the usefulness of veriT on Isabelle problems. The current proof rules [40] should accommodate the more expressive logic.

Acknowledgment We would like to thank Haniel Barbosa for his support with the implementation in veriT. We also thank Haniel Barbosa, Jasmin Blanchette, Pascal Fontaine, Daniela Kaufmann, Petar Vukmirović, and the anonymous reviewers for many fruitful discussions and suggesting many textual improvements. The first and third authors have received funding from the European Research Council (ERC) under the European Union's Horizon 2020 research and innovation program (grant agreements No. 713999, Matryoshka, and No. 830927, Concordia). The second author is supported by the LIT AI Lab funded by the State of Upper Austria. The training presented in this paper was carried out using the Grid'5000 testbed, supported by a scientific interest group hosted by Inria and including CNRS, RENATER and several Universities as well as other organizations (see https://www.grid5000.fr).

References

1. Reliable Reconstruction of Fine-Grained Proofs in a Proof Assistant. Zenodo (Apr 2021). https://doi.org/10.5281/zenodo.4727349
2. Abdulaziz, M., Paulson, L.C.: An Isabelle/HOL formalisation of Green's theorem. Archive of Formal Proofs (Jan 2018), https://isa-afp.org/entries/Green.html, formal proof development
3. Abdulaziz, M., Paulson, L.C.: An Isabelle/HOL formalisation of Green's theorem. Journal of Automated Reasoning **63**(3), 763–786 (Nov 2019). https://doi.org/10.1007/s10817-018-9495-z
4. Armand, M., Faure, G., Grégoire, B., Keller, C., Théry, L., Werner, B.: A modular integration of SAT/SMT solvers to Coq through proof witnesses. In: Jouannaud, J.P., Shao, Z. (eds.) CPP 2011. LNCS, vol. 7086, pp. 135–150. Springer Berlin Heidelberg (2011). https://doi.org/10.1007/978-3-642-25379-9_12
5. Assaf, A., Burel, G., Cauderlier, R., Delahaye, D., Dowek, G., Dubois, C., Gilbert, F., Halmagrand, P., Hermant, O., Saillard, R.: Expressing theories in the $\lambda\pi$-calculus modulo theory and in the Dedukti system. In: TYPES: Types for Proofs and Programs. Novi SAd, Serbia (May 2016)
6. Barbosa, H.: Efficient instantiation techniques in SMT (work in progress). vol. 1635, pp. 1–10. CEUR-WS.org (Jul 2016), http://ceur-ws.org/Vol-1635/#paper-01
7. Barbosa, H., Blanchette, J.C., Fleury, M., Fontaine, P.: Scalable fine-grained proofs for formula processing. Journal of Automated Reasoning (Jan 2019). https://doi.org/10.1007/s10817-018-09502-y
8. Barbosa, H., Fontaine, P., Reynolds, A.: Congruence closure with free variables. In: Legay, A., Margaria, T. (eds.) TACAS 2017. LNCS, vol. 10206, pp. 214–230. Springer Berlin Heidelberg (2017). https://doi.org/10.1007/978-3-662-54580-5_13
9. Barbosa, H., Reynolds, A., Ouraoui, D.E., Tinelli, C., Barrett, C.W.: Extending SMT solvers to higher-order logic. In: Fontaine, P. (ed.) CADE 27. LNCS, vol. 11716, pp. 35–54. Springer International Publishing (2019). https://doi.org/10.1007/978-3-030-29436-6_3
10. Barrett, C., Conway, C.L., Deters, M., Hadarean, L., Jovanović, D., King, T., Reynolds, A., Tinelli, C.: CVC4. In: Gopalakrishnan, G., Qadeer, S. (eds.) CAV 2011. LNCS, vol. 6806, pp. 171–177. Springer Berlin Heidelberg (2011). https://doi.org/10.1007/978-3-642-22110-1_14
11. Barrett, C., Fontaine, P., Tinelli, C.: The SMT-LIB Standard: Version 2.6. Tech. rep., Department of Computer Science, The University of Iowa (2017), available at www.SMT-LIB.org
12. Barrett, C.W., Tinelli, C.: Satisfiability modulo theories. In: Clarke, E.M., Henzinger, T.A., Veith, H., Bloem, R. (eds.) Handbook of Model Checking, pp. 305–343. Springer International Publishing, Cham (2018). https://doi.org/10.1007/978-3-319-10575-8_11
13. Becker, H., Blanchette, J.C., Waldmann, U., Wand, D.: Formalization of Knuth–Bendix orders for lambda-free higher-order terms. Archive of Formal Proofs (Nov 2016), https://isa-afp.org/entries/Lambda_Free_KBOs.html, formal proof development
14. Blanchette, J.C., Böhme, S., Fleury, M., Smolka, S.J., Steckermeier, A.: Semi-intelligible Isar proofs from machine-generated proofs. Journal of Automated Reasoning **56**(2), 155–200 (2016). https://doi.org/10.1007/s10817-015-9335-3

15. Blanchette, J.C., Böhme, S., Paulson, L.C.: Extending Sledgehammer with smt solvers. In: Bjørner, N., Sofronie-Stokkermans, V. (eds.) CADE 23. LNCS, vol. 6803, pp. 116–130. Springer Berlin Heidelberg (2011). https://doi.org/10.1007/978-3-642-22438-6_11

16. Böhme, S.: Proving Theorems of Higher-Order Logic with SMT Solvers. Ph.D. thesis, Technische Universität München (2012), http://mediatum.ub.tum.de/node?id=1084525

17. Böhme, S., Nipkow, T.: Sledgehammer: Judgement day. In: Giesl, J., Hähnle, R. (eds.) IJCAR 2010. pp. 107–121. Springer Berlin Heidelberg (2010). https://doi.org/10.1007/978-3-642-14203-1_9

18. Böhme, S., Weber, T.: Fast LCF-style proof reconstruction for Z3. In: Kaufmann, M., Paulson, L.C. (eds.) ITP 2010. LNCS, vol. 6172, pp. 179–194. Springer Berlin Heidelberg (2010). https://doi.org/10.1007/978-3-642-14052-5_14

19. Bouton, T., de Oliveira, D.C.B., Déharbe, D., Fontaine, P.: veriT: An open, trustable and efficient SMT-solver. In: Schmidt, R.A. (ed.) CADE 22. LNCS, vol. 5663, pp. 151–156. Springer Berlin Heidelberg (2009). https://doi.org/10.1007/978-3-642-02959-2_12

20. Déharbe, D., Fontaine, P., Guyot, Y., Voisin, L.: SMT solvers for Rodin. In: Derrick, J., Fitzgerald, J.A., Gnesi, S., Khurshid, S., Leuschel, M., Reeves, S., Riccobene, E. (eds.) ABZ 2012. LNCS, vol. 7316, pp. 194–207. Springer Berlin Heidelberg (Jun 2012). https://doi.org/10.1007/978-3-642-30885-7_14

21. Dutertre, B., de Moura, L.: Integrating simplex with DPLL(T). Tech. rep., SRI International (May 2006), http://www.csl.sri.com/users/bruno/publis/sri-csl-06-01.pdf

22. Eberl, M.: Elementary facts about the distribution of primes. Archive of Formal Proofs (Feb 2019), https://isa-afp.org/entries/Prime_Distribution_Elementary.html, formal proof development

23. Eberl, M., Paulson, L.C.: The prime number theorem. Archive of Formal Proofs (Sep 2018), https://isa-afp.org/entries/Prime_Number_Theorem.html, formal proof development

24. Ekici, B., Mebsout, A., Tinelli, C., Keller, C., Katz, G., Reynolds, A., Barrett, C.W.: SMTCoq: A plug-in for integrating SMT solvers into Coq. In: Majumdar, R., Kuncak, V. (eds.) CAV 2017. LNCS, vol. 10427, pp. 126–133. Springer International Publishing (2017). https://doi.org/10.1007/978-3-319-63390-9_7

25. Fleury, M., Schurr, H.: Reconstructing veriT proofs in Isabelle/HOL. In: Reis, G., Barbosa, H. (eds.) PxTP 2019. EPTCS, vol. 301, pp. 36–50 (2019). https://doi.org/10.4204/EPTCS.301.6

26. Gordon, M.J.C., Milner, R., Wadsworth, C.P.: Edinburgh LCF: A Mechanised Logic of Computation, LNCS, vol. 78. Springer Berlin Heidelberg (1979). https://doi.org/10.1007/3-540-09724-4

27. Immler, F.: Re: [isabelle] Isabelle2019-RC2 sporadic smt failures. Email (May 2019), https://lists.cam.ac.uk/pipermail/cl-isabelle-users/2019-May/msg00130.html

28. Kühlwein, D., Blanchette, J.C., Kaliszyk, C., Urban, J.: Mash: Machine learning for Sledgehammer. In: ITP. LNCS, vol. 7998, pp. 35–50. Springer (2013)

29. Leino, K.R.M., Pit-Claudel, C.: Trigger selection strategies to stabilize program verifiers. In: Chaudhuri, S., Farzan, A. (eds.) CAV 2016. LNCS, vol. 9779, pp. 361–381. Springer International Publishing (2016). https://doi.org/10.1007/978-3-319-41528-4_20

30. Marić, F., Spasić, M., Thiemann, R.: An incremental simplex algorithm with unsatisfiable core generation. Archive of Formal Proofs (Aug 2018), https://isa-afp.org/entries/Simplex.html, formal proof development
31. McLaughlin, S., Barrett, C., Ge, Y.: Cooperating theorem provers: A case study combining HOL-Light and CVC Lite. Electronic Notes in Theoretical Computer Science **144**(2), 43–51 (2006). https://doi.org/10.1016/j.entcs.2005.12.005
32. McMillan, K.L.: Interpolants from Z3 proofs. In: FMCAD 2011. pp. 19–27. FMCAD Inc, Austin, Texas (2011)
33. Meng, J., Paulson, L.C.: Lightweight relevance filtering for machine-generated resolution problems. J. Appl. Log. **7**(1), 41–57 (2009)
34. de Moura, L., Bjørner, N.: Z3: An efficient SMT solver. In: Ramakrishnan, C.R., Rehof, J. (eds.) TACAS 2008. LNCS, vol. 4963, pp. 337–340. Springer Berlin Heidelberg (2008). https://doi.org/10.1007/978-3-540-78800-3_24
35. Reynolds, A., Barbosa, H., Fontaine, P.: Revisiting enumerative instantiation. In: Beyer, D., Huisman, M. (eds.) TACAS 2018. LNCS, vol. 10806, pp. 112–131. Springer International Publishing (2018). https://doi.org/10.1007/978-3-319-89963-3_7
36. Reynolds, A., Tinelli, C., de Moura, L.: Finding conflicting instances of quantified formulas in SMT. In: FMCAD 2014. pp. 195–202. IEEE (2014). https://doi.org/10.1109/FMCAD.2014.6987613
37. Schlichtkrull, A., Blanchette, J.C., Traytel, D., Waldmann, U.: Formalization of Bachmair and Ganzinger's ordered resolution prover. Archive of Formal Proofs (Jan 2018), https://isa-afp.org/entries/Ordered_Resolution_Prover.html, formal proof development
38. Schulz, S.: E - a brainiac theorem prover. AI Communications **15**(2-3), 111–126 (2002), http://content.iospress.com/articles/ai-communications/aic260
39. Stump, A., Oe, D., Reynolds, A., Hadarean, L., Tinelli, C.: SMT proof checking using a logical framework. Formal Methods in System Design **42**(1), 91–118 (Feb 2013). https://doi.org/10.1007/s10703-012-0163-3
40. The veriT Team and Contributors: Proofonomicon: A reference of the veriT proof format. Software Documentation (2021), https://www.verit-solver.org/documentation/proofonomicon.pdf, last Accessed: April 2021

Open Access This chapter is licensed under the terms of the Creative Commons Attribution 4.0 International License (http://creativecommons.org/licenses/by/4.0/), which permits use, sharing, adaptation, distribution and reproduction in any medium or format, as long as you give appropriate credit to the original author(s) and the source, provide a link to the Creative Commons license and indicate if changes were made.

The images or other third party material in this chapter are included in the chapter's Creative Commons license, unless indicated otherwise in a credit line to the material. If material is not included in the chapter's Creative Commons license and your intended use is not permitted by statutory regulation or exceeds the permitted use, you will need to obtain permission directly from the copyright holder.

An Automated Approach to the Collatz Conjecture*

Emre Yolcu[1] , Scott Aaronson[2], and Marijn J. H. Heule[1,3]

[1] Carnegie Mellon University, Pittsburgh, PA 15213, USA
{emreyolcu,marijn}@cmu.edu
[2] University of Texas at Austin, Austin, TX 78712, USA
scott@scottaaronson.com
[3] Amazon Scholar

Abstract. We explore the Collatz conjecture and its variants through the lens of termination of string rewriting. We construct a rewriting system that simulates the iterated application of the Collatz function on strings corresponding to mixed binary–ternary representations of positive integers. Termination of this rewriting system is equivalent to the Collatz conjecture. To show the feasibility of our approach in proving mathematically interesting statements, we implement a minimal termination prover that uses the automated method of matrix/arctic interpretations and we perform experiments where we obtain proofs of nontrivial weakenings of the Collatz conjecture. Finally, we adapt our rewriting system to show that other open problems in mathematics can also be approached as termination problems for relatively small rewriting systems. Although we do not succeed in proving the Collatz conjecture, we believe that the ideas here represent an interesting new approach.

1 Introduction

Let $\mathbb{N} = \{0, 1, 2, \ldots\}$ denote the natural numbers and $\mathbb{N}^+ = \{1, 2, 3, \ldots\}$ denote the positive integers. We define the *Collatz function* $C \colon \mathbb{N}^+ \to \mathbb{N}^+$ as

$$C(n) = \begin{cases} n/2 & \text{if } n \equiv 0 \pmod 2 \\ 3n + 1 & \text{if } n \equiv 1 \pmod 2. \end{cases}$$

Given a function f and a number $k \in \mathbb{N}$, the function f^k denotes the kth iterate of f. The well-known *Collatz conjecture* is the following:

Conjecture 1. For all $n \in \mathbb{N}^+$, there exists some $k \in \mathbb{N}$ such that $C^k(n) = 1$.

This is a longstanding open problem and there is a vast literature dedicated to its study. For its history, we refer the reader to the comprehensive surveys by Lagarias [17–19].

Definition 1 (Convergent function). *Consider a function $f \colon X \to X$. Given $x \in X$, the sequence of iterates $f_\tau(x) := (x, f(x), f^2(x), \ldots)$ is called the f-trajectory of x. For some designated element $z \in X$, if for all $x \in X$ the trajectory $f_\tau(x)$ contains z, the function f is called* convergent.

---

* The full version is available at https://www.cs.cmu.edu/~eyolcu/research/rewriting-collatz.pdf.

© The Author(s) 2021
A. Platzer and G. Sutcliffe (Eds.): CADE 2021, LNAI 12699, pp. 468–484, 2021.
https://doi.org/10.1007/978-3-030-79876-5_27

In this paper, we describe an approach based on termination of string rewriting to automatically search for a proof of the Collatz conjecture. Although trying to prove the Collatz conjecture via automated deduction is clearly a moonshot goal, there are two recent technological advances that provide reasons for optimism that at least some interesting variants of the problem might be solvable. First, the invention of the method of matrix interpretations and its variants such as arctic interpretations turns the quest of finding a ranking function to witness termination into a problem that is suitable for systematic search. Second, the progress in satisfiability (SAT) solving makes it possible to solve many seemingly difficult combinatorial problems efficiently in practice. Their combination, i.e., using SAT solvers to find interpretations, has so far been effective in solving challenging termination problems. We make the following contributions:

- We show how a generalized Collatz function can be expressed as a rewriting system that is terminating if and only if the function is convergent.
- We show that translations into rewriting systems that use non-unary representations of numbers are empirically more amenable to automation compared with their previously and more commonly studied counterparts that use unary representations.
- We automatically prove various weakenings of the Collatz conjecture and observe that only relatively large matrix/arctic interpretations exist for some generalized Collatz functions. Existing termination tools often limit their default strategies to search for small interpretations as they are tailored for the setting where the task is to quickly solve a large quantity of relatively easy problems. We make the point that, given more resources, the interpretation method has the potential to scale.
- We observe that the phase-saving heuristic used in modern SAT solvers degrades the performance of CDCL solvers on formulas encoding the existence of matrix/arctic interpretations, whereas using negative branching improves solver performance.
- We present adaptations of our rewriting system that allow reformulating several more open problems in mathematics as termination problems of small size.

2 Preliminaries

2.1 String Rewriting Systems

Definition 2 (String rewriting system). *Let Σ be an alphabet, i.e., a set of symbols. A string rewriting system (SRS) over Σ is a relation $R \subseteq \Sigma^* \times \Sigma^*$. Elements $(\ell, r) \in R$ are called* rewrite rules *and are usually written as $\ell \to r$. The system R induces a* rewrite relation $\to_R := \{(s\ell t, srt) \mid s, t \in \Sigma^*, \ \ell \to r \in R\}$ *on the set Σ^* of strings.*

Definition 3 (Termination). *A relation $\to$ on A is* terminating *(denoted $\mathrm{SN}(\to)$) if there is no infinite sequence $s_0, s_1, \ldots \in A$ such that $s_i \to s_{i+1}$ for all $i \geq 0$.*

We conflate an SRS R with the rewrite relation it induces, writing "R is terminating" instead of "$\to_R$ is terminating". The following is a useful generalization of termination:

Definition 4 (Relative termination). *For SRSs R and S, the system R is said to be* terminating relative to S *(denoted $\mathrm{SN}(R/S)$) if every sequence of rewrites for the system $R \cup S$ applies the rules from R at most finitely many times.*

Relative termination allows proofs to be broken into steps as codified by the following.

Lemma 1 (Rule removal [29, Theorem 1]). *Let R be an SRS. If there exists a subset $T \subseteq R$ such that $\mathrm{SN}(T/R)$ and $\mathrm{SN}(R \setminus T)$, then $\mathrm{SN}(R)$.*

This lemma allows us to "remove rules" in the following way. When proving $\mathrm{SN}(R)$, if we succeed at finding a subset T satisfying $\mathrm{SN}(T/R)$, the proof obligation becomes weakened to $\mathrm{SN}(R \setminus T)$, where the rules of T are no longer present. This removal of rules can be repeated until no rules remain, thus producing a stepwise proof of termination.

Another useful technique is reversal:

Lemma 2 (Rule reversal [29, Lemma 2]). *For a string $s = s_1 \ldots s_n \in \Sigma^*$, denote $s^{\mathrm{rev}} := s_n \ldots s_1$ and define the reversal of an SRS R as $R^{\mathrm{rev}} := \{\ell^{\mathrm{rev}} \to r^{\mathrm{rev}} \mid \ell \to r \in R\}$. For SRSs R and S, we have $\mathrm{SN}(R/S)$ if and only if $\mathrm{SN}(R^{\mathrm{rev}}/S^{\mathrm{rev}})$.*

Reversal is of interest because methods for proving termination are not necessarily invariant under reversal, that is, a given technique may fail to show termination of a system R while succeeding for its reversal R^{rev}.

Yet another important notion is top termination:

Definition 5 (Top termination). *Let R be an SRS over Σ. The top rewrite relation induced by R is defined as $\to_{R_{\mathrm{top}}} := \{(\ell s, rs) \mid s \in \Sigma^*, \ell \to r \in R\}$. If $\to_{R_{\mathrm{top}}}$ is terminating, R is said to be top terminating.*

In plain language, top termination allows rewrites to be performed only at the leftmost end of a string. As we will see in the next section (Theorem 1), top termination problems can admit proofs of a more relaxed form compared to termination. Relative top termination, i.e., proving $\mathrm{SN}(R_{\mathrm{top}}/S)$ for SRSs R and S, is a crucial component in the dependency pair approach [1] which reduces a termination problem to a relative top termination problem that is often easier to solve. In order to avoid requiring familiarity with the dependency pair approach, we omit its discussion, and instead prove a self-contained result (Lemma 4) that encapsulates dependency pairs in a more elementary manner for the specific rewriting systems that we consider in this paper.

2.2 Interpretation Method

We state (at a high level) the key results on matrix/arctic interpretations that we use in our implementation. For more details we refer the reader to existing work [2,6,10,15,26]. With the interpretation method, the main idea is to find a ranking function that assigns a value to each string such that it decreases strictly when the string is modified by an application of a rewrite rule. If for all strings the value is bounded from below, then it cannot decrease indefinitely, ruling out the existence of an infinite sequence of rewrites. Formally, we search for an instance of the following:

Definition 6 (Extended/weakly monotone algebra). *Let Σ be an alphabet, A a set, $[\sigma]: A \to A$ an interpretation for every $\sigma \in \Sigma$, $>$ and $\gtrsim$ order relations over A such that $>$ is well-founded and $\gtrsim$ satisfies $> \cdot \gtrsim \subseteq >$. Letting $[\cdot]_\Sigma := \{[\sigma] \mid \sigma \in \Sigma\}$, the structure $(A, [\cdot]_\Sigma, >, \gtrsim)$ is a weakly monotone Σ-algebra if for every $\sigma \in \Sigma$ the interpretation $[\sigma]$ is monotone with respect to $\gtrsim$. It is an extended monotone Σ-algebra if, additionally, for every $\sigma \in \Sigma$ the interpretation $[\sigma]$ is monotone with respect to $>$.*

We extend the interpretation from symbols to strings $s = s_1 \ldots s_n \in \Sigma^*$ as $[s] :=$ $[s_1] \circ \cdots \circ [s_n]$. The following general theorem characterizes relative termination (resp. top termination) as the existence of extended (resp. weakly) monotone algebras.

Theorem 1 ([6, Theorem 2]). *Let R and S be SRSs over the alphabet Σ. We have* $\mathrm{SN}(R/S)$ *(resp.* $\mathrm{SN}(R_{\mathrm{top}}/S)$*) if and only if there exists an extended (resp. weakly) monotone Σ-algebra* $(A, [\cdot]_\Sigma, >, \gtrsim)$ *such that*
 - *for each rule $\ell \to r \in R$ we have $[\ell](x) > [r](x)$ for all $x \in A$,*
 - *for each rule $\ell \to r \in S$ we have $[\ell](x) \gtrsim [r](x)$ for all $x \in A$.*

An effective way to prove relative (top) termination is to try to satisfy the conditions of the above theorem by fixing $(A, >, \gtrsim)$ and algorithmically searching for appropriate interpretations of symbols. Matrix interpretations is an instance of this method. We fix a dimension d, set $A = \mathbb{N}^d$, define $\vec{x} \gtrsim \vec{y} \iff x_i \geq y_i$ for all $i \in \{1, \ldots, d\}$, and define $\vec{x} > \vec{y} \iff \vec{x} \gtrsim \vec{y} \wedge x_1 > y_1$. For interpreting each symbol $\sigma \in \Sigma$, we consider an affine function $[\sigma](\vec{x}) = M_\sigma \vec{x} + v_\sigma$. In this way, the structure $(\mathbb{N}^d, [\cdot]_\Sigma, >, \gtrsim)$ satisfies the requirements of Definition 6 for a weakly monotone algebra. Additionally setting $(M_\sigma)_{1,1} = 1$ satisfies the requirements for an extended monotone algebra. Matrix interpretations can also be adapted to the max–plus algebra of arctic numbers $\mathbb{A} := \mathbb{N} \cup \{-\infty\}$ as coefficients with different arithmetic operations and order relations [15,26].

Example 1. Let $R = \{aa \to aba\}$ and $S = \{b \to bb\}$. The following functions constitute a matrix interpretations proof that shows $\mathrm{SN}(R/S)$.

$$[a](\vec{x}) = \begin{bmatrix} 1 & 1 \\ 0 & 0 \end{bmatrix} \vec{x} + \begin{bmatrix} 0 \\ 1 \end{bmatrix} \qquad [b](\vec{x}) = \begin{bmatrix} 1 & 0 \\ 0 & 0 \end{bmatrix} \vec{x} + \begin{bmatrix} 0 \\ 0 \end{bmatrix}$$

It can be checked that the above interpretations give an extended monotone algebra and that they satisfy the following for all $\vec{x} \in \mathbb{N}^2$, which implies $\mathrm{SN}(R/S)$ via Theorem 1.

$$[aa](\vec{x}) = \begin{bmatrix} 1 & 1 \\ 0 & 0 \end{bmatrix} \vec{x} + \begin{bmatrix} 1 \\ 1 \end{bmatrix} > \begin{bmatrix} 1 & 1 \\ 0 & 0 \end{bmatrix} \vec{x} + \begin{bmatrix} 0 \\ 1 \end{bmatrix} = [aba](\vec{x})$$

$$[b](\vec{x}) = \begin{bmatrix} 1 & 0 \\ 0 & 0 \end{bmatrix} \vec{x} + \begin{bmatrix} 0 \\ 0 \end{bmatrix} \gtrsim \begin{bmatrix} 1 & 0 \\ 0 & 0 \end{bmatrix} \vec{x} + \begin{bmatrix} 0 \\ 0 \end{bmatrix} = [bb](\vec{x})$$

In order to automate the search for the interpretations given a rewriting system R, an effective approach is to encode all of the aforementioned constraints as a propositional formula in CNF and use a SAT solver to look for a satisfying assignment. This additionally involves fixing a finite domain for the coefficients that can occur in the interpretations and encoding arithmetic over the chosen finite domain using propositional variables.

2.3 Generalized Collatz Functions

We consider instances of the following generalization of the Collatz function. Its variants have commonly appeared in the literature [3, 12, 14, 16, 21, 24, 27].

Definition 7 (Generalized Collatz function). *Let X be one of $\mathbb{N}$, $\mathbb{N}^+$, or $\mathbb{Z}$ and define* $X_\perp := X \cup \{\perp\}$. *A function $f \colon X_\perp \to X_\perp$ is a generalized Collatz function if $f(\perp) =$*

$\perp$ *and there exist an integer* $d \geq 2$ *and rational numbers* $q_0, \ldots, q_{d-1}, r_0, \ldots, r_{d-1}$
such that for all $0 \leq i \leq d - 1$ *and all* $n \in X$, *we have*

$$f(n) = q_i n + r_i \quad if \, n \equiv i \pmod{d}$$
$$or \quad f(n) = \perp \quad if \, n \equiv i \pmod{d}.$$

In the above, we allow the representation of a partially defined function by mapping to $\perp$ in the undefined cases. We call a partial f convergent if all f-trajectories contain $\perp$.

Note that the Collatz function corresponds to a generalized one with $d = 2, q_0 = 1/2$, $r_0 = 0, q_1 = 3, r_1 = 1$. Although the Collatz function is by far the most widely studied case, there are several other concrete examples of generalized Collatz functions the convergence of which is worth studying due to their connections to open problems in number theory and computability theory. We discuss these cases in Section 5.

3 Rewriting the Collatz Function

We start with systems that use unary representations and then demonstrate via examples that mixed base representations can be more suitable for use with automated methods.

3.1 Rewriting in Unary

The following system of Zantema [29] simulates iterated application of the Collatz function to a number represented in unary, and terminates upon reaching 1.

Example 2. $\mathcal{Z}$ denotes the following SRS, consisting of 5 symbols and 7 rules.

$$h11 \to 1h \qquad 11h\diamond \to 11s\diamond \qquad h1\diamond \to t11\diamond$$
$$1s \to s1 \qquad 1t \to t111$$
$$\diamond s \to \diamond h \qquad \diamond t \to \diamond h$$

This system can be seen as encoding the execution of a Turing machine with cells that can be contracted/expanded. The symbols 1 and $\diamond$ (blank) form the tape alphabet, while the symbols h (half), s (shift), t (triple) indicate the head along with the state of the machine. Through the following result, the Collatz conjecture can be reformulated as termination of string rewriting.

Theorem 2 ([29]). $\mathcal{Z}$ *is terminating if and only if the Collatz conjecture holds.*

While the forward direction of the above theorem is easy to see (since $\diamond h1^{2n}\diamond \to_{\mathcal{Z}}^*$ $\diamond h1^n\diamond$ for $n > 1$ and $\diamond h1^{2n+1}\diamond \to_{\mathcal{Z}}^* \diamond h1^{3n+2}\diamond$ for $n \geq 0$), the backward direction is far from obvious because not every string corresponds to a valid configuration of the underlying machine.

As another example, consider the system $\mathcal{W} = \{h11 \to 1h, 1h\diamond \to 1t\diamond, 1t \to t111, \diamond t \to \diamond h\}$ (originally due to Zantema[4]). Termination of this system has yet to be proved via automated methods. Nevertheless, there is a simple reason for its termination:

---

[4] https://www.lri.fr/~marche/tpdb/tpdb-2.0/SRS/Zantema/z079.srs

It simulates iterated application of a partial generalized Collatz function $W: \mathbb{N}_\perp^+ \to \mathbb{N}_\perp^+$ defined as follows, which is easily seen to be convergent.

$$W(n) = \begin{cases} 3n/2 & \text{if } n \equiv 0 \pmod 2 \\ \perp & \text{if } n \equiv 1 \pmod 2 \end{cases}$$

If a proof of the Collatz conjecture is to be produced by some automated method that relies on rewriting, then that method better be able to prove a statement as simple as the convergence of W. With this in mind, we describe an alternative rewriting system that simulates the Collatz function and terminates upon reaching 1. We then provide examples where the alternative system is more suitable for use with termination tools (for instance allowing an automated proof of the convergence of W).

3.2 Rewriting in Mixed Base

In the mixed base scheme, the overall idea is as follows. Given a number $n \in \mathbb{N}^+$, we write a mixed binary–ternary representation for it (noting that this representation is not unique). With this representation, as long as the least significant digit is binary, the parity of the number can be recognized by checking only this digit, as opposed to scanning the entire string when working in unary. This allows us to easily determine the correct case when applying the Collatz function. If the least significant digit is ternary, then the representation is rewritten (while preserving its decimal value) to make this digit binary. Afterwards, since computing $n/2$ corresponds to erasing a trailing binary 0 and computing $3n + 1$ corresponds to inserting a trailing ternary 1, applying the Collatz function takes a single rewrite step. We explain this scheme more formally below.

A mixed base numeral system is a numeral system where the base changes across positions, which we define as follows. Note that unary is not a positional numeral system, so we require the bases to be greater than 1.

Definition 8 (Mixed base representation). *Let $B \subseteq \mathbb{N}_{>1}$ be a set of bases and let $N = n_{1b_1} n_{2b_2} \ldots n_{kb_k}$ be a string where $n_i \in \mathbb{N}$. If we have for each $1 \le i \le k$ that $b_i \in B$ and $0 \le n_i < b_i$, then N is called a* mixed B-ary representation.

The string N from above represents the decimal number $N_{10} = \sum_{i=1}^{k} n_i \prod_{j=i+1}^{k} b_j$. Observing that the addition of leading zeros to a string does not change its decimal value, we may assume without loss of generality that $n_1 > 0$. Furthermore, b_1 does not affect the decimal value of the string, so we may omit it.

Now, define $\beta_b^n(x) := bx + n$. After rearranging, we see that the decimal value of the B-ary string $N = n_1 n_{2b_2} \ldots n_{kb_k}$ may also be written as $N_{10} = (\beta_{b_k}^{n_k} \circ \beta_{b_{k-1}}^{n_{k-1}} \circ \cdots \circ \beta_{b_2}^{n_2})(n_1)$. This gives us a string and a function view of the same representation, and we will switch between them as appropriate. In doing so, we also conflate the symbols and the corresponding functions, referring to β_b^n as n_b.

As the last ingredient before describing the rewriting system, we observe that we can write $(\beta_b^n \circ \beta_c^m)(x) = bcx + bm + n$ equivalently as another composition $(\beta_c^{m'} \circ \beta_b^{n'})(x) = cbx + cn' + m'$ for some suitable $0 \le n' < b$ and $0 \le m' < c$. This allows us to swap the bases of adjacent positions while preserving the decimal value of the string.

From this point on, we constrain ourselves to the mixed $\{2, 3\}$-ary (binary–ternary) representations as we shift our focus to simulating the Collatz function (noting that it is possible to adapt the rewriting system that we will end up with to other instances of the general case). More precisely, we simulate the following redefinition of the Collatz function where the odd case incorporates an additional division by 2.

$$T(n) = \begin{cases} \frac{n}{2} & \text{if } n \equiv 0 \pmod 2 \\ \frac{3n+1}{2} & \text{if } n \equiv 1 \pmod 2 \end{cases}$$

We will describe an SRS $\mathcal{T}$ over the symbols $\{f, t, 0, 1, 2, \triangleleft, \triangleright\}$ that simulates iterated application of the Collatz function and terminates upon reaching 1. The symbols f, t correspond to binary digits $0_2, 1_2$; and $0, 1, 2$ to ternary digits $0_3, 1_3, 2_3$. The symbol $\triangleleft$ marks the beginning of a string while also standing for the most significant digit (without loss of generality assumed to be 1) and $\triangleright$ marks the end of a string. Consider the functional view of these symbols:

$$
\begin{array}{lll}
f(x) = 2x & \begin{array}{l} 0(x) = 3x \\ 1(x) = 3x + 1 \\ 2(x) = 3x + 2 \end{array} & \begin{array}{l} \triangleleft(x) = 1 \\ \triangleright(x) = x \end{array}
\end{array}
\tag{1}
$$
$$t(x) = 2x + 1$$

Each positive natural number can be expressed as some composition of these functions, which corresponds to a string as per our previous discussion.

Example 3. Allowing the inclusion of a redundant trailing symbol $\triangleright$ to mixed base representations, we can write $19 = (\triangleleft 0f1\triangleright)_{10} = \triangleright(1(f(0(\triangleleft(x)))))$. The string representation ends with a ternary symbol, so we will rewrite it. With the function view, we have $1(f(x)) = 3(2x) + 1 = 6x + 1 = 2(3x) + 1 = t(0(x))$. This shows that we could also write $19 = (\triangleleft 00t\triangleright)_{10}$, which now ends with the binary digit 1_2. This gives us the rewrite rule $f1 \to 0t$. We can now apply the Collatz function to this representation by rewriting only the rightmost two symbols of the string since $T(\triangleright(t(x))) = \frac{3(2x+1)+1}{2} = \frac{6x+4}{2} = 3x + 2 = (\triangleright(2(x)))$. This gives us the rewrite rule $t\triangleright \to 2\triangleright$. After applying this rule, we indeed obtain $T(19) = 29 = (\triangleleft 002\triangleright)_{10}$.

In the manner of the above example, we compute all the necessary transformations and obtain the following 11-rule SRS $\mathcal{T}$.

$$
\mathcal{D}_T = \left\{ \begin{array}{l} f\triangleright \to \triangleright \\ t\triangleright \to 2\triangleright \end{array} \right\} \quad
\mathcal{A} = \left\{ \begin{array}{ll} f0 \to 0f & t0 \to 1t \\ f1 \to 0t & t1 \to 2f \\ f2 \to 1f & t2 \to 2t \end{array} \right\} \quad
\mathcal{B} = \left\{ \begin{array}{l} \triangleleft 0 \to \triangleleft t \\ \triangleleft 1 \to \triangleleft ff \\ \triangleleft 2 \to \triangleleft ft \end{array} \right\}
$$

This SRS is split into subsystems $\mathcal{D}_T$ (dynamic rules for T) and $\mathcal{X} = \mathcal{A} \cup \mathcal{B}$ (auxiliary rules). The two rules in $\mathcal{D}_T$ encode the application of the Collatz function T, while the rules in $\mathcal{X}$ serve to push binary symbols towards the rightmost end of the string by swapping the bases of adjacent positions without changing the represented value.

Example 4 (Rewrite sequence of $\mathcal{T}$). Consider the string $s = \triangleleft ff0\triangleright$ that represents the number 12. Below is a possible rewrite sequence of $\mathcal{T}$ that starts from s, with the corresponding decimal values (under the interpretations from (1)) displayed above the strings. Underlines indicate the parts of the strings where the rules are applied.

$$\begin{array}{ccccccc} 12 & 12 & 6 & 6 & 3 & 3 & 5 \\ \vartriangleleft f\underline{f0}\vartriangleright \to_{\mathcal{A}} & \vartriangleleft f\underline{0f}\vartriangleright \to_{\mathcal{D}_T} & \vartriangleleft\underline{f0}\vartriangleright \to_{\mathcal{A}} & \vartriangleleft\underline{0f}\vartriangleright \to_{\mathcal{D}_T} & \vartriangleleft\underline{0}\vartriangleright \to_{\mathcal{B}} & \vartriangleleft\underline{t}\vartriangleright \to_{\mathcal{D}_T} & \vartriangleleft\underline{2}\vartriangleright \end{array}$$

$$\begin{array}{ccccccc} 5 & 8 & 8 & 8 & 4 & 2 & 1 \\ \to_{\mathcal{B}} \vartriangleleft f\underline{t}\vartriangleright & \to_{\mathcal{D}_T} \vartriangleleft\underline{f2}\vartriangleright & \to_{\mathcal{A}} \vartriangleleft\underline{1f}\vartriangleright & \to_{\mathcal{B}} \vartriangleleft f\underline{f}f\vartriangleright & \to_{\mathcal{D}_T} \vartriangleleft f\underline{ff}\vartriangleright & \to_{\mathcal{D}_T} \vartriangleleft\underline{f}f\vartriangleright & \to_{\mathcal{D}_T} \vartriangleleft\vartriangleright \end{array}$$

The trajectory of T continues upon reaching 1, however, in order to be able to formulate the Collatz conjecture as a termination problem, $\mathcal{T}$ is made in such a way that its rewrite sequences stop upon reaching the string representation $\vartriangleleft\vartriangleright$ of 1 since no rule is applicable.

Termination of the subsystems of $\mathcal{T}$ with $\mathcal{B}$ or $\mathcal{D}_T$ removed is easily seen. However, since we have matrix interpretations at our disposal, let us give a compact proof.

Lemma 3. $\mathrm{SN}(\mathcal{T} \setminus \mathcal{B})$ and $\mathrm{SN}(\mathcal{T} \setminus \mathcal{D}_T)$.

Proof. It is easily checked that the interpretations below show $\mathrm{SN}((\mathcal{T} \setminus \mathcal{B})^{\mathrm{rev}})$, which implies $\mathrm{SN}(\mathcal{T} \setminus \mathcal{B})$ by Lemma 2.

$$[f](x) = [t](x) = 2x + 1 \qquad [\vartriangleright] = x \qquad [0](x) = [1](x) = [2](x) = 2x$$

Below interpretations show $\mathrm{SN}((\mathcal{T} \setminus \mathcal{D}_T)^{\mathrm{rev}})$, which implies $\mathrm{SN}(\mathcal{T} \setminus \mathcal{D}_T)$ by Lemma 2.

$$[f](x) = [t](x) = [\vartriangleleft](x) = x + 1 \qquad [0](x) = [1](x) = [2](x) = 4x \qquad \square$$

As a whole, the system $\mathcal{T}$ simulates the iterated application of T (except at 1).

Theorem 3. $\mathcal{T}$ *is terminating if and only if* T *is convergent.*

Proof (sketch). We observe that the rules of $\mathcal{T}$ do not change the number of occurrences of $\vartriangleleft$ or $\vartriangleright$ in a string and that the rewrite sequences operate strictly on one side of these symbols. Thus, we may view a given string as split into blocks delimited by $\vartriangleleft$ or $\vartriangleright$ and consider the termination of each block separately. In this way, we conclude that there exists a nonterminating rewrite sequence for a string if and only if it contains a block of the *canonical form* $\vartriangleleft(f|t|0|1|2)^*\vartriangleright$ that can be rewritten indefinitely, since the rewrite sequences that start on blocks of all other forms are already seen to terminate by Lemma 3. Furthermore, under the interpretations in (1), the sequences of values attained by the rewrites of the blocks in canonical form correspond directly to Collatz trajectories, since the rules in $\mathcal{X}$ do not change the value of the block and the rules in $\mathcal{D}_T$ change the value of the block in exactly the same way as the Collatz function T. $\square$

When trying to remove a rule in $\mathcal{D}_T$ or $\mathcal{B}$ it suffices to show relative top termination, allowing us to use weakly (instead of extended) monotone algebras when applying Theorem 1 and take advantage of the more relaxed constraints when searching for matrix/arctic interpretations. The lemma below encapsulates dependency pairs, and it can in fact be automatically proved via the dependency pair framework [9].

Lemma 4. *For each subset* $\mathcal{R} \subseteq \mathcal{B}$, *if* $\mathrm{SN}(\mathcal{R}_{\mathrm{top}}/\mathcal{T})$ *then* $\mathrm{SN}(\mathcal{R}/\mathcal{T})$. *And, for each subset* $\mathcal{R} \subseteq \mathcal{D}_T$, *if* $\mathrm{SN}(\mathcal{R}_{\mathrm{top}}^{\mathrm{rev}}/\mathcal{T}^{\mathrm{rev}})$ *then* $\mathrm{SN}(\mathcal{R}^{\mathrm{rev}}/\mathcal{T}^{\mathrm{rev}})$.

Proof (sketch). Without loss of generality, assume we start with a string of the canonical form $\lhd(f|t|0|1|2)^*\rhd$ (resp. its reversal). Then, the rules in $\mathcal{B}$ (resp. $\mathcal{D}_T{}^{\mathrm{rev}}$) can only be applied at the top level. As we know from Lemma 3 that $\mathcal{T} \setminus \mathcal{B}$ (resp. $\mathcal{T} \setminus \mathcal{D}_T$) is terminating, any infinite sequence of rewrites in $\mathcal{T}$ (resp. its reversal) would require infinitely many applications of the rules from $\mathcal{B}$ (resp. $\mathcal{D}_T{}^{\mathrm{rev}}$). As these rules can only be applied at the top level, this would imply relative top nontermination. □

4 Automated Proofs

We adapt the rewriting system $\mathcal{T}$ to different generalized Collatz functions to explore the effectiveness of the mixed base scheme on weakened variants of the Collatz conjecture. The rewriting systems, scripts to reproduce the experiments, and our implementation of a termination prover are available at https://github.com/emreyolcu/rewriting-collatz.

Most top-tier termination tools, such as AProVE, Matchbox, and T$_T$T$_2$, use the SAT solver MiniSat [5] to search for matrix/arctic interpretations. This choice is somewhat surprising as MiniSat has not been updated since 2008 and the performance of SAT solvers has improved significantly in the last decade. The use of MiniSat in these provers is motivated by its observed effectiveness in finding interpretations. We investigated the reason for this, which turned out to be a heuristic that MiniSat disables in its default configuration. MiniSat uses negative branching [5], which explores the "false" branch first for all decision variables. Modern SAT solvers use phase-saving [22] which first explores the branch corresponding to the truth value to which the variable was forced to most recently during unit propagation. In our case, enabling negative branching improves solver performance for formulas that encode the existence of interpretations.

4.1 Convergence of W

With the mixed binary–ternary scheme, the function W from Section 3.1 can be seen to be simulated by the system $\mathcal{W}' = \{f\rhd \to 0\rhd\} \cup \mathcal{X}$. A small matrix interpretations proof is found for this system in less than a second, in contrast to its variant $\mathcal{W}$ that uses unary representations for which no automated proof is known.

Theorem 4. SN($\mathcal{W}'$).

Proof. The interpretations below prove SN($\{\rhd f \to \rhd 0\}/\mathcal{X}^{\mathrm{rev}}$):

$$[f](\vec{x}) = \begin{bmatrix} 1 & 0 \\ 0 & 1 \end{bmatrix}\vec{x} + \begin{bmatrix} 1 \\ 1 \end{bmatrix} \qquad [t](\vec{x}) = \begin{bmatrix} 1 & 0 \\ 0 & 0 \end{bmatrix}\vec{x} + \begin{bmatrix} 1 \\ 0 \end{bmatrix}$$

$$[\lhd](\vec{x}) = \begin{bmatrix} 1 & 0 \\ 0 & 0 \end{bmatrix}\vec{x} \qquad [\rhd](\vec{x}) = \begin{bmatrix} 1 & 2 \\ 0 & 0 \end{bmatrix}\vec{x}$$

$$[0](\vec{x}) = \begin{bmatrix} 1 & 0 \\ 0 & 1 \end{bmatrix}\vec{x} + \begin{bmatrix} 2 \\ 0 \end{bmatrix} \qquad [1](\vec{x}) = \begin{bmatrix} 1 & 0 \\ 1 & 0 \end{bmatrix}\vec{x} + \begin{bmatrix} 2 \\ 2 \end{bmatrix} \qquad [2](\vec{x}) = \begin{bmatrix} 1 & 0 \\ 1 & 0 \end{bmatrix}\vec{x} + \begin{bmatrix} 2 \\ 2 \end{bmatrix}$$

By Lemmas 3 and 2, $\mathcal{X}^{\mathrm{rev}}$ is terminating. As a result, $\mathcal{W}'^{\mathrm{rev}}$ is terminating, which by Lemma 2 implies that $\mathcal{W}'$ is terminating. □

4.2 Farkas' Variant

Let $2\mathbb{N} + 1 = \{1, 3, 5, \ldots\}$ denote the odd natural numbers. Farkas [8] studied a slight modification $F' \colon 2\mathbb{N} + 1 \to 2\mathbb{N} + 1$ of the Collatz function which can be proved convergent via induction. We consider automatically proving the convergence of this function as another test case for the mixed base scheme that is easier than the Collatz conjecture without being entirely trivial. We refer the reader to [8] for the original definition of F'. Below, we define another function $F \colon \mathbb{N} \to \mathbb{N}$ that resembles the Collatz function more closely than Farkas' F' (with respect to the definitions of the cases) while being equivalent to F' in terms of convergence. This variant is obtained by introducing an additional case in the Collatz function for $n \equiv 1 \pmod 3$ and applying T otherwise. Its definition and a set $\mathcal{D}_F$ of dynamic rules are shown below.

$$
F(n) = \begin{cases} \frac{n-1}{3} & \text{if } n \equiv 1 \pmod 3 \\ \frac{n}{2} & \text{if } n \equiv 0 \text{ or } n \equiv 2 \pmod 6 \\ \frac{3n+1}{2} & \text{if } n \equiv 3 \text{ or } n \equiv 5 \pmod 6 \end{cases} \qquad \mathcal{D}_F = \begin{Bmatrix} 1\triangleright & \to & \triangleright \\ 0f\triangleright & \to & 0\triangleright \\ 1f\triangleright & \to & 1\triangleright \\ 1t\triangleright & \to & 12\triangleright \\ 2t\triangleright & \to & 22\triangleright \end{Bmatrix}
$$

Termination of the rewriting system $\mathcal{F} = \mathcal{D}_F \cup \mathcal{X}$ is equivalent to the convergence of F. The proof of the equivalence is essentially the same as that of Theorem 3. Farkas gave an inductive proof of convergence for F' via case analysis, and we found an automated proof that $\mathcal{F}$ is terminating via arctic interpretations. It is worth mentioning that the default configurations of the existing termination tools (e.g., AProVE, Matchbox) are too conservative to prove termination of this system, but after their authors tweaked the strategies they were also able to find automated proofs via arctic interpretations.

Theorem 5. *For all $n \in \mathbb{N}^+$, the trajectory $F_\tau(n)$ contains 1.*

Proof. We will show $\mathrm{SN}(\mathcal{F})$. By Lemmas 3 and 2, we have $\mathrm{SN}(\mathcal{X}^{\mathrm{rev}})$. The arctic interpretations below (with the empty cells standing for $-\infty$) prove $\mathrm{SN}(\mathcal{D}_{F\,\mathrm{top}}^{\mathrm{rev}}/\mathcal{X}^{\mathrm{rev}})$ by Theorem 1, which implies $\mathrm{SN}(\mathcal{D}_F^{\mathrm{rev}}/\mathcal{X}^{\mathrm{rev}})$ by Lemma 4. As we know $\mathcal{X}^{\mathrm{rev}}$ is terminating, by Lemma 1 we conclude $\mathrm{SN}(\mathcal{D}_F^{\mathrm{rev}} \cup \mathcal{X}^{\mathrm{rev}})$, implying $\mathrm{SN}(\mathcal{F})$ via Lemma 2.

$$
[f](\vec{x}) = \begin{bmatrix} & & 2 \\ & 2 & 0 \\ 2 & & \end{bmatrix} \vec{x} + \begin{bmatrix} 0 \\ \\ \end{bmatrix} \qquad [t](\vec{x}) = \begin{bmatrix} & & 2 & \\ 0 & 2 & 0 & 0 \\ 2 & & 2 & \end{bmatrix} \vec{x} + \begin{bmatrix} 0 \\ \\ \end{bmatrix}
$$

$$
[\triangleleft](\vec{x}) = \begin{bmatrix} 0 \\ 2 \\ \\ 4 \end{bmatrix} \qquad [\triangleright](\vec{x}) = \begin{bmatrix} 0 \\ \\ \end{bmatrix} \vec{x}
$$

$$
[0](\vec{x}) = \begin{bmatrix} 0 & 4 & 0 \\ & 4 & \\ & 4 & 0 \\ 0 & 3 & 0 \end{bmatrix} \vec{x} \qquad [1](\vec{x}) = \begin{bmatrix} 1 & & \\ & 4 & 0 \\ & 4 & 0 \\ 0 & & \\ 0 & 3 & 0 \end{bmatrix} \vec{x} \qquad [2](\vec{x}) = \begin{bmatrix} 0 & 0 & \\ & 4 & \\ 0 & 1 & 0 \\ 0 & 0 & 0 \end{bmatrix} \vec{x}
$$

4.3   Subsets of $\mathcal{T}$

It is also interesting to consider whether we can automatically prove terminations of proper subsets of $\mathcal{T}$. Specifically, we considered the 11 subsystems obtained by leaving out a single rewriting rule from $\mathcal{T}$, and we found proofs via matrix/arctic interpretations for all of the 11 subproblems. The reason for our interest in these problems is threefold:

1. Termination of $\mathcal{T}$ implies the terminations of all of its subsystems, so proving its termination is at least as difficult a task as proving terminations of the 11 subsystems. Therefore, the subproblems serve as additional sanity checks that an automated approach aspiring to succeed for the Collatz conjecture ought to be able to pass.
2. When proving termination in a stepwise manner, we solve a sequence of relative termination problems. Having proved the terminations of all 11 subsystems is a partial solution to the full problem, since it implies that for any single rule $\ell \to r \in \mathcal{T}$, proving $\mathrm{SN}(\{\ell \to r\}/\mathcal{T})$ settles the Collatz conjecture.
3. After the removal of a rule, the termination of the remaining system still encodes a valid mathematical question about the Collatz trajectories. The question of termination of a proper subset is equivalent to asking if every corresponding Collatz trajectory that does not require the use of the left-out rule is convergent.

Example 5. As an instance of leaving out a rule, consider the subsystem $\mathcal{T} \setminus \{f1 \to 0t\}$. There is a single-step matrix interpretations proof that this system is terminating:

$$[f](\vec{x}) = \begin{bmatrix} 1 & 1 \\ 1 & 0 \end{bmatrix} \vec{x} \qquad [t](\vec{x}) = \begin{bmatrix} 1 & 3 \\ 3 & 4 \end{bmatrix} \vec{x} + \begin{bmatrix} 1 \\ 1 \end{bmatrix}$$

$$[\lhd](\vec{x}) = \begin{bmatrix} 1 & 5 \\ 0 & 0 \end{bmatrix} \vec{x} \qquad [\rhd](\vec{x}) = \begin{bmatrix} 1 & 0 \\ 1 & 0 \end{bmatrix} \vec{x} + \begin{bmatrix} 1 \\ 1 \end{bmatrix}$$

$$[0](\vec{x}) = \begin{bmatrix} 7 & 2 \\ 2 & 5 \end{bmatrix} \vec{x} + \begin{bmatrix} 2 \\ 1 \end{bmatrix} \qquad [1](\vec{x}) = \begin{bmatrix} 2 & 1 \\ 1 & 1 \end{bmatrix} \vec{x} + \begin{bmatrix} 1 \\ 0 \end{bmatrix} \qquad [2](\vec{x}) = \begin{bmatrix} 2 & 2 \\ 2 & 4 \end{bmatrix} \vec{x} + \begin{bmatrix} 0 \\ 2 \end{bmatrix}$$

With the above interpretations, we can show for instance that the Collatz trajectory starting at 3 (represented as $\lhd t \rhd$) is convergent, because the missing rule is not used in any derivation of 1 ($\lhd \rhd$) from 3. Below is an example derivation along with the decimal values each string represents and a vector value of each string under the interpretations above (setting $\vec{x} = (0,0)$ for the purpose of demonstration). We omit the subscripts from the rewrite relations and simply write $\to$.

3	5	5	8	8	8	4	2	1
$\lhd t \rhd$	$\to \lhd 2 \rhd$	$\to \lhd f t \rhd$	$\to \lhd f 2 \rhd$	$\to \lhd 1 f \rhd$	$\to \lhd f f f \rhd$	$\to \lhd f f \rhd$	$\to \lhd f \rhd$	$\to \lhd \rhd$
$\begin{bmatrix} 79 \\ 0 \end{bmatrix} >$	$\begin{bmatrix} 78 \\ 0 \end{bmatrix} >$	$\begin{bmatrix} 68 \\ 0 \end{bmatrix} >$	$\begin{bmatrix} 62 \\ 0 \end{bmatrix} >$	$\begin{bmatrix} 41 \\ 0 \end{bmatrix} >$	$\begin{bmatrix} 40 \\ 0 \end{bmatrix} >$	$\begin{bmatrix} 26 \\ 0 \end{bmatrix} >$	$\begin{bmatrix} 14 \\ 0 \end{bmatrix} >$	$\begin{bmatrix} 12 \\ 0 \end{bmatrix}$

Table 1 shows the parameters for the proofs that we found for the termination of each subsystem. For each rule $\ell \to r$ that is left out, we searched for a stepwise proof to show that $\mathcal{B} \setminus \{\ell \to r\}$ is terminating relative to $\mathcal{T} \setminus \{\ell \to r\}$ (freely utilizing weakly monotone

Table 1. Smallest proofs found for terminations of subsystems of $\mathcal{T}$ in under 120 seconds. The columns show the matrix dimension d and the maximum number v of distinct coefficients that appear in the matrices, along with the median time to find an entire termination proof across 10 repetitions for the fixed d and v.

Rule removed	Matrix			Arctic			Rule removed	Matrix			Arctic		
	d	v	Time	d	v	Time		d	v	Time	d	v	Time
f▷ → ▷	3	4	4s	3	5	19s	f0 → 0f	4	2	1s	3	4	3s
t▷ → 2▷	1	2	<1s	1	3	<1s	f1 → 0t	1	3	1s	1	4	1s
◁0 → ◁t	2	2	<1s	2	3	<1s	f2 → 1f	1	2	<1s	1	3	<1s
◁1 → ◁ff	3	3	1s	3	4	1s	t0 → 1t	4	3	2s	3	4	1s
◁2 → ◁ft	4	4	8s	4	3	4s	t1 → 2f	5	2	1s	4	3	1s
							t2 → 2t	4	4	28s	2	5	1s

algebras due to Lemma 4). Such a proof requires at most three steps since there are at most three rules in $\mathcal{B} \setminus \{\ell \to r\}$. On the table, we report the smallest parameters (in terms of matrix dimension) that work for all of these steps. As we already know that $\mathrm{SN}(\mathcal{T} \setminus \mathcal{B})$ holds (by Lemma 3), the interpretations found allow us to conclude the termination of each subsystem. This is not the only way to prove the terminations of the subsystems, however, we chose this uniform strategy for the sake of comparison.

4.4 Odd Trajectories

In the originally defined Collatz function C, applying $2n + 1 \mapsto 6n + 4$ produces an even number, so we incorporate a single division by 2 into the definition of the odd case and obtain the function T with the same overall dynamics as C. Taking this idea further by performing as many divisions by 2 as possible leads to the so-called Syracuse function $\mathrm{Syr} \colon 2\mathbb{N} + 1 \to 2\mathbb{N} + 1$, defined as $\mathrm{Syr}(n) = \frac{3n+1}{2^k}$ where $k = \max\{k \in \mathbb{N}^+ \mid 2^k \text{ divides } 3n + 1\}$.

Expressing the Syracuse function as a generalized Collatz function would require infinitely many cases to account for all of the possible appearances of 2^k as the denominator with different values of k. As a result, we are unable to simulate it with a finite rewriting system. Nevertheless, we may compromise and accelerate the Collatz function by a constant amount. We first observe that if $n \equiv 1 \pmod 8$ then $\mathrm{Syr}(n) = \frac{3n+1}{4}$ and if $n \equiv 3 \pmod 4$ then $\mathrm{Syr}(n) = \frac{3n+1}{2}$. Furthermore, for any $n \in \mathbb{N}$ we have $\mathrm{Syr}(8n + 5) = \mathrm{Syr}(2n + 1)$ since $3(8n + 5) + 1 = 24n + 16 = 4(6n + 4) = 4(3(2n + 1) + 1)$. Putting these observations together, we can define a generalized Collatz function $S \colon 2\mathbb{N} + 1 \to 2\mathbb{N} + 1$ as follows.

$$S(n) = \begin{cases} \frac{3n+1}{4} & \text{if } n \equiv 1 \pmod 8 \\ \frac{n-1}{4} & \text{if } n \equiv 5 \pmod 8 \\ \frac{3n+1}{2} & \text{if } n \equiv 3 \pmod 4 \end{cases}$$

S is convergent if and only if C (or T) is convergent, and the number of steps that S takes to converge is between that of T and Syr. In a manner similar to before, we

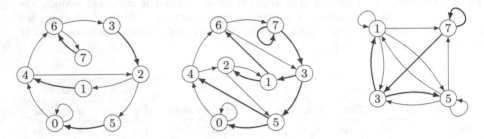

Fig. 1. Transition graphs of the iterates in the Collatz trajectories across residue classes modulo 8 for the functions C (left), T (middle), S (right). For each function f, the edge $u \to v$ is part of its transition graph if and only if there exists some $n \equiv u \pmod 8$ such that $f(n) \equiv v \pmod 8$. Bold edges indicate transitions where $f(n) > n$.

can translate S into a rewriting system $\mathcal{S} = \{ff\bullet \to 0\bullet, tf\bullet \to \bullet, t\bullet \to 2\bullet\} \cup \mathcal{X}$. Since we are working with odd numbers we used a new symbol $\bullet$ to mark the end of a string, viewed functionally as $\bullet(x) = 2x + 1$. Termination of the rewriting system $\mathcal{S}$ is equivalent to the convergence of S. Similar to $\mathcal{T}$, proving the termination of $\mathcal{S}$ is currently beyond our reach, although it may potentially be an easier path to the Collatz conjecture (compared to proving $\mathrm{SN}(\mathcal{T})$). Failing to prove the termination of $\mathcal{S}$ itself, we considered the subsystems of $\mathcal{S}$ as we did for $\mathcal{T}$ in Section 4.3. With matrix/arctic interpretations, the terminations of all but two of the 11-rule subsystems of $\mathcal{S}$ were automatically proved. Despite devoting thousands of CPU hours, we were not able to find interpretations to prove that $\mathcal{S}_1 = \mathcal{S} \setminus \{ff\bullet \to 0\bullet\}$ or $\mathcal{S}_2 = \mathcal{S} \setminus \{tf\bullet \to \bullet\}$ is terminating, so we leave them as challenges for automated termination proving.

4.5   Collatz Trajectories Modulo 8

Let m be a power of 2. Given $k \in \{0, 1, \dots, m - 1\}$, is it the case that all nonconvergent Collatz trajectories contain some $n \equiv k \pmod m$? For several values of k this can be proved to hold by inspecting the transitions of the iterates in the Collatz trajectories across residue classes modulo m (shown on Figure 1 for $m = 8$). These questions can also be formulated as the terminations of some rewriting systems. With this approach we found automated proofs for several cases:

Theorem 6. *If there exists a nonconvergent Collatz trajectory, it cannot avoid the residue classes of* 2, 3, 4, 6 *modulo* 8.

It remains open whether the above holds for the residue classes of 0, 1, 5, 7 modulo 8.

5   More Problems to Approach via Rewriting

Mahler's 3/2 Problem. Let $\xi \in \mathbb{R}_{>0}$ be a real number. It is called a *Z-number* if for all $k \in \mathbb{N}$ we have $\mathrm{frac}\left(\xi\left(\frac{3}{2}\right)^k\right) < \frac{1}{2}$, where $\mathrm{frac}(\cdot)$ denotes the fractional part of the number. Mahler [20] conjectured that there are no Z-numbers. Moreover, he considered a generalized Collatz function $M \colon \mathbb{N}^+ \to \mathbb{N}^+$, defined as follows.

$$M(n) = \begin{cases} \frac{3n}{2} & \text{if } n \equiv 0 \pmod 2 \\ \frac{3n+1}{2} & \text{if } n \equiv 1 \pmod 4 \\ \bot & \text{if } n \equiv 3 \pmod 4 \end{cases}$$

He related the behaviors of M-trajectories to the existence of Z-numbers:

Theorem 7. *For $n \in \mathbb{N}^+$, if a Z-number exists in the interval $[n, n+1)$, then there is no $k \in \mathbb{N}$ for which $M^k(n) \equiv 3 \pmod 4$.*

Thus, the nonexistence of Z-numbers can be established by proving that M is convergent, which is equivalent to the termination of $\mathcal{M} = \{\texttt{f}\triangleright \to 0\triangleright, \texttt{ft}\triangleright \to 10\triangleright\} \cup \mathcal{X}$. In order to ensure termination at the case $n \equiv 3 \pmod 4$, there is no rule with the LHS $\texttt{tt}\triangleright$.

Halting Problem for Busy Beaver-5. The busy beaver problem concerns finding binary-alphabet Turing machines with n states that, when given an input tape of all 0s, write the largest number of 1s on the tape upon halting. For each n, the machine that achieves this is called the "Busy Beaver-n". Note that this definition only requires the machines to halt on all-0 inputs, leaving the behavior on other inputs unspecified and allowing them not to halt in general. Michel [21] observed that for $n \in \{2, 3, 4\}$, the busy beaver machines are all *total Turing machines*, i.e., they halt on all inputs, and moreover proved that they all simulate some generalized Collatz function. It is an open problem whether all busy beavers are total. In particular, it is unknown whether the current Busy Beaver-5 candidate is total. Michel showed that the Busy Beaver-5 candidate simulates the following generalized Collatz function.

$$B(n) = \begin{cases} \frac{5n+18}{3} & \text{if } n \equiv 0 \pmod 3 \\ \frac{5n+22}{3} & \text{if } n \equiv 1 \pmod 3 \\ \bot & \text{if } n \equiv 2 \pmod 3 \end{cases}$$

Convergence of the above function can be studied via the termination of a rewriting system obtained by a mixed $\{3, 5\}$-ary (ternary–quinary) translation scheme. We were unable to prove the termination of the resulting system.

Ternary Expansions of 2^n. Erdős [7] asked: When does the ternary expansion of 2^n omit the digit 2? This is the case for $2^0 = (1)_3$, $2^2 = (11)_3$, and $2^8 = (100111)_3$. He conjectured that it does not happen for $n > 8$. This conjecture can be proved by showing that the rewriting system $\mathcal{E} = \{0\triangleright \to \triangleright, 1\triangleright \to \triangleright, \triangleleft\triangleright \to \triangleleft\triangleright\} \cup \{r \to \ell \mid \ell \to r \in \mathcal{X}\}$ is terminating on all initial strings of the form $\triangleleft \texttt{f}^8 \texttt{f}^+\triangleright$. Given a string that corresponds to the binary representation of a power of 2, this system essentially rewrites the string into ternary by pushing ternary symbols to the right without altering the value that the string represents, and removes the occurrences of the ternary digits 0 and 1 (but not 2). If the ternary expansion does not contain the digit 2 then all digits will be removed, resulting in the string $\triangleleft\triangleright$ that can then be rewritten to itself indefinitely. This problem, as described, is an instance of "local termination" [28] since it is concerned with termination on not all possible strings but a subset of them. We have not performed experiments with this system or local termination yet and we leave this for future work.

6   Related Work

To our knowledge, Zantema [29], with his system $\mathcal{Z}$ that we saw in Section 3.1, was the first to attempt using an automated method and string rewriting to search for a proof of the Collatz conjecture. In addition, although we independently discovered the mixed binary–ternary system described in Section 3.2, Scollo [25] had essentially the same idea, the difference being that he adopted a functional view of the digits that is slightly different than in (1). Scollo was not concerned with proving termination, though, and proposed rewriting primarily as a formalism that forgoes the arithmetic interpretation of the iterates and instead emphasizes its dynamic/computational behavior.

De Mol [4] showed the existence of a small 2-tag system [23] with the following rules that simulates the iterated application of the Collatz function given a unary representation: $\{1 \rightharpoonup \triangleleft\triangleright, \triangleleft \rightharpoonup 1, \triangleright \rightharpoonup 111\}$. This tag system halts if and only if the Collatz conjecture holds, giving yet another formulation of the problem.

Kari [11] designed 1D cellular automata that perform multiplication by 3 and 3/2 in base 6, and reformulated both the Collatz conjecture and Mahler's 3/2 problem as sets of constraints to be satisfied by the space-time diagrams of these cellular automata.

Kauffman [13] developed a formalism to perform arithmetic that he called *string arithmetic*, and expressed the Collatz conjecture within it. This formalism works with unary representations of numbers, and uses the three symbols 1, $\triangleleft$, $\triangleright$. Letting ϵ denote the empty string and N be any string representing a number, string arithmetic consists of the following bidirectional rewrite rules (or "identities") to convert between different strings representing the same number: $\{\triangleright\triangleleft \leftrightarrow \epsilon, 11 \leftrightarrow \triangleleft 1\triangleright, 1N \leftrightarrow N1\}$. Then, the Collatz function is encoded by the following two rules: $\{\triangleleft N\triangleright \rightarrow N, \triangleleft N\triangleright 1 \rightarrow \triangleleft N1\triangleright N\}$. The Collatz conjecture is equivalent to the question of whether for strings of 1s of all lengths there exists a rewrite sequence using the five rules above to reach the string 1.

7   Future Work

Several extensions to this work can further our understanding of the potential of rewriting techniques for answering mathematical questions. For instance, although matrix/arctic interpretations lead to automated proofs of several weakened variants discussed in this paper, it might still be the case that there exists no matrix/arctic interpretation to establish the termination of the Collatz system $\mathcal{T}$. Proving nonexistence would provide guidance as to where to focus our efforts when searching for a proof. Another issue is the matter of representation, specifically, it is worth exploring whether there exists a suitable translation of the Collatz conjecture into a term, instead of string, rewriting system since many automated termination proving techniques are generalized to term rewriting. Finally, injecting problem-specific knowledge into the rewriting systems or the termination techniques would be helpful as there exists a wealth of information about the Collatz conjecture that could simplify proof search.

Acknowledgments. We thank Jeffrey Lagarias, Florian Frohn, Johannes Waldmann, Carsten Fuhs, Jürgen Giesl, Luke Schaeffer, and Chris Lynch for discussions. We thank Jeremy Avigad, Jasmin Blanchette, and reviewers of CADE for their detailed comments on an earlier draft. This work was supported by NSF under grant CCF-2006363.

References

1. Arts, T., Giesl, J.: Termination of term rewriting using dependency pairs. Theoretical Computer Science **236**(1), 133–178 (2000)
2. Baader, F., Nipkow, T.: Term Rewriting and All That. Cambridge University Press (1998)
3. Buttsworth, R.N., Matthews, K.R.: On some Markov matrices arising from the generalized Collatz mapping. Acta Arithmetica **55**(1), 43–57 (1990)
4. De Mol, L.: Tag systems and Collatz-like functions. Theoretical Computer Science **390**(1), 92–101 (2008)
5. Eén, N., Sörensson, N.: An extensible SAT-solver. In: Giunchiglia, E., Tacchella, A. (eds.) Theory and Applications of Satisfiability Testing (SAT), Lecture Notes in Computer Science, vol. 2919, pp. 502–518. Springer (2004)
6. Endrullis, J., Waldmann, J., Zantema, H.: Matrix interpretations for proving termination of term rewriting. Journal of Automated Reasoning **40**(2), 195–220 (2008)
7. Erdős, P.: Some unconventional problems in number theory. Mathematics Magazine **52**(2), 67–70 (1979)
8. Farkas, H.M.: Variants of the $3N + 1$ conjecture and multiplicative semigroups. In: Geometry, Spectral Theory, Groups, and Dynamics, Contemporary Mathematics, vol. 387, pp. 121–127. American Mathematical Society (2005)
9. Giesl, J., Thiemann, R., Schneider-Kamp, P., Falke, S.: Mechanizing and improving dependency pairs. Journal of Automated Reasoning **37**(3), 155–203 (2006)
10. Hofbauer, D., Waldmann, J.: Termination of string rewriting with matrix interpretations. In: Pfenning, F. (ed.) Term Rewriting and Applications (RTA), Lecture Notes in Computer Science, vol. 4098, pp. 328–342. Springer (2006)
11. Kari, J.: Cellular automata, the Collatz conjecture and powers of 3/2. In: Yen, H., Ibarra, O.H. (eds.) Developments in Language Theory (DLT), Lecture Notes in Computer Science, vol. 7410, pp. 40–49. Springer (2012)
12. Kaščák, F.: Small universal one-state linear operator algorithm. In: Havel, I.M., Koubek, V. (eds.) Mathematical Foundations of Computer Science (MFCS), Lecture Notes in Computer Science, vol. 629, pp. 327–335. Springer (1992)
13. Kauffman, L.H.: Arithmetic in the form. Cybernetics and Systems **26**(1), 1–57 (1995)
14. Kohl, S.: Wildness of iteration of certain residue-class-wise affine mappings. Advances in Applied Mathematics **39**(3), 322–328 (2007)
15. Koprowski, A., Waldmann, J.: Max/plus tree automata for termination of term rewriting. Acta Cybernetica **19**(2), 357–392 (2009)
16. Lagarias, J.C.: The $3x + 1$ problem and its generalizations. The American Mathematical Monthly **92**(1), 3–23 (1985)
17. Lagarias, J.C.: The Ultimate Challenge: The $3x + 1$ Problem. American Mathematical Society (2010)
18. Lagarias, J.C.: The $3x + 1$ problem: An annotated bibliography (1963–1999) (2011), arXiv:math/0309224
19. Lagarias, J.C.: The $3x + 1$ problem: An annotated bibliography, II (2000–2009) (2012), arXiv:math/0608208
20. Mahler, K.: An unsolved problem on the powers of 3/2. Journal of the Australian Mathematical Society **8**(2), 313–321 (1968)
21. Michel, P.: Problems in number theory from busy beaver competition. Logical Methods in Computer Science **11**(4:10), 1–35 (2015)
22. Pipatsrisawat, K., Darwiche, A.: A lightweight component caching scheme for satisfiability solvers. In: Marques-Silva, J., Sakallah, K.A. (eds.) Theory and Applications of Satisfiability Testing (SAT), Lecture Notes in Computer Science, vol. 4501, pp. 294–299. Springer (2007)

23. Post, E.L.: Formal reductions of the general combinatorial decision problem. American Journal of Mathematics **65**(2), 197–215 (1943)
24. Rawsthorne, D.A.: Imitation of an iteration. Mathematics Magazine **58**(3), 172–176 (1985)
25. Scollo, G.: ω-rewriting the Collatz problem. Fundamenta Informaticae **64**(1-4), 405–416 (2005)
26. Sternagel, C., Thiemann, R.: Formalizing monotone algebras for certification of termination and complexity proofs. In: Dowek, G. (ed.) Rewriting and Typed Lambda Calculi (RTA-TLCA), Lecture Notes in Computer Science, vol. 8560, pp. 441–455. Springer (2014)
27. Wagon, S.: The Collatz problem. The Mathematical Intelligencer **7**(1), 72–76 (1985)
28. Waldmann, J., de Vrijer, R., Endrullis, J.: Local termination: Theory and practice. Logical Methods in Computer Science **6**(3) (2010)
29. Zantema, H.: Termination of string rewriting proved automatically. Journal of Automated Reasoning **34**(2), 105–139 (2005)

Open Access This chapter is licensed under the terms of the Creative Commons Attribution 4.0 International License (http://creativecommons.org/licenses/by/4.0/), which permits use, sharing, adaptation, distribution and reproduction in any medium or format, as long as you give appropriate credit to the original author(s) and the source, provide a link to the Creative Commons license and indicate if changes were made.

The images or other third party material in this chapter are included in the chapter's Creative Commons license, unless indicated otherwise in a credit line to the material. If material is not included in the chapter's Creative Commons license and your intended use is not permitted by statutory regulation or exceeds the permitted use, you will need to obtain permission directly from the copyright holder.

Verified Interactive Computation of Definite Integrals

Runqing Xu[1,2] , Liming Li[1] , Bohua Zhan[1,2(✉)]

[1]SKLCS, Institute of Software, Chinese Academy of Sciences, Beijing, China
[2]University of Chinese Academy of Sciences, Beijing, China
{xurq, lilm, bzhan}@ios.ac.cn

Abstract. Symbolic computation is involved in many areas of mathematics, as well as in analysis of physical systems in science and engineering. Computer algebra systems present an easy-to-use interface for performing these calculations, but do not provide strong guarantees of correctness. In contrast, interactive theorem proving provides much stronger guarantees of correctness, but requires more time and expertise. In this paper, we propose a general framework for combining these two methods, and demonstrate it using computation of definite integrals. It allows the user to carry out step-by-step computations in a familiar user interface, while also verifying the computation by translating it to proofs in higher-order logic. The system consists of an intermediate language for recording computations, proof automation for simplification and inequality checking, and heuristic integration methods. A prototype is implemented in Python based on HolPy, and tested on a large collection of examples at the undergraduate level.

Keywords: Symbolic integration, User interface, Proof automation

1   Introduction

Symbolic computation is an important tool in mathematics, science, and engineering. It forms a key part of many mathematical proofs. On the engineering side, justifications for the design of signal processing and control systems contain extensive symbolic computations [6,33], involving derivatives and integrals, Laplace and Fourier transforms, and various special functions.

Typically, these computations can be performed using computer algebra systems such as Mathematica, Maple, and Maxima. Given the complexity of the task, it is not surprising that even the best of these systems are liable to errors. One famous example is $\int_{-1}^{1} \sqrt{x^2}\, dx$, which an early version of Maple evaluates to zero [23] (the error has been fixed in the more recent versions). Bugs in Mathematica have also been observed by mathematicians [15], including evaluation of determinants of matrices with large integer entries, and several evaluations of integrals (also fixed in the most recent version). While some errors are simply implementation mistakes, more systematic errors in symbolic computation

ⓒ The Author(s) 2021
A. Platzer and G. Sutcliffe (Eds.): CADE 2021, LNAI 12699, pp. 485–503, 2021.
https://doi.org/10.1007/978-3-030-79876-5_28

may arise due to neglect of checking side conditions, involving concepts such as well-definedness of expressions, singularities, convergence, and so on. While individual bugs can be reported and fixed, completely eliminating the possibility of error would require a more systematic approach.

Formalization of mathematics in interactive theorem provers promises to eventually achieve this goal. There is already a lot of work on formalization of analysis and linear algebra in interactive theorem provers, as well as verified computations based on the formalized theories. They provide much stronger guarantees of correctness, and also allow users to specify more detailed steps, enabling computations that are too difficult to be found automatically by computer algebra systems. However, a major disadvantage (for now) is that interactive theorem proving requires a great deal of time and expertise on the part of the user, making it difficult to apply on a much larger scale.

It is therefore natural to try to combine the advantages of computer algebra systems with theorem proving. There have already been many works in this direction. A common approach, proposed by Harrison and Théry [20,23], is to invoke a computer algebra system for computations that are difficult to perform, but whose results can be verified more easily. This greatly extends the capability of proof assistants for tasks such as factorization [23], linear arithmetic [28], etc. However, to use such a system, the user still needs expertise in the use of proof assistants, and the range of applicability is limited by the simple proof automation that is available for checking results.

In this paper, we propose a more general framework for verified symbolic computation in theorem provers, and demonstrate it using computation of definite integrals. The resulting system allows users to perform calculations of definite integrals step-by-step, in a user interface similar to that of a computer algebra system, but with the computations verified by automatic translation to proofs in higher-order logic. We choose definite integration for demonstration purposes, due to the great variety of techniques that can be used, but we intend the idea to be applicable to other kinds of symbolic computations.

The framework consists of several components. At the top, a graphical user interface displays the current computation and allows user actions. The user interface produces computations in a standard format. Next, proof automation is used to reconstruct from the computation a proof in higher-order logic. Finally, the proof depends on theorems in mathematics, e.g. (in the case of definite integration) those concerning continuity, derivatives, and integrals.

We implement a prototype based on HolPy, a new interactive theorem prover written in Python [49]. The SymPy package for symbolic computation in Python is used at various places for untrusted computations. The user interface is written in JavaScript as a web application, using Python as backend for convenient invocation of HolPy and SymPy libraries. The underlying theorems in analysis are mostly translated to HolPy from HOL Light (with some modifications). Their proofs have not been fully formalized in HolPy, hence the statements of these theorems still need to be trusted.

We now give an outline for the rest of this paper. Section 2 presents the overall framework. Section 3 describes the intermediate format for recording computations of definite integrals. In Section 4 and 5, we describe respectively the user interface and the proof reconstruction process. In Section 6 we present an evaluation of the system, along with some interesting examples. Finally, we conclude in Section 7 with discussion of possible future work.

Related work. There is a huge body of work on formal verification of continuous and hybrid systems, based on reachability checking [4], computation of invariants [36,41], deductive methods [34,35,47], and so on. In particular, KeYmaera X [18] provides a user interface for verifying hybrid systems using differential dynamic logic, with automatic generation of proofs checkable in Isabelle [9]. Most of this work focuses on automatic verification and/or logical formalisms. Our work can be seen as complementary, focusing on verifying symbolic reasoning about mathematical concepts such as special functions and integration, which can also form a part of the justification of control systems.

Harrison and Théry proposed the "skeptical" approach for combining theorem provers with computer algebra systems [20,23]. Some common applications include factorization of polynomials, which is further applied to verify antiderivatives involving sine and cosine [23]. More recently, this technique is used by Chyzak et al. to formalize the proof of irrationality of $\zeta(3)$ [14], and by Harrison to verify proofs of hypergeometric sums found using the WZ method [22]. Similar approaches are implemented in Isabelle [8], PVS [3] and Lean [28]. Compared to this work, we present more complex proof automation for reconstructing proofs, as well as a user interface for allowing users to perform multi-step computations in a more familiar setting. Other user interfaces for proof assistants with support for displaying mathematical computations include Theorema [11] and jsCoq [5].

The theory of integration has been formalized in every major proof assistant [12,24,31,40,43]. Recently, more advanced concepts that are important in science and engineering have been formalized, including the work by Hasan et al. on Fourier and Laplace transforms [37,38,46], and Immler et al. on ordinary differential equations [25,26]. Work has also been done on formalizing advanced concepts in linear algebra [29], with applications in analyzing mechanical systems [13,44]. Of course, formalized symbolic computation can be applied in many other domains. For example, Selsam et al. [42] verified in Lean the correctness of stochastic backpropagation, an important algorithm in deep learning.

Slagle initiated the study of automatic integration with a heuristic method [45]. Later research focused more on methods that are complete for certain types of integrands, such as Risch's algorithm [19]. More recently, Rubi (rule-based integration) has been demonstrated to be a powerful technique [39]. However, none of these work focuses on formal verification. A verified computation of asymptotics for real-valued functions is implemented by Eberl [16]. Verified *numerical* computation of definite integrals is implemented by Mahboubi et al. [30].

Acknowledgements. This work was partially supported by the National Natural Science Foundation of China under Grant Nos. 62002351, 62032024, and the

Chinese Academy of Sciences Pioneer 100 Talents Program under Grant No. Y9RC585036.

2   Overall Architecture

In this section, we describe the overall architecture of the system, leaving descriptions of its components to the following sections. We focus on definite integrals of continuous functions in one variable over closed intervals. In particular, we consider expressions given by the following syntax:

$$e := v \mid c \mid e_1 \; op \; e_2 \mid f(e) \mid \mathsf{Deriv}(e, v) \mid \mathsf{Integral}(e, v, a, b)$$

Here v is a variable; c is a constant (either a rational number or π); op is an arithmetic operation ($+, -, \times, \div$ and exponentiation); f is a special function (such as logarithms, exponentials, or trigonometric functions); $\mathsf{Deriv}(e, v)$ denotes the derivative of e with respect to variable v; $\mathsf{Integral}(e, v, a, b)$ denotes the definite integral of e with respect to variable v over the interval $[a, b]$. In the rest of this paper, we will use both concrete syntax and LaTeX form of expressions. We use *locations* to point to particular subexpressions. A location is given by a sequence of natural numbers (written in the form $n_1.n_2 \ldots n_k$, with each n_i starting from zero), specifying the path to a subtree in the abstract syntax tree of an expression. For example, in the expression

$$1 + \mathsf{Integral}(1 + \sin^3(x), x, 0, 1)$$

the location of $\sin^3(x)$ is given by 1.0.1.

A computation is represented as a list of steps, with each step specifying a rewriting of the current expression. Each step should provide sufficient information so that both checking its correctness and proof generation can be performed relatively easily. A computation begins with the integral to be evaluated, and ends with an expression in simplified closed form. Each step contains the name of the rule used, the location in the expression at which it is applied, and the expected result of applying the step. A step may contain additional parameters and certificates needed for verification. Rules of integration include substitution, integration by parts, use of a trigonometric identity, and so on (described in detail in Section 3). For example, integration by parts takes as parameters two expressions u and v, such that $f \cdot dx = u \cdot dv$ where f is the integrand of the integral at the given location.

A graphical user interface allows the user to specify a computation in ways similar to using a computer algebra system. The user interface displays the computation in LaTeX or in text form. At each step, the user selects part of the current expression to focus on, then selects an action from the menu. Depending on the selected action, the user may need to enter some of the parameters, while the other parameters are automatically inferred by the system. After checking validity of inputs, the user interface computes the result of the action. A package for symbolic computation may be invoked at this step.

There are many side conditions that need to hold in order for a computation step to be correct, some of which may not be caught at the user interface. Translation of the computation to proofs in higher-order logic greatly increases our confidence in the computation and can point out potential errors. In this work, we translate the computation to higher-order logic proofs in HolPy. One main difficulty is implementing sufficiently powerful proof automation for simplification of expressions, inequality checking, and other side conditions. We demonstrate that the API for proof automation in HolPy is sufficiently powerful for this purpose. However, note the representation of a computation is independent from any particular proof assistant, so additional proof translation may be implemented for other proof assistants.

Finally, various algorithms for integration (such as Slagle's method [45]) may be implemented to perform several steps of computation at once. We implemented Slagle's method and have it as one of the options at the user interface.

The overall framework is shown in the following diagram.

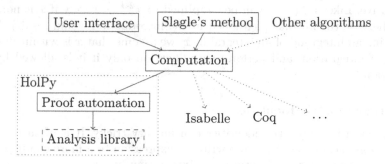

Here solid boxes and arrows indicate parts that are implemented for this paper. The analysis library is only partially formalized. Dotted arrows indicate possible future extensions.

This layered design can be viewed as a separation of concerns. At the top, the user only need to think about how to evaluate an integral in general mathematical terms. The implementation of integration algorithms only involves computer algebra. Proof automation involves algorithms for constructing proofs in the underlying logic. Finally, building a library in analysis involves working with a proof assistant. All these are put together to enable verification of potentially difficult symbolic integration by producing proofs in higher-order logic or other logical formalisms. In the following three sections, we describe the top three layers of the system in more detail.

3   Integration Rules

Rules of integration define the language for recording computations. Each rule may take additional parameters (as described below), as well as a location parameter specifying the subexpression the rule is applied on.

3.1   Simplification

The rule **Simplification** rewrites an expression to an equivalent simpler form. The details of simplification depends on the implementation. Here we only specify in broad terms what is and is not simplified. These choices are made mainly considering the ease of performing simplifications, and having a clearly defined "simplified form". We do expand products of polynomials and combine terms (e.g. from $(x+1)(x-1)$ to x^2-1). We do not reduce quotients of polynomials (e.g. from $(x^3+1)/(x^2+1)$ to $x-(x-1)/(x^2+1)$, and from $2/(x^2-1)$ to $1/(x-1)-1/(x+1)$). We do not automatically expand powers (e.g. $(x+1)^5$). We do simplify values of trigonometric functions (e.g. from $\sin(\frac{\pi}{4})$ to $\sqrt{2}/2$, and from $\sin(\frac{\pi}{2}-x)$ to $\cos x$), but do not use other trigonometric identities. We do evaluate derivatives and apply a fixed list of basic integrals, including linearity, powers, sine, cosine, exponential, and derivatives of trigonometric functions.

One complication is that certain rewrite rules contain side conditions. For example, it is only possible to simplify $\sqrt{xy}$ to $\sqrt{x} \cdot \sqrt{y}$ when both x and y are nonnegative. Likewise $(x^2)^{\frac{1}{2}}$ can be simplified to $x^{2 \cdot \frac{1}{2}} = x$ only if x is nonnegative (otherwise the mistake mentioned in the introduction would result). When simplifying an integrand of an integral in x, we assume that x is within the open domain of integration, and perform simplification only if it is allowed by this assumption.

3.2   Trigonometric Identities

Application of trigonometric identities can be very tricky. It is often necessary to use trigonometric identities to rewrite an expression to a more complex form, in order to prepare for a substitution or integration by parts.

We use the classification of trigonometric identities by Fu et al. [17], which is implemented in SymPy (sympy.simplify.fu). In this scheme, trigonometric identities are classified into several groups with names of the form TRi. Some commonly used groups are shown below (rewriting from left to right):

- TR5: $\sin^2 x = 1 - \cos^2 x$.
- TR6: $\cos^2 x = 1 - \sin^2 x$.
- TR7: $\cos^2 x = \frac{1}{2}(1 + \cos 2x)$.
- TR9: $\sin x + \sin y = 2 \sin\left(\frac{x+y}{2}\right) \cos\left(\frac{x-y}{2}\right)$, etc.
- TR11: $\sin 2x = 2 \sin x \cos x$, $\cos 2x = \cos^2 x - \sin^2 x$, etc.

The **Rewrite trigonometric** rule rewrites using one group of trigonometric identities, followed by simplification. It takes a parameter *rule* which specifies the name of the rule used. For example, applying with *rule* = TR5 on $2 - 2\sin^2 x$ yields $2\cos^2 x$.

3.3   Substitution

Substitution makes use of the following theorem known from first-year calculus:

$$\int_a^b f(g(x))g'(x)\,dx = \int_{g(a)}^{g(b)} f(u)\,du.$$

There are two possible directions for applying the theorem, corresponding to two rules **Substitution I** and **Substitution II**.

Forward substitution. The rule **Substitution I** assumes the integral is in the form $f(g(x))g'(x)$. Typically in informal writing, only $g(x)$ is provided, and $f(x)$ is found by a sometimes magical process. To see the possible complexity involved, consider the integral

$$\int_{\frac{3}{4}}^{1} \frac{1}{\sqrt{1-x}-1}\, dx$$

The required substitution is $u = \sqrt{1-x}$. The usual explanation continues as follows. Compute $du = -\frac{1}{2}(1-x)^{-1/2}\, dx = -\frac{1}{2}u^{-1}\, dx$. So $dx = -2u \cdot du$. The values of u at the boundary points are $\frac{1}{2}$ and 0. So the integral can be rewritten as $\int_{1/2}^{0} -2u/(u-1)\, du = \int_{0}^{1/2} 2u/(u-1)\, du$.

Heurstic methods are needed for finding a suitable function f. Hence, we require the **Substitution I** rule to specify both f and g as parameters. The rule checks that $f(g(x))g'(x)$ and the original integrand become the same after simplification. We also restrict g to be monotonic (equivalently $g'(x) \geq 0$ or $g'(x) \leq 0$ in the open interval (a, b))[1]. For example, the previous substitution is given by $f(u) = 2u/(u-1)$ and $g(x) = \sqrt{1-x}$.

Backward substitution. The rule **Substitution II** applies substitution in the other direction. In informal writing, it is usually expressed as substituting x by some expression $g(t)$. Then f is the original integrand, but the values of a and b need to be found by the reader. Our rule requires specifying a and b so that $g(a)$ and $g(b)$ equals the original limits of integration, and g is monotonic in the range (a, b). For example, the step

$$\int_{0}^{1} \sqrt{1-x^2}\, dx = \int_{0}^{\frac{\pi}{2}} \sqrt{1-\sin^2 t}\, \cos t\, dt$$

is represented as $g = \sin(t), a = 0$ and $b = \pi/2$.

3.4   Integration by Parts

The **Integration by parts** rule applies the theorem

$$\int_{a}^{b} u(x)v'(x)\, dx = u(x)v(x)|_{a}^{b} - \int_{a}^{b} u'(x)v(x)\, dx$$

Typically in informal writing, both u and v are provided. These are recorded as parameters of the rule. The rule checks that $f \cdot dx = u \cdot dv$, where f is the original integrand. For example, the step

$$\int_{-1}^{2} xe^x\, dx = xe^x|_{-1}^{2} - \int_{-1}^{2} e^x\, dx$$

is represented as $u = x$ and $v = e^x$.

---

[1] It is possible to relax this assumption, but the process for reconstructing the proof would be more involved.

3.5   Rewriting

The **Rewrite** rule provides more flexibility for rewriting than simplification. It allows rewriting an expression to any equivalent form as the preparation for applying other rules. The rule takes a parameter *rhs* specifying the intended right side of the rewrite, and another expression *denom*, defaulting to 1. The rule checks that *denom* is nonzero in the domain of integration, and the original expression and *rhs* have the same simplification after multiplying by *denom*.

The presence of *denom* means polynomial division and partial fraction decomposition can be specified. For example, when integrating $x^3/(x^2+1)$, the first step is to divide the numerator by the denominator, yielding $x - x/(x^2+1)$. Simplification as we have implemented is not strongly enough to show their equivalence. However, after multiplying both sides by $denom = x^2 + 1$, the expressions x^3 and $x(x^2+1) - x$ become the same after simplification.

3.6   Splitting an Integral

Sometimes it is necessary to split the domain of integration into two or more parts. This is needed to deal with absolute values, and non-monotonic functions g in a substitution. The rule **Split region** takes a parameter c satisfying $a \leq c \leq b$, and split the integral $\int_a^b f(x)\,dx$ into $\int_a^c f(x)\,dx + \int_c^b f(x)\,dx$. For example, when integrating $\int_{-1}^1 \sqrt{x^2}\,dx$ (the example from the introduction), the first step is to split with $c = 0$, resulting in $\int_{-1}^0 \sqrt{x^2}\,dx + \int_0^1 \sqrt{x^2}\,dx$, which can then be simplified to $\int_{-1}^0 -x\,dx + \int_0^1 x\,dx$.

3.7   Solving Equations

One particularly interesting technique for integration involves solving for the value of the integral in an equation[2]. If an integral I can be written in the form $X - cI$, where X is any expression (containing no or simpler integrals), and c is a constant not equal to -1, then we can solve the equation $I = X - cI$ to obtain $I = X/(c+1)$. Common uses of this technique include integrating expressions of the form $e^{ax}\sin bx$ and $e^{ax}\cos bx$ (apply integration by parts twice, then solve equation). The rule **Solve equation** is applied only to the whole expression, and takes two parameters: the index *id* of a previous step and a coefficient *coeff*. Let I be the integral before step *id*. The rule adds $coeff \cdot I$ to the current expression, then divide by $coeff + 1$ and simplify. For example, in the evaluation of $\int_0^{\pi/2} e^{2x}\cos x\,dx$, after some steps we get $-2 + e^\pi - 4\int_0^{\pi/2} e^{2x}\cos x\,dx$. Then, applying **Solve equation** with $id = 1$ and $coeff = 4$ yields the answer $\frac{1}{5}(-2+e^\pi)$.

4   User Interface

Above the level of representation of a computation, the graphical user interface helps the user to specify a computation in several ways. Compared to editing a computation directly, the user interface provides the following conveniences:

---

[2] This is valid as long as the integral exists. In our setting this holds as long as the integrand is continuous.

- Display of all expressions in LATEX format.
- Selection of actions and subexpressions to perform the action on.
- Automatically generate some parameters of steps.
- Access to automatic integration algorithms such as Slagle's method.

In the remainder of this section, we describe the last two functionalities in more detail. A screenshot of the user interface is shown in Figure 1.

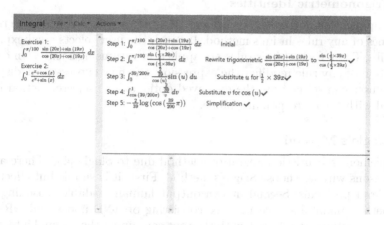

Fig. 1. Screenshot of the user interface, showing the computation of Example 2 in Section 6.

4.1 Substitution

As discussed in Section 3.3, the **Substitution I** rule requires both f and g as parameters, while typically only g is specified in informal arguments. Finding the function f can be a nontrivial process. We try two heuristic methods for finding f. First, if the substitution $u = g(x)$ can be solved for x, yielding a function h such that $x = h(u)$, then f can be found by dividing the integrand by $g'(x)$, then substituting $h(u)$ for x and simplify. Both solving and simplification can be done without checking well-definedness of intermediate expressions, since in the end one only need $f(g(x))g'(x)$ to equal the integrand. For the implementation, we use SymPy's solve function to attempt to find h. The second heuristic simply replaces all expressions equal to $g(x)$ by u, then hope that all remaining occurrences of x is in a single $g'(x)$ in the numerator. Note that the user can always first rewrite the expression into a form where the second heuristic can be applied.

4.2 Rational Functions

Polynomial division or partial fraction decomposition is a common first step for integrating rational functions. From the user interface, the user can invoke these actions. Then SymPy's apart method is used to obtain the results, For example, starting from the integral $\int_{1/3}^{1/2} \frac{x}{1-x^4} \, dx$, the user may choose partial fraction decomposition from the menu, which turns the integral into $\int_{1/3}^{1/2} \frac{x}{2(x^2+1)} - \frac{1}{4(x+1)} - \frac{1}{4(x-1)} \, dx$. The **Rewrite** rule with appropriate *denom* parameter is generated from this step.

4.3   Trigonometric Identities

For the application of trigonometric identities, the user does not need to remember names of any rules in Fu's method. Instead, the user selects a subexpression to rewrite. Then, each of Fu's rules are applied in turn using SymPy. In case the application of any rule modifies the expression, the new expression is displayed, and the user can select from the displayed options. The selected action is then recorded with the corresponding name.

4.4   Slagle's Method

We implement a heuristic integration method due to Slagle [45]. There are two main reasons why we choose Slagle's method. First, it is simple but effective for college-level problems. Second, it can output human-readable reasoning steps. This method maintains a search tree consisting of AND-nodes and OR-nodes. Each node contains an integral, with the root containing the original integral. An AND-node specifies that the integral at the node would be solved if each of its child nodes are solved. An OR-node specifies that the integral at the node would be solved if one of its child nodes is solved. The method iteratively expands the tree using a list of *algorithmic* and *heuristic* rules. Algorithmic rules involve basic normalization operations such as simplification and polynomial division, they are always applied to each node. In contrast, heuristic rules are more exploratory, such as guessing potential expressions for substitution, and count as one step in the search.

Our implementation is mostly faithful to the original presentation [45], with some modifications to fit better with our framework. The output of Slagle's method (if successful) is a list of applications of algorithmic and heuristic rules. Each rule can then be converted to one or more computation steps described in Section 3.

5   Proof Translation

We now describe the process for translating a computation to a proof in higher-order logic. This requires sufficiently strong proof automation for verifying the application of each integration rule. The main components of the automation include showing two expressions are equal by simplification, inequality checking, and showing continuity, differentiability, and integrability of functions. The proof automation is implemented in Python based on HolPy. However, it should be possible to implement it in other proof assistants, and one aim of this section is to provide details to facilitate this process.

5.1 Introduction to HolPy

HolPy [49] is a new system for interactive theorem proving implemented in Python. Like Isabelle [32], HOL Light [21], and HOL4 [1], it uses higher-order logic as the logical foundation. The design of HolPy centers around explicit proof terms that can be generated and checked as Python objects, and written to a file in JSON format. Macros are used pervasively to control the size of proof terms. An API for proof automation facilitates implementation of procedures generating proof terms, in a manner similar to writing proof automation in the ML family of languages, but in the setting of an imperative programming language.

5.2 Background Library

For the background library in analysis, we ported statements of over a thousand theorems from HOL Light, of which about 40% are proved using the point-and-click based user interface [49]. However, major parts of the theory are yet to be formalized, including the construction of real numbers, the gauge integral, and the fundamental theorem of calculus. At present, the statements of the theorems need to be trusted. Finishing the formalization of the analysis library is planned as future work.

5.3 Structure of Proof Automation

The procedure for translating a computation is as follows. For each step in the computation, all expressions involved are first translated into terms in higher-order logic. Depending on the rule used, the automation applies the appropriate conversion to the input term, with the parameters of the rule serving as additional arguments to the conversion. Next, the automation attempts to show the equality between the result of the conversion and the expected output of the step by simplifying both sides. Hence, there does not need to be perfect agreement in the expected output and what is computed by proof automation. The translation is successful as long as proof automation is able to show their equivalence. In this way, we allow additional flexibility in the implementations.

We now discuss the overall structure of proof automation, which bears some similarity to the structure of auto and simp tactics in Isabelle [48]. We maintain two tables: a table of proof rules and a table of simplification rules. Each table is indexed by the head of the predicate or term the rule expects. There may be multiple rules associated to the same head term.

- A *prove* rule for a predicate p takes as input a goal whose head is p and a list of assumptions, and attempts to prove the goal. A simple way to specify a prove rule is from a list of theorems whose conclusion matches the given predicate. The corresponding prove rule attempts to apply each of the theorems in order. In case a theorem has assumptions, it recursively applies the overall **prove** procedure (described below) to discharge each assumption.

– A *simplification* rule for a function f takes as input a term whose head is f and a list of assumptions, and computes the simplification of the term under these assumptions. A simple way to specify a simplification rule is from a list of theorems whose conclusion is an equality, where the left side has head f. The corresponding simplification rule attempts to rewrite using each of the equalities in order. Assumptions in the theorem are discharged by recursive calls to prove as in the previous case.

The overall procedure is defined as a mutual recursion between two functions prove and norm. The norm function receives a term and a list of assumptions as input. It first recursively applies itself to the subterms of the term. Next, it looks for simplification rules associated to the head of the term and applies them in turn. If the head changes, the process is repeated. Note the prove function may be called to discharge assumptions of rewrite rules. This continues until the term is not changed by the simplification rules. The prove function takes a goal and a list of assumptions as input. It first simplifies the goal, then look for prove rules associated to the head term and applies each of them in turn. The case where the goal is an equality reduces to simplifying both sides and then comparing whether they are the same.

5.4   Inequality Checking

A major task of proof automation is checking inequalities in one variable x constrained to lie in an interval $[a, b]$ or (a, b). For example, if one wishes to simplify $\sqrt{f(x)^2}$ to $f(x)$ in the integrand, where the integral is from a to b, one needs to check $f(x) \geq 0$ in the open interval (a, b). Here f may involve the usual arithmetic operations, as well as logarithm, exponential, and trigonometric functions.

The general problem of inequality checking is undecidable when special functions are involved. Hence, we can only hope for methods that can solve most of the inequality goals that appear in practice. There are many heuristic methods [7] as well as decision procedures for inequalities. For our purposes, we found the following, which can be considered as a simplified version of interval arithmetic, to be both simple and effective: starting from the assumption that x lies in a certain interval, iteratively deduce the intervals constraining each of the subterms in the expression. The derivation for each subterm depends on the head of the subterm. Of course, this method is incomplete as it tends to over-approximate the intervals of terms formed from binary operators. Implementation of more advanced inequality checking methods is a goal for the future.

5.5   Simplification

Simplification for arithmetic operations follows the same principle as in Section 3.1: expand the expression into polynomial form, but do not expand powers. We also do not reduce rational functions. This is similar to the normalization of polynomials in other implementations of proof automation [7].

More precisely, define a monomial to be a term of the form $c \cdot (a_1^{p_1} a_2^{p_2} \cdots a_k^{p_k})$, where c is a rational number, and each a_i is either a prime number or a term whose head is not an arithmetic operator. If a_i is a prime number, then the corresponding p_i must be either non-constant or a rational number between 0 and 1 exclusive. The a_i's are distinct and sorted in a pre-determined order. A rational number is a special case of a monomial, with $k = 0$. We call c the coefficient of a monomial and $a_1^{p_1} a_2^{p_2} \cdots a_k^{p_k}$ its body. A polynomial is a sum of monomials, whose bodies are all distinct and in sorted order. It is clear that any expression can be simplified into this form. For example, $\sqrt{6}\sqrt{2}(x + 3^{2/3})$ is simplified to

$$6^{1/2}2^{1/2}x + 6^{1/2}2^{1/2}3^{2/3} = 2^{1/2}3^{1/2}2^{1/2}x + 2^{1/2}3^{1/2}2^{1/2}3^{2/3} = 2 \cdot 3^{1/2}x + 6 \cdot 3^{1/6}$$

Simplification of polynomials is implemented in the simplification rules for $+$, $\times$ and power. $a - b$ and a/b are simply reduced to $a + (-1) \cdot b$ and $a \cdot b^{-1}$, respectively.

For logarithms and exponentials, we apply the standard simplification rules $\log 1 = 0, \log(e^x) = x$ and $e^0 = 1, x > 0 \longrightarrow e^{\log x} = x$. Simplifying trigonometric functions applied to special values is trickier, as we may need to add or subtract multiples of π. For example, $\cos \frac{7\pi}{3}$ is first rewritten to $\cos \frac{\pi}{3}$ and then to $\frac{1}{2}$.

When simplifying an integral over the closed interval $[a, b]$, we apply the following congruence rule:

$$\forall x \in (a, b). \ f(x) = g(x) \longrightarrow \int_a^b f(x)\, dx = \int_a^b g(x)\, dx.$$

This allows us to assume $x \in (a, b)$ when simplifying $f(x)$.

5.6 Applying Theorems

For proving continuity and differentiability, we set up the corresponding prove rules using lists of introduction rules. Some of these rules require assumptions that are discharged recursively. For example, the introduction rule for division is as follows:

$$[\![\text{continuous\_on } S \ f, \ \text{continuous\_on } S \ g, \ \forall x \in S. \ g(x) \neq 0]\!]$$
$$\longrightarrow \text{continuous\_on } S \ (\lambda x. \ f(x)/g(x))$$

Application of this rule involves recursively proving the three assumptions, including the use of inequality checking from Section 5.4.

Substitution and integration by parts are implemented by applying the corresponding theorems. This is simple because the parameters of the rule already contain instantiations for all function variables.

6 Evaluation and Examples

We evaluated our prototype implementation[3] on problems taken from exam preparation books (Tongji), online problem lists by D. Kouba [27] (Kouba) and

---

[3] The code and examples are available online at https://github.com/bzhan/holpy.

the MIT Integration Bee [2] (MIT). We also compared our results with Maple and WolframAlpha. Statistics from the evaluation are shown in Table 1.

Problem set	Total	Solved	Ratio	Slagle	Ratio	Maple	WolframAlpha
Tongji	36	36	100%	26	72%	32	35
Kouba/Substitution	18	17	94%	13	72%	18	18
Kouba/Exponentials	12	7	58%	7	58%	12	11
Kouba/Trigonometric	27	22	81%	11	41%	18	22
Kouba/ByParts	23	22	96%	17	74%	23	23
Kouba/LogArcTangent	22	21	95%	13	59%	21	21
Kouba/PartialFraction	20	16	80%	8	40%	18	20
MIT/2013	25	20	80%	14	56%	20	24
Total	183	161	88%	109	60%	162	174

Table 1. Statistics on the problem lists. "Solved" indicates the number of problems for which proofs can be successfully reconstructed from human-provided computations. "Slagle" indicates the number of problems that can be solved by Slagle's method, with successful proof reconstruction. "Maple" represents the number of problems solved by Maple. "WolframAlpha" represents the number of problems which WolframAlpha can give step-by-step solutions without exceeding its time limit.

The Kouba problem lists are divided into different categories based on techniques used. With human-provided computation steps, we can reconstruct proofs for all of the Tongji problems, most of the problems in D. Kouba's list, while problems from the MIT Integration Bee are more challenging (with the later years increasing in difficulty). Most of the failures are due to unable to show equality after simplification, and during inequality checking. Some are due to unsupported functions.

We show two interesting examples from our case studies. SymPy (version 1.5) returns a wrong answer on the first example and times out on the second. The second example takes a long time even for Mathematica, and cannot be solved by its online version WolframAlpha. These examples demonstrate that our system avoids the common errors, and since the user can guide the computation step-by-step, is also able to verify integrals that are difficult even for sophisticated computer algebra systems.

The first example (Tongji, #27) demonstrates the splitting of domain of integration, as well as use of trigonometric identities. The integral is

$$\int_0^\pi \sqrt{1 + \cos 2x}\, dx$$

This integral is incorrectly evaluated by SymPy as 0. It is correctly evaluated by Mathematica almost instantly.

The evaluation begins with application of trigonometric identities, rewriting the integrand to $\sqrt{1 + \cos^2 x - \sin^2 x}$ and then to $\sqrt{2 \cos^2 x}$. For this, the user simply needs to select $\cos 2x$ and then $\sin^2 x$, and choose the desired rewrite targets. The resulting situation is similar to the example given in the introduction. It is then necessary to split the domain of integration where $\cos x = 0$. The system is able to automatically determine $x = \frac{\pi}{2}$. The full computation is:

$$I = \int_0^\pi \sqrt{1 + \cos^2 x - \sin^2 x}\, dx \quad \text{(Rewrite trig. rule TR11)}$$

$$= \int_0^\pi \sqrt{2\cos^2 x}\, dx = \sqrt{2} \int_0^\pi |\cos x|\, dx \quad \text{(Rewrite trig. rule TR5, Simplification)}$$

$$= \sqrt{2} \left(\int_0^{\frac{\pi}{2}} |\cos x|\, dx + \int_{\frac{\pi}{2}}^\pi |\cos x|\, dx \right) \quad \text{(Split region with } c = \frac{\pi}{2})$$

$$= 2\sqrt{2} \quad \text{(Elim absolute value, Simplification)}$$

The second example comes from MIT Integration Bee 2019, problem #14:

$$I = \int_0^{\pi/100} \frac{\sin(20x) + \sin(19x)}{\cos(20x) + \cos(19x)}\, dx$$

It is simple if one notices to apply the sum-to-product identity first, but almost impossible otherwise. WolframAlpha fails to find the symbolic answer. Using Mathematica offline, it takes about 15 seconds to return an answer, which is however much more complicated than necessary.

The full computation using our tool is:

$$I = \int_0^{\pi/100} \frac{\sin\left(\frac{39}{2}x\right)}{\cos\left(\frac{39}{2}x\right)}\, dx \quad \text{(Rewrite trigonometric, rule TR9)}$$

$$= \int_{\cos\left(\frac{39\pi}{200}\right)}^1 \frac{2}{39}\frac{1}{t}\, dt \quad \text{(Substitution I with } g = \cos\left(\frac{39}{2}x\right))$$

$$= -\frac{2}{39} \log\left(\cos\frac{39\pi}{200}\right) \quad \text{(Simplification)}.$$

7   Conclusion

In this paper, we proposed a framework for verifying symbolic computation of definite integrals, where the user can perform computations in an interface familiar from computer algebra systems, but with results verified by automatic translation to proofs in higher-order logic. The design of the framework follows a layered approach, with each layer focusing on a different aspect of the problem: methods for solving integrals, computer algebra, and proof reconstruction. We implemented a prototype system based on HolPy, and evaluated it on a test suite consisting of publicly available problem lists at the undergraduate level, showing its effectiveness on a large majority of cases.

One immediate piece of future work is to secure the foundation of the higher-order logic proof, by formalizing the proofs of the required theorems. Another gap is the arithmetic computation and comparison of real constants, which, in the case of comparisons, would require approximation techniques [10].

Our prototype implementation focuses on definite integrals of one-variable functions. However, the idea can be applied more generally, by suitably extending the language of integration rules. For applications in the engineering domain, some extensions that would be of high value include linear algebra, improper integrals (including Laplace and Fourier transforms), and vector calculus.

References

1. The HOL 4 system. http://hol.sourceforge.net/
2. MIT Integration Bee. http://www.mit.edu/~pax/integrationbee.html, accessed: 2020-1-22
3. Adams, A., Dunstan, M., Gottliebsen, H., Kelsey, T., Martin, U., Owre, S.: Computer algebra meets automated theorem proving: Integrating Maple and PVS. In: Boulton, R.J., Jackson, P.B. (eds.) Theorem Proving in Higher Order Logics. Lecture Notes in Computer Science, vol. 2152, pp. 27–42. Springer Berlin Heidelberg, Berlin, Heidelberg (2001)
4. Althoff, M., Frehse, G., Girard, A.: Set propagation techniques for reachability analysis. Annual Review of Control, Robotics, and Autonomous Systems **4**(1) (2021)
5. Arias, E.J.G., Pin, B., Jouvelot, P.: jsCoq: Towards hybrid theorem proving interfaces. In: Autexier, S., Quaresma, P. (eds.) Proceedings of the 12th Workshop on User Interfaces for Theorem Provers, UITP 2016, Coimbra, Portugal, 2nd July 2016. EPTCS, vol. 239, pp. 15–27 (2016)
6. Aström, K.J., Murray, R.M.: Feedback Systems: An Introduction for Scientists and Engineers. Princeton University Press, Princeton (2008)
7. Avigad, J., Lewis, R.Y., Roux, C.: A heuristic prover for real inequalities. J. Autom. Reasoning **56**(3), 367–386 (2016)
8. Ballarin, C., Homann, K., Calmet, J.: Theorems and algorithms: An interface between Isabelle and Maple. In: Levelt, A.H.M. (ed.) Proceedings of the 1995 International Symposium on Symbolic and Algebraic Computation. p. 150–157. ISSAC '95, Association for Computing Machinery, New York, NY, USA (1995)
9. Bohrer, B., Rahli, V., Vukotic, I., Völp, M., Platzer, A.: Formally verified differential dynamic logic. In: Bertot, Y., Vafeiadis, V. (eds.) Proceedings of the 6th ACM SIGPLAN Conference on Certified Programs and Proofs, CPP 2017, Paris, France, January 16-17, 2017. pp. 208–221 (2017)
10. Bréhard, F., Mahboubi, A., Pous, D.: A certificate-based approach to formally verified approximations. In: Harrison, J., O'Leary, J., Tolmach, A. (eds.) 10th International Conference on Interactive Theorem Proving, ITP 2019, September 9-12, 2019, Portland, OR, USA. LIPIcs, vol. 141, pp. 8:1–8:19 (2019)
11. Buchberger, B., Jebelean, T., Kutsia, T., Maletzky, A., Windsteiger, W.: Theorema 2.0: Computer-assisted natural-style mathematics. J. Formaliz. Reason. **9**(1), 149–185 (2016)
12. Butler, R.W.: Formalization of the integral calculus in the PVS theorem prover. J. Formalized Reasoning **2**(1), 1–26 (2009)
13. Chen, S., Wang, G., Li, X., Zhang, Q., Shi, Z., Guan, Y.: Formalization of camera pose estimation algorithm based on rodrigues formula. Formal Aspects Comput. **32**(4-6), 417–437 (2020)
14. Chyzak, F., Mahboubi, A., Sibut-Pinote, T., Tassi, E.: A computer-algebra-based formal proof of the irrationality of $\zeta(3)$. In: Klein, G., Gamboa, R. (eds.) Interactive Theorem Proving. Lecture Notes in Computer Science, vol. 8558, pp. 160–176. Springer International Publishing, Cham (2014)
15. Durán, A.J., Pérez, M., Varona, J.L.: The misfortunes of a trio of mathematicians using computer algebra systems. can we trust in them? Notices Amer. Math. Soc. **61**(10), 1249–1252 (2014)
16. Eberl, M.: Verified real asymptotics in Isabelle/HOL. In: Davenport, J.H., Wang, D., Kauers, M., Bradford, R.J. (eds.) Proceedings of the 2019 on International

Symposium on Symbolic and Algebraic Computation, ISSAC 2019, Beijing, China, July 15-18, 2019. pp. 147–154. ACM (2019)

17. Fu, H., Zhong, X., Zeng, Z.: Automated and readable simplification of trigonometric expressions. Mathematical and Computer Modelling **44**(11-12), 1169–1177 (2006)

18. Fulton, N., Mitsch, S., Quesel, J., Völp, M., Platzer, A.: KeYmaera X: an axiomatic tactical theorem prover for hybrid systems. In: Felty, A.P., Middeldorp, A. (eds.) Automated Deduction - CADE-25 - 25th International Conference on Automated Deduction, Berlin, Germany, August 1-7, 2015, Proceedings. Lecture Notes in Computer Science, vol. 9195, pp. 527–538 (2015)

19. Geddes, K.O., Czapor, S.R., Labahn, G.: The Risch Integration Algorithm, pp. 511–573. Springer US, Boston, MA (1992)

20. Harrison, J.: Theorem proving with the real numbers. CPHC/BCS distinguished dissertations, Springer (1998)

21. Harrison, J.: HOL Light: An overview. In: Berghofer, S., Nipkow, T., Urban, C., Wenzel, M. (eds.) Theorem Proving in Higher Order Logics. Lecture Notes in Computer Science, vol. 5674, pp. 60–66. Springer Berlin Heidelberg, Berlin, Heidelberg (2009)

22. Harrison, J.: Formal proofs of hypergeometric sums - dedicated to the memory of Andrzej Trybulec. J. Autom. Reasoning **55**(3), 223–243 (2015)

23. Harrison, J., Théry, L.: A skeptic's approach to combining HOL and Maple. J. Autom. Reason. **21**(3), 279–294 (1998)

24. Hölzl, J., Heller, A.: Three chapters of measure theory in Isabelle/HOL. In: van Eekelen, M., Geuvers, H., Schmaltz, J., Wiedijk, F. (eds.) Interactive Theorem Proving - Second International Conference, ITP 2011, Berg en Dal, The Netherlands, August 22-25, 2011. Proceedings. Lecture Notes in Computer Science, vol. 6898, pp. 135–151 (2011)

25. Immler, F.: A verified ODE solver and the Lorenz attractor. J. Autom. Reason. **61**(1-4), 73–111 (2018)

26. Immler, F., Traut, C.: The flow of ODEs. In: Blanchette, J.C., Merz, S. (eds.) Interactive Theorem Proving - 7th International Conference, ITP 2016, Nancy, France, August 22-25, 2016, Proceedings. Lecture Notes in Computer Science, vol. 9807, pp. 184–199 (2016)

27. Kouba, D.A.: The calculus page problems list. https://www.math.ucdavis.edu/~kouba/ProblemsList.html, accessed: 2020-1-22

28. Lewis, R.Y.: An extensible ad hoc interface between Lean and Mathematica. In: Dubois, C., Paleo, B.W. (eds.) Proceedings of the Fifth Workshop on Proof eXchange for Theorem Proving, PxTP 2017, Brasília, Brazil, 23-24 September 2017. EPTCS, vol. 262, pp. 23–37 (2017)

29. Li, L., Shi, Z., Guan, Y., Zhang, Q., Li, Y.: Formalization of geometric algebra in HOL Light. J. Autom. Reasoning **63**(3), 787–808 (2019)

30. Mahboubi, A., Melquiond, G., Sibut-Pinote, T.: Formally verified approximations of definite integrals. J. Autom. Reason. **62**(2), 281–300 (2019)

31. Mhamdi, T., Hasan, O., Tahar, S.: On the formalization of the Lebesgue integration theory in HOL. In: Kaufmann, M., Paulson, L.C. (eds.) Interactive Theorem Proving, First International Conference, ITP 2010, Edinburgh, UK, July 11-14, 2010. Proceedings. Lecture Notes in Computer Science, vol. 6172, pp. 387–402 (2010)

32. Nipkow, T., Paulson, L.C., Wenzel, M.: Isabelle/HOL - A Proof Assistant for Higher-Order Logic, Lecture Notes in Computer Science, vol. 2283. Springer (2002)

33. Oppenheim, A.V., Willsky, A.S.: Signals and Systems. Prentice Hall, Upper Saddle River, New Jersey (1996)
34. Platzer, A.: Differential dynamic logic for hybrid systems. J. Autom. Reason. **41**(2), 143–189 (2008)
35. Platzer, A.: A complete uniform substitution calculus for differential dynamic logic. J. Autom. Reason. **59**(2), 219–265 (2017)
36. Prajna, S., Jadbabaie, A.: Safety verification of hybrid systems using barrier certificates. In: Alur, R., Pappas, G.J. (eds.) Hybrid Systems: Computation and Control, 7th International Workshop, HSCC 2004, Philadelphia, PA, USA, March 25-27, 2004, Proceedings. Lecture Notes in Computer Science, vol. 2993, pp. 477–492 (2004)
37. Rashid, A., Hasan, O.: On the formalization of Fourier transform in higher-order logic. In: Blanchette, J.C., Merz, S. (eds.) Interactive Theorem Proving. Lecture Notes in Computer Science, vol. 9807, pp. 483–490. Springer International Publishing, Cham (2016)
38. Rashid, A., Hasan, O.: Formal analysis of continuous-time systems using Fourier transform. J. Symb. Comput. **90**, 65–88 (2019)
39. Rich, A.D., Scheibe, P., Abbasi, N.M.: Rule-based integration: An extensive system of symbolic integration rules. J. Open Source Softw. **3**(32), 1073 (2018)
40. Richter, S.: Formalizing integration theory with an application to probabilistic algorithms. In: Slind, K., Bunker, A., Gopalakrishnan, G. (eds.) Theorem Proving in Higher Order Logics, 17th International Conference, TPHOLs 2004, Park City, Utah, USA, September 14-17, 2004, Proceedings. Lecture Notes in Computer Science, vol. 3223, pp. 271–286 (2004)
41. Sankaranarayanan, S., Sipma, H., Manna, Z.: Constructing invariants for hybrid systems. In: Alur, R., Pappas, G.J. (eds.) Hybrid Systems: Computation and Control, 7th International Workshop, HSCC 2004, Philadelphia, PA, USA, March 25-27, 2004, Proceedings. Lecture Notes in Computer Science, vol. 2993, pp. 539–554 (2004)
42. Selsam, D., Liang, P., Dill, D.L.: Developing bug-free machine learning systems with formal mathematics. In: Precup, D., Teh, Y.W. (eds.) Proceedings of the 34th International Conference on Machine Learning, ICML 2017, Sydney, NSW, Australia, 6-11 August 2017. Proceedings of Machine Learning Research, vol. 70, pp. 3047–3056 (2017)
43. Shi, Z., Gu, W., Li, X., Guan, Y., Ye, S., Zhang, J., Wei, H.: The gauge integral theory in HOL4. J. Applied Mathematics **2013**, 160875:1–160875:7 (2013)
44. Shi, Z., Wu, A., Yang, X., Guan, Y., Li, Y., Song, X.: Formal analysis of the kinematic Jacobian in screw theory. Formal Aspects Comput. **30**(6), 739–757 (2018)
45. Slagle, J.R.: A heuristic program that solves symbolic integration problems in freshman calculus. J. ACM **10**(4), 507–520 (1963)
46. Taqdees, S.H., Hasan, O.: Formalization of Laplace transform using the multivariable calculus theory of HOL-Light. In: McMillan, K., Middeldorp, A., Voronkov, A. (eds.) Logic for Programming, Artificial Intelligence, and Reasoning - 19th International Conference, LPAR-19, Stellenbosch, South Africa, December 14-19, 2013. Proceedings. Lecture Notes in Computer Science, vol. 8312, pp. 744–758 (2013)
47. Wang, S., Zhan, N., Zou, L.: An improved HHL prover: An interactive theorem prover for hybrid systems. In: Butler, M., Conchon, S., Zaïdi, F. (eds.) Formal Methods and Software Engineering - 17th International Conference on Formal Engineering Methods, ICFEM 2015, Paris, France, November 3-5, 2015, Proceedings. Lecture Notes in Computer Science, vol. 9407, pp. 382–399 (2015)

48. Wenzel, M.: The Isabelle/Isar reference manual. `http://isabelle.in.tum.de/doc/isar-ref.pdf`
49. Zhan, B., Ji, Z., Zhou, W., Xiang, C., Hou, J., Sun, W.: Design of point-and-click user interfaces for proof assistants. In: Ait-Ameur, Y., Qin, S. (eds.) Formal Methods and Software Engineering - 21st International Conference on Formal Engineering Methods, ICFEM 2019, Shenzhen, China, November 5-9, 2019, Proceedings. Lecture Notes in Computer Science, vol. 11852, pp. 86–103 (2019)

Open Access This chapter is licensed under the terms of the Creative Commons Attribution 4.0 International License (`http://creativecommons.org/licenses/by/4.0/`), which permits use, sharing, adaptation, distribution and reproduction in any medium or format, as long as you give appropriate credit to the original author(s) and the source, provide a link to the Creative Commons license and indicate if changes were made.

The images or other third party material in this chapter are included in the chapter's Creative Commons license, unless indicated otherwise in a credit line to the material. If material is not included in the chapter's Creative Commons license and your intended use is not permitted by statutory regulation or exceeds the permitted use, you will need to obtain permission directly from the copyright holder.

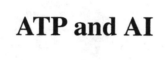

ATP and AI

Confidences for Commonsense Reasoning

Tanel Tammet[1]([⊠])(iD), Dirk Draheim[2](iD), and Priit Järv[1](iD)

[1] Applied Artificial Intelligence Group,
Tallinn University of Technology, Tallinn, Estonia
{tanel.tammet,priit.jarv1}@taltech.ee
[2] Information Systems Group, Tallinn University of Technology, Tallinn, Estonia
dirk.draheim@taltech.ee

Abstract. Commonsense reasoning has long been considered one of the holy grails of artificial intelligence. Our goal is to develop a logic-based component for hybrid – machine learning plus logic – commonsense question answering systems. A critical feature for the component is estimating the confidence in the statements derived from knowledge bases containing uncertain contrary and supporting evidence obtained from different sources. Instead of computing exact probabilities or designing a new calculus we focus on extending the methods and algorithms used by the existing automated reasoners for full classical first-order logic. The paper presents the CONFER framework and implementation for confidence estimation of derived answers.

1 Introduction

The mainstream approaches for "commonsense reasoning" (CSR) before this century focused on rule based reasoning and building suitable logical systems. During the last ten years the focus has switched to machine learning and neural networks. Both of these approaches appear to be limited. A promising approach to practical question answering is building hybrid systems like Watson [17] which complement the current machine learning systems for natural language with logic-based reasoning systems specialized for CSR. In particular, hybrid systems have a good potential for progress towards explainable A.I. See Marcus [26] for an overview of the current work in the area. Our goal is to build upon the existing theory and reasoning systems for first order logic (FOL) to develop a framework and practical systems using FOL reasoners which could be incorporated into a hybrid system containing both machine learning components and rule-based reasoning components. This approach will also provide step-by-step proofs for the answers found, useful for building explainable systems.

We will present the design and implementation of the CONFER framework for extending existing automated reasoning systems with confidence calculation capabilities. We will not focus on other, arguably even more critical issues for CSR and question answering, like handling natural language itself, dialogues,

© The Author(s) 2021
A. Platzer and G. Sutcliffe (Eds.): CADE 2021, LNAI 12699, pp. 507–524, 2021.
https://doi.org/10.1007/978-3-030-79876-5_29

rules with exceptions and default logic [31] or circumscription, knowledge representation for space/time, epistemic reasoning, using context, building and collecting suitable rules, machine learning etc.

The specific CSR task targeted by the current paper is *question answering*: given either a knowledge base of facts and rules or a large corpora of texts (or both), plus optionally a situation description (assumptions) for the questions, answer questions posed either in logic or natural language.

Historically, the longest-going CSR project has been the logic-based CYC project [25], already in 1985 stating the focus on CSR. Despite several successes, the approach taken in the CYC project has often been viewed as problematic ([8], [10]) and has been repeatedly used as an argument against logic-based methods in CSR. Beltagy et al [5] experiment with Markov Logic Network for combining logical and distributional representations of natural language meaning. Domingos et al note in [13] that the CYC project has used Markov Logic for making a part of their knowledge base probabilistic. Khot et al [24] experiment with Markov Logic Networks for NLP question answering. Furbach et al [20] describe research and experiments with a system for natural language question answering, converting natural language sentences to logic and then performing proof search, using different existing FOL knowledge bases. The authors note a number of difficulties, with the most crucial being the lack of sufficiently rich FOL knowledge bases. The closest current approach to ours appears to be the Braid system [23] built by the team previously involved with the Watson system.

2   Interpretation and Encoding of Uncertainty

Reasoning under uncertainty has been thoroughly investigated for at least a century, leading to a proliferation of different theories and mechanisms. A classic example is the MYCIN system [6]. For newer approaches see, for example, [32] and [9]. Each of these is well suited for certain kinds of problems and ill-suited for other kinds. Underlying this is the philosophical complexity of interpreting probability: see [22] for an overview, see also [16], pp. 5-7.

Most of the previous work on combining logic with uncertainty has targeted propositional logic. First order logic is then handled by creating a finite set of weighted ground instances of formulas. This is the approach taken, for example, by the probabilistic logic programming systems ProbLog2 [18], PRISM [34] and the implementation of Markov Logic Networks [12,11] by the Alchemy 2 system [1]. These systems pose different restrictions to the FOL formulas and while well-suited for small domains in cases the restrictions can be followed, the approach becomes unfeasible if the domain is large or formulas complex. For example, neither the ProbLog 2 nor Alchemy 2 implementations manage to answer queries like `1.0::p(a). 1.0::p(i(a,b)). 1.0::p(Y) :- p(X), p(i(X,Y)).` `query(p(b)).` The implementation of ProbLog2 [29] fails, presumably due to infinite recursion in searching for possible groundings for the variables, while Alchemy 2 does not allow function terms in grounded facts.

Previous approaches to full first order logic tend to fall into one of the three camps: either using fuzzy logic [41], representing probabilities as an interval (see [15] for the axiomatic derivation of Dempster-Schafer rules) or interpreting probabilities via many worlds similarly to modalities [4].

For the sake of this work, we largely follow the *subjective interpretation* of probability as a degree of belief, originating from Ramsey and De Finetti. We use the word *confidence* to denote our rough adherence to this interpretation. We avoid using complex measures such as intervals, distributions or fuzzy functions.

In the context of question answering we assume that confidences are typically used for sorting a list of candidate answers by their calculated confidence and optionally applying a filter to eliminate answers with a confidence under a certain threshold. Answers provided may be also annotated with a confidence number. If we are given or can calculate several different confidences for the same answer, we always prefer the higher confidence. The question of calculating a correct probability rarely arises or is considered to be unfeasible.

2.1   Sources, Representation and Meaning of Statements, Confidences and Dependencies

We assume that the confidence in a fact or rule in our common sense knowledge base (KB in the following) typically arises from a large number of human users via crowd-sourcing like in ConceptNet [35,7], NLP-analyzed scraped text from the web like NELL [27], and/or combining different knowledge bases with weights like in [14] and [7] or assigned to the equivalence of name pairs in the vocabulary like in [28] and [19]. There is recent progress towards making knowledge bases for common sense reasoning where the relation strengths (typicality, saliency) have been empirically evaluated [7,33].

To each FOL statement S we will assign both a confidence c and a set L of unique identifiers of (non-derived) input statements used for deriving this statement: a triple $\langle S, c, L \rangle$. Lists of such triples are then treated as sets. The dependency lists L are used in the formula estimating the cumulated confidence. The algorithm for calculating confidences c for derivations will be presented later.

To be more exact, we will not allow assigning confidences to arbitrary statements. Instead, we will assume that the FOL statements are converted to a conjunctive normal form: a conjunction of Skolemized disjunctions, where each disjunction only consists of atomic statements (a predicate applied to arguments) or negations of atomic statements. Such disjunctions are called *clauses*. We will not allow nested triples, i.e. S is always a pure FOL clause not containing any confidence or dependency information usable by the presented algorithms. However, for each single FOL clause S there may be many different derivable triples $\langle S, c, L \rangle$ for different c and L, stemming from different derivation trees of S. They are assumed to be independent statements, possibly allowing the calculation of the cumulative confidence for S higher than $max(c, c')$ where c and c' come from different triples.

A KB may contain logical contradictions and identical FOL clauses with different confidences given by different sources. For example, the following is a logically contradictory KB containing several copies of the same clause with different confidences. The CONFER algorithm presented later gives us the confidence of $bird(a) : 0.682$ from this KB:

$$\langle bird(X), 0.1, L_1 \rangle, \langle bird(a), 0.8, L_2 \rangle, \langle bird(a), 0.9, L_3 \rangle, \langle \neg bird(a), 0.3, L_4 \rangle$$

We interpret the confidence as estimating the lower limit of the probability of a statement, i.e., $\langle S, c, L \rangle$ is interpreted as "statements L support the claim that $probability(S) \geq c$". Thus two different confidence statements for the same clause are never contradictory, even if given by the same source.

3   The CONFER Extension Framework for CSR

In the following we will present the CONFER framework of extensions to the mainstream resolution-based search methods. We expect that the same framework can be adapted to search methods different from resolution, i.e. the specific aspects of resolution are not relevant for the main principles of the approach.

The intuition behind CONFER is preserving first order classical logic (FOL) intact as an underlying machinery for derivations in CSR. The core methods of automated reasoning used by most of the high-performance automated reasoning systems remain usable as core methods for CSR. Essentially, FOL with the resolution method produces all combinations of derivable sentences (modulo simplifications like subsumption) which could lead to a proof. The main difference between strict FOL and CONFER extensions is in the handling of constructed proof trees: the outcome of a CONFER reasoner is a set of combined FOL proofs with the confidence measures added.

Importantly, the framework does not generally calculate the exact maximal confidence for derived statements, since this is, in nontrivial cases, either impossible or unfeasible. Our goal is to give a practically useful estimation of the maximal confidence without causing a large overhead on the FOL proof search and avoiding combinatorial explosion while calculating the confidences.

3.1   Resolution Method

In the following we will assume that the underlying first order reasoner uses the resolution method, see [3] for details. The rest of the paper assumes familiarity with the basic concepts, terminology and algorithms of the resolution method.

3.2   Queries and Answers

We assume the question posed is in one of two forms: *(1)* Is the statement Q true? *(2)* Find values V for existentially bound variables in Q so that Q is true. For simplicity's sake we will assume that the statement Q is in the prefix form, i.e., no quantifiers occur in the scope of other logical connectives.

In the second case, it could be that several different value vectors can be assigned to the variables, essentially giving different answers. We also note that an answer could be a disjunction, giving possible options instead of a single definite answer. However, as shown in [38], in case a single definite answer exists, it will be derived eventually.

A widely used machinery in resolution-based theorem provers for extracting values of existentially bound variables in Q is to use a special *answer predicate*, converting a question statement Q to a formula

$$\exists X_1, ..., \exists X_n (Q(X_1, ..., X_n) \& \neg answer(X_1, ..., X_n))$$

for existentially quantified variables in Q [21]. Whenever a clause is derived which consists of only answer predicates, it is treated as a contradiction (essentially, answer) and the arguments of the answer predicate are returned as the values looked for. A common convention is to call such clauses *answer clauses*. We will require that the proof search does not stop whenever an answer clause is found, but will continue to look for new answer clauses until a predetermined time limit is reached. See [37] for a framework of extracting multiple answers.

We also assume that queries take a general form $(KB\&A) \Rightarrow Q$ where KB is a commonsense knowledge base, A is an optional set of precondition statements for this particular question and Q is a question statement.

Since we assume the use of the resolution method for proof search, the whole general query form is negated and converted to clauses, i.e., disjunctions of literals (positive or negative atoms). We will call the clauses stemming from the question statement *question clauses*.

3.3   Top Level of the Algorithm

Calculating confidences for question answering requires, at least, the ability to calculate (a) the decreasing confidence of a conjunction of clauses as performed by the resolution and paramodulation rule, (b) the increasing confidence of a disjunction of clauses for cumulating evidence, (c) the decreasing confidence of considering negative evidence for a clause.

While the systems based on, say, Bayes networks and Markov logic, perform these operations in a combined manner, our framework will split the whole search into separate phases for each. First we perform a modified resolution search we call *c-resolution* calculating the decreasing confidence and potentially giving a large number of different answers and proofs. Next we will combine the different proofs using the cumulation operation. Finally we will collect negative evidence for all the answers obtained so far, separately for each individual answer. The latter search is also split into the c-resolution phase and the cumulating phase. Since we assume the use of full FOL, the c-resolution search will not necessarily terminate, thus we will use a time limit. The top level of the algorithm is presented in the following section as Algorithm 1.

Algorithm 1 CONFER algorithm

Input: Common sense knowledge base KB, question Q, time limit t.
Output: Set of answers R with attached confidences.

1: Let R={}.
2: Find a set of initial positive answers with confidences and dependencies
   IPA={$\langle A_1, c_1, L_1 \rangle, ..., \langle A_p, c_p, L_p \rangle$} for Q from KB using c-resolution with the time
   limit $t/2$.
3: Calculate a set of cumulative positive answers CPA={$\langle B_1, d_1, E_1 \rangle, ..., \langle B_r, d_r, E_r \rangle$}
   from IPA.
4: Let $i = 1$.
5: **while** $i <= r$ **do**
6:     Form the negated question NQ_i from $\neg Q$ with a substition s given by B_i
7:     Find a set of initial negative answers N_i with confidences and dependencies for
       NQ_i from KB using c-resolution with the time limit $t/(2*r)$.
8:     **if** N_i is empty **then**
9:         Let $nc_i = 0$.
10:    **else**
11:        Calculate the cumulative negative confidence nc_i from N_i.
12:    **end if**
13:    Add a pair $\langle B_i, (c_i - nc_i) \rangle$ to R.
14:    Let $i = i + 1$.
15: **end while**
16: For each pair $\langle B_i, d_i \rangle$, $\langle B_j, d_j \rangle$ in R where $i \neq j$, $B_i = B_j$ and $d_i >= d_j$, remove
    $B_j : d_j$ from R.
17: Remove from R all elements $\langle B_i, d_i \rangle$ where $d_i <= 0$.
18: **return** the set of answers with confidences R.

3.4   C-Resolution

The core part of the algorithm described above is c-resolution: a relatively simple modification of the resolution method calculating and keeping track of the (multiplied) confidences of premises of each step along with the union of their dependencies.

Definition 1 (C-Resolution). *A modification of the resolution method computing an ever-increasing set of different proofs for different answers (substitutions to the question clauses) while employing the relevance filter (definition 2), performing basic confidence calculation for resolution steps (definition 3), assigning the union of the dependency lists of premises to each derived clause, restricting subsumption to c-subsumption (definition 5) and restricting simplification steps according to c-subsumption.*

Inconsistencies. A KB with a nontrivial structure may contain inconsistencies in the sense that a contradiction can be derived from the KB. Looking at existing KBs mentioned earlier, we observe that they either are already inconsistent (for example, the largest FOL version of OpenCyc [30] in TPTP [40] is inconsistent) or would become inconsistent in case intuitively valid inequalities are added, for example, inequalities of classes such as "a cat is not a dog", "a male is not a female" or default rules such as "birds can fly", "dead birds cannot fly", "penguins cannot fly". We note that several large existing KBs do not contain such inequalities explicitly, although they are necessary for nontrivial question answering under the open-world assumption.

Since classical FOL allows to derive anything from a contradiction, it is clearly unsuitable for a large subset of KB-s. Two possible ways of overcoming this issue are: (a) using some version of relevance logic or other paraconsistent logics or (b) defining a filter for eliminating irrelevant classical proofs. We argue that despite a lot of theoretical work in the area, only little work has been done in automated proving for relevance logic, thus using it directly is likely to create significant complexities. Instead, we introduce a simple relevance filter:

Definition 2 (Relevance Filter). *Each resolution derivation of a contradiction not containing any answer clauses is discarded.*

Since a standard resolution derivation of a contradiction does not lead to any further derivations, this filter is completeness-preserving in the sense that all resolution derivations containing an answer clause are still found.

Confidences of Derived Clauses. We take the approach of (a) providing a simple sensible baseline algorithm for calculating confidences of derived clauses, and (b) leaving open ways to modify this algorithm for specific cases as need arises. We will use a single rational number in the range 0...1 as a measure of a confidence of a clause, with 1 standing for perfect confidence and 0 standing for no information. Confidence of an atomic clause not holding is represented as a confidence of the negation of the clause.

As a baseline we use the standard approach of computing uncertainties of clauses derived from independent parent clauses A and B as:

$$P(A \wedge B) = P(A) * P(B)$$

Notice that for dependent parent clauses this formula *under-estimates* the confidence of the result.

Definition 3 (Basic Confidence Calculation for Resolution Steps). *For binary resolution and paramodulation steps, the confidence of a result is obtained by multiplying the confidences of the premises. For the factorization step, the confidence of the result is the confidence of the premise, unchanged. Question clauses have a confidence 1.*

A simple example employing forward reasoning (concretely, *negative ordered resolution*):

```
0.8:: bird(tweety).
0.9:: bird(X) => canfly(X).
0.7:: canfly(X) => fast(X).
1.0:: fast(X) => answer(X).
```

leads to a sequential derivation of

```
0.72:: canfly(tweety).
0.504:: fast(tweety).
0.504:: answer(tweety).
```

Recall that the confidences are assumed to be lower bounds of probabilities. Notice that the possible dependence of the premises could be taken into account, as in the following section for cumulative evidence. This would result in higher confidence numbers for derivations with dependent premises. Consider the following example:

```
0.9:: bird(X) => canfly(X).
0.1:: -bird(X) => canfly(X).
```

Using the basic calculation step we can derive that anything can fly: 0.09:: `canfly(X)`. However, since anything is either a bird or is not a bird, the confidence of `canfly(X)` should be at least 0.1, and possibly higher, depending on the ratio of birds to non-birds.

Generally, we can use the minimization operation leading to a higher confidence value than the multiplication of the confidences of premises in the following special case. The standard resolution inference rule used by a large class of automated reasoners is defined as

$$\frac{A_1 \vee A_2 \vee ... \vee A_n \qquad \neg B_1 \vee B_2 \vee ... \vee B_m}{(A_2 \vee ... \vee A_n \vee B_2 \vee ... \vee B_m)\sigma}$$

where σ is the most general unifier of A_1 and B_1. A clause A *subsumes* a clause B if the literals of $A\delta$ are a subset of literals of B for some substitution δ.

Definition 4 (Extended Confidence Calculation for Resolution Steps).
If $(A_2 \vee ... \vee A_n)\sigma$ subsumes $(B_2 \vee ... \vee B_m)\sigma$ in the resolution inference defined above then the confidence of the result is the minimum of the confidences of premises.

C-Subsumption and Simplifications. Since standard subsumption used by resolution provers to clean up search space may remove clauses with a higher confidence or fewer dependencies than the subsuming clause, it may cause the prover to lose derivations potentially leading to a higher confidence. Thus we use *c-subsumption* instead of the standard subsumption:

Definition 5 (C-Subsumption).   *A triple $T_1 = \langle A_1, c_1, L_1 \rangle$ consisting of a clause A_1, confidence c_1 and a dependency list L_1 c-subsumes a triple $T_2 = \langle A_2, c_2, L_2 \rangle$ if and only if A_1 subsumes A_2, $c_1 \geq c_2$ and $L_1 \subseteq L_2$.*

We can prove the following lemma:

Lemma 1 (C-Subsumption Preserves Completeness).   *When a c-resolution proof can be found without using subsumption, it can be also found with c-subsumption.*

The proof holds for strategies of resolution for which standard subsumption is complete for ordinary proof search without confidences.

We restrict the simplification operations like demodulation and subsuming resolution accordingly: a derivation step must keep the original premiss P if the result has a lower confidence or a longer list of dependencies than P.

3.5 Cumulative Confidence

We will now look at the situation with additional evidence for the derived answer. In our context, using additional evidence is possible if a clause C can be derived in different ways, giving two different derivations d_1 and d_2 with confidences c_1 and c_2. In case the derivations d_1 and d_2 are independent, we could apply the standard formula

$$P(A \vee B) = P(A) + P(B) - P(A \wedge B)$$

to c_1 and c_2 to calculate the cumulative confidence for C.

What would it mean for derivations to be "independent"? In the context of commonsense reasoning we cannot expect to have an exact measure of independence. However, suppose the derivations d_1 and d_2 consist of exactly the same initial clauses, but used in a different order. In this case $c_1 = c_2$ and the cumulative confidence should intuitively be also just c_1: no additional evidence is provided. On the other hand, in case that the non-question input clauses of d_1 are d_2 are mutually disjoint, then the derivations are also independent (assuming all the input clauses are mutually independent), and we should apply the previous rule for $P(A \vee B)$ for computing the cumulative confidence.

We will estimate the independence i of two derivations d_1 and d_2 simply as

$$1 - \frac{\text{number of shared input clauses of } d_1 \text{ and } d_2}{\text{total number of input clauses in } d_1 \text{ and } d_2} \tag{1}$$

Thus, if no clauses are shared between d_1 and d_2, then $i = 1$ and if all the clauses are shared, then $i = 0$.

In addition, we also know that it is highly unlikely that all the input clauses are mutually independent. Again, lacking a realistic way to calculate the dependencies, we give a heuristic estimate h in the range 0...1 to the overall independence of the input clause set, where 1 stands for total independence and 0 for total dependence.

Finally, we will calculate the overall independence of two derivations d_1 and d_2 as $i * h$. Next, we will postulate a heuristic rule for the combination of these two independence measures as follows.

Definition 6 (Confidence Calculation for Cumulative Evidence). *Given two derivations d_1 and d_2 of the search result C with confidences c_1 and c_2, calculate the updated confidence of C as*

$$max(c_1 + c_2 * i * h, \ c_1 * i * h + c_2) - c_1 * c_2 * i * h$$

where

- *independence of derivations i is defined as 1 above,*
- *h is the heuristic estimate of the independence of the total set of input clauses from 1 for total independence to 0 for total dependence.*

The formula satisfies the following *intuitive requirements for cumulative evidence*:

- If d_1 and d_2 do not share non-question input clauses and all the input clauses are mutually independent, $i * h = 1$ and the formula turns into $c_1 + c_2 - (c_1 * c_2)$.
- If d_1 and d_2 have the same non-question input clauses or the total set of input clauses is mutually totally dependent, $i * h = 0$ and the formula turns into $max(c_1, c_2)$.

3.6   Negative Evidence

Recall the standard mechanism employed in FOL provers for finding concrete answers: transforming existentially quantified goal clauses to clauses containing a special **answer** predicate and treating clauses containing only **answer** predicates as actual answers to the question found.

Once negation is present, the reasoning system using the CONFER framework has to attempt to find both positive and negative evidence for any potential answer. This cannot be easily done in a single proof search run.

Observe that giving a general search question containing variables like $bird(X) \lor answer(X)$ may produce a different set of answers than the positive question $\neg bird(X) \lor answer(X)$. Also observe that the potential set of answers may be huge for both positive and negative answers: in a large KB there may be millions of statements about birds and our reasoning system will be able to derive only a small fraction of potential answers in any given time slot. Thus, even if negative evidence is potentially derivable for some positive answer, the system is unlikely to find it.

A reasonable solution to this problem is to run the searches for negative evidence only for the concrete instances of positive answers found. More concretely, we conduct additional proof search for the negations of two types of questions Q: *(a)* If Q contains no existentially quantified variables, is the statement $\neg Q$ true? *(b)* For all i vectors of values $C_1 i, ..., C_n i$ found for existentially bound variables $X_1, ... X_n$ in Q making Q true, is $\neg Q$ true when we substitute the values in $C_1 i, ..., C_n i$ for corresponding variables in Q?. The final confidence of an answer to Q is calculated by subtracting from the confidence of the positive answer the confidence of the answer to the corresponding negated instance of the question.

Using negative evidence may lead to unexpected results. Consider the following trivial example in the ProbLog syntax:

```
0.5::bird(a).  0.5::not bird(a).  query(bird(a)).
```

CONFER gives us confidence 0, which we interpret as "no information", not as "false". However, ProbLog2 gives confidence 0.25, which is explained by one of the authors in private correspondence thus: an atom (head) is satisfied if any of the rules that make it true fire and none of the rules that make it false fire. In this example ProbLog2 gets $0.5 * (1 - 0.5) = 0.25$. On the other hand, the three different algorithms of the Alchemy 2 system – MC-SAT explained in [12], exact and approximate probabilistic theorem proving explained in [11] – give answers 0.015, 0 and 0.082, respectively. To be concrete, we are using the Alchemy 2 versions from [2]. For this and the following Alchemy 2 examples we prepared an MLN file with no weights and a training data file with some generated facts for each example. Then we ran the *learnwts* program with default parameters, which created the MLN file with weights for each example.

Next, consider a previous example augmented with the "birds fly" rule:

```
0.5::bird(a).   0.5::not bird(a).   0.9:: flies(X) :- bird(X).
query(flies(_)).
```

Here CONFER gives us 0.45, which is inconsistent with the result of the previous example. ProbLog2, on the other hand, gives 0.225, which is unintuitive, but consistent with the unintuitive result of ProbLog2 in the previous example. The three algorithms of Alchemy 2 mentioned above give us 0.047, 0 and 0.98. The issue arising in this example is similar to nonmonotonic reasoning like default logic: adding negative evidence to being a bird should block previously derivable facts. We know that since FOL is not decidable, such checks would make derivation steps generally not computable. As a final twist to the example we augment the ruleset by giving more details about the distribution:

```
0.5::bird(a).   0.5::not bird(a).   0.9:: flies(X) :- bird(X).
0.1:: not flies(X) :- bird(X).
%% 0.1:: flies(X) :- not bird(X). %% commented out
0.9:: not flies(X) :- not bird(X).
query(flies(_)).
```

Here CONFER gives us an acceptable 0.014 (positive evidence 0.490 and negative evidence 0.476), while ProbLog2 gives 0.2025. The results of Alchemy 2 are 0.047, 0 and 0.976. Adding the rule we have commented out makes CONFER to give -0.008 while ProbLog2 complains that the example is not acceptable. Alchemy 2 gives us 0.056, 0 and 0.509.

4   Implementation and Experimental Results

The first author has implemented the CONFER framework as an extended version of his high-performance open-source automated reasoning system gkc [39] for FOL, performing fairly well in the yearly CASC competition for automated reasoners [36], see http://www.tptp.org/CASC/. The implementation is written in C like gkc. The compiled executable can be downloaded from http://logictools.org/confer/ along with a number of examples.

Several algorithms, strategies and optimizations present in the gkc system are currently switched off, due to the need for additional modifications and testing.

In particular, parallel processing is switched off, as well as the crucial algorithms for selecting a list of suitable search strategies and performing search by batches with iteratively increasing time limits.

Importantly, we have not yet implemented any specialized strategies for using the attached confidences and dependencies for directing and optimizing search. It is clear that the added information gives ample potential opportunities for directing the search.

We will give an overview of the experiments with the implementation in two sections. First we will look at the confidences calculated and compare these, where possible, with the values given by ProbLog2 and Alchemy 2. Next we will look at the performance of the system on nontrivial problems.

The inputs and outputs for the CONFER implementation and the systems compared to are given on the web page http://logictools.org/confer/. The set of examples given contains over 30 case studies and can be run using the command-line implementation provided on the same web page as a single executable file. The implementation is self-contained, not dependent on other systems or external libraries. It should run on any 64-bit Linux system.

4.1   Comparing Confidences

We will compare the confidences calculated by CONFER on small selected examples with these of ProbLog2 and Alchemy 2. The first two are presented in the ProbLog2 tutorial. When CONFER can perform neither cumulation nor collection of evidence, the values calculated are the same as of ProbLog2. The cumulation operation of CONFER produces, as expected, slightly different values than ProbLog2 or Alchemy 2. For the following examples the overall independence estimate h is assigned 1 (maximum). Since the principles of handling negative evidence are fundamentally different between the two systems, this operation causes the most significant changes. It is worth noticing that more often than not, the results of ProbLog2 and Alchemy 2 also differ.

First, a simple version of the well-known social networks of smokers example in the ProbLog syntax. CONFER uses a different syntax, but the clauses and confidences given are exactly the same. We have also built the corresponding data- and rulesets for Alchemy 2, which uses a fairly different input method than CONFER or ProbLog.

```
0.8::stress(ann).              0.4::stress(bob).
0.6::influences(ann,bob).      0.2::influences(bob,carl).
smokes(X) :- stress(X).
smokes(X) :- influences(Y,X), smokes(Y).
query(smokes(carl)).
```

For this example, ProbLog2 gives an answer 0.1376 and CONFER gives 0.1201, cumulating values 0.096 and 0.08. The three different algorithms of Alchemy 2 – MC-SAT inference (see [12]), exact and approximate lifted inference explained in [11] – give 0.135, 0 and 0.741, respectively. In the following tables we

will refer to these three as *Alch i*, *Alch e* and *Alch a*. Removing the input clause
0.4::stress(bob) also removes the cumulation possibility and both CONFER
and ProbLog2 give 0.096 as an answer.

Next, the well-known earthquake example. CONFER performs both cumulation and collecting negative evidence.

```
person(john).     person(mary).
0.7::burglary.    0.2::earthquake.
0.9::alarm :- burglary, earthquake.
0.8::alarm :- burglary, \+earthquake.
0.1::alarm :- \+burglary, earthquake.
0.8::calls(X) :- alarm, person(X).
0.1::calls(X) :- \+alarm, person(X).
evidence(calls(john),true).
evidence(calls(mary),true).
query(burglary).
query(earthquake).
```

We will present the ProbLog2 and CONFER results with both the positive
and negative evidence components (columns CONFER + and CONFER -) given
by CONFER. Importantly, by default CONFER will try to find up to 10 different
proofs: increasing or decreasing these limits has a noticeable effect on the results
as well as running time.

query	CONFER	CONFER +	CONFER -	Problog	Alch i	Alch e	Alch a
burglary	0.8713	0.97650	0.1051	0.9819	0.709	0	0.905095
earthquake	0.1648	0.8854	0.7206	0.2268	0.204	0	0.888

Finally we bring the famous penguin example from default logic. We will
formulate it using confidences instead of defaults. We state that penguins form
a tiny subset of birds. The CONFER implementation collects both positive and
negative evidence, but there are no cumulation possibilities.

```
1.0::bird(tweety).     1.0::penguin(pennie).
1.0:: bird(X) :- penguin(X).
0.001:: penguin(X) :- bird(X).
0.9:: flies(X) :- bird(X).
1.0:: not flies(X) :- penguin(X).
query(flies(_)).
```

query	CONFER	CONFER +	CONFER -	Problog	Alch i	Alch e	Alch a
flies(pennie)	-0.1	0.9	1.0	0	0.00001	0	0
flies(tweety)	0.899	0.9	0.001	0.8991	0.064	0	0.873

4.2   Performance

We will investigate the performance of our CONFER implementation on the following nontrivial example FOL problems from the TPTP collection [40]. Due to restrictions in the language or the principles of the search algorithm, ProbLog2 cannot handle any of these examples even if they are converted to clauses in ProbLog syntax. Thus we will compare the performance of the CONFER system on several modifications of the problems against the conventional FOL prover gkc used as a base for building the CONFER system.

The results are given for the following problems with the TPTP identifier and ratings: 0 means all the provers tested by the TPTP maintaners find a proof, 1 means no prover manages to find a proof. *Steamroller* (PUZ031+1, rating 0) is a puzzle without equality. *Dreadbury* (PUZ001+2.p, rating 0.23) is a puzzle using also equality. *Lukasiewicz* (LCL047-1.p, rating 0) is an example in logical calculi. Commonsense reasoning problems from CYC are taken from the largest consistent CYC version in TPTP: *CSR025+5*, *CSR035+5*, *CSR045+5*, *CSR055+5* (ratings 0.67, 0.83, 0.97, 0.87).

The CYC problems CSR025+5 ... CSR055+5 contain ca half a million formulae, but the proofs are relatively short. The first three problems are relatively small, but their proofs are significantly longer. The Steamroller, Dreadbury and the CYC CSR035+5 problems have been augmented with a question asking for answer substitutions, while for the other CYC problems and the Lukasiewicz problems the conjectures do not contain the existence quantifier, thus we just try to prove these. For comparison purposes the CONFER proof searches are restricted to finding only the first answer (thus no cumulation is possible) and not collecting negative evidence.

We consider both the versions of problems with all clauses assigned a confidence between 0.6 ... 0.99 cyclically with a step 0.01 (column CONFER in the following table) and all the confidences assigned 1.0 (column CONFER 1.0). It is important to note that the CONFER system uses conventional subsumption and simplification for clauses with the confidence 1.0, i.e. in the "CONFER 1" column proof search is reduced to the ordinary resolution search. The gkc column gives the pure search time of the gkc prover used as a base for building the CONFER system, for the original TPTP versions (without a question of substitutions being asked). As a special case, variations 0 ... 4 of the Lukasiewicz problem are formed by attaching confidences below 1 to respectively 1 ... 4 input clauses and letting other confidences have value 1.0. (the Lukasiewicz problem consists of five clauses, one of these being the clause to be proved).

The columns CONFER ... "gkc pure" contain the pure proof search time in seconds using negative ordered resolution for all the problems except CYC and the set of support resolution for CYC. The gkc column gives the pure search time for the gkc prover used as a base for building the CONFER system, for the original TPTP versions (without a question of substitutions being asked). Pure search time does not include printing, parsing and clausifying the problem and indexing the formed clauses. The final column "gkc full" gives full wall clock time for gkc.

Problem	CONFER	CONFER 1.0	gkc pure	gkc full
Steamroller	0.0018	0.0015	0.001	0.06
Dreadbury	0.0017	0.0011	0.001	0.06
Lukasz 0		0.0916	0.093	0.22
Lukasz 1	0.913			
Lukasz 2	23			
Lukasz 3	19			
Lukasz 4	16			
CSR025+5	0.0004	0.0001	0.0001	4.5
CSR035+5	0.0001	0.0001	0.07	4.6
CSR045+5	3.418	1.4	1.3	5.8
CSR055+5	0.0001	0.0001	0.0001	4.5

We can observe that the confidence and dependency collecting calculations along with the restricted c-subsumption do not have a noticeable effect on performance for most of these problems. However, adding confidences below 1 to the Lukasziewicz problem do incur a significant penalty, which – surprisingly – diminishes somewhat when all the clauses have such confidences. The confidences incur a noticeable penalty to CSR045+5, which has the longest proof among our CYC examples. Our hypotheses is that for these examples the c-subsumption along with restricted simplification changes the direction of the search significantly.

5   Summary and Future Work

We have presented a novel framework CONFER along with the implementation for reasoning with approximate confidences for full, unrestricted first order logic. The presented examples demonstrate that the confidences found by our implementation are similar to the confidences found by the leading probabilistic Prolog and Markov logic implementations ProbLog2 [18] and Alchemy 2 [1]. CONFER is based on conventional first order theorem proving theory and algorithms not requiring saturation, differently from the systems using weighted ground saturation of FOL formulas like ProbLog2 and Alchemy 2. We have shown that this enables the CONFER implementation to efficiently solve large nontrivial FOL problems with attached confidences.

We plan to continue work on the CONFER implementation in several directions: finding and removing bugs, improving the functionality and devising search strategies specialized for the FOL formulas with associated confidences. We expect to integrate machine learning approaches, in particular using semantic similarities for reasoning with analogies and estimating the relevance of input clauses for proof search guidance. The goal of this work is creating a practically usable component for logic-based question answering from large commonsense knowledge bases.

References

1. Alchemy 2 system. https://code.google.com/archive/p/alchemy-2/
2. Alchemy 2 system repository. https://github.com/PhDP/alchemy2
3. Bachmair, L., Ganzinger, H.: Resolution theorem proving. In: Robinson, A., Voronkov, A. (eds.) Handbook of Automated Reasoning, vol. I, ch. 2. pp. 19–99. Elsevier (2001)
4. Baltag, A., Smets, S.: Keep changing your beliefs, aiming for the truth. Erkenntnis **75**(2), 255–270 (2011)
5. Beltagy, I., Chau, C., Boleda, G., Garrette, D., Erk, K., Mooney, R.: Montague meets Markov: Deep semantics with probabilistic logical form. In: Diab, M., Baldwin, T., Baroni, M. (eds.) Proc. of *SEM'12 – the 2nd Joint Conference on Lexical and Computational Semantics. pp. 11–21. Association for Computational Linguistics (2013)
6. Buchanan, B., Shortliffe, E.: Rule-Based Expert Systems: The MYCIN Experiments of the Stanford Heuristic Programming Project. Addison Wesley (1984)
7. Chalier, Y., Razniewski, S., Weikum, G.: Joint reasoning for multi-faceted commonsense knowledge. CoRR abs/2001.04170 (2020), https://arxiv.org/abs/2001.04170
8. Conesa, J., Storey, V., Sugumaran, V.: Usability of upper level ontologies: The case of ResearchCyc. Data and Knowledge Engineering **69**(4), 343–356 (2010)
9. de Salvo Braz, R., Amir, E., Roth, D.: Lifted first-order probabilistic inference. In: Kaelbling, L.P., Saffiotti, A. (eds.) Proc. of IJCAI'05 – the 19th Intl. Joint Conf. on Artificial intelligence. pp. 1319–1325. Professional Book Center (2005)
10. Domingos, P.: The Master Algorithm: How the Quest for the Ultimate Learning Machine Will Remake Our World. Basic Books (2015)
11. Domingos, P., Gogate, V.: Probabilistic theorem proving. In: Cozman, F., Pfeffer, A. (eds.) Proc. of UAI'11 – the 27th Conf. on Uncertainty in Artificial Intelligence. pp. 256–265. AUAI (2011)
12. Domingos, P., Kok, S., Poon, H., Richardson, M., Singla, P.: Unifying logical and statistical AI. In: Cohn, A. (ed.) Proc. of AAAI'06 – the 21st National Conf. on Artificial Intelligence. pp. 2–9. AAAI (2006)
13. Domingos, P.M. amd Kok, S., Lowd, D., Poon, H., Richardson, M., Singla, P.: Markov Logic. In: De Raedt, L., Frasconi, P., Kersting, K., Muggleton, S. (eds.) Probabilistic Inductive Logic Programming: Theory and Applications. LNCS, vol. 4911, pp. 92–117. Springer (2008)
14. Dong, X., Gabrilovich, E., Heitz, G., Horn, W., Lao, N., Murphy, K., Strohmann, T., Sun, S., Zhang, W.: Knowledge vault: a Web-scale approach to probabilistic knowledge fusion. In: Macskassy, S.A., Perlich, C., Leskovec, J., Wang, W., Ghani, R. (eds.) Proc. of KDD'14 – the 20th ACM SIGKDD Intl. Conf. on Knowledge Discovery and Data Mining. pp. 601–610. ACM (2014)
15. Draheim, D., Tammet, T.: From sensors to Dempster-Shafer theory and back: The axiom of ambiguous sensor correctness and its applications. In: Hartmann, S., Küng, J., Kotsis, G., Tjoa, A.M., Khalil, I. (eds.) Proc. of DEXA'2020 – the 31st Intl. Conf. on Database and Expert Systems Applications. LNCS, vol. 12391, pp. 3–19. Springer (2020)
16. Draheim, D.: Generalized Jeffrey Conditionalization – A Frequentist Semantics of Partial Conditionalization. Springer (2017)
17. Ferrucci, D.A.: Introduction to "This is Watson". IBM Journal of Research and Development **56**(3.4), 1–15 (2012)

18. Fierens, D., den Broeck, V., G., Renkens, J., Shterionov, D., Gutmann, D., Thon, I., Janssens, G., De Raedt, L.: Inference and learning in probabilistic logic programs using weighted Boolean formulas. Theory and Practice of Logic Programming **15**(3), 358–401 (2015)
19. Formato, F., Gerla, G., Sessa, M.: Similarity-based unification. Fundamenta Informaticae **41**(4), 393–414 (2000)
20. Furbach, U., Krämer, T., Schon, C.: Names are not just sound and smoke: Word embeddings for axiom selection. In: Fontaine, P. (ed.) Proc. of CADE'2019 – the 27th Intl. Conf. on Automated Deduction. LNCS, vol. 11716, pp. 250–268. Springer (2019)
21. Green, C.: Theorem proving as a basis for question-answering systems. Machine Intelligence **4**, 183–205 (1969)
22. Hájek, A.: Interpretations of Probability. In: Stanford Encyclopedia of Philosophy (2019), https://plato.stanford.edu/entries/probability-interpret/
23. Kalyanpur, A., Breloff, T., Ferrucci, D.A., Lally, A., Jantos, J.: Braid: Weaving symbolic and statistical knowledge into coherent logical explanations. CoRR abs/2011.13354 (2020), https://arxiv.org/abs/2011.13354
24. Khot, T., Balasubramanian, N., Gribkoff, E., Sabharwal, E., Clark, P., Etzioni, O.: Exploring Markov Logic Networks for question answering. In: Màrquez, L., Callison-Burch, C., Su, J. (eds.) Proc. of EMNLP'2015 – the 2015 Conference on Empirical Methods in Natural Language Processing. pp. 685–694. Association for Computational Linguistics (2015)
25. Lenat, D., Prakash, M., Shepherd, M.: Using common sense knowledge to overcome brittleness and knowledge acquisition bottlenecks. AI Magazine **6**(4), 65–85 (1985)
26. Marcus, G.: The next decade in AI: four steps towards robust artificial intelligence. CoRR abs/2002.06177 (2020), https://arxiv.org/abs/2002.06177
27. Mitchell, T., Cohen, W., Hruschka, E., Talukdar, P., Yang, B., Betteridge, J., Carlson, A., Dalvi, B., Gardner, M., Kisiel, B.: Never-ending learning. Communications of the ACM **61**(5), 103–115 (2018)
28. Pileggi, S.F.: Web of similarity. Journal of Computational Science **36**(100578), 1–7 (2019)
29. Problog2. https://dtai.cs.kuleuven.be/problog/
30. Ramachandran, D., Reagan, P., Goolsbey, K.: First-orderized researchcyc: Expressivity and efficiency in a common-sense ontology. In: AAAI workshop on contexts and ontologies: theory, practice and applications. pp. 33–40 (2005)
31. Reiter, R.: A logic for default reasoning. Artificial Intelligence **13**(1–2), 81–132 (1980)
32. Richardson, M., Domingos, P.: Markov Logic Networks. Machine Learning **62**(1–2), 107–136 (2006)
33. Romero, J., Razniewski, S., Pal, K., Pan, J.Z., Sakhadeo, A., Weikum, G.: Commonsense properties from query logs and question answering forums. In: Zhu, W., Tao, D., Cheng, X., Cui, P., Rundensteiner, E.A., Carmel, D., He, Q., Yu, J.X. (eds.) Proc. of CIKM'19 – the 28th ACM Intl. Conf. on Information and Knowledge Management. pp. 1411–1420. ACM (2019)
34. Sato, T.: Generative modeling by PRISM. In: Hill, P.M., Warren, D.S. (eds.) Proc. ICLP'2009 – the 25th Intl. Conf. on Logic Programming. LNCS, vol. 5649, pp. 24–35. Springer (2009)
35. Speer, R., Chin, J., Havasi, C.: ConceptNet 5.5: An open multilingual graph of general knowledge. In: Singh, S.P., Markovitch, S. (eds.) Proc. of AAAI'2017 – the 31st AAAI Conf. on Artificial Intelligence. pp. 4444–4451. AAAI (2017)

36. Sutcliffe, G.: The CADE ATP system competition – CASC. AI Magazine **37**(2), 99–101 (2016)
37. Sutcliffe, G., Yerikalapudi, A., Trac, S.: Multiple answer extraction for question answering with automated theorem proving systems. In: Lane, H.C., Guesgen, H.W. (eds.) Proc. of FLAIRS'22 – the 22nd Intl. Florida Artificial Intelligence Research Society Conference. AAAI (2009)
38. Tammet, T.: Completeness of resolution for definite answers. Journal of Logic and Computation **5**(4), 449–71 (1995)
39. Tammet, T.: GKC: A reasoning system for large knowledge bases. In: Fontaine, P. (ed.) Proc. of CADE'2019 – the 27th Intl. Conf. on Automated Deduction. LNCS, vol. 11716, pp. 538–549. Springer (2019)
40. TPTP homepage. http://www.tptp.org
41. Zadeh, L.: Fuzzy logic. Computer **21**(4), 94–102 (1988)

Open Access This chapter is licensed under the terms of the Creative Commons Attribution 4.0 International License (http://creativecommons.org/licenses/by/4.0/), which permits use, sharing, adaptation, distribution and reproduction in any medium or format, as long as you give appropriate credit to the original author(s) and the source, provide a link to the Creative Commons license and indicate if changes were made.

The images or other third party material in this chapter are included in the chapter's Creative Commons license, unless indicated otherwise in a credit line to the material. If material is not included in the chapter's Creative Commons license and your intended use is not permitted by statutory regulation or exceeds the permitted use, you will need to obtain permission directly from the copyright holder.

Neural Precedence Recommender

Filip Bártek[1,2] and Martin Suda[1]

[1] Czech Institute of Informatics, Robotics and Cybernetics
[2] Faculty of Electrical Engineering
Czech Technical University in Prague, Czech Republic
{filip.bartek,martin.suda}@cvut.cz

Abstract. The state-of-the-art superposition-based theorem provers for first-or-der logic rely on simplification orderings on terms to constrain the applicability of inference rules, which in turn shapes the ensuing search space. The popular Knuth-Bendix simplification ordering is parameterized by *symbol precedence*—a permutation of the predicate and function symbols of the input problem's signature. Thus, the choice of precedence has an indirect yet often substantial impact on the amount of work required to complete a proof search successfully.

This paper describes and evaluates a symbol precedence recommender, a machine learning system that estimates the best possible precedence based on observations of prover performance on a set of problems and random precedences. Using the graph convolutional neural network technology, the system does not presuppose the problems to be related or share a common signature. When coupled with the theorem prover Vampire and evaluated on the TPTP problem library, the recom-mender is found to outperform a state-of-the-art heuristic by more than 4 % on unseen problems.

Keywords: saturation-based theorem proving · simplification ordering · symbol precedence · machine learning · graph convolutional network

1 Introduction

Modern saturation-based Automatic Theorem Provers (ATPs) such as E [34], SPASS [40], or Vampire [21] employ the superposition calculus [4,24] as their underlying in-ference system. Integrating the flavors of resolution [5], paramodulation [30], and the unfailing completion [3], superposition is a powerful calculus with native support for equational reasoning. The calculus is parameterized by a simplification ordering on terms and uses it to constrain the applicability of inferences, with a significant impact on performance.

Both main classes of simplification orderings used in practice, the Knuth-Bendix ordering [19] and the lexicographic path ordering [16], are specified with the help of a *symbol precedence*, an ordering on the signature symbols. While the superposition calculus is refutationally complete for any simplification ordering [4], the choice of the precedence has a significant impact on how long it takes to solve a given problem.

It is well known that giving the highest precedence to the predicate symbols in-troduced as sub-formula names during clausification [25] can immediately make the saturation produce the exponential set of clauses that the transformation is designed to

© The Author(s) 2021
A. Platzer and G. Sutcliffe (Eds.): CADE 2021, LNAI 12699, pp. 525–542, 2021.
https://doi.org/10.1007/978-3-030-79876-5_30

avoid [29]. Also, certain orderings help to make the superposition a decision procedure on specific fragments of first-order logic (see, e.g., [11,14]). However, the precise way by which the choice of a precedence influences the follow-up proof search on a general problem is extremely hard to predict.

Several general-purpose precedence generating schemes are available to ATP users, such as the successful `invfreq` scheme in E [33], which orders the symbols by the number of occurrences in the input problem. However, experiments with random precedences indicate that the existing schemes often fail to come close to the optimum precedence [28], suggesting room for further improvements.

In this work, we propose a machine learning system that learns to predict for an ATP whether one precedence will lead to a faster proof search on a given problem than another. Given a previously unseen problem, it can then be asked to recommend the best possible precedence for an ATP to run with. Relying only on the logical structure of the problems, the system generalizes the knowledge about favorable precedences across problems with different signatures.

Our recommender uses a relational graph convolutional neural network [32] to represent the problem structure. It learns from the ATP performance on selected problems and pairs of randomly sampled precedences. This information is used to train a *symbol cost model*, which then realizes the recommendation by simply sorting the problem's symbols according to the obtained costs.

This work strictly improves on our previous experiments with linear regression models and simple hand-crafted symbol features [6] and is, to the best of our knowledge, the first method able to propose good symbol precedences automatically using a non-linear transformation of the input problem structure.

The rest of this paper is organized as follows. Section 2 exposes the basic terminology used throughout the remaining sections. Section 3 proposes a structure of the precedence recommender that can be trained on pairs of symbol precedences, as described in Sect. 4. Section 5 summarizes and discusses experiments performed using an implementation of the precedence recommender. Section 6 compares the system proposed in this work with notable related works. Section 7 concludes the investigation and outlines possible directions for future research.

2 Preliminaries

2.1 Saturation-Based Theorem Proving

A *first-order logic (FOL) problem* consists of a set of axiom formulas and a conjecture formula. In a *refutation-based automated theorem prover (ATP)*, proving that the axioms entail the conjecture is reduced to proving that the axioms together with the negated conjecture entail a *contradiction*. The most popular first-order logic (FOL) automated theorem provers (ATPs), such as Vampire [21], E [34], or SPASS [40], start the proof search by converting the input FOL formulas to an equisatisfiable representation in *clause normal form (CNF)* [25,13]. We denote the problem in clause normal form (CNF) as $P = (\Sigma, Cl)$, where Σ is a list of all non-logical (predicate and function) *symbols* in the problem called the *signature*, and Cl is the set of clauses of the problem (including the negated conjecture).

Given a problem P in CNF, a *saturation-based* ATP searches for a refutational proof by iteratively applying the *inference rules* from the given *calculus* to infer new clauses entailed by Cl. As soon as the empty clause, denoted by $\square$, is inferred, the prover concludes that the premises entail the conjecture. The sequence of those inferences leading up from the input clauses Cl to the discovered $\square$ constitutes a proof. If the premises do not entail the conjecture, the proof search continues until the set of inferred clauses is saturated with respect to the inference rules. In the standard setting of time-restricted proof search, a time limit may end the process prematurely.

Since the space of derivable clauses is typically very large, the efficacy of the prover depends on the order in which the inferences are applied. The standard saturation-based ATPs order the inferences by maintaining two classes of inferred clauses: processed and unprocessed [34]. In each *iteration of the saturation loop*, one clause (so-called *given clause*) is combined with all the processed clauses for inferences. The resulting new clauses and the given clause are added to the unprocessed set and the processed set, respectively. Finishing the proof in few iterations of the saturation loop is important because the number of inferred clauses typically grows exponentially during the proof search.

2.2 Superposition Calculus

The *superposition calculus* is of particular interest because it is used in the most successful contemporary FOL ATPs. A *simplification ordering on terms* [4] constrains the inferences of the superposition calculus.

The simplification ordering on terms influences the superposition calculus in two ways. First, the inferences on each clause are limited to the selected literals. In each clause, either a negative literal or all maximal literals are selected. The maximality is evaluated according to the simplification ordering. Second, the simplification ordering orients some of the equalities to prevent superposition and equality factoring from inferring redundant complex conclusions. In each of these two roles, the simplification ordering may impact the direction and, in effect, the length of the proof search.

The *Knuth-Bendix ordering (KBO)* [19], a commonly used simplification ordering scheme, is parameterized by symbol weights and a *symbol precedence*, a permutation[3] of the non-logical symbols of the input problem. In this work, we focus on the task of finding a symbol precedence which leads to a good performance of an ATP when plugged into the Knuth-Bendix ordering (KBO), leaving all the symbol weights at the default value 1 as set by the ATP Vampire.

2.3 Neural Networks

A *feedforward artificial neural network* [12] is a directed acyclic graph of *modules*. Each module is an operation that consumes a numeric (input) *vector* and outputs a numeric vector. Each of the components of the output vector is called a *unit* of the

---

[3] The definition of KBO does not require the precedence to be total. However, for use in ATPs, the more symbols and thus also terms we can compare, the better.

module. The output of each module is differentiable with respect to the input almost everywhere.

The standard modules include the *fully connected layer*, which performs an affine transformation, and non-linear *activation functions* such as the *Rectified Linear Unit (ReLU)* or *sigmoid*.[4] A fully connected layer with a single unit is called the *linear unit*.

Some of the modules are parameterized by numeric *parameters*. For example, the fully connected layer that transforms the input x by the affine transformation $Wx + b$ is parameterized by the weight matrix W and the bias vector b. If the output of a module is differentiable with respect to a parameter, that parameter is considered *trainable*.

In a typical scenario, the neural network is trained by *gradient descent* on a *training set* of *examples*. In such a setting, the network outputs a single numeric value called *loss* when evaluated on a *batch* of examples. The loss of a batch is typically computed as a weighted sum of the losses of the individual examples. Since each of the modules is differentiable with respect to its input and trainable parameters, the gradient of the loss with respect to all trainable parameters of the neural network can be computed using the *back-propagation* algorithm [12]. The trainable parameters are then updated by taking a small step against the gradient—in the direction that is expected to reduce the loss. An *epoch* is a sequence of iterations that updates the trainable parameters using each example in the training set exactly once.

A *graph convolutional network (GCN)* is a special case of feedforward neural network. The modules of a GCN transform messages that are passed along the edges of a graph encoded in the input example. A particular architecture of a GCN used prominently in this work is discussed in Sect. 3.2.

3   Architecture

A *symbol precedence recommender* is a system that takes a CNF problem $P = (\Sigma, Cl)$ as the input, and produces a precedence π^* over the symbols Σ as the output. For the recommender to be useful, it should produce a precedence that likely leads to a quick search for a proof. In this work, we use the number of iterations of the saturation loop as a metric describing the effort required to find a proof.

The recommender described in this section first uses a neural network to compute a cost value for each symbol of the input problem, and then orders the symbols by their costs in a non-increasing order. In this manner, the task of finding good precedences is reduced to the task of training a good symbol cost function, as discussed in Sect. 4.

The recommender consists of modules that perform specific sub-tasks, each of which is described in detail in one of the following sections (see also Fig. 1).

3.1   Graph Constructor: From CNF to Graphs

As the first step of the recommender processing pipeline, the input problem is converted from a CNF representation to a *heterogeneous (directed) graph* [41]. Each of the nodes of the graph is labeled with a node type, and each edge is labeled with an edge type,

---

[4] These are, respectively, $f(x) = \max\{0, x\}$ and $g(x) = \frac{1}{1+e^{-x}}$.

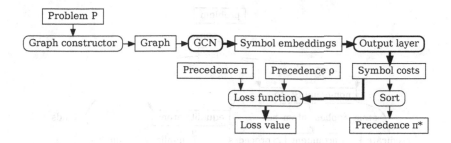

Fig. 1. Recommender architecture overview. When recommending a precedence, the input is problem P and the output is precedence π^*. When training, the input is problem P and precedences π and ρ, and the output is the loss value. The trainable modules and the edges along which the loss gradient is propagated are emphasized by bold lines.

defining the heterogeneous nature of the graph. Each node corresponds to one of the elements that constitute the CNF formula, such as a clause, an atom, or a predicate symbol. Each such category of elements corresponds to one node type. The edges represent the (oriented) relations between the elements, for example, the incidence relation between a clause and one of its (literals') atoms, or the relation between an atom and its predicate symbol. $\mathcal{R}$ denotes the set of all relations in the graph. Figure 2 shows the types of nodes and edges used in our graph representation. Figure 3 shows an example of a graph representation of a simple problem.

The graph representation exhibits, namely, the following properties:

- Lossless: The original problem can be faithfully reconstructed from the corresponding graph representation (up to logical equivalence).
- Signature agnostic: Renaming the symbols and variables in the input problem yields an isomorphic graph.
- For each relation $r \in \mathcal{R}$, its inverse r^{-1} is also present in the graph, typically represented by a different edge type.
- The polarity of the literals is expressed by the type of the edge (pos or neg) connecting the respective atom to the clause it occurs in.
- For every non-equality atom and term, the order of its arguments is captured by a sequence of argument nodes chained by edges [27].
- The two operands of equality are not ordered. This reflects the symmetry of equality.
- Sub-expression sharing [8,26,27]: Identical atoms and terms share a node representation.

3.2 GCN: From Graphs to Symbol Embeddings

For each symbol in the input problem P, we seek to find a vector representation, i.e., an *embedding*, that captures the symbol's properties that are relevant for correctly ranking the symbol in the symbol precedences over P.

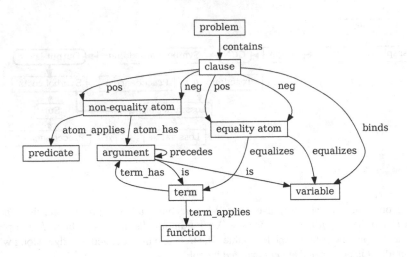

Fig. 2. CNF graph schema

The symbol embeddings are output by a *relational graph convolutional network (R-GCN)* [32], which is a stack of *graph convolutional layers*. Each layer consists of a collection of differentiable modules—one module per edge type. The computation of the GCN starts with assigning each node an initial embedding and then iteratively updates the embeddings by passing them through the convolutional layers.

The initial embedding $h_a^{(0)}$ of a node a is a concatenation of two vectors: a *feature vector* specific for that node (typically empty) and a trainable vector shared by all nodes of the same type. In our particular implementation, feature vectors are used in nodes that correspond to clauses and symbols. Each clause node has a feature vector with a one-hot encoding of the role of the clause, which can be either axiom, assumption, or negated conjecture [38,36]. Each symbol node has a feature vector with two bits of data: whether the symbol was introduced into the problem during preprocessing (most notably during clausification), and whether the symbol appears in a conjecture clause.

One pass through the convolutional layer updates the node embeddings by passing a message along each of the edges. For an edge of type $r \in \mathcal{R}$ going from source node s to destination node d at layer l, the message is composed by converting the embedding of the source node $h_s^{(l)}$ using the module associated with the edge type r. In the simple case that the module is a fully connected layer with weight matrix $W_r^{(l)}$ and bias vector $b_r^{(l)}$, the message is $W_r^{(l)} h_s^{(l)} + b_r^{(l)}$. Each message is then divided by the normalization constant $c_{s,d} = \sqrt{|\mathcal{N}_s^r|}\sqrt{|\mathcal{N}_d^r|}$ [18], where $\mathcal{N}_a^r$ is the set of neighbors of node a under the relation r.

Once all messages are computed, they are aggregated at the destination nodes to form new node embeddings. Each node d aggregates all the incoming messages of a given edge type r by summation, then passes the sum through an activation function

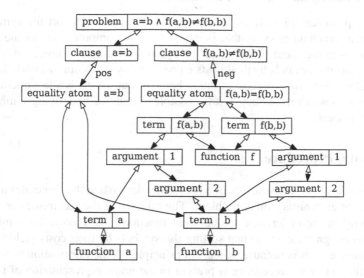

Fig. 3. Graph representation of the CNF formula $a = b \wedge f(a,b) \neq f(b,b)$

σ such as the ReLU, and finally aggregates the messages across the edge types by summation, yielding the new embedding $h_d^{(l+1)}$.

The following formula captures the complete update of the embedding of node d by layer l:

$$h_d^{(l+1)} = \sum_{r \in \mathcal{R}} \sigma \left(\sum_{s \in \mathcal{N}_d^r} \frac{1}{c_{s,d}} (W_r^{(l)} h_s^{(l)} + b_r^{(l)}) \right)$$

3.3 Output Layer: From Symbol Embeddings to Symbol Costs

The symbol cost of each symbol is computed by passing the symbol's embedding through a linear output unit, which is an affine transformation with no activation function.

It is possible to use a more complex output layer in place of the linear unit, e.g., a feedforward network with one or more hidden layers. Our experiments showed no significant improvement when a hidden layer was added, likely because the underlying GCN learns a sufficiently complex transformation.

Let θ denote the vector of all parameters of the whole neural network consisting of the GCN and the output unit. Given an input problem P with signature $\Sigma = (s_1, \ldots, s_n)$, we denote the cost of symbol s_i predicted by the network as $c(i, P; \theta)$. In the rest of this text, we refer to the predicted cost of s_i simply as $c(i)$ because the problem P and the parameters θ are fixed in each respective context.

3.4 Sort: From Symbol Costs to Precedence

The symbol precedence heuristics commonly used in the ATPs sort the symbols by some numeric syntactic property that is inexpensive to compute, such as the number of occurrences in the input problem, or the symbol arity. In our precedence recommender, we sort the symbols by their costs c produced by the neural network described in Sects. 3.2 and 3.3. An advantage of this scheme is that sorting is a fast operation.

Moreover, as we show in Sect. 4, it is possible to train the underlying symbol costs by gradient descent.

4   Training Procedure

In Sect. 3 we described the structure of a recommender system that generates a symbol precedence for an arbitrary input problem. The efficacy of the recommender depends on the quality of the underlying symbol cost function c. In theory, the symbol cost function can assign the costs so that sorting the symbols by their costs yields an optimum precedence. This is because, at least in principle, all the information necessary to determine the optimum precedence is present in the graph representation of the input problem thanks to the lossless property of the graph encoding. Our approach to defining an appropriate symbol cost function is based on statistical learning from executions of an ATP on a set of problems with random precedences.

To train a useful symbol cost function c, we define a precedence cost function C using the symbol cost function c in a manner that ensures that minimizing C corresponds to sorting the symbols by c. Finding a precedence that minimizes C can then be done efficiently and precisely. We proceed to train C on the proxy task of ranking the precedences.

4.1   Precedence Cost

We extend the notion of cost from symbols to precedences by taking the sum of the symbol costs weighted by their positions in the given precedence π:

$$C(\pi) = Z_n \sum_{i=1}^{n} i \cdot c(\pi(i))$$

$Z_n = \frac{2}{n(n+1)}$ is a normalization factor that ensures the commensurability of precedence costs across signature sizes. More precisely, normalizing by Z_n makes the expected value of the precedence cost on a given problem independent of the problem's signature size n, provided the expected symbol cost $\mathbb{E}_i[c(i)]$ does not depend on n:

$$\mathbb{E}_\pi[C(\pi)] = \mathbb{E}_\pi\left[Z_n \sum_{i=1}^{n} i \cdot c(\pi(i)) \right] = Z_n \sum_{i=1}^{n} i \cdot \mathbb{E}_\pi[c(\pi(i))]$$

$$= Z_n \left(\sum_{i=1}^{n} i \right) \mathbb{E}_i[c(i)] = \frac{2}{n(n+1)} \frac{n(n+1)}{2} \mathbb{E}_i[c(i)] = \mathbb{E}_i[c(i)]$$

When C is defined in this way, the precedence produced by the recommender (see Sect. 3.4) minimizes C.

Lemma 1. *The precedence cost C is minimized by any precedence that sorts the symbols by their costs in non-increasing order:*

$$\operatorname*{argmin}_{\rho} C(\rho) = \operatorname{argsort}^{-}(c(1), \dots, c(n))$$

where $\operatorname{argmin}_{\rho} C(\rho)$ is the set of all precedences that minimize precedence cost C for a given symbol cost c, and $\operatorname{argsort}^{-}(x)$ is the set of all permutations π that sort vector x in non-increasing order $(x_{\pi(1)} \geq x_{\pi(2)} \geq \dots \geq x_{\pi(n)})$.

Proof. We prove direction "$\operatorname{argmin}_{\rho} C(\rho) \subseteq \operatorname{argsort}^{-}(c(1), \dots, c(n))$" by contradiction. Let π minimize C and let π not sort the costs in non-increasing order. Then there exist $k < l$ such that $c(\pi(k)) < c(\pi(l))$. Let $\bar{\pi}$ be a precedence obtained from π by swapping the elements k and l. Then we obtain

$$
\begin{aligned}
\frac{C(\bar{\pi}) - C(\pi)}{Z_n} &= kc(\bar{\pi}(k)) + lc(\bar{\pi}(l)) - kc(\pi(k)) - lc(\pi(l)) \\
&= kc(\pi(l)) + lc(\pi(k)) - kc(\pi(k)) - lc(\pi(l)) \\
&= k(c(\pi(l)) - c(\pi(k))) - l(c(\pi(l)) - c(\pi(k))) \\
&= (k - l)(c(\pi(l)) - c(\pi(k))) \\
&< 0
\end{aligned}
$$

The final inequality is due to $k - l < 0$ and $c(\pi(l)) - c(\pi(k)) > 0$. Clearly, $Z_n > 0$ for any $n \geq 0$. Thus, $C(\bar{\pi}) < C(\pi)$, which contradicts the assumption that π minimizes C.

To prove the other direction of the equality, first observe that all precedences π that sort the symbol costs in a non-increasing order necessarily have the same precedence cost $C(\pi)$. Since $\emptyset \neq \operatorname{argmin}_{\rho} C(\rho) \subseteq \operatorname{argsort}^{-}(c(1), \dots, c(n))$, each of the precedences in $\operatorname{argsort}^{-}(c(1), \dots, c(n))$ has the cost $\min_{\rho} C(\rho)$. It follows that $\operatorname{argsort}^{-}(c(1), \dots, c(n)) \subseteq \operatorname{argmin}_{\rho} C(\rho)$. □

4.2 Learning to Rank Precedences

Our ultimate goal is to train the precedence cost function C so that it is minimized by the best precedence, measuring the quality of a precedence by the number of iterations of the saturation loop taken to solve the problem.

Approaching this task directly, as a regression problem, runs into the difficulty of establishing sensible target cost values for the precedences in the training dataset, especially when a wide variety of input problems is covered. Approaching the task as a binary classification of precedences seems possible, but it is not clear which precedences should be a priori labeled as positive and which as negative, to give a guarantee that a precedence minimizing the precedence cost (i.e. the one obtained by sorting) would be among the best in any good sense.

We cast the task as an instance of score-based ranking problem [23,7] by training a classifier to decide which of a *pair* of precedences is better based on their costs. We train the classifier in a way that ensures that better precedences are assigned lower costs. The motivation for learning to order pairs of precedences is that it allows learning on easy problems, and that it may allow the system to generalize to precedences that are better than any of those seen during training.

Training Data. Each training example has the form (P, π, ρ), where $P = (\Sigma, Cl)$ is a problem and π, ρ are precedences over Σ such that the prover using π solves P in fewer iterations of the saturation loop than with ρ, denoted as $\pi \prec_P \rho$.

Loss Function. Let (P, π, ρ) be a training example ($\pi \prec_P \rho$). The precedence cost classifies this example correctly if $C(\pi) < C(\rho)$, or alternatively $S(\pi, \rho) = C(\rho) - C(\pi) > 0$. We approach this problem as an instance of binary classification with the logistic loss [23], a loss function routinely used in classification tasks in machine learning:

$$\ell(P, \pi, \rho) = -\log \text{sigmoid}\, S(\pi, \rho) = -\log \text{sigmoid}(C(\rho) - C(\pi))$$

$$= -\log \text{sigmoid}\, Z_n \sum_{i=1}^{n} i(c(\rho(i)) - c(\pi(i)))$$

Note that the classifier cannot simply train S to output a positive number on all pairs of precedences because S is defined as a difference of two precedence costs. Intuitively, by training on the example (P, π, ρ) we are pushing $C(\pi)$ down and $C(\rho)$ up.

The loss function is clearly differentiable with respect to the symbol costs, and the symbol cost function c is differentiable with respect to its trainable parameters. This enables the use of gradient descent to find the values of the parameters of c that locally minimize the loss value.

Figure 1 shows how the loss function is plugged into the recommender for training.

5   Experimental Evaluation

To demonstrate the capacity of the trainable precedence recommender described in Sects. 3 and 4, we performed a series of experiments. In this section, we describe the design and configuration of the experiments, and then compare the performance of several trained models to a baseline heuristic.

The scripts that were used to generate the training data and to train and evaluate the recommender are available online.[5]

5.1   Environment

System. All experiments were run on a computer with the CPU Intel Xeon Gold 6140 (72 cores @ 2.30 GHz) and 383 GiB RAM.

---

[5] https://github.com/filipbartek/vampire-ml/tree/cade28

Solver. The empirical evaluation was performed using a modified version of the ATP Vampire 4.3.0 [21]. The prover was used to generate the training data and to evaluate the trained precedence recommender. To generate the training data, Vampire was modified to output CNF representations of the problems and annotated problem signatures in a machine-readable format. For the evaluation of the precedences generated by the recommender, Vampire was modified to allow the user to supply explicit predicate and function symbol precedences for the proof search (normally, the user only picks a precedence generation heuristic). The modified version of Vampire is available online.[6]

We run Vampire with a fixed strategy[7] and a time limit of 10 seconds. To increase the potential impact of predicate precedences, we used a simple transfinite Knuth-Bendix ordering (TKBO) [22,20] that compares atoms according to the predicate precedence first, using the regular KBO to break ties between atoms and to compare terms (using the Vampire option `--literal_comparison_mode predicate`).

5.2   Dataset Preparation

The training data consists of examples of the form (P, π, ρ), where P is a CNF problem and π, ρ are precedences of symbols of problem P such that out of the two precedences, π yields a proof in fewer iterations of the saturation loop (see Sect. 2.1).

Since the TKBO never compares a predicate symbol with a function symbol, two separate precedences can be considered for each problem: a predicate precedence and a function precedence. We trained a predicate precedence recommender separately from a function precedence recommender to simplify the training process and to isolate the effects of the predicate and function precedences. This section describes how the training data for the case of training a *predicate* precedence recommender was generated. Data for training the function precedence recommender was generated analogously.

Base Problem Set. The input problems were assumed to be specified in the CNF or the first-order form (FOF) fragment of the TPTP language [36]. FOF problems were first converted into equisatisfiable CNF problems by Vampire.

We used the problem library TPTP v7.4.0 [36] as the source of problems for training and evaluation of the recommender. We denote the set of all problems available for training and evaluation as $\mathcal{P}_0$ ($|\mathcal{P}_0| = 17\,053$).

Node Feature Extraction. In addition to the signature and the structure of the problem, some metadata was extracted from the input problem to allow training a more efficient recommender. First, each clause was annotated with its role in the problem, which could be either axiom, assumption, or negated conjecture. Second, each symbol was annotated with two bits of data: whether the symbol was introduced into the problem during preprocessing, and whether the symbol appeared in a conjecture clause. This metadata was used to construct the initial embeddings of the respective nodes in the graph representation of the problem (see Sect. 3.2).

---

[6] https://github.com/filipbartek/vampire/tree/cade28
[7] Saturation algorithm: DISCOUNT, age to weight ratio: 1:10, AVATAR [39]: disabled, literal comparison mode: predicate; all other options left at their default values.

Examples Generation. The examples were generated by an iterative sampling of $\mathcal{P}_0$. In each iteration, a problem $P \in \mathcal{P}_0$ was chosen and Vampire was executed twice on P with two (uniformly) random predicate precedences and one common random function precedence. The "background" random function precedence served as additional noise (in addition to the variability contained in TPTP) and made sure that the predicate precedence recommender would not be able to rely on any specificity that would come from fixing function precedences in the training data.

The two executions were compared in terms of performance: the predicate precedence π was recognized as better than the predicate precedence ρ, denoted as $\pi \prec_P \rho$, if the proof search finished successfully with π and if the number of iterations of the saturation loop with π was smaller than with ρ. If one of the two precedences was recognized as better, the example (P, π, ρ) would be produced, where π was the better precedence, and ρ was the other precedence. Otherwise, for example, if the proof search timed out on both precedences, we would go back to sampling another problem.

To ensure the efficiency of the sampling, we interpreted the process as an instance of the Bernoulli multi-armed bandit problem [37], with the reward of a trial being 1 in case an example is produced, and 0 otherwise.

We employed adaptive sampling to balance exploring problems that have been tried relatively scarcely and exploiting problems that have yielded examples relatively often. For each problem $P \in \mathcal{P}_0$, the generator kept track of the number of times the problem has been tried n_P, and the number of examples generated from that problem s_P. The ratio $\frac{s_P}{n_P}$ corresponded to the average reward of problem P observed so far. The problems were sampled using the allocation strategy UCB1 [1] with a parallelizing relaxation.

First, the values of n_P and s_P for each problem P were bootstrapped by sampling the problem a number of times equal to a lower bound on the final value of n_P (at least 1).[8] In each subsequent iteration, the generator sampled the problem P that maximized $\frac{s_P}{n_P} + \sqrt{\frac{2 \ln n}{n_P}}$, where $n = \sum_{P \in \mathcal{P}_0} n_P$ was the total number of tries on all problems. The parallelizing relaxation means that the s_P values were only updated once in 1000 iterations, allowing up to 2000 parallel solver executions.

The sampling continued until 1 000 000 examples were generated when training a predicate precedence recommender, or 800 000 examples in the case of a function precedence recommender. For example, while generating 1 000 000 examples for the predicate precedence dataset, 5349 out of the 17 053 problems yielded at least one example, while the least explored problem was tried 19 times, and the most exploited problem 504 times.

Validation Split. The 17 053 problems in $\mathcal{P}_0$ were first split roughly in half to form the training set and the validation set. Next, both training and validation sets were restricted to problems whose graph representation consisted of at most 100 000 nodes to limit the memory requirements of the training. Approximately 90 % of the problems fit into this limit and there were 7648 problems in the resulting validation set $\mathcal{P}_{\text{val}}$. The training

---

[8] The number of tries each problem was bootstrapped with is $n_0 = \lceil \frac{2 \log N}{(1+\sqrt{\frac{2 \log N |\mathcal{P}_0|}{N}})^2} \rceil$, where N is the final number of examples to be generated. For example, if $N = 1\,000\,000$ and $|\mathcal{P}_0| = 17\,053$, then $n_0 = 10$.

set $\mathcal{P}_{\text{train}}$ was further restricted to problems that correspond to at least one training example, resulting in 2571 problems when training a predicate precedence recommender, and 1953 problems when training a function precedence recommender.

5.3 Hyperparameters

We used a GCN described in Sect. 3.2 with depth 4, message size 16, ReLU activation function, skip connections [41], and layer normalization [2]. We tuned the hyperparameters by a small manual exploration.

5.4 Training Procedure

A symbol cost model was trained by gradient descent on the precedence ranking task (see Sect. 4.2) using the examples generated from $\mathcal{P}_{\text{train}}$. To avoid redundant computations, all examples generated from any given problem were processed in the same training batch. Thus, each training batch contained up to 128 problems and all examples generated from these problems. The symbol cost model was trained using the Adam optimizer [17]. The learning rate started at 1.28×10^{-3} and was halved each time the loss on $\mathcal{P}_{\text{train}}$ stagnated for 10 consecutive epochs.

The examples were weighted. Each of the examples of problem P contributed to the training with the weight $\frac{1}{s_P}$, where s_P was the number of examples of problem P in the training set. This ensured that each problem contributed to the training to the same degree irrespective of the relative number of examples.

We continued the training until the validation accuracy stopped increasing for 100 consecutive epochs.

5.5 Final Evaluation

After the training finished, we performed a final evaluation of the most promising intermediate trained model on the whole $\mathcal{P}_{\text{val}}$. The model that manifested the best solver performance on a sample of 1000 validation problems was taken as the most promising.

5.6 Results

A predicate precedence recommender was trained on approximately 500 000 examples, and a function precedence recommender was trained on approximately 400 000 examples. For each problem $P \in \mathcal{P}_{\text{val}}$, a predicate and a function precedences were generated by the respective trained recommender, and Vampire was run using these precedences with a wall clock time limit of 10 seconds. The results are averaged over 5 runs to reduce the effect of noise due to the wall clock time limit. As a baseline, the performance of Vampire with the `frequency` precedence heuristic[9] was evaluated with the same time limit. For comparison, the two trained recommenders were evaluated separately, with the predicate precedence recommender using the `frequency` heuristic to generate the function precedences, and vice versa.

---

[9] This is Vampire's analogue of the `invfreq` scheme in E [33].

To generate a precedence for a problem, the recommender first converts the problem to a machine-friendly CNF format, then converts the CNF to a graph, then predicts symbol costs using the GCN model and finally orders the symbols by their costs to produce the precedence. To simplify the experiment, the time limit of 10 seconds was only imposed on the Vampire run, excluding the time taken by the recommender to generate the precedence. When run with 2 threads, the preprocessing of a single problem took at most 1.26 seconds for 80 % of the problems by extrapolation from a sample of 1000 problems.[10] Table 1 shows the results of the final evaluation.

Table 1. Results of the evaluation of symbol precedence heuristics based on various symbol cost models on $\mathcal{P}_{val}$ ($|\mathcal{P}_{val}| = 7648$). Means and standard deviations over 5 runs are reported. The GCN models were trained according to the description in Sects. 3 to 5. The model Simple is the final linear model from our previous work [6]. The models that used machine learning only for the predicate precedence used the `frequency` heuristic for the function precedence, and vice versa. The frequency model uses the standard `frequency` heuristic for both predicate and function precedence.

Symbol cost model	Successes on $\mathcal{P}_{val}$		Improvement over baseline	
	Mean	Std	Absolute	Relative
GCN (predicate and function)	3951.6	1.62	+182.0	1.048
GCN (predicate only)	3923.6	2.24	+154.0	1.041
GCN (function only)	3874.2	1.83	+104.6	1.028
Simple (predicate only)	3827.2	1.94	+57.6	1.015
Frequency (baseline)	3769.6	3.07	0.0	1.000

The results show that the GCN-based model outperformed the `frequency` heuristic by a significant margin. Since the predicate precedence recommender was trained with randomly distributed function precedences, it was expected to perform well irrespective of the function precedence heuristic it is combined with, and conversely. Combining the trained recommenders for predicate and function precedences manifested better performance than any of the two in combination with the standard `frequency` heuristic, outperforming the `frequency` heuristic by approximately 4.8 %.

We have confirmed our earlier conjecture [6] that using a graph neural network (GNN) may outperform the "simple" linear predicate precedence heuristic trained in [6].[11]

6 Related Work

Our previous text [6] marked the initial investigation of applying techniques of machine learning to generating good symbol precedences. The neural recommender presented here uses a GNN to model symbol costs, while [6] used a linear combination of symbol features readily available in the ATP Vampire. The GNN-based approach yields more performant precedences at the cost of longer training and preprocessing time.

---

[10] The remaining 20 % of the problems either finished preprocessing within 5 seconds, or were omitted from preprocessing due to exceeding the node count limit.

[11] The measurements presented in Table 1 are not directly comparable with those reported in [6] due to differences in the validation problem sets and the computation environments.

In [26], [15] and [27], the authors propose similar GNN architectures to solve tasks on FOL problems. They use the GNNs to solve classification tasks such as premise selection. While our system is trained on a proxy classification task, the main task it is evaluated on is the generation of useful precedences.

The problem of learning to rank objects represented by scores trainable by gradient descent was explored in [7]. Our work can be seen to apply the approach of [7] to rank permutations represented by weighted sums of symbol costs.

7 Conclusion and Future Work

We have described a system that extracts useful symbol precedences from the graph representations of CNF problems. Comparison with a conventional symbol precedence heuristic shows that using a GCN to consider the whole structure of the input problem is beneficial.

A manual analysis of the trained recommender could produce new insights into how the choice of the symbol precedence influences the proof search, which could in turn help design new efficient precedence generating schemes. Indeed, a trained cost model summarizes the observed behaviors of an ATP with random precedences and is able to discover patterns in them (as we know implicitly from its accuracy) despite their seemingly chaotic behavior as perceived by a human observer. The challenge is to extract these patterns in a human-understandable form.

In addition to the symbol precedence, KBO is determined by symbol *weights*. In this work, we keep the symbol weights fixed to the value 1. Learning to recommend symbol weights in addition to the precedences represents an interesting avenue for future research.

The same applies to the idea of learning to recommend both the predicate and function precedences using a single GCN. The joint learning, although more complex to design, could additionally discover interdependencies between the effects of function precedence and predicate precedence on the proof search, while the current setup implicitly assumes that the effects are independent. Finally, a higher training data efficiency could be achieved by considering all pairs of measured executions on a problem in one training batch.

Acknowledgments

This work was generously supported by the Czech Science Foundation project no. 20-06390Y (JUNIOR grant), the project RICAIP no. 857306 under the EU-H2020 programme, and the Grant Agency of the Czech Technical University in Prague, grant no. SGS20/215/OHK3/3T/37.

References

1. Auer, P., Cesa-Bianchi, N., Fischer, P.: Finite-time analysis of the multi-armed bandit problem. Machine Learning 47(2-3), 235–256 (May 2002). https://doi.org/10.1023/A:1013689704352

2. Ba, J.L., Kiros, J.R., Hinton, G.E.: Layer normalization (Jul 2016), http://arxiv.org/abs/1607.06450
3. Bachmair, L., Derschowitz, N., Plaisted, D.A.: Completion without failure. In: Aït-Kaci, H., Nivat, M. (eds.) Rewriting Techniques, pp. 1–30. Academic Press (1989). https://doi.org/10.1016/B978-0-12-046371-8.50007-9
4. Bachmair, L., Ganzinger, H.: Rewrite-based equational theorem proving with selection and simplification. J. Log. Comput. **4**(3), 217–247 (1994). https://doi.org/10.1093/logcom/4.3.217
5. Bachmair, L., Ganzinger, H.: Resolution theorem proving. In: Robinson and Voronkov [31], pp. 19–99. https://doi.org/10.1016/b978-044450813-3/50004-7
6. Bártek, F., Suda, M.: Learning precedences from simple symbol features. In: Fontaine et al. [10], pp. 21–33, http://ceur-ws.org/Vol-2752/paper2.pdf
7. Burges, C., Shaked, T., Renshaw, E., Lazier, A., Deeds, M., Hamilton, N., Hullender, G.: Learning to rank using gradient descent. In: ICML 2005 - Proceedings of the 22nd International Conference on Machine Learning. pp. 89–96. ACM Press, New York, New York, USA (2005). https://doi.org/10.1145/1102351.1102363
8. Chvalovský, K., Jakubův, J., Suda, M., Urban, J.: ENIGMA-NG: Efficient neural and gradient-boosted inference guidance for E. In: Fontaine [9]. https://doi.org/10.1007/978-3-030-29436-6_12
9. Fontaine, P. (ed.): Automated Deduction - CADE 27, LNCS, vol. 11716. Springer, Cham (2019). https://doi.org/10.1007/978-3-030-29436-6
10. Fontaine, P., Korovin, K., Kotsireas, I.S., Rümmer, P., Tourret, S. (eds.): Joint Proceedings of the 7th Workshop on Practical Aspects of Automated Reasoning (PAAR) and the 5th Satisfiability Checking and Symbolic Computation Workshop (SC-Square) Workshop, 2020 co-located with the 10th International Joint Conference on Automated Reasoning (IJCAR 2020). No. 2752 in CEUR Workshop Proceedings, CEUR-WS.org, Aachen (2020), http://ceur-ws.org/Vol-2752
11. Ganzinger, H., de Nivelle, H.: A superposition decision procedure for the guarded fragment with equality. In: 14th Annual IEEE Symposium on Logic in Computer Science. pp. 295–303. IEEE Computer Society (1999). https://doi.org/10.1109/LICS.1999.782624
12. Goodfellow, I.J., Bengio, Y., Courville, A.C.: Deep Learning. Adaptive computation and machine learning, MIT Press (2016), http://www.deeplearningbook.org/
13. Harrison, J.: Handbook of Practical Logic and Automated Reasoning. Cambridge University Press, Cambridge (2009). https://doi.org/10.1017/CBO9780511576430
14. Hustadt, U., Konev, B., Schmidt, R.A.: Deciding monodic fragments by temporal resolution. In: Nieuwenhuis, R. (ed.) Automated Deduction – CADE-20. LNCS, vol. 3632, pp. 204–218. Springer, Berlin, Heidelberg (2005). https://doi.org/10.1007/11532231_15
15. Jakubův, J., Chvalovský, K., Olšák, M., Piotrowski, B., Suda, M., Urban, J.: ENIGMA Anonymous: Symbol-independent inference guiding machine (system description). In: Peltier, N., Sofronie-Stokkermans, V. (eds.) Automated Reasoning. LNCS, vol. 12167, pp. 448–463. Springer, Cham (Jul 2020). https://doi.org/10.1007/978-3-030-51054-1_29
16. Kamin, S.N., Lévy, J.: Two generalizations of the recursive path ordering (1980), http://www.cs.tau.ac.il/~nachumd/term/kamin-levy80spo.pdf, unpublished letter to Nachum Dershowitz
17. Kingma, D.P., Ba, J.: Adam: A method for stochastic optimization (Dec 2014), http://arxiv.org/abs/1412.6980
18. Kipf, T.N., Welling, M.: Semi-supervised classification with graph convolutional networks. In: 5th International Conference on Learning Representations, ICLR 2017 (Sep 2017), https://openreview.net/forum?id=SJU4ayYgl
19. Knuth, D.E., Bendix, P.B.: Simple word problems in universal algebras. In: Siekmann and Wrightson [35], pp. 342–376. https://doi.org/10.1007/978-3-642-81955-1_23

20. Kovács, L., Moser, G., Voronkov, A.: On transfinite Knuth-Bendix orders. In: Bjørner, N., Sofronie-Stokkermans, V. (eds.) Automated Deduction – CADE-23. LNCS, vol. 6803, pp. 384–399. Springer, Berlin, Heidelberg (2011). https://doi.org/10.1007/978-3-642-22438-6_29

21. Kovács, L., Voronkov, A.: First-order theorem proving and Vampire. In: Sharygina, N., Veith, H. (eds.) Computer Aided Verification. LNCS, vol. 8044, pp. 1–35. Springer, Berlin, Heidelberg (2013). https://doi.org/10.1007/978-3-642-39799-8_1

22. Ludwig, M., Waldmann, U.: An extension of the Knuth-Bendix ordering with LPO-like properties. In: Dershowitz, N., Voronkov, A. (eds.) Logic for Programming, Artificial Intelligence, and Reasoning. LNCS, vol. 4790, pp. 348–362. Springer, Berlin, Heidelberg (Oct 2007). https://doi.org/10.1007/978-3-540-75560-9_26

23. Mohri, M., Rostamizadeh, A., Talwalkar, A.: Foundations of Machine Learning. MIT Press, 2 edn. (2018), https://cs.nyu.edu/~mohri/mlbook/

24. Nieuwenhuis, R., Rubio, A.: Paramodulation-based theorem proving. In: Robinson and Voronkov [31], pp. 371–443. https://doi.org/10.1016/b978-044450813-3/50009-6

25. Nonnengart, A., Weidenbach, C.: Computing small clause normal forms. In: Robinson and Voronkov [31], pp. 335–367. https://doi.org/10.1016/b978-044450813-3/50008-4

26. Olšák, M., Kaliszyk, C., Urban, J.: Property invariant embedding for automated reasoning. In: Giacomo, G.D., Catalá, A., Dilkina, B., Milano, M., Barro, S., Bugarín, A., Lang, J. (eds.) ECAI 2020 – 24th European Conference on Artificial Intelligence. Frontiers in Artificial Intelligence and Applications, vol. 325, pp. 1395–1402. IOS Press (2020). https://doi.org/10.3233/FAIA200244

27. Rawson, M., Reger, G.: Directed graph networks for logical reasoning (extended abstract). In: Fontaine et al. [10], pp. 109–119, http://ceur-ws.org/Vol-2752/paper8.pdf

28. Reger, G., Suda, M.: Measuring progress to predict success: Can a good proof strategy be evolved? In: AITP 2017. pp. 20–21 (2017), http://aitp-conference.org/2017/aitp17-proceedings.pdf

29. Reger, G., Suda, M., Voronkov, A.: New techniques in clausal form generation. In: Benzmüller, C., Sutcliffe, G., Rojas, R. (eds.) GCAI 2016. 2nd Global Conference on Artificial Intelligence. EPiC Series in Computing, vol. 41, pp. 11–23. EasyChair (2016). https://doi.org/10.29007/dzfz

30. Robinson, G., Wos, L.: Paramodulation and theorem-proving in first-order theories with equality. In: Siekmann and Wrightson [35], pp. 298–313. https://doi.org/10.1007/978-3-642-81955-1_19

31. Robinson, J.A., Voronkov, A. (eds.): Handbook of Automated Reasoning (in 2 volumes). Elsevier and MIT Press (2001)

32. Schlichtkrull, M.S., Kipf, T.N., Bloem, P., van den Berg, R., Titov, I., Welling, M.: Modeling relational data with graph convolutional networks. In: Gangemi, A., Navigli, R., Vidal, M., Hitzler, P., Troncy, R., Hollink, L., Tordai, A., Alam, M. (eds.) The Semantic Web. LNCS, vol. 10843, pp. 593–607. Springer, Cham (2018). https://doi.org/10.1007/978-3-319-93417-4_38

33. Schulz, S.: E 2.4 user manual. EasyChair preprint no. 2272, Manchester (2020), https://easychair.org/publications/preprint/8dss

34. Schulz, S., Cruanes, S., Vukmirović, P.: Faster, higher, stronger: E 2.3. In: Fontaine [9], pp. 495–507. https://doi.org/10.1007/978-3-030-29436-6_29

35. Siekmann, J.H., Wrightson, G. (eds.): Springer, Berlin, Heidelberg (1983)

36. Sutcliffe, G.: The TPTP problem library and associated infrastructure. Journal of Automated Reasoning 59(4) (Dec 2017). https://doi.org/10.1007/s10817-017-9407-7

37. Sutton, R.S., Barto, A.G.: Reinforcement Learning: An Introduction. The MIT Press, 2 edn. (2018), http://incompleteideas.net/book/the-book-2nd.html

542   F. Bártek, M. Suda

38. TPTP syntax, `http://www.tptp.org/TPTP/SyntaxBNF.html`
39. Voronkov, A.: AVATAR: The architecture for first-order theorem provers. In: Biere, A., Bloem, R. (eds.) Computer Aided Verification. LNCS, vol. 8559, pp. 696–710. Springer, Cham (2014). https://doi.org/10.1007/978-3-319-08867-9_46
40. Weidenbach, C., Dimova, D., Fietzke, A., Kumar, R., Suda, M., Wischnewski, P.: SPASS version 3.5. In: Schmidt, R.A. (ed.) Automated Deduction - CADE-22. LNCS, vol. 5663, pp. 140–145. Springer, Berlin, Heidelberg (2009). https://doi.org/10.1007/978-3-642-02959-2_10
41. Zhou, J., Cui, G., Zhang, Z., Yang, C., Liu, Z., Wang, L., Li, C., Sun, M.: Graph neural networks: A review of methods and applications (Dec 2018), `http://arxiv.org/abs/1812.08434`

Open Access This chapter is licensed under the terms of the Creative Commons Attribution 4.0 International License (`http://creativecommons.org/licenses/by/4.0/`), which permits use, sharing, adaptation, distribution and reproduction in any medium or format, as long as you give appropriate credit to the original author(s) and the source, provide a link to the Creative Commons license and indicate if changes were made.

The images or other third party material in this chapter are included in the chapter's Creative Commons license, unless indicated otherwise in a credit line to the material. If material is not included in the chapter's Creative Commons license and your intended use is not permitted by statutory regulation or exceeds the permitted use, you will need to obtain permission directly from the copyright holder.

Improving ENIGMA-style Clause Selection while Learning From History

Martin Suda ⓘ

Czech Technical University in Prague, Prague, Czech Republic
`martin.suda@cvut.cz`

Abstract. We re-examine the topic of machine-learned clause selection guidance in saturation-based theorem provers. The central idea, recently popularized by the ENIGMA system, is to learn a classifier for recognizing clauses that appeared in previously discovered proofs. In subsequent runs, clauses classified positively are prioritized for selection. We propose several improvements to this approach and experimentally confirm their viability. For the demonstration, we use a recursive neural network to classify clauses based on their derivation history and the presence or absence of automatically supplied theory axioms therein. The automatic theorem prover Vampire guided by the network achieves a 41 % improvement on a relevant subset of SMT-LIB in a real time evaluation.

Keywords: Saturation-based theorem proving · Clause Selection · Machine Learning · Recursive Neural Networks.

1 Introduction

The idea to improve the performance of saturation-based automatic theorem provers (ATPs) with the help of machine learning (ML), while going back at least to the early work of Schulz [8, 30], has recently been enjoying a renewed interest. Most notable is the ENIGMA system [16, 17] extending the ATP E [31] by machine learned clause selection guidance. The architecture trains a binary classifier for recognizing as positive those clauses that appeared in previously discovered proofs and as negative the remaining selected ones. In subsequent runs, clauses classified positively are prioritized for selection.

A system such as ENIGMA needs to carefully balance the expressive power of the used ML model with the time it takes to evaluate its advice. For example, Loos et al. [22], who were the first to integrate state-of-the-art neural networks with E, discovered their models to be too slow to simply replace the traditional clause selection mechanism. In the meantime, the data-hungry deep learning approaches motivate researchers to augment training data with artificially crafted theorems [1]. Yet another interesting aspect is what features we allow the model to learn from. One could speculate that the recent success of ENIGMA on the Mizar dataset [7, 18] can at least partially be explained by the involved problems sharing a common source and encoding. It is still open whether some new form of general "theorem proving knowledge" could be learned to improve the performance of an ATP across, e.g., the very diverse TPTP library.

© The Author(s) 2021

A. Platzer and G. Sutcliffe (Eds.): CADE 2021, LNAI 12699, pp. 543–561, 2021.
https://doi.org/10.1007/978-3-030-79876-5_31

In this paper, we propose several improvements to ENIGMA-style clause selection guidance and experimentally test their viability in a novel setting:

- We lay out a set of possibilities for integrating the learned advice into the ATP and single out the recently developed layered clause selection [10,11,36] as particularly suitable for the task.
- We speed up evaluation by a new lazy evaluation scheme under which many generated clauses need not be evaluated by the potentially slow classifier.
- We demonstrate the importance of "positive bias", i.e., of tuning the classifier to rather err on the side of false positives than on the side of false negatives.
- Finally, we propose the use of "negative mining" for improving learning from proofs obtained while relying on previously learned guidance.

To test these ideas, we designed a recursive neural network to classify clauses based solely on their derivation history and the presence or absence of automatically supplied theory axioms therein. This allows us to test here, as a byproduct of the conducted experiments, whether the human-engineered heuristic for controlling the amount of theory reasoning presented in our previous work [11] can be matched or even overcome by the automatically discovered neural guidance.

The rest of the paper is structured as follows. Sect. 2 recalls the necessary ATP theory, explains clause selection and how to improve it using ML. Sect. 3 covers layered clause selection and the new lazy evaluation scheme. In Sect. 4, we describe our neural architecture and in Sect. 5 we bring everything together and evaluate the presented ideas, using the prover Vampire as our workhorse and a relevant subset of SMT-LIB as the testing grounds. Finally, Sect. 6 concludes.

2   ATPs, Clause Selection, and Machine Learning

The technology behind the modern automatic theorem provers (ATPs) for first-order logic (FOL), such as E [31], SPASS [40], or Vampire [21], can be roughly outlined by using the following three adjectives.

Refutational: The task of the prover is to check whether a given conjecture G logically follows from given axioms $A_1, \ldots, A_n$, i.e. whether

$$A_1, \ldots, A_n \models G, \tag{1}$$

where G and each A_i are FOL formulas. The prover starts by negating the conjecture G and transforming $\neg G, A_1, \ldots, A_n$ into an equisatisfiable set of clauses $\mathcal{C}$. It then applies a sound logical calculus to iteratively derive further clauses, logical consequence of $\mathcal{C}$, until the obvious contradiction in the form of the empty clause $\bot$ is derived. This *refutes* the assumption that $\neg G, A_1, \ldots, A_n$ could be satisfiable and thus confirms (1).

Superposition-based: The most popular calculus used in this context is superposition [3,23], an extension of ordered resolution [4] with a built-in support for handling equality. It consists of several inference rules, such as the resolution rule, factoring, subsumption, superposition, or demodulation.

Inference rules in general determine how to derive new clauses from old ones, where by old clauses we mean either the initial clauses C or clauses derived previously. The clauses that need to be present for a rule to be applicable are called the *premises* and the newly derived clause is called the *conclusion*. By applying the inference rules the prover gradually constructs a *derivation*, a directed acyclic (hyper-)graph (DAG), with the initial clauses forming the leaves and the derived clauses (labeled by the respective applied rules) forming the internal nodes. A *proof* is the smallest sub-DAG of a derivation containing the final empty clause and for every derived clause the corresponding inference and its premises.

Saturation-based: A saturation algorithm is the concrete way of organizing the process of deriving new clauses, such that every applicable inference is eventually considered. Modern saturation-based ATPs employ some variant of the *given-clause algorithm*, in which clauses are selected for inferences one by one [27].

The process employs two sets of clauses, often called the *active* set A and the *passive* set P. At the beginning all the initial clauses are put to the passive set. Then in every iteration, the prover *selects* and removes a clause C from P, inserts it into A, and performs all the applicable inferences with premises in A such that at least one of the premises is C. The conclusions of these inferences are then inserted into P. This way the prover maintains (at the end of each iteration) the invariant that inferences among the clauses in the active set have been performed. The selected clause C is sometimes also called the "given clause".

During a typical prover run, P grows much faster than A (the growth is roughly quadratic). Analogously, although for different reasons, when a proof is discovered, its clauses constitute only a fraction of A. Notice that every clause $C \in A$ that is in the end *not* part of the proof did not need to be selected and represents a wasted effort. This explains why *clause selection*, i.e. the procedure for picking in each iteration the next clause to process, is one of the main heuristic decision points in the prover, which hugely affects its performance [32].

2.1   Traditional Approaches to Clause Selection

There are two basic criteria that have been identified as generally correlating with the likelihood of a clause contributing to the yet-to-be discovered proof.

One is clause's *age* or, more precisely, its "date of birth", typically implemented as an ever increasing timestamp. Preferring for selection old clauses to more recently derived ones corresponds to a breadth-first strategy and ensures fairness. The other criterion is clause's size, referred to as *weight* in the ATP lingo, and is realized by some form of symbol counting. Preferring for selection small clauses to large ones is a greedy strategy, based on the observation that small conclusions typically belong to inferences with small premises and that the ultimate conclusion—the empty clause—is the smallest of all. The best results are achieved when these two criteria (or their variations) are combined [32].

To implement efficient clause selection by numerical criteria such as age and weight, an ATP represents the passive set P as a set of priority queues. A queue contains (pointers to) the clauses in P ordered by its respective criterion. Selection typically alternates between the available queues under a certain ratio.

A successful strategy is, for instance, to select 10 clauses by weight for every clause selected by age, i.e., with an *age-to-weight* ratio of 1:10.

2.2   ENIGMA-style Machine-Learned Clause Selection Guidance

The idea to improve clause selection by learning from previous prover experience goes, to the best of our knowledge, back to Schulz [8,30] and has more recently been successfully employed by the ENIGMA system and others [7,15–17,22].

The experience is collected from successful prover runs, where each selected clause constitutes a training example and the example is marked as *positive*, if the clause ended-up in the discovered proof, and *negative* otherwise. A machine learning (ML) algorithm is then used to *fit* this data and produce a *model* $\mathcal{M}$ for *classifying* clauses into positive and negative, accordingly. A good learning algorithm produces a model $\mathcal{M}$ which not only accurately classifies the training data but also *generalizes* well to unseen examples. The computational costs of both training and evaluation are also important.

While clauses are logical formulas, i.e., discrete objects forming a countable set, ML algorithms, rooted in mathematical statistics, are primarily equipped to dealing with fixed-seized real-valued vectors. Thus the question of how to *represent* clauses for the learning is the first obstacle that needs to be overcome, before the whole idea can be made to work. In the beginning, the authors of ENIGMA experimented with various forms of hand-crafted numerical clause *features* [16,17]. An attractive alternative explored in later work [7,15,22] is the use of artificial *neural networks*, which can be understood as extracting the most relevant features automatically.

An important distinction can in both cases be made between approaches which have access to the concrete identity of predicate and function symbols (i.e., the signature) that make up the clauses, and those that do not. For example: Is the ML algorithm allowed to assume that the symbol grp_mult is used to represent the multiplication operation in a group or does it only recognize a general binary function? The first option can be much more powerful, but we need to ensure that the signature symbols are *aligned* and used consistently across the problems in our benchmark. Otherwise the learned advice cannot meaningfully cary over to previously unsolved problems. While the assumption of aligned signature has been employed by the early systems [16,22], the most recent version of ENIGMA [15,24] can work in a "signature agnostic" mode.

In this work we represent clauses solely by their derivation history, deliberately ignoring their logical content. Thus we do not require the assumption of an aligned signature, per se. However, we rely on a fixed set of distinguished axioms to supply features in the derivation leaves.

2.3   Integrating the Learned Advice

Once we have a trained model $\mathcal{M}$, an immediate possibility for integrating it into the clause selection procedure is to introduce a new queue that will order the clauses using $\mathcal{M}$. Two basic versions of this idea have been described:

"Priority":   The ordering puts all the clauses classified by $\mathcal{M}$ as positive before those classified negatively. Within the two classes, older clauses are preferred.

Let us for the purposes of future reference denote this scheme $\mathcal{M}^{1,0}$. It has been successfully used by the early ENIGMAs [7, 16, 17].

"Logits":   Even models officially described as binary classifiers typically internally compute a real-valued estimate L of how much "positive" or "negative" an example appears to be and only turn this estimate into a binary decision in the last step, by comparing it against a fixed threshold t, most often 0. A machine learning term for this estimate L is the *logit*.[1]

The second version orders the clauses on the new queue by the "raw" logits produced by a model. We denote it $\mathcal{M}^{-\mathbb{R}}$ to stress that clauses with high L are treated as small from the perspective of the selection and therefore preferred. This scheme has been used by Loos et al. [22] and in the latest ENGIMA [15, 37].

Combining with a traditional strategy.   While it is possible to rely exclusively on selection governed by the model, it turns out to be better [7] to combine it with the traditional heuristics. The most natural choice is to take $\mathcal{S}$, the original strategy that was used to generate the training data, and extend it by adding the new queue, be it $\mathcal{M}^{1,0}$ or $\mathcal{M}^{-\mathbb{R}}$, next to the already present queues. We then again supply a ratio under which the original selection from $\mathcal{S}$ and the new selection based on $\mathcal{M}$ get alternated. We will denote this kind of combination with the original strategy as $\mathcal{S} \oplus \mathcal{M}^{1,0}$ and $\mathcal{S} \oplus \mathcal{M}^{-\mathbb{R}}$, respectively.

3   Layered Clause Selection and Lazy Model Evaluation

Layered clause selection (LCS) is a recently developed method [10, 11, 36] for smoothly incorporating a categorical preference for certain clauses into a base clause selection strategy $\mathcal{S}$. In this paper, we will readily use it in combination with the binary classifier advice from a trained model $\mathcal{M}$.

When we instantiate LCS to our particular case,[2] its function can be summarized by the expression

$$\mathcal{S} \oplus \mathcal{S}[\mathcal{M}^1].$$

In words, the base selection strategy $\mathcal{S}$ is alternated with $\mathcal{S}[\mathcal{M}^1]$, the same selection scheme $\mathcal{S}$ but applied only to clauses classified positively by $\mathcal{M}$. Implicit here is a convention that whenever there is no positively classified passive clause, a fallback to plain $\mathcal{S}$ occurs. Additionally, we again specify a "second-level" ratio to govern the alternation between pure $\mathcal{S}$ and $\mathcal{S}[\mathcal{M}^1]$.

The main advantage of LCS, compared to the options outlined in the previous section, is that the original, typically well-tuned, base selection mechanism $\mathcal{S}$ is also applied to $\mathcal{M}^1$, the clauses classified positively by $\mathcal{M}$.

---

[1]   A logit can be turned into a (formal) probability, i.e. a value between 0 and 1, by passing it, as is typically done, through the *sigmoid* function $\sigma(x) = 1/(1 + e^{-x})$.

[2]   We rely here on the *monotone* mode of split; there is also a *disjoint* mode [10].

3.1   Lazy Model Evaluation

It is often the case that evaluating a clause by the model $\mathcal{M}$ is a relatively expensive operation [22]. As we explain here, however, this operation can be avoided in many cases, especially when using LCS to integrate the advice.

We propose the following *lazy evaluation approach* to be used with $\mathcal{S} \oplus \mathcal{S}[\mathcal{M}^1]$. Every clause entering the passive set $\mathcal{P}$ is initially inserted to both $\mathcal{S}$ and $\mathcal{S}[\mathcal{M}^1]$ *without* being evaluated by $\mathcal{M}$. Then, whenever (as governed by the second-level ratio) it is the moment to select a clause from $\mathcal{S}[\mathcal{M}^1]$, the algorithm

1. picks (as usual, according to $\mathcal{S}$) the best clause C in $\mathcal{S}[\mathcal{M}^1]$,
2. only then evaluates C by $\mathcal{M}$, and
3. if C gets classified as negative, it forgets C, a goes back to 1.

This repeats until the first positively classified clause is found, which is then returned. Note that this way the "observable behaviour" of $\mathcal{S}[\mathcal{M}^1]$ is preserved.

The power of lazy evaluation lies in the fact that not every clause needs to be evaluated before a proof is found. Indeed, recall the remark that the passive set $\mathcal{P}$ is typically much larger than the active set $\mathcal{A}$, which also holds on a typical successful termination. Every clause left in passive at that moment is a clause that did not need to be evaluated by $\mathcal{M}$ thanks to lazy evaluation.

We remark that lazy evaluation can similarly be used with the integration mode $\mathcal{M}^{1,0}$ based on priorities.

We experimentally demonstrate the effect of the technique in Sect. 5.4.

4   A Neural Classification of Clause Derivations

In this work we choose to represent a clause, for the purpose of learning, solely by its derivation history. Thus a clause can only be distinguished by the axioms from which it was derived and by the precise way in which these axioms interacted with each other through inferences in the derivation. This means we deliberately ignore the clause's logical content.

We decided to focus on this representation, because it promises to be fast. Although an individual clause's derivation history may be large, it is a simple function of its parents' histories (just one application of an inference rule). Moreover, before a clause with a complicated history can be selected, most of its ancestors will have been selected already.[3] This guarantees the amortised cost of evaluating a single clause to be constant.

A second motivation comes from our recent work [11], where we have shown that theory reasoning facilitated by automatically adding theory axioms for axiomatising theories, while in itself a powerful technique, often leads the prover to unpromising parts of the search space. We developed a heuristic for controlling the amount of theory reasoning in the derivation of a clause [11]. Our goal here is to test whether a similar or even stronger heuristic can be automatically discovered by a neural network.

---

[3]   Exceptions are caused by simplifying inferences applied eagerly outside of the governance of the main clause selection mechanism.

Examples of axioms that Vampire uses to axiomatise theories include the commutativity or associativity axioms for the arithmetic operations, an axiomatization of the theory of arrays [6] or of the theory of term algebras [20]. For us it is mainly important that the axioms are introduced internally by the prover and can therefore be consistently identified across individual problems.

4.1 Recursive Neural Networks

A recursive neural network (RvNN) is a network created by *recursively* composing a finite set of neural building blocks over a structured input [12]. A general neural block is a function $N_\theta : \mathbb{R}^k \to \mathbb{R}^l$ depending on a vector of parameters θ that can be optimized during training (see below in Section 4.3).

In our case, the structured input is a clause derivation, i.e. a DAG with nodes identified with the derived clauses. To enable a recursion, an RvNN represents each node C by a real vector v_C (of a fixed dimension n) called a (learnable) *embedding*. During training a network learns to embed the space of derivable clauses into $\mathbb{R}^n$ in some a priori unknown, but still useful way.

We assume that each initial clause C, a leaf of the derivation DAG, is labeled as belonging to one of the automatically added theory axioms or coming from the user input. Let these labels form a finite set of *axiom origin labels* $\mathcal{L}_A$. Furthermore, let the applicable inference rules that label the internal nodes of the DAG form a finite set of *inference rule labels* $\mathcal{L}_R$. The specific building blocks of our neural architecture are the following three (indexed families of) functions:

- for every axiom label $l \in \mathcal{L}_A$, a nullary *init* function $I_l \in \mathbb{R}^n$ which to an initial clause C labeled by l assigns its embedding $v_C := I_l$,
- for every inference rule $r \in \mathcal{L}_R$, a *deriv* function, $D_r : \mathbb{R}^n \times \cdots \times \mathbb{R}^n \to \mathbb{R}^n$ which to a conclusion clause C_c derived by r from premises $(C_1, \ldots, C_k)$ with embeddings $v_{C_1}, \ldots, v_{C_k}$ assignes the embedding $v_{C_c} := D_r(v_{C_1}, \ldots, v_{C_k})$,
- and, finally, a single *eval* function $E : \mathbb{R}^n \to \mathbb{R}$ which evaluates an embedding v_C such that the corresponding clause C is classified as *positive* whenever $E(v_C) \geq t$, with the threshold t set, by default, to 0.

By recursively composing the init and deriv functions, any derived clause C can be assigned an embedding v_C and also evaluated by E to see whether the network recommends it as positive, that should be preferred in proof search.

4.2 Architecture Details

Here we outline the details of our architecture for the benefit of neural network practitioners. All the used terminology is standard (see, e.g., [13]).

We realized each init function I_l as an independent learnable vector. Similarly, each deriv function D_r was independently defined. For a rule of arity two, such as resolution, we used:

$$D_r(v_1, v_2) = \text{LayerNorm}(y), \quad y = W_2^r \cdot x + b_2^r, \quad x = \text{ReLU}(W_1^r \cdot [v_1, v_2] + b_1^r),$$

where $[\cdot, \cdot]$ denotes vector concatenation, ReLU is the rectified linear unit nonlinearity $(f(x) = \max\{0, x\})$ applied component-wise, and the learnable matrices

W_1^r, W_2^r and vectors b_1^r, b_2^r are such that $x \in \mathbb{R}^{2n}$ and $y \in \mathbb{R}^n$. (We took inspiration from Sandler et al. [29] for doubling the embedding size before applying the non-linearity.) Finally, LayerNorm is a *layer normalization* [2] module, without which training often became numerically unstable for deeper derivation DAGs.[4]

For unary inference rules, such as factoring, we used an equation analogous to the above, except for the concatenation operation. We did not need to model an inference rule with a variable number of premises, but one option would be to arbitrarily "bracket" its arguments into a tree of binary applications.

Finally, the eval function was $E(v) = W_2 \cdot \text{ReLU}(W_1 \cdot v + b) + c$ with trainable $W_1 \in \mathbb{R}^{n \times n}, b \in \mathbb{R}^n, W_2 \in \mathbb{R}^{1 \times n}$, and $c \in \mathbb{R}$.

4.3   Training the Network

To train a network means to find values for the trainable parameters such that it accurately classifies the training data and ideally also generalises to unseen future cases. We follow a standard methodology for training our RvNN.

In particular, we use the gradient descent (GD) optimization algorithm (with the Adam optimiser [19]) minimising the typical binary cross-entropy *loss*, composed as a sum of contributions, for every selected clause C, of the form

$$-y_C \cdot \log(\sigma(E(v_C))) - (1 - y_C) \cdot \log(1 - \sigma(E(v_C))),$$

with $y_C = 1$ for the positive and $y_C = 0$ for the negative examples.

These contributions are weighted such that each derivation DAG (corresponding to a prover run on a single problem) receives equal weight. Moreover, within each DAG we re-scale the influence of positive versus the negative examples such that these two categories contribute evenly. The scaling is important as our training data is highly unbalanced (cf. Sect. 5.1).

We split the available successful derivations into a *training* set and a *validation* set, and only train on the first set using the second to observe generalisation to unseen examples. As the GD algorithm progresses, iterating over the training data in rounds called *epochs*, we evaluate the loss on the validation set and stop the process early if this loss does not decrease for a specified period. This *early stopping* criterion was important to produce a model that generalizes well.

As another form of regularisation, i.e. a technique for preventing overfitting to the training data, we employ *dropout* [35] (independently for each "read" of a clause embedding by one of the deriv or eval functions). Dropout means that at training time each component v_i of the embedding v has a certain probability of being zero-ed out. This "voluntary brain damage" makes the network more robust as it prevents neurons from forming too complex co-adaptations [35].

Finally, we experimented with using non-constant learning rates as suggested by Smith et al. [33,34]. In the end, we used a schedule with a linear warmup for the first 50 epochs followed by a hyperbolic cooldown [38] (cf. Fig. 1 in Sect. 5.2).

---

[4]   We also tried to skip LayerNorm and replace ReLU by the hyperbolic tangent function. This restores stability, but does not train or classify so well.

4.4 An Abstraction for Compression and Caching

Since our representation of clauses deliberately discards information, we end up encountering distinct clauses indistinguishable from the perspective of the network. For example, every initial clause C originating from the input problem (as opposed to being added as a theory axiom) receives the same embedding $v_C = I_{input}$. Indistinguishable clauses also arise as conclusions of an inference that can be applied in more than one way to certain premises.

Mathematically, we deal with an equivalence relation $\sim$ on clauses based on "having the same derivation tree": $C_1 \sim C_2 \leftrightarrow derivation(C_1) = derivation(C_2)$. The "fingerprint" $derivation(C)$ of a clause could be defined as a formal expression recording the derivation history of C using the labels from $\mathcal{L}_A$ as nullary operators and those from $\mathcal{L}_R$ as operators with arities of the corresponding inference rules. For example: $Resolution(thax\_inverse\_assoc, Factoring(input))$.

We made use of this equivalence in our implementation in two places:

1. When preparing the training data. We "compressed" each derivation DAG as a factorisation by $\sim$, keeping only one representative of each class. A class containing a positive example was marked as a positive example.
2. When interfacing the trained model from the ATP. We cached the embeddings (and evaluated logits) for the already encountered clauses under their class identifier. Sect. 5.4 evaluates the effect of this technique.

5 Experiments

We implemented the infrastructure for training an RvNN clause derivation classifier (as described in Sect. 4) in Python, relying on the PyTorch (version 1.7) library [25] and its TorchScript extension for interfacing the trained model from C++. We modified the automatic theorem prover Vampire (version 4.5.1) to (1) optionally record to a log file the constructed derivation, including information on selected clauses and clauses found in the discovered proof (the *logging-mode*), (2) to be able to load a trained TorchScript model and use it for clause selection guidance under various modes of integration (detailed in Sects. 2.3 and 3).[5]

We took the same subset of 20 795 problems from the SMT-LIB library [5] as in previous work [11]: formed as the largest set of problems in a fragment supported by Vampire, excluding problems known to be satisfiable and those provable by Vampire's default strategy in 10 s either without adding theory axioms or while performing clause selection by age only.

As the baseline strategy S we took Vampire's implementation of the DISCOUNT saturation loop under the age-to-weight ratio 1:10 (which typically performs well with DISCOUNT), keeping all other settings default, including the enabled AVATAR architecture. We later enhanced this S with various forms of guidance. All the benchmarking was done using a 10 s time limit.[6]

---

[5] Supplementary materials can be found at https://git.io/JtHNl.
[6] Running on an Intel(R) Xeon(R) Gold 6140 CPUs @ 2.3 GHz server with 500 GB RAM, using no more than 30 of the available 72 cores to reduce mutual influence.

5.1   Data Preparation

During an initial run, the baseline strategy $\mathcal{S}$ was able to solve 734 problems under the 10 s time limit. We collected the corresponding successful derivations using the logging-mode (and lifting the time limit, since the logging causes a non-negligible overhead) and processed them into a form suitable for training a neural model. The derivations contained approximately 5.0 million clauses in total (the overall context), out of which 3.9 million were selected[7] (the training examples) and 30 thousand of these appeared in a proof (the positive examples). In these derivations, Vampire used 31 distinct theory axioms to facilitate theory reasoning. Including the "user input" label for clauses coming from the actual problem files, there were in total 32 distinct labels for the derivation leaves. In addition, we recorded 15 inference rules, such as resolution, superposition, backward and forward demodulation or subsumption resolution and including one rule for the derivation of a component clause in AVATAR [26,39]. Thus we obtained 15 distinct labels for the internal nodes.

We compressed these derivations identifying clauses with the same "abstract derivation history" dictated by the labels, as described in Sect. 4.4. This reduced the derivation set to 0.7 million nodes (i.e. abstracted clauses) in total. Out of the 734 derivations 242 were still larger than 1000 nodes (the largest had 6426 nodes) and each of these gave rise to a separate "mini-batch". We grouped the remaining 492 derivations to obtain an approximate size of 1000 nodes per mini-batch (the maximum was 12 original derivations grouped in one mini-batch). In total, we obtained 412 mini-batches and randomly singled out 330 (i.e., 80 %) of these for training, keeping 82 aside for validation.

5.2   Training

Since the size of the training set is relatively small, we instantiated the architecture described in Sect. 4.2 with embedding size $n = 64$ and dropout probability $p = 0.3$. We trained for 100 epochs, with a non-constant learning rate peaking at $\alpha = 2.5 \times 10^{-4}$ in epoch 50. Every epoch we computed the loss on the validation set and selected the model which minimizes this quantity. This was the model from epoch 45 in our case, which we will denote $\mathcal{M}$ here.

The development of the training and validation loss throughout training, as well as that of the learning rate, is plotted in Fig. 1. Additionally, the right side of the figure allows us to compare the validation loss—an ML estimate of the model's ability to generalize—with the ultimate metric of practical generalization, namely the number of in-training-unseen problems solved by Vampire equipped with the corresponding model for guidance.[8] We can see that the "proxy" (i.e. the minimisation of the validation loss) and the "target" (i.e. the maximisation of ATP performance) correspond quite well, at least to the degree that we measured the highest ATP gain with the validation-loss-minimizing $\mathcal{M}$.

---

[7] Ancestors of selected clauses are sometimes not selected clauses themselves if they arise through immediate simplifications or through reductions.

[8] Integrated using the layered scheme with a second level ratio 2:1 (cf. Sect. 5.3).

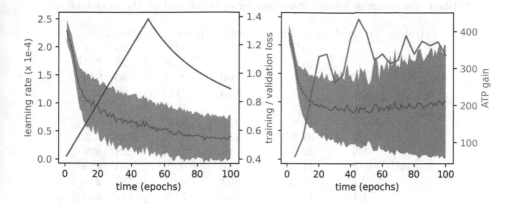

Fig. 1. Training the neural model. Red: the training (left) and validation (right) loss as a function training time; shaded: per problem weighted standard deviations. Blue (left): the supplied non-constant learning rate (cf. Sect. 4.3). Green (right): in training unseen problems solved by Vampire equipped with the corresponding model.

We remark that this assurance was not cheap to obtain. While the whole 100 epoch training took 45 minutes to complete (using 20 workers and 1 master process in a parallel training setup), each of the 20 ATP evaluation data points corresponds to approximately 2 hours of 30 core computation.

5.3   Advice Integration

In this part of the experiment we tested the various ways of integrating the learnt advice as described in Sects. 2.3 and 3. Let us recall that these are the single queue schemes $\mathcal{M}^{-\mathbb{R}}$ and $\mathcal{M}^{1,0}$ based on the raw logits and the binary decision, respectively, their combinations $\mathcal{S} \oplus \mathcal{M}^{-\mathbb{R}}$ and $\mathcal{S} \oplus \mathcal{M}^{1,0}$ with the base strategy $\mathcal{S}$ under some second level ratio, and, finally, $\mathcal{S} \oplus \mathcal{S}[\mathcal{M}^1]$, the integration of the guidance by the layered clause selection scheme.

Our results are shown in Table 1. It starts by reporting on the performance of the baseline strategy $\mathcal{S}$ and then compares it to the other strategies (the gained and lost columns are w.r.t. the original run of $\mathcal{S}$).[9] We can see that the two single queue approaches are quite weak, with the better $\mathcal{M}^{1,0}$ solving only 25 % of the baseline. Nor can the combination $\mathcal{S} \oplus \mathcal{M}^{-\mathbb{R}}$ be considered a success, as it only solves more problems when less and less advice is taken, seemingly approaching the performance of $\mathcal{S}$ from below. This trend repeats with $\mathcal{S} \oplus \mathcal{M}^{1,0}$, although here an interesting number of problems not solved by the baseline is gained by strategies which rely on the advice more than half of the time.

With our model $\mathcal{M}$, only the layered clause selection integration $\mathcal{S} \oplus \mathcal{S}[\mathcal{M}^1]$ is able to improve on the performance of the baseline strategy $\mathcal{S}$. In fact, it

---

[9]   We had to switch to a different machine after producing the training data. There, a rerun of $\mathcal{S}$ gave a slightly better performance than the 734 solved problems used for training. We still used the original run's results to compute the gained and lost values here; the percentage solved is with respect to the new run of $\mathcal{S}$.

Table 1. Performance results of various forms of integrating the model advice.

strategy	ratio	$\mathcal{M}$ eval. time%	#solved (percent $\mathcal{S}$)		gained	lost
$\mathcal{S}$	–	0%	756	100%	26	4
$\mathcal{M}^{-\mathbb{R}}$	–	25%	55	7%	25	704
$\mathcal{M}^{1,0}$	–	13%	**190**	25%	**30**	574
$\mathcal{S} \oplus \mathcal{M}^{-\mathbb{R}}$	5:1	57%	**543**	71%	86	277
	2:1	48%	445	58%	78	367
	1:1	41%	335	44%	54	453
	1:2	32%	248	32%	39	525
	1:5	32%	140	18%	28	622
$\mathcal{S} \oplus \mathcal{M}^{1,0}$	10:1	11%	**686**	90%	80	**128**
	2:1	14%	602	79%	112	244
	1:1	14%	555	73%	111	290
	1:2	14%	519	68%	**132**	347
	1:10	14%	520	68%	**132**	346
$\mathcal{S} \oplus \mathcal{S}[\mathcal{M}^1]$	2:1	27%	855	113%	210	**89**
	1:1	32%	1032	136%	411	113
	1:2	33%	**1036**	137%	**430**	128
	1:3	30%	1026	135%	428	136
	1:5	25%	989	130%	405	150

Table 2. Performance decrease caused by turning off abstraction caching and lazy evaluation, and both; demonstrated on $\mathcal{S} \oplus \mathcal{S}[\mathcal{M}^1]$ under the second level ratio 1:2.

	$\mathcal{M}$ eval. time%	#solved (percent $\mathcal{S}$)	
both techniques enabled	33%	1036	137%
without abstraction caching	45%	1007	133%
without lazy evaluation	58%	905	119%
both techniques disabled	73%	782	103%

improves on it very significantly: with the second level ratio of 1:2 we achieve 137% performance of the baseline and gain 430 problems unsolved by $\mathcal{S}$.

5.4   Evaluation Speed, Lazy Evaluation, and Abstraction Caching

Table 1 also shows the percentage of computation time the individual strategies spent evaluating the advice, i.e. interfacing $\mathcal{M}$.

A word of warning first. These number are hard to interpret across different strategies. It is because different guidance steers the prover to different parts of the search space. For example, notice the seemingly paradoxical situation most pronounced with $\mathcal{S} \oplus \mathcal{M}^{-\mathbb{R}}$, where the more often is the advice from $\mathcal{M}$ nominally requested, the less time the prover spends interfacing $\mathcal{M}$. Looking closely at a few problems, we discovered that in strategies relying a lot on $\mathcal{M}^{-\mathbb{R}}$, such as $\mathcal{S} \oplus \mathcal{M}^{-\mathbb{R}}$ under the ratio 1:5, most of the time is spent performing forward subsumption. An explanation is that the guidance becomes increasingly bad and the prover slows down, processing larger and larger clauses for which the subsumption checks are expensive and dominate the runtime.[10]

---

[10] A similar experience with bad guidance has been made by the authors of ENIGMA.

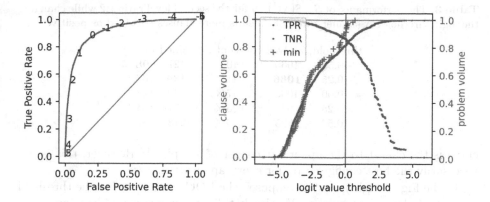

Fig. 2. The receiver operating characteristic curve (left) and a related plot with explicit threshold (right) for the selected model $\mathcal{M}$; both based on validation data.

When the guidance is the same, however, we can use the eval. time percentage to estimate the efficiency of the integration. The results shown in Table 1 were obtained using both lazy evaluation[11] and abstraction caching (as described in sections 3.1 and 4.4). Taking the best performing $\mathcal{S} \oplus \mathcal{S}[\mathcal{M}^1]$ under the second level ratio 1:2, we selectively disabled: first abstraction caching, then lazy evaluation and finally both techniques, obtaining the values shown in Table 2.

We can see that the techniques considerably contribute to the overall performance. Indeed, without them Vampire would spend the whole 73 % of computation time evaluating the network (compared to only 33 %) and the strategy would barely match (with 103 %) the performance of the baseline $\mathcal{S}$.

5.5   Positive Bias

Two important characteristics, from a machine learning perspective, of an obtained model are the *true positive rate* (TPR) (also called sensitivity) and the *true negative rate* (TNR) (also specificity). TPR is defined as the fraction of positively labeled examples which the model also classifies as such. TNR is, analogously, the fraction of negatively labeled examples. Our model $\mathcal{M}$ achieves (on the validation set) 86 % TPR and 81 % TNR.

The final judgement of a neural classifier follows from a comparison to a threshold value t, set by default to $t = 0$ (recall Sect. 4.1). Changing this threshold allows us to trade TPR for TNR and vice versa in straightforward way. The interdependence of these two values on the varied threshold is traditionally captured by the so called *receiver operating characteristic* (ROC) curve, shown for our model in Fig. 2 (left). The tradition dictates that the x axis be labeled by the false positive rate (FPR) (also called fall-out) which is simply $1 - TNR$. Under such presentation, one generally strives to pick a threshold value at which the

---

[11] With the exception of the $\mathcal{M}^{-\mathbb{R}}$ guidance, with which it is incompatible.

Table 3. The performance of $\mathcal{S} \oplus \mathcal{S}[\mathcal{M}^1]$ under the second level ratio 1:2 while changing the logit threshold. A smaller threshold means more clauses classified as positive.

threshold	#solved	(percent $\mathcal{S}$)	gained	lost
−0.50	1063	140 %	427	**98**
−0.25	**1066**	141 %	**439**	107
0.00	1036	137 %	430	128
0.25	945	125 %	375	164
0.50	825	109 %	278	187

curve is the closest to the upper left corner of the plot.[12] However, this is not necessarily the best configuration for every application.

In the Fig. 2 (right), we "decompose" the ROC curve by using the threshold t for the independent axis x. We also highlight, for every problem (again, in the validation set), what is the minimal logit value across all positively labeled examples belonging to that problem. In other words, what is the logit of the "least positively classified" clause from the problem's proof. We can see that for the majority of the problems these minima are below the threshold $t = 0$. This means that for those problems at least one clause from the original proof is getting classified as negative by $\mathcal{M}$ under $t = 0$.

These observations motivated us to experiment with non-zero values of the threshold in an ATP evaluation. Particularly promising seemed the use of a threshold t smaller than zero with the intention of classifying more clauses as positive. The results of the experiment are in shown Table 3. Indeed, we could further improve the best performing strategy from Table 1 with both $t = −0.25$ and $t = −0.5$. It can be seen that smaller values lead to fewer problems lost, but even the ATP gain is better with $t = −0.25$ than with the default $t = 0$, leading to the overall best improvement of 141 % with respect to the baseline $\mathcal{S}$.

5.6   Learning from Guided Proofs and Negative Mining

As previously unsolved problems get proven with the help of the trained guidance, the new proofs can be used to enrich the training set and potentially help obtaining even better models. This idea of alternating the training and the ATP evaluation steps in a reinforcing *loop* has been proposed and successfully realized by the authors of ENIGMA on the Mizar dataset [18]. Here we propose an enhancement of the idea and repeat an analogous experiment in our setting.

By collecting proofs discovered by a selection of 8 different configurations tested in the previous sections, we grew our set of solved problems from 734 to 1528. We decided to keep one proof per problem, strictly extending the original training set. We then repeated the same training procedure as described in Sect. 5.2 on this new set and on an extension of this set obtained as follows.

Negative mining: We suspected that the successful derivations obtained with the help of $\mathcal{M}$ might not contain enough "typical wrong decisions" from the

---

[12] Minimizing the standard cross entropy loss should actually automatically "bring the curve" close to that corner for the threshold $t = 0$.

Table 4. The performance of new models learned from guided proofs. $\mathcal{U}$ is the set of 1528 problems used for the training. The gained and lost counts are here w.r.t. $\mathcal{U}$.

	#solved	(percent $\mathcal{S}$)	(percent $|\mathcal{U}|$)	gained	lost
plain	1268	167 %	82 %	90	350
with negative mining	**1394**	**184 %**	91 %	**140**	**274**

perspective of $\mathcal{S}$ to provide for good enough training. We therefore logged the *failing* runs of $\mathcal{S}$ on the $(1528 - 734)$ problems only solved by one of the guided strategies and augmented the corresponding derivations with these.[13]

Table 4 confirms[14] that negative mining indeed helps to produce a better model. Mainly, however, it shows that training from additional derivations further dramatically improves the performance of the obtained strategy.

6   Conclusion

We revisited the topic of ENIGMA-style clause selection guidance by a machine learned binary classifier and proposed four improvements to previous work: (1) the use of layered clause selection for integrating the advice, (2) the lazy evaluation trick to reduce the overhead of interfacing a potentially expensive model, (3) the "positive bias" idea suggesting to be really careful not to discard potentially useful clauses, and (4) the "negative mining" technique to provide enough negative examples when learning from proofs obtained with previous guidance.

We have also shown that a strong advice can be obtained by looking just at the derivation history to discriminate a clause. The automatically discovered neural guidance significantly improves upon the human-engineered heuristic [11] under identical conditions. Rerunning $\mathcal{S}$ with the theory heuristic enabled in its default form [10] resulted here in 816 (107 %) solved problems.

By deliberately focusing of the representation of clauses by their derivations, we obtained some nice properties, such as relative speed of evaluation. However, in situations where theory reasoning by automatically added theory axioms is not prevalent, such as on most of the TPTP library, we expect guidance based on derivations with just a single axiom origin label, the *input*, to be quite weak.

Still, we see a great opportunity in using statistical methods for analyzing ATP behaviour; not only for improving prover performance with a black box guidance, but also as a tool for discovering regularities that could be exploited to improve our understanding of the technology on a deeper level.

Acknowledgement

This work was supported by the Czech Science Foundation project 20-06390Y and the project RICAIP no. 857306 under the EU-H2020 programme. We also thank the anonymous reviewers for suggesting numerous improvements.

---

[13] Negative mining has, for instance, been previously used when training deep models for the premise selection task [14].

[14] The ATP eval was again integrating via $\mathcal{S} \oplus \mathcal{S}[\mathcal{M}^1]$ under the second level ratio 1:2.

References

1. Aygün, E., Ahmed, Z., Anand, A., Firoiu, V., Glorot, X., Orseau, L., et al.: Learning to prove from synthetic theorems. CoRR **abs/2006.11259** (2020)
2. Ba, L.J., Kiros, J.R., Hinton, G.E.: Layer normalization. CoRR **abs/1607.06450** (2016)
3. Bachmair, L., Ganzinger, H.: Rewrite-based equational theorem proving with selection and simplification. J. Log. Comput. **4**(3), 217–247 (1994). https://doi.org/10.1093/logcom/4.3.217
4. Bachmair, L., Ganzinger, H.: Resolution theorem proving. In: Robinson and Voronkov [28], pp. 19–99. https://doi.org/10.1016/b978-044450813-3/50004-7
5. Barrett, C., Fontaine, P., Tinelli, C.: The Satisfiability Modulo Theories Library (SMT-LIB) (2016), www.SMT-LIB.org
6. Bradley, A.R., Manna, Z., Sipma, H.B.: What's decidable about arrays? In: Emerson, E.A., Namjoshi, K.S. (eds.) Verification, Model Checking, and Abstract Interpretation, 7th International Conference, VMCAI 2006, Charleston, SC, USA, January 8-10, 2006, Proceedings. LNCS, vol. 3855, pp. 427–442. Springer (2006). https://doi.org/10.1007/11609773_28
7. Chvalovský, K., Jakubuv, J., Suda, M., Urban, J.: ENIGMA-NG: efficient neural and gradient-boosted inference guidance for E. In: Fontaine [9], pp. 197–215. https://doi.org/10.1007/978-3-030-29436-6_12
8. Denzinger, J., Schulz, S.: Learning Domain Knowledge to Improve Theorem Proving. In: McRobbie, M., Slaney, J. (eds.) Proc. of the 13th CADE, New Brunswick. pp. 62–76. No. 1104 in LNAI, Springer (1996)
9. Fontaine, P. (ed.): Automated Deduction - CADE 27 - 27th International Conference on Automated Deduction, Natal, Brazil, August 27-30, 2019, Proceedings, LNCS, vol. 11716. Springer (2019). https://doi.org/10.1007/978-3-030-29436-6
10. Gleiss, B., Suda, M.: Layered clause selection for saturation-based theorem proving. In: Fontaine, P., Korovin, K., Kotsireas, I.S., Rümmer, P., Tourret, S. (eds.) Joint Proceedings of the 7th Workshop on Practical Aspects of Automated Reasoning (PAAR) and the 5th Satisfiability Checking and Symbolic Computation Workshop (SC-Square), co-located with the 10th International Joint Conference on Automated Reasoning (IJCAR 2020), Paris, France, June-July, 2020 (Virtual). CEUR Workshop Proceedings, vol. 2752, pp. 34–52. CEUR-WS.org (2020), http://ceur-ws.org/Vol-2752/paper3.pdf
11. Gleiss, B., Suda, M.: Layered clause selection for theory reasoning - (short paper). In: Peltier, N., Sofronie-Stokkermans, V. (eds.) Automated Reasoning - 10th International Joint Conference, IJCAR 2020, Paris, France, July 1-4, 2020, Proceedings, Part I. LNCS, vol. 12166, pp. 402–409. Springer (2020). https://doi.org/10.1007/978-3-030-51074-9_23
12. Goller, C., Küchler, A.: Learning task-dependent distributed representations by backpropagation through structure. In: Proceedings of International Conference on Neural Networks (ICNN'96), Washington, DC, USA, June 3-6, 1996. pp. 347–352. IEEE (1996). https://doi.org/10.1109/ICNN.1996.548916
13. Goodfellow, I.J., Bengio, Y., Courville, A.C.: Deep Learning. Adaptive computation and machine learning, MIT Press (2016), http://www.deeplearningbook.org/
14. Irving, G., Szegedy, C., Alemi, A.A., Eén, N., Chollet, F., Urban, J.: Deepmath - deep sequence models for premise selection. In: Lee, D.D., Sugiyama, M., von Luxburg, U., Guyon, I., Garnett, R. (eds.) Advances in Neural Information Processing Systems 29: Annual Conference on Neural Information Processing Systems 2016, December 5-10, 2016, Barcelona,

Spain. pp. 2235–2243 (2016), https://proceedings.neurips.cc/paper/2016/hash/f197002b9a0853eca5e046d9ca4663d5-Abstract.html

15. Jakubuv, J., Chvalovský, K., Olšák, M., Piotrowski, B., Suda, M., Urban, J.: ENIGMA anonymous: Symbol-independent inference guiding machine (system description). In: Peltier, N., Sofronie-Stokkermans, V. (eds.) Automated Reasoning - 10th International Joint Conference, IJCAR 2020, Paris, France, July 1-4, 2020, Proceedings, Part II. LNCS, vol. 12167, pp. 448–463. Springer (2020). https://doi.org/10.1007/978-3-030-51054-1_29

16. Jakubuv, J., Urban, J.: ENIGMA: efficient learning-based inference guiding machine. In: Geuvers, H., England, M., Hasan, O., Rabe, F., Teschke, O. (eds.) Intelligent Computer Mathematics - 10th International Conference, CICM 2017, Edinburgh, UK, July 17-21, 2017, Proceedings. LNCS, vol. 10383, pp. 292–302. Springer (2017). https://doi.org/10.1007/978-3-319-62075-6_20

17. Jakubuv, J., Urban, J.: Enhancing ENIGMA given clause guidance. In: Rabe, F., Farmer, W.M., Passmore, G.O., Youssef, A. (eds.) Intelligent Computer Mathematics - 11th International Conference, CICM 2018, Hagenberg, Austria, August 13-17, 2018, Proceedings. LNCS, vol. 11006, pp. 118–124. Springer (2018). https://doi.org/10.1007/978-3-319-96812-4_11

18. Jakubuv, J., Urban, J.: Hammering Mizar by learning clause guidance (short paper). In: Harrison, J., O'Leary, J., Tolmach, A. (eds.) 10th International Conference on Interactive Theorem Proving, ITP 2019, September 9-12, 2019, Portland, OR, USA. LIPIcs, vol. 141, pp. 34:1–34:8. Schloss Dagstuhl - Leibniz-Zentrum für Informatik (2019). https://doi.org/10.4230/LIPIcs.ITP.2019.34

19. Kingma, D.P., Ba, J.: Adam: A method for stochastic optimization. In: Bengio, Y., LeCun, Y. (eds.) 3rd International Conference on Learning Representations, ICLR 2015, San Diego, CA, USA, May 7-9, 2015, Conference Track Proceedings (2015), http://arxiv.org/abs/1412.6980

20. Kovács, L., Robillard, S., Voronkov, A.: Coming to terms with quantified reasoning. In: Castagna, G., Gordon, A.D. (eds.) Proceedings of the 44th ACM SIGPLAN Symposium on Principles of Programming Languages, POPL 2017, Paris, France, January 18-20, 2017. pp. 260–270. ACM (2017). https://doi.org/10.1145/3009837.3009887

21. Kovács, L., Voronkov, A.: First-order theorem proving and Vampire. In: Sharygina, N., Veith, H. (eds.) Computer Aided Verification - 25th International Conference, CAV 2013, Saint Petersburg, Russia, July 13-19, 2013. Proceedings. LNCS, vol. 8044, pp. 1–35. Springer (2013). https://doi.org/10.1007/978-3-642-39799-8_1

22. Loos, S.M., Irving, G., Szegedy, C., Kaliszyk, C.: Deep network guided proof search. In: Eiter, T., Sands, D. (eds.) LPAR-21, 21st International Conference on Logic for Programming, Artificial Intelligence and Reasoning, Maun, Botswana, May 7-12, 2017. EPiC Series in Computing, vol. 46, pp. 85–105. EasyChair (2017). https://doi.org/10.29007/8mwc

23. Nieuwenhuis, R., Rubio, A.: Paramodulation-based theorem proving. In: Robinson and Voronkov [28], pp. 371–443. https://doi.org/10.1016/b978-044450813-3/50009-6

24. Olšák, M., Kaliszyk, C., Urban, J.: Property invariant embedding for automated reasoning. In: Giacomo, G.D., Catalá, A., Dilkina, B., Milano, M., Barro, S., Bugarín, A., Lang, J. (eds.) ECAI 2020 - 24th European Conference on Artificial Intelligence, 29 August-8 September 2020, Santiago de Compostela, Spain, August 29 - September 8, 2020 - Including 10th Conference on Prestigious Applications of Artificial Intelligence (PAIS 2020). Frontiers in Artifi-

cial Intelligence and Applications, vol. 325, pp. 1395–1402. IOS Press (2020). https://doi.org/10.3233/FAIA200244

25. Paszke, A., Gross, S., Massa, F., Lerer, A., Bradbury, J., Chanan, G., et al.: Pytorch: An imperative style, high-performance deep learning library. In: Wallach, H., Larochelle, H., Beygelzimer, A., dAlché-Buc, F., Fox, E., Garnett, R. (eds.) Advances in Neural Information Processing Systems 32, pp. 8024–8035. Curran Associates, Inc. (2019), http://papers.neurips.cc/paper/9015-pytorch-an-imperative-style-high-performance-deep-learning-library.pdf

26. Reger, G., Suda, M., Voronkov, A.: Playing with AVATAR. In: Felty, A.P., Middeldorp, A. (eds.) Automated Deduction - CADE-25 - 25th International Conference on Automated Deduction, Berlin, Germany, August 1-7, 2015, Proceedings. LNCS, vol. 9195, pp. 399–415. Springer (2015). https://doi.org/10.1007/978-3-319-21401-6_28

27. Riazanov, A., Voronkov, A.: Limited resource strategy in resolution theorem proving. J. Symb. Comput. 36(1-2), 101–115 (2003). https://doi.org/10.1016/S0747-7171(03)00040-3

28. Robinson, J.A., Voronkov, A. (eds.): Handbook of Automated Reasoning (in 2 volumes). Elsevier and MIT Press (2001)

29. Sandler, M., Howard, A.G., Zhu, M., Zhmoginov, A., Chen, L.: Mobilenetv2: Inverted residuals and linear bottlenecks. In: 2018 IEEE Conference on Computer Vision and Pattern Recognition, CVPR 2018, Salt Lake City, UT, USA, June 18-22, 2018. pp. 4510–4520. IEEE Computer Society (2018). https://doi.org/10.1109/CVPR.2018.00474

30. Schulz, S.: Learning Search Control Knowledge for Equational Deduction. No. 230 in DISKI, Akademische Verlagsgesellschaft Aka GmbH Berlin (2000)

31. Schulz, S., Cruanes, S., Vukmirovic, P.: Faster, higher, stronger: E 2.3. In: Fontaine [9], pp. 495–507. https://doi.org/10.1007/978-3-030-29436-6_29

32. Schulz, S., Möhrmann, M.: Performance of clause selection heuristics for saturation-based theorem proving. In: Olivetti, N., Tiwari, A. (eds.) Automated Reasoning - 8th International Joint Conference, IJCAR 2016, Coimbra, Portugal, June 27 - July 2, 2016, Proceedings. LNCS, vol. 9706, pp. 330–345. Springer (2016). https://doi.org/10.1007/978-3-319-40229-1_23

33. Smith, L.N.: Cyclical learning rates for training neural networks. In: 2017 IEEE Winter Conference on Applications of Computer Vision, WACV 2017, Santa Rosa, CA, USA, March 24-31, 2017. pp. 464–472. IEEE Computer Society (2017). https://doi.org/10.1109/WACV.2017.58

34. Smith, L.N., Topin, N.: Super-convergence: Very fast training of residual networks using large learning rates. CoRR **abs/1708.07120** (2017)

35. Srivastava, N., Hinton, G.E., Krizhevsky, A., Sutskever, I., Salakhutdinov, R.: Dropout: a simple way to prevent neural networks from overfitting. J. Mach. Learn. Res. **15**(1), 1929–1958 (2014), http://dl.acm.org/citation.cfm?id=2670313

36. Tammet, T.: GKC: A reasoning system for large knowledge bases. In: Fontaine [9], pp. 538–549. https://doi.org/10.1007/978-3-030-29436-6_32

37. Urban, J.: personal communication

38. Vaswani, A., Shazeer, N., Parmar, N., Uszkoreit, J., Jones, L., Gomez, A.N., et al.: Attention is all you need. In: Guyon, I., von Luxburg, U., Bengio, S., Wallach, H.M., Fergus, R., Vishwanathan, S.V.N., Garnett, R. (eds.) Advances in Neural Information Processing Systems 30: Annual Conference on Neural Information Processing Systems 2017, December 4-9, 2017, Long Beach, CA, USA. pp. 5998–6008 (2017), https://proceedings.neurips.cc/paper/2017/hash/3f5ee243547dee91fbd053c1c4a845aa-Abstract.html

39. Voronkov, A.: AVATAR: the architecture for first-order theorem provers. In: Biere, A., Bloem, R. (eds.) Computer Aided Verification - 26th International Conference, CAV 2014, Held as Part of the Vienna Summer of Logic, VSL 2014, Vienna, Austria, July 18-22, 2014. Proceedings. LNCS, vol. 8559, pp. 696–710. Springer (2014). https://doi.org/10.1007/978-3-319-08867-9_46

40. Weidenbach, C., Dimova, D., Fietzke, A., Kumar, R., Suda, M., Wischnewski, P.: SPASS version 3.5. In: Schmidt, R.A. (ed.) Automated Deduction - CADE-22, 22nd International Conference on Automated Deduction, Montreal, Canada, August 2-7, 2009. Proceedings. LNCS, vol. 5663, pp. 140–145. Springer (2009). https://doi.org/10.1007/978-3-642-02959-2_10

Open Access This chapter is licensed under the terms of the Creative Commons Attribution 4.0 International License (http://creativecommons.org/licenses/by/4.0/), which permits use, sharing, adaptation, distribution and reproduction in any medium or format, as long as you give appropriate credit to the original author(s) and the source, provide a link to the Creative Commons license and indicate if changes were made.

The images or other third party material in this chapter are included in the chapter's Creative Commons license, unless indicated otherwise in a credit line to the material. If material is not included in the chapter's Creative Commons license and your intended use is not permitted by statutory regulation or exceeds the permitted use, you will need to obtain permission directly from the copyright holder.

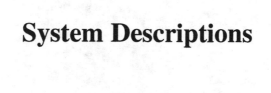

System Descriptions

A Normative Supervisor for Reinforcement Learning Agents

Emery Neufeld[1], Ezio Bartocci[1], Agata Ciabattoni[1], and Guido
Governatori[2]

^{1} TU Wien, Vienna, Austria
^{2} Data61, CSIRO, Melbourne, Australia

Abstract. We introduce a modular and transparent approach for augmenting the ability of reinforcement learning agents to comply with a
given norm base. The normative supervisor module functions as both
an event recorder and real-time compliance checker w.r.t. an external
norm base. We have implemented this module with a theorem prover for
defeasible deontic logic, in a reinforcement learning agent that we task
with playing a "vegan" version of the arcade game Pac-Man.

1 Introduction

Autonomous agents are an increasingly integral part of modern life. While
performing activities formerly reserved for human agents, they must possess
the ability to adapt to (potentially unpredictable) changes in their environment;
reinforcement learning (RL) has proven a successful method for teaching agents
this behaviour (see, e.g. [16,13]). Performing human roles further requires that
agents align themselves with the ethical standards their human counterparts are
subject to, introducing a requirement for ethical reasoning. RL has been employed
to enforce such standards as well (see, e.g., [14]); agents can be trained to act
in line with further rewards/penalties assigned according to the performance
of ethical/unethical behaviour through a reward function. However, this does
not provide a guarantee of the desired behaviour. Moreover, such techniques are
not well equipped to handle the complexities of ethical reasoning. In general,
like other black-box machine learning methods, RL cannot transparently explain
why a certain policy is compliant or not. Additionally, when the ethical values
are embedded in the learning process, a small change in their definition would
require us to retrain the policy from scratch.

To obviate the limitations of RL to represent ethical norms, the approach
we follow in this paper combines RL with Deontic Logic, the branch of formal
logic that is concerned with prescriptive statements; we implement a normative
supervisor to inform a trained RL agent of the ethical requirements in force in a
given situation. Since the pioneering works [17,15], it has been well understood
that Deontic Logic can be applied to model ethical norms; the difference between
ethical and legal norms is indeed only on how they emerge, not what normative
consequences are entailed by them. We implement our normative supervisor using

---

^{1} This work was partially supported by WWTF project MA16-28 and the DC-RES run by the TU
Wien's Faculty of Informatics and the FH-Technikum Wien.

© The Author(s) 2021
A. Platzer and G. Sutcliffe (Eds.): CADE 2021, LNAI 12699, pp. 565–576, 2021.
https://doi.org/10.1007/978-3-030-79876-5_32

defeasible deontic logic [8,9]. This is a simple and computationally feasible, yet expressive, logic allowing for defeasible reasoning, and can easily accommodate changes to the norm base, should the ethical requirements become more complex (see Sect. 3.4 for a brief walk-through). Moreover, the constructive nature of this logic allows us to determine how a given conclusion has been reached.

By embedding the normative supervisor into the RL agent architecture, the agent can follow near-optimal learned policies while enforcing ethical actions in a modular and transparent way. The supervisor functions as both an event recorder and real-time compliance checker; it corrects the choice of a given action from the policy only when this violates a norm. It is furthermore used as an event logger to identify and extract new sets of (ethical) norms to promote particular goals. We demonstrate our approach on an RL agent that plays a "vegan" version of *Pac-Man*, with an "ethical" constraint forbidding Pac-Man from eating ghosts. Already used as a case study in [14,10], the *Pac-Man* game is a closed environment for testing with clearly defined game mechanics and parameters which are easy to isolate, manipulate, and extend with variably intricate rule sets. We successfully evaluated our approach with several tests, consisting of "vegan" games and a "vegetarian" version of the game where the agent can eat only one type of ghost. The achievement of full compliance in the latter case was possible with the introduction of additional norms identified via the event recorder.

Related Work. The papers [14] and [10] on Pac-Man motivated our work. The former employs multi-objective RL with policy orchestration to impose normative constraints on vegan Pac-Man. It seamlessly combines ethically compliant behaviour and learned optimal behaviour; however, the ethical reasoning performed is still to a degree implicit, it does not provide justifications for the choices made, and it is not clear how the approach would remain reasonably transparent with more complex norm sets. [10] takes steps to integrate more complex constraints on a RL agent, but as they are embedded in the learned policy, it lacks the transparency of a logic-based implementation. [1] and [2] address the problem of transparency in the implementation of ethical behaviours in AI, but their approach has not been implemented and tested yet. Symbolic reasoning for implementing ethically compliant behaviour in autonomous agents has been used in many frameworks, such as [5], which models the behaviour from a BDI perspective. This approach does not allow for defeasible reasoning, and focuses on avoiding ethical non-compliance at the planning level. Non-monotonic logic-based approaches that extend BDI with a normative component appear in [6,9], whose solutions remain only at the theoretical level. These papers belong to the related field of Normative Multi-Agent Systems, which is not specifically concerned with the ethical behaviour of agents [3], and whose introduced formalisms and tools (e.g. [12]) have not yet been used in combination with RL.

2   Background

Normative Reasoning. Normative reasoning differs from the reasoning captured by classical logic in that the focus is not on true or false statements, but rather the imposition of norms onto such statements.

We will deal with two types of norms: constitutive and regulative norms (see [4] for the terminology). Regulative norms describe obligations, prohibitions and permissions. Constitutive norms regulate instead the creation of institutional facts as well as the modification of the normative system itself; their content is a relation between two concepts, and they will typically take the form "in context c, concept x counts as concept y", where x refers to a more concrete concept (e.g., walking) and y to a more abstract one (e.g., moving). We say concept x is at a lower level of abstraction than concept y in context c if there is a constitutive norm with context c asserting that x counts as y (henceforth denoted $\mathbf{C}(x, y)$).

Reinforcement Learning (RL). RL refers to a class of algorithms specialized in learning how an agent should act in its environment to maximize the expected cumulative reward. Given a function that assigns rewards/penalties to each state and successor state pair (or state-action pairs), the RL algorithm learns an optimal policy, a function from states to actions that can govern its behaviour.

In our case study we chose Q-learning [18] with function approximation as a RL algorithm. In Q-learning, the RL algorithm first learns a function $Q(s, a)$ to predict the expected cumulative reward (Q-value) from state s taking action a. The learned policy picks the action $argmax_{a \in possible} \ Q(s, a)$ with the highest Q-value over a list of possible actions. The function Q is approximated as a linear function which is the weighted sum of features describing some elements of the environment (e.g., the distance between the agent and object X); the features which are most relevant to predicting the agent success are weighted most heavily.

Vegan Pac-Man. In the arcade game *Pac-Man*, an eponymous agent is situated inside a maze over a grid, where some cells contain a 'food pellet' which Pac-Man will eat if it moves inside the cell. Pac-Man's goal is to maximize his score; when Pac-Man eats a food pellet he gains a reward (+10 points), but there is also a time penalty (−1 point for every time step). Pac-Man wins when he has eaten all the food pellets in the maze (resulting in +500 points), and he loses if he collides with one of the ghost agents wandering around the maze (resulting in −500 points). However, after eating a 'power pellet' (of which there are two), the ghosts become 'scared', and Pac-Man can eat them (for +200 points).

Inspired by [14], we consider a variation of the UC Berkeley AI Pac-Man implementation [7], where Pac-Man cannot eat ghosts (only blue ghosts in the vegetarian version). Our Pac-Man agent utilizes a Q-learning policy; for the utility function we use the game's score, and we take the game states as states. We use the same game layout as in [14]; this is a 20×11 maze populated with 97 food pellets and two ghosts (blue and orange) which follow random paths, where the maximum score available is 2170, and 1370 when eating ghosts is forbidden.

3   The Normative Supervisor

The key component of our approach is a *normative supervisor* whose architecture is illustrated in Fig. 1. This module consists of a normative reasoning engine (we use the SPINdle theorem prover [11]), and of other components that encode the

norms and environmental data into defeasible deontic logic rules, and translate
the conclusions of the reasoning engine into instructions for the agent.

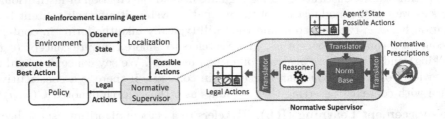

Fig. 1. Key components and placement of the Normative Supervisor.

We place the normative supervisor in the already-trained agent's control loop
between the localization and policy module. The localization module identifies
the current agent's state with respect to its environment and returns a list of
possible actions to the normative supervisor. This module filters out all the
actions that are not compliant with the norms. The policy will then identify,
among the pool of the compliant actions, the optimal one for generating the next
game state. If there are no available compliant actions the normative supervisor
will select the 'lesser evil' action. This module additionally enables the logging of
events during the game for later scrutiny.

3.1   Configuring the Norm Base

We start with a simple normative prescription, consisting only of the behavioral
constraint proposed in [14] that "Pac-Man must not eat ghosts"[2], represented as
$vegan : \mathbf{F}(eat(pacman, ghost))$, where $\mathbf{F}$ denotes prohibition.

If this norm base is to inform our agent's actions, it needs to reference concepts
that correspond to the information directly processed by the agent, which is
limited to the locations of game entities and the actions that Pac-Man can
perform, which we denote as *North, South, East, West*, and *Stop*. The only
way $eat(pacman, ghost)$ can be done is if (a) the ghost is in a 'scared' state,
and (b) Pac-Man and the ghost move into the same cell. These are expressed
as $scared(ghost)$ and $inRange(pacman, ghost)$ respectively. Pac-Man does not
know which direction the ghost will move in, but we will assume a "cautious"
model of action where Pac-Man is not to perform any action that *could* constitute
eating a ghost; that is, if Pac-Man takes an action that could reasonably lead
to him violating a norm, we will consider that norm violated. Since Pac-Man's
next action determines what is in range, we will actually need five entities
to express $inRange(pacman, ghost)$, one corresponding to each action. These
concepts are used to construct a constitutive norm, or a kind of strategy, regarding
eating, $strategy_{North} : \mathbf{C}(North, eat(pacman, ghost))$, which is applicable in
the context $\{scared(ghost), inNorthRange(pacman, ghost)\}$.

---

[2] For the time being we generalize the blue and the orange ghosts as *ghost*.

For $inNorthRange(pacman, ghost)$, we have access to the positions of Pac-Man and the ghosts, so we can create another set of constitutive norms for this, which apply in the context $\{pacman(i,j)\}$, $range_{North}$: $\mathbf{C}(ghost(k,l)$, $inNorthRange(pacman, ghost))$, where (k,l) has a Manhattan distance of one or fewer cells from $(i, j + 1)$.

Finally, we need to consider additional relationships between norms and concepts. For this norm base, we only have one regulative norm, so a mechanism for conflict resolution is not needed. However, as Pac-Man can only execute one action at a time, we have a non-concurrence relation between every action. This amounts to an inability to comply with multiple obligations over distinct actions. However, since Vegan Pac-Man does not deal with any obligations, additional rules will not be needed.

Representing the Norm Base. We need a formal language – equipped with an automated theorem prover – capable of effectively representing and reasoning with the norm base; we chose defeasible deontic (propositional) logic (DDPL for short) [8]. DDPL is defined over literals and modal literals, and the key ingredient is the rules we can construct from them. For the purposes of this paper we only consider one deontic modality (obligation $\mathbf{O}$) and define prohibition and permission as $\mathbf{F}(p) \equiv \mathbf{O}(\neg p)$ and $\mathbf{P}(p) \equiv \neg\mathbf{O}(\neg p)$.

Definition 1. *A rule is an expression* $r : A(r) \hookrightarrow_* N(r)$ *where r is a label uniquely identifying the rule,* $A(r) = \{a_1, ..., a_n\}$ *is the antecedent,* $N(r)$ *is the consequent,* $\hookrightarrow_* \in \{\rightarrow_*, \Rightarrow_*, \rightsquigarrow_*\}$, *and the mode of each rule is designated with* $* \in \{C, O\}$.

Rules labelled by C and O are constitutive and regulative rules, respectively. *Strict rules* $(\rightarrow_*)$ are rules where the consequent strictly follows from the antecedent without exception. *Defeasible rules* $(\Rightarrow_*)$ are rules where the consequent typically follows from the antecedent, unless there is evidence to the contrary. *Defeaters* $(\rightsquigarrow_*)$ are rules that only prevent a conclusion from being reached by a defeasible rule; regulative defeaters are used to encode permissive rules (see [8]).

The central concept of DDPL (and our application of it) is:

Definition 2. *A defeasible theory* D *is a tuple* $\langle F, R_O, R_C, > \rangle$, *where* F *is a set of literals (facts),* R_O *and* R_C *are sets of regulative and constitutive rules, and* $>$ *is a superiority relation over rules.*

These tools will be utilized to map Pac-Man's to a defeasible theory; the environment translated to a set of facts and the norm base to a set of rules.

3.2 Automating Translation

We are now dealing with three kinds of syntax: our informal representation of the norm base, the input and output of the host process, and the formal language of the reasoner (DDPL and its theorem prover SPINdle [11]). If we frame the reasoner as a central reasoning facility, the agent as a front-end, and the norm base as a back-end, we can implement this dynamic as a translator with two faces, one front-facing and one back-facing, feeding information into the reasoner from the agent and the norm base respectively.

Front End Translation. The front-end translator will be continuously in use, sending new data to be translated and requiring translated proposed actions as the environment changes. This will be an algorithm that transforms input data from the agent into propositions which assert facts about the agent or the environment, and then logical conclusions into instructions the agent will understand. Each cell of the Pac-Man grid can contain characters (Pac-Man or one of the ghosts), an object (a wall or a food pellet), or nothing at all. Walls are accounted for during the localization stage of Pac-Man's algorithm and food pellets are not an entity that appears in the norm base, so we will need to reason only about the characters. Hence we have two sets of variables in each game; $pacman_{i,j}$ and $ghost_{i,j}$ (along with $scared(ghost)$ if the ghost is in a scared state) assert the current coordinates of Pac-Man and of each ghost, and appear in a set $Facts$ in the defeasible theory $GameState = \langle Facts, R_C, R_O, > \rangle$.

Actions will be represented as deontic literals, in the set

$$Actions = \{North, South, East, West, Stop\}$$

A query from Pac-Man to the reasoner will be accompanied by a representation of the current game state, along with a list of possible actions, $possible$, which will be translated to the corresponding literal in $Actions$.

Back End Translation. In this critical task it is crucial to ensure that norms dictate the same behaviour once translated into this language. Besides making sure that each component of the norm can be represented by the language, we must also analyse our translated norm base with respect to how the available metadata is accommodated by the reasoner's rules of inference.

We represent the regulative norm of Vegan Pac-Man ($vegan$) as:

$$\Rightarrow_O \neg eat_{pacman,ghost} \in R_O$$

where defeasibility is given as a precautionary measure, in case we want to add (potentially conflicting) norms later.

Note that if moving North counts as eating a ghost, an obligation to go North counts as being obligated to eat a ghost, and a prohibition to eat a ghost implies a prohibition to move North. So we can rewrite $strategy_{North}$ as $\mathbf{C}(\mathbf{O}(\neg eat(pacman, ghost)), \mathbf{O}(\neg North))$, or with the applicable context as:

$$scared_{ghost}, inNorthRange_{pacman,ghost}, \mathbf{O}(\neg eat_{pacman,ghost}) \Rightarrow_O \neg North \in R_O$$

Note that though this a constitutive rule, in DDPL it will be in R_O. This will work for all of the constitutive norms attached to a prohibited action, where we place the context and the prohibition in question in the antecedent, and the prohibition of the concrete action in the strategy is the consequent.

For the remaining constitutive norms, we have a rather simple conversion. These norms will be generated w.r.t. the input from the agent; for example, if the agent (Pac-Man) tells us that he is at $(2, 3)$, the rule $range_{North}$ will be:

$$pacman_{2,3}, ghost_{2,4} \rightarrow_C inNorthRange_{pacman,ghost} \in R_C$$

We have found that it is more time-efficient to generate these constitutive norms anew whenever the fact set changes, instead of generating every possible constitutive norm ahead of time, and having SPINdle deal with all at once.

3.3   Classify and Assess Conclusions

Once we understand how various concepts are represented in the reasoner language, we need to parse the possible outputs of the reasoning engine into indicators as to which actions in the agent's arsenal are compliant with the norm base.

Compliant Solutions. Ideally, we will want to locate a compliant solution – an action that constitutes a possible course of action for the agent that does not violate any norms – from the conclusions yielded by the reasoner.

Definition 3. *A set of compliant solutions is: (1) non-empty, and consisting only of (2) solutions composed of possible actions, (3) solutions that do not violate any norms, and (4) solutions that are internally consistent.*

The manner in which we construct such a set is heavily influenced by the output (conclusions) yielded by SPINdle. Conclusions in DDPL are established over proofs and can be classified as defeasible or definite, and positive or negative. A positive conclusion means that the referenced literal holds, while a negative indicates that this literal has been refuted. A definite conclusion is obtained by using only strict rules and facts using forward chaining of rules. A conclusion holds defeasibly (denoted by $+\partial_C$ for a factual conclusion and $+\partial_O$ for an obligation) if there is an applicable rule for it and the rules for the opposite cannot be applied or are defeated. Over the course of a proof, each rule will be classified as either applicable (i.e., the antecedent holds and the consequent follows), discarded (i.e., the rule is not applied because the antecedent doesn't fully hold), or defeated by a defeater or a higher priority rule. For a set of rules R, $R[p]$, R_O and R^{sd} are, respectively, the subsets of: the rules for p, regulative rules, and strict or defeasible rule. The definition of provability for defeasible obligations [8] (we define only defeasible conclusions, because in our formalization regulative norms were expressed as defeasible rules) is:

Definition 4. *Given a defeasible theory D, if $D \vdash +\partial_O p$, then:*
1. $\exists r \in R_O^{sd}[p]$ *that is applicable defeasible, and*
2. $\forall s \in R_O[\neg p]$ *either: (a) s is discarded, or (b) $s \in R^{sd}$ and $\exists t \in R_O[p]$ s.t. t is applicable, t > s, or (c) s is a defeater, $\exists t \in R_O^{sd}[p]$ s.t. t is applicable, t > s*

A derivation in DDPL has a three phase argumentation structure, where arguments are simply applicable rules: (1) we need an argument for the conclusion we want to prove, (2) we analyse all possible counter-arguments, and (3) we rebut the counter-arguments. An argument can be rebutted when it is not applicable or when it is defeated by a stronger applicable argument. If we exclude the undercut case, in every phase the arguments attack the arguments in the previous phase. A rule attacks another rule if the conclusions of the two rules are contradictory (note that $\mathbf{P}(q)$ and $\mathbf{P}(\neg q)$ are not a deontic contradiction). Accordingly, any regulative rule for q attacks a strict or defeasible regulative rule for $\neg q$. However, a regulative defeater for q is not attacked by a regulative defeater for $\neg q$ (condition 2(c) above).

We parse out a solution set by: (1) if we do not receive a full set of conclusions from SPINdle, we return an empty set; (2) we remove all conclusions that do not reference a literal in *possible*; (3) any action corresponding to a defeasibly proved positive literal occurs in every solution; and (4) any action corresponding to a defeasibly proved negative literal is discarded from every solution.

Claim: the above procedure yields either an empty set or a compliant solution. *Proof sketch:* If our solution is not internally consistent, we can prove both $+\delta_O\ a$ and $+\delta_O\neg a$ for some action a. In this case SPINdle will return neither, and the above procedure leads to an empty set in step (1). Only possible actions will occur in a solution as per step (2), and any solutions which fail to comply with an obligation or prohibition will be excluded through step (3) and (4) respectively.

'Lesser of two Evils' Solutions. If the above procedure leaves us with an empty solution set, we want to identify which non-compliant actions constitute the "best" choice (i.e. are minimally non-compliant). Our characterization of degrees of non-compliance depends on the way the reasoner constructs solutions, and what information it logs during this process. SPINdle has an inference logger that classifies every rule in the theory as discarded, applicable, or defeated. For our agent, the chosen degree is a score derived from the of norms that have been applied versus those that have been defeated (discarded norms are ignored):

$$score := \#complied - \#violated = \#applied - \#defeated$$

This score is computed through the theory $GameState_a$, which is constructed by adding a fact $\mathbf{O}(a)$ to $GameState$. Recall that a rule will be defeated when its defeasible theory includes a fact that conflicts with the head of this rule. So when we add $\mathbf{O}(a)$ to $GameState$, all norms that prescribed $\mathbf{F}(a) = \mathbf{O}(\neg a)$ for $GameState$ are defeated and any prescribing $\mathbf{O}(a)$ is applied. To compute the score, we use SPINdle in a rather unconventional way, ignoring conclusions yielded and checking the inference log to count which rules have been applied during reasoning ($\#applied$) and which were defeated ($\#defeated$) and set $score = \#applied - \#defeated$. This procedure is completed for every action in *possible*, and we select the action(s) with the highest score. If there are multiple actions with a highest score, we send multiple solutions to the agent and it will pick the best action according to its policy.

Claim: computing scores for all possible actions is completed in polynomial time. *Proof sketch:* As shown in [8], conclusions in DDPL can be computed in linear time with respect to the the number of literal occurrences plus the number of the rules in the theory. The claim holds since every action in *possible* is a literal, and the above procedure is completed $|possible|$ times.

3.4   Revising the Norm Base

We demonstrate the advantages of our approach – modularity, configurability, and capability as an event recorder – through revising our norm base.

Inherent to Pac-Man's environment is the possibility of encountering a state where no compliant action is possible; in this section we explore how to address cases like this through adding or removing rules to the norm base.

When playing "vegan" Pac-Man, we may encounter the case depicted in Fig. 2(a). In absence of additional information Pac-Man will eat whichever ghost

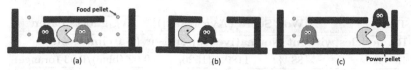

Fig. 2. Pac-Man trapped between two ghosts (a) or in a corner (b). In (c) Pac-Man consumes the power pellet and eats the ghost at the same time.

the policy indicates it should, and a violation report is generated. Each violation report is saved as a timestamped file accompanied with the representation of the current game state. This report can be used to retroactively examine the context in which violations occur, and we can thereby revise our norm base which is independent from the agent's RL policy. In the case of "vegan" Pac-Man, these reports make it clear that this version of the game will be susceptible to somewhat regular violations in the form of Fig. 2(a).

If we consider instead "vegetarian" Pac-Man, we can restrict our norm base to the *vegan* rule only applied to the blue ghost. However, situations in which compliance is not possible can still occur; for instance the one depicted in Fig. 2(b), or the case where Pac-Man consumes a power pellet and the blue ghost at the same time, as shown in Fig. 2(c). In the latter case, the violation occurs because, prior to Pac-Man's consumption of the power pellet, the blue ghost is not scared and Pac-Man's strategy to comply with *vegan* will not be triggered. This is roughly analogous to an agent committing an unethical act because it has no way of recognizing that it is unethical.

Summarily, the violation reports show that there are four points in the maze where Pac-Man, potentially, cannot comply, given the information he has access to; in response, we add a norm *danger* steering Pac-Man away from these areas:

$$\Rightarrow_O \neg enter_{pacman,danger}$$

which is accompanied by constitutive norms defining the abstract action of "entering danger" (for some pre-defined location denoted as *danger*), such as:

$$inNorthRange_{pacman,danger}, inRange_{ghost,danger} \Rightarrow_O \neg North$$

4 Evaluation and Conclusion

We have presented a modular and transparent approach that enables an autonomous agent in pursuing ethical goals, while still running an RL policy that maximizes its cumulative reward. Our approach was evaluated on six tests[3], in batches of 100 games. The results are displayed in the following table and discussed below; we give data on both game performance (average score and % games won) and ethical performance (ghosts eaten). Refer to Sec. 2 for a thorough description of the testing environment.

The first two *baseline* tests measured the performance of Pac-Man using two different (ethically agnostic) RL policies without the normative supervisor; this establishes a baseline for Pac-Man's game performance. We refer to the first

---

[3] We use a laptop with Intel i5-8250U CPU (4 cores, 1.60 GHz) and 8GB RAM, running Ubuntu 18.04, Java 8, Python 2.7.

Test	Won	Score (Avg [Max])	Avg ghosts eaten
RL policies without Normative Supervisor (Baseline tests)			
1a – Safe	88 %	1189.4 [1526]	0.02 (blue)/0.03 (orange)
1b – Hungry	87 %	1503.5 [2133]	0.89 (blue)/ 0.81 (orange)
RL policies with Normative Supervisor			
2a – SafeVegan	89 %	1193.39 [1526]	0.01 (blue)/0.02 (orange)
2b – HungryVegan	92 %	1211.67 [1350]	0.00 (blue)/0.00 (orange)
3 – Vegetarian	94 %	1413.8 [1742]	0.01 (blue)/0.79 (orange)
4 – SafeVegetarian	87 %	1336.2 [1747]	0.00 (blue)/0.88 (orange)

RL policy (in Test 1a) as *safe* because the algorithm used to train it does not differentiate between regular ghosts and scared ghosts, learning how to avoid them altogether. We refer to the other RL policy (in Test 1b) as *hungry* because the corresponding algorithm differentiates between regular ghosts and scared ghosts, and the agent learns how to eat the scared ghosts. The results for Test 1b (average score of 1503.5 maximum score of 2133) were comparable to the baseline version in [14] (average score of 1675.9, max score of 2144).

Tests 2a, 2b, 3, and 4 make use of the normative supervisor. In 2a and 2b, we subject Pac-Man to a "vegan" norm base, prohibiting eating all ghosts (for both the *safe* and *hungry* policies respectively). The results obtained for test 2a were comparable to those in [14]: the average number of violations was the same in both tests (0.03 ghosts), and our average score was only slightly smaller (1193.39 instead of 1268.5). Compared with the baseline, the game performance did not suffer. For test 2b we obtained instead full compliance. Test 3 and 4 both use the *hungry* policy. In test 3 we subject Pac-Man to a "vegetarian" norm base, where only eating blue ghosts is forbidden. Allowing Pac-Man to eat one of the ghosts allows him to further maximize his score and avoid the violations depicted in Fig. 2(a). Test 4 addresses the two edge cases of non-compliance occurring in Test 3 as depicted in Fig. 2(b) and Fig. 2(c) by adding the new rules defined in Sec. 3.4, steering Pac-Man away from entering the "dangerous" areas. Here, violations were completely eliminated.

These tests, along with the analysis of the violation reports created in non-compliant cases, yielded several insights. The module did not cause Pac-Man's game performance to suffer, and could successfully identify non-compliant behaviour. It implemented compliant behaviour in most cases, with the exception of situations where compliance *was not possible*. The violation reports allowed us to identify such situations with ease.

The game used in this paper offers limited opportunities to work with meaningful (ethical) norms. We aim to explore alternative case studies with more options to define multiple (and possibly conflicting) ethical goals to test the interactions between RL and a normative supervisor based on DDPL.

References

1. Aler Tubella, A., Dignum, V.: The glass box approach: Verifying contextual adherence to values. In: Proc. of AISafety@IJCAI: Workshop on Artificial Intelligence Safety co-located with the 28th International Joint Conference on Artificial Intelligence. CEUR Workshop Proceedings, vol. 2419. CEUR-WS.org (2019), http://ceur-ws.org/Vol-2419/paper_18.pdf
2. Aler Tubella, A., Theodorou, A., Dignum, F., Dignum, V.: Governance by glass-box: Implementing transparent moral bounds for AI behaviour. In: Proc. of IJCAI 2019: the 28th International Joint Conference on Artificial Intelligence. pp. 5787–5793. ijcai.org (2019). https://doi.org/10.24963/ijcai.2019/802
3. Andrighetto, G., Governatori, G., Noriega, P., van der Torre, L.W.N. (eds.): Normative Multi-Agent Systems, Dagstuhl Follow-Ups, vol. 4. Schloss Dagstuhl - Leibniz-Zentrum fuer Informatik (2013), http://drops.dagstuhl.de/opus/portals/dfu/index.php?semnr=13003
4. Boella, G., van der Torre, L.: Regulative and constitutive norms in normative multiagent systems. In: Proc. of KR 2004: the 9th International Conference on Principles of Knowledge Representation and Reasoning. pp. 255–266. AAAI Press (2004), http://www.aaai.org/Library/KR/2004/kr04-028.php
5. Bremner, P., Dennis, L.A., Fisher, M., Winfield, A.F.T.: On proactive, transparent, and verifiable ethical reasoning for robots. Proc. IEEE **107**(3), 541–561 (2019). https://doi.org/10.1109/JPROC.2019.2898267
6. Broersen, J., Dastani, M., Hulstijn, J., Huang, Z., van der Torre, L.: The boid architecture: conflicts between beliefs, obligations, intentions and desires. In: Proceedings of the fifth international conference on Autonomous agents. pp. 9–16 (2001)
7. DeNero, J., Klein, D.: UC Berkeley CS188 intro to AI – course materials (2014)
8. Governatori, G., Olivieri, F., Rotolo, A., Scannapieco, S.: Computing strong and weak permissions in defeasible logic. Journal of Phil. Logic **42**(6), 799–829 (2013). https://doi.org/10.1007/s10992-013-9295-1
9. Governatori, G., Rotolo, A.: BIO logical agents: Norms, beliefs, intentions in defeasible logic. Journal of Autonomous Agents and Multi Agent Systems **17**(1), 36–69 (2008). https://doi.org/10.1007/s10458-008-9030-4
10. Hasanbeig, M., Kantaros, Y., Abate, A., Kroening, D., Pappas, G.J., Lee, I.: Reinforcement learning for temporal logic control synthesis with probabilistic satisfaction guarantees. In: Proc. of CDC 2019: the 58th IEEE Conference on Decision and Control. pp. 5338–5343 (2019). https://doi.org/10.1109/CDC40024.2019.9028919
11. Lam, H.P., Governatori, G.: The making of SPINdle. In: Proc. of RuleML 2009: International Symposium on Rule Interchange and Applications. LNCS, vol. 5858, pp. 315–322. Springer, Heidelberg (2009). https://doi.org/10.1007/978-3-642-04985-9
12. Lam, H.P., Governatori, G.: Towards a model of UAVs navigation in urban canyon through defeasible logic. Journal of Logic and Computation **23**(2), 373–395 (2013). https://doi.org/10.1007/978-3-642-04985-9
13. Levine, S., Finn, C., Darrell, T., Abbeel, P.: End-to-end training of deep visuomotor policies. Journal of Machine Learning Research **17**, 39:1–39:40 (2016), http://jmlr.org/papers/v17/15-522.html
14. Noothigattu, R., Bouneffouf, D., Mattei, N., Chandra, R., Madan, P., Varshney, K.R., Campbell, M., Singh, M., Rossi, F.: Teaching ai agents ethical values using reinforcement learning and policy orchestration. In: Proceedings of the Twenty-Eighth International Joint Conference on Artificial Intelligence, IJCAI-19. pp. 6377–

6381. International Joint Conferences on Artificial Intelligence Organization (7 2019). https://doi.org/10.24963/ijcai.2019/891, https://doi.org/10.24963/ijcai.2019/891

15. Nowell-Smith, P.H., Lemmon, E.J.: Escapism: The logical basis of ethics. Mind **69**(275), 289–300 (1960)

16. Silver, D., Schrittwieser, J., Simonyan, K., Antonoglou, I., Huang, A., Guez, A., Hubert, T., Baker, L., Lai, M., Bolton, A., Chen, Y., Lillicrap, T.P., Hui, F., Sifre, L., van den Driessche, G., Graepel, T., Hassabis, D.: Mastering the game of Go without human knowledge. Nature **550**(7676), 354–359 (2017). https://doi.org/10.1038/nature24270

17. Von Wright, G.H.: An essay in deontic logic and the general theory of action. Acta Philosophica Fennica **21** (1968)

18. Watkins, C.J.C.H.: Learning from Delayed Rewards. Ph.D. thesis, King's College, Cambridge, UK (May 1989), http://www.cs.rhul.ac.uk/~chrisw/new_thesis.pdf

Open Access This chapter is licensed under the terms of the Creative Commons Attribution 4.0 International License (http://creativecommons.org/licenses/by/4.0/), which permits use, sharing, adaptation, distribution and reproduction in any medium or format, as long as you give appropriate credit to the original author(s) and the source, provide a link to the Creative Commons license and indicate if changes were made.

The images or other third party material in this chapter are included in the chapter's Creative Commons license, unless indicated otherwise in a credit line to the material. If material is not included in the chapter's Creative Commons license and your intended use is not permitted by statutory regulation or exceeds the permitted use, you will need to obtain permission directly from the copyright holder.

Automatically Building Diagrams for Olympiad Geometry Problems

Ryan Krueger[1], Jesse Michael Han[2], and Daniel Selsam[3]

[1] University of Oxford, Oxford, UK
[2] University of Pittsburgh, Pittsburgh PA, USA
[3] Microsoft Research, Redmond WA, USA

Abstract. We present a method for automatically building diagrams for olympiad-level geometry problems and implement our approach in a new open-source software tool, the Geometry Model Builder (GMB). Central to our method is a new domain-specific language, the Geometry Model-Building Language (GMBL), for specifying geometry problems along with additional metadata useful for building diagrams. A GMBL program specifies (1) how to parameterize geometric objects (or sets of geometric objects) and initialize these parameterized quantities, (2) which quantities to compute directly from other quantities, and (3) additional constraints to accumulate into a (differentiable) loss function. A GMBL program induces a (usually) tractable numerical optimization problem whose solutions correspond to diagrams of the original problem statement, and that we can solve reliably using gradient descent. Of the 39 geometry problems since 2000 appearing in the International Mathematical Olympiad, 36 can be expressed in our logic and our system can produce diagrams for 94% of them on average. To the best of our knowledge, our method is the first in automated geometry diagram construction to generate models for such complex problems.

1 Introduction

Automated theorem provers for Euclidean geometry often use numerical models (*i.e.* diagrams) for heuristic reasoning, *e.g.* for conjecturing subgoals, pruning branches, checking non-degeneracy conditions, and selecting auxiliary constructions. However, modern solvers rely on diagrams that are either supplied manually [7,24] or generated automatically via methods that are severely limited in scope [12]. Motivated by the IMO Grand Challenge, an ongoing effort to build an AI that can win a gold medal at the International Mathematical Olympiad (IMO), we present a method for expressing and solving olympiad-level systems of geometric constraints.

Historically, algebraic methods are the most complete and performant for automated geometry diagram construction but suffer from degenerate solutions

© The Author(s) 2021
A. Platzer and G. Sutcliffe (Eds.): CADE 2021, LNAI 12699, pp. 577–588, 2021.
https://doi.org/10.1007/978-3-030-79876-5_33

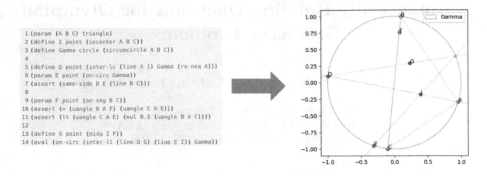

```
1 (param (A B C) triangle)
2 (define I point (incenter A B C))
3 (define Gamma circle (circumcircle A B C))
4
5 (define D point (inter-lc (line A I) Gamma (rs-neq A)))
6 (param E point (on-circ Gamma))
7 (assert (same-side D E (line B C)))
8
9 (param F point (on-seg B C))
10 (assert (= (uangle B A F) (uangle C A E)))
11 (assert (lt (uangle C A E) (mul 0.5 (uangle B A C))))
12
13 (define G point (midp I F))
14 (eval (on-circ (inter-ll (line D G) (line E I)) Gamma))
```

Fig. 1: An example GMBL program and corresponding diagram generated by the GMB for IMO 2010 Problem 2.

and, in the numerical case, non-convexity. These methods are restricted to relatively simple geometric configurations as poor local minima arise via large numbers of parameters. Moreover, degenerate solutions manifest as poor distributions for the vertices of geometric objects (*e.g.* a non-sensical triangle) as well as intersections of objects at more than one point (*e.g.* lines and circles, circles and circles).

We constructed a domain-specific language (DSL), the Geometry Model-Building Language (GMBL), to express geometry problems whose semantics induce tractable numerical optimization problems. The GMBL includes a set of commands with which users introduce geometric objects and constraints between these objects. There is a direct interpretation from these commands to the parameterization of geometric objects, the computation of geometric quantities from existing ones, and additional numerical constraints. The GMBL employs *root selector* declarations to disambiguate multiple solution problems, *reparameterizations* both to reduce the number of parameters and increase uniformity in model variance, and *joint distributions* for geometric objects that are susceptible to degeneracy (*i.e.* triangles and polygons). Our DSL treats points, lines, and circles as first-class citizens, and the language can be easily extended to support additional high-level features in terms of these primitives.

We provide an implementation of our method, the Geometry Model Builder (GMB), that compiles GMBL programs into Tensorflow computation graphs [1] and generates models via off-the-shelf, gradient-based optimization. Figure 2 demonstrates an overview of this implementation. Experimentally, we find that the GMBL sufficiently reduces the parameter space and mitigates degeneracy to make our target geometry amenable to numerical optimization. We tested our method on all IMO geometry problems since 2000 ($n = 39$), of which 36 can be expressed as GMBL programs. Using default parameters, the GMB finds a single model for 94% of these 36 problems in an average of 27.07 seconds. Of the problems for which our program found a model and the goal of the problem could be stated in our DSL, the goal held in the final model 86% of the time.

All code is available on GitHub[4] with which users can write GMBL programs and generate diagrams. Our program can be run both as a command-line tool for integration with theorem provers or as a locally-hosted web server.

2 Background

Here we provide an overview of olympiad-level geometry problem statements, as well as several challenges presented by the associated constraint problems.

2.1 Olympiad-Level Geometry Problem Statements

IMO geometry problems are stated as a sequential introduction of potentially-constrained geometric objects, as well as additional constraints between entities. Such constraints can take one of two forms: (1) *geometric* constraints describe the relative position of geometric entities (*e.g.* two lines are parallel) while (2) *dimensional* constraints enforce specific numerical values (*e.g.* angle, radius). Lastly, problems end with a goal (or set of goals) typically in the form of geometric or dimensional constraints. The following is an example from IMO 2009:

> Let ABC be a triangle with circumcentre O. The points P and Q are interior points of the sides CA and AB, respectively. Let K, L, and M be the midpoints of the segments BP, CQ, and PQ, respectively, and let Γ be the circle passing through K, L, and M. Suppose that the line PQ is tangent to the circle Γ. Prove that $OP = OQ$.

(IMO 2009 P2)

This problem introduces ten named geometric objects and has a single goal.

Note that this class of problems does not admit a mathematical description but rather is defined empirically (*i.e.* as those problems selected for olympiads). The overwhelming majority of these problems are of a particular type – plane geometry problems that can be expressed as problems in nonlinear real arithmetic (NRA). However, while NRA is technically decidable, olympiad problems tend to be littered with order constraints and complex constructions (*e.g.* mixtilinear incenter) and be well beyond the capability of existing algebraic methods. On the other hand, they are selected to admit elegant, human-comprehensible proofs. It is this class of problems for which the GMBL was designed to express; though rare, any particular olympiad geometry problem is not guaranteed to be of this type and therefore is not necessarily expressible in the GMBL.

2.2 Challenge: Globally Coupled Constraints

A naïve approach to generate models would incrementally instantiate objects via their immediate constraints. For (IMO 2009 P2), this would work as follows:

1. Sample points A, B, and C.

---

[4] https://github.com/rkruegs123/geo-model-builder

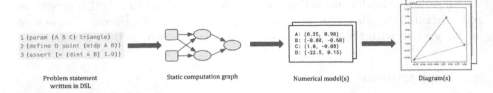

Problem statement   Static computation graph   Numerical model(s)   Diagram(s)
written in DSL

Fig. 2: An overview of our method. Our program takes as input a GMBL program and translates it to a set of real-valued parameters and differentiable losses in the form of a static computation graph. We then apply gradient-based optimization to obtain numerical models and display them as diagrams.

2. Compute O as the circumcenter of $\triangle ABC$.
3. Sample P and Q on the segments CA and AB, respectively.
4. Compute K, L, and M as the midpoints of BP, CQ, and PQ, respectively.
5. Compute Γ as the circle defined by K, L, and M.

Immediately we see a problem – there is no guarantee that PQ is tangent to Γ in the final model. Indeed, the constraints of (IMO 2009 P2) are quite globally coupled – the choice of P partially determines the circle Γ to which PQ must be tangent, and every choice of $\triangle ABC$ does not even admit a pair P and Q satisfying this constraint. This is an example of the frequent *non-constructive* nature of IMO geometry problems. When there is no obvious reparameterization to avoid downstream effects, all constraints must be considered *simultaneously* rather than incrementally or as a set of smaller local optimization problems.

2.3   Challenge: Root Resolution

Even in the constructive case, local optimization is not necessarily sufficient given that multiple solutions can exist for algebraic constraints. More specifically, two circles or a circle and a line intersect at up to two distinct points and in a problem that specifies each distinct intersection point, the correct root to assign is generally not locally deducible. Without global information, this can lead to poor initializations becoming trapped in local minima. The GMBL accounts for this by including a set of explicit *root selectors* as described in Section 3.3. These root selectors provide global information for selecting the appropriate point from a set of multiple solutions to a system of equations.

3   Methods

In this section we present the GMBL and GMB in detail. In our presentation, we make use of the following notation and definitions:

– The `type` of a geometric object can be one of (1) `point`, (2) `line`, or (3) `circle`. We denote the `type` of a real-valued number as `number`.
– We use `<>` to denote an instance of a type.
– A `name` is a string value that refers to a geometric object.

3.1   GMBL: Overview

The GMBL is a DSL for expressing olympiad-level geometry problems that loss-lessly induces a numerical optimization problem. It consists of four *commands*, each of which has a direct interpretation regarding the accumulation of (1) real-valued parameters and (2) differentiable losses in terms of these parameters:

1. `param`: assigns a `name` to a new geometric object parameterized either by a default or optionally supplied parameterization
2. `define`: assigns a `name` to an object computed in terms of existing ones
3. `assert`: imposes an additional constraint (*i.e.* differentiable loss value)
4. `eval`: evaluates a given constraint in the final model(s)

Table 1 provides a summary of their usage. The GMBL includes an extensible library of *functions* and *predicates* with which commands are written. Notably, this library includes a notion of *root selection* to explicitly resolve the selection of roots to systems of equations with multiple solutions.

3.2   GMBL: Commands

In the following, we describe in more detail the usage of each command and their roles in constructing a tractable numerical optimization problem.

   `param` accepts as arguments a `string`, a `type`, and an *optional* parameter-ization. This introduces a geometric object that is parameterized either by the default parameterization for `<type>` or by the supplied method. Each primitive geometric type has the following default parameterization:

- `point`: parameterized by its x- and y-coordinates
- `line`: parameterized by two points that define the line
- `circle`: parameterized by its origin and radius

Optional parameterizations embody our method's use of *reparameterization* to decrease the number of parameters and increase model diversity. For example, consider a point C on the line $\overleftrightarrow{AB}$ that is subject to additional constraints. Rather than optimizing over the x- and y-coordinates of C, we can express C in terms of a single value z that scales C's placement on the line $\overleftrightarrow{AB}$.

   In addition to the standard usage of `param` outlined above, the GMBL in-cludes an important variant of this command to introduce sets of points that form triangles and polygons. This variant accepts as arguments (1) a *list* of point names, and (2) a *required* parameterization (see Table 1). This *joint* parameter-ization of triangles and polygons further prevents degeneracy. For example, to initialize a triangle $\triangle ABC$, we can sample the vertices from normal distribu-tions with means at distinct thirds of the unit circle. This method minimizes the sampling of triangles with extreme angle values, as well as allows for explicit con-trol over the distribution of acute vs. obtuse triangles by adjusting the standard deviations. Appendix C includes a list of all available parameterizations.[5]

---

[5] All appendices can be found in the long version of this paper [15].

Table 1: An overview of usage for the four commands.

Command	Usage
param	(param \<string\> \<type\> \<optional-parameterization\>) or (param (\<string\>, ..., \<string\>) \<parameterization\>)
define	(define \<string\> \<type\> \<value\>)
assert	(assert \<predicate\>)
eval	(eval \<predicate\>)

define accepts as arguments a string, a type, and a value that is one of \<point\>, \<line\>, or \<circle\>. This command serves as a basic assignment operator and is useful for caching commonly used values. The functions described in Section 3.3 are used to construct \<value\> from existing geometric objects.

assert accepts a single predicate and imposes it as an additional constraint on the system. This is achieved by translating the predicate to a set of algebraic values and registering them as losses. This command does not introduce any *new* geometric objects and can only refer to those already introduced by param or define. Notably, dimensional constraints and negations are always enforced via assert. Detail on supported predicates is presented in Section 3.3.

eval, like assert, accepts a single predicate and therefore does not introduce any new geometric objects. However, unlike assert, the corresponding algebraic values are evaluated and returned with the final model rather than registered as losses and enforced via optimization. This command is most useful for those interested in integrating the GMBL with theorem provers.

3.3 GMBL: Functions and Predicates

The second component of our DSL is a set of functions and predicates for constructing arguments to the commands outlined above. Functions construct new geometric objects and numerical values whereas predicates describe relationships between them. Our DSL includes high-level abstractions for common geometric concepts in olympiad geometry (*e.g.* excircle, isotomic conjugate).

Functions in the GMBL employ a notion of *root selectors* to address the "multiple solutions problem" described in Section 2.3. In plane geometry, this problem typically manifests with multiple candidate point solutions, such as the intersection between a line and a circle. Root selectors control for this by allowing users to specify the appropriate point for functions with multiple solutions. Figure 3 demonstrates their usage in the functions inter-lc (intersection of a line and circle) and inter-cc (intersection of two circles).

Importantly, arguments to predicates and functions can be specified with functions rather than named geometric objects. For a list of supported functions, predicates, and root selectors, refer to Appendices A, B, and C, respectively.

```
1 (param Gamma circle)
2 (param l line)
3
4 ;; Intersection points of l and Gamma
5 (define A point (inter-lc l Gamma rs-arbitrary))
6 (define B point (inter-lc l Gamma (rs-neq A)))
7
8 ;; Intersection points of l and Omega
9 (param Omega circle)
10 (define C point (inter-lc l Omega (rs-closer-to-p A)))
11 (define D point (inter-lc l Omega (rs-neq C)))
12
13 ;; Intersection points of Gamma and Omega
14 (define E point (inter-cc Gamma Omega (rs-closer-to-l l)))
15 (define F point (inter-cc Gamma Omega (rs-neq E)))
```

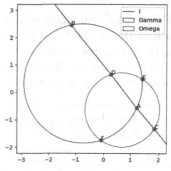

(a) A GMBL program that uses root selectors.   (b) A corresponding diagram.

Fig. 3: An example usage of root selectors to resolve the intersections of lines and circles, and circles and circles.

3.4 Auxiliary Losses

The optimization problem encoded by a GMBL progran includes three additional loss values. Foremost, for every instance of a circle intersecting a line or other circle, we impose a loss value that ensures the two geometric objects indeed intersect. The final two, albeit opposing losses are intended to minimize global degeneracy. We impose one loss that minimizes the mean of all point norms to prevent exceptionally separate objects and a second to enforce a sufficient distance between points to maintain distinctness.

3.5 Implementation

We built the GMB, an open-source implementation that compiles GMBL programs to optimization problems and generates models. The GMB takes as input a GMBL program and processes each command in sequence to accumulate real-valued parameters and differentiable losses in a Tensorflow computation graph. After registering auxiliary losses , we apply off-the-shelf gradient-based local optimization to produce models of the constraint system. In summary, to generate N numerical models, our optimization procedure works as follows:

1. Construct computation graph by sequentially processing commands.
2. Register auxiliary losses.
3. Sample sets of initial parameter values and rank via loss value.
4. Choose (next) best initialization and optimize via gradient descent.
5. Repeat (4) until obtaining N models or the maximum # of tries is reached.

Our program accepts as arguments (1) the # of models desired (default = 1), (2) the # of initializations to sample (default = 10), and (3) the max # of optimization tries (default = 3). Our program also accepts the standard suite of parameters for training a Tensorflow model, including an initial learning rate (default = 0.1), a decay rate (default = 0.7), the max # of iterations (default = 5000), and an epsilon value (default = 0.001) to determine stopping criteria.

Table 2: An evaluation of our method's ability to generate a single model for each of the 36 IMO problems encoded in our DSL. For each problem, 10 sets of initial parameters were sampled over which our program optimized up to three. All data shown are the average of three trials. The first row demonstrates results using default parameters ($\epsilon = 0.001$, learning rate $= 0.1$, # iterations $= 5,000$).

ϵ	Learning Rate	Iterations	% Success	% Goal Satisfaction	Time per Problem (s)		
					All	Fail	Success
0.001	0.1	5,000	93.52	85.84	27.07	223.51	14.72
0.01	0.1	5,000	92.60	84.71	26.86	229.71	14.43
0.001	0.01	5,000	88.88	86.32	27.54	137.85	14.33
0.001	0.1	10,000	92.59	86.02	34.78	287.51	15.43

4 Results

In this section, we present an evaluation of our method's proficiency in three areas of expressing and solving olympiad-level geometry problems:

1. Expressing olympiad-level geometry problems as GMBL programs.
2. Generating models for these programs.
3. Preserving truths (up to tolerance) that are not directly optimized for.

Table 2 contains a summary of our results.

Our evaluation considers all 39 IMO geometry problems since 2000. Of these 39 problems, 36 can be expressed in our DSL. Those that we cannot encode involve variable numbers of geometric objects. For 32 of these 36 problems, we can express the goals as `eval` commands in the corresponding GMBL programs. The goals of the additional four problems are not expressible in our DSL, *e.g.* our DSL cannot express goals of the form "Find all possible values of $\angle ABC$."

To evaluate (2) and (3), we conducted three trials in which we ran our program on each of the 36 encodings with varying sets of arguments. With default arguments, our program generated a single model for (on average) 94% of these problems. Our program ran for an average of 27.07 seconds for each problem but there is a stark difference between time to success and time to failure (14.72 vs 223.51 seconds) as failure entails completing all optimization attempts whereas successful generation of a model terminates the program. We achieve similar success rates with more forgiving training arguments or a higher tolerance.

For use in automated theorem proving, it is essential that models generated by our tool not only satisfy the constraint problem up to tolerance but *also* any other truths that follow from the set of input constraints. The most immediate example of such a truth is the *goal* of a problem statement. Therefore, we used the goals of IMO geometry problems as a proxy for this ability by only checking the satisfaction of the goal in the final model (*i.e.* with an `eval` statement) rather than directly optimizing for it. In our experiments, we considered such a goal satisfied if it held up to $\epsilon * 10$ as it is reasonable to expect slightly higher floating-point error without explicit optimization. Using default parameters, the goal held up to tolerance in 86% of problems for which we found a model and could express the goal. This rate was similar across all other sets of arguments.

5   Future Work

Here we discuss various opportunities for improvement of our method.

Firstly, improvements could be made to our method of numerical optimization. While Tensorflow offers a convenient way of caching terms via a static computation graph and optimizing directly over this representation, there is not explicit support for *constrained* optimization. Because of this, arbitrary weights have to be assigned to each loss value. Though rare, this can result in false positives and negatives for the satisfaction of a constraint. Using an explicit constrained-optimization method (*e.g.* SLSQP) would enable the separation of soft constraints (*e.g.* maximizing the distance between points) and hard constraints (*e.g.* those enforced by `assert`), removing the need for arbitrary weights.

Secondly, cognitive overhead could be reduced as users are currently required to determine degrees of freedom; it would be far easier to write problem statements using only declarations of geometric objects and constraints between them, *e.g.* using only `assert`. This could be accomplished by treating our DSL as a low-level "instruction set" to which a higher-level language could be compiled. The main challenge of such a compiler would be appropriately identifying opportunities to reduce the degrees of freedom. To achieve this, the compiler would require a decision procedure for line and circle membership.

Lastly, we could improve our current treatment of distinctness. To prevent degenerate solutions, our method optimizes for object distinctness and rejects models with duplicates. However, there is the occasional problem for which a local optimum encodes two provably distinct points as equal up to floating point tolerance. There are many techniques that could be applied to this problem (*e.g.* annealing) though we do not consider them here as the issue is rare.

6   Related Work

Though many techniques for mechanized geometry diagram construction have been introduced over the decades, no method, to the best of our knowledge, can produce models for more than a negligible fraction of olympiad problems. There exist many systems, built primarily for educational purposes, for interactively generating diagrams using ruler-and-compass constructions, *e.g.* GCLC [13], GeoGebra [11], Geometer's Sketchpad [20], and Cinderella [19]. There are also non-interactive methods for deriving such constructions, *e.g.* GeoView [2] and program synthesis [9,12]. However, as discussed in Section 2.2, very few olympiad problems can be described in such a form. Alternatively, Penrose is an early-stage system for translating mathematical descriptions to diagrams that relies on constrained numerical optimization and therefore does not suffer from this expressivity limitation [25]. However, this system lacks support for constraints with multiple roots, *e.g.* intersecting circles. There are more classical methods that similarly depart from constructive geometry. MMP/Geometer [8] translates the problem to a set of algebraic equations and uses numerical optimization (*e.g.* BFGS) and GEOTHER [22, 23] first translates a predicate specification into polynomial equations, decomposes this system into representative triangular sets, and obtains solutions for each set numerically. Neither of these programs are available to evaluate though we did test similar approaches using modern libraries (specifically: `sympy` [17] and `scipy` [21]) and both numerical and symbolic methods would almost always timeout on relatively simple olympiad problems.

Generating models for systems of geometric constraints is also a challenge in computer-aided design (CAD) for engineering diagram drawing. Recent efforts focus on graph-based synthetic methods, a subset of techniques concerned with ruler-and-compass constructions [3, 5, 6, 10, 14, 16, 18]. Most relevant to our method are Bettig and Shah's "solution selectors" which, similar to root selectors in the GMBL, allow users to specify the configuration of a CAD model [4]. However, these solution selectors are purpose-built and do not generalize.

7   Conclusion

It is standard in GTP to rely on diagrams for heuristic reasoning but the scale of automatic diagram construction is limited. To enable efforts to build a solver for IMO geometry problems, we developed a method for building diagrams for olympiad-level geometry problems. Our method is based on the GMBL, a DSL for expressing geometry problems that induces (usually) tractable numerical optimization problems. The GMBL includes a set of commands that have a direct interpretation for accumulating real-valued parameters and differentiable losses. Arguments to these commands are constructed with a library of functions and predicates that includes notions of root selection, joint distributions, and reparameterizations to minimize degeneracy and the number of parameters. We implemented our approach in an open-source tool that translates GMBL programs to diagrams. Using this program, we evaluated our method on all IMO geometry problems since 2000. Our implementation reliably produces models; moreover, known truths that are not directly optimized for typically hold up to tolerance. By handling configurations of this complexity, our system clears a roadblock in GTP and provides a critical tool for undertakers of the IMO Grand Challenge.

References

1. M. Abadi, P. Barham, J. Chen, Z. Chen, A. Davis, J. Dean, M. Devin, S. Ghemawat, G. Irving, M. Isard, et al. Tensorflow: A system for large-scale machine learning. In *12th USENIX symposium on operating systems design and implementation (OSDI 16)*, pages 265–283, 2016.

2. Y. Bertot, F. Guilhot, and L. Pottier. Visualizing geometrical statements with GeoView. *Electronic Notes in Theoretical Computer Science*, 103:49–65, 2004.
3. B. Bettig and C. M Hoffmann. Geometric constraint solving in parametric computer-aided design. *Journal of computing and information science in engineering*, 11(2), 2011.
4. B. Bettig and J. Shah. Solution selectors: a user-oriented answer to the multiple solution problem in constraint solving. *J. Mech. Des.*, 125(3):443–451, 2003.
5. B. N. Freeman-Benson, J. Maloney, and A. Borning. An incremental constraint solver. *Communications of the ACM*, 33(1):54–63, 1990.
6. I. Fudos. *Constraint solving for computer aided design*. PhD thesis, Verlag nicht ermittelbar, 1995.
7. W. Gan, X. Yu, T. Zhang, and M. Wang. Automatically proving plane geometry theorems stated by text and diagram. *International Journal of Pattern Recognition and Artificial Intelligence*, 33(07):1940003, 2019.
8. X.-S. Gao and Q. Lin. Mmp/geometer–a software package for automated geometric reasoning. In *International Workshop on Automated Deduction in Geometry*, pages 44–66. Springer, 2002.
9. S. Gulwani, V. A. Korthikanti, and A. Tiwari. Synthesizing geometry constructions. *ACM SIGPLAN Notices*, 46(6):50–61, 2011.
10. C. M. Hoffmann and R. Joan-Arinyo. Parametric modeling. In *Handbook of computer aided geometric design*, pages 519–541. Elsevier, 2002.
11. M. Hohenwarter and M. Hohenwarter. GeoGebra.
12. S. Itzhaky, S. Gulwani, N. Immerman, and M. Sagiv. Solving geometry problems using a combination of symbolic and numerical reasoning. In *International Conference on Logic for Programming Artificial Intelligence and Reasoning*, pages 457–472. Springer, 2013.
13. P. Janičić. GCLC—a tool for constructive euclidean geometry and more than that. In *International Congress on Mathematical Software*, pages 58–73. Springer, 2006.
14. G. A. Kramer. Solving geometric constraint systems. In *AAAI*, pages 708–714, 1990.
15. R. Krueger, J. M. Han, and D. Selsam. Automatically Building Diagrams for Olympiad Geometry Problems. *arXiv preprint arXiv:2012.02590*, 2020.
16. R. S. Latham and A. E. Middleditch. Connectivity analysis: a tool for processing geometric constraints. *Computer-Aided Design*, 28(11):917–928, 1996.
17. A. Meurer, C. P. Smith, M. Paprocki, O. Čertík, S. B. Kirpichev, M. Rocklin, A. Kumar, S. Ivanov, J. K. Moore, S. Singh, et al. SymPy: symbolic computing in Python. *PeerJ Computer Science*, 3:e103, 2017.
18. J. C. Owen. Algebraic solution for geometry from dimensional constraints. In *Proceedings of the first ACM symposium on Solid modeling foundations and CAD/-CAM applications*, pages 397–407, 1991.
19. J. Richter-Gebert and U. H. Kortenkamp. *The Cinderella. 2 Manual: Working with The Interactive Geometry Software*. Springer Science & Business Media, 2012.
20. D. Scher. Lifting the curtain: The evolution of the Geometer's Sketchpad. *The Mathematics Educator*, 10(2), 1999.
21. P. Virtanen, R. Gommers, T. E. Oliphant, M. Haberland, T. Reddy, D. Courna-peau, E. Burovski, P. Peterson, W. Weckesser, J. Bright, et al. SciPy 1.0: fundamental algorithms for scientific computing in Python. *Nature methods*, 17(3):261–272, 2020.
22. D. Wang. Geother 1.1: Handling and proving geometric theorems automatically. In *International Workshop on Automated Deduction in Geometry*, pages 194–215. Springer, 2002.

23. D. Wang. Automated generation of diagrams with Maple and Java. In *Algebra, Geometry and Software Systems*, pages 277–287. Springer, 2003.
24. K. Wang and Z. Su. Automated geometry theorem proving for human-readable proofs. In *Twenty-Fourth International Joint Conference on Artificial Intelligence*, 2015.
25. K. Ye, W. Ni, M. Krieger, D. Ma'ayan, J. Wise, J. Aldrich, J. Sunshine, and K. Crane. Penrose: from mathematical notation to beautiful diagrams. *ACM Transactions on Graphics (TOG)*, 39(4):144–1, 2020.

Open Access This chapter is licensed under the terms of the Creative Commons Attribution 4.0 International License (http://creativecommons.org/licenses/by/4.0/), which permits use, sharing, adaptation, distribution and reproduction in any medium or format, as long as you give appropriate credit to the original author(s) and the source, provide a link to the Creative Commons license and indicate if changes were made.

The images or other third party material in this chapter are included in the chapter's Creative Commons license, unless indicated otherwise in a credit line to the material. If material is not included in the chapter's Creative Commons license and your intended use is not permitted by statutory regulation or exceeds the permitted use, you will need to obtain permission directly from the copyright holder.

The Fusemate Logic Programming System

Peter Baumgartner(iD)

Data61/CSIRO and The Australian National University, Canberra, Australia
Peter.Baumgartner@data61.csiro.au

Abstract. Fusemate is a logic programming system that implements the possible model semantics for disjunctive logic programs. Its input language is centered around a weak notion of stratification with comprehension and aggregation operators on top of it. Fusemate is implemented as a shallow embedding in the Scala programming language. This enables using Scala data types natively as terms, a tight interface with external systems, and it makes model computation available as an ordinary container data structure constructor. The paper describes the above features and implementation aspects. It also demonstrates them with a non-trivial use-case, the embedding of the description logic $\mathcal{ALCIF}$ into Fusemate's input language.

1 Introduction

Fusemate[1] is a logic programming system for computing possible models of disjunctive logic programs [23,24]. A Fusemate logic program consists of (typically) non-ground if-then rules with stratified default negation in the body [21]. Stratification entails that a true default-negated body literal remains true in the course of deriving new conclusions.

Fusemate was introduced in [7] for modelling systems that evolve over time and for analysing their current state based on the events so far. Such tasks are often subsumed under the terms of stream processing, complex event recognition, and situational awareness, and have been addressed (also) with logic-based approaches [2,9,4,5].

To my knowledge, Fusemate is unique among all these and other logic programming systems [12,1,13,26,16] (and theorem provers) in the way it is implemented. Fusemate is implemented by shallow embedding in a full-fledged programming language, Scala [25]. Essentially, the user writes a syntactically sugared Scala program utilizing familiar logic programming notation, and the program's execution returns models. This has advantages and disadvantages. The main disadvantages is that it is more difficult to implement performance boosting measures like term indexing. The main advantage is that interfacing with data structure libraries and with external systems is easy, an aspect whose importance has been emphasized for virtually all of the above systems. In fact, Fusemate is motivated in parts by exploring how far the embedding approach can be pushed and to what benefit.

The earlier Fusemate paper [7] focused on the model computation calculus with a belief revision operator as the main novelty. It utilized a certain notion of *stratification*

---

[1] Fusemate is available at https://bitbucket.csiro.au/users/bau050/repos/fusemate/.

© The Author(s) 2021
A. Platzer and G. Sutcliffe (Eds.): CADE 2021, LNAI 12699, pp. 589–601, 2021.
https://doi.org/10.1007/978-3-030-79876-5_34

by time (SBT) for making the calculus effective and useful in the intended application areas. This system description focuses on the advantages of the shallow embedding approach as boosted by new language features introduced here. These new language features are (a) non-standard comprehension and aggregation operators, among others, and (b) a weaker notion of *stratification by time and predicates (SBTP)*. In brief, SBTP is a lexicographic combination of stratification by time and the standard stratification in terms of the call-graph of the program. Section 5 has an example that demonstrates the need for (a) and (b) in combination, and Section 4 discusses the shallow embedding approach and its advantages on a more general level.

Here is an excerpt from a Fusemate program that previews some of the new features:

```
1  type Time = java.time.LocalDateTime
2  val allIds = 1 to 10
3  case class Change(time:Time, id:Int, color:String) extends Atom
4  case class State(time:Time, id:Int, color:String) extends Atom
5  case class FullState(time:Time, drive:Set[Int], stop:Set[Int]) extends Atom
6  State(time, id, color) :- Now(time), CHOOSE(id:Int, allIds), Change(t <= time, id, color)
7  FullState(time, drive.toSet, stop.toSet) :- State(time,_,_),
8    COLLECT(drive:List[Int], id STH State(time, id, "green")),
9    COLLECT(stop:List[Int], id STH (State(time, id, color), color=="red" || color=="yellow"))
10 MovingState(time) :- FullState(time, drive, stop), stop.size < drive.size
11 Faulty(time, id, since) :- State(time, id, "red"), Change(since < time, id, "green"),
12   NOT (Change(t, id, "yellow"), since < t, t < time)
```

The scenario comprises traffic lights identified by numbers 1 to 10 (line 2). In the course of time the traffic lights change their colors, and each such event is recorded as a corresponding Change atom (line 3). The rule on line 6 computes a State at a current time Now(time) as a snapshot of the current colors of all traffic lights. For that, the comprehension Change(t <=time,id,color) on line 6 finds the latest Change event before or at time for a fixed id chosen from allIds, and binds that time to the (unused) variable t. A FullState aggregates the separate State facts at a time partitioned as (Scala) sets of ids of "drive" and "stop" colors. In that, the COLLECT special form collects in a Scala List-typed variable the specified terms that satisfy the body behind STH. Notice that all atoms in FullState refer to the same time, yet the program is SBTP because State comes before FullState in predicate stratification. (Predicate stratification is computed automatically by Fusemate with Tarjan's algorithm.) The rule on line 10 demonstrates the use of the Scala Set method size in the body. Line 11 demonstrates the use of default negation in combination with comprehension. When applied to a given sequence of Change events, Fusemate computes models, one-at-a-time, each as Scala set of atoms.

2 Fusemate Programs

For the purpose of this paper, a brief summary of the syntactic notions underlying Fusemate programs is sufficient; see [7] for details. Terms and atoms of a given signature are defined as usual. Let $var(z)$ denote the set of variables occurring in an expression z. We say that z is *ground* if $var(z) = \emptyset$. We write $z\sigma$ for applying a substitution σ to

z. The domain of σ is denoted by $dom(\sigma)$. A substitution γ is a *grounding substitution for z* iff $dom(\gamma) = var(z)$ and $z\gamma$ is ground. In this case we simply say that γ *is for z*.

Let $\mathbb{T}$ be a countably infinite discrete set of *time points* equipped with a total strict ordering $<$ ("earlier than"), e.g., the integers. Assume that the time points, comparison operators $=$ and $\leq$, and a successor time function $+1$ are part of the signature and interpreted in the intended way. A *time term* is a (possibly non-ground) term over the sub-signature $\mathbb{T} \cup \{+1\}$.

The signature may contain other "built-in" predicate and function symbols for pre-defined types such as strings, arithmetic data types, sets, etc. We only informally assume that all terms are built in a well-sorted way and that built-in operators over ground terms can be evaluated effectively.

An *ordinary atom (with time term t)* is of the form $p(t, t_1, \ldots, t_n)$ where p is an ordinary predicate (i.e., neither a time predicate nor built-in), t is a time term and $t_1, \ldots, t_n$ terms. A *(Fusemate) rule* is an implication written in Prolog-like syntax as

$$H \text{ :- } b_1, \ldots, b_k, \text{not } \vec{b}_{k+1}, \ldots, \text{not } \vec{b}_n \ . \tag{1}$$

In (1), a rule *head* H is either (a) a disjunction $h_1 \vee \cdots \vee h_m$ of ordinary atoms, for some $m \geq 1$, or (b) the expression **fail**.[2] In case (a) the rule is *ordinary* and in case (b) it is a *fail rule*. A rule *body* B, the part to the right of :-, is defined by mutual recursion as follows. A *positive body literal* is one of the following: (a) an ordinary atom, (b) a *comprehension atom (with time term x)* of the form $p(x \circ t, t_1, \ldots, t_n)$ **sth** B, where x is a variable, $\circ \in \{<, \leq, >, \geq\}$ and B is a body, (c) a built-in call , i.e., an atom with a built-in predicate symbol, or (d) a *special form* **let**(x, t), **choose**(x, ts), **match**(t, s) or **collect**$(x, t$ **sth** $B)$ where x is a variable, s, t are terms, ts is a list of terms, and B is a body. A *positive body* is a list $\vec{b} = b_1, \ldots, b_k$ of positive body literals with $k \geq 0$. If $k = 0$ then $\vec{b}$ is *empty* otherwise it is *non-empty*. A *negative body literal* is an expression of the form **not** $\vec{b}$, where $\vec{b}$ is a non-empty positive body. A *body* is a list $B = b_1, \ldots, b_k, \text{not } \vec{b}_{k+1}, \ldots, \text{not } \vec{b}_n$ comprised of a (possibly empty) positive body and (possibly zero) negative body literals. It is *variable free* if $var(b_1, \ldots, b_k) = \emptyset$.

Let r be a rule (1). We say that r is *range-restricted* iff $var(H) \subseteq var(\vec{b})$. Compared to the usual notion of range-restrictedness [18], Fusemate rules may contain extra variables in negative body literals. For example, $p(t, x) \text{ :- } q(t, x), \text{not}(s < t, r(s, x, y))$ is range-restricted in our sense with extra variables s and y. The extra variables are implicitly existentially quantified within the **not** expression. The example corresponds to the formula $q(t, x) \wedge \neg \exists s, y.(s < t \wedge r(s, x, y)) \rightarrow p(t, x)$. Semantically and operationally this will cause no problems thanks to stratification, introduced next.

Fusemate programs – sets of rules – need to be "stratified by time and by predicates" (SBTP). The standard notion of stratification by predicates means that the call graph of the program contains no cycles going through negative body literals. The edges of this call graph are the "depends on" relation between predicate symbols such that p positively (negatively) depends on q if there is a rule with a p-atom in its head and a q-atom in its positive (negative) body. For disjunctive heads, all head predicates are

---

[2] This definition of head is actually simplified as Fusemate offers an additional head operator for belief revision, see [7]. This is ignored here.

defined to depend positively on each other. Every strongly connected component of the call graph is called a stratum, and in predicate stratified programs negative body literals can occur only in strata lower than the head stratum.

SBTP is defined as follows: for every rule (1) in a given program, (a) there is a variable *time* that is the time term of some ordinary $b \in \vec{b}$, (b) if H is an ordinary head then every head literal must have a time term constrained to be $\geq$ than *time*, and (c) for all rule bodies B occurring in the rule:

(i) the time term of every ordinary or comprehension body literal in B must be constrained to be $\leq$ than *time*, and
(ii) for every negative body literal **not** $\vec{b}$ in B (including the top-level body of (1)) and every ordinary or comprehension literal $b \in \vec{b}$, the time term of b must constrained to be (i) $<$ than *time* or (ii) $\leq$ than *time* and the predicate symbol of b is in a lower stratum than H.

For the purpose of this paper we only informally assume that all rules contain constraints for enforcing the required time ordering properties. There are similar stratification requirements for comprehension atoms and special forms so that their evaluation satisfies the counterpart of condition (ii) (see below for **collect**). A fully formal definition could be given by modifying the spelled-out definition of SBT in [7].

As an example, if r belongs to a lower stratum than p then the following five rules all are SBTP, while only the first two rules are SBT.

$$p(time, x) :- q(time, x), r(t, y), t \leq time \qquad (2)$$

$$p(time, x) :- q(time, x), \textbf{not}(r(t, y), t < time) \qquad (3)$$

$$p(time, x) :- q(time, x), \textbf{not}(r(t, y), t \leq time) \qquad (4)$$

$$p(time + 1, x) :- q(time, x), \textbf{not}(r(t, y), t \leq time) \qquad (5)$$

$$p(time, x) :- q(time, x), (p(t < time, y) \textbf{ sth } q(t, y)), r(t, y) \qquad (6)$$

Finally, a *(Fusemate) program* is a set of range-restricted rules that is SBTP.

3   Model Computation

The possible model semantics of disjunctive logic programs [23,24] associates to a given disjunctive program a certain set of normal programs (i.e., without disjunctive heads) and takes the intended model(s) of these normal programs as the possible models of the given program. These "split" programs represent all possible ways of making one or more head literals true, for every disjunctive rule. As a propositional example, the program $\{a :- b, a \lor c :- b, b :- \}$ is associated to the split programs $\{a :- b, b :- \}$ and $\{a :- b, c :- b, b :- \}$. The possible models, hence, are $\{a, b\}$ and $\{a, b, c\}$

Fusemate computes possible models by bottom-up fixpoint computation and dynamic grounding the program rules in the style of hyper tableaux [8]. The model computation procedure is implemented as a variant of the well-known given-clause algorithm, which seeks to avoid deriving the same conclusion from the same premises twice. It exhausts inferences in an outer loop/inner loop fashion according to the given program's stratification by time and by predicates. The main data structure is a set of paths, where each path represents a partial model candidate computed so far (see [7] for more details). Paths are selected, extended, split and put back into the set until exhausted, for a depth-first, left-to right inference strategy. Paths carry full status information, which is instrumental for implementing incrementality, such that facts with current or later time can be added at any stage without requiring model recomputation from scratch. This, however, necessitated keeping already exhausted paths for continued inferences later.

The proof procedure's core operation is computing a *body matcher*, i.e., a substitution γ for a rule's positive body variables so that the rule body becomes satisfied in the current partial model candidate. Formally, let I be a set of ordinary ground atoms, representing the obvious interpretation that assigns true to exactly the members of I. Let B be a body. A *body matcher for B* is a substitution γ for the positive body of B , written as $I, \gamma \models B$, such that the following holds (b, B means the sequence of head b and rest body B):

$$I, \varepsilon \models \epsilon \qquad (\epsilon \text{ is the empty body and } \varepsilon \text{ is the empty substitution})$$

$$I, \gamma\sigma \models b, B \qquad \text{iff } \gamma \text{ is for } b, b\gamma \in I \text{ and } I, \sigma \models B\gamma, \text{ with } b \text{ ordinary atom}$$

$$I, \gamma\sigma \models (p(x \overset{\leq}{<} t, t_1, \ldots, t_n) \text{ sth } C), B \text{ iff } \gamma \text{ is for } p(x, t_1, \ldots, t_n) \text{ and}$$

(1) $p(x, t_1, \ldots, t_n)\gamma \in I, x\gamma < t$ and $I, \delta \models C\gamma$ for some δ,

(2) there is no γ' for $p(x, t_1, \ldots, t_n)$ and no δ such that

$$p(x, t_1, \ldots, t_n)\gamma' \in I, x\gamma < x\gamma' \overset{\leq}{<} t \text{ and } I, \delta \models C\gamma', \text{ and}$$

(3) $I, \sigma \models B\gamma$

$$I, \sigma \models a, B \qquad \text{iff } a \text{ evaluates to true and } I, \sigma \models B \text{ where } a \text{ is ground built-in}$$

$$I, \gamma\sigma \models \text{let}(x, t), B \text{ iff } \gamma = [x \mapsto t] \text{ and } I, \sigma \models B\gamma$$

$$I, \gamma\sigma \models \text{choose}(x, ts), B \text{ iff } \gamma = [x \mapsto t] \text{ and } I, \sigma \models B\gamma \text{ for some } t \in ts$$

$$I, \gamma\sigma \models \text{match}(t, s), B \text{ iff } \gamma \text{ is for } t, t\gamma = s \text{ and } I, \sigma \models B\gamma$$

$$I, \gamma\sigma \models \text{collect}(x, t \text{ sth } C), B \text{ iff } \gamma = [x \mapsto \{t\delta \mid I, \delta \models C\}] \text{ and } I, \sigma \models B\gamma$$

$$I, \sigma \models \text{not } \vec{b}, B \qquad \text{iff there is no } \delta \text{ such that } I, \delta \models \vec{b}, \text{ and } A, \sigma \models B$$

A *comprehension atom* $p(x \circ t, t_1, \ldots, t_n)$ sth B stands for the subset of all ground p-instances in I such that B is satisfied and with a time x as close as possible to t wrt. $<$ or $\leq$. The cases for $>$ and $\geq$ are dual and not spelled out above to save space. The **collect** special form collects in the variable x the set of all instances of term t such that the body C is satisfied in I. We require comprehension atoms and **collect**s to be used in a stratified way, so that their results do not change later in a derivation when I is extended. The requirements are the same as with **not** and can be enforced by ordering constraints.

The definition above extends the earlier definition of body matchers in [7] with the new comprehension construct and the **let, choose, match, collect** operators. It now also enforces left-to-right evaluation of B because the new binding operators depend on a fixed order guarantee to be useful. An example is the (nonsensical) body **CHOOSE** (x: Int, List(1, 2, 3)), **LET**(xxx: Int, 3*x), xxx % 2 ==0 which relies on this order. Undefined cases, e.g., when evaluation of a non-ground built-in is attempted, or when a binder variable has already been used before are detected as compile time syntax errors.

4 Shallow Embedding in Scala

Fusemate is implemented as a shallow embedding into Scala [25]. It has three conceptual main components: a signature framework, a Scala compiler plugin, and an inference engine for fixpoint computation as explained in Section 3. The signature framework provides a set of Scala class definitions as the syntactical basis for writing Fusemate programs. It is parameterized in a type Time, which can be any Scala or Java type that is equipped with an ordering and an addition function for time increments, for example Int or java.time.OffsetDataTime. The programmer then refines an abstract class Atom of the Time-instantiated signature framework with definitions of predicate symbols and their (Scala-)sorted arities. See lines (3)-(5) in the program in the introduction for an example. These atoms then can be used in Fusemate rules, see lines (6)–(12) in the example.

While written in convenient syntax, rules are syntactically ill-formed Scala. This problem is solved by the compiler plugin, which intercepts the compilation of the input file at an early stage and transforms the rules into valid Scala source code.[3] More precisely, a rule is transformed into a curried partial function that is parameterized in an interpretation context I. The curried parameters are Scala guarded pattern matching expression and correspond to the rule's positive body literals, in order. For example, the Faulty rule on lines (11) and (12), with the condition since < time ignored, for simplicity, is (roughly) translated into the function f

```
1   (I: Interpretation) => { case State(time, id, "red") => {
2     case Change(since, id1, "green") if id == id1 &&
3     ({ case Change(t, id2, "yellow") if id == id2 && since < t && t < time => FAIL} failsOn I) =>
4        Faulty(time, id, since) } }
```

Notice the renaming of repeated occurrences of the id variable, which is needed for the correct semantics. Notice also that a Scala Boolean-valued expression in an ordinary body literal position (e.g., t < time) simply becomes a guard in a pattern.

The code above can be understood with body matcher computation in mind. Suppose the inference engine selects an interpretation I from the current set of paths. For exhausting f on I, the inference engine combinatorially chooses literals $l_1, l_2 \in I$ and collects the evaluation results of $f(I)(l_1)(l_2)$, if defined. Observe that by the transformation into Scala pattern matching, body matchers are only implicitly computed by the Scala runtime system. Each evaluation result, hence, is a body-matcher instantiated head.

The rule's negative body literal is translated into the code on line (3) and conjoined to the guard of the preceding ordinary literal. In general, a negative literal **NOT** *body* is treated by translating **FAIL :- NOT** *body* and evaluating the resulting Scala code on I by means of the failsOn method. If **FAIL** is not derivable then **NOT** *body* is satisfied. Again, appropriate bindings for the variables bound outside of *body* are held implicitly by the Scala runtime system. The translation of the special forms and comprehension is not explained here for space reasons. Fusemate can show the generated code, though.

---

[3] Early experiments showed it is cumbersome and error-prone to write the Scala code by hand, so this was not an option. The compiler plugin is written in Scala and operates at the abstract syntax tree level. This was conveniently be done thanks to a sophisticated quasiquote mechanism.

Properties and Advantages

The shallow embedding approach enables introspection capabilities and interfacing between the rule language and the host language beyond what is implemented in other systems. In Fusemate, the terms of the logical language are nothing but Scala objects. As a consequence, any available Scala type or library data structure can be used as a built-in without extending an "interface" to an extension language – simply because there is none. Dually, the embedding of the rule language into the host language Scala is equally trivial because rules, atoms and interpretations are Scala objects, too.

It is this "closed loop" that makes an aggregation operator (**collect**) possible that returns a list of Scala objects as specified by the programmer, e.g., a list of terms or atoms.[4] This list can be further analysed or manipulated by the rules. See the description logic embedding in Section 5, which critically depends on this feature. This introspection capability stands out in comparison to the logic programming systems mentioned in the introduction. For instance, aggregation in systems like DLV [1], and IDB [12] is limited to predefined integer-valued aggregates for sum, count, times, max and min.

Most logic programming systems can be called from a (traditional) host programming language and can call external systems or utilize libraries for data structures. The DLV system, for instance, interfaces with C++ and Python [22], Prova [16] with Java, and IDP with the Lua scripting language. Systems based on grounding (e.g., DLV and IDP) face the problem of "value invention" by external calls, i.e., having to deal with terms that are not part of the input specification [10].

The main issue, however, from the Fusemate perspective is that these systems' external interfaces are rather heavy-handed (boilerplate code, mapping logic terms to/from the host language, String representation of logic programs) and/or limited to a predefined set of data structures. In contrast, Fusemate's seamless integration with Scala encourages a more integrated and experimental problem solving workflow. The following Scala program demonstrates this point with the traffic light example:

```scala
1  List("2020-07-02T10:00:00,1,green", .., "2020-07-02T10:02:15,2,red")
2      .map { _.split(",") } // Split CSVs intos triple, represented as Java array
3      .map { // Convert String triple to positive Change literals
4          case Array(date,id,color) => Change(LocalDateTime.parse(date), id.toInt, color) }
5      .saturate { rules } // saturate is the Fusemate call, computes all models of the rules
6      .head // Select the first model
7      .toList // Convert to Scala List because we want to sort elements by time:
8      .sortBy { _.time }
9      .flatMap { // Analyze literals in model and retain only Faulty ones as CSV
10         case Faulty(time, id, since) => List(s"$time,$id,$since")
11         case _ => List() }
```

From a workflow perspective, this program integrates Fusemate as a list operator (on a list of Change instances) in an otherwise unremarkable functional program.

---

[4] Technically, this is possible because the current interpretation is available in the rule body through the parameter I (see the transformation example above). One could directly access I, e.g., as in **CHOOSE**(a: atom, I), **MATCH**(State(t,3,c), a), t>10, c !="red"

For a more realistically sized experiment I tried a combined Fusemate/Scala work-flow for analysing the data of the DEBS 2015 Grand Challenge.[5] The data comprises two millions taxi rides in New York City in terms of start/end times, and start/end GPS coordinates, among others. The problem considered was to detect anomalies where a taxi driver drivers away from a busy hotspot without a passenger. Solving the problem required clustering locations by pickup/drop-off activity for determining hotspots, and then analysing driver behavior given their pickups/drop-offs at these hotspots.

Two million data points were too much for Fusemate alone and required Scala preprocessing, e.g., for filling a grid abstraction of New York coordinates, data cleansing and filtering out little active drivers. Fusemate was used for computing clusters with rules similar to transitive closure computation. Input to Fusemate calls were Scala precomputed point clouds. The computed clusters were used to analyze Scala prefiltered taxi rides for anomaly detection based on the clusters. This involved three moderately complex rules, for first identifying gaps and then analysing them. The comprehension operator was useful to find "the most recent ride predating a given start", among others. The longest Fusemate run was 0.31sec for 64 rides (with 39 clusters fixed), most other runs took less than 0.15sec. Fusemate's performance was perfectly acceptable in this experiment thanks to a *combined* workflow.

5 Embedding Description Logic $\mathcal{ALCIF}$

$\mathcal{ALCIF}$ is the well-known description logic $\mathcal{ALC}$ extended with inverse roles and functional roles. (See [3] for background on description logics.) This section describes how to translate an $\mathcal{ALCIF}$ knowledge base to Fusemate rules and facts for satisfia-bility checking.

This is our example knowledge base, TBox on the left, ABox on the right:

$$Person \sqsubseteq Rich \sqcup Poor \qquad\qquad Anne : Person \sqcap Poor$$
$$Person \sqsubseteq \exists father.Person \qquad (Anne, Fred) : father$$
$$Rich \sqsubseteq \forall father^{-1}.Rich \qquad\qquad Bob : Person$$
$$Rich \sqcap Poor \sqsubseteq \bot \qquad\qquad (Bob, Fred) : father$$

The father role is declared as functional, i.e., as a right-unique relation, and $father^{-1}$ denotes its inverse "child" relation. The third GCI says that all children of a rich father are rich as well. In all models of the knowledge base Fred is Poor. This follows from the given fact that his child Anne is poor, functionality of father and the third CGI. However, there are models where Bob is Rich and models where Bob is Poor.

Translating description logic into rule-based languages has been done in many ways, see e.g. [20,17,14,11]. An obvious starting point is taking the FOL version of a given knowledge base. Concept names become unary predicates, role names become binary predicates, and GCIs (general concept inclusions) are translated into implications. By polynomial transformations, the implications can be turned into clausal form (if-then rules over literals), except for existential quantification in a positive context, which

---

[5] http://www.debs2015.org/call-grand-challenge.html

causes unbounded Skolem terms in derivations when treated naively (for example, the third CGI above is problematic in this sense). This is why many systems and also the transformation to Fusemate below avoid Skolemization.

The first GCI corresponds to the clause $\text{Person}(x) \rightarrow \text{Rich}(x) \lor \text{Poor}(x)$, and the second corresponds to the "almost" clause $\text{Person}(x) \rightarrow \exists y.(\text{father}(x, y) \land \text{Person}(y))$. Fusemate works with the reified rule versions of these, with an IsA-predicate for concept instances, and a HasA-predicate for role instances. For the whole TBox one obtains the following, where RN stands for "role name" and CN stands for "concept name".[6]

1 IsA(x, Exists(RN("father"), CN("Person")), time) :- IsA(x, CN("Person"), time)
2 IsA(x, CN("Rich"), time) **OR** IsA(x, CN("Poor"), time) :- IsA(x, CN("Person"), time)
3 IsA(x, Forall(Inv(RN("father")), CN("Rich")), time) :- IsA(x, CN("Rich"), time)
4 **FAIL** :- IsA(x, CN("Poor"), time), IsA(x, CN("Rich"), time)
5 functionalRoles = Set(RN("father"))

Every GCI can be converted into rules like the above without problems. For that, starting from its NNF, $\exists$-quantifications in the premise of a rule can be expanded in place, and $\forall$-quantifications can be moved to the head as the $\exists$-quantification of the NNF of the negated formula. Similarly for negated concept names. See [20] for such transformation methods. The ABox is represented similarly. Its first element, for instance, is IsA(Name("Anne"), And2(CN("Person"), CN("Poor")), 0).

In addition, some more general "library" rules for the tableau calculus are needed:

1 IsA(x, c1, time) **AND** IsA(x, c2, time) :- IsA(x, And2(c1, c2), time)
2 IsA(x, c1, time) **OR** IsA(x, c2, time) :- IsA(x, Or2(c1, c2), time)
3 // Expansion rules for quantifiers
4 IsA(y, c, time) :- Neighbour(x, r, y, time), IsA(x, Forall(r, c), time)
5 HasA(x, r, rSuccOfx, time+1) **AND** IsA(rSuccOfx, c, time+1): @preds("TimePlus1") :-
6   IsA(x, Exists(r, c), time), ! (functionalRoles contains r),
7   **NOT**(Neighbour(x, r, y, time), IsA(y, c, time)), **NOT**(Blocked(x, _, time)),
8   **LET**(rSuccOfx: Individual, Succ(r, x))

10 HasA(x, r, rSuccOfx, time+1) **AND** IsA(rSuccOfx, c, time+1): @preds("TimePlus1") :- (
11   IsA(x, Exists(r, c), time), functionalRoles contains r,
12   **NOT**(Neighbour(x, r, y, time)), **NOT**(Blocked(x, _, time)),
13   **LET**(rSuccOfx: Individual, Succ(r, x))

15 IsA(y, c, time) :-
16   IsA(x, Exists(r, c), time), functionalRoles contains r,
17   Neighbour(x, r, y, time)

The expansion rules on lines 1 and 2 deal with the $\mathcal{ALC}$ binary Boolean connectives And2 and Or2 in the obvious way. Supposing NNF of embedded formulas, no other cases can apply. The remaining rules can be understood best with the standard tableau algorithm for $\mathcal{ALCIN}$ in mind, which includes blocking to guarantee termination. They follow the terminology in [6, Chapter 4]. The Neighbour relation abstracts from the HasA relation, left away for space reasons. The expansion rule for $\exists$ comes for three cases. The first case (line 5), for example, applies to non-functional roles as per the Scala builtin test on line 6. The expansion of the given $\exists$-formula only happens if it

---

[6] See the Fusemate web page for the full, runnable code.

is not yet satisfied and in a non-blocked situation (line 7). In this case the rule derives a Skolem object defined on line 8 for satisfying the ∃-formula. Notice the annotation @preds("TimePlus1") which makes sure that the head is on the highest stratum. This way, the rule will be applied after, in particular, the rules for blocking. Furthermore, with the time stamp time +1 the Skolem object is kept separate from the computations in the current iteration time. The blocking rules are defined as follows:

```
1  // Collect all concepts that an individual x isA, at a given time
2  Label(x, cs.toSet, time) :- IsA(x, _, time), COLLECT(cs: List[Concept], c STH IsA(x, c, time))
3  // Ancestor relation of Skolem objects introduced by exists-right
4  Anc(x, Succ(r, x), time) :- HasA(x, r, Succ(r, x), time)
5  Anc(x, Succ(r, z), time) :- HasA(z, r, Succ(r, z), time), Step(time, prev), Anc(x, z, prev)
6  // Blocked case 1: y is blocked by some individual x
7  Blocked(y, x, time) :- Label(y, yIsAs, time), Anc(x, y, time), Label(x, xIsAs, time), yIsAs == xIsAs
8  // Blocked case 2: y is blocked by some ancestor
9  Blocked(y, x, time) :- Anc(x, y, time), Blocked(x, _, time)
```

Some additional rules are needed for dealing with basic inconsistencies and for carrying over IsA and HasA facts between iterations. They are not shown here.

The expansion rules and blocking rules follow the tableau calculus description in [6, Chapter 4]. One important detail is that the expansion rule for ∃ must be applied with lowest priority. This is straightforward thanks to Fusemate's stratification and aggregation construct. Equally important is the access to (Scala) data structures via built-ins and using them as terms of the logical language. This made it easy to program Skolemization and the Label relation for collecting sets of concepts of an individual.

6   Conclusions

This paper described recent developments around the Fusemate logic programming system. It included new technical improvements for a weaker form of stratification, which enabled useful aggregation and comprehension language constructs. It also argued for the advantages of the tight integration with Fusemate's host language, Scala, in terms of data structures and usability.

Answer set solvers like DLV and SModels are designed to solve NP-complete or higher complexity search problems as fast as possible. Fusemate is not motivated as a competitive such system, it is motivated for "well-behaved" knowledge representation applications, similarly to description logic reasoners, whose (often) NExpTime complete solving capabilities are not expected to be typically needed. (Some more work is needed, though, e.g., on improving the current term indexing techniques to speed up model computation.) More specifically, the main intended application of Fusemate is for the runtime analysis of systems that evolve over time. The taxi rides data experiment explained in Section 4 is an example for that. It suggests that Fusemate is currently best used in a combined problem solving workflow if scalability is an issue.

As for future work, the next steps are to make the description logic reasoner of Section 5 callable from within Fusemate rules in a DL-safe way [19] and to embed a temporal reasoning formalism. The event calculus [15] seems to be a good fit.

Acknowledgements.   I am grateful to the reviewers for their helpful comments.

References

1. Alviano, M., Faber, W., Leone, N., Perri, S., Pfeifer, G., Terracina, G.: The Disjunctive Datalog System DLV. In: de Moor, O., Gottlob, G., Furche, T., Sellers, A.J. (eds.) Datalog Reloaded - First International Workshop, Datalog 2010, Oxford, UK, March 16-19, 2010. Revised Selected Papers. Lecture Notes in Computer Science, vol. 6702, pp. 282–301. Springer (2010). https://doi.org/10.1007/978-3-642-24206-9_17
2. Artikis, A., Skarlatidis, A., Portet, F., Paliouras, G.: Logic-Based Event Recognition. Knowledge Engineering Review **27**(4), 469–506 (2012). https://doi.org/10.1017/S0269888912000264
3. Baader, F., Calvanese, D., McGuinness, D., Nardi, D., Patel-Schneider, P. (eds.): Description Logic Handbook. Cambridge University Press (2002)
4. Baader, F., Bauer, A., Baumgartner, P., Cregan, A., Gabaldon, A., Ji, K., Lee, K., Rajaratnam, D., Schwitter, R.: A Novel Architecture for Situation Awareness Systems. In: Giese, M., Waaler, A. (eds.) Automated Reasoning with Analytic Tableaux and Related Methods (TABLEAUX 2009). LNAI, vol. 5607, pp. 77–92. Springer (July 2009). https://doi.org/10.1007/978-3-642-02716-1_7
5. Baader, F., Borgwardt, S., Lippmann, M.: Temporal Conjunctive Queries in Expressive Description Logics with Transitive Roles. In: Pfahringer, B., Renz, J. (eds.) AI 2015: Advances in Artificial Intelligence - 28th Australasian Joint Conference, Canberra, ACT, Australia, November 30 - December 4, 2015, Proceedings. Lecture Notes in Computer Science, vol. 9457, pp. 21–33. Springer (2015). https://doi.org/10.1007/978-3-319-26350-2_3
6. Baader, F., Horrocks, I., Lutz, C., Sattler, U.: An Introduction to Description Logic. Cambridge University Press (2017)
7. Baumgartner, P.: Possible Models Computation and Revision – A Practical Approach. In: Peltier, N., Sofronie-Stokkermans, V. (eds.) International Joint Conference on Automated Reasoning. LNAI, vol. 12166, pp. 337–355. Springer International Publishing, Cham (2020). https://doi.org/10.1007/978-3-030-51074-9_19
8. Baumgartner, P., Furbach, U., Niemelä, I.: Hyper Tableaux. In: Logics in Artificial Intelligence (JELIA '96). Lecture Notes in Artificial Intelligence, vol. 1126. Springer (1996)
9. Beck, H., Dao-Tran, M., Eiter, T.: LARS: A Logic-based framework for Analytic Reasoning over Streams. Artificial Intelligence **261**, 16–70 (2018). https://doi.org/10.1016/j.artint.2018.04.003
10. Calimeri, F., Cozza, S., Ianni, G.: External sources of knowledge and value invention in logic programming. Annals of Mathematics and Artificial Intelligence **50**, 333–361 (08 2007). https://doi.org/10.1007/s10472-007-9076-z
11. Carral, D., Krötzsch, M.: Rewriting the Description Logic ALCHIQ to Disjunctive Existential Rules. In: Bessiere, C. (ed.) Proceedings of the Twenty-Ninth International Joint Conference on Artificial Intelligence, IJCAI 2020. pp. 1777–1783. ijcai.org (2020). https://doi.org/10.24963/ijcai.2020/246
12. Cat, B.D., Bogaerts, B., Bruynooghe, M., Janssens, G., Denecker, M.: Predicate logic as a modeling language: the IDP system. In: Michael Kifer and Yanhong Annie Liu (ed.) Declarative Logic Programming: Theory, Systems, and Applications, pp. 279–323. ACM / Morgan & Claypool (2018). https://doi.org/10.1145/3191315.3191321
13. Gebser, M., Kaminski, R., Kaufmann, B., Schaub, T.: Clingo = ASP + Control: Preliminary Report. CoRR **abs/1405.3694** (2014), http://arxiv.org/abs/1405.3694
14. Grosof, B.N., Horrocks, I., Volz, R., Decker, S.: Description Logic Programs: Combining Logic Programs with Description Logic. In: Hencsey, G., White, B., Chen, Y.R., Kovács, L., Lawrence, S. (eds.) Proceedings of the Twelfth International World Wide Web Conference, WWW 2003, Budapest, Hungary, May 20-24, 2003. pp. 48–57. ACM (2003). https://doi.org/10.1145/775152.775160

15. Kowalski, R.A., Sergot, M.J.: A Logic-based Calculus of Events. New Generation Computing **4**(1), 67–95 (1986). https://doi.org/10.1007/BF03037383

16. Kozlenkov, A., Peñaloza, R., Nigam, V., Royer, L., Dawelbait, G., Schroeder, M.: Prova: Rule-Based Java Scripting for Distributed Web Applications: A Case Study in Bioinformatics. In: EDBT Workshops. LNCS, vol. 4254, pp. 899–908. Springer (2006). https://doi.org/10.1007/11896548_68

17. Lukácsy, G., Szeredi, P.: Efficient description logic reasoning in Prolog: The DLog system. Theory and Practice of Logic Programming **9**(3), 343–414 (2009). https://doi.org/10.1017/S1471068409003792

18. Manthey, R., Bry, F.: SATCHMO: a theorem prover implemented in Prolog. In: Lusk, E., Overbeek, R. (eds.) Proceedings of the 9th Conference on Automated Deduction, Argonne, Illinois, May 1988. Lecture Notes in Computer Science, vol. 310, pp. 415–434. Springer (1988)

19. Motik, B., Sattler, U., Studer, R.: Query Answering for OWL-DL with Rules. In: McIlraith, S.A., Plexousakis, D., van Harmelen, F. (eds.) The Semantic Web – ISWC 2004. pp. 549–563. Springer Berlin Heidelberg, Berlin, Heidelberg (2004)

20. Motik, B., Shearer, R., Horrocks, I.: Hypertableau Reasoning for Description Logics. Journal of Artificial Intelligence Research **36**, 165–228 (2009). https://doi.org/10.1613/jair.2811

21. Przymusinski, T.C.: On the Declarative Semantics of Deductive Databases and Logic Programs. In: Minker, J. (ed.) Foundations of Deductive Databases and Logic Programming, pp. 193 – 216. Morgan Kaufmann (1988). https://doi.org/10.1016/B978-0-934613-40-8.50009-9

22. Redl, C.: The DLVHEX System for Knowledge Representation: Recent Advances (System Description). Theory and Practice of Logic Programming **16** (07 2016). https://doi.org/10.1017/S1471068416000211

23. Sakama, C.: Possible Model Semantics for Disjunctive Databases. In: Kim, W., Nicholas, J.M., Nishio, S. (eds.) Proceedings First International Conference on Deductive and Object-Oriented Databases (DOOD-89). pp. 337–351. Elsevier Science Publishers B.V. (North–Holland) Amsterdam (1990)

24. Sakama, C., Inoue, K.: An Alternative Approach to the Semantics of Disjunctive Logic Programs and Deductive Databases. Journal of Automated Reasoning **13**, 145–172 (1994)

25. The Scala Programming Language, https://www.scala-lang.org

26. Syrjänen, T., Niemelä, I.: The Smodels System. In: Eiter, T., Faber, W., Truszczynski, M. (eds.) Logic Programming and Nonmonotonic Reasoning, 6th International Conference, LPNMR 2001, Vienna, Austria, September 17-19, 2001, Proceedings. Lecture Notes in Computer Science, vol. 2173, pp. 434–438. Springer (2001). https://doi.org/10.1007/3-540-45402-0_38

Open Access This chapter is licensed under the terms of the Creative Commons Attribution 4.0 International License (http://creativecommons.org/licenses/by/4.0/), which permits use, sharing, adaptation, distribution and reproduction in any medium or format, as long as you give appropriate credit to the original author(s) and the source, provide a link to the Creative Commons license and indicate if changes were made.

The images or other third party material in this chapter are included in the chapter's Creative Commons license, unless indicated otherwise in a credit line to the material. If material is not included in the chapter's Creative Commons license and your intended use is not permitted by statutory regulation or exceeds the permitted use, you will need to obtain permission directly from the copyright holder.

Twee: An Equational Theorem Prover

Nicholas Smallbone

Department of Computer Science and Engineering,
Chalmers University of Technology, Gothenburg, Sweden
nicsma@chalmers.se

Abstract. Twee is an automated theorem prover for equational logic. It implements unfailing Knuth-Bendix completion with ground joinability testing and a connectedness-based redundancy criterion. It came second in the UEQ division of CASC-J10, solving some problems that no other system solved. This paper describes Twee's design and implementation.

Keywords: Automated theorem proving · unit equality · completion

1 Introduction

Twee is an automated theorem prover for equational logic, available as open-source software [17]. It features good performance (coming second in the UEQ division of CASC-J10), low memory use, and human-readable proof output.

Twee's general architecture is quite traditional: it uses a DISCOUNT loop [7] implementing unfailing Knuth-Bendix completion [3]. However, it has a few characteristics which are unusual in a high-performance theorem prover:

Fixed heuristics. Twee does not adjust its strategy based on the input problem. It uses a fixed term order, a fixed critical pair scoring function, and so on. Rather than detecting the kind of problem, Twee uses general-purpose strategies that work for all sorts of problems (Section 2).

Strong redundancy tests. Rather than using special strategies for associative-commutative functions, Twee builds in strong redundancy tests, based on ground joinability and connectedness (Section 3). These handle not just AC functions but many kinds of unorientable equations, in particular permutative ones (where both sides are almost the same but with variables in a different order).

A high-level language. Twee consists of 5300 lines of Haskell code, whereas for example Waldmeister [12] is 65000 lines of C. As such, it is easy to experiment with. Despite the choice of programming language, Twee is quite fast at raw deduction steps, thanks to careful coding of low-level term operations (Section 4).

Despite the fixed heuristics and high-level language, Twee comes close in performance to E [14] and Waldmeister [12]. It is strong in many problem classes,

© The Author(s) 2021
A. Platzer and G. Sutcliffe (Eds.): CADE 2021, LNAI 12699, pp. 602–613, 2021.
https://doi.org/10.1007/978-3-030-79876-5_35

including LAT (lattices) and REL (relation algebra) from TPTP, which feature many commutative operators where Twee's redundancy tests shine, and on unusual problems, where no prover has special heuristics. Twee is however poor at RNG (rings), where it seems important to choose a good term order. The rest of the paper describes Twee's design in detail, focusing on the three aspects above.

Notation. We use $t \equiv u$ to mean that t and u are syntactically equal.

2   Architecture

Twee natively supports only unit equality problems with ground goals, but the frontend also supports arbitrary quantification, Horn formulas, and many-sorted logic. These features are eliminated using the external tool Jukebox [16], which:

- Clausifies the problem to eliminate conjunction and quantifiers.
- Encodes Horn clauses as equations [5].
- Encodes sorts using extra functions [4].

At this point, the goal can still contain existentially-quantified variables, which must be eliminated. To do so, we use an old trick, also used by Waldmeister: if the goal $t = u$ is non-ground, we add new function symbols *eq*, *true* and *false*, and two axioms $\forall X.\ eq(X, X) = true$ and $eq(t, u) = false$, and replace the goal with *true* = *false*. Now we have a unit equality problem with a ground goal.

The main proof loop is shown in Algorithm 1. It implements unfailing completion [3] using a DISCOUNT loop [7]. The state consists of R, a set of rewrite rules and unorientable equations (the *active set*, initially empty); Q, the set of unprocessed critical pairs formed from R (the *passive set*, initially containing all the axioms); J, a set of ground joinable equations used for subsumption checking (following [1]); and the goal. The main loop removes the best critical pair from Q (see below), and if it is not redundant, adds it to R (oriented if possible) and adds all its critical pairs to Q. Every so often, the rules in R are reduced with respect to one another and redundant rules are removed. The goal is kept normalised with respect to R and the prover succeeds if the goal becomes trivial.[1]

The passive set is normally quadratic in the size of the active set: typical numbers are $|R| \approx 10,000$ and $|Q| \approx 10,000,000$. Hence we must process each passive critical pair at high speed, but can spend time on each new rewrite rule.

Term ordering. We always use KBO, with all functions having weight 1, and ordered so that more frequently-occuring functions are smaller.

Critical pair selection. When a critical pair is added to Q, it is first normalised and then assigned a score; the proof loop selects the critical pair with the lowest score. The score function's job is to pick out promising critical pairs, and the choice of score function can make or break the prover. However, as it is applied to every critical pair, it also needs to be fast. We compute scores as follows:

---

[1] An equation is considered trivial if it is of the form $t = t$.

Algorithm 1 The main proof loop

$(R, J, Q) = (\emptyset, \emptyset, A)$
while $Q \neq \emptyset$ **do**
    P = remove lowest-scoring element of Q
    if P's parent rules are still present in R **then**
        normalise P using R to get $t = u$
        if $t \not\equiv u$ and $t = u$ is not connected and $t = u$ is not subsumed by J **then**
            if $t = u$ is ground joinable **then**
                add $t = u$ to J
            else
                orient $t = u$ and add it to R
                for all critical pairs cp of $t = u$ and R **do**
                    normalise cp using only the oriented rules in R
                    if cp is non-trivial **then** add cp to Q **end if**
                end for
                normalise goal using R
                if goal is trivial **then return** "theorem" **end if**
                simplify rules in R wrt each other, but limit this step to 5% of total runtime
            end if
        end if
    end if
end while
return "countersatisfiable"

- We start with a weighted sum of the size of the two terms. By default we take $4 \, \text{weight}(t) + \text{weight}(u)$, where t is the bigger term and u the smaller. In other words, the size of the bigger term is most important. Variables are weighted slightly less than function symbols, to encourage finding more general rules.
- To encourage Twee to use all the axioms, we add the critical pair's *depth*, where axioms have depth 0, critical pairs of the axioms have depth 1, etc.
- If a term contains the same subterm multiple times, only one occurrence of that subterm is counted; the other occurrences get a nominal weight of one symbol. In effect we measure the weight as if the term was a DAG rather than a tree. The idea is that identical subterms form the same critical pairs, and tend to get rewritten at the same time: they come and go together.
- Finally, any critical pair of the form $eq(v, w) = \textit{false}$ (where eq is the function used to encode existential goals) with v and w unifiable is given a fixed cost of 1, because selecting it will immediately prove the goal. This trick is also used by Waldmeister, and is vital in practice for existential goals.

Proof production and checking. Twee uses an LCF-style kernel [9] to guarantee soundness. Every member of the active set comes with a proof object, which is verified by a trusted proof checker (consisting of about a page of code). The proofs are low-level and thus easy to check: the only proof steps allowed are reflexivity, symmetry, transitivity, congruence and applying an axiom or lemma. It is not possible to add a rule to the active set without supplying a proof, and any invalid proof step causes a fatal runtime error. The key to making this fast is that only the active set, not the passive set, includes proof objects.

Once the goal is proved, we transform the proof object into a human-readable proof, consisting of a flat sequence of rewrite steps. We also introduce lemmas, to avoid exponentially-sized proofs: any active rewrite rule is a candidate lemma. Our approach is similar to [8], but simpler as our proof steps are smaller; but their lemma selection strategy is smarter than ours and produces fewer lemmas.

Goal transformation. Twee's frontend can optionally transform the problem to make the prover more goal-directed. The transformation is simple, but strange. For every function term $f(\ldots)$ appearing in the goal, we introduce a fresh constant symbol a and add the axiom $f(\ldots) = a$. For example, if the goal is $f(g(a), b) = h(c)$, we add the axioms $f(g(a), b) = d_1$, $g(a) = d_2$, and $h(c) = d_3$. Simplification will rewrite the first axiom to $f(d_2, b) = d_1$ and the goal to $d_1 = d_3$.

By doing this transformation, (1) any subterm of the goal gets normalised to a constant, so critical pairs containing goal terms get a lower score, and (2) new critical pairs involving these constants appear, which are likely to be relevant to the goal. We evaluate this transformation in Section 5.

Weak rewrite rules. Completion sometimes deduces equations where both sides have a variable not occurring on the other side, such as $f(x, y) = g(x, z)$. Such equations are awkward for rewriting: suppose we want to use this equation to rewrite the term $f(t, u)$—what value should we choose for z?

Twee splits this equation into nicely-behaved rewrite rules instead. To do so, we introduce the concept of a *weak rewrite rule*. A weak rewrite rule $t \rightsquigarrow u$ is like an ordinary rewrite rule, except that it only satisfies $t \geqslant u$, not $t > u$.[2] Weak rewrite rules form critical pairs and participate in rewriting just like any other rewrite rule, except that to ensure termination, we may only perform the rewrite step $t\sigma \rightsquigarrow u\sigma$ if $t\sigma \not\equiv u\sigma$, i.e. $t\sigma$ and $u\sigma$ are syntactically different terms.[3]

Using weak rewrite rules, Twee splits $f(x, y) = g(x, z)$ into the two rules $f(x, y) \rightarrow g(x, \perp)$ and $g(x, z) \rightsquigarrow g(x, \perp)$, where $\perp$ is the *minimal* term in the term ordering. Note that $g(x, z) \rightsquigarrow g(x, \perp)$ is a valid weak rewrite rule because $g(x, z) \geqslant g(x, \perp)$, with equality exactly when $z \equiv \perp$.

As another example, the equation $f(x, x, y, z) = g(x, y, y, w)$ is split into $f(x, x, y, \perp) = g(x, y, y, \perp)$, $f(x, x, y, z) \rightsquigarrow f(x, x, y, \perp)$ and $g(x, y, y, w) \rightsquigarrow g(x, y, y, \perp)$. In this case, we are still left with an unorientable rule afterwards, but since it has the same variables on both sides it is unproblematic for rewriting.

It is always possible and safe to split an equation into an equivalent set of:
- ordinary rewrite rules $t \rightarrow u$ with $t > u$,
- weak rewrite rules $t \rightsquigarrow u$ with $t \geqslant u$, and
- unorientable equations $t = u$ where both sides have the same set of variables.

Twee does this whenever an equation is about to be added to R.

---

[2] $t \geqslant u$ means: for all grounding substitutions σ, either $t\sigma > u\sigma$ or $t\sigma \equiv u\sigma$.

[3] This is different from e.g. constrained rewriting: we can perform the rewrite even if t and u are unifiable, as long as they are not the same term right now.

3   Redundancy Criteria

The basic redundancy criterion of Knuth-Bendix completion is *joinability*: a critical pair can be discarded if both sides normalise to the same term. Joinability runs into problems when we have unorientable equations. For example, consider a rewrite system for an associative-commutative operator "+":

$$x + y = y + x \tag{1}$$
$$(x + y) + z \to x + (y + z) \tag{2}$$
$$x + (y + z) = y + (x + z) \tag{3}$$

From (1) and (2) we get the critical pair $x + (y + z) \xleftarrow{(2)} (x + y) + z \xrightarrow{(1)} z + (x + y)$, which cannot be rewritten any further so it is not joinable. However, the critical pair is redundant, because the above rewrite system is ground confluent. We would like to detect redundant but non-joinable critical pairs.

This section presents the redundancy criteria that Twee uses to handle unorientable equations: our take on the well-known approach of ground joinability testing [6], and a novel (we believe) approach based on connectedness [2]. Unlike the standard techniques for associative-commutative functions [1], our criteria handle any kind of permutative equation; we evaluate our approach in Section 5.

3.1   Ground Joinability Testing

Although the critical pair $x + (y + z) \leftarrow (x + y) + z \to z + (x + y)$ is not joinable, all ground instances of it are joinable, and we say that the critical pair is ground joinable. For example, the instance $a + (b + c) \leftarrow (a + b) + c \to c + (a + b)$, with $a < b < c$, can be joined since $c + (a + b) \xrightarrow{(3)} a + (c + b) \xrightarrow{(1)} a + (b + c)$. Any ground joinable critical pair is redundant.

Martin and Nipkow [13] suggest an approach for checking ground joinability:

– Consider all possible orderings between the variables of the critical pair, such as $x < y < z$, $y < x \equiv z$, $x \equiv y < z$, and so on.
– For each ordering, show that the critical pair is joinable when the variables have that order. Formally, this means showing that all ground instances satisfying the ordering are joinable. For example, the rewrite proof above shows our critical pair joinable for any ground instance satisfying $x < y < z$.

Their algorithm effectively does a case analysis on all possible variable orderings, but it is inefficient because there are so many possible orderings.

Our algorithm is similar, but tries to minimise the number of cases it considers. It does so by allowing orderings that: (1) constrain only a subset of the variables, such as $x < y$, and (2) use $\leqslant$, as in $x \leqslant y < z$. It works as follows:

1. Choose a strict total order on *all* the variables, using *only* $<$; e.g., $x < y < z$.
2. Show that the critical pair is joinable under that ordering. Formally, we show that all *ground instances* satisfying the ordering are joinable.

3. We have now shown that the critical pair is joinable in one specific case. Now *generalise* that case, by: (1) removing variables from the ordering, and (2) replacing $<$ with $\leqslant$ in the ordering, as long as the critical pair is joinable under the resulting ordering. (This may e.g. generalise $x < y < z$ to $x \leqslant z$.)
4. Repeat, but pick an ordering that is not covered by any of the cases so far.
5. When all variable orderings involving only $<$ have been covered, all the ones that remain must involve $\equiv$. For each such ordering, take the critical pair, unify all equal variables, and recursively call the ground joinability check.

Example. Take the critical pair $x + (y+z) \leftarrow (x+y) + z \rightarrow z + (x+y)$ and suppose that we choose the ordering $x < y < z$. It can be joined when this order holds, as for any instance where $x < y < z$, we have $z + (x+y) \xrightarrow{(3)} x + (z+y) \xrightarrow{(1)} x + (y+z)$.

Having joined the critical pair in one case, we now generalise the case. We first try to remove each variable in turn, i.e. to join the critical pair in the three cases $x < y$, $y < z$, and $x < z$ in turn. None of these attempts succeeds.

Now we try replacing a $<$ with a $\leqslant$, to get $x < y \leqslant z$. We must check if all ground instances satisfying $x < y \leqslant z$ are joinable, but how? We might think of splitting this into two cases $x < y < z$ and $x < y \equiv z$, but instead we are going to find *one rewrite proof* that works for both.

Consider the rewrite proof above. In it, the step $x + (z + y) \rightarrow x + (y + z)$ is fine if $y < z$, but does not seem to be allowed if $y \equiv z$. But in fact it is fine: if $y \equiv z$, the terms $x + (z + y)$ and $x + (y + z)$ are identical, so this rewrite step does nothing and can just be dropped. That is, the proof works both when $x < y < z$ and $x < y \equiv z$, and shows joinability for the case $x < y \leqslant z$. We generalise the other $<$ similarly, showing that the critical pair is joinable in the case $x \leqslant y \leqslant z$.

Next, we pick another total order on the variables, but not one in which $x \leqslant y \leqslant z$. We might pick, for example, $z < y < x$. The process repeats: we show ground joinability under this ordering, and generalise it to $z \leqslant y \leqslant x$. We repeat until all cases are covered, and the ground joinability test succeeds.

Although our algorithm can be expensive in theory, in practice it needs to consider only a few orderings, and a small number of variables. Step (5) can occasionally be expensive, but by generalising $<$ to $\leqslant$ we can usually avoid it.

The general case. Here is how we test joinability under a given variable ordering. First, we parameterise our term order. Given an ordering C, we define $t \geqslant_C u$ to mean that, for all grounding substitutions σ, if σ satisfies C then $t\sigma \geqslant u\sigma$.

In the example, we weakened a $<$ to a $\leqslant$. To do so, we used a rewrite step that, in some ground instances, rewrote a term to *the same term*. To allow these kind of steps, we loosen our definition of rewriting: we may perform a rewrite $t \rightarrow u$ under C as long as $t \geqslant_C u$ and $t \not\equiv u$. Rewriting terminates because given a rewrite proof $t \geqslant_C u \geqslant_C v \geqslant_C \ldots$, there is always a ground instance where $t' >_C u' >_C v' >_C \ldots$, since C was constructed as a strict order in step (1).

With this definition, normalising $z + (x+y)$ using the ordering $C := x \leqslant y \leqslant z$ yields $z + (x + y) \rightarrow x + (z + y) \rightarrow x + (y + z)$, where e.g. the first step is allowed because $z + x \geqslant_C x + z$ and $z + x \not\equiv x + z$. Thus we can join our example critical pair under a given variable ordering just by normalising both sides, as we want.

The last ingredient is to implement a test for $t \succcurlyeq_C u$, which we have done for KBO. The tricky part is checking whether $\mathrm{weight}(t) \geqslant \mathrm{weight}(u)$, which can be solved by taking the expression $\mathrm{weight}(t) - \mathrm{weight}(u)$, a linear combination of the weights of t's and u's variables, and computing its minimum possible value.

One nice property is that the rest of the ground joining code is independent of the term order. To support e.g. LPO, one just needs to implement $\succcurlyeq_C$ for it.

Why not allow arbitrary ordering constraints? Some critical pairs can only be ground joined by using ordering constraints on arbitrary terms (e.g. $x + y \prec z$). We do not support these, as they make everything enormously more complex:

- The number of possible orderings becomes infinite. You can get stuck enumerating more and more cases of a case split which never ends. In our design, there are finitely many orderings and the algorithm clearly terminates.
- Computing $\succcurlyeq_C$ for KBO becomes NP-complete [10]. In our setting, it takes polynomial time, and we expect it can be done in linear time following [11].

3.2   Connectedness

Ground joinability testing is rather heavyweight, constructing and analysing a sometimes large case split, and sometimes it fails because it only supports case splits on variables. Twee also supports a simpler, complementary method that works well when an unorientable equation is applied *under* another function.

The method makes use of *connectedness*. A critical pair $s \leftarrow t \rightarrow u$ is *connected* if there is a rewrite proof $s = t_1 = \ldots = t_n = u$ such that each t_i is strictly less than t [2]. In Knuth-Bendix completion, any connected critical pair is redundant. In other words, when joining $s \leftarrow t \rightarrow u$, we can do rewrite steps that *increase* the term, as long as the result is always strictly less than t.

Here is how we use connectedness. Let σ be a substitution that grounds s and u. When joining $s \leftarrow t \rightarrow u$, we may want to perform a rewrite step $v \rightarrow w$ using an unoriented equation, but we don't know if $v \geqslant w$. We allow the rewrite step $v \rightarrow w$ as long as: (1) $w \prec t$, and (2) $v\sigma \succ w\sigma$. Condition (1) ensures connectedness, and condition (2) ensures that rewriting eventually terminates.

For example, suppose we take the earlier rules for "$+$" and add a function f:

$$f(x + y, z + w) \rightarrow f(x, f(z, f(y, w))) \tag{4}$$
$$f(x, f(y, z)) = f(y, f(x, z)) \tag{5}$$

Assume KBO with both f and $+$ having weight 1. One critical pair is
$$f(y, f(z, f(x, w))) \xleftarrow{(4)} f(y + x, z + w) \xleftarrow{(1)} f(x + y, z + w) \xrightarrow{(4)} f(x, f(z, f(y, w))).$$
We can show this to be connected using $\sigma = \{x \mapsto a, y \mapsto b, z \mapsto c, w \mapsto d\}$, $a \prec b \prec c \prec d$. The left term $f(y, f(z, f(x, w)))$ rewrites to $f(y, f(x, f(z, w)))$ using (5), because $f(y, f(x, f(z, w))) \prec f(x + y, z + w)$ (connectedness) and $f(b, f(c, f(a, d))) \succ f(b, f(a, f(c, d)))$ (termination); and that rewrites to $f(x, f(y, f(z, w)))$ similarly. The right term $f(x, f(z, f(y, w)))$ also rewrites to $f(x, f(y, f(z, w)))$. Thus the critical pair is redundant.

In general we try two choices of σ: one where the first variable in $s = u$ is mapped to a_1, the second to a_2, and so on (with $a_1 \prec \ldots \prec a_n$); and another where the variables are mapped in reverse order. The critical pair is redundant if either choice of σ works. This is not a principled choice—most likely, some critical pairs need a different σ—but we do not know how to find the "best" σ.

4   Implementation

Twee consists of 5300 lines of Haskell code, comprising: terms, unification etc. (1150 lines); the frontend (850 lines); proof output (700 lines); general data structures (700 lines); the main proof loop (600 lines); joining, ground joining and connectedness (500 lines); critical pairs and the passive set (400 lines); term indexing (250 lines); and KBO (150 lines). This does not include TPTP parsing, clausification, etc., which are provided by the 4000-line Jukebox [16] program.

Most of Twee is written in a high-level, Haskell-idiomatic, somewhat inefficient style. Performance-critical parts (term manipulation, term indexing, and the passive set) are coded more carefully, and are described below. The bottleneck is usually normalising the many millions of critical pairs that are generated.

4.1   Terms

The simplest way to represent terms in Haskell, as trees, is not ideal: it creates pressure on the garbage collector, and core operations such as matching and unification become heavily recursive and needlessly slow.

Instead, we represent terms as *flatterms*—the term is flattened into a list of symbols and stored in an array. In order to preserve the structure of the term, each symbol is paired with a number giving the size of the subterm rooted at that symbol. For example, the term $f(x, g(x, y))$ is represented as:

$f : 5$	$x : 1$	$g : 3$	$x : 1$	$y : 1$

where e.g. $g : 3$ indicates a subterm with root g that is 3 symbols long (g, x, y).

In addition, each function and variable has an *ID number*, and the term stores those ID numbers, rather than a pointer to the function or variable. So, in the array above, the "f" really means the ID number of f. Functions have positive ID numbers, and variables negative, so they can be easily told apart, and there is a separate global array which maps ID numbers to functions. This design allows us to represent a term as a simple array of integers, so that pressure on the garbage collector is reduced. Also, comparing two terms for equality just amounts to a bytewise comparison of the arrays (a C `memcmp`). What's more, by using array slicing, we can view a term's subterms as flatterms in their own right.

On top of this we build a higher-level API. There are two types, terms and termlists, both implemented as flatterms. With the help of Haskell's user-defined patterns, they are exposed to the user as ordinary algebraic datatypes. We can use normal pattern matching to e.g. check if a term is a function or variable, access its children (as a termlist), iterate through it a symbol or subterm at a time, etc. All these operations turn into a few machine instructions. Matching and unification are implemented using this API as efficient tail-recursive loops.

4.2 Indexing

Rewriting uses a perfect discrimination tree [15], including Waldmeister's refinements [12]. The implementation takes care not to create backtracking points unless needed. There is no unification index, since this is not usually a bottleneck.

4.3 The Passive Set

Early versions of Twee often ran out of memory after about 30 minutes. The reason is the passive set—it grows quadratically in the number of active rules, because any pair of rules can have a critical pair. In typical prover runs it contains anywhere between a million and a hundred million critical pairs.

Twee now uses a space-efficient passive set representation adapted from Waldmeister [12]. The main idea is to throw away all terms involved in the critical pair, and only remember: (1) the ID numbers of the two rules involved, (2) the position of the overlap, and (3) the score of the critical pair. When a critical pair is selected, the ID numbers and position are used to reconstruct the critical pair. This design uses about 12 bytes of memory per critical pair, so Twee can run for many hours without running out of memory.

5 Evaluation

In this section we report on two evaluations: one investigating the effect of the different redundancy criteria of Section 3, and one comparing the performance of Twee against E 2.5 and Waldmeister. In both cases we ran Twee on all 981 unsatisfiable UEQ problems from TPTP 7.4.0, with a time limit of 5 minutes.

Redundancy criteria. Figure 1a shows how the performance of Twee varies depending on which redundancy criteria are enabled. The x-axis shows the number of problems solved (starting from problem 600) and the y-axis shows the runtime for that problem. The combination of ground joinability testing and connectedness is much stronger than either on their own—it seems that each catches cases that the other misses. It is clearly best to have both switched on.

The figure also includes a variant of Twee which implements the heuristic for AC functions described in [1] (and no other redundancy criterion), which solves fewer problems than our approach. This is perhaps not surprising, as our approach handles a wider class of functions.

Twee, E, Waldmeister. Figure 1b compares Twee's performance against E and Waldmeister. Twee is run in three variations: with and without the goal-directed transformation from Section 2, and as a timesliced version which runs the other two versions for 150s each. By far the best choice for Twee is to timeslice, when it comes close to Waldmeister's performance. This suggests that Twee with and without the goal transformation solve somewhat different sets of problems.

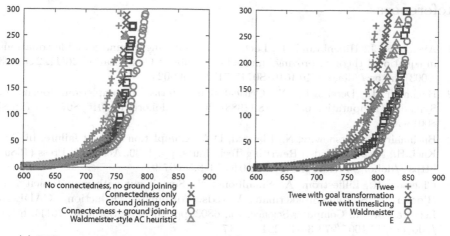

(a) Different redundancy criteria.   (b) Compared against Waldmeister and E.

Fig. 1: Benchmarks.

6   Future Work

Knuth-Bendix completion pays little attention to the goal: it simply completes the rewrite system until the goal becomes trivial. We plan to search for ways to make Twee more goal-directed, for example by rewriting the goal backwards somewhat in the style of [18]. The success of the goal transformation shows that goal direction ought to be important.

Twee uses a fixed term ordering, which is clearly a weakness on certain problem kinds such as RNG. We do not want to choose a term order based on syntactic analysis of the problem, but would like to choose it dynamically based on the state of the proof, perhaps by incorporating ideas from MædMax [19].

7   Conclusion

Twee is a unit equality prover implemented in 5300 lines of Haskell code. Its performance is good, thanks to a careful implementation, strong redundancy criteria and a transformation to help goal-directness. It performs particularly strongly on problems involving permutative laws, such as those in LAT and REL. Its main weaknesses are that it always uses a fixed term order, and has only weak goal direction. We hope that a future version of Twee, with real goal direction and a smart choice of term order, will be even stronger.

Acknowledgements. This work was supported by the Swedish Research Council (VR) grant 2016-06204, *Systematic Testing of Cyber-Physical Systems (SyTeC)*. We thank the reviewers for their many helpful comments.

References

1. Avenhaus, J., Hillenbrand, T., Löchner, B.: On using ground joinable equations in equational theorem proving. Journal of Symbolic Computation 36(1), 217–233 (2003), https://doi.org/10.1016/S0747-7171(03)00024-5

2. Bachmair, L., Dershowitz, N.: Critical pair criteria for completion. Journal of Symbolic Computation 6(1), 1–18 (1988), https://doi.org/10.1016/S0747-7171(88)80018-X

3. Bachmair, L., Dershowitz, N., Plaisted, D.A.: Completion without failure. In: Aït-Kaci, H., Nivat, M. (eds.) Rewriting Techniques, pp. 1–30. Academic Press (1989), https://doi.org/10.1016/B978-0-12-046371-8.50007-9

4. Claessen, K., Lillieström, A., Smallbone, N.: Sort it out with monotonicity. In: Bjørner, N., Sofronie-Stokkermans, V. (eds.) Automated Deduction – CADE-23. Lecture Notes in Computer Science, vol. 6803, pp. 207–221. Springer (2011), https://doi.org/10.1007/978-3-642-22438-6_17

5. Claessen, K., Smallbone, N.: Efficient encodings of first-order Horn formulas in equational logic. In: Galmiche, D., Schulz, S., Sebastiani, R. (eds.) Automated Reasoning - 9th International Joint Conference, IJCAR 2018, Held as Part of the Federated Logic Conference, FloC 2018, Oxford, UK, July 14-17, 2018, Proceedings. Lecture Notes in Computer Science, vol. 10900, pp. 388–404. Springer (2018), https://doi.org/10.1007/978-3-319-94205-6_26

6. Comon, H., Narendran, P., Nieuwenhuis, R., Rusinowitch, M.: Deciding the confluence of ordered term rewrite systems. ACM Transactions on Computational Logic 4(1), 33–55 (Jan 2003), https://doi.org/10.1145/601775.601777

7. Denzinger, J., Kronenburg, M., Schulz, S.: DISCOUNT - a distributed and learning equational prover. Journal of Automated Reasoning 18(2), 189–198 (Apr 1997), https://doi.org/10.1023/A:1005879229581

8. Denzinger, J., Schulz, S.: Recording and analysing knowledge-based distributed deduction processes. Journal of Symbolic Computation 21(4), 523–541 (1996), https://doi.org/10.1006/jsco.1996.0029

9. Gordon, M.J., Milner, R., Wadsworth, C.P.: Edinburgh LCF. A mechanised logic of computation. Springer, Berlin, Heidelberg (1979), https://doi.org/10.1007/3-540-09724-4

10. Korovin, K., Voronkov, A.: A decision procedure for the existential theory of term algebras with the Knuth-Bendix ordering. In: Proceedings of the 15th Annual IEEE Symposium on Logic in Computer Science. pp. 291–302. LICS '00, IEEE Computer Society, Los Alamitos, CA, USA (2000), https://doi.org/10.1109/LICS.2000.855777

11. Löchner, B.: Things to know when implementing KBO. Journal of Automated Reasoning 36(4), 289–310 (Apr 2006), https://doi.org/10.1007/s10817-006-9031-4

12. Löchner, B., Hillenbrand, T.: A phytography of WALDMEISTER. AI Communications 15(2,3), 127–133 (Aug 2002)

13. Martin, U., Nipkow, T.: Ordered rewriting and confluence. In: Stickel, M.E. (ed.) 10th International Conference on Automated Deduction. pp. 366–380. Springer Berlin Heidelberg, Berlin, Heidelberg (1990), https://doi.org/10.1007/3-540-52885-7_100

14. Schulz, S., Cruanes, S., Vukmirović, P.: Faster, higher, stronger: E 2.3. In: Fontaine, P. (ed.) Automated Deduction – CADE 27. pp. 495–507. Springer International Publishing, Cham (2019), https://doi.org/10.1007/978-3-030-29436-6_29

15. Sekar, R., Ramakrishnan, I., Voronkov, A.: Chapter 26 - Term indexing. In: Robinson, A., Voronkov, A. (eds.) Handbook of Automated Reasoning, pp. 1853–1964. Handbook of Automated Reasoning, North-Holland, Amsterdam (2001), https://doi.org/10.1016/B978-044450813-3/50028-X
16. Smallbone, N.: Jukebox. https://github.com/nick8325/jukebox/ (2018)
17. Smallbone, N.: Twee, an equational theorem prover. https://nick8325.github.io/twee/ (2021)
18. Socher-Ambrosius, R.: A goal oriented strategy based on completion. In: Kirchner, H., Levi, G. (eds.) Algebraic and Logic Programming. pp. 435–445. Springer Berlin Heidelberg, Berlin, Heidelberg (1992), https://doi.org/10.1007/BFb0013842
19. Winkler, S., Moser, G.: MædMax: A maximal ordered completion tool. In: Galmiche, D., Schulz, S., Sebastiani, R. (eds.) Automated Reasoning. pp. 472–480. Springer International Publishing, Cham (2018), https://doi.org/10.1007/978-3-319-94205-6_31

Open Access This chapter is licensed under the terms of the Creative Commons Attribution 4.0 International License (http://creativecommons.org/licenses/by/4.0/), which permits use, sharing, adaptation, distribution and reproduction in any medium or format, as long as you give appropriate credit to the original author(s) and the source, provide a link to the Creative Commons license and indicate if changes were made.

The images or other third party material in this chapter are included in the chapter's Creative Commons license, unless indicated otherwise in a credit line to the material. If material is not included in the chapter's Creative Commons license and your intended use is not permitted by statutory regulation or exceeds the permitted use, you will need to obtain permission directly from the copyright holder.

The Isabelle/Naproche Natural Language Proof Assistant

Adrian De Lon[1], Peter Koepke[1], Anton Lorenzen[1], Adrian Marti[1],
Marcel Schütz[1], and Makarius Wenzel[2]

[1] University of Bonn, Bonn, Germany, https://www.math.uni-bonn.de/ag/logik
[2] Augsburg, Germany, https://sketis.net

Abstract Naproche is an emerging *natural proof assistant* that accepts
input in the controlled natural language ForTheL. Naproche is included
in the current version of the Isabelle/PIDE which allows comfortable
editing and asynchronous proof-checking of ForTheL texts. The `.tex`
dialect of ForTheL can be typeset by LATEX into documents that approximate the language and appearance of ordinary mathematical texts.

1 Introduction

Naproche (for Natural Proof Checking) is an emerging *natural* proof assistant
that accepts input in a controlled natural language, approximating ordinary
mathematical language and texts. The system uses

- the dedicated input language ForTheL (Formula Theory Language),
- natural language processing for texts with symbolic material,
- strong automatic theorem proving (ATP) for filling in implicit or obvious
  proof steps.

The current version of Naproche also introduces a LATEX dialect of ForTheL so
that high-quality mathematical typesetting is readily available. Naproche allows
the formalization and proof-checking of advanced mathematics in a style that is
immediately readable by mathematicians. Example formalizations from various
domains of undergraduate mathematics are included.

Naproche ships as a component in the latest release of the Isabelle prover
platform [8]. When editing a ForTheL file in Isabelle/jEdit Prover IDE (PIDE),
there is an auxiliary Naproche server in the background to quickly answer requests for checking ForTheL texts, with an internal cache to avoid repeated
checking of unchanged text segments. The implementation uses programming interfaces of Isabelle/PIDE that allow user-defined file formats to participate in the
concurrent document model. A second auxiliary server allows the Naproche program to run external prover processes under the control of Isabelle, with explicit
timeouts. This works reliably on the usual platforms (Linux, Windows, macOS)

© The Author(s) 2021
A. Platzer and G. Sutcliffe (Eds.): CADE 2021, LNAI 12699, pp. 614–624, 2021.
https://doi.org/10.1007/978-3-030-79876-5_36

by re-using external provers of Isabelle/Sledgehammer [17]. From the perspective of logic, there is *no connection* of Naproche with Isabelle/Sledgehammer or any other Isabelle/HOL tools.

In this paper we briefly discuss the need for *natural* proof assistants, provide some general information on Isabelle/Naproche, and give an overview of methods employed in the system, using an excerpt from a formalization of Euclid's infinitude of primes as a running example. To conclude we compare Naproche to other projects in formal mathematics with natural language input and indicate ways to further extend Naproche's naturalness and efficiency.

2 Natural Proof Assistants

While state-of-the-art interactive theorem provers have been successfully used to prove and certify highly non-trivial research mathematics, they are still, according to Lawrence Paulson [16] "unsuitable for mathematics. Their formal proofs are unreadable."

Natural proof assistants intend to bridge the wide gap between intuitive mathematical texts and the formal rigour of logical calculi. We propose the following criteria for natural proof assistants:

- Input languages should be close to the mathematical vernacular, including support for common grammatical conventions and symbolic expressions. These languages should support familiar text structurings, such as the usual definition-theorem-proof style.
- Proofs should consist of natural argumentative phrases for various proof tactics, allowing for a more declarative style.
- The system should use familiar logics and mathematical ontologies.
- Tedious details and obvious proof gaps should be filled in automatically.
- An intuitive editor should allow for interactive text and theory development, where incremental proof checking can guide the formalization.

We expect that naturalness will be crucial for the adoption of formal mathematics by the wider mathematical community. This is in line with some ongoing large-scale projects in formal mathematics. For instance, the *ALEXANDRIA* project by Paulson [16] stipulates:

> *ALEXANDRIA will be based on legible structured proofs. Formal proofs should be not mere code, but a machine-checkable form of communication between mathematicians.*

The *Formal Abstracts* project of Thomas Hales [5] intends to

- *give a statement of the main theorem of each published mathematical paper in a language that is both human and machine readable,*
- *link each term in theorem statements to a precise definition of that term (again in human/machine readable form).*

3   Isabelle/Naproche

The Naproche proof assistant stems from two long-term efforts aiming towards naturalness: the Evidence Algorithm (EA) and System for Automated Deduction (SAD) projects at the universities of Kiev and Paris [14,15,20,21], and the Naproche project at Bonn [1,2,3,10]. Naproche extends the input language ForTheL of SAD and embeds it into LATEX, allowing mathematical typesetting; the original proof-checking mechanisms of SAD have been made more efficient and varied.

The first experimental integration of the then Naproche-SAD prover into the Isabelle Prover IDE was done in 2018 by Frerix and Wenzel [23, §1.2]. The current (refined and extended) version has now become a bundled component of Isabelle2021 [8]. After downloading and unpacking the Isabelle distribution, Isabelle/Naproche becomes immediately accessible in the *Documentation* panel, section *Examples*, entry $ISABELLE_NAPROCHE/Intro.thy. Isabelle and its add-on components work directly without manual installation, but this comes at the cost of substantial resource requirements: on Linux the total size is 1.2 GB, which includes Java 15 (330 MB), E prover 2.5 (30 MB), and Naproche (20 MB). The bulk of other Isabelle components are required for Isabelle/HOL theory and proof development, but Naproche has no logical connection to that.

The Naproche prover is invoked automatically when editing ForTheL files with .ftl or .ftl.tex extensions. Further examples and an introductory tutorial are linked in the Isabelle theory file $ISABELLE_NAPROCHE/Intro.thy: as usual for Isabelle/jEdit and other IDEs, following a link works by a mouse click combined with the keyboard modifier CTRL (Linux, Windows) or CMD (macOS). The examples deal with results from undergraduate number theory, geometry, and set theory; most are available in the classic ASCII style as well as in LATEX style and typeset in PDF.

The ForTheL library FLib [13] contains a variety of formalizations for earlier versions of Naproche. Some substantial texts have been written as undergraduate student projects and cover, e.g., group theory up to Sylow theorems, initial chapters from Walter Rudin's *Analysis*, or set theory up to Silver's theorem in cardinal arithmetic. These texts will soon be upgraded to the new version of Naproche and included in an interlinked formalized library of readable and proof-checked mathematical texts.

4   Formalizing in ForTheL

4.1   Example

The following screenshot shows a proof of the infinitude of prime numbers in the Isabelle/Naproche Prover IDE taken from the bundled tutorial which itself is a proof-checked ForTheL text:

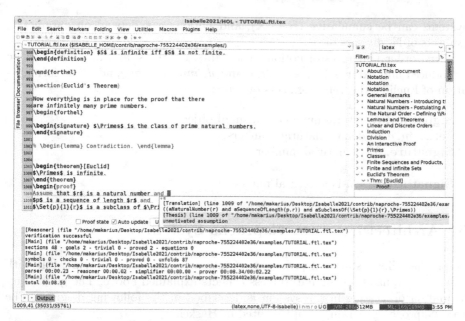

The editor buffer contains the ForTheL source, which also happens to conform to standard LATEX format. (The "Contradiction" lemma, now deactivated by a %, is a left-over of a typical check for hidden inconsistencies in the axiomatic setup.) The Output panel contains feedback from the Naproche prover about the source document: "verification successful" and some statistics; the most relevant messages are also shown in-line over the source as squiggly underline with popup on mouse-hovering. The Sidekick/latex structure overview is provided by standard plugins of the underlying text editor. This piece of mathematics is typeset by LATEX as follows:

Euclid's Theorem

Signature. $\mathbb{P}$ is the class of prime natural numbers.
Theorem. $\mathbb{P}$ is infinite.
Proof. Assume that r is a natural number and p is a sequence of length r and $\{p_1, \ldots, p_r\}$ is a subclass of $\mathbb{P}$. [...]   □

4.2   The ForTheL Language

The mathematical controlled language ForTheL has been developed over several decades in the Evidence Algorithm (EA) / System for Automated Deduction (SAD) project. It is carefully designed to approximate the weakly typed natural language of mathematics whilst being efficiently translatable to first-order logic. In ForTheL, standard mathematical types are called *notions*, and these are internally represented as predicates with a distinguished variable, which are treated as unary predicates with the other variables used as parameters ("types as predicates"). This leads to a flexible dependent type system where number systems can be cumulative ($\mathbb{N} \subseteq \mathbb{R}$), and notions can depend on parameters (subsets of $\mathbb{N}$, divisors of n).

First-order languages of notions, constants, relations, and functions can be introduced and extended by *signature* and *definition* commands. The formalization of Euclid's theorem, e.g., sets out like:

Signature. A natural number is a small object.
Let $\ldots m, n \ldots$ denote natural numbers.
Signature. 0 is a natural number.
$\ldots$
Signature. $m + n$ is a natural number.

---

5 Architecture of the Naproche System

Naproche follows standard principles of interactive theorem proving, but with a strong emphasis on the naturalness aspects explained above. The general information processing in the system is described in the following diagram. The core Naproche program is implemented in Haskell.

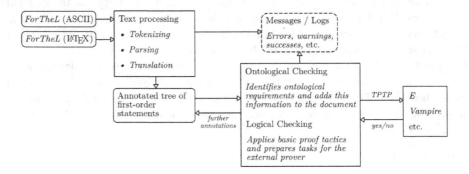

In the sequel we shall describe main components of Naproche.

5.1 Tokenizing and Parsing

Naproche uses a standard tokenizing algorithm for cutting text up into a list of meaningful tokens, with precise source positions to enable PIDE messages and markup, e.g., by colours for free and bound variables. When using LATEX syntax, the tokenizer also takes care of expanding certain TEX commands (see the next subsection).

Parsing is carried out in Haskell's monadic style with parser combinators. We allow ambiguous parsing, since it better fits natural language. Currently the translation into tagged first-order logic is already part of the parsing process. The following translation of our example snippet was obtained by running Naproche from the command line with the -T (translate) option:

```
......
hypothesis.
  assume forall v0 ((HeadTerm :: v0 = Primes) implies
  (aClass(v0) and forall v1 (aElementOf(v1,v0)
  iff (aNaturalNumber(v1) and isPrime(v1))))).

conjecture Euclid.
  isInfinite(Primes).
  proof.
    assume ((aNaturalNumber(r) and aSequenceOfLength(p,r)) and
    aSubsetOf(Set{p}{1}{r},Primes)).
    n = Prod{p}{1}{r}+1.
......
```

In order to make Naproche more versatile we plan on parsing into an abstract syntax tree instead, so that different logical back-ends could translate into different logics. We have already made some experiments on translating ForTheL to Lean [12].

Moreover, with the input language growing, we shall eventually turn to some grammatical framework to speed up language development without hard-coding vocabulary or grammar rules into the Naproche code.

5.2 LATEX Processing

We have extended Naproche to support a .ftl.tex format, in addition to the original .ftl format. Files in .ftl.tex format are intended to be readable by both Naproche for logical checking and by LATEX for typesetting.

The LATEX tokenizer ignores the whole document, except what is inside forthel environments of the form

```
\begin{forthel}
  % Insert what you want Naproche to process here
\end{forthel}
```

In a forthel environment, standard LATEX syntax can be used for declaring text environments for theorems and definitions.

In Naproche, users can define their own operators and phrases by defining linguistic and symbolic *patterns*. This mechanism has been adapted to allow LATEX constructs in patterns. In the Euclid text we use the pattern \Set{p}{1}{r} for the finite set $\{p_1, \ldots, p_r\}$. By defining \Set as a LATEX macro we can arrange that the ForTheL pattern will be printed in the familiar set notation:

```
\newcommand{\Set}[3]{\{#1_{#2},\dots,#1_{#3}\}}
```

There are some primitive concepts in Naproche, such as the logical operators $\vee$, $\wedge$, $\exists$ that are directly recognized in the LATEX source and expanded to corresponding internal tokens.

The current release of Naproche does not differentiate between math mode and text mode in LaTeX, since it re-uses much of the parsing machinery of the original .ftl format. Future releases shall make such a distinction to increase the robustness of the parser, improve error messages and resolve some ambiguities in the current grammar.

5.3   Logical Processing

The first-order formulas derived from ForTheL statements are put into an internal **ProofText** data type consisting of blocks of formulae, arranged in a tree-like fashion. The tree structure mirrors the logical structure of a text, where a statement can be seen as a node to which a subtext, e.g., its proof is attached. Since statements in a proof can have their own subproofs this leads to a recursive tree structure, on which the further checking is performed along a depth-first left-to-right traversal.

5.4   Ontological Checking by the Naproche Reasoner

An innocent mathematical statement like $a^2 + b^2 = c^2$ contains a number of implicit proof tasks, even if the whole statement is not to be proved, but part of a definition or an assumption. One has to check that a, b, c are (numerical) terms to which the squaring operation can be applied, and that the resulting squares can be subjected to addition and equality. These checks are called "ontological", and they roughly correspond to type checking in type-orientated systems. The situation here is however more complicated, as types (i.e. notions) and operations may involve first-order definitions with preconditions, which cannot be decided during the parsing process but only during proof-checking. So in the checking process each node of the aforementioned tree is first checked *ontologically*; if the node formula itself is marked as a conjecture, it is *logically* checked.

5.5   Logical Checking by the Naproche Reasoner

The various checks are organized by the Naproche reasoner module. In simple cases the reasoner itself can supply a proof; if not, the reasoner constructs proof tasks for the ATP. Since definitions in first-order logic are formally symmetric equivalences, they may lead to circularities in proof searches. Instead definitions are successively unfolded by replacing the definiendum by the definiens. This process may be iterated when proof attempts fail.

The ATP is given certain timeouts to search for proofs. Ontological checking is supposed to be easier than proper mathematical proving. So the default time for each ontological check is set to 1 sec, whereas proving gets 3 sec and can be iterated for several rounds of definition unfolding.

5.6   Communication with an External ATP

Proof tasks are translated into the generic TPTP first-order format for ATPs. These can be viewed in the Output window of Isabelle/jEdit, after inserting the directive [dump on] into the ForTheL source. The final proof task in checking Euclid's proof ends with the TPTP lines:

```
fof(m_,hypothesis,( ! [W0] : (aClass(W0) =>
    (isInfinite(W0) <=> ( ~ isFinite(W0)))))).
fof(m_,hypothesis,(aClass(szPzrzizmzezs) &
    ( ! [W0] : (aElementOf(W0,szPzrzizmzezs)
    <=> (aNaturalNumber(W0) & isPrime(W0)))))).
fof(m__,conjecture,
    ......
    (aElementOf(W4,szSzeztlcdtrclcz1rclcdtrc(W0,W1)) <=>
    (aNaturalNumber(W4) & isPrime(W4)))))))))))) =>
    isInfinite(szPzrzizmzezs))).
```

By default Naproche uses E prover [19] as external ATP, but one may switch to other provers available in the Isabelle distribution.

6   Integration into Isabelle

The initial integration of Naproche into the Isabelle Prover IDE happened in 2018 and is briefly reported as an example in the PIDE overview article [23] based on Isabelle2019 (June 2019). The main idea was to turn the existing Haskell command-line program into a TCP server that can answer concurrent requests for checking ForTheL texts in a purely functional manner, with proper handling of cancel messages (for interrupts caused by user editing); this required to remove a few low-level system operations, like reading physical files or **exit** of the process. Afterwards, the semantic operation **forthel_file** in Isabelle – to check ForTheL text and produce markup messages according to the PIDE protocol – was implemented as Isabelle/Isar command in Isabelle/ML as usual, but the main work is delegated to the Naproche server. Its implementation uses the Isabelle/Haskell library for common Isabelle/PIDE message formats, source positions, markup etc. – it is maintained within the Isabelle distribution.

The current version of Isabelle/Naproche refines this approach in various respects. In particular, Isabelle2021 now provides a standard mechanism for user-defined *Isabelle/Scala services*: this is both relevant for Isabelle command-line tools to build and test Isabelle/Naproche, and the Prover IDE support of ForTheL files to connect the Isabelle/jEdit front-end to the Naproche back-end.

Moreover, the Java process running the Prover IDE provides an additional TCP server to launch external provers that are already distributed with Isabelle (thanks to Isabelle/Sledgehammer): Naproche applications mainly use the current E prover 2.5 [19], but SPASS and Vampire are available for experiments.

The existing management of processes in Isabelle/Scala involves considerable efforts to robustly support interrupts and timeouts in a concurrent environment; this works on all platforms supported by Isabelle (using special tricks for Windows/Cygwin, and macOS/Rosetta on Apple Silicon).

The documentation file $ISABELLE_NAPROCHE/Intro.thy gives further hints on implementation near the end, with hyperlinks to the sources. A lot of technical Isabelle infrastructure is re-used by Isabelle/Naproche, but there is presently no connection to Isabelle/HOL, which is a much larger and better-known application of the same Isabelle framework [18].

7 Related and Future Work

Bridging the gap between mathematical practice and fully formal methods has always been a central concern in formal mathematics. The development of the Mizar system [11] was accompanied or even driven by the stepwise adaptation of its language to standard mathematical proof methods and logical foundations. In contrast, most interactive theorem provers feature formal tactic languages, with tactics scripts that can hardly be understood without stepwise tracing and reconstructing internal logical states.

The Mizar language has been a role model for other proof languages. There are, e.g., "Mizar modes" for HOL [6,25] and Coq [4] and the widely used Isar language for Isabelle [24,22]. These language can be read by mathematicians, with some effort, but they retain a strong bias toward computer science customs. A survey of input languages for formalization on a scale between formal and natural can be found in [9].

Only a few formal mathematics projects have aimed at processing actual mathematical language. These projects have operated in isolation and seem to be mostly inactive now. The paper [7] by Muhammad Humayoun and Christophe Raffalli, e.g., describes the MathNat project and also surveys other related attempts.

The Naproche approach can be viewed in the Mizar tradition: use a rich controlled language for mathematics, increase the proving capabilities by strong automated theorem proving, and, eventually, create an extensive library of basic mathematics and specialized theories, which simultaneously can be used as a library for human readers.

The readability and naturalness of texts which proof-check in the Naproche system motivate significant further extensions of the project where ad hoc methods are to be replaced by principled and established approaches:

1. the input language ForTheL has to be extended for wide mathematical coverage; ForTheL needs an extensive formal grammar and vocabulary to be processed by strong linguistic methods; the vocabulary may also encompass standard LaTeX symbols and semantic information;

2. methods of type derivation and elaboration should be provided;

3. Isabelle/Sledgehammer-like methods should lead to efficient premise selection in large texts and theories;

4. the creation of libraries of ForTheL documents requires import and export mechanisms corresponding to quoting and referencing in the mathematical literature;

5. the natural text processing of Naproche should be interfaced with other proof assistants to leverage their strengths and libraries. We shall in particular work on a "Naproche mode" for Isabelle.

References

1. Cramer, M.: Proof-checking mathematical texts in controlled natural language. Ph.D. thesis, University of Bonn (2013), http://hdl.handle.net/20.500.11811/5780
2. Cramer, M., Koepke, P., Kühlwein, D., Schröder, B.: The Naproche system (2009), https://citeseerx.ist.psu.edu/viewdoc/summary?doi=10.1.1.211.3401
3. Frerix, S., Koepke, P.: Automatic proof-checking of ordinary mathematical texts. Proceedings of the Workshop Formal Mathematics for Mathematicians (2018), http://ceur-ws.org/Vol-2307/paper13.pdf
4. Giero, M., Wiedijk, F.: MMode, a Mizar mode for the proof assistant Coq (2003), https://www.cs.ru.nl/~freek/mmode/mmode.pdf
5. Hales, T.: Formal abstracts (2020), https://formalabstracts.github.io
6. Harrison, J.: A Mizar mode for HOL. In: von Wright, J., Grundy, J., Harrison, J. (eds.) Theorem Proving in Higher Order Logics: 9th International Conference, TPHOLs'96. Lecture Notes in Computer Science, vol. 1125, pp. 203–220. Springer-Verlag, Turku, Finland (1996)
7. Humayoun, M., Raffalli, C.: MathNat - mathematical text in a controlled natural language. Journal on Research in Computing Science **46** (2010)
8. Isabelle contributors: The Isabelle2021 release (2021), https://isabelle.in.tum.de
9. Kaliszyk, C., Rabe, F.: A survey of languages for formalizing mathematics. In: Benzmüller, C., Miller, B. (eds.) Intelligent Computer Mathematics. pp. 138–156. Springer International Publishing, Cham (2020). https://doi.org/10.1007/978-3-030-53518-6_9
10. Koepke, P.: Textbook mathematics in the Naproche-SAD system. In: Brady, E., Davenport, J., Farmer, W.M., Kaliszyk, C., Kohlhase, A., Kohlhase, M., Müller, D., Pąk, K., Coen, C.S. (eds.) Joint Proceedings of the FMM and LML Workshops (2019), http://ceur-ws.org/Vol-2634/FMM4.pdf
11. Mizar, http://www.mizar.org/
12. de Moura, L.M., Kong, S., Avigad, J., van Doorn, F., von Raumer, J.: The Lean Theorem Prover (system description). In: Felty, A.P., Middeldorp, A. (eds.) Automated Deduction – CADE-25 – 25th International Conference on Automated Deduction, Berlin, Germany, August 1-7, 2015, Proceedings. Lecture Notes in Computer Science, vol. 9195, pp. 378–388. Springer (2015). https://doi.org/10.1007/978-3-319-21401-6_26
13. Naproche contributors: FLib, https://github.com/naproche-community/FLib
14. Paskevich, A.: Méthodes de formalisation des connaissances et des raisonnements mathématiques: aspects appliqués et théoriques. Ph.D. thesis, Université Paris 12 (2007), http://tertium.org/papers/thesis-07.fr.pdf
15. Paskevich, A.: The syntax and semantics of the ForTheL language (2007), http://nevidal.org/download/forthel.pdf
16. Paulson, L.C.: ALEXANDRIA: Large-scale formal proof for the working mathematician, https://www.cl.cam.ac.uk/~lp15/Grants/Alexandria

17. Paulson, L.C., Blanchette, J.C.: Three years of experience with Sledgehammer, a practical link between automatic and interactive theorem provers. In: Sutcliffe, G., Schulz, S., Ternovska, E. (eds.) IWIL 2010. The 8th International Workshop on the Implementation of Logics. EPiC Series in Computing, vol. 2, pp. 1–11. EasyChair (2012). https://doi.org/10.29007/36dt
18. Paulson, L.C., Nipkow, T., Wenzel, M.: From LCF to Isabelle/HOL. Formal Aspects of Computing **31**, 675–698 (September 2019), https://doi.org/10.1007/s00165-019-00492-1, Springer, London
19. Schulz, S.: The E Theorem Prover, https://eprover.org
20. Verchinine, K., Lyaletski, A., Paskevich, A.: System for automated deduction (SAD): a tool for proof verification. Automated Deduction–CADE-21 pp. 398–403 (2007). https://doi.org/10.1007/978-3-540-73595-3_29
21. Verchinine, K., Lyaletski, A., Paskevich, A., Anisimov, A.: On correctness of mathematical texts from a logical and practical point of view. In: Autexier, S., Campbell, J., Rubio, J., Sorge, V., Suzuki, M., Wiedijk, F. (eds.) International Conference on Intelligent Computer Mathematics. pp. 583–598. Springer (2008). https://doi.org/10.1007/978-3-540-85110-3_47
22. Wenzel, M.: The Isar proof language in 2016 (2016), http://sketis.net/wp-content/uploads/2016/08/Isabelle_Workshop_2016_Isar.pdf
23. Wenzel, M.: Interaction with formal mathematical documents in Isabelle/PIDE. In: Kaliszyk, C., Brady, E., Kohlhase, A., Sacerdoti Coen, C. (eds.) Intelligent Computer Mathematics (CICM 2019). Lecture Notes in Artificial Intelligence, vol. 11617. Springer (2019). https://doi.org/10.1007/978-3-030-23250-4_1
24. Wenzel, M.: Isar — a generic interpretative approach to readable formal proof documents. In: Bertot, Y., Dowek, G., Théry, L., Hirschowitz, A., Paulin, C. (eds.) Theorem Proving in Higher Order Logics. pp. 167–183. Springer Berlin Heidelberg, Berlin, Heidelberg (1999)
25. Wiedijk, F.: Mizar light for HOL light. In: Boulton, R.J., Jackson, P.B. (eds.) TPHOLs: International Conference on Theorem Proving in Higher Order Logics. pp. 378–393. Springer (2001)

Open Access This chapter is licensed under the terms of the Creative Commons Attribution 4.0 International License (http://creativecommons.org/licenses/by/4.0/), which permits use, sharing, adaptation, distribution and reproduction in any medium or format, as long as you give appropriate credit to the original author(s) and the source, provide a link to the Creative Commons license and indicate if changes were made.

The images or other third party material in this chapter are included in the chapter's Creative Commons license, unless indicated otherwise in a credit line to the material. If material is not included in the chapter's Creative Commons license and your intended use is not permitted by statutory regulation or exceeds the permitted use, you will need to obtain permission directly from the copyright holder.

The Lean 4 Theorem Prover and Programming Language

Leonardo de Moura[1]([✉]) [iD] and Sebastian Ullrich[2][iD]

[1] Microsoft Research, Redmond WA, USA
`leonardo@microsoft.com`
[2] Karlsruhe Institute of Technology, Karlsruhe, Germany
`sebastian.ullrich@kit.edu`

Abstract. Lean 4 is a reimplementation of the Lean interactive theorem prover (ITP) in Lean itself. It addresses many shortcomings of the previous versions and contains many new features. Lean 4 is fully extensible: users can modify and extend the parser, elaborator, tactics, decision procedures, pretty printer, and code generator. The new system has a hygienic macro system custom-built for ITPs. It contains a new typeclass resolution procedure based on tabled resolution, addressing significant performance problems reported by the growing user base. Lean 4 is also an efficient functional programming language based on a novel programming paradigm called *functional but in-place*. Efficient code generation is crucial for Lean users because many write custom proof automation procedures in Lean itself.

1 Introduction

The Lean project[3] started in 2013 [9] as an interactive theorem prover based on the Calculus of Inductive Constructions [4] (CIC). In 2017, using Lean 3, a community of users with very different backgrounds started the Lean mathematical library project mathlib [13]. At the time of this writing, mathlib has roughly half a million lines of code, and contains many nontrivial mathematical objects such as Schemes [2]. Mathlib is also the foundation for the *Perfectoid Spaces in Lean* project [1], and the *Liquid Tensor* challenge [11] posed by the renowned mathematician Peter Scholze. Mathlib contains not only mathematical objects but also Lean metaprograms that extend the system [5]. Some of these metaprograms implement nontrivial proof automation, such as a ring theory solver and a decision procedure for Presburger arithmetic. Lean metaprograms in mathlib also extend the system by adding new top-level command and features not related to proof automation. For example, it contains a package of semantic linters that alert users to many commonly made mistakes [5]. Lean 3 metaprograms have

---

[3] `http://leanprover.github.io`

© The Author(s) 2021
A. Platzer and G. Sutcliffe (Eds.): CADE 2021, LNAI 12699, pp. 625–635, 2021.
https://doi.org/10.1007/978-3-030-79876-5_37

been also instrumental in building standalone applications, such as a SQL query equivalence checker [3].

We believe the Lean 3 theorem prover's success is primarily due to its extensibility capabilities and metaprogramming framework [6]. However, users cannot modify many parts of the system without changing Lean 3 source code written in C++. Another issue is that many proof automation metaprograms are not competitive with similar proof automation implemented in programming languages with an efficient compiler such as C++ and OCaml. The primary source of inefficiency in Lean 3 metaprograms is the virtual machine interpretation overhead.

Lean 4 is a reimplementation of the Lean theorem prover in Lean itself[4]. It is an extensible theorem prover and an efficient programming language. The new compiler produces C code, and users can now implement efficient proof automation in Lean, compile it into efficient C code, and load it as a plugin. In Lean 4, users can access all internal data structures used to implement Lean by merely importing the `Lean` package. Lean 4 is also a platform for developing efficient domain-specific automation. It has a more robust and extensible elaborator, and addresses many other shortcomings of Lean 3. We expect the Lean community to extend and add new features without having to change the Lean source code. We released Lean 4 at the beginning of 2021, it is open source, the community is already porting mathlib, and the number of applications is quickly growing. It includes a translation verifier for Reopt[5], a package for supporting inductive-inductive types[6], and a car controller[7].

2   Lean by Example

In this section, we introduce the Lean language using a series of examples. The source code for the examples is available at `https://github.com/leanprover/lean4/blob/cade2021/doc/BoolExpr.lean`. For additional details and installation instructions, we recommend the reader consult the online manual[8].

We define functions by using the `def` keyword followed by its name, a parameter list, return type, and body. The parameter list consists of successive parameters that are separated by spaces. We can specify an explicit type for each parameter. If we do not specify a specific argument type, the elaborator tries to infer the function body's type. The Boolean `or` function is defined by pattern-matching as follows

```
def or (a b : Bool) :=
  match a with
  | true  => true
  | false => b
```

---

[4] http://github.com/leanprover/lean4
[5] https://github.com/GaloisInc/reopt-vcg
[6] https://github.com/javra/iit
[7] https://github.com/GaloisInc/lean4-balance-car
[8] http://leanprover.github.io/lean4/doc

We can use the command `#check <term>` to inspect the type of term, and `#eval <term>` to evaluate it.

```
#check or true false -- Bool (this is a comment in Lean)
#eval  or true false -- true
```

Lean has a hygienic macro system and comes equipped with many macros for commonly used idioms. For example, we can also define the function or using

```
def or : Bool → Bool → Bool
| true, _  => true
| false, b => b
```

The notation above is a macro that expands into a `match`-expression. In Lean, a theorem is a definition whose result type is a proposition. For an example, consider the following simple theorem about the definition above

```
theorem or_true (b : Bool) : or true b = true :=
  rfl
```

The constant `rfl` has type ∀ {α : Sort u} {a : α}, a = a, the curly braces indicate that the parameters α and a are *implicit* and should be inferred by solving typing constraints. In the example above, the inferred values for α and a are Bool and or true b, respectively, and the resulting type is or true b = or true b. This is a valid proof because or true b is *definitionally equal* to b. In dependent type theory, every term has a computational behavior, and supports a notion of reduction. In principle, two terms that reduce to the same value are called definitionally equal. In the following example, we use pattern matching to prove that or b b = b

```
theorem or_self : ∀ (b : Bool), or b b = b
| true  => rfl
| false => rfl
```

Note that or b b does not reduce to b, but after pattern matching we have that or true true (or false false) reduces to true (false).

In the following example, we define the recursive datatype `BoolExpr` for representing Boolean expressions using the command `inductive`.

```
inductive BoolExpr where
| var (name : String)
| val (b : Bool)
| or  (p q : BoolExpr)
| not (p : BoolExpr)
```

This command generates constructors `BoolExpr.var`, `BoolExpr.val`, `BoolExpr.or`, and `BoolExpr.not`. The Lean kernel also generates an inductive principle for the new type `BoolExpr`. We can write a basic "simplifier" for Boolean expressions as follows

```
def simplify : BoolExpr → BoolExpr
| BoolExpr.or p q => mkOr (simplify p) (simplify q)
| BoolExpr.not p  => mkNot (simplify p)
```

```
  | e                    => e
where
  mkOr : BoolExpr → BoolExpr → BoolExpr
    | p, BoolExpr.val true   => BoolExpr.val true
    | p, BoolExpr.val false  => p
    | BoolExpr.val true, p   => BoolExpr.val true
    | BoolExpr.val false, p  => p
    | p, q                   => BoolExpr.or p q

  mkNot : BoolExpr → BoolExpr
    | BoolExpr.val b => BoolExpr.val (not b)
    | p              => BoolExpr.not p
```

The function `simplify` is a simple bottom-up simplifier. We use the `where` clause to define two local auxiliary functions `mkOr` and `mkNot` for constructing "simplified" or and not expressions respectively. Their global names are `simplify.mkOr` and `simplify.mkNot`.

Given a context that maps variable names to Boolean values, we define a "denotation" function (or evaluator) for Boolean expressions. We use an association list to represent the context.

```
abbrev Context := AssocList String Bool

def denote (ctx : Context) : BoolExpr → Bool
  | BoolExpr.or p q => denote ctx p || denote ctx q
  | BoolExpr.not p  => !denote ctx p
  | BoolExpr.val b => b
  | BoolExpr.var x => if let some b := ctx.find? x then b else false
```

In the example above, `p || q` is notation for `or p q`, `!p` for `not p`, and `if let p := t then a else b` is a macro that expands into `match t with | p => a | _ => b`. The term `ctx.find? x` is syntax sugar for `AssocList.find? ctx x`.

As in previous versions, we can use tactics for constructing proofs and terms. We use the keyword `by` to switch into *tactic mode*. Tactics are user-defined or built-in procedures that construct various terms. They are all implemented in Lean itself. The `simp` tactic implements an extensible simplifier, and is one of the most popular tactics in `mathlib`. Its implementation [9] can be extended and modified by Lean users.

```
...
@[simp] theorem denote_mkOr (ctx : Context) (p q : BoolExpr)
       : denote ctx (simplify.mkOr p q) = denote ctx (or p q) :=
  ...
def denote_simplify (ctx : Context) (p : BoolExpr)
     : denote ctx (simplify p) = denote ctx p :=
  by induction p with
  | or p q ih₁ ih₂ => simp [ih₁, ih₂]
```

---

[9] https://github.com/leanprover/lean4/blob/cade21/src/Lean/Meta/Tactic/Simp/Main.lean.

```
| not p ih      => simp [ih]
| _             => rfl
```

In the example above, we use the `induction` tactic, its syntax is similar to a `match`-expression. The variables ih_1 and ih_2 are the induction hypothesis for `p` and `q` in the first alternative for the case `p` is a `BoolExpr.or`. The `simp` tactic uses any theorem marked with the `@[simp]` attribute as a rewriting rule (e.g., `denote_mkOr`). We explicitly provide the induction hypotheses as additional rewriting rules inside square brackets.

Typeclass Resolution. Typeclasses [16] provide an elegant and effective way of managing ad-hoc polymorphism in both programming languages and interactive proof assistants. Then we can declare particular elements of a typeclass to be *instances*. These provide hints to the elaborator: any time the elaborator is looking for an element of a typeclass, it can consult a table of declared instances to find a suitable element. What makes typeclass inference powerful is that one can *chain* instances, that is, an instance declaration can in turn depend on other instances. This causes class inference to recurse through instances, backtracking when necessary. The Lean typeclass resolution procedure can be viewed as a simple λ-Prolog interpreter [8], where the Horn clauses are the user declared instances.

For example, the standard library defines a typeclass `Inhabited` to enable typeclass inference to infer a "default" or "arbitrary" element of types that contain at least one element.

```
class Inhabited (α : Sort u) where
  default : α

def arbitrary [Inhabited α] : α :=
  Inhabited.default
```

The annotation `[Inhabited α]` at `arbitrary` indicates that this implicit parameter should be synthesized from instance declarations using typeclass resolution. We can define an instance for our `BoolExpr` type defined earlier as follows

```
instance : Inhabited BoolExpr where
  default := BoolExpr.val false
```

This instance specifies that the "default" element for `BoolExpr` is `BoolExpr.val false`. The following declaration shows that if two types α and β are inhabited, then so is their product:

```
instance [Inhabited α] [Inhabited β] : Inhabited (α × β) where
  default := (arbitrary, arbitrary)
```

The standard library has many builtin classes such as `Repr` α and `DecidableEq` α. The class `Repr` α is similar to Haskell's `Show` α typeclass, and `DecidableEq` α is a typeclass for types that have decidable equality. Lean 4 also provides code synthesizers for many builtin classes. The command `deriving` instructs Lean to auto-generate an instance.

```
deriving instance DecidableEq for BoolExpr
```

```
#eval decide (BoolExpr.val true = BoolExpr.val false)
```
-- *false*

In the example above, the `deriving` command generates the instance

```
(a b : BoolExpr) → Decidable (a = b)
```

The function `decide` evaluates decidable propositions. Thus, the last command returns `false` since `BoolExpr.val true` is not equal to `BoolExpr.val false`.

The increasingly sophisticated uses of typeclasses in mathlib have exposed a few limitations in Lean 3: unnecessary overhead due to the lack of term indexing techniques, and exponential running times in the presence of diamonds. Lean 4 implements a new procedure [12], tabled typeclass resolution, that solves these problems by using discrimination trees[10] for better indexing and tabling, which is a generalization of memoizing introduced initially to address similar limitations of early logic programming systems[11].

The hygienic macro system. In interactive theorem provers (ITPs), Lean included, extensible syntax is not only crucial to lower the cognitive burden of manipulating complex mathematical objects, but plays a critical role in developing reusable abstractions in libraries. Lean 3 support such extensions in the form of restrictive "syntax sugar" substitutions and other ad hoc mechanisms, which are too rudimentary to support many desirable abstractions. As a result, libraries are littered with unnecessary redundancy. The Lean 3 tactic languages is plagued by a seemingly unrelated issue: accidental name capture, which often produces unexpected and counterintuitive behavior. Lean 4 takes ideas from the Scheme family of programming languages and solves these two problems simultaneously by use of a *hygienic*, i.e. capture-avoiding, macro system custom-built for ITPs [15].

Lean 3's "mixfix" notation system is still supported in Lean 4, but based on the much more general macro system; in fact, the Lean 3 `notation` keyword itself has been reimplemented as a macro, more specifically as a *macro-generating macro*. By providing such a tower of abstractions for writing syntax sugars, of which we will see more levels below, we want to enable users to work in the simplest model appropriate for their respective use case while always keeping open the option to switch to a lower, more expressive level.

As an example, we define the infix notation $\Gamma \vdash p$, with precedence 50, for the function `denote` defined earlier.

```
infix:50 "⊢" => denote
```

The `infix` command expands to

```
notation:50 Γ "⊢" p:50 => denote Γ p
```

---

[10] https://github.com/leanprover/lean4/blob/cade21/src/Lean/Meta/DiscrTree.lean.

[11] https://github.com/leanprover/lean4/blob/cade21/src/Lean/Meta/SynthInstance.lean.

which itself expands to the macro declaration

```
macro:50 Γ:term "⊢" p:term:50  : term => `(denote $Γ $p)
```

where the *syntactic category* (term) of placeholders and of the entire macro is
now specified explicitly, implying that macros can also be written for/using other
categories such as the top-level command. The right-hand side uses an explicit
syntax quasiquotation to construct the syntax tree, with syntax placeholders
(*antiquotations*) prefixed with $. As suggested by the explicit use of quotations,
the right-hand side may now be an arbitrary Lean term computing a syntax
object, allowing for *procedural* macros as well.

macro itself is another command-level macro that, for our notation example,
expands to two commands

```
syntax:50 term "⊢" term:50 : term
macro_rules
  | `($Γ ⊢ $e) => `(denote $Γ $e)
```

that is, a pair of parser extension and syntax transformer. By separating these
two steps at this abstraction level, it becomes possible to define (mutually) recursive macros and to reuse syntax between macros. Using macro_rules, users
can even extend existing macros with new rules. In general, separating parsing and expansion means that that we can obtain a well-structured syntax tree
pre-expansion, i.e. a *concrete* syntax tree, and use it to implement source code
tooling such as auto-completion, go-to-definition, and refactorings.

We can use the syntax command for defining embedded domain-specific languages. In simple cases, we can reuse existing syntactic categories for this but
assign them new semantics, such as in the following notation for constructing
BoolExpr objects.

```
syntax "`[BExpr|" term "]" : term
macro_rules
  | `(`[BExpr| true])     => `(BoolExpr.val true)
  | `(`[BExpr| false])    => `(BoolExpr.val false)
  | `(`[BExpr| $x:ident]) => `(BoolExpr.var $(quote x.getId.toString))
  | `(`[BExpr| $p ∨ $q])  => `(BoolExpr.or `[BExpr| $p] `[BExpr| $q])
  | `(`[BExpr| ¬ $p])     => `(BoolExpr.not `[BExpr| $p])

#check `[BExpr| p ∨ true]
-- BoolExpr.or (BoolExpr.var "p") (BoolExpr.val true) : BoolExpr
```

The macro_rules command above specifies how to convert a subset of the builtin
syntax for terms into constructor applications for BoolExpr. The term $(quote
x.getId.toString) converts the identifier x into a string literal.

As a final example, we modify the notation Γ ⊢ p. In the following version, Γ
is not an arbitrary term anymore, but a comma-separated sequence of entries of
the form var ↦ value, and the right-hand side is now interpreted as a BoolExpr
term by reusing our macro from above.

```
syntax entry := ident " ↦ " term:max
syntax entry,* "⊢" term : term
```

```
macro_rules
  | `( $[$xs:ident ↦ $vs:term],* ⊢ $p:term ) =>
    let xs := xs.map fun x => quote x.getId.toString
    `(denote (List.toAssocList [$[( $xs , $vs )],*]) `[BExpr| $p])
#eval a ↦ false, b ↦ true ⊢ b ∨ a  -- true
```

We use the *antiquotation splice* $[$xs:ident ↦ $vs:term],* to deconstruct the sequence of entries into two arrays xs and vs containing the variable names and values, respectively, adjust the former array, and combine them again in a second splice.

3   The Code Generator

The Lean 4 code generator produces efficient C code. It is useful for building both efficient Lean extensions and standalone applications. The code generator performs many transformations, and many of them are based on techniques used in the Haskell compiler GHC [7]. However, in contrast to Haskell, Lean is a strict language. We control code inlining and specialization using the attributes @[inline] and @[specialize]. They are crucial for eliminating the overhead introduced by the towers of abstractions used in our source code. Before emitting C code, we erase proof terms and convert Lean expressions into an intermediate representation (IR). The IR is a collection of Lean data structures,[12] and users can implement support for backends other than C by writing Lean programs that import Lean.Compiler.IR. Lean 4 also comes with an interpreter for the IR, which allows for rapid incremental development and testing right from inside the editor. Whenever the interpreter calls a function for which native, ahead-of-time compiled code is available, it will switch to that instead, which includes all functions from the standard library. Thus the interpretation overhead is negligible as long as e.g. all expensive tactics are precompiled.

Functional but in-place. Most functional languages rely on garbage collection for automatic memory management. They usually eschew reference counting in favor of a tracing garbage collector, which has less bookkeeping overhead at runtime. On the other hand, having an exact reference count of each value enables optimizations such as destructive updates [14]. When performing functional updates, objects often die just before creating an object of the same kind. We observe a similar phenomenon when we insert a new element into a purely functional data structure, such as binary trees, a theorem prover rewrites formulas, a compiler applies optimizations by transforming abstract syntax trees, or the function simplify defined earlier. We call it the *resurrection hypothesis*: many objects die just before creating an object of the same kind. The Lean memory manager uses reference counting and takes advantage of this hypothesis, and enables pure code to perform destructive updates in all scenarios described

---

[12] https://github.com/leanprover/lean4/blob/cade21/src/Lean/Compiler/IR/Basic.lean

above when objects are not shared. It also allows a novel programming paradigm that we call *functional but in-place* (FBIP) [10]. Our preliminary experimental results demonstrate our new compiler produces competitive code that often outperforms the code generated by high-performance compilers such as ocamlopt and GHC [14]. As an example, consider the function map f as that applies a function f to each element of a list as. In this example, [] denotes the empty list, and a::as the list with head a followed by the tail as.

```
def map : (α → β) → List α → List β
  | f, []    => []
  | f, a::as => f a :: map f as
```

If the list referenced by as is not shared, the code generated by our compiler does not allocate any memory. Moreover, if as is a nonshared list of list of integers, then map (map inc) as will not allocate any memory either. In contrast to static linearity systems, allocations are also avoided even if only a prefix of the list is not shared. FBIP also allows Lean users to use data structures, such as arrays and hashtables, in pure code without any performance penalty when they are not shared. We believe this is an attractive feature because hashtables are frequently used to implement decision procedures and nontrivial proof automation.

4   The User Interface

Our system implements the Language Server Protocol (LSP) using the task abstraction provided by its standard library. The Lean 4 LSP server is incremental and is continuously analyzing the source text and providing semantic information to editors implementing LSP. Our LSP server implements most LSP features found in advanced IDEs, such as hyperlinks, syntax highlighting, type information, error handling, auto-completion, etc. Many editors implement LSP, but VS Code is the preferred editor by the Lean user community. We provide extensions for visualizing the intermediate proof states in interactive tactic blocks, and we want to port the Lean 3 widget library for constructing interactive visualizations for their proofs and programs.

5   Conclusion

Lean 4 aims to be a fully extensible interactive theorem prover and functional programming language. It has an expressive logical foundation for writing mathematical specifications and proofs and formally verified programs. Lean 4 provides many new unique features, including a hygienic macro-system, an efficient typeclass resolution procedure based on tabled resolution, efficient code generator, and abstractions for sealing low-level optimizations. The new elaboration procedure is more general and efficient than those implemented in previous versions. Users may also extend and modify the elaborator using Lean itself. Lean has a relatively small trusted kernel, and the rich API allows users to export their developments to other systems and implement their own reference checkers. Lean is an ongoing and long-term effort, and future plans include integration with external SMT solvers and first-order theorem provers, new compiler backends, and porting the Lean 3 Mathematical Library.

Acknowledgments. We are grateful to Marc Huisinga and Wojciech Nawrocki for developing the LSP server, Daniel Selsam for working with us on the new typeclass resolution procedure and interesting design discussions, Daan Leijen, Nikhil Swamy, Sebastian Graf, Simon Peyton Jones, and Max Wagner for advice and design discussions, Joe Hendrix, Andrew Kent, Rob Dockins, and Simon Winwood from Galois Inc for being early Lean 4 adopters, and providing useful feedback and suggestions, and the whole Lean community for all their excitement and pushing Lean forward.

References

1. Buzzard, K., Commelin, J., Massot, P.: Formalising Perfectoid Spaces. In: Proceedings of the 9th ACM SIGPLAN International Conference on Certified Programs and Proofs. p. 299–312. CPP 2020, New York, NY, USA (2020). https://doi.org/10.1145/3372885.3373830, https://doi.org/10.1145/3372885.3373830

2. Buzzard, K., Hughes, C., Lau, K., Livingston, A., Mir, R.F., Morrison, S.: Schemes in Lean. https://arxiv.org/abs/2101.02602 (2021), arXiv:2101.02602

3. Chu, S., Murphy, B., Roesch, J., Cheung, A., Suciu, D.: Axiomatic foundations and algorithms for deciding semantic equivalences of SQL queries. Proc. VLDB Endow. 11(11), 1482–1495 (Jul 2018). https://doi.org/10.14778/3236187.3236200, https://doi.org/10.14778/3236187.3236200

4. Coquand, T., Huet, G.: The calculus of constructions. Inform. and Comput. 76(2-3), 95–120 (1988)

5. van Doorn, F., Ebner, G., Lewis, R.Y.: Maintaining a library of formal mathematics. In: Benzmüller, C., Miller, B. (eds.) Intelligent Computer Mathematics. pp. 251–267. Springer International Publishing, Cham (2020)

6. Ebner, G., Ullrich, S., Roesch, J., Avigad, J., de Moura, L.: A metaprogramming framework for formal verification. Proc. ACM Program. Lang. 1(ICFP) (Sep 2017). https://doi.org/http://dx.doi.org/10.1145/3110278

7. Jones, S.L.P.: Compiling Haskell by program transformation: a report from the trenches. In: In Proc. European Symp. on Programming. pp. 18–44. Springer-Verlag (1996)

8. Miller, D., Nadathur, G.: Programming with Higher-Order Logic. Cambridge (2012)

9. de Moura, L., Kong, S., Avigad, J., Van Doorn, F., von Raumer, J.: The Lean theorem prover. In: International Conference on Automated Deduction. pp. 378–388. Springer (2015)

10. Reinking, A., Xie, N., de Moura, L., Leijen, D.: Perceus: Garbage free reference counting with reuse. Tech. Rep. MSR-TR-2020-42, Microsoft Research (2020)

11. Scholze, P.: Liquid tensor experiment. https://xenaproject.wordpress.com/2020/12/05/liquid-tensor-experiment (2020), project repository https://github.com/leanprover-community/lean-liquid

12. Selsam, D., Ullrich, S., de Moura, L.: Tabled typeclass resolution. https://arxiv.org/abs/2001.04301 (2020), arXiv:2001.04301

13. The mathlib Community: The Lean mathematical library. In: Proceedings of the 9th ACM SIGPLAN International Conference on Certified Programs and Proofs. p. 367–381. CPP 2020, New York, NY, USA (2020). https://doi.org/10.1145/3372885.3373824, https://doi.org/10.1145/3372885.3373824

14. Ullrich, S., de Moura, L.: Counting immutable beans: Reference counting optimized for purely functional programming. In: 31st Symposium on Implementation and Application of Functional Languages (2019)

15. Ullrich, S., de Moura, L.: Beyond notations: Hygienic macro expansion for theorem proving languages. In: Peltier, N., Sofronie-Stokkermans, V. (eds.) Automated Reasoning. pp. 167–182. Cham (2020)

16. Wadler, P., Blott, S.: How to make ad-hoc polymorphism less ad hoc. In: Proceedings of the 16th ACM SIGPLAN-SIGACT symposium on Principles of programming languages. pp. 60–76. ACM (1989)

Open Access This chapter is licensed under the terms of the Creative Commons Attribution 4.0 International License (http://creativecommons.org/licenses/by/4.0/), which permits use, sharing, adaptation, distribution and reproduction in any medium or format, as long as you give appropriate credit to the original author(s) and the source, provide a link to the Creative Commons license and indicate if changes were made.

The images or other third party material in this chapter are included in the chapter's Creative Commons license, unless indicated otherwise in a credit line to the material. If material is not included in the chapter's Creative Commons license and your intended use is not permitted by statutory regulation or exceeds the permitted use, you will need to obtain permission directly from the copyright holder.

Harpoon: Mechanizing Metatheory Interactively

Jacob Errington⬭, Junyoung Jang⬭, and Brigitte Pientka⬭

McGill University, Montreal, Canada
{jacob.errington, junyoung.jang}@mail.mcgill.ca, bpientka@cs.mcgill.ca

Abstract. BELUGA is a proof checker that provides sophisticated infrastructure for implementing formal systems with the logical framework LF and proving metatheoretic properties as total, recursive functions transforming LF derivations. In this paper, we describe HARPOON, an interactive proof engine built on top of BELUGA. It allows users to develop proofs interactively using a small, fixed set of high-level *actions* that safely transform a subgoal. A sequence of actions elaborates into a (partial) *proof script* that serves as an intermediate representation describing an assertion-level proof. Last, a proof script translates into a BELUGA program which can be type-checked independently. HARPOON is available on GitHub. We have used HARPOON to replay a wide array of examples covering all features supported by BELUGA. In particular, we have used it for normalization proofs, including the recently proposed POPLMark reloaded challenge.

1 Introduction

Mechanizing formal systems and proofs about them plays an important role in establishing trust in programming languages and verifying software systems in general. Key questions in this setting are how to represent variables, (simultaneous) substitutions, assumptions, and derivations that depend on assumptions. Higher-order abstract syntax (HOAS) provides an elegant and unifying answer to these questions, relieving users from having to write boilerplate code.

BELUGA is a proof checker with built-in support for HOAS encodings of formal systems based on the logical framework LF [13]. Metatheoretic inductive proofs are implemented as recursive, dependently-typed functions that manipulate and transform HOAS representations [21,4,25]. In this paper, we describe the interactive proof engine HARPOON which is built on top of BELUGA. A HARPOON user modularly and incrementally develops a metatheoretic proof by solving independent subgoals via a fixed set of high-level *actions*. An action eliminates the subgoal on which it is executed, filling it with a proof that possibly contains new subgoals to be resolved. The actions we support are: introduction of assumptions, case-analysis, inductive reasoning, and both forward and backward reasoning styles.

© The Author(s) 2021
A. Platzer and G. Sutcliffe (Eds.): CADE 2021, LNAI 12699, pp. 636–648, 2021.
https://doi.org/10.1007/978-3-030-79876-5_38

While our fixed set of actions is largely inspired by similar systems such as Twelf [20,28,27] and Abella [11], HARPOON advances the state of the art in interactively developing mechanized proofs about HOAS representations in two ways: 1. We treat subgoals as first-class and characterize them using contextual types that pair their goal types together with the contexts in which they are meaningful; a contextual substitution property guarantees that each step of proof development correctly refines the partial proof under construction [8]. 2. Rather than simply record the sequence of actions given by the user, we elaborate this sequence into an assertion-level proof [15], represented as what we call a *proof script*. The proof script is what we record as output of an interactive session. It can be both typechecked directly and translated into a BELUGA program.

We have used HARPOON (see https://beluga-lang.readthedocs.io/) on a wide range of representative examples from the BELUGA library: normalization proofs for the simply-typed lambda calculus [6], benchmarks for reasoning about binders [9,10], and the recent POPLMark Reloaded challenge [1]. These examples involve numerous concerns that arise in proof development, and cover all the domain-specific abstractions that BELUGA provides. Our experience shows that HAR-POON lowers the entry barrier for users: they only need to understand how to represent formal systems and derivations using HOAS encodings and can then manipulate the HOAS representations directly via the high-level actions which correspond closely to how proofs are developed on paper. As such, we believe that HARPOON eases the task of proving metatheoretic statements.

2   Proof Development in Harpoon

We introduce the main features of HARPOON by interactively developing the proof of two lemmas that play a central role in the proof of weak normalization of the simply-typed lambda calculus. For a more detailed description, see [6].

2.1   Initial setup: encoding the language

We begin by defining the simply-typed lambda-calculus in the logical framework LF [13] using an intrinsically typed encoding. In typical HOAS style, lambda abstraction takes an LF function representing the abstraction of a term over a variable. There is no case for variables, as they are treated implicitly. We remind the reader that this is a weak, representational function space – there is no case analysis or recursion, so only genuine lambda terms can be represented.

```
LF tp : type =              LF tm : tp → type =
 | unit: tp                  | lam : (tm T1 → tm T2) → tm (arr T1 T2)
 | arr : tp → tp → tp;       | app : tm (arr T1 T2) → tm T1 → tm T2;
```

Free variables such as T1 and T2 are implicitly universally quantified (see [23]) and programmers subsequently do not supply arguments for implicitly quantified parameters when using a constructor.

Next, we define a small-step operational semantics for the language. For simplicity, we use a call-by-name reduction strategy and do not reduce under lambda-abstractions. Note that we use LF application to encode the object-level substitution in the s_beta rule.

```
LF step : tm T → tm T → type =        LF steps : tm T → tm T → type =
 | s_app : step M M'                    | next : step M M' → steps M' N
          → step (app M N) (app M' N)           → steps M N
 | s_beta: step (app (lam M) N) (M N);  | refl: steps M M;
```

Using this definition, we define a notion of termination: a term halts if it reduces to a value. This is captured by the constructor halts/m.

```
LF val : tm T → type = v_lam: val (lam M);
LF halts : tm T → type = halts/m : val V → steps M V → halts M;
```

2.2   Termination Property: intros, split, unbox, and solve

As the first short lemma, we show the Termination property: if M' is known to halt and steps M M', then M also halts. We start our interactive proof session by loading the signature and defining the name of the theorem and the statement that we want to prove.

```
Name of theorem: halts_step
Statement of theorem: [ ⊢ step M M'] → [ ⊢ halts M'] → [ ⊢ halts M]
```

We pair each LF object such as step M M' together with the LF context in which it is meaningful [21,26,19]. We refer to such an object as a *contextual object* and embed contextual types, written as _ ⊢ _ , into Beluga types using the "box" syntax. In this example, the LF context, written on the left of ⊢ , is empty, as we consider closed LF objects. As before, the free variables M and M' are implicitly quantified at the outside. They themselves stand for contextual objects and have contextual type (⊢ tm T). The *theorem statements* are hence *statements about contextual LF objects* and directly correspond to BELUGA types.

The proof begins with a single subgoal whose type is simply the statement of the theorem under no assumptions. Since this subgoal has a function type, HARPOON will automatically apply the intros action, which introduces assumptions as follows: First, the (implicitly) universally quantified variables M, M' are added to the *meta-context*. This context collects parameters introduced by universal quantifiers. This is in contrast with the *computational context*, which collects assumptions introduced by the simple function space. In particular, the second phase of the intros action adds the assumptions s : [⊢ step M M'] and h : [⊢ halts M'] to the computational context. Observe that since M and M' have type tm T, intros also adds T to the meta-context, although it is implicit in the definitions of step and halts and is not visible at all in the theorem statement (see the meta-context Fig. 1 step 1).

The proof proceeds by inversion on h. Using the split action, we add the two new assumptions S:(⊢ steps M' M2) and V:(⊢ val M2) to the meta-context

Step 1	Step 2	Step 3
Meta-context:	Meta-context:	Meta-context:
T : (⊢ tp)	T : (⊢ tp)	T : (⊢ tp)
M : (⊢ tm T)	M : (⊢ tm T)	M : (⊢ tm T)
M' : (⊢ tm T)	M' : (⊢ tm T)	M' : (⊢ tm T)
	M2 : (⊢ tm T)	M2 : (⊢ tm T)
	S : (⊢ steps M' M2)	S : (⊢ steps M' M2)
	V : (⊢ val M2)	V : (⊢ val M2)
		S' : (⊢ step M M')
Computational context:	Computational context:	Computational context:
s : [⊢ step M M']	s : [⊢ step M M']	s : [⊢ step M M']
h : [⊢ halts M']	h : [⊢ halts M']	h : [⊢ halts M']
[⊢ halts M]	[⊢ halts M]	[⊢ halts M]
> split h	> unbox s as S'	> solve [⊢ halts/m (next S' S) V]

Fig. 1. Interactive session of the proof for the `halts_step` lemma.

(see Fig. 1, step 1.). To build a proof for [⊢ halts M], we need to show that there is a step from M to some value M2. To build such a derivation, we use first the **unbox** action on the computation-level assumption s to obtain an assumption S' in the meta-context which is accessible to the LF layer (inside a box) (see Fig. 1, step 2.). Finally, we can finish the proof by supplying the term [⊢ **halts/m** (**next** S' S) V] with the **solve** action (see Fig. 1, step 3). This is similar to the exact tactic in Coq.

The resulting proof script is given below. Assertions are written in boldface and curly braces denote new scopes, listing the full meta-context and the full computational context. Using an erasure we can then generate a translated program in the external syntax, i.e. the syntax a user would use when implementing the proof directly, rather than the internal syntax. It is hence much more compact than the actual proof script. This program can then be seamlessly combined with hand-written BELUGA programs and can also independently type-checked.

Theorem halts_step: [⊢ step M M'] → [⊢ halts M'] → [⊢ halts M]

Proof Script

```
intros
{ T : ( ⊢ tp), M : ( ⊢ tm T), M' : ( ⊢ tm T)
| s : [ ⊢ step M M'], h : [ ⊢ halts M']
; split h as
  case halts/m:
  { T : ( ⊢ tp), M : ( ⊢ tm T), M' : ( ⊢ tm T),
    M2 : ( ⊢ tm T), S : ( ⊢ steps M' M2), V : ( ⊢ val M2)
  | s : [ ⊢ step M M'], h : [ ⊢ halts M']
  ; by s as S' unboxed
  ; solve [ ⊢ halts/m (next S' S) V]
  }
}
```

Erased program (external syntax)

```
fn s => fn h =>
  let [ ⊢ halts/m S V] = h in
  let [ ⊢ S'] = s in
  [ ⊢ halts/m (next S' S) V]
```

2.3 Setup continued: reducibility

We now consider one of the key lemmas in the weak normalization proof, called the backwards closed lemma, i.e. if M' is reducible at some type T and M steps to

M', then M is also reducible at T. We begin to define a set of terms *reducible* at a type T. All reducible terms are required to halt, and reducible terms at an arrow type are required to produce reducible output given reducible input. Concretely, a term M is reducible at type (**arr** T1 T2), if for all terms N:tm T1 where N is reducible at type T1, then (**app** M N) is reducible at type T2. Reducibility cannot be directly encoded on the LF layer, as it is not merely describing the syntax of an expression or derivation. Instead, we encode the set of reducible terms using the stratified type Reduce which is recursively defined on the type T in BELUGA (see [16]). Note that we write { } for explicit universal quantification over contextual objects.

```
stratified Reduce : {T : (⊢ tp)} [⊢ tm T] → ctype =
  | Unit: [⊢ halts M] → Reduce [⊢ unit] [⊢ M]
  | Arr : [⊢ halts M]
          → ({N:(⊢ tm T1)} Reduce [⊢ T1] [⊢ N] → Reduce [⊢ T2] [⊢ app M N])
          → Reduce [⊢ arr T1 T2] [⊢ M];
```

2.4 Backwards Closed Property: msplit, suffices, and by

We can now state the backwards closed lemma formally as follows: if M' is reducible at some type T and M steps to M', then M is also reducible at T. We prove this lemma by induction on T. This is specified by referring to the position of the induction variable in the statement.

```
Name of theorem: bwd_closed
Statement of theorem:
    {T : (⊢ tp)} {M : (⊢ tm T)} {M' : (⊢ tm T)}
    [⊢ step M M'] → Reduce [⊢ T] [⊢ M'] → Reduce [⊢ T] [⊢ M]
Induction order: 1
```

After HARPOON automatically introduces the metavariables T, M, and M' together with an assumption s : [⊢ step M M'] and r : Reduce [⊢ T] [⊢ M'], we use **msplit** T to split the proof into two cases (see Fig. 2, step 1). Whereas **split** case analyzes a BELUGA type, **msplit** considers the cases for a (contextual) LF type. In reality, **msplit** is implemented in terms of the **split** action.

The case for T = **unit** is straightforward (see Fig. 2, steps 2 and 3). First, we use the **split** action to invert the premise r : Reduce [⊢ unit] [⊢ M']. Then, we use the **by** action to invoke the halts_step lemma (see Sec. 2.2) to obtain an assumption h : [⊢ halts M]. We **solve** this case by supplying the term **Unit** h (see Fig. 2 step 3).

In the case for T = **arr** T1 T2, we begin similarly by inversion on r using the **split** action (see Fig. 3 step 4). We observe that the goal type is Reduce [⊢ arr T1 T2] [⊢ M], which can be produced by using the **Arr** constructor if we can construct a proof for each of the user-specified types, [⊢ halts M] and {N:(⊢ tm T1)} Reduce [⊢ T1] [⊢ N] → Reduce [⊢ T2] [⊢ app M N]. Such *backwards reasoning* is accomplished via the **suffices** action. The user supplies a term representing an implication whose conclusion is compatible with the current goal and proceeds to prove its premises as specified (see Fig.3 step 5).

Step 1

```
Meta-context:
  T : ( ⊢ tp )
  M : ( ⊢ tm T )
  M' : ( ⊢ tm T )
Computational context:
  s : [⊢ step M M']
  r : Reduce [⊢ T] [⊢ M']
```
```
Reduce [⊢ T] [⊢ M]
> msplit T
```

Step 2

```
Meta-context:
  M : ( ⊢ tm unit )
  M': ( ⊢ tm unit )
Computational context:
  s : [⊢ step M M']
  r : Reduce [⊢ unit] [⊢ M']
```
```
Reduce [⊢ unit] [⊢ M]
> split r
```

Step 3

```
Meta-context:
  M : ( ⊢ tm unit )
  M': ( ⊢ tm unit )
Computational context:
  s : [⊢ step M M']
  h': [⊢ halts M' ]
  r : Reduce [⊢ unit] [⊢ M']
```
```
Reduce [⊢ unit] [⊢ M]
> by halts_step s h' as h;
  solve Unit h
```

Fig. 2. Backwards Closed Lemma. Step 1: Case analysis of the type T; Steps 2 and 3: Base case (T = unit).

To prove the first premise, we apply the `halts_step` lemma (see Fig. 3 step 6). As for the second premise, HARPOON first automatically introduces the variable N:(⊢ tm T1) and the assumption r1:Reduce [⊢ T1] [⊢ N], so it remains to show Reduce [⊢ T2] [⊢ app M N]. We deduce r':Reduce [⊢ T2] [⊢ app M' N] using the assumption rn. Using s:[⊢ step M M'], we build a derivation s':[⊢ step (app M N) (app M' N)] using s_app. Finally, we appeal to the induction hypothesis. Using the **by** action, we refer to the recursive call to complete the proof (see Fig. 3 step 7). The resulting proof script (of around 70 lines) can again be translated into a compact program.

Note that HARPOON allows users to use underscores to stand for arguments that are uniquely determined (see HARPOON Proof 3 step 7). We enforce that these underscores stand for uniquely determined objects in order to guarantee that the contexts and the goal type of every subgoal are closed. This ensures modularity: solving one subgoal does not affect any other open subgoals. As a consequence, users are not restricted in their proof development. As they would on paper, users can work on goals in any order, mix forward and backward reasoning, erase wrong parts, and replace them by correct steps.

Using the explained actions, one can now prove the fundamental lemma and the weak normalization theorem. For a more detailed description of this proof in BELUGA see [5,6].

Additional actions. HARPOON supports some additional features not discussed in this paper; see https://beluga-lang.readthedocs.io/ for a complete list of actions. In general, these actions add no expressive power, but enable more precise expression of a user's intent. For example, the **invert** action splits on the type of a given term, ensuring that there is a unique case to consider. It is implemented simply as the **split** action followed by an additional check.

3   Implementation of Harpoon

HARPOON is a front end that allows users to construct a proof for a theorem statement represented as a BELUGA type. Types in BELUGA include universal

Step 4

Meta-context:
```
  T1 : (⊢ tp)
  T2 : (⊢ tp)
  M  : (⊢ tm (arr T1 T2))
  M' : (⊢ tm (arr T1 T2))
```
Computational context:
```
  s  : [⊢ step M M']
  r  : Reduce [⊢ arr T1 T2][⊢ M']
```

```
Reduce [⊢ arr T1 T2][⊢ M]
> split r
```

Step 5

Meta-context:
```
  T1 : (⊢ tp)
  T2 : (⊢ tp)
  M  : (⊢ tm (arr T1 T2))
  M' : (⊢ tm (arr T1 T2))
```
Computational context:
```
  s  : [⊢ step M M']
  rn : {N : ( ⊢ tm T)}Reduce [⊢ N][⊢ T]
         → Reduce [⊢ T2] [⊢ app M' N]
  h' : [⊢ halts M']
  r  : Reduce [⊢ arr T1 T2][⊢ M']
```

```
Reduce [⊢ arr T1 T2][⊢ M]
> suffices by Arr toshow
  [⊢ halts M],
  {N : ( ⊢ tm T1)}Reduce [⊢ T1][⊢ N]
       → Reduce [⊢ T2][⊢ app M N]
```

Step 6

Meta-context:
```
  T1 : (⊢ tp)
  T2 : (⊢ tp)
  M  : (⊢ tm (arr T1 T2))
  M' : (⊢ tm (arr T1 T2))
```

Computational context:
```
  s  : [⊢ step M M']
  rn : {N : ( ⊢ tm T)} Reduce [⊢ N][⊢ T]
       → Reduce [⊢ T2] [⊢ app M' N]
  h' : [⊢ halts M']
  r  : Reduce [⊢ arr T1 T2][⊢ M']
```

```
[⊢ halts M]
> by halts_step s h' as h
```

Step 7

Meta-context:
```
  T1 : (⊢ tp)
  T2 : (⊢ tp)
  M  : (⊢ tm (arr T1 T2))
  M' : (⊢ tm (arr T1 T2))
  N  : (⊢ tm T1)
```
Computational context:
```
  s  : [⊢ step M M']
  rn : {N : ( ⊢ tm T)} Reduce [⊢ N][⊢ T]
       → Reduce [⊢ T2] [⊢ app M' N]
  h' : [⊢ halts M']
  r  : Reduce [⊢ arr T1 T2][⊢ M']
  r1 : Reduce [⊢ T1] [⊢  N]
```

```
Reduce [⊢ T2] [⊢ app M N]
> by (rn [⊢ N] r1) as r';
  unbox s as S;
  by (bwd_closed _ _ _ [⊢ s_app S] r') as ih
```

Fig. 3. Backwards Closed Lemma: Step Case

quantification over contextual types (dependent function space, written with curly braces), implications (simple function space), boxed contextual types, and stratified/recursive types (written as $\mathbf{c}\ \overrightarrow{C}$ where C stands for a contextual object). In addition, BELUGA supports quantification over LF contexts and even LF substitutions relating two LF contexts. We omit these below for simplicity, although they are also supported in HARPOON. In essence, BELUGA types correspond to statements in first-order logic over a domain consisting of contextual objects, LF contexts, and LF substitutions. We can view $\mathbf{c}\ \overrightarrow{C}$ and $[\Psi \vdash A]$ as atomic propositions.

$$\begin{array}{lll}
\text{Types} & \tau ::= \mathbf{c}\ \overrightarrow{C} \mid [\Psi \vdash A] \mid \{X{:}(\Psi \vdash A)\}\,\tau \mid \tau_1 \to \tau_2 \\
\text{Meta-Context} & \Delta ::= \cdot \mid \Delta, X{::}(\Psi \vdash A) \\
\text{Context} & \Gamma ::= \cdot \mid \Gamma, x{:}\tau
\end{array}$$

Users construct a natural deduction proof for a theorem statement where Γ, the *computation context*, contains hypotheses introduced from the simple function space and where Δ, the *meta-context*, holds parameters introduced from the universal quantifier (curly-brace syntax) or by lifting an assumption $[\Psi \vdash A]$ from Γ (box-elimination rule).

A subgoal in HARPOON is a typed hole in the proof that remains to be filled by the user. Such a hole is represented by a *subgoal variable*, the type of which is a contextual type $(\Delta; \Gamma \vdash \tau)$ that captures the typechecking state at the point the variable occurs [19,3]: it remains to construct a proof for τ with the parameters from Δ and the assumptions from Γ. Subgoal variables in the proof script are collected into a *subgoal context* and substitution of subgoal variables is type-preserving [8]. Interactive actions are implemented with subgoal substitutions, so the correctness of interactive proof refinement is a consequence of the subgoal substitution property. Note that a subgoal's type cannot itself contain subgoals – the subgoal type must be fully determined, so solving one subgoal cannot affect any other subgoal. Furthermore, subgoal variables may be introduced only in positions where we must construct a normal term (written e); these are terms that we must *check* against a given type. This given type becomes part of the subgoal's type. Subgoal variables stand thus in contrast with ordinary variables, which are neutral terms (written i). (See [14,26,16] for examples of this so-called *bi-directional* characterization of normal and neutral proof terms in BELUGA.)

An action is executed on a subgoal to eliminate it, while possibly introducing new subgoals. Actions emphasize the bi-directional nature of interactive proof construction: some demand normal terms e and others demand neutral terms i. To execute an action, the system synthesizes a proof script fragment from it, and substitutes that fragment for the current subgoal. Any subgoal variables present in the fragment become part of the subgoal context, and the user will have to solve them later. When no subgoals remain, the proof script is closed and can be translated straightforwardly to a BELUGA program in internal (fully elaborated) syntax. We employ an erasure to display the program to the user. These are the essential actions for proof development, omitting our so-called "administrative" actions (such as **undo**):

Actions $\alpha ::=$ intros | solve e | by i as x | unbox i as X | split i | suffices i by $\vec{\tau}$

intros introduces all assumptions from function types in the current goal; solve closes the current subgoal with a given a normal term, introducing no new subgoals. This action trivially makes HARPOON complete, as a full BELUGA program could be given via solve to eliminate the initial subgoal of any proof. The action by enables introducing an intermediate result, often from a lemma or an induction hypothesis, demanding a neutral term i and binding it to a given name; unbox is the same as by, but it binds the result as a variable in the *meta-context*; split considers a covering set of cases for a neutral term (typically a variable) and generates possible induction hypotheses based on the specified induction order, (for details on coverage, see [24]); suffices allows programmers to reason backwards by supplying a neutral term i of function type and the types $\vec{\tau}$ of arguments to construct for this function.

4 Empirical evaluation of Harpoon

We give a summary of representative case studies that we replayed using HAR-POON in Table 1. In porting these proofs to HARPOON, we use **solve** e only when e is atomic, i.e. it describes either a contextual LF term or a constant applied to all its arguments (either $e = M$, $e = [C]$ or $e = c\ \overrightarrow{C}\ e_1 \ldots e_n$). We list in the table the number of commands used to complete the proof and what particular features made the selected case study interesting for testing HARPOON. The first

Case study	Main feature tested
MiniML value soundness	Automatic solving of trivial goals
MiniML compilation completeness	Unboxing program variables
STLC type preservation	Automatic solving of trivial goals
STLC type uniqueness [22]	Open term manipulation; (Contexts, Parameter variables)
STLC weak normalization [6]	Case analysis on LF contexts, substitution variables, parameter variables, and inductive and stratified types.
STLC strong normalization [1]	Larger development (310 commands), all forms of case analysis as above.
STLC alg. equality completeness [6]	Larger development (180 commands), all forms of case analysis as above.

Table 1. Summary of proofs ported to HARPOON from BELUGA.

four examples proceed by straightforward induction, but the remaining examples are less direct since they feature logical relations. The STLC strong normalization and algorithmic equality completeness examples are larger developments, totalling 38 and 26 theorems respectively. Crucially, these case studies make use of BELUGA's domain-specific abstractions, by splitting on contexts, reasoning about object-language variables, and exploiting the built-in equational theory of substitutions. We have since used HARPOON to replay the meta-theoretic proofs about Standard ML from [18].

This evaluation gives us confidence in the robustness and expressive power of HARPOON.

5 Related work

There are several approaches to specify and reason about formal systems.

BELUGA and hence HARPOON belong to the lineage of the Twelf system [20], which also implements the logical framework LF. Metatheoretic proofs in Twelf are implemented as *relations*. Totality checking then ensures that these relations correspond to actual proofs. As Twelf is limited to proving Π_1 formulas ("forall-exists" statements), normalization proofs using logical relations cannot be directly encoded. Although HARPOON's actions are largely inspired by the internal actions of Twelf's (experimental) fully-automated metatheorem prover [28,27], HARPOON supports user interaction, more expressive theorem statements, and generation of proof witnesses, in the form of both the generated proof script and BELUGA program resulting from translation.

The Abella system [11] also provides an interactive theorem prover for reasoning about specifications using HOAS. First, its theoretical basis is quite different from BELUGA's: Abella's reasoning logic extends first-order logic with a ∇ quantifier [12] that is used to express properties about variables. Second, Abella's interactive mode provides a fixed set of *tactics*, similar to the actions we describe in this paper. However, these tactics only loosely connect to the actual theoretical foundation of Abella and no proof terms are generated as witnesses by the Abella system.

We can also reason about formal systems in general purpose proof assistants such as Coq. The general philosophy in such systems is that users should be in the position of writing complex domain-specific tactics to facilitate proof construction using languages such as LTac [7] or MTac(2) [29,17]. Although this is an extremely flexible approach, we believe that the tactic-centric view often obscures the actual line of reasoning in the proof. The proofs themselves can often be illegible and incomprehensible. Further, strong static guarantees about interactive proof construction are lacking; for example, *dynamic* checks enforce variable dependencies. In contrast, our goal is to enable mechanized proof development in a style close to that of a proof on paper. Thus we provide a fixed set of tactics suitable for a wide array of proofs, so users can concentrate on proof development instead of tactic development. As such, our work draws inspiration from [2] where the authors describe high-level actions within the tutorial proof checker Tutch. Our work extends and adapts this view to the mechanization of inductive metatheoretic proofs based on HOAS representations.

6 Conclusion

We have presented HARPOON, an interactive command-driven front-end of BELUGA for mechanizing meta-theoretic proofs based on high-level actions. The sequence of interactive actions is elaborated into a proof script behind the scenes that represents an assertion-level proof. Last, proof scripts can soundly be translated to BELUGA programs. We have evaluated HARPOON on several case-studies, ranging from purely syntactic arguments to proofs by logical relations. Our experience is that HARPOON lowers the entry barrier for users to develop meta-theoretic proofs about HOAS encodings.

In the future, we aim to extend HARPOON with additional high-level actions that support further automation. A natural first step is to support an action trivial which would attempt to automatically close an open sub-goal.

Acknowledgments. Jacob Errington and Junyoung Jang acknowledge support from Fonds de Recherche du Québec – Nature et technologies (FRQNT). Brigitte Pientka acknowledges support from National Science and Engineering Research Council (NSERC).

References

1. Abel, A., Allais, G., Hameer, A., Pientka, B., Momigliano, A., Schäfer, S., Stark, K.: POPLMark Reloaded: Mechanizing Proofs by Logical Relations. J. Funct. Program. **29**, e19 (2019). https://doi.org/10.1017/S0956796819000170

2. Abel, A., Chang, B.Y.E., Pfenning, F.: Human-readable machine-verifiable proofs for teaching constructive logic. In: Egly, U., Fiedler, A., Horacek, H., Schmitt, S. (eds.) Proceedings of the Workshop on Proof Transformation and Presentation and Proof Complexities (PTP'01). pp. 33–48. Siena, Italy (2001), http://www2.tcs.ifi.lmu.de/~abel/ptp01.pdf

3. Boespflug, M., Pientka, B.: Multi-level contextual modal type theory. In: Nadathur, G., Geuvers, H. (eds.) 6th International Workshop on Logical Frameworks and Meta-languages: Theory and Practice (LFMTP'11). Electronic Proceedings in Theoretical Computer Science (EPTCS), vol. 71, pp. 29–43 (2011)

4. Cave, A., Pientka, B.: Programming with binders and indexed data-types. In: 39th ACM SIGPLAN-SIGACT Symposium on Principles of Programming Languages (POPL'12). pp. 413–424. ACM Press (2012)

5. Cave, A., Pientka, B.: First-class substitutions in contextual type theory. In: 8th ACM SIGPLAN International Workshop on Logical Frameworks and Meta-Languages: Theory and Practice (LFMTP'13). pp. 15–24. ACM Press (2013)

6. Cave, A., Pientka, B.: Mechanizing Proofs with Logical Relations – Kripke-style. Mathematical Structures in Computer Science **28**(9), 1606–1638 (2018). https://doi.org/10.1017/S0960129518000154

7. Delahaye, D.: A tactic language for the system Coq. In: Parigot, M., Voronkov, A. (eds.) 7th International Conference on Logic for Programming and Automated Reasoning (LPAR'00). Lecture Notes in Computer Science, vol. 1955, pp. 85–95. Springer (2000). https://doi.org/10.1007/3-540-44404-1_7

8. Errington, J.: Mechanizing metatheory interactively. Master's thesis, McGill University (2020)

9. Felty, A.F., Momigliano, A., Pientka, B.: Benchmarks for reasoning with syntax trees containing binders and contexts of assumptions. Math. Struct. in Comp. Science **28**(9), 1507–1540 (2018). https://doi.org/10.1017/S0960129517000093

10. Felty, A.P., Momigliano, A., Pientka, B.: The next 700 challenge problems for reasoning with higher-order abstract syntax representations: Part 2 - a survey. Journal of Automated Reasoning **55**(4), 307–372 (2015). https://doi.org/10.1007/s10817-015-9327-3

11. Gacek, A.: The Abella interactive theorem prover (System Description). In: Armando, A., Baumgartner, P., Dowek, G. (eds.) 4th International Joint Conference on Automated Reasoning. Lecture Notes in Artificial Intelligence, vol. 5195, pp. 154–161. Springer (2008)

12. Gacek, A., Miller, D., Nadathur, G.: Combining generic judgments with recursive definitions. In: Pfenning, F. (ed.) 23rd Symposium on Logic in Computer Science. IEEE Computer Society Press (2008)

13. Harper, R., Honsell, F., Plotkin, G.: A framework for defining logics. Journal of the ACM **40**(1), 143–184 (January 1993)

14. Heilala, S., Pientka, B.: Bidirectional decision procedures for the intuitionistic propositional modal logic is4. In: Pfenning, F. (ed.) 21st International Conference on Automated Deduction (CADE'07). pp. 116–131. Lecture Notes in Computer Science (LNCS 4603), Springer (2007)

15. Huang, X.: Reconstruction proofs at the assertion level. In: Bundy, A. (ed.) Proceedings of the 12th International Conference on Automated Deduction (CADE-12). Lecture Notes in Computer Science, vol. 814, pp. 738–752. Springer (1994). https://doi.org/10.1007/3-540-58156-1_53

16. Jacob-Rao, R., Pientka, B., Thibodeau, D.: Index-stratified types. In: Kirchner, H. (ed.) 3rd International Conference on Formal Structures for Computation and Deduction (FSCD'18). pp. 19:1–19:17. LIPIcs, Schloss Dagstuhl - Leibniz-Zentrum für Informatik (January 2018)

17. Kaiser, J., Ziliani, B., Krebbers, R., Régis-Gianas, Y., Dreyer, D.: Mtac2: typed tactics for backward reasoning in coq. Proc. ACM Program. Lang. 2(ICFP), 78:1–78:31 (2018). https://doi.org/10.1145/3236773

18. Lee, D.K., Crary, K., Harper, R.: Towards a mechanized metatheory of Standard ML. In: 34th ACM SIGPLAN-SIGACT Symposium on Principles of Programming Languages (POPL'07). pp. 173–184. ACM Press (2007)

19. Nanevski, A., Pfenning, F., Pientka, B.: Contextual modal type theory. ACM Transactions on Computational Logic 9(3), 1–49 (2008)

20. Pfenning, F., Schürmann, C.: System description: Twelf — A Meta-Logical Framework for Deductive Systems. In: Ganzinger, H. (ed.) 16th International Conference on Automated Deduction (CADE-16). pp. 202–206. Lecture Notes in Artificial Intelligence (LNAI 1632), Springer (1999)

21. Pientka, B.: A type-theoretic foundation for programming with higher-order abstract syntax and first-class substitutions. In: 35th ACM SIGPLAN-SIGACT Symposium on Principles of Programming Languages (POPL'08). pp. 371–382. ACM Press (2008)

22. Pientka, B.: Programming inductive proofs: a new approach based on contextual types. In: Siegler, S., Wasser, N. (eds.) Verification, Induction, Termination Analysis - Festschrift for Christoph Walther on the Occasion of his 60th Birthday. pp. 1–16. Lecture Notes in Computer Science (LNCS 6463), Springer (2010)

23. Pientka, B.: An insider's look at LF type reconstruction: Everything you (n)ever wanted to know. Journal of Functional Programming 1(1–37) (2013)

24. Pientka, B., Abel, A.: Structural recursion over contextual objects. In: Altenkirch, T. (ed.) 13th International Conference on Typed Lambda Calculi and Applications (TLCA'15). pp. 273–287. Leibniz International Proceedings in Informatics (LIPIcs) of Schloss Dagstuhl (2015)

25. Pientka, B., Cave, A.: Inductive Beluga: Programming Proofs (System Description). In: Felty, A.P., Middeldorp, A. (eds.) 25th International Conference on Automated Deduction (CADE-25). pp. 272–281. Lecture Notes in Computer Science (LNCS 9195), Springer (2015)

26. Pientka, B., Dunfield, J.: Programming with proofs and explicit contexts. In: ACM SIGPLAN Symposium on Principles and Practice of Declarative Programming (PPDP'08). pp. 163–173. ACM Press (2008)

27. Schürmann, C.: Automating the Meta Theory of Deductive Systems. Ph.D. thesis, Department of Computer Science, Carnegie Mellon University (2000), CMU-CS-00-146

28. Schürmann, C., Pfenning, F.: Automated theorem proving in a simple meta-logic for LF. In: Kirchner, C., Kirchner, H. (eds.) Proceedings of the 15th International Conference on Automated Deduction (CADE-15). pp. 286–300. Springer-Verlag Lecture Notes in Computer Science (LNCS) 1421, Lindau, Germany (Jul 1998)

29. Ziliani, B., Dreyer, D., Krishnaswami, N.R., Nanevski, A., Vafeiadis, V.: Mtac: A monad for typed tactic programming in Coq. Journal of Functional Programming 25 (2015)

648   J. Errington et al.

Open Access This chapter is licensed under the terms of the Creative Commons Attribution 4.0 International License (http://creativecommons.org/licenses/by/4.0/), which permits use, sharing, adaptation, distribution and reproduction in any medium or format, as long as you give appropriate credit to the original author(s) and the source, provide a link to the Creative Commons license and indicate if changes were made.

The images or other third party material in this chapter are included in the chapter's Creative Commons license, unless indicated otherwise in a credit line to the material. If material is not included in the chapter's Creative Commons license and your intended use is not permitted by statutory regulation or exceeds the permitted use, you will need to obtain permission directly from the copyright holder.

Author Index

Printed in the United States
by Baker & Taylor Publisher Services

Printed in the United States
by Baker & Taylor Publisher Services